# American Casebook Series
# Hornbook Series and Basic Legal Texts
# Nutshell Series

of

## WEST PUBLISHING COMPANY
P.O. Box 3526
St. Paul, Minnesota 55165
December, 1979

---

### ACCOUNTING

Fiflis and Kripke's Teaching Materials on Accounting for Business Lawyers, 2nd Ed., 684 pages, 1977 (Casebook)

### ADMINISTRATIVE LAW

Davis' Cases, Text and Problems on Administrative Law, 6th Ed., 683 pages, 1977 (Casebook)

Davis' Basic Text on Administrative Law, 3rd Ed., 617 pages, 1972 (Text)

Davis' Police Discretion, 176 pages, 1975 (Text)

Gellhorn's Administrative Law and Process in a Nutshell, 336 pages, 1972 (Text)

Mashaw and Merrill's Introduction to the American Public Law System, 1095 pages, 1975, with 1978 Supplement (Casebook)

Robinson and Gellhorn's The Administrative Process, 928 pages, 1974 (Casebook)

### ADMIRALTY

Healy and Sharpe's Cases and Materials on Admiralty, 875 pages, 1974 (Casebook)

### AGENCY—PARTNERSHIP

Crane and Bromberg's Hornbook on Partnership, 695 pages, 1968 (Text)

Henn's Cases and Materials on Agency, Partnership and Other Unincorporated Business Enterprises, 396 pages, 1972 (Casebook)

Reuschlein and Gregory's Hornbook on the Law of Agency and Partnership, 625 pages, 1979 (Text)

Seavey's Hornbook on Agency, 329 pages, 1964 (Text)

Seavey and Hall's Cases on Agency, 431 pages, 1956 (Casebook)

### AGENCY—PARTNERSHIP—Continued

Seavey, Reuschlein and Hall's Cases on Agency and Partnership, 599 pages, 1962 (Casebook)

Steffen and Kerr's Cases and Materials on Agency-Partnership, 4th Ed., approximately 860 pages, December, 1979 (Casebook)

Steffen's Agency-Partnership in a Nutshell, 364 pages, 1977 (Text)

### ANTITRUST LAW

Gellhorn's Antitrust Law and Economics in a Nutshell, 406 pages, 1976 (Text)

Oppenheim and Weston's Cases and Comments on Federal Antitrust Laws, 3rd Ed., 952 pages, 1968, with 1975 Supplement (Casebook)

Oppenheim and Weston's Price and Service Discrimination under the Robinson-Patman Act, 3rd Ed., 258 pages, 1974 (Casebook—reprint from Oppenheim and Weston's Cases and Comments on Federal Antitrust Laws, 3rd Ed., 1968)

Posner's Cases and Economic Notes on Antitrust, 885 pages, 1974 (Casebook)

Sullivan's Handbook of the Law of Antitrust, 886 pages, 1977 (Text)

See also Regulated Industries, Trade Regulation

### BANKING LAW

See Regulated Industries

### BUSINESS PLANNING

Painter's Problems and Materials in Business Planning, 791 pages, 1975, with 1978 Supplement (Casebook)

### CIVIL PROCEDURE

Casad's Res Judicata in a Nutshell, 310 pages, 1976 (Text)

## CIVIL PROCEDURE—Continued

Cound, Friedenthal and Miller's Cases and Materials on Civil Procedure, 2nd Ed., 1186 pages, 1974 with 1978 Supplement (Casebook)

Cound, Friedenthal and Miller's Cases on Pleading, Discovery and Joinder, 643 pages, 1968 (Casebook)

Ehrenzweig and Louisell's Jurisdiction in a Nutshell, 3rd Ed., 291 pages, 1973 (Text)

Federal Rules of Civil-Appellate-Criminal Procedure—West Law School Edition, 342 pages, 1979

Hodges, Jones and Elliott's Cases and Materials on Texas Trial and Appellate Procedure, 2nd Ed., 745 pages, 1974 (Casebook)

Hodges, Jones and Elliott's Cases and Materials on the Judicial Process Prior to Trial in Texas, 2nd Ed., 871 pages, 1977 (Casebook)

Kane's Civil Procedure in a Nutshell, 271 pages, 1979 (Text)

Karlen's Procedure Before Trial in a Nutshell, 258 pages, 1972 (Text)

Karlen and Joiner's Cases and Materials on Trials and Appeals, 536 pages, 1971 (Casebook)

Karlen, Meisenholder, Stevens and Vestal's Cases on Civil Procedure, 923 pages, 1975 (Casebook)

Koffler and Reppy's Hornbook on Common Law Pleading, 663 pages, 1969 (Text)

McBaine's Cases on Introduction to Civil Procedure, 399 pages, 1950 (Casebook)

McCoid's Cases on Civil Procedure, 823 pages, 1974 (Casebook)

Park's Computer-Aided Exercises on Civil Procedure, 118 pages, 1976 (Coursebook)

Shipman's Hornbook on Common-Law Pleading, 3rd Ed., 644 pages, 1923 (Text)

Siegel's Hornbook on New York Practice, 1011 pages, 1978 (Text)

See also Federal Jurisdiction and Procedure

## CIVIL RIGHTS

Abernathy's Cases and Materials on Civil Rights, approximately 665 pages, January 1980 (Casebook)

Lockhart, Kamisar and Choper's Cases on Constitutional Rights and Liberties, 4th Ed., 1244 pages plus Appendix, 1975, with 1979 Supplement (Casebook)—reprint from Lockhart, et al. Cases on Constitutional Law, 4th Ed., 1975

Vieira's Civil Rights in a Nutshell, 279 pages, 1978 (Text)

## COMMERCIAL LAW

Bailey's Secured Transactions in a Nutshell, 377 pages, 1976 (Text)

Epstein and Martin's Basic Uniform Commercial Code Teaching Materials, 599 pages, 1977 (Casebook)

Henson's Hornbook on Secured Transactions under the U.C.C., 2nd Ed., 504 pages, 1979 with 1979 P.P. (Text)

Murray's Commercial Law, Problems and Materials, 366 pages, 1975 (Coursebook)

Nordstrom and Clovis' Problems and Materials on Commercial Paper, 458 pages, 1972 (Casebook)

Nordstrom and Lattin's Problems and Materials on Sales and Secured Transactions, 809 pages, 1968 (Casebook)

Nordstrom's Hornbook on Sales, 600 pages, 1970 (Text)

Selected Commercial Statutes, 1277 pages, 1979

Speidel, Summers and White's Teaching Materials on Commercial and Consumer Law, 2nd Ed., 1475 pages, 1974 (Casebook)

Stone's Uniform Commercial Code in a Nutshell, 507 pages, 1975 (Text)

Uniform Commercial Code, Official Text with Comments, 994 pages, 1978

UCC Article Nine Reprint, 128 pages, 1976

Weber's Commercial Paper in a Nutshell, 2nd Ed., 361 pages, 1975 (Text)

White and Summers' Hornbook on the Uniform Commercial Code, 2nd Ed., approximately 1202 pages, January, 1980 (Text)

## COMMUNITY PROPERTY

Huie's Texas Cases and Materials on Marital Property Rights, 681 pages, 1966 (Casebook)

Verrall's Cases and Materials on California Community Property, 3rd Ed., 547 pages, 1977 (Casebook)

## COMPARATIVE LAW

Langbein's Comparative Criminal Procedure: Germany, 172 pages, 1977 (Casebook)

## CONFLICT OF LAWS

Cramton, Currie and Kay's Cases-Comments-Questions on Conflict of Laws, 2nd Ed., 1021 pages, 1975 (Casebook)

Ehrenzweig's Treatise on Conflict of Laws, 824 pages, 1962 (Text)

Ehrenzweig's Conflicts in a Nutshell, 3rd Ed., 432 pages, 1974 (Text)

# LAW SCHOOL PUBLICATION—Continued

## CONFLICT OF LAWS—Continued

Goodrich and Scoles' Hornbook on Conflict of Laws, 4th Ed., 483 pages, 1964 (Text)

Scoles and Weintraub's Cases and Materials on Conflict of Laws, 2nd Ed., 966 pages, 1972, with 1978 Supplement (Casebook)

## CONSTITUTIONAL LAW

Engdahl's Constitutional Power in a Nutshell: Federal and State, 411 pages, 1974 (Text)

Ginsburg's Constitutional Aspects of Sex-Based Discrimination, 129 pages, 1974 (Casebook)—reprint from Davidson, Ginsburg and Kay's Cases on Sex-Based Discrimination, 1974

Lockhart, Kamisar and Choper's Cases-Comments-Questions on Constitutional Law, 4th Ed., 1664 pages plus Appendix, 1975, with 1979 Supplement (Casebook)

Lockhart, Kamisar and Choper's Cases-Comments-Questions on the American Constitution, 4th Ed., 1249 pages plus Appendix, 1975, with 1979 Supplement (Casebook)—reprint from Lockhart, et al. Cases on Constitutional Law, 4th Ed., 1975

Lockhart, Kamisar and Choper's Cases and Materials on Constitutional Rights and Liberties, 4th Ed., 1244 pages plus Appendix, 1975, with 1979 Supplement (Casebook)—reprint from Lockhart, et al. Cases on Constitutional Law, 4th Ed., 1975

Miller's Presidential Power in a Nutshell, 328 pages, 1977 (Text)

Nowak, Rotunda and Young's Hornbook on Constitutional Law, 974 pages, 1978, with 1979 pocket part (Text)

Vieira's Civil Rights in a Nutshell, 279 pages, 1978 (Text)

William's Constitutional Analysis in a Nutshell, 388 pages, 1979 (Text)

## CONSUMER LAW

Epstein's Consumer Protection in a Nutshell, 322 pages, 1976 (Text)

Kripke's Text-Cases-Materials on Consumer Credit, 454 pages, 1970 (Casebook)

McCall's Consumer Protection, Cases, Notes and Materials, 594 pages, 1977, with 1977 Statutory Supplement (Casebook)

Schrag's Cases and Materials on Consumer Protection, 2nd Ed., 197 pages, 1973 (Casebook)—reprint from Cooper, et al. Cases on Law and Poverty, 2nd Ed., 1973

Selected Commercial Statutes, 1277 pages, 1979

## CONSUMER LAW —Continued

Spanogle and Rohner's Cases and Materials on Consumer Law, 693 pages, 1979 (Casebook)

Uniform Consumer Credit Code, Official Text with Comments, 218 pages, 1974

## CONTRACTS

Calamari & Perillo's Cases and Problems on Contracts, 1061 pages, 1978 (Casebook)

Calamari and Perillo's Hornbook on Contracts, 2nd Ed., 878 pages, 1977 (Text)

Corbin's Text on Contracts, One Volume Student Edition, 1224 pages, 1952 (Text)

Freedman's Cases and Materials on Contracts, 658 pages, 1973 (Casebook)

Fuller and Eisenberg's Cases on Basic Contract Law, 3rd Ed., 1043 pages, 1972 (Casebook)

Jackson's Cases on Contract Law in Modern Society, 1404 pages, 1973 (Casebook)

Keyes' Government Contracts in a Nutshell, 423 pages, 1979 (Text)

Reitz's Cases on Contracts as Basic Commercial Law, 763 pages, 1975 (Casebook)

Schaber and Rohwer's Contracts in a Nutshell, 307 pages, 1975 (Text)

Simpson's Hornbook on Contracts, 2nd Ed., 510 pages, 1965 (Text)

## COPYRIGHT

Nimmer's Cases and Materials on Copyright and Other Aspects of Law Pertaining to Literary, Musical and Artistic Works, Illustrated, 2nd Ed., 1023 pages, 1979 (Casebook)

See also Patent Law

## CORPORATIONS

Hamilton's Cases on Corporations—Including Partnerships and Limited Partnerships, 998 pages, 1976, with 1979 Case and Statutory Supplement (Casebook)

Henn's Cases on Corporations, 1279 pages, 1974, with 1974 Statutes, Forms and Case Study Supplement (Casebook)

Henn's Hornbook on Corporations, 2nd Ed., 956 pages, 1970 (Text)

Jennings and Buxbaum's Cases and Materials on Corporations, 5th Ed., 1156 pages, 1979 (Casebook)

## CORRECTIONS

Krantz's Cases and Materials on the Law of Corrections and Prisoners' Rights, 1130 pages, 1973, with 1977 Supplement (Casebook)

## CORRECTIONS—Continued

Krantz's Law of Corrections and Prisoners' Rights in a Nutshell, 353 pages, 1976 (Text)

Model Rules and Regulations on Prisoners' Rights and Responsibilities, 212 pages, 1973

Popper's Post-Conviction Remedies in a Nutshell, 360 pages, 1978 (Text)

## CREDITOR'S RIGHTS

Epstein's Debtor-Creditor Law in a Nutshell, 2nd Ed., approximately 322 pages, December, 1979 (Text)

Epstein and Landers' Debtors and Creditors: Cases and Materials, 722 pages, 1978, with 1979 Supplement (Casebook)

Riesenfeld's Cases and Materials on Creditors' Remedies and Debtors' Protection, 3rd Ed., 795 pages, 1979 with 1979 Statutory Supplement (Casebook)

Selected Bankruptcy Statutes, 351 pages, 1979

## CRIMINAL LAW AND CRIMINAL PROCEDURE

Cohen and Gobert's Problems in Criminal Law, 297 pages, 1976 (Problem book)

Davis' Police Discretion, 176 pages, 1975 (Text)

Dix and Sharlot's Cases and Materials on Criminal Law, 2nd Ed., 756 pages, 1979 (Casebook)

Federal Rules of Civil-Appellate-Criminal Procedure—West Law School Edition, 342 pages, 1979

Grano's Problems in Criminal Procedure, 171 pages, 1974 (Problem book)

Heymann and Kenety's The Murder Trial of Wilbur Jackson: A Homicide in the Family, 340 pages, 1975 (Case Study)

Israel and LaFave's Criminal Procedure in a Nutshell, 2nd Ed., 404 pages, 1975 (Text)

Johnson's Criminal Law: Cases, Materials and Text on Substantive Criminal Law in its Procedural Context, 878 pages, 1975, with 1977 Supplement (Casebook)

Kamisar, LaFave and Israel's Cases, Comments and Questions on Modern Criminal Procedure, 4th ed., 1572 pages, plus Appendix, 1974, with 1980 Supplement (Casebook)

Kamisar, LaFave and Israel's Cases, Comments and Questions on Basic Criminal Procedure, 4th Ed., 790 pages, 1974, with 1980 Supplement (Casebook)—reprint from Kasimar, et al. Modern Criminal Procedure, 4th ed., 1974

LaFave's Modern Criminal Law: Cases, Comments and Questions, 789 pages, 1978 (Casebook)

LaFave and Scott's Hornbook on Criminal Law, 763 pages, 1972 (Text)

## CRIMINAL LAW AND CRIMINAL PROCEDURE—Continued

Loewy's Criminal Law in a Nutshell, 302 pages, 1975 (Text)

Saltzburg's American Criminal Procedure, Cases and Commentary, approx. 1270 pages, December, 1979 (Casebook)

Uniform Rules of Criminal Procedure—Approved Draft, 407 pages, 1974

Uviller's The Processes of Criminal Justice: Adjudication, 2nd Ed., 700 pages, 1979. Soft-cover reprint from Uviller's The Processes of Criminal Justice: Investigation and Adjudication, 2nd Ed. (Casebook)

Uviller's The Processes of Criminal Justice: Investigation and Adjudication, 2nd Ed., 1320 pages, 1979 with 1979 Statutory Supplement (Casebook)

Uviller's The Processes of Criminal Justice: Investigation, 2nd Ed., 650 pages, 1979. Soft-cover reprint from Uviller's The Processes of Criminal Justice: Investigation and Adjudication, 2nd Ed. (Casebook)

Vorenberg's Cases on Criminal Law and Procedure, 1044 pages, 1975, with 1979 Supplement (Casebook)

See also Corrections, Juvenile Justice

## DECEDENTS ESTATES

See Wills, Trusts and Estates

## DOMESTIC RELATIONS

Clark's Cases and Problems on Domestic Relations, 2nd Ed., 918 pages, 1974, with 1977 Supplement (Casebook)

Clark's Hornbook on Domestic Relations, 754 pages, 1968 (Text)

Kay's Sex-Based Discrimination in Family Law, 305 pages, 1974 (Casebook)—reprint from Davidson, Ginsburg and Kay's Cases on Sex-Based Discrimination, 1974

Krause's Cases and Materials on Family Law, 1132 pages, 1976, with 1978 Supplement (Casebook)

Krause's Family Law in a Nutshell, 400 pages, 1977 (Text)

Paulsen's Cases and Selected Problems on Family Law and Poverty, 2nd Ed., 200 pages, 1973 (Casebook)—reprint from Cooper, et al. Cases on Law and Poverty, 2nd Ed., 1973

## EDUCATION LAW

Morris' The Constitution and American Education, 833 pages, 1974 (Casebook)

## EMPLOYMENT DISCRIMINATION

Cooper, Rabb and Rubin's Fair Employment Litigation: Text and Materials for Student and Practitioner, 590 pages, 1975 (Coursebook)

# LAW SCHOOL PUBLICATION—Continued

## EMPLOYMENT DISCRIMINATION —
Continued

Player's Cases and Materials on Employment Discrimination Law, approximately 825 pages, December, 1979 (Casebook)

Player's Federal Law of Employment Discrimination in a Nutshell, 336 pages, 1976 (Text)

Sovern's Cases and Materials on Racial Discrimination in Employment, 2nd Ed., 167 pages, 1973 (Casebook)— reprint from Cooper et al. Cases on Law and Poverty, 2nd Ed., 1973

See also Women and the Law

## ENVIRONMENTAL LAW

Currie's Cases and Materials on Pollution, 715 pages, 1975 (Casebook)

Federal Environmental Law, 1600 pages, 1974 (Text)

Hanks, Tarlock and Hanks' Cases on Environmental Law and Policy, 1242 pages, 1974, with 1976 Supplement (Casebook)

Rodgers' Hornbook on Environmental Law, 956 pages, 1977 (Text)

See also Natural Resources and Water Law

## EQUITY

See Remedies

## ESTATE PLANNING

Casner and Stein's Estate Planning under the Tax Reform Act of 1976, 456 pages, 1978 (Coursebook)

Lynn's Introduction to Estate Planning, in a Nutshell, 2nd Ed., 378 pages, 1978 (Text)

## EVIDENCE

Broun and Meisenholder's Problems in Evidence, 130 pages, 1973 (Problem book)

Cleary and Strong's Cases, Materials and Problems on Evidence, 2nd Ed., 1124 pages, 1975 (Casebook)

Federal Rules of Evidence for United States Courts and Magistrates, 325 pages, 1979

Kimball's Programmed Materials on Problems in Evidence, 380 pages, 1978 (Problem book)

Lempert and Saltzburg's A Modern Approach to Evidence: Text, Problems, Transcripts and Cases, 1231 pages, 1977 (Casebook)

Lilly's Introduction to the Law of Evidence, 486 pages, 1978 (Text)

McCormick, Elliott and Sutton's Cases and Materials on Evidence, 4th Ed., 1088 pages, 1971 (Casebook)

McCormick's Hornbook on Evidence, 2nd Ed., 938 pages, 1972, with 1978 pocket part (Text)

## EVIDENCE—Continued

Rothstein's Evidence in a Nutshell, 406 pages, 1970 (Text)

## FEDERAL JURISDICTION AND PROCEDURE

Currie's Cases and Materials on Federal Courts, 2nd Ed., 1040 pages, 1975, with 1978 Supplement (Casebook)

Currie's Federal Jurisdiction in a Nutshell, 228 pages, 1976 (Text)

Federal Rules of Civil-Appellate-Criminal Procedure—West Law School Edition, 342 pages, 1979

Forrester and Moye's Cases and Materials on Federal Jurisdiction and Procedure, 3rd Ed., 917 pages, 1977 (Casebook)

Merrill and Vetri's Problems on Federal Courts and Civil Procedure, 460 pages, 1974 (Problem book)

Wright's Hornbook on Federal Courts, 3rd Ed., 818 pages, 1976 (Text)

## FUTURE INTERESTS

See Wills, Trusts, and Estates

## HOUSING AND URBAN DEVELOPMENT

Berger's Cases and Materials on Housing, 2nd Ed., 254 pages, 1973 (Casebook)—reprint from Cooper et al. Cases on Law and Poverty, 2nd Ed., 1973

See also Land Use

## INDIAN LAW

Getches, Rosenfelt and Wilkinson's Cases on Federal Indian Law, 660 pages, 1979 (Casebook)

## INSURANCE

Keeton's Cases on Basic Insurance Law, 2nd Ed., 1086 pages, 1977

Keeton's Basic Text on Insurance Law, 712 pages, 1971 (Text)

Keeton's Case Supplement to Keeton's Basic Text on Insurance Law, 334 pages, 1978 (Casebook)

Keeton's Programmed Problems in Insurance Law, 243 pages, 1972 (Text Supplement)

## INTERNATIONAL LAW

Friedmann, Lissityzyn and Pugh's Cases and Materials on International Law, 1205 pages, 1969, with 1972 Supplement (Casebook)

Jackson's Legal Problems of International Economic Relations, 1097 pages, 1977, with Statutory Supplement (Casebook)

Kirgis' International Organizations in Their Legal Setting, 1016 pages, 1977 (Casebook)

# LAW SCHOOL PUBLICATION—Continued

## INTRODUCTION TO LAW

Dobbyn's So You Want to go to Law School, Revised First Edition, 206 pages, 1976 (Text)

Kinyon's Introduction to Law Study and Law Examinations in a Nutshell, 389 pages, 1971 (Text)

See also Legal Method and Legal System

## JUDICIAL ADMINISTRATION

Carrington, Meador and Rosenberg's Justice on Appeal, 263 pages, 1976 (Casebook)

Nelson's Cases and Materials on Judicial Administration and the Administration of Justice, 1032 pages, 1974 (Casebook)

## JURISPRUDENCE

Christie's Text and Readings on Jurisprudence—The Philosophy of Law, 1056 pages, 1973 (Casebook)

## JUVENILE JUSTICE

Fox's Cases and Materials on Modern Juvenile Justice, 1012 pages, 1972 (Casebook)

Fox's Juvenile Courts in a Nutshell, 2nd Ed., 275 pages, 1977 (Text)

## LABOR LAW

Gorman's Labor Law-Unionization and Collective Bargaining, 914 pages, 1976 (Text)

Leslie's Labor Law in a Nutshell, 403 pages, 1979 (Text)

Nolan's Labor Arbitration Law and Practice in a Nutshell, 358 pages, 1979 (Text)

Oberer, Hanslowe and Anderson's Cases and Materials on Labor Law—Collective Bargaining in a Free Society, 2nd Ed., 1168 pages, 1979, with 1979 Statutory Supplement (Casebook)

See also Employment Discrimination, Social Legislation

## LAND FINANCE—PROPERTY SECURITY

Bruce's Real Estate Finance in a Nutshell, 292 pages, 1979 (Text)

Maxwell, Riesenfeld, Hetland and Warren's Cases on California Security Transactions in Land, 2nd Ed., 584 pages, 1975 (Casebook)

Nelson and Whitman's Cases on Real Estate Finance and Development, 1064 pages, 1976 (Casebook)

Osborne's Cases and Materials on Secured Transactions, 559 pages, 1967 (Casebook)

Osborne, Nelson and Whitman's Hornbook on Real Estate Finance Law, 3rd Ed., 885 pages, 1979 (Text)

## LAND USE

Beuscher, Wright and Gitelman's Cases and Materials on Land Use, 2nd Ed., 1133 pages, 1976 (Casebook)

Hagman's Cases on Public Planning and Control of Urban and Land Development, 1208 pages, 1973, with 1976 Supplement (Casebook)

Hagman's Hornbook on Urban Planning and Land Development Control Law, 706 pages, 1971 (Text)

Wright and Webber's Land Use in a Nutshell, 316 pages, 1978 (Text)

See also Housing and Urban Development

## LAW AND ECONOMICS

Manne's The Economics of Legal Relationships—Readings in the Theory of Property Rights, 660 pages, 1975 (Text)

See also Regulated Industries

## LAW AND MEDICINE—PSYCHIATRY

King's The Law of Medical Malpractice in a Nutshell, 340 pages, 1977 (Text)

Sharpe, Fiscina and Head's Cases on Law and Medicine, 882 pages, 1978 (Casebook)

## LEGAL RESEARCH AND WRITING

Cohen's Legal Research in a Nutshell, 3rd Ed., 415 pages, 1978 (Text)

How to Find the Law With Special Chapters on Legal Writing, 7th Ed., 542 pages, 1976. Problem book available (Coursebook)

Rombauer's Legal Problem Solving—Analysis, Research and Writing, 3rd Ed., 352 pages, 1978 (Casebook)

Statsky's Legal Research, Writing and Analysis: Some Starting Points, 180 pages, 1974 (Text)—reprint from Statsky's Introduction to Paralegalism, 1974

Statsky and Wernet's Case Analysis and Fundamentals of Legal Writing, 576 pages, 1977 (Text)

Weihofen's Legal Writing Style, 2nd Ed., 332 pages, 1980 (Text)

## LEGAL CLINICS

Freeman and Weihofen's Cases and Text on Clinical Law Training—Interviewing and Counseling, 506 pages, 1972 (Casebook)

## LEGAL PROFESSION

Aronson's Problems in Professional Responsibility, 280 pages, 1978 (Problem book)

Mallen and Levit's Legal Malpractice, 727 pages, 1977 (Coursebook)

# LAW SCHOOL PUBLICATION—Continued

## LEGAL PROFESSION—Continued

Mellinkoff's The Conscience of a Lawyer, 304 pages, 1973 (Text)

Mellinkoff's Lawyers and the System of Justice, 983 pages, 1976 (Casebook)

Pirsig and Kirwin's Cases and Materials on Professional Responsibility, 3rd Ed., 667 pages, 1976, with 1977 Supplement (Casebook)

## LEGAL HISTORY

See Legal Method and Legal System

## LEGAL METHOD AND LEGAL SYSTEM

Aldisert's Readings, Materials and Cases in the Judicial Process, 948 pages, 1976 (Casebook)

Fryer and Orentlicher's Cases and Materials on Legal Method and Legal System, 1043 pages, 1967 (Casebook)

Greenberg's Judicial Process and Social Change, 666 pages, 1977 (Coursebook)

Kempin's Historical Introduction to Anglo-American Law in a Nutshell, 2nd Ed., 280 pages, 1973 (Text)

Kimball's Historical Introduction to the Legal System, 610 pages, 1966 (Casebook)

Leflar's Appellate Judicial Opinions, 343 pages, 1974 (Text)

Mashaw and Merrill's Introduction to the American Public Law System, 1095 pages, 1975, with 1978 Supplement (Casebook)

Murphy's Cases and Materials on Introduction to Law—Legal Process and Procedure, 772 pages, 1977 (Casebook)

Smith's Cases and Materials on the Development of Legal Institutions, 757 pages, 1965 (Casebook)

Statsky's Legislative Analysis: How to Use Statutes and Regulations, 216 pages, 1975 (Text)

## LEGISLATION

Davies' Legislative Law and Process in a Nutshell, 279 pages, 1975 (Text)

Nutting and Dickerson's Cases and Materials on Legislation, 5th Ed., 744 pages, 1978 (Casebook)

Statsky's Legislative Analysis: How to Use Statutes and Regulations, 216 pages, 1975 (Text)

## LOCAL GOVERNMENT

McCarthy's Local Government Law in a Nutshell, 386 pages, 1975 (Text)

Michelman and Sandalow's Cases-Comments-Questions on Government in Urban Areas, 1216 pages, 1970, with 1972 Supplement (Casebook)

Stason and Kauper's Cases and Materials on Municipal Corporations, 3rd Ed., 692 pages, 1959 (Casebook)

## LOCAL GOVERNMENT—Continued

Valente's Cases and Materials on Local Government Law, 928 pages, 1975 (Casebook)

## MASS COMMUNICATION LAW

Gillmor and Barron's Cases and Comment on Mass Communication Law, 3rd Ed., 988 pages, 1979 (Casebook)

Ginsburg's Regulation of Broadcasting: Law and Policy Towards Radio, Television and Cable Communications, 741 pages, 1979 (Casebook)

Zuckman and Gayne's Mass Communications Law in a Nutshell, 431 pages, 1977 (Text)

## MORTGAGES

See Land Finance—Property Security

## NATURAL RESOURCES LAW

Rodger's Cases on Energy and Natural Resources Law, 995 pages, 1979 (Casebook)

See also Environmental Law & Water Law

## OFFICE PRACTICE

Binder and Price's Legal Interviewing and Counseling: A Client-Centered Approach, 232 pages, 1977 (Text)

Edwards and White's Problems, Readings and Materials on the Lawyer as a Negotiator, 484 pages, 1977 (Casebook)

Freeman and Weihofen's Cases and Text on Clinical Law Training—Interviewing and Counseling, 506 pages, 1972 (Casebook)

Shaffer's Legal Interviewing and Counseling in a Nutshell, 353 pages, 1976 (Text)

Strong and Clark's Law Office Management, 424 pages, 1974 (Casebook)

## OIL AND GAS

Hemingway's Hornbook on Oil and Gas, 486 pages, 1971, with 1978 pocket part (Text)

Huie, Woodward and Smith's Cases and Materials on Oil and Gas, 2nd Ed., 955 pages, 1972 (Casebook)

See also Natural Resources

## PARTNERSHIP

See Agency—Partnership

## PATENT LAW

Choate's Cases and Materials on Patent Law, 1060 pages, 1973 (Casebook)

See also Copyright

## POVERTY LAW

Brudno's Poverty, Inequality, and the Law: Cases-Commentary-Analysis, 934 pages, 1976 (Casebook)

# LAW SCHOOL PUBLICATION—Continued

## POVERTY LAW—Continued

Brudno's Cases on Income Redistribution Theories and Programs, 480 pages, 1977 (Casebook)—reprint from Brudno's Cases on Poverty, Inequality and the Law, 1976

Cooper, Dodyk, Berger, Paulsen, Schrag and Sovern's Cases and Materials on Law and Poverty, 2nd Ed., 1208 pages, 1973 (Casebook)

LaFrance, Schroeder, Bennett and Boyd's Hornbook on Law of the Poor, 558 pages, 1973 (Text)

See also Social Legislation

## PRODUCTS LIABILITY

Noel and Phillips' Cases on Products Liability, 836 pages, 1976 (Casebook)

Noel and Phillips' Products Liability in a Nutshell, 365 pages, 1974 (Text)

## PROPERTY

Aigler, Smith and Tefft's Cases on Property, 2 volumes, 1339 pages, 1960 (Casebook)

Bernhardt's Real Property in a Nutshell, 425 pages, 1975 (Text)

Browder, Cunningham, Julin and Smith's Cases on Basic Property Law, 3rd Ed., 1447 pages, 1979 (Casebook)

Burby's Hornbook on Real Property, 3rd Ed., 490 pages, 1965 (Text)

Chused's A Modern Approach to Property: Cases-Notes-Materials, 1069 pages, 1978 (Casebook)

Cohen's Materials for a Basic Course in Property, 526 pages, 1978 (Casebook)

Donahue, Kauper and Martin's Cases on Property, 1501 pages, 1974 (Casebook)

Hill's Landlord and Tenant Law in a Nutshell, 319 pages, 1979 (Text)

Moynihan's Introduction to Real Property, 254 pages, 1962 (Text)

Phipps' Titles in a Nutshell, 277 pages, 1968 (Text)

Smith and Boyer's Survey of the Law of Property, 2nd Ed., 510 pages, 1971 (Text)

Uniform Land Transactions Act, Uniform Simplification of Land Transfers Act, Uniform Condominium Act, 1978 Official Text with Comments, 462 pages, 1978

See also Housing and Urban Development, Land Finance, Land Use

## REAL ESTATE

See Land Finance

## REGULATED INDUSTRIES

Morgan's Cases and Materials on Economic Regulation of Business, 830 pages, 1976, with 1978 Supplement (Casebook)

## REGULATED INDUSTRIES—Continued

Pozen's Financial Institutions: Cases, Materials and Problems on Investment Management, 844 pages, 1978 (Casebook)

White's Teaching Materials on Banking Law, 1058 pages, 1976, with 1976 Statutory Supplement (Casebook)

See also Mass Communication Law

## REMEDIES

Cribbet's Cases and Materials on Judicial Remedies, 762 pages, 1954 (Casebook)

Dobbs' Hornbook on Remedies, 1067 pages, 1973 (Text)

Dobbs' Problems in Remedies, 137 pages, 1974 (Problem book)

Dobbyn's Injunctions in a Nutshell, 264 pages, 1974 (Text)

McClintock's Hornbook on Equity, 2nd Ed., 643 pages, 1948 (Text)

McCormick's Hornbook on Damages, 811 pages, 1935 (Text)

O'Connell's Remedies in a Nutshell, 364 pages, 1977 (Text)

Van Hecke, Leavell and Nelson's Cases and Materials on Equitable Remedies and Restitution, 2nd Ed., 717 pages, 1973 (Casebook)

York and Bauman's Cases and Materials on Remedies, 3rd Ed., 1250 pages, 1979 (Casebook)

## REVIEW MATERIALS

Ballantine's Problems
Smith's Review

## SECURITIES REGULATION

Ratner's Securities Regulation: Materials for a Basic Course, 2nd Ed., approximately 1062 pages, December, 1979, with 1979 Supplement (Casebook)

Ratner's Securities Regulation in a Nutshell, 300 pages, 1978 (Text)

## SOCIAL LEGISLATION

Brudno's Income Redistribution Theories and Programs: Cases-Commentary-Analysis, 480 pages, 1977 (Casebook)—reprint from Brudno's Poverty, Inequality and the Law, 1976

Cohen's Cases and Materials on Law and Social Control: The Processes of Deprivation of Liberty, approximately 825 pages, December, 1979 (Casebook)

Cooper and Dodyk's Cases and Materials on Income Maintenance, 2nd Ed., 449 pages, 1973 (Casebook)—reprint from Cooper et al. Cases on Law and Poverty, 2nd Ed., 1973

LaFrance's Welfare Law: Structure and Entitlement in a Nutshell, 455 pages, 1979 (Text)

## SOCIAL LEGISLATION—Continued

Malone, Plant and Little's Cases on the Employment Relation, 1055 pages, 1974, with 1977 Supplement (Casebook)

See also Poverty Law

## SURETYSHIP

Osborne's Cases on Suretyship, 221 pages, 1966 (Casebook)

Simpson's Hornbook on Suretyship, 569 pages, 1950 (Text)

## TAXATION

Chommie's Hornbook on Federal Income Taxation, 2nd Ed., 1051 pages, 1973 (Text)

Chommie's Review of Federal Income Taxation, 90 pages, 1973 (Text)

Hellerstein and Hellerstein's Cases on State and Local Taxation, 4th Ed., 1041 pages, 1978 (Casebook)

Kahn and Gann's Corporate Taxation and Taxation of Partnerships and Partners, 1107 pages, 1979 (Casebook)

Kragen and McNulty's Cases and Materials on Federal Income Taxation, 3rd Ed., Vol. 1, 1270 pages, 1979 (Casebook)

Kramer and McCord's Problems for Federal Estate and Gift Taxes, 206 pages, 1976 (Problem book)

Lowndes, Kramer and McCord's Hornbook on Federal Estate and Gift Taxes, 3rd Ed., 1099 pages, 1974 (Text)

McCord's 1976 Estate and Gift Tax Reform-Analysis, Explanation and Commentary, 377 pages, 1977 (Text)

McNulty's Federal Estate and Gift Taxation in a Nutshell, 2nd Ed., 488 pages, 1979 (Text)

McNulty's Federal Income Taxation of Individuals in a Nutshell, 2nd Ed., 422 pages, 1978 (Text)

Rice's Problems and Materials in Federal Estate and Gift Taxation, 3rd Ed., 474 pages, 1978 (Casebook)

Rice and Solomon's Problems and Materials in Federal Income Taxation, 3rd Ed., 675 pages, 1979 (Casebook)

Rose and Raskind's Advanced Federal Income Taxation: Corporate Transactions-Cases, Materials and Problems, 955 pages, 1978 (Casebook)

Selected Federal Taxation Statutes and Regulations, 1415 pages, 1979

Sobeloff's Federal Income Taxation of Corporations and Stockholders in a Nutshell, 374 pages, 1978 (Text)

## TORTS

Green, Pedrick, Rahl, Thode, Hawkins, Smith and Treece's Cases and Materials on Torts, 2nd Ed., 1360 pages, 1977 (Casebook)

## TORTS—Continued

Green, Pedrick, Rahl, Thode, Hawkins, Smith, and Treece's Advanced Torts: Injuries to Business, Political and Family Interests, 544 pages, 1977 (Casebook)—reprint from Green, et al. Cases and Materials on Torts, 2nd Ed., 1977

Keeton's Computer-Aided and Workbook Exercises on Tort Law, 164 pages, 1976 (Coursebook)

Keeton and Keeton's Cases and Materials on Torts, 2nd Ed., 1200 pages, 1977 (Casebook)

Kionka's Torts in a Nutshell: Injuries to Persons and Property, 434 pages, 1977 (Text)

Malone's Torts in a Nutshell: Injuries to Family, Social and Trade Relations, 340 pages, 1979 (Text)

Prosser's Hornbook on Torts, 4th Ed., 1208 pages, 1971 (Text)

Shapo's Cases on Tort and Compensation Law, 1244 pages, 1976 (Casebook)

See also Products Liability

## TRADE REGULATION

Oppenheim and Weston's Cases and Materials on Unfair Trade Practices and Consumer Protection, 3rd Ed., 1065 pages, 1974, with 1977 Supplement (Casebook)

See also Antitrust, Regulated Industries

## TRIAL ADVOCACY

Bergman's Trial Advocacy in a Nutshell, 402 pages, 1979 (Text)

Hegland's Trial and Practice Skills in a Nutshell, 346 pages, 1978 (Text)

Jean's Trial Advocacy (Student Edition), 473 pages, 1975 (Text)

McElhaney's Effective Litigation, 457 pages, 1974 (Casebook)

## TRUSTS

See Wills, Trusts and Estates

## WATER LAW

Trelease's Cases and Materials on Water Law, 3rd Ed., 828 pages, 1979 (Casebook)

See also Natural Resources & Environmental Law

## WILL, TRUSTS AND ESTATES

Atkinson's Hornbook on Wills, 2nd Ed., 975 pages, 1953 (Text)

Averill's Uniform Probate Code in a Nutshell, 425 pages, 1978 (Text)

Bogert's Hornbook on Trusts, 5th Ed., 726 pages, 1973 (Text)

Clark, Lusky and Murphy's Cases and Materials on Gratuitous Transfers, 2nd Ed., 1102 pages, 1977 (Casebook)

# LAW SCHOOL PUBLICATION—Continued

## WILL, TRUSTS AND ESTATES
### —Continued

Gulliver's Cases and Materials on Future Interests, 624 pages, 1959 (Casebook)

Gulliver's Introduction to the Law of Future Interests, 87 pages, 1959 (Casebook)

Halbach (Editor)—Death, Taxes, and Family Property: Essays and American Assembly Report, 189 pages, 1977 (Text)

Mennell's Cases and Materials on California Decedent's Estates, 566 pages, 1973 (Casebook)

Mennell's Wills and Trusts in a Nutshell, 392 pages, 1979 (Text)

Powell's Cases on Trusts and Wills, 639 pages, 1960 (Casebook)

Simes' Hornbook on Future Interests, 2nd Ed., 355 pages, 1966 (Text)

## WILL, TRUSTS AND ESTATES
### —Continued

Turrentine's Cases and Text on Wills and Administration, 2nd Ed., 483 pages, 1962 (Casebook)

Uniform Probate Code, 5th Ed., Official Text With Comments, 384 pages, 1977

## WOMEN AND THE LAW

Davidson, Ginsburg and Kay's Text, Cases and Materials on Sex-Based Discrimination, 1031 pages, 1974, with 1978 Supplement (Casebook)

See also Employment Discrimination

## WORKMEN'S COMPENSATION

See Social Legislation

*

# THE CONSTITUTION

## AND

# AMERICAN EDUCATION

### Second Edition

By

**ARVAL A. MORRIS**
Professor of Law
Adjunct Professor of Education
University of Washington

**AMERICAN CASEBOOK SERIES**

ST. PAUL, MINN.
WEST PUBLISHING CO.
1980

**Library of Congress Cataloging in Publication Data**

Morris, Arval A
   The Constitution and American education.
   (American casebook series)
   Includes index.
   1.  Educational law and legislation—United States—Cases.  2.  United States—
Constitutional law—Cases.  3.  Education and state—United States.
I.  Title.  II.  Series.
KF4118.M67      1980        344.73'07        79–28177

**ISBN** 0–8299–2080–3

Morris—Const. & Am. Educ. 2d ACB

FOR

LAURA

AND

HAL

SINE QUIBUS NON . . . .

*

# PREFACE

Authors or editors have views of their subjects that inform their work, and I am no exception. I set forth my views here in the belief they may help a reader evaluate this book.

The basic commitment of the American people is to their Constitution. The First Amendment to the Constitution of the United States plainly lays down the injunction that Congress shall make no law abridging the right of the people to freedom of speech or press. This provision simultaneously guarantees the right, and encourages every citizen to exercise his right, to express opinions on all aspects of public affairs. The underlying constitutional commitments are to a republican form of constitutional democracy in which the basic postulates are: (1) that the people of the United States are to be self-governing, controlling their government and not vice-versa, and (2) that the people are fully to engage in discussion and argument about the proper course of state in order to identify policies they want their representatives to follow for their common welfare. This vision lies at the core of the set of constitutional ideas expressed by the founding fathers, and their vision cannot be realized without an educated people. Citizens must be sufficiently educated in order to be able to think; to think clearly and discriminately, and to think independently for themselves. Thus, in outline form, it is possible to identify the constitutional criteria that are fundamental to the American political community and that are fundamental to the constituent elements of the concept of good citizenship. These criteria are also sufficient to identify a community consensus that will justify a system of American education.

Clearly, every American child must be educated in such a way that he is effectively afforded the opportunity to be the kind of citizen required by the First Amendment. At the very minimum this means that American schools must equip all students (1) with the tools of learning; (2) with curious minds that are open to new and different worlds in which they may live, and (3) with precise minds such that they can have a keen and profound understanding of their cultural heritage. These requirements go both to subject matter and to teaching methods. Moreover, although the First Amendment does not require that the people agree with each other, indeed it is assumed that they will not, it is essential that the people understand and communicate with each other. This means that the people must first learn to listen to one another, and hence another function of the American school can be identified.

XVII

# PREFACE

It can be seen that the primary goals of the First Amendment are two, and that they are interconnected: to encourage the development in each citizen of the maximum amount of intelligent personality, and consequently, social diversity, within a social order that encourages the maximum amount of community citizenship, and consequently social unity. Obviously, the educational system has a vital role to play in helping the American people to realize these constitutional ideals. In this context then, the basic justification for an American school system is that it educate the next generation intelligently for good citizenship, as the concept of good citizenship is contemplated by the Constitution of the United States. In a profound sense, therefore, American education is involved with the law.

Every college or university through its College of Education, Law or Arts and Sciences, should offer at least one basic course on the intersections of law and education. That course, The Constitution And American Education, should concentrate on fundamentals. It should analyze the basic constitutional framework within which law and education must function by critically focussing on constitutional issues presented in education cases and by focussing on the constitutional processes through which constitutional ideals are brought to bear on the resolution of the issues. When taught in the College of Education, discussion emphasis can be on the educational wisdom of legal decisions. In a law school context, emphasis will be more narrowly technical, and in the College of Arts and Sciences, the course can emphasize law as a liberal art. In every situation, the basic course has the advantage of its subject matter, because higher education students have had considerable experience with K–12 educational institutions. They can bring that experience to bear when evaluating the adequacy of a legal decision.

In addition to the basic course on law and education, a College of Education should, I believe, offer at least two more: (1) School Law For Administrators and Teachers, and (2) Law And Higher Education. Both courses should presuppose the basic course. The one for administrators and teachers should focus on more specific legal detail by exploring the law in relation to such educational subjects as the contract and tort liability of school districts, school officials and teachers; necessary school board procedures, e. g., notice, voting, public nature and recording requirements; school elections, e. g., petitions and notice for elections, ballots, qualifications for voting, and a detailed analysis of the state and local administrative structures over education. The course on the Law of Higher Education should also concentrate on legal detail and particularly on the legal problems that are peculiar to higher education.

This book presents materials and other information necessary for the first, or basic, course on the Constitution and American Education.

# PREFACE

The book is designed to serve as a general introduction to a broad and fundamental area of law for those persons who have had no prior exposure to the subject. Although the emphasis is primarily on the ways in which the U. S. Constitution controls public education, the book also includes pedagogical, sociological and other materials necessary for a first, basic course. I have tried to avoid presenting snippets of materials and over-editing cases, because I believe it important for students to have a quantity of material sufficient for them to analyze and compare competing value premises and modes of reasoning.

The basic reasoning behind the organization of the book is this. The thrust of the initial chapter is orientation. It introduces the reader to the American legal system and related matters such as suggestions on how to read and analyze cases. Thereafter, the book turns to law and education proper. I have presented materials responding to certain fundamental questions.

The first fundamental question that the book deals with is in Chapter II: whether, under our Constitution, the state has constitutional power to restrict the physical liberty of a child and limit the right of a parent to raise his child in order to educate him? This question necessarily raises additional questions about the constitutional legitimacy of compulsory attendance laws, and if they are, whether a state must permit alternatives other than attendance at a government school to satisfy its attendance requirements? Also, it raises additional questions such as whether liberty interests ever outweigh a state's interest in compulsory education and whether a state is legally bound to exchange a quid pro quo—a quality education—for the restriction of a child's liberty and parental rights?

The second fundamental question the book confronts, in Chapters III, IV and V, parallels the first, and focusses on a child's freedom of mind. Assuming a state has the constitutional power to require its children to attend school, what can it do to their minds once they are there? What, if any, constitutional provisions limit a state's power to mold the minds of its youth either by excluding materials, thereby keeping them in ignorance or by confronting them with materials and requiring a mastery of them? Does a teacher have a constitutional right to make decisions about content or method of courses? Is there a hidden curriculum? If so, what are its values? These and similar questions are considered in Chapter III where the concentration is on a school's formal curriculum, and again in Chapter IV, where the concentration is on non-curricular affairs. Because of its importance and because it makes a separate unit unto itself, religion and whether it legally may be used to affect a student's mind, both in curricular and non-curricular affairs, appears in Chapter V. The book's first basic question concerns the physical liberty of a child, and the second fundamental question, found in Chapters III, IV and V,

PREFACE

concerns a child's freedom of thought.  Nevertheless, they are related
because questions about a state's power to mold a child's thought are
heavily influenced by legal considerations about a state's power to
compel school attendance in the first place.

Materials responding to a third set of questions, found in Chapter
VI, focus on how and the extent to which, if at all, a state may control a child's behavior when he is at school.  Here the concern is not
so much on freedom of the student's mind as on his privacy and related matters.  Does a state have power to require students to shave,
to cut their hair in a district-prescribed style, not to wear jeans, or to
search his locker or his clothing when looking for drugs?  Also, what
types of disciplinary sanctions may a student be subjected to, and
what constitutionally required procedures must be observed before
disciplining a student?

Materials in Chapter VII explore the life of teachers in school.
Can teachers be subjected to a district's grooming code?  Do teachers
have constitutional rights to speak out publicly about school matters?
What are the grounds for which teachers may be discharged, and what
constitutionally required procedures must be observed before dismissing them?  And what about teacher unions?  Can teachers be fired
if they strike?

A final group of chapters center on the concept of equality, and
particularly on the idea of equal educational opportunity.  The basic
question is: what is an equal educational opportunity?  Is it to be
judged by an input standard—the resources a state makes available for
each student—or by an output standard—the educational development
of a student?  If a Black child goes to an all-Black school, does that
show inequality?  If a school only has a girls' volleyball team, and no
boy may participate on it, is that inequality?  If, due to a handicap,
some children learn more slowly than others, must the state supply
them additional educational resources in order to treat them equally?
Questions about equal educational opportunity are explored in the last
three chapters: Chapter VIII, where the focus is on race; Chapter
IX, where the focus is on sex, and Chapter X, where the focus primarily is on handicapped, exceptional and gifted children.

Before concluding these prefatory remarks I should like to thank
some of the people who have helped make this book possible.  I cannot trace my intellectual debts fully, but on any account I am especially indebted to Professors Ray O. Werner and Douglas J. Mertz of The
Colorado College who thoroughly awakened my intellectual interests,
and to Professors Rueben A. Zubrow and Morris Garnsey of the University of Colorado and Myres S. McDougal of the Yale Law School
who, along with Professor Harold D. Evjen of Colorado, and Profes-

# PREFACE

sors Arthur Bestor and Melvin Rader of the University of Washington, have helped me sustain my intellectual interests and curiosity. Finally, I am indebted to the late Gordon C. Lee who, as Dean of the College of Education at the University of Washington, introduced me to the importance of the impact of constitutional ideals on educational affairs. I also thank my students who have patiently suffered through experimental classes with these materials and particularly the persons who, in various ways, have made direct contributions to this book, especially Michael E. Andrews, John Humphrie and Steve Katz. Furthermore, I thank Viola Bird, Eleanor Barrows, Maxine Dowd, Mary Hubert, Flora Meyerson, Genevieve Grove, Victoria Northington, Ann Van Hassel and Marian Gallagher for rendering their usual excellent library services. Of course, none of the persons named above is responsible for any of the shortcomings of this book. Finally, and especially, I thank Gail Creager, Melody Walker and Diane Coleman who labored mightily and typed the entire manuscript and parts of it twice.

ARVAL A. MORRIS

Seattle, Washington
December, 1979

*

# SUMMARY OF CONTENTS

*

# TABLE OF CONTENTS

# TABLE OF CONTENTS

TABLE OF CONTENTS

CHAPTER III: CONSTITUTIONAL LIMITATIONS ON GOVERNMENTAL POWER TO CONTROL THE EXPRESSION OF IDEAS WITHIN THE CURRICULUM—Continued

# TABLE OF CONTENTS

# TABLE OF CONTENTS

# TABLE OF CONTENTS

TABLE OF CONTENTS

# TABLE OF CONTENTS

# TABLE OF CONTENTS

# TABLE OF CONTENTS

# TABLE OF CONTENTS

## CHAPTER X: CONSTITUTIONAL FREEDOM AND EQUAL EDUCATIONAL OPPORTUNITY—Cont'd

\*

# TABLE OF CASES

The principal cases are in italic type. Cases cited or discussed are in roman type. References are to Pages.

# TABLE OF CASES

# TABLE OF CASES

# TABLE OF CASES

# TABLE OF CASES

# TABLE OF CASES

# THE CONSTITUTION

## AND

# AMERICAN EDUCATION

---

## THE CONSTITUTION OF THE UNITED STATES OF AMERICA

---

We the people of the United States, in Order to form a more perfect Union, establish Justice, insure domestic Tranquility, provide for the common defence, promote the general Welfare, and secure the Blessings of Liberty to ourselves and our Posterity, do ordain and establish this Constitution for the United States of America.

### ARTICLE I

SECTION 1.   All legislative Powers herein granted shall be vested in a Congress of the United States, which shall consist of a Senate and House of Representatives.

SECTION 2.   The House of Representatives shall be composed of Members chosen every second Year by the People of the several States, and the Electors in each State shall have the Qualifications requisite for Electors of the most numerous Branch of the State Legislature.

No person shall be a Representative who shall not have attained to the Age of twenty-five Years, and been seven Years a Citizen of the United States, and who shall not, when elected, be an Inhabitant of that State in which he shall be chosen.

Representatives and direct Taxes shall be apportioned among the several States which may be included within this Union, according to their respective Numbers, which shall be determined by adding to the whole Number of free Persons, including those bound to Service for a Term of Years, and excluding Indians not taxed, three fifths of all other Persons.   The actual Enumeration shall be made within three Years after the first Meeting of the Congress of the United States, and within every subsequent Term of ten Years, in such Manner as they shall by Law direct.   The Number of Representatives shall not exceed one for every thirty Thousand, but each State shall have at Least one Representative;  and until such enumeration shall be made, the State of New Hampshire shall be entitled to chuse three. Massachusetts eight, Rhode Island and Providence Plantations one, Connecticut five, New York six, New Jersey four, Pennsylvania eight, Delaware one, Maryland six, Virginia ten, North Carolina five, South Carolina five, and Georgia three.

When vacancies happen in the Representation from any State, the Executive Authority thereof shall issue Writs of Election to fill such Vacancies.

The House of Representatives shall chuse their Speaker and other Officers; and shall have the sole Power of Impeachment.

SECTION 3.   The Senate of the United States shall be composed of two Senators from each State, chosen by the Legislature thereof, for six Years; and each Senator shall have one Vote.

Immediately after they shall be assembled in Consequence of the first Election, they shall be divided as equally as may be into three Classes.   The Seats of the Senators of the first Class shall be vacated at the Expiration of the second Year, of the second Class at the Expiration of the fourth Year, and of the third Class at the Expiration of the sixth Year, so that one third may be chosen every second Year; and if Vacancies happen by Resignation, or otherwise, during the Recess of the Legislature of any State, the Executive thereof may make temporary Appointments until the next Meeting of the Legislature, which shall then fill such Vacancies.

No Person shall be a Senator who shall not have attained to the Age of thirty Years, and been nine Years a Citizen of the United States, and who shall not, when elected, be an Inhabitant of that State for which he shall be chosen.

The Vice President of the United States shall be President of the Senate, but shall have no Vote, unless they be equally divided.

The Senate shall chuse their other Officers, and also a President pro tempore, in the absence of the Vice President, or when he shall exercise the Office of President of the United States.

The Senate shall have the sole Power to try all Impeachments. When sitting for that Purpose, they shall be on Oath or Affirmation. When the President of the United States is tried, the Chief Justice shall preside: And no Person shall be convicted without the Concurrence of two thirds of the Members present.

Judgment in Cases of Impeachment shall not extend further than to removal from Office, and disqualification to hold and enjoy any Office of honor, Trust or Profit under the United States: but the Party convicted shall nevertheless be liable and subject to Indictment, Trial, Judgment and Punishment, according to Law.

SECTION 4.   The Times, Places and Manner of holding Elections for Senators and Representatives, shall be prescribed in each State by the Legislature thereof;  but the Congress may at any time by Law make or alter such Regulations, except as to the Places of Chusing Senators.

The Congress shall assemble at least once in every Year, and such Meeting shall be on the first Monday in December, unless they shall by Law appoint a different Day.

SECTION 5. Each House shall be the Judge of the Elections, Returns and Qualifications of its own Members, and a Majority of each shall constitute a Quorum to do Business; but a smaller Number may adjourn from day to day, and may be authorized to compel the Attendance of absent Members, in such Manner, and under such Penalties as each House may provide.

Each House may determine the Rules of its Proceedings, punish its Members for disorderly Behavior, and, with the Concurrence of two thirds, expel a Member.

Each House shall keep a Journal of its Proceedings, and from time to time publish the same, excepting such Parts as may in their Judgment require Secrecy; and the Yeas and Nays of the Members of either House on any question shall, at the Desire of one fifth of those Present, be entered on the journal.

Neither House, during the Session of Congress, shall, without the Consent of the other, adjourn for more than three days, nor to any other Place than that in which the two Houses shall be sitting.

SECTION 6. The Senators and Representatives shall receive a Compensation for their Services, to be ascertained by Law, and paid out of the Treasury of the United States. They shall in all Cases, except Treason, Felony and Breach of the Peace, be privileged from Arrest during their Attendance at the Session of their respective Houses, and in going to and returning from the same; and for any Speech or Debate in either House, they shall not be questioned in any other Place.

No Senator or Representative shall, during the Time for which he was elected, be appointed to any civil Office under the Authority of the United States, which shall have been created, or the Emoluments whereof shall have been encreased during such time; and no Person holding any Office under the United States, shall be a Member of either House during his Continuance in Office.

SECTION 7. All Bills for raising Revenue shall originate in the House of Representatives; but the Senate may propose or concur with Amendments as on other Bills.

Every Bill which shall have passed the House of Representatives and the Senate, shall, before it become a Law, be presented to the President of the United States; If he approve he shall sign it, but if not he shall return it, with his Objections to that House in which it shall have originated, who shall enter the Objections at large on their Journal, and proceed to reconsider it.  If after such Reconsideration two thirds of that House shall agree to pass the Bill, it shall be sent, together with the Objections, to the other House, by which it shall likewise be reconsidered, and if approved by two thirds of that House, it shall become a Law.  But in all such Cases the Votes of both Houses shall be determined by Yeas and Nays, and the Names of the Persons voting for and against the Bill shall be entered on the Journal of each House respectively.  If any Bill shall not be returned by the President within ten Days (Sundays excepted) after it shall have been presented to him, the Same shall be a Law, in like Manner as if he had signed it, unless the Congress by their Adjournment prevent its Return, in which Case it shall not be a Law.

Every Order, Resolution, or Vote to which the Concurrence of the Senate and House of Representatives may be necessary (except on a question of Adjournment) shall be presented to the President of the United States;  and before the Same shall take Effect, shall be approved by him, or being disapproved by him, shall be repassed by two thirds of the Senate and House of Representatives, according to the Rules and Limitations prescribed in the Case of a Bill.

SECTION 8.   The Congress shall have Power To lay and collect Taxes, Duties, Imposts and Excises, to pay the Debts and provide for the common Defence and general Welfare of the United States;  but all Duties, Imposts and Excises shall be uniform throughout the United States;

To borrow Money on the Credit of the United States;

To regulate Commerce with foreign Nations, and among the several States, and with the Indian Tribes;

To establish an uniform Rule of Naturalization, and uniform Laws on the subject of Bankruptcies throughout the United States;

To coin Money, regulate the Value thereof, and of foreign Coin, and fix the Standard of Weights and Measures;

To provide for the Punishment of counterfeiting the Securities and current Coin of the United States;

To establish Post Offices and post Roads;

To promote the Progress of Science and useful Arts, by securing for limited Times to Authors and Inventors the exclusive Right to their respective Writings and Discoveries;

To constitute Tribunals inferior to the supreme Court;

To define and punish Piracies and Felonies committed on the high Seas, and Offenses against the Law of Nations:

To declare War, grant Letters of Marque and Reprisal, and make Rules concerning Captures on Land and Water;

To raise and support Armies, but no Appropriation of Money to that Use shall be for a longer Term than two Years;

To provide and maintain a Navy;

To make Rules for the Government and Regulation of the land and naval Forces;

To provide for calling forth the Militia to execute the Laws of the Union, suppress Insurrections and repel Invasions;

To provide for organizing, arming, and disciplining the Militia, and for governing such Part of them as may be employed in the Service of the United States, reserving to the States respectively, the Appointment of the Officers, and the Authority of training the Militia according to the discipline prescribed by Congress.

To exercise exclusive Legislation in all Cases whatsoever, over such District (not exceeding ten Miles square) as may, by Cession of particular States, and the acceptance of Congress, become the Seat of the Government of the United States, and to exercise like Authority over all Places purchased by the Consent of the Legislature of the State in which the Same shall be, for the Erection of Forts, Magazines, Arsenals, dock-Yards, and other needful Buildings;—And

To make all Laws which shall be necessary and proper for carrying into Execution the foregoing Powers, and all other Powers vested by this Constitution in the Government of the United States, or in any Department or Officer thereof.

SECTION 9.  The Migration or Importation of such Persons as any of the States now existing shall think proper to admit, shall not be prohibited by the Congress prior to the Year one thousand eight hundred and eight, but a Tax or duty may be imposed on such Importation, not exceeding ten dollars for each Person.

The privilege of the Writ of Habeas Corpus shall not be suspended, unless when in Cases of Rebellion or Invasion the public Safety may require it.

No Bill of Attainder or ex post facto Law shall be passed.

No capitation, or other direct, Tax shall be laid, unless in Proportion to the Census or Enumeration herein before directed to be taken.

No Tax or Duty shall be laid on Articles exported from any State.

No Preference shall be given by any Regulation of Commerce or Revenue to the Ports of one State over those of another; nor shall Vessels bound to, or from, one State, be obliged to enter, clear, or pay Duties in another.

No Money shall be drawn from the Treasury, but in Consequence of Appropriations made by Law; and a regular Statement and Account of the Receipts and Expenditures of all public Money shall be published from time to time.

No Title of Nobility shall be granted by the United States: And no Person holding any Office of Profit or Trust under them, shall, without the Consent of the Congress, accept of any present, Emolument, Office, or Title, of any kind whatever, from any King, Prince, or foreign State.

SECTION 10.   No State shall enter into any Treaty, Alliance, or Confederation; grant Letters of Marque and Reprisal; coin Money; emit Bills of Credit; make any Thing but gold and silver Coin a Tender in Payment of Debts; pass any Bill of Attainder, ex post facto Law, or Law impairing the Obligation of Contracts, or grant any Title of Nobility.

No State shall, without the Consent of the Congress, lay any Imposts or Duties on Imports or Exports, except what may be absolutely necessary for executing its inspection Laws: and the net Produce of all Duties and Imposts, laid by any State on Imports or Exports, shall be for the Use of the Treasury of the United States; and all such Laws shall be subject to the Revision and Controul of the Congress.

No State shall, without the Consent of Congress, lay any duty of Tonnage, keep Troops, or Ships of War in time of Peace, enter into any Agreement or Compact with another State, or with a foreign Power, or engage in War, unless actually invaded, or in such imminent Danger as will not admit of delay.

## ARTICLE II

SECTION 1.   The executive Power shall be vested in a President of the United States of America.   He shall hold his Office during the Term of four Years, and, together with the Vice President, chosen for the same Term, be elected, as follows

Each State shall appoint, in such Manner as the Legislature thereof may direct, a Number of Electors, equal to the whole Number of Senators and Representatives to which the State may be entitled in the Congress: but no Senator or Representative, or Person holding an Office of Trust or Profit under the United States, shall be appointed an Elector.

The Electors shall meet in their respective States, and vote by Ballot for two persons, of whom one at least shall not be an Inhabitant of the same State with themselves.   And they shall make a List of all the Persons voted for, and of the Number of Votes for each; which List they shall sign and certify, and transmit sealed to the Seat of the Government of the United States, directed to the President of the Senate.   The President of the Senate shall, in the Presence of the Senate and House of Representatives, open all the Certificates, and the Votes shall then be counted.   The Person having the greatest Number of Votes shall be the President, if such Number be a Majority of the whole Number of Electors appointed; and if there be more than one who have such Majority, and have an equal Number of Votes, then the House of Representatives shall immediately chuse by Ballot one of them for President; and if no Person have a Majority, then from the five highest on the List the said House shall in like Manner chuse the President. But in chusing the President, the Votes shall be taken by States, the Representation from each State having one Vote; A quorum for this Purpose shall consist of a Member or Members from two thirds of the States, and a Majority of all the States shall be necessary to a Choice. In every Case, after the Choice of the President, the Person having the greatest Number of Votes of Electors shall be the Vice President. But if there should remain two or more who have equal Votes, the Senate shall chuse from them by Ballot the Vice President.

The Congress may determine the Time of chusing the Electors, and the Day on which they shall give their Votes; which Day shall be the same throughout the United States.

No person except a natural born Citizen, or a Citizen of the United States, at the time of the Adoption of this Constitution, shall be eligible to the Office of President; neither shall any Person be eligible to that Office who shall not have attained to the Age of thirty-five Years, and been fourteen Years a Resident within the United States.

In Case of the Removal of the President from Office, or of his Death, Resignation, or Inability to discharge the Powers and Duties of the said Office, the same shall devolve on the Vice President, and the Congress may by Law provide for the Case of Removal, Death, Resignation or Inability, both of the President and Vice President, declaring what Officer shall then act as President, and such Officer shall act accordingly, until the Disability be removed, or a President shall be elected.

The President shall, at stated Times, receive for his Services, a Compensation, which shall neither be encreased nor diminished during the Period for which he shall have been elected, and he shall not receive within that Period any other Emolument from the United States, or any of them.

Before he enter on the Execution of his Office, he shall take the following Oath or Affirmation: "I do solemnly swear (or affirm) that I will faithfully execute the Office of President of the United States, and will to the best of my Ability, preserve, protect and defend the Constitution of the United States."

SECTION 2. The President shall be Commander in Chief of the Army and Navy of the United States, and of the Militia of the several States, when called into the actual Service of the United States; he may require the Opinion in writing, of the principal Officer in each of the executive Departments, upon any subject relating to the Duties of their respective Offices, and he shall have Power to Grant Reprieves and Pardons for Offenses against the United States, except in Cases of Impeachment.

He shall have Power, by and with the Advice and Consent of the Senate, to make Treaties, provided two thirds of the Senators present concur; and he shall nominate, and by and with the Advice and Consent of the Senate, shall appoint Ambassadors, other public Ministers and Consuls, Judges of the supreme Court, and all other Officers of the United States, whose Appointments are not herein otherwise provided for, and which shall be established by Law: but the Congress may by Law vest the Appointment of such inferior Officers, as they think proper, in the President alone, in the Courts of Law, or in the Heads of Departments.

The President shall have Power to fill up all Vacancies that may happen during the Recess of the Senate, by granting Commissions which shall expire at the End of their next Session.

SECTION 3.   He shall from time to time give to the Congress Information of the State of the Union, and recommend to their Consideration such Measures as he shall judge necessary and expedient; he may, on extraordinary Occasions, convene both Houses, or either of them, and in Case of Disagreement between them, with Respect to the Time of Adjournment, he may adjourn them to such Time as he shall think proper; he shall receive Ambassadors and other public Ministers; he shall take Care that the Laws be faithfully executed, and shall Commission all the Officers of the United States.

SECTION 4.   The President, Vice President and all civil Officers of the United States, shall be removed from Office on Impeachment for, and Conviction of, Treason, Bribery, or other high Crimes and Misdemeanors.

## ARTICLE III

SECTION 1.   The judicial Power of the United States, shall be vested in one supreme Court, and in such inferior Courts as the Congress may from time to time ordain and establish.  The Judges, both of the supreme and inferior Courts, shall hold their Offices during good Behaviour, and shall, at stated Times, receive for their Services a Compensation which shall not be diminished during their Continuance in Office.

SECTION 2.   The judicial Power shall extend to all Cases, in Law and Equity, arising under this Constitution, the Laws of the United States, and Treaties made, or which shall be made, under their Authority;—to all Cases affecting Ambassadors, other public Ministers and Consuls;—to all Cases of admiralty and maritime Jurisdiction; —to Controversies to which the United States shall be a Party;—to Controversies between two or more States;—between a State and Citizens of another State;—between Citizens of different States;—between Citizens of the same State claiming Lands under Grants of different States, and between a State, or the Citizens thereof, and foreign States, Citizens or Subjects.

In all Cases affecting Ambassadors, other public Ministers and Consuls, and those in which a State shall be Party, the supreme Court shall have original Jurisdiction. In all the other Cases before mentioned, the supreme Court shall have appellate Jurisdiction, both as to Law and Fact, with such Exceptions, and under such Regulations as the Congress shall make.

The trial of all Crimes, except in Cases of Impeachment, shall be by Jury; and such Trial shall be held in the State where the said Crimes shall have been committed; but when not committed within any State, the Trial shall be at such Place or Places as the Congress may by Law have directed.

SECTION 3. Treason against the United States, shall consist only in levying War against them, or in adhering to their Enemies, giving them Aid and Comfort. No Person shall be convicted of Treason unless on the Testimony of two Witnesses to the same overt Act, or on Confession in open Court.

The Congress shall have power to declare the Punishment of Treason, but no Attainder of Treason shall work Corruption of Blood, or Forfeiture except during the Life of the Person attainted.

## ARTICLE IV

SECTION 1. Full Faith and Credit shall be given in each State to the public Acts, Records, and judicial Proceedings of every other State. And the Congress may by general Laws prescribe the Manner in which such Acts, Records and Proceedings shall be proved, and the Effect thereof.

SECTION 2. The Citizens of each State shall be entitled to all Privileges and Immunities of Citizens in the several States.

A Person charged in any State with Treason, Felony, or other Crime, who shall flee from Justice, and be found in another State, shall on demand of the executive Authority of the State from which he fled, be delivered up, to be removed to the State having Jurisdiction of the Crime.

No Person held to Service or Labour in one State, under the Laws thereof, escaping into another, shall, in Consequence of any Law or Regulation therein, be discharged from such Service or Labour, but shall be delivered up on Claim of the Party to whom such Service or Labour may be due.

SECTION 3. New States may be admitted by the Congress into this Union; but no new State shall be formed or erected within the

Jurisdiction of any other State; nor any State be formed by the Junction of two or more States, or parts of States, without the Consent of the Legislatures of the States concerned as well as of the Congress.

The Congress shall have Power to dispose of and make all needful Rules and Regulations respecting the Territory or other Property belonging to the United States; and nothing in this Constitution shall be so construed as to Prejudice any Claims of the United States, or of any particular State.

SECTION 4. The United States shall guarantee to every State in this Union a Republican Form of Government, and shall protect each of them against Invasion; and on Application of the Legislature, or of the Executive (when the Legislature cannot be convened) against domestic Violence.

## ARTICLE V

The Congress, whenever two thirds of both Houses shall deem it necessary, shall propose Amendments to this Constitution, or, on the Application of the Legislatures of two thirds of the several States, shall call a Convention for proposing Amendments, which, in either Case, shall be valid to all Intents and Purposes, as part of this Constitution, when ratified by the Legislatures of three fourths of the several States, or by Conventions in three fourths thereof, as the one or the other Mode of Ratification may be proposed by the Congress; Provided that no Amendment which may be made prior to the Year One thousand eight hundred and eight shall in any Manner affect the first and fourth Clauses in the Ninth Section of the first Article; and that no State, without its Consent, shall be deprived of its equal Suffrage in the Senate.

## ARTICLE VI

All Debts contracted and Engagements entered into, before the Adoption of this Constitution, shall be as valid against the United States under this Constitution, as under the Confederation.

This Constitution, and the Laws of the United States which shall be made in Pursuance thereof; and all Treaties made, or which shall be made, under the Authority of the United States, shall be the supreme Law of the Land; and the Judges in every State shall be bound thereby, any Thing in the Constitution or Laws of any State to the Contrary notwithstanding.

The Senators and Representatives before mentioned, and the Members of the several State Legislatures, and all executive and judicial Officers, both of the United States and of the several States, shall be bound by Oath or Affirmation, to support this Constitution; but no religious Test shall ever be required as a Qualification to any Office or public Trust under the United States.

## ARTICLE VII

The Ratification of the Conventions of nine States shall be sufficient for the Establishment of this Constitution between the States so ratifying the Same.[a]

Done in Convention by the Unanimous Consent of the States present the Seventeenth Day of September in the Year of our Lord one thousand seven hundred and Eighty seven and of the Independence of the United States of America the Twelfth. In Witness whereof We have hereunto subscribed our Names. [Signatures omitted.]

ARTICLES IN ADDITION TO, AND AMENDMENT OF, THE CONSTITUTION OF THE UNITED STATES OF AMERICA, PROPOSED BY CONGRESS, AND RATIFIED BY THE LEGISLATURES OF THE SEVERAL STATES, PURSUANT TO THE FIFTH ARTICLE OF THE ORIGINAL CONSTITUTION.

## AMENDMENT I

Congress shall make no law respecting an establishment of religion, or prohibiting the free exercise thereof; or abridging the freedom of speech, or of the press; or the right of the people peaceably to assemble, and to petition the Government for a redress of grievances.

## AMENDMENT II

A well regulated Militia, being necessary to the security of a free State, the right of the people to keep and bear Arms, shall not be infringed.

## AMENDMENT III

No Soldier shall, in time of peace be quartered in any house, without the consent of the Owner, nor in time of war, but in a manner to be prescribed by law.

## AMENDMENT IV

The right of the people to be secure in their persons, houses, papers, and effects, against unreasonable searches and seizures, shall not be violated, and no Warrants shall issue, but upon probable cause, supported by Oath or affirmation, and particularly describing the place to be searched, and the persons or things to be seized.

[a] By July 26, 1788, eleven states had ratified the Constitution. On September 13, 1788, the Continental Congress (which had continued to function at irregular intervals) passed a resolution to put the new Constitution into operation. The first Wednesday, or January 17, 1789, was fixed as the day for choosing presidential electors, the first Wednesday of February for the meeting of electors, and the first Wednesday of March, i. e., March 4, 1789, for the opening of the new Congress.—Ed.

## AMENDMENT V

No person shall be held to answer for a capital, or otherwise infamous crime, unless on a presentment or indictment of a Grand Jury, except in cases arising in the land or naval forces, or in the Militia, when in actual service in time of War or public danger; nor shall any person be subject for the same offence to be twice put in jeopardy of life or limb; nor shall be compelled in any criminal case to be a witness against himself, nor be deprived of life, liberty, or property, without due process of law; nor shall private property be taken for public use, without just compensation.

## AMENDMENT VI

In all criminal prosecutions, the accused shall enjoy the right to a speedy and public trial, by an impartial jury of the State and district wherein the crime shall have been committed, which district shall have been previously ascertained by law, and to be informed of the nature and cause of the accusation; to be confronted with the witnesses against him; to have compulsory process for obtaining witnesses in his favor, and to have the Assistance of Counsel for his defence.

## AMENDMENT VII

In suits at common law, where the value in controversy shall exceed twenty dollars, the right of trial by jury shall be preserved, and no fact tried by a jury, shall be otherwise re-examined in any Court of the United States, than according to the rules of the common law.

## AMENDMENT VIII

Excessive bail shall not be required, nor excessive fines imposed, nor cruel and unusual punishments inflicted.

## AMENDMENT IX

The enumeration in the Constitution, of certain rights, shall not be construed to deny or disparage others retained by the people.

## AMENDMENT X

The powers not delegated to the United States by the Constitution, nor prohibited by it to the States, are reserved to the States respectively, or to the people.

## AMENDMENT XI [1798]

The Judicial power of the United States shall not be construed to extend to any suit in law or equity, commenced or prosecuted against one of the United States by Citizens of another State, or by Citizens or Subjects of any Foreign State.

## AMENDMENT XII [1804]

The Electors shall meet in their respective states and vote by ballot for President and Vice President, one of whom, at least, shall not
be an inhabitant of the same state with themselves; they shall name
in their ballots the person voted for as President, and in distinct ballots the person voted for as Vice President, and they shall make distinct lists of all persons voted for as President, and of all persons
voted for as Vice President, and of the number of votes for each,
which lists they shall sign and certify, and transmit sealed to the seat
of the government of the United States, directed to the President of
the Senate;—The President of the Senate shall, in presence of the
Senate and House of Representatives, open all the certificates and the
votes shall then be counted;—The person having the greatest number
of votes for President, shall be the President, if such number be a
majority of the whole number of Electors appointed; and if no person
have such majority, then from the persons having the highest numbers not exceeding three on the list of those voted for as President,
the House of Representatives shall choose immediately, by ballot,
the President. But in choosing the President, the votes shall be taken
by states, the representation from each state having one vote; a
quorum for this purpose shall consist of a member or members from
two-thirds of the states, and a majority of all the states shall be necessary to a choice. And if the House of Representatives shall not
choose a President whenever the right of choice shall devolve upon
them, before the fourth day of March next following, then the Vice
President shall act as President, as in the case of the death or other
constitutional disability of the President.—The person having the
greatest number of votes as Vice President, shall be the Vice President, if such number be a majority of the whole number of Electors
appointed, and if no person have a majority, then from the two highest numbers on the list, the Senate shall choose the Vice President;
a quorum for the purpose shall consist of two-thirds of the whole
number of Senators, and a majority of the whole number shall be
necessary to a choice. But no person constitutionally ineligible to
the office of President shall be eligible to that of Vice President of the
United States.

## AMENDMENT XIII [1865]

SECTION 1. Neither slavery nor involuntary servitude, except
as a punishment for crime whereof the party shall have been duly
convicted, shall exist within the United States, or any place subject
to their jurisdiction.

SECTION 2. Congress shall have power to enforce this article by
appropriate legislation.

## AMENDMENT XIV [1868]

SECTION 1.   All persons born or naturalized in the United States, and subject to the jurisdiction thereof, are citizens of the United States and of the State wherein they reside.   No State shall make or enforce any law which shall abridge the privileges or immunities of citizens of the United States;  nor shall any State deprive any person of life, liberty, or property, without due process of law;  nor deny to any person within its jurisdiction the equal protection of the laws.

SECTION 2.   Representatives shall be apportioned among the several States according to their respective numbers, counting the whole number of persons in each State, excluding Indians not taxed. But when the right to vote at any election for the choice of electors for President and Vice President of the United States, Representatives in Congress, the Executive and Judicial officers of a State, or the members of the Legislature thereof, is denied to any of the male inhabitants of such State, being twenty-one years of age, and citizens of the United States, or in any way abridged, except for participation in rebellion, or other crime, the basis of representation therein shall be reduced in the proportion which the number of such male citizens shall bear to the whole number of male citizens twenty-one years of age in such State.

SECTION 3.   No person shall be a Senator or Representative in Congress, or elector of President and Vice President, or hold any office, civil or military, under the United States, or under any State, who, having previously taken an oath, as a member of Congress, or as an officer of the United States, or as a member of any State legislature, or as an executive or judicial officer of any State, to support the Constitution of the United States, shall have engaged in insurrection or rebellion against the same, or given aid or comfort to the enemies thereof.   But Congress may by a vote of two-thirds of each House, remove such disability.

SECTION 4.   The validity of the public debt of the United States, authorized by law, including debts incurred for payment of pensions and bounties for services in suppressing insurrection or rebellion shall not be questioned.   But neither the United States nor any State shall assume or pay any debt or obligation incurred in aid of insurrection or rebellion against the United States, or any claim for the loss or emancipation of any slaves;  but all such debts, obligations and claims shall be held illegal and void.

SECTION 5.   The Congress shall have power to enforce, by appropriate legislation, the provisions of this article.

## AMENDMENT XV [1870]

SECTION 1.  The right of citizens of the United States to vote shall not be denied or abridged by the United States or by any State on account of race, color, or previous condition of servitude.

SECTION 2.  The Congress shall have power to enforce this article by appropriate legislation.

## AMENDMENT XVI [1913]

The Congress shall have power to lay and collect taxes on incomes, from whatever source derived, without apportionment among the several States, and without regard to any census or enumeration.

## AMENDMENT XVII [1913]

The Senate of the United States shall be composed of two Senators from each State, elected by the people thereof, for six years; and each Senator shall have one vote.  The electors in each State shall have the qualifications requisite for electors of the most numerous branch of the State legislatures.

When vacancies happen in the representation of any State in the Senate, the executive authority of such State shall issue writs of election to fill such vacancies: *Provided,* That the legislature of any State may empower the executive thereof to make temporary appointments until the people fill the vacancies by election as the legislature may direct.

This amendment shall not be so construed as to affect the election or term of any Senator chosen before it becomes valid as part of the Constitution.

## AMENDMENT XVIII [1919]

SECTION 1.  After one year from the ratification of this article the manufacture, sale, or transportation of intoxicating liquors within, the importation thereof into, or the exportation thereof from the United States and all territory subject to the jurisdiction thereof for beverage purposes is hereby prohibited.

SECTION 2.  The Congress and the several States shall have concurrent power to enforce this article by appropriate legislation.

SECTION 3.  This article shall be inoperative unless it shall have been ratified as an amendment to the Constitution by the legislatures of the several States, as provided in the Constitution, within seven years from the date of the submission hereof to the States by the Congress.

## AMENDMENT XIX [1920]

The right of citizens of the United States to vote shall not be denied or abridged by the United States or by any State on account of sex.

Congress shall have power to enforce this article by appropriate legislation.

## AMENDMENT XX [1933]

SECTION 1.   The terms of the President and Vice President shall end at noon on the 20th day of January, and the terms of Senators and Representatives at noon on the 3d day of January, of the years in which such terms would have ended if this article had not been ratified; and the terms of their successors shall then begin.

SECTION 2.   The Congress shall assemble at least once in every year, and such meeting shall begin at noon on the 3d day of January, unless they shall by law appoint a different day.

SECTION 3.   If, at the time fixed for the beginning of the term of the President, the President elect shall have died, the Vice President elect shall become President.   If a President shall not have been chosen before the time fixed for the beginning of his term, or if the President elect shall have failed to qualify, then the Vice President elect shall act as President until a President shall have qualified; and the Congress may by law provide for the case wherein neither a President elect nor a Vice President elect shall have qualified, declaring who shall then act as President, or the manner in which one who is to act shall be selected, and such person shall act accordingly until a President or Vice President shall have qualified.

SECTION 4.   The Congress may by law provide for the case of the death of any of the persons from whom the House of Representatives may choose a President whenever the right of choice shall have devolved upon them, and for the case of the death of any of the persons from whom the Senate may choose a Vice President whenever the right of choice shall have devolved upon them.

SECTION 5.   Sections 1 and 2 shall take effect on the 15th day of October following the ratification of this article.

SECTION 6.   This article shall be inoperative unless it shall have been ratified as an amendment to the Constitution by the legislatures of three-fourths of the several States within seven years from the date of its submission.

## AMENDMENT XXI [1933]

SECTION 1.   The eighteenth article of amendment to the Constitution of the United States is hereby repealed.

SECTION 2.  The transportation or importation into any State, Territory, or Possession of the United States for delivery or use therein of intoxicating liquors, in violation of the laws thereof, is hereby prohibited.

SECTION 3.  This article shall be inoperative unless it shall have been ratified as an amendment to the Constitution by conventions in the several States, as provided in the Constitution, within seven years from the date of the submission hereof to the States by the Congress.

## AMENDMENT XXII [1951]

SECTION 1.  No person shall be elected to the office of the President more than twice, and no person who has held the office of President, or acted as President, for more than two years of a term to which some other person was elected President shall be elected to the office of the President more than once.  But this Article shall not apply to any person holding the office of President when this Article was proposed by the Congress, and shall not prevent any person who may be holding the office of President, or acting as President, during the term within which this Article becomes operative from holding the office of President or acting as President during the remainder of such term.

SECTION 2.  This article shall be inoperative unless it shall have been ratified as an amendment to the Constitution by the legislatures of three-fourths of the several States within seven years from the date of its submission to the States by the Congress.

## AMENDMENT XXIII [1961]

SECTION 1.  The District constituting the seat of Government of the United States shall appoint in such manner as Congress may direct:

A number of electors of President and Vice President equal to the whole number of Senators and Representatives in Congress to which the District would be entitled if it were a State, but in no event more than the least populous State; they shall be in addition to those appointed by the States, but they shall be considered, for the purposes of the election of President and Vice President, to be electors appointed by a State; and they shall meet in the District and perform such duties as provided by the twelfth article of amendment.

SECTION 2.  The Congress shall have power to enforce this article by appropriate legislation.

## AMENDMENT XXIV [1964]

SECTION 1.  The right of citizens of the United States to vote in any primary or other election for President or Vice President, for electors for President or Vice President, or for Senator or Representative in Congress, shall not be denied or abridged by the United States or any State by reason of failure to pay any poll tax or other tax.

SECTION 2. The Congress shall have power to enforce this article by appropriate legislation.

## AMENDMENT XXV [1967]

SECTION 1. In case of the removal of the President from office or of his death or resignation, the Vice President shall become President.

SECTION 2. Whenever there is a vacancy in the office of the Vice President, the President shall nominate a Vice President who shall take office upon confirmation by a majority vote of both Houses of Congress.

SECTION 3. Whenever the President transmits to the President pro tempore of the Senate and the Speaker of the House of Representatives his written declaration that he is unable to discharge the powers and duties of his office, and until he transmits to them a written declaration to the contrary, such powers and duties shall be discharged by the Vice President as Acting President.

SECTION 4. Whenever the Vice President and a majority of either the principal officers of the executive departments or of such other body as Congress may by law provide, transmit to the President pro tempore of the Senate and the Speaker of the House of Representatives their written declaration that the President is unable to discharge the powers and duties of his office, the Vice President shall immediately assume the powers and duties of the office as Acting President.

Thereafter, when the President transmits to the President pro tempore of the Senate and the Speaker of the House of Representatives his written declaration that no inability exists, he shall resume the powers and duties of his office unless the Vice President and a majority of either the principal officers of the executive department or of such other body as Congress may by law provide, transmit within four days to the President pro tempore of the Senate and the Speaker of the House of Representatives their written declaration that the President is unable to discharge the powers and duties of his office. Thereupon Congress shall decide the issue, assembling within forty-eight hours for that purpose if not in session. If the Congress, within twenty-one days after receipt of the latter written declaration, or, if Congress is not in session, within twenty-one days after Congress is required to assemble, determines by two-thirds vote of both Houses that the President is unable to discharge the powers and duties of his office, the Vice President shall continue to discharge the same as Acting President; otherwise, the President shall resume the powers and duties of his office.

## AMENDMENT XXVI [1971]

SECTION 1. The right of citizens of the United States, who are eighteen years of age or older, to vote shall not be denied or abridged by the United States or by any State on account of age.

SECTION 2. The Congress shall have power to enforce this article by appropriate legislation.

## AMENDMENT XXVII (Proposed)

SECTION 1. Equality of rights under the law shall not be denied or abridged by the United States or by any state on account of sex.

SECTION 2. The Congress shall have the power to enforce, by appropriate legislation, the provisions of this article.

SECTION 3. This amendment shall take effect two years after the date of ratification.

## NOTES AND QUESTIONS

1. What is the structural organization of the original document of 1787? Is it that basically, but not completely, each of the seven articles has its own subject area? Write out a brief description of the basic subject area for each of the seven articles.

2. Did the framers provide any one place where they set forth the entire powers of the states and their governments? The powers of the federal government? What are the likely consequences of such an apportionment of powers?

3. The framers divided the federal government into three separate and independent branches—the legislative, the excutive and the judiciary—and assigned a particular group of powers to each division. Identify the powers to be exercised by each branch of government. What reason accounts for the "separation of powers"? Distinguish the "separation of powers" from "checks and balances." Are these wise ideas? If you were creating a government, how would you do it? Why?

4. It is sometimes said that with one very important exception congress has no legislative powers except those that expressly are "herein granted" by the constitution. Explain the constitutional reasons why a person would make this statement and identify the "one very important exception." Do you agree?

5. Describe the way in which a bill would become a constitutionally valid law in the actual course of legislation. To what extent is the "separation of powers" involved? Indicate as many as you can of the president's functions in the legislative process. The judiciary's.

6. Give examples of cases that come under the jurisdiction of the federal courts. What, exactly, is the "judicial power"?

7. Article IV basically provides for constitutional relations between the states and the federal government and between the states themselves. What relations are provided? What are some of the limitations on the

"full faith and credit" clause? What procedure must Puerto Rico follow in order to become a state?

8. Article V basically provides two ways of amending the constitution. Describe each. Has each method been used in the past? Why or why not?

9. Article VI basically provides for the vindication of federal law. What methods are set forth? Are they adequate? "The powers of the national government are limited, but within the field of its power it is supreme, and this supremacy the state courts are bound to uphold." Explain the constitutional meaning and the importance of this quotation.

10. What are the limitations on the powers of the federal government that are found in the original constitution of 1787? What is the difference between a bill of attainder and an ex post facto law? What is a "writ of habeas corpus" and how does it function?

11. The first ten amendments—the Bill of Rights—were added on December 15, 1791. Analyze them carefully. Which amendments provide "substantive" protections and which provide "procedural" protections? Is the use of wire taps by police to obtain evidence a violation of any amendment; why or why not? Electronic eavesdropping?

12. Analyze the tenth amendment and the constitutional validity and significance of the statement: "The federal government is a government having only specifically delegated powers." What is the meaning of the statement: "The constitution sets up a limited government"? What are the constitutional limitations on government?

13. Evaluate the constitutional validity of this statement: "The fundamental civil and political rights of citizens stem from their State and not from their United States citizenship."

14. There are four fundamental categories relevant to the constitutional scheme of allocating power: (1) powers to be exercised exclusively by the federal government; (2) powers that may be exercised concurrently by the states and federal government; (3) powers to be exercised exclusively by the states, and (4) the denial of power and prohibiting their exercise by either federal governments, the states, or both. Identify the powers (or denials) that fall into each of the four categories and give your reasons for classifying each of them.

# Chapter I

# THE SUPREME COURT AND THE AMERICAN
# LEGAL SYSTEM

---

## INTRODUCTION

---

The legal systems of the United States baffle most foreign visitors. And not a few American citizens stand in awe of them. There is such a multiplicity of courts, laws and jurisdictions that even the perceptive observer frequently becomes lost in the legal maze. There are the legal systems, and subsystems, of the Fifty States. Then, of course, there are the Federal Court jurisdictions, the Federal administrative agencies and also the Military. Legal terminology appears impenetrable, and the law books foreboding. But, to some, what appears even more bewildering is the profuse expansion of American law, intruding during the last 100 years into almost every facet of everyday life. This has become particularly true with the rise of modern administrative agencies, some would say bureaucracies, which make their appearances at all levels: federal, state, and local.

The task of harnessing the fifty state-court systems and the federal court system, plus all the administrative agencies, state and federal, into a unified whole is difficult indeed. Yet, somehow, the American legal systems do manage to resolve their manifold complexities and to preserve the inner dynamics of an evolving American society. However, the niceties and refinements of the legal machinery must be fully comprehended to understand its total pervasiveness. But, an attempt to reduce the intricacies of the legal systems to one accurate summary would require many books and is a task fraught with peril. Perhaps, instead, a canvass of a few highpoints will suffice for the purposes at hand.

The Constitution's first three articles are devoted to setting up the federal legislature, the executive and the judiciary. These are the separate and coordinate branches of American government. The founding fathers were careful to provide for a separate and independent court system for the new federal government. Equally important, they determined that Congress might shape its contours to meet changing needs of the day. Early experiences, first in the colonies, and then under the Articles of Confederation, had taught them the wisdom of this course.

The following selection presents a simplified description of our federal court system. One reason why it is essential that students understand our court systems is that they can better evaluate the law cases that follow.

---

## THE UNITED STATES COURTS

Committee on the Judiciary, 1975.
House of Representatives, U.S. Congress.

The position of the United States courts in our governmental organization is not difficult to understand when that organization is seen as a whole. Our government is a dual one—Federal and State—and the Federal Government in turn has three separate branches—the Legislative, the Executive, and the Judicial. The United States courts constitute the Judicial Branch of the Federal Government. Thus, the powers of the United States courts are first of all limited as Federal powers—they can exercise only those powers granted by the United States Constitution to the Federal Government—and secondly are limited as judicial—they cannot exercise powers belonging to the Legislative or Executive Branches of the Government.

### THE JUDICIAL BRANCH

The Constitution assures the equality and independence of the Judicial Branch from the Legislative and Executive Branches. Although Federal judges are appointed by the President of the United States with the advice and consent of the Senate, and although funds for the operation of the courts are appropriated by the Congress, the independence of the United States courts is provided for in three respects:

*First,* under the Constitution these courts can be called upon to exercise only judicial powers and to perform only judicial work. Judicial power and judicial work involve essentially the application and interpretation of the law in the decision of real differences, that is, in the language of the Constitution, the decision of "Cases" and "Controversies." The courts cannot be called upon to make laws—the function of the Legislative Department—nor to enforce and execute laws—the function of the Executive Department.

*Second,* Federal judges "hold their Office during good Behavior" that is, as long as they desire to be judges and perform their work. They can be removed from office against their will only by impeachment.

*Third,* the Constitution provides that the "Compensation" of Federal judges "shall not be diminished during their continuance in office." Neither the President nor the Congress can reduce the salary of a Federal judge.

These three provisions—for judicial work only, for holding office during good behavior, and for undiminished compensation—are designed to assure judges of independence from outside influence so that their decisions may be completely impartial.

## STATE AND UNITED STATES COURT SYSTEMS

Throughout the United States there are two sets of judicial systems. One set is that of the State and local courts established in each State under the authority of the State government. The other is that of the United States courts set up under the authority of the Constitution by the Congress of the United States.

The State courts have general, unlimited power to decide almost every type of case, subject only to the limitations of State law. They are located in every town and county and are the tribunals with which citizens most often have contact. The great bulk of legal business concerning divorce and the probate of estates and all other matters except those assigned to the United States courts is handled by these State courts.

The United States courts, on the other hand, have power to decide only those cases in which the Constitution gives them authority. They are located principally in the larger cities. The controversies in only a few carefully selected types of cases set forth in the Constitution can be heard in the United States courts.

## CASES WHICH THE UNITED STATES
## COURTS CAN DECIDE

The controversies which can be decided in the United States courts are set forth in section 2 of Article III of the United States Constitution. These are first of all "Controversies to which the United States shall be a party," that is, cases in which the United States Government itself or one of its officers is either suing someone else or is being sued by another party. Obviously it would be inappropriate that the United States Government depend upon the State governments for the courts in which to decide controversies to which it is a party.

Secondly, the United States courts have power to decide cases where State courts are inappropriate or might be suspected of partiality. Thus, Federal judicial power extends "to Controversies between two or more States; between a State and Citizens of another State; between Citizens of different States; between Citizens of the same State claiming Lands under Grants of different States, . . .." If the State of Missouri sues the State of Illinois for pollution of the Mississippi River, the courts of either Missouri or Illinois would be inappropriate and perhaps not impartial forums. These suits may be decided in the United States courts. At various times State feeling in our country has run high, and it has seemed better to avoid any

Morris—Const. & Am.Educ. 2d ACB—3

suspicion of favoritism by vesting power to decide these controversies in the United States courts.

State courts are also inappropriate in "Cases affecting Ambassadors, other public Ministers and Consuls" and in cases "between a State, or the Citizens thereof, and foreign States, Citizens, or Subjects." The United States Government has responsibility for our relations with other nations, and cases involving their representatives or their citizens may affect our foreign relations so that such cases should be decided in the United States courts.

And, thirdly the Constitution provides that the judicial power extends "to all Cases, in Law and Equity, arising under this Constitution, the Laws of the United States, and Treaties made, or which shall be made, under their Authority" and "to all Cases of admiralty and maritime jurisdiction." Under these provisions the United States courts decide cases involving the Constitution, laws enacted by Congress, treaties, or laws relating to navigable waters.

The Constitution declares what cases may be decided in the United States courts. The Congress can and has determined that some of these cases may also be tried in State courts and that others may be tried only in the United States courts. Thus Congress has provided that, with some exceptions, cases arising under the Constitution or laws of the United States or between citizens of different States may be tried in the United States courts only if the amount involved exceeds $10,000 and even then may be tried in either the State or the United States courts. The Congress has also provided that maritime cases and suits against consuls can be tried only in the United States courts. When a State court decides a case involving Federal law, it in a sense acts as a United States court, and its decision on Federal law may be reviewed by the United States Supreme Court.

In any event this discussion should make it clear that the United States courts cannot decide every case which arises, but only those which the Constitution and the laws enacted by the Congress allot to them. And as you may suspect from the length of this discussion, whether a case is one which may be decided by the United States courts is an extremely technical and complicated matter which lawyers and judges frequently spend a great deal of time resolving.

## THE UNITED STATES COURT SYSTEM

The United States court system to which decision of the types of cases just discussed has been entrusted has varied a great deal throughout the history of our country. The Constitution merely provides: "The Judicial Power of the United States, shall be vested in one supreme Court, and in such inferior Courts as the Congress may from time to time ordain and establish." Thus, the only indispensable court is the Supreme Court, and the Congress has from time to time established and abolished various other United States courts.

At the present time the United States court system may be likened to a pyramid. At the apex of the pyramid stands the Supreme Court of the United States, the highest court in the land. On the next level stand the United States courts of appeals, 11 in all. On the next level stand the United States district courts, 94 in all, including the United States District Courts for the District of Columbia and Puerto Rico and the district courts in the Canal Zone, Guam, and the Virgin Islands. The United States Tax Court and, in a sense, certain administrative agencies may be included here because the review of their decisions may be directly in the courts of appeals. Some agency reviews, however, are handled by the district courts.

A person involved in a suit in a United States court may thus proceed through three levels of decision. His case will be heard and decided by one of the courts or agencies on the lower level. If either party is dissatisfied with the decision rendered, he may usually have review of right in one of the courts of appeals. Then, if he is still dissatisfied, but usually only if his case involves a matter of great national importance, he may obtain review in the Supreme Court of the United States.

This pyramidal organization of the courts serves two purposes. First, the Supreme Court and the courts of appeals can correct errors which have been made in the decisions in the trial courts. Secondly, these higher courts can assure uniformity of decision by reviewing cases where two or more lower courts have reached different results. The chart on page 3 shows the organization of the United States courts.

## The Supreme Court

The highest court is the Supreme Court of the United States. It consists of nine Justices, appointed for life by the President with the advice and consent of the United States Senate. One Justice is designated the Chief Justice and he receives a salary of $62,500 a year. The other justices receive $60,000 a year. The officers appointed by the Court include a Clerk to keep its records, a Marshal to maintain order and supervise the administrative affairs of the Court, a Reporter to publish its opinions, and a Librarian to serve the justices and the lawyers of the Supreme Court bar. Additionally the Chief Justice is authorized to appoint an Administrative Assistant.

The court meets on the first Monday of October each year. It continues in session usually until June and receives and disposes of about 5,000 cases each year. Most of these cases are disposed of by the brief decision that the subject matter is either not proper or not of sufficient importance to warrant full Court review. But each year between 200 and 250 cases of great importance and interest are decided on the merits. About half of these decisions are announced in full published opinions.

The official address of the Supreme Court is: The Supreme Court of the United States, Washington, D.C. 20543.

## Courts of Appeals

The intermediate appellate courts in the United States judicial system are the courts of appeals in 11 circuits. Each circuit includes three or more States, except the District of Columbia Circuit. The States of Alaska and Hawaii and the territory of Guam are included in the ninth circuit, Puerto Rico is included in the first circuit, the Virgin Islands in the third circuit, and the Canal Zone in the fifth circuit. Each court consists of between 3 and 15 judges depending upon the amount of work in the circuit, and the judge with the longest service, who has not reached his 70th birthday, is the chief judge. Each judge receives a salary of $42,500 a year. There are now 97 circuit judges.

The 11 United States courts of appeals currently are receiving about 16,500 cases every year. A disappointed suitor in a district court usually has a right to have the decision of his case reviewed by the court of appeals of his circuit. In addition to appeals from the district courts, the courts of appeals receive many cases to review actions of the tax court and various Federal administrative agencies for errors of law.

## District Courts

The United States courts where cases are initially tried and decided are the district courts. There are 94 of these courts, 89 in the 50 States, and one each in the District of Columbia, the Canal Zone, Guam, Puerto Rico, and the Virgin Islands. Each State has at least one court; but many States have two or three districts, and California, Texas, and New York have four districts each. A district itself may be divided into divisions and may have several places where the court hears cases. Each district has from 1 to 27 judges depending upon the volume of cases which must be decided. For each district there is a clerk's office, a United States marshal's office, and one or more bankruptcy judges, United States magistrates, probation officers and court reporters. In addition, there is a United States attorney's office in each district. Further each district court has a plan under which lawyers are provided for poor defendants in criminal cases. To assure adequate service full-time public defenders are appointed in those courts where criminal cases are numerous.

Four hundred district judgeships are authorized by law, and the salary of each judge is $40,000 a year. In districts having two or more judges, the judge senior in service who has not reached 70 years of age is the chief judge. The district courts are currently receiving about 103,500 civil cases, 38,000 criminal cases, and 189,000 bankruptcy cases every year.

Some district courts, namely those in the Canal Zone, Guam, and the Virgin Islands, have jurisdiction over local cases as well as those arising under Federal law. These courts thus differ in several respects from the other 91 United States districts courts. In these places the Federal Government does not share the judicial power as it does with the State governments in the several States, with the local government of the District of Columbia, and with the Commonwealth Government in Puerto Rico. Thus, these courts are not limited to the types of cases defined in the Constitution as part of the Federal judicial power, but decide all types of cases as do State courts. Then, too, the judges in the Canal Zone, Guam and the Virgin Islands are not appointed for life, but for terms of 8 years, and are not protected against diminution of their salaries during their terms of office. These courts may also be given duties which are not strictly judicial in nature.

Because of these differences, territorial courts have been called "legislative courts" to distinguish them from the "constitutional courts." The name indicates that these courts have been created, not in the exercise of Congress' power to establish courts under the judiciary article of the Constitution, but under its powers in the legislative article over the Territories and other fields of Federal authority.

## LAW AND PROCEDURE IN THE UNITED STATES COURTS

The organization of the United States courts set up to handle the types of cases designated in the Constitution for decision by the Judicial Branch of the Federal Government has been described. For many years there was much confusion as to whether these types of cases were merely to be decided by a different court system or whether in addition they were to be decided according to different rules of law and a different procedure.

The question of the rule of law to apply in these types of cases was largely determined by the supremacy clause making the Constitution, statutes, and treaties of the United States Government the supreme law of the land. However, until 1938, the United States courts in suits between citizens of different States also purported to apply a general law, not the law of any State; but now it is settled that the law applied in the United States courts is the same as the law which would be applied in a State court in similar cases.

The question of procedure, conversely, was long governed by the rule that the United States courts, except where Federal statutes otherwise provided, followed the procedure of the courts in the State where they were sitting. However, again in 1938, Rules of Civil Procedure prepared by an advisory committee and approved by the Supreme Court became effective to give the United States courts their own rules of practice. And in 1946 Federal Rules of Criminal Procedure prepared in a similar fashion became effective. Both rules of practice have adopted the simplest, most modern, and best procedure and have been models for procedural reform in the States. In 1966 these Rules of Civil and Criminal Procedure were extensively revised and up-dated. Then in 1968 the Supreme Court adopted uniform Rules of Federal Appellate Procedure for the United States Courts of Appeals. The Supreme Court has also approved new Rules of Evidence governing the trial of civil and criminal cases in the United States district courts, and new comprehensive Rules of Procedure in Bankruptcy cases. Rules adopted by the Court must be approved by Congress before they become effective. Thus, today the United States courts decide cases involving citizens of different States according to the same rules of law as would govern the case in a State court, but decide them by Federal procedure.

### Illustration: An Automobile Accident

This whole rather complex problem of the various cases that may be tried in the United States courts may be illustrated for you by the story of an automobile collision. Bill Smith from Chicago, driving his car on an Illinois road, has a collision with another vehicle. Ordinarily no suit arising out of that accident could be tried in a United States court; it would be heard and decided in a State court. But if the other vehicle were an army truck driven by a soldier, Bill Smith may want to sue the United States, or the United States may decide to sue Bill Smith. In either event Bill Smith or the United States may commence a suit in the United States district court in Illinois.

If the other vehicle belonged to a private person who lived in Illinois, Bill Smith or the other owner may sue only in the State court, unless under certain circumstances the suit involved some provision of the Federal statutes or the Federal Constitution. If, on the other hand, the other vehicle belonged to John Jones who lived in St. Louis, Mo., then either John Jones or Bill Smith may sue in a United States district court because they were from different States.

These possible suits have been civil cases brought to compensate the parties for damage done, and it is unlikely that a criminal case brought by the Government would arise. Yet, if either Bill Smith or the other driver had been handling his car so recklessly as to warrant a criminal prosecution for reckless driving, manslaughter, etc., the suit would be brought by the State of Illinois in the State court. Let us suppose, however, that the other driver was in a car which he had stolen in Indiana and had driven into Illinois. Then that driver might be prosecuted by the United States Government in the United States district court under Federal law for transporting a stolen automobile from one State into another.

If either Bill Smith or his adversary is dissatisfied with the decision of the United States district court, he may appeal to a United States court of appeals, and if still dissatisfied after a decision by that court, he may seek review in the United States Supreme Court on questions of Federal law which arose in the proceedings. So you can see how an accident usually gives rise to suits which can be tried in State courts only, but which under special circumstances may be tried or reviewed in the United States courts. . . .

---

## JUDICIAL REVIEW

---

The Supreme Court has the power to make the final decisions in all cases presenting substantial questions about federal law, including constitutional law, whether or not the case involves an interpretation of the law or its proper application. It makes no difference whether the lawsuit was started in the state or federal courts, nor does it matter whether the federal law involved is the Constitution or treaty, or a law passed pursuant to the Constitution or a treaty, or an administrative or executive ruling. The Supreme Court of the United States is the final authority on all questions of federal law. For example, in a case about the marriage of A and B which involved a racially discriminatory state law, the Supreme Court would have to review the work product of a state legislature as well as that of a state court which had earlier passed on the same question, to see whether the statute and its interpretation were unconstitutional. This procedure is known as judicial review because it involves a judicial review of the laws passed by a legislature, either Congress or state, to determine whether they are unconstitutional. Since the Supreme Court has power only to decide "cases," judicial review can be exercised only when the proper "case" is brought before it. Judicial review is practiced by state and federal courts.

Judicial review is one of our bedrock ideas. Thus, it is most important to note that courts in the American legal systems really perform two prime, and different, functions. On the one hand, they decide individual lawsuits granting redress to private parties, or perhaps, punishing violators of law. This type of case constitutes their usual daily fare, and most of the lawsuits simply involve a selection of the governing law and an application of it to the facts of the case. But, on the other hand, the courts also decide cases in which an argument has been made that the law itself is not in keeping with the Constitution, or that the Constitution precludes a particular application of a law. In this second type of case, the courts perform a radically different function, they must determine whether a particular branch of government, say the legislature or the executive, has acted beyond the ambit of its constitutional powers. In these instances, the courts perform a supervisory function over the branches of government. This latter activity is known as judicial review. The court having the power to make the final decision on all questions concerning state constitutional questions is, of course, the highest state court, and the Court having the power to make the final decision on all questions concerning the United States Constitution is, of course, the Supreme Court of the United States. State constitutions, of course, must be consistent with our national Constitution and the United States Supreme Court can decide the cases where there is a conflict between the two. Thus a study of American Constitutional Law tends also to be a study of the Supreme Court of the United States.

The essence of judicial review has been cogently stated by Professor Charles L. Black of the Yale Law School in his interesting book, THE PEOPLE AND THE COURT. He says:

> In the course of a judicial proceeding, it may happen that one of the litigants relies on a statute or other governmental pronouncement which the other litigant contends to be repugnant to some provision of the Constitution. It is the task of the court to determine what the law is. If the Constitution is a law of superior status, then the rule of the Constitution, and not the rule of the statute or other governmental pronouncement, is the correct rule of law for application to the case before the court. The Court, under our system, therefore considers itself bound to follow the rule of the Constitution, and so to treat the other rule as a nullity. (p. 12.) © Charles L. Black, Jr. 1960, The Mac-Millan Company, New York (1960).

Simply put, these notions are the hallmarks of judicial review. Whatever the final consensus of historical opinion about the American civilization, the role of the judiciary in interpreting and applying the Constitution to limit the powers of government will surely be a prime consideration for comment. Judicial review—that is, the power of American courts to set aside national and state legislation as unconstitutional—is one of the outstanding contributions of the United States to the science and art of government. Fundamentally, judicial review really accomplishes three things, each of which is vitally important. First, although the Supreme Court may say only that a law is "not unconstitutional," the public tends to believe that the Court places the stamp of legitimacy upon any law or practice that successfully passes its muster. Secondly, courts serve as a check on the otherwise unbridled power of the other branches of government whenever they seek to trespass onto territory forbidden them by the Constitution as it is interpreted by the Supreme Court. Thirdly, by fearlessly upholding a humane interpretation of our Constitution, the Supreme Court preserves, and requires the other branches of government to observe our great constitutional ideal of human dignity which otherwise might be forgotten.

## WHAT STANDARD OF JUDICIAL REVIEW?

A question about courts declaring laws or governmental actions unconstitutional has troubled some people. Simply put, the question is: what should be the appropriate standard of judicial review whenever a court makes a declaration of unconstitutionality? The usual rule is that legislation is *presumed* to be constitutional by courts, and the person attacking the constitutionality of a law has the burden of showing that the law is unconstitutional. But, according to what standard of unconstitutionality? Should the Supreme Court, or any court be willing to declare laws or governmental actions unconstitutional whenever they *may possibly* be unconstitutional, or when they *may* tend to be; or when they *actually tend* to be; or when, on close balance, they *preponderate* to be; or when they are *clearly and convincingly* shown to be; or only when there can be *absolutely no doubt* that the law or governmental action in question is unconstitutional— "so clear that it is not open to rational question"? Obviously, the role of the courts in our system of government would vary considerably depending which one of these standards is used. For example, courts would be most active under the first standard, declaring many laws and governmental actions unconstitutional, but they would be least active under the last standard when a court would not declare a law or act unconstitutional if there were any possible doubt. Under the last standard, so long as the government's choice could be shown to be rational then that choice would be constitutional. The question is: which standard should be used?

In times past, especially in the nineteenth century, most scholars, and the Supreme Court itself, argued for the last standard—a court should never make a declaration of unconstitutionality unless the matter is "so clear that it is not open to rational question." This rule and the presumption that a law is constitutional permit the widest latitude to other divisions of government, and, it is argued, that this rule is the only appropriate one for judicial review in a democracy. The people elect Congressmen and Presidents, but not Supreme Court Justices; therefore, it is argued, if America is to be ruled by a democracy, rather than by the Supreme Court, the Supreme Court, and other courts too, should declare governmental actions unconstitutional only when they are so clearly unconstitutional that the matter is not open to rational question. There is some merit in this view, but it is not the whole story.

This view has merit because the Constitution does give many powers to the various branches of government, and they are expected to use those powers for the general human welfare of all Americans. It would be intolerable for the Supreme Court to sit in judgment of

every action, trying desperately to find something that was unconstitutional. It simply doesn't do this, and the other branches of government are allowed to interpret their constitutionally delegated powers broadly.

But, the American Constitutional scheme consists of more than a
simple delegation of powers to government. In addition, there are
certain matters which have not been delegated to government, but
which have been retained by the people. There are many "no trespass-
ing" signs in our constitution—areas where government is not allowed.
Indeed, the Constitution expressly denies many powers to government, and that is the whole point of a Bill of Rights. Among others,
it says that the people shall have certain constitutional rights—to
speak, write, publish, read and associate freely—that is, without any
governmental interference. In short, these rights are treasured rights.
Shall the Supreme Court, when reviewing governmental actions dealing with these areas, especially freedom of thought and conscience,
allow the governmental action to stand unless it is so clearly unconstitutional that the matter is not open to rational question? Or should
some other standard of review be used by the Supreme Court in cases
dealing with an American's fundamental rights and liberties?

It is obvious that two general types of issues are presented to the
Supreme Court because of Constitutional structure. First, there is
the type of case where the question is whether the Constitution has
delegated a power to government to deal with a particular subject
matter. For example, under Article I, section 8, of the Constitution
a question can arise whether Congress has power to incorporate a national bank, or to tax gambling, or to regulate business and agriculture
or to pass a law forbidding racial discrimination by motels and restaurants that are serving interstate travellers. The question in each
of these cases is the reach of the delegated constitutional power: does
it include this particular subject matter? Or is this subject matter
solely for state legislation? In this first type of situation the political
process can be relied upon. Lobbyists function and the elected politicians come from the state and are responsive to the people of the
states. For this type of case the standard of review perhaps can appropriately be that the Supreme Court will declare a governmental action
unconstitutional only when the matter is not open to rational question.

But, of course, a second general type of issue is presented to the
Supreme Court. There are cases where the question for decision is
whether an exercise of governmental power, state or federal, is contrary to a person's individual rights and liberties as they are set forth
and protected by the Constitution? For example, the question may be
whether governmental action infringes upon a person's rights to speak,
to read, to publish, or to associate. In these cases, unlike the first
type, the ordinary political processes cannot be relied upon. In a pure
democracy the majority governs. For example, if the majority want-

ed to take away from some citizens the rights of free speech, press and association, then in a pure democracy, the majority can do so. But, that is not possible under the American Constitution. No American's rights to life, liberty, freedom of speech, press, association or worship can be submitted to a majority vote; no right protected by the Bill of Rights depends merely upon a political election. These rights have been withdrawn from the vicissitudes of everyday politics, and placed beyond the reach of simple majorities and elected or appointed officials. What is needed is a non-elected body; one not subject to the shifting winds of majority vote to protect these constitutional rights, and that is a primary task of all our courts, especially the Supreme Court.

Since the political process cannot be fully relied upon in this second type of case, and more reliance is placed on courts, the Supreme Court is justified in using a different standard of review and being more active. Its standard for reviewing governmental actions that allegedly invade fundamental liberties must be different. If the Court is to fulfill its role in this area it must act frequently and forcefully. It has done so; for example, it sometimes has relaxed the presumption of constitutionality or it has created a presumption against the constitutional validity of government actions alleged to invade fundamental American rights and liberties. This trend started with a famous footnote by Mr. Justice Stone:

> "There may be narrower scope for operation of the presumption of constitutionality when legislation appears on its face to be within a specific prohibition of the Constitution such as those of the first ten amendments, which are deemed equally specific when held to be embraced within the Fourteenth." (U. S. v. Carolene Products, 304 U.S. 144, 58 S.Ct. 778, 82 L.Ed. 1234 (1938)).

James Madison, the "father of our constitution," saw that American courts must necessarily play a more active role in cases involving human liberties and welfare than in other types of cases. During the Congressional deliberations in the first American Congress when the Bill of Rights was being formulated, James Madison said:

> If they are incorporated into the Constitution, independent tribunals of justice will consider themselves in a peculiar manner the guardians of those rights; they will be an impenetrable bulwark against every assumption of power in the Legislative or Executive; they will be naturally led to resist every encroachment upon rights expressly stipulated for in the Constitution by the declaration of rights. (Irving Brant, The Madison Heritage, 35 N.Y.U. LAW REV. 882, 889–900.)

This role of the Supreme Court has caused some people to call it "activist." But would we want our liberties protected by a "passive" Court; one that would do so only when the unconstitutionality of the matter is not open to any rational question? Surely not. When dealing with this second general type of case, the Supreme Court, in a sense, acts as the constitutional conscience of our country, and rightly so. Recently, our courts, and especially the Supreme Court, have been dealing more and more with this second type of case involving human liberty, and less with the first type. Frequently, but not always, the Supreme Court and other courts have upheld our constitutional ideals of human liberty and human dignity with the result that they are greatly respected by the overwhelming majority of the American people. In doing so, the Supreme Court and the other courts are fulfilling their proper role in American society, and they are held in high esteem.

## THE SUPREME COURT

The Supreme Court has not always been held in high esteem. On February 1, 1790, when the Supreme Court of the United States first convened in the Royal Exchange Building in New York City, it found that it had nothing to do. There were no cases to decide; so the Court adjourned. The next annual term of Court was held in Philadelphia's new City Hall. But again, there were no cases to decide; so after admitting some lawyers to practice before it, the Court adjourned. The Congress legislated, and the president administered, but the Court adjourned. During that ten-year period to 1800, it decided only fifty-six cases, and a scant few of them were of major significance. The importance of a Justice of the Supreme Court was not recognized, and it lay inchoate. The Court's role was slow to emerge.

In those days, being a Justice of the United States Supreme Court was seen by some people as having so little value and reward that John Jay, the Court's first Chief Justice, resigned to run for governor of the State of New York. His decision is really not surprising. It is understandable when one considers the nature of the early Court and its work, including the fact that the first courtroom in the Nation's capitol was so inadequate that it later became the office for the Marshal of the Court. In addition, these were the times when the Justices were required to "ride circuit" in order to handle certain aspects of judicial administration. Because of the inconveniences of transportation in those days Justice Iredell termed himself a "travelling postboy." His "circuit riding" necessitated a twice-a-year tour of Georgia and North and South Carolina plus a gruelling journey of two thousand miles twice a year, to and from Philadelphia. Riding circuit was so onerous and formidable that one of the early Justices, Johnson, resigned because of it. The rigors of this practice persisted well into the nineteenth century.

In 1800, an act of Congress created the District of Columbia and also created much work for the Supreme Court. The reason is simple. The Court now became the place of final resolution for all of the run-of-the-mill legal disputes of the people who lived in the District. Thus, the total business of the Supreme Court increased, but it tended to function more like a state court, rather than as the Supreme Court of the United States. This act of Congress pushed the Court towards becoming just another typical court of law deciding cases of contested wills, real estate and divorce. This state of affairs could not long endure for the pulse of America increased its beat.

Not only was the business of the Supreme Court to change, but so was its number of Justices. The Court has not always had nine Justices. When the Supreme Court first met in 1789 it had only five Justices, although six were authorized, and the next year it was expanded to six. The six Justices became seven in 1807; nine in 1834, and reached a historical high number of ten in 1863. The Court continued to have ten Justices until 1865 when Mr. Justice Catron died and his position was abolished by Congress, as was that of Mr. Justice Wayne who died in 1867. The reason Congress abolished both positions was to prevent President Johnson from filling them. In 1869, Congress created a new position making the Supreme Court consist of nine Justices, and nine has remained the number of Justices for over one hundred years. It is unlikely that the future will see a change in the number of Justices on the Court.

The nineteenth century saw the American people conquer a continent, spanning it by rail from coast-to-coast and creating new states where previously there had been territories. During the middle and latter portions of the nineteenth century thirty-five million uprooted immigrants migrated to these shores from Europe and Asia at great personal loss and suffering. With them came a new series of complicated legal problems wrapped together with all the constitutional issues inherent in a dynamic, and ofttimes exploitative, industrialism. And, of course, these were days of great domestic issues, generating their own constitutional problems, which culminated in the Civil War. No institution of government could fail to reverberate under the pulse of such pressure. The Supreme Court responded.

Long before 1875 the Court ceased to meet only to adjourn. That year it heard almost two hundred cases. That number is surely the maximum that can be heard and fully explored by nine Justices. These were important cases, befitting an expanding nation with its growing industrialism. Many of them involved the scope and nature of the freedom to be allowed interstate commerce; others dealt with Congressional powers to take lands previously in private ownership and develop them for public purposes, and other cases dealt with the right to trial by jury.  In fact, the flow of cases came to be so great that Congress, in 1891, established the federal Courts of Appeal, thereby relieving the Supreme Court of what had grown to be an oppressive workload.

But, the pressures were relentless.  By 1925, the total business of the Court had grown to such an extent that once again something had to be done about it.  That something was known as the Judges' Bill because members of the Court prepared it, and Congress enacted it into law.  Under the Act of 1925 the obligatory appeals jurisdiction was contracted and the Supreme Court was given almost complete discretion to choose among the many cases which compete to come to its courtroom either by way of appeal or certiorari.  To a significant extent, this measure has been successful.  The net result has been the establishment of a case selection process which has tended to stabilize the business of the Supreme Court, allowing the Court to hear and decide the most important constitutional, and other, cases of wide public interest.  Occasionally, the Court uses its discretion not to consider a crucially important case, and it has been criticized for this practice. But, generally, the Supreme Court exercises its discretion to consider the most significant cases.  This last point is not sufficiently understood and accounts for much of the popular ignorance.  This selective process can produce an abnormal number of cases with stirring, controversial issues.  The Court is repeatedly confronted with cases cluttered over with vested interests and in which public emotions run deep and prejudices are pronounced.  In sum, then, these are controversial cases.  It is no wonder that the Court frequently becomes a storm center for public discussion, and sometimes abuse, which defies quantitative description.  Yet, only by deciding controversial cases can the Court continue to make its highest contribution to American life. That is its job, and this point is frequently overlooked by those who criticize the decision-making of the Court.

One point should be made clear.  It concerns the cases in which the petitions have asked the Court for a hearing, but the Court refused; that is, *certiorari* has been denied.  In these cases the decisions of the lower courts are not disturbed.  It is important to note that the decisions are not "disturbed," and that the Supreme Court gave no view on the substantive merits or demerits of the lower court's decision, and that the only proper inference to be drawn is that the request for Court review of the case did not get the necessary four votes.  No one knows exactly why the Justices refuse to vote to grant a full hearing to a case, and surely they can, and do, vote for different, and perhaps conflicting, reasons.  The important point to remember is that a denial of certiorari does not mean that the Supreme Court agrees with the result reached by a lower federal or state court.  Contrary to what might be reported by the media, a denial of certiorari means only that the case failed to get the necessary four votes for reasons that are unknown.

A slightly different circumstance prevails when the Supreme Court deals with a case that has come to it by appeal, rather than by certiorari. In the case of certiorari, the lawyers, in a sense, are standing outside petitioning the Court to open its doors to them and grant them a full hearing. Thus, a refusal to grant certiorari simply means that the case failed to get the necessary four votes to open the door and to get inside the Court. On the other hand, cases on appeal are, so to speak, already inside the Court, but the question is whether they can stay there and get a full hearing plus a decision on the merits. Cases on appeal contain the necessary federal question for obligatory appeals jurisdiction. But, many cases on appeal, like those on certiorari, border on the frivolous and represent a last-gasp attempt. If the federal question is insignificant or frivolous, the Court may not grant a full hearing to the case. Instead, it may dismiss the appeal for want of a substantial federal question, or perhaps, because the decision below was correct. In such circumstances the decision of the lower court is final, but the Supreme Court has also said that the federal question presented to it is "insubstantial." It did not say this in the cases that were denied certiorari. In appeals, also, as with certiorari, the final result is the same. The court has considerable leeway to pick and choose the cases which it will grant a full hearing, and then decide on the merits.

Currently, Supreme Court review is essentially as follows:

ON APPEAL (a review by right):

From state courts

1. Where a state court has held a federal statute or treaty provision unconstitutional.

2. Where a state court has upheld a state law or state constitutional provision arguably in conflict with the federal Constitution, laws, or treaties.

From federal courts of appeals

1. Where a federal law or treaty is held unconstitutional.

2. Where a state law or state constitutional provision is held invalid because it conflicts with a federal law, treaty, or constitutional provision.

From federal district courts (Direct appeal to Supreme Court)

1. Where a federal statute having a criminal penalty is held unconstitutional.

2. Where judgment has been rendered to enforce antitrust laws, the Interstate Commerce Act, or Title II of the Federal Communications Act.

3. Where a three-judge district court grants or denies an injunction restraining enforcement of state statutes or federal statutes, or orders of certain federal agencies.

ON CERTIORARI (a discretionary review granted or denied by vote of the Supreme Court):

From state courts

1. In cases involving federal questions where the decision was favorable to the federal claim made under federal law or Constitutional provisions.

From courts of appeals

1. Where a decision interprets or applies the Constitution or federal laws or treaties.

2. Where state laws or state constitutional provisions have been challenged as contrary to federal law, and the court of appeals has upheld the state provisions.

Decision-making by the Supreme Court is a group process. Solo performances are unknown. No single member, be he the Chief or Associate Justice, dictates his private reason or personal views to his independent-minded brethren. Individually and independently they work together to arrive at a group decision for the Court. The fact that the decisions of the Supreme Court are group decisions is trite, but easily overlooked. It is highly important and carries with it some interesting and frequently beneficial consequences. For example, one easily ignored implication is that a group decision probably produces a final judgment having a viewpoint of greater breadth and depth, and fewer extremes, than most individual decisions. This point is particularly applicable when one considers the quality of the individual members of the Supreme Court. When Justices are endowed with high-quality intellects and breadth of understanding, they can collectively bring to bear an awesome combination of sweeping brain power and extensive learning on a legal question.

Another feature frequently associated with the group decision process is that of stability. Because of this, the Supreme Court decisions tend to conform to the configurations of the past more than they otherwise might. Radical breaks with history seem not to appear often. Any Justice can raise a point of constitutional tradition and demand that it be met by his colleagues. Collectively, they can record doubts and qualifications which a person, working alone, can easily overlook. The fact that the Court must write group opinions, satisfactory to each member of the majority, although, perhaps, not fully satisfactory to each Justice entirely; the fact that the Court must justify its decisions within the framework of the constitution, and the fact that dissents to these opinions are freely filed, all go a long way toward insuring the integrity and reliability of the group decision process. This process can produce court opinions which are not fully satisfactory to the probing minds of legal scholars because the opinions must sometimes represent a compromise among some Justices, with no one Justice's view completely and rigorously followed. Occasionally, therefore, the group decision process can produce an unaesthetic opinion. But the group decision process also aids the Court to produce stable and, frequently, wise decisions which, in turn, are beneficial to our Nation and which can withstand the fickle breezes of a changing wind. One must always keep in mind: the judicial process in the Supreme Court is a group process. The Court does not function by using either committees or panels of Justices. Unless he disqualifies himself for some reason, each Justice passes on each case that seeks a hearing and on the merits of each case after the hearing has been held. The Constitution puts the judicial power in only one Supreme Court, not in its committees, panels or sections. One invariant rule prevails: judging is always an individual matter for each Justice and is never delegated; yet, too, the judicial process of the Supreme Court results in a group process.

What are the outlines of this judicial process? This question intrigues almost everyone who is seriously interested in the Supreme Court, and its answer is somewhat frustrating. The only honest answer is that no one, outside the Court members themselves, can be absolutely sure of everything that takes place inside the chambers. The reason for this situation is a simple one—the actual deliberations and intellectual interchanges of the Justices while they are in conference are, quite properly, not released to the press and are not made the subject of public curiosity. However, a few things are known, and they, in turn, allow some reasonable speculations regarding others.

A term of Court is well known, although its actual duration may vary slightly. It usually lasts about thirty-six weeks with the first session day being the first Monday of each October and continuing in session usually until about July 1. This means then, that, since the average Justice works six days a week and between eight and ten hours per day, each member of the Court puts in about 1,800 total hours per court term on court business. These hours are spent listening to lawyer arguments on cases, discussing court business in conference sessions, writing or studying opinions, reading other types of petitions, reading the briefs submitted by attorneys, and engaging in other collateral matters affecting the Court.

Officially, when the courtroom is open, the Court is in session only four days a week, Monday through Thursday, and the Justices listen to arguments only four hours per day. This schedule is usually followed by a recess period of about two weeks. During the days of argument the cases are called promptly, and the formal argument is held. Each case is usually given one hour for oral argument, one-half hour for each side. This is a critical time for the lawyer. He cannot read his argument to the Court. He must be able to pull together his side of a complex case, and to present it in a coherent and convincing way. Yet, there is a constant hurdle for him because he must also answer the probing questions which Justices ask, interrupting his argument, and which are based on their reading of the written materials in the case; that is, the briefs and other materials submitted by the attorneys. After hearing arguments, the Court recesses for two or three weeks for purposes of studying briefs, writing opinions and passing on other petitions.

One day has special significance for a student of the Supreme Court. Each Friday of the oral argument weeks finds the members of the Court in conference. During the usual conference session, the members of the Court spend most of their time discussing and voting, although they sometimes go over final drafts of opinions. The bulk of time in conference is probably spent on the cases which recently have been orally argued on their merits. Yet, the Court also must pass on those cases in which lawyers have asked that its discretion be exercised and that the case be granted a hearing by the Court. In these cases, the lawyers have asked that the Court grant their cases a hearing; that is, they have filed a petition requesting a grant of *certiorari,* or if the case is on appeal, they have filed a petition in support of the Court's jurisdiction over the case. The conference sessions begin sharply at eleven o'clock on Friday morning and last until five-thirty. One might be curious about what goes on in the conference.

On Fridays, at eleven, the Justices meet at their conference room which is a beautifully oak paneled chamber with one side lined with books from the floor to the ceiling. An exquisite marble fireplace is at one end of the chamber and over it hangs the only adornment in the room—a portrait of Mr. Chief Justice Marshall, the "Great Chief Justice." There is a rectangular table that stands in the middle of the conference room. The Justices are called to the conference by a buzzer that rings in each Justice's chamber about five minutes before the appointed hour. Religiously, the Justices follow a long held tradition. Meeting near Chief Justice Marshall's portrait, they greet each other in a friendly fashion and shake hands all around before beginning their work. The reason for this rite is that it helps to maintain the necessary working friendships among the Justices when they take up the court business which usually consists of very difficult and controversial cases. The observance is important. It shows that a harmony of aims if not views is the guiding principle of the Court. One should always remember that an independent Justice can be the possessor of a mind which has been honed to a keen cutting edge like a scalpel's, and, occasionally, he may have a rapier tongue to match. But reason prevails, and the Court deliberations seem not to get out of hand, despite the burning issues found in a case and the courage and convictions about them which a Justice may have. After cordialities have been exchanged, the members of the Court seat themselves around a large conference table. The session ensues.

Seated at the head of the table is the Chief Justice and directly across from him, at the other end of the table, sits the Senior Associate Justice. The rest of the members sit on either side of the table according to their rank in seniority, descending in seniority away from the Chief Justice. No one else ever is allowed in the room, and, if necessary, the most recently appointed Justice serves as a "messenger boy," carrying messages in and out of the conference room. This is a security device. It insures a full, frank and free discussion of all issues and ideas with the complete assurance of privacy. Consequently, no one, other than the Justices, really knows the substantive content of what actually transpires during a conference. However, it is known that each Justice has an agenda of the day's cases; that the Chief Justice calls the items on for discussion and that he has the first opportunity to discuss the matter, if he so chooses. Discussion of the matter under consideration then passes from Justice to Justice according to his seniority, those having more seniority speaking first, until each of them has said all that he wishes. After discussion, the Chief Justice calls for the vote. If the case is one that has already been accepted by the Court and has had its hearing it takes a majority vote, usually five of the nine votes, to dispose of the case on its merits. But, if the case is one in which the question is whether the Court will grant a full hearing, it takes only four votes to bring the case to the Court for its initial hearing. Thus, a vote of four Justices is necessary to fix the cases onto the calendar of the Supreme Court and a majority vote, usually a vote of five Justices, is necessary to decide the merits of the case removing it from the Court's calendar. If a Justice disqualifies himself in a case which has had a full hearing and if the remaining eight Justices split in their vote four-to-four, then the decision of the majority in the lower court is affirmed by the Supreme Court. While such a decision is binding on the parties, it does not become a precedent. Interestingly, the voting proceeds by an order opposite to that of the discussion. The first vote is cast by the Justice who has most recently been appointed to the Court and so on up the seniority ladder with the Chief Justice voting last. This procedure has been designed to eliminate the influence of a senior Justice's vote on a junior Justice. It should be noted that the discussion preceding the vote need not indicate the way a senior Justice will vote, but rather, it may very well consist only of an analytical and dispassionate discussion of the problems involved in a case as they have been seen by a Justice.

After the voting is concluded the case must be assigned to a Justice for opinion writing. This assignment is made by the Chief Justice if he has voted with the majority. If not, then the senior Justice voting with the majority assigns the case to a Justice for an opinion. The Justices are notified that evening by messenger of their assignments. No official assignments are made for dissenting or concurring opinions. These lie solely within the discretion of the Justices, and are freely filed. When the majority opinion has been written, to the satisfaction of the individual Justice doing the initial work, it is then circulated to the other members of the Court, majority and dissenting Justices, for their comments. This is a time of agonizing scrutiny. The cracks, crevices and loopholes of an opinion are revealed to its author by the discerning views of his brethren who pass on them with piercing eyes. Frequently, with due contrition, the opinion must be drastically rewritten by its original author and sent again upon its journey to the Justices. The dissenting opinions are also fully circulated among the Justices, and sometimes the dissenting opinions will change votes, occasionally enough votes to make that opinion the majority opinion. Before each Justice finally makes up his mind there has been a constant interchange among them by memoranda, telephone and at the lunch table. Majority opinions have been rewritten as many as ten to twenty times before final agreement was reached. Finally, after receiving approval from the majority, the opinion accompanied by its dissents, is filed in open court. Thus, in summary, it can be seen that the work of the Supreme Court Justices falls into four broad categories: reading various papers (petitions for certiorari, motions, etc.), listening to oral arguments, the conference and tentative voting, and writing opinions and ultimate decision.

Following is a description in quantitative terms of the business of the Supreme Court during the 1977 term. It provides another dimension showing the current workload of the Court. No attempt will be made to describe the legal complexity of any case, nor its controversial character. During that term, reaching roughly from October, 1977 to mid-1978, a record number of 3,854 cases were listed upon the Court's docket. The Court, as a unit, wrote full opinions, some of them from fifty to a hundred pages, or more, and, in addition, the individual Justices produced concurring and dissenting opinions. All in all, there were 159 full-blown Opinions of the Court written during the 1977 term. To gain a full perspective of the amount of work necessary to produce these opinions one should view them in the context of the additional demands upon members of the Court. Primarily, these additional demands are those of reading the briefs and petitions for certiorari, etc., which have been submitted; of hearing arguments; of participating in the deliberative sessions; and of researching and writing opinions. When these considerations are added to the other duties of a Justice, such as supervising a circuit, contributing to the legal education of both law students and members of the practicing bar, as well as conducting his private research and scholarly writing which is incidental to his own personal interests, then, it is clear that, once again, we have reached a point beyond which we cannot reasonably expect more.

## CHART, FEDERAL COURT STRUCTURE AND FLOW OF CASES TO THE UNITED STATES SUPREME COURT

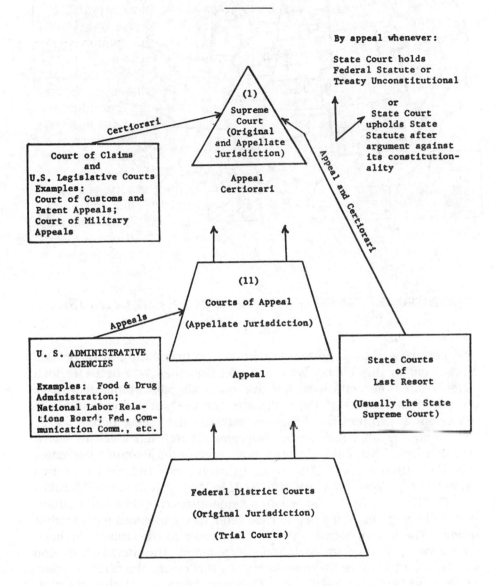

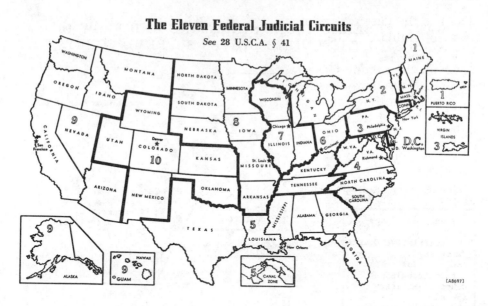

A NOTE ON FINDING AND READING CASE OPINIONS

You may want to go to a law library and read the full reports of cases cited in this book. How will you find them? Legal citations differ from other citations, but are quite simple. Generally, cases are given the names of the parties to the law suit. An example is Adamson v. California. Adamson was the defendant in the lower court and the appellant in the Supreme Court, and since it was a criminal case, the State of California, represented by the prosecutor, was the other party. Civil cases usually carry the names of two persons; e. g., Baggett v. Bullitt, 377 U.S. 360, 84 S.Ct. 1316, 12 L.Ed. 2d 377 (1964), with the appellant's name appearing first. The numbers following the name of the case refer to volume and page in that order. The letters between the numbers refer to the title of the book where the opinion may be found. Frequently, the identical opinion can be found in more than one book. In this event, the official report of the case is always cited first. Thus, for Baggett v. Bullitt, the citation is to volume 377 of the official United States reports where the opinion is printed at page 360; it also refers you to volume 84 of the Supreme Court reporter (sometimes cited as S.Ct.), a publication of the West Publishing Company, where the identical opinion is printed at page 1316, and to volume 13 of the United States Supreme Court Reports, Lawyers Edition, second series, another private reporting company, where the identical opinion is printed at page 377. Finally,

(1964) is the date when the case was decided.  The citations to state cases are similar.  Books are cited similarly to cases: first comes the volume number, but only if the book has more than one volume, followed by the name of the author, then the title of the book, page, and finally the date of publication.  Articles are similar: first is the name of the author, followed by the article's title, the volume number, then the title of the journal, followed by the page number, and lastly the date of publication.

Once you have found the opinion, whether in this book or the law library, what do you do with it?  One suggestion comes from Karl Llewellyn's book, THE BRAMBLE BUSH, 1960, excerpts are from pp. 41–55:

".   .   .   The first thing to do with an opinion, then, is read it. The next thing is to get clear the actual decision, the judgment rendered.  Who won, the plaintiff or defendant?  And watch your step here.  You are after in first instance the plaintiff and defendant *below,* in the trial court.  In order to follow through what happened you must therefore first know the outcome *below;* else you do not see what was appealed from, nor by whom.  You now follow through in order to see exactly what *further* judgment has been rendered on appeal.  The stage is then cleared of form—although of course you do not yet know all that these forms mean, that they imply.  You can turn now to what you want peculiarly to know.  Given the actual judgments below and above as your indispensable framework—what has the case decided, and what can you derive from it as to what will be decided later?

"You will be looking, in the opinion, or in the preliminary matter plus the opinion, for the following: a statement of the facts the court assumes;  a statement of the precise way the question has come before the court—which includes what the plaintiff wanted below, and what the defendant did about it, the judgment below, and what the trial court did that is complained of;  then the outcome on appeal, the judgment;  and finally the reasons this court gives for doing what it did. This does not look so bad.  But it is much worse than it looks.

"For all our cases are decided, all our opinions are written, all our predictions, all our arguments are made, on certain four assumptions. They are the first presuppositions of our study.  They must be rutted into you till you can juggle with them standing on your head and in your sleep.

1) *The court must decide the dispute that is before it*.  It cannot refuse because the job is hard, or dubious, or dangerous.

2) *The court can decide* only *the particular dispute which is before it*.  When it speaks to that question it speaks ex cathedra, with authority, with finality, with an almost magic power.  When it speaks to the question before it, it announces *law,* and if what it announces is new, it legislates, it *makes* the law.  But when it speaks to any other

question at all, it says mere words, which no man needs to follow. Are such words worthless? They are not. We know them as judicial *dicta;* when they are wholly off the point at issue we call them *obiter dicta*—words dropped along the road, wayside remarks. Yet even wayside remarks shed light on the remarker. They may be very useful in the future to him, or to us. But he will not feel bound to them, as to his ex cathedra utterance. They came not hallowed by a Delphic frenzy. He may be slow to change them; but not so slow as in the other case.

3) *The court can decide the particular dispute only according to a general rule which covers a whole class of like disputes.* Our legal theory does not admit of single decisions standing on their own. If judges are free, are indeed forced, to decide new cases for which there is no rule, they must at least make a new rule as they decide. So far, good. But how wide, or how narrow, is the general rule in this particular case? That is a troublesome matter. The practice of our case-law, however, is I think fairly stated thus: it pays to be suspicious of general rules which look too wide; it pays to go slow in feeling *certain* that a wide rule has been laid down at all, or that, if seemingly laid down, it will be followed. For there is a fourth accepted canon:

4) *Everything, everything, everything, big or small, a judge may say in an opinion, is to be read with primary reference to the particular dispute, the particular question before him.* You are not to think that the words mean what they might if they stood alone. You are to have your eye on the case in hand, and to learn how to interpret all that has been said *merely* as a reason for deciding *that* case *that* way. . . .

"What now of preparation for your case class? Your cases are assigned. Before they can be used they have to be digested. Experience shows that it is well to brief them. Briefing is valuable if only for the impending discussion. Briefing is well nigh essential when it comes to the review. . . .

". . . Briefing is also the saddest trap that ever awaited a law student, if he does not watch his step. For the practice under pressure of time, as eyes grow tired in the evening, or the movies lure, is to brief cases, *one by one,* and therefore blindly. Now if I have made one point in this discussion it should be this: that a case read by itself is meaningless, is nil, is blank, is blah . . . Briefing, I say again, is a problem of putting down what in the one case bears upon the problem stated by the other cases. Each brief should be in terms of *what this case adds to what I already know about* this subject. . . . What does the case *add, what difference does it make,* to what I already know? This is the keynote of the brief. . . .

"What, now, should a brief contain? (1) First, as a finder: the title and its page in the casebook. (2) Second, to orient it in the law, the state and date. From now on, the order becomes largely immaterial. I give you one possible and useful order. (3) What, precisely, did the plaintiff want? What did he ask for? This is one most vital and one almost regularly overlooked feature of a brief. This is the first start in coming to the *question*. (4) Contrariwise, what did the defendant want and how did the case come to an issue? (5) What did the trial court do; that is, what was the judgment below? (6) Finally, what action of the trial court is complained of? When you have these things in your brief, and only then, are you prepared tc look for either relevant facts or relevant rules of law. When you have found these things, and only then, have you your cross-lines laid to spot *the question* in the case. (7) I find it useful to put down next the outcome of appeal. You see why that is useful. It at once makes clear whether the language of the court in a given passage was or was not necessary to the decision. (8) Then come the facts of the case as assumed by the court. I warn you, I warn you strongly, against cutting the facts down too far. If you cherish any hope of insight into *what difference the rules make* to people, you will have to keep an eye out to some of the more striking details of the facts, as the court gives them. I know you will lose patience with them. But observe this, my friends. *You will be impatient with the facts to the precise extent to which you need them.* If you do not need them, if you already have some knowledge of the background of the case, the facts will not be boring; they will interest you. If they pester and upset you, that is a sign that you know so little about what the case means in life that these facts need desperate study.

"Which facts, then, are significant? I recur again to my proposition. One case will not tell you. Only the group of cases will give you any start at solving that. The more cases you read, therefore, before you brief any, the better off you are, provided only that you brief them each one in the light of all.

"And finally, remember this: it is where the facts (as illumined, as *selected*, as *classified* in the light of other cases) *cross* with the issue given by the procedural set-up, that the narrow-issue question of the case is found. *And only there.*

(9) After the facts, the ratio decidendi, phrased preferably substantially along the lines taken by the court. (10) If you do not like the language of the court, in the light of the other cases, here is the place to note down how you think it should have phrased the rule.

"Beyond this, notes are a matter of discretion. (11) I have always found it useful to indicate something of the line of argument the court indulged in, for reasons which I hope to make appear. (12) A beginning law student, moreover, finds in the cases many remarks as to the law, which although they have no bearing on the subject he is studying, are highly interesting and informative. It was my practice when a student to note those down, but to note them by themselves, where they helped memory but did not get in the way of review.

"So much for the brief. And if you follow this advice you will discover that by the time the last brief is made the class is well prepared. . . ."

Mechanically, a brief of a case could have eight parts: (1) the name and date of the case, and the name of the court that decided it; (2) the significant facts; i. e., those on which the court's decision is based; (3) to the extent possible, a statement of the case's procedural details; i. e., what relief was sought, the nature of the legal controversy in the lower court and the disposition there; (4) the issue or issues on appeal; (5) the arguments of the parties on the issue(s); (6) the decision of the appeal court; (7) the reasoning of the court in support of its decision; and (8) a statement of the rule(s) of law that the decision in the case stands for. It would probably prove helpful to prepare a separate brief for each major case in this book.

## A NOTE ON THE BILL OF RIGHTS AND THE FOURTEENTH AMENDMENT

The Bill of Rights became part of the Constitution of the United States because of the strong demands that were made for it in the several states during the ratification debates. These first ten amendments along with certain of the provisions of the original Constitution —the prohibitions on bills of attainder, ex post facto laws, impairment of the obligation of contract, suspension of the writ of habeas corpus (see, Art. I, secs. 9 and 10), plus careful procedures for, and a precise and narrow definition of, treason—were, and are, viewed as the fundamental liberties of a free people. They are viewed as fundamental freedoms because they place limitations on the powers of government. Because of these provisions government simply cannot do certain things; for example, it cannot pass a law abridging the freedom of speech; thus, the people constitutionally are free of government controls and within constitutional limits can speak freely, if they so choose. Initially, the Bill of Rights placed limitations only on the powers of the federal government, not on state governments. This view was the foundation of a ruling by the Supreme Court of the United States in Barron v. Baltimore, 7 Pet. 243, 8 L.Ed. 672 (1833). The basic idea was that the national Bill of Rights functioned as a limitation only on federal powers and the state bills of rights functioned as limitations on state powers; the national Bill of Rights did not control the states.

State bills of rights, while highly similar, are not uniform. More importantly, if a state fails to abide by its bill of rights there is little that can be done about it. One can appeal to the state courts that they enforce their limitations upon the powers of their state governments. But, if state courts do not enforce their bills of rights limiting state powers, then that is the end of the matter. Federal courts have no jurisdiction solely to enforce a state bill of rights against that state government. The state courts have the final word when construing and applying their state laws and constitutions, so long as no question of federal law is presented. Thus, when dealing with its own residents in situations not involving federal law, and when unchecked by state courts that fail to enforce their state bills of rights, a state can invade the liberties of its peoples with impunity.

The adoption of the Fourteenth Amendment in 1868 significantly changed this state of affairs by extending federal constitutional controls over the acts of the governments of the states. That amendment applies directly to the states declaring, among other matters, that "No state shall make or enforce any law which shall abridge the privileges or immunities of citizens of the United States; nor shall any State deprive any person of life, liberty or property, without due process of law; nor deny to any person within its jurisdiction the equal protection of the laws." By section five Congress is given power to pass all laws appropriate to implementing this provision. Since the Fourteenth Amendment and all of Congress' statutes under it are federal laws, they can be enforced directly by either state or federal courts having the proper jurisdiction.

One of the important problems posed for the Supreme Court by this amendment is its relationship to the national Bill of Rights. Basically, the Court has had to specify the meaning of the words "liberty" and "due process of law" in the provision of the Fourteenth Amendment declaring that no state shall "deprive any person of life, liberty or property, without due process of law." This provision is frequently referred to as the "due process" clause. But, what is the substantive content of this "liberty" and "due process," and does the Bill of Rights have some special relationship with the "liberty" and "due process" provisions of the Fourteenth Amendment? Five views of the proper relationship between the Bill of Rights and the Fourteenth Amendment have been expressed by Justices of the Supreme Court. They are. (1) The Fundamental Rights View; (2) The Complete Incorporation View, and (3) The Selective Incorporation View. The individual merits of each view have been debated at length, usually in dissenting or concurring opinions, and in the critical literature on the subject. Two additional views—The Complete Incorporation Plus Fundamental Rights View and The Selective Incorporation Plus Fundamental Rights View—set forth the possible breadth of the words "liberty" and "due process" of the Fourteenth Amendment.

## THE SELECTIVE INCORPORATION PLUS FUNDAMENTAL
## RIGHTS VIEW

———

This is the current overall view of the Supreme Court on the "liberty" and "due process" provisions of the Fourteenth Amendment. This view holds that the "liberty" provision of the Fourteenth Amendment selectively incorporates those provisions of the Bill of Rights deemed "fundamental" or "implicit in the concept of ordered liberty," and it also includes other "fundamental rights" that are not expressly set forth in the Constitution. The additional "fundamental rights" are considered to have such a character that they cannot be denied without also violating the fundamental principles of justice that lie at the base of our civil and political institutions. When considering the validity of this view, one should recall the ninth amendment stating that the "enumeration in the Constitution, of certain rights, shall not be construed to deny or disparage others retained by the people." An example of this view is Roe v. Wade, 410 U.S. 113, 93 S.Ct. 705, 35 L.Ed.2d 147 (1973) in which the Supreme Court held certain anti-abortion laws unconstitutional:

".  .  . the Court has recognized that a right of personal privacy, or a guarantee of certain areas or zones of privacy, does exist under the Constitution. In varying contexts the Court of individual Justices have indeed found at least the roots of that right in the First Amendment, *Stanley v. Georgia,* 394 U.S. 557, 564 (1969); in the Fourth and Fifth Amendments, *Terry v. Ohio,* 392 U.S. 1, 8–9 (1968), *Katz v. United States,* 389 U.S. 347, 350 (1967), *Boyd v. United States,* 116 U.S. 616 (1886), see *Olmstead v. United States,* 277 U.S. 438, 478 (1928) (Brandeis, J., dissenting); in the penumbras of the Bill of Rights, *Griswold v. Connecticut,* 381 U.S. 479, 484–485 (1965); in the Ninth Amendment, *id.,* at 486 (Goldberg, J., concurring); or in the concept of liberty guaranteed by the first section of the Fourteenth Amendment, see *Meyer v. Nebraska,* 262 U.S. 390, 399 (1923). These decisions make it clear that only personal rights that can be deemed 'fundamental' or 'implicit in the concept of ordered liberty,' *Palko v. Connecticut,* 302 U.S. 319, 325 (1937), are included in this guarantee of personal privacy. They also make it clear that the right has some extension to activities relating to marriage, *Loving v. Virginia,* 388 U.S. 1, 12 (1967), procreation, *Skinner v. Oklahoma,* 316 U.S. 535, 541–542 (1942), contraception, *Eisenstadt v. Baird,* 405 U.S. 438, 453–454 (1972); *id.,* at 460, 463–465 (White, J., concurring), family relationships, *Prince v. Massachusetts,* 321 U.S.

158, 166 (1944), and child rearing and education, *Pierce v. Society of Sisters*, 268 U.S. 510, 535 (1925), *Meyer v. Nebraska, supra.*

"This right of privacy, whether it be founded in the Fourteenth Amendment's concept of personal liberty and restrictions upon state action, as we feel it is, or, as the District Court determined, in the Ninth Amendment's reservation of rights to the people, is broad enough to encompass a woman's decision whether or not to terminate her pregnancy."

---

## DUNCAN v. LOUISIANA

Supreme Court of the United States, 1968.
391 U.S. 145, 88 S.Ct. 1444, 20 L.Ed.2d 491, rehearing denied 392 U.S. 947, 88 S.Ct. 2270, 20 L.Ed.2d 1412.

Mr. Justice WHITE delivered the opinion of the Court.  .  .  .

The Fourteenth Amendment denies the States the power to "deprive any person of life, liberty, or property, without due process of law."  In resolving conflicting claims concerning the meaning of this spacious language, the Court has looked increasingly to the Bill of Rights for guidance; many of the rights guaranteed by the first eight Amendments to the Constitution have been held to be protected against state action by the Due Process Clause of the Fourteenth Amendment. That clause now protects the right to compensation for property taken by the State;[4] the rights of speech, press, and religion covered by the First Amendment;[5] the Fourth Amendment rights to be free from unreasonable searches and seizures and to have excluded from criminal trials any evidence illegally seized;[6] the right guaranteed by the Fifth Amendment to be free of compelled self-incrimination;[7] and the Sixth Amendment rights to counsel,[8] to a speedy [9] and public [10] trial, to confrontation of opposing witnesses,[11] and to compulsory process for obtaining witnesses.[12]

The test for determining whether a right extended by the Fifth and Sixth Amendments with respect to federal criminal proceedings

[4] Chicago, B. & Q. R. Co. v. Chicago, 166 U.S. 226 (1897).

[5] See, e. g., Fiske v. Kansas, 274 U.S. 380 (1927).

[6] See Mapp v. Ohio, 367 U.S. 643 (1961).

[7] Malloy v. Hogan, 378 U.S. 1 (1964).

[8] Gideon v. Wainwright, 372 U.S. 335 (1963).

[9] Klopfer v. North Carolina, 386 U.S. 213 (1967).

[10] In re Oliver, 333 U.S. 257 (1948).

[11] Pointer v. Texas, 380 U.S. 400 (1965).

[12] Washington v. Texas, 388 U.S. 14 (1967).

is also protected against state action by the Fourteenth Amendment has been phrased in a variety of ways in the opinions of this Court. The question has been asked whether a right is among those " 'fundamental principles of liberty and justice which lie at the base of all our civil and political institutions,' " Powell v. Alabama, 287 U.S. 45, 67 (1932);[13] whether it is "basic in our system of jurisprudence," In re Oliver, 333 U.S. 257, 273 (1948); and whether it is "a fundamental right, essential to a fair trial," Gideon v. Wainwright, 372 U.S. 335, 343–344 (1963); Malloy v. Hogan, 378 U.S. 1, 6 (1964); Pointer v. Texas, 380 U.S. 400, 403 (1965). The claim before us is that the right to trial by jury guaranteed by the Sixth Amendment meets these tests. The position of Louisiana, on the other hand, is that the Constitution imposes upon the States no duty to give a jury trial in any criminal case, regardless of the seriousness of the crime or the size of the punishment which may be imposed. Because we believe that trial by jury in criminal cases is fundamental to the American scheme of justice, we hold that the Fourteenth Amendment guarantees a right of jury trial in all criminal cases which—were they to be tried in a federal court—would come within the Sixth Amendment's guarantee.[14] Since

[13] Quoting from Hebert v. Louisiana, 272 U.S. 312, 316 (1926).

[14] In one sense recent cases applying provisions of the first eight Amendments to the States represent a new approach to the "incorporation" debate. Earlier the Court can be seen as having asked, when inquiring into whether some particular procedural safeguard was required of a State, if a civilized system could be imagined that would not accord the particular protection. For example, Palko v. Connecticut, 302 U.S. 319, 325 (1937), stated: "The right to trial by jury and the immunity from prosecution except as the result of an indictment may have value and importance. Even so, they are not of the very essence of a scheme of ordered liberty. . . . Few would be so narrow or provincial as to maintain that a fair and enlightened system of justice would be impossible without them." The recent cases, on the other hand, have proceeded upon the valid assumption that state criminal processes are not imaginary and theoretical schemes but actual systems bearing virtually every characteristic of the common-law system that has been developing contemporaneously in England and in this country. The question thus is whether given this kind of system a particular procedure is fundamental—whether, that is, a procedure is necessary to an Anglo-American regime of ordered liberty. It is this sort of inquiry that can justify the conclusions that state courts must exclude evidence seized in violation of the Fourth Amendment, Mapp v. Ohio, 367 U.S. 643 (1961); that state prosecutors may not comment on a defendant's failure to testify, Griffin v. California, 380 U.S. 609 (1965); and that criminal punishment may not be imposed for the status of narcotics addiction, Robinson v. California, 370 U.S. 660 (1962). Of immediate relevance for this case are the Court's holdings that the States must comply with certain provisions of the Sixth Amendment, specifically that the States may not refuse a speedy trial, confrontation of witnesses, and the assistance, at state expense if necessary, of counsel. See cases cited in nn. 8–12, supra. Of each of these determinations that a constitutional provision originally written to bind the Federal Government should bind the States as well it might be said that the limitation in question is not necessarily fundamental to fairness in every criminal system that might be imagined but is fundamental in the context of the criminal processes maintained by the American States.

When the inquiry is approached in this way the question whether the States can impose criminal punishment without granting a jury trial appears quite different from the way it appeared in the

we consider the appeal before us to be such a case, we hold that the Constitution was violated when appellant's demand for a jury trial was refused.

## A NOTE ON STATE ACTION

Except for the first sentence, the rest of the first section of the Fourteenth Amendment is expressly qualified by a requirement that "state action" must be present before that amendment can apply; for example, ". . . nor shall any state deprive any person of life, liberty, or property, without due process of law. . . ." It does not apply to acts that are purely "private." But is the distinction so clear? What is "state action"?

State action is present whenever a state legislature passes a statute, or when a municipal legislature passes an ordinance, or whenever a State Board of Education or a Local School Board passes a rule or regulation applying to the operation of the public schools. State action is also present whenever a governor of a state acts, or whenever a superintendent, principal or, perhaps, a teacher acts pursuant to prior authorization by a state legislature or a school board. Thus, when in the classroom, the public-school teacher may be engaging in state action. Also, the teacher engages in state action whenever he or she carries out additional duties pursuant to a state law or a rule or regulation of a school board. The teacher is acting as an agent of the state, and his acts are "state action." But, does a teacher engage in state action if, when teaching class, he or she, without authorization, should suddenly hit a student with a club, yardstick or ruler? Or does a teacher engage in state action if while driving to school in the morning before classes, he stops his car four blocks from school and breaks up a fist fight between two pupils who are on their way to school? Is the teacher acting as a private citizen or as an agent of the state? Suppose he breaks up the fist fight after school hours and after the pupils have returned to their homes and have gone outside to play? Suppose the record reveals that a teacher systematically gives lower grades to minority pupils, is that teacher's grading subject to Fourteenth Amendment controls?

older cases opining that States might abolish jury trial. See, e. g., Maxwell v. Dow, 176 U.S. 581 (1900). A criminal process which was fair and equitable but used no juries is easy to imagine. It would make use of alternative guarantees and protections which would serve the purposes that the jury serves in the English and American systems. Yet no American State has undertaken to construct such a system. Instead, every American State, including Louisiana, uses the jury extensively, and imposes very serious punishments only after a trial at which the defendant has a right to a jury's verdict. In every State, including Louisiana, the structure and style of the criminal process—the supporting framework and the subsidiary procedures—are of the sort that naturally complement jury trial, and have developed in connection with and in reliance upon jury trial.

One case from the Supreme Court of the United States indicates that "private" schools, under certain circumstances, might possibly engage in "state action," with the result that the Fourteenth Amendment applies to them. In Burton v. Wilmington Parking Authority, 365 U.S. 715, 81 S.Ct. 856, 6 L.Ed.2d 45 (1961), a "private" restaurant obtained a twenty-year lease of some space within a building used for off-street automobile parking and which was owned and operated by the Wilmington Parking Authority, an agency of the State of Delaware. The "private" restaurant spent $220,000 of its money for improvements, redecorations and furnishings, all of which became the property of the Parking Authority; its main and marked public entrance was on the street, and there was no public entrance directly from the parking garage; the Delaware Supreme Court found only "private" action presented and that "the only connection Eagle [restaurant] has with the public facility  .   .   . is the furnishing of the sum of $28,700 annually in the form of rent which is used by the Authority to defray a portion of the operating expenses of an otherwise unprofitable enterprise." Eagle restaurant practiced racial discrimination by refusing to serve Black people, and argued that it had a constitutional right to do so because it was "private," and the Fourteenth Amendment's prohibition of racial discrimination applied only to "state action." On appeal, the Supreme Court said: "  .   .   . we cannot say that the [factual considerations] lead inescapably to the conclusion that state action is not present. Their persuasiveness is diminished when evaluated in the context of other factors which must be acknowledged.

"The land and building were publicly owned. As an entity, the building was dedicated to 'public uses' in performance of the Authority's 'essential governmental functions.'  .   .   . The costs of land acquisition, construction, and maintenance are defrayed entirely from donations by the City of Wilmington, from loans and revenue bonds and from the proceeds of rentals and parking services out of which the loans and bonds were payable. Assuming that the distinction would be significant, cf. Derrington v. Plummer, 240 F.2d 922, 925, (5th Cir. 1956), the commercially leased areas were not surplus state property, but constituted a physically and financially integral and, indeed, indispensable part of the State's plan to operate its project as a self-sustaining unit. Upkeep and maintenance of the building, including necessary repairs, were responsibilities of the Authority and were payable out of public funds. It cannot be doubted that the peculiar relationship of the restaurant to the parking facility in which it is located confers on each an incidental variety of mutual benefits. Guests of the restaurant are afforded a convenient place to park their automobiles, even if they cannot enter the restaurant directly from the parking area. Similarly, its convenience for diners may well provide additional demand for the Authority's parking facilities. Should any improvements effected in the leasehold by Eagle become part of the realty, there is no possibility of increased taxes being passed on to it since the fee is held by a tax-exempt government agency. Neither can it be ignored, especially in view of Eagle's affirmative allegation that for it to serve Negroes would injure its business, that profits earned by discrimination not only contribute to, but also are indispensable elements in, the financial success of a governmental agency.

"Addition of all these activities, obligations and responsibilities of the Authority, the benefits mutually conferred, together with the obvious fact that the restaurant is operated as an integral part of a public building devoted to a public parking service, indicates that degree of state participation and involvement in discriminatory action which it was the design of the Fourteenth Amendment to condemn. It is irony amounting to grave injustice that in one part of a single building, erected and maintained with public funds by an agency of the State to serve a public purpose, all persons have equal rights, while in another portion, also serving the public, a Negro is a second-class citizen, offensive because of his race, without rights and unentitled to service, but at the same time fully enjoys equal access to nearby restaurants in wholly privately owned buildings. As the Chancellor pointed out, in its lease with Eagle the Authority could have affirmatively required Eagle to discharge the responsibilities under the Fourteenth Amendment imposed upon the private enterprise as a consequence of state participation. But no State may effectively abdicate its responsibilities by either ignoring them or by merely failing to discharge them whatever the motive may be. It is of no consolation to an individual denied the equal protection of the laws that it was done in good faith. Certainly the conclusions drawn in similar cases by the various Courts of Appeals do not depend upon such a distinction. By its inaction, the Authority, and through it the State, has not only made itself a party to the refusal of service, but has elected to place its power, property and prestige behind the admitted discrimination. The State has so far insinuated itself into a position of interdependence with Eagle that it must be recognized as a joint participant in the challenged activity, which, on that account, cannot be considered to have been so 'purely private' as to fall without the scope of the Fourteenth Amendment.

"Because readily applicable formulae may not be fashioned, the conclusions drawn from the facts and circumstances of this record are by no means declared as universal truths on the basis of which every state leasing agreement is to be tested. Owing to the very 'largeness' of government, a multitude of relationships might appear to some to fall within the Amendment's embrace, but that, it must be remembered, can be determined only in the framework of the peculiar facts or circumstances present. Therefore respondents' prophecy of nigh universal application of a constitutional precept so peculiarly dependent for its invocation upon appropriate facts fails to take into account

'Differences in circumstances [which] beget appropriate differences in law,' Whitney v. Tax Comm'n, 309 U.S. 530, 542. Specifically defining the limits of our inquiry, what we hold today is that when a State leases public property in the manner and for the purpose shown to have been the case here, the proscriptions of the Fourteenth Amendment must be complied with by the lessee as certainly as though they were binding covenants written into the agreement itself.

"The judgment of the Supreme Court of Delaware is reversed and the cause remanded for further proceedings consistent with this opinion.

"REVERSED AND REMANDED."

## PROBLEM

Consider the following hypothetical set of facts in light of the Supreme Court's decision and reasoning in Burton v. Wilmington Parking Authority, supra. The Sacred Heart Academy is a parochial school approved by the State Superintendent of Education for offering common-school education in grades one through twelve. There is no doubt that the education offered has been certified by the State Superintendent of Education to serve a public purpose, and that the state has relied upon this instruction to service the educational needs of a large percentage of its school-age children; thus, the Academy is an integral part of the state's educational plan. The Academy has two main buildings, one of which was recently built. One, the recently constructed High School building, was constructed and furnished after the Board of Directors of the Sacred Heart Academy received a loan from the United States Office of Health, Education and Welfare to cover the entire cost of land acquisition, construction and furnishing. The loan carries the low interest rate of 1% per year, and is part of our Nation's policy of making low-interest funds available for school construction purposes. The High School is fully equipped with a modern science center which was also purchased and is maintained with the money received from another loan for educational purposes from the federal government, and which carries .5% interest per year. Evidence shows that the Sacred Heart Academy receives tax exemptions from state, county and local property taxation; that it is exempt from Federal income taxation; that some of its required textbooks are supplied free of charge to its students by the State Office of Education; that its high school was constructed after receiving a zoning variance from the City Planning Commission which allowed the structure as an exception to the local zoning code, and that all of its teachers must, and do, have certification under state laws. It cannot be doubted that the relationship between the Academy and the state is one which confers on each a variety of mutual benefits. The Academy's successes or failures are indispensable elements in the overall success or failure of the state's attempt to educate its children. The Sacred Heart Academy insists on teaching the scriptures of one religion as the revealed truth and as part of its required courses, and it admits all children except that it refuses to admit any children who themselves, or their parents, are of the Black Muslim faith or who are militant atheists. The Academy argues that its policies of discrimination on religious grounds and of promoting and furthering one specific religion are justifiable and are not subject to the Fourteenth Amendment because it is a "private" not a "public" school. Assume that you are the judge, what decision is proper? Would your decision be any different if the state also supplied and paid the salaries of all the science and mathematics teachers who taught at the Academy? If not, what more facts would be necessary before you would conclude that "state action" is present? Why? Assuming that you decide that "state action" is present at the Academy, at least with reference to the high school, would the Congress, the state legislature, or if properly authorized, the state board of education have power to enact rules and regulations controlling and prescribing the admission, and other, practices of the Sacred Heart Academy?

# Chapter II

# CONSTITUTIONAL FREEDOM AND COMPULSORY SCHOOLING: A CONTRADICTION?

## INTRODUCTION

Chapter I of this book has been devoted primarily to sketching the structure of America's court system and the constitutional framework within which courts decide cases affecting education. We turn now to the legal materials themselves. In this chapter the primary focus will be on the problems attendant to the constitutionality of the legal requirements creating America's system of *compulsory* schooling. Compulsory attendance requirements are currently found in all but two states, and those two states provide free public schooling on a voluntary rather than compulsory attendance basis. Massachusetts enacted the first compulsory school attendance in 1852, and by 1918 all states had followed suit, Louisiana (1910), Alabama (1915), Florida (1915), South Carolina (1915), Georgia (1916), and Mississippi (1918), being the last. A close relationship existed between the compulsory school attendance movement and the humanitarian drive to eliminate child labor from American manufacture and industry. A typical young American in 1898 could expect to receive only five years of schooling, until age eleven or twelve. Extensions upward of the age requirements of compulsory schooling laws to sixteen or eighteen years effectively eliminated the exploitation of child labor by American business and agriculture. See, generally, M. Katz, A History of Compulsory Education Laws (1976); Burgess, "The Goddess, the School Book, and Compulsion," 46 Harv.Ed.Rev. 199 (1976); Tyack, The One Best System (1974), and Steinhilber and Sokolowski, State Law On Compulsory Attendance (Office of Ed., Dept. of HEW, 1966). But, these age extensions also raise an important question: Whether such a long educational period, which necessarily involves the compulsory loss of freedom, is constitutionally permissible? Before considering legal materials on problems related to this question, a word of advice is offered.

When considering the remainder of the materials it is always worthwhile to ask all of the searching and embarrassing questions, even if they are not asked in the book. Do our schools actually correspond to their professed legal justifications, or is there a gap between a school's social reality and its justifying rhetoric of good, legal intentions?  Also, is the justifying rationale adequate?  Judges may know little about educational processes, yet because of their office they must decide cases affecting those processes.  When doing so, their reasons and decisions become the legal requirements to which schools must conform.  But, judicial decisions are not always "correct."  Judicial decisions and reasoning should always be scrutinized and challenged to identify whether they, themselves, meet the tests of good and sufficient reason.

The political democracy of the United States, its long-term national security, the competitive power of the economy, the integrity of church, family and other social institutions, and the human well-being of individuals are all vitally dependent upon the excellence and effectiveness of America's schools.  If our schools fail to meet the demands that are currently being made upon them, or that will be made upon them in the foreseeable future, the American people will be unable to achieve their individual, family, community and national goals.  A free, democratic and vital society must depend on its schools to produce humane, responsible, rational and effective citizens.  These goals cannot be achieved unless the legal rationale justifying what takes place in our schools is adequate to meet the needs of our day, and those of the foreseeable future, and unless the historical reality in our schools actually conforms to that justifying rationale.  That is why we, as students, must always seek out and ask all the searching and embarrassing questions.

The legal importance of education is revealed by the fact that forty-eight of the 50 states have state constitutional provisions requiring that the state legislature create a system of public education.  On the other hand, only one state (New York) has a constitutional provision requiring that the state provide a service other than education (welfare).  Less than half of the state constitutions make specific reference to services, other than education, that a state may elect to provide.  Thus, one can see the importance with which education is held, but the question remains: education for what?  The answer from the state constitutions is that education is considered to be a vital part of the democratic process, so much so that without education the American political system could not function properly.  Virginia, for example, historically recognized the special relationship between effective voting and education by its provision requiring that two-thirds of its poll tax be used "exclusively in aid of the free public schools."  Constitution of Virginia, Article VIII, § 173, and see Harper v. Virginia Board of Elections, 383 U.S. 663, 664, 86 S.Ct. 1079, 1080, 16 L.Ed.2d 169 (1966).  Minnesota's provision is not untypical:

> The stability of a republican form of government depending mainly upon the intelligence of the people, it shall be the duty of the legislature to establish a general and uniform

system of public schools. (Constitution of Minnesota, Article VIII, § 1).

A citizen's willingness and ability to participate effectively in the social, civil and political life of the United States is uniquely dependent upon education.

The dominant purposes of compulsory education today are the development of good citizenship and the development of sufficient intellectual skills such that those capable of continuing on to higher education can do so; they can then supply the intellectual leadership needed for our society by becoming scholars, intellectuals and members of the learned professions. The overall goal seems to be the development of sufficient mind and character that will enable a person to know how to live and participate effectively in American democracy. "The modern public school derived from a philosophy of freedom reflected in the First Amendment," wrote Mr. Justice Frankfurter, adding that "the evolution of colonial education . . . into the public school system of today is the story of changing conceptions regarding the American democratic society, of the functions of State-maintained education in such a society and of the role therein of the free exercise of religion by the people." McCollum v. Bd. of Ed., 333 U.S. 203, 214, 68 S.Ct. 461, 466–467, 92 L.Ed. 649, 659–660 (1948):

> "The non-sectarian or secular public school was the means of reconciling freedom in general with religious freedom. The sharp confinement of the public schools to secular education was a recognition of the need of a democratic society to educate its children, insofar as the State undertook to do so, in an atmosphere free from pressures in a realm in which pressures are most resisted and where conflicts are most easily and most bitterly engendered. Designed to serve as perhaps the most powerful agency for promoting cohesion among a heterogeneous democratic people, the public school must keep scrupulously free from entanglement in the strife of sects. . . . This development of the public school as a symbol of our secular unity was not a sudden achievement nor attained without violent conflict." Id. at 216–217, 468, 661.

## STATE AND FEDERAL CONTROL OF EDUCATION

Before the adoption of the Constitution of the United States, a child's education was the responsibility of his parents. This is the common-law rule—that parental control over a child extends to control the education of that child—and this rule of parental control still exists in the limited number of situations where it has not been modified by federal or state law.  The United States Constitution is completely silent on the whole subject.  It fails to make any direct references about education.  Consequently, there is no specific constitutional directive about the purposes of education, nor are there any direct references about which of the two divisions of government, state or federal, shall have exclusive or shared constitutional responsibilities for education.  The result has been that states primarily control and regulate public education for the following reasons.

In legal theory the federal government is looked upon as one of specifically delegated powers.  Thus, for example, Congress can pass laws only by exercising the specific powers granted to it.  The bulk of Congress' powers are set forth in Article I, Section 8, of the Constitution, and direct power over education is not among them.  On the other hand, legal theory holds that the situation of a state government is just the opposite of that of the federal government.  A state government possesses all the powers that are not specifically prohibited to it by either the federal or state constitutions.  This broad, general reservoir of power that is possessed by a state is frequently referred to as the "police power," but the Supreme Court of the United States has never fully defined its scope and limits.  In Mayor of the City of New York v. Miln, 11 Pet. 102, 9 L.Ed. 648 (1837), the Supreme Court said: "It [the police power] embraces every law which concerns the welfare of the whole people of the state or any individual within it, whether it relates to their rights or duties, whether it respects them as men or citizens of the state, whether in their public or private relations, whether it relates to the rights of persons or property of the whole people of the state or of any individual within it."  In Hannibal & St. J. R. Co. v. Husen, 95 U.S. 465, 24 L.Ed. 527 (1877), it said: "The police power of a state extends to the protection of the lives, limbs, health, comfort, and quiet of all persons, and to the protection of all property, within the state, and hence to the making of all regulations promotive of domestic order, morals, health, and safety."  The result is that state legislatures can legislate directly on the subject of education unless their state constitutions forbid them, because nothing in the federal constitution precludes state authority.  The constitutions of most states require that their state legislatures create a system of public schools.  This means then, that state legislatures generally have the power to see to it that schools are built; to require that certain persons attend school and to prescribe the curriculum, methods and goals of education.  And state legislatures have exercised their powers extensively, establishing uniform, statewide systems of public education.

The traditional view that a state has extensive state power over education was set forth long ago, and has been reiterated by the Supreme Court of Indiana in State ex rel. Clark v. Haworth, 122 Ind. 462, 23 N.E. 946 (1890).  The primary question presented to the court was whether jurisdiction over public education was a state or local governmental matter.

"  .   .   .   Essentially and intrinsically, the schools in which are educated and trained the children who are to become the rulers of the commonwealth are matters of state, and not of local, jurisdiction.  In such matters the state is a unit, and the legislature the source of power.  The authority over schools and school affairs is not necessarily a distributive one, to be exercised by local instrumentalities;  but, on the contrary, it is a central power residing in the legislature of the state.  It is for the law-making power to determine whether the authority shall be exercised by a state board of education, or distributed to county, township, or city organizations throughout the state.  With that determination the judiciary can no more rightfully interfere than can the legislature with a decree or judgment pronounced by a judicial tribunal.  The decision is as conclusive and inviolable in the one case as in the other;  and an interference with the legislative judgment would be a breach of the constitution which no principle would justify, nor any precedent excuse. .   .   .   Judge Cooley has examined the question with care, and discussed it with ability;  and he declares that the legislature has plenary power over the subject of the public schools.  He says in the course of his discussion, that 'to what degree the legislature shall provide for the education of the people at the cost of the state, or of its municipalities, is a question which, except as regulated by the constitution, addresses itself to the legislative judgment exclusively.'  Again, he says, 'The governing school boards derive all their authority from the statute and can exercise no powers except those expressly granted and those which result by necessary implication from the grant.'  Const.Lim. (5th Ed.) p. 225, note 1.  No case has been cited by counsel, and none has been discovered by us,—although we have searched the reports with care,—which denies the doctrine that the regulation of the public schools is a state matter, exclusively within the dominion of the legislature.   .   .   . "

"As the [state] power over schools is a legislative one, it is not exhausted by exercise.  The legislature, having tried one plan, is not precluded from trying another.  It has a choice of methods, and may change its plans as often as it deems necessary or expedient;  and for mistakes or abuses it is answerable to the people, but not to the courts.  It is clear, therefore, that, even if it were true that the legislature had uniformly intrusted the management of school affairs to local organizations, it would not authorize the conclusion that it might not change the system. To deny the power to change, is to affirm that progress is impossible, and that we must move forever 'in the dim footsteps of antiquity.' But the legislative power moves in a constant stream, and is not exhausted by its exercise in any number of instances, however great. It is not true, however, that the authority over schools was originally regarded as a local one. On the contrary, the earlier cases asserted that the legislature could not delegate the power to levy taxes for school purposes to local organizations, but must itself directly exercise the power; thus denying, in the strongest possible form, the theory of local control. . . . All the public schools have been established under legislative enactments, and all rules and regulations have been made pursuant to statutory authority. Every school that has been established owes its existence to legislation, and every school officer owes his authority to the statute.

"It is impossible to conceive of the existence of a uniform system of common schools without power lodged somewhere to make it uniform; and, even in the absence of express constitutional provisions, that power must necessarily reside in the legislature. If it does reside there, then that body must have, as an incident of the principal power, the authority to prescribe the course of study, and the system of instruction, that shall be pursued and adopted, as well as the books which shall be used. This general doctrine is well entrenched by authority. Hovey v. State, 119 Ind. 395, 21 N.E. Rep. 21; Hovey v. Riley, 119 Ind. 386, 21 N.E.Rep. 890; State v. Hawkins, 44 Ohio St. 98, 5 N.E.Rep. 228; State v. Harmon, 31 Ohio St. 250. Having this authority, the legislature may not only prescribe regulations for using such books, but it may also declare how the books shall be obtained and distributed. If it may do this, then it may provide that they shall be obtained through the medium of a contract awarded to the best or lowest bidder, since, if it be true, as it unquestionably is, that the power is legislative, it must also be true that the legislature has an unrestricted discretion, and an unfettered choice of methods. It cannot be possible that the courts can interfere with this legislative power, and adjudge that the legislature shall not adopt this method or that method; for, if the question is at all legislative, it is so in its whole length and breadth."

Finally, with respect to overall state authority over schools and school districts, Nebraska's Supreme Court said:

" . . . we have often held that the state is supreme in the creation and control of school districts, and may, if it thinks proper, modify or withdraw any of their powers, or destroy such school districts without the consent of the legal voters or even over their protests." Kosmicki v. Kowalski, 184 Neb. 639, 171 N.W.2d 172 (1969).

Must a state legislature having power over education exercise that power and create public schools? In the absence of a constitutional requirement to create schools a state legislature need not act. In such circumstances a state may have private schools but no public schools.

The constitutions of some states require their state legislatures to create a school system. Article 9, Section 5 of California's Constitution provides an example of a constitutional duty: "The legislature shall provide for a system of common schools by which a free school shall be kept up and supported in each district at least six months in every year, after the first year in which a school has been established." When it is not defined by either constitution or statute, questions frequently arise concerning the scope and meaning of the term "common schools". They are the schools that the legislature is obligated to establish. The distinctive elements of common schools are "that they are free schools, open to all the children of proper school age residing in the locality, and affording, so long as the term lasts, equal opportunity for all to acquire the learning taught in the various common school branches." City of Louisville v. Commonwealth, 134 Ky. 488, 121 S.W. 411 (1909), and see 47 Am.Jur., Schools, § 3, p. 298. Included in the term "common schools" are the public elementary and secondary grade schools, one through twelve. For example, the Supreme Court of Idaho in Paulson v. Minidoka County School Dist., 93 Idaho 469, 463 P.2d 935 (1970), stated: "We hold that Minidoka County High School is a 'common school' within the meaning . . . of the Idaho Constitution. Because the appellants' high school is a 'common school' it must, by constitutional command, be 'free'." On whether required textbooks and other needed materials must be supplied freely to pupils at state expense, see Bond v. Ann Arbor School Dist., 18 Mich.App. 506, 171 N.W.2d 557 (1969) and Johnson v. New York State Ed. Department, 449 F.2d 871 (2d Cir. 1971). Courts have held that the term "common school" does not include kindergartens, Los Angeles County v. Kirk, 148 Cal. 385, 83 P. 250 (1905), nor schools for adults or special education schools, such as a school for the blind, Walls v. Board of Ed., 195 Ark. 955, 116 S.W.2d 354 (1938). The duty of the legislature under this type of state constitutional provision extends only to establishing "common schools." On the other hand, while not required by its state constitution to do so, if it chooses to use it a state legislature has the power to establish free kindergartens, In re Kindergarten Schools, 18 Colo. 234, 32 P. 422 (1893), free special education schools, or a free system of higher education. State Bank of Commerce of Brockport v. Stone, 261 N.Y. 175, 184 N.E. 750 (1933).

State legislatures do not administer the daily affairs of the public schools. That would be an enormously unwieldly task, and legislatures would be free to do little else. Instead, state legislatures create administrative agencies such as State Boards of Education; a chief executive office commonly called the "State Superintendent of Public Schools," and local school boards, and then delegate certain powers to these sub-agencies to enable them to run the schools. The exact statutory pattern varies from state to state. Courts refuse to allow state legislatures to delegate their legislative powers to these administrative agencies because the state constitutions place the pure legislative power solely in the legislatures. The result is that so long as state legislatures, by law, set forth clear and concise standards to guide their administrative agencies, courts will allow legislatures to delegate the authority necessary to enable administrative agencies to make rules and regulations for running the day-to-day operations of the schools. The power delegated includes the authority to perform legislative, executive and quasi-judicial functions. The State Board of Education usually functions as the legislative body that makes school policy; the State Superintendent usually functions as the highest administrative officer for the school system, and both may exercise quasi-judicial functions. Enactment of various rules and regulations is discretionary with the State Boards of Education. But, if rules or regulations are enacted, they must be made pursuant to, and be consistent with, the standards set forth by statute by the legislature.

So long as it follows the legislative standards and stays within its delegated powers, and it doesn't violate a constitutional limitation on them, the highest administrative agency, usually a State Board of Education, has the final authority on all matters of educational policy and on the ultimate administrative practices of a state's public schools. Its policy and administrative judgments will not be reviewed, nor reversed, by the courts unless bad faith, fraud or breach of trust can be shown as having been the basis for the policy of administrative judgments. The same situation prevails generally in the case of quasi-judicial rulings not involving a pure question of law. On the other hand, a State Board of Education cannot have the final word if only a pure question of law is involved, such as the proper interpretation of the law setting forth its controlling standards. The latter is a pure judicial function and there is no presumption in favor of a State Board's ruling; finality rests with the courts. See, Wilson v. Board of Ed., 234 Md. 561, 200 A.2d 67 (1964). But, when a case does not involve a pure question of law, a strong presumption favors the State Board's decision, and the courts generally will not substitute their decisions for those of State Boards by reversing the quasi-judicial rulings of a State Board of Education unless those rulings are arbitrary or capricious. This means that in all matters within its legal discretion that fairly and honestly admit of two or more opinions, the opinion of the State Board of Education is final and conclusive. For example, the Board of Trustees of a local Texas school district found the Superintendent of that district guilty of withholding, mishandling and misapplying school district funds, and ordered that he be discharged. The Superintendent of the district appealed the order to the State Superintendent of Public Instruction who, after a hearing, reversed the decision of the Board of Trustees and ordered that the Superintendent be reinstated. The Board of Trustees then appealed the State Superintendent's decision to the State Board of Education which reversed the State Superintendent's decision and affirmed the original order of the Board of Trustees calling for the discharge of the district Superintendent, who then brought an action in a court seeking to have his discharge order set aside. On appeal, the Court of Civil Appeals for Texas refused, stating:

"The question before the school board and the State Board of Education in the instant case was one of fact relating to the manner in which appellant was performing his duties as superintendent of schools in connection with the handling and application of the finances of the school district which had been entrusted to his care. There was no implication in the findings made by the school board that appellant had been guilty of an intentional misapplication of the funds belonging to the school district, or of an intention on his part to appropriate the funds of the school to his own use and benefit. The board simply found as a fact that appellant had 'withheld, mishandled and misapplied funds belonging to the Trinity Independent School District' which had been entrusted to his custody as superintendent of its schools and that he had 'failed to divulge material information relative to the handling of said funds to the trustees of the school district.' The question as to whether appellant should have been discharged for one or more of the reasons set out in the charges preferred against him were, we think, matters of fact relating to the internal affairs of the school and the efficient management thereof and 'came within the purview of the matters committed by the Legislature to such board for its determination' and the decision of the State Board that appellant had been properly discharged was final on that issue.

"Appellant's contention that the State Board of Education acted arbitrarily, capriciously, or fraudulently in affirming the judgment of the Board of Trustees of the Trinity Independent School District cannot be sustained. As stated by The Supreme Court in the case of Railroad Commission of Texas v. Shell Oil Co., Inc., et al., supra, it is generally recognized that where the order of the agency under attack involves the exercise of the sound judgment and discretion of the agency in a matter committed to it by the Legislature, the court will sustain the order if the action of the agency in reaching such conclusion is reasonably supported by substantial evidence, and, at the time such order was entered by the agency, there then existed sufficient facts to justify the entry of the order." Blair v. Board of Trustees, 161 S.W.2d 1030 (Texas, 1942).

A local government unit, such as a city or a town, has power over education only to the extent that the authority specifically has been delegated to it either by a statute of the state legislature or directly by the state constitution. "If a power is not given it is said it does not exist." Mosier v. Thompson, 216 Tenn. 655, 393 S.W.2d 734 (1965). Moreover, a state legislature can compel cities to levy taxes for school purposes in order "to supplement the fund paid to the [local school] district out of the state money" because education is a state, not a local, function. City of Louisville v. Commonwealth, 134 Ky. 488, 121 S.W. 411 (1909). A school district is also a local unit separate from a city or town, and it also is a creature of the state; thus, the state constitution and legislative statute creating the school district are the sources of that local district's powers. Its school board has no others. "A school district derives its existence and powers wholly from the General Assembly" said the Illinois court. Dato v. Village of Vernon Hills, 62 Ill.App.2d 274, 210 N.E.2d 626 (1965). A legislature can delegate certain broadly defined powers over education to a local school board. In such situations the school board is said to have discretionary authority within which it can make decisions or adopt additional rules and regulations that it deems necessary and wise, so long as they fall within the scope of the broadly defined powers delegated by the legislature. For example, it may have discretion to decide which teacher to hire or where to locate a school building. In addition to discretionary powers which require the exercise of judgment, a legislature can also require that a local (or state) school board act in very specific ways—ways that are ministerial and do not involve the exercise of judgment. For example, a local school board might be required to prepare a budget or accept the lowest bid on a contract. Thus, the powers of a local and state school board can be classified as discretionary or ministerial. Since education is primarily a state function and since members of state and local boards of education derive their offices and powers from the state, courts hold that members of State and local boards of education are state officers. Board of Ed. v. Society of Alumni of Louisville Male High, Ky., 239 S.W.2d 931 (1951).

Although the legal control of education is primarily a state function, no state legislature is absolutely free to do anything and everything with education that it may choose. Usually the courts will not interfere. But if a state should act in a manner that contravenes a constitutional limitation on its powers—say a provision of the Bill of Rights that has been incorporated into the Fourteenth Amendment—then courts do interfere. Also, Congress has vast power to regulate and control certain matters even though they might impinge upon education. If Congress properly exercises its constitutional powers and that exercise conflicts with a state constitution or statute, then that state law must give way because the federal law is the "Supreme Law of the Land." Moreover, Congress has power to affect education by taxing and then making the money available to the states for educational purposes so long as the states agree to comply with certain conditions set by Congress. Congress' power over these grant-in-aid programs derives from Article 1, Section 8, clause 1, of the Constitution of the United States which grants power to Congress "to lay and collect taxes, duties, imposts, and excises, to pay the debts and provide for the common defense and general welfare of the United States." Congress' powers to tax and to provide for "the general welfare" includes the power to provide for education through such means as making grants of funds available so long as the states agree to meet certain conditions. The result is that a complicated network of constitutional provisions, state and federal laws control or affect public education. A capsule description of one federal spending program follows. It is one example of the way in which Congress has affected education.

Congress enacted the Elementary and Secondary Education Act (ESEA) in 1965 (Pub.L.No. 89–10, 79 Stat. 27 (1965)). It is one of the most comprehensive attempts at the federal level to provide federal aid to elementary and secondary schools, public and private. There may be questions about the constitutionality of some of its provisions. Title I of ESEA sets up the largest and most pervasive program of the Act that has been funded by Congress. Under it, millions of students have received billions in federal aid. This title provides needed funds to the states for distribution to their local educational agencies for the creation and supplementation of programs to meet the special needs of educationally deprived children. However, before a state can distribute funds to one of its educational agencies, provision must first be made in that particular program for full participation of private schools, including parochial schools, that have deprived children in attendance. Title II of the Act provides funds to states to acquire textbooks, library resources and other instructional materials for the use of children in public and private, including parochial, elementary and secondary schools. Title III authorizes the Commissioner of Education to make direct grants to local educational agencies within a state for the construction and operation of educational centers, but first he must determine that the program of the local educational agency provides for the participation of children attending non-profit private schools as well as public schools. Title IV authorizes the Commissioner of Education to make grants to universities and colleges, including non-profit institutions for the purpose of advancing research in education.

## NOTES AND QUESTIONS

1.  Is the ultimate control over public education primarily a local function, a state function or a federal function? Why?

2.  Does the state legislature have power to change or to abolish the system of public schools?

3.  Does the state legislature have power to prescribe the curriculum and to select the books for public schools?

4.  Does the state legislature have power to require that cities of a certain class, or counties, lay taxes and build and maintain public schools, even without a vote of the citizens within that city or county?

5.  What is a "common school"? Is a community college a "common school"? A pre-school? A kindergarten? A school for the blind? A school for economically deprived children? A university?

6.  What is "the police power"? If the legislature exercises its "police power" within its constitutional authority, will courts determine whether the legislation is good or bad, or wise or unwise?

7.  If the State Constitution does not require its legislature to create a kindergarten, does it have power to do so? Could a legislature create a system of free community colleges?

8.  Does the Constitution of the United States grant direct power over education to Congress? To the states? To municipalities?

9.  When a school board adopts a curriculum plan is it exercising ministerial or discretionary powers?

10. Describe, in detail, the legal controls over the legislative and administrative structure of education in your state.

## THE STATUTORY REQUIREMENT OF COMPULSORY SCHOOLING

———

The common-law responsibility of a parent for his child's education is owed not only to the child but to the state as well. The reason is that the state has an interest in having its children educated so that they can become good citizens and make up a body politic capable of solving new social problems in an intelligent and democratic way. To achieve these ends the common-law parental responsibility has been supplemented by state constitutional provisions and laws that apply to every child living within the state. Their overall constitutionality has been upheld. California's constitution provides an illustration, Article 9, Section 1, states: "A general difference of knowledge and intelligence being essential to the preservation of the rights and liberties of the people, the legislature shall encourage by all suitable means the promotion of intellectual, scientific, moral and agricultural improvement." These measures commonly provide for compulsory school attendance of children of specified ages and place an obligation upon parents, or their substitutes, to see to it that their children attend school regularly. By law, public school attendance officers have the duty of enforcing mandatory attendance at public and private schools. If parents should fail to meet their obligation by refusing to send a child to school, they can be subjected to civil or criminal penalties. If a child is sent to school but refuses to attend regularly thereby becoming an incorrigible truant, then states commonly provide that the child can be made a ward of the juvenile court to be supervised by a juvenile probation officer. Thus, state coercion is applied to enforce the duty to attend school. On this analysis, the common-school, public education provided for children by a state is primarily a duty imposed on the children and parents for the public good, and secondarily an individual right that they possess. Washington's law provides a typical example of the obligation to attend school.

"All parents, guardians and other persons in this state having custody of any child eight years of age and under fifteen years of age, or of any child fifteen years of age and under eighteen years of age not regularly and lawfully engaged in some useful and remunerative occupation or attending part-time school in accordance with the provisions of chapter 28A.28 RCW or excused from school attendance thereunder, shall cause such child to attend the public school of the district in which the child resides for the full time when such school may be in session or to attend a private school for the same time, unless the school district superintendent of the district in which the child resides shall have excused such child from such attendance because the child is physically or mentally unable to attend school or has already attained a reasonable proficiency in the branches required by law to be taught in the first nine grades of the public schools of this state. Proof of absence from any public or private school shall be prima facie evidence of a violation of this section. Private school for the purposes of this section shall be one approved or accredited under regulations established by the state board of education." RCW 28A.27.010.

## WHAT IS THE PURPOSE OF COMPULSORY SCHOOLING?

A carefully written legal obligation requiring that children attend public schools or their legal equivalent may be constitutionally valid. But, questions remain about the proper goals of public education. Is "schooling" properly to be distinguished from "education"? Clearly, the dominant political community should be required to justify its legal obligation to attend school and the prolonged detention of its children-citizens in a system of public, or equivalent, education. What then is the justifying purpose of modern compulsory schooling? A fair question is whether public education is any longer useful, and, if so, on what terms and conditions seeking what specific goals, and if not, then what is the alternative?

In McCollum v. Bd. of Ed., Mr. Justice Frankfurter stated that "the public school is at once the symbol of our democracy and the most pervasive means for promoting our common destiny." Frankfurter's belief, like Thomas Jefferson's before him, was that the two dominant purposes of compulsory public education are (1) to make the people capable of being guardians of their own liberties, and (2) to provide our society with intellectual leadership. The first purpose goes to effective citizenship. Compulsory public education should provide everybody with the intellectual resources, and particularly an effective command of the language, needed to separate public truths from half-truths or lies and thereby enabling everyone to participate effectively in the political processes and to defend themselves against demagogues and tyrants. Is one of the primary goals of modern education that of creating a political community, and, if so, how should that political community be defined? The second purpose of compulsory public education is to impart enough intellectual skills to students such that those capable of continuing can become scholars, intellectuals and members of the learned professions. This probably implies an elitist notion: that higher, non-compulsory education should be made available to men and women from all social classes, but only to those persons having a pronounced taste for intellectual matters; who are qualified for it, and who are committed to spending their lives in intellectual pursuits. Has the dream of making culture available to the masses, by making higher education widely available, failed? If so or if not, what are the implications for compulsory education in the "common schools"? Are the above two purposes the proper goals of compulsory education today?

What are the correct answers to the following questions? They are reprinted with permission from p. 18 of the April, 1973, issue of the *Center Report*, a publication of the Center for the Study of Democratic Institutions, Santa Barbara, California:

"I    Should the primary concern of education be the creation of a political community?  If so, how shall the political community be conceived?  As primarily economic, concerned mainly with the livelihoods of its members and with the productivity of the whole, or as requiring additional dimensions?

"A.    Questions regarding education in the context of a strict conception of political community:

"1.    Are universal literacy and numericity of sufficient importance in this decade to deserve the substantial share of educational funds and energies?  Or should there be, for all students, a broader range of outcomes?

"2.    How shall the terminal point of public education be determined?

"3.    How shall assessed national needs and individual aspirations and propensities be reconciled when they are incongruent?

"4.    Are schools the appropriate institutions for career education (job training)?  Or should training be on-the-job or in specially equipped and specially timed institutions supplementary to the schools?

"5.    Shall maximizing the educability of the deprived, least-schooled segments of our population be a matter of first priority?  If so, what environmental deprivations are most deleterious and most capable of correction: e. g., parental expectations and rewards vs. richness of sensory imput in earliest years?

"6.    If the answer to question 5 is affirmative, is it also desirable that education of the less-deprived and the talented be refurbished and nurtured in the midst of emphasis on the deprived?  If so, how maintain a maximum of the propinquities among socioeconomic classes and ethnic groups, if these are threatened by this dual emphasis?

"B.    Questions regarding education in the context of a broad conception of political community:

"1.    Shall schools be concerned with recast of values and loyalties and reformation of character?  If so, should the aim be one body of values, loyalties, and characteral traits or should a diversity be sought?  What are the components of the most desirable bodies of values, loyalties, character traits?

"2.    If this task is held inappropriate to the public schools, should it be undertaken at all?  If so, by what other means?

"3.    Shall the schools be concerned with imparting the arts of the 'practical,' i. e., the processes by which statute, moral precept, and scientific generality are brought to bear on concrete, particular situations, and consensus obtained?  Or should other instrumentalities for service be sought?   Or should these arts be left to those who seek them out in experience?

"4.   Concerning a common language, history, and culture: to what extent and in what form shall these be pursued?   What degree and form of patriotism?   How shall religion be treated?

"5.   What, if any, requirements of the community justify compulsory attendance?   To what age?

"6.   What, if any community requirements justify grades and credentials?

"7.   If the community believed that education (study) should be lifelong and made adequate provision for it, what would be the effect on all the preceding questions?

"II   Shall the public schools disavow restriction to political community narrowly conceived and concern itself as well with development of a wide range of human potentialities?   Should these potentialities be conceived as contributions to political community, as an added category of goods, or as the larger category within which membership in political community is one part?

"A.   Shall the public schools deepen their working definition of literacy to include perception of the terms, distinctions, and commitments to methods and principles which render a solution to a complex problem only one solution among several?   If pursued effectively, such a deepening of the notion of literacy will tend to blur the distinction between expert and layman, hence between ruler and ruled.   Is this wise?

"B.   Shall there be concern for individually different talents for satisfying activities unrelated to careers, e. g., appreciation and production of fine and applied arts?   If so, how can these individual differences be identified early?   What means are there for transforming fantasies about such activities, and limitations of the child's view of them imposed by limited experience, into trials of less fantastic and more varied resources of satisfaction?   How can such transformations be obtained while yet honoring individual differences in these respects?

"C.   If there shall be concern for individually different outcomes of education, what are the means for integrating individualized goals common to most or all recipients of education?

"D.   Should the schools, at every level, visibly as well as in fact, promise to each student a contribution to a then-felt want or need?

"E.   What of the educational responsibilities of other institutions: church, family, industry, the professions, institutions yet to be devised?"

Robert Hutchins, a noted educator and former President of the Center for the Study of Democratic Institutions, advanced the following thoughts about "Political Maturity." Do they also identify the overall purpose of compulsory schooling, so that it is not inconsistent with effective and meaningful education? Completely? If Hutchins' views are not adequate, in what way should they be supplemented in order to identify the purpose of compulsory schooling?

## ROBERT M. HUTCHINS, ON POLITICAL MATURITY

It is not necessary for the people of this country or for the world to agree upon anything or to agree with one another. That would be too much to expect and it could also turn out to be very boring. But it is necessary, I think, if we are to survive, that we understand one another. At the moment it would be very difficult to say (and, in fact, I haven't heard anybody say it) that we have a political community in this country. We can't communicate with one another, inside the academy or out.

A common educational program once thought indispensable has disappeared, and over the last five years many books have received much acclaim for recommending that our public schools be abolished. They have shown not the slightest interest in the consequences of such action on the formation or maintenance of the political community. Their interest has been in gratifying the whims of individuals, and this could only lead to the kind of amoral egotism disclosed by the Watergate transcripts.

I have always thought that the basic requirements for the formation of a political community is a common liberal education, an education that is appropriate to a community of free men. This has nothing to do with vocational training or with what is called career education, whatever that may mean. The liberal arts are the arts of communication and the arts of using the mind. They are the arts indispensable to further learning, for they are the arts of reading, writing, speaking, listening, figuring. They have a timeless quality, for they are indispensable no matter what happens in any state of the world. They are, in fact, the arts of becoming human. The object of liberal or basic education may be said to be the transformation of young animals into human beings.

I believe in liberal education for everybody. Nor have I ever seen any evidence that it is beyond the reach of everybody, nor any evidence that educational institutions are incapable of imparting it if only they will. But often they don't.

I became an academic administrator in 1923. For more than 51 years, I have seen educational institutions from the kindergarten up settle their programs by logrolling, by public relations, by political pressure and most of all by asking where the money is. I have met with committees of great universities to discuss education and research, and I have found them talking about those mystic initials ADA and FTE, average daily attendance and fulltime equivalents This is what they wanted to talk about because manipulating these letters produces the revenue, through a kind of mystical algebra, derived from the state. What this led to was public relations as determinant of policy. They tried to think of courses that would attract students. It mattered not whether these courses had any intellectual content. Things have not changed.

In these meetings, there was a general fear expressed that courses with intellectual content would for that reason alone frighten students. Hence it would defeat the economic purpose the university had in view.

The purpose of the educational system as a whole is to form and maintain the political community and to equip the citizen (I emphasize the word "citizen" because citizens are what we seem to lack) with the means of going on learning all his life. This is an enormous task. And the job of educational leaders is not to think up educational gimmicks that will deceive the public into supporting things not worth doing, but to explain to the people what education is, why it is important, why it is as important as the founding fathers thought, and even more, why in a technological age the rapidity of change makes current fads the least effective of all educational programs. The trouble with current fads is that they won't stay current for very long.

---

## THE CONSTITUTIONAL COMPROMISE

---

## PIERCE v. SOCIETY OF THE SISTERS OF THE HOLY NAMES OF JESUS AND MARY
## PIERCE v. HILL MILITARY ACADEMY

Supreme Court of the United States, 1925.
268 U.S. 510, 45 S.Ct. 571, 69 L.Ed. 1070.

Mr. Justice McREYNOLDS delivered the opinion of the Court.

These appeals are from decrees, based upon undenied allegations, which granted preliminary orders restraining appellants from threatening or attempting to enforce the Compulsory Education Act adopted November 7, 1922, under the initiative provision of her Constitution by the voters of Oregon. Jud.Code, § 266. They present the same points of law; there are no controverted questions of fact. Rights said to be guaranteed by the federal Constitution were specially set up, and appropriate prayers asked for their protection.

The challenged Act, effective September 1, 1926, requires every parent, guardian or other person having control or charge or custody of a child between eight and sixteen years to send him "to a public school for the period of time a public school shall be held during the current year" in the district where the child resides; and failure to do so is declared a misdemeanor. There are exemptions—not specially important here—for children who are not normal, or who have completed the eighth grade, or who reside at considerable distances from any public school, or whose parents or guardians hold special permits from the County Superintendent. The manifest purpose is to compel general attendance at public schools by normal children, between eight and sixteen, who have not completed the eighth grade. And without doubt enforcement of the statute would seriously impair, perhaps destroy, the profitable features of appellees' business and greatly diminish the value of their property.

Appellee, the Society of Sisters, is an Oregon corporation, organized in 1880, with power to care for orphans, educate and instruct the youth, establish and maintain academies or schools, and acquire necessary real and personal property. It has long devoted its property and effort to the secular and religious education and care of children, and has acquired the valuable good will of many parents and guardians. It conducts interdependent primary and high schools and junior colleges, and maintains orphanages for the custody and control of children between eight and sixteen. In its primary schools many children between those ages are taught the subjects usually pursued in Oregon public schools during the first eight years. Systematic religious instruction and moral training according to the tenets of the Roman Catholic Church are also regularly provided. All courses of study, both temporal and religious, contemplate continuity of training under appellee's charge; the primary schools are essential to the system and the most profitable. It owns valuable buildings, especially constructed and equipped for school purposes. The business is remunerative—the annual income from primary schools exceeds thirty thousand dollars—and the successful conduct of this requires long time contracts with teachers and parents. The Compulsory Education Act of 1922 has already caused the withdrawal from its schools of children who would otherwise continue, and their income has steadily declined. The appellants, public officers, have proclaimed their purpose strictly to enforce the statute.

After setting out the above facts the Society's bill alleges that the enactment conflicts with the right of parents to choose schools where their children will receive appropriate mental and religious training, the right of the child to influence the parents' choice of a school, the right of schools and teachers therein to engage in a useful business or profession, and is accordingly repugnant to the Constitution and void. And, further, that unless enforcement of the measure is enjoined the corporation's business and property will suffer irreparable injury.

Appellee, Hill Military Academy, is a private corporation organized in 1908 under the laws of Oregon, engaged in owning, operating and conducting for profit an elementary, college preparatory and military training school for boys between the ages of five and twenty-one years. The average attendance is one hundred, and the annual fees received for each student amount to some eight hundred dollars. The elementary department is divided into eight grades, as in the public schools; the college preparatory department has four grades, similar to those of the public high schools; the courses of study conform to the requirements of the State Board of Education. Military instruction and training are also given, under the supervision of an Army officer. It owns considerable real and personal property, some useful only for school purposes. The business and incident good will are very valuable. In order to conduct its affairs long time contracts must be made for supplies, equipment, teachers and pupils. Appellants, law officers of the State and County, have publicly announced that the Act of November 7, 1922, is valid and have declared their intention to enforce it. By reason of the statute and threat of enforcement appellee's business is being destroyed and its property depreciated; parents and guardians are refusing to make contracts for the future instruction of their sons, and some are being withdrawn.

The Academy's bill states the foregoing facts and then alleges that the challenged Act contravenes the corporation's right guaranteed by the Fourteenth Amendment and that unless appellants are restrained from proclaiming its validity and threatening to enforce it irreparable injury will result. The prayer is for an appropriate injunction.

No answer was interposed in either cause, and after proper notices they were heard by three judges (Jud.Code § 266) on motions for preliminary injunctions upon the specifically alleged facts. The court ruled that the Fourteenth Amendment guaranteed appellees against the deprivation of their property without due process of law consequent upon the unlawful interference by appellants with the free choice of patrons, present and prospective. It declared the right to conduct schools was property and that parents and guardians, as part of their liberty, might direct the education of children by selecting reputable teachers and places. Also, that these schools were not unfit or harmful to the public, and that enforcement of the challenged statute would unlawfully deprive them of patronage and thereby destroy their owners' business and property. Finally, that the threats to enforce the Act would continue to cause irreparable injury; and the suits were not premature.

No question is raised concerning the power of the State reasonably to regulate all schools, to inspect, supervise and examine them, their teachers and pupils; to require that all children of proper age attend some school, that teachers shall be of good moral character and patriotic disposition, that certain studies plainly essential to good citizenship must be taught, and that nothing be taught which is manifestly inimical to the public welfare.

The inevitable practical result of enforcing the Act under consideration would be destruction of appellees' primary schools, and perhaps all other private primary schools for normal children within the State of Oregon. These parties are engaged in a kind of undertaking not inherently harmful, but long regarded as useful and meritorious. Certainly there is nothing in the present records to indicate that they have failed to discharge their obligations to patrons, students or the State. And there are no peculiar circumstances or present emergencies which demand extraordinary measures relative to primary education.

Under the doctrine of Meyer v. Nebraska, 262 U.S. 390, we think it entirely plain that the Act of 1922 unreasonably interferes with the liberty of parents and guardians to direct the upbringing and education of children under their control. As often heretofore pointed out, rights guaranteed by the Constitution may not be abridged by legislation which has no reasonable relation to some purpose within the competency of the State. The fundamental theory of liberty upon which all governments in this Union repose excludes any general power of the State to standardize its children by forcing them to accept instruction from public teachers only. The child is not the mere creature of the State; those who nurture him and direct his destiny have the right, coupled with the high duty, to recognize and prepare him for additional obligations.

Appellees are corporations and therefore, it is said, they cannot claim for themselves the liberty which the Fourteenth Amendment guarantees. Accepted in the proper sense, this is true.   .   .   .   But they have business and property for which they claim protection. These are threatened with destruction through the unwarranted compulsion which appellants are exercising over present and prospective patrons of their schools. And this court has gone very far to protect against loss threatened by such action. Truax v. Raich, 239 U.S. 33; Truax v. Corrigan, 257 U.S. 312; Terrace v. Thompson, 263 U.S. 197.

The courts of the State have not construed the Act, and we must determine its meaning for ourselves. Evidently it was expected to have general application and cannot be construed as though merely intended to amend the charters of certain private corporations, as in Berea College v. Kentucky, 211 U.S. 45. No argument in favor of such view has been advanced.

Generally it is entirely true, as urged by counsel, that no person in any business has such an interest in possible customers as to enable him to restrain exercise of proper power of the State upon the ground that he will be deprived of patronage. But the injunctions here sought are not against the exercise of any *proper* power. Plaintiffs asked protection against arbitrary, unreasonable and unlawful interference with their patrons and the consequent destruction of their business and property. Their interest is clear and immediate, within the rule approved in Truax v. Raich, Truax v. Corrigan and Terrace v. Thompson, supra, and many other cases where injunctions have issued to protect business enterprises against interference with the freedom of patrons or customers.   .   .   .

The suits were not premature. The injury to appellees was present and very real, not a mere possibility in the remote future. If no relief had been possible prior to the effective date of the Act, the injury would have become irreparable. Prevention of impending injury by unlawful action is a well recognized function of courts of equity.

The decrees below are affirmed.


### NOTES AND QUESTIONS

1. Pierce v. Society of Sisters is a basic case because it establishes the fundamental constitutional framework within which states may regulate education. We learn from Pierce's compromise that no state government has constitutional power to dictate educational choice completely; no state can require that all its children be educated exclusively in its public schools. But, Pierce does not tell us whether a state has general constitutional power to require some compulsory school attendance. That was assumed: "No question is raised concerning the power of the State reasonably   .   .   .   to require that all children of proper age attend some school."

   However, compulsory education laws have not gone unchallenged. In Compulsory Mis-Education (1964), Paul Goodman wrote that they have "become a universal trap" and are "no good" because "many of the youth, both poor and middle-class, might be better off if the system simply did not exist, even if they then had no formal schooling at all." Ivan Illich has proposed that "the first article of a bill of rights for a modern, humanist society would correspond to the First Amendment of the U. S. Constitution: 'The State shall make no law with respect to the establishment of education.' There shall be no ritual obligatory for all." I. Illich, Deschooling Society (1970). See also, B. & R. Gross (eds.), Radical School Reform (1969), and J. Holt, Freedom and Beyond (1972). What, if any, are the valid educational arguments against compulsory schooling?

2. Should the Court have decided (rather than assumed) whether a state has constitutional power to require any compulsory public schooling of its children? What are the considerations relevant to a constitutional

decision in favor or against the state power? Is compulsory schooling compatible with human liberty? Do you agree with John Stuart Mill:

> If the government would make up its mind to require for every child a good education, it might save itself the trouble of providing one. It might leave to parents to obtain the education where and how they pleased, and content itself with helping to pay the school fees of the poorer classes of children. . . . The objections which are urged with reason against state education do not apply to the enforcement of all education by the state, but to the state's taking upon itself to direct that education [standardize its children?] . . . . . A general state education is a mere contrivance for molding people to be exactly like one another. . . . An education established and controlled by the state should exist, if it exists at all, as one among competing experiments, carried on for the purpose of example and stimulus, to keep the others up to a certain standard of excellence." (W. Levi, ed., Six Great Humanistic Essays of John Stuart Mill 1963)

What are the differences, if any, between Mill's views and Pierce? Would Mill have voted with the majority in Pierce if he had been a Justice on the Supreme Court at the time of decision? Would you? Why or why not?

3.  When deciding Pierce the Supreme Court could have refused to compromise and could have ruled completely in favor of the states, giving them full monopoly powers over all of education, or the Court could have ruled just the opposite, i. e., that states have no power whatsoever to compel school attendance, thereby leaving educational matters with the family and with the state to provide only voluntary school attendance programs. Is the latter Mill's position? Instead, the Supreme Court compromised. It assumed a state constitutionally can compel attendance at some school, but it left the choice to parents to decide between a public or a private school: "The child is not the mere creature of the State; those who nurture him and direct his destiny have the right, coupled with the high duty, to recognize and prepare him for additional obligations." Why should parents have this right? Where is it found in the constitution? Is Pierce an example of a "fundamental rights" approach to constitutional interpretation? What are some examples of the "additional obligations" that parents may prepare their children for? Do your examples necessarily involve parents choosing values for their children? Does Pierce hold that schools cannot choose values for their students? As a matter of educational or social policy or of constitutional law, should parental value choices for their children concern us more or less than value choices by schools?

4.  Is Pierce a case requiring a separation of church and state or one requiring a separation of school and state? Although religious freedom is not the articulated basis of the decision, some critics have suggested that if Pierce were decided today, the Court would base its decision on the First Amendment's clause guaranteeing the free exercise of religion; see, Pollak, Public Prayers and Public Schools, 77 Harv.L.Rev.

62, 75, note 48 (1963). That might be true if the rights of the parents and children of the Society of Sisters were the only rights involved. But what about the rights of parents and children involved with the Hill Military Academy? It was a non-sectarian, private school and cannot qualify for protection under the guarantee of the free exercise of religion. The parents and children involved with the Hill Military Academy can claim constitutional protection for their rights under the free speech provision of the First Amendment because the Supreme Court has ruled that the "conjunction of liberties is not peculiar to religious activity and institutions alone. The First Amendment gives freedom of the mind the same security as freedom of conscience." Thomas v. Collins, 323 U.S. 516, 531, 65 S.Ct. 315, 323 (1945). On this analysis, freedom of mind and conscience (which will necessarily lead to cultural diversity and pluralism) were the values protected against state control and "standardization" by Pierce. Thus, the core of Pierce's decision lies in the meaning of these words: "The fundamental theory of liberty upon which all governments in this Union repose excludes any general power of the State to standardize its children by forcing them to accept instruction from public teachers only." This analysis also informs the nature of the choices parents constitutionally can make when preparing their children for "additional obligations." If this analysis is correct, then Pierce has both a religious and non-religious component. See, Arons, The Separation of School and State: Pierce Reconsidered, 46 Harv.Ed.Rev. 76 (1976). Do you believe this interpretation of Pierce is correct?

5. Writing for the Court in Griswold v. Connecticut, 381 U.S. 479, 85 S.Ct. 1678, 14 L.Ed.2d 510 (1965), Mr. Justice Douglas stated that "by Pierce . . . the right to educate one's children as one chooses is made applicable to the states by force of the First and Fourteenth Amendments." Do you agree that that statement is the ruling of Pierce?

6. Does Pierce establish either (1) that private schools, including parochial schools, have a constitutional right to exist, or (2) that states cannot control curricula of private schools to the same extent that they can control public school curricula, or (3) that parents have a right to prepare their child "for additional obligations" by substituting parental education at home for public or private school education?

7. Is achieving the "melting pot" inconsistent with achieving the plurality that comes from Pierce's protection of parental, private value choices? In McCollum v. Board of Educ., supra, Mr. Justice Frankfurter stated that America's public schools were "designed to serve as perhaps the most powerful agency for promoting cohesion among a heterogeneous democratic people" and that "this development of the public school as a symbol of our secular unity was not a sudden achievement nor attained without violent conflict." Is Frankfurter's view consistent with Pierce? Should Pierce be overruled because of the requirements of Brown v. Board of Educ., 347 U.S. 483, 74 S.Ct. 686, 98 L.Ed. 873 (1954)? If only a desegregated, unitary state school system meets constitutional requirements, should a state be constitutionally permitted, under Pierce, to allow private schools to exist within its borders, especially racially-

discriminatory private schools? Furthermore, shouldn't all parents and all children, including all children now attending all private schools, whether parochial or whether racially discriminatory or not, have to share equally in the tasks of producing an integrated society? See, Norwood v. Harrison, infra, Chapter VIII.

# CONSTITUTIONAL LIMITATIONS ON THE OBLIGATION TO ATTEND SCHOOL

## WISCONSIN v. YODER

Supreme Court of the United States, 1972.
406 U.S. 205, 92 S.Ct. 1526, 32 L.Ed.2d 15.

Mr. Chief Justice BURGER delivered the opinion of the Court.

On petition of the State of Wisconsin, we granted the writ in this case to review a decision of the Wisconsin Supreme Court holding that respondents' convictions for violating the State's compulsory school attendance law were invalid under the Free Exercise Clause of the First Amendment to the United States Constitution made applicable to the State by the Fourteenth Amendment. For the reasons hereafter stated we affirm the judgment of the Supreme Court of Wisconsin.

Respondents Jonas Yoder and Adin Yutzy are members of the Old Order Amish Religion, and respondent Wallace Miller is a member of the Conservative Amish Mennonite Church. They and their families are residents of Green County, Wisconsin. Wisconsin's compulsory school attendance law required them to cause their children to attend public or private school until reaching age 16 but the respondents declined to send their children, ages 14 and 15, to public school after completing the eighth grade. [The children, Frieda Yoder, aged 15, Barbara Miller, aged 15, and Vernon Yutzy, aged 14, were all graduates of the eighth grade of public school.] The children were not enrolled in any private school, or within any recognized exception to the compulsory attendance law, and they are conceded to be subject to the Wisconsin statute.

On complaint of the school district administrator for the public schools, respondents were charged, tried, and convicted of violating the compulsory attendance law in Green County Court and were fined the sum of $5 each. Respondents defended on the ground that the application of the compulsory attendance law violated their rights under the First and Fourteenth Amendments. [The First Amendment provides: "Congress shall make no law respecting an establishment of religion, or prohibiting the Free exercise thereof. . . . "] The trial testimony showed that respondents believed, in accordance with the tenets of Old Order Amish communities generally, that their children's attendance at high school, public or private, was contrary to the Amish religion and way of life. They believed that by sending their children to high school, they would not only expose themselves to the danger of the censure of the church community, but, as found by the county court, endanger their own salvation and that of their children. The State stipulated that respondents' religious beliefs were sincere.

.  .  .  The history of the Amish sect was given in some detail, beginning with the Swiss Anabaptists of the 16th century who rejected institutionalized churches and sought to return to the early, simple, Christian life de-emphasizing material success, rejecting the competitive spirit, and seeking to insulate themselves from the modern world. As a result of their common heritage, Old Order Amish communities today are characterized by a fundamental belief that salvation requires life in a church community separate and apart from the world and worldly influence. This concept of life aloof from the world and its values is central to their faith.

A related feature of Old Order Amish communities is their devotion to a life in harmony with nature and the soil, as exemplified by the simple life of the early Christian era which continued in America during much of our early national life. Amish beliefs require members of the community to make their living by farming or closely related activities. Broadly speaking, the Old Order Amish religion pervades and determines the entire mode of life of its adherents. Their conduct is regulated in great detail by the *Ordnung*, or rules, of the church community. Adult baptism, which occurs in late adolescence, is the time at which Amish young people voluntarily undertake heavy obligations, not unlike the Bar Mitzvah of the Jews, to abide by the rules of the church community.

Amish objection to formal education beyond the eighth grade is firmly grounded in these central religious concepts. They object to the high school and higher education generally because the values it teaches are in marked variance with Amish values and the Amish way of life; they view secondary school education as an impermissible exposure of their children to a "worldly" influence in conflict with their beliefs. The high school tends to emphasize intellectual and scientific accomplishments, self-distinction, competitiveness, worldly success, and social life with other students. Amish society emphasizes informal learning-through-doing, a life of "goodness," rather than a life of intellect, wisdom, rather than technical knowledge, community welfare rather than competition, and separation, rather than integration with contemporary worldly society.

Formal high school education beyond the eighth grade is contrary to Amish beliefs not only because it places Amish children in an environment hostile to Amish beliefs with increasing emphasis on competition in class work and sports and with pressure to conform to the styles, manners and ways of the peer group, but because it takes them away from their community, physically and emotionally, during the crucial and formative adolescent period of life. During this period, the children must acquire Amish attitudes favoring manual work and self-reliance and the specific skills needed to perform the adult role of an Amish farmer or housewife. They must learn to enjoy physical labor. Once a child has learned basic reading, writing, and elementary mathematics, these traits, skills, and attitudes admittedly fall within the category of those best learned through example and "doing" rather than in a classroom. And, at this time in life, the Amish child must also grow in his faith and his relationship to the Amish community if he is to be prepared to accept the heavy obligations imposed by adult baptism. In short, high school attendance with teachers who are not of the Amish faith—and may even be hostile to it—interposes a serious barrier to the integration of the Amish child into the Amish religious community. Dr. John Hostetler, one of the experts on Amish society, testified that the modern high school is not equipped, in curriculum or social environment, to impart the values promoted by Amish society.

The Amish do not object to elementary education through the first eight grades as a general proposition because they agree that their children must have basic skills in the "three R's" in order to read the Bible, to be good farmers and citizens and to be able to deal with non-Amish people when necessary in the course of daily affairs. They view such a basic education as acceptable because it does not significantly expose their children to worldly values or interfere with their development in the Amish community during the crucial adolescent period. . . .

On the basis of such considerations, Dr. Hostetler testified that compulsory high school attendance could not only result in great psychological harm to Amish children, because of the conflicts it would produce, but would, in his opinion, ultimately result in the destruction of the Old Order Amish church community as it exists in the United States today. The testimony of Dr. Donald A. Erickson, an expert witness on education, also showed that the Amish succeed in preparing their high school age children to be productive members of the Amish community. He described their system of learning-through-doing the skills directly relevant to their adult roles in the Amish community as "ideal" and perhaps superior to ordinary high school education. The evidence also showed that the Amish have an excellent record as law-abiding and generally self-sufficient members of society.

. . . The Wisconsin Supreme Court, however, sustained respondents' claim under the Free Exercise Clause of the First Amendment and reversed the convictions.  A majority of the court was of the opinion that the State had failed to make an adequate showing that its interest in "establishing and maintaining an education system overrides the defendants' right to the free exercise of their religion."

## I

There is no doubt as to the power of a State, having a high responsibility for education of its citizens, to impose reasonable regulations for the control and duration of basic education.  See, e. g., Pierce v. Society of Sisters,   .  .  .   Providing public schools ranks at the very apex of the function of a State.  Yet even this paramount responsibility was, in *Pierce*, made to yield to the right of parents to provide an equivalent education in a privately operated system. There the Court held that Oregon's statute compelling attendance in a public school from age eight to age 16 unreasonably interfered with the interest of parents in directing the rearing of their offspring including their education in church-operated schools.  As that case suggests, the values of parental direction of the religious upbringing and education of their children in their early and formative years have a high place in our society.   .  .  .   Thus, a State's interest in universal education, however highly we rank it, is not totally free from a balancing process when it impinges on other fundamental rights and interests, such as those specifically protected by the Free Exercise Clause of the First Amendment and the traditional interest of parents with respect to the religious upbringing of their children so long as they, in the words of *Pierce*, "prepare [them] for additional obligations."   .  .  .

It follows that in order for Wisconsin to compel school attendance beyond the eighth grade against a claim that such attendance interferes with the practice of a legitimate religious belief, it must appear either that the State does not deny the free exercise of religious belief by its requirement, or that there is a state interest of sufficient magnitude to override the interest claiming protection under the Free Exercise Clause.   .  .  .

The essence of all that has been said and written on the subject is that only those interests of the highest order and those not otherwise served can overbalance legitimate claims to the free exercise of religion.  We can accept it as settled, therefore, that however strong the State's interest in universal compulsory education, it is by no means absolute to the exclusion or subordination of all other interests.

.  .  .

## II

We come then to the quality of the claims of the respondents concerning the alleged encroachment of Wisconsin's compulsory school attendance statute on their rights and the rights of their children to the free exercise of the religious beliefs they and their forebears have adhered to for almost three centuries. In evaluating those claims we must be careful to determine whether the Amish religious faith and their mode of life are, as they claim, inseparable and interdependent. A way of life, however virtuous and admirable, may not be interposed as a barrier to reasonable state regulation of education if it is based on purely secular considerations; to have the protection of the Religion Clauses, the claims must be rooted in religious belief. Although a determination of what is a "religious" belief or practice entitled to constitutional protection may present a most delicate question, the very concept of ordered liberty precludes allowing every person to make his own standards on matters of conduct in which society as a whole has important interests. Thus, if the Amish asserted their claims because of their subjective evaluation and rejection of the contemporary secular values accepted by the majority, much as Thoreau rejected the social values of his time and isolated himself at Walden Pond, their claim would not rest on a religious basis. Thoreau's choice was philosophical and personal rather than religious, and such belief does not rise to the demands of the Religion Clause.

Giving no weight to such secular considerations, however, we see that the record in this case abundantly supports the claim that the traditional way of life of the Amish is not merely a matter of personal preference, but one of deep religious conviction, shared by an organized group, and intimately related to daily living. That the Old Order Amish daily life and religious practice stems from their faith is shown by the fact that it is in response to their literal interpretation of the Biblical injunction from the Epistle of Paul to the Romans, "Be not conformed to this world. . . . " This command is fundamental to the Amish faith. Moreover, for the Old Order Amish, religion is not simply a matter of theocratic belief. As the expert witnesses explained, the Old Order Amish religion pervades and determines virtually their entire way of life, regulating it with the detail of the Talmudic diet through the strictly enforced rules of the church community.

The record shows that the respondents' religious beliefs and attitude toward life, family, and home have remained constant—perhaps some would say static—in a period of unparalleled progress in human knowledge generally and great changes in education. The respondents freely concede, and indeed assert as an article of faith, that their religious beliefs and what we would today call "life style" has not altered in fundamentals for centuries. Their way of life in a church-oriented community, separated from the outside world and "worldly" influences, their attachment to nature and the soil, is a way inherently simple and uncomplicated, albeit difficult to preserve against the pressure to conform. Their rejection of telephones, automobiles, radios, and television, their mode of dress, of speech, their habits of manual work do indeed set them apart from much of contemporary society; these customs are both symbolic and practical.

As the society around the Amish has become more populous, urban, industrialized, and complex, particularly in this century, government regulation of human affairs has correspondingly become more detailed and pervasive. The Amish mode of life has thus come into conflict increasingly with requirements of contemporary society exerting a hydraulic insistence on conformity to majoritarian standards. So long as compulsory education laws were confined to eight grades of elementary basic education imparted in a nearby rural schoolhouse, with a large proportion of students of the Amish faith, the Old Order Amish had little basis to fear that school attendance would expose their children to the worldly influence they reject. But modern compulsory secondary education in rural areas is now largely carried on in a consolidated school, often remote from the student's home and alien to his daily home life. As the record so strongly shows, the values and programs of the modern secondary school are in sharp conflict with the fundamental mode of life mandated by the Amish religion; modern laws requiring compulsory secondary education have accordingly engendered great concern and conflict. The conclusion is inescapable that secondary schooling, by exposing Amish children to worldly influences in terms of attitudes, goals and values contrary to beliefs, and by substantially interfering with the religious development of the Amish child and his integration into the way of life of the Amish faith community at the crucial adolescent state of development, contravenes the basic religious tenets and practice of the Amish faith, both as to the parent and the child.

The impact of the compulsory attendance law on respondents' practice of the Amish religion is not only severe, but inescapable, for the Wisconsin law affirmatively compels them, under threat of criminal sanction, to perform acts undeniably at odds with fundamental tenets of their religious beliefs. See Braunfeld v. Brown, 366 U.S. 599, 605 (1961). Nor is the impact of the compulsory attendance law confined to grave interference with important Amish religious tenets from a subjective point of view. It carries with it precisely the kind of objective danger to the free exercise of religion which the First Amendment was designed to prevent. As the record shows, compulsory school attendance to age 16 for Amish children carries with it a very real threat of undermining the Amish community and religious practice as it exists today; they must either abandon belief and be assimilated into society at large, or be forced to migrate to some other and more tolerant region.

In sum, the unchallenged testimony of acknowledged experts in education and religious history, almost 300 years of consistent practice, and strong evidence of a sustained faith pervading and regulating respondents' entire mode of life support the claim that enforcement of the State's requirement of compulsory formal education after the eighth grade would gravely endanger if not destroy the free exercise of respondents' religious beliefs.

### III

.   .   .   Wisconsin concedes that under the Religion Clauses religious beliefs are absolutely free from the State's control, but it argues that "actions," even though religiously grounded, are outside the protection of the First Amendment.   But our decisions have rejected the idea that religiously grounded conduct is always outside the protection of the Free Exercise Clause.   It is true that activities of individuals, even when religiously based, are often subject to regulation by the States in the exercise of their undoubted power to promote the health, safety, and general welfare, or the Federal Government in the exercise of its delegated powers.   .   .   .   But to agree that religiously grounded conduct must often be subject to the broad police power of the State is not to deny that there are areas of conduct protected by the Free Exercise Clause of the First Amendment and thus beyond the power of the State to control, even under regulations of general applicability.   .   .   .   This case, therefore, does not become easier because respondents were convicted for their "actions" in refusing to send their children to the public high school; in this context belief and action cannot be neatly confined in logic-tight compartments.   .   .   .

Nor can this case be disposed of on the grounds that Wisconsin's requirement for school attendance to age 16 applies uniformly to all citizens of the State and does not, on its face, discriminate against religions or a particular religion, or that it is motivated by legitimate secular concerns.   A regulation neutral on its face may, in its application, nonetheless offend the constitutional requirement for governmental neutrality, if it unduly burdens the free exercise of religion.
.   .   .   The Court must not ignore the danger that an exception from a general obligation of citizenship on religious grounds may run afoul of the Establishment Clause, but that danger cannot be allowed to prevent any exception no matter how vital it may be to the protection of values promoted by the right of free exercise.   By preserving doctrinal flexibility and recognizing the need for a sensible and realistic application of the Religion Clauses

> "we have been able to chart a course that preserved the autonomy and freedom of religious bodies while avoiding any semblance of established religion.   This is a 'tight rope' and one we have successfully traversed."   Walz v. Tax Commission, 397 U.S., at 672.

We turn, then to the State's broader contention that its interest in its system of compulsory education is so compelling that even the established religious practices of the Amish must give way. Where fundamental claims of religious freedom are at stake, however, we cannot accept such a sweeping claim; despite its admitted validity in the generality of cases, we must searchingly examine the interests which the State seeks to promote by its requirement for compulsory education to age 16, and the impediment to those objectives that would flow from recognizing the claimed Amish exemption. . . .

The State advances two primary arguments in support of its system of compulsory education. It notes, as Thomas Jefferson pointed out early in our history, that some degree of education is necessary to prepare citizens to participate effectively and intelligently in our open political system if we are to preserve freedom and independence. Further, education prepares individuals to be self-reliant and self-sufficient participants in society. We accept these propositions.

However, the evidence adduced by the Amish in this case is persuasively to the effect that an additional one or two years of formal high school for Amish children in place of their long established program of informal vocational education would do little to serve those interests. Respondents' experts testified at trial, without challenge, that the value of all education must be assessed in terms of its capacity to prepare the child for life. It is one thing to say that compulsory education for a year or two beyond the eighth grade may be necessary when its goal is the preparation of the child for life in modern society as the majority live, but it is quite another if the goal of education be viewed as the preparation of the child for life in the separated agrarian community that is the keystone of the Amish faith. . . .

The State attacks respondents' position as one fostering "ignorance" from which the child must be protected by the State. No one can question the State's duty to protect children from ignorance but this argument does not square with the facts disclosed in the record. Whatever their idiosyncrasies as seen by the majority, this record strongly shows that the Amish community has been a highly successful social unit within our society even if apart from the conventional "mainstream." Its members are productive and very law-abiding members of society; they reject public welfare in any of its usual modern forms. The Congress itself recognized their self-sufficiency by authorizing exemption of such groups as the Amish from the obligation to pay social security taxes.

It is neither fair nor correct to suggest that the Amish are opposed to education beyond the eighth grade level. What this record shows is that they are opposed to conventional formal education of the type provided by a certified high school because it comes at the child's crucial adolescent period of religious development. Dr. Donald Erickson, for example, testified that their system of learning-by-doing was an "ideal system" of education in terms of preparing Amish children for life as adults in the Amish community, and that "I would be inclined to say they do a better job in this than most of the rest of us do." As he put it, "these people aren't purporting to be learned people, and it seems to me that the self-sufficiency of the community is the best evidence I can point to—whatever is being done seems to function well."

We must not forget that in the Middle Ages important values of the civilization of the western world were preserved by members of religious orders who isolated themselves from all worldly influences against great obstacles. There can be no assumption that today's majority is "right" and the Amish and others like them are "wrong." A way of life that is odd or even erratic but interferes with no rights or interests of others is not to be condemned because it is different.

The State, however, supports its interest in providing an additional one or two years of compulsory high school education to Amish children because of the possibility that some such children will choose to leave the Amish community, and that if this occurs they will be ill-equipped for life. The State argues that if Amish children leave their church they should not be in the position of making their way in the world without the education available in the one or two additional years the State requires. However, on this record, that argument is highly speculative. There is no specific evidence of the loss of Amish adherents by attrition, nor is there any showing that upon leaving the Amish community Amish children, with their practical agricultural training and habits of industry and self-reliance would become burdens on society because of educational shortcomings. Indeed, this argument of the State appears to rest primarily on the State's mistaken assumption, already noted, that the Amish do not provide any education for their children beyond the eighth grade, but allow them to grow in "ignorance." To the contrary, not only do the Amish accept the necessity for formal schooling through the eighth grade level, but continue to provide what has been characterized by the undisputed testimony of expert educators as an "ideal" vocational education for their children in the adolescent years.

There is nothing in this record to suggest that the Amish qualities of reliability, self-reliance, and dedication to work would fail to find ready markets in today's society. Absent some contrary evidence supporting the State's position, we are unwilling to assume that persons possessing such valuable vocational skills and habits are doomed to become burdens on society should they determine to leave the Amish faith, nor is there any basis in the record to warrant a finding that an additional one or two years of formal school education beyond the eighth grade would serve to eliminate any such problem that might exist.

Insofar as the State's claim rests on the view that a brief additional period of formal education is imperative to enable the Amish to participate effectively and intelligently in our democratic process, it must fall. The Amish alternative to formal secondary school education has enabled them to function effectively in their day-to-day life under self-imposed limitations on relations with the world, and to survive and prosper in contemporary society as a separate, sharply identifiable and highly self-sufficient community for more than 200 years in this country. In itself this is strong evidence that they are capable of fulfilling the social and political responsibilities of citizenship without compelled attendance beyond the eighth grade at the price of jeopardizing their free exercise of religious belief. . . .

The requirement for compulsory education beyond the eighth grade is a relatively recent development in our history. Less than 60 years ago, the educational requirements of almost all of the States were satisfied by completion of the elementary grades, at least where the child was regularly and lawfully employed. The independence and successful social functioning of the Amish community for a period approaching almost three centuries and more than 200 years in this country is strong evidence that there is at best a speculative gain, in terms of meeting the duties of citizenship, from an additional one or two years of compulsory formal education. Against this background it would require a more particularized showing from the State on this point to justify the severe interference with religious freedom such additional compulsory attendance would entail.

We should also note that compulsory education and child labor laws find their historical origin in common humanitarian instincts, and that the age limits of both laws have been coordinated to achieve their related objectives. In the context of this case, such considerations, if anything, support rather than detract from respondents' position. The origins of the requirement for school attendance to age 16, an age falling after the completion of elementary school but before completion of high school, are not entirely clear. But to some extent such laws reflected the movement to prohibit most child labor under age 16 that culminated in the provisions of the Federal Fair Labor Standards Act of 1938. It is true, then, that the 16-year child labor age limit may to some degree derive from a contemporary impression that children should be in school until that age. But at the same time, it cannot be denied that, conversely, the 16-year education limit reflects, in substantial measure, the concern that children under that age not be employed under conditions hazardous to their health, or in work that should be performed by adults.

The requirement of compulsory schooling to age 16 must therefore be viewed as aimed not merely at providing educational opportunities for children, but as an alternative to the equally undesirable consequence of unhealthful child labor displacing adult workers, or, on the other hand, forced idleness. The two kinds of statutes—compulsory school attendance and child labor laws—tend to keep children of certain ages off the labor market and in school; this in turn provides opportunity to prepare for a livelihood of a higher order than that children could perform without education and protects their health in adolescence.

In these terms, Wisconsin's interest in compelling the school attendance of Amish children to age 16 emerges as somewhat less substantial than requiring such attendance for children generally.  For, while agricultural employment is not totally outside the legitimate concerns of the child labor laws, employment of children under parental guidance and on the family farm from age 14 to age 16 is an ancient tradition which lies at the periphery of the objectives of such laws.  There is no intimation that the Amish employment of their children on family farms is in any way deleterious to their health or that Amish parents exploit children at tender years.  Any such inference would be contrary to the record before us.  Moreover, employment of Amish children on the family farm does not present the undesirable economic aspects of eliminating jobs which might otherwise be held by adults.

## IV

Finally, the State, on authority of Prince v. Massachusetts, argues that a decision exempting Amish children from the State's requirement fails to recognize the substantive right of the Amish child to a secondary education, and fails to give due regard to the power of the State as *parens patriae* to extend the benefit of secondary education to children regardless of the wishes of their parents.  .  .  .

Contrary to the suggestion of the dissenting opinion of Mr. Justice DOUGLAS, our holding today in no degree depends on the assertion of the religious interest of the child as contrasted with that of the parents.  It is the parents who are subject to prosecution here for failing to cause their children to attend school, and it is their right of free exercise, not that of their children, that must determine Wisconsin's power to impose criminal penalties on the parent.  The dissent argues that a child who expresses a desire to attend public high school in conflict with the wishes of his parents should not be prevented from doing so.  There is no reason for the Court to consider that point since it is not an issue in the case.  The children are not parties to this litigation.  The State has at no point tried this case on the theory that respondents were preventing their children from attending school against their expressed desires, and indeed the record is to the contrary.  [The only relevant testimony in the record is to the effect that the wishes of the one child who testified corresponded with those of her parents.  Testimony of Frieda Yoder, Tr. 92–94, to the effect that her personal religious beliefs guided her decision to discontinue school attendance after the 8th grade.  The other children were not called by either side.]  The State's position from the outset has been that it is empowered to apply its compulsory attendance law to Amish parents in the same manner as to other parents—that is, without regard to the wishes of the child. That is the claim we reject today.

Our holding in no way determines the proper resolution of possible competing interests of parents, children, and the State in an appropriate state court proceeding in which the power of the State is asserted on the theory that Amish parents are preventing their minor children from attending high school despite their expressed desires to the contrary. . . .

The State's argument proceeds without reliance on any actual conflict between the wishes of parents and children. It appears to rest on the potential that exemption of Amish parents from the requirements of the compulsory education law might allow some parents to act contrary to the best interests of their children by foreclosing their opportunity to make an intelligent choice between the Amish way of life and that of the outside world. The same argument could, of course, be made with respect to all church schools short of college. There is nothing in the record or in the ordinary course of human experience to suggest that non-Amish parents generally consult with children up to ages 14–16 if they are placed in a church school of the parents' faith.

Indeed it seems clear that if the State is empowered, as *parens patriae,* to "save" a child from himself or his Amish parents by requiring an additional two years of compulsory formal high school education, the State will in large measure influence, if not determine, the religious future of the child. Even more markedly than in *Prince,* therefore, this case involves the fundamental interest of parents, as contrasted with that of the State, to guide the religious future and education of their children. The history and culture of western civilization reflect a strong tradition of parental concern for the nurture and upbringing of their children. This primary role of the parents in the upbringing of their children is now established beyond debate as an enduring American tradition. If not the first, perhaps the most significant statements of the Court in this area are found in Pierce v. Society of Sisters, in which the Court observed:

> "Under the doctrine of Meyer v. Nebraska, 262 U.S. 390, we think it entirely plain that the Act of 1922 unreasonably interferes with the liberty of parents and guardians to direct the upbringing and education of children under their control. As often heretofore pointed out, rights guaranteed by the Constitution may not be abridged by legislation which has no reasonable relation to some purpose within the competency of the State. The fundamental theory of liberty upon which all governments in this Union repose excludes any general power of the State to standardize its children by forcing them to accept instruction from public teachers only. The

child is not the mere creature of the State; those who nurture him and direct his destiny have the right, coupled with the high duty, to recognize and prepare him for additional obligations." 268 U.S., at 534–535.

The duty to prepare the child for "additional obligations," referred to by the Court, must be read to include the inculcation of moral standards, religious beliefs and elements of good citizenship. *Pierce,* of course, recognized that where nothing more than the general interest of the parent in the nurture and education of his children is involved, it is beyond dispute that the State acts "reasonably" and constitutionally in requiring education to age 16 in some public and private school meeting the standards prescribed by the State.

However read, the Court's holding in *Pierce* stands as a charter of the rights of parents to direct the religious upbringing of their children. And, when the interests of parenthood are combined with a free exercise claim of the nature revealed by this record, more than merely a "reasonable relation to some purpose within the competency of the state" is required to sustain the validity of the State's requirement under the First Amendment. To be sure, the power of the parent, even when linked to a free exercise claim, may be subject to limitation under *Prince* if it appears that parental decisions will jeopardize the health or safety of the child, or have a potential for significant social burdens. But in this case, the Amish have introduced persuasive evidence undermining the arguments the State has advanced to support its claims in terms of the welfare of the child and society as a whole. The record strongly indicates that accommodating the religious objections of the Amish by foregoing one, or at most two, additional years of compulsory education will not impair the physical or mental health of the child, nor result in an inability to be self-supporting, or to discharge the duties and responsibilities of citizenship, or in any other way materially detract from the welfare of society.

In the face of our consistent emphasis on the central values underlying the Religion Clauses in our constitutional scheme of government, we cannot accept a *parens patriae* claim of such all-encompassing scope and with such sweeping potential for broad and unforeseeable application as that urged by the State.

V

For the reasons stated we hold, with the Supreme Court of Wisconsin, that the First and Fourteenth Amendments prevent the State from compelling respondents to cause their children to attend formal high school to age 16. Our disposition of this case, however, in no way alters our recognition of the obvious fact that courts are not school boards or legislatures, and are ill-equipped to determine the "necessity" of discrete aspects of a State's program of compulsory education. This should suggest that courts must move with great circumspection in performing the sensitive and delicate task of weighing a State's legitimate social concern when faced with religious claims for exemption from generally applicable educational requirements.  It cannot be over-emphasized that we are not dealing with a way of life and mode of education by a group claiming to have recently discovered some "progressive" or more enlightened process for rearing children for modern life.

Aided by a history of three centuries as an identifiable religious sect and a long history as a successful and self-sufficient segment of American society, the Amish in this case have convincingly demonstrated the sincerity of their religious beliefs, the interrelationship of belief with their mode of life, the vital role which belief and daily conduct play in the continued survival of Old Order Amish communities and their religious organization, and the hazards presented by the State's enforcement of a statute generally valid as to others.  Beyond this, they have carried the even more difficult burden of demonstrating the adequacy of their alternative mode of continuing informal vocational education in terms of precisely those overall interests that the State advances in support of its program of compulsory high school education.  In light of this convincing showing, one which probably few other religious groups or sects could make, and weighing the minimal difference between what the State would require and what the Amish already accept, it was incumbent on the State to show with more particularity how its admittedly strong interest in compulsory education would be adversely affected by granting an exemption to the Amish.  Sherbert v. Verner.   .   .   .

Nothing we hold is intended to undermine the general applicability of the State's compulsory school attendance statutes or to limit the power of the State to promulgate reasonable standards that, while not impairing the free exercise of religion, provide for continuing agricultural vocational education under parental and church guidance by the Old Order Amish or others similarly situated.  The States have had a long history of amicable and effective relationships with church-sponsored schools, and there is no basis for assuming that, in this related context, reasonable standards cannot be established concerning the content of the continuing vocational education of Amish children under parental guidance, provided always that state regulations are not inconsistent with what we have said in this opinion.

Affirmed.

Mr. Justice POWELL and Mr. Justice REHNQUIST took no part in the consideration or decision of this case.

Mr. Justice WHITE, with whom Mr. Justice BRENNAN and Mr. Justice STEWART join, concurring.   *   *   *

This would be a very different case for me if respondents' claim were that their religion forbade their children from attending any school at any time and from complying in any way with the educational standards set by the State. * * * There is evidence in the record that many children desert the Amish faith when they they come of age. A State has a legitimate interest not only in seeking to develop the latent talents of its children but in seeking to prepare them for the life style which they may later choose or at least to provide them with an option other than the life they have led in the past. In the circumstances of this case, although the question is close, I am unable to say that the State has demonstrated that Amish children who leave school in the eighth grade will be intellectually stultified or unable to acquire new academic skills later. * * *

Decision in cases such as this and the administration of an exemption for Old Order Amish from the State's compulsory school attendance laws will inevitably involve the kind of close and perhaps repeated scrutiny of religious practices, as exemplified in today's opinion, which the Court has heretofore been anxious to avoid. But such entanglement does not create a forbidden establishment of religion where it is essential to implement free exercise values threatened by an otherwise neutral program instituted to foster some permissible, nonreligious state objective. I join the Court because the sincerity of the Amish religious policy here is uncontested, because the potential adverse impact of the state requirement is great and because the State's valid interest in education has already been largely satisfied by the eight years the children have already spent in school.

Mr. Justice DOUGLAS, dissenting in part.

I

I agree with the Court that the religious scruples of the Amish are opposed to the education of their children beyond the grade schools, yet I disagree with the Court's conclusion that the matter is within the dispensation of parents alone. The Court's analysis assumes that the only interests at stake in the case are those of the Amish parents on the one hand, and those of the State on the other. The difficulty with this approach is that, despite the Court's claim, the parents are seeking to vindicate not only their own free exercise claims, but also those of their high-school-age children.

It is argued that the right of the Amish children to religious freedom is not presented by the facts of the case, as the issue before the Court involves only the Amish parents' religious freedom to defy a state criminal statute imposing upon them an affirmative duty to cause their children to attend high school.

First, respondents' motion to dismiss in the trial court expressly asserts, not only the religious liberty of the adults, but also that of the children, as a defense to the prosecutions. . . .

Second, . . . no analysis of religious liberty claims can take place in a vacuum. If the parents in this case are allowed a religious exemption, the inevitable effect is to impose the parents' notions of religious duty upon their children.  Where the child is mature enough to express potentially conflicting desires, it would be an invasion of the child's rights to permit such an imposition without canvassing his views.  .  .  .  As the child has no other effective forum, it is in this litigation that his rights should be considered.  And, if an Amish child desires to attend high school, and is mature enough to have that desire respected, the State may well be able to override the parents' religiously motivated objections.

Religion is an individual experience.  It is not necessary, nor even appropriate, for every Amish child to express his views on the subject in a prosecution of a single adult.  Crucial, however, are the views of the child whose parent is the subject of the suit.  Frieda Yoder has in fact testified that her own religious views are opposed to high-school education.  I therefore join the judgment of the Court as to respondent Jonas Yoder.  But Frieda Yoder's views may not be those of Vernon Yutzy or Barbara Miller.  I must dissent, therefore, as to respondents Adin Yutzy and Wallace Miller as their motion to dismiss also raised the question of their children's religious liberty.

## II

This issue has never been squarely presented before today.  Our opinions are full of talk about the power of the parents over the child's education.  .  .  .  Recent cases, however, have clearly held that the children themselves have constitutionally protectible interests.

These children are "persons" within the meaning of the Bill of Rights.  We have so held over and over again.  In Haley v. Ohio, 332 U.S. 596, we extended the protection of the Fourteenth Amendment in a state trial of a 15-year-old boy.  In In re Gault, 387 U.S. 1, 13, we held that "neither the Fourteenth Amendment nor the Bill of Rights is for adults alone."  In In re Winship, 397 U.S. 358, we held that a 12-year-old boy, when charged with an act which would be a crime if committed by an adult, was entitled to procedural safeguards contained in the Sixth Amendment.

In Tinker v. Des Moines School Dist., 393 U.S. 503, we dealt with 13-year-old, 15-year-old, and 16-year-old students who wore armbands to public schools and were disciplined for doing so.  We gave them relief, saying that their First Amendment rights had been abridged.

"Students in school as well as out of school are 'persons' under our Constitution.  They are possessed of fundamental rights which the State must respect, just as they themselves must respect the obligations to the State."  .  .  .

.  .  .  On this important and vital matter of education, I think the children should be entitled to be heard.  While the parents, absent dissent, normally speak for the entire family, the education of the child is a matter on which the child will often have decided views. He may want to be a pianist or an astronaut or an ocean geographer. To do so he will have to break from the Amish tradition.

It is the future of the student, not the future of the parents, that is imperilled in today's decision. If a parent keeps his child out of school beyond the grade school, then the child will be forever barred from entry into the new and amazing world of diversity that we have today. The child may decide that that is the preferred course, or he may rebel. It is the student's judgment, not his parent's, that is essential if we are to give full meaning to what we have said about the Bill of Rights and of the right of students to be masters of their own destiny. If he is harnessed to the Amish way of life by those in authority over him and if his education is truncated, his entire life may be stunted and deformed. The child, therefore, should be given an opportunity to be heard before the State gives the exemption which we honor today.

The views of the two children in question were not canvassed by the Wisconsin courts. The matter should be explicitly reserved so that new hearings can be held on remand of the case.


### III

I think the emphasis of the Court on the "law and order" record of this Amish group of people is quite irrelevant. A religion is a religion irrespective of what the misdemeanor or felony records of its members might be. I am not at all sure how the Catholics, Episcopalians, the Baptists, Jehovah's Witnesses, the Unitarians, and my own Presbyterians would make out if we were subjected to such a test. It is, of course, true that if a group or society was organized to perpetuate crime and if that is its motif, we would have rather startling problems akin to those that were raised when some years back a particular sect was challenged here as operating on a fraudulent basis. United States v. Ballard, 322 U.S. 78. But no such factors are present here, and the Amish, whether with a high or low criminal record, certainly qualify by all historic standards as a religion within the meaning of the First Amendment.

The Court rightly rejects the notion that actions, even though religiously grounded, are outside the protection of the Free Exercise Clause of the First Amendment. . . .

In another way, however, the Court retreats when in reference to Henry Thoreau it says his "choice was philosophical and personal rather than religious, and such belief does not rise to the demands of the Religion Clause." That is contrary to what we held in United States v. Seeger, 380 U.S. 163, where we were concerned with the meaning of the words "religious training and belief" in the Selective

Service Act, which were the basis of many conscientious objector claims. We said:

> ". . . Within that phrase would come all sincere religious beliefs which are based upon a power or being, or upon a faith, to which all else is subordinate or upon which all else is ultimately dependent. The test might be stated in these words: A sincere and meaningful belief which occupies in the life of its possessor a place parallel to that filled by the God of those admittedly qualifying for the exemption comes within the statutory definition. This construction avoids imputing to Congress an intent to classify different religious beliefs, exempting some and excluding others, and is in accord with the well-established congressional policy of equal treatment for those whose opposition to service is grounded in their religious tenets." Id., 176.

Welsh v. United States, 398 U.S. 333, was in the same vein, the Court saying:

> ". . . In this case, Welsh's conscientious objection to war was undeniably based in part on his perception of world politics. In a letter to his local board, he wrote:
>
> > " 'I can only act according to what I am and what I see. And I see that the military complex wastes both human and material resources, that it fosters disregard for (what I consider a paramount concern) human needs and ends; I see that the means we employ to "defend" our "way of life" profoundly change that way of life. I see that in our failure to recognize the political, social, and economic realities of the world, we, *as a nation,* fail our responsibility *as a nation.*' " Id., 342.

The essence of Welsh's philosophy on the basis of which we held he was entitled to an exemption was in these words:

> "I believe that human life is valuable in and of itself; in its living; therefore, I will not injure or kill another human being. This belief (and the corresponding 'duty' to abstain from violence toward another person) is not 'superior to those arising from any human relation.' On the contrary: *it is essential to every human relation.* I cannot, therefore, conscientiously comply with the Government's insistence that I assume duties which I feel are immoral and totally repugnant." Id., 343.

I adhere to these exalted views of "religion" and see no acceptable alternative to them now that we have become a Nation of many religions and sects, representing all of the diversities of the human race. 380 U.S., at 192–193.

## NOTES AND QUESTIONS

1.　Yoder presents only the case of the Amish parents, not that of the Amish children, and poses the question the Supreme Court assumed in Pierce: Does a state have constitutional power to require compulsory school attendance of all its children through high school? Unlike Pierce, the Amish parents did not object merely to public schooling beyond the eighth grade, but they objected to all formal schooling beyond that grade. The Court seeks to answer the constitutional question by using a balancing test. It places the religious interests of the Amish parents on one side of the balancing scale and all the interests of the state in its compulsory attendance laws on the other, and then favors the weightier set of interests. The interests of the Amish children are not weighed in the balance because, although affected, the children were not parties to the law suit. Can you identify precisely the exact set of interests the Court places on each side of its balancing scale? Do you agree with the Court on which set of interests is the weightier?

2.　Wisconsin argued that its two interests "in its system of compulsory education [are] so compelling that even the established religious practices of the Amish must give away." The two state interests were: (1) "that some degree of education is necessary to prepare citizens to participate effectively and intelligently in our open political system if we are to preserve freedom and independence," and (2) "education prepares individuals to be self-reliant and self-sufficient participants in society." Are these statements valid? Does compulsory school attendance actually achieve these ends or are the statements merely rhetoric without corresponding social reality? The Supreme Court stated: "We accept these propositions."

Are these two state interests really satisfied, so far as the Court is concerned, by formal schooling only through the eighth grade? By all children or only by Amish children? The Court states that "it is one thing to say that compulsory education for a year or two beyond the eighth grade may be necessary when its goal is the preparation of the child for life in modern society as the majority live, but it is quite another if the goal of education be viewed as the preparation of the child for life in the separated agrarian community that is the keystone of the Amish faith." The Court noted that a state's bona fide interest in eliminating the exploitation of child labor through compulsory school attendance of children to age 16 was "less substantial [for Amish children] than requiring such attendance for children generally" because "there is no intimation that Amish employment of their children on family farms is in any way deleterious to their health or that Amish parents exploit children at tender years," and moreover, "employment of Amish children on the family farm does not present the undesirable economic aspects of eliminating jobs which might otherwise be held by adults." Does this line of reasoning mean that the Amish parents escaped punishment precisely because their practices were viewed to be "decent," "law abiding," "productive," "sincere" and no threat to jobs in the economy? What is Douglas' view on this point? Can you think of any other group who might weaken the state's bona-fide interests as the Amish did?

Could American Indians, Eskimos or Chicanos similarly weaken the state's interests? Could any cultural or religious group other than the Amish?

Did Wisconsin fail to present one of its critical state interests? Should it have argued that it had a compelling state interest in compulsory high school attendance of Amish children as a means of racially integrating a large community within American society? See, Kurland, The Supreme Court, Compulsory Education, and the First Amendment's Religion Clauses, 75 W.Va.Law Rev. 213 (1973). If Wisconsin had made this argument, would it have changed the Supreme Court's decision? Should it have?

3.  The interests of the Amish parents was that of religious freedom. Their Amish religious "beliefs require members . . . to make their living by farming or closely related activities." The parents objected to formal education beyond eighth grade because "the values [high school] teach are in marked variance with Amish values and the Amish way of life" which "emphasizes informal learning-through-doing, a life of 'goodness,' rather than a life of intellect, wisdom rather than technical knowledge, community welfare rather than competition, and separation rather than integration with contemporary worldly society." In other words, the Amish parents were fearful of high schools as socializing agents, that their children would become socialized into the American national community and that that would mean the destruction of the Amish. The Amish parents claimed that their right to religious freedom weighed heavier in the constitutional balance than the state's interests in compulsory schooling, and the Supreme Court agreed. Do you? Why?

The Court states that the Amish have "convincingly demonstrated the sincerity of their religious beliefs." What elements of "sincerity" does the Court consider? Is this judgment one Courts ought to make? What role does it play in the decision? What factors led the Court to judge that the Amish religious beliefs and their way of life was "inseparable and interdependent?" How important is this judgment to the decision in Yoder? Suppose an old and well-established Indian religious order sincerely believed that members would be religiously purified by public dancing at noon with rattlesnakes in their mouths, and kept a supply of rattlesnakes for this purpose, would the acts of public dancing (in a bar? on a sidewalk?) constitutionally be susceptible to state regulation or prohibition? The beliefs? If government could regulate or prohibit the act of public dancing with a rattlesnake in one's mouth, but not the religious belief, in what way is the use of governmental power here to be distinguished from its attempted use in Yoder?

Suppose a case were presented in which the Amish believed that it was religiously improper to educate their children beyond the sixth grade, or third grade, would the Yoder decision control this new case? How should it be decided?

4.  In Yoder, the Supreme Court, but not Justice Douglas, avoids the possibility of a clash between the interests of the Amish parents and those of their children. The Court avoids the clash with Amish parental in-

terests at the cost of depriving the Amish children of sufficient high-school value socialization and technical intellectual development that would equip them to make an intelligent decision on whether to remain within the Amish community.  Should the Court have done as Justice Douglas suggested:  required the Wisconsin court to canvass the opinions of the Amish children on whether they wanted to go to high school?  Should the Amish children have the opportunity to choose to be a modern college-educated person?  How realistic is that opportunity for a person who after reaching adulthood without a high school education, decides he wants to go to college?  Suppose the Court had followed Douglas's suggestion and now there is evidence showing that 20% of the Amish children want to go to high school, 50% do not, and 30% do not care one way or the other, would the Supreme Court's decision have been different?

5.  Does Yoder mark a beginning opening of the constitutional door for equivalent, but not formal school, education?  The Court states that "it is neither fair nor correct to suggest that the Amish are opposed to education beyond the eighth grade level," but rather "that they are opposed to conventional formal education of the type provided by a certified high school  .  .  .".  The Amish "continue to provide what has been characteristic by the undisputed testimony  .  .  .  as an 'ideal' vocational education for their children in the adolescent years."  Is the Amish education "vocational" in the sense of learning a trade that is useful in modern life or "vocational" in the sense of learning a separate and different way of life?  In what sense is the vocational-type education provided by the Amish equivalent to that provided by the state in its public schools?  The Court recognized that "the history and culture of western civilization reflect a strong tradition of parental concern for the nurture and upbringing of their children.  This primary role of the parents in the upbringing of their children is now established beyond debate as an enduring American tradition" and "the most significant statements of the Court in this area are found in Pierce  .  .  .".  Does this line of analysis lead to the conclusion that a parent may have a constitutional right not to obey a state's compulsory schooling law and not to send his child to any school, but to educate the child at home, so long as the child's home education is equivalent to that which the child would obtain in a public school under the standards prescribed by the state?

The Court also stated that "Pierce stands as a charter of the rights of parents to direct the religious upbringing of their children."  Is that all Pierce stands for?  "Pierce, of course, recognized that where nothing more than the general interest of the parent in the nurture and education of his children is involved, it is beyond dispute that the State acts  .  .  .  constitutionally in requiring education to age 16 in some public and (sic) private school meeting the standards prescribed by the State."  Considering the Amish way of life, do the above quotes mean that a parent can avoid compulsory schooling laws for his child if the parent's religious practices sincerely reflect the values of an eighteenth or nineteenth century way of rural life, but that the laws cannot be avoided if the parent's way of life is modern and urban, or do they mean that the "progressive" and "enlightened" parent may also avoid the compulsory schooling laws by providing his child with alternative, equivalent education?

6.  Are there other constitutionally justifiable reasons for not obeying a state's compulsory school attendance laws? Some courts have recognized the right of parents to refuse to send their children to dangerous schools or along dangerous roads to school. For example, the New York Supreme Court ruled that parents reasonably could refuse to have their child, under 16, walk 1½ miles alone alongside a poorly maintained, unfenced and lonely road to a bus stop. In re Richards, 255 App.Div. 922, 7 N.Y.S.2d 722 (1938). More recently, Pennsylvania's Supreme Court ruled "that a parent is justified in withdrawing his child from a school where the health and welfare of the child is threatened," even though the state has a compulsory schooling law and the local school board demands that the child be sent to an unsafe and dangerous school. Zebra v. School Dist., 449 Pa. 432, 296 A.2d 748 (1972); also see, Bichrest v. School Dist., 346 F.Supp. 249, 252–53 (E.D.Pa.1972).

---

### COMMONWEALTH v. BEY

Superior Court of Pennsylvania, 1950.
166 Pa.Super. 136, 70 A.2d 693.

RENO, Judge. Appellants, husband and wife, were convicted in a summary proceeding before an alderman and on appeal in the court below of violating the compulsory attendance provisions of the School Code. . . .

The provision that children shall attend "continuously through the entire term" recognizes the obvious fact that each day's school work is built upon the lessons taught on the preceding day. It is virtually impossible properly to educate a child who is absent one day a week. Friday's instruction is the foundation for understanding Monday's lesson. By such regularly recurring absences the child loses not only one-fifth of the instruction, but the continuity of the course of study is broken and the pupil is not able to keep pace with his classmates. . . .

Appellants are Mohammedans, and they have persistently refused to send their children of compulsory attendance age to school on Fridays, the sacred day of that religion. They have sent them to the public schools on all other days except Friday. They invoke the guarantees of religious freedom contained in the State and Federal constitutions. Appellants were convicted for the same offense in 1943 and 1944. . . .

Judgment and sentence affirmed.

### NOTES AND QUESTIONS

1.  Assume Commonwealth v. Bey, supra, has been appealed to the Supreme Court of the United States and you are a Justice. In light of Wiscon-

sin v. Yoder, what decision must be rendered? Why? See also, In re Currence, 42 Misc.2d 418, 248 N.Y.S.2d 251 (1963) (for religious sabbath reasons parents wanted to keep their child out of school on Wednesdays and Thursdays), and Commonwealth v. Renfrew, 332 Mass. 492, 126 N.E.2d 109 (1955) (Buddist parents not wanting their child exposed to Christian doctrines wanted to teach their child at home).

2. In Elkins v. Moreno, 435 U.S. 647, 98 S.Ct. 1338, 55 L.Ed.2d 614 (1978), the United States Supreme Court ruled that a nonimmigrant alien student, legally within this country with his parents, constitutionally must be given the opportunity to prove under state law that he is a "resident" for in-state tuition purposes at the state university. Younger, K through 12, alien children, legally within the country, most likely could not be excluded from public school by local school boards. See, Hosier v. Evans, 314 F.Supp. 316 (D.C. Virgin Islands, 1970). Can a school board exclude from public schools all the K–12 children of aliens who are illegally in the United States? Can either the alien parents who are legally within this country or those illegally in the United States lawfully refuse to obey a state's compulsory schooling law and not send their children to public schools? If so, on what grounds?

3. Can all parents avoid compulsory schooling laws by refusing to send their child to school if they live a considerable distance away and no free transportation is provided by the School Board? Or, must the School Board provide the transportation in which case parents must send their child to school? Consider these questions in relation to the following problem.

# PROBLEM

---

## R. MANJARES v. DR. R. E. NEWTON

Supreme Court of California, 1966.
64 Cal.2d 365, 49 Cal.Rptr. 805, 411 P.2d 901.

"Plaintiffs live just off a county road in the Paloma Creek area of Monterey County. This is in the southeast corner of the school district, about 30 miles from the junior high school and about half that distance from the elementary school to which the children were assigned. For many years the district has provided bus transportation to students along certain county roads. The closest stop to plaintiffs' homes is at the Hastings Reservation, 6.2 miles away. The controversy between the parties involves the question whether the board is required to authorize transportation for this approximate six-mile distance.

"Each year the board reviews existing routes and decides whether to curtail, maintain, or extend them. In the three years prior to 1963, when plaintiffs moved into the area, there was a trend toward curtailing the routes for reasons of economy. The board's policy regarding transportation is contained in section 16B of its rules and regulations, which provides that, while it is the responsibility of students and their parents to arrange the daily travel between home and school, the board may assist in transporting pupils who live beyond two miles from a bus stop if road conditions, pupil density, or hazardous walking conditions make it advantageous, but that some areas will not be served by buses for reasons of safety. The section also provides that, if the distance from a regular bus stop to a student's home exceeds two miles, payments of six cents per additional mile may be authorized in lieu of transportation.

"As a result of plaintiffs' inability to provide transportation, the children did not attend school for the remainder of the 1963–64 school year. The district superintendent recommended to the county superintendent of schools that they be excused from compulsory school attendance under section 12153 of the Education Code, which provides that students residing more than two miles from school shall be exempted from compulsory attendance on the written approval of the county superintendent.

"In their complaint plaintiffs, after alleging their inability to secure transportation and the details of the Wallace proposal, asserted that the board's action resulted in excluding the minor plaintiffs from the public schools and in depriving them of their constitutional rights of due process of law and equal protection. They prayed for a restraining order compelling the board to furnish them with transportation to and from school."

Assume you are the Judge, what decision would you render in this case; following what precedents, and for what reasons?

On appeal the Supreme Court of California held:
Where, as here, it is shown without question that eight children are being totally deprived of an education because the board refuses to authorize transportation to school and the district is in the financial position to extend the existing bus system to include them, it is arbitrary and unreasonable to refuse to do so simply because it may be more expensive to transport these children than others in the district. 411 P.2d at p. 908.

Query: Should the decision have been different (1) if the family had been sufficiently wealthy to pay for the transportation, or (2) if the family had the ability to provide "equivalent education" in the home or if the Board were in a poor financial position?

## NOTES AND QUESTIONS

1. What is the operational difference between not providing public transportation to students in order to enable them to receive a free public education and not providing specialized public education to students suffering from congenital or environmental learning disabilities such that they cannot take advantage of the usual curriculum of public education? Is the state legally obliged to provide the special education? Should it

be? Who should bear its cost? Why? Should a school be legally obliged to provide for gifted children by creating "ability groups" or "tracking" within its curriculum? See, Hobson v. Hansen, infra.

## EQUIVALENT EDUCATION

Pierce v. Society of Sisters indicates that "the child is not the mere creature of the State," but that parents "who nurture him and direct his destiny have the right, coupled with the high duty, to recognize and prepare him for additional obligations." Thus, the state has no power to compel schooling of its children solely in its public schools. Presumably, parents have "the right, coupled with the high duty," to send their children to private schools that otherwise meet all valid state regulations.

But, suppose parents individually or in small groups, choose to prepare their children for Pierce's "additional obligations" by educating them in their homes rather than sending them to any school, public or private. Does Pierce recognize that right as a matter of constitutional law? Or, does Pierce only recognize a lesser right of parents to educate their children in approved private, rather than public, schools? Washington's statute, supra, for example, is silent on home education but permits private school attendance to satisfy its compulsory requirement, and defines a private school as "one approved or acredited under regulations established by the state board of education." In an early case, Washington v. Cournort, 69 Wash. 361, 124 P. 910 (1912), in which parents, who were experienced teachers, claimed the right to teach their children at home, and without prior state permission, Washington's Supreme Court ruled:

"We have no doubt many parents are capable of instructing their own children, but to permit such parents to withdraw their children from the public schools without permission from the superintendent of schools, and to instruct them at home, would be to disrupt our common school system and destroy its value to the state. This statute recognizes that adequate private schools may be maintained in any district to which parents may send their children without any violation of the law, and it would be a good defense to show attendance at such private school for the required time. We do not think that the giving of instruction by a parent to a child, conceding the competency of the parent to fully instruct the child in all that is taught in the public schools, is within the meaning of the law 'to attend a private school.' Such a requirement means more than home instruction; it means the same character of school as the public school, a regular, organized and existing institution making a business of instructing children of school age in the required studies and for the full time required by the laws of this state. The only difference between the two schools is the nature of the institution. One is a public institution, organized and maintained as one of the institutions of the state. The other is a private institution, organized and maintained by private individuals or corporations. There may be a difference in institution and government, but the purpose and end of both public and private schools must be the same—the education of children of school age. The parent who teaches his children at home, whatever be his reason for desiring to do so, does not maintain such a school. Undoubtedly a private school may be maintained in a private home in which the children of the instructor may be pupils. This provision of the law is not to be determined by the place where the school is maintained, nor the individuality or number of the pupils who attend it. It is to be determined by the purpose, intent and character of the endeavor. The evidence of the state was to the effect that appellant maintained no school at his home; that his two little girls could be seen playing about the house at all times during the ordinary school hours. No effort was made to refute this testimony. Appellant seemed to be impressed with the belief that, if he was a competent and qualified teacher and gave instruction to his children at his home, he maintained a private school within the meaning of the law. Such is not a compliance with the law. . . ."

Is this ruling consistent with the basic premises and reasoning the Supreme Court relied upon when deciding Pierce and Yoder? In order to comply with the constitution must state law permit home instruction?

Many states try to avoid any possible constitutional question by passing laws permitting home instruction. Many of them, like New York [see, N.Y.Educ.Law § 3204 (McKinney 1979) and In re Franz Children, 55 A.D.2d 424, 390 N.Y.S.2d 940 (1977)] and New Jersey, permit home instruction, so long as it is "equivalent" to the instruction a child would otherwise receive in a public school. To this end, some states require that the home instructors be tutors "who meet all requirements prescribed by law . . . for private tutors" [Fla. Stat. § 232.02(4) (1975) or be regularly certified teachers (Cal.Educ. Code §§ 44865, 87433)]. Yet, other states expressly permit home instruction by parents. Are these laws wise from a substantive, educational point of view? For exceptional children? Ordinary children? What are the relevant considerations that a judge should weigh when deciding whether the home instruction is actually "equivalent" education? Compare the following two cases on this last question.

## STEPHENS v. BONGART

Juvenile and Domestic Relations Court of New Jersey, 1937.
15 N.J.Misc. 80, 189 A. 131.

SIEGLER, Judge. Helen Stephens, attendance officer of the school district of the town of West Orange in the county of Essex, filed her complaint against Gertrude R. Bongart and Benno Bongart, the defendants in this action, charging that they reside within the school district of the town of West Orange, and being the parents and having custody and control of William Bongart, aged twelve, and Robert Bongart, aged eleven, their children, have, since the 5th day of April 1936, failed to cause their said children regularly to attend the public schools of the school district of the said town of West Orange; further charging said defendants having neither caused said children to attend a day school in which there is given instruction equivalent to that provided in the public schools for children of similar grades and attainments, nor have they received equivalent instruction elsewhere than at school, contrary to the provisions of an act of the Legislature of the state of New Jersey entitled, "An Act to establish a thorough and efficient system of free public schools, and to provide for the maintenance, support and management thereof," . . . .

The act upon which these proceedings are based . . . reads as follows: "Every parent, guardian or other person having custody and control of a child between the ages of seven and sixteen years shall cause such child regularly to attend the public schools of such district or to attend a day school in which there is given instruction equivalent to that provided in the public schools for children of similar grades and attainments or to receive equivalent instruction elsewhere than at school unless such child is above the age of fourteen years. . . . Such regular attendance shall be during all the days and hours that the public schools are in session in said school district, unless it shall be shown to the satisfaction of the board of education of said school district that the mental condition of the child is such that he or she cannot benefit from instruction in the school or hat the bodily condition of the child is such as to prevent his or her attendance at school."

. . . .

The second point for determination is whether or not the defendants provided instruction for their children equivalent to that provided in the public schools for children of similar grades and attainments.

This necessitates an analysis of the testimony. The proof is that the defendants' children, William, twelve, and Robert, eleven, were in the sixth and fifth grades, respectively, in the Washington Street School, West Orange, until April 3, 1936. From that date, these children failed to attend a public or day school, although proper notice was served upon the defendants to return the children to a school.

The defendants admit they caused the children's withdrawal from the Washington School.

Since that time, the defendants claim that they instructed their children in their own home in the subjects taught in fifth and sixth grades.  This instruction, they claim, is equivalent to that provided in the public schools for children of similar grades and attainments. The case turns on this factual situation.  2 Words and Phrases, Second Series, p. 312, defines the word equivalent as follows:

> " 'Equivalent' means 'equal in worth or value, force, power effect, import and the like.' "

Quite definitely, the term refers to the giving of instruction equal in value and effect to that given in a public school.  In determining this question, consideration must be given, first, to the matter of the ability of the parents to provide equivalent instruction, and, secondly, to a comparison of the quality, character, and methods of teaching employed by the defendants and that of the West Orange public school system.  Mrs. Bongart was graduated from the Eastern District High School, New York City, in 1911.  In 1917 she was a special student at Hunter College, evening course.  This required three or four evenings a week, which she carried on for only two years.  She studied economics, psychology, art, portrait work, charcoal work and painting; she majored in home economics.  Mrs. Bongart had no teaching experience.  She was married about fifteen years ago, and her chief employment was that of housewife.  Mr. Bongart is a graduate of the University of Strassbourg, in the field of electrical and mechanical engineering.  He never trained for teaching, but did have employment as a teacher at the New York Aerial School, Newark Technical School, and the Newark Junior High School until recently.  He taught subjects in mechanical drawing and electrical engineering. The teachers in the elementary grades of the public schools, particularly the fifth and sixth grades in the West Orange school system, must have at least a high school education and three years at an approved normal school in the state of New Jersey.

The normal school curriculum includes a type of training and education intended to qualify students to teach in the elementary class in the subjects of English, history, science, sociology, civics, mathematics, hygiene, geography, art, music, and physical education.  The major aim is to give the teachers training in techniques of presentation of material to elementary school students.  That involves the proper selection of material, knowledge of children, and the organization of their work, so that every teacher should know the results which must be achieved in terms of knowledge, habits, skills, attitudes, and appreciations.  Her training should qualify her to develop individuality and the personality of each child under her supervision. One of the major aims of our public school to-day is to teach the way in which the individual must fit into the social group.  The evidence establishes that the teachers in the fifth and sixth grades of Washington School possess this training and qualify in these courses.

It is clear, upon comparison, that there is a substantial variance between the training, qualifications, and experience of the defendants and those obtaining in the public school system of West Orange.

Now, what was the instruction given by the defendants at their home? The children assemble, one in the dining room and the other in the front room, each morning at 9 o'clock, and continue until 12; they resume at 1 o'clock, and recess at 3 o'clock in the afternoon. They receive instruction in arithmetic, spelling, history, geography, language, and music. In the evening, the father instructs them in science between 7 and 9 o'clock.

In the study of arithmetic a text-book is used by Stone and Millis, dated 1914. There were no text-books for spelling, language, music, civics, hygiene, and art; while the text-books used were outmoded and outdated, the latest published in 1921 and the oldest in 1881, and all certainly of questionable value in the instruction of children. Spelling was taught without a book, the mother giving twenty words at random each week, which the children had to learn and place in a notebook. The other subjects were taught by assigning periods of 30 or 35 minutes for each. Language was taught largely through the reading of newspapers, the Literary Digest and the Saturday Evening Post. Poetry was principally taught by the use of an occasional piece of poetry out of the Sunday Times and the New York Daily News, a tabloid newspaper. No poems were memorized. Music was taught by listening to radio concerts. There were no song books or singing exercises. Mechanical drawing and current events were given by the father in the evening. The Newark Evening News and some other periodicals were sources from which current events were drawn for discussion. The Bible was read once in a while. The flag of the country was exhibited in front of the house on patriotic occasions. The mother spoke to them about hygiene and the danger of alcoholic beverages, but no hygiene textbook was used. There were no instructions in observance of patriotic holidays, and no observance of Arbor Day. There was no physical training except that which they got outside in the ordinary course of their play. They had membership in the Y.M.C.A., but failed to attend during September and October. Of this default the parents had no knowledge.

The instruction was interrupted from time to time by the mother's household duties, occasional shopping tours, and house callers. The defendants had no definite schedule for daily instruction. The evidence indicates that the boys obtained from children in school, periodically, information as to the subjects they were studying in school, and transmitted that information to the mother, who guided herself in instructing the children, to some extent, by it. They had no marks for their work. There were no daily work papers, tests, or examinations; at least, there were none presented in evidence. In fact, the mother admits she had no standard by which to determine whether the children were absorbing the instruction she was attempting to give. There was no organized supervision over the teaching that the defendants gave; the work of the children, and the results accomplished, were never submitted to any other competent authority for supervision, criticism, or approval.

A summary of the methods of instruction at the Washington School of West Orange will be useful for comparative purposes. The elementary grades are supervised by a specially trained person, who has complete supervision over the courses of study, the textbooks used, and the methods employed by the teachers in transmitting knowledge and the building and developing of the personalities of the children. The school is organized as a miniature community center, a sort of city, where each child considers himself a citizen, with duties toward the community as is required on the outside. The educational structure thus developed is in the nature of a group enterprise, where the children work together for the common good. The teacher creates the atmosphere and becomes the guiding influence. A high discipline is maintained by strict attention to the development of habits, skills and attitudes. There is group discussion. The children bring in articles from the outside. They study the biographies of great men, and discuss their achievements. In the fifth and sixth grades, reading, writing, spelling, arithmetic, English, history, geography, civics, hygiene, safety education, music, art, and penmanship are taught. The children are taught to use the dictionary. The norm for instruction may be found in several monographs on each subject, provided by the state board of education, and strict adherence is required. In the fifth grade, there are seven text-books in daily use to cover the subjects. In the sixth grade, there are also seven text-books, supplemented by thirteen reference and reading books used in connection with their courses, and, in addition, the school library is available to them. Every text, reading, and reference book, 26 in number, produced in evidence, is carefully selected in accordance with the regulations of the state board of education and approved by the supervisor of the elementary grades and by the board of education of West Orange. There is a student schedule for the fifth and sixth grades, which provides for instruction from 8:45 a. m. until 3 p. m. from Monday to Friday, inclusive. The curriculum provides for instruction in the development of abilities, habits, and skills. Instruction is also given by way of travel lectures, picture studies, art and music, so that every child has something to talk about. Thus, an audience situation is created for the children, where each child is required to rise and speak to the entire group. This creates self-confidence, and tends to adjust the child to the social group.

One poem a week, and appreciation for the beauties of nature and literature are taught. Besides teaching arithmetic from texts, they instruct in practical matters requiring arithmetic. Geography is taught to meet life situations by creating interest in world travel and training the children to visualize, in their reading, places that they have studied. In music, each child is allowed to develop whatever talent he may possess. In art, each child learns the harmony of color in dress, interior decoration, and everyday life. Every morning the children have a reading from the Bible and recite the Lord's Prayer. They salute the flag and sing patriotic songs. They observe Arbor Day and all patriotic holidays. A course in safety education and fire prevention is pursued. The month of June is devoted to review. They have physical education four periods each week under a special supervisor. In the civics course, the children are on the lookout for all material in current events. There are three school magazines. Washington School has a monthly newspaper, and all children are eligible to participate in its columns.

From this comparison and analysis of the evidence, I find (1) that the education, training, and equipment of the defendants are substantially inadequate, as compared with those of the public school teacher; (2) that the schedule of study and the program of activities of the defendant are irregular, uncertain, and without form, while the public school curriculum is definite and allots a specified time and, in most cases, a special teacher for every subject studied in the fifth and sixth grades; (3) that the instruction given by the defendants is without proper or modern text-books, lacks supervision by competent authorities of pupil and teacher, lacks a method, standard, or other means of determining the progress or attainments of the child; none of which deficiencies are present in the public school; (4) that the teaching of discipline and health habits lacks plan and a trained method, fixing responsibility on the child for its execution; while, at the school, it is part of a definite program of character education; (5) that the defendants cannot provide for group or class teaching, and lack the ability to develop attitudes and create a social setting so that the children may be trained to deal with their playmates and friends as a part of a social group; (6) that the public school system provides such social groups and lays emphasis on its development, and stresses the adjustment of the child to group life and group activity and a course of living that he will be required to follow and meet as he goes out into the world.

The primary function of education is to get an understanding and interpretation of modern civilization. In the early days of the Republic, the idea that an educated citizenship lies at the very foundation of a democratic government has defined our philosophy of national development. For these reasons, the maintenance of an adequate system of public education for youth is a fundamental responsibility of any commonwealth. The public school system of New Jersey embodies the highest ideals of American democracy, and has developed a program which offers unusual opportunities to the children of our state. All citizens have a deep interest in our public schools, and should take pride in the high rank which they occupy in the nation. To deny children instruction seems as unnatural as to withhold their necessary subsistence. Education is brought, as it were, to the very door of all classes of society, and ignorance is quite inexcusable. The failure of the parents to provide the child with the benefits of that opportunity should be a matter of great concern when at issue. The education of youth is of such vast importance and of such singular utility in the journey of life that it obviously carries its own recommendation with it, for on it, in a great measure, depends all that we ever hope to be; every perfection that a generous and well-disposed mind would gladly arrive at. It is this that usually renders one man preferable to another. And, as the great end of learning is to teach man to know himself and to fit him for life, so he who knows most is enabled to practice best and to be an example for those who know but little.

The schools, whose function frequently is thought of solely in material terms, have a far more important responsibility. They must aid parents, not simply in the training of their children for the trades and professions, whose criterion of success too often is the amount of money they can make, but, rather, the training and development of men and women of character; men and women whose minds have been trained to the understanding of basic principles and ideals, with the courage and strength of will to live up to and apply them in their daily lives.

I incline to the opinion that education is no longer concerned merely with the acquisition of facts; the instilling of worthy habits, attitudes, appreciations, and skills is far more important than mere imparting of subject-matter. A primary objective of education to-day is the development of character and good citizenship. Education must impart to the child the way to live. This brings me to the belief that, in a cosmopolitan area such as we live in, with all the complexities of life, and our reliance upon others to carry out the functions of education, it is almost impossible for a child to be adequately taught in his home. I cannot conceive how a child can receive in the home instruction and experiences in group activity and in social outlook in any manner or form comparable to that provided in the public school. To give him less than that is depriving the child of the training and development of the most necessary emotions and instincts of life. I cannot accept the theory asserted by Mr. Bongart that, "I am not interested in method, but in results." That theory is archaic, mechanical, and destructive of the finer instincts of the child. It does seem to me, too, quite unlikely that this type of instruction could produce a child with all the attributes that a person of education, refinement, and character should possess.

I have carefully observed the defendants' children in court, their demeanor, their responses under examination, and their reaction to the proceedings while in court, and there is clear evidence that it is their belief that they are on a "grand holiday," free from the restraints, discipline, and responsibility of other children in school attendance. All of this seems to me to be attributable to the course adopted and pursued by the parents. I have also carefully examined all the evidence and exhibits, and it is my opinion that the defendants have failed to give their children instruction equivalent to that provided with the public schools in the fifth and sixth grades, but, rather, have engaged in a haphazard and hit-or-miss kind of instruction, not calculated to conform with the provisions of the statute, and that both defendants actively and independently participated in causing their children not to go to the public school or a day school. I have been satisfied beyond a reasonable doubt by the evidence of the guilt of both defendants as charged. Both defendants are hereby deemed to be disorderly persons.

## NOTES AND QUESTIONS

1. In this case Judge Siegler makes six findings of fact from which the court concludes that the defendant parents are criminally liable for keeping their children out of school while attempting to teach them at home. Are all six of the court's findings necessary to the result in the case? Which, if any, of the six findings of fact provide the strongest argument for bussing of school children to provide a racial balance?

2. Shirley Temple was a child actress who made films in Hollywood, California at an age when most other children were in a common school. The usual custom in the case of child actors who spent their days on the movie set instead of in a classroom is to provide special tutors, academically qualified, to educate such children. Would such a scheme meet the approval of Judge Siegler?

3. True or false? Judge Siegler believed that the primary purpose of public education was to prepare one for later employment?

4. Could a child ever receive an adequate education at home in Judge Siegler's view? In yours? Explain.

5. Would Judge Siegler have ruled in favor of the Bongart parents if they could have shown that their children attended public school during morning hours and then returned home for the remainder of the day when home instruction occurred? Should this solution be accepted? Is this solution possible under existing compulsory schooling laws? Most of them do not permit state boards of education to authorize pupil instruction on a part-time basis? Should the laws be changed?

## STATE OF NEW JERSEY v. MASSA

Morris County Court, New Jersey, 1967.
95 N.J.Super. 382, 231 A.2d 252.

COLLINS, J. C. C. This is a trial *de novo* on appeal from the Pequannock Township Municipal Court. Defendants were charged and convicted with failing to cause their daughter Barbara, aged 12, regularly to attend the public schools of the district and further for failing to either send Barbara to a private school or provide an equivalent education elsewhere than at school, contrary to the provisions of N.J.S.A. 18:14–14. The municipal magistrate imposed a fine of $2490 for both defendants.

Mr. and Mrs. Massa appeared *pro se*. Mrs. Massa conducted the case; Mr. Massa concurred.

Mrs. Massa testified that she had taught Barbara at home for two years before September 1965. Barbara returned to school in September 1965, but began receiving her education at home again on April 25, 1966.

Mrs. Massa said her motive was that she desired the pleasure of seeing her daughter's mind develop. She felt she wanted to be with her child when the child would be more alive and fresh. She also maintained that in school much time was wasted and that at home a student can make better use of her time.

Mrs. Massa is a high school graduate. Her husband is an interior decorator. Neither holds a teacher's certificate. However, the State stipulated that a child may be taught at home and also that Mr. or Mrs. Massa need not be certified by the State of New Jersey to so teach. The sole issue in this case is one of equivalency. Have defendants provided their daughter with an education equivalent to that provided by the Pequannock Township School System?

Mrs. Massa introduced into evidence 19 exhibits. Five of these exhibits, in booklet form, are condensations of basic subjects, are concise and seem to contain all the basic subject material for the respective subjects. Mrs. Massa also introduced textbooks which are used as supplements to her own compilations as well as for test material and written problems.

Mrs. Massa introduced English, spelling and mathematics tests taken by her daughter at the Pequannock School after she had been taught for two years at home. The lowest mark on these tests was a B.

Other exhibits included one of over 100 geography booklets prepared by Mrs. Massa from National Geographic Magazine, each containing articles and maps concerning the topography and societies of a particular part of the world; a 1' wide and 30' long scroll depicting the evolution of life on earth commencing five billion years ago and continuing to the present, which appears to be a good visual aid not merely for children but adults as well; a series of 27 maps for study and memorization; textbooks used to supplement defendant's material; examples of books used as either references or historical reading, and photographs to show that the Massa family lives a normal, active, wholesome life. The family consists of the parents, three sons, (Marshall, age 16 and Michael, age 15, both attend high school; and William, age 6) and daughter Barbara.

There is also a report by an independent testing service of Barbara's scores on standard achievement tests. They show that she is considerably higher than the national median except in arithmetic.

Mrs. Massa satisfied this court that she has an established program of teaching and studying. There are definite times each day for the various subjects and recreation. She evaluates Barbara's progress through testing. If Barbara has not learned something which has been taught, Mrs. Massa then reviews that particular area.

Barbara takes violin lessons and attends dancing school. She also is taught art by her father, who has taught this subject in various schools.

Mrs. Massa called Margaret Cordasco as a witness. She had been Barbara's teacher from September 1965 to April 1966. She testified basically that Barbara was bright, well behaved and not different from the average child her age except for some trouble adjusting socially.

The State called as a witness David MacMurray, the Assistant Superintendent of Pequannock Schools. He testified that the defendants were not giving Barbara an equivalent education. Most of his testimony dealt with Mrs. Massa's lack of certification and background for teaching and the lack of social development of Barbara because she is being taught alone.

He outlined procedures which Pequannock teachers perform, such as evaluation sheets, lesson plans and use of visual aids. He also stressed specialization since Pequannock schools have qualified teachers for certain specialized subjects. He did not think the defendants had the specialization necessary to teach all basic subjects. He also testified about extra-curricular activity, which is available but not required.

The State placed six exhibits in evidence. These included a more recent mathematics book than is being used by defendants, a sample of teacher evaluation, a list of visual aids, sample schedules for the day and lesson plans, and an achievement testing program.

Leslie Rear, the Morris County Superintendent of Schools, then testified for the State. His testimony, like that of MacMurray, dealt primarily with social development of the child and Mrs. Massa's qualifications. He felt that Barbara was not participating in the learning process since she had not participated in the development of the material. Mrs. Massa, however, testified that these materials were used as an outline from which she taught her daughter and as a reference for her daughter to use in review—not as a substitute for all source material.

N.J.S.A. 18:14–14 provides:

"Every parent, guardian or other person having custody and control of a child between the ages of 6 and 16 years shall cause such child regularly to attend the public schools of the district or a day school in which there is given instruction equivalent to that provided in the public schools for children of similar grades and attainments *or to receive equivalent instruction elsewhere than at school.*" (Emphasis added)

State v. Vaughn, 44 N.J. 142, 207 A.2d 537 (1965), interpreted the above statute to permit the parent having charge and control of the child to elect to substitute one of the alternatives for public school. It is then incumbent upon the parent to introduce evidence showing one of the alternatives is being substituted. "If there is such evidence in the case, then the ultimate burden of persuasion remains with the State,"  .   .   .

N.J.S.A. 18:14–39 provides for the penalty for violation of N.J.S.A. 18:14–14:

"A parent, guardian or other person having charge and control of a child between the ages of 6 and 16 years, who shall fail to comply with any of the provisions of this article relating to his duties shall be deemed a disorderly person and shall be subject to a fine of not more than $5.00 for a first offense and not more than $25.00 for each subsequent offense, in the discretion of the court."

The statute subjects the defendants to conviction as a disorderly person, a quasi-criminal offense. In quasi-criminal proceedings the burden of proof is beyond a reasonable doubt.

This case presents two questions on the issue of equivalency for determination. What does the word "equivalent" mean in the context of N.J.S.A. 18:14–14? And, has the State carried the required burden of proof to convict defendants?

In Knox v. O'Brien, 7 N.J.Super. 608, 72 A.2d 389 (1950), the County Court interpreted the word "equivalent" to include not only academic equivalency but also the equivalency of social development. This interpretation appears untenable in the face of the language of our own statute and also the decisions in other jurisdictions.

If the interpretation in *Knox,* were followed, it would not be possible to have children educated outside of school. Under the *Knox* rationale, in order for children to develop socially it would be necessary for them to be educated in a group. A group of students being educated in the same manner and place would constitute a *de facto* school. Our statute provides that children may receive an equivalent education elsewhere than at school. What could have been intended by the Legislature by adding this alternative?

The Legislature must have contemplated that a child could be educated alone provided the education was equivalent to the public schools. Conditions in today's society illustrate that such situations exist. Examples are the child prodigy whose education is accelerated by private tutoring, or the infant performer whose education is provided by private tutoring. If group education is required by our statute, then these examples as well as all education at home would have to be eliminated.

The court in State v. Peterman, 32 Ind.App. 665, 70 N.E. 550, 551, . . . commented on the nature of a school, stating, "We do not think that the number of persons whether one or many, makes a place where instruction is imparted any less or more a school." That case held that a child attending the home of a private tutor was attending a private school within the meaning of the Indiana statute.

This court agrees with the above decision that the number of students does not determine a school and, further, that a certain number of students need not be present to attain an equivalent education.

Perhaps the New Jersey Legislature intended the word "equivalent" to mean taught by a certified teacher elsewhere than at school. However, I believe there are teachers today teaching in various schools in New Jersey who are not certified. The prosecutor stipulated, as stated above, that the State's position is that a child may be taught at home and that a person teaching at home is not required to be certified as a teacher by the State for the purpose of teaching his own children. Had the Legislature intended such a requirement, it would have so provided.

The case of Commonwealth v. Roberts, 159 Mass. 372, 34 N.E. 402 . . . dealt with a statute similar to New Jersey's. The Massachusetts statute permitted instruction in school or academies in the same town or district, or instruction by a private tutor or governess, or by the parents themselves provided it is given in good faith and is sufficient in extent. The court stated that under this statute the parents may show that the child has been sufficiently and properly instructed. The object of the statute was stated to be that all children shall be educated, not that they shall be educated a particular way.

It is in this sense that this court feels the present case should be decided. The purpose of the law is to insure the education of all children. In State v. Peterman, supra, the court stated:

> "The law was made for the parent, who does not educate his child, and not for the parent . . . [who] places within the reach of the child the opportunity and means of acquiring an education equal to that obtainable in the public schools of the state." . . .

Faced with exiguous precedent in New Jersey and having reviewed the above cited cases in other states, this court holds that the language of the New Jersey statute, N.J.S.A. 18:14–14, providing for "equivalent education elsewhere than at school," requires only a showing of academic equivalence. As stated above, to hold that the statute requires equivalent social contact and development as well would emasculate this alternative and allow only group education, thereby eliminating private tutoring or home education. A statute is to be interpreted to uphold its validity in its entirety if possible. . . . This is the only reasonable interpretation available in this case which would accomplish this end.

Having determined the intent of the Legislature as requiring only equivalent academic instruction, the only remaining question is whether the defendants provided their daughter with an education equivalent to that available in the public schools. After reviewing the evidence presented by both the State and the defendants, this court finds that the State has not shown beyond a reasonable doubt that defendants failed to provide their daughter with an equivalent education.

The majority of testimony of the State's witnesses dealt with the lack of social development.

The other point pressed by the State was Mrs. Massa's lack of teaching ability and techniques based upon her limited education and experience. However, this court finds this testimony to be inapposite to the actual issue of equivalency under the New Jersey statute and the stipulations of the State. In any case, from my observation of her while testifying and during oral argument, I am satisfied that Mrs. Massa is self-educated and well qualified to teach her daughter the basic subjects from grades one through eight.

The remainder of the testimony of the State's witnesses dealt primarily with the child's deficiency in mathematics. This alone, however, does not establish an educational program unequivalent to that in the public schools in the face of the evidence presented by defendants.

Defendants presented a great deal of evidence to support their position, not the least of which was their daughter's test papers taken in the Pequannock school after having been taught at home for two years. The results speak for themselves. The evidence of the State which was actually directed toward the issue of equivalency in this case fell short of the required burden of proof.

The Massa family, all of whom were present at each of the hearings, appeared to be a normal, well-adjusted family. The behavior of the four Massa children in the courtroom evidenced an exemplary upbringing.

It is the opinion of this court that defendants' daughter has received and is receiving an education equivalent to that available in the Pequannock public schools. There is no indication of bad faith or improper motive on defendants' part. Under a more definite statute with sufficient guidelines or a lesser burden of proof, this might not necessarily be the case. However, within the framework of the existing law and the nature of the stipulations by the State, this court finds the defendant not guilty and reverses the municipal court conviction.

In view of the fact that defendants appeared pro se, the court suggests that the prosecutor draw an order in accordance herewith.

## NOTES AND QUESTIONS

1. Why did Massa's home education qualify as "equivalent academic instruction" under the New Jersey statute but that of Bongart did not? Was the requirement of a "certified teacher" determinative? Peer socialization? Was the same meaning of the term "equivalent academic instruction" applied equally in the two cases? If not, and the meaning of the term varied between the two cases, what were the differences in meaning?

2. Did the court find as a fact that Mrs. Bongart was not and that Mrs. Massa was developing the individuality, personality and mentality of each child under her supervision? Do you agree? Why or why not? Was this consideration relevant in the same way to the decision in Massa? Should it have been?

3. Does the court's decision in Stephens v. Bongart ultimately rest on the view that home education is not equivalent to school education because home education fails to teach the individual how to fit into social groups? If so, could New Jersey's statute providing for "equivalent" education ever be satisfied by home education? Is the court consistent in Massa?

4. Do you agree that the factual distinctions between the Massa and the Bongart cases justified the different results? What precise facts? Why or why not?

5. Would the court's decision in the Massa case have been the same if there had been no evidence of the child's success on external examinations used by the public schools or by an independent testing service? Can there be true home education if the child is required to take periodic tests at a school?

6. Why didn't the Washington Court in State v. Counort, supra, consider the quality of the home education? Should it have? Why or why not? If so, what are the specific criteria that make equivalent home instruction into a "private school"? Is association with other children from all walks of life a requirement?

7. Do you agree with the decisions and the reasoning in the Bongart, Massa and Counort cases? Which shows more insight into education? Why?

8. Why does the court in Massa require that the state carry the burden of proof? Why in Massa was the required standard of proof that the state had to meet the standard of "beyond a reasonable doubt" rather than the standard of "by a fair preponderance of the evidence"? What is the difference between these standards? Which would you require if you were the judge, and why?

9. Which of the decisions in the three cases is most promotive of and compatible with the views that "an educated citizenship lies at the very foundation of a democratic government" and that "a primary objective of education today is the development of character and good citizenship"? How can these objectives be achieved in school? In the home?

10. In Matter of Thomas H, 78 Misc.2d 412, 357 N.Y.S.2d 384 (1974) three children aged 13, 12 and 10, were taught at home by their parents who followed a nongraded curriculum which aimed to teach skills through "instruction in a total environment." New York's family court ruled that the home instruction was not "equivalent instruction" because of a lack of compliance with "the daily hours of attendance required under [New York's] Education Law," and because of "a lack of consistent quality in subject instruction, if not an absence of instruction in some areas and it shows an absence of a systematic approach to the course of study of the branches specified in the statute and regulations." Does this ruling mean that home instruction must be conducted in the class-after-class, lock-step style of public schools? If so, would that be consistent with Yoder in the case of religious parents who want their children to learn a different life-style?

11. For discussion of state controls over private schools see, J. Elson, "State Regulation Of Nonpublic Schools: The Legal Framework," printed in D. A. Erickson (ed.), Public Control Of Nonpublic Schools (1969).

## "HOST" POWER AND COMPULSORY SCHOOLING

———

Compulsory schooling laws have the consequence of producing large numbers of children in America's public schools. A public school board's powers over its children are governed by statute, but, generally, they can be divided into two basic categories: (1) powers directly related to education itself, and (2) powers related to the fact that schools are "host" institutions for children. The first category of powers will be the subject of later chapters.  The second category of powers simply recognizes the basic facts that education takes place in buildings which must be maintained in a good state of repair and free of vandalism;  that large groups of children congregated together in schools necessarily involve health considerations, and that individuals making up these congregations must be protected from harming each other.  But, regardless which category of powers a school board may exercise, it must exercise them in accordance with the constitution and with the purposes for which state statutes granted those powers.  For further discussion, see, Goldstein, The Scope and Source of School Board Authority To Regulate Student Conduct and Status: A Nonconstitutional Analysis, 117 U. of Pa.L.Rev. 373 (1969).  Does the following case reveal a proper constitutional exercise of school board host powers in relation to the compulsory obligation of parents to send their children to school?  Is the case consistent with Pierce?  Yoder?

## VACCINATION

---

### ARCHIE CUDE v. ARKANSAS

Supreme Court of Arkansas, 1964.
237 Ark. 927, 377 S.W.2d 816.

ROBINSON, Justice.  The issue is the authority of the courts to appoint a guardian for children between the ages of 7 and 15, inclusive, who are not attending school, and to give the guardian custody of the children with directions to have them vaccinated to facilitate school attendance.

Appellants, Archie Cude and his wife, Mary Frances, are the parents of eight children, three of whom are between the ages of 7 and 15, inclusive.  The children are Wayne Monroe, age 12, Delia Marie, 10, and Linda May, 8.  Wayne went only to the second grade;  the other two have not attended school at all.  The children are not in school for the reason that the school authorities will not permit them to attend school because they have not been vaccinated against smallpox.  The Cudes will not permit such vaccinations;  they contend that it is contrary to their religion.

This litigation was commenced by Ben Core, Prosecuting Attorney for the Ninth Judicial District of the State of Arkansas, filing in the Probate Court of Polk County, on behalf of the State, a petition alleging that the three Cude children were not attending school;  that the father, Archie Cude, had been fined on three occasions for violating the law requiring that parents send their children to school, and he has persisted in his refusal to have the children vaccinated so that they can attend school, and that the father has avowed that he will never permit the children to be vaccinated; that unless the children are removed from the custody of the natural parents they will not have all the benefits and advantages of a school education. The petition asks that the children be placed in the custody of the Child Welfare Division of the State Welfare Department.

The appellants responded, contending first, that the probate court did not have jurisdiction, and further, that vaccination of the children was against respondents' religious beliefs. There was a full scale hearing; it was shown that the children were not attending school because they had not been vaccinated; that the appellants would not permit them to be vaccinated because of their religious beliefs, and appellant, Archie Cude, testified that if the children were taken from him and vaccinated he would not accept them back.

The court appointed Miss Ruth Johnston, Director of the Child Welfare Division of the State Welfare Department, as guardian of the children. The order further provides: "Said guardian is authorized and directed to file a petition in the Chancery Court of Polk County, Arkansas, for the purpose of obtaining the physical control and custody of the children for the purpose of having such children properly vaccinated and immunized against the disease of smallpox, and thereafter enrolled in the public schools of this State, all in accordance with the laws of this State, and all to be done by qualified and licensed and practicing physicians of this State as soon as is reasonably possible after the said children are in the custody of said guardian. After the immunization of the said children, the guardian shall offer, through the office of the Prosecuting Attorney for the 9th Judicial Circuit, to deliver the said children back into the custody of the Defendants, and the guardian is authorized and directed to do so, and if the Defendants shall not accept the said children back into the home of the Defendants, then the said guardian is hereby authorized and empowered to consent to the subsequent adoption of the said children by a party or parties acceptable to the Guardian and to the Probate Court which may consent."

Pursuant to the foregoing order, the guardian, Ruth Johnston, filed a petition in the chancery court asking for custody of the children. Over appellants' protest the petition was granted. The Cudes have appealed.

Actually, there are two appeals; one from the order of the probate court appointing the guardian; the other from the order of the chancery court giving Miss Johnston custody of the children. The cases have been consolidated on appeal.

For the purposes of the appeal, we will assume that the Cudes, in good faith because of their religious beliefs, will not permit the children to be vaccinated. Then the question is whether they have the legal right to prevent vaccination. The answer is that they do not have such right.

There is no question that the laws of this State require parents to send to school their children between the ages of 7 and 15, inclusive. Ark.Stat.Ann. § 80–1502 (Repl.1960) provides: "Every parent, guardian, or other person residing within the State of Arkansas and having in custody or charge any child or children between the ages of seven [7] and fifteen [15], (both inclusive) shall send such child or children to a public, private, or parochial school under such penalty for noncompliance with this section as hereinafter provided."

The school administrative authorities of the State of Arkansas have adopted a regulation requiring vaccination as follows: "No person shall be entered as a teacher, employee or pupil in a public or private school in this state without having first presented to the principal in charge or the proper authorities, a certificate from a licensed and competent physician of this State certifying that the said teacher, employee or pupil has been successfully vaccinated; or in lieu of a certificate of successful vaccination, a certificate certifying a recent vaccination done in a proper manner by a competent physician; or a certificate showing immunity from having had smallpox. * * *" There is no question about the validity of this regulation. . . .

It is clear that the law requires that the children attend school, and a valid regulation requires that they be vaccinated. The next question is: Are appellants, because of their religion, exempt from the law and the regulation requiring that the children be vaccinated so that they can go to school? It will be remembered that appellants do not object to the children going to school; it is the vaccination that is objectionable to them. But, according to a valid regulation, the children are not permitted to go to school without having been vaccinated.

Article 2, Sec. 24 of the Constitution of Arkansas provides: "All men have a natural and indefeasible right to worship Almighty God according to the dictates of their own consciences; no man can, of right, be compelled to attend, erect or support any place of worship; or to maintain any ministry against his consent. No human authority can, in any case or manner whatsoever, control or interfere with the right of conscience; and no preference shall ever be given, by law, to any religious establishment, denomination or mode of worship above any other." The foregoing provision of the Constitution means that anyone has the right to worship God in the manner of his own choice, but it does not mean that he can engage in religious practices inconsistent with the peace, safety and health of the inhabitants of the State, and it does not mean that parents, on religious grounds, have the right to deny their children an education.

The U. S. Supreme Court said in Prince v. Commonwealth of Massachusetts, 321 U.S. 158, 64 S.Ct. 438, 88 L.Ed. 645: "The right to practice religions freely does not include liberty to expose the community or the child to communicable disease or the latter to ill health or death. * * * Parents may be free to become martyrs themselves. But it does not follow they are free, in identical circumstances, to make martyrs of their children before they have reached the age of full and legal discretion when they can make that choice for themselves."

It is a matter of common knowledge that prior to the development of protection against smallpox by vaccination, the disease, on occasion, ran rampant and caused great suffering and sickness throughout the world. According to the great weight of authority, it is within the police power of the State to require that school children be vaccinated against smallpox, and that such requirement does not violate the constitutional rights of anyone, on religious grounds or otherwise. In fact, this principle is so firmly settled that no extensive discussion is required.

In the early case of Reynolds v. United States, 98 U.S. 145, 25 L.Ed. 244, the issue was whether a Mormon who believed in polygamy was immune from the operation of the statute forbidding the practice of multiple marriage. There, the court said: " * * * the only question which remains is, whether those who make polygamy a part of their religion are excepted from the operation of the statute. If they are, then those who do not make polygamy a part of their religious belief may be found guilty and punished, while those who do, must be acquitted and go free. This would be introducing a new element into criminal law. Laws are made for the government of actions, and while they cannot interfere with mere religious belief and opinions, they may with practices. Suppose one believed that human sacrifices were a necessary part of religious worship, would it be seriously contended that the civil government under which he lived could not interfere and prevent a sacrifice? Or if a wife religiously believed it was her duty to burn herself upon the funeral pile of her dead husband, would it be beyond the power of the civil government to prevent her carrying her belief into practice?"

In cases too numerous to mention, it has been held, in effect, that a person's right to exhibit religious freedom ceases where it overlaps and transgresses the rights of others. We cite a few cases upholding the validity of statutes requiring vaccination, and affirming orders of courts authorizing blood transfusions, etc. In Re Whitmore, Dom. Rel.Ct.N.Y., 47 N.Y.S.2d 143; vaccination of school child. Sadlock v. Board of Education, 137 N.J.L. 85, 58 A.2d 218; vaccination of school child. State v. Perricone, 37 N.J. 463, 181 A.2d 751; giving blood transfusion to infant. City of New Braunfels v. Waldschmidt, 109 Tex. 302, 207 S.W. 303; vaccination of school child. Mosier v. Barren County Board of Health, 308 Ky. 829, 215 S.W.2d 967; vaccination of school child; Board of Education of Mountain Lakes v. Maas, 56 N.J. Super. 245, 152 A.2d 394; vaccination of school child. In Re Clark,

Ohio Com.Pl., 185 N.E.2d 128; blood transfusion for three year old child.

This court said in Seubold v. Fort Smith Special School District, 218 Ark. 560, 237 S.W.2d 884: "In Jacobson v. Commonwealth of Massachusetts, 197 U.S. 11, 25 S.Ct. 358, 49 L.Ed. 643, the Supreme Court of the United States considered the matter of compulsory vaccination as infringing on rights claimed under the United States Constitution, and held that a State law requiring compulsory vaccination did not deprive a citizen of liberty guaranteed by the United States Constitution. More recently, in the case of Zucht v. King, 260 U.S. 174, 43 S.Ct. 24, 25, 67 L.Ed. 194, the United States Supreme Court again considered the matter of compulsory vaccination; and Mr. Justice Brandeis, speaking for the Court said: ' * * * Long before this suit was instituted, Jacobson v. Massachusetts, 197 U.S. 11, 25 S.Ct. 358, 49 L.Ed. 643, 3 Ann.Cas. 765, had settled that it is within the police power of a state to provide for compulsory vaccination.' "

Appellant contends that in the circumstances of this case the probate court does not have jurisdiction to appoint a guardian. The Constitution of Arkansas, Article 7, Sec. 34 provides: "In each county the Judge of the court having jurisdiction in matters of equity shall be judge of the court or probate, and have such exclusive original jurisdiction in matters relative to * * * guardians * * *. *The judge of the probate court shall try all issues of law and of facts arising in causes or proceedings within the jurisdiction of said court, and therein pending.*" (Our italics).

It will be noticed that the above provision of the Constitution gives probate courts jurisdiction in matters relative to guardians, and provides that the probate court shall try all issues of law and facts in causes within the jurisdiction of the court and pending therein. . . .

The issue of whether the three children of appellants were neglected was before the probate court in the proceeding for the appointment of a guardian, and the court had jurisdiction to determine that fact. The evidence that the parents would not permit vaccination and thereby enable the children to attend school is sufficient to base a finding of neglect. . . .

Appellants argue that Archie Cude has been fined on three occasions for not sending the children to school, and that the State has no other remedy. This action was not instituted for the purpose of punishing Cude, but to enable the children to obtain a reasonable education. The fact that Cude has been fined for violation of the law in not sending his children to school in no way benefited the children. It did not bring about the desired result of the children being sent to school. . . .

Affirmed.

JOHNSON, Justice (dissenting).

The only penalty which the legislature saw fit to provide for the failure to compel certain children to attend school is contained in Ark.Stat.Ann. § 80–1508 (Repl.1960) as follows:

> "Each day such persons violate the provisions of this act shall constitute a separate offense, and the penalty for the violation of such provision shall be a fine not to exceed ten dollars [$10.00] for each offense."

This penalty has been administered against appellants not because they have refused to comply with the compulsory attendance law but because they have refused to comply with an administrative regulation which resulted in the school authorities prohibiting their children's attendance.

It is well settled that penal statutes are to be strictly construed in favor of the accused and courts are not permitted to enlarge the punishment provided by the legislature either directly or by implication. . . .

While much of the logic contained in the majority opinion from a sociological standpoint appears to be unanswerable, nevertheless from a legal standpoint I have found no way to escape the conclusion that the trial court and this court on trial de novo on appeal are enlarging the penalty for failure to comply with the compulsory attendance law to an extent never dreamed of by the proper lawmaking body. In the absence of legislation to the contrary, I as a judge am not willing now or ever to say as a matter of law that the failure to comply with this one simple regulation of school administrative authorities constitutes such neglect of children so as to warrant the state administering the cruel and unusual punishment of depriving such children of their natural parents and depriving the natural parents of their children.

Some consolation may be derived from the fact that the children in the case at bar will be offered back to their parents when the State Welfare Department carries out the orders of the court. Even so, the precedent set here that permits the taking of the children *at all* is the vice that opens a Pandora's box which may haunt this court for years to come. In my view, one of the forseeable spectres is the unfettered interference by the State Welfare Department in areas where it has no legal standing whatsoever. In its apparent zeal to protect the immuned from the unimmuned I believe the majority has given meaning to the word *neglect* which no amount of rationalization can justify. This is the door that has been left open. History reveals that once a door is open to an administrative agency that door is not easily closed. Whose children under what pretext will be taken next? Will they be kept forever? For the reasons stated, I respectfully dissent.

NOTES AND QUESTIONS

1. In Mannis v. Arkansas, 240 Ark. 42 (1966), the Supreme Court of Arkansas applied and extended the *Cude* case, supra, holding that a parochial school was a "private school" within the meaning of its state laws requiring smallpox vaccinations of children attending public or private schools. What, if any, is the relationship between being vaccinated and obtaining an education?

2. North Carolina, like some other states, allows a statutory exemption for "members of a recognized religious organization whose teachings are contrary to the . . . [practice of vaccination]." See, State v. Miday, 263 N.C. 747, 140 S.E.2d 325 (1965). Is this desirable legislation? Why? What criteria should be used to determine which group is a "recognized religious" group?

3. As the *Cude* case demonstrates, parents do not have the legal right to prevent vaccination unless a law gives it to them. In the *Cude* case a school administrative authority adopted the regulation requiring the vaccination. By what authority do school boards or health boards have the power to adopt regulations requiring vaccinations as a condition precedent for school attendance? Was the act of the school administrative authority discretionary or ministerial? Could the school administrative authority adopt a regulation allowing an exemption from vaccination for certain members of religious faiths?

4. Could a state legislature, a school administrative authority or a state health board constitutionally require children to take an I.Q. test as a condition of entrance to a school? A personality test? Submit to a physical examination? To sex education? To the cutting of long hair? To blood sampling and typing? Would a board of education properly exercise its "host" powers if it passed rules prohibiting name-calling, fighting and similar types of student behavior? Prohibit high school girls and boys from wearing shoes with sharp spike-heels or metal taps that damage floors? Requiring seeing and hearing tests? See, Streich v. Board of Educ., 34 S.D. 169, 147 N.W. 779 (1914), and also see Mathews v. Kalamazoo Board of Educ., 127 Mich. 530, 86 N.W. 1036 (1901) and Goldstein, "The Scope and Source of School Board Authority to Regulate Student Conduct and Status: A Nonconstitutional Analysis," 117 U. of Pa.Law Rev. 373, 387–411 (1969).

5. Is the decision in the *Cude* case consistent with the decision in Wisconsin v. Yoder?

## SHOULD COMPULSORY SCHOOLING LAWS IMPLY A QUID PRO QUO?

State compulsory schooling laws result in a vast deprivation of the liberty of children who are required to attend school; perhaps it is a greater deprivation of liberty than that occurring under our criminal laws. Compulsory schooling laws not only deprive a child of his liberty, but also they deprive a parent of his right to control his child's upbringing and development. If children fail to receive an education adequate to their needs, what can be the constitutional justification for a state depriving its children and their parents of their rights and liberty? In this situation, parents, but especially children, have been harmed by the state without their having received an equally compensating benefit to offset their losses. This situation raises the issue whether a parent or a student can sue and recover for their loss of rights and liberty and for the student's failure to learn; i. e., his failure to receive an adequate education that would have offset his loss of liberty?

There is virtually no settled law in this area. A federal law, 42 U.S.C. § 1983, authorizes law suits to be brought in federal courts if the claim is that a state agent deprived a plaintiff of his constitutional rights. The character of the issue that any law suit might present to a court will differ depending upon who the defendant may be and what constitutional right is relied upon by parent or student plaintiffs. In Monell v. Department of Social Services, 436 U.S. 658, 98 S.Ct. 2018, 56 L.Ed.2d 611 (1978), the U. S. Supreme Court ruled that "local governmental bodies [such as state or local school boards] can be sued directly under Section 1983 for monetary, declaratory, or injunctive relief where . . . the action that is alleged to be unconstitutional implements or executes a policy statement, ordinance, regulation, or decision officially adopted by that body's officers . . .". But, the Supreme Court continued, a local governmental agency "cannot be held liable solely because it employs a tortfeasor— or, in other words, a municipality cannot be held liable under Section 1983 on a respondeat superior theory." Thus, a school board can be sued under 42 U.S.C. § 1983 but only when it acts under some official policy, such as a mandatory school attendance policy, and thereby "causes" an employee, such as incompetent teachers or administrators, to violate another's constitutional rights. A school board would not be responsible under § 1983 for injuries to children and deprivations of their liberties inflicted by its employees if the injuries were not "caused" by school board policy. Virtually all of classroom instruction and compulsory class attendance is "caused" by school board policy. The Supreme Court reserved decision on whether a school board, as a board, should have any kind of qualified immunity from suit. Section 1983 also applies to individual agents of local and state government, including public school administrators, teachers and individual school board members, see, Carey v. Piphus, 435 U.S. 247, 98 S.Ct. 1042, 55 L.Ed.2d 252 (1978). To date, no case involving § 1983 and a claim of unjustified deprivation of liberty or parental right because of compulsory schooling laws has been found, but it is clear that a school board and its employees are subject to suit in a federal court. Any recovery would necessarily depend upon the merits of the specific case.

The few decided cases do not involve loss of liberty claims under § 1983, but involve tort claims under the regular tort law of a state—such as educational malpractice or teacher or administrator negligence. In a public school context the issue presented by the tort cases is whether courts may provide a remedy to public school students who were compelled to attend classes but suffered loss of educational benefits because administrators and/or teachers intentionally or negligently failed to observe minimum standards of competency practiced by others in the same or similar circumstances. This failure harms students because they do not reach the levels of educational attainment that they probably would have reached if the administrators and/or teachers had performed at minimum professional competency levels. The specific harm is the loss of the difference made by a professionally competent administrator and/or teacher. Under a tort theory, a plaintiff-student theoretically might ask the court to award one or more of at least three types of relief: (1) removal of an incompetent administrator or teacher (this one is relatively cost-free); (2) remedial instruction either provided by or paid for by the administrator, teacher or school board; and (3) a money payment equal to reasonably expected but now diminished future income, e. g., a student is relegated to low-income, menial jobs because of his inferior education but would have had a higher income if properly educated. In order to win an educational malpractice law suit and be entitled to relief, a plaintiff-student would have to prove (1) that defendant (teacher?) owed a duty to the student to conform to a certain standard of conduct, i. e., a duty of care; (2) that the specific content of the standard of conduct owed to the student is to be measured by the professional level of teacher competency actually practiced by other teachers in same or similar circumstances within the community; (3) that the defendant (teacher?) failed to conform to the actual level of professional competency; i. e., was incompetent (negligent) in the circumstances; (4) that educational harm was suffered by plaintiff-student; and (5) that the harm was caused by the incompetent defendant (teacher). Assuming the truth of Mr. Joseph Nocera's following statement ("Saving Our Schools From The Teachers' Unions," The Wash. Monthly, May, 1979, p. 16), and considering the above criteria, would an undereducated student in Washington D. C.'s public school system have a valid case:

> Washington [D. C.'s] schools are in enough trouble that no one connected with them tries to gloss over the problems. Such denials would look foolish in the face of what is simply overwhelming evidence: high school seniors who can't read; whole classes of tenth graders doing sixth and seventh grade work; graduates of the D. C. school system who aren't even able to understand bus signs. These are not isolated cases— the breakdown in education here has been on a massive scale. "In the math department of DCTC [D. C. Teachers College,

a school filled almost entirely with graduates of the D. C. public school system]," reported *The Washington Post* a few years ago, "more than 80 per cent of incoming freshmen score so low on an arithmetic exam that they are required to take remedial courses, starting with work normally taught in fifth and sixth grades."   (Until it merged with two other colleges to form the University of D. C., this was the school that trained most of the people who ended up teaching in the D. C. school system.)

———

## PETER W. v. SAN FRANCISCO UNIFIED SCHOOL DIST.

California Court of Appeals, 1976.
60 Cal.App.3d 814, 131 Cal.Rptr. 854.

[In 1972, a young man, identified here as Peter W., having an average class attendance record in San Francisco's public schools for twelve years, and also having an average or an above average IQ, was graduated from high school and awarded a diploma.  His reading ability was, perhaps, at the fifth-grade level.  During Peter W.'s twelve years of attending public school, his parents repeatedly tried to obtain information about his academic progress, and they were repeatedly assured that he was performing at or near grade level. After graduation from high school and after learning the truth, that he was only marginally employable and that he may not qualify for enlistment into the armed services, Peter W. brought this law suit against the school district and its employees.  He alleged that his inability to read and write was "proximately caused" by the "negligence" of his teachers and by other district employees.  He asked for $500,000 damages.  The trial court judge dismissed Peter W.'s complaint without permitting any trial and without rendering an opinion. The case is now on appeal presenting only questions of law about the legal adequacy of the allegations made in Peter W.'s complaint.  The question, in other words, is one that assumes he can prove everything he has alleged in his complaint, and asks whether the law in California is that such Peter W. actually had rights which were invaded, as alleged, and that therefore, he had pleaded a legally sound case? If the answer is "yes" then he could go back to the trial court and present his evidence in proof of his allegations.]

RATTIGAN, Associate Justice.

The novel—and troublesome—question on this appeal is whether a person who claims to have been inadequately educated, while a student in a public school system, may state a cause of action in tort against the public authorities who operate and administer the system. We hold that he may not.

The appeal reaches us upon plaintiff's first amended complaint (hereinafter the "complaint"), which purports to state seven causes of action. Respondent (San Francisco Unified School District, its superintendent of schools, its governing board, and the individual board members) appeared to it by filing general demurrers to all seven counts; we hereinafter refer to them as "defendants."

## THE FIRST CAUSE OF ACTION

The first count, which is the prototype of the others (each of which incorporates all of its allegations by reference), sounds in negligence. . . .

"XI. Defendant school district, its agents and employees, negligently and carelessly failed to provide plaintiff with adequate instruction, guidance, counseling and/or supervision in basic academic skills such as reading and writing, although said school district had the authority, responsibility and ability . . . [to do so]. . . ."

In five enumerated subsections which follow in the same paragraph . . . plaintiff alleges that the school district and its agents and employees, "negligently and carelessly" in each instance, (1) failed to apprehend his reading disabilities, (2) assigned him to classes in which he could not read "the books and other materials," (3) allowed him "to pass and advance from a course or grade level" with knowledge that he had not achieved either its completion or the skills "necessary for him to succeed or benefit from subsequent courses," (4) assigned him to classes in which the instructors were unqualified or which were not "geared" to his reading level, and (5) permitted him to graduate from high school although he was "unable to read above the eighth grade level, as required by Education Code . . . thereby depriving him of additional instruction in reading and other academic skills."

. . .

In the closing paragraphs of the first count, plaintiff alleges general damages based upon his "permanent disability and inability to gain meaningful employment"; special damages incurred as the cost of compensatory tutoring allegedly required by reason of the "negligence, acts and omissions of defendants". . . .

According to the familiar California formula, the allegations requisite to a cause of action for negligence are (1) facts showing a duty of care in the defendant, (2) negligence constituting a breach of the duty, and (3) injury to the plaintiff as a proximate result. The present parties do not debate the adequacy of plaintiff's first count with respect to the elements of negligence, proximate cause, and injury; they focus exclusively upon the issue (which we find dispositive, as will appear) of whether it alleges facts sufficient to show that defendants owed him a "duty of care."

The facts which it shows in this respect—or not—appear in its allegations that he had been a student undergoing academic instruction in the public school system operated and administered by defendants. He argues that these facts alone show the requisite "duty of care" upon three judicially recognized theories, for which he cites authorities, pertaining to the public schools.

According to the first theory, "[a]ssumption of the function of instruction of students imposes the duty to exercise reasonable care in its discharge." . . . The [precedential] decisions he cites for his first theory have no application here . . . .

Plaintiff's second theory is that "[t]here is a special relationship between students and teachers which supports [the teachers'] duty to exercise reasonable care." He cites for this theory a wide-ranged array of decisions which enforced or addressed various "rights," "opportunities," or privileges of public school students (particularly in equal protection contexts), but none of which involved the question whether the school authorities owed them a "duty of care" in the process of their academic education. The third theory is that the "[d]uty of teachers to exercise reasonable care in instruction and supervision of students is recognized in California." The decisions cited here are inapplicable because they establish only that public school authorities have a duty to exercise reasonable care for the *physical safety* of students under their supervision.

For want of relevant authority in each instance, plaintiff's allegations of his enrollment and attendance at defendants' schools do not plead the requisite "duty of care," relative to his academic instruction, upon any of the three theories he invokes. Of course, no reasonable observer would be heard to say that these facts did not impose upon defendants a "duty of care" within any common meaning of the term; given the commanding importance of public education in society, we state a truism in remarking that the public authorities who are dutybound to educate are also bound to do it with "care." But the truism does not answer the present inquiry, in which "duty of care" is not a term of common parlance; it is instead a legalistic concept of "duty" which will sustain liability for negligence in its breach, and it must be analyzed in that light.

The concept reflects the longstanding language of decisions in which the existence of a "duty of care," in a defendant, has been repeatedly defined as a requisite element of his liability for negligence. The concept has not been treated as immutable . . . .

Despite changes in the concept, several constants are apparent from its evolution. One is that the concept itself is still an essential factor in any assessment of liability for negligence. Another is that whether a defendant owes the requisite "duty of care," in a given factual situation, presents a question of law which is to be determined by the courts alone. A third, and the one most important in the present case, is that judicial recognition of such duty in the defendant, with the consequence of his liability in negligence for its breach, is initially to be dictated or precluded by considerations of public policy.

. . .

"An affirmative declaration of duty [of care] simply amounts to a statement that two parties stand in such relationship that the law will impose on one a responsibility for the exercise of care toward the other. Inherent in this simple description are various and sometimes delicate *policy judgments*. The social utility of the activity out of which the injury arises, compared with the risks involved in its conduct; the kind of person with whom the actor is dealing; the workability of a rule of care, especially in terms of the parties' relative ability to adopt practical means of preventing injury; the relative ability of the parties to bear the financial burden of injury and the availability of means by which the loss may be shifted or spread; the body of statutes and judicial precedents which color the parties' relationship; the prophylactic effect of a rule of liability; in the case of a public agency defendant, the extent of its powers, the role imposed upon it by law and the limitations imposed upon it by budget and finally, the moral imperatives which judges share with their fellow citizens—such are the factors which play a role in the determination of duty. Occasions for judicial determination of a duty of care are infrequent, because in 'run of the mill' accident cases the existence of a duty may be—and usually is—safely assumed. Here the problem is squarely presented."

In Rowland v. Christian (1968) 69 Cal.2d 108, 70 Cal.Rptr. 97, 443 P.2d 561, the Supreme Court used similar terminology in defining various public policy considerations as exceptional factors which might alone warrant *non*liability for negligence. The court declared that the foundation of *all* negligence liability in this state was Civil Code section 1714, paraphrased the section in terms of duty of care (as expressing the principle that "[a]ll persons are required to use ordinary care to prevent others being injured as the result of their conduct"), and stated that liability was to flow from this "fundamental principle" in all cases except where a departure from it was *"clearly supported by public policy."* The court then described the pertinent factors of public policy, and their role, as follows:

"A departure from this fundamental principle involves the balancing of a number of considerations; the major ones are the foreseeability of harm to the plaintiff, the degree of certainty that the plaintiff suffered injury, the closeness of the connection between the defendant's conduct and the injury suffered, the moral blame attached to the defendant's conduct, the policy of preventing future harm, the extent of the burden to the defendant and consequences to the community of imposing a duty to exercise care with resulting liability for breach, and the availability, cost, and prevalence of insurance for the risk involved."

Such policy factors, and their controlling role in the determination whether a defendant owes a "duty of care" which will underlie his liability for negligence in its breach, have been similarly defined in other decisions. Some have been classified as "administrative factors" which involve such considerations as the possibility of "feigned claims," and the difficulty of proof, of a particular injury; others, as "socio-economic and moral factors" involving the prospect of limitless liability for the same injury.

It has also been pointed out that the concept of "duty" may actually focus upon the rights of the injured plaintiff rather than upon the obligations of the defendant, but that the same public policy considerations will control whether the one may state a cause of action for negligence, against the other, in a given factual situation. . . .

On occasions when the Supreme Court has opened or sanctioned new areas of tort liability, it has noted that the wrongs and injuries involved were both comprehensible and assessable within the existing judicial framework. This is simply not true of wrongful conduct and injuries allegedly involved in educational malfeasance. Unlike the activity of the highway or the marketplace, classroom methodology affords no readily acceptable standards of care, or cause, or injury. The science of pedagogy itself is fraught with different and conflicting theories of how or what a child should be taught, and any layman might—and commonly does—have his own emphatic views on the subject. The "injury" claimed here is plaintiff's inability to read and write. Substantial professional authority attests that the achievement of literacy in the schools, or its failure, are influenced by a host of factors which affect the pupil subjectively, from outside the formal teaching process, and beyond the control of its ministers. They may be physical, neurological, emotional, cultural, environmental; they may be present but not perceived, recognized but not identified.

We find in this situation no conceivable "workability of a rule of care" against which defendants' alleged conduct may be measured, no reasonable "degree of certainty that . . . plaintiff suffered injury" within the meaning of the law of negligence, and no such perceptible "connection between the defendant's conduct and the injury suffered," as alleged, which would establish a causal link between them within the same meaning.

These recognized policy considerations alone negate an actionable "duty of care" in persons and agencies who administer the academic phases of the public educational process. Others, which are even more important in practical terms, command the same result. Few of our institutions, if any, have aroused the controversies, or incurred the public dissatisfaction, which have attended the operation of the public schools during the last few decades. Rightly or wrongly, but widely, they are charged with outright failure in the achievement of their educational objectives; according to some critics, they bear responsibility for many of the social and moral problems of our society at large. Their public plight in these respects is attested in the daily media, in bitter governing board elections, in wholesale rejections of school bond proposals, and in survey upon survey. To hold them to an actionable "duty of care," in the discharge of their academic functions, would expose them to the tort claims—real or imagined—of disaffected students and parents in countless numbers. They are already beset by social and financial problems which have gone to major litigation, but for which no permanent solution has yet appeared. The ultimate consequences, in terms of public time and money, would burden them—and society—beyond calculation.

Upon consideration of the role imposed upon the public schools by law and the limitations imposed upon them by their publicly-supported budgets, and of the just-cited "consequences to the community of imposing [upon them] a duty to exercise care with resulting liability for breach," we find no such "duty" in the first count of plaintiff's complaint. As this conclusion is dispositive, other problems presented by the pleading need not be discussed: it states no cause of action.

## THE LAST FIVE CAUSES OF ACTION

In each of his last five counts (the third through the seventh, inclusive), plaintiff repleads all the allegations of the first one. He further alleges, in each, that he had incurred "the damages alleged herein" "as a direct and proximate result" of a specified violation, by one or more of the defendants and as to him, of a respectively described "duty" (or "mandatory duty") allegedly imposed upon them by an express provision of law. The theory of each count is that it states a cause of action for breach of a "mandatory duty  . . .."

If it be assumed that each of these counts effectively pleads the district's failure to have exercised "reasonable diligence to discharge the duty" respectively alleged, as mentioned in the statute none states a cause of action. This is because the statute imposes liability for failure to discharge only such "mandatory duty" as is "imposed by an enactment that is designed to protect against the risk of a particular kind of injury." The various "enactments" cited in these counts are not so "designed." We have already seen that the failure of educational achievement may not be characterized as an "injury" within the meaning of tort law.  . . .

## THE SECOND CAUSE OF ACTION

Plaintiff's second count requires separate treatment because the theory of liability invoked in it is materially different from those reflected in the others. After incorporating into it all the allegations of the first count, he further alleges as follows:

"Defendant school district, its agents and employees, falsely and fraudulently represented to plaintiff's mother and natural guardian that plaintiff was performing at or near grade level in basic academic skills such as reading and writing. . . ." The representations were false. The charged defendants knew that they were false, or had no basis for believing them to be true. "As a direct and proximate result of the intentional or negligent misrepresentation made . . ., plaintiff suffered the damages set forth herein."

For the public policy reasons heretofore stated with respect to plaintiff's first count, we hold that this one states no cause of action for *negligence* in the form of the "misrepresentation" alleged. The possibility of its stating a cause of action for *intentional* misrepresentation, to which it expressly refers in the alternative, is assisted by judicial limitations placed upon the scope of the governmental immunity which is granted, as to liability for "misrepresentation," by Government Code section 818.8.

The second count nevertheless does not state a cause of action, for intentional misrepresentation, because it alleges no facts showing the requisite element of *reliance* upon the "misrepresentation" it asserts. . . .

The judgment of dismissal is affirmed.

## NOTES AND QUESTIONS

1. The court relied on public policy reasons to rule that the complaint stated no legal cause of action for negligence because the law did not recognize a duty of academic care and concern running from defendants to plaintiff Peter W. In deciding whether such a duty of care exists, the court indicated that the proper approach is to balance the policy reasons favoring such a duty against policy reasons disfavoring the duty. Can you identify and state the policy reasons the court placed on either side of its judicial balancing scale? Are all the policy reasons balanced? Are the right ones on the scale?

2. Did the court balance Peter W.'s constitutional interest in liberty? If not, why not? Would that interest be weighed in the balance if the law suit had been brought under § 1983 instead of, or in addition to, alleging negligence and/or emotional injury?

3. If it is true, as the court asserts, "that the achievement of literacy in the schools, or its failure, are influenced by a host of factors which affect the pupil subjectively," is it only part of the whole truth? Does not public school instruction directly affect "the achievement of literacy"? If so, why does the court fail to recognize that fact and to deal with its necessary implications for finding a duty of care? If, on the other hand, school instruction does not influence literacy, then what is the justification for compulsory schooling laws?

4.  Should the effectiveness and competency of a teacher be judged by his academic degrees or, like any other worker, by his results? If, for example, one fourth grade teacher consistently at the end of the year brings in most of his students above grade level in reading, but another fourth grade teacher, with the same student mix, consistently ends his year with dispirited, bewildered students, most of whom are reading below grade level, then is one competent and the other not, even though they hold the same degrees? Couldn't the same judgment be made of principals of comparable schools, one with declining overall reading scores and one with rising scores? Why shouldn't educators have to document their competency, not by their degrees, but by the academic records of their students?

5.  If in some other state, a school district adopted a minimum competency testing program for grade advancement purposes, would such a program enable a court to identify enough workable standards so that it would rule opposite to Peter W.?

6.  Some courts have tended to agree with the Peter W. case. See, e. g., Donohue v. Copiague Union Free School Dist., 64 A.D.2d 29, 407 N.Y.S.2d 874 (1978), but compare, Pierce v. Board of Educ., 44 Ill.App. 3d 324, 3 Ill.Dec. 67, 358 N.E.2d 67 (1976) in which a court ruled that if the school district knew, or should have known, that a K–12 student had a learning disability, and if the district refused requests to test the student, or to notify the superintendent of public instruction of the student's need for special education, then the school board could properly be held liable in tort for the emotional trauma and other emotional injury done to the student without there having to be any accompanying physical injuries. Query, how would the Peter W. case have been decided in Illinois if in addition to negligence, Peter W. also had alleged that he suffered emotional injury? Generally see, Comment, Educational Malpractice, 124 U. of Pa.L.Rev. 755 (1976) and Note, Educational Malpractice, 13 Suff.L.Rev. 27 (1979).

7.  In Peter W.'s case the court stated that his final allegation did "not state a cause of action, for intentional misrepresentation, because it alleges no facts showing the requisite element of *reliance* upon the 'misrepresentation' it asserts." Suppose Peter W.'s lawyer had alleged reliance on the school's misrepresentations, would a trial then have taken place? If so, and the allegations were proved, would Peter W. win?

8.  In Hoffman v. Board of Educ., 64 A.D.2d 369, 410 N.Y.S.2d 99 (1978) the Appellate Division of New York's Supreme Court ruled that a student was entitled to recover $500,000.00 in damages from the Board of Education because of his diminished intellectual development. The student was of normal intelligence but had been misclassified for eleven years into classes for children of retarded mental development. The court said that the student's diminished intellectual development was caused by the negligence of School Board employees when they failed to follow the school psychologist's advice that the student be re-evaluated within two years after originally being placed in the class. In an important sense, was Peter W. "misclassified"?

9.    Reconsider this problem and the possible use of Section 1983 in rela-
      tion to the equal protection and due process doctrines developed in sub-
      sequent chapters.

10.   In Brown v. Board of Educ., (reproduced in chapter VIII) the Supreme
      Court ruled that racially "separate educational facilities are inherently
      unequal" and deprive children of equal educational opportunity.  Gen-
      erally, it is the responsibility of a school board, not courts, to direct
      that children have equal educational opportunities for a quality educa-
      tion.  In a segregated setting many techniques can deny equal educa-
      tional oportunity, such as discriminatory testing, discriminatory coun-
      seling and inferior teaching.  To remedy such circumstances, and to
      guard against resegregation, courts sometimes deem it essential to
      mandate that educational components be part of a desegregation plan,
      including such things as comprehensive and remedial reading programs,
      vocational training, in-house teacher training programs that insure
      desegregation, and other measures.  What is the real reason why courts
      mandate educational components as part of a desegregation plan?
      Could it be that underlying it all is the view that students who have
      been subjected to segregation have received inferior educations;
      i. e., they have not received a quid pro quo for their loss of liberty due
      to a state's compulsory schooling laws, and that is partially why "sepa-
      rate educational facilities are inherently unequal"?  If so, is segrega-
      tion by race the only reason why some students receive inferior educa-
      tions, depriving them of their quid pro quos?

------

## MILLIKEN v. BRADLEY

Supreme Court of the United States, 1977.
433 U.S. 267, 97 S.Ct. 2749, 53 L.Ed.2d 745.

Mr. Chief Justice BURGER delivered the opinion of the Court.

We granted certiorari in this case to consider  .  .  .  whether
a District Court can, as part of a desegregation decree, order compensatory or remedial educational programs for schoolchildren who
have been subjected to past acts of *de jure* segregation  .  .  .  .

I

This case is before the Court for the second time it marks the
culmination of seven years of litigation over *de jure* school segregation in the Detroit public school system.  For almost six years, the
litigation has focused exclusively on the appropriate remedy to correct
official acts of racial discrimination committed by both the Detroit
School Board and the State of Michigan.  No challenge is now made
by the State or the local school board to the prior findings of *de jure*
segregation.

      .  .  .  the District Court on August 11, 1975, approved, in prin-
ciple, the Detroit Board's inclusion of remedial and compensatory
educational components in the desegregation plan.

"We find that the majority of the educational components included in the Detroit Board plan are essential for
a school district undergoing desegregation.  While it is true
that the delivery of quality desegregated educational services
is the obligation of the school board, nevertheless this court
deems it essential to mandate educational components where
they are needed to remedy effects of past segregation, to assure a successful desegregative effort and to minimize the
possibility of resegregation."

The District Court [also] expressly found that two components
of testing and counseling, as then administered in Detroit's schools,
were infected with the discriminatory bias of a segregated school system:

"In a segregated setting many techniques deny equal
protection to black students, such as discriminatory testing
[and] discriminatory counseling  . . . ."

The District Court also found that, to make desegregation work, it
was necessary to include remedial reading programs and in-service
training for teachers and administrators:

"In a system undergoing desegregation, teachers will
require orientation and training for desegregation. . . .
Additionally, we find that  . . .  comprehensive reading
programs are essential  . . .  to a successful desegregative effort."

Having established these general principles, the District Court
formulated several "remedial guidelines" to govern the Detroit Board's
development of a final plan.  Declining "to substitute its authority
for the authority of elected state and local officials to decide which
educational components are beneficial to the school community," the
District Judge laid down the following guidelines with respect to each
of the four educational components at issue here:

(a) *Reading*.  Concluding that "[t]here is no educational component more directly associated with the process of desegregation
than reading," the District Court directed the General Superintendent
of Detroit's schools to institute a remedial reading and communications skills program "[t]o eradicate the effects of past discrimination  . . . ."  The content of the required program was not prescribed by the court; rather, formulation and implementation of the
program was left to the Superintendent and to a committee to be selected by him.

(b) *In-Service Training*.  The court also directed the Detroit
Board to formulate a comprehensive in-service teacher training pro-
gram, an element "essential to a system undergoing desegregation."
In the District Court's view, an in-service training program for teach-

ers and administrators, to train professional and instructional personnel to cope with the desegregation process in Detroit, would tend to ensure that all students in a desegregated system would be treated equally by teachers and administrators able, by virtue of special training, to cope with special problems, presented by desegregation, and thereby facilitate Detroit's conversion to a unitary system.

(c) *Testing.* Because it found, based on record evidence, that Negro children "are especially affected by biased testing procedures," the District Court determined that, frequently, minority students in Detroit were adversely affected by discriminatory testing procedures. Unless the school system's tests were administered in a way "free from racial, ethnic and cultural bias," the District Court concluded that Negro children in Detroit might thereafter be impeded in their educational growth. Accordingly, the court directed the Detroit Board and the State Department of Education to institute a testing program along the lines proposed by the local school board in its original desegregation plan.

(d) *Counseling and Career Guidance.* Finally, the District Court addressed what expert witnesses had described as psychological pressures on Detroit's students in a system undergoing desegregation. Counselors were required, the court concluded, both to deal with the numerous problems and tensions arising in the change from Detroit's dual system, and, more concretely, to counsel students concerning the new vocational and technical school programs available under the plan through the cooperation of state and local officials.

Nine months later, on May 11, 1976, the District Court entered its final order. Emphasizing that it had "been careful to order only what is essential for a school district undergoing desegregation," the court ordered the Detroit Board and the state defendants to institute comprehensive programs as to the four educational components by the start of the September 1976 school term. The cost of these four programs, the court concluded, was to be equally borne by the Detroit School Board and the State. To carry out this cost sharing, the court directed the local board to calculate its highest budget allocation in any prior year for the several educational programs and, from that base, any excess cost attributable to the desegregation plan was to be paid equally by the two groups of defendants responsible for prior constitutional violations, i. e., the Detroit Board and the state defendants.

. . .

The state defendants then sought review in this Court, challenging only those portions of the District Court's comprehensive remedial order dealing with the four educational components and with the State's obligation to defray the costs of those programs. We granted certiorari, and we affirm.

## II

This Court has not previously addressed directly the question whether federal courts can order remedial education programs as part of a school desegregation decree. However, the general principles governing our resolution of this issue are well settled by the prior decisions of this Court. In the first case concerning federal courts' remedial powers in eliminating *de jure* school segregation, the Court laid down the basic rule which governs to this day: "In fashioning and effectuating the [desegregation] decrees, the courts will be guided by equitable principles." Brown v. Board of Education, 349 U.S. 294, 300 (1955) (*Brown II*).

### A

Application of those "equitable principles," we have held, requires federal courts to focus upon three factors. In the first place, like other equitable remedies, the nature of the desegregation remedy is to be determined by the nature and scope of the constitutional violation. The remedy must therefore be related to "the *condition* alleged to offend the Constitution. . . ." Second, the decree must indeed be *remedial* in nature, that is, it must be designed as nearly as possible "to restore the victims of discriminatory conduct to the position they would have occupied in the absence of such conduct." Third, the federal courts in devising a remedy must take into account the interests of state and local authorities in managing their own affairs, consistent with the Constitution. In *Brown II* the Court squarely held that "[s]chool authorities have the *primary* responsibility for elucidating, assessing, and solving these problems. . . ." If, however, "school authorities fail in their affirmative obligations . . . judicial authority may be invoked." Once invoked, "the scope of a district court's equitable powers to remedy past wrongs is broad, for breadth and flexibility are inherent in equitable remedies."

### B

The well-settled principle that the nature and scope of the remedy are to be determined by the violation means simply that federal-court decrees must directly address and relate to the constitutional violation itself. Because of this inherent limitation upon federal judicial authority, federal-court decrees exceed appropriate limits if they are aimed at eliminating a condition that does not violate the Constitution or does not flow from such a violation, or if they are imposed upon governmental units that were neither involved in nor affected by the constitutional violation. But where, as here, a constitutional violation has been found, the remedy does not "exceed" the violation if the remedy is tailored to cure the " '*condition* that offends the Constitution.' "

The "condition" offending the Constitution is Detroit's *de jure* segregated school system, which was so pervasively and persistently segregated that the District Court found that the need for the educational components flowed directly from constitutional violations by both state and local officials.   These specific educational remedies, although normally left to the discretion of the elected school board and professional educators, were deemed necessary to restore the victims of discriminatory conduct to the position they would have enjoyed in terms of education had these four components been provided in a nondiscriminatory manner in a school system free from pervasive *de jure* racial segregation.

.   .   .   In a word, discriminatory student assignment policies can themselves manifest and breed other inequalities built into a dual system founded on racial discrimination.   Federal courts need not, and cannot, close their eyes to inequalities, shown by the record, which flow from a longstanding segregated system.

C

In light of the mandate of *Brown I* and *Brown II*, federal courts have, over the years, often required the inclusion of remedial programs in desegregation plans to overcome the inequalities inherent in dual school systems.   In 1966, for example, the District Court for the District of South Carolina directed the inclusion of remedial courses to overcome the effects of a segregated system:

> "Because the weaknesses of a dual school system may have already affected many children, the court would be remiss in its duty if any desegregation plan were approved which did not provide for remedial education courses.   They shall be included in the plan."

In 1967, the Court of Appeals for the Fifth Circuit, then engaged in overseeing the desegregation of numerous school districts in the South, laid down the following requirement in an en banc decision:

> "The defendants shall provide remedial education programs which permit students attending or who have previously attended segregated schools *to overcome past inadequacies* in their education."

.   .   .   Two years later, the Fifth Circuit again adhered to the rule that District Courts could properly seek to overcome the built-in inadequacies of a segregated educational system:

> "The trial court concluded that the school board must establish remedial programs to assist students who previously attended all-Negro schools when those students transfer to formerly all-white schools.   .   .   .   The *remedial programs   .   .   .   are an integral part of a program for com-*

*pensatory education to be provided Negro students who have long been disadvantaged* by the inequities and discrimination inherent in the dual school system. The requirement that the School Board institute remedial programs so far as they are feasible is a proper exercise of the court's discretion."

Our reference to these cases is not to be taken as necessarily approving holdings not reviewed by this Court. However, they demonstrate that the District Court in the case now before us did not break new ground in approving the School Board's proposed plan. . . . In so doing, the District Court was adopting specific programs proposed by local school authorities, who must be presumed to be familiar with the problems and the needs of a system undergoing desegregation.

We do not, of course, imply that the order here is a blueprint for other cases. That cannot be; in school desegregation cases, "[t]here is no universal answer to complex problems . . .; there is obviously no one plan that will do the job in every case." On this record, however, we are bound to conclude that the decree before us was aptly tailored to remedy the consequences of the constitutional violation. Children who have been thus educationally and culturally set apart from the larger community will inevitably acquire habits of speech, conduct, and attitudes reflecting their cultural isolation. They are likely to acquire speech habits, for example, which vary from the environment in which they must ultimately function and compete, if they are to enter and be a part of that community. This is not peculiar to race; in this setting, it can affect any children who, as a group, are isolated by force of law from the mainstream.

Pupil assignment alone does not automatically remedy the impact of previous, unlawful educational isolation; the consequences linger and can be dealt with only by independent measures. In short, speech habits acquired in a segregated system do not vanish simply by moving the child to a desegregated school. The root condition shown by this record must be treated directly by special training at the hands of teachers prepared for that task. This is what the District Judge in the case drew from the record before him as to the consequences of Detroit's *de jure* system, and we cannot conclude that the remedies decreed exceeded the scope of the violations found.

Nor do we find any other reason to believe that the broad and flexible equity powers of the court were abused in this case. The established role of local school authorities was maintained inviolate, and the remedy is indeed remedial. The order does not punish anyone, nor does it impair or jeopardize the educational system in Detroit.

The judgment of the Court of Appeals is therefore affirmed.

Affirmed.

Mr. Justice MARSHALL, concurring.

I wholeheartedly join The Chief Justice's opinion for the Court.

What is, to me, most tragic about this case is that in all relevant respects it is in no way unique. That a northern school board has been found guilty of intentionally discriminatory acts is, unfortunately, not unusual. That the academic development of black children has been impaired by this wrongdoing is to be expected. And, therefore, that a program of remediation is necessary to supplement the primary remedy of pupil reassignment is inevitable.

Mr. Justice POWELL, concurring in the judgment.

Normally, the plaintiffs in this type of litigation are students, parents, and supporting organizations who desire to desegregate a school system alleged to be the product, in whole or in part, of *de jure* segregative action by the public school authorities. The principal defendant is usually the local board of education or school board. Occasionally the state board of education and state officials are joined as defendants. This protracted litigation commenced in 1970 in this conventional mold. In the intervening years, however, the posture of the litigation has changed so drastically as to leave it largely a friendly suit between the plaintiffs (respondents Bradley et al.) and the original principal defendant, the Detroit School Board. These parties, antagonistic for years, have now joined forces apparently for the purpose of extracting funds from the state treasury. As between the original principal parties—the plaintiffs and the Detroit School Board—no case or controversy remains on the issues now before us. The Board enthusiastically supports the entire desegregation decree even though the decree intrudes deeply on the Board's own decision-making powers. Indeed, the present School Board *proposed* most of the educational components included in the District Court's decree.

. . .

Thus the only complaining party is the State of Michigan (acting through state officials) and its basic complaint concerns *money*, not desegregation. It has been ordered to pay about $5,800,000 to the Detroit School Board. This is one-half the estimated "excess cost" of 4 of the 11 educational components included in the desegregation decree: remedial reading, in-service training of teachers, testing, and counseling.

Given the foregoing unique circumstances, it seems to me that the proper disposition of this case is to dismiss the writ of certiorari as improvidently granted. But as the Court has chosen to decide the case here, I join in the judgment as a result less likely to prolong the disruption of education in Detroit than a reversal or remand. Despite wide-ranging dicta in the Court's opinion, the only issue decided is that the District Court's findings as to specific constitutional violations justified the four remedial educational components included in the desegregation decree.  .  .  .    The majority views the record as justifying the conclusion that "the need for educational components flowed directly from constitutional violations by both state and local officials."   On that view of the record, our settled doctrine requiring that the remedy be carefully tailored to fit identified constitutional violations is reaffirmed by today's result.   I therefore concur in the judgment.

## Chapter III

# CONSTITUTIONAL LIMITATIONS ON GOVERNMEN-
# TAL POWER TO CONTROL THE EXPRESSION
# OF IDEAS WITHIN THE CURRICULUM

## INTRODUCTION

Materials in Chapter II considered several aspects of the most basic question lying at the foundation of all governmentally organized, K–12 education in this country: Does the state have constitutional power to restrict the rights of parents and the liberties of children in order to educate them? This basic question was broken into several distinct ones: whether a state's compulsory attendance laws are constitutional; whether a state must allow its compulsory schooling laws to be satisfied by private school attendance or by equivalent home instruction; whether a state's compulsory schooling laws must ever yield to parental rights or to a child's interests in liberty, and whether compulsory education laws imply a quid pro quo?

Among other things, it was discovered, from Pierce and Yoder, that a state's compulsory teaching powers constitutionally can be asserted only in a weak form. Oregon claimed a strong form in Pierce; i. e., that *all* the teaching power is fully vested in the state and is to be exercised exclusively by authorized agencies of government. On Oregon's strong view of a state's teaching power, non-governmental institutions, and parental rights in the area of education, must give way for they had no constitutional existence. If they existed at all, they existed solely out of state tolerance or out of state considerations of policy. Inherent in Oregon's strong version of its claim to an exclusive teaching power was an alien conception of unitary sovereignty which underlies the unified and centralized sovereignties of such nations as France, Cuba or the U.S.S.R. The Supreme Court rejected Oregon's strong claim, and its underlying notion of unitary sovereignty. It approved of a weak version of a state's schooling power. The Supreme Court's view was that a state's teaching power, to be constitutional, can not be exclusive. At best, a state is only one claimant of the teaching power among others, and a state enjoys neither a monopoly nor a priority in the field. This weak constitutionally required version might support a state requirement that all children be educated to a certain level, but not that they all be educated in government classrooms. The weak constitutional version of a state's teaching power found in Pierce and Yoder is consistent with the theory of democratic pluralism underlying the American state. Query: Does this line of constitutional analysis imply that, to be constitutional, a state's public school curriculum should also be consistent with a pluralistic conception of American society?

This chapter considers the second most fundamental question: Assuming a state can compel schooling of its children, can it school children in any way it wishes, choosing whatever it considers fit for molding a child's mind and excluding all the rest, or are there constitutional limitations on a state's power to mold children's minds? In other words, the basic question in this chapter concerns the constitutional limitations on a state's power to dictate the curriculum. This fundamental question breaks down into many other questions: what constitutional provisions limit state authority; where does education end and propagandizing begin; whether it is consistent with Pierce and the theory of a pluralistic state for parents to have rights to select courses from the public school curriculum for their children, and under what circumstances, if ever, must a teacher's choice of course content and teaching methods be respected by school authorities? Then, in addition to a school's formal curriculum, there is the hidden curriculum. A school teaches much by its example as well as by the communicated word. Value-laden procedures are found in classrooms and in other processes; for example, if a school approves and follows a corporal punishment policy, is it thereby teaching students that violence is an appropriate way for adults to solve problems since that is the way in which its adults solve some of the school's problems? Some of these, and related, questions will be considered in later chapters.

The focus in this chapter will be on the constitutional provisions directly limiting a state's power to mold a child's developing mind. The First Amendment has been fully incorporated into the Fourteenth Amendment and because of this the First Amendment applies to states, their subdivisions and their public schools, limiting their powers. First Amendment limitations on state powers fall into two broad divisions: (1) the religious expression provisions, and (2) the non-religious or "secular" free expression provisions, which include a person's constitutional rights to freedom of speech, press, assembly, and to petition government for a redress of grievances. Because of the uniqueness of some of the problems and because of the volume of litigation, with few exceptions, the religious limitations on state power will be considered separately in a later chapter after first considering the "secular" free speech limitations on state powers. This chapter will explore the requirements of the First Amendment's guarantees of freedom of secular expression and then consider them as they have been applied in an educational context, especially as they limit state power to mold a child's mind whether by prescribing a curriculum or by promoting an official orthodoxy in its public schools.

A fundamental cleavage exists regarding the ultimate purpose of education between those persons who, above all else, regard education as a means of instilling and propagating certain proper and officially approved or tolerated ideas, beliefs and values and those other people who, above all else, regard education as a means of producing a person with a disciplined and critical mind having the power of independent judgment and capable of choosing his own ideas, beliefs and values. The latter view is fully consistent with the requirements of a constitutional democracy, and it is helpful in defining the concept of "good citizenship." There is no reason to equate an "open mind" with an "empty mind".

Freedom in America implies a trust in the individual. The person is expected to think for himself and to come to his own conclusions. There is to be no censor of thoughts in America, and the founding fathers placed their trust in the ordinary person. They rejected forever the establishment of any authority over a person's mind or his conscience. A person's constitutional freedom to believe, and to say what he believes, does not depend upon what he believes or upon the rightness of what he believes, or upon obtaining prior permission from some superior authority. The American proposition of freedom is that a person is free to find and speak the truth that is in him and that the official views come afterward. The American trust is in the free individual. On that we have staked our all.

This is not to say that the state can never place restraints on schools. We know that a complete absence of all restraints on all aspects of human liberty leads ultimately to the severest of restraints because the strong enslave the weak, and power, not reason, rules with the usual result that the powerfully intolerant destroy the tolerant and tolerance itself. On the other hand, it is to say that when the state places a restraint upon liberty that restraint, itself, must be justified before it can be allowed. Freedom is the fundamental preference and the basic postulate. Limitations on it must be justified and can be no broader than their justifications.

The next section contains several selections setting forth the fundamental theory of free expression generally, without special reference to education. They should be studied carefully, and after mastering their intrinsic merits, one should consider their implications for education. Two of the important questions are: (1) whether government has any power to suppress any substantive idea, and (2) whether government has any power to prohibit certain acts of free expression? These questions involving the substance of ideas should be distinguished from questions of procedure such as: Does the government have power fairly to regulate the time, place and manner of expressing ideas? Procedural regulations may not deny expression to any substantive idea or act, but may only regulate them. After all, it is difficult, if not impossible, to locate constitutional justification for a huge demonstration that seeks to express an idea, or protest a policy, at the busiest intersection of a community during the commuter rush hour. The community might justifiably require that the demonstration take place at another place or time, or perhaps, in another manner. But would the community, through its government, be justified in suppressing the idea in its entirety?

## THE GENERAL THEORY OF FREE EXPRESSION

### DECLARATION OF INDEPENDENCE
#### July 4, 1776.

When in the Course of human events, it becomes necessary for one people to dissolve the political bands, which have connected them with another, and to assume, among the powers of the earth, the separate and equal station, to which the Laws of Nature and of Nature's God entitle them, a decent respect to the Opinions of mankind requires that they should declare the causes which impel them to the separation.—We hold these truths to be self-evident, that all men are created equal, that they are endowed by their Creator with certain unalienable Rights, that among these are Life, Liberty and the pursuit of Happiness.—That to secure these rights, Governments are instituted among Men, deriving their just powers from the consent of the governed,—That whenever any Form of Government becomes destructive of these ends, it is the Right of the People to alter or to abolish it, and to institute new Government, laying its foundation on such principles and organizing its powers in such form, as to them shall seem most likely to effect their Safety and Happiness. Prudence, indeed, will dictate that Governments long established should not be changed for light and transient causes; and accordingly all experience hath shewn, that mankind are more disposed to suffer, while evils are sufferable, than to right themselves by abolishing the forms to which they are accustomed. But when a long train of abuses and usurpations, pursuing invariably the same Object evinces a design to reduce them under absolute Despotism, it is their right, it is their duty to throw off such Government, and to provide new Guards for their future security.—Such has been the patient sufferance of these Colonies; and such is now the necessity which constrains them to alter their former Systems of Government.

### CONSTITUTION OF THE UNITED STATES

#### Preamble

We the People of the United States, in Order to form a more perfect Union, establish Justice, insure domestic Tranquility, provide for the common defence, promote the general Welfare, and secure the Blessings of Liberty to ourselves and our Posterity, do ordain and establish this Constitution for the United States of America. (March 4, 1789).

### AMENDMENT I

Congress shall make no law  .  .  .  abridging the freedom of speech, or of the press; or the right of the people peaceably to assemble, and to petition the Government for a redress of grievances. (December 15, 1791).

### AMENDMENT XIV

All persons born or naturalized in the United States, and subject to the jurisdiction thereof, are citizens of the United States and of the State wherein they reside.  No State shall make or enforce any law which shall abridge the privileges or immunities of citizens of the United States;  nor shall any State deprive any person of life, liberty or property, without due process of law, nor deny to any person within its jurisdiction the equal protection of the laws.  (July 28, 1868).

## JOHN STUART MILL, ON LIBERTY, 1859

———

.  .  .  The object of this Essay is to assert one very simple principle, as entitled to govern absolutely the dealings of society with the individual in the way of compulsion and control, whether the means used be physcial force in the form of legal penalties, or the moral coercion of public opinion.  That principle is, that the sole end for which mankind are warranted, individually or collectively, in interfering with the liberty of action of any of their number is self-protection.  That the only purpose for which power can be rightfully exercised over any member of a civilized community, against his will, is to prevent harm to others.  His own good, either physical or moral, is not a sufficient warrant.  He cannot rightfully be compelled to do or forbear because it will be better for him to do so, because it will make him happier, because, in the opinions of others, to do so would be wise, or even right.  These are good reasons for remonstrating with him, or reasoning with him, or persuading him or entreating him, but not for compelling him, or visiting him with any evil, in case he do otherwise.  To justify that, the conduct from which it is desired to deter him must be calculated to produce evil to someone else.  The only part of the conduct of any one, for which he is amenable to society, is that which concerns others.  In the part which merely concerns himself, his independence is, of right, absolute.  Over himself, over his own body and mind, the individual is sovereign.

It is, perhaps, hardly necessary to say that this doctrine is meant to apply only to human beings in the maturity of their faculties. We are not speaking of children, or of young persons below the age which the law may fix as that of manhood or womanhood.  Those who are still in a state to require being taken care of by others, must be protected against their own actions as well as against external injury.  .  .  .  But as soon as mankind have attained the capacity of being guided to their own improvement by conviction or persuasion (a period long since reached in all nations with whom we need here concern ourselves), compulsion, either in the direct form or in that of pains and penalties for non-compliance, is no longer admissible as a means to their own good, and justifiable only for the security of others.  .  .  .

.  .  .  The only freedom which deserves the name, is that of pursuing our own good in our own way, so long as we do not attempt to deprive others of theirs, or impede their efforts to obtain it.  .  .

Though this doctrine is anything but new, and, to some persons, may have the air of a truism, there is no doctrine which stands more directly opposed to the general tendency of existing opinion and practice.  Society has expended fully as much effort in the attempt (according to its lights) to compel people to conform to its notions of personal, as of social excellence.  .  .  .

.  .  .  If all mankind minus one, were of one opinion, and only one person were of the contrary opinion, mankind would be no more justified in silencing that one person, than he, if he had the power, would be justified in silencing mankind.  Were an opinion a personal possession of no value except to the owner; if to be obstructed in the enjoyment of it were simply a private injury, it would make some difference whether the injury was inflicted only on a few persons or on many.  But the peculiar evil of silencing the expression of an opinion is, that it is robbing the human race; posterity as well as the existing generation; those who dissent from the opinion, still more than those who hold it.  If the opinion is right, they are deprived of the opportunity of exchanging error for truth: if wrong, they lose, what is almost as great a benefit, the clearer perception and livelier impression of truth, produced by its collision with error.

It is necessary to consider separately these two hypotheses, each of which has a distinct branch of the argument corresponding to it. We can never be sure that the opinion we are endeavoring to stifle is a false opinion; and if we were sure, stifling it would be an evil still.

First: the opinion which it is attempted to suppress by authority may possibly be true.  Those who desire to suppress it, of course deny its truth; but they are not infallible.  They have no authority to decide the question for all mankind, and exclude every other person from the means of judging.   To refuse a hearing to an opinion, because they are sure that it is false, is to assume that *their* certainty is the same thing as *absolute* certainty.   All silencing of discussion is an assumption of infallibility.   Its condemnation may be allowed to rest on this common argument, not the worse for being common. .   .   .

.   .   .   There is the greatest difference between presuming an opinion to be true because, with every opportunity for contesting it, it has not been refuted, and assuming its truth for the purpose of not permitting its refutation.   Complete liberty of contradicting and disproving our opinion, is the very condition which justifies us in assuming its truth for purposes of action; and on no other terms can a being with human faculties have any rational assurance of being right.   .   .   .

But, indeed, the dictum that truth always triumphs over persecution, is one of those pleasant falsehoods which men repeat after one another till they pass into commonplaces, but which all experience refutes.   History teems with instances of truth put down by persecution.   If not suppressed forever, it may be thrown back for centuries.   .   .   .   It is a piece of idle sentimentality that truth, merely as truth, has any inherent power denied to error, of prevailing against the dungeon and the stake.   Men are not more zealous for truth than they often are for error, and a sufficient application of legal or even of social penalties will generally succeed in stopping the propagation of either.   The real advantage which truth has, consists in this, that when an opinion is true, it may be extinguished once, twice, or many times, but in the course of ages there will generally be found persons to rediscover it, until some one of its reappearances falls on a time when from favorable circumstances it escapes persecution until it has made such head as to withstand all subsequent attempts to suppress it.   .   .   .

Let us now pass to the second division of the argument, and dismissing the supposition that any of the received opinions may be false, let us assume them to be true, and examine into the worth of the manner in which they are likely to be held, when their truth is not freely and openly canvassed.   However unwillingly a person who has a strong opinion may admit the possibility that his opinion may be false, he ought to be moved by the consideration that however true it may be, if it is not fully, frequently, and fearlessly discussed, it will be held as a dead dogma, not a living truth.

There is a class of persons   .   .   .   who think it enough if a person assents undoubtingly to what they think true, though he has no knowledge whatever of the grounds of the opinion, and could not make a tenable defence of it against the most superficial objections. Such persons, if they can once get their creed taught from authority, naturally think that no good, and some harm, comes of its being allowed to be questioned.  Where their influence prevails, they make it nearly impossible for the received opinion to be rejected wisely and considerately, though it may still be rejected rashly and ignorantly;  for to shut out discussion entirely is seldom possible, and when it once gets in, beliefs not grounded on conviction are apt to give way before the slightest semblance of an argument.  Waiving, however, this possibility—assuming that the true opinion abides in the mind, but abides as a prejudice, a belief independent of, and proof against, argument—this is not the way in which truth ought to be held by a rational being.  This is not knowing the truth.  Truth, thus held, is but one superstition the more, accidentally clinging to the words which enunciate a truth.

If the intellect and judgment of mankind ought to be cultivated .  .  . on what can these faculties be more appropriately exercised by any one, than on the things which concern him so much that it is considered necessary for him to hold opinions on them?  If the cultivation of the understanding consists in one thing more than in another, it is surely in learning the grounds of one's own opinions.  Whatever people believe, on subjects on which it is of the first importance to believe rightly, they ought to be able to defend against at least the common objections.  .  .  .

If, however, the mischievous operation of the absence of free discussion, when the received opinions are true, were confined to leaving men ignorant of the grounds of those opinions, it might be thought that this, if an intellectual, is no moral evil, and does not affect the worth of the opinions, regarded in their influence on the character.  The fact, however, is, that not only the grounds of the opinion are forgotten in the absence of discussion, but too often the meaning of the opinion itself.  .  .  .  The great chapter in human history which this fact occupies and fills, cannot be too earnestly studied and meditated on.  .  .  .

It still remains to speak of one of the principal causes which make diversity of opinion advantageous, and will continue to do so until mankind shall have entered a stage of intellectual advancement which at present seems at an incalculable distance.  We have hitherto considered only two possibilities: that the received opinion may be false, and some other opinion, consequently, true; or that, the received opinion being true, a conflict with the opposite error is essential to a clear apprehension and deep feeling of its truth.  But there is a commoner case than either of these; when the conflicting doctrines, instead of being one true and the other false, share the truth between them; and the nonconforming opinion is needed to supply the remainder of the truth, of which the received doctrine embodies only a part.  Popular opinions, on subjects not palpable to sense, are often true, but seldom or never the whole truth.  They are a part of the truth; sometimes a greater, sometimes a smaller part, but exaggerated, distorted, and disjoined from the truths by which they ought to be accompanied and limited. Heretical opinions, on the other hand, are generally some of these suppressed and neglected truths, bursting the bonds which kept them down, and either seeking reconciliation with the truth contained in the common opinion, or fronting it as enemies, and setting themselves up, with similar exclusiveness, as the whole truth. The latter case is hitherto the most frequent, as, in the human mind, one-sidedness has always been the rule, and many-sidedness the exception. Hence, even in revolutions of opinion, one part of the truth usually sets while another rises. Even progress, which ought to superadd, for the most part only substitutes one partial and incomplete truth for another; improvement consisting chiefly in this, that the new fragment of truth is more wanted, more adapted to the needs of the time, than that which it displaces. Such being the partial character of prevailing opinions, even when resting on a true foundation; every opinion which embodies somewhat of the portion of truth which the common opinion omits, ought to be considered precious, with whatever amount of error and confusion that truth may be blended. No sober judge of human affairs will feel bound to be indignant because those who force on our notice truths which we should otherwise have overlooked, overlook some of those which we see. Rather, he will think that so long as popular truth is one-sided, it is more desirable than otherwise that unpopular truth should have one-sided asserters too; such being usually the most energetic, and the most likely to compel reluctant attention to the fragment of wisdom which they proclaim as if it were the whole.   .   .   .

.   .   .   Before quitting the subject of freedom of opinion, it is fit to take some notice of those who say, that the free expression of all opinions should be permitted, on condition that the manner be temperate, and do not pass the bounds of fair discussion. Much might be said on the impossibility of fixing where these supposed bounds are to be placed; for if the test be offence to those whose opinion is attacked, I think experience testifies that this offence is given whenever the attack is telling and powerful, and that every opponent who pushes them hard, and whom they find it difficult to answer, appears to them, if he shows any strong feeling on the subject, an intemperate opponent. But this, though an important consideration in a practical point of view, merges in a more fundamental objection. Undoubtedly the manner of asserting an opinion, even though it be a true one, may be very objectionable, and may justly incur severe censure. But the principal offences of the kind are such as it is mostly impossible, unless by accidental self-betrayal, to bring home to conviction. The gravest of them is, to argue sophistically, to suppress facts or arguments, to misstate the elements of the case, or misrepresent the opposite opinion. But all this, even to the most aggravated degree, is so continually done in perfect good faith, by persons who are not considered, and in many other respects may not deserve to be considered, ignorant or incompetent, that it is rarely possible on adequate grounds conscientiously to stamp the misrepresentation as morally culpable; and still less could law presume to interfere with this kind of controversial misconduct. With regard to what is commonly meant by intemperate discussion, namely, invective, sarcasm, personality, and the like, the denunciation of these weapons would deserve more sympathy if it were ever proposed to interdict them equally to both sides; but it is only desired to restrain the employment of them against the prevailing opinion: against the unprevailing they may not only be used without general disapproval, but will be likely to obtain for him who uses them the praise of honest zeal and righteous indignation. Yet whatever mischief arises from their use, is greatest when they are employed against the comparatively defenceless; and whatever unfair advantage can be derived by any opinion from this mode of asserting it, accrues almost exclusively to received opinions. The worst offence of this kind which can be committed by a polemic, is to stigmatize those who hold the contrary opinion as bad and immoral men. To calumny of this sort, those who hold any unpopular opinion are peculiarly exposed, because they are in general few and uninfluential, and nobody but themselves feels much interest in seeing justice done them; but this weapon is, from the nature of the case, denied to those who attack a prevailing opinion: they can neither use it with safety to themselves, nor, if they could, would it do anything but recoil on their own cause. In general, opinions contrary to those commonly received can only obtain a hearing by studied moderation of language, and the most cautious avoidance of unnecessary offence, from which they hardly ever deviate even in a slight degree without losing ground: while unmeasured vituperation employed on the side of the prevailing opinion, really does deter people from professing contrary opinions, and from listening to those who profess them. For the interest, therefore, of truth and justice, it is far more important to restrain this employment of vituperative language than the other   .   .   .

The liberty of the individual must be thus far limited; he must not make himself a nuisance to other people. But if he refrains from molesting others in what concerns them, and merely acts according to his own inclination and judgment in things which concern himself, the same reasons which show that opinion should be free, prove also that he should be allowed, without molestation, to carry his opinions into practice at his own cost. That mankind are not infallible; that their truths, for the most part, are only half-truths; that unity of opinion, unless resulting from the fullest and freest comparison of opposite opinions, is not desirable, and diversity not an evil, but a good, until mankind are much more capable than at present of recognizing all sides of the truth, are principles applicable to men's modes of action, not less than to their opinions. As it is useful that while mankind are imperfect there should be different experiments of living; that free scope should be given to varieties of character, short of injury to others; and that the worth of different modes of life should be proved practically, when any one thinks fit to try them. It is desirable, in short, that in things which do not primarily concern others, individuality should assert itself. Where, not the person's own character, but the traditions or customs of other people are the rule of conduct, there is wanting one of the principal ingredients of human happiness, and quite the chief ingredient of individual and social progress.

\*    \*    \*

He who lets the world, or his own portion of it, choose his plan of life for him, has no need of any other faculty than the ape-like one of imitation. He who chooses his plan for himself, employs all his faculties. He must use observation to see, reasoning and judgment to foresee, activity to gather materials for decision, discrimination to decide, and when he has decided, firmness and self-control to hold to his deliberate decision. And these qualities he requires and exercises exactly in proportion as the part of his conduct which he determines according to his own judgment and feelings is a large one. It is possible that he might be guided in some good path, and kept out of harm's way, without any of these things. But what will be his comparative worth as a human being? It really is of importance, not only what men do, but also what manner of men they are that do it  Among the works of man, which human life is rightly employed in perfecting and beautifying, the first in importance surely is man himself. Supposing it were possible to get houses built, corn grown, battles fought, causes tried, and even churches erected and prayers said, by machinery—by automatons in human form—it would be a considerable loss to exchange for these automatons even the men and women who at present inhabit the more civilized parts of the world, and who assuredly are but starved specimens of what nature can and will produce. Human nature is not a machine to be built after a model, and set to do exactly the work prescribed for it, but a tree, which requires to grow and develop itself on all sides, according to the tendency of the inward forces which make it a living thing. . . .

---

## ABRAMS v. UNITED STATES

Supreme Court of the United States, 1919.
250 U.S. 616, 629–631, 40 S.Ct. 17, 22, 63 L.Ed. 1173, 1180.

HOLMES, J.   .   .   .   In this case sentences of twenty years imprisonment have been imposed for the publishing of two leaflets that I believe the defendants had as much right to publish as the Government has to publish the Constitution of the United States now vainly invoked by them. Even if I am technically wrong and enough can be squeezed from these poor and puny anonymities to turn the color of legal litmus paper; I will add, even if what I think the necessary intent were shown; the most nominal punishment seems to me all that possibly could be inflicted, unless the defendants are to be made to suffer not for what the indictment alleges but for the creed that they avow—a creed that I believe to be the creed of ignorance and immaturity when honestly held, as I see no reason to doubt that it was held here, but which, although made the subject of examination at the trial, no one has a right even to consider in dealing with the charges before the Court.

Persecution for the expression of opinions seems to me perfectly logical. If you have no doubt of your premises or your power and want a certain result with all your heart you naturally express your wishes in law and sweep away all opposition. To allow opposition by speech seems to indicate that you think the speech impotent, as when a man says that he has squared the circle, or that you do not care whole-heartedly for the result, or that you doubt either your power or your premises. But when men have realized that time has upset many fighting faiths, they may come to believe even more than they believe the very foundations of their own conduct that the ultimate good desired is better reached by free trade in ideas—that the best test of truth is the power of the thought to get itself accepted in the competition of the market, and that truth is the only ground upon which their wishes safely can be carried out. That at any rate is the theory of our Constitution. It is an experiment, as all life is an experiment. Every year if not every day we have to wager our salvation upon some prophecy based upon imperfect knowledge. While that experiment is part of our system I think that we should be eternally vigilant against attempts to check the expression of opinions that we loathe and believe to be fraught with death, unless they so imminently threaten immediate interference with the lawful and pressing purposes of the law that an immediate check is required to save the country. I wholly disagree with the argument of the Government that the First Amendment left the common law as to seditious libel in force. History seems to me against the notion. I had conceived that the United States through many years had shown its repentance for the Sedition Act of 1798, by repaying fines that it imposed. Only the emergency that makes it immediately dangerous to leave the correction of evil counsels to time warrants making any exception to the sweeping command, "Congress shall make no law  .  .  . abridging the freedom of speech." Of course I am speaking only of expressions of opinion and exhortations, which were all that were uttered here, but I regret that I cannot put into more impressive words my belief that in their conviction upon this indictment the defendants were deprived of their rights under the Constitution of the United States.　.　.　.

———

## WHITNEY v. CALIFORNIA

Supreme Court of the United States, 1927.
274 U.S. 357, 375–76, 47 S.Ct. 641, 648, 71 L.Ed. 1095, 1105–1106.

BRANDEIS, J.　.　.　.　Those who won our independence believed that the final end of the State was to make men free to develop their faculties; and that in its government the deliberative forces should prevail over the arbitrary.　They valued liberty both as an end and as a means.　They believed liberty to be the secret of happiness and courage to be the secret of liberty.　They believed that freedom to think as you will and to speak as you think are means indispensable to the discovery and spread of political truth; that without free speech and assembly discussion would be futile; that with them, discussion affords ordinarily adequate protection against the dissemination of noxious doctrine; that the greatest menace to freedom is an inert people; that public discussion is a political duty; and that this should be a fundamental principle of the American government.[2]　They recognized the risks to which all human institutions are subject.　But they knew that order cannot be secured merely through fear of punishment for its infraction; that it is hazardous to discourage thought, hope and imagination; that fear breeds repression; that repression breeds hate; that hate menaces stable government; that the path of safety lies in the opportunity to discuss freely supposed grievances and proposed remedies; and that the fitting remedy for evil counsels is good ones.　Believing in the power of reason as applied through public discussion, they eschewed silence coerced by law—the argument of force in its worst form.　Recognizing the occasional tyrannies of governing majorities, they amended the Constitution so that free speech and assembly should be guaranteed.

Fear of serious injury cannot alone justify suppression of free speech and assembly.　Men feared witches and burnt women.　It is the function of speech to free men from the bondage of irrational fears.　To justify suppression of free speech there must be reasonable ground

[2] Compare Thomas Jefferson: "We have nothing to fear from the demoralizing reasonings of some, if others are left free to demonstrate their errors and especially when the law stands ready to punish the first criminal act produced by the false reasonings; these are safer corrections than the conscience of the judge." Quoted by Charles A. Beard, The Nation, July 7, 1926, vol. 123, p. 8. Also in first Inaugural Address: "If there be any among us who would wish to dissolve this union or change its republican form, let them stand undisturbed as monuments of the safety with which error of opinion may be tolerated where reason is left free to combat it."

to fear that serious evil will result if free speech is practiced. There must be reasonable ground to believe that the danger apprehended is imminent. There must be reasonable ground to believe that the evil to be prevented is a serious one. Every denunciation of existing law tends in some measure to increase the probability that there will be violation of it. Condonation of a breach enhances the probability. Expressions of approval add to the probability. Propagation of the criminal state of mind by teaching syndicalism increases it. Advocacy of law-breaking heightens it still further. But even advocacy of violation, however reprehensible morally, is not a justification for denying free speech where the advocacy falls short of incitement and there is nothing to indicate that the advocacy would be immediately acted on. The wide difference between advocacy and incitement, between preparation and attempt, between assembling and conspiracy, must be borne in mind. In order to support a finding of clear and present danger it must be shown either that immediate serious violence was to be expected or was advocated, or that the past conduct furnished reason to believe that such advocacy was then contemplated.

Those who won our independence by revolution were not cowards. They did not fear political change. They did not exalt order at the cost of liberty. To courageous, self-reliant men, with confidence in the power of free and fearless reasoning applied through the processes of popular government, no danger flowing from speech can be deemed clear and present, unless the incidence of the evil apprehended is so imminent that it may befall before there is opportunity for full discussion. If there be time to expose through discussion the falsehood and fallacies, to avert the evil by the processes of education, the remedy to be applied is more speech, not enforced silence. Only an emergency can justify repression. Such must be the rule if authority is to be reconciled with freedom. Such, in my opinion, is the command of the Constitution.   .   .   .

———

## THOMAS I. EMERSON, THE SYSTEM OF FREEDOM OF EXPRESSION

Copyright © by Thomas I. Emerson, 1970.
Selections from pages 6–15.

.   .   .   The system of freedom of expression in a democratic society rests upon four main premises. These may be stated, in capsule form, as follows:

First, freedom of expression is essential as a means of assuring individual self-fulfillment. The proper end of man is the realization of his character and potentialities as a human being. For the achievement of this self-realization the mind must be free. Hence suppression of belief, opinion, or other expression is an affront to the dignity of man, a negation of man's essential nature. Moreover, man in his capacity as a member of society has a right to share in the common decisions that affect him. To cut off his search for truth, or his expression of it, is to elevate society and the state to a despotic command over him and to place him under the arbitrary control of others.

Second, freedom of expression is an essential process for advancing knowledge and discovering truth. An individual who seeks knowledge and truth must hear all sides of the question, consider all alternatives, test his judgment by exposing it to opposition, and make full use of different minds. Discussion must be kept open no matter how certainly true an accepted opinion may seem to be; many of the most widely acknowledged truths have turned out to be erroneous. Conversely, the same principle applies no matter how false or pernicious the new opinion appears to be; for the unaccepted opinion may be true or partially true and, even if wholly false, its presentation and open discussion compel a rethinking and retesting of the accepted opinion. The reasons which make open discussion essential for an intelligent individual judgment likewise make it imperative for rational social judgment.

Third, freedom of expression is essential to provide for participation in decision making by all members of society. This is particularly significant for political decisions. Once one accepts the premise of the Declaration of Independence—that governments "derive their just powers from the consent of the governed"—it follows that the governed must, in order to exercise their right of consent, have full freedom of expression both in forming individual judgments and in forming the common judgment. The principle also carries beyond the political realm. It embraces the right to participate in the building of the whole culture, and includes freedom of expression in religion, literature, art, science, and all areas of human learning and knowledge.

Finally, freedom of expression is a method of achieving a more adaptable and hence a more stable community, of maintaining the precarious balance between healthy cleavage and necessary consensus. This follows because suppression of discussion makes a rational judgment impossible, substituting force for reason; because suppression promotes inflexibility and stultification, preventing society from adjusting to changing circumstances or developing new ideas; and because suppression conceals the real problems confronting a society, diverting public attention from the critical issues. At the same time the process of open discussion promotes greater cohesion in a society because people are more ready to accept decisions that go against them if they have a part in the decision-making process. Moreover, the state at all times retains adequate powers to promote unity and to suppress resort to force. Freedom of expression thus provides a framework in which the conflict necessary to the progress of a society can take place without destroying the society. It is an essential mechanism for maintaining the balance between stability and change.

The validity of the foregoing premises has never been proved or disproved, and probably could not be. Nevertheless our society is based upon the faith that they hold true and, in maintaining a system of freedom of expression, we act upon that faith. The considerations just outlined thus represent the values we seek in a system of freedom of expression and the functions that system is intended to perform. It should be added that, while our current system of freedom of expression is a product of constitutional liberalism, the values and functions which underlie it are essential to any open society regardless of the particular form its political, economic and social institutions may take.

Two basic implications of the theory underlying our system of freedom of expression need to be emphasized. The first is that it is not a general measure of the individual's right to freedom of expression that any particular exercise of that right may be thought to promote or retard other goals of the society. The theory asserts that freedom of expression, while not the sole or sufficient end of society, is a good in itself, or at least an essential element in a good society. The society may seek to achieve other or more inclusive ends—such as virtue, justice, equality, or the maximum realization of the potentialities of its members. These are not necessarily gained by accepting the rules for freedom of expression. But, as a general proposition, the society may not seek them by suppressing the beliefs or opinions of individual members. To achieve these other goals it must rely upon other methods: the use of counter-expression and the regulation or control of conduct which is not expression. Hence the right to control individual expression, on the ground that it is judged to promote good or evil, justice or injustice, equality or inequality, is not, speaking generally, within the competence of the good society.

The second implication, in a sense a corollary of the first, is that the theory rests upon a fundamental distinction between belief, opinion, and communication of ideas on the one hand, and different forms of conduct on the other. For shorthand purposes we refer to this distinction hereafter as one between "expression" and "action." As just observed, in order to achieve its desired goals, a society or the state is entitled to exercise control over action—whether by prohibiting or compelling it—on an entirely different and vastly more extensive basis. But expression occupies an especially protected position. In this sector of human conduct, the social right of suppression or compulsion is at its lowest point, in most respects nonexistent. A majority of one has the right to control action, but a minority of one has the right to talk.

This marking off of the special status of expression is a crucial ingredient of the basic theory for several reasons. In the first place, thought and communication are the fountainhead of all expression of the individual personality. To cut off the flow at the source is to dry up the whole stream. Freedom at this point is essential to all other freedoms. Hence society must withhold its right of suppression until the stage of action is reached. Secondly, expression is normally conceived as doing less injury to other social goals than action. It generally has less immediate consequences, is less irremediable in its impact. Thirdly, the power of society and the state over the individual is so pervasive, and construction of doctrines, institutions, and administrative practices to limit this power so difficult, that only by drawing such a protective line between expression and action is it possible to strike a safe balance between authority and freedom.

### The Dynamics of Limitation

In constructing and maintaining a system of freedom of expression the major controversies have arisen not over acceptance of the basic theory, but in attempting to fit its values and functions into a more comprehensive scheme of social goals. These issues have revolved around the question of what limitations, if any, ought to be imposed upon freedom of expression in order to reconcile that interest with other individual and social interests sought by the good society. Most of our efforts in the past to formulate rules for limiting freedom of expression have been seriously defective through failure to take into consideration the realistic context on which such limitations are administered. The crux of the problem is that the limitations, whatever they may be, must be applied by one group of human beings to other human beings.

First of all, it is necessary to recognize the powerful forces that impel men towards the elimination of unorthodox expression. Most men have a strong inclination, for rational or irrational reasons, to suppress opposition. On the other hand, persons who stand up against society and challenge the traditional view usually have similarly strong feelings about the issues they raise. Thus dissent often is not pitched in conventional terms, nor does it follow customary standards of polite expression. Moreover, the forces of inertia within a society ordinarily resist the expression of new ideas or the pressures of the underprivileged who seek a change. And the longer-run logic of the traditional theory may not be immediately apparent to untutored participants in the conflict. Suppression of opinion may thus seem an entirely plausible course of action; tolerance a weakness or a foolish risk.

Thus it is clear that the problem of maintaining a system of freedom of expression in a society is one of the most complex any society has to face. Self-restraint, self-discipline, and maturity are required. The theory is essentially a highly sophisticated one. The members of the society must be willing to sacrifice individual and short-term advantage for social and long-range goals. And the process must operate in a context that is charged with emotion and subject to powerful conflicting forces of self-interest.

These considerations must be weighed in attempting to construct a theory of limitations. A system of free expression can be successful only when it rests upon the strongest possible commitment to the positive right and the narrowest possible basis for exceptions. And any such exceptions must be clear-cut, precise, and readily controlled. Otherwise the forces that press toward restriction will break through the openings, and freedom of expression will become the exception and suppression the rule.

A second major consideration in imposing restrictions upon expression is the difficulty of framing precise limitations. The object of the limitation is usually not the expression itself but its feared consequences. Repression of expression is thus purely a preventive measure and, like all preventive measures, cuts far more widely and deeply than is necessary to control the ensuing conduct. Moreover, the infinite varieties and subtleties of language and other forms of communication make it impossible to construct a limitation upon expression in definite terms. Thus a wide area of expression is brought within reach of the limitation and enormous discretionary power placed in the hands of those who administer it.

## NOTES AND QUESTIONS

1. Mr. Justice Holmes' opinion in Abrams emphasizes the Millsian idea that "truth" is important and must be allowed to flourish in an open society without censorship so that in the long run the "truth" will be "accepted in the competition of the market" and an informed citizenry will then act according to the dictates of that known "truth." Are men such rational creatures after all? How would B. F. Skinner react to Holmes' views in Abrams? See B. F. Skinner, BEYOND FREEDOM AND DIGNITY (1971), chapters 1 and 2. For a discussion of anti-intellectualism in the twentieth century see Richard Hofstadter, ANTI-INTELLECTUALISM IN AMERICAN LIFE (1962) and Crane Brinton, IDEAS AND MEN—THE STORY OF WESTERN THOUGHT (1950), chapter 14. See also L. J. Henderson, PARETO'S GENERAL SOCIOLOGY (1935) for an exposition of human behavior at odds with the premise set out by J. S. Mill in ON LIBERTY.

2. In the Whitney case the defendant was convicted under a state syndicalism statute for forming an organization advocating violent overthrow of the government. The Supreme Court, speaking through Mr. Justice Sanford, affirmed with Mr. Justice Brandeis concurring in result. But, Brandeis disagreed with the majority's rationale that mere advocacy of violent overthrow of the government, standing alone, was sufficient to warrant the suppression of free speech. Is the Brandeis test for suppressing free speech reasonable? Workable? How could one know before hand whether his speech was protected

or not under the Brandeis test? What difference does it make whether one knows if his speech will be protected? Whitney v. California was overruled in Brandenburg v. Ohio, 395 U.S. 444, 89 S.Ct. 1827, 23 L.Ed.2d 430 (1969), and Justice Brandeis' rationale for suppressing free speech is the current view of the Supreme Court.

3. The individual's right to freedom of speech is protected by the Constitution. But its contours might be defined, in part, by the public function of freedom of speech. The First Amendment protects the major public interest of self-governance requiring an integrated scheme of First Amendment freedoms: "The First Amendment does not protect a 'freedom to speak.' It protects the freedom of those activities of thought and communication by which we 'govern.' It is concerned, not with a private right, but with a public power, a governmental responsibility." A. Meiklejohn, The First Amendment Is an Absolute, 1961 Sup.Ct.Rev. 245, 255, and see, Brennan, The Supreme Court and the Meiklejohn Interpretation of the First Amendment, 79 Harv.L.Rev. 1 (1965). Meiklejohn first published his views at a period in our political history when "McCarthyism," then in its incipient stages, gave birth to the House of Representatives Committee on Unamerican Activities. A. Meiklejohn, Political Freedom (1948). What exactly is an "Unamerican Activity?" How do you suppose Meiklejohn viewed the McCarthy era? For a narrowing construction of the meaning of "unamerican activities" as it is used in the House of Representatives Unamerican Activities Committee see Barenblatt v. United States, 360 U.S. 109, 79 S.Ct. 1081, 3 L.Ed.2d 1115 (1960), and compare Watkins v. U. S., 354 U.S. 178, 77 S.Ct. 1173, 1 L.Ed.2d 1273 (1957).

## CONSTITUTIONAL PROTECTION OF THE RIGHT TO ACADEMIC FREEDOM

### SWEEZY v. NEW HAMPSHIRE

Supreme Court of the United States, 1957.
354 U.S. 234, 77 S.Ct. 1203, 1 L.Ed.2d 1311.

[Paul Sweezy, a former professor of economics at Harvard, describes himself as a "classical Marxist" and "Socialist." He has written books and articles on the general theme of the inevitable collapse of capitalism and rise of socialism. He was invited to the University of New Hampshire where he gave several lectures expressing his views. New Hampshire's Revised Statutes, 1955, ch. 588, § 1, provided, " 'Subversive person' means any person who commits, attempts to commit, or aids in the commission, or advocates, abets, advises or teaches, by any means any person to commit, attempt to commit, or aid in the commission of any act intended to overthrow, destroy or alter, or to assist in the overthrow, destruction or alteration of, the constitutional form of the government of the United States, or of the state of New Hampshire, or any political subdivision of either of them, by force, or violence; or who is a member of a subversive organization or a foreign subversive organization."

"Pursuant to an investigation of subversive activities authorized by a joint resolution of both houses of the New Hampshire Legislature, the State Attorney General subpoenaed petitioner [Sweezy] before him on January 8, 1954, for extensive questioning. Among the matters about which petitioner was questioned were: details of his career and personal life, whether he was then or ever had been a member of the Communist Party, whether he had ever attended its meetings, whether he had ever attended meetings that he knew were also attended by Party members, whether he knew any Communists in or out of the State, whether he knew named persons with alleged connections with organizations either on the United States Attorney General's list or cited by the Un-American Activities Committee of the United States House of Representatives or had ever attended meetings with them, whether he had ever taught or supported the overthrow of the State by force or violence or had ever known or assisted any persons or groups that had done so, whether he had ever been connected with organizations on the Attorney General's list, whether he had supported or written in behalf of a variety of allegedly subversive, named causes, conferences, periodicals, petitions, and attempts to raise funds for the legal defense of certain persons, whether he knew about the Progressive Party, what positions he had held in it, whether he had been a candidate for Presidential Elector for that Party, whether certain persons were in that Party, whether Communists had influenced or been members of the Progressive Party, whether he had sponsored activities in behalf of the candidacy of Henry A. Wallace, whether he advocated replacing the capitalist system with another economic system, whether his conception of socialism involved force and violence, whether by his writings and actions he had ever attempted to advance the Societ Union's 'propaganda line,' whether he had ever attended meetings of the Liberal Club at the University of New Hampshire, whether the magazine of which he was co-editor was 'a Communist-line publication,' and whether he knew named persons.

"[Sweezy] answered most of these questions, making it very plain that he had never been a Communist, never taught violent overthrow of the Government, never knowingly associated with Communists in the State, but was a socialist believer in peaceful change who had at one time belonged to certain organizations on the list of the United States Attorney General (which did not include the Progressive Party) or cited by the House Un-American Activities Committee. He declined to answer as irrelevant or violative of free speech guarantees certain questions about the Progressive Party and whether he knew particular persons. He stated repeatedly, however, that he had no knowledge of Communists or of Communist influence in the

Progressive Party, and he testified that he had been a candidate for that Party, signing the required loyalty oath, and that he did not know whether an alleged Communist leader was active in the Progressive Party.

"Despite the exhaustive scope of this inquiry, the Attorney General again subpoenaed [Sweezy] to testify on June 3, 1954, and the interrogation was similarly sweeping.  Petitioner again answered virtually all questions, including those concerning the relationship of named persons to the Communist Party or other causes deemed subversive under state laws, alleged Communist influence on all organizations with which he had been connected including the Progressive Party, and his own participation in organizations other than the Progressive Party and its antecedent, the Progressive Citizens of America.  He refused, however, to answer certain questions regarding (1) a lecture given by him at the University of New Hampshire, (2) activities of himself and others in the Progressive political organizations, and (3) 'opinions and beliefs,' invoking the constitutional guarantees of free speech.

"The Attorney General then petitioned the Superior Court to order petitioner to answer questions in these categories.  The court ruled that petitioner had to answer those questions pertaining to the lectures and to the Progressive Party and its predecessor but not those otherwise pertaining to 'opinions and beliefs.'  Upon petitioner's refusal to answer the questions sanctioned by the court, he was found in contempt of court and ordered committed to the county jail until purged of contempt.

"The Supreme Court of New Hampshire affirmed the order of the Superior Court.  It held that the questions at issue were relevant and that no constitutional provision permitted petitioner to frustrate the State's demands. . . .

"The questions that petitioner refused to answer regarding the university lecture, the third given by him in three years at the invitation of the faculty for humanities, were:

> 'What was the subject of your lecture?'
>
> 'Didn't you tell the class at the University of New Hampshire on Monday, March 22, 1954, that Socialism was inevitable in this country?'
>
> 'Did you advocate Marxism at that time?'
>
> 'Did you express the opinion, or did you make the statement at that time that Socialism was inevitable in America?'
>
> 'Did you in this last lecture on March 22 or in any of the former lectures espouse the theory of dialectical materialism?'

'I have in the file here a statement from a person who attended your class, and I will read it in part because I don't want you to think I am just fishing. "His talk this time was on the inevitability of the Socialist program. It was a glossed-over interpretation of the materialistic dialectic." Now, again I ask you the original question.'

"In response to the first question of this series, petitioner had said at the hearing:

'I would like to say one thing in this connection, Mr. Wyman. I stated under oath at my last appearance that, and I now repeat it, that I do not advocate or in any way further the aim of overthrowing constitutional government by force and violence. I did not so advocate in the lecture I gave at the University of New Hampshire. In fact I have never at any time so advocated in a lecture anywhere. Aside from that I have nothing I want to say about the lecture in question.'

"The New Hampshire Supreme Court, although recognizing that such inquiries 'undoubtedly interfered with the defendant's free exercise' of his constitutionally guaranteed right to lecture, justified the interference on the ground that it would occur 'in the limited area in which the legislative committee may reasonably believe that the overthrow of existing government by force and violence is being or has been taught, advocated or planned, an area in which the interest of the State justifies this intrusion upon civil liberties.' . . . According to the court, the facts that made reasonable the Committee's belief that petitioner had taught violent overthrow in his lecture were that he was a Socialist with a record of affiliation with groups cited by the Attorney General of the United States or the House Un-American Activities Committee and that he was co-editor of an article stating that, although the authors hated violence, it was less to be deplored when used by the Soviet Union than by capitalist countries.

"[Sweezy] stated, in response to questions at the hearing, that he did not know of any Communist interest in, connection with, influence over, activity in, or manipulation of the Progressive Party. He refused to answer, despite court order, the following questions on the ground that, by inquiring into the activities of a lawful political organization, they infringed upon the inviolability of the right to privacy in his political thoughts, actions and associations:

'Was she, Nancy Sweezy, your wife, active in the formation of the Progressive Citizens of America?'

'Was Nancy Sweezy then working with individuals who were then members of the Communist Party?'

'Was Charles Beebe active in forming the Progressive Citizens of America?'

'Did he work with your present wife—Did Charles Beebe work with your present wife in 1947?'

'Did it [a meeting at the home of one Abraham Walenko] have anything to do with the Progressive Party?'

"The Supreme Court of New Hampshire justified this intrusion upon his freedom on the same basis that it upheld questioning about the university lecture, namely, that the restriction was limited to situations where the Committee had reason to believe that violent overthrow of the Government was being advocated or planned. . . ."].

Mr. Chief Justice WARREN announced the judgment of the Court, and delivered an opinion in which Mr. Justices BLACK, DOUGLAS and BRENNAN joined.

. . . The State Supreme Court thus conceded without extended discussion that petitioner's right to lecture and his right to associate with others were constitutionally protected freedoms which had been abridged through this investigation. These conclusions could not be seriously debated. Merely to summon a witness and compel him, against his will, to disclose the nature of his past expressions and associations is a measure of governmental interference in these matters. These are rights which are safeguarded by the Bill of Rights and the Fourteenth Amendment. We believe that there unquestionably was an invasion of petitioner's liberties in the areas of academic freedom and political expression—areas in which government should be extremely reticent to tread.

The essentiality of freedom in the community of American universities is almost self-evident. No one should underestimate the vital role in a democracy that is played by those who guide and train our youth. To impose any strait jacket upon the intellectual leaders in our colleges and universities would imperil the future of our Nation. No field of education is so thoroughly comprehended by man that new discoveries cannot yet be made. Particularly is that true in the social sciences, where few, if any, principles are accepted as absolutes. Scholarship cannot flourish in an atmosphere of suspicion and distrust. Teachers and students must always remain free to inquire, to study and to evaluate, to gain new maturity and understanding; otherwise our civilization will stagnate and die.

Equally manifest as a fundamental principle of a democratic society is political freedom of the individual. Our form of government is built on the premise that every citizen shall have the right to engage in political expression and association. This right was enshrined in the First Amendment of the Bill of Rights. Exercise of these basic freedoms in America has traditionally been through the media of political associations.  Any interference with the freedom of a party is simultaneously an interference with the freedom of its adherents.  All political ideas cannot and should not be channeled into the programs of our two major parties.  History has amply proved the virtue of political activity by minority, dissident groups, who innumerable times have been in the vanguard of democratic thought and whose programs were ultimately accepted.  Mere unorthodoxy or dissent from the prevailing mores is not to be condemned.  The absence of such voices would be a symptom of grave illness in our society.

Notwithstanding the undeniable importance of freedom in the areas, the Supreme Court of New Hampshire did not consider that the abridgment of petitioner's rights under the Constitution vitiated the investigation.  In the view of that court, "the answer lies in a determination of whether the object of the legislative investigation under consideration is such as to justify the restriction thereby imposed upon the defendant's liberties."  100 N.H., at 113–114, 121 A.2d, at 791–792.  It found such justification in the legislature's judgment, expressed by its authorizing resolution, that there exists a potential menace from those who would overthrow the government by force and violence.  That court concluded that the need for the legislature to be informed on so elemental a subject as the self-preservation of government outweighed the deprivation of constitutional rights that occurred in the process.

We do not now conceive of any circumstance wherein a state interest would justify infringement of rights in these fields.  But we do not need to reach such fundamental questions of state power to decide this case.  The State Supreme Court itself recognized that there was a weakness in its conclusion that the menace of forcible overthrow of the government justified sacrificing constitutional rights.  There was a missing link in the chain of reasoning.  The syllogism was not complete.  There was nothing to connect the questioning of petitioner with this fundamental interest of the State.  .  .  .

The respective roles of the legislature and the investigator thus revealed are of considerable significance to the issue before us.  It is eminently clear that the basic discretion of determining the direction of the legislative inquiry has been turned over to the investigative agency.  .  .  .

Instead of making known the nature of the data it desired, the legislature has insulated itself from those witnesses whose rights may be vitally affected by the investigation.  Incorporating by reference provisions from its subversive activities act, it has told the Attorney General, in effect to screen the citizenry of New Hampshire to bring to light anyone who fits into the expansive definitions.

Within the very broad area thus committed to the discretion of the Attorney General there may be many facts which the legislature might find useful. There would also be a great deal of data which that assembly would not want or need. In the classes of information that the legislature might deem it desirable to have, there will be some which it could not validly acquire because of the effect upon the constitutional rights of individual citizens. Separating the wheat from the chaff, from the standpoint of the legislature's object, is the legislature's responsibility because it alone can make that judgment. In this case, the New Hampshire legislature has delegated that task to the Attorney General.

As a result, neither we nor the state courts have any assurance that the questions petitioner refused to answer fall into a category of matters upon which the legislature wanted to be informed when it initiated this inquiry. The judiciary are thus placed in an untenable position. Lacking even the elementary fact that the legislature wants certain questions answered and recognizing that petitioner's constitutional rights are in jeopardy, we are asked to approve or disapprove his incarceration for contempt.

In our view, the answer is clear. No one would deny that the infringement of constitutional rights of individuals would violate the guarantee of due process where no state interest underlies the state action. Thus, if the Attorney General's interrogation of petitioner were in fact wholly unrelated to the object of the legislature in authorizing the inquiry, the Due Process Clause would preclude the endangering of constitutional liberties. We believe that an equivalent situation is presented in this case. The lack of any indications that the legislature wanted the information the Attorney General attempted to elicit from petitioner must be treated as the absence of authority. It follows that the use of the contempt power, notwithstanding the interference with constitutional rights, was not in accordance with the due process requirements of the Fourteenth Amendment. . . .

The judgment of the Supreme Court of New Hampshire is

Reversed.

Mr. Justice FRANKFURTER, whom Mr. Justice HARLAN joins, concurring in the result.

. . . When weighed against the grave harm resulting from governmental intrusion into the intellectual life of a university, such justification for compelling a witness to discuss the contents of his lecture appears grossly inadequate. Particularly is this so where the witness has sworn that neither in the lecture nor at any other time did he ever advocate overthrowing the Government by force and violence.

Progress in the natural sciences is not remotely confined to findings made in the laboratory. Insights into the mysteries of nature are born of hypothesis and speculation. The more so is this true in the pursuit of understanding in the groping endeavors of what are called the social sciences, the concern of which is man and society. The problems are that the respective preoccupations and anthropology, economics, law, psychology, sociology and related areas of scholarship are merely departmentalized dealing, by way of manageable division of analysis, with interpenetrating aspects of holistic perplexities. For society's good—if understanding be an essential need of society—inquiries into these problems, speculations about them, stimulation in others of reflection upon them, must be left as unfettered as possible. Political power must abstain from intrusion into this activity of freedom, pursued in the interest of wise government and the people's well-being, except for reasons that are exigent and obviously compelling.

These pages need not be burdened with proof, based on the testimony of a cloud of impressive witnesses, of the dependence of a free society on free universities. This means the exclusion of governmental intervention in the intellectual life of a university. It matters little whether such intervention occurs avowedly or through action that inevitably tends to check the ardor and fearlessness of scholars, qualities at once so fragile and so indispensable for fruitful academic labor. One need only refer to the address of T. H. Huxley at the opening of Johns Hopkins University, the Annual Reports of President A. Lawrence Lowell of Harvard, the Reports of the University Grants Committee in Great Britain, as illustrative items in a vast body of literature. Suffice it to quote the latest expression on this subject. It is also perhaps the most poignant because its plea on behalf of continuing the free spirit of the open universities of South Africa has gone unheeded.

"In a university knowledge is its own end, not merely a means to an end. A university ceases to be true to its own nature if it becomes the tool of Church or State or any sectional interest. A university is characterized by the spirit of free inquiry, its ideal being the ideal of Socrates—'to follow the argument where it leads.' This implies the right to examine, question, modify or reject traditional ideas and beliefs. Dogma and hypothesis are incompatible, and the concept of an immutable doctrine is repugnant to the spirit of a university. The concern of its scholars is not merely to add and revise facts in relation to an accepted framework, but to be ever examining and modifying the framework itself.

.   .   .   .   .   .   .   .   .

"Freedom to reason and freedom for disputation on the basis of observation and experiment are the necessary conditions for the advancement of scientific knowledge. A sense of freedom is also necessary for creative work in the arts which, equally with scientific research, is the concern of the university.

.   .   .   .   .   .   .   .   .

". . . It is the business of a university to provide that atmosphere which is most conducive to speculation, experiment and creation. It is an atmosphere in which there prevail 'the four essential freedoms' of a university—to determine for itself on academic grounds who may teach, what may be taught, how it shall be taught, and who may be admitted to study." The Open Universities in South Africa 10–12. (A statement of a conference of senior scholars from the University of Cape Town and the University of the Witwatersrand, including A. v. d. S. Centlivres and Richard Feetham, as Chancellors of the respective universities.)

I do not suggest that what New Hampshire has here sanctioned bears any resemblance to the policy against which this South African remonstrance was directed. I do say that in these matters of the spirit inroads on legitimacy must be resisted at their incipiency. This kind of evil grows by what it is allowed to feed on. The admonition of this Court in another context is applicable here. "It may be that it is the obnoxious thing in its mildest and least repulsive form; but illegitimate and unconstitutional practices get their first footing in that way, namely, by silent approaches and slight deviations from legal modes of procedure." . . .

In the political realm, as in the academic, thought and action are presumptively immune from inquisition by political authority. It cannot require argument that inquiry would be barred to ascertain whether a citizen had voted for one or the other of the two major parties either in a state or national election. Until recently, no difference would have been entertained in regard to inquiries about a voter's affiliations with one of the various so-called third parties that have had their day, or longer, in our political history. . . . The implications of the United States Constitution for national elections and "the concept of ordered liberty" implicit in the Due Process Clause of the Fourteenth Amendment as against the States, Palko v. Connecticut, . . . were not frozen as of 1789 or 1868, respectively. While the language of the Constitution does not change, the changing circumstances of a progressive society for which it was designed yield new and fuller import to its meaning. . . . Whatever, on the basis of massive proof and in the light of history, of which this Court may well take judicial notice, be the justification for not regarding the Communist Party as a conventional political party, no such justification has been afforded in regard to the Progressive Party. A foundation in fact and reason would have to be established far weightier than the intimations that appear in the record to warrant such a view of the Progressive Party. This precludes the questioning that petitioner resisted in regard to that Party.*

. . .

## NOTES AND QUESTIONS

1. Was there a unifying rationale for the Court in the Sweezy case? How can one tell? Why is this an important question? Was the portent of Sweezy realized in the Keyishian case, infra?

2. In Shelton v. Tucker, 364 U.S. 479, 81 S.Ct. 247, 5 L.Ed.2d 231 (1960), all public school teachers were placed under an obligation by an Arkansas statute to file, each year, an affidavit listing all organizations to which they contributed funds and to which they belonged during the past five years. This law was declared unconstitutional because it was overly broad:

"The unlimited and indiscriminate sweep of the statute now before us brings it within the ban of our prior cases. The statute's comprehensive interference with associational freedom goes far beyond what might be justified in the exercise of the State's legitimate inquiry into the fitness and competence of its teachers." Moreover, the Supreme Court said:

"It is not disputed that to compel a teacher to disclose his every associational tie is to impair that teacher's right of free association, a right closely allied to freedom of speech and a right which, like free speech, lies at the foundation of a free society. . . . Such interference with personal freedom is conspicuously accented when the teacher serves at the absolute will of those to whom the disclosure must be made—those who any year can terminate the teacher's employment without bringing charges, without notice, without a hearing, without affording an opportunity to explain.

"The statute does not provide that the information it requires be kept confidential. Each school board is left free to deal with the information as it wishes. The record contains evidence to indicate that fear of public disclosure is neither theoretical nor groundless. Even if there were no disclosure to the general public, the pressure upon a teacher to avoid any ties which might displease those who control his professional destiny would be constant and heavy. Public exposure, bringing with it the possibility of public pressures upon school boards to discharge teachers who belong to unpopular or minority organizations, would simply operate to widen and aggravate the impairment of constitutional liberty.

"The vigilant protection of constitutional freedoms is nowhere more vital than in the community of American schools. . . ."

3.   In Elfbrandt v. Russell, 384 U.S. 11, 86 S.Ct. 1238, 16 L.Ed.2d 321 (1966), Arizona required an oath of all state employees, including all school teachers, reading as follows:

"I, (type or print name) do solemnly swear (or affirm) that I will support the Constitution of the United States and the Constitution and laws of the State of Arizona; that I will bear true faith and allegiance to the same, and defend them against all enemies, foreign and domestic, and that I will faithfully and impartially discharge the duties of the office of (name of office) according to the best of my ability, so help me God (or so I do affirm)."   Elfbrandt, a teacher and a Quaker, decided she could not in good conscience take the oath, not knowing what it meant and not having the opportunity for a hearing at which its precise scope and meaning could be determined.   The Supreme Court held the oath requirement unconstitutional as an infringement of the First Amendment.

".   .   .    One who subscribes to this Arizona oath and who is, or thereafter becomes, a knowing member of an organization which has as 'one of its purposes' the violent overthrow of the government, is subject to immediate discharge and criminal penalties.   Nothing in the oath, the statutory gloss, or the construction of the oath and statutes given by the Arizona Supreme Court, purports to exclude association by one who does not subscribe to the organization's unlawful ends.   Here as in Baggett v. Bullitt, [377 U.S. 360] the 'hazard of being prosecuted for knowing but guiltless behavior' (id., at 373) is a reality.   People often label as 'communist' ideas which they oppose; and they often make up our juries.   '[P]rosecutors too are human.'   Cramp v. Board of Public Instruction, 368 U.S. 278, 287.   Would a teacher be safe and secure in going to a Pugwash Conference?   Would it be legal to join a seminar group predominantly Communist and therefore subject to control by those who are said to believe in the overthrow of the Government by force and violence?   Juries might convict though the teacher did not subscribe to the wrongful aims of the organization.   And there is apparently no machinery provided for getting clearance in advance.

"Those who join an organization but do not share its unlawful purposes and who do not participate in its unlawful activities surely pose no threat, either as citizens or as public employees.   Laws such as this which are not restricted in scope to those who join with the 'specific intent' to further illegal action impose, in effect a conclusive presumption that the member shares the unlawful aims of the organization.   See Aptheker v. Secretary of State, [378 U.S. 500].   The unconstitutionality of this Act follows a fortiori from Speiser v. Randall, 357 U.S. 513, where we held that a State may not even place on an applicant for a tax exemption the burden of proving that he has not engaged in criminal advocacy.

"This Act threatens the cherished freedom of association protected by the First Amendment, made applicable to the States through the Fourteenth Amendment. . . . A statute touching those protected rights must be 'narrowly drawn to define and punish specific conduct as constituting a clear and present danger to a substantial interest of the State.' Cantwell v. Connecticut, 310 U.S. 296, 311. Legitimate legislative goals 'cannot be pursued by means that broadly stifle fundamental personal liberties when the end can be more narrowly achieved.' Shelton v. Tucker, 364 U.S. 479, 488. . . . A law which applies to membership without the 'specific intent' to further the illegal aims of the organization infringes unnecessarily on protected freedoms. It rests on the doctrine of 'guilt by association' which has no place here. . . . Such a law cannot stand."

4.  In Barenblatt v. U. S., 360 U.S. 109, 79 S.Ct. 1081, 3 L.Ed.2d 1115 (1959), an investigation case involving the then named House Committee on Un-American Activities, currently renamed the House Internal Security Committee, the Supreme Court recognized: "Of course, broadly viewed, inquiries cannot be made into the teaching that is pursued at any of our educational institutions. When academic teaching-freedom and its corollary learning-freedom, so essential to the well-being of the Nation, are claimed, this Court will always be on the alert against intrusion by Congress into this constitutionally protected domain."

---

## KEYISHIAN v. BOARD OF REGENTS

Supreme Court of the United States, 1967.
385 U.S. 589, 87 S.Ct. 675, 17 L.Ed.2d 629.

Mr. Justice BRENNAN delivered the opinion of the Court.

. . . As faculty members of the State University [appellants] continued employment was conditioned upon their compliance with a New York plan, formulated partly in statutes and partly in administrative regulations, which the State utilizes to prevent the appointment or retention of "subversive" persons in state employment.

. . . Each . . . refused to sign, as regulations then in effect required, a certificate that he was not a Communist, and that if he had ever been a Communist, he had communicated that fact to the President of the State University of New York. Each was notified that his failure to sign the certificate would require his dismissal.

. . .

Appellants brought this action for declaratory and injunctive relief, alleging that the state program violated the Federal Constitution in various respects. . . .

We considered some aspects of the constitutionality of the New York plan 15 years ago in Adler v. Board of Education, 342 U.S. 485.

That litigation arose after New York passed the Feinberg Law which added § 3022 to the Education Law. The Feinberg Law was enacted to implement and enforce two earlier statutes. The first was a 1917 law, now § 3021 of the Education Law, under which "the utterance of any treasonable or seditious word or words or the doing of any treasonable or seditious act" is a ground for dismissal from the public school system. The second was a 1939 law which . . . is now § 105 of that law. This law disqualifies from the civil service and from employment in the educational system any person who advocates the overthrow of government by force, violence, or any unlawful means, or publishes material advocating such overthrow or organizes or joins any society or group of persons advocating such doctrine.

The Feinberg Law charged the State Board of Regents with the duty of promulgating rules and regulations providing procedures for the disqualification or removal of persons in the public school system who violate the 1917 law or who are ineligible for appointment to or retention in the public school system under the 1939 law. The Board of Regents was further directed to make a list, after notice and hearing, of "subversive" organizations, defined as organizations which advocate the doctrine of overthrow of government by force, violence, or any unlawful means. Finally, the Board was directed to provide in its rules and regulations that membership in any listed organization should constitute prima facie evidence of disqualification for appointment to or retention in any office or position in the public schools of the State.

The Board of Regents thereupon promulgated rules and regulations containing procedures to be followed by appointing authorities to discover persons ineligible for appointment or retention under the 1939 law, or because of violation of the 1917 law. The Board also announced its intention to list "subversive" organizations after requisite notice and hearing, and provided that membership in a listed organization after the date of its listing should be regarded as constituting prima facie evidence of disqualification, and that membership prior to listing should be presumptive evidence that membership has continued, in the absence of a showing that such membership was terminated in good faith. Under the regulations, an appointing official is forbidden to make an appointment until after he has first inquired of an applicant's former employers and other persons to ascertain whether the applicant is disqualified or ineligible for appointment. In addition, an annual inquiry must be made to determine whether an appointed employee has ceased to be qualified for retention, and a report of findings must be filed.

*Adler* . . . held, in effect, that there was no constitutional infirmity in former § 12–a [the predecessor to § 105] or in the Feinberg Law on their faces and that they were capable of constitutional application. But the contention urged in this case that both § 3021 and § 105 are unconstitutionally vague was not heard or decided.

.   .   .   Appellants in this case timely asserted below the unconstitutionality of all these sections on grounds of vagueness and that question is now properly before us for decision.   Moreover, to the extent that *Adler* sustained the provision of the Feinberg Law constituting membership in an organization advocating forceful overthrow of government a ground for disqualification, pertinent constitutional doctrines have since rejected the premises upon which that conclusion rested.   *Adler* is therefore not dispositive of the constitutional issues we must decide in this case.   .   .   .

Section 3021 requires removal for "treasonable or seditious" utterances or acts.   The 1958 amendment to § 105 of the Civil Service Law, now subdivision 3 of that section, added such utterances or acts as a ground for removal under that law also.   The same wording is used in both statutes—that "the utterance of any treasonable or seditious word or words or the doing of any treasonable or seditious act or acts" shall be ground for removal.   But there is a vital difference between the two laws.   Section 3021 does not define the terms "treasonable or seditious" as used in that section;   in contrast, subdivision 3 of § 105 of the Civil Service Law provides that the terms "treasonable word or act" shall mean "treason" as defined in the Penal Law and the terms "seditious word or act" shall mean "criminal anarchy" as defined in the Penal Law.   .   .   .

Even assuming that "treasonable" and "seditious" in § 3021 and § 105, subd. 3, have the same meaning, the uncertainty is hardly removed.   .   .   .   The difficulty centers upon the meaning of "seditious."   Subdivision 3 equates the term "seditious" with "criminal anarchy" as defined in the Penal Law.   Is the reference only to Penal Law § 160, defining criminal anarchy as "the doctrine that organized government should be overthrown by force or violence, or by assassination of the executive head or of any of the executive officials of government, or by any unlawful means"?   But that section ends with the sentence "The advocacy of such doctrine either by word of mouth or writing is a felony."   Does that sentence draw into § 105, Penal Law § 161, proscribing "advocacy of criminal anarchy"?   If so, the possible scope of "seditious" utterances or acts has virtually no limit.   For under Penal Law § 161, one commits the felony of advocating criminal anarchy if he   "   .   .   .   publicly displays any book   .   .   . containing or advocating, advising or teaching the doctrine that organized government should be overthrown by force, violence or any unlawful means."   Does the teacher who carries a copy of the Communist Manifesto on a public street thereby advocate criminal anarchy?   It is no answer to say that the statute would not be applied in such a case.   We cannot gainsay the potential effect of this obscure wording on "those with a conscientious and scrupulous regard for such undertakings."   Baggett v. Bullitt, 377 U.S. 360, 374.   Even were it certain that the definition referred to in § 105 was solely Penal Law § 160, the scope of § 105 still remains indefinite.   The teacher cannot know the extent, if any, to which a "seditious" utterance must transcend mere statement about abstract doctrine, the extent to which it must be intended to and tend to indoctrinate or incite to action in furtherance of the defined doctrine.  The crucial consideration is that no teacher can know just where the line is drawn between "seditious" and nonseditious utterances and acts.   .   .   .

Similar uncertainty arises as to the application of subdivision 1(b) of § 105.  That subsection requires the disqualification of an employee involved with the distribution of written material "containing or advocating, advising or teaching the doctrine" of forceful overthrow, and who himself "advocates, advises, teaches, or embraces the duty, necessity or propriety of adopting the doctrine contained therein."  Here again, mere advocacy of abstract doctrine is apparently included.  And does the prohibition of distribution of matter "containing" the doctrine bar histories of the evolution of Marxist doctrine or tracing the background of the French, American, or Russian revolutions?  The additional requirement, that the person participating in distribution of the material be one who "advocates, advises, teaches, or embraces the duty, necessity or propriety of adopting the doctrine" of forceful overthrow, does not alleviate the uncertainty in the scope of the section, but exacerbates it.  Like the language of § 105, subd. 1(a), this language may reasonably be construed to cover mere expression of belief.  For example, does the university librarian who recommends the reading of such materials thereby "advocate .   .   . the   .   .   . propriety of adopting the doctrine contained therein"?

.   .   .   In light of the intricate administrative machinery for its enforcement, this is not surprising.  The very intricacy of the plan and the uncertainty as to the scope of its proscriptions make it a highly efficient *in terrorem* mechanism.  It would be a bold teacher who would not stay as far as possible from utterances or acts which might jeopardize his living by enmeshing him in this intricate machinery.  The uncertainty as to the utterances and acts proscribed increases that caution in "those who believe the written law means what it says."  Baggett v. Bullitt, supra, at 374.  The result must be to stifle "that free play of the spirit which all teachers ought especially to cultivate and practice.   .   .   ."  That probability is enhanced by the provisions requiring an annual review of every teacher to determine whether any utterance or act of his, inside the classroom or out, came within the sanctions of the laws.  For a memorandum warns employees that under the statutes "subversive" activities may take the form of "[t]he writing of articles, the distribution of pamphlets, the endorsement of speeches made or articles written or acts performed by others," and reminds them "that it is a primary duty of the school authorities in each school district to take positive action to eliminate from the school system any teacher in whose case there is evidence that he is guilty of subversive activity.  School authorities are under obligation to proceed immediately and conclusively in every such case."   .   .   .

Our Nation is deeply committed to safeguarding academic freedom which is of transcendent value to all of us and not merely to the teachers concerned.  That freedom is therefore a special concern of the First Amendment, which does not tolerate laws that cast a pall of orthodoxy over the classroom.  "The vigilant protection of constitutional freedoms is nowhere more vital than in the community of American schools."  Shelton v. Tucker,   .   .   .   The classroom is peculiarly the "marketplace of ideas."  The Nation's future depends upon leaders trained through wide exposure to that robust exchange of ideas which discovers truth "out of a multitude of tongues, [rather] than through any kind of authoritative selection."   .   .   .   In Sweezy v. New Hampshire,   .   .   .   we said:

> "The essentiality of freedom in the community of American universities is almost self-evident.  No one should underestimate the vital role in a democracy that is played by those who guide and train our youth.  To impose any strait jacket upon the intellectual leaders in our colleges and universities would imperil the future of our Nation.  No field of education is so thoroughly comprehended by man that new discoveries cannot yet be made.  Particularly is that true in the social sciences, where few, if any, principles are accepted as absolutes.  Scholarship cannot flourish in an atmosphere of suspicion and distrust.  Teachers and students must always remain free to inquire, to study and to evaluate, to gain new maturity and understanding;  otherwise, our civilization will stagnate and die."

We emphasize once again that "[p]recision of regulation must be the touchstone in an area so closely touching our most precious freedoms," N. A. A. C. P. v. Button, 317 U.S. 415, 438; "[f]or standards of permissible statutory vagueness are strict in the area of free expression.   .   .   .   Because First Amendment freedoms need breathing space to survive, government may regulate in the area only with narrow specificity."   .   .   .   New York's complicated and intricate scheme plainly violates that standard.  When one must guess what conduct or utterance may lose him his position, one necessarily will "steer far wider of the unlawful zone.   .   .   ."  Speiser v. Randall, 357 U.S. 513, 526.  For "[t]he threat of sanctions may deter   .   .   .   almost as potently as the actual application of sanctions." N. A. A. C. P. v. Button, supra, at 433.  The danger of that chilling effect upon the exercise of vital First Amendment rights must be guarded against by sensitive tools which clearly inform teachers what is being proscribed.   .   .   .

The regulatory maze created by New York is wholly lacking in "terms susceptible of objective measurement."  Cramp v. Board of

Public Instruction, supra, at 286. It has the quality of "extraordinary ambiguity" found to be fatal to the oaths considered in Cramp and Baggett v. Bullitt. "[M]en of common intelligence must necessarily guess at its meaning and differ as to its application. . . . " . . . Vagueness of wording is aggravated by prolixity and profusion of statutes, regulations, and administrative machinery, and by manifold cross-references to interrelated enactments and rules.

We therefore hold that § 3021 of the Education Law and subdivisions 1(a), 1(b) and 3 of § 105 of the Civil Service Law as implemented by the machinery created pursuant to § 3022 of the Education Law are unconstitutional.

Appellants have also challenged the constitutionality of the discrete provisions of subdivision 1(c) of § 105 and subdivision 2 of the Feinberg Law, which make Communist Party membership, as such, prima facie evidence of disqualification. . . . Subdivision 2 of the Feinberg Law was, however, before the Court in *Adler* and its constitutionality was sustained. But constitutional doctrine which has emerged since that decision has rejected its major premise. That premise was that public employment, including academic employment, may be conditioned upon the surrender of constitutional rights which could not be abridged by direct government action. Teachers, the Court said in *Adler,* "may work for the school system upon the reasonable terms laid down by the proper authorities of New York. If they do not choose to work on such terms, they are at liberty to retain their beliefs and associations and go elsewhere." 342 U.S., at 492. The Court also stated that a teacher denied employment because of membership in a listed organization "is not thereby denied the right of free speech and assembly. His freedom of choice between membership in the organization and employment in the school system might be limited, but not his freedom of speech or assembly, except in the remote sense that limitation is inherent in every choice." . . .

We proceed then to the question of the validity of the provisions of subdivision 1(c) of § 105 and subdivision 2 of § 3022, barring employment to members of listed organizations. Here again constitutional doctrine has developed since *Adler.* Mere knowing membership without a specific intent to further the unlawful aims of an organization is not a constitutionally adequate basis for exclusion from such positions as those held by appellants.

In Elfbrandt v. Russell, 384 U.S. 11, we said, "Those who join an organization but do not share its unlawful purposes and who do not participate in its unlawful activities surely pose no threat, either as citizens or as public employees." . . . We there struck down a statutorily required oath binding the state employee not to become a member of the Communist Party with knowledge of its unlawful purpose, on threat of discharge and perjury prosecution if the oath were violated. We found that "[a]ny lingering doubt that proscription of mere knowing membership, without any showing of 'specific intent,' would run afoul of the Constitution was set at rest by our decision in Aptheker v. Secretary of State, 378 U.S. 500." . . . In *Aptheker* we held that Party membership, without knowledge of the Party's unlawful purposes *and* specific intent to further its unlawful aims, could not constitutionally warrant deprivation of the right to travel abroad. As we said in Schneiderman v. United States, 320 U.S. 118, 136, "[U]nder our traditions beliefs are personal and not a matter of mere association, and . . . men in adhering to a political party or other organization . . . do not subscribe unqualifiedly to all of its platforms or asserted principles." "A law which applies to membership without the 'specific intent' to further the illegal aims of the organization infringes unnecessarily on protected freedoms. It rests on the doctrine of 'guilt by association' which has no place here." . . . Thus mere Party membership, even with knowledge of the Party's unlawful goals, cannot suffice to justify criminal punishment, see Scales v. United States, 367 U.S. 203; Noto v. United States, 367 U.S. 290; Yates v. United States, 354 U.S. 298; nor may it warrant a finding of moral unfitness justifying disbarment. Schware v. Board of Bar Examiners, 353 U.S. 232. . . .

Measured against this standard, both Civil Service Law § 105, subd. 1(c), and Education Law § 3022, subd. 2, sweep overbroadly into association which may not be proscribed. The presumption of disqualification arising from proof of mere membership may be rebutted, but only by (a) a denial of membership, (b) a denial that the organization advocates the overthrow of government by force, or (c) a denial that the teacher has knowledge of such advocacy. . . . Thus proof of nonactive membership or a showing of the absence of intent to further unlawful aims will not rebut the presumption and defeat dismissal. This is emphasized in official administrative interpretations. For example, it is said in a letter addressed to prospective appointees by the President of the State University, "You will note that . . . both the Law and regulations are very specifically directed toward the elimination and nonappointment of 'Communists' from or to our teaching ranks. . . . " The Feinberg Certificate was even more explicit: "Anyone who is a *member* of the Communist Party or of any organization that advocates the violent overthrow of the Government of the United States or of the State of New York or any political subdivision thereof cannot be employed by the State University." . . . This official administrative interpretation is supported by the legislative preamble to the Feinberg Law, § 1, in which the legislature concludes as a result of its findings that "it is essential that the laws prohibiting persons who are *members* of subversive groups, such as the communist party and its affiliated organizations, from obtaining or retaining employment in the public schools, be rigorously enforced." . . .

Thus § 105, subd. 1(c), and § 3022, subd. 2, suffer from impermissible "overbreadth." . . . They seek to bar employment both for association which legitimately may be proscribed and for association which may not be proscribed consistently with First Amendment rights. Where statutes have an overbroad sweep, just as where they are vague, "the hazard of loss or substantial impairment of those precious rights may be critical," . . . since those covered by the statute are bound to limit their behavior to that which is unquestionably safe. As we said in Shelton v. Tucker, . . . "The breadth of legislative abridgment must be viewed in the light of less drastic means for achieving the same basic purpose."

We therefore hold that Civil Service Law § 105, subd. 1(c), and Education Law § 3022, subd. 2, are invalid insofar as they proscribe mere knowing membership without any showing of specific intent to further the unlawful aims of the Communist Party of the United States or of the State of New York.

The judgment of the District Court is reversed and the case is remanded for further proceedings consistent with this opinion.

Reversed and remanded.

Mr. Justice CLARK, with whom Mr. Justice HARLAN, Mr. Justice STEWART and Mr. Justice WHITE join, dissenting.

The blunderbuss fashion in which the majority couches "its artillery of words," together with the morass of cases it cites as authority and the obscurity of their application to the question at hand, makes it difficult to grasp the true thrust of its decision. . . .

It is clear that the Feinberg Law, in which this Court found "no constitutional infirmity" in 1952, has been given its death blow today. Just as the majority here finds that there "can be no doubt of the legitimacy of New York's interest in protecting its education system from subversion" there can also be no doubt that "the be-all and end-all" of New York's effort is here. And, regardless of its correctness, neither New York nor the several States that have followed the teaching of Adler v. Board of Education, 342 U.S. 485, for some 15 years, can ever put the pieces together again. No court has ever reached out so far to destroy so much with so little.

Our late Brother Minton wrote for the Court:

"A teacher works in a sensitive area in a schoolroom. There he shapes the attitude of young minds towards the society in which they live. In this, the state has a vital concern. It must preserve the integrity of the schools. That the school authorities have the right and the duty to screen the officials, teachers, and employees as to their fitness to maintain the integrity of the schools as a part of ordered society, cannot be doubted. . . .

The majority says that the Feinberg Law is bad because it has an "over-broad sweep." I regret to say—and I do so with deference —that the majority has by its broadside swept away one of our most precious rights, namely, the right of self-preservation. Our public educational system is the genius of our democracy. The minds of our youth are developed there and the character of that development will determine the future of our land. Indeed, our very existence depends upon it. The issue here is a very narrow one. It is not freedom of speech, freedom of thought, freedom of press, freedom of assembly, or of association, even in the Communist Party. It is simply this: May the State provide that one who, after a hearing with full judicial review, is found to have wilfully and deliberately advocated, advised, or taught that our Government should be overthrown by force or violence or other unlawful means; or to have wilfully and deliberately printed, published, etc., any book or paper that so advocated *and to have personally* advocated such doctrine himself; or to have wilfully and deliberately become a member of an organization that advocates such doctrine, is prima facie disqualified from teaching in its university?    My answer, in keeping with all of our cases up until today, is "Yes"!

I dissent.

## NOTES AND QUESTIONS

1. In a dissent to the Adler decision, supra, which decision was overruled in Keyishian, Mr. Justice Douglas, joined by Mr. Justice Black, wrote:

"The Constitution guarantees freedom of thought and expression to everyone in our society. All are entitled to it; and none needs it more than the teacher.

"The public school is in most respects the cradle of our democracy. . . . the impact of this kind of censorship in the public school system illustrates the high purpose of the First Amendment in freeing speech and thought from censorship. . . .

"The very threat of such a procedure is certain to raise havoc with academic freedom. . . . Fearing condemnation, [the teacher] will tend to shrink from any association that stirs controversy. In that manner freedom of expression will be stifled. . . .

"There can be no real academic freedom in that environment. Where suspicion fills the air and holds scholars in line for fear of their jobs, there can be no exercise of the free intellect. . . .

"This system of spying and surveillance with its accompanying reports and trials cannot go hand in hand with academic freedom. It produces standardized thought, not the pursuit of truth. Yet it was the pursuit of truth which the First Amendment was designed to protect. . . . We need be bold and adventuresome in our thinking to survive. . . . The Framers knew the danger of dogmatism; they also knew the strength that comes when the mind is free, when ideas may be pursued wherever they lead. We forget

these teachings of the First Amendment when we sustain this law."
Adler v. Board of Education, 342 U.S. 485 at 508–11, 72 S.Ct. 380
at 392–94, 96 L.Ed. 517 at 532–34 (1952), *passim*.

Mr. Justice Frankfurter dissented on jurisdictional grounds but
made special reference to "the teacher's freedom of thought, inquiry, and expression," and to "the freedom of thought and activity,
and especially  .  .  .  the feeling of such freedom, which are, as
I suppose no one would deny, part of the necessary professional
equipment of teachers in a free society."  Id. at 504–05.

2.   In the same year that it decided the Adler case, the Supreme Court
held unconstitutional an Oklahoma statute requiring all state employees, including teachers, to take a loyalty oath to the effect that
for the preceding five years they were not members of organizations
listed as "subversive" or "communist front" by the United States
Attorney General.   Mr. Justice Frankfurter wrote a concurring opinion joined by Mr. Justice Douglas:

".  .  .  to require such an oath, on pain of a teacher's loss
of his position in case of refusal to take the oath, penalizes a teacher for exercising a right of association peculiarly characteristic of
our people.  .  .  .   Such joining is an exercise of the rights of
free speech and free inquiry.  By limiting the power of the States
to interfere with freedom of speech and freedom of inquiry and
freedom of association, the Fourteenth Amendment protects all persons, no matter what their calling.  But, in view of the nature of the
teacher's relation to the effective exercise of the rights which are
safeguarded by the Bill of Rights and by the Fourteenth Amendment, inhibition of freedom of thought, and of action upon thought,
in the case of teachers brings the safeguards of those amendments
vividly into operation.  Such unwarranted inhibition upon the free
spirit of teachers affects not only those who, like the appellants, are
immediately before the Court.  It has an unmistakable tendency to
chill that free play of the spirit which all teachers ought especially
to cultivate and practice;  it makes for caution and timidity in their
associations by potential teachers.  .  .  .

"That our democracy ultimately rests on public opinion is a
platitude of speech but not a commonplace in action.  Public opinion
is the ultimate reliance of our society only if it be disciplined and
responsible.  It can be disciplined and responsible only if habits of
open-mindedness and of critical inquiry are acquired in the formative years of our citizens.  The process of education has naturally
enough been the basis of hope for the perdurance of our democracy
on the part of all our great leaders, from Thomas Jefferson onwards.

"To regard teachers—in our entire educational system, from
the primary grades to the university—as the priests of our democracy is therefore not to indulge in hyperbole.  It is the special task
of teachers to foster those habits of open-mindedness and critical
inquiry which alone make for responsible citizens, who, in turn,
make possible an enlightened and effective public opinion.  Teachers
must fulfill their function by precept and practice, by the very
atmosphere which they generate;  they must be exemplars of open-

mindedness and free inquiry. They cannot carry out their noble task if the conditions for the practice of a responsible and critical mind are denied to them. They must have the freedom of responsible inquiry, by thought and action, into the meaning of social and economic ideas, into the checkered history of social and economic dogma. They must be free to sift evanescent doctrine, qualified by time and circumstance, from that restless, enduring process of extending the bounds of understanding and wisdom, to assure which the freedoms of thought, of speech, of inquiry, of worship are guaranteed by the Constitution of the United States against infraction by national or state government.

"The functions of educational institutions in our national life and the conditions under which alone they can adequately perform them are at the basis of these limitations upon state and national power." Wieman v. Updegraff, 344 U.S. 183 at 195–97, 73 S.Ct. 215 at 220–21, 97 L.Ed. 216 at 224–25 (1952).

3. Do these cases mean that public school teachers can no longer be disqualified from their jobs for any expression or association for which they could not be punished criminally?

4. May school administrators today constitutionally require a non-communist loyalty oath of teachers? May they inquire into a teacher's associations? With the communist party? Should a teacher be fired if he refuses to answer whether he is a communist or a member of the communist party? Why or why not? Why should secret membership in the communist party receive constitutional protection? Does it?

5. What, precisely, is the substantive content of the concept of Academic Freedom that is protected by the Constitution, and to whom does it apply and in what circumstances? Write it out on paper.

6. Should schools focus their teaching on those ideas that have won in the competition of the marketplace" or should they focus only on the ideas that have won the acceptance of scholars, or both? Why? What are the implications of your answer for the curriculum and teaching methods of a school?

7. Do "subversive activities" present special problems for schools justifying restraints on academic freedom? Is the problem any different for the "common schools" than for higher education?

8. It is sometimes asserted that academic freedom stops with the university and does not extend to the common schools. What are the reasons that lead to this view? Is the view valid? Can it not be asserted that, properly viewed, the common school teacher and the university research scholar share the same ultimate faith and that the common school teacher, when teaching, like the university professor, should be a living functioning example of academic freedom? The task of the effective teacher is not only to disseminate available knowledge, but, more importantly, to teach the methods and criteria of objective inquiry and responsible evaluation. Of even greater importance is the task of the teacher to bring student awareness into full and profound appreciation and respect for objective fact and value and for intellectual

clarity and integrity. How can these goals be achieved unless the K–12 teacher enjoys academic freedom in the classroom commensurate with his needs? Conceived properly, the aims of effective teaching are in harmony with those of the research scholar. Properly conceived and executed, teaching gives an enriched meaning to the life of the student. But it does more than this: it also is indispensable to achieving the proper goals of the university, and constitutes the means for achieving effective training for responsible citizenship and leadership in a free and democratic society. It should be noted that both research and teaching can be done excellently, or either can be done poorly, depending upon the abilities and talents of the person. But, while academic freedom might apply a bit differently to each of the grades of a common school, reason appears to insist that academic freedom should extend throughout our school system—to the common schools as well as to the university. Generally see, Note, Developments in the Law: Academic Freedom, 81 Harv.Law Rev. 1045 (1968), and Nordin, The Legal Protection of Academic Freedom, in C. Hooker (ed.), THE COURTS AND EDUCATION (1978).

## PROBLEM

In light of all the preceding materials, do you believe that any part of the following statute from Florida is unconstitutional? If so, which part or parts? Why or why not?

Americanism vs. communism; required high school course

"(1) The legislature of the state hereby finds it to be a fact that

(a) The political ideology commonly known and referred to as communism is in conflict with and contrary to the principles of constitutional government of the United States as epitomized in its national constitution,

(b) The successful exploitation and manipulation of youth and student groups throughout the world today are a major challenge which the free world forces must meet and defeat, and

(c) The best method of meeting this challenge is to have the youth of the state and nation throughly and completely informed as to the evils, dangers and fallacies of communism by giving them a thorough understanding of the entire communist movement, including its history, doctrines, objectives and techniques.

"(2) The public high schools shall each teach a complete course of not less than thirty hours, to all students enrolled in said public high schools entitled "Americanism versus communism."

"(3) The course shall provide adequate instruction in the history, doctrines, objectives and techniques of communism and shall be for the primary purpose of instilling in the minds of the students a greater appreciation of democratic processes, freedom under law, and the will to preserve that freedom.

"(4) The course shall be one of orientation in comparative governments and shall emphasize the free-enterprise-competitive economy of the United States as the one which produces higher wages, higher standards of living, greater personal freedom and liberty than any other system of economics on earth.

"(5) The course shall lay particular emphasis upon the dangers of communism, the ways to fight communism, the evils of communism, the fallacies of communism, and the false doctrines of communism.

"(6) The state textbook council and the department of education shall take such action as may be necessary and appropriate to prescribe suitable textbook and instructional material as provided by state law, using as one of their guides the official reports of the house committee on un-American activities and the senate internal security subcommittee of the United States congress.

"(7) No teacher or textual material assigned to this course shall present communism as preferable to the system of constitutional government and the free-enterprise-competitive economy indigenous to the United States." Fla.Stat. § 233.064.

## DIRECT GOVERNMENTAL POWERS OVER THE CURRICULUM

### INTRODUCTION

The term "curriculum" can be used in at least two senses. One sense refers to the studies prescribed for a given grade, the successful completion of which leads ultimately to a high school diploma. A second sense of the term refers to the whole life-experience program of the school; that is, "all of the experiences for which the school accepts responsibility." W. B. Ragan, MODERN ELEMENTARY CURRICULUM 5 (1966), and see, J. D. Mohler & E. C. Bolmeier, LAW OF EXTRACURRICULAR ACTIVITIES IN SECONDARY SCHOOLS (1968). In this sense, a school can be responsible for extra-curricular as well as curricular programs. Courts generally use the term "curriculum" in both senses, and indeed, occasionally in a third, and broader sense. They have infrequently used the term to apply to whatever happens in school, whether the authorities want to accept responsibility for it or not.

The federal government exerts considerable force on the curriculum by making grants of money available to states so long as they agree to provide certain programs.  But the federal government has no direct control over the school curriculum.  Within constitutional limitations, the state legislature has the power to control and to prescribe the subject matter of the curriculum, methods of instruction, and books to be used.  The Supreme Courts of North Carolina and Tennessee have provided statements of the legislature's power:

> The General Assembly has the power, which we think cannot be questioned to prescribe by statute the subjects to be taught and the methods of instruction to be followed in the public schools of the state, whether such public schools be included within the uniform system required to be maintained by the Constitution, or whether they be public schools established for certain districts formed under the general school law by the state or under specific statutes.  Posey v. Bd. of Ed., 199 N.C. 306, 154 S.E. 393 (1930).

> .  .  .  That the state may establish a uniform series of books to be taught in the schools, which it provides and controls, seems to be a proposition as evident as that it may provide a uniform system of schools, which we take it is not now an open question;  and while the selection of text-books may, in the earlier and cruder stages of the law, have been left to, and exercised by, local superintendents, directors, and teachers, it was not for want of authority in the state to prescribe a uniform system, but rather because the system had not reached that stage of development and progress that made it advisable, in the opinion of the legislature, to so provide.  .  .  .  We think it clear that the state itself might, if it saw proper, publish the books to be used in its public schools.

> .  .  .

> .  .  .  The authority of the state over schools is a legislative one, and it is difficult to see how a uniform system can be maintained which will confer equal benefits upon all sections of the state, unless it is done by legislative action.  If the authority to regulate and control schools is legislative, then it must have an unrestricted right to prescribe methods, and the courts cannot interfere with it, unless some scheme is devised which is contrary to other provisions of the constitution.  .  .  .  Leeper v. State, 103 Tenn. 500, 53 S.W. 962 (1899).

## Methods of Instruction

State legislatures seldom prescribe the teaching methods that must be used in classroom teaching, leaving matters of pedagogy to school personnel.  But, legislatures may speak to the subject generally, requiring that teachers carry out the prescribed teaching methods and courses of study;  for example, Washington provides that

"Certificated employees shall faithfully enforce in the common schools the course of study and regulations prescribed, whether regulations of the district, the superintendent of public instruction, or the state board of education, and shall furnish promptly all information relating to the common schools which may be requested by the county or intermediate district superintendent.

"Any certificated employee who wilfully refuses or neglects to enforce the course of study or the rules and regulations as above in this section required, shall not be allowed by the directors any warrant for salary due until said person shall have complied with said requirements."  RCW 28A.-67.060.

Moreover, without reference to subject matter legislatures frequently direct teachers to impress certain values onto the minds of their students.  Again Washington provides a not unusual example:

"It shall be the duty of all teachers to endeavor to impress on the minds of their pupils the principles of morality, truth, justice, temperance, humanity and patriotism;  to teach them to avoid idleness, profanity and falsehood;  to instruct them in the principles of free government, and to train them up to the true comprehension of the rights, duty and dignity of American citizenship."  RCW 28A.67.110.

"No person, whose certificate or permit authorizing him to teach in the common schools of this state has been revoked due to his failure to endeavor to impress on the minds of his pupils the principles of patriotism, or to train them up to the true comprehension of the rights, duty and dignity of American citizenship, shall be permitted to teach in any common school in this state."  RCW 28A.67.030.

Can the above two statutes be enforced constitutionally?

The highest court in Massachusetts has sustained the right of school authorities to prescribe the teaching methods to be used in classroom teaching in a case involving a girl whose father refused to allow her to attend a bookkeeping class because she became upset when the teacher selected a rival pupil to aid in the correction of homework, and after a week's work on a problem the rival pupil marked her answer "wrong," but the teacher later marked it "correct":

The real and vital question is not whether the plaintiff was guilty of misconduct in refusing to attend her class, but whether a parent has the right to say a certain method of teaching any given course of study shall be pursued. The question answers itself. Were it otherwise, should several parents hold diverse opinions all must yield to one or confusion and failure inevitably follow. The determination of the procedure and the management and direction of pupils and studies in this Commonwealth rests in the wise discretion and sound judgment of teachers and school committee, whose action in these respects is not subject to the supervision of this court.

The case at bar is one purely of administrative detail and its exercise violates no legal right of pupil or parent. The plaintiff was without right in requiring that the principal personally should attend to the supervision of her individual work, perhaps to the neglect of more important duties. Wulf v. Wakefield, 221 Mass. 427, 109 N.E. 358 (1915).

Qualified school administrators equally can have power over classroom teaching methods, but generally, members of boards of education do not.

The law does not contemplate that the members of a board of education shall supervise the professional work of teachers, principals, and superintendents. They are not teachers, and ordinarily, not qualified to be such. Generally they do not possess qualifications to pass upon methods of instruction and discipline. The law clearly contemplated that professionally trained teachers, principals, and superintendents shall have exclusive control of these matters. State ex rel. Rogers v. Board of Education, 125 W.Va. 579, 25 S.E.2d 537 (1943).

Generally, courts will not review a prescribed teaching method unless it raises a constitutional question or is "arbitrary or capricious," or raises other legal problems. For example, in State v. Avoyelles Parish School Bd., 147 So.2d 729 (La.1962), Louisiana's Supreme Court said that "It is not the function of a court to sit in judgment on the propriety of school curriculum, methods of teaching and demonstrations which school officials have determined necessary and proper."

## Subjects Taught

The legislatures do not restrict themselves to prescribing "academic" subjects. Legislatures also require that pupils engage in the study of thrift, Security Nat. Bank v. Bagley, 202 Iowa 701, 210 N.W. 947 (1926), driver education, Acorn Auto Driving School v. Board of

Education, 27 Ill.2d 93, 187 N.E.2d 722 (1963) and health and physical education:

> Various sections of our school law recognize the scope of physical training, or education; it has for many years formed a definite and integral part of the curriculum of the public schools. The school law . . . includes, in the course of study prescribed for the elementary public schools of the Commonwealth, instruction in 'health, including physical training,' as one of the required branches. For high schools, the State Council of Education determines the subjects to be taught based on statutory authority . . . . Physical training includes organized sports and athletic exercises. Athletics are important to the moral, physical and mental development of students. Appeal of Ganoposki, 332 Pa. 550, 2 A.2d 742 (1938).

Moreover, the sexism perhaps notwithstanding, a state legislature apparently can require that commercial and vocational courses be part of the curriculum:

> If this were a question of common school education, the proposition would probably not be questioned. But the power of the legislature to impose a system of public school education upon local communities is not limited to common branches alone. It is the judgment of the legislature that this state should now require public education in something more than the common branches; that it should provide for the public education of boys in that which pertains to successful agriculture, and of girls in that which pertains to successful housekeeping. The question whether the population and wealth of the state are such as to warrant such measures is a legislative and not a judicial question, a question of legislative policy, and not of legislative power. Associated Schools of Independent School Dist. No. 63 v. School Dist. No. 83, 122 Minn. 254, 142 N.W. 325 (1913).

What is the relationship of these subjects to "good citizenship"?

In practice, state legislatures mandate various subjects, requiring that they constitute a minimum part of the school curriculum, and then delegate powers to either State Boards of Education or Local School Boards, enabling them to prescribe and shape the remainder of the curriculum. Occasionally, an attempt will be made by either the legislature or school board to indoctrinate pupils into blindly holding only one point of view. At least three types of situations involving constitutional freedom can arise: (1) the situation of official indoctrination whereby either the legislature or school board not only requires that a certain subject be taught, but that it be taught uncritically or that only certain received "truths" be allowed; (2) the situation of official ignorance which is the converse of the situation of official indoctrination, whereby the legislature or school board disallows the teaching of a certain subject; e. g., man's evolution, usually because it is contrary to the received "truth," and finally (3) the rather common ambiguous situation in which no prior decision is made by the legislature or school board, but, for example, by a teacher who selects a book for a course or a method of teaching which is later attacked and sought to be suppressed because it is "dirty," or "improper" etc.

## CONSTITUTIONAL LIMITATIONS ON GOVERNMENTAL POWERS OVER THE CURRICULUM

Education is an attempt by the community to form beliefs and habits that are consonant with the highest standards of knowledge and the best ideals of behavior. True as this statement is, it does not mean that schools are properly directed toward indoctrination or toward the preservation of the existing culture or any one political point of view. To hold that schools are to promote one, or a few, officially approved view, or views, is to hold to the totalitarian position, and that position is inconsistent with a democratic society. On the other hand, it is as unrealistic as it is evasive to hold that the curriculum and teachers must hold fast to neutrality whenever a controversial issue is presented, leaving the matter for the individual to decide. Diversity exists within America's democratic community, and it gives rise to controversial issues. A school is supposed to prepare the student for life in American democracy, and a school that failed openly to explore controversial questions would be a failure. It would not be a school at all, but more akin to a prison.

Yet, education necessarily involves some indoctrination. However, education is more than indoctrination, and not all indoctrination is inconsistent with the requirements of a democratic society. Indoctrination has at least two meanings. In one sense, indoctrination means the careful teaching of the fundamentals of a branch of knowledge as the basic principles have come to be accepted by scholars in that field of knowledge. Positive teaching may involve some indoctrination in this sense. In the beneficial use of the term the students are not equally competent as judges and a teacher's knowledge is to be conveyed. Yet, even here, the subject matter should be taught within an open atmosphere of challenge and criticism by students. The goal is a critical and curious mind. "Indoctrination" can be used in a second, and obnoxious, sense, applying to a situation where there is a difference of opinion between equally competent judges on a matter of opinion such as religion. This is the area that needs a clear treatment showing a profound respect for matters of fact and value, and the methods of competent inquiry. It is a golden opportunity for the curriculum. In the obnoxious sense, indoctrination can occur when only one side of the matter is presented, or when the alternative sides are presented inadequately. Moreover, if there is not sufficient time for full exploration and development of the issue then obnoxious indoctrination will inevitably occur.

An indispensable function of the curriculum of the common school is to educate for good citizenship. In the American democracy this means education that is directed toward producing a mentality in all students such that they can distinguish fact from value and can critically evaluate values and rationally choose their own. It is education directed toward achieving a responsible freedom. Specifically it means that the educational process must itself respect the principles of the American constitution while teaching those principles, especially the principles and procedures of the American Bill of Rights. An educational curriculum based on these principles is not a catechism nor indoctrination in the obnoxious sense. This curriculum allows for differences of opinions where views can differ, and it would include a fair amount of discussion about political theory, alternative economic systems, government, contemporary affairs and literature. Its primary goal is the realization of the social purposes of American democratic society as they have been set forth in the Bill of Rights which constitutionally protects diversity. For further discussion see, I. B. Berkson, The Ideal And The Community 253–64 (1958).

## THE BASIC POSTULATE: FREEDOM OF THE MIND

---

## WEST VIRGINIA STATE BOARD OF EDUCATION
### v. BARNETTE

Supreme Court of the United States, 1943.
319 U.S. 624, 63 S.Ct. 1178, 87 L.Ed. 1628.

Mr. Justice JACKSON delivered the opinion of the Court.

Following the decision of this Court on June 3, 1940, in Minersville School District v. Gobitis, 310 U.S. 586, the West Virginia legislature amended its statutes to require all schools therein to conduct courses of instruction in history, civics, and in the Constitutions of the United States and of the State "for the purpose of teaching, fostering and perpetuating the ideals, principles and spirit of Americanism, and increasing the knowledge of the organization and machinery of the government." Appellant Board of Education was directed, with advice of the State Superintendent of Schools, to "prescribe the courses of study covering these subjects" for public schools. The

Act made it the duty of private, parochial and denominational schools to prescribe courses of study "similar to those required for the public schools."

The Board of Education on January 9, 1942, adopted a resolution containing recitals taken largely from the Court's *Gobitis* opinion and ordering that the salute to the flag become "a regular part of the program of activities in the public schools," that all teachers and pupils "shall be required to participate in the salute honoring the Nation represented by the Flag; provided, however, that refusal to salute the Flag be regarded as an act of insubordination, and shall be dealt with accordingly."

The resolution originally required the "commonly accepted salute to the Flag" which it defined. Objections to the salute as "being too much like Hitler's" were raised by the Parent and Teachers Association, the Boy and Girl Scouts, the Red Cross, and the Federation of Women's Clubs. Some modification appears to have been made in deference to these objections, but no concession was made to Jehovah's Witnesses. What is now required is the "stiff-arm" salute, the saluter to keep the right hand raised with palm turned up while the following is repeated: "I pledge allegiance to the Flag of the United States of America and to the Republic for which it stands; one Nation, indivisible, with liberty and justice for all."

Failure to conform is "insubordination" dealt with by expulsion. Readmission is denied by statute until compliance. Meanwhile the expelled child is "unlawfully absent" and may be proceeded against as a delinquent. His parents or guardians are liable to prosecution, and if convicted are subject to fine not exceeding $50 and jail term not exceeding thirty days.

Appellees, citizens of the United States and of West Virginia, brought suit in the United States District Court for themselves and others similarly situated asking its injunction to restrain enforcement of these laws and regulations against Jehovah's Witnesses. The Witnesses are an unincorporated body teaching that the obligation imposed by law of God is superior to that of laws enacted by temporal government. Their religious beliefs include a literal version of Exodus, Chapter 20, verses 4 and 5, which says: "Thou shalt not make unto thee any graven image, or any likeness of anything that is in heaven above, or that is in the earth beneath, or that is in the water under the earth; thou shalt not bow down thyself to them nor serve them." They consider that the flag is an "image" within this command. For this reason they refuse to salute it.

Children of this faith have been expelled from school and are threatened with exclusion for no other cause. Officials threaten to send them to reformatories maintained for criminally inclined juveniles.   Parents of such children have been prosecuted and are threatened with prosecutions for causing delinquency.

The Board of Education moved to dismiss the complaint setting forth these facts and alleging that the law and regulations are an unconstitutional denial of religious freedom, and of freedom of speech, and are invalid under the "due process" and "equal protection" clauses of the Fourteenth Amendment to the Federal Constitution.   .   .   .

This case calls upon us to reconsider a precedent decision, as the Court throughout its history often has been required to do.   Before turning to the *Gobitis* case, however, it is desirable to notice certain characteristics by which this controversy is distinguished.

The freedom asserted by these appellees does not bring them into collision with rights asserted by any other individual.   It is such conflicts which most frequently require intervention of the State to determine where the rights of one end and those of another begin. But the refusal of these persons to participate in the ceremony does not interfere with or deny rights of others to do so.   Nor is there any question in this case that their behavior is peaceable and orderly.   The sole conflict is between authority and rights of the individual.   The State asserts power to condition access to public education on making a prescribed sign and profession and at the same time to coerce attendance by punishing both parent and child.   The latter stand on a right of self-determination in matters that touch individual opinion and personal attitude.

As the present CHIEF JUSTICE said in dissent in the *Gobitis* case, the State may "require teaching by instruction and study of all in our history and in the structure and organization of our government, including the guaranties of civil liberty, which tend to inspire patriotism and love of country."   .   .   .   Here, however, we are dealing with a compulsion of students to declare a belief.   They are not merely made acquainted with the flag salute so that they may be informed as to what it is or even what it means.   The issue here is whether this slow and easily neglected route to aroused loyalties constitutionally may be short-cut by substituting a compulsory salute and slogan.   .   .   .

There is no doubt that, in connection with the pledges, the flag salute is a form of utterance.   Symbolism is a primitive but effective way of communicating ideas.   The use of an emblem or flag to symbolize some system, idea, institution, or personality, is a short cut from mind to mind.   Causes and nations, political parties, lodges and ecclesiastical groups seek to knit the loyalty of their followings to a flag or banner, a color or design.   The State announces rank, function, and authority through crowns and maces, uniforms and black robes; the church speaks through the Cross, the Crucifix, the altar and shrine, and clerical raiment.   Symbols of State often convey political ideas just as religious symbols come to convey theological ones.   Associated with many of these symbols are appropriate gestures of acceptance or respect: a salute, a bowed or bared head, a bended knee. A person gets from a symbol the meaning he puts into it, and what is one man's comfort and inspiration is another's jest and scorn.

Over a decade ago Chief Justice Hughes led this Court in holding that the display of a red flag as a symbol of opposition by peaceful and legal means to organized government was protected by the free speech guaranties of the Constitution. Stromberg v. California, 283 U.S. 359. Here it is the State that employs a flag as a symbol of adherence to government as presently organized. It requires the individual to communicate by word and sign his acceptance of the political ideas it thus bespeaks. Objection to this form of communication when coerced is an old one, well known to the framers of the Bill of Rights.

It is also to be noted that the compulsory flag salute and pledge requires affirmation of a belief and an attitude of mind. It is not clear whether the regulation contemplates that pupils forego any contrary convictions of their own and become unwilling converts to the prescribed ceremony or whether it will be acceptable if they simulate assent by words without belief and by a gesture barren of meaning. It is now a commonplace that censorship or suppression of expression of opinion is tolerated by our Constitution only when the expression presents a clear and present danger of action of a kind the State is empowered to prevent and punish. It would seem that involuntary affirmation could be commanded only on even more immediate and urgent grounds than silence. But here the power of compulsion is invoked without any allegation that remaining passive during a flag salute ritual creates a clear and present danger that would justify an effort even to muffle expression. To sustain the compulsory flag salute we are required to say that a Bill of Rights which guards the individual's right to speak his own mind, left it open to public authorities to compel him to utter what is not in his mind.

Whether the First Amendment to the Constitution will permit officials to order observance of ritual of this nature does not depend upon whether as a voluntary exercise we would think it to be good, bad or merely innocuous. Any credo of nationalism is likely to include what some disapprove or to omit what others think essential, and to give off different overtones as it takes on different accents or interpretations. If official power exists to coerce acceptance of any patriotic creed, what it shall contain cannot be decided by courts, but must be largely discretionary with the ordaining authority, whose power to prescribe would no doubt include power to amend. Hence validity of the asserted power to force an American citizen publicly to profess any statement of belief or to engage in any ceremony of assent to one, presents questions of power that must be considered independently of any idea we may have as to the utility of the ceremony in question.

Nor does the issue as we see it turn on one's possession of particular religious views or the sincerity with which they are held. While religion supplies appellees' motive for enduring the discomforts of making the issue in this case, many citizens who do not share these religious views hold such a compulsory rite to infringe constitutional liberty of the individual. It is not necessary to inquire whether nonconformist beliefs will exempt from the duty to salute unless we first find power to make the salute a legal duty.

The *Gobitis* decision, however, *assumed*, as did the argument in that case and in this, that power exists in the State to impose the flag salute discipline upon school children in general. The Court only examined and rejected a claim based on religious beliefs of immunity from an unquestioned general rule. The question which underlies the flag salute controversy is whether such a ceremony so touching matters of opinion and political attitude may be imposed upon the individual by official authority under powers committed to any political organization under our Constitution. We examine rather than assume existence of this power and, against this broader definition of issues in this case, reexamine specific grounds assigned for the *Gobitis* decision.

1. It was said that the flag-salute controversy confronted the Court with "the problem which Lincoln cast in memorable dilemma: 'Must a government of necessity be too *strong* for the liberties of its people, or too *weak* to maintain its own existence?' " and that the answer must be in favor of strength. . . .

We think these issues may be examined free of pressure or restraint growing out of such considerations.

It may be doubted whether Mr. Lincoln would have thought that the strength of government to maintain itself would be impressively vindicated by our confirming power of the State to expel a handful of children from school. Such oversimplification, so handy in political debate, often lacks the precision necessary to postulates of judicial reasoning. If validly applied to this problem, the utterance cited would resolve every issue of power in favor of those in authority and would require us to override every liberty thought to weaken or delay execution of their policies.

Government of limited power need not be anemic government. Assurance that rights are secure tends to diminish fear and jealousy of strong government, and by making us feel safe to live under it makes for its better support. Without promise of a limiting Bill of Rights it is doubtful if our Constitution could have mustered enough strength to enable its ratification. To enforce those rights today is not to choose weak government over strong government. It is only to adhere as a means of strength to individual freedom of mind in preference to officially disciplined uniformity for which history indicates a disappointing and disastrous end.

The subject now before us exemplifies this principle. Free public education, if faithful to the ideal of secular instruction and political neutrality, will not be partisan or enemy of any class, creed, party, or faction. If it is to impose any ideological discipline, however, each party or denomination must seek to control, or failing that, to weaken the influence of the educational system. Observance of the limitations of the Constitution will not weaken government in the field appropriate for its exercise.

2. It was also considered in the *Gobitis* case that functions of educational officers in States, counties and school districts were such that to interfere with their authority "would in effect make us the school board for the country."  . . .

The Fourteenth Amendment, as now applied to the States, protects the citizen against the State itself and all of its creatures—Boards of Education not excepted. These have, of course, important, delicate, and highly discretionary functions, but none that they may not perform within the limits of the Bill of Rights. That they are educating the young for citizenship is reason for scrupulous protection of Constitutional freedoms of the individual, if we are not to strangle the free mind at its source and teach youth to discount important principles of our government as mere platitudes.

Such Boards are numerous and their territorial jurisdiction often small. But small and local authority may feel less sense of responsibility to the Constitution, and agencies of publicity may be less vigilant in calling it to account. The action of Congress in making flag observance voluntary and respecting the conscience of the objector in a matter so vital as raising the Army contrasts sharply with these local regulations in matters relatively trivial to the welfare of the nation. There are village tyrants as well as village Hampdens, but none who acts under color of law is beyond reach of the Constitution.

3. The *Gobitis* opinion reasoned that this is a field "where courts possess no marked and certainly no controlling competence," that it is committed to the legislatures as well as the courts to guard cherished liberties and that it is constitutionally appropriate to "fight out the wise use of legislative authority in the forum of public opinion and before legislative assemblies rather than to transfer such a contest to the judicial arena," since all the "effective means of inducing political changes are left free."  . . .

The very purpose of a Bill of Rights was to withdraw certain subjects from the vicissitudes of political controversy, to place them beyond the reach of majorities and officials and to establish them as legal principles to be applied by the courts. One's right to life, liberty, and property, to free speech, a free press, freedom of worship and assembly, and other fundamental rights may not be submitted to vote; they depend on the outcome of no elections.

In weighing arguments of the parties it is important to distinguish between the due process clause of the Fourteenth Amendment as an instrument for transmitting the principles of the First Amendment and those cases in which it is applied for its own sake. The test of legislation which collides with the Fourteenth Amendment, because it also collides with the principles of the First, is much more definite than the test when only the Fourteenth is involved. Much of the vagueness of the due process clause disappears when the specific prohibitions of the First become its standard. The right of a State to regulate, for example, a public utility may well include, so far as the due process test is concerned, power to impose all of the restrictions which a legislature may have a "rational basis" for adopting. But freedoms of speech and of press, of assembly, and of worship may not be infringed on such slender grounds. They are susceptible of restriction only to prevent grave and immediate danger to interests which the State may lawfully protect. It is important to note that while it is the Fourteenth Amendment which bears directly upon the State it is the more specific limiting principles of the First Amendment that finally govern this case.

Nor does our duty to apply the Bill of Rights to assertions of official authority depend upon our possession of marked competence in the field where the invasion of rights occurs. True, the task of translating the majestic generalities of the Bill of Rights, conceived as part of the pattern of liberal government in the eighteenth century, into concrete restraints on officials dealing with the problems of the twentieth century, is one to disturb self-confidence. These principles grew in soil which also produced a philosophy that the individual was the center of society, that his liberty was attainable through mere absence of governmental restraints, and that government should be entrusted with few controls and only the mildest supervision over men's affairs. We must transplant these rights to a soil in which the *laissez-faire* concept or principle of non-interference has withered at least as to economic affairs, and social advancements are increasingly sought through closer integration of society and through expanded and strengthened governmental controls. These changed conditions often deprive precedents of reliability and cast us more than we would choose upon our own judgment. But we act in these matters not by authority of our competence but by force of our commissions. We cannot, because of modest estimates of our competence in such specialties as public education, withhold the judgment that history authenticates as the function of this Court when liberty is infringed.

4. Lastly, and this is the very heart of the *Gobitis* opinion, it reasons that "National unity is the basis of national security," that the authorities have "the right to select appropriate means for its attainment," and hence reaches the conclusion that such compulsory measures toward "national unity" are constitutional. . . . Upon the verity of this assumption depends our answer in this case.

National unity as an end which officials may foster by persuasion and example is not in question. The problem is whether under our Constitution compulsion as here employed is a permissible means for its achievement.

Struggles to coerce uniformity of sentiment in support of some end thought essential to their time and country have been waged by many good as well as by evil men. Nationalism is a relatively recent phenomenon but at other times and places the ends have been racial or territorial security, support of a dynasty or regime, and particular plans for saving souls. As first and moderate methods to attain unity have failed, those bent on its accomplishment must resort to an ever-increasing severity. As governmental pressure toward unity becomes greater, so strife becomes more bitter as to whose unity it shall be. Probably no deeper division of our people could proceed from any provocation than from finding it necessary to choose what doctrine and whose program public educational officials shall compel youth to unite in embracing. Ultimate futility of such attempts to compel coherence is the lesson of every such effort from the Roman drive to stamp out Christianity as a disturber of its pagen unity, the Inquisition, as a means to religious and dynastic unity, the Siberian exiles as a means of Russian unity, down to the fast failing efforts of our present totalitarian enemies. Those who begin coercive elimination of dissent soon find themselves exterminating dissenters. Compulsory unification of opinion achieves only the unanimity of the graveyard.

It seems trite but necessary to say that the First Amendment to our Constitution was designed to avoid these ends by avoiding these beginnings. There is no mysticism in the American concept of the State or of the nature or origin of its authority. We set up government by consent of the governed, and the Bill of Rights denies those in power any legal opportunity to coerce that consent. Authority here is to be controlled by public opinion, not public opinion by authority.

The case is made difficult not because the principles of its decision are obscure but because the flag involved is our own. Nevertheless, we apply the limitations of the Constitution with no fear that freedom to be intellectually and spiritually diverse or even contrary will disintegrate the social organization. To believe that patriotism will not flourish if patriotic ceremonies are voluntary and spontaneous instead of a compulsory routine is to make an unflattering estimate of the appeal of our institutions to free minds. We can have intellectual individualism and the rich cultural diversities that we owe to exceptional minds only at the price of occasional eccentricity and abnormal attitudes. When they are so harmless to others or to the State as those we deal with here, the price is not too great. But freedom to differ is not limited to things that do not matter much. That would be a mere shadow of freedom. The test of its substance is the right to differ as to things that touch the heart of the existing order.

If there is any fixed star in our constitutional constellation, it is that no official, high or petty, can prescribe what shall be orthodox in politics, nationalism, religion, or other matters of opinion or force citizens to confess by word or act their faith therein. If there are any circumstances which permit an exception, they do not now occur to us.

We think the action of the local authorities in compelling the flag salute and pledge transcends constitutional limitations on their power and invades the sphere of intellect and spirit which it is the purpose of the First Amendment to our Constitution to reserve from all official control.

The decision of this Court in Minersville School District v. Gobitis and the holdings of those few *per curiam* decisions which preceded and foreshadowed it are overruled, and the judgment enjoining enforcement of the West Virginia Regulation is
    Affirmed.

### NOTES AND QUESTIONS

1.  Is West Va. v. Barnette a religion case? The Court indicates that its decision in this case would have been no different if the plaintiffs had not been Jehovah's Witnesses: "Nor does the issue as we see it turn on one's possession of particular religious views or the sincerity with which they are held" and "It is not necessary to inquire whether nonconformist beliefs will exempt from the duty to salute unless we first find power to make the salute a legal duty." Thus, a non-religious student or even a teacher could have challenged the flag salute if it had been made part of his teaching duties. See, Russo v. Central School Dist., 469 F.2d 623 (2d Cir. 1972), cert. den., 411 U.S. 932, 93 S.Ct. 1899, 36 L.Ed.2d 391. If Barnette is not a religion case, then what do you think is a precise description of the interest put forth by plaintiffs and protected by the Court from invasion by the state's compulsory flag salute?

2.  The Court assumes that an essential feature of speech is that it is an expression of the mind; thus, in this sense, speech acts are mental acts. "The compulsory flag salute and pledge requires affirmation of a belief and an attitude of mind." If the state can compel a person to commit speech acts, perhaps, in time, the state will come to control part of that person's mind, but state control of citizens' minds is unconstitutional: "If there is any fixed star in our constitutional constellation, it is that no official, high or petty, can prescribe what shall be orthodox in politics, nationalism, religion, or other matters of opinion or force citizens to confess by word or act their faith therein." The state's compulsory flag salute sought to achieve "the compulsory unification of opinion [which the Court believed] achieves only the unanimity of the graveyard." The Court thought it "trite but necessary to say that the First Amendment to our Constitution was designed to avoid these ends by avoiding these beginnings."

3.  Does Barnette adumbrate a constitutional theory and method of education about controversial issues that is based on a profound respect for a child's developing mind and on the theory of pluralism underlying

Pierce? The Court expressly approved state power to reach the end sought by the flag salute: "the state may 'require teaching by instruction and study of all in our history and in the structure and organization of our government, including the guarantees of civil liberty, which tend to inspire patriotism and love of country.'" The means was the problem: the "issue here is whether this slow and easily neglected route to aroused loyalties constitutionally may be short-cut by substituting a compulsory salute and slogan." What is it that is unconstitutionally lost when the state takes such a short-cut? Is the constitutional difference between a "slow and easily neglected route to aroused loyalties" and the short-cut of a compulsory flag salute that of respect for a student's developing mind; i. e., a constitutionally required respect that permits teachers and schools, when dealing in controversial areas of "politics, nationalism, religion or other matters of opinion," to present facts and ideas to a student's mind but prohibits teachers and schools from requiring a student to declare his belief in any specific but debatable opinion? In other words, the student has a constitutional right to develop his own opinions and cannot be compelled by the state to hold any particular opinion. Does this analysis distinguish a compulsory flag salute from compulsory instruction in American civics? What are the implications of Barnette for the ways in which teachers of history, political science, social studies and other similar subjects should present and examine over their materials?

4.  Is it important to the decision in Barnette to distinguish between a person's action that affects others and a person's action that does not and concerns only that person's claim of free expression against the government? Why? Would the decision have been different if the flag salute were optional rather than compulsory? Does government have constitutional power to prescribe an optional or discretionary "voluntary" flag salute? The lower federal court in Barnette "restrained enforcement [of the flag salute requirement] as to the plaintiffs and those of that class"; i. e., all students who object to the flag salute and not just Jehovah's Witnesses. The U. S. Supreme Court ruled that "the judgment enjoining enforcement of the West Virginia Regulation is affirmed." What does this mean? If, as set forth above, the vice of the flag salute was compulsory indoctrination, why should the Court leave open the possibility of a voluntary flag salute? Isn't it likely that the non-objecting students need constitutional protection from indoctrination more than objecting students? Can there really be a purely "voluntary" flag salute? If the flag salute is compulsory, and a student or teacher refuses to salute the flag, can school authorities require that he leave the room or stand silently during the ceremony? See, Goetz v. Ansell, 477 F.2d 636 (2nd Cir. 1973); Frain v. Baron, 307 F.Supp. 27 (E.D.N.Y.1969); Banks v. Bd. of Public Instruction, 314 F.Supp. 285 (S.D.Fla.1970) precluding expulsion of a student who refused to stand silently during the pledge of allegiance, and Sheldon v. Fannin, 221 F.Supp. 766 (D.Ariz.1963) precluding expulsion of student who refused to stand during singing of National Anthem.

5.  Must a school's "Hidden Curriculum" respond to Barnette's general premises against compulsory indoctrination? A public school is a social institution in the same sense that hospitals, state universities and

prisons are. Each has a set of defined social purposes and a set of fundamental rules that create a framework within which people work to achieve the institution's purposes. One author, S. Sarason, in THE CULTURE OF THE SCHOOL AND THE PROBLEM OF CHANGE (1971), states that although the curricular importance of the under-lying framework by the rules for a school is easily overlooked, because it cannot be seen physically, it can be a powerful teaching mechanism, especially in elementary school. For example, those who instruct are powerful and are adults and those who should receive instruction are powerless and are children. The standing, adult teacher dominates the classroom asking seated, children questions which they must respond to, but children, in return, are permitted to ask very few questions of the teacher. Adults are to be left alone with other adults except when they are obliged to be in the class or lunchrooms, and children must line up or wait for recess or for the word of an adult to go to the bathroom or to be dismissed. The teacher decides what the children will do; the teacher evaluates their performances, including evaluation of such things as "cooperates" or "listens attentively" or "follows rules" or "is courteous and considerate" or "has good citizenship," and maintains order and discipline, especially where student-teacher ratios are excessive.

All of this may be necessary, but it does convey a set of values which children must absorb and master *before* successfully getting on to their primary educational business in a school. The messages conveyed by the hidden curriculum are that life, at least in school, is properly structured hierarchically with a leader at the top (the totalitarian model?); that decisions and orders properly flow from those people at the top (adults) to those at the bottom, and that those children who do not conform (e. g., to line up) can be punished, perhaps physically, while those who do conform are rewarded. Often, a child who fails to master the hidden curriculum withdraws. A teacher may report the withdrawal of a child as his not even trying to do his "spelling," and he is, therefore, unmotivated, when, in truth, the child has withdrawn because he has not mastered the hidden curriculum, or may be fearful of its reward system. Children who successfully master the hidden curriculum may have deeply internalized a set of values more in harmony with totalitarian rather than democratic structures. Consider whether a school's hidden curriculum is consistent with Barnette's theories and with those theories found in other cases in this chapter? (For general discussion, see Jackson, The Student's World, 66 Elementary School J. 345 (1966)).

6. The U. S. Supreme Court reaffirmed its decision in Barnette in Wooley v. Maynard, 430 U.S. 705, 97 S.Ct. 1428, 51 L.Ed.2d 752 (1977). Jehovah's Witnesses objected to New Hampshire's law requiring passenger automobiles to carry license plates which displayed the state motto: "Live Free or Die." Analogizing this situation to Barnette's compulsory flag-salute, the Supreme Court struck down New Hampshire's law, ruling that the first amendment's protection of freedom of thought "includes both the right to speak freely and the right to refrain from speaking at all" and that both rights are "complementary components of a broader concept of 'individual freedom of mind.'"

## FREEDOM FROM GOVERNMENTALLY COMPELLED
## IGNORANCE

---

### MEYER v. NEBRASKA

Supreme Court of the United States, 1923.
262 U.S. 390, 43 S.Ct. 625, 67 L.Ed. 1042.

Mr. Justice McREYNOLDS delivered the opinion of the Court.

Plaintiff in error [Meyer] was tried and convicted in the District Court for Hamilton County, Nebraska, under an information which charged that on May 25, 1920, while an instructor in Zion Parochial School, he unlawfully taught the subject of reading in the German language to Raymond Parpart, a child of ten years, who had not attained and successfully passed the eighth grade. The information is based upon "An act relating to the teaching of foreign languages in the State of Nebraska," . . .

"Section 1. No person, individually or as a teacher, shall, in any private, denominational, parochial or public school, teach any subject to any person in any language other than the English language.

"Sec. 2. Languages, other than the English language, may be taught as languages only after a pupil shall have attained and successfully passed the eighth grade as evidenced by a certificate of graduation issued by the county superintendent of the county in which the child resides.

"Sec. 3. Any person who violates any of the provisions of this act shall be deemed guilty of a misdemeanor and upon conviction, shall be subject to a fine of not less than twenty-five dollars ($25), nor more than one hundred dollars ($100) or be confined in the county jail for any period not exceeding thirty days for each offense.

"Sec. 4. Whereas, an emergency exists, this act shall be in force from and after its passage and approval."

The Supreme Court of the State affirmed the judgment of conviction. . . . It declared the offense charged and established was "the direct and intentional teaching of the German language as a distinct subject to a child who had not passed the eighth grade," in the parochial school maintained by Zion Evangelical Lutheran Congregation, a collection of Biblical stories being used therefor. And it held that the statute forbidding this did not conflict with the Fourteenth Amendment, but was a valid exercise of the police power. The following excerpts from the opinion sufficiently indicate the reasons advanced to support the conclusion.

"The salutary purpose of the statute is clear. The legislature had seen the baneful effects of permitting foreigners, who had taken residence in this country, to rear and educate their children in the language of their native land. The result of that condition was found to be inimical to our own safety. To allow the children of foreigners, who had emigrated here, to be taught from early childhood the language of the country of their parents was to rear them with that language as their mother tongue. It was to educate them so that they must always think in that language, and, as a consequence, naturally inculcate in them the ideas and sentiments foreign to the best interests of this country. The statute, therefore, was intended not only to require that the education of all children be conducted in the English language, but that, until they had grown into that language and until it had become a part of them, they should not in the schools be taught any other language. The obvious purpose of this statute was that the English language should be and become the mother tongue of all children reared in this state. The enactment of such a statute comes reasonably within the police power of the state. . . .

"It is suggested that the law is an unwarranted restriction, in that it applies to all citizens of the state and arbitrarily interferes with the rights of citizens who are not of foreign ancestry, and prevents them, without reason, from having their children taught foreign languages in school. That argument is not well taken, for it assumes that every citizen finds himself restrained by the statute. The hours which a child is able to devote to study in the confinement of school are limited. It must have ample time for exercise or play. Its daily capacity for learning is comparatively small. A selection of subjects for its education, therefore, from among the many that might be taught, is obviously necessary. The legislature no doubt had in mind the practical operation of the law. The law affects few citizens, except those of foreign lineage. Other citizens, in their selection of studies, except perhaps in rare instances, have never deemed it of importance to teach their children foreign languages before such children have reached the eighth grade. In the legislative mind, the salutary effect of the statute no doubt outweighed the restriction upon the citizens generally, which, it appears, was a restriction of no real consequence."

The problem for our determination is whether the statute as construed and applied unreasonably infringes the liberty guaranteed to the plaintiff in error by the Fourteenth Amendment. "No State shall . . . deprive any person of life, liberty, or property, without due process of law."

While this Court has not attempted to define with exactness the liberty thus guaranteed, the term has received much consideration and some of the included things have been definitely stated. Without doubt, it denotes not merely freedom from bodily restraint but also the right of the individual to contract, to engage in any of the common occupations of life, to acquire useful knowledge, to marry, establish a home and bring up children, to worship God according to the dictates of his own conscience, and generally to enjoy those privileges long recognized at common law as essential to the orderly pursuit of happiness by free men.   .   .   .   The established doctrine is that this liberty may not be interfered with, under the guise of protecting the public interest, by legislative action which is arbitrary or without reasonable relation to some purpose within the competency of the State to effect.   Determination by the legislature of what constitutes proper exercise of police power is not final or conclusive but is subject to supervision by the courts.   .   .   .

The American people have always regarded education and acquisition of knowledge as matters of supreme importance which should be diligently promoted.   The Ordinance of 1787 declares, "Religion, morality, and knowledge being necessary to good government and the happiness of mankind, schools and the means of education shall forever be encouraged."   Corresponding to the right of control, it is the natural duty of the parent to give his children education suitable to their station in life;  and nearly all the States, including Nebraska, enforce this obligation by compulsory laws.

Practically, education of the young is only possible in schools conducted by especially qualified persons who devote themselves thereto.   The calling always has been regarded as useful and honorable, essential, indeed, to the public welfare.   Mere knowledge of the German language cannot reasonably be regarded as harmful.   Heretofore it has been commonly looked upon as helpful and desirable.   Plaintiff in error taught this language in school as part of his occupation.   His right thus to teach and the right of parents to engage him so to instruct their children, we think, are within the liberty of the Amendment.

The challenged statute forbids the teaching in school of any subject except in English;  also the teaching of any other language until the pupil has attained and successfully passed the eighth grade, which is not usually accomplished before the age of twelve.   The Supreme Court of the State has held that "the so-called ancient or dead languages" are not "within the spirit or the purpose of the act."   .   .   .   Latin, Greek, Hebrew are not proscribed;  but German, French, Spanish, Italian and every other alien speech are within the ban.   Evidently the legislature has attempted materially to interfere with the calling of modern language teachers, with the opportunities of pupils to acquire knowledge, and with the power of parents to control the education of their own.

It is said the purpose of the legislation was to promote civic development by inhibiting training and education of the immature in foreign tongues and ideals before they could learn English and acquire American ideals;  and "that the English language should be and become the mother tongue of all children reared in this State." It is also affirmed that the foreign born population is very large, that certain communities commonly use foreign words, follow foreign leaders, move in a foreign atmosphere, and that the children are thereby hindered from becoming citizens of the most useful type and the public safety is imperiled.

That the State may do much, go very far, indeed, in order to improve the quality of its citizens, physically, mentally and morally, is clear; but the individual has certain fundamental rights which must be respected. The protection of the Constitution extends to all, to those who speak other languages as well as to those born with English on the tongue. Perhaps it would be highly advantageous if all had ready understanding of our ordinary speech, but this cannot be coerced by methods which conflict with the Constitution—a desirable end cannot be promoted by prohibited means.

For the welfare of his Ideal Commonwealth, Plato suggested a law which should provide: "That the wives of our guardians are to be common, and their children are to be common, and no parent is to know his own child, nor any child his parent. . . . The proper officers will take the offspring of the good parents to the pen or fold, and there they will deposit them with certain nurses who dwell in a separate quarter; but the offspring of the inferior, or of the better when they chance to be deformed, will be put away in some mysterious, unknown place, as they should be." In order to submerge the individual and develop ideal citizens, Sparta assembled the males at seven into barracks and intrusted their subsequent education and training to official guardians. Although such measures have been deliberately approved by men of great genius, their ideas touching the relation between individual and State were wholly different from those upon which our institutions rest; and it hardly will be affirmed that any legislature could impose such restrictions upon the people of a State without doing violence to both letter and spirit of the Constitution.

The desire of the legislature to foster a homogeneous people with American ideals prepared readily to understand current discussions of civic matters is easy to appreciate. Unfortunate experiences during the late war and aversion toward every characteristic of truculent adversaries were certainly enough to quicken that aspiration. But the means adopted, we think, exceed the limitations upon the power of the State and conflict with rights assured to plaintiff in error. The interference is plain enough and no adequate reason therefor in time of peace and domestic tranquility has been shown.

The power of the State to compel attendance at some school and to make reasonable regulations for all schools, including a requirement that they shall give instructions in English, is not questioned. Nor has challenge been made of the State's power to prescribe a curriculum for institutions which it supports. Those matters are not within the present controversy. Our concern is with the prohibition approved by the Supreme Court.   .   .   .   No emergency has arisen which renders knowledge by a child of some language other than English so clearly harmful as to justify its inhibition with the consequent infringement of rights long freely enjoyed. We are constrained to conclude that the statute as applied is arbitrary and without reasonable relation to any end within the competency of the State.

As the statute undertakes to interfere only with teaching which involves a modern language, leaving complete freedom as to other matters, there seems no adequate foundation for the suggestion that the purpose was to protect the child's health by limiting his mental activities. It is well known that proficiency in a foreign language seldom comes to one not instructed at an early age, and experience shows that this is not injurious to the health, morals or understanding of the ordinary child.

The judgment of the court below must be reversed and the cause remanded for further proceedings not inconsistent with this opinion.

Reversed.

Mr. Justice HOLMES, with whom Mr. Justice SUTHERLAND concurred, dissented. His opinion appears in a companion case, Bartels v. Iowa, 262 U.S. 407   .   .   .

"We all agree, I take it, that it is desirable that all the citizens of the United States should speak a common tongue, and therefore that the end aimed at by the statute is a lawful and proper one. The only question is whether the means adopted deprive teachers of the liberty secured to them by the Fourteenth Amendment. It is with hesitation and unwillingness that I differ from my brethren with regard to a law like this but I cannot bring my mind to believe that in some circumstances, and circumstances existing it is said in Nebraska, the statute might not be regarded as a reasonable or even necessary method of reaching the desired result. The part of the act with which we are concerned deals with the teaching of young children. Youth is the time when familiarity with a language is established and if there are sections in the State where a child would hear only Polish or French or German spoken at home I am not prepared to say that it is unreasonable to provide that in his early years he shall hear and speak only English at school. But if it is reasonable it is not an undue restriction of the liberty either of teacher or scholar. No one would doubt that a teacher might be forbidden to teach many things, and the only criterion of his liberty under the Constitution that I can think of is 'whether, considering the end in view, the statute passes the bounds of reason and assumes the character of a merely arbitrary fiat.'   .   .   .   I think I appreciate the objection to the law but it appears to me to present a question upon which men reasonably might differ and therefore I am unable to say that the Constitution of the United States prevents the experiment being tried."

## NOTES AND QUESTIONS

1.  In Farrington v. T. Tokushige, 273 U.S. 284, 47 S.Ct. 406, 71 L.Ed. 646 (1927) the Supreme Court held unconstitutional the Foreign Language School Act of Hawaii which applied to private schools and which was similar to Nebraska's. See also, Mo Hock Ke Lok Po v. Stainback, 74 F.Supp. 852 (D.Hawaii 1947) which held unconstitutional subsequent legislation prohibiting the teaching of a foreign language to children below a specified age or grade, reversed on other grounds, 336 U.S. 368, 69 S.Ct. 606, 93 L.Ed. 741 (1949). What is the extent to which a state might regulate the curriculum of a private school? State v. Williams, 253 N.C. 337, 117 S.E.2d 444 (1960) is one of the rare recent cases considering constitutional limitations on a state's power to regulate private schools. For general discussion, see, J. Elson, "State Regulation of Nonpublic Schools: The Legal Framework," in Erickson (ed.), PUBLIC CONTROLS FOR PUBLIC SCHOOLS (1969).

2.  In *Meyer,* the Court refers to (1) the constitutional liberty of a teacher to pursue his profession; (2) the constitutional liberty of children to obtain useful information and education, and (3) the constitutional liberty of parents to direct the education of their children. Are these three freedoms consistent and interrelated? In all instances? Compare the underlying theory of *Meyer* with that of *Pierce.* Each case, it appears, is ultimately grounded in a constitutional theory of democratic pluralism that denies the state unified and sole sovereign control over its citizens. Looked at this way, Meyer's three liberties (that of a teacher's, a student's and his parents) can be consistent and harmonious in many instances. But, does Meyer yield guidance in situations where the teacher's liberty conflicts with that of the parents' regarding the education of a child; for example, if a teacher seeks to introduce sex education topics into a speech class and a parent objects? Does Meyer tell us which of the three constitutional liberties should prevail?

3.  The Meyer case involved a private school, and was decided before the First Amendment was incorporated into the Fourteenth. If it were decided today, it probably would be decided on First Amendment academic freedom grounds. Does Meyer apply to the public schools? Could a public school discharge a teacher who injected prohibited materials into his course? Does the Meyer case lay a constitutional foundation for parents to select courses for their children from the elective portions of a public school's curriculum? Most fundamentally, if a state legislature passed a law just like Nebraska's and it applied only to the public schools, would the law be ruled unconstitutional? When answering this question consider Meyer, Pierce and the following case.

## EPPERSON v. ARKANSAS

Supreme Court of the United States, 1968.
393 U.S. 97, 89 S.Ct. 266, 21 L.Ed.2d 228.

Mr. Justice FORTAS delivered the opinion of the Court.

This appeal challenges the constitutionality of the "anti-evolution" statute which the State of Arkansas adopted in 1928 to prohibit the teaching in its public schools and universities of the theory that man evolved from other species of life. The statute was a product of the upsurge of "fundamentalist" religious fervor of the twenties. The Arkansas statute was an adaption of the famous Tennessee "monkey law" which that State adopted in 1925. The constitutionality of the Tennessee law was upheld by the Tennessee Supreme Court in the celebrated *Scopes* case in 1927.

The Arkansas law makes it unlawful for a teacher in any state-supported school or university "to teach the theory or doctrine that mankind ascended or descended from a lower order of animals," or "to adopt or use in any such institution a textbook that teaches" this theory. Violation is a misdemeanor and subjects the violator to dismissal from his position.

The present case concerns the teaching of biology in a high school in Little Rock. According to the testimony, until the events here in litigation, the official textbook furnished for the high school biology course did not have a section on the Darwinian Theory. Then, for the academic year 1965–1966, the school administration, on recommendation of the teachers of biology in the school system, adopted and prescribed a textbook which contained a chapter setting forth "the theory about the origin   *   *   *   of man from a lower form of animal."

Susan Epperson, a young woman who graduated from Arkansas' school system and then obtained her master's degree in zoology at the University of Illinois, was employed by the Little Rock school system in the fall of 1964 to teach 10th grade biology at Central High School. At the start of the next academic year, 1965, she was confronted by the new textbook (which one surmises from the record was not unwelcome to her). She faced at least a literal dilemma because she was supposed to use the new textbook for classroom instruction and presumably to teach the statutorily condemned chapter; but to do so would be a criminal offense and subject her to dismissal.

She instituted the present action in the Chancery Court of the State, seeking a declaration that the Arkansas statute is void and enjoining the State and the defendant officials of the Little Rock school system from dismissing her for violation of the statute's provisions. H. H. Blanchard, a parent of children attending the public schools, intervened in support of the action.

The Chancery Court, in an opinion by Chancellor Murray O. Reed, held that the statute violated the Fourteenth Amendment to the United States Constitution. The court noted that this Amendment encompasses the prohibitions upon state interference with freedom of speech and thought which are contained in the First Amendment. Accordingly, it held that the challenged statute is unconstitutional because, in violation of the First Amendment, it "tends to hinder the quest for knowledge, restrict the freedom to learn, and restrain the freedom to teach." In this perspective, the Act, it held, was an unconstitutional and void restraint upon the freedom of speech guaranteed by the Constitution.

On appeal, the Supreme Court of Arkansas reversed [in a two sentence opinion]. . . . It sustained the statute as an exercise of the State's power to specify the curriculum in public schools. It did not address itself to the competing constitutional considerations. . . .

. . . It is of no moment whether the law is deemed to prohibit mention of Darwin's theory, or to forbid any or all of the infinite varieties of communication embraced within the term "teaching." Under either interpretation, the law must be stricken because of its conflict with the constitutional prohibition of state laws respecting an establishment of religion or prohibiting the free exercise thereof. The overriding fact is that Arkansas' law selects from the body of knowledge a particular segment which it proscribes for the sole reason that it is deemed to conflict with a particular religious doctrine; that is, with a particular interpretation of the Book of Genesis by a particular religious group.

The antecedents of today's decision are many and unmistakable. They are rooted in the foundation soil of our Nation. They are fundamental to freedom. . . .

Judicial interposition in the operation of the public school system of the Nation raises problems requiring care and restraint. Our courts, however, have not failed to apply the First Amendment's mandate in our educational system where essential to safeguard the fundamental values of freedom of speech and inquiry and of belief. By and large, public education in our Nation is committed to the control of state and local authorities. Courts do not and cannot intervene in the resolution of conflicts which arise in the daily operation of school systems and which do not directly and sharply implicate basic constitutional values. On the other hand, "[t]he vigilant protection of constitutional freedoms is nowhere more vital than in the community of American schools," Shelton v. Tucker, . . . As this Court said in Keyishian v. Board of Regents, the First Amendment "does not tolerate laws that cast a pall of orthodoxy over the classroom." . . .

The earliest cases in this Court on the subject of the impact of constitutional guarantees upon the classroom were decided before the Court expressly applied the specific prohibitions of the First Amendment to the States.  But as early as 1923, the Court did not hesitate to condemn under the Due Process Clause "arbitrary" restrictions upon the freedom of teachers to teach and of students to learn.  In that year, the Court, in an opinion by Justice McReynolds, held unconstitutional an Act of the State of Nebraska making it a crime to teach any subject in any language other than English to pupils who had not passed the eighth grade.  The State's purpose in enacting the law was to promote civic cohesiveness by encouraging the learning of English and to combat the "baneful effect" of permitting foreigners to rear and educate their children in the language of the parents' native land.  The Court recognized these purposes, and it acknowledged the State's power to prescribe the school curriculum, but it held that these were not adequate to support the restriction upon the liberty of teacher and pupil.  The challenged statute it held, unconstitutionally interfered with the right of the individual, guaranteed by the Due Process Clause, to engage in any of the common occupations of life and to acquire useful knowledge.  Meyer v. Nebraska,  . . .

There is and can be no doubt that the First Amendment does not permit the State to require that teaching and learning must be tailored to the principles or prohibitions of any religious sect or dogma.  . . .

. . .  The State's undoubted right to prescribe the curriculum for its public schools does not carry with it the right to prohibit, on pain of criminal penalty, the teaching of a scientific theory or doctrine where that prohibition is based upon reasons that violate the First Amendment.  It is much too late to argue that the State may impose upon the teachers in its schools any conditions that it chooses, however restrictive they may be of constitutional guarantees.  Keyishian v. Board of Regents,  . . .

In the present case, there can be no doubt that Arkansas has sought to prevent its teachers from discussing the theory of evolution because it is contrary to the belief of some that the Book of Genesis must be the execlusive source of doctrine as to the origin of man.  No suggestion has been made that Arkansas' law may be justified by considerations of state policy other than the religious views of some of its citizens.  It is clear that fundamentalist sectarian conviction was and is the law's reason for existence.  Its antecedent, Tennessee's "monkey law," candidly stated its purpose: to make it unlawful "to teach any theory that denies the story of the Divine Creation of man as taught in the Bible, and to teach instead that man has descended from a lower order of animals."  Perhaps the sensational publicity attendant upon the *Scopes* trial induced Arkansas to adopt less explicit language.  It eliminated Tennessee's reference to "the story of the Divine Creation of man" as taught in the Bible, but there is no doubt that the motivation for the law was the same: to suppress the teaching of a theory which, it was thought, "denied" the divine creation of man.

Arkansas' law cannot be defended as an act of religious neutrality. Arkansas did not seek to excise from the curricula of its schools and universities all discussion of the origin of man. The law's effort was confined to an attempt to blot out a particular theory because of its supposed conflict with the Biblical account, literally read. Plainly, the law is contrary to the mandate of the First, and in violation of the Fourteenth, Amendment to the Constitution.

The judgment of the Supreme Court of Arkansas is reversed.

Reversed.

Mr. Justice BLACK, concurring.  .  .  .

It is plain that a state law prohibiting all teaching of human development or biology is constitutionally quite different from a law that compels a teacher to teach as true only one theory of a given doctrine. It would be difficult to make a First Amendment case out of a state law eliminating the subject of higher mathematics, or astronomy, or biology from its curriculum. And, for all the Supreme Court of Arkansas has said, this particular Act may prohibit that and nothing else. This Court, however, treats the Arkansas Act as though it made it a misdemeanor to teach or to use a book that teaches that evolution is true. But it is not for this Court to arrogate to itself the power to determine the scope of Arkansas statutes. Since the highest court of Arkansas has deliberately refused to give its statute that meaning, we should not presume to do so.

It seems to me that in this situation the statute is too vague for us to strike it down on any ground but that: vagueness. Under this statute as construed by the Arkansas Supreme Court, a teacher cannot know whether he is forbidden to mention Darwin's theory, at all or only free to discuss it as long as he refrains from contending that it is true. It is an established rule that a statute which leaves an ordinary man so doubtful about its meaning that he cannot know when he has violated it denies him the first essential of due process.  .  .  .  Holding the statute too vague to enforce would not only follow long-standing constitutional precedents but it would avoid having this Court take unto itself the duty of a State's highest court to interpret and mark the boundaries of the State's laws. And, more important, it would not place this Court in the unenviable position of violating the principle of leaving the States absolutely free to choose their own curriculums for their own schools so long as their action does not palpably conflict with a clear constitutional command.  .  .  .

Mr. Justice STEWART, concurring in the result.

The States are most assuredly free "to choose their own curriculums for their own schools." A State is entirely free, for example, to decide that the only foreign language to be taught in its public school system shall be Spanish.  But would a State be constitutionally free to punish a teacher for letting his students know that other languages are also spoken in the world?  I think not.

It is one thing for a State to determine that "the subject of higher mathematics, or astronomy, or biology" shall or shall not be included in its public school curriculum.  It is quite another thing for a State to make it a criminal offense for a public school teacher so much as to mention the very existence of an entire system of respected human thought.  That kind of criminal law, I think, would clearly impinge upon the guarantees of free communication contained in the First Amendment, and made applicable to the States by the Fourteenth.

The Arkansas Supreme Court has said that the statute before us may or may not be just such a law.  The result, as Mr. Justice BLACK points out, is that "a teacher cannot know whether he is forbidden to mention Darwin's theory at all."  Since I believe that no State could constitutionally forbid a teacher "to mention Darwin's theory at all," and since Arkansas may, or may not, have done just that, I conclude that the statute before us is so vague as to be invalid under the Fourteenth Amendment.

## NOTES AND QUESTIONS

1.  The first case was Scopes v. Tennessee, 154 Tenn. 105, 289 S.W. 363 (1927) (the "Monkey Trial" case) which drew world attention.  William Jennings Bryan and Clarence Darrow were the two lawyers pitted against each other.  Scopes was tried for having taught "a certain theory [of evolution] that denied the story of the divine creation of man, as taught in the Bible  .  .  .".  H. L. Mencken referred to the trial as an example of "American boobery."  Scopes was convicted, but his conviction was reversed on appeal; however, as Epperson shows, the issue did not disappear.

2.  The usual presumption attendant upon a statute is that it is constitutional, and it is necessary for the party asserting its unconstitutionality to carry the burden of proof.  In Epperson, the Court assumed that the statute in question had a religious purpose and the burden of proving its constitutionality fell upon the state.  Why should the Court reverse the presumption of constitutionality in this case?

3.  Religious freedom is the justifying rationale of the Supreme Court for its decision in Epperson.  The First Amendment's guarantee of religious freedom requires a state to be neutral toward religion, neither aiding nor hindering it.  In what way did Arkansas' statute aid religion?

4.  In 1973 Tennessee's legislature passed the following law (73 Tenn.Pub. Acts, Ch. 377):

     Any biology textbook used for teaching in the public schools, which expresses an opinion of, or relates a theory about origins or creation of man and his world shall be prohibited from being used as a textbook in such system unless it specifically states that it is a theory as to the origin and creation of man and his world and is not represented to be scientific fact.  Any textbook so used in the public education system which expresses an opinion or relates to a theory or theories shall give in the same textbook and under the same subject commensurate attention to, and an equal amount of emphasis on, the origins and creation of man and his world as the same is recorded in other theories, including, but not limited to, the Genesis account in the Bible.  .   .   . The teaching of all occult or satanical beliefs of human origin is expressly excluded from this Act.  Provided, however, that the Holy Bible shall not be defined as a textbook, but is hereby declared to be a reference work and shall not be required to carry the disclaimer above provided for textbooks.

Does this statute meet the requirements of Epperson?  It came before the Court of Appeals for the Sixth Circuit in Daniel v. Waters, 515 F.2d 485 (6th Cir., 1975), which ruled:

".   .   . the statute complained of does not directly forbid the teaching of evolution.  It does, however, prohibit the selection of any textbook which teaches evolution unless it also contains a disclaimer stating that such doctrine is 'a theory as to the origin and creation of man and his world and is not represented to be scientific fact.'  And the same statute expressly requires the inclusion of the Genesis version of creation (if any version at all is taught) while permitting that version alone to be printed without the above disclaimer.

"We believe that in several respects the statute under consideration is unconstitutional on its face.  .   .   .

"First, the statute requires that any textbook which expresses an opinion about the origin of man 'shall be prohibited from being used' unless the book specifically states that the opinion is 'a theory' and 'is not represented to be scientific fact.'  The statute also requires that the Biblical account of creation (and other theories of creation) be printed at the same time, with commensurate attention and equal emphasis.  As to all such theories, except only the Genesis theory, the textbook must print the disclaimer quoted above.  But the proviso in Section 2 would allow the printing of the Biblical account of creation as set forth in Genesis without any such disclaimer.  The result of this legislation is a clearly defined preferential position for a Biblical version of creation as opposed to any account of the development of man based on scientific research and reasoning.  For a state to seek to enforce such a preference by law is to seek to accomplish the very establishment of religion which the First Amendment to the Constitution of the United States squarely forbids.

"We believe the provisions of the Tennessee statute are obviously in violation of the First Amendment prohibition on any law 'respecting the establishment of religion' as that phrase has been authoritatively interpreted in Epperson v. Arkansas.  .   .   .

".   .   . the requirement of preferential treatment of the Bible clearly offends the Establishment Clause of the First Amendment, the exclusion at the end of Section 1 of the statute would inextricably involve the State Textbook Commission in the most difficult and hotly disputed of theological arguments. . . . Throughout human history the God of some men has frequently been regarded as the Devil incarnate by men of other religious persuasions.   It would be utterly impossible for the Tennessee Textbook Commission to determine which religious theories were 'occult' or 'satanical' without seeking to resolve the theological arguments which have embroiled and frustrated theologians through the ages.

"The requirement that some religious concepts of creation, adhered to presumably by some Tennessee citizens, be excluded on such grounds in favor of the Bible of the Jews and the Christians represents still another method of preferential treatment of particular faiths by state law and, of course, is forbidden by the Establishment Clause of the First Amendment.

"We deem the two constitutional violations described above to be patent and obvious on the face of the statute  .  .  .. Under these circumstances, we find no need to determine whether the terms 'occult' and 'satanical' are, as claimed by appellants, also void for vagueness under the Due Process Clause of the Fourteenth Amendment.   Nor for the same reason do we feel it is necessary or desirable to pass on appellants' claims that the statute as drawn represents violation of the Freedom of Speech and Press Clauses of the First Amendment."

5.  A student teacher who, in response to questions from his students, stated that Darwin's theory of the origin of specie and the evolution of life is a valid one, and who stated he did not attend church, believe in life after death, nor in heaven or hell, was summarily discharged after a complaint had been lodged by parents.   The court granted the teacher a judgment against school authorities ruling that the discharge was a violation of the establishment clause of the First Amendment.   Moore v. Gaston County Bd. of Educ., 357 F.Supp. 1037 (W.D.N.C.1973).

6.  Would all the requirements of Epperson be met if, today, the Arkansas legislature passed a law completely prohibiting all teaching in its public schools about any aspect of the origins of man?   Can a local school board in a racially mixed and highly urbanized city, in an attempt to contribute to racial peace and harmony, constitutionally prohibit its teachers from mentioning or otherwise informing their students of any theory about inherent genetic differences in intelligence among racial groups?   Could a "social policy and current events" teacher in the public schools be penalized if he assigned and discussed with his students materials that analyzed the validity of such theories, or would his rights to academic freedom protect him?

## FREEDOM FROM ARBITRARY CENSORSHIP OF CLASS MATERIALS

### KEEFE v. GEANAKOS

United States Court of Appeals, 1969.
418 F.2d 359 (1st Cir.).

ALDRICH, Chief Judge. . . . The plaintiff is the head of the English department and coordinator for grades 7 through 12 for the Ipswich (Massachusetts) Public School System, with part-time duties as a teacher of English. He has tenure, . . .

On the opening day of school in September 1969 the plaintiff gave to each member of his senior English class a copy of the September 1969 Atlantic Monthly magazine, a publication of high reputation, and stated that the reading assignment for that night was the first article therein. September was the educational number, so-called, of the Atlantic, and some 75 copies had been supplied by the school department. Plaintiff discussed the article, and a particular word that was used therein, and explained the word's origin and context, and the reasons the author had included it. The word, admittedly highly offensive, is a vulgar term for an incestuous son. Plaintiff stated that any student who felt the assignment personally distasteful could have an alternative one.

The next evening the plaintiff was called to a meeting of the school committee and asked to defend his use of the offending word. Following his explanation, a majority of the members of the committee asked him informally if he would agree not to use it again in the classroom. Plaintiff replied that he could not, in good conscience, agree. His counsel states, however, without contradiction, that in point of fact plaintiff has not used it again. No formal action was taken at this meeting. Thereafter plaintiff was suspended, as a matter of discipline, and it is now proposed that he should be discharged.

Reduced to fundamentals, the substance of plaintiff's position is that as a matter of law his conduct which forms the basis of the charge did not warrant discipline. Accordingly, he argues, there is no ground for any hearing. He divides this position into two parts. The principal one is that his conduct was within his competence as a teacher, as a matter of academic freedom, whether the defendants approved of it or not. The second is that he had been given inadequate prior warning by such regulations as were in force, particularly in the light of the totality of the circumstances known to him, that his actions would be considered improper, so that an ex post facto ruling would, itself, unsettle academic freedom. The defendants, essentially, deny plaintiff's contentions. They accept the existence of a principle of academic freedom to teach, but state that it is limited to proper classroom materials as reasonably determined by the school committee in the light of pertinent conditions, of which they cite in particular the age of the students.   Asked by the court whether a teacher has a right to say to the school committee that it is wrong if, in fact, its decision was arbitrary, counsel candidly and commendably (and correctly) responded in the affirmative.   This we consider to be the present issue.   In reviewing the denial of interlocutory injunctive relief, the test that we of course apply is whether there is a probability that plaintiff will prevail on the merits.

The Lifton article [The Young and the Old by Robert J. Lifton, psychiatrist and professor at Yale's Medical School] which we have read in its entirety, has been described as a valuable discussion of "dissent, protest, radicalism and revolt."   It is in no sense pornographic.  We need no supporting affidavits to find it scholarly, thoughtful and thought-provoking.   The single offending word, although repeated a number of times, is not artificially introduced, but, on the contrary, is important to the development of the thesis and the conclusions of the author.   Indeed, we would find it difficult to disagree with plaintiff's assertion that no proper study of the article could avoid consideration of this word.   It is not possible to read the article, either in whole or in part, as an incitement to libidinous conduct, or even thoughts.   If it raised the concept of incest, it was not to suggest it, but to condemn it;  the word was used, by the persons, described as as a superlative of opprobrium.   We believe not only that the article negatived any other concept, but that an understanding of it would reject, rather than suggest, the word's use.

With regard to the word itself, we cannot think that it is unknown to many students in the last year of high school, and we might well take judicial notice of its use by young radicals and protesters from coast to coast.   No doubt its use genuinely offends the parents of some of the students—therein, in part, lay its relevancy to the article.

Hence the question in this case is whether a teacher may, for demonstrated educational purposes, quote a "dirty" word currently used in order to give special offense, or whether the shock is too great for high school seniors to stand.   If the answer were that the students must be protected from such exposure, we would fear for their future. We do not question the good faith of the defendants in believing that some parents have been offended.   With the greatest of respect to such parents, their sensibilities are not the full measure of what is proper education.

We of course agree with defendants, that what is to be said or read to students is not to be determined by obscenity standards for adult consumption.   .   .   .   At the same time, the issue must be one of degree.   A high school senior is not devoid of all discrimination or resistance.   Furthermore, as in all other instances, the offensiveness of language and the particular propriety or impropriety is dependent on the circumstances of the utterance.

Apart from cases discussing academic freedom in the large, not surprisingly we find no decisions closely in point. . . . We accept the conclusion of the court below that "some measure of public regulation of classroom speech is inherent in every provision of public education." But when we consider the facts at bar as we have elaborated them, we find it difficult not to think that its application to the present case demeans any proper concept of education. The general chilling effect of permitting such rigorous censorship is even more serious.

We believe it equally probable that the plaintiff will prevail on the issue of lack of any notice that a discussion of this article with the senior class was forbidden conduct. The school regulation upon which defendants rely, although unquestionably worthy, is not apposite. It does not follow that a teacher may not be on notice of impropriety from the circumstances of a case without the necessity of a regulation. In the present case, however, the circumstances would have disclosed that no less than five books, by as many authors, containing the word in question were to be found in the school library. It is hard to think that any student could walk into the library and receive a book, but that his teacher could not subject the content to serious discussion in class.

Such inconsistency on the part of the school has been regarded as fatal. We, too, would probably so regard it. At the same time, we prefer not to place our decision on this ground alone, lest our doing so diminish our principal holding, or lead to a bowdlerization of the school library.

Finally, we are not persuaded by the district court's conclusion that no irreparable injury is involved because the plaintiff, if successful, may recover money damages. Academic freedom is not preserved by compulsory retirement, even at full pay.

The immediate question before us is whether we should grant interlocutory relief pending appeal. This question, as defendants point out, raises the ultimate issue of the appeal itself. The matter has been extensively briefed and argued by both sides. We see no purpose in taking two bites. . . . The order of the district court denying an interlocutory injunction pending a decision on the merits is reversed and the case is remanded for further proceedings consistent herewith.

## PARDUCCI v. RUTLAND

United States District Court, 1970.
316 F.Supp. 352 (M.D.Ala.).

JOHNSON, Chief Judge.

Plaintiff, a probationary teacher, was dismissed from her position as a high school teacher in the Montgomery public schools for assigning a certain short story to her junior (eleventh grade) English classes. In her complaint, which was filed with this Court on April 27, 1970, plaintiff alleges that defendants, in ordering her dismissal, violated her First Amendment right to academic freedom and her Fourteenth Amendment right to due process of law. . . .

On April 21, 1970, plaintiff assigned as outside reading to her junior English classes a story, entitled "Welcome to the Monkey House." The story, a comic satire, was selected by plaintiff to give her students a better understanding of one particular genre of western literature—the short story. The story's author, Kurt Vonnegut, Jr., is a prominent contemporary writer who has published numerous short stories and novels, including *The Cat's Cradle* and a recent best seller, *Slaughter-House Five*.

The following morning, plaintiff was called to Principal Rutland's office for a conference with him and the Associate Superintendent of the school system. Both men expressed their displeasure with the content of the story, which they described as "literary garbage", and with the "philosophy" of the story, which they construed as condoning, if not encouraging, "the killing off of elderly people and free sex." They also expressed concern over the fact that three of plaintiff's students had asked to be excused from the assignment and that several disgruntled parents had called the school to complain. They then admonished plaintiff not to teach the story in any of her classes.

Plaintiff retorted that she was bewildered by their interpretation of and attitude toward the story, that she still considered it to be a good literary work, and that, while not meaning to cause any trouble, she felt that she had a professional obligation to teach the story. . . .

. . . The School Board hearing . . . was held, and on May 6, the School Board notified plaintiff that she had been dismissed from her job for assigning materials which had a "disruptive" effect on the school and for refusing "the counselling and advice of the school principal." The School Board also advised the plaintiff that one of the bases for her dismissal was "insubordination" by reason of a statement that she made to the Principal and Associate Superintendent that "regardless of their counselling" she "would continue to teach the eleventh grade English class at the Jeff Davis High School by the use of whatever material" she wanted "and in whatever manner" she thought best. . . .

At the outset, it should be made clear that plaintiff's teaching ability is not in issue. The Principal of her school has conceded that plaintiff was a good teacher and that she would have received a favorable evaluation from him at the end of the year but for the single incident which led to her dismissal.

Plaintiff asserts in her complaint that her dismissal for assigning "Welcome to the Monkey House" violated her First Amendment right to academic freedom.

That teachers are entitled to First Amendment freedoms is an issue no longer in dispute. "It can hardly be argued that either students or teachers shed their constitutional rights to freedom of speech or expression at the schoolhouse gate." . . . These constitutional protections are unaffected by the presence or absence of tenure under state law.

Although academic freedom is not one of the enumerated rights of the First Amendment, the Supreme Court has on numerous occasions emphasized that the right to teach, to inquire, to evaluate and to study is fundamental to a democratic society. In holding a New York loyalty oath statute unconstitutionally vague, the Court stressed the need to expose students to a robust exchange of ideas in the classroom:

> Our nation is deeply committed to safeguarding academic freedom, which is of transcendant value to all of us and not merely to the teachers concerned. That freedom is therefore a special concern of the First Amendment, which does not tolerate laws that cast a pall of orthodoxy over the classroom. . . . The classroom is peculiarly the "marketplace of ideas."

Furthermore, the safeguards of the First Amendment will quickly be brought into play to protect the right of academic freedom because any unwarranted invasion of this right will tend to have a chilling effect on the exercise of the right by other teachers.

The right to academic freedom, however, like all other constitutional rights, is not absolute and must be balanced against the competing interests of society. This Court is keenly aware of the state's vital interest in protecting the impressionable minds of its young people from *any* form of extreme propagandism in the classroom.

> A teacher works in a sensitive area in a schoolroom. There he shapes the attitudes of young minds towards the society in which they live. In this, the state has a vital concern.

While the balancing of these interests will necessarily depend on the particular facts before the Court, certain guidelines in this area were provided by the Supreme Court . . . :

> [T]he forbidden conduct would *"materially* and *substantially* interfere with the requirements of appropriate discipline in the operation of the school".

The Court was, however, quick to caution the student that:

> [Any] conduct  .  .  .  in class or out of it, which for any reason—whether it stems from time, place or type of behavior—materially disrupts classwork or involves substantial disorder or invasion of the rights of others is, of course, not immunized by the constitutional guarantee of freedom of speech.

Thus, the first question to be answered is whether "Welcome to the Monkey House" is inappropriate reading for high school juniors. While the story contains several vulgar terms and a reference to an involuntary act of sexual intercourse, the Court, having read the story very carefully, can find nothing that would render it obscene  .    .  . .

The slang words are contained in two short rhymes which are less ribald than those found in many of Shakespeare's plays.   The reference in the story to an act of sexual intercourse is no more descriptive than the rape scene in Pope's "Rape of the Lock".   As for the theme of the story, the Court notes that the anthology in which the story was published was reviewed by several of the popular national weekly magazines, none of which found the subject matter of any of the stories to be offensive.   It appears to the Court, moreover, that the author, rather than advocating the "killing off of old people," satirizes the practice to symbolize the increasing depersonalization of man in society.

The Court's finding as to the appropriateness of the story for high school students is confirmed by the reaction of the students themselves.   Rather than there being a threatened or actual substantial disruption to the educational processes of the school, the evidence reflects that the assigning of the story was greeted with apathy by most of the students.   Only three of plaintiff's students asked to be excused from the assignment.   On this question of whether there was a material and substantial threat of disruption, the Principal testified at the School Board hearing that there was no indication that any of plaintiff's other 87 students were planning to disrupt the normal routine of the school.   This Court now specifically finds and concludes that the conduct for which plaintiff was dismissed was not such that "would materially and substantially interfere with" reasonable requirements of discipline in the school.

Since the defendants have failed to show either that the assignment was inappropriate reading for high school juniors, or that it created a significant disruption to the educational processes of this school, this Court concludes that plaintiff's dismissal constituted an unwarranted invasion of her First Amendment right to academic freedom.

The English Department at Jefferson Davis High School publishes "English Reading Lists" for the benefit of its teachers and students. Each list (the lists are compiled separately for each grade) contains the names of approximately twenty-five recommended works.

One of the recommended novels on the "Junior English Reading List" is J. D. Salinger's *Catcher in The Rye*. This novel, while undisputedly a classic in American literature, contains far more offensive and descriptive language than that found in plaintiff's assigned story. The "Senior English Reading List" contains a number of works such as Huxley's *Brave New World* and Orwell's *1984* which have highly provocative and sophisticated themes. Furthermore, the school library contains a number of books with controversial words and philosophies.

This situation illustrates how easily arbitrary discrimination can occur when public officials are given unfettered discretion to decide what books should be taught and what books should be banned. While not questioning either the motives or good faith of the defendants, this Court finds their inconsistency to be not only enigmatic but also grossly unfair.

With these several basic constitutional principles in mind it inevitably follows that the defendants in this case cannot justify the dismissal of this plaintiff under the guise of insubordination. The facts are clear that plaintiff's "insubordination" was not insubordination in any sense and was not, in reality, a reason for the School Board's action.

In accordance with the foregoing, it is the order, judgment and decree of this Court that the plaintiff be reinstated as a teacher for the duration of her contract, with the same rights and privileges which attached to her status prior to her illegal suspension.

It is further ordered that plaintiff be paid her regular salary for both the period during which she was suspended and for the remaining period of her contract.

It is further ordered that defendants expunge from plaintiff's employment records and transcripts any and all references relating to her suspension and dismissal.

## NOTES AND QUESTIONS

1. What are the proper judicial standards of "appropriateness" that courts should apply to the teaching materials in these kinds of cases? "Welcome to the Monkey House" contains language like "kick him in the balls" and "mourn my pecker purple daughter," while Lifton's Atlantic Monthly article made frequent reference to "motherfuckers." Do you agree with Judges Johnson and Aldrich that literature such as this is not inappropriate for high school juniors and seniors? Why shouldn't high schools respect the decisions of parents who do not want their children exposed to such literature?

2. Do these two cases stand for the proposition that teachers have complete freedom to select classroom materials? What are the limitations on the cases? Would the issues in the two cases have been different and would the cases have been decided differently if, in each, a school board rule generally allowed teacher selection of materials but prohibited classroom use of the specific materials in question, and had been in effect well before the beginning date of the course, with each teacher being personally aware of the rule? Would the cases have been decided differently if, in each, the school board prohibited teacher choice and prescribed the materials to be used in the courses, but for which the teachers substituted their different choices of materials, and that gave rise to the problems?

3. Identify what precise characteristic of the school board's actions regarding the teaching materials was held to be constitutionally defective in each case?

## FREEDOM FROM ARBITRARY TEACHING METHODS

---

## WASILEWSKI v. BOARD OF SCHOOL DIRECTORS OF THE CITY OF MILWAUKEE

Supreme Court of Wisconsin, 1961.
14 Wis.2d 243, 111 N.W.2d 198.

CURRIE, Justice.   .   .   .   May a teacher, such as relator, having tenure   .   .   .   be discharged for his conduct, in discussing matters of sex in his classes, which is alleged to transgress "good behavior" when the teacher has violated no rule promulgated by the superintendent or the board, and has received no advance warning that such conduct was disapproved by the school authorities?   .   .   .

Under the provisions of sec. 38.24(18), Stats., a teacher having tenure, such as relator, may only be discharged for conduct which transgresses the bounds of good behavior or constitutes inefficiency. The first issue to be considered is concerned only with the question of what bad behavior would be sufficient cause for discharge.   .   .

.   .   .   relator argues that the board's action in discharging him for interjecting matters of sex education into his speech classes was arbitrary, oppressive, and unreasonable. However, such argument fails to recognize that the issue is not whether it was improper conduct for relator to discuss sex in his speech classes, but rather whether his handling of this topic was such a violation of recognized standards of propriety as to constitute bad behavior. Thus, if relator's discourses on sex in his speech classes had been conducted in such a manner as to constitute proper conduct in a biology class, they would not automatically have been converted into misconduct warranting discharge by the happenstance that they took place in a speech class, absent any rule of the school authorities prohibiting the same or any specific warning to relator from the principal or superintendent that sex was not to be a subject of discussion in speech classes. However, if relator's manner of discoursing on the topic of sex in his speech classes exceeded the bounds of the recognized standards of propriety, we deem that it constituted bad conduct which would warrant a discharge even though there was no express rule prohibiting it and he had received no warning to desist therefrom. As an intelligent person trained to teach at the high school level, relator should have realized that such conduct was improper. . . .

In reviewing this record we are satisfied that the following findings as to relator's acts in his speech classes, establish conduct transcending the contemporary standards of propriety of the community in which he taught: (1) That relator walked from desk to desk during a discussion of houses of prostitution and indicated to each student whether, in his opinion, such student was of such apparent age as to gain admittance to a house of prostitution; (2) that he told the "Schultz" and "cow" vulgar stories; (3) that he described the act of breaking the hymen of a virgin in such a manner as to give his students the impression that he was describing a personal experience— being an unmarried man he thereby may well have given the impression that he considered it proper conduct to violate the criminal statutes prohibiting fornication; (4) that in discussing pre-marital sex relations, he indicated to his students that he believed in the same, although he qualified this view by stating that such relations might be objectionable under certain circumstances, such as where this practice violated religious beliefs; and (5) that he discussed pre-marital sex relations without pointing out to the students that there were state statutes prohibiting the same.

In arriving at this conclusion we are unmindful of the fact that relator's speech classes were composed entirely of senior boys, and that the ages of such boys were from seventeen to nineteen years, inclusive.

There are sound reasons of policy why such conduct, by transcending the bounds of the standards of propriety of the contemporary community, constituted misconduct under sec. 38.24(18), Stats. As was well pointed out by the learned trial court in his memorandum opinion, a teacher exerts considerable influence in moulding the social and moral outlook of his students by his own precept, deportment, and example. This is especially true of a popular and effective teacher such as the record in this case discloses relator to have been. The importance of the teacher in moulding the social and moral views of his students is well stated in one of the texts on education as follows:

> "If we agree that the moral virtues are not taught and learned in the usual way, or at least not in the same way in which reading and writing and arithmetic are taught and

learned, then they are incorporated into the pupil's system of values through practice, example, and emulation. With respect to moral formation the role of the teacher may not be minimized, for he is the chief creator of the student's educational environment and the main source of his inspiration."

In considering the immediately preceding issue, we have set forth certain conduct of the relator which has been determined to constitute misconduct warranting the discharge. Relator attacks the sufficiency of the evidence to sustain the findings of fact, whereby these enumerated activities were found to have occurred, as well as other additional findings of fact.

Our review of the testimony given at the hearing causes us to conclude that the board could reasonably make the findings which it did even though in some respects this court might have reached the opposite conclusion if it had been the trier of the facts. The applicable principle of law is well stated in State ex rel. Morehouse v. Hunt, 1940, 235 Wis. 358, 367, 291 N.W. 745, 749, as follows:

> "The case is *certiorari*. When *certiorari* is invoked to review the action of an administrative board, the findings of the board upon the facts before it are conclusive if in any reasonable view the evidence sustains them."

The testimony relating to certain of the matters covered in the findings is in sharp dispute. We can perceive of no useful purpose which would be served by recounting the testimony of the various witnesses.

. . .

MARTIN, Chief Justice, and HALLOWS, Justice (concurring).

We concur in the result but do not agree with much of the dicta and the reasoning of the majority. Much of what has been said would have been better off unsaid. We especially object to the proposition advanced that a teacher certified to teach history, English and speech can discuss a controversial subject of sex in his speech class as a teacher certified to teach biology might discuss it in a biology class in the absence of any rule of the school authorities or any specific warning that sex was not to be the subject of discussion in speech classes.

A teacher is hired for his competency to teach certain subjects. Sex education is a subject matter for which a teacher should be especially competent to teach. A parent and the school authorities have a right to expect that children are not going to be exposed to comments, discussions, and personal opinions of a teacher on sex who had not been certified to teach such subject in classes which do not relate to such subjects. There need be no rule of school authorities prohibiting the same or any specific warning to the teacher not to discuss sex in his classroom unless specifically authorized.

The majority opinion fails to recognize the right of the parent to determine whether his child shall be taught about sex in the public schools. The subject is optional. The concern of the parent as to who is to teach the subject and what his or her background and qualifications are, and the parent's right to visit the class in which the subject is discussed, are all ignored in the majority opinion. Only one qualified and so certified by the proper authorities should be allowed to undertake to teach this delicate subject and only in a class expressly held for that purpose.

A parent has the right to visit such a class to determine how such instructions are being given, who is giving the instructions, and in general know of the existing conditions. A parent should not be forced to visit each and every class which his child attends to determine whether sex education is being given and if it is, how it is being handled.

What has happened in this case may well be taken as an example of what we may expect if sex education is being given in classes other than those designated for that purpose.

Under the majority opinion, an unqualfied, unauthorized person, entirely unfit, may have his fling at teaching or instructing in sex education with little fear of the consequences, except perhaps a mild censure, unless the school board adopts a rule prohibiting such activity. It seems to us to be bad in itself, not bad because it is prohibited, mala in se, not mala prohibita.

## NOTES AND QUESTIONS

1. Does the reasoning of the concurring opinion suggest that a teacher of history would be forbidden to discuss the moral decay of the Roman Catholic Church in Europe prior to and during the Reformation because he isn't certified by the state to teach religion? Aren't school curriculum disciplines abstract categories which are compartmentalized for pedagogical purposes only? In fact, don't such disciplines flow into and affect each other so that a discussion about economics, for example, requires a knowledge of psychology, political science, mathematics and history? Could an economics teacher adequately teach economics without discussing the alternative and competing economic systems such as capitalism, socialism, communism? Would an economics teacher who discussed the economic system of communism be "teaching communism"?

2. California's law resolves the sex education question this way:

"No governing board of a public elementary or secondary school may require pupils to attend any class in which human reproductive organs and their functions and processes are described, illustrated or discussed, whether such class be part of a course designated "sex education" or "family life education" or by some similar term, or part of any other course which pupils are required to attend.

"If classes are offered in public elementary and secondary schools in which human reproductive organs and their functions and processes are described, illustrated or discussed, the parent or guardian of each pupil enrolled in such class shall first be notified in writing of the class.   Sending the required notice through the regular United States mail, or any other method which such local school district commonly uses to communicate individually in writing to all parents, meets the notification requirements of this paragraph.

"Opportunity shall be provided to each parent or guardian to request in writing that his child not attend the class.   Such requests shall be valid for the school year in which they are submitted but may be withdrawn by the parent or guardian at any time.   No child may attend a class if a request that he not attend the class has been received by the school.

"Any written or audiovisual material to be used in a class in which human reproductive organs and their functions and processes are described, illustrated, or discussed shall be available for inspection by the parent or guardian at reasonable times and places prior to the holding of a course which includes such classes.   The parent or guardian shall be notified in writing of his opportunity to inspect and review such materials.

"This section shall not apply to description or illustration of human reproductive organs which may appear in a textbook, adopted pursuant to law, on physiology, biology, zoology, general science, personal hygiene, or health.

"Nothing in this section shall be construed as encouraging the description, illustration, or discussion of human reproductive organs and their functions and processes in the public elementary and secondary schools.

"The certification document of any person charged with the responsibility of making any instructional material available for inspection under this section or who is charged with the responsibility of notifying a parent or guardian of any class conducted within the purview of this section, and who knowingly and willfully fails to make instructional material available for inspection or to notify such parent or guardian, may be revoked or suspended because of such act.   The certification document of any person who knowingly and willfully requires a pupil to attend a class within the purview of this section when a request that the pupil not attend has been received from the parent or guardian may be revoked or suspended because of such act."   West's Ann.Educ.Code of Calif. § 51550.

What are the merits and demerits of this statute?  If you had been a California legislator would you have voted for this statute?  Why or why not?  Would it have been relevant to the decisions in the Wasilewski and Mailloux cases if it had been the law of those states at the time of decision?  Why or why not?

## MAILLOUX v. KILEY

United States District Court, 1971.
323 F.Supp. 1387 (D.Mass.), affirmed 448 F.2d 1242 (1st Cir., 1971).

WYZANSKI, Chief Judge. This case involves an action by a public high school teacher against the City of Lawrence, the members of its school committee, the superintendent of its schools, and the principal of its high school. Plaintiff claims that in discharging him for his classroom conduct in connection with a taboo word the school committee deprived him of his rights under the First and Fourteenth Amendments to the United States Constitution, and that, therefore he has a cause of action under 42 U.S.C.A. § 1983 within this court's jurisdiction under 28 U.S.C.A. § 1343(3).

These are the facts as found by this court after a full hearing.

. . . Defendant principal assigned plaintiff to teach basic English to a class of about 25 students, boys and girls 16 and 17 years of age, all in the junior class or 11th grade.

Plaintiff assigned to the class for outside reading chapters in a novel, The Thread That Runs So True, by Jesse Stuart. The novel describes an incident based on the experiences of the author as a young country school teacher in rural Kentucky. He had taken over a one-room school in which the class had been seated with boys on one side, and girls on the other side, of the room. He intermingled the sexes for seating. Some parents objected on the ground the new teacher was running a "courting school." Nowhere in the novel is there the word "fuck."

October 1, 1970, during a discussion of the book in class, some students thought the protest against changing the seating in the Kentucky classroom was ridiculous. Plaintiff said that other things today are just as ridiculous. He then introduced the subject of society and its ways, as illustrated by taboo words. He wrote the word "goo" on the board and asked the class for a definition. No one being able to define it, plaintiff said that this word did not exist in English but in another culture it might be a taboo word. He then wrote on the blackboard the word "fuck," and, in accordance with his customary teaching methods of calling for volunteers to respond to a question, asked the class in general for a definition. After a couple of minutes a boy volunteered that the word meant "sexual intercourse." Plaintiff, without using the word orally, said, "we have two words, sexual intercourse, and this word on the board * * * one * * * is acceptable by society * * * the other is not accepted. It is a taboo word." After a few minutes of discussion of other aspects of taboos, plaintiff went on to other matters.

At all times in the discussion plaintiff was in good faith pursuing what he regarded as an educational goal. He was not attempting to probe the private feelings, or attitudes, or experiences of his students, or to embarrass them.

October 2, 1970, the parent of a girl in the class, being erroneously informed that plaintiff had called upon a particular girl in the class to define the taboo word, complained to the principal. He asked Miss Horner, the head of the English department, to investigate the incident. Plaintiff did admit that he had written on the board the taboo word. He also said he had "probably" called upon a specific girl to define the word. But this court is persuaded by all the testimony that he did not in fact call on any girl individually and that his statement to Miss Horner, repeated later to the union, of what he "probably" did is not an accurate statement of what he actually did. At his meeting with Miss Horner, plaintiff did not refer to the novel which the class had been discussing.

After plaintiff had been interviewed by Miss Horner, defendant superintendent on October 13, 1970 suspended him for seven days with pay.

Plaintiff engaged counsel who requested a hearing before the school committee, and a bill of particulars. The committee furnished particulars alleging that:

" *  *  * Mr. Mailloux did write a list of words on the chalk-board.

One of the words was 'fuck'."

A female student was asked to define the word 'fuck'."

"When confronted with the incident by the head of the department, Mr. Mailloux admitted that the incident was true." . . .

The committee gave plaintiff and his counsel a hearing on October 20, 1970.

October 21, 1970 the committee dismissed plaintiff on the general charge of "conduct unbecoming a teacher." It made no finding as to any specific particular.

Following his discharge, plaintiff brought this action seeking temporary and permanent relief. . . .

. . . Upon the basis of [two] hearings this court makes the following additional findings.

1. The topic of taboo words had a limited relevance to the Stuart novel which plaintiff's class was discussing, but it had a high degree of relevance to the proper teaching of eleventh grade basic English even to students not expecting to go to college and therefore placed in a "low track."

2. The word "fuck" is relevant to a discussion of taboo words. Its impact effectively illustrates how taboo words function.

3.   Boys and girls in an eleventh grade have a sophistication sufficient to treat the word from a serious educational viewpoint. While at first they may be surprised and self-conscious to have the word discussed, they are not likely to be embarrassed or offended.

4.   Plaintiff's writing the word did not have a disturbing effect. A class might be less disturbed by having the word written than if it had been spoken. Most students had seen the word even if they had not used it.

5.   Plaintiff's calling upon the class for a volunteer to define the word was a technique that was reasonable and was in accordance with customs in plaintiff's class. It avoided implicating anyone who did not wish to participate.

6.   The word "fuck" is in books in the school library.

7.   In the opinion of experts of significant standing, such as members of the faculties of the Harvard University School of Education and of Massachusetts Institute of Technology, the discussion of taboo words in the eleventh grade, the way plaintiff used the word "fuck," his writing of it on the blackboard, and the inquiry he addressed to the class, were appropriate and reasonable under the circumstances and served a serious educational purpose. In the opinion of other qualified persons plaintiff's use of the word was not under the circumstances reasonable, or appropriate, or conducive to a serious educational purpose. It has not been shown what is the preponderant opinion in the teaching profession, or in that part of the profession which teaches English.

The parties have not relied upon any express regulation of the Lawrence School Committee or the Lawrence High School. The regulations set forth in an attachment to the complaint have no general or specific provisions relevant to this case.

We now turn to questions of ultimate fact and of law.  .   .   .

The Fourteenth Amendment recognizes that a public school teacher has not only a civic right to freedom of speech both outside .   .   .   the schoolhouse, but also some measure of academic freedom as to his in-classroom teaching.  .   .   .

.   .   .   cases  .   .   .   [uphold] two kinds of academic freedom: the substantive right of a teacher to choose a teaching method which in the court's view served a demonstrated educational purpose; and the procedural right of a teacher not to be discharged for the use of a teaching method which was not proscribed by a regulation, and as to which it was not proven that he should have had notice that its use was prohibited.  .   .   .

The teaching methods plaintiff used were obviously not "necessary" to the proper teaching of the subject and students assigned to him, in the sense that a reference to Darwinian evolution might be thought necessary to the teaching of biology.  See the concurrence of Mr. Justice Stewart in Epperson v. Arkansas, 393 U.S. 97, 116,

. . .

Here we have the use of teaching methods which divide professional opinion.  There is substantial support from expert witnesses of undoubted competence that the discussion of taboo words was relevant to an assigned book, and, whether or not so relevant, was at least relevant to the subject of eleventh grade English, that "fuck" was an appropriate choice of an illustrative taboo word, and that writing it on the board and calling upon the class to define it were appropriate techniques.  Yet there was also substantial evidence, chiefly from persons with experience as principals but also from the head of the English department at plaintiff's school, that it was inappropriate to use the particular word under the circumstances of this case.  The weight of the testimony offered leads this court to make an ultimate finding that plaintiff's methods served an educational purpose, in the sense that they were relevant and had professional endorsement from experts of significant standing.  But this court has not implied that the weight of opinion in the teaching profession as a whole, or the weight of opinion among English teachers as a whole, would be that plaintiff's methods were within limits that, even if they would not themselves use them, they would regard as permissible for others.  To make a finding on that point would have required a more thorough sampling, especially of younger teachers, than the record offers.

. . .

Nor is this case, like *Keefe* or *Parducci,* one where the court, from its own evaluation of the teaching method used, may conclude that, even if the court would not use the method, it is plainly permissible for others to use it, at least in the absence of an express proscription. *Keefe* indicated that the use in the classroom of the word "fuck" is not impermissible under all circumstances—as, for example when it appears in a book properly assigned for student reading.  But a teacher who uses a taboo sexual word must take care not to transcend his legitimate professional purpose.  When a male teacher asks a class of adolescent boys and girls to define a taboo sexual word the question must not go beyond asking for verbal knowledge and become a titillating probe of privacy.  He must not sacrifice his dignity to join his pupils as "frére et cochon."  Here, it should be stated unequivocally, there is no evidence that this plaintiff transcended legitimate professional purposes.  Indeed, the court has specifically found he acted in good faith.  But the risk of abuse involved in the technique of questioning students precludes this court from concluding that the method was *plainly* permissible.  Too much depends on the context and the teacher's good faith.

Where, as here, a secondary school teacher chooses a teaching method that is not necessary for the proper instruction of his class, that is not shown to be regarded by the weight of opinion in his profession as permissible, that is not so transparently proper that a court can without expert testimony evaluate it as proper, but that is relevant to his subject and students and, in the opinion of experts of significant standing, serves a serious educational purpose, it is a heretofore undecided question whether the Constitution gives him any right to use the method or leaves the issue to the school authorities. Note, Developments in the Law of Academic Freedom, 81 Harv.L.Rev. 1050, Van Alstyne, The Constitutional Rights of Teachers and Professors, 1970 Duke Law Journal, p. 841.

.   .   .

In support of a qualified right of a teacher, even at the secondary level, to use a teaching method which is relevant and in the opinion of experts of significant standing has a serious educational purpose is the central rationale of academic freedom. The Constitution recognizes that freedom in order to foster open minds, creative imaginations, and adventurous spirits. Our national belief is that the heterodox as well as the orthodox are a source of individual and of social growth. We do not confine academic freedom to conventional teachers or to those who can get a majority vote from their colleagues. Our faith is that the teacher's freedom to choose among options for which there is any substantial support will increase his intellectual vitality and his moral strength. The teacher whose responsibility has been nourished by independence, enterprise, and free choice becomes for his student a better model of the democratic citizen. His examples of applying and adapting the values of the old order to the demands and opportunities of a constantly changing world are among the most important lessens he gives to youth.

Yet the secondary school situation is distinguishable from higher levels of education.   .   .   . There are constitutional considerations of magnitude which, predictably, might warrant a legal conclusion that the secondary school teacher's constitutional right in his classroom is only to be free from discriminatory religious, racial, political and like measure. Epperson v. Arkansas, supra, and from state action which is unreasonable, or perhaps has not even a plausible rational basis.   .   .   .

The secondary school more clearly than the college or university acts *in loco parentis* with respect to minors. It is closely governed by a school board selected by a local community. The faculty does not have the independent traditions, the broad discretion as to teaching methods, nor usually the intellectual qualifications, of university professors. Among secondary school teachers there are often many persons with little experience. Some teachers and most students have limited intellectual and emotional maturity. Most parents, students, school boards, and members of the community usually expect the secondary school to concentrate on transmitting basic information, teaching "the best that is known and thought in the world," training by established techniques, and, to some extent at least, indoctrinating in the *mores* of the surrounding society.  While secondary schools are not rigid disciplinary institutions, neither are they open forums in which mature adults, already habituated to social restraints, exchange ideas on a level of parity.  Moreover, it cannot be accepted as a premise that the student is voluntarily in the classroom and willing to be exposed to a teaching method which, though reasonable, is not approved by the school authorities or by the weight of professional opinion.  A secondary school student, unlike most college students, is usually required to attend school classes, and may have no choice as to his teacher.

Bearing in mind these competing considerations, this court rules that when a secondary school teacher uses a teaching method which he does not prove has the support of the preponderant opinion of the teaching profession or of the part of it to which he belongs, but which he merely proves is relevant to his subject and students, is regarded by experts of significant standing as serving a serious educational purpose, and was used by him in good faith the state may suspend or discharge a teacher for using that method but it may not resort to such drastic sanctions unless the state proves he was put on notice either by a regulation or otherwise that he should not use that method. This exclusively procedural protection is afforded to a teacher not because he is a state employee, or because he is a citizen, but because in his teaching capacity he is engaged in the exercise of what may plausibly be considered "vital First Amendment rights."  Keyishian v. Board of Regents.  In his teaching capacity he is not required to "guess what conduct or utterance may lose him his position," (Ibid). If he did not have the right to be warned before he was discharged, he might be more timid than it is in the public interest that he should be, and he might steer away from reasonable methods with which it is in the public interest to experiment.  Ibid.

In the instant case it is not claimed that any regulation warned plaintiff not to follow the methods he chose.  Nor can it be said that plaintiff should have known that his teaching methods were not permitted.  There is no substantial evidence that his methods were contrary to an informal rule, to an understanding among school teachers of his school or teachers generally, to a body of disciplinary precedents, to precise canons of ethics, or to specific opinions expressed in professional journals or other publications.  This was not the kind of unforeseeable outrageous conduct which all men of good will would, once their attention is called to it, immediately perceive to be forbidden.  On this last point it is sufficient to refer to the testimony given by faculty members of Harvard University and M. I. T. who had prepared their students for secondary school teaching careers.

Finally, in the face of the record of judicial uncertainty in this case it cannot be held that it was self-evident that a teacher should not have used the methods followed by plaintiff. . . .

Inasmuch as at the time he acted plaintiff did not know, and there was no reason that he should have known, that his conduct was proscribed, it was a violation of due process for the defendants to suspend or discharge him on that account. . . .

. . . .

Plaintiff, in accordance with Parducci v. Rutland, is entitled to a judgment directing:

    1.  All defendants to continue plaintiff in employment

. . . .

    2.  All defendants to expunge from their employment records and transcripts all references to plaintiff's suspension and discharge.

    3.  The City of Lawrence, as his employer, and the school committee members, as the persons who discharged him, to compensate him for the salary loss he suffered,

. . . .

The court is not unmindful that both the opinion and the judgment cover not only plaintiff's discharge without compensation but also his suspension with pay. The reason that the suspension is covered is because in the circumstances of this case the superintendent and all others treated is as a penalty. Nothing herein suggests that school authorities are not free after they have learned that the teacher is using a teaching method of which they disapprove, and which is not appropriate to the proper teaching of the subject, to suspend him until he agrees to cease using the method.

---

## MAILLOUX v. KILEY

United States Court of Appeals, 1971.
448 F.2d 1242 (1st Cir.).

PER CURIAM.

This case is back after trial, following our earlier decision in regard to a preliminary injunction. In the light of defendants' present argument we may have there indicated a departure from Keefe v. Geanakos, that we did not intend. On the facts of that case we held that the teacher's conduct could not properly subject him to suspension, on both substantive First Amendment and procedural due process grounds. We also recognized, however, that free speech does not grant teachers a license to say or write in class whatever they may feel like, and that the propriety of regulations or sanctions must depend on such circumstances as the age and sophistication of the students, the closeness of the relation between the specific technique used and some concededly valid educational objective, and the context and manner of presentation.

With all respect to the district court's sensitive effort to devise guidelines for weighing those circumstances, we suspect that any such formulation would introduce more problems than it would resolve. At present we see no substitute for a case-by-case inquiry into whether the legitimate interests of the authorities are demonstrably sufficient to circumscribe a teacher's speech. Here, however, in weighing the findings below we confess that we are not of one mind as to whether plaintiff's conduct fell within the protection of the First Amendment.

However, we find the ground relied on below as dispositive as both sound and sufficient. Defendants point to a statement in the Code of Ethics of the Education Profession that the teacher "recognizes the supreme importance of the pursuit of the truth, devotion to excellence and the nurture of democratic citizenship." As notice to the plaintiff that he should not have engaged in the act in question, this standard, although laudable, is impermissibly vague. It cannot justify a post facto decision by the school authorities that the use of a particular teaching method is ground for discharge, or other serious sanction, simply because some educators disapprove of it. The district court found that the plaintiff's conduct was within standards responsibly, although not universally recognized, and that he acted in good faith and without notice that these defendants, as his superiors, were not of that view. Sanctions in this circumstance would be a denial of due process.

Affirmed.

## NOTES AND QUESTIONS

1. Does Mailloux provide procedural or substantive protection for academic freedom? What guidelines are provided by Judge Wyzanski? Did the Court of Appeals accept his guidelines, in part or whole?

2. If, in Mailloux, a school regulation known to the teacher had, in effect, warned him "not to follow the methods he chose," what would have been the decision of the courts? Why? Suppose a teaching method actually used by a teacher can also be "proved" to have "the support of the preponderant opinion of the teaching profession," but school regulations, nevertheless, prohibit using the method, and the teacher is dismissed, does such "opinion proof" control the court's decisions?

3. The Court of Appeals, in Mailloux, stated that the validity of any such regulation "must depend on such circumstances as the age and the sophistication of the students, the closeness of the relation between the specific technique used and some concededly valid educational objective, and the context and manner of presentation" and that it could see "no substitute for case-by-case inquiry into whether the legitimate interests of the authorities are demonstrably sufficient to circumscribe a teacher's speech." Is the proper inference of these quotes that no

general guidelines regarding academic freedom can be, or should be, created? Even so, do not the last two sentences of the Court of Appeals approve guidelines for situations like Mailloux? Can you prepare a set of guidelines for the future guidance of teachers? This appellate court also decided Keefe, has it changed its position on academic freedom between Keefe and Mailloux? Do the court's decisions rest on a teacher's right to teach or a student's right to know, or both? What difference would it make?

4.  In Ahern v. Board of Educ., 456 F.2d 399 (8th Cir. 1972), in an attempt to maintain discipline, a substitute teacher slapped a student. When informed of the incident on her return, the regular teacher's "reaction [in front of her students] was one of anger, which manifested itself in the following statement: 'That bitch. I hope if this happens again all of you will walk out.'" The teacher apparently saw the substitute teacher's attempt to maintain discipline as creating classroom structures contrary to those needed by her teaching methods which "had the effect of shifting to students many decisions customarily made by teachers."

"The slapping incident immediately became the focus of Miss Ahern's economics classes, her goal being to assist her students in formulating and having effected a school regulation regarding corporal punishment. On Wednesday, March 19, Miss Ahern was called to a conference which was attended by Dr. Eugene Miller, the high school principal, and by the assistant principal and Miss Ahern's department chairman. Dr. Miller reprimanded Miss Ahern during the course of the meeting for calling the substitute teacher a bitch in front of her students. He also directed her to teach economics (rather than politics) in her economics classes and to return to more conventional teaching methods. Miss Ahern also was instructed to restore order promptly in her classes and not to discuss the slapping incident with students or other teachers. Finally, Dr. Miller warned Miss Ahern that she could be suspended from her teaching position for the remainder of the year if she did not comply with his directions.

"Miss Ahern deliberately ignored Dr. Miller's directions in the interests of preserving rapport with her students and of guarding her academic freedom to select the method of teaching to be employed in her classrooms. At least some of Miss Ahern's classes continued to discuss the slapping incident and, on Thursday, March 20, a copy of a proposed corporal punishment regulation was sent by messenger from one of her classes to Dr. Miller's office. Accompanying the regulation was a note requesting that the principal come to the classroom to discuss the proposal. Dr. Miller declined that invitation and a subsequent one made by Miss Ahern via a telephone in her classroom.

"Before classes began on Friday morning, March 21, a large number of students held a non-disruptive protest meeting in the student lounge. Although the meeting was adjourned at the request of administrators in time for participating students to attend their first classes, several students were tardy. Dr. Miller summoned Miss Ahern to a meeting (which was recorded and later transcribed) at approximately eight o'clock that morning, and made the following statement:

> Miss Ahern, I have some statements to make. I ask you to listen and then you will be given an opportunity to speak. Since our meeting on Wednesday morning, you have failed to return to your classes and teach economics as directed. Instead, you have continued to discuss with students, students' rights and teachers' rights and non-rights to the students, and in addition have aided students in preparing slips of paper advocating a protest meeting in the Senior Lounge this morning. For these reasons and the reasons that we gave you on Wednesday morning, I am suspending you from all teaching duties here at Senior High, effective immediately, until at which time you will be given an opportunity for a hearing before the Board of Education. Dr. Lundstrom, the Superintendent of Schools, will notify you as to the time, day, and place of this hearing. At this time, I am asking you to turn in your keys and any personal belongings that you have in the room you may obtain between the hours of nine and ten, tomorrow morning. . . .
>
> Yes, your suspension will be with pay, your status will be determined at the Board of Education hearing."

Ms. Ahern was fired for insubordination. Was her dismissal constitutionally permissible or does she have a valid academic freedom defense? How would the Keefe and Mailloux Court probably rule on the case?

5.  Does an adequate distinction exist between classroom teaching and the materials of a school library such that Keefe and Mailloux should not apply to the library?

## PARENTAL RIGHTS TO ELIMINATE COURSES FROM THE CURRICULUM FOR THEIR CHILD

In Meyer the U. S. Supreme Court indicated that "it hardly will be affirmed that any legislature" can impose restrictions upon its people designed "to submerge the individual and [to] develop ideal citizens" without "doing violence to both letter and spirit of the Constitution." The Court returned to this theme in Pierce saying that the "fundamental theory of liberty upon which all governments in this Union repose excludes any general power of the state to standardize its children by forcing them to accept instruction from public teachers only." Thus, the Court ruled that parents who nurture and direct their child's destiny "have the right . . . to recognize and prepare him for additional obligations" by sending him to an approved private school of their choice. But, that may be too expensive. Do parents also have the right "to prepare their child for additional obligations" by precluding their child from taking courses in a public school's curriculum that they believe conflict with his preparation for "additional obligations"? To qualify, must the "additional obligations" be religious obligations?

---

### STATE ex rel. KELLEY v. FERGUSON

Supreme Court of Nebraska, 1914.
95 Neb. 63, 144 N.W. 1039.

FAWCETT, J. . . . [The allegations are that] prior to December 17, 1912, plaintiff had instructed his daughter Eunice Kelley "not to go to the class in domestic science; that said class was conducted in a building more than a mile distant from the Saratoga school which she was attending, and that the time consumed by said class was almost a half day, thereby causing the said Eunice Kelley to fall behind in her other studies for lack of time; that the respondents wrongfully and unlawfully and against the protests of relator required said Eunice Kelley to take said course in domestic science, and on the 17th day of December, 1912, the respondents wrongfully, unlawfully, and without cause therefor dismissed said Eunice Kelley from said school and refused and have ever since refused to allow her to attend school of said district, although since said time relator has several times made demand upon the said school board and its officers to reinstate her." The answer admits the formal allegations in the petition and alleges: That in the course of study adopted by the school district of Lincoln, which, it is alleged, is substantially the same as the courses of study in all other municipal school districts of the United States, there are eight grades below the high school; that Eunice Kelley is 12 years old and is a sixth grade pupil attending the Saratoga school; that all subjects in the sixth grade are required subjects, and one of these is domestic science; that no pupils are excused from taking any subjects in said grade except for good cause; that no cause was shown and none existed for excusing the said Eunice from attending said class; that the demand of the relator was arbitrary, unreasonable, and without just basis; that respondents could not comply with such arbitrary and unreasonable demand without undermining and destroying the discipline of the schools; that industrial training is essential to the welfare of the public, and it is the function of the state to require courses to be given affording industrial training; that in the exercise of this function a course in domestic science was prescribed for the sixth grade in the schools of the district; that in requiring attendance in classes in which this subject was taught the board of education was acting within its powers, and it could not excuse any pupils from taking said course unless a good and sufficient reason for such excuse was shown. The court found the facts as alleged . . . and awarded the writ. . . .

The issue presented by the pleadings and decided by the district court is clean cut and raises the single question: Can the parent of a child in a city graded school decide the question as to whether or not such child shall be required to carry any particular study which has been prescribed by the board of education; or does the power to make such decision rest entirely in such board?  Or, to state it another way, has the parent a right to make a reasonable selection from the prescribed studies for his child to pursue, and, having done so, must this selection be respected by the board of education?  If the parent has such right, and judgment in this case must be affirmed, for we do not think a case could be presented where a selection made by a parent would more clearly be a reasonable selection than the one attempted to be made in this case.  The relator's child was a girl 12 years of age. She was in the sixth grade.  The study which the relator directed her not to take was that of cooking, which is required under the subject of domestic science.  The other studies which she was required to take and was taking were reading, spelling, arithmetic, geography, general lessons, drawing, and writing.  The testimony of the father is that at the time the disagreement arose the daughter was studying music, which required not less than two hours a day.  If the relator desired to have his daughter study music, he had the unquestionable right to have her do so, and if he thought that the taking of lessons in music, in addition to the studies she was taking in school, as above set out, was all she was able to carry, then, if he had a right to make a selection at all, it must be conceded that it was reasonable for him to select the lesson in domestic science, which took substantially one-tenth of her entire school time, as the lesson to be dropped, in order that she might continue her music.  It is contended that this selection was not made by the relator in good faith but was made because of the fact that the school authorities declined to permit his daughter, at the close of the cooking lesson at the Capital school, to which the class were taken in a body by the teacher from the Saratoga school, to return to her home on the Seventeenth Street car line instead of requiring her to return with the entire class to the Saratoga school and to be there dismissed.  We do not think this fact, even if it were the cause which finally impelled relator to make his attempted selection, is very material.  The important question to the school board and to parents generally is that of the right of a parent to make a reasonable selection from the prescribed studies for his child to pursue.

The question is not a new one.  It was considered and decided by this court in State ex rel. Sheibley v. School District, 31 Neb. 552, 48 N.W. 393.  In that case the father expressed a desire to have his daughter study grammar instead of rhetoric.  His wish was respected and the change made.  Subsequently he objected to her studying grammar and demanded that she be excused from continuing the study.  When asked what reason he had for not wanting his daughter to pursue the study, he informed the board "that said study was not taught in said school as he had been instructed when he went to school."  That was the only reason he would offer for not wanting his daughter to pursue the study. Under his direction the daughter refused to pursue the study, and as a result of such refusal she was expelled. An original application for mandamus was made in this court, and the writ awarded. The syllabus holds: "The school trustees of a high school have authority to classify and grade the scholars in the district and cause them to be taught in such departments as they may deem expedient; they may also prescribe the courses of study and textbooks for the use of the school and such reasonable rules and regulations as they may think needful. They may also require prompt attendance, respectful deportment, and diligence in study. The parent, however, has a right to make a reasonable selection from the prescribed studies for his child to pursue, and this selection must be respected by the trustees, as the right of the parent in that regard is superior to that of the trustees and the teachers." . . . Now who is to determine what studies she shall pursue in school, a teacher, who has a mere temporary interest in her welfare, or her father, who may reasonably be supposed to be desirous of pursuing such course as will best promote the happiness of his child? The father certainly possesses superior opportunities of knowing the physical and mental capabilities of his child. It may be apparent that all the prescribed course of studies is more than the strength of the child can undergo; or he may be desirous, as is frequently the case, that his child, while attending school, should also take lessons in music, painting, etc., from private teachers. This he has a right to do. The right of the parent, therefore, to determine what studies his child shall pursue is paramount to that of the trustees or teacher. Schools are provided by the public in which prescribed branches are taught, which are free to all within the district between certain ages. But no pupil attending the school can be compelled to study any prescribed branch against the protest of the parent that the child shall not study such branch, and any rule or regulation that requires the pupil to continue such studies is arbitrary and unreasonable. There is no good reason why the failure of one or more pupils to study one or more prescribed branches should result disastrously to the proper discipline, efficiency, and well-being of the school. Such pupils are not idle but merely devoting their attention to other branches; and so long as the failure of the students, thus excepted, to study all the branches of the prescribed course does not prejudice the equal rights of other students, there is no cause for complaint." . . .

Wherever education is most general, there life and property are the most safe, and civilization of the highest order. The public school is one of the main bulwarks of our nation, and we would not knowingly do anything to undermine it; but we should be careful to avoid permitting our love for this noble institution to cause us to regard it as "all in all" and destroy both the God-given and constitutional right of a parent to have some voice in the bringing up and education of his children. We believe in the doctrine of the greatest good to the greatest number, and that the welfare of the individual must give way to the welfare of society in general. The whole current of modern thought and agitation is "onward." The people are beginning to realize as never before that, if we continue to jog along in the ruts our fathers before us have made, little will be accomplished in the way of national and social improvement. The state is more and more taking hold of the private affairs of individuals and requiring that they conduct their business affairs honestly and with due regard for the public good. All this is commendable and must receive the sanction of every good citizen. But in this age of agitation, such as the world has never known before, we want to be careful lest we carry the doctrine of governmental paternalism too far, for, after all is said and done, the prime factor in our scheme of government is the American home.   .   .   .

The judgment of the district court is therefore affirmed.

## NOTES AND QUESTIONS

1. In Pierce v. Society of Sisters, supra, the Court stated: " . . . we think it entirely plain that the Act of 1922 unreasonably interferes with the liberty of parents and guardians to direct the upbringing and education of children under their control," and "The child is not the mere creature of the State; those who nurture him and direct his destiny have the right, coupled with the high duty, to recognize and prepare him for additional obligations." This view was strongly reinforced in Meyer v. Nebraska, supra. Does Pierce or Meyer or Wisconsin v. Yoder provide the constitutional foundation for a parental right to control and select classes for their children?

2. Suppose a parent decided that his child should not participate in one of the following classes: reading, mathematics, chemistry, physical or sex education, would Kelley v. Ferguson be determinative? What limitations are suggested by these two cases on the parental right to control and direct a child's education? Under the rule of this case could a parent refuse to allow his child to be taught "the essentials of good citizenship?" If not, is this then, the primary goal of the public schools? Who determines what subjects are essential for good citizenship? What were the conceptions of the political community and good citizenship that the Supreme Court allowed the Amish in Wisconsin v. Yoder? Is the conception the same or different in Pierce and Kelley v. Ferguson?

3. On the right of parents to control education, see generally, School Board Dist. No. 18 v. Thompson, 24 Okl. 1, 103 P. 578 (1909); Hardwick v. Board of School Trustees, 54 Cal.App. 696, 205 P. 49 (1921); Sheibley v. School Dist., 31 Neb. 552, 48 N.W. 393 (1891) and compare, Samuel Benedict Memorial School v. Bradford, 111 Ga. 801, 36 S.E. 920 (1900), and State ex rel. Andrews v. Webber, 108 Ind. 31, 8 N.E. 708 (1886).

4. On the right of a parent to inspect his child's school records, see, Van Allen v. McCleary, 27 Misc.2d 81, 211 N.Y.S.2d 501 (1961).

## CENSORSHIP AND THE LIBRARY

### MINARCINI v. STRONGSVILLE SCHOOL DIST.

United States Court of Appeals, 1976.
541 F.2d 577 (6th Cir.).

EDWARDS, Circuit Judge.

This record presents a vivid story of heated community debate over what sort of books should be (1) selected as high school text books, (2) purchased for a high school library, (3) removed from a high school library, or (4) forbidden to be taught or assigned in a high school classroom. The setting of this controversy is the high school in Strongsville, Ohio, a suburb of Cleveland.

This case originated as a class action brought under 42 U.S.C.A. § 1983 against the Strongsville City School District, the members of the Board of Education and the Superintendent of the school district by five public high school students through their parents, as next friends. The suit claimed violation of First and Fourteenth Amendment rights in that the school board, disregarding the recommendation of the faculty, refused to approve Joseph Heller's *Catch 22* and Kurt Vonnegut's *God Bless You, Mr. Rosewater* as texts or library books, ordered Vonnegut's *Cat's Cradle* and Heller's *Catch 22* to be removed from the library, and issued resolutions which served to prohibit teacher and student discussion of these books in class or their use as supplemental reading.

## I. THE BOARD'S DECISION NOT TO APPROVE OR PURCHASE CERTAIN TEXTS

It appears clear to this court that the State of Ohio has specifically committed the duty of selecting and purchasing textbooks to local boards of education. O.R.C. § 3329.07 (1975) provides as follows:

The board of education of each city, exempted village, and local school district shall cause it to be ascertained and at a regular meeting determine which, and the number of each of the textbooks the schools under its charge require. The clerk at once shall order the books agreed upon from the publisher, who on receipt of such order must ship them to the clerk without delay. He forthwith shall examine the books, and, if found right and in accordance with the order, remit the amount to the publisher. The board must pay for the books so purchased and in addition all charges for the transportation of the books out of the general fund of said district or out of such other funds as it may have available for such purchase of textbooks. If such board at any time can secure from the publishers books at less than such maximum price, they shall do so, and without unnecessary delay may make effort to secure such lower price before adopting any particular textbooks.

Clearly, discretion as to the selection of textbooks must be lodged somewhere and we can find no federal constitutional prohibition which prevents its being lodged in school board officials who are elected representatives of the people. To the extent that this suit concerns a question as to whether the school faculty may make its professional choices of textbooks prevail over the considered decision of the Board of Education empowered by state law to make such decisions, we affirm the decision of the District Judge in dismissing that portion of plaintiffs' complaint. In short, we find no federal constitutional violation in this Board's exercise of curriculum and textbook control as empowered by the Ohio statute.

Nor do we think that the Board's decisions in selecting texts were arbitrary and capricious or offended procedural due process. There was a Board committee appointed to make recommendations on textbooks. It met with the faculty committee and with a citizens' committee to discuss the books recommended by the faculty before the Board received its committee's recommendations and acted thereon. As to the appellants' complaints of arbitrary and capricious action, we again affirm the District Court.

## II. THE REMOVAL OF CERTAIN BOOKS FROM THE SCHOOL LIBRARY

In his opinion the District Judge held that "the novels *Catch 22* by Joseph Heller, *God Bless You, Mr. Rosewater* and *Cat's Cradle* by Kurt Vonnegut, Jr., are not on trial in this proceeding." Further he stated, "Literary value of the three novels [has] been conceded by the parties . . ." and that "obscenity as defined in the Supreme Court's pronouncements is eliminated as an issue herein by agreement of counsel." These holdings do not appear to be disputed on this appeal, and we accept them.

The District Judge, in dismissing the complaint concerning removal from the library of Heller's *Catch 22* and Vonnegut's *Cat's Cradle*, relied strongly upon a Second Circuit opinion in Presidents Council, District 25 v. Community School Board No. 25, 457 F.2d 289 (2nd Cir.), cert. denied, 409 U.S. 998, 93 S.Ct. 308, 34 L.Ed.2d 260 (1972). In that case, after noting, as we have above, that some authorized body has to make a determination as to the choice of books for texts or for the library, the Second Circuit continued by discussing a parallel right on the part of a board to "winnow" the library:

> The administration of any library, whether it be a university or particularly a public junior high school, involves a constant process of selection and winnowing based not only

on educational needs but financial and architectural realities. To suggest that the shelving or unshelving of books presents a constitutional issue, *particularly where there is no showing of a curtailment of freedom of speech or thought,* is a proposition we cannot accept. (Emphasis added.)

The District Judge in our instant case appears to have read this paragraph as upholding an absolute right on the part of this school board to remove from the library and presumably to destroy any books it regarded unfavorably without concern for the First Amendment. We do not read the Second Circuit opinion so broadly (see qualifying clause italicized above). If it were unqualified, we would not follow it.

A library is a storehouse of knowledge. When created for a public school it is an important privilege created by the state for the benefit of the students in the school. That privilege is not subject to being withdrawn by succeeding school boards whose members might desire to "winnow" the library for books the content of which occasioned their displeasure or disapproval. Of course, a copy of a book may wear out. Some books may become obsolete. Shelf space alone may at some point require some selection of books to be retained and books to be disposed of. No such rationale is involved in this case however.

The sole explanation offered by this record is provided by the School Board's minutes of July 17, 1972, which read as follows:

Mrs. Wong reviewed the Citizens Committee report regarding adoption of "God Bless You Mr. Rosewater".

Dr. Cain presented the following minority report:

> 1. It is recommended that *God Bless You Mr. Rosewater* not be purchased, either as a textbook, supplemental reading book or library book. The book is completely sick. One secretary read it for one-half hour and handed it back to the reviewer with the written comment, "GARBAGE".

> 2. Instead, it is recommended that the autobiography of Captain Eddie Rickenbacker be purchased for use in the English course. It is modern and it fills the need of providing material which will inspire and educate the students as well as teach them high moral values and provide the opportunity to learn from a man of exceptional ability and understanding.

> 3. For the same reason, it is recommended that the following books be purchased for immediate use as required supplemental reading in the high school social studies program:

> *Herbert Hoover,* a biography by Eugene Lyons; *Reminiscences of Douglas MacArthur*

4. It is also recommended in the interest of a balanced program that *One Day in The Life of Ivan Denisovich* by A. I. Solzhenitsyn, be purchased as a supplemental reader for the high school social studies program.

5. It is also recommended that copies of all of the above books be placed in the library of each secondary school.

6. It is also recommended that *Cats Cradle,* which was written by the same character (Vennegutter) who wrote, using the term loosely, *God Bless You Mr. Rosewater,* and which has been used as a textbook, although never legally adopted by the Board, be withdrawn immediately and all copies disposed of in accordance with statutory procedure.

7. Finally, it is recommended that the McGuffy Readers be bought as supplemental readers for enrichment program purposes for the elementary schools, since they seem to offer so many advantages in vocabulary, content and sentence structure over the drivel being pushed today.

While we recognize that the minute quoted above is designated as a "minority report," we find it significant in view of intervenor Cain's active role in the removal process and the fact that it offers the only official clue to the reasons for the School Board majority's two book removal motions. The Board's silence is extraordinary in view of the intense community controversy and the expressed professional views of the faculty favorable to the books concerned.

In the absence of any explanation of the Board's action which is neutral in First Amendment terms, we must conclude that the School Board removed the books because it found them objectionable in content and because it felt that it had the power, unfettered by the First Amendment, to censor the school library for subject matter which the Board members found distasteful.

Neither the State of Ohio nor the Strongsville School Board was under any federal constitutional compulsion to provide a library for the Strongsville High School or to choose any particular books. Once having created such a privilege for the benefit of its students, however, neither body could place conditions on the use of the library which were related solely to the social or political tastes of school board members.

The Supreme Court long ago said: "It is too late in the day to doubt that the liberties of religion and expression may be infringed by the denial of or placing conditions upon a benefit or privilege."

A public school library is also a valuable adjunct to classroom discussion. If one of the English teachers considered Joseph Heller's

*Catch 22* to be one of the more important modern American novels (as, indeed, at least one did), we assume that no one would dispute that the First Amendment's protection of academic freedom would protect both his right to say so in class and his students' right to hear him and to find and read the book. Obviously, the students' success in this last endeavor would be greatly hindered by the fact that the book sought had been removed from the school library. The removal of books from a school library is a much more serious burden upon freedom of classroom discussion than the action found unconstitutional in Tinker v. Des Moines Independent Community School District, 393 U.S. 503, 89 S.Ct. 733, 21 L.Ed.2d 731 (1969).

Further, we do not think this burden is minimized by the availability of the disputed book in sources outside the school. Restraint on expression may not generally be justified by the fact that there may be other times, places, or circumstances available for such expression.

A library is a mighty resource in the free marketplace of ideas. It is specially dedicated to broad dissemination of ideas. It is a forum for silent speech.

We recognize of course, that we deal here with a somewhat more difficult concept than a direct restraint on speech. Here we are concerned with the right of students to receive information which they and their teachers desire them to have. First Amendment protection of the right to know has frequently been recognized in the past. Nonetheless, we might have felt that its application here was more doubtful absent a very recent Supreme Court case. In Virginia State Board of Pharmacy v. Virginia Citizens Consumers Council, Inc., 425 U.S. 748, 96 S.Ct. 1817, 1823, 48 L.Ed.2d 346 (1976), Mr. Justice Blackmun wrote for the Court:

> Freedom of speech presupposes a willing speaker. But where a speaker exists, as is the case here, the protection afforded is to the communication, to its source and to its recipients both. This is clear from the decided cases. In Lamont v. Postmaster General, the Court upheld the First Amendment rights of citizens to receive political publications sent from abroad. More recently, in Kleindienst v. Mandel, we acknowledged that this Court has referred to a First Amendment right to "receive information and ideas," and that freedom of speech " 'necessarily protects the right to receive.' " And in Procunier v. Martinez, where censorship of prison inmates' mail was under examination, we thought it unnecessary to assess the First Amendment rights of the inmates themselves, for it was reasoned that such censorship equally infringed the rights of noninmates to whom correspondence was addressed. There are numerous other expressions to the same effect in the Court's decisions. If there is a right to ad-

vertise, there is a reciprocal right to receive the advertising, and it may be asserted by these appellees.

We believe that the language just quoted, plus the recent cases of Kleindienst v. Mandel, supra, and Procunier v. Martinez, supra, serve to establish firmly both the First Amendment right to know which is involved in our instant case and the standing of the student plaintiffs to raise the issue.

As to this issue, we must reverse.

## NOTES AND QUESTIONS

1. Suppose a book is attacked by a Black because it sought to show the low I.Q. and inherent, constitutional inferiority of Blacks, what result?

2. The Supreme Court denied certiorari in Presidents Council v. Community School Board, 409 U.S. 998, 93 S.Ct. 308, 34 L.Ed.2d 260 (1973); Mr. Justice Douglas dissented:

> "A book entitled Down These Main Streets by Piri Thomas was purchased by the librarians of three junior high schools in School District 25 in Queens, New York. The novel describes in graphic detail sexual and drug related activities that are a part of everyday life for those who live in Spanish Harlem. Its purpose was to acquaint the youth of Queens with the problems of their contemporaries in this social setting. The book was objected to by some parents and after a public meeting the School Board by a vote of 5–3 banned it from the libraries. A later vote by the Board amended the order so the book is now kept on the shelves for direct loan to any parent who wants his or her children to have access to it. No child can borrow it directly.

> "This suit was brought on behalf of a principal, a librarian, and various parents and children who request that the court declare the resolution adopted by the Board unconstitutional, and order the defendants to place the book on normal circulation in the libraries and enjoin them from interfering with other school libraries within their jurisdiction which desire to purchase the book.

> "Actions of school boards are not immune from constitutional scrutiny, . . . The First Amendment involves not only the right to speak and publish but also the right to hear, to learn, to know. . . . And this Court has recognized that this right to know is 'nowhere more vital than in our schools and universities,' . . . The book involved is not alleged to be obscene either under the standards of Roth v. United States, 354 U.S. 476 (1957); or under the stricter standards for minors set forth in Ginsberg v. New York, 390 U.S. 629 (1968).

> "The Board, however, contends that a book with such vivid accounts of sordid and perverted occurrences is not good for junior high students. At trial both sides produced expert witnesses to prove the value and/or harm of the novel. At school the children

are allowed to discuss the contents of the book and the social problems it portrays. They can do everything but read it. This in my mind lessens somewhat the contention that the subject matter of the book is not proper.

"The First Amendment is a preferred right and is of great importance in the schools. In *Tinker*, the Court held that the First Amendment can only be restricted in the schools when a disciplinary problem is raised. No such allegation is asserted here. What else can the School Board now decide it does not like? How else will its sensibilities be offended? Are we sending children to school to be educated by the norms of the School Board or are we educating our youth to shed the prejudices of the past, to explore all forms of thought, and to find solutions to our world's problems?

"Another requirement of the First Amendment is that any statute that imposes restrictions on the freedoms it protects must be narrowly drawn so as to impose any limitation in only the least restrictive way. § 2590e(3) gives the Board power to 'determine matters relating to the instruction of students, including the selection of textbooks and other instructional materials  .  .  .,' provided they are approved by the Chancellor. The Commissioners' regulation says that secondary school book collections 'shall consist of books approved as satisfactory for (1) supplementing the curriculum (2) reference and general information (3) appreciation and (4) pleasure reading,' 8 N.Y.Code, Rules & Regs.Educ., § 91.1(b) (1966). Even a casual reading of these regulations show they contain no discreet limitations of the type spoken of in Cantwell v. Conn., Speiser v. Randall, or Shelton v. Tucker.

"Because the issues raised here are crucial to our national life, I would hear argument in this case.

"Mr. Justice STEWART would also grant the petition for certiorari and set the case for oral argument."

Assuming that the court had granted certiorari; what would have been the decision on the merits of this case and for what reasons?

3. The Minarcini case is ultimately grounded in the First Amendment's protection of a student's right to know. Is this view unique to protection for the library or does it extend to the curriculum? This view should be compared to those found in the *Keefe, Parducci* and *Mailloux* cases, supra. Are those three cases ultimately based on a student's right to know or on an independent right of teachers to academic freedom? Or is the teacher's right to academic freedom really only a derivative right from a student's right to know? For discussion see, Van Alstyne, The Constitutional Rights of Teachers and Professors, 1970 Duke L.J. 841. What difference does it make? The right to know presupposes a willing communicant, and if none exists, then the right to know is not operative. Thus, the right to know might protect a teacher's right to speak but not his right not to speak. Suppose a school board orders that certain materials be taught in a prescribed way, drawing certain prescribed conclusions, such as those prescribed by Florida's found

at the end of the materials on academic freedom, supra, would a teacher's right derived from a student's right to know, by itself, protect a teacher who refused to teach as ordered? Wouldn't a student's right to know entitle him to have the school board's materials taught as prescribed? Or, suppose a school board ordered that certain materials, such as any reference to the origins of man, be excised from the curriculum, would a student's right to know protect a teacher who informed his students about the existence of Darwin's theory? Does the right to know protect against official exclusion of ideas from the curriculum? Suppose in Minarcini the question was not whether the books should be removed from the library, but whether the books should be purchased at all, would a student's right to know justify a court ordering a school board to buy the books?

---

## THE LIBRARY BILL OF RIGHTS

Printed with permission of The American Library Association.

The Council of the American Library Association reaffirms its belief in the following basic policies which should govern the services of all libraries.

1. As a responsibility of library service, books and other library materials selected should be chosen for values of interest, information and enlightenment of all the people of the community. In no case should library materials be excluded because of the race or nationality or the social, political, or religious views of the authors.

2. Libraries should provide books and other materials presenting all points of view concerning the problems and issues of our times; no library materials should be proscribed or removed from libraries because of partisan or doctrinal disapproval.

3. Censorship should be challenged by libraries in the maintenance of their responsibility to provide public information and enlightenment.

4. Libraries should cooperate with all persons and groups concerned with resisting abridgment of free expression and free access to ideas.

5. The rights of an individual to the use of a library should not be denied or abridged because of his race, religion, national origins or social or political views.

6. As an institution of education for democratic living, the library should welcome the use of its meeting rooms for socially useful and cultural activities and discussion of current public questions. Such meeting places should be available on equal terms to all groups in the community regardless of the beliefs and affiliations of their members, providing that the meetings be open to the public.

(Adopted June 18, 1948. Amended February 2, 1961, and June 27, 1967, by the American Library Association Council).

## PROBLEM

1. California's law provides:

No instructional materials shall be adopted by any governing board for use in the schools which, in its determination, contains:

(a) Any matter reflecting adversely upon persons because of their race, color, creed, national origin, ancestry, sex or occupation.

(b) Any sectarian or denominational doctrine or propaganda contrary to law. West's Ann.Educ.Code of Calif. § 60044.

If you had been a member of California's legislature would you have voted for this statute? Why or why not? Is it constitutional?

# Chapter IV

## CONSTITUTIONAL LIMITATIONS ON GOVERN-MENTAL CONTROL OF IDEAS IN NON–CURRICULAR AFFAIRS

### INTRODUCTION

This chapter and the next one continue the exploration of First-Amendment themes introduced in the last chapter. But the focus of this chapter is different. The focus here is on the constitutional protection for free expression of ideas in noncurricular areas. In an important sense, this chapter indirectly comments on a subject area only slightly touched on by the previous materials: What are the constitutionally correct criteria against which a school's governance system should be judged? Should a school's internal governance system conform to the premises of democratic pluralism that are basic to the decisions in Meyer and Pierce?

There are many models of proper school governance. Professor Ladd has identified two of the most important—the paternalistic-authoritarian model and the democratic model. (See, Ladd, Regulating Student Behavior Without Ending Up In Court, 54 Phi Delta Kappan 304 (1973) and Alleged Disruptive Student Behavior and The Legal Authority of Public School Officials, 19 J.Pub.Law 209 (1970)). The paternalistic-authoritarian model has been the historical choice. It emphasizes strict and comprehensive discipline and functions hierarchically with authority found in the school's administrative structure. Extensive regulation of student conduct is practiced. Students are seen as immature persons who properly can be coerced in certain circumstances. Students have privileges awarded them by the administration but no rights. And school governance is characterized by "discipline first" and "adults-know-best" attitudes. The democratic model of governance sees students and adults as equal participants in some but not all school activities. It justifies student participation on the ground that learning is more efficient and effective in a democratic context. The administration retains ultimate authority, but emphasis is on a respectful, pleasant and considerate learning environment for the student, rather than on a strict code of discipline. The school is characterized by an absence of emphasis on comprehensive regulation of student conduct and by a strong emphasis on a "learning-must-come-first" attitude.

Legal conflict over appropriate governance models often takes the form of claims about "students rights." The outcome of these legal conflicts can be crucially important because schools are an important socializing force, and a school's governance system is a powerful socializing tool. Our constitution is not neutral in these conflicts because it protects free expression, privacy, equality and other rights. They are critical to a person's human dignity and serve as basic ingredients in our representative democracy. Frequently, students may challenge a school rule by arguing that, as applied to them, the rule violates their "constitutional rights." Thus, many cases in this chapter are "student rights" cases. But since this chapter is limited to free expression of *ideas* in non-curricular areas, and does not address constitutional protection of privacy and other rights, it does not exhaust either the "student rights" cases or the theme of proper school governance. That theme is picked up again, but without First Amendment emphasis on the expression of ideas, in chapter VI which follows immediately after the next chapter (V) on religious freedom.

Although our constitution protects the free expression of ideas, its protection varies from context to context. It may permit some restrictions on freedom in a school context. Yet, any state power restricting the free expression of ideas must be fully justified before it can pass constitutional muster. In the materials that follow, try to identify the precise ground relied upon by the state for limiting the free expression of ideas and then identify why the state's ground was, or was not, held by the courts to provide a constitutionally adequate basis. Then, describe the constitutional right involved in each of the cases and the type of a school governance system that would be effective yet protective of that right.

## IN THE CLASSROOM

---

## TINKER v. DES MOINES INDEPENDENT COMMUNITY SCHOOL DISTRICT

Supreme Court of the United States, 1969.
393 U.S. 503, 89 S.Ct. 733, 21 L.Ed.2d 731.

Mr. Justice FORTAS delivered the opinion of the Court.

Petitioner John F. Tinker, 15 years old, and petitioner Christopher Eckhardt, 16 years old, attended high schools in Des Moines, Iowa. Petitioner Mary Beth Tinker, John's sister, was a 13-year-old student in junior high school.

In December 1965, a group of adults and students in Des Moines held a meeting at the Eckhardt home. The group determined to publicize their objections to the hostilities in Vietnam and their support for a truce by wearing black armbands during the holiday season and by fasting on December 16 and New Year's Eve. Petitioners and their parents had previously engaged in similar activities, and they decided to participate in the program.

The principals of the Des Moines schools became aware of the plan to wear armbands. On December 14, 1965, they met and adopted a policy that any student wearing an armband to school would be asked to remove it, and if he refused he would be suspended until he returned without the armband. Petitioners were aware of the regulation that the school authorities adopted.

On December 16, Mary Beth and Christopher wore black armbands to their schools. John Tinker wore his armband the next day. They were all sent home and suspended from school until they would come back without their armbands. They did not return to school until after the planned period for wearing armbands had expired— that is, until after New Year's Day.

This complaint was filed in the United States District Court by petitioners, through their fathers, . . . It prayed for an injunction restraining the respondent school officials and the respondent members of the board of directors of the school district from disciplining the petitioners, and it sought nominal damages. . . . [T]he District Court dismissed the complaint. It upheld the constitutionality of the school authorities' action on the ground that it was reasonable in order to prevent disturbance of school discipline. . . . The court referred to but expressly declined to follow the Fifth Circuit's holding in a similar case that the wearing of symbols like the armbands cannot be prohibited unless it "materially and substantially interfere[s] with the requirements of appropriate discipline in the operation of the school." Burnside v. Byars, 363 F.2d 744, 749 (5th Cir. 1966). [But compare, Blackwell v. Issaquena Cty. Bd. of Education, 363 F.2d 749 (5th Cir. 1966).]

On appeal, the Court of Appeals for the Eighth Circuit considered the case *en banc*. The court was equally divided, and the District Court's decision was accordingly affirmed, without opinion. . . . We granted certiorari. . . .

The District Court recognized that the wearing of an armband for the purpose of expressing certain views is the type of symbolic act that is within the Free Speech Clause of the First Amendment. See West Virginia State Board of Education v. Barnette, . . . As we shall discuss, the wearing of armbands in the circumstances of this case was entirely divorced from actually or potentially disruptive conduct by those participating in it. It was closely akin to "pure speech" which, we have repeatedly held, is entitled to comprehensive protection under the First Amendment. . . .

First Amendment rights, applied in light of the special characteristics of the school environment, are available to teachers and students. It can hardly be argued that either students or teachers shed their constitutional rights to freedom of speech or expression at the school-house gate. This has been the unmistakable holding of this Court for almost 50 years. In Meyer v. Nebraska, . . . this Court, . . . held that the Due Process Clause of the Fourteenth Amendment prevents States from forbidding the teaching of a foreign language to young students. Statutes to this effect, the Court held, unconstitutionally interfere with the liberty of teacher, student, and parent. . . .

. . . On the other hand, the Court has repeatedly emphasized the need for affirming the comprehensive authority of the States and of school officials, consistent with fundamental constitutional safeguards, to prescribe and control conduct in the schools. . . . Our problem lies in the area where students in the exercise of First Amendment rights collide with the rules of the school authorities.

The problem posed by the present case does not relate to regulation of the length of skirts or the type of clothing, to hair style, or deportment. . . . It does not concern aggressive, disruptive action or even group demonstrations. Our problem involves direct, primary First Amendment rights akin to "pure speech."

The school officials banned and sought to punish petitioners for a silent, passive expression of opinion, unaccompanied by any disorder or disturbance on the part of petitioners. There is here no evidence whatever of petitioners' interference, actual or nascent, with the schools' work or of collision with the rights of other students to be secure and to be let alone. Accordingly, this case does not concern speech or action that intrudes upon the work of the schools or the rights of other students.

Only a few of the 18,000 students in the school system wore the black armbands. Only five students were suspended for wearing them. There is no indication that the work of the schools or any class was disrupted. Outside the classrooms, a few students made hostile remarks to the children wearing armbands, but there were no threats or acts of violence on school premises.

The District Court concluded that the action of the school authorities was reasonable because it was based upon their fear of a disturbance from the wearing of the armbands. But, in our system, undifferentiated fear or apprehension of disturbance is not enough to overcome the right to freedom of expression. Any departure from absolute regimentation may cause trouble. Any variation from the majority's opinion may inspire fear. Any word spoken, in class, in the lunchroom, or on the campus, that deviates from the views of another person may start an argument or cause a disturbance. But our Constitution says we must take this risk . . . and our history says that it is this sort of hazardous freedom—this kind of openness—that is the basis of our national strength and of the independence and vigor of Americans who grow up and live in this relatively permissive, often disputatious, society.

In order for the State in the person of school officials to justify prohibition of a particular expression of opinion, it must be able to show that its action was caused by something more than a mere desire to avoid the discomfort and unpleasantness that always accompany an unpopular viewpoint. Certainly where there is no finding and no showing that engaging in the forbidden conduct would "materially and substantially interfere with the requirements of appropriate discipline in the operation of the school," the prohibition cannot be sustained. . . .

In the present case, the District Court made no such finding, and our independent examination of the record fails to yield evidence that the school authorities had reason to anticipate that the wearing of the armbands would substantially interfere with the work of the school or impinge upon the rights of other students. Even an official memorandum prepared after the suspension that listed the reasons for the ban on wearing the armbands made no reference to the anticipation of such disruption.

On the contrary, the action of the school authorities appears to have been based upon an urgent wish to avoid the controversy which might result from the expression, even by the silent symbol of armbands, of opposition to this Nation's part in the conflagration in Vietnam. It is revealing, in this respect, that the meeting at which the school principals decided to issue the contested regulation was called in response to a student's statement to the journalism teacher in one of the schools that he wanted to write an article on Vietnam and have it published in the school paper. (The student was dissuaded.)

It is also relevant that the school authorities did not purport to prohibit the wearing of all symbols of political or controversial significance. The record shows that students in some of the schools wore buttons relating to national political campaigns, and some even wore the Iron Cross, traditionally a symbol of Nazism. The order prohibiting the wearing of armbands did not extend to these. Instead, a particular symbol—black armbands worn to exhibit opposition to this Nation's involvement in Vietnam—was singled out for prohibition. Clearly, the prohibition of expression of one particular opinion, at least without evidence that it is necessary to avoid material and substantial interference with schoolwork or discipline, is not constitutionally permissible.

In our system, state-operated schools may not be enclaves of totalitarianism. School officials do not possess absolute authority over their students. Students in school as well as out of school are "persons" under our Constitution. They are possessed of fundamental rights which the State must respect, just as they themselves must respect their obligations to the State. In our system, students may not be regarded as closed-circuit recipients of only that which the State chooses to communicate. They may not be confined to the expression of those sentiments that are officially approved. In the absence of a specific showing of constitutionally valid reasons to regulate their speech, students are entitled to freedom of expression of their views. As Judge Gewin, speaking for the Fifth Circuit, said, school officials cannot suppress "expressions of feelings with which they do not wish to contend." Burnside v. Byars, supra, 363 F.2d at 749.

In Meyer v. Nebraska, supra, . . . Mr. Justice McReynolds expressed this Nation's repudiation of the principle that a State might so conduct its schools as to "foster a homogeneous people." He said:

> "In order to submerge the individual and develop ideal citizens, Sparta assembled the males at seven into barracks and intrusted their subsequent education and training to official guardians. Although such measures have been deliberately approved by men of great genius, their ideas touching the relation between individual and State were wholly different from those upon which our institutions rest; and it hardly will be affirmed that any Legislature could impose such restrictions upon the people of a state without doing violence to both letter and spirit of the Constitution."

This principle has been repeated by this Court on numerous occasions during the intervening years. In Keyishian v. Board of Regents, . . . Justice Brennan, speaking for the Court, said:

> " 'The vigilant protection of constitutional freedoms is nowhere more vital than in the community of American schools.' Shelton v. Tucker, . . . The classroom is peculiarly the 'marketplace of ideas.' The Nation's future depends upon leaders trained through wide exposure to that robust exchange of ideas which discovers truth 'out of a multitude of tongues, [rather] than through any kind of authoritative selection.' "

The principle of these cases is not confined to the supervised and ordained discussion which takes place in the classroom. The principal use to which the schools are dedicated is to accommodate students during prescribed hours for the purpose of certain types of activities. Among those activities is personal intercommunication among the students. This is not only an inevitable part of the process of attending school; it is also an important part of the educational process. A student's rights, therefore, do not embrace merely the classroom hours. When he is in the cafeteria, or on the playing field, or on the campus during the authorized hours, he may express his opinions, even on controversial subjects like the conflict in Vietnam, if he does so without "materially and substantially interfer[ing] with the requirements of appropriate discipline in the operation of the school" and without colliding with the rights of others. . . . But conduct by the student, in class or out of it, which for any reason—whether it stems from time, place, or type of behavior—materially disrupts classwork or involves substantial disorder or invasion of the rights of others is, of course, not immunized by the constitutional guarantee of freedom of speech. . . .

Under our Constitution, free speech is not a right that is given only to be so circumscribed that it exists in principle but not in fact. Freedom of expression would not truly exist if the right could be exercised only in an area that a benevolent government has provided as a safe haven for crackpots. The Constitution says that Congress (and the States) may not abridge the right to free speech. This provision means what it says. We properly read it to permit reasonable regulation of speech-connected activities in carefully restricted circumstances. But we do not confine the permissible exercise of First Amendment rights to a telephone booth or the four corners of a pamphlet, or to supervised and ordained discussion in a school classroom.

If a regulation were adopted by school officials forbidding discussion of the Vietnam conflict, or the expression by any student of opposition to it anywhere on school property except as part of a prescribed classroom exercise, it would be obvious that the regulation would violate the constitutional rights of students, at least if it could not be justified by a showing that the students' activities would materially and substantially disrupt the work and discipline of the school. . . . In the circumstances of the present case, the prohibition of the silent, passive "witness of the armbands," as one of the children called it, is no less offensive to the Constitution's guarantees.

As we have discussed, the record does not demonstrate any facts which might reasonably have led school authorities to forecast substantial disruption of or material interference with school activities, and no disturbances or disorders on the school premises in fact occurred. These petitioners merely went about their ordained rounds in school. Their deviation consisted only in wearing on their sleeve a band of black cloth, not more than two inches wide. They wore it to exhibit their disapproval of the Vietnam hostilities and their advocacy of a truce, to make their views known, and, by their example, to influence others to adopt them. They neither interrupted school activities nor sought to intrude in the school affairs or the lives of others. They caused discussion outside of the classrooms, but no interference with work and no disorder. In the circumstances, our Constitution does not permit officials of the State to deny their form of expression. . . .

Reversed and remanded.

Mr. Justice STEWART, concurring.

Although I agree with much of what is said in the Court's opinion, and with its judgment in this case, I cannot share the Court's uncritical assumption that, school discipline aside, the First Amendment rights of children are co-extensive with those of adults. Indeed, I had thought the Court decided otherwise just last Term in Ginsberg v. New York, 390 U.S. 629, . . . I continue to hold the view I expressed in that case: "[A] State may permissibly determine that, at least in some precisely delineated areas, a child—like someone in a captive audience—is not possessed of that full capacity for individual choice which is the presupposition of First Amendment guarantees." Id., at 649–650, . . .

Mr. Justice WHITE, concurring.

While I join the Court's opinion, I deem it appropriate to note, first, that the Court continues to recognize a distinction between communicating by words and communicating by acts or conduct which sufficiently impinges on some valid state interest; and, second, that I do not subscribe to everything the Court of Appeals said about free speech in its opinion in Burnside v. Byars, . . . a case relied upon by the Court in the matter now before us.

Mr. Justice BLACK, dissenting.

The Court's holding in this case ushers in what I deem to be an entirely new era in which the power to control pupils by the elected "officials of state supported public schools * * *" in the United States is in ultimate effect transferred to the Supreme Court. The Court brought this particular case here on a petition for certiorari urging that the First and Fourteenth Amendments protect the right of school pupils to express their political views all the way "from kindergarten through high school." Here the constitutional right to "political expression" asserted was a right to wear black armbands during school hours and at classes in order to demonstrate to the other students that the petitioners were mourning because of the death of United States soldiers in Vietnam and to protest that war which they were against. Ordered to refrain from wearing the armbands in school by the elected school officials and the teachers vested with state authority to do so, apparently only seven out of the school system's 18,000 pupils deliberately refused to obey the order. One defying pupil was Paul Tinker, 8 years old, who was in the second grade; another, Hope Tinker, was 11 years old and in the fifth grade; a third member of the Tinker family was 13, in the eighth grade; and a fourth member of the same family was John Tinker, 15 years old, an 11th grade high school pupil. Their father, a Methodist minister without a church, is paid a salary by the American Friends Service Committee. Another student who defied the school order and insisted on wearing an armband in school was Christopher Eckhardt, an 11th grade pupil and a petitioner in this case. His mother is an official in the Women's International League for Peace and Freedom.
. . . .

Assuming that the Court is correct in holding that the conduct of wearing armbands for the purpose of conveying political ideas is protected by the First Amendment, . . . the crucial remaining questions are whether students and teachers may use the schools at their whim as a platform for the exercise of free speech—"symbolic" or "pure"—and whether the courts will allocate to themselves the function of deciding how the pupils' school day will be spent. While I have always believed that under the First and Fourteenth Amendments neither the State nor the Federal Government has any authority to regulate or censor the content of speech, I have never believed that any person has a right to give speeches or engage in demonstrations where he pleases and when he pleases. This Court has already rejected such a notion. . . .

While the record does not show that any of these armband students shouted, used profane language, or were violent in any manner, detailed testimony by some of them shows their armbands caused comments, warnings by other students, the poking of fun at them, and a warning by an older football player that other, non-protesting students had better let them alone. There is also evidence that a teacher of mathematics had his lesson period practically "wrecked" chiefly by disputes with Mary Beth Tinker, who wore her armband for her "demonstration." Even a casual reading of the record shows that this armband did divert students' minds from their regular lessons, and that talk, comments, etc., made John Tinker "self-conscious" in attending school with his armband. . . . And I repeat that if the time has come when pupils of state-supported schools, kindergartens, grammer schools, or high schools, can defy and flout orders of school officials to keep their minds on their own schoolwork, it is the beginning of a new revolutionary era of permissiveness in this country fostered by the judiciary. The next logical step, it appears to me, would be to hold unconstitutional laws that bar pupils under 21 or 18 from voting, or from being elected members of the boards of education. . . .

In my view, teachers in state-controlled public schools are hired to teach there. Although Mr. Justice McReynolds may have intimated to the contrary in Meyer v. Nebraska, supra, certainly a teacher is not paid to go into school and teach subjects the State does not hire him to teach as a part of its selected curriculum. Nor are public school students sent to the schools at public expense to broadcast political or any other views to educate and inform the public. The original idea of schools, which I do not believe is yet abandoned as worthless or out of date, was that children had not yet reached the point of experience and wisdom which enabled them to teach all of their elders. It may be that the Nation has outworn the old-fashioned slogan that "children are to be seen not heard," but one may, I hope, be permitted to harbor the thought that taxpayers send children to school on the premise that at their age they need to learn, not teach. . . .

Change has been said to be truly the law of life but sometimes the old and the tried and true are worth holding. The schools of this Nation have undoubtedly contributed to giving us tranquility and to making us a more law abiding people. Uncontrolled and uncontrollable liberty is an enemy to domestic peace. We cannot close our eyes to the fact that some of the country's greatest problems are crimes committed by the youth, too many of school age. School discipline, like parental discipline, is an integral and important part of training our children to be good citizens—to be better citizens. Here a very small number of students have crisply and summarily refused to obey a school order designed to give pupils who want to learn the opportunity to do so. One does not need to be a prophet or the son of a prophet to know that after the Court's holding today some students in Iowa schools and indeed in all schools will be ready, able, and willing to defy their teachers on practically all orders. This is the more unfortunate for the schools since groups of students all over the land are already running loose, conducting break-ins, sit-ins, lie-ins, and smash-ins. Many of these student groups, as is all too familiar to all who read the newspapers and watch the television news programs, have already engaged in rioting, property seizures, and destruction. They have picketed schools to force students not to cross their picket lines and have too often violently attacked earnest but frightened students who wanted an education that the pickets did not want them to get. Students engaged in such activities are apparently confident that they know far more about how to operate public school systems than do their parents, teachers, and elected school officials. It is no answer to say that the particular students here have not yet reached such high points in their demands to attend classes in order to exercise their political pressures. Turned loose with lawsuits for damages and injunctions against their teachers as they are here, it is nothing but wishful thinking to imagine that young, immature students will not soon believe it is their right to control the schools rather than the right of the States that collect the taxes to hire the teachers for the benefit of the pupils. This case, therefore, wholly without constitutional reasons in my judgment, subjects all the public schools in the country to the whims and caprices of their loudest-mouthed, but maybe not their brightest, students. I, for one, am not fully persuaded that school pupils are wise enough, even with this Court's expert help from Washington, to run the 23,390 public school systems in our 50 States.   .   .   .   I dissent.

Mr. Justice HARLAN, dissenting.

.   .   .   I would, in cases like this, cast upon those complaining the burden of showing that a particular school measure was motivated by other than legitimate school concerns—for example, a desire to prohibit the expression of an unpopular point of view, while permitting expression of the dominant opinion.

Finding nothing in this record which impugns the good faith of respondents in promulgating the armband regulation, I would affirm the judgment below.

## NOTES AND QUESTIONS

1. What is the Supreme Court's ultimate rationale for its decisions that students have First Amendment rights to free expression and that they can be exercised in the classroom during the class instruction period? The Court stated that "In our system, students may not be regarded as closed-circuit recipients of only that which the state chooses to communicate" and that students "may not be confined to the expression of those sentiments that are officially approved." The Court also said that "state operated schools may not be enclaves of totalitarianism" and that "school officials do not possess absolute authority over their students." At another point the Court stated that "the principal use to which the schools are dedicated is to accommodate students during prescribed hours for the purpose of certain types of activity. Among these activities is personal intercommunication among the students. This is not only an inevitable part of the process of attending. It is also an important part of the educational process . . .". Do these quotations reveal the ultimate rationale of Tinker? If so, is that rationale consistent with those of Meyer, Pierce and West Va. v. Barnette? Does Tinker eventually rest on the theory of democratic pluralism? See generally, Comment, Academic Freedom In The High School Classroom, 15 J.Fam.L. 706 (1976–77), and Nahmod, Beyond Tinker: The High School As An Educational Public Forum, 5 Harv.Civ.Rights-Civ.Lib. L.Rev. 278 (1970).

2. The Court recognized that certain kinds of student expression would not be protected: "conduct by the student, in class or out of it, which for any reason—whether it stems from time, place or type of behavior—materially disrupts classwork or involves substantial disorder or invasion of the rights of others is, of course, not immunized by the constitutional guarantee of freedom of speech." What was the evidence relied upon by the state in its attempt to come within this quote and restrict student free expression? Why did the Court find the state's evidence inadequate? What evidence is necessary to prove substantial disruption?

Suppose other students in the class had friends and relatives in Vietnam, some of whom had been killed, and they disapproved of the black armbands and began to hoot and engage the Tinker children in a fistfight. Surely, that would be a disruption involving "substantial disorder." Would that be sufficient for the principal to insist that the armbands be removed? Even if the disruption was not caused by the symbolic speech itself but by the response of other students to the speech? Should it ever be permissible to silence a non-disruptive speaker? Why should a heckler have a veto? Generally see, Melton v. Young, 465 F.2d 1332 (6th Cir. 1972), certiorari denied, 411 U.S. 951, 93 S.Ct. 1926, 36 L.Ed.2d 414 (1973), and Nahmod, Controversy In the Classroom: The High School Teacher and Freedom of Expression, 39 Geo.Wash.L.Rev. 1032 (1971).

Does Tinker require actual disruption or only a reasonable forecast of disruption? If it only requires a reasonable forecast of substantial disruption what evidence is sufficient? A verbal disagreement between students? Between a teacher and students? Loud inappropriate laughter? Lack of attention?

3.  Would the Tinker decision have been decided differently if teachers rather than students were involved? Why or why not? See, James v. Board of Educ., 461 F.2d 566 (2d Cir. 1972), rehearing denied 409 U.S. 1042, 93 S.Ct. 529, 34 L.Ed.2d 491. Suppose a local Board of Education passed a regulation prohibiting teachers from wearing political campaign buttons or armbands or any other similar type of insignia in the classroom, would this regulation be upheld? Consider the implications of the views of Mr. Justice Harlan as compared with those of the majority. What difference do they make? Which view do you agree with? Why?

Was the symbolic speech in Tinker the free choice of the students or were they being "used" to further a "cause"? Should this consideration make any difference in a court's decision?

Suppose the school board had adopted a regulation to the effect that the wearing of armbands would be allowed on playfields, in the cafeteria and hallways, but not in the classrooms, would this regulation of the expression have been upheld?

4.  The Supreme Court refused to grant certiorari to review Barker v. Hardway, Mr. Justice Fortas specifically stating:

> "I agree that certiorari should be denied. The petitioners were suspended from college not for expressing their opinions on a matter of substance, but for violent and destructive interference with the rights of others. An adequate hearing was afforded them on the issue of suspension. The petitioners contend that their conduct was protected by the First Amendment, but the findings of the District Court, which were accepted by the Court of Appeals, establish that the petitioners here engaged in an aggressive and violent demonstration and not in peaceful, nondisruptive expression, such as was involved in [Tinker]. The petitioners' conduct was therefore clearly not protected by the First and Fourteenth Amendments." Barker v. Hardway, 394 U.S. 905, 89 S.Ct. 1009, 22 L.Ed.2d 217 (1969).

5.  When deciding this type of a case, should a court distinguish between disruptions of a school's curricular activities and disruptions of its extra-curricular activities? If so, why? Assuming that it is proper to distinguish curricular from extra-curricular activities, would that distinction have made any difference in the decision of this case?

6.  The Court stated that the problem posed by Tinker "does not relate to regulation of the length of skirts or the type of clothing, to hair style or deportment." These problems will be considered in the chapter after next. But, does Tinker's problem relate to school newspapers? Suppose a fight had broken out between the Tinker children and students who had relatives killed in Vietnam and the student newspaper wanted to comment on it in a general article on "The Morality of America's War in Vietnam," would Tinker apply?

## PROBLEM

"The Court finds from this undisputed evidence that all of the plaintiffs are of Mexican descent and are referred to variously as 'Mexicans', 'Hispanos' and 'Chicanos'. In August of 1969, the plaintiff, Hernandez, spokesman for the plaintiffs, asked if plaintiffs would be permitted to wear black berets and long hair while in school. As reasons for the request, it was stated that the wearing of the berets would be a symbol of their Mexican culture; it would show unity among Mexicans; it would be a symbol of respect, and a symbol of their dissatisfaction with society's treatment of their race, and their desire to improve that treatment.

"Mr. Shannon, himself of Mexican descent, told the plaintiffs that he was a part of the same culture to which they referred and that he was sympathetic with their desire to generate respect for the Mexican culture. He told the plaintiffs that their request to wear long hair and black berets was new, but they would be permitted to do so and 'we would try and see if we could live with it.'

"In September, the plaintiffs requested permission to extend into the school system, a celebration of Independence Day of the Republic of Mexico (September 16) by having a walkout of students to participate in a parade and demonstration. Although this caused considerable apprehension among school officials and some students and parents, due to the fact that the previous spring, a demonstration at West High School in the Denver system had resulted in violence, destruction of property, and confrontations between students and police; nonetheless, Mr. Shannon not only granted the request, but he also arranged for assemblies at the school to explain the reason for and significance of the celebration on September 16 and to present appropriate Mexican entertainment.

" . . . The plaintiffs walked in the hallways during class time talking in loud voices and from time to time, shouting, 'Chicano power'; during passing periods, they congregated in the hallways to block the same from free passage by other students; they refused to give their names to the teachers and explain what they were doing in the hallways during class time; . . . when a teacher supervising the hallways gave some students directions, one of the plaintiffs stated: 'Don't listen to that old bag—the berets will take care of her'; . . . they attempted to induce students in class to leave the classrooms and join them in the hallways; and they refused to obey a requirement of the School Board that material to be distributed on school property be submitted in advance to the principal." See Hernandez v. School District No. 1, 315 F.Supp. 289 (D.Colo.1970).

Assume that the plaintiffs have been suspended and that you are a judge, on the basis of all the materials studied, what decision would you make on the substantive merits and for what reasons? Compare Burnside v. Byars, 363 F.2d 744 (5th Cir. 1966) with Blackwell v. Issaquena County Bd. of Education, 363 F.2d 749 (5th Cir. 1966), and see also, Guzick v. Drebus, 305 F.Supp. 472 (N.D.Ohio 1969), aff'd 431 F.2d 594, cert. den. 401 U.S. 948.

## NEWSPAPERS

---

## PAPISH v. BOARD OF CURATORS OF UNIVERSITY OF MISSOURI

Supreme Court of the United States, 1973.
410 U.S. 667, 93 S.Ct. 1197, 35 L.Ed.2d 618.

PER CURIAM.

Petitioner, a graduate student in the University of Missouri School of Journalism, was expelled for distributing on campus a newspaper "containing forms of indecent speech" in violation of the By-Laws of the Board of Curators. The newspaper, the Free Press Underground, had been sold on this state university campus for more than four years pursuant to an authorization obtained from the University Business Office. The particular newspaper issue in question was found to be unacceptable for two reasons. First, on the front cover the publishers had reproduced a political cartoon previously printed in another newspaper depicting policeman raping the Statue of Liberty and the Goddess of Justice. The caption under the cartoon read: " . . . With Liberty and Justice for All." Secondly, the issue contained an article entitled M_____ f_____ Acquitted," which discussed the trial and acquittal on an assault charge of a New York City youth who was a member of an organization known as "Up Against the Wall, M_____ f_____."

Following a hearing, the Student Conduct Committee found that petitioner had violated Paragraph B of Art. A of the General Standards of Student Conduct which requires students "to observe generally accepted standards of conduct" and specifically prohibits "indecent conduct or speech." [2] Her dismissal, after affirmance first by the Chancellor of the University and then by its Board of Curators, was made effective in the middle of the spring semester. Although she was then permitted to remain on campus until the end of the sem-

---

[2] In pertinent part, the By-Law states: "Students enrolling in the University assume an obligation and are expected by the University to conduct themselves in a manner compatible with the University's functions and missions as an educational institution. For that purpose students are required to observe generally accepted standards of conduct . . . . [I]ndecent conduct or speech . . . are examples of conduct which would contravene this standard . . . ." 464 F.2d, at 138.

ester, she was not given credit for the one course in which she made a passing grade. . . . She claimed that her dismissal was improperly premised on activities protected by the First Amendment. The District Court denied relief, 331 F.Supp. 1321, and the Court of Appeals affirmed, one judge dissenting. 464 F.2d 136. . . .

The District Court's opinion rests, in part, on the conclusion that the banned issue of the newspaper was obscene. The Court of Appeals found it unnecessary to decide that question. Instead, assuming that the newspaper was not obscene and that its distribution in the community at large would be protected by the First Amendment, the court held that on a university campus "freedom of expression" could properly be "subordinated to other interests such as, for example, the conventions of decency in the use and display of language and pictures." . . . The court concluded that "[t]he Constitution does not compel the University [to allow] such publications as the one in litigation to be publicly sold or distributed on its open campus."

This case was decided several days before we handed down Healy v. James, 408 U.S. 169, 92 S.Ct. 2338, 33 L.Ed.2d 266 (1972), in which, while recognizing a state university's undoubted prerogative to enforce reasonable rules governing student conduct, we reaffirmed that "state colleges and universities are not enclaves immune from the sweep of the First Amendment." . . . See Tinker v. Des Moines Independent School District. . . . We think *Healy* makes it clear that the mere dissemination of ideas—no matter how offensive to good taste—on a state university campus may not be shut off in the name alone of "conventions of decency." Other recent precedents of this Court make it equally clear that neither the political cartoon nor the headline story involved in this case can be labelled as constitutionally obscene or otherwise unprotected. . . . There is language in the opinion below which suggests that the University's action here could be viewed as an exercise of its legitimate authority to enforce reasonable regulations as to the time, place, and manner of speech and its dissemination. While we have repeatedly approved such regulatory authority, . . . the facts set forth in the opinions below show clearly that petitioner was dismissed because of the disapproved *content* of the newspaper rather than the time, place, or manner of its distribution.

Since the First Amendment leaves no room for the operation of a dual standard in the academic community with respect to the content of speech, and because the state University's action here cannot be justified as a nondiscriminatory application of reasonable rules governing conduct, the judgments of the courts below must be reversed. Accordingly the petition for a writ of certiorari is granted, the case is remanded to the District Court, and that court is instructed to order the University to restore to petitioner any course credits she earned for the semester in question and, unless she is barred from reinstatement for valid academic reasons, to reinstate her as a student in the graduate program.

Reversed and remanded.

Mr. Chief Justice BURGER, dissenting.

I join the dissent of Justice REHNQUIST which follows and add a few additional observations. . . .

In theory, at least, a university is not merely an arena for the discussion of ideas by students and faculty; it is also an institution where individuals learn to express themselves in acceptable, civil terms. We provide that environment to the end that students may learn the self-restraint necessary to the functioning of a civilized society and understand the need for those external restraints to which we must all submit if group existence is to be tolerable.

. . . Students are, of course, free to criticize the university, its faculty, or the government in vigorous or even harsh terms. But it is not unreasonable or violative of the Constitution to subject to disciplinary action those individuals who distribute publications which are at the same time obscene and infantile. To preclude a university or college from regulating the distribution of such obscene materials does not protect the values inherent in the First Amendment; rather, it demeans those values. The anomaly of the Court's holding today is suggested by its use of the now familiar "code" abbreviation for the petitioner's foul language. . . .

Mr. Justice REHNQUIST, with whom THE CHIEF JUSTICE and Mr. Justice BLACKMUN join, dissenting. . . .

I continue to adhere to the dissenting views expressed in Rosenfeld v. New Jersey, 408 U.S. 901, 92 S.Ct. 2479, 33 L.Ed.2d 321 (1972), that the public use of the word "M\_\_\_\_\_ f\_\_\_\_\_" is "lewd and obscene" . . . A state university is an establishment for the purpose of educating the State's young people, supported by the tax revenues of the State's citizens. The notion that the officials lawfully charged with the governance of the university have so little control over the environment for which they are responsible that they may not prevent the public distribution of a newspaper on campus which contained the language described in the Court's opinion is quite unacceptable to me and I would suspect would have been equally unacceptable to the Framers of the First Amendment. This is indeed a case where the observation of a unanimous Court in *Chaplinski* that "such utterances are no essential part of any exposition of ideas and are of such slight social value as a step to truth that any benefit that may be derived from them is clearly outweighed by the social interest in order and morality" applies with compelling force.

The Court cautions that "disenchantment with Miss Papish's performance, understandable as it may have been, is no justification for denial of constitutional rights." Quite so. But a wooden insistence on equating, for constitutional purposes, the authority of the State to criminally punish with its authority to exercise even a modicum of control over the University which it operates, serves neither the Constitution nor public education well. There is reason to think that the "disenchantment" of which the Court speaks may, after this decision, become widespread among taxpayers and legislators. The system of tax supported public universities which has grown up in this country is one of its truly great accomplishments; if they are to continue to grow and thrive to serve an expanding population, they must have something more than the grudging support of taxpayers and legislators. But one can scarcely blame the latter, if told by the Court that their only function is to supply tax money for the operation of the University, the "disenchantment" may reach such a point that they doubt the game is worth the candle.

----

### FUJISHIMA v. BOARD OF EDUCATION

United States Court of Appeals, 1972.
460 F.2d 1355 (7th Cir.).

SPRECHER, Circuit Judge. This suit challenges the constitutionality of section 6–19 of the rules of the Chicago Board of Education:

No person shall be permitted  .  .  .  to distribute on the school premises any books, tracts, or other publications, .  .  . unless the same shall have been approved by the General Superintendent of Schools.

Plaintiffs are three high school students who were disciplined for violation of section 6–19. On behalf of themselves and of a class of all high school students in Chicago school districts, they sought declaratory and injunctive relief. They also asked for actual and exemplary damages.

Plaintiffs Burt Fujishima and Richard Peluso were seniors at Lane Technical High School. They were suspended for four and seven days respectively for distributing about 350 copies of *The Cosmic Frog*, an "underground" newspaper they and another student published. The papers were distributed free both before and between classes and during lunch breaks.

Plaintiff Robert Balanoff, a sophomore at Bowen High School, was suspended for two days for giving another student an unsigned copy of a petition calling for "teach-ins" concerning the war in Viet Nam. The exchange occurred in May of 1970 in a school corridor between classes.

In October 1970, Balanoff was suspended for five days for distributing leaflets about the war to 15 or 20 students. This distribution took place during a fire drill, while Balanoff and his classmates were in their assigned places across the street from the school. . . .

. . . Defendants' primary theory on the appeal is that section 6–19 is constitutionally permissible because it does not require approval of the *content* of a publication before it may be distributed. Unfortunately for defendants' theory, that is neither what the rule says nor how defendants have previously interpreted it. The superintendent must approve "the same," which refers back to "any books, tracts, or other publications." The superintendent cannot perform his duty under the rule without having the publication submitted to him. The principals believed the rule requires approval of the publication itself: the Fujishima and Peluso suspensions were for "distribution of unauthorized material in the school"; the Balanoff suspensions were for "distribution of unauthorized materials in the school building" and for "distributing unapproved literature in class during fire drill."

Because section 6–19 requires prior approval of publications, it is unconstitutional as a prior restraint in violation of the First Amendment. This conclusion is compelled by combining the holdings of Near v. Minnesota, 283 U.S. 697, . . . and Tinker v. Des Moines Independent Community School District, . . . *Tinker* held that, absent a showing of material and substantial interference with the requirements of school discipline, schools may not restrain the full First-Amendment rights of their students. *Near* established one of those rights, freedom to distribute a publication without prior censorship.

Other courts have held unconstitutional similar restraints on student distribution of underground newspapers and political literature.[3] In Riseman v. School Committee, 439 F.2d 148 (1st Cir. 1971), a rule directed against advertising and promoting on school grounds was used to deny permission to a student to distribute political literature. The First Circuit invalidated the rule as vague, overbroad and impermissible as a prior restraint. The court said the school might regulate the time, manner and place of distribution, but could not require advance approval of the content of the material.

---

[3] In harmony with the cases cited in the text are these analogous cases: Antonelli v. Hammond, 308 F.Supp. 1329 (D. Mass.1970) (board could not require prior submission of material to be printed in college newspaper); Dickey v. Alabama State Board of Education, 273 F.Supp. 613 (M.D.Ala.1967) (student editor could not be expelled for inserting "CENSORED" across blank columns where disapproved editorial was to have run); Zuck-er v. Panitz, 299 F.Supp. 102 (S.D.N.Y. 1969) (students could purchase ad in high school paper to express feelings against the war); Brooks v. Auburn University, 296 F.Supp. 188 (M.D.Ala.), aff'd, 412 F.2d 1171 (5th Cir. 1969), and Snyder v. Board of Trustees, 286 F.Supp. 927 (N.D.Ill.1968) (banning certain speakers from appearing on campus was an unconstitutional prior restraint).

The Fourth Circuit in Quarterman v. Byrd, 453 F.2d 54 (1971), enjoined the enforcement of a rule which required prior permission from the principal before distributing any material. The court in Sullivan v. Houston Independent School District, 333 F.Supp. 1149 (S.D.Tex.1971), refused to permit the school to give even a one-day review to the principal; the school could not justify imposition of any prior restraint on distribution of underground newspapers.

The district court in Eisner v. Stamford Board of Education, 314 F.Supp. 832 (D.Conn.1970), reached the same result in invalidating a rule which required prior approval. On appeal the Second Circuit affirmed the invalidation, but modified the lower court's opinion so extensively as to obliterate it. 440 F.2d 803 (1971). The court allowed prior submission of publications if accompanied by elaborate procedural safeguards.

We believe that the court erred in *Eisner* in interpreting *Tinker* to allow prior restraint of publication—long a constitutionally prohibited power—as a tool of school officials in "forecasting" substantial disruption of school activities. In proper context, Mr. Justice Fortas' use of the word "forecast" in *Tinker* means a prediction by school officials that existing conduct, such as the wearing of arm bands—if allowed to continue—will probably interfere with school discipline. . . . *Tinker* in no way suggests that students may be required to announce their intentions of engaging in certain conduct beforehand so school authorities may decide whether to prohibit the conduct. Such a concept of prior restraint is even more offensive when applied to the long-protected area of publication.

This interpretation of the *Tinker* forecast rule is supported by this court's opinion in Scoville v. Board of Education, 425 F.2d 10 (7th Cir.), cert. denied, 400 U.S. 826, 91 S.Ct. 51, 27 L.Ed.2d 55 (1970). There the court applied the rule to a decision made by school officials three days after publication and distribution of the newspaper. Even though *Grass High* contained articles critical of the school administration, this court found that the board could not reasonably have forecast substantial disruption and therefore could not expel the student authors.

The *Tinker* forecast rule is properly a formula for determining when the requirements of school discipline justify *punishment* of students for exercise of their First-Amendment rights. It is not a basis for establishing a system of censorship and licensing designed to *prevent* the exercise of First-Amendment rights.

Because we believe *Eisner* is unsound constitutional law, and because defendants in effect concede that they cannot require submission of publications before approval of distribution, we declare section 6–19 unconstitutional and remand the case for entry of an injunction against its enforcement.

Such injunction will not prevent defendants from promulgating reasonable, specific regulations setting forth the time, manner and place in which distribution of written materials may occur. This does not mean, as defendants' brief suggests, that the board may require a student to obtain administrative approval of the time, manner and place of the particular distribution he proposes. The board has the burden of telling students when, how and where they may distribute materials. *See* Sullivan v. Houston Independent School District, 307 F.Supp. 1328, 1340 (S.D.Tex.1969). The board may then punish students who violate those regulations. Of course, the board may also establish a rule punishing students who publish and distribute on school grounds obscene or libelous literature.

Plaintiff Balanoff's second suspension remains on his record. He was punished under section 6–19 for distributing leaflets to classmates during a fire drill. Because the rule is unconstitutional, his suspension under it cannot stand.

Defendants argue that the justification for the suspension is "self-evident" from the record. All that appears in the record are the following allegations by plaintiffs:

At no time during the fire drill was there any disorder. The distribution of said leaflets did not disrupt classes; nor did it interfere with any other proper school activity, including the fire drill. At no time during the distribution was the Plaintiff asked to stop distributing the leaflets by any member of the Bowen faculty or administration.

Neither in the district court nor on appeal have defendants suggested that evidence exists to challenge those factual assertions.

The district court speculated that students might use a fire drill, or might even instigate one, to engage in disruptive activities. His error was similar to the district court's in Scoville v. Board of Education, . . . "No reasonable inference of [a showing that the action was taken on a reasonable forecast of a substantial disruption of school activity] can be drawn from the complaint. . . ."

The board might issue a rule prohibiting distribution of literature during a fire drill as a regulation of time and place, but it could not apply such a rule *ex post facto* to Balanoff.

The district court's order shall include a direction to expunge Balanoff's second suspension from his record.

### NOTES AND QUESTIONS

1. Explain carefully the significance and different implications for a system of free expression between a subsequent punishment for engaging in expression and a prior restraint on that expression. Which is more dangerous? Which was involved in each case?

2. The Fujishima case applied Tinker to strike down a "prior restraint" requirement that students submit publications to school authorities for approval before distributing them in schools. Do you agree with the Fujishima court statement that the "Tinker forecast rule is properly a formula for determining when the requirements of school discipline justify *punishment* of students for exercise of their First Amendment rights" and that it "is not a basis for establishing a system of censorship and licensing designed to *prevent* the exercise of First Amendment rights"? When judging whether to approve the publication for distribution, what standard should the school authorities use? Does Fujishima hold that all prior review regulations are per se unconstitutional, or does Fujishima hold unconstitutional only those prior review regulations that do not have procedural safeguards and adequate standards for the guidance of school authority decisions? For example, in Baughman v. Freienmuth, 478 F.2d 1345 (4th Cir. 1973), the U. S. Court of Appeals held the Montgomery Bd. of Education's "prior restraint regulation" unconstitutional and advanced the following propositions:

(a) Secondary school children are within the protection of the First Amendment, although their rights are not coextensive with those of adults.

(b) Secondary school authorities may exercise reasonable prior restraint upon the exercise of students' First Amendment rights.

(c) Such prior restraints must contain precise criteria sufficiently spelling out what is forbidden so that a reasonably intelligent student will know what he may write and what he may not write.

(d) A prior restraint system, even though precisely defining what may not be written is nevertheless invalid unless it provides for:

(1) A definition of 'Distribution' and its application to different kinds of material;

(2) Prompt approval or disapproval of what is submitted;

(3) Specification of the effect of failure to act promptly; and,

(4) An adequate and prompt appeal procedure.

Is this case consistent with Fujishima v. Board of Educ?

3. If Fujishima had been decided after Papish instead of before it, would Papish, a university case, have been a controlling precedent? Is Papish limited to "indecent speech"? Would Justice Rehnquist's views in Papish be more persuasive in a K–12 context whenever publication of profanity is involved? Would Papish permit school authorities to censor the content of a student newspaper in order to prevent a "substantial disruption"? In order to protect students from obscenity?

4. California's law provides:

"Students of the public schools shall have the right to exercise freedom of speech and of the press including, but not limited to, the use of bulletin boards, the distribution of printed materials or petitions, the wearing of buttons, badges, and other insignia, and the right of expression in official publications, whether or not such publications or other means of expression are supported financially by the school or by use of school facilities, except that expression shall be prohibited which is obscene, libelous, or slanderous. Also prohibited shall be material which so incites students as to create a clear and present danger of the commission of unlawful acts on school premises or the violation of lawful school regulations, or the substantial disruption of the orderly operation of the school.

"Each government board of a school district and each county board of education shall adopt rules and regulations in the form of a written publications code, which shall include reasonable provisions for the time, place, and manner of conducting such activities within its respective jurisdiction.

"Student editors of official school publications shall be responsible for assigning and editing the news, editorial and feature content of their publications subject to the limitations of this section. However, it shall be the responsibility of a journalism advisor or advisors of student publications within each school to supervise the production of the student staff, to maintain professional standards of English and journalism, and to maintain the provisions of this section.

"There shall be no prior restraint of material prepared for official school publications except insofar as it violates this section. School officials shall have the burden of showing justification without undue delay prior to any limitation of student expression under this section.

" 'Official school publications,' shall refer to material produced by students in the journalism, newspaper, yearbook, or writing classes and distributed to the student body either free or for a fee.

"Nothing in this section shall prohibit or prevent any governing board of a school district to adopt otherwise valid rules and regulations relating to oral communication by students upon the premises of each school." West's Ann.Educ.Code of Calif. § 48916.

Is any part of this statute unconstitutional? Why or why not?

5. In Leibner v. Sharbaugh, 429 F.Supp. 744 (E.D.Va.1977) a high school student was suspended for unauthorized distribution of an underground newspaper, The Green Orange, which was described as "a showcase of bad taste." The reasons for the suspension were: "(1) the newspaper was distributed without receiving prior approval as required by the Student Responsibility and Rights Policy; (2) the publication did not identify the author as required by the school rules; and (3) the newspaper was of questionable taste, decency, and journalistic standards." The Leibner court ruled that the high school's regulations were unconstitutional formulating the general rule as: "In general, school regulations which act as a prior restraint on the distribution of student literature are constitutionally permissible *only* where the substantive justifications for such restraint are precisely defined and the procedures for making these determinations and the review of any decision to restrain distribution are adequate."

Applying that general rule the court concluded that "in this case, both the substantive standards and procedural safeguards are facially inadequate." Does this general rule meet all the requirements of Tinker? Fujishima? Also see, Pliscou v. Holtville School Dist., 411 F.Supp. 842 (S.D.Cal.1976). For further discussion see, Letwin, Administrative Censorship of the Independent Student Press—Demise of the Double Standard? 28 So.Carolina L.Rev. 565 (1977).

6. The Papish, Fujishima and Leibner cases involved attempts to distribute private or "underground" newspapers without prior restraint. Would the school authorities have prevailed in the cases if school newspapers had been involved? Do school authorities have greater power to control the substance of school newspapers?

---

## ZUCKER v. PANITZ

United States District Court, 1969.
299 F.Supp. 102 (S.D.N.Y.).

MEZTNER, District Judge. This action concerns the right of high school students to publish a paid advertisement opposing the war in Vietnam in their school newspaper. . . .

A group of New Rochelle High School students, led by plaintiff Richard Orentzel, formed an Ad Hoc Student Committee Against the War in Vietnam. The group sought to publish an advertisment in opposition to the war in the student newspaper, The Huguenot Herald, in November 1967, offering to pay the standard student rate. The text of the proposed advertisement is as follows: "The United States government is pursuing a policy in Viet Nam which is both repugnant to moral and international law and dangerous to the future of humanity. We can stop it. We must stop it." The editorial board of the newspaper, which was then headed by plaintiff Laura Zucker, approved publication of the advertisement, but the principal of the school, Dr. Adolph Panitz, directed that the advertisement not be published. The affidavit of plaintiff Orentzel alleges that the committee still desires to publish the advertisement and has been informed that the newspaper would accept it but for the directive of the principal.

The gravamen of the dispute concerns the function and content of the school newspaper. Plaintiffs allege that the purpose of the Huguenot Herald is *inter alia,* "to provide a forum for the dissemination of ideas and information by and to the students of New Rochelle High School." Therefore, prohibition of the advertisement constitutes a constitutionally proscribed abridgement of their freedom of speech.

The defendants take issue with this characterization of the newspaper. They advance the theory that the publication "is not a newspaper in the usual sense" but is a "beneficial educational device" developed as part of the curriculum and intended to inure primarily to the benefit of those who compile, edit and publish it.[1] They assert a long-standing policy of the school administration which limits news items and editorials to matters pertaining to the high school and its activities. Similarly, "no advertising will be permitted which expresses a point of view on any subject not related to New Rochelle High School." Even paid advertising in support of student government nominees is prohibited and only purely commercial advertising is accepted. This policy is alleged to be reasonable and necessary to preserve the journal as an educational device and prevent it from becoming mainly an organ for the dissemination of news and views unrelated to the high school.

In sum, defendants' main factual argument is that the war is not a school-related activity, and therefore not qualified for news, editorial and advertising treatment. They have submitted issues of the newspaper from September 1968 to April 1969 to illustrate school-related subjects and the absence of other than purely commercial advertising.

If the Huguenot Herald's contents were truly as flaccid as the defendants' argument implies, it would indeed be a sterile publication. Furthermore, its function as an educational device surely could not be served if such were the content of the paper. However, it is clear that the newspaper is more than a mere activity time and place sheet. The factual core of defendants' argument falls with a perusal of the newspapers submitted to the court. They illustrate that the newspaper is being used as a communications media regarding controversial topics and that the teaching of journalism includes dissemination of such ideas. Such a school paper is truly an educational device.

For instance, on October 18, 1968, an article on draft board procedures, including discussion of the basis for graduate deferments as well as problems of initial registration appeared, as well as an article concerning a poll of high school students on national political candidates and the war. On January 31, 1969, the paper included an item that the principal had placed literature on the draft in the school library. On April 25, 1969, the paper reported on a draft information assembly and informed its readers of the availability of draft counseling outside the school. Moreover, items have appeared on the following: the grant of money by the students' General Organization to Eldridge Cleaver to speak at Iona College (vetoed by the principal); school fund-raising activities for Biafra; federal aid for preschool through high school education; meeting of a YMCA-sponsored group whose purpose is discussion of such issues as racial change, violence

[1] Defendants' argument that the journal would be just as valuable an educational tool if it were compiled and then consigned to the files without publication is without merit, since in fact the paper is published and sold at 10 cents per copy or $2 per subscription. Moreover, the paper includes letters to the editor, clearly a part of the journalistic experience which would be truncated were the newspaper merely a dummy.

and political action possibilities; a state assemblyman's proposal for an elected Board of Education; the proposal of several educators for community involvement as part of the educational process; types of narcotics and their effects; high school drug use; community treatment facilities; establishment of a new anti-Establishment high school newspaper; and a letter to the editor that a poll should be held to determine whether the newspaper should serve more than its present function and become an instrument and advocate of student power.

The presence of articles concerning the draft and student opinion of United States participation in the war shows that the war is considered to be a school-related subject. This being the case, there is no logical reason to permit news stories on the subject and preclude student advertising.

Defendants further argue that since no advertising on political matters is permitted, the plaintiffs have no cause for discontent. It is undisputed that no such advertising has been permitted, but this is not dispositive. In Wirta v. Alameda-Contra Costa Transit District, 68 Cal.2d 51, 64 Cal.Rptr. 430, 434 P.2d 982 (1967) (en banc) (rehearing denied 1968), the court held that where motor coaches were a forum for commercial advertising, refusal to accept a proposed peace message violated the First Amendment guarantee of free speech. It said:

> "[D]efendants, having opened a forum for the expression of ideas by providing facilities for advertisements on its buses, cannot for reasons of administrative convenience decline to accept advertisements expressing opinions and beliefs within the ambit of First Amendment protection."
>
> . . .
>
> "Not only does the district's policy prefer certain classes of protected ideas over others but it goes even further and affords total freedom of the forum to mercantile messages while banning the vast majority of opinions and beliefs extant which enjoy First Amendment protection because of their noncommercialism."

Defendants would have the court find that the school's action is protected because plaintiffs have no right of access to the school newspaper. They argue that the recent Supreme Court case of Tinker v. Des Moines Independent Community School District held only that students have the same rights inside the schoolyard that they have as citizens. Therefore, since citizens as yet have no right of access to the private press, plaintiffs are entitled to no greater privilege.

In *Tinker,* the plaintiffs were suspended from school for wearing black armbands to protest the war in Vietnam. The Court held that the wearing of armbands was closely akin to pure speech and that First Amendment rights, *"applied in light of the special characteris-*

*tics of the school environment,* are available to teachers and students." The principle of free speech is not confined to classroom discussion:

> "The principal use to which the schools are dedicated is to accommodate students during prescribed hours for the purpose of certain types of activities. Among those activities is personal intercommunication among the students. This is not only an inevitable part of the process of attending school. *It is also an important part of the educational process.* A student's rights therefore, do not embrace merely the classroom hours. When he is in the cafeteria, or on the playing field, or on the campus during the authorized hours, he may express his opinions, even on controversial subjects like the conflict in Vietnam, if he does so without 'materially and substantially interfer[ing] with the requirement of appropriate discipline in the operation of the school' and without colliding with the rights of others." (emphasis added).

Defendants have told the court that the Huguenot Herald is not a newspaper in the usual sense, but is part of the curriculum and an educational device. However, it is inconsistent for them to also espouse the position that the school's action is protected because there is no general right of access to the private press.

We have found, from review of its contents, that within the context of the school and educational environment, it is a forum for the dissemination of ideas. Our problem then, as in *Tinker,* "lies in the area where students in the exercise of First Amendment rights collide with the rules of the school authorities." Here, the school paper appears to have been open to free expression of ideas in the news and editorial columns as well as in letters to the editor. It is patently unfair in light of the free speech doctrine to close to the students the forum which they deem effective to present their ideas. The rationale of *Tinker* carries beyond the facts in that case.

*Tinker* also disposes of defendants' contention that cases involving advertising in public facilities are inapposite because a school and a school newspaper are not public facilities in the same sense as buses and terminals (see *Writa, Kissinger* and *Wolin,* cited herein)—that is, they invite only a portion of the public.

This lawsuit arises at a time when many in the educational community oppose the tactics of the young in securing a political voice. It would be both incongruous and dangerous for this court to hold that students who wish to express their views on matters intimately related to them, through traditionally accepted nondisruptive modes of communication, may be precluded from doing so by that same adult community.

Plaintiffs' motion for summary judgment is granted. Settle order.

NOTES AND QUESTIONS

1. What is the basic premise of Zucker? It appears to be that where schools make public resources and access to a captive audience available to selected students as part of an approved school program, then that activity constitutes "state action" and is controlled by the Constitution in the same way in which official school authorities are controlled.

2. The court ruled that "within the context of the school and educational environment, it [the school newspaper] is a forum for the dissemination of ideas." What is the meaning of this finding that a school newspaper is "a forum for the dissemination of ideas"? Must the school paper be open to all subjects? Does Zucker hold that a high school constitutionally may not have a policy strictly limiting what appears in its school paper to news items and editorials pertaining to the high school and its activities and that is why the student advertisement against the Vietnam war could not be prohibited? Or does the holding of Zucker rest on notions of free speech and equality; i. e., that a school may restrict the contents of its school paper to school-related subjects, but the U.S. participation in the Vietnam war was a school-related subject, and that, therefore, "there is no logical reason to permit news stories on the subject and preclude student advertising"?

3. Suppose the school paper had accepted and published the advertisement and because of it school authorities now want to withdraw all school support, can they do so constitutionally? Joyner v. Whiting, 477 F.2d 456 (4th Cir. 1973), is relevant:

> "Johnnie Edward Joyner, editor of the Campus Echo, the official student newspaper of North Carolina Central University, and Harvey Lee White, president of the university's student government association, appeal from an order of the district court, which (a) denied their application for declaratory and injunctive relief to secure reinstatement of financial support for the Echo, and (b) permanently enjoined Albert N. Whiting, president of the university, and his successors in office, from granting future financial support to any campus newspaper. Joyner and White assert that the decree violates the First and Fourteenth Amendments. President Whiting urges affirmance on the ground that the paper's segregationist editorial policy violate the Fourteenth Amendment and the Civil Rights Act of 1964. [The paper espoused keeping NCCU an all Black institution.] We reverse because the president's irrevocable withdrawal of financial support from the Echo and the court's decree reinforcing this action abridge the freedom of the press in violation of the First Amendment.

> "Censorship of constitutionally protected expression cannot be imposed by suspending the editors, suppressing circulation, requiring imprimatur of controversial articles, excising repugnant material, withdrawing financial support, or asserting any other form of censorial oversight based on the institution's power of the purse  .  .  .  the freedom of the press enjoyed by students

is not absolute or unfettered.  Students, like all other citizens, are forbidden advocacy which 'is directed to inciting or producing imminent lawless action and is likely to incite or produce such action.'  .  .  .  Tinker v. Des Moines School Dist., expressly limits the free and unrestricted expression of opinion in schools to instances where it does not 'materially and substantially interfere with the requirements of appropriate discipline in the operation of the school.'  We previously considered these limitations in Quarterman v. Byrd, 453 F.2d 54, 58 (4th Cir. 1971):

> 'Specifically, school authorities may by appropriate regulation, exercise prior restraint upon publications distributed on school premises during school hours in those special circumstances where they can "reasonably 'forecast substantial disruption of or material interference with school activities' " on account of the distribution of such printed material.'

"Censorship of the paper cannot be sustained on the court's theory.  The record contains no proof that the editorial policy of the paper incited harassment, violence, or interference with white students and faculty.  At the most, the editorial comments advocated racial segregation contrary to the Fourteenth Amendment and the Civil Rights Act of 1964.  The court's rationale disregards the distinction between the First Amendment's clause prohibiting the establishment of religion and its clause protecting freedom of the press.  Neither federal nor state governments may expend funds to establish a religion.  The First Amendment, however, contains no similar ban against speech or press.  Both governments may spend money to publish the positions they take on controversial subjects.  The speeches and publications that originate in government offices attest to the diversity of views that are freely expounded.  But under the rule that President Whiting urges us to affirm, no state official could use his office to criticize, as the editor of the Echo did, government policy on race relations with which he disagrees.  We need not decide whether the Echo is a state agency; it is enough to say that even if it were, it would not be prohibited from expressing its hostility to racial integration.  The Fourteenth Amendment and the Civil Rights Act proscribe state action that denies the equal protection of the laws, not state advocacy.  To be sure, the line between action and advocacy may sometimes be difficult to draw, but it is clear that nothing written in the Echo crossed it.

"The president, emphasizing that the students are still free to publish and circulate a newspaper on the campus without university support, protests that the denial of financial support cannot be considered censorship because it is permanent.  Permanency, he suggests, does not link the ebb and flow of funds with disapproval or approval of editorial policy.  Absent this correlation, he claims, there is no censorship.  But this argument overlooks the fact that one of the reasons for the president's withdrawal of funds was his displeasure with the paper's editorial policy.  The abridgement of freedom of the press is nonetheless real because it is permanent.  Freedom of the press cannot be preserved, as Mr. Justice Frankfurter noted, by prohibitions calculated 'to burn the house to roast the pig.' The president has failed to carry the 'heavy burden of showing justification for the imposition of' a prior restraint on expression. He has proved only that he considers the paper's editorial comment to be abhorrent, contrary to the university's policy, and inconsistent with constitutional and statutory guarantees of equality. This is plainly insufficient."

4. The facts of Bayer v. Kinzler, 383 F.Supp. 1164 (E.D.N.Y.1974), affirmed 515 F.2d 504 (2d Cir. 1975) were these:

"The October 25, 1974 issue of the Farmingdale High School student newspaper contains a sex information supplement. One plaintiff is an editor of the newspaper. A second plaintiff is a student who states that she wishes to receive the supplement. The four page supplement is primarily composed of articles dealing with contraception and abortion. The articles are serious in tone and obviously intended to convey information rather than appeal to prurient interests. It is conceded the articles are not obscene. On October 25, 1974, defendant principal ordered the seizure of 700 undistributed copies of the newspaper. He also ordered that there be no further distribution of the newspaper and supplement. Defendants have expressed, however, a willingness to release the newspapers without the supplements. This proposal is not satisfactory to plaintiffs."

Citing the *Tinker* case the court stated "that a school regulation prohibiting expression of a particular opinion is impermissible . . . without evidence that the regulation is 'necessary to avoid material and substantial interference with schoolwork or discipline.'" It recognized that "Tinker is factually distinguishable [from Bayer] because it involved expression of an opinion rather than publication of factual information," but concluded that Tinker's "test seems equally valid in this case." Applying Tinker the court concluded that "it is extremely unlikely that distribution of the supplement will cause material and substantial interference with schoolwork and discipline. Accordingly, the court finds that seizure of the supplement and refusal to allow distribution were not reasonably necessary to avoid material and substantial interference with schoolwork or discipline."

## SOLICITATION

### TRACHTMAN v. ANKER

United States Court of Appeals, 1977.
563 F.2d 512 (2d Cir.).

LUMBARD, Circuit Judge. These are cross appeals from a judgment of the Southern District, Constance Baker Motley, Judge, entered on December 16, 1976, which enjoined defendants from restraining plaintiffs' attempts to distribute a sex questionnaire to eleventh and twelfth-grade students at Stuyvesant High School in New York City and to publish the results in the student publication, "The Stuyvesant Voice."

This controversy began when Jeff Trachtman [editor] and Robert Marks, a staff member of the "Voice," submitted a plan to survey the sexual attitudes of Stuyvesant students and publish the results in the "Voice" to the school's principal, defendant Fabricante. Initially, the plan contemplated oral interviews of a "cross section" of the student population to be conducted by a group of student researchers. Mr. Fabricante denied the students permission to conduct the survey . . . .

The students sought review . . . by Chancellor Anker. By this time the focus of the proposed survey had shifted from oral interviews to a questionnaire. Thus, in their letter to Anker, dated December 24, 1975, Trachtman and Marks submitted for review a questionnaire consisting of twenty-five questions, which, they advised, was to be used as a means for obtaining information for an article on "Sexuality in Stuyvesant" to appear in the "Voice." The questions, which the district court described as "requiring rather personal and frank information about the student's sexual attitudes, preferences, knowledge and experience," covered such topics as pre-marital sex, contraception, homosexuality, masturbation and the extent of students' "sexual experience." The questionnaire included a proposed cover letter which described the nature and purpose of the survey; it stressed the importance of honest and open answers but advised the student that, "[y]ou are not required to answer any of the questions and if you feel particularly uncomfortable—don't push yourself."

The students sought permission to distribute the questionnaire on school grounds on a random basis. The answers were to be returned anonymously and were to be kept "confidential." The students were to tabulate the results and publish them in an article in the "Voice," which would also attempt to interpret the results.

Having received no reply from Chancellor Anker, on January 13, 1976 Marks and Trachtman wrote to Harold Siegel, Secretary of the Board of Education, and requested approval of their plan. Siegel responded in a letter dated February 27, 1976, to which he attached the decision of the Board. The decision advised the students that the survey could not be conducted stating, "Freedom of the press must be affirmed; however no inquiry should invade the rights of other persons." The decision indicated that the type of survey proposed could be conducted only by professional researchers, with the consent of the students' parents. The decision noted that "[m]atters dealing with sexuality could have serious consequences for the well being of the individual," and pointed out that the students lacked the requisite expertise to conduct such a survey and that the survey proposed made no provision for parental consent and did not guarantee the anonymity of those who answered.

Mr. Siegel responded to a request for reconsideration by indicating that the Board believed that many students would be harmed if confronted with the questions propounded by the questionnaire.

Plaintiffs commenced this action on August 26, 1976, seeking declaratory and injunctive relief under 42 U.S.C.A. § 1983, on the ground that the defendants' actions in prohibiting the dissemination of the questionnaire and publication of its results violated the First Amendment.

. . .

Judge Motley found that permission to distribute the questionnaire could be denied consistently with the First Amendment only if defendants could prove that "there is a strong possibility the distribution of the questionnaire would result in significant psychological harm to members of Stuyvesant High School." She found that the "thrust" of defendants' evidence was that many high school students were only beginning to develop sexual identities and that the questionnaire would force emotionally immature individuals to confront difficult issues prematurely and become "quite apprehensive or even unstable as a result of answering this questionnaire." The court found this argument convincing with respect to thirteen and fourteen year old students; however, as to older students, the court found the claims of potential emotional damage unconvincing and concluded that the psychological and educational benefits to be gained from distribution of the questionnaire to this group of students outweighed any potential harm. Accordingly, the court held that defendants could not prohibit the students from distributing the questionnaire to eleventh and twelfth-grade students and from publishing the results in the "Voice." The court also found that certain safeguards should guide distribution of the questionnaire and ordered that the students and school officials should negotiate a plan to implement distribution and to provide for "both confidential and public discussion groups for students who would like to talk with school personnel after the distribution of the survey and publication of the results in the *Voice*."

On appeal both parties agree that the defendants' restraint of the students' efforts to collect and disseminate information and ideas involves rights protected by the First Amendment. Essentially, resolution of the issues here turns upon a narrow question: What was it necessary for the defendants to prove to justify the prohibition of the distribution of the questionnaire and did the defendants meet this burden of proof?

Our inquiry must begin with *Tinker*. Essentially, the defendants' position is that the students here seek not only to communicate an idea but to utilize school facilities to solicit a response that will invade the rights of other students by subjecting them to psychological pressures which may engender significant emotional harm. Plaintiffs do not question defendants' authority to protect the physical and psychological well being of students while they are on school grounds; rather, they contend that defendants have not made a sufficient showing to justify infringement of the students' rights to speech and expression.

In interpreting the standard laid down in *Tinker,* this court has held that in order to justify restraints on secondary school publications, which are to be distributed within the confines of school property, school officials must bear the burden of demonstrating "a reasonable basis for interference with student speech, and . . . courts will not rest content with officials bare allegation that such a basis existed." At the same time, it is clear that school authorities need not wait for a potential harm to occur before taking protective action. Although this case involves a situation where the potential disruption is psychological rather than physical, *Tinker* and its progeny hold that the burden is on the school officials to demonstrate that there was reasonable cause to believe that distribution of the questionnaire would have caused significant psychological harm to some of the Stuyvesant students.

In support of their argument that students confronted with the questionnaire could suffer serious emotional harm, defendants submitted affidavits from four experts in the fields of psychology and psychiatry. Florence Halpern, professor of psychology at the New York University School of Medicine, stated that many adolescents are anxious about the "whole area of sex" and that attempts to answer the questionnaire by such students "would be very likely" to create anxiety and feelings of self-doubt; further, she stated that there were almost certainly some students with a "brittle" sexual adjustment and that for "such adolescents, the questionnaire might well be the force that pushes them into a panic state or even a psychosis." She concluded that distribution of the questionnaire was a "potentially dangerous" act that was "likely to result in serious injury to at least some of the students."

Dr. Aaron H. Esman, chief psychiatrist at the Jewish Board of Guardians (an organization providing mental health treatment to emotionally disturbed children) and an associate in psychiatry at the Columbia University College of Physicians and Surgeons, indicated that a number of the questions (particularly those dealing with homosexuality, masturbation, and "sexual experience") were "highly inappropriate," particularly for children ages twelve through fourteen; such questions, in Dr. Esman's opinion, were "likely to arouse considerable anxiety and tension," which "might well lead to serious emotional difficulties."

Vera S. Paster, a psychologist and assistant director of the Bureau of Child Guidance (the mental health agency for the New York City school system) asserted that there were a "large number" of high school students who would need help dealing with the anxiety reactions caused by confronting the questionnaire and that the proposed methodology of the survey would make it impossible to provide "back up support or protection" for such students.

Dr. Ingram Cohen, chief school psychiatrist of the Bureau of Child Guidance, indicated that there are wide discrepancies in the physical and psychological development of adolescent students, even among students of the same age. Dr. Cohen also pointed out that the survey made no provision for assistance to students who reacted adversely to it and concluded that it had a sufficient potential for harm to justify prohibiting its dissemination.

The record shows that the curriculum at Stuyvesant includes various courses on sex and sexuality and that professionally supervised peer-group discussions are sponsored by the school. The defendants have consistently treated the topic of sexuality as an important part of students' lives, which requires special treatment because of its sensitive nature. Thus, the school system has provided several courses on the physical and emotional aspects of sex; such courses are taught by teachers with special qualifications and administrative materials emphasize the sensitive nature of the topic. Further, the Board has consistently taken the position that even professional researchers may not conduct "sexual surveys" of students without meeting certain specific requirements.

Plaintiffs offered statements from five experts, including Gilbert Trachtman, who is a professor of educational psychology at New York University. Plaintiffs' experts questioned the possibility that any emotional harm could be caused by students' attempts to answer the questionnaire, pointed out that the survey might be of substantial benefit to many students, and expressed the opinion that "squelching" the survey could have deleterious effects. They indicated that the topics covered in the questionnaire are of normal interest to adolescents and are common subjects of conversation; further, some of these experts emphasized that students in Manhattan are bombarded with sexually explicit materials and that it was highly unlikely that any student could be harmed by answering the questionnaire. It is noteworthy, however, that at least two of plaintiffs' experts, one of whom was Gilbert Trachtman, recognized that there was some possibility that some students would suffer emotional damage as a result of answering the questionnaire.

. . . .

In determining the constitutionality of restrictions on student expression such as are involved here, it is not the function of the courts to reevaluate the wisdom of the actions of state officials charged with protecting the health and welfare of public school students. The inquiry of the district court should have been limited to determining whether defendants had demonstrated a substantial basis for their conclusion that distribution of the questionnaire would result in significant harm to some Stuyvesant students. In this regard, we must keep in mind the repeated emphasis of the Supreme Court that,

Judicial interposition in the operation of the public school system of the Nation raises problems requiring care and restraint. . . . By and large, public education in our Nation is committed to the control of state and local authorities.

We believe that the school authorities did not act unreasonably in deciding that the proposed questionnaire should not be distributed because of the probability that it would result in psychological harm to some students. The district court found this to be so with respect to ninth and tenth-grade students. We see no reason why the conclusion of the defendants that this was also true of eleventh and twelfth-grade students was not within their competence. Although psychological diagnoses of the type involved here are by their nature difficult of precision, we do not think defendants' inability to predict with certainty that a certain number of students in all grades would be harmed should mean that defendants are without power to protect students against a foreseen harm. We believe that the school authorities are sufficiently experienced and knowledgeable concerning these matters, which have been entrusted to them by the community; a federal court ought not impose its own views in such matters where there is a rational basis for the decisions and actions of the school authorities. Their action here is not so much a curtailment of any First Amendment rights; it is principally a measure to protect the students committed to their care, who are compelled by law to attend the school, from peer contacts and pressures which may result in emotional disturbance to some of those students whose responses are sought. The First Amendment right to express one's views does not include the right to importune others to respond to questions when there is reason to believe that such importuning may result in harmful consequences. Consequently where school authorities have reason to believe that harmful consequences might result to students, while they are on the school premises, from solicitation of answers to questions, then prohibition of such solicitation is not a violation of any constitutional rights of those who seek to solicit.

In sum, we conclude that the record established a substantial basis for defendants' belief that distribution of the questionnaire would result in significant emotional harm to a number of students throughout the Stuyvesant population. Accordingly, the judgment is reversed insofar as it restrains defendants from prohibiting distribution of the questionnaire to eleventh and twelfth-grade students at Stuyvesant and the case is remanded with instructions to dismiss the complaint.

GURFEIN, Circuit Judge, concurring:

First, while the passing out of the several questionnaires might not provoke a breach of the peace, a blow to the psyche may do more permanent damage than a blow to the chin. "Invasion of the rights of others is, of course, not immunized by the constitutional guarantee of freedom of speech." Tinker v. Des Moines School Dist.

Second, whether such a traumatic effect can be foreseen is the subject of dispute among recognized psychiatrists, as Judge Mansfield notes. I think such dispute is better resolved by professional educators than by federal judges even when they find the credentials of plaintiffs' experts "more impressive". This is not a case where there is no evidence to support the school officials.

Lastly, this is not a case involving "distribution of sexual material in school." It is, as Judge Lumbard states, a case that involves individual responses to various aspects of sex from the point of view of personal history, a matter different from the simple dissemination of reading matter dealing with sex, which the majority opinion does not purport to ban. See footnote 2. That deserves further emphasis in response to the dissenting opinion, lest the majority decision serve as an unintended precedent in derogation of First Amendment right.

MANSFIELD, Circuit Judge (dissenting):

With due respect I must dissent for the reason that in my view the defendants have completely failed to sustain their burden of showing that they are justified in depriving plaintiffs of their First Amendment right to engage in constitutionally protected freedom of expression by distributing to students the questionnaire regarding sex attitudes.

There is no suggestion of any danger that the questionnaire would disrupt school activities or lead to a breach of the peace, which are the type of "substantive evils" that might justify a prior restraint. Instead the majority, relying upon dicta in Tinker v. Des Moines School District, to the effect that school authorities may prohibit speech "that intrudes upon . . . the rights of other students," or "involves . . . an invasion of the rights of others" would include in these amorphous terms the dissemination to others of non-disruptive, non-defamatory and non-obscene material because it might cause some kind of "psychological" harm to an undefined number of students. With this I disagree. It represents an entirely too vague and nebulous extension of the concept of "rights" to support the drastic type of censorship and prior restraint sought by the defendants.

. . . Where physical disruption or violence is threatened, some inroads on free expression are tolerable because the interests of students and school officials are relatively specific and lend themselves to concrete evaluation. But a general undifferentiated fear of emotional disturbance on the part of some student readers strikes me as too nebulous and as posing too dangerous a potential for unjustifiable destruction of constitutionally protected free speech rights to support a prior restraint. A public school's premises are the very "marketplace of ideas" where personal intercommunication between students, in or out of the classroom, is "an important part of the educational process" even though some students may experience a degree of mental trauma in that process.   If school officials are permitted to ban a questionnaire of the type here at issue because of possible "psychological" harm, they could prohibit the dissemination of a broad range of other articles on school premises on the same theory, even though the publications were readily available elsewhere and the information in them was instructive.   Within the last few years, for instance, the New York Times, which represents that it publishes "All the News That's Fit to Print," has published numerous articles on the very matters that are the subject of plaintiffs' questionnaire, including items regarding the number of pregnant girls in public schools, the operation by New York City of a separate school for pregnant schoolgirls attended by up to 2,000 students annually, sexual activity among American teenagers, and the results of a nationwide study of adolescent sexuality.   Under the majority's decision, distribution of these items among students would be prohibited as posing a psychological danger to some.   The possibilities for harmful censorship under the guise of "protecting" the rights of students against emotional strain are sufficiently numerous to be frightening.

Even accepting arguendo the majority's thesis to the effect that other students' rights include the right to be free of any emotional stress, defendants have failed to sustain their burden of showing that the First Amendment values in the present case are outweighed by the risk of psychological harm.   The right of a newspaper to conduct a survey on a controversial topic and to publish the results represents the very quintessence of activity protected by the First Amendment. In a school environment, moreover, there is a positive value in the students' exercise of responsibilities associated with the publication of a newspaper, which gives them a greater appreciation for the true meaning and value of the Bill of Rights than they might otherwise possess.

The majority's holding that the values inherent in these basic rights are outweighed by the potential psychological harm which the questionnaire might cause to some students is based on conclusory and speculative opinions of a few psychologists, which are expressed in short affidavits, hypothetical rather than supported by any factual bases, untested by cross-examination, and flatly controverted by contrary affidavit opinions of other experts who possess equal if not superior qualifications as psychologists.   All of the affidavits submitted by defendants, moreover, assume that a student possessed of fragile sensibilities would not only read the questionnaire but make an intensive effort to answer it, notwithstanding the statement on its face that "The survey is random and completely confidential.—You are not required to answer any of the questions and if you feel particularly uncomfortable—don't push yourself."   Some of the defendants' affidavits appear to be concerned principally with an issue not before the court—the methodology used by the questionnaire and its invalidity from a scientific statistical viewpoint,—rather than its psychological impact on students.

.   .   . In this day and age, when children in New York City are literally bombarded with explicit sex materials on public newsstands on the way to and from school, when they are encouraged openly and frankly to discuss sex topics and problems in "rap sessions" sponsored by their schools (which, unlike the questionnaire at issue are face-to-face and not anonymous), when the children actually do discuss sex with their peers at school, when the number of teenage pregnancies in New York City's public high schools such as Stuyvesant is so high that the City has operated a special high school for pregnant high school girls attended by up to 2,000 pregnant teenagers annually, when adolescent sexuality is openly discussed in New York newspapers, I believe the defendants have failed completely to demonstrate any reasonable likelihood that the questionnaire poses any substantial harm to any appreciable number of high school students.

The picture drawn by the defendants of high school freshmen and sophomores (to say nothing of juniors and seniors) as fragile, budding egos flushed with the delicate rose of sexual naivety, is so unreal and out of touch with contemporary facts of life as to lead one to wonder whether there has been a communications breakdown between them and the next generation.  Yet the defendants' sponsorship of "rap sessions" among students to discuss these very matters indicates not only an awareness of the high school student's knowledge and insight into sex matters but a strange inconsistency with the defendants' attitude toward the questionnaire.  If face-to-face, non-anonymous discussions between students of the very matters that are the subject of the questionnaire causes no psychological harm to those involved, I cannot believe that an anonymous questionnaire, which states right on its face that the recipient need not answer it but is free to throw it away, would do so, I can only conclude that the defendants are more concerned about the structure and methodology of the questionnaire than about its alleged psychological impact.

Other courts, when faced with substantially the same problem, have not hesitated to find that distribution of sexual material in school to students is protected by the First Amendment and that school authorities failed to sustain their heavy burden of demonstrating that prohibition of such distribution was reasonably necessary to guard against harm to the students' rights.  See, e. g., Shanley v. Northeast Independent School Dist., 462 F.2d 960 (5th Cir. 1972) (school newspaper article discussing birth control).  Indeed, in Bayer v. Kinzler, 383 F.Supp. 1164 (E.D.N.Y.), aff'd, 515 F.2d 504 (2d Cir. 1974), we affirmed a district court decision finding that the distribution of a sex information supplement to a school newspaper was constitutionally protected.  I fail to find any significant legal distinction between these holdings and the present case.

## NOTES AND QUESTIONS

1.  Dissenting Judge Mansfield failed "to find any significant legal distinction between [Bayer v. Kinzler, supra] and the present case." In a footnote the majority distinguished Bayer saying that here "plaintiffs' desire to use Stuyvesant students as research subjects distinguishes this case from . . . Bayer v. Kinzler" and that the "questionnaire does not seek to convey information but to obtain it in a manner that school officials contend may result in psychological damage." Who is correct? Does the majority's distinction rest on an assumption "that there is a qualitative difference between a reader's psychic reaction to a questionnaire and to an advocative or informational speech or article on the same subject".? (Comment, Behind The Schoolhouse Gate: Sex and The Student Pollster, 54 N.Y.U.L.Rev. 161 (1979)). Is there a principled basis for holding that a monologue should be more protected than a dialogue? Is this really a school newspaper case, a questionnaire case, or is it a solicitation case? Should the Tinker rule apply irrespective of what type of case it is so long as speech is involved?

2.  Did the majority opinion actually apply the Tinker case? Was there any evidence of "substantial disruption" or "material interference" with the school's work or discipline?

The majority suggested that banning the distribution of the questionnaire might not constitute a prohibition of substantive speech about sex, but only a procedural time, place or manner regulation, because students could still discuss the subject in sex education classes and informally among themselves. Is this view consistent with Tinker? Didn't Tinker hold that a school could not confine the discussion of a subject solely to one place; i. e., to the classroom and then only as part of the regular curriculum? But the majority did not rest its decision on procedural time-place-or-manner reasoning. The majority stated that, under Tinker, "in order to justify restraints on secondary school publications . . . school officials must bear the burden of demonstrating 'a reasonable basis for interference with student speech, and . . . courts will not rest content with officials bare allegation that such a basis existed." Is this an accurate restatement of the Tinker rule? If not, what are the differences? The majority stated that "a federal court ought not impose its own views in such matters where there is a rational basis for the decisions and actions of the school authorities." Is this deference to school officials consistent with Tinker? The majority then applied its deferential "rational basis" rule. What testimony did the majority accept as constituting the "rational basis" in support of the decision of the school authorities? Can you identify the precise nature of psychological harm in question? Was the occurrence of this psychological harm probable? Most probable? Slightly probable? Or only feared? Is it correct for a court to equate psychological harm with Tinker's "material disruption" or "substantial interference" tests? Is the "rational basis" rule and the Tinker rule one and the same? Can school authorities prohibit the wearing of black armbands if there is some "rational basis" for their action such as the fact that armbands, when they communicate successfully, must distract student attention from their classwork and other activities? Tinker also indicated that speech might be regulated if it threatened substantial "invasion of the rights of others." Does the majority identify any "rights of others" that would be invaded if the questionnaire were distributed?

3. Should the Tinker rule apply to this case if it is viewed as a solicitation case? Does a solicitation case have fundamentally different features from Tinker? Was the Tinker rule created with a solicitation-type problem in mind?

4. Suppose the student paper, "The Voice," took the questionnaire and published it in the newspaper and, on learning that the student paper was about to be distributed, the school authorities prohibited school distribution of that issue. If the student editors asked a court to order school authorities to permit the distribution, what would be the court's decision and opinion? Would the court apply the "rational basis" or the Tinker rule?

---

## KATZ v. McAULAY

United States Court of Appeals, 1971.
438 F.2d 1058 (2d Cir.) cert. den. 405 U.S. 933, 92 S.Ct. 930, 30 L.Ed.2d 809.

ANDERSON, Circuit Judge. The New York Board of Regents has a rule, some forty-seven years old, which prohibits "soliciting funds from the pupils in the public schools." Plaintiffs, four students at Ardsley High School, a public school in Westchester County, New York, brought this civil rights action for anticipatory relief against enforcement of that rule. Their action arose when school officials threatened plaintiffs with expulsion if they distributed on school premises leaflets soliciting funds from their fellow students.

More specifically, on February 6 and 9, 1970, plaintiffs distributed in the high school corridors a one-page leaflet entitled "Join the Conspiracy." In it they decried the prosecution of eight defendants then on trial in the District Court for the Northern District of Illinois and solicited funds for the "activists' " defense. The leaflet stated:

"More than $33,000 per month is spent on their defense. Money is desperately needed to give these people a just trial. Money is needed to pay for transcripts. PLEASE contribute and/or buy a button from Jane Katz, Carey Marvin, Greg Gottlieb or anyone else who is helping out."

The dissemination of leaflets occurred before the school day began, and the affidavits of school officials contain no evidence of a specific instance of interference by the plaintiffs with the operation of the school or of any demonstration collision with the rights of other students to be let alone. Nonetheless, school officials warned plaintiffs that their circulation of leaflets violated the Board of Regents rule and a local Board of Education rule forbidding any "outside organization    *    *    *    to use this School    *    *    *    for the dissemination or release of information by flyers    *    *    *"    without first obtaining written approval of the Board.

Asserting the First Amendment overbreadth of both rules, plaintiffs sought a declaratory judgment declaring that "the policies, regulations and actions of the defendants    *    *    *    are unconstitutional" and preliminary and permanent injunctions restraining defendants from taking disciplinary action against students distributing this leaflet or any other leaflet soliciting funds for causes involving "matters of public interest."    .    .    .

An application for a preliminary injunction is addressed to the judicial discretion of the district court, and this court will not set aside the disposition of such an application unless erroneous as a matter of law or the result of an abuse of judicial discretion.    .    .    . We therefore go no further into the merits of this action than is necessary to determine whether the trial court's assessment of the relative importance, on the one hand, of the rights asserted and, on the other, of the governmental interest the rule purports to protect, constituted an abuse of discretion.    In this connection consideration must be given to the irreparable nature of the injury allegedly flowing from the denial of preliminary relief and the likelihood of the applicants' ultimate success on the merits.    .    .    .

The constitutional guarantee of free speech limits state power to regulate the personal intercommunication of secondary school pupils. Tinker v. Des Moines Independent Community School District,    .    .    . From this premise plaintiffs contend the distribution of leaflets which "communicat[e] thoughts between citizens, and discuss    .    .    . public questions,"    .    .    . is protected expression and that such expression is no less protected by virtue of the fact that solicitation of contributions is an integral part thereof.    .    .    .

Assuming that plaintiffs' activity was "speech" within the meaning of the First Amendment, school officials had the burden of showing governmental interests which might justify their interference with that "speech."    .    .    .    The Supreme Court has repeatedly affirmed that such an interest lies in the implementation of "the comprehensive authority of the States and of school officials, consistent with fundamental constitutional safeguards, to prescribe and control conduct in the schools."    .    .    .    The exercise of such authority may not, however, abridge the free expression of students in the public high schools unless that expression "materially and substantially interfere[s] with the requirements of appropriate discipline in the operation of the school."    .    .    .

Though the skeletal evidentiary matter before the trial court disclosed minimal potential interference at most, the probability that plaintiffs' overbreadth contention would prevail at trial is so slight that the denial of preliminary relief cannot be held to have constituted an abuse of discretion. . . . the Board of Regents' rule articulated its proscription in terms of those non-expressive features of student conduct which raise a sufficiently high probability of harm—i. e. the pressures upon students of multiple solicitations—to justify the Board's interference with such communicative conduct.

Pupils are on school premises in response to the statutory requirement that they attend school for the purpose of formal education. Where outside organizations or individuals espousing various causes seek to take advantage of the required assemblage of secondary school pupils, as a captive audience, to solicit funds, either directly or through the agency of some of the pupils, for their particular project or cause, they are in effect in competition for the time, attention and interest of the pupils with those who are seeking to administer the school system. Whether it is done a few minutes before school opens or a few minutes after, its effect is not so limited in time and it is plainly harmful to the operation of the public schools. If there is no regulation against it, literally dozens of organizations and causes may importune pupils to solicit on their behalf; and it is foreseeable that pressure groups within the student body are likely to use more than polite requests to get contributions even from those who are in disagreement with the particular cause or who are, in truth, too poor to afford a donation. The Board's regulation appears to be reasonable and proper and has a rational relationship to the orderly operation of the school system.

The rule's focus upon a demonstrable harm rather than an undifferentiated fear of disturbance distinguishes plaintiffs' action from Scoville v. Board of Education, 425 F.2d 10 (7 Cir. 1970). There, the complaint of students disciplined by school authorities, who were unable to prove a reasonable likelihood of substantial disruption which would follow the students' distribution of an underground newspaper, was held to state a claim for damages and declarative and injunctive relief. Though the underground newspaper was sold to students, the defendant school authorities did not act pursuant to an anti-solicitation regulation comparable to the Board of Regents' rule. . . .

Affirmed.

J. JOSEPH SMITH, Circuit Judge (dissenting):

I respectfully dissent. I agree that there are possibilities of embarrassment and disruption of school functions in solicitation of school students which might justify regulation not sustainable as to the public at large. But I think that when related to public issues such as that involved in this case, solicitation of funds is an integral part of the propagandizing, as in the case of the religious colporteurs, and freedom to do one includes freedom to do the other, at least in the absence of a showing of gross disruption, so that complete prohibition as opposed to reasonable regulation, as of time and place, cannot be sustained.  See Cantwell v. Connecticut, 310 U.S. 296, 306–307, 60 S.Ct. 900, 84 L.Ed. 1213 (1940).  "[T]he pamphlets of Thomas Paine were not distributed free of charge."  Murdock v. Pennsylvania, 319 U.S. 105, 111, 63 S.Ct. 870, 874, 87 LEd. 1292 (1943).  So I think on a showing such as this the courts must protect the students in their efforts to communicate, misguided as we may consider them.  I would reverse for issuance of a temporary injunction.

## NOTES AND QUESTIONS

1.  How important to the decision of this case is it that its context is of a request for a preliminary injunction?

2.  Suppose instead of asking for a preliminary injunction, plaintiffs had solicited the funds and then had been expelled from school because of that solicitation, would the decision have been the same?  Why or why not?

3.  Suppose the rule of the Board of Regents had been modified to permit solicitation of funds by the Jr. Red Cross and Neighbors In Need, a local group devoted to providing food for the hungry, would these factors have altered the decision of the Court?  Should they?  Why or why not?

4.  Suppose plaintiffs wanted to distribute copies of an "underground" newspaper at ten cents a copy, and the newspaper carried the same language as did the leaflet in this case, plus a statement that all the money collected from the sale of this issue of the newspaper would be sent to the defense fund, what decision would you render and for what reasons?

5.  California's law provides:

"During school hours, and within one hour before the time of opening and within one hour after the time of closing of school, pupils of the public school shall not be solicited on school premises by teachers or others to subscribe or contribute to the funds of, to become members of, or to work for, any organization not directly under the control of the school authorities, unless the organization is a non-partisan, charitable organization organized for charitable purposes by an act of Congress or under the laws of the state, the purpose of the solicitation is non-partisan and charitable, and the solicitation has been approved by the county board of education or by the governing board of the school district in which the school is located.

"No person shall solicit any other person to contribute to any fund or to purchase any item of personal property, upon the representation that the money received is to be used wholly or in part for the benefit of any public school or the student body of any public school, unless such person obtains the prior written approval of either the governing board of the school district in which such solicitation is to be made or the governing board of the school district having jurisdiction over the school or student body represented to be benefited by such solicitation, or the designee of either of such boards.

"The prohibitions of this section shall not apply with respect to any solicitation or contribution the total proceeds of which are delivered to a public school, nor to a solicitation of a transfer to be effected by a testamentary act." West's Ann.Educ. Code of California §§ 51520, 51521.

Is any part of these statutes unconstitutional? Why or why not?

6. This case, *Bayer* and the *Trachtman* case, were decided by the Second Circuit United States Court of Appeals. Are they consistent? Did the court alter its position? Did the court apply the Tinker rule in the cases? The "rational basis" rule?

---

## BONNER–LYONS v. SCHOOL COMMITTEE OF BOSTON

United States Court of Appeals, 1973.
480 F.2d 442 (1st Cir.).

McENTEE, Circuit Judge. Plaintiffs, members of The Ad Hoc Parents' Committee for Quality Education, alleging violations of their first amendment and equal protection rights, initiated this action under 42 U.S.C.A. § 1983 to enjoin defendants, the members of the School Committee of the City of Boston, from using the internal distribution system of the City's schools to disseminate notices opposing the use of bussing to achieve school integration. In the alternative, plaintiffs sought an order compelling defendants to allow them to use this same system to distribute communications publicizing pro-bussing rallies. The trial court denied repeated requests for preliminary injunctive relief and this appeal followed. Since we conclude that by disseminating the notices in question the defendants utilized the school distribution system to support and promote the views of one group while denying the use of this system to groups representing other points of view, we reverse and grant the injunctive relief specified below.

The following facts are not in dispute. On March 29, 1973, defendants adopted an official resolution authorizing the distribution of notices to all Boston parents urging them to support a march and rally to be held at the Massachusetts State House on April 3. The purpose of this rally was to express opposition to the retention of the Massachusetts "Racial Imbalance Law," 9 M.G.L.A. c. 71, §§ 37C–37D, and to the use of forced bussing as a tool to achieve racial integration in the schools. When plaintiffs requested defendants either to abandon this planned distribution or to permit the dissemination of pro-bussing notices, defendants refused to agree to either alternative. Plaintiffs then filed this suit and sought a temporary restraining order against the distribution. Thereafter, pursuant to defendants' resolution, on March 30 the following notice was distributed by means of the school system's "fan-out" distribution procedure to the approximately 97,000 students in the Boston system.[1]

[1] According to plaintiffs' counsel's affidavit, the system's "fan-out" distribution procedure operates in the following manner. A message which is ready for distribution is first transmitted by telephone from the Deputy Superintendent to six

"Dear Parents:

At a meeting on March 29, 1973, a resolution of the School Committee to support the Parents' March on the State House on Tuesday, April 3, 1973, at 10:00 A.M. was passed unanimously.

The purpose of the meeting is to inform the Governor and members of the Legislature that parents and the Boston School Committee stand united in opposition to forced busing and redistricting now being considered by the State Board of Education.

All parents are encouraged to write the Governor, the Senators and the Representatives in support of House Bill 3439 which opposes busing without the written consent of the parents."

On April 3 the anti-bussing rally was held as scheduled and, on the following day, plaintiffs' initial appeal from the denial of a temporary restraining order to prevent the distribution of these notices was dismissed as moot. On April 13, 1973, however, plaintiffs filed a further motion for injunctive relief seeking in particular an order requiring defendants to make the school distribution system available for the dissemination of notices concerning a pro-bussing rally tentatively set for late April. Due to difficulties in obtaining a hearing, however, this motion was not heard until April 30 and the proposed rally had to be postponed and ultimately cancelled. Thereafter, the trial court, finding, *inter alia,* that plaintiffs had failed to establish either that defendants had interfered with their first amendment rights or that a federal question was presented, issued a brief order denying the requested preliminary injunction.

On this background we find ourselves unable to agree with this disposition. As we read the March 30 notice, it seems apparent that this message tended to lend support and to mobilize opinion in favor of the position of those private parties who sponsored the April 3 "Parents' March on the State House." Under these circumstances, we conclude that defendants, by authorizing this distribution, sanctioned the use of the school distribution system as a forum for discussion of at least those issues which were treated in this notice.[2]

area Assistant Superintendents and then by them to the individual schools in their charge. At the schools the message is typed, reproduced, and distributed to teachers who then deliver it to each individual student.

[2] We are further buttressed in our conclusion that defendants have made available the school distribution system as a forum for the discussion of the possible repeal of the "Racial Imbalance Act" and the forced bussing of school children by the indication in the record that on April 30, 1973, defendants apparently authorized the distribution of a second set of notices, publicizing an anti-bussing rally scheduled to be held on May 2. While the record has not been fully developed with regard to this incident, we note that defendants state that these notices were not prepared by them but rather by the Home and School Association which they describe as "a private group." If these

When defendants' refusal to allow plaintiffs access to this system is considered in light of this conclusion, the trial court's error becomes manifest since it is well settled that once a forum is opened for the expression of views, regardless of how unusual the forum, under the dual mandate of the first amendment and the equal protection clause neither the government nor any private censor may pick and choose between those views which may or may not be expressed.  See, e. g., Police Department of Chicago v. Mosley  .  .  .  National Socialist White People's Party v. Ringers, 473 F.2d 1010, infra.

Under these circumstances and particularly in light of the fact that defendants refused to represent either in the trial court or in oral argument on appeal that no further notices of this type would be distributed, we remand with directions that the defendants, their agents, servants, or employees be enjoined from causing or directing administrators or teachers employed in the Boston Public Schools from distributing, in classrooms or on school premises during the hours of required school attendance, to pupils enrolled in said schools, notices calling the attention of their parents or others to or inviting them to attend particular rallies, meetings or other activities designed to support a particular viewpoint on so-called racial imbalance legislation now pending in the General Court, or soliciting them to engage in letter-writing or activity in support of a particular viewpoint on such legislation, unless fair and reasonable timely opportunity is afforded to others having differing views to use the same channels to invite attendance at or call attention to rallies and activity in furtherance of such differing views.

Remanded for proceedings, consistent with this opinion.

## FREEDOM OF ASSOCIATION

### HEALY v. JAMES

Supreme Court of the United States, 1972.
408 U.S. 169, 92 S.Ct. 2338, 33 L.Ed.2d 266.

Mr. Justice POWELL delivered the opinion of the Court.  .  .  .

Petitioners are students attending Central Connecticut State College (CCSC), a state-supported institution of higher learning.  In September 1969 they undertook to organize what they then referred to as a "local chapter" of Students for a Democratic Society (SDS). Pursuant to procedures established by the College, petitioners filed a request for official recognition as a campus organization with the Student Affairs Committee, a committee composed of four students, three faculty members and the Dean of Student Affairs.  The request

representations are found to be true, a clearer example of an impermissible selective opening of a forum to a group whose views are favored is difficult to imagine.

specified three purposes for the proposed organization's existence. It would provide "a forum of discussion and self-education for students developing an analysis of American society"; it would serve as "an agency for integrating thought with action so as to bring about constructive changes"; and it would endeavor to provide "a coordinating body for relating the problems of leftist students" with other interested groups on campus and in the community. The Committee, while satisfied that the statement of purposes was clear and unobjectionable on its face, exhibited concern over the relationship between the proposed local group and the National SDS organization. In response to inquiries, representatives of the proposed organization stated that they would not affiliate with any national organization and that their group would remain "completely independent."

In response to other questions asked by Committee members concerning SDS's reputation for campus disruption, the applicants made the following statements, which proved significant during the later stages of these proceedings:

"Q.   How would you respond to issues of violence as other S.D.S. chapters have?

"A.   Our action would have to be dependent upon each issue.

"Q.   Would you use any means possible?

"A.   No I can't say that; would not know until we know what the issues are.

"Q.   Could you envision the S.D.S. interrupting a class?

"A.   Impossible for me to say."

With this information before it, the Committee requested an additional filing by the applicants, including a formal statement regarding affiliations. The amended application filed in response stated flatly that "CCSC Students for a Democratic Society are not under the dictates of any National organization."   .   .   .

By a vote of six to two the Committee ultimately approved the application and recommended to the President of the College, Dr. James, that the organization be accorded official recognition.   .   .   .

Several days later, the President rejected the Committee's recommendation, and issued a statement indicating that petitioners' organization was not to be accorded the benefits of official campus recognition. His accompanying remarks, which are set out in full in the margin, indicate several reasons for his action. He found that the organization's philosophy was antithetical to the school's policies, and that the group's independence was doubtful. He concluded that approval should not be granted to any group that "openly repudiates" the College's dedication to academic freedom.   .   .   .

Their efforts to gain recognition having proved ultimately unsuccessful, and having been made to feel the burden of nonrecognition, petitioners resorted to the courts.   .   .   .

At the outset we note that state colleges and universities are not enclaves immune from the sweep of the First Amendment. "It can hardly be argued that either students or teachers shed their constitutional rights to freedom of speech or expression at the schoolhouse gate." Tinker v. Des Moines Independent Community School District, . . . Of course, as Mr. Justice Fortas made clear in *Tinker*, First Amendment rights must always be applied "in light of the special characteristics of the . . . environment" in the particular case. . . . And, where state-operated educational institutions are involved, this Court has long recognized "the need for affirming the comprehensive authority of the States and of school officials, consistent with fundamental constitutional safeguards, to prescribe and control conduct in the schools." . . . Yet, the precedents of this Court leave no room for the view that, because of the acknowledged need for order, First Amendment protections should apply with less force on college campuses than in the community at large. Quite to the contrary, "[t]he vigilant protection of constitutional freedoms is nowhere more vital than in the community of American schools." Shelton v. Tucker, . . . The college classroom with its surrounding environs is peculiarly the "market place of ideas" and we break no new constitutional ground in reaffirming this Nation's dedication to safeguarding academic freedom. Keyishian v. Board of Regents, . . .

Among the rights protected by the First Amendment is the right of individuals to associate to further their personal beliefs. While the freedom of association is not explicitly set out in the Amendment, it has long been held to be implicit in the freedoms of speech, assembly and petition. . . . There can be no doubt that denial of official recognition, without justification, to college organizations burdens or abridges that associational right. The primary impediment to free association flowing from nonrecognition is the denial of use of campus facilities for meetings and other appropriate purposes. The practical effect of nonrecognition was demonstrated in this case when, several days after the President's decision was announced, petitioners were not allowed to hold a meeting in the campus coffee shop because they were not an approved group.

Petitioners' associational interests also were circumscribed by the denial of the use of campus bulletin boards and the school newspaper. If an organization is to remain a viable entity in a campus community in which new students enter on a regular basis, it must possess the means of communicating with these students. Moreover, the organization's ability to participate in the intellectual give and take of campus debate, and to pursue its stated purposes, is limited by denial of access to the customary media for communicating with the administration, faculty members, and other students. Such impediments cannot be viewed as insubstantial.

Respondents and the courts below appear to have taken the view that denial of official recognition in this case abridged no constitutional rights. The District Court concluded that

> "President James' discretionary action in denying this application cannot be legitimately magnified and distorted into a constitutionally cognizable interference with the personal ideas or beliefs of any segment of the college students; neither does his action deter in any material way the individual advocacy of their personal beliefs; nor can his action be reasonably construed to be an invasion of, or having a chilling effect on academic freedom."

In that court's view all that was denied petitioners was the "administrative seal of official college respectability." . . . A majority of the Court of Appeals agreed that petitioners had been denied only the "college's stamp of approval." . . .

We do not agree with the characterization by the courts below of the consequences of nonrecognition. We may concede . . . that the administration "has taken no direct action . . . to restrict the rights of petitioners' members to associate freely." But the Constitution's protection is not limited to direct interference with fundamental rights. The requirement in *Patterson* that the NAACP disclose its membership lists was found to be an impermissible, though indirect, infringement of the members' associational rights. Likewise, in this case, the group's possible ability to exist outside the campus community does not ameliorate significantly the disabilities imposed by the President's action. We are not free to disregard the practical realities. Mr. Justice Stewart has made the salient point: "Freedoms such as these are protected not only against heavy-handed frontal attack, but also from being stifled by more subtle governmental interference." . . .

The opinions below also assumed that petitioners had the burden of showing entitlement to recognition by the College. While petitioners have not challenged the procedural requirement that they file an application in conformity with the rules of the College, they do question the view of the courts below that final rejection could rest on their failure to convince the administration that their organization was unaffiliated with the National SDS. For reasons to be stated later in this opinion, we do not consider the issue of affiliation to be a controlling one. But apart from any particular issue, once petitioners had filed an application in conformity with the requirements, the burden was upon the College administration to justify its decision of rejection. . . . It is to be remembered that the effect of the College's denial of recognition was a form of prior restraint, denying to petitioners' organization the range of associational activities described above. While a college has a legitimate interest in preventing disruption on the campus, which under circumstances requiring the safeguarding of that interest may justify such restraint, a "heavy burden" rests on the college to demonstrate the appropriateness of that action.

These fundamental errors—discounting the existence of a cognizable First Amendment interest and misplacing the burden of proof— require that the judgments below be reversed. But we are unable to conclude that no basis exists upon which nonrecognition might be appropriate. Indeed, based on a reasonable reading of the ambiguous facts of this case, there appears to be at least one potentially acceptable ground for a denial of recognition. Because of this ambiguous state of the record we conclude that the case should be remanded and, in an effort to provide guidance to the lower courts upon reconsideration, it is appropriate to discuss the several bases of President James' decision. Four possible justifications for nonrecognition, all closely related, might be derived from the record and his statements. Three of those grounds are inadequate to substantiate his decision: a fourth, however, has merit.

A

From the outset the controversy in this case has centered in large measure around the relationship, if any, between petitioners' group and the National SDS. The Student Affairs Committee meetings, as reflected in its minutes, focused considerable attention on this issue; the court-ordered hearing also was directed primarily to this question. Despite assurances from petitioners and their counsel that the local group was in fact independent of the National organization, it is evident that President James was significantly influenced by his apprehension that there was a connection. Aware of the fact that some SDS chapters had been associated with disruptive and violent campus activity, he apparently considered that affiliation itself was sufficient justification for denying recognition.

Although this precise issue has not come before the Court heretofore, the Court has consistently disapproved governmental action imposing criminal sanctions or denying rights and privileges solely because of a citizen's association with an unpopular organization. . . . In these cases it has been established that "guilt by association alone, without [establishing] that an individual's association poses the threat feared by the Government," is an impermissible basis upon which to deny First Amendment rights. United States v. Robel, 389 U.S., at 265, . . . The Government has the burden of establishing a knowing affiliation with an organization possessing unlawful aims and goals and a specific intent to further those illegal aims.

Students for a Democratic Society, as conceded by the College and the lower courts, is loosely organized, having various factions and promoting a number of diverse social and political views only some of which call for unlawful action. Not only did petitioners proclaim their complete independence from this organization, but they also indicated that they shared only some of the beliefs its leaders have expressed.

On this record it is clear that the relationship was not an adequate ground for the denial of recognition.

## B

Having concluded that petitioners were affiliated with, or at least retained an affinity for, National SDS, President James attributed what he believed to be the philosophy of that organization to the local group. He characterized the petitioning group as adhering to "some of the major tenets of the national organization," including a philosophy of violence and disruption. Understandably, he found that philosophy abhorrent. In an article signed by President James in an alumni periodical, and made a part of the record below, he announced his unwillingness to "sanction an organization that openly advocates the destruction of the very ideals and freedoms upon which the academic life is founded." He further emphasized that the petitioners' "philosophies" were "counter to the official policy of the college."

The mere disagreement of the President with the group's philosophy affords no reason to deny it recognition. As repugnant as these views may have been, especially to one with President James' responsibility, the mere expression of them would not justify the denial of First Amendment rights. Whether petitioners did in fact advocate a philosophy of "destruction" thus becomes immaterial. The College, acting here as the instrumentality of the State, may not restrict speech or association simply because it finds the views expressed by any group to be abhorrent. As Mr. Justice Black put it most simply and clearly:

> "I do not believe that it can be too often repeated that the freedoms of speech, press, petition and assembly guaranteed by the First Amendment must be accorded to the ideas we hate or sooner or later they will be denied to the ideas we cherish." Communist Party v. Subversive Activities Control Bd., 367 U.S. 1, 137 (1961).

## C

As the litigation progressed in the District Court, a third rationale for President James' decision—beyond the questions of affiliation and philosophy—began to emerge. His second statement, issued after the court-ordered hearing, indicates that he based rejection on a conclusion that this particular group would be a "disruptive influence at CCSC." This language was underscored in the second District Court opinion. In fact, the [lower] Court concluded that the President had determined that CCSC–SDS's "prospective campus activities were likely to cause a disruptive influence at CCSC." . . .

If this reason, directed at the organization's activities rather than its philosophy, were factually supported by the record, this Court's prior decisions would provide a basis for considering the propriety of nonrecognition. The critical line heretofore drawn for determining the permissibility of regulation is the line between mere advocacy and advocacy "directed to inciting or producing imminent lawless action and . . . likely to incite or produce such action." Brandenburg v. Ohio, 395 U.S. 444, 447. . . . In the context of the "special characteristics of the school environment," the power of the government to prohibit "lawless action" is not limited to acts of a criminal nature. Also prohibitable are actions which "materially and substantially disrupt the work and discipline of the school." Tinker v. Des Moines Independent Community School District, . . . Associational activities need not be tolerated where they infringe reasonable campus rules, interrupt classes or substantially interfere with the opportunity of other students to obtain an education.

The "Student Bill of Rights" at CCSC, upon which great emphasis was placed by the President, draws precisely this distinction between advocacy and action. It purports to impose no limitations on the right of college student organizations "to examine and discuss *all* questions of interest to them." But it also states that students have no right (1) "to deprive others of the opportunity to speak or be heard," (2) "to invade the privacy of others," (3) "to damage the property of others," (4) "to disrupt the regular and essential operation of the college," or (5) "to interfere with the rights of others." The line between permissible speech and impermissible conduct tracks the constitutional requirement, and if there were an evidential basis to support the conclusion that CCSC–SDS posed a substantial threat of material disruption in violation of that command the President's decision should be affirmed.

The record, however, offers no substantial basis for that conclusion. . . .

## D

These same references in the record to the group's equivocation regarding how it might respond to "issues of violence" and whether it could ever "envision . . . interrupting a class," suggest a fourth possible reason why recognition might have been denied to these petitioners. These remarks might well have been read as announcing petitioners' unwillingness to be bound by reasonable school rules governing conduct. The College's Statement of Rights, Freedoms and Responsibilities of Students, contains, as we have seen, an explicit statement with respect to campus disruption. The regulation, carefully differentiating between advocacy and action, is a reasonable one, and petitioners have not questioned it directly. Yet their statements raise considerable question whether they intend to abide by the prohibitions contained therein.

As we have already stated in Parts B and C, the critical line for First Amendment purposes must be drawn between advocacy, which is entitled to full protection, and action, which is not. Petitioners may, if they so choose, preach the propriety of amending or even doing away with any or all campus regulations. They may not, however, undertake to flout these rules. Mr. Justice Blackmun, at the time he was a circuit judge on the Eighth Circuit, stated:

> "We . . . hold that a college has the inherent power to promulgate rules and regulations; that it has the inherent power properly to discipline; that it has power appropriately to protect itself and its property; that it may expect that its students adhere to generally accepted standards of conduct."

. . .

Just as in the community at large, reasonable regulations with respect to the time, the place, and the manner in which student groups conduct their speech-related activities must be respected. A college administration may impose a requirement, such as may have been imposed in this case, that a group seeking official recognition affirm in advance its willingness to adhere to reasonable campus law. Such a requirement does not impose an impermissible condition on the students' associational rights. Their freedom to speak out, to assemble, or to petition for changes in school rules is in no sense infringed. It merely constitutes an agreement to conform with reasonable standards respecting conduct. This is a minimal requirement, in the interest of the entire academic community, of any group seeking the privilege of official recognition.

Petitioners have not challenged in this litigation the procedural or substantive aspects of the College's requirements governing applications for official recognition. Although the record is unclear on this point, CCSC may have, among its requirements for recognition, a rule that prospective groups affirm that they intend to comply with reasonable campus regulations. Upon remand it should first be determined whether the College recognition procedures contemplate any such requirement. If so, it should then be ascertained whether petitioners intend to comply. Since we do not have the terms of a specific prior affirmation rule before us, we are not called on to decide whether any particular formulation would or would not prove constitutionally acceptable. Assuming the existence of a valid rule, however, we do conclude that the benefits of participation in the internal life of the college community may be denied to any group that reserves the right to violate any valid campus rules with which they disagree.

We think the above discussion establishes the appropriate framework for consideration of petitioners' request for campus recognition. Because respondents failed to accord due recognition to First Amendment principles, the judgment below approving respondents' denial of recognition must be reversed. Since we cannot conclude from this record that petitioners were willing to abide by reasonable campus rules and regulations, we order the case remanded for reconsideration.

. . .

Reversed and remanded.

Mr. Chief Justice BURGER, concurring.

. . . It is within . . . the academic community that problems such as these should be resolved. The courts, state or federal, should be a last resort. Part of the educational experience of every college student should be an experience in responsible self-government and this must be a joint enterprise of students and faculty. It should not be imposed unilaterally from above, nor can the terms of the relationship be dictated by students. . . .

The relatively placid life of the college campus of the past has not prepared either administrators or students for their respective responsibilities in maintaining an atmosphere in which divergent views can be asserted vigorously, but civilly, to the end that those who seek to be heard accord the same right to all others. The "Statement of Rights, Freedoms and Responsibilities of Students," sometimes called the "College Bill of Rights," in effect on this campus, and not questioned by petitioners, reflected a rational adjustment of the competing interests. But it is impossible to know from the record in this case whether the student group was willing to acknowledge an obligation to abide by that "Bill of Rights." . . .

Mr. Justice DOUGLAS

While I join the opinion of the Court, I add a few words.

. . . the status quo of the college or university is the governing body (trustees or overseers), administrative officers, who include caretakers and the police, and the faculty. Those groups have well-defined or vaguely inferred values to perpetuate. The customary technique has been to conceive of the minds of students as receptacles for the information which the faculty have garnered over the years. Education is commonly thought as the process of filling the receptacles with what the faculty in its wisdom deems fit and proper.

Many inside and out of faculty circles realize that one of the main problems of faculty members is their own re-education or re-orientation. Some have narrow specialties that are hardly relevant to modern times. History has passed others by, leaving them interesting relics of a by-gone day. More often than not they represent those who withered under the pressures of McCarthyism or other forces of conformity and represent but a timid replica of those who once brought distinction to the ideal of academic freedom.

The confrontation between them and the oncoming students has often been upsetting. The problem is not one of choosing sides. Students—who by reason of the Twenty-sixth Amendment become eligible to vote when 18 years of age—are adults who are members of the college or university community. Their interests and concerns are often quite different from those of the faculty. They often have values, views, and ideologies that are at war with the ones which the college has traditionally espoused or indoctrinated. When they ask for change, they, the students, speak in the tradition of Jefferson and Madison and the First Amendment.

The First Amendment does not authorize violence. But it does authorize advocacy, group activities, and espousal of change.

The present case is miniscule in the events of the 60's and 70's. But the fact that it has to come here for ultimate resolution, indicates the sickness of our academic world, measured by First Amendment standards. Students as well as faculty are entitled to credentials in their search for truth. If we are to become an integrated, adult society, rather than a stubborn status quo opposed to change, students and faculties should have communal interests in which each age learns from the other. Without ferment of one kind or another, a college or university (like a federal agency or other human institution) becomes a useless appendage to a society which traditionally has reflected the spirit of rebellion. . . .

Mr. Justice REHNQUIST, concurring in the result.

While I do not subscribe to some of the language in the Court's opinion, I concur in the result that it reaches. . . .

I find the implication clear from the Court's opinion that the constitutional limitations on the government acting as administrator of a college differ from the limitations on the government acting as sovereign to enforce its criminal laws. The Court's quotations from Tinker v. Des Moines Independent Community School District, . . . to the effect that First Amendment rights must always be applied "in light of the special characteristics of the . . . environment," and from Esteban v. Central Missouri State College, 415 F.2d 1077, 1089 (CA8, 1969), to the effect that a college "may expect that its students adhere to generally accepted standards of conduct," emphasize this fact.

Cases such as United Public Workers v. Mitchell, 330 U.S. 75, . . . and Pickering v. Board of Education etc., 391 U.S. 563, . . . make it equally clear that the government in its capacity as employer also differs constitutionally from the government in its capacity as the sovereign executing criminal laws. The Court in *Pickering* said:

> "The problem in any case is to arrive at a balance between the interests of the teacher, as a citizen, in commenting upon matters of public concern and the interest of the State, as an employer, in promoting the efficiency of the public services it performs through its employees." . . .

Because of these acknowledged distinctions of constitutional dimension based upon the role of the government, I have serious doubt as to whether cases dealing with the imposition of criminal sanctions . . . are properly applicable to this case dealing with the government as college administrator. I also doubt whether cases dealing with the prior restraint imposed by injunctive process of a court, . . .

are precisely comparable to this case, in which a typical sanction imposed was the requirement that the group abandon its plan to meet in the college coffee shop.

Prior cases dealing with First Amendment rights are not fungible goods, and I think the doctrine of these cases suggests two important distinctions. The government as employer or school administrator may impose upon employees and students reasonable regulations that would be impermissible if imposed by the government upon all citizens. And there can be a constitutional distinction between the infliction of criminal punishment, on the one hand, and the imposition of milder administrative or disciplinary sanctions, on the other, even though the same First Amendment interest is implicated by each.

Because some of the language used by the Court tends to obscure these distinctions, which I believe to be important, I concur only in the judgment.

## NOTES AND QUESTIONS

1.  Would this case have been decided differently if (1) a "common school" rather than a university were involved, or if (2) the organization denied recognition were a teacher's organization rather than student? If so, why? In Dixon v. Beresh, 361 F.Supp. 253 (E.D.Mich.1973), high school officials "refused to afford recognition to student organizations known and the Mumford Committee to End Stress and the Mumford Young Socialist Alliance" because of a policy that "forbids the school from affording recognition to student groups which advocate 'controversial' ideas or which 'stress one side' of issues." The principal, in his unfettered discretion, decided what was controversial. Citing Tinker, the court ruled: "Absent a threat to the orderly operation of the school, to deny recognition to a student group for the reason that it advocates 'controversial' ideas is patently unconstitutional" and that the student organizations "are to be granted recognition immediately."

2.  What are the constitutional rules governing school recognition of student organizations? Is Healy a prior restraint case? Must the campus be open to student association? Did the Court decide that a rule prohibiting all student organizations or associations would be unconstitutional or does Healy decide only an equal protection issue; namely, that where some student organizations are recognized by school authorities then recognition cannot be denied to the SDS on the grounds advanced by President James?

John Jones, a public high school student, joined an organization that frequently met during school hours. Jones attended the group's meetings, rather than class, and he was charged with truancy. Does Jones have, or should he have, a valid truancy defense if he claims that the state's compulsory attendance laws, including their truancy provisions, violate his constitutional right to free association?

3.  Healy deals with the constitutional right to recognition of continuing association. The constitution also protects the right to (non-continuing) association; i. e., an individual meeting. Suppose a public high school adopted a rule that "no student nor any student club, organization or

association, nor any part of the student body, shall celebrate, parade or demonstrate on school grounds without prior approval from the principal." The rule is silent making no distinction between disruptive or violent and non-disruptive or non-violent demonstrations. After Healy and Tinker, is this rule constitutional? Could it be applied constitutionally to a demonstration inside the school buildings?

4. Suppose high school (or college) authorities refused to permit "gay dances" or to recognize a student group known as "The Gay Lib," giving the following separate and independent reasons for the refusal: (1) official recognition would tend to expand and increase homosexual behavior which will, in turn, cause increased violations of the state's anti-sodomy law; (2) the mere presence of homosexual groups disrupts and interferes with the institution's educational function; (3) recognition incorrectly implies in the public mind institutional approval of homosexuality, and (4) recognition is inconsistent with the school's task of presenting moral education. Was any of these grounds the subject of discussion in the *Healy* case? Would any of the three grounds suffice for non-recognition? Ratchford v. Gay Lib, 434 U.S. 1080, 98 S. Ct. 1276, 55 L.Ed.2d 789 (1978) involved similar facts. A divided U. S. Court of Appeals held the ban against recognition unconstitutional, and the Supreme Court refused to review the case. Dissenting from the Court's denial of review, Mr. Justice Rehnquist, joined by Justice Blackmun, insisted that "Healy v. James did not directly address" the question of non-recognition of homosexual groups. Do you agree? Justice Rehnquist thought it important that expert psychological testimony had "established the fact that the meeting together of individuals who consider themselves homosexual in an officially recognized university organization can have a distinctly different effect from the mere advocacy of repeal of the State's sodomy statute." Justice Rehnquist pointed out that "some speech that has a propensity to induce action prohibited by the criminal laws may itself be prohibited," and he continued: "A fortiori, speech and conduct combined which have that effect may surely be placed off limits of a university campus without doing violence to the [First Amendment]." Would, or should, the same views be applied to meetings of heterosexual groups in a state having laws against fornication and adultery? For further discussion, see, Comment, Beyond Tinker and Healy: Applying The First Amendment To Student Activities, 78 Col.L.Rev. 1700 (1978).

5. Healy indicates that the educational institution had to provide students with at least two ingredients of associational freedom—a place to meet and a place to publicize meetings. The Court deliberately left open the question whether some funding also had to be provided as part of the right to associational freedom. The Healy rationale strongly suggests that students have no right to direct funding, but indirect funding may raise a different issue. Suppose an educational institution charged student groups for the rental value of meeting rooms and the costs involved in publicizing the groups' meetings in the school newspaper and on bulletin boards, do the students have a constitutionally valid complaint against the charges? What does the rationale of Healy suggest?

6. What kind of school governance system is implied by Healy?

7. Does this case apply to secret societies? Would the decision have been different if a secret society were involved?

Assume you are the judge, and in light of Healy v. James, supra, would you have decided the following case differently than did Oregon's Supreme Court? If so, are the Oregon decision and its opinion fully consistent with Healy v. James? If not, where do they differ? Are these differings justifiable? Why or why not? Identify all the rulings advanced by Judge Lusk (such as "they [students] have no constitutional right to be members of clubs organized in the high schools, and composed of children attending different high schools, and which the school board may have substantial reason for believing to be inimical to the discipline and effective operation of the schools") and analyze each against the rationale of Healy.

---

## BURKITT v. SCHOOL DIST. NO. 1

Supreme Court of Oregon, 1952.
195 Or. 471, 246 P.2d 566.

LUSK, Justice. Since 1909 secret societies in the high schools of this state have been prohibited by law. The statute in O.C.L.A. so providing reads:

> § 111–3004. "Secret societies of every kind and character, including fraternities and sororities, so called, which may now or hereafter exist among the pupils of any of the public schools of this state, including high schools, either local or country, are hereby declared unlawful."

> § 111–3005. "It is hereby made the duty of each school board within the state, to examine, from time to time, into the condition of all schools under its charge and to suppress all secret societies therein, and for this purpose such boards are hereby authorized to suspend or expel from school, in their discretion, all pupils who engage in the organization or maintenance of such societies."

> § 111–3006. "This act shall not apply to either the state agricultural college or the state university." . . .

. . . the statute appears to have been more honored in the breach than the observance. Until 1936 the school authorities seem to have done little if anything to discharge their statutory duty to "suppress all secret societies" in the high schools, although there were for many years in the high schools of Portland a number of secret fraternities and sororities, some of the former being local chapters of national organizations. In 1936 a pledge system was inaugurated under which pupils and their parents were required to sign a pledge that the pupil was not and would not become a member of any such society.

If it was discovered that a pupil had violated the pledge he was suspended; afterward he and a parent could come to the superintendent's office and agree that the pupil would resign from the organization, whereupon the suspension would be lifted.  The system was found only partially effective.  Sometimes, when the issue arose, parents protested that the particular organization involved was not a secret society and that it was not operating in the schools.  In 1943 and 1944 the school authorities, because of these protests from parents and their own feeling of uncertainty as to how far they could go in the enforcement of the law, abandoned the pledge system, and adopted a policy of ignoring the societies as long as they kept their activities out of the schools.  This did not work either; the pupils then began to wear fraternity and sorority pins openly and to engage in pledging, "dogging," and other activities peculiar to their organizations, in the schools.

It was against this background of experience with a problem which, as Mr. Jonathan W. Edwards, deputy superintendent of schools testified, "has existed in our schools for the last 35 or 40 years," and with the purpose of discharging the duty imposed upon them by law, that the board of directors of the school district on or about October 27, 1949, adopted a resolution by which were promulgated certain regulations prescribing the conditions under which clubs could be organized and conducted in the high schools of the district.  .   .   .

The resolution contains the following recitals:

"Whereas, secret societies of every kind and character, including fraternities and sororities, so called, are contrary to state law, and

"Whereas, the state law imposes upon the School Board the duty of suppressing such organizations within the public schools of this district and to that end authorizes the School Board to suspend or expel from schools in its discretion all pupils who engage in the organization or maintenance of such societies, and

"Whereas, clubs and organizations other than secret societies, organized and maintained by school pupils can become and be inimical to the best interest of the school pupils, the community or the effective operation of the schools."

The superintendent of schools is then directed to suppress secret societies "and also clubs and organizations other than secret societies which the Superintendent in his discretion considers inimical to the best interest of the school pupils, the community, or the effective operation of the schools, by suspending or expelling" pupils who are members thereof.  It was further resolved that school clubs should not be banned which have been approved and chartered by the high school principal on conditions established by the superintendent of schools. These provisions are followed by what are termed "tentative conditions," which provide that all organizations of pupils must be approved by the central school administration and chartered by the particular school from which organized; that the application for a charter must show the sponsoring group, adult supervisor or advisors, the purposes of the organization and standards for membership, a list of officers and members, a copy of any ceremonial or initiation, and a pledge against secrecy. Then follow 18 rules designed to keep the school authorities advised of the membership and financial condition, and to regulate the activities of these chartered organizations. It is required that at all functions of the organizations adult advisors approved by the school principal shall be present; any initiation ceremonies not approved by the principal are prohibited, and such ceremonies are required to be open to the school staff and parents of inductees; no more than a two-thirds vote shall be required for admission to membership; hazing, "dogging" and all other types of pre-initiation activities, rush periods, and post-bid screening of members are prohibited. Membership in an organization not chartered is made a ground for suspension or expulsion.

The particular rule, however, which is involved in this case is No. 7, which reads as follows:

> "Members of any chartered organizations shall be regularly enrolled high school students from one high school student body. Graduates or students who have dropped from school shall not be permitted to retain membership. Public school students who were bona fide members of an interschool club prior to October 27, 1949, may retain membership in any such club that qualifies for a charter."

The validity of this rule is the principal question in the case.

Plaintiffs are three adults and four minors. Of the adults one has a son and a daughter attending Lincoln High School, a public school of the district; another has a daughter attending St. Helen's Hall, a private school in Portland; and another has two daughters attending St. Mary's Academy in Portland, erroneously referred to in the record as a parochial school, actually a private school under Catholic auspices. The two private schools give a high school education. Each of the children of the adult plaintiffs is a member of one or another of the four organizations named in the complaint whose status is here involved. Plaintiffs refer to these organizations as "unincorporated clubs," defendants and intervenors as sororities and fraternities. We shall call them simply "clubs." Each of the minor plaintiffs is a pupil of a Portland public high school and a member and officer or representative of one or another of the following named clubs: Alpha Sigma, Joma Joma, Wiki and Pierrette, and they appear on behalf, not only of themselves, but of the clubs named and all other clubs similarly situated.   The defendants are the school district, its board of directors, and school clerk.   .   .   .

The plaintiffs do not deny that there are secret societies in the Portland high schools, or at least that there were on February 28, 1950, the day their complaint was filed.   .   .   .

The circuit judge found in his opinion that at least some of the plaintiff clubs were secret societies.   We think there is justification in the evidence for that finding.   Moreover, the evidence shows that in organization, officers, types of records kept, rushing, pledging, initiation (with necessary variations as between fraternities and sororities) all the members of the Big Six followed somewhat of a pattern, and that three members of the Big Six were chapters of national fraternities.   We are inclined to the opinion that some elements of secrecy were likewise common to all the Big Six societies.   Indeed, if the secret societies admitted to exist are not to be found among the unchartered members of the Big Six, we are at a loss to know where to look for them.   But in the view we take of the actual question for decision, it is not necessary to determine which clubs are secret societies or whether the plaintiff clubs are among them.   Much testimony was adduced upon that subject, and there has been extensive argument respecting it.   The basic questions, however, are whether there is a secret society problem in the high schools of Portland, and, if so, whether, by the adoption of Rule 7, along with the other so-called "tentative conditions," the school board exceeded its authority;   or whether, on the other hand, Rule 7 is a reasonable regulation appropriate to accomplish the end expressed in the resolution of October 27, 1949, namely, the suppression of secret societies in the high schools.   .   .   .

This court would be the last to sanction any unlawful interference with "the liberty of parents and guardians to direct the upbringing and education of children under their control."   Pierce v. Society of the Sisters,   .   .   .

The plaintiffs also rely on West Virginia State Board of Education v. Barnette,   .   .   .   Of course, no such question [of a compulsory flag salute] is involved here.

There is nothing in Rule 7, nor in any other of the rules adopted by the school board, which prevents the minor plaintiffs from assembling and associating freely at any time and place, outside of school hours, approved by their parents, with children from other high schools, public or private.   This is their constitutional right.   But they have no constitutional right to be members of clubs organized in the high schools, and composed of children attending different high schools, and which the school board may have substantial reason for believing to be inimical to the discipline and effective operation of the schools.   .   .   .   Nor does it make any difference that the minor plaintiffs may be required by law to attend some school, either public or private. . . . That obligation is likewise their opportunity to receive an education. . . . When they avail themselves of that opportunity they must, in the nature of things, submit to the discipline of the schools and to regulations reasonably calculated to promote such discipline and the high purpose for which the schools are established— the education of youth, which is not limited to the imparting of knowledge, but includes as well the development of character and preparation for the assumption of the responsibilities of citizenship in a democracy. To attain these ends not the least in value of the lessons to be learned are the lessons of self-restraint, self-discipline, tolerance, and respect for duly constituted authority. In this regard parents and the schools have their respective rights and duties, which complement one another, and may be exercised and discharged in cooperation for the welfare of the child and the state.

Here, as it seems to us, for the court to interfere with the action of the school authorities now challenged would be little less than to constitute ourselves a school board for all the schools of the state. This is something we have neither the right nor the inclination to do.

The provision of the resolution which invests the superintendent with the power to suppress nonsecret societies which in his discretion he considers inimical to the best interests of the school pupils, the community, or the effective operation of the schools, is attacked as a delegation of "unconstrained authority." In connection with this claim attention is called to the fact that the superintendent has exempted from the ban clubs sponsored by national fraternal organizations, by religious organizations, national youth organizations, and civic organizations such as the Kiwanis Club. . . . If at any time the superintendent should be guilty of applying the regulation with "an unequal and oppressive mind," as in Yick Wo v. Hopkins, [118 U.S. 356] then the rule of that case could be invoked. We are unable to say from the record in this case that he has done so thus far. . . .

The foregoing considerations lead us to the conclusion that the defendant School Board, in adopting the regulations here in question, acted within its authority, and that the regulations, particularly Rule 7, are reasonable and constitute a measure taken in good faith for the purpose of stamping out secret societies in the high schools under the Board's jurisdiction, in accordance with the duty imposed upon it by law . . .

## NOTES AND QUESTIONS

1. Is it possible that the statute and rule number 7 in this case if sought to be applied to adults would be an unconstitutional abridgment of the right to free and continuing secret association protected by the first amendment? See, NAACP v. Alabama, 357 U.S. 449, 78 S.Ct. 1163, 2 L.Ed.2d 1488 (1958). Cf. People of the State of New York ex rel.

Bryant v. Zimmerman, 278 U.S. 63, 49 S.Ct. 61, 73 L.Ed. 184 (1928). What is the justification for the school district to ban secret associations? Is the statute and rule 7 overbroad?

2. Does the rationale of the court penalize students for their *status* as secret society members rather than for any *acts* as such members? Does the fact that their membership was voluntary affect your answer? Should it?

3. Should a constitutional distinction be drawn between public and secret association?

## OFF THE SCHOOL PREMISES

### GRAYNED v. CITY OF ROCKFORD

Supreme Court of United States, 1972.
408 U.S. 104, 92 S.Ct. 2294, 33 L.Ed.2d 222.

Mr. Justice MARSHALL delivered the opinion of the Court.

Appellant Richard Grayned was convicted for his part in a demonstration in front of West Senior High School in Rockford, Illinois. Negro students at the school had first presented their grievances to school administrators. When the principal took no action on crucial complaints, a more public demonstration of protest was planned. On April 25, 1969, approximately 200 people—students, their family members, and friends—gathered next to the school grounds. Appellant, whose brother and twin sisters were attending the school, was part of this group. The demonstrators marched around on a sidewalk about 100 feet from the school building, which was set back from the street. Many carried signs which summarized the grievances: "Black cheerleaders to cheer too"; "Black history with black teachers"; "Equal rights, Negro counselors." Others, without placards, made the "power to the people" sign with their upraised and clenched fists.

In other respects, the evidence at appellant's trial was sharply contradictory. Government witnesses reported that the demonstrators repeatedly cheered, chanted, baited policemen, and made other noise that was audible in the school; that hundreds of students were distracted from their school activities and lined the classroom windows to watch the demonstration; that some demonstrators successfully yelled to their friends to leave the school building and join the demonstration; that uncontrolled latenesses after period changes in the school were far greater than usual, with late students admitting that they had been watching the demonstration; and that, in general, orderly school procedure was disrupted. Defense witnesses claimed that the demonstrators were at all times quiet and orderly; that they did not seek to violate the law, but only to "make a point"; that the only noise was made by policemen using loudspeakers; that almost no students were noticeable at the schoolhouse windows; and that orderly school procedure was not disrupted.

After warning the demonstrators, the police arrested 40 of them, including appellant. For participating in the demonstration, Grayned was tried and convicted of violating two Rockford ordinances, hereinafter referred to as the "anti-picketing" ordinance and the "anti-noise" ordinance. A $25 fine was imposed for each violation. . . .

I

At the time of appellant's arrest and conviction, Rockford's anti-picketing ordinance provided that

"A person commits disorderly conduct when he knowingly:

. . . . . . . . .

"(i) Pickets or demonstrates on a public way within 150 feet of any primary or secondary school building while the school is in session and one-half hour before the school is in session and one-half hour after the school session has been concluded, provided that this subsection does not prohibit the peaceful picketing of any school involved in a labor dispute . . . ."

With the exception of two unimportant words, this ordinance is identical to the Chicago disorderly conduct ordinance we have today considered in Police Department of Chicago v. Mosley, ante. For the reasons given in *Mosley*, we agree with the dissenting Justice Schaefer below, and hold that § 18.1(i) violates the Equal Protection Clause of the Fourteenth Amendment. Appellant's conviction under this invalid ordinance must be reversed.

II

The anti-noise ordinance reads, in pertinent part, as follows:

"[N]o person, while on public or private grounds adjacent to any building in which a school or any class thereof is in session, shall willfully make or assist in the making of any noise or diversion which disturbs or tends to disturb the peace or good order of such school session or class thereof . . . ." Code of Ordinances, c. 28, § 19.2(a).

Appellant claims that, on its face, this ordinance is both vague and overboard, and therefore unconstitutional. We conclude, however, that the ordinance suffers from neither of these related infirmities.

A. Vagueness

It is a basic principle of due process that an enactment is void for vagueness if its prohibitions are not clearly defined. Vague laws offend several important values. First, because we assume that man is free to steer between lawful and unlawful conduct, we insist that laws give the person of ordinary intelligence a reasonable opportunity to know what is prohibited, so that he may act accordingly. Vague laws may trap the innocent by not providing fair warning. Second, if arbitrary and discriminatory enforcement is to be prevented, laws must provide explicit standards for those who apply them. A vague law impermissibly delegates basic policy matters to policemen, judges, and juries for resolution on an *ad hoc* and subjective basis, with the attendant dangers of arbitrary and discriminatory application. Third, but related, where a vague statute "abut[s] upon sensitive areas of basic First Amendment freedoms," it "operates to inhibit the exercise of [those] freedoms." Uncertain meanings inevitably lead citizens to " 'steer far wider of the unlawful zone'  . . . than if the boundaries of the forbidden areas were clearly marked."

Although the question is close, we conclude that the anti-noise ordinance is not impermissibly vague. The court below rejected appellant's arguments "that proscribed conduct was not sufficiently specified and that police were given too broad a discretion in determining whether conduct was proscribed."  . . .

. . .  we find no unconstitutional vagueness in the anti-noise ordinance. Condemned to the use of words, we can never expect mathematical certainty from our language. The words of the Rockford ordinance are marked by "flexibility and reasonable breadth, rather than meticulous specificity,"  . . .  but we think it is clear what the ordinance as a whole prohibits. Designed, according to its preamble, "for the protection of Schools," the ordinance forbids deliberately noisy or diversionary activity which disrupts or is about to disrupt normal school activities. It forbids this willful activity at fixed times—when school is in session—and at a sufficiently fixed place—"adjacent" to the school. Were we left with just the words of the ordinance, we might be troubled by the imprecision of the phrase "tends to disturb." However,  . . .  the Supreme Court of Illinois construed a Chicago ordinance prohibiting, *inter alia*, a "diversion tending to disturb the peace," and held that it permitted conviction only where there was "*imminent* threat of violence."  . . .  we think it proper to conclude that the Supreme Court of Illinois would interpret the Rockford ordinance to prohibit only actual or imminent interference with the "peace or good order" of the school.

Although the prohibited quantum of disturbance is not specified in the ordinance, it is apparent from the statute's announced purpose that the measure is whether normal school activity has been or is about to be disrupted. We do not have here a vague, general "breach of the peace" ordinance, but a specific statute for the school context, where the prohibited disturbances are easily measured by their impact on the normal activities of the school. Given this "particular context," the ordinance gives "fair notice to whom [it] is directed." . . .

## B.  Overbreadth

A clear and precise enactment may nevertheless be "overbroad" if in its reach it prohibits constitutionally protected conduct.  Although appellant does not claim that, as applied to him, the anti-noise ordinance has punished protected expressive activity, he claims that the ordinance is overbroad on its face.  Because overbroad laws, like vague ones, deter privileged activity, our cases firmly establish appellant's standing to raise an overbreadth challenge.  The crucial question, then, is whether the ordinance sweeps within its prohibitions what may not be punished under the First and Fourteenth Amendments.  Specifically, appellant contends that the Rockford ordinance unduly interferes with First and Fourteenth Amendment rights to picket on a public sidewalk near a school.  We disagree.

"In considering the right of a municipality to control the use of public streets for the expression of religious [or political] views, we start with the words of Mr. Justice Roberts that 'Wherever the title of streets and parks may rest, they have immemorially been held in trust for the use of the public and, time out of mind, have been used for purposes of assembly, communicating thoughts between citizens, and discussing public questions.' . . ."  The right to use a public place for expressive activity may be restricted only for weighty reasons.

Clearly, government has no power to restrict such activity because of its message.  Our cases make equally clear, however, that reasonable "time, place and manner" regulations may be necessary to further significant governmental interests, and are permitted.  For example, two parades cannot march on the same street simultaneously, and government may allow only one. . . .  Subject to such reasonable regulation, however, peaceful demonstrations in public places are protected by the First Amendment.  Of course, where demonstrations turn violent, they lose their protected quality as expression under the First Amendment.

The nature of a place, "the pattern of its normal activities, dictates the kinds of regulations of time, place, and manner that are reasonable."  Although a silent vigil may not unduly interfere with a public library, . . . making a speech in the reading room almost certainly would.  That same speech should be perfectly appropriate in a park.  The crucial question is whether the manner of expression is basically incompatible with the normal activity of a particular place at a particular time.  Our cases make clear that in assessing the reasonableness of regulation, we must weigh heavily the fact that communication is involved; the regulation must be narrowly tailored to further the State's legitimate interest.  "Access to [the streets, sidewalks, parks, and other similar public places] for the purpose of exercising [First Amendment rights] cannot constitutionally be denied broadly  .  .  .  ."  Free expression "must not, in the guise of regulation, be abridged or denied."

In light of these general principles, we do not think that Rockford's ordinance is an unconstitutional regulation of activity around a school.  Our touchstone is Tinker v. Des Moines  .  .  .  in which we considered the question of how to accommodate First Amendment rights with the "special characteristics of the school environment."  .  .  .  *Tinker* held that the Des Moines School District could not punish students for wearing black armbands to school in protest of the Vietnam War.  Recognizing that "wide exposure to  .  .  .  robust exchange of ideas" is an "important part of the educational process" and should be nurtured,  .  .  .  we concluded that free expression could not be barred from the school campus. We made clear that "undifferentiated fear or apprehension of disturbance is not enough to overcome the right to freedom of expression,"  .  .  .  and that particular expressive activity could not be prohibited because of a "mere desire to avoid the discomfort and unpleasantness that always accompany an unpopular viewpoint,"  .  .  . But we nowhere suggested that students, teachers, or anyone else has an absolute constitutional right to use all parts of a school building or its immediate environs for his unlimited expressive purposes. Expressive activity could certainly be restricted, but only if the forbidden conduct "materially disrupts classwork or involves substantial disorder or invasion of the rights of others."  .  .  .  The wearing of armbands was protected in *Tinker* because the students "neither interrupted school activities nor sought to intrude in the school affairs or the lives of others.  They caused discussion outside of the classrooms, but no interference with work and no disorder."  .  .  .

Just as *Tinker* made clear that school property may not be declared off-limits for expressive activity by students, we think it clear that the public sidewalk adjacent to school grounds may not be declared off-limits for expressive activity by members of the public. But in each case, expressive activity may be prohibited if it "materially disrupts classwork or involves substantial disorder or invasion of the rights of others."  .  .  .

We would be ignoring reality if we did not recognize that the public schools in a community are important institutions, and are often the focus of significant grievances.  Without interfering with normal school activities, daytime picketing and handbilling on public grounds near a school can effectively publicize those grievances to pedestrians, school visitors, and deliverymen, as well as to teachers, administrators, and students.  Some picketing to that end will be quiet and peaceful, and will in no way disturb the normal functioning of the school.  For example, it would be highly unusual if the classic expressive gesture of the solitary picketer disrupts anything related to the school, at least on a public sidewalk open to pedestrians. On the other hand, schools could hardly tolerate boisterous demonstrators who drown out classroom conversation, make studying impossible, block entrances, or incite children to leave the schoolhouse.

Rockford's anti-noise ordinance goes no further than *Tinker* says a municipality may go to prevent interference with its schools. It is narrowly tailored to further Rockford's compelling interest in having an undisrupted school session conducive to the students' learning, and does not unnecessarily interfere with First Amendment rights. . . . Rockford punishes only conduct which disrupts or is about to disrupt normal school activities. That decision is made, as it should be, on an individualized basis, given the particular fact situation. Peaceful picketing which does not interfere with the ordinary functioning of the school is permitted. And the ordinance gives no license to punish anyone because of what he is saying.

We recognize that the ordinance prohibits some picketing which is neither violent nor physically obstructive. Noisy demonstrations which disrupt or are incompatible with normal school activities are obviously within the ordinance's reach. Such expressive conduct may be constitutionally protected at other places or other times, . . . but next to a school, while classes are in session, it may be prohibited. The anti-noise ordinance imposes no such restriction on expressive activity before or after the school session, while the student/faculty "audience" enters and leaves the school.

. . . Rockford's modest restriction on some peaceful picketing represents a considered and specific legislative judgment that some kinds of expressive activity should be restricted at a particular time and place, here in order to protect the schools. Such a reasonable regulation is not inconsistent with the First and Fourteenth Amendments. The anti-noise ordinance is not invalid on its face.

Mr. Justice BLACKMUN joins in the judgment and in Part I of the opinion of the Court. He concurs in the result as to Part II of the opinion.

Mr. Justice DOUGLAS, dissenting in part [II].

. . . We held in Cox v. Louisiana, 379 U.S. 536, 544–545, 85 S.Ct. 453, 458–459, 13 L.Ed.2d 471, that a State could not infringe a person's right of free speech and free assembly by convicting him under a "disturbing the peace" ordinance where all that the students in that case did was to protest segregation and discrimination against Blacks by peaceably assemblying and marching to the courthouse where they sang, prayed, and listened to a speech, but where there was no violence, no rioting, no boisterous conduct.

The school where the present picketing occurred was the center of a racial conflict. Most of the picketers were indeed students in the school.  The dispute doubtless disturbed the school; and the blaring of the loudspeakers of the police was certainly a "noise or diversion" in the meaning of the ordinance.  But there was no evidence that appellant was noisy or boisterous or rowdy.  He walked quietly and in an orderly manner.  As I read this record the disruptive force loosened at this school was an issue dealing with race—an issue that is preeminently one for solution by First Amendment means.  That is all that was done here; and the entire picketing, including appellant's part in it, was done in the best First Amendment tradition.

### NOTES AND QUESTIONS

1.  The ordinance involved in Part I of the Court's opinion exempted "peaceful picketing of any school involved in a labor dispute."  This ordinance was viewed as unconstitutionally denying the equal protection of the laws on the authority of Police Dept. of Chicago v. Mosley, 408 U.S. 92, 92 S.Ct. 2286, 33 L.Ed.2d 212 (1972).  Mosley involved a virtually identical ordinance also exempting "peaceful labor picketing."  The Supreme Court said:  "The question we consider here is whether this selective exclusion from a public place is permitted.  Our answer is 'No.'"  The Court continued:  "Chicago's ordinance imposes a selective restriction on expressive conduct far 'greater than is essential to the furtherance of [a substantial governmental] interest,'" and "the discrimination among pickets is based on the content of their expression.  Therefore, under the Equal Protection Clause, it may not stand."  For comment see, Black, Equal But Inadequate Protection:  A Look at Mosley and Grayned, 8 Harv.Civ.Rights & Civ.Lib.L.Rev. 469 (1973).

## AFTER HOUR USE OF SCHOOL FACILITIES

### NATIONAL SOCIALIST WHITE PEOPLE'S PARTY
### v. RINGERS

United States Court of Appeals, 1973.
473 F.2d 1010 (4th Cir.).

The facts underlying this controversy have been stipulated by the parties:  The Party, a successor to the American Nazi Party, is a non-profit corporation, incorporated in Virginia.  A charter purpose of the Party is to gain political power by all legal and non-violent means, including the elective process.  Party membership is limited only to whites of any religion who embrace its views.  No Negro has ever held membership in the Party.

The Board, an arm of the State of Virginia, has responsibility for schools, grounds, and related property.  State law permits the Board to rent high school auditoriums during non-school hours "for any legal assembly,"  .  .  .  "as will not impair the efficiency of the schools."
.  .  .  Pursuant to this statutory authority, the Board has promulgated regulations under which it leases school property to organiza-

tions in "good standing."   By regulation, an organization possesses "good standing" if it has "no previous record of abuse of school facilities."   The Board has for some time, and on a regular basis, granted permits to use the auditorium to a wide variety of public and private groups on a first-come first-served basis.  The Board has granted such permits to organizations which exclude certain racial, religious, or sexual groups.  Except for a few instances involving groups which had previously damaged school property, no group has been denied the use of an available auditorium except the Party.

The Board has consistently refused to rent available auditoriums to the Party, although the Party has no previous record of abuse to school property.  .  .  .

The Board's repeated exercise of its discretionary authority to rent the Yorktown High School auditorium for a nominal fee during non-school hours to public and private groups for public and private meetings on a first-come first-served basis, to the extent that the auditorium is not needed for school purposes and that non-school uses will not endanger the property, constitutes, in our view an effective dedication of the auditorium for the exercise of the first amendment rights of freedom of speech, association and assembly.  This partial dedication as a forum for the exercise of first amendment rights makes the school auditorium conceptually indistinguishable for first amendment purposes as a "public place" from streets and parks, which too, are acquired and maintained at public expense.  There can be little doubt that streets and parks are recognized forums for the exercise of first amendment rights.  In Hague v. C. I. O.   .   .   .   Mr. Justice Roberts wrote:

> Wherever the title of streets and parks may rest, they have immemorially been held in trust for the use of the public and, time out of mind, have been used for purposes of assembly, communicating thoughts between citizens, and discussing public questions.   Such use of the streets and *public places* has, from ancient times, been a part of the privileges, immunities, rights, and liberties of citizens.   The privilege of a citizen of the United States to use the streets and parks for communication of views on national questions may be regulated in the interest of all;  it is not absolute, but relative, and must be exercised in subordination to the general comfort and convenience, and in consonance with peace and good order;  but it must not, in the guise of regulation, be abridged or denied.   (emphasis added).

By the same token, we conclude that the school auditorium, since it has effectively been partially dedicated for first amendment uses, may be used for purposes of assembly, communicating thoughts between citizens and discussing public questions.  In a public place regularly used for the exercise of free speech and the exchange of ideas, we do not see how walls and a roof can insulate against the reach of the first amendment's commands. That amendment's protections cannot be made to turn on the structural distinctions between, for example, an open public park, a public amphitheatre, a public stadium, or an enclosed public auditorium. While limitations on its use as a forum to permit it to serve its prime function (school purposes), to serve the general comfort and convenience, and to preserve peace and good order, including the protection of property, may be sustained, a regulation which limits the exercise of first amendment guarantees should be stricken down.

There is no dispute that the first amendment protects from state interference the expression in a public place of the unpopular as well as the popular and the right to assemble peaceably in a public place in the interest and furtherance of the unpopular as well as the popular. Specifically, the expression of racist and anti-semitic views in a public place and the right to assemble in a public place for the purpose of communicating and discussing racist and anti-semitic views are protected activities and may not be circumscribed by the state, except where "advocacy is directed to inciting or producing imminent lawless action and is likely to incite or produce such action." Brandenburg v. Ohio . . . or where "there are special, limited circumstances in which speech is so interlaced with burgeoning violence that it is not protected by the broad guarantee of the First Amendment," Carroll v. Princess Anne, 393 U.S. 175, . . . Under the stipulated facts, the Party presented no such danger.

Certainly the ability to meet in public places is fundamental to the exercise of first amendment freedoms. If the state denies that opportunity to an unpopular group, the first amendment will be substantially emasculated. The very recent case of Healy v. James . . . held that the first amendment requires a state-supported college to recognize a student political group (SDS) and to afford it the use of campus facilities for communication and association, unless it was shown that the group, in addition to mere advocacy of radical doctrines, would likely "infringe reasonable campus rules, interrupt classes or substantially interfere with the opportunity of other students to obtain an education." . . . The basis of the Court's reasoning was the inescapable link between the denial of campus facilities for communication and assembly and prior restraint of unpopular ideas. Thus, the Court stressed that: "Among the rights protected by the First Amendment is the right of individuals to associate to further their personal beliefs. . . . There can be no doubt that denial of official recognition, without justification, to college organizations burdens or abridges that associational right. The primary impediment to free association flowing from nonrecognition is the denial of use of campus facilities for meetings and other appropriate purposes." . . . Later, the Court expressed the point more directly: "It is to be remembered that the effect of the College's denial of recognition was a form of prior restraint, denying to petitioners' organization the range of associational activities described above." . . .

Since the first amendment prohibits the state from interfering with the expression of unpopular, indeed, offensive, views, and with assembly and association for the purpose of exchanging and furthering them, we think that the first amendment protects the expression of such views in those public places dedicated to the exercise of first amendment rights by groups which implement them by restrictive membership policies. We therefore, conclude that the School Board's denial of the use of a public forum because of the Party's discriminatory membership policies constitutes as much of an invalid prior restraint as if it had denied the Party the use of the forum on the basis of the controversial beliefs which the Party would express at that place. . . .

We are confident that if the high school auditorium is made available to all groups, the very diversity and complexity of the views expressed, taken in bulk, will cure any incidental official identification attendant upon the use of the building for the articulation of extreme or abusive speech. At least that is the principle on which we have staked our all. As Mr. Justice Brandeis said years ago, "If there be time to expose through discussion the falsehood and fallacies, to avert the evil by the processes of education, the remedy to be applied is more speech, not enforced silence." . . . We conclude therefore that, considering all the factors in this case, the School Board has not overcome the "heavy presumption" against its effective prior restraint on the Party's right to free speech. . . .

BUTZNER, Circuit Judge (concurring in part and dissenting in part).

. . . Were this case concerned solely with prior restraint on freedom of speech and assembly, I would not dissent. But this appeal does not turn on the right to preach racial hatred and religious bigotry. The first amendment clearly grants this right whether the speech is made in a park, on a street, or in a building that has been designated as a public forum. It is the Party's exclusion of black citizens, not its message, that justified the Board's refusal to rent the auditorium.

Contrary to the Party's assertion, its first amendment rights are not so overriding that its racially discriminatory membership policy is irrelevant. Freedom of speech, assembly, and association are guaranteed by the first amendment to political organizations. Healy v. James, . . . Indeed, these rights are indispensable to a democracy. Nevertheless, the guarantee of first amendment freedoms does not compel a state to nurture racially discriminatory political parties. Just the opposite is true.

In a long line of cases, the Supreme Court has construed the fourteenth and fifteenth amendments to prohibit a wide variety of devices designed to keep black citizens from participating in political parties and the election process. As the abolition of white primaries attests, the state, acting through political parties or political associations, cannot abridge the right of a citizen to vote on account of race or deny him the equal protection of the laws. While some of these cases involve the fourteenth amendment and others the fifteenth, the distinction is not critical to this appeal because both amendments bar discrimination that is tainted by state action. These cases demonstrate that careful scrutiny of the state's involvement is demanded when the state aids political associations that discriminate on racial grounds. They teach, albeit implicitly, that when state action is united with a political party or association that bars black people from full participation in its affairs, the union is illegal despite the first amendment rights possessed by white members of the organization. These cases provide no valid distinction between a political party which has enjoyed success and one that has not. To permit the Party to use the school auditorium now, but to refuse it access in the future when it achieves success is simply locking the barn door after the horse has been stolen. . . .

Less my dissent provoke misunderstanding, I repeat that it is based on the racially discriminatory practices of the Party, not its speeches. A political party's rhetoric cannot be equated with its rules. Though politicians of every persuasion are entitled to freedom of speech and assembly, their exclusion of people from party membership on account of race is a tactic that has been expressly condemned by the Supreme Court. The Constitution's requirement of unrestricted membership is calculated to encourage, not suppress, free discussion and association. By declaring that political parties must be open to all citizens, the Court has wisely assigned priority to the political rights secured by the fourteenth and fifteenth amendments. Experience has shown this primacy affords ample accommodation for first amendment rights, and I see no reason in this appeal to encroach upon it. The Party's exclusion of black citizens from membership is the decisive step beyond advocacy that justified the district court's dismissal of its complaint.

# Chapter V

# CONSTITUTIONAL FREEDOM AND RELIGION

## INTRODUCTION

This chapter continues and completes the exploration of First Amendment themes as they serve to protect the freedom of mind and conscience. This chapter's focus is on religion. The basic question is whether the state can mold a child's mind into a religious way of thinking either by introducing religious matter into its public schools or by providing tax funds to religious schools?

The First Amendment prohibits any law "respecting an establishment of religion, or prohibiting the free exercise thereof." It has been incorporated into the Fourteenth Amendment and applies to the states and all their subdivisions. The religious ban is complete, barring government from aiding and enhancing or inhibiting and hindering religion. In other words, with respect to religion, government must be neutral. When fully implemented, these two clauses of the First Amendment will produce a separation of church and state in the United States. Thus, Americans enjoy freedom of religion and only they, themselves, and not their government, are responsible for the growth or decline of religion in the United States. But, government need not be neutral with respect to freedom of expression. The First Amendment prohibits government only from "abridging the freedom of speech, or of the press; or the right of the people peaceably to assemble, and to petition the government for a redress of grievances." It does not prohibit government from establishing freedom of speech as it does prohibit government from establishing religion.

One definition of "religion" is that any "individual or group belief is religious if it occupies the same place in the lives of its adherents that orthodox beliefs occupy in the lives of their adherents. Four characteristics should be present: (1) a belief regarding the meaning of life; (2) a psychological commitment by the individual adherent (or if a group, by the members generally) to this belief; (3) a system of moral practice resulting from adherence to this belief; and (4) an acknowledgement by its adherents that the belief (or belief system) is their exclusive or supreme system of ultimate beliefs." Note, Defining Religion, 32 U. of Chi.L.Rev. 533, 550–51 (1965).

Religion can be a strong force, and it can serve either to unify or to divide a people. If a country is strongly of one predominating faith, and if there is a union of church and state, that faith frequently, but not always, functions as a unifying societal force. But the United States does not rely upon any one religious viewpoint. There is no one "official" religion. In the United States church and state are separate, and many different religions are represented on its soil. Thus, religions in America coexist with each other within a secular state. This is the American Heritage, and while harmony usually prevails, it is sometimes a heritage of friction.

Some religions have chosen to establish separate and independent parochial school systems. Pierce v. Society of Sisters, supra, clearly recognizes that religious and other private groups have a constitutional right to establish separate, private schools, so long as they comply with the constitutional regulations of the schools set by state legislatures and state boards of education.

In an educational context three general types of constitutional law problems have arisen, and they will be covered in this chapter. The first two are "establishment" problems and the last is a problem of the "free exercise of religion": (1) problems concerning attempts to prescribe religion as part of public school activities, curricular or otherwise; (2) problems concerning attempts to channel public funds into the support of parochial schools, and (3) problems of conflict between a pupil's (or parent's) claim to free exercise of religion and the curricular requirements of a school.

## THE SEPARATION OF CHURCH AND STATE

-------

## THE HERITAGE

-------

### EVERSON v. BOARD OF EDUCATION

Supreme Court of the United States, 1947.
330 U.S. 1, 67 S.Ct. 504, 91 L.Ed. 711, rehearing denied 330 U.S. 855, 67 S.Ct. 962, 91 L.Ed. 1297.
[The majority opinion in this case is printed infra, at p. 410].

Mr. Justice RUTLEDGE, with whom Mr. Justice FRANKFURTER, Mr. Justice JACKSON and Mr. Justice BURTON agree, dissenting.

"Congress shall make no law respecting an establishment of religion, or prohibiting the free exercise thereof. . . ." U.S.Const., Amend. I. . . .

This case forces us to determine squarely for the first time what was "an establishment of religion" in the First Amendment's conception. . . .

Not simply an established church, but any law respecting an establishment of religion is forbidden. The Amendment was broadly but not loosely phrased. It is the compact and exact summation of its author's views formed during his long struggle for religious freedom. In Madison's own words characterizing Jefferson's Bill for Establishing Religious Freedom, the guaranty he put in our national charter, like the bill he piloted through the Virginia Assembly, was "a Model of technical precision, and perspicuous brevity." Madison could not have confused "church" and "religion," or "an established church" and "an establishment of religion."

The Amendment's purpose was not to strike merely at the official establishment of a single sect, creed or religion, outlawing only a formal relation such as had prevailed in England and some of the colonies. Necessarily it was to uproot all such relationships. But the object was broader than separating church and state in this narrow sense. It was to create a complete and permanent separation of the spheres of religious activity and civil authority by comprehensively forbidding every form of public aid or support for religion. In proof the Amendment's wording and history unite with this Court's consistent utterances whenever attention has been fixed directly upon the question.

"Religion" appears only once in the Amendment. But the word governs two prohibitions and governs them alike. It does not have two meanings, one narrow to forbid "an establishment" and another, much broader, for securing "the free exercise thereof." "Thereof" brings down "religion" with its entire and exact content, no more and no less, from the first into the second guaranty, so that Congress and now the states are as broadly restricted concerning the one as they are regarding the other.

No one would claim today that the Amendment is constricted, in "prohibiting the free exercise" of religion, to securing the free exercise of some formal or creedal observance, of one sect or of many. It secures all forms of religious expression, creedal, sectarian or non-sectarian, wherever and however taking place, except conduct which trenches upon the like freedoms of others or clearly and presently endangers the community's good order and security. For the protective purposes of this phase of the basic freedom, street preaching, oral or by distribution of literature, has been given "the same high estate under the First Amendment as . . . worship in the churches and preaching from the pulpits." And on this basis parents have been held entitled to send their children to private, religious schools. Pierce v. Society of Sisters, 268 U.S. 510. Accordingly, daily religious education commingled with secular is "religion" within the guaranty's comprehensive scope. So are religious training and teaching in whatever form. The word connotes the broadest content, determined not by the form or formality of the teaching or where it occurs, but by its essential nature regardless of those details.

"Religion" has the same broad significance in the twin prohibition concerning "an establishment." The Amendment was not duplicitous. "Religion" and "establishment" were not used in any formal or technical sense. The prohibition broadly forbids state support, financial or other, of religion in any guise, form or degree. It outlaws all use of public funds for religious purposes.

II

No provision of the Constitution is more closely tied to or given content by its generating history than the religious clause of the First Amendment. It is at once the refined product and the terse summation of that history. The history includes not only Madison's authorship and the proceedings before the First Congress, but also the long and intensive struggle for religious freedom in America, more especially in Virginia, of which the Amendment was the direct culmination. In the documents of the times, particularly of Madison, who was leader in the Virginia struggle before he became the Amendment's sponsor, but also in the writings of Jefferson and others and in the issues which engendered them is to be found irrefutable confirmation of the Amendment's sweeping content.

For Madison, as also for Jefferson, religious freedom was the crux of the struggle for freedom in general. . . . Madison was coauthor with George Mason of the religious clause in Virginia's great Declaration of Rights of 1776. He is credited with changing it from a mere statement of the principle of tolerance to the first official legislative pronouncement that freedom of conscience and religion are inherent rights of the individual. He sought also to have the Declaration expressly condemn the existing Virginia establishment. But the forces supporting it were then too strong.

Accordingly Madison yielded on this phase but not for long. At once he resumed the fight, continuing it before succeeding legislative sessions. As a member of the General Assembly in 1779 he threw his full weight behind Jefferson's historic Bill for Establishing Religious Freedom. That bill was a prime phase of Jefferson's broad program of democratic reform undertaken on his return from the Continental Congress in 1776 and submitted for the General Assembly's consideration in 1779 as his proposed revised Virginia code. With Jefferson's departure for Europe in 1784, Madison became the Bill's prime sponsor. Enactment failed in successive legislatures from its introduction in June, 1779, until its adoption in January, 1786. But during all this time the fight for religious freedom moved forward in Virginia on various fronts with growing intensity. Madison led throughout, against Patrick Henry's powerful opposing leadership until Henry was elected governor in November, 1784.

The climax came in the legislative struggle of 1784–1785 over the Assessment Bill. . . . This was nothing more nor less than a taxing measure for the support of religion, designed to revive the payment of tithes suspended since 1777. So long as it singled out a particular sect for preference it incurred the active and general hostility of dissentient groups. It was broadened to include them, with the result that some subsided temporarily in their opposition. As altered, the bill gave to each taxpayer the privilege of designating which church should receive his share of the tax.  In default of designation the legislature applied it to pious uses.  But what is of the utmost significance here, "in its final form the bill left the taxpayer the option of giving his tax to education."

Madison was unyielding at all times, opposing with all his vigor the general and nondiscriminatory as he had the earlier particular and discriminatory assessments proposed.  The modified Assessment Bill passed second reading in December, 1784, and was all but enacted. Madison and his followers, however, maneuvered deferment of final consideration until November, 1785.  And before the Assembly reconvened in the fall he issued his historic Memorial and Remonstrance.

This is Madison's complete, though not his only, interpretation of religious liberty.  It is a broadside attack upon all forms of "establishment" of religion, both general and particular, nondiscriminatory or selective.  Reflecting not only the many legislative conflicts over the Assessment Bill and the Bill for Establishing Religious Freedom but also, for example, the struggles for religious incorporations and the continued maintenance of the glebes, the Remonstrance is at once the most concise and the most accurate statement of the views of the First Amendment's author concerning what is "an establishment of religion."  Because it behooves us in the dimming distance of time not to lose sight of what he and his coworkers had in mind when, by a single sweeping stroke of the pen, they forbade an establishment of religion and secured its free exercise, the text of the Remonstrance is appended at the end of this opinion for its wider current reference, together with a copy of the bill against which it was directed.

The Remonstrance, stirring up a storm of popular protest, killed the Assessment Bill.  It collapsed in committee shortly before Christmas, 1785.  With this, the way was cleared at last for enactment of Jefferson's Bill for Establishing Religious Freedom.  Madison promptly drove it through in January of 1786, seven years from the time it was first introduced.  This dual victory substantially ended the fight over establishments, settling the issue against them.

The next year Madison became a member of the Constitutional Convention.  Its work done, he fought valiantly to secure the ratification of its great product in Virginia as elsewhere, and nowhere else more effectively.  Madison was certain in his own mind that under the Constitution "there is not a shadow of right in the general government to intermeddle with religion" and that "this subject is, for the honor of America, perfectly free and unshackled.  The government has no jurisdiction over it.  . . ."  Nevertheless he pledged that he would work for a Bill of Rights, including a specific guaranty of religious freedom, and Virginia, with other states, ratified the Constitution on this assurance.

Ratification thus accomplished, Madison was sent to the first Congress.  There he went at once about performing his pledge to establish freedom for the nation as he had done in Virginia. Within a little more than three years from his legislative victory at home he had proposed and secured the submission and ratification of the First Amendment as the first article of our Bill of Rights.

All the great instruments of the Virginia struggle for religious liberty thus became warp and woof of our constitutional tradition, not simply by the course of history, but by the common unifying force of Madison's life, thought and sponsorship. He epitomized the whole of that tradition in the Amendment's compact, but nonetheless comprehensive, phrasing.

As the Remonstrance discloses throughout, Madison opposed every form and degree of official relation between religion and civil authority. For him religion was a wholly private matter beyond the scope of civil power either to restrain or to support. Denial or abridgment of religious freedom was a violation of rights both of conscience and of natural equality. State aid was no less obnoxious or destructive to freedom and to religion itself than other forms of state interference. "Establishment" and "free exercise" were correlative and coextensive ideas, representing only different facets of the single great and fundamental freedom. The Remonstrance, following the Virginia statute's example, referred to the history of religious conflicts and the effects of all sorts of establishments, current and historical, to suppress religion's free exercise. With Jefferson, Madison believed that to tolerate any fragment of establishment would be by so much to perpetuate restraint upon that freedom. Hence he sought to tear out the institution not partially but root and branch, and to bar its return forever.

In no phase was he more unrelentingly absolute than in opposing state support or aid by taxation. Not over "three pence" contribution was thus to be exacted from any citizen for such a purpose . . . Tithes had been the lifeblood of establishment before and after other compulsions disappeared. Madison and his coworkers made no exceptions or abridgments to the complete separation they created. Their objection was not to small tithes. It was to any tithes whatsoever. "If it were lawful to impose a small tax for religion, the admission would pave the way for oppressive levies." Not the amount but "the principle of assessment was wrong." And the principle was as much to prevent "the interference of law in religion" as to restrain religious intervention in political matters. In this field the authors of our freedom would not tolerate "the first experiment on our liberties" or "wait till usurped power had strengthened itself by exercise, and entangled the question in precedents. " . . .

In view of this history no further proof is needed that the Amendment forbids any appropriation, large or small, from public funds to aid or support any and all religious exercises. But if more were called for, the debates in the First Congress and this Court's consistent expressions, whenever it has touched on the matter directly, supply it.

By contrast with the Virginia history, the congressional debates on consideration of the Amendment reveal only sparse discussion, reflecting the fact that the essential issues had been settled. Indeed the matter had become so well understood as to have been taken for granted in all but formal phrasing. Hence, the only enlightening reference shows concern, not to preserve any power to use public funds in aid of religion, but to prevent the Amendment from outlawing private gifts inadvertently by virtue of the breadth of its wording. . . .

## ATTEMPTS TO ESTABLISH RELIGION IN PUBLIC SCHOOLS

---

[In addition to the materials appearing in this section, consider also, Epperson v. Arkansas printed supra.]

### McCOLLUM v. BOARD OF EDUCATION

Supreme Court of the United States, 1948.

333 U.S. 203, 68 S.Ct. 461, 92 L.Ed. 649.

Mr. Justice BLACK delivered the opinion of the Court.

This case relates to the power of a state to utilize its tax-supported public school system in aid of religious instruction insofar as that power may be restricted by the First and Fourteenth Amendments to the Federal Constitution.

The appellant, Vashti McCollum, began this action for mandamus against the Champaign Board of Education in the Circuit Court of Champaign County, Illinois. Her asserted interest was that of a resident and taxpayer of Champaign and of a parent whose child was then enrolled in the Champaign public schools. Illinois has a compulsory education law which, with exceptions, requires parents to send their children, aged seven to sixteen, to its tax-supported public schools where the children are to remain in attendance during the hours when the schools are regularly in session. Parents who violate this law commit a misdemeanor punishable by fine unless the children attend private or parochial schools which meet educational standards fixed by the State. District boards of education are given general supervisory powers over the use of the public school buildings within the school districts. . . .

Although there are disputes between the parties as to various inferences that may or may not properly be drawn from the evidence concerning the religious program, the following facts are shown by the record without dispute. In 1940 interested members of the Jewish, Roman Catholic, and a few of the Protestant faiths formed a voluntary association called the Champaign Council on Religious Education. They obtained permission from the Board of Education to offer classes in religious instruction to public school pupils in grades four to nine inclusive. Classes were made up of pupils whose parents signed print-ed cards requesting that their children be permitted to attend; they were held weekly, thirty minutes for the lower grades, forty-five minutes for the higher. The council employed the religious teachers at no expense to the school authorities, but the instructors were sub-ject to the approval and supervision of the superintendent of schools. The classes were taught in three separate religious groups by Protes-tant teachers, Catholic priests, and a Jewish rabbi, although for the past several years there have apparently been no classes instructed in the Jewish religion. Classes were conducted in the regular classrooms of the school building. Students who did not choose to take the re-ligious instruction were not released from public school duties; they were required to leave their classrooms and go to some other place in the school building for pursuit of their secular studies. On the other hand, students who were released from secular study for the religious instructions were required to be present at the religious classes. Re-ports of their presence or absence were to be made to their secular teachers.

The foregoing facts, without reference to others that appear in the record, show the use of tax-supported property for religious instruction and the close cooperation between the school authorities and the re-ligious council in promoting religious education. The operation of the state's compulsory education system thus assists and is integrated with the program of religious instruction carried on by separate re-ligious sects. Pupils compelled by law to go to school for secular ed-ucation are released in part from their legal duty upon the condition that they attend the religious classes. This is beyond all question a utilization of the tax-established and tax-supported public school sys-tem to aid religious groups to spread their faith. And it falls squarely under the ban of the First Amendment . . . "Neither a state nor the Federal Government can set up a church. Neither can pass laws which aid one religion, aid all religions, or prefer one religion over another. Neither can force or influence a person to go to or to remain away from church against his will or force him to profess a belief or disbelief in any religion. No person can be punished for entertaining or professing religious beliefs or disbeliefs, for church attendance or non-attendance. No tax in any amount, large or small can be levied to support any religious activities or institutions, what-ever they may be called, or whatever form they may adopt to teach or practice religion. Neither a state nor the Federal Government can, openly or secretly, participate in the affairs of any religious organ-izations or groups and *vice versa*. In the words of Jefferson, the clause against establishment of religion by law was intended to erect 'a wall of separation between church and State'." . . .

To hold that a state cannot consistently with the First and Four-teenth Amendments utilize its public school system to aid any or all religious faiths or sects in the dissemination of their doctrines and ideals does not, as counsel urge, manifest a governmental hostility to religion or religious teachings.  A manifestation of such hostility would be at war with our national tradition as embodied in the First Amendment's guaranty of the free exercise of religion.  For the First Amendment rests upon the premise that both religion and government can best work to achieve their lofty aims if each is left free from the other within its respective sphere.  .  .  .  the First Amendment has erected a wall between Church and State which must be kept high and impregnable.

Here not only are the State's tax-supported public school buildings used for the dissemination of religious doctrines.  The State also affords sectarian groups an invaluable aid in that it helps to provide pupils for their religious classes through use of the State's compulsory public school machinery.  This is not separation of Church and State.

The cause is reversed and remanded to the State Supreme Court for proceedings not inconsistent with this opinion.

Reversed and remanded.*

---

### ZORACH v. CLAUSON

Supreme Court of the United States, 1952.
343 U.S. 306, 72 S.Ct. 679, 96 L.Ed. 954.

Mr. Justice DOUGLAS delivered the opinion of the Court.

New York City has a program which permits its public schools to release students during the school day so that they may leave the school buildings and school grounds and go to religious centers for religious instruction or devotional exercises.  A student is released on written request of his parents.  Those not released stay in the classrooms.  The churches make weekly reports to the schools, sending a list of children who have been released from public school but who have not reported for religious instruction.

This "released time" program involves neither religious instruction in public school classrooms nor the expenditure of public funds.  All costs, including the application blanks, are paid by the religious organizations.  The case is therefore unlike McCollum v. Board of Education, 333 U.S. 203, which involved a "released time" program from Illinois.  In that case the classrooms were turned over to religious instructors.  We accordingly held that the program violated the First Amendment which (by reason of the Fourteenth Amendment) prohibits the states from establishing religion or prohibiting its free exercise.

* The concurring opinions of Mr. Jus-  dissenting opinion of Mr. Justice Reed
tices Frankfurter and Jackson and the  are omitted.

Appellants, who are taxpayers and residents of New York City and whose children attend its public schools, challenge the present law, contending it is in essence not different from the one involved in the *McCollum* case. Their argument, stated elaborately in various ways, reduces itself to this: the weight and influence of the school is put behind a program for religious instruction; public school teachers police it, keeping tab on students who are released; the classroom activities come to a halt while the students who are released for religious instruction are on leave; the school is a crutch on which the churches are leaning for support in their religious training; without the cooperation of the schools this "released time" program, like the one in the *McCollum* case, would be futile and ineffective. . . .

The briefs and arguments are replete with data bearing on the merits of this type of "released time" program. Views *pro* and *con* are expressed, based on practical experience with these programs and with their implications. We do not stop to summarize these materials nor to burden the opinion with an analysis of them. For they involve considerations not germane to the narrow constitutional issue presented. They largely concern the wisdom of the system, its efficiency from an educational point of view, and the political considerations which have motivated its adoption or rejection in some communities. Those matters are of no concern here, since our problem reduces itself to whether New York by this system has either prohibited the "free exercise" of religion or has made a law "respecting an establishment of religion" within the meaning of the First Amendment.

It take obtuse reasoning to inject any issue of the "free exercise" of religion into the present case. No one is forced to go to the religious classroom and no religious exercise or instruction is brought to the classrooms of the public schools. A student need not take religious instruction. He is left to his own desires as to the manner of time of his religious devotions, if any.

There is a suggestion that the system involves the use of coercion to get public school students into religious classrooms. There is no evidence in the record before us that supports that conclusion. The present record indeed tells us that the school authorities are neutral in this regard and do no more than release students whose parents so request. If in fact coercion were used, if it were established that any one or more teachers were using their office to persuade or force students to take the religious instruction, a wholly different case would be presented. Hence we put aside that claim of coercion both as respects the "free exercise" of religion and "an establishment of religion" within the meaning of the First Amendment.

Moreover, apart from that claim of coercion, we do not see how New York by this type of "released time" program has made a law respecting an establishment of religion within the meaning of the First Amendment. There is much talk of the separation of Church and State in the history of the Bill of Rights and in the decisions clustering around the First Amendment. . . . There cannot be the slightest doubt that the First Amendment reflects the philosophy that Church and State should be separated. And so far as interference with the "free exercise" of religion and an "establishment" of religion are concerned, the separation must be complete and unequivocal. The First Amendment within the scope of its coverage permits no exception; the prohibition is absolute. The First Amendment, however, does not say that in every and all respects there shall be a separation of Church and State. Rather, it studiously defines the manner, the specific ways, in which there shall be no concert or union or dependency one on the other. That is the common sense of the matter. Otherwise the state and religion would be aliens to each other—hostile, suspicious, and even unfriendly. Churches could not be required to pay even property taxes. Municipalities would not be permitted to render police or fire protection to religious groups. Policemen who helped parishioners into their places of worship would violate the Constitution. Prayers in our legislative halls; the appeals to the Almighty in the messages of the Chief Executive; the proclamations making Thanksgiving Day a holiday; "so help me God" in our courtroom oaths —these and all other references to the Almighty that run through our laws, our public rituals, our ceremonies would be flouting the First Amendment. A fastidious atheist or agnostic could even object to the supplication with which the Court opens each session: "God save the United States and this Honorable Court."

We would have to press the concept of separation of Church and State to these extremes to condemn the present law on constitutional grounds. The nullification of this law would have wide and profound effects. A Catholic student applies to his teacher for permission to leave the school during hours on a Holy Day of Obligation to attend a mass. A Jewish student asks his teacher for permission to be excused for Yom Kippur. A Protestant wants the afternoon off for a family baptismal ceremony. In each case the teacher, in order to make sure the student is not a truant, goes further and requires a report from the priest, the rabbi, or the minister. The teacher in other words cooperates in a religious program to the extent of making it possible for her students to participate in it. Whether she does it occasionally for a few students, regularly for one, or pursuant to a systematized program designed to further the religious needs of all the students does not alter the character of the act.

We are a religious people whose institutions presuppose a Supreme Being. We guarantee the freedom to worship as one chooses. We make room for as wide a variety of beliefs and creeds as the spiritual needs of man deem necessary. We sponsor an attitude on the part of government that shows no partiality to any one group and that lets each flourish according to the zeal of its adherents and the appeal of its dogma. When the state encourages religious instruction or cooperates with religious authorities by adjusting the schedule of public events to sectarian needs, it follows the best of our traditions. For it then respects the religious nature of our people and accommodates the public service to their spiritual needs. To hold that it may not would be to find in the Constitution a requirement that the government show a callous indifference to religious groups. That would be preferring those who believe in no religion over those who do believe. Government may not finance religious groups nor undertake religious instruction nor blend secular and sectarian education nor use secular institutions to force one or some religion on any person. But we find no constitutional requirement which makes it necessary for government to be hostile to religion and to throw its weight against efforts to widen the effective scope of religious influence. The government must be neutral when it comes to competition between sects. It may not thrust any sect on any person. It may not make a religious observance compulsory. It may not coerce anyone to attend church, to observe a religious holiday, or to take religious instruction. But it can close its doors or suspend its operations as to those who want to repair to their religious sanctuary for worship or instruction. No more than that is undertaken here.

This program may be unwise and improvident from an educational or a community viewpoint. That appeal is made to us on a theory, previously advanced, that each case must be decided on the basis of "our own prepossessions." See McCollum v. Board of Education, supra. Our individual preferences, however, are not the constitutional standard. The constitutional standard is the separation of Church and State. The problem, like many problems in constitutional law, is one of degree. . . .

In the *McCollum* case the classrooms were used for religious instruction and the force of the public school was used to promote that instruction. Here, as we have said, the public schools do no more than accommodate their schedules to a program of outside religious instruction. We follow the *McCollum* case. But we cannot expand it to cover the present released time program unless separation of Church and State means that public institutions can make no adjustments of their schedules to accommodate the religious needs of the people. We cannot read into the Bill of Rights such a philosophy of hostility to religion.

Affirmed.

Mr. Justice BLACK, dissenting.

McCollum ex rel. Illinois v. Board of Education, 333 U.S. 203, held invalid as an "establishment of religion" an Illinois system under which school children, compelled by law to go to public schools, were freed from some hours of required school work on condition that they attend special religious classes held in the school buildings. Although the classes were taught by sectarian teachers neither employed nor paid by the state, the state did use its power to further the program by releasing some of the children from regular class work, insisting that those released attend the religious classes, and requiring that those who remained behind do some kind of academic work while the others received their religious training.  We said this about the Illinois system:

> "Pupils compelled by law to go to school for secular education are released in part from their legal duty upon the condition that they attend the religious classes.  This is beyond all question a utilization of the tax-established and tax-supported public school system to aid religious groups to spread their faith.  And it falls squarely under the ban of the First Amendment.  .   .   ."   McCollum v. Board of Education, supra.

I see no significant difference between the invalid Illinois system and that of New York here sustained.  Except for the use of the school buildings in Illinois, there is no difference between the systems which I consider even worthy of mention.  In the New York program, as in that of Illinois, the school authorities release some of the children on the condition that they attend the religious classes, get reports on whether they attend, and hold the other children in the school building until the religious hour is over.  As we attempted to make categorically clear, the *McCollum* decision would have been the same if the religious classes had not been held in the school buildings.  We said:

> "Here *not only* are the State's tax-supported public school buildings used for the dissemination of religious doctrines.  The State *also* affords sectarian groups an invaluable aid in that it helps to provide pupils for their religious classes through use of the State's compulsory public school machinery.  *This* is not separation of Church and State."  (Emphasis supplied.)   McCollum v. Board of Education, supra.

*McCollum* thus held that Illinois could not constitutionally manipulate the compelled classroom hours of its compulsory school machinery so as to channel children into sectarian classes.  Yet that is exactly what the Court holds New York can do.

I am aware that our *McCollum* decision on separation of Church and State has been subjected to a most searching examination throughout the country.  Probably few opinions from this Court in recent years have attracted more attention or stirred wider debate.  Our insistence on "a wall between Church and State which must be kept high and impregnable" has seemed to some a correct exposition of the philosophy and a true interpretation of the language of the First Amendment to which we should strictly adhere.  With equal conviction and sincerity, others have thought the *McCollum* decision fundamentally wrong and have pledged continuous warfare against it.  The opinions in the court below and the briefs here reflect these diverse viewpoints. In dissenting today, I mean to do more than give routine approval to our *McCollum* decision. . . .

The Court's validation of the New York system rests in part on its statement that Americans are "a religious people whose institutions presuppose a Supreme Being." This was at least as true when the First Amendment was adopted; and it was just as true when eight Justices of this Court invalidated the released time system in *McCollum* on the premise that a state can no more "aid all religions" than it can aid one. It was precisely because Eighteenth Century Americans were a religious people divided into many fighting sects that we were given the constitutional mandate to keep Church and State completely separate. Colonial history had already shown that, here as elsewhere zealous sectarians entrusted with governmental power to further their causes would sometimes torture, maim and kill those they branded "heretics," "atheists" or "agnostics." The First Amendment was therefore to insure that no one powerful sect or combination of sects could use political or governmental power to punish dissenters whom they could not convert to their faith. Now as then, it is only by wholly isolating the state from the religious sphere and compelling it to be completely neutral, that the freedom of each and every denomination and of all nonbelievers can be maintained. It is this neutrality the Court abandons today when it treats New York's coercive system as a program which *merely* "encourages religious instruction or cooperates with religious authorities." The abandonment is all the more dangerous to liberty because of the Court's legal exaltation of the orthodox and its derogation of unbelievers.

Under our system of religious freedom, people have gone to their religious sanctuaries not because they feared the law but because they loved their God. The choice of all has been as free as the choice of those who answered the call to worship moved only by the music of the old Sunday morning church bells. The spiritual mind of man has thus been free to believe, disbelieve, or doubt, without repression, great or small, by the heavy hand of government. Statutes authorizing such repression have been stricken. Before today, our judicial opinions have refrained from drawing invidious distinctions between those who believe in no religion and those who do believe. The First Amendment has lost much if the religious follower and the atheist are no longer to be judicially regarded as entitled to equal justice under law.

State help to religion injects political and party prejudices into a holy field. It too often substitutes force for prayer, hate for love, and persecution for persuasion. Government should not be allowed, under cover of the soft euphemism of "co-operation," to steal into the sacred area of religious choice. . . .

Mr. Justice JACKSON, dissenting.

This released time program is founded upon a use of the State's power of coercion, which, for me, determines its unconstitutionality.

Stripped to its essentials, the plan has two stages: first, that the State compel each student to yield a large part of his time for public secular education; and, second, that some of it be "released" to him on condition that he devote it to sectarian religious purposes.

No one suggests that the Constitution would permit the State directly to require this "released" time to be spent "under the control of a duly constituted religious body." This program accomplishes that forbidden result by indirection. If public education were taking so much of the pupils' time as to injure the public or the students' welfare by encroaching upon their religious opportunity, simply shortening everyone's school day would facilitate voluntary and optional attendance at Church classes. But that suggestion is rejected upon the ground that if they are made free many students will not go to the Church. Hence, they must be deprived of freedom for this period, with Church attendance put to them as one of the two permissible ways of using it.

The greater effectiveness of this system over voluntary attendance after school hours is due to the truant officer who, if the youngster fails to go to the Church school, dogs him back to the public schoolroom. Here schooling is more or less suspended during the "released time" so the nonreligious attendants will not forge ahead of the churchgoing absentees. But it serves as a temporary jail for a pupil who will not go to Church. It takes more subtlety of mind than I possess to deny that this is governmental constraint in support of religion. It is as unconstitutional, in my view, when exerted by indirection as when exercised forthrightly.

As one whose children, as a matter of free choice, have been sent to privately supported Church schools, I may challenge the Court's suggestion that opposition to this plan can only be antireligious, atheistic, or agnostic. My evangelistic breathren confuse an objection to compulsion with an objection to religion. It is possible to hold a faith with enough confidence to believe that what should be rendered to God does not need to be decided and collected by Caesar.

The day that this country ceases to be free for irreligion it will cease to be free for religion—except for the sect that can win political power. The same epithetical jurisprudence used by the Court today to beat down those who oppose pressuring children into some religion can devise as good epithets tomorrow against those who object to pressuring them into a favored religion. And, after all, if we concede to the State power and wisdom to single out "duly constituted religious" bodies as exclusive alternatives for compulsory secular instruction, it would be logical to also uphold the power and wisdom to choose the true faith among those "duly constituted." We start down a rough road when we begin to mix compulsory public education with compulsory godliness.

A number of Justices just short of a majority of the majority that promulgates today's passionate dialectics joined in answering them in McCollum ex rel. Illinois v. Board of Education, 333 U.S. 203. The distinction attempted between that case and this is trivial, almost to the point of cynicism, magnifying its nonessential details and disparaging compulsion which was the underlying reason for invalidity. A reading of the Court's opinion in that case along with its opinion in this case will show such difference of overtones and undertones as to make clear that the *McCollum* case has passed like a storm in a tea-cup. The wall which the Court was professing to erect between Church and State has become even more warped and twisted than I expected. Today's judgment will be more interesting to students of psychology and of the judicial processes than to students of constitutional law.*

## NOTES AND QUESTIONS

1.  What were the precise facts on which the Court based its decision in McCollum v. Board of Educ.? Does its decision rest on the power of the state to compel school attendance? If so, how can the decision in Zorach v. Clauson be reconciled with it? If it cannot, what were the decisions in *McCollum* and *Zorach* based upon? Are the two cases hopelessly in conflict? What importance should be attached to the facts that Mr. Justice Black delivered the opinion for the Court in *McCollum* but dissented in *Zorach*?

2.  Under the decisions in these two cases would a religious program be constitutional if it were conducted on a voluntary basis, in the school during school hours but during the time when the students would otherwise be "released" if the religions paid the school for the use of the facilities? Why or why not? Suppose the program took place in the school immediately after the end of the required school day and payment were made for use of the facilities? Reconsider your answers to these questions in light of the following materials in this section.

3.  In a town with two schools, one parochial and one public, would it be constitutional for the two schools to have joint graduation ceremonies, including religious services, in the auditorium of the public high school? Why or why not? Suppose the parochial high school had no auditorium, could it constitutionally use the public school auditorium during or after the required public school hours for its functions, many involving religious services? Why or why not?

4.  According to the Supreme Court, which is the First Amendment's purpose: (1) to forbid government from preferring one religion over another, or (2) to forbid impartial governmental aid to all religions? Why?

5.  Are the basic theories of the First Amendment the same in McCollum and Zorach? Or does one case promote a "neutralist" theory and the other an "accommodation of religion" theory? If so, which case does

---

* A dissenting opinion by Mr. Justice Frankfurter is omitted.

what? In what way do these two theories of the First Amendment differ from a "secularist" theory, if at all? Which theory is correct? Why?

6. A "shared time" (dual enrollment) arrangement is one whereby some students attend part-time at a public school, e. g., for the science and mathematics courses, and are then "released" to spend the remainder of the school day at a private school; the remaining students attend the public school full-time. Is such a program constitutional? A regulation under the Federal Elementary and Secondary Education Act of 1965 defines "dual enrollment" as a "shared use of public facilities for instructional purposes under public auspices by teachers or students from public and private nonprofit schools" (45 C.F.R. 118.1), and the act provides funds to states for certain programs if they will participate in the shared-time programs, can they do so constitutionally? Does the Federal Act incorporate a "neutralist," a "secularist" or an "accommodationist" theory of the First Amendment?

----

## ENGEL v. VITALE

Supreme Court of the United States, 1962.
370 U.S. 421, 82 S.Ct. 1261, 8 L.Ed.2d 601.

Mr. Justice BLACK delivered the opinion of the Court.

The respondent Board of Education of Union Free School District No. 9, New Hyde Park, New York, acting in its official capacity under state law, directed the School District's principal to cause the following prayer to be said aloud by each class in the presence of a teacher at the beginning of each school day:

> "Almighty God, we acknowledge our dependence upon Thee,
> and we beg Thy blessings upon us, our parents, our teachers,
> and our Country."

This daily procedure was adopted on the recommendation of the State Board of Regents, a governmental agency created by the State Constitution to which the New York Legislature has granted broad supervisory, executive, and legislative powers over the State's public school system. These state officials composed the prayer which they recommended and published as a part of their "Statement on Moral and Spiritual Training in the Schools," saying: "We believe that this Statement will be subscribed to by all men and women of good will, and we call upon all of them to aid in giving life to our program."

Shortly after the practice of reciting the Regents' prayer was adopted by the School District, the parents of ten pupils brought this action in a New York State Court insisting that use of this official prayer in the public schools was contrary to the beliefs, religions, or religious practices of both themselves and their children. Among other things, these parents challenged the constitutionality of both the state law authorizing the School District to direct the use of prayer in public schools and the School District's regulation ordering the recitation of this particular prayer on the ground that these actions of official governmental agencies violate that part of the First Amendment of the Federal Constitution which commands that "Congress shall make no law respecting an establishment of religion"—a command which was "made applicable to the State of New York by the Fourteenth Amendment of the said Constitution." . . .

We think that by using its public school system to encourage recitation of the Regents' prayer, the State of New York has adopted a practice wholly inconsistent with the Establishment Clause. There can, of course, be no doubt that New York's program of daily classroom invocation of God's blessings as prescribed in the Regents' prayer is a religious activity. It is a solemn avowal of divine faith and supplication for the blessings of the Almighty. The nature of such a prayer has always been religious, none of the respondents has denied this and the trial court expressly so found:

> "The religious nature of prayer was recognized by Jefferson and has been concurred in by theological writers, the United States Supreme Court and State courts and administrative officials, including New York's Commissioner of Education. A committee of the New York Legislature has agreed.

> "The Board of Regents as *amicus curiae*, the respondents and intervenors all concede the religious nature of prayer, but seek to distinguish this prayer because it is based on our spiritual heritage. . . . "

    . . . It is a matter of history that this very practice of establishing governmentally composed prayers for religious services was one of the reasons which caused many of our early colonists to leave England and seek religious freedom in America. The Book of Common Prayer, which was created under governmental direction and which was approved by Acts of Parliament in 1548 and 1549, set out in minute detail the accepted form and content of prayer and other religious ceremonies to be used in the established, tax-supported Church of England. The controversies over the Book and what should be its content repeatedly threatened to disrupt the peace of that country as the accepted forms of prayer in the established church changed with the views of the particular ruler that happened to be in control at the time. Powerful groups representing some of the varying religious views of the people struggled among themselves to impress their particular views upon the Government and obtain amendments of the Book more suitable to their respective notions of how religious services should be conducted in order that the official religious establishment would advance their particular religious beliefs. Other groups, lacking the necessary political power to influence the Government on the matter, decided to leave England and its established church and seek freedom in America from England's governmentally ordained and supported religion.

It is an unfortunate fact of history that when some of the very groups which had most strenuously opposed the established Church of England found themselves sufficiently in control of colonial governments in this country to write their own prayers into law, they passed laws making their own religion the official religion of their respective colonies.  Indeed, as late as the time of the Revolutionary War, there were established churches in at least eight of the thirteen former colonies and established religions in at least four of the other five.  But the successful Revolution against English political domination was shortly followed by intense opposition to the practice of establishing religion by law.  This opposition crystallized rapidly into an effective political force in Virginia where the minority religious groups such as Presbyterians, Lutherans, Quakers and Baptists had gained such strength that the adherents to the established Episcopal Church were actually a minority themselves.  In 1785–1786, those opposed to the established Church, led by James Madison and Thomas Jefferson, who, though themselves not members of any of these dissenting religious groups, opposed all religious establishments by law on grounds of principle, obtained the enactment of the famous "Virginia Bill for Religious Liberty" by which all religious groups were placed on an equal footing so far as the State was concerned.  Similar though less far-reaching legislation was being considered and passed in other States.

By the time of the adoption of the Constitution, our history shows that there was widespread awareness among many Americans of the dangers of a union of Church and State.  These people knew, some of them from bitter personal experience, that one of the greatest dangers to the freedom of the individual to worship in his own way lay in the Government's placing its official stamp of approval upon one particular kind of prayer or one particular form of religious services.  They knew the anguish, hardship and bitter strife that could come when zealous religious groups struggled with one another to obtain the Government's stamp of approval from each King, Queen, or Protector that came to temporary power.  The Constitution was intended to avert a part of this danger by leaving the government of this country in the hands of the people rather than in the hands of any monarch.  But this safeguard was not enough.  Our Founders were no more willing to let the content of their prayers and their privilege of praying whenever they pleased be influenced by the ballot box than they were to let these vital matters of personal conscience depend upon the succession of monarchs.  The First Amendment was added to the Constitution to stand as a guarantee that neither the power nor the prestige of the Federal Government would be used to control, support or influence the kinds of prayer the American people can say—that the people's religions must not be subjected to the pressures of government for change each time a new political administration is elected to office.   Under that Amendment's prohibition against governmental establishment of religion, as reinforced by the provisions of the Fourteenth Amendment, government in this country, be it state or federal, is without power to prescribe by law any particular form of prayer which is to be used as an official prayer in carrying on any program of governmentally sponsored religious activity.

There can be no doubt that New York's state prayer program officially establishes the religious beliefs embodied in the Regents' prayer.   The respondents' argument to the contrary, which is largely based upon the contention that the Regents' prayer is "non-denominational" and the fact that the program, as modified and approved by state courts, does not require all pupils to recite the prayer but permits those who wish to do so to remain silent or be excused from the room, ignores the essential nature of the program's constitutional defects.   Neither the fact that the prayer may be denominationally neutral nor the fact that its observance on the part of the students is voluntary can serve to free it from the limitations of the Establishment Clause, as it might from the Free Exercise Clause, of the First Amendment, both of which are operative against the States by virtue of the Fourteenth Amendment.   Although these two clauses may in certain instances overlap, they forbid two quite different kinds of governmental encroachment upon religious freedom.   The Establishment Clause, unlike the Free Exercise Clause, does not depend upon any showing of direct governmental compulsion and is violated by the enactment of laws which establish an official religion whether those laws operate directly to coerce nonobserving individuals or not.   This is not to say, of course, that laws officially prescribing a particular form of religious worship do not involve coercion of such individuals.   When the power, prestige and financial support of government is placed behind a particular religious belief, the indirect coercive pressure upon religious minorities to conform to the prevailing officially approved religion is plain.   But the purposes underlying the Establishment Clause go much further than that.   Its first and most immediate purpose rested on the belief that a union of government and religion tends to destroy government and to degrade religion.   The history of governmentally established religion, both in England and in this country, showed that whenever government had allied itself with one particular form of religion, the inevitable result had been that it had incurred the hatred, disrespect and even contempt of those who held contrary beliefs.   That same history showed that many people had lost their respect for any religion that had relied upon the support of government to spread its faith.   The Establishment Clause thus stands as an expression of principle on the part of the Founders of our Constitution that religion is too personal, too sacred, too holy, to permit its "unhallowed perversion" by a civil magistrate.   Another purpose of the Establishment Clause rested upon an awareness of the historical fact that governmentally established religions and religious persecutions go hand in hand. The Founders knew that only a few years after the Book of Common Prayer became the only accepted form of religious services in the established Church of England, an Act of Uniformity was passed to compel all Englishmen to attend those services and to make it a criminal offense to conduct or attend religious gatherings of any other kind—a law which was consistently flouted by dissenting religious groups in England and which contributed to widespread persecutions of people like John Bunyan who persisted in holding "unlawful [religious] meetings  .   .   . to the great disturbance and distraction of the good subjects of this kingdom.  .   .   ." And they knew that similar persecutions had received the sanction of law in several of the colonies in this country soon after the establishment of official religions in those colonies. It was in large part to get completely away from this sort of systematic religious persecution that the Founders brought into being our Nation, our Constitution, and our Bill of Rights with its prohibition against any governmental establishment of religion. The New York laws officially prescribing the Regents' prayer are inconsistent both with the purposes of the Establishment Clause and with the Establishment Clause itself.

It has been argued that to apply the Constitution in such a way as to prohibit state laws respecting an establishment of religious services in public schools is to indicate a hostility toward religion or toward prayer. Nothing, of course, could be more wrong. The history of man is inseparable from the history of religion. And perhaps it is not too much to say that since the beginning of that history many people have devoutly believed that "More things are wrought by prayer than this world dreams of." It was doubtless largely due to men who believed this that there grew up a sentiment that caused men to leave the cross-currents of officially established state religions and religious persecution in Europe and come to this country filled with the hope that they could find a place in which they could pray when they pleased to the God of their faith in the language they chose. And there were men of this same faith in the power of prayer who led the fight for adoption of our Constitution and also for our Bill of Rights with the very guarantees of religious freedom that forbid the sort of governmental activity which New York has attempted here. These men knew that the First Amendment, which tried to put an end to governmental control of religion and of prayer, was not written to destroy either. They knew rather that it was written to quiet well-justified fears which nearly all of them felt arising out of an awareness that governments of the past had shackled men's tongues to make them speak only the religious thoughts that government wanted them to speak and to pray only to the God that government wanted them to pray to. It is neither sacrilegious nor antireligious to say that each separate government in this country should stay out of the business of writing or sanctioning official prayers and leave that purely religious function to the people themselves and to those the people choose to look to for religious guidance.

It is true that New York's establishment of its Regents' prayer as an officially approved religious doctrine of that State does not amount to a total establishment of one particular religious sect to the exclusion of all others—that, indeed, the governmental endorsement of that prayer seems relatively insignificant when compared to the governmental encroachments upon religion which were commonplace 200 years ago. To those who may subscribe to the view that because the Regents' official prayer is so brief and general there can be no danger to religious freedom in its governmental establishment, however, it may be appropriate to say in the words of James Madison, the author of the First Amendment:

> "[I]t is proper to take alarm at the first experiment on our liberties. . . . Who does not see that the same authority which can establish Christianity, in exclusion of all other Religions, may establish with the same ease any particular sect of Christians, in exclusion of all other Sects? That the same authority which can force a citizen to contribute three pence only of his property for the support of any one establishment, may force him to conform to any other establishment in all cases whatsoever?"

The judgment of the Court of Appeals of New York is reversed and the cause remanded for further proceedings not inconsistent with this opinion.

Reversed and remanded*

---

## ABINGTON SCHOOL DIST. v. SCHEMPP

### MURRAY v. CURLETT

Supreme Court of the United States, 1963.
374 U.S. 203, 83 S.Ct. 1560, 10 L.Ed.2d 844.

Mr. Justice CLARK delivered the opinion of the Court.

[The Schempp case (No. 142) involved a Pennsylvania law that required: "At least ten verses from the Holy Bible shall be read, without comment, at the opening of each public school on each school day. Any child shall be excused from such Bible reading, or attending such Bible reading, upon the written request of his parent or guardian." The Schempp family were members of the Unitarian Church and objected to recitations of the Lord's Prayer and readings from the

---

\* The concurring opinion of Mr. Justice
Douglas and dissenting opinion of Mr.
Justice Stewart are omitted.

Bible. Mrs. Murray and her son, in case No. 119, were "professed atheists." They attacked a Baltimore school rule requiring the "reading, without comment, of a chapter in the Holy Bible and/or the use of the Lord's Prayer." Baltimore also excused children from the exercise on the request of parent or guardian.]

The interrelationship of the Establishment and the Free Exercise Clauses was first touched upon by Mr. Justice Roberts for the Court in Cantwell v. Connecticut, [310 U.S. 296] at 303–304, where it was said that their "inhibition of legislation" had

> "a double aspect. On the one hand, it forestalls compulsion by law of the acceptance of any creed or the practice of any form of worship. Freedom of conscience and freedom to adhere to such religious organization or form of worship as the individual may choose cannot be restricted by law. On the other hand, it safeguards the free exercise of the chosen form of religion. Thus the Amendment embraces two concepts,— freedom to believe and freedom to act. The first is absolute but, in the nature of things, the second cannot be." . . .

The wholesome "neutrality" of which this Court's cases speak thus stems from a recognition of the teachings of history that powerful sects or groups might bring about a fusion of governmental and religious functions or a concert or dependency of one upon the other to the end that official support of the State or Federal Government would be placed behind the tenets of one or of all orthodoxies. This the Establishment Clause prohibits. And a further reason for neutrality is found in the Free Exercise Clause, which recognizes the value of religious training, teaching and observance and, more particularly, the right of every person to freely choose his own course with reference thereto, free of any compulsion from the state. This the Free Exercise Clause guarantees. Thus, as we have seen, the two clauses may overlap. As we have indicated, the Establishment Clause has been directly considered by this Court eight times in the past score of years and, with only one Justice dissenting on the point, it has consistently held that the clause withdrew all legislative power respecting religious belief or the expression thereof. The test may be stated as follows: what are the purpose and the primary effect of the enactment? If either is the advancement or inhibition of religion then the enactment exceeds the scope of legislative power as circumscribed by the Constitution. That is to say that to withstand the strictures of the Establishment Clause there must be a secular legislative purpose and a primary effect that neither advances nor inhibits religion. . . .
The Free Exercise Clause, likewise considered many times here, withdraws from legislative power, state and federal, the exertion of any restraint on the free exercise of religion. Its purpose is to secure religious liberty in the individual by prohibiting any invasions thereof by civil authority. Hence it is necessary in a free exercise case for one

to show the coercive effect of the enactment as it operates against him
in the practice of his religion.   The distinction between the two clauses
is apparent—a violation of the Free Exercise Clause is predicated on
coercion while the Establishment Clause violation need not be so attended.

Applying the Establishment Clause principles to the cases at bar
we find that the States are requiring the selection and reading at the
opening of the school day of verses from the Holy Bible and the recitation of the Lord's Prayer by the students in unison.   These exercises
are prescribed as part of the curricular activities of students who are
required by law to attend school.   They are held in the school buildings
under the supervision and with the participation of teachers employed
in those schools.   None of these factors, other than compulsory school
attendance, was present in the program upheld in Zorach v. Clauson.
The trial court in No. 142 has found that such an opening exercise is
a religious ceremony and was intended by the State to be so.   We agree
with the trial court's finding as to the religious character of the exercises.   Given that finding, the exercises and the law requiring them
are in violation of the Establishment Clause.

There is no such specific finding as to the religious character of
the exercises in No. 119, and the State contends (as does the State in
No. 142) that the program is an effort to extend its benefits to all public school children without regard to their religious belief.   Included
within its secular purposes, it says, are the promotion of moral values,
the contradiction to the materialistic trends of our times, the perpetuation of our institutions and the teaching of literature.   The case came
up on demurrer, of course, to a petition which alleged that the uniform
practice under the rule had been to read from the King James version
of the Bible and that the exercise was sectarian.   The short answer,
therefore, is that the religious character of the exercise was admitted
by the State.   But even if its purpose is not strictly religious, it is
sought to be accomplished through readings, without comment, from
the Bible.   Surely the place of the Bible as an instrument of religion
cannot be gainsaid, and the State's recognition of the pervading religious character of the ceremony is evident from the rule's specific
permission of the alternative use of the Catholic Douay version as well
as the recent amendment permitting nonattendance at the exercises.
None of these factors is consistent with the contention that the Bible
is here used either as an instrument for nonreligious moral inspiration or as a reference for the teaching of secular subjects.

The conclusion follows that in both cases the laws require religious
exercises and such exercises are being conducted in direct violation of
the rights of the appellees and petitioners.   Nor are these required exercises mitigated by the fact that individual students may absent themselves upon parental request, for that fact furnishes no defense to a
claim of unconstitutionality under the Establishment Clause.   .   .   .
Further, it is no defense to urge that the religious practices here may

be relatively minor encroachments on the First Amendment. The breach of neutrality that is today a trickling stream may all too soon become a raging torrent and, in the words of Madison, "it is proper to take alarm at the first experiment on our liberties." . . .

It is insisted that unless these religious exercises are permitted a "religion of secularism" is established in the schools. We agree of course that the State may not establish a "religion of secularism" in the sense of affirmatively opposing or showing hostility to religion, thus "preferring those who believe in no religion over those who do believe." . . . We do not agree, however, that this decision in any sense has that effect. In addition, it might well be said that one's education is not complete without a study of comparative religion or the history of religion and its relationship to the advancement of civilization. It certainly may be said that the Bible is worthy of study for its literary and historic qualities. Nothing we have said here indicates that such study of the Bible or of religion, when presented objectively as part of a secular program of education, may not be effected consistently with the First Amendment. But the exercises here do not fall into those categories. They are religious exercises, required by the States in violation of the command of the First Amendment that the Government maintain strict neutrality, neither aiding nor opposing religion.

Finally, we cannot accept that the concept of neutrality, which does not permit a State to require a religious exercise even with the consent of the majority of those affected, collides with the majority's right to free exercise of religion. While the Free Exercise Clause clearly prohibits the use of state action to deny the rights of free exercise to *anyone*, it has never meant that a majority could use the machinery of the State to practice its beliefs. Such a contention was effectively answered by Mr. Justice Jackson for the Court in West Virginia Board of Education v. Barnette, 319 U.S. 624, 638 (1943):

"The very purpose of a Bill of Rights was to withdraw certain subjects from the vicissitudes of political controversy, to place them beyond the reach of majorities and officials and to establish them as legal principles to be applied by the courts. One's right to . . . freedom of worship . . . and other fundamental rights may not be submitted to vote; they depend on the outcome of no elections."

The place of religion in our society is an exalted one, achieved through a long tradition of reliance on the home, the church and the inviolable citadel of the individual heart and mind. We have come to recognize through bitter experience that it is not within the power of government to invade that citadel, whether its purpose or effect be to aid or oppose, to advance or retard. In the relationship between man and religion, the State is firmly committed to a position of neutrality. . . .*

## NOTES AND QUESTIONS

1. Is the text of neutrality, that is, the "purpose and primary effect" test, clear? Can you use it? Present some hypothetical examples demonstrating its application. How can you determine the "purpose" of an enactment? How do you determine which effect is a statute's primary effect?

2. Would the decision in *Engel* have been any different if the prayer had not been composed by the New York Regents? Would it be constitutional for an elementary school to require its pupils each morning to utter the following verse:

> "We thank you for the flowers so sweet;
>
> "We thank you for the food we eat;
>
> "We thank you for the birds that sing;
>
> "We thank you for everything."

What decision under Engel and the "purpose and primary effect" test? Why? See, DeSpain v. DeKalb Comm. School Dist., 255 F. Supp. 655 (N.D.Ill.1966) cert. den. 390 U.S. 906 and Stein v. Oshinsky, 348 F.2d 999 (2d Cir. 1965).

3. What are the differences between the Abington and Murray cases? Should the differences have required differing applications of the neutrality test? Does an atheist have any claim under the First Amendment? If so, why? Which theory of the First Amendment supports an atheist's claim and which does not?

4. Assuming there is no state law or school regulation on the subject, can a teacher constitutionally begin class with prayers or a reading from the Bible? Can the teacher do so constitutionally if there is a state law or school regulation requiring the exercises?

5. After these cases, can a teacher constitutionally conduct a silent prayer in school? Is the following practice constitutional?
   ". . . in order to provide for a working accommodation, the School Board changed "the bell and beginning of school timing" as illustrated by the procedure inaugurated in the Sandy Hill School: at 8:40 A.M. a warning bell sounds, followed by another bell at 8:45 A.M. to indicate that the home rooms are open for the use of those children desiring to pray. At 8:50 A.M. a third bell rings, signifying the end of the voluntary prayer period and additionally, that school is about to begin. At 9:00 A.M. a bell signifying the actual start of the class day is rung.

   "Plaintiffs object to these practices. . . .

   "The policy initially proposed by defendants purported to establish a position of neutrality on the part of the Board of Education with respect to religion." See, Reed v. Van Hoven, 237 F.Supp. 48 (W.D.Mich.1965).

---

* Concurring opinions of Mr. Justices Douglas, Brennan and Goldberg are omit- ted as is a dissenting opinion by Mr. Justice Stewart.

6. Can the Bible constitutionally be part of the public school's library? If so, which version? May the Bible be distributed during school hours to all pupils who want a copy? May the Bible be used in the curriculum of public schools; if so, how?

7. In Meltzer v. Board of Public Instruction, 548 F.2d 559 (5th Cir. 1977) the Court of Appeals ruled that distribution of Gideon Bibles to K–12 students was distribution to a "captive audience," and amounted to placing a "stamp of approval upon the Gideon version of the Bible, thus creating an unconstitutional preference for one religion over another."

8. In an extensive opinion, Judge H. Curtis Meanor of the U.S. District Court in New Jersey held that the Establishment Clause is violated by teaching the "Science of Creative Intelligence/Transcendental Meditation" in New Jersey's public schools. After analyzing SCI/TM's concepts, Judge Meanor found them to be in a "field of pure creative intelligence" and in an "unmanifest field of life which is perfect, pure and infinite." As such, he stated, the concepts were religious in nature. He also noted that students learning Transcendental Meditation were compelled to attend a religious ceremony, the "Puja." Malnak v. Yogi, 440 F.Supp. 1284 (D.N.J.1977).

--------

## JOHNSON v. HUNTINGTON BEACH UNION HIGH SCHOOL DIST.

California Court of Appeals, Fourth District, 1977.
68 Cal.App.3d 1, 137 Cal.Rptr. 43, certiorari denied 434 U.S. 877,
98 S.Ct. 228, 54 L.Ed.2d 156.

TAMURA, Associate Justice. Plaintiffs (high school students) sought judicial relief from a refusal of the Huntington Beach Union High School District (district) to permit a voluntary student Bible study club to meet and conduct its activities on the school campus during the school day. The trial court sustained the district's action and denied plaintiffs the relief sought.

The operative facts set forth in the stipulated facts on which the cause was heard and submitted may be summarized as follows: The district is charged with supervising and establishing rules and regulations for high schools within the district. Plaintiffs are students at Edison High School, a public tax-supported secondary school under the jurisdiction of the district.

Pursuant to statutory authority, the district has provided for recognition of student clubs and has prescribed regulations under which such clubs may operate on high school campuses. Under the district's rules, student organizations may not have free use of classrooms or school facilities other than by applying for and receiving recognition, i. e., official approval to operate on the campus as a student club. For many years the district has permitted and still permits high schools under its jurisdiction to grant recognition to student clubs and to permit such clubs to use classrooms and other space for club meetings and to publicize their activities through the school newspaper and school bulletin boards. The district did not, however, permit student religious clubs to meet on the school campus during the school day.

Plaintiffs filed suit for injunctive and declaratory relief to establish their claimed rights to official club recognition, to use school classrooms and other space during the school day for club meetings, to use bulletin boards and similar facilities for the posting of club activities, and to have access to the school newspaper for purposes of publicizing club events. The cause was heard on the pleadings and stipulated facts. . . . Judgment was entered decreeing that the district was prohibited from recognizing plaintiffs' Bible study club or from assisting plaintiffs in their efforts to form a religious club and that the school's posture of nonrecognition did not violate plaintiffs' free exercise or other First Amendment guarantees. Plaintiffs appeal from that judgment.

Plaintiffs do not challenge either the district's authority to promulgate rules for the operation of student clubs on campus or the validity of the existing rules. They attack the judgment below on the ground that there are no federal or state constitutional proscriptions against school authorities permitting plaintiffs' Bible club to meet and conduct its activities on campus during the school day on the same footing as other student clubs and that refusal to grant such permission violates plaintiffs' First and Fourteenth Amendment rights. From the analysis which follows, we have concluded that the issues were correctly resolved by the trial court and that the judgment should be affirmed.

The First Amendment to the United States Constitution provides in relevant part: "Congress shall make no law respecting an establishment of religion, or prohibiting the free exercise thereof . . . ." In erecting a wall of separation between church and state, the framers of our Constitution acted upon the belief " 'that a union of government and religion tends to destroy government and to degrade religion.' [Citation.] When government . . . allies itself with one particular form of religion, the inevitable result is that it incurs 'the hatred, disrespect and even contempt of those who held contrary beliefs.' " (Abington School District v. Schempp, quoting Engel v. Vitale,). Provisions of the First Amendment, including the Establishment Clause, are subsumed under the Due Process Clause of the Fourteenth Amendment and govern state action.

Preservation of religious liberty and the maintenance of governmental neutrality have undergone their severest test in the context of religious exercises within school corridors. In quick succession the Supreme Court of the United States passed upon two "release time" programs which were challenged as violative of the Establishment Clause. Illinois ex rel. McCollum v. Board of Education, put before the court a program whereby the school turned over its classrooms during the school day to religious groups which, one day a week for 30 minutes, substituted religious training for the secular education provided under the compulsory education law. The court held that the use of tax-supported property for religious instruction during a time when students were compelled by law to attend school resulted in the state becoming an active participant in religious affairs and thereby violated its constitutional obligation of neutrality.

Sensitive to the religious needs of its pupils but cognizant of its constitutional duties, New York devised a release time program whereby students were released from school to receive spiritual training at the church of their belief. Students were released only upon written request of their parents; those not released remained in the classroom. This program withstood constitutional scrutiny in Zorach v. Clauson. The court noted that while it is the philosophy of the First Amendment to erect a citadel where neither state nor church would invade the precinct of the other, not all cooperation between the secular and the religious is condemned. As much as the state must remain neutral in the affairs of religion, neither can it assume a posture of hostility. Thus, a course of accommodation involving nothing more than school officials adjusting educational schedules to meet sectarian needs of its students was found consistent with constitutional precepts.

A state policy of accommodation, however, can overstep constitutional limits and becomes an impermissible form of aid to religion. In Abington School District v. Schempp, supra, school officials instituted a practice whereby passages of the Bible were read without comment at the beginning of each school day. Those students not wishing to participate were permitted to absent themselves. The court noted that although our heritage and culture is in part grounded in the belief in the almighty the Constitution mandates governmental neutrality which neither prefers one religion over another nor advances all religion but instead creates a sanctuary where all religions may flourish without governmental interference. Governmental neutrality and religious freedom, the court observed, can be preserved only by the segregation of secular activity from religious pursuit through the banishment of all governmental allegiance with religion. The court concluded that state sponsorship of Bible reading during the school day violated the principle of neutrality, placed the state behind religious inculcation and infringed the free exercise rights of nonbelievers.

In Lemon v. Kurtzman, the high court announced a tripartite test, synthesized from criteria developed by prior decisions, for determining whether state action involves a violation of the Establishment Clause. To pass constitutional muster the state activity must satisfy three conditions: (1) It must have a secular legislative purpose; (2)

its primary effect must neither advance nor inhibit religion; and (3) it must not foster excessive governmental entanglement with religion. . . . Failure to meet any one of the three conditions is fatal to the constitutionality of state action.

No test, however, can be applied with precision in determining where the line between church and state should be drawn; the problem, like many in constitutional adjudication, is one of degree. The high court has cautioned that the tripartite *Lemon* test is to be viewed, not as a formula prescribing the precise scope of constitutional inquiry, but as a touchstone with which to identify instances where the objectives of the Establishment Clause have been compromised. The primary evils the Clause was intended to protect against are "sponsorship, financial support, and active involvement of the sovereign in religious activity." We proceed to apply the foregoing precepts to the case at bench.

The precise question we must decide is whether school officials of a tax-supported high school of the district may permit plaintiffs' Bible study club to meet and conduct its activities on the school campus during the school day under regulations governing student clubs. The administrative action which plaintiffs seek would constitute state action and as such must withstand constitutional scrutiny under the guidelines enunciated in Lemon v. Kurtzman, supra.

To the extent that the first prong of the tripartite test may be applicable it is only necessary to observe that the exercise of the power to permit student organizations to conduct their activities on school campuses during the school day in accordance with district rules and regulations is in the abstract secular in nature.

However, in adjudging whether the "primary effect" of the state action sought by plaintiffs advances religion, we must examine its consequence not in the abstract but as applied to the Bible study club. In this regard, the Supreme Court has cautioned that the crucial inquiry is not whether some benefit accrues to a religious institution as a consequence of state action, but whether its primary effect advances religion. Aid may be said to have an impermissible primary effect of advancing religion "when it funds a specifically religious activity in an otherwise substantially secular setting."

Plaintiffs do not dispute the fact that the club's mission, "to enable those participating to know God better so that they will be better persons . . . by prayerfully studying the Bible," is religious in nature. It is also apparent that if the club is permitted to meet and conduct its activities on the school campus as a student club as demanded by plaintiffs, state financial support would flow directly to the club. It would be entitled to use classroom space rent free, receive heat and light and would be monitored by a paid faculty sponsor. The district would also be obligated at its expense to audit club finances. One of the factors differentiating *McCollum* from *Zorach* was the free use of school facilities, classrooms, heat and light. Thus this financial subsidy alone may be sufficient to compel constitutional condemnation of the requested state action.

We do not rest our decision, however, on financial aid alone. The "primary effect" test bespeaks not only of financial assistance but also necessarily inquired whether the consequence of state action is to place its imprimatur upon the religious activity. This aspect of the effect test reaches the essence of the Establishment Clause proscription. In Abington School District v. Schempp, supra, the court cogently observed: " 'The [First] Amendment's purpose was not to strike merely at the official establishment of a single sect, creed or religion, outlawing only a formal relation such as had prevailed in England and some of the colonies. Necessarily it was to uproot all such relationships. But the object was broader than separating church and state in this narrow sense. It was to create a complete and permanent separation of the spheres of religious activity and civil authority by comprehensively forbidding every form of public aid or support for religion.' " The point is that impermissible governmental support is present when the weight of secular authority is behind the dissemination of religious tenets.

It is in the foregoing respect that permitting plaintiffs' Bible study club to meet and operate on the school campus during the school day most offends establishment principles. Under the district's rules and regulations, the club will become an entity "sponsored by the school" and as such will be entitled to use the school name in connection with its activities, to free use of school premises and property, to access to the school newspaper and school posting facilities to advertise its activities, and to solicit contributions on campus during the school day. Thus, the consequence of permitting the club to operate on campus as a recognized student organization is to place school support and sponsorship behind the religious objectives of the club. The Bible study club would implicitly become an integral part of the school's extracurricular program conducted during the school day when students are compelled by law to attend the school.

The state action which plaintiffs seek would also run afoul of the third prong of the *Lemon* test. The school would be required to supply a "faculty sponsor" who would be required to attend all club functions and approve all club activities. The school would also be required to audit the club's financial accounts and review membership procedures to ensure they are neither secret nor discriminatory. Thus, permitting the Bible study club to operate on campus would foster excessive state entanglement with religion.

An additional factor which cannot be ignored in the context of the Establishment Clause is the potential for divisiveness in matters of religion which the requested state action to be evaluated may engender. Students who are members of less orthodox religions may be unable to organize a club because of insufficient student support or unavilability of a faculty sponsor. In such event, the free exercise rights of the minority might well be infringed by the pressure upon them to conform to the beliefs of the recognized religious club. Even if we assume that the spectrum of religious beliefs present in the national community is represented at the school, there is a real possibility that competing sects or beliefs will vie for school permission to operate on campus. Manifestly this could engender student divisiveness in matters of religious beliefs.

In sum, the school machinery implicated in permitting the student Bible study club to meet on campus under the district's rules and regulations goes far beyond the accommodation endorsed in *Zorach*. There the school cooperated with religious institutions only to the extent of adjusting its schedule to make it possible for the students who wished to do so to repair to their respective houses of worship to partake in religious activities off campus. The teachers did not sponsor, participate in, or monitor the religious function. Religion must be a private matter wholly untouched by state involvement or sponsorship. The school permission sought by plaintiffs would meld the secular with the sectarian and would empower the Bible study club members to use the prestige and authority of the school in proselytizing their beliefs among students whose presence on the campus is compelled by law and who may be vulnerable to the pressure of an officially recognized student religious organization. This, the First Amendment will not permit. . . .

Judgment is affirmed.

GARDNER, P. J., concurs.

McDANIEL, Associate Justice (dissenting).

I dissent. . . .

. . . I would hold that the recognition here sought by the plaintiffs would result only in an *accommodation* of the religious views and activities of the plaintiffs as permitted under Zorach v. Clauson, supra, 343 U.S. 306, 72 S.Ct. 679, 96 L.Ed. 954; and would not be impermissible *sponsorship* which I construe under the cases to mean affirmatively to require the religious activity challenged.

As a postscript of this portion of the dissent, I must respectfully observe that the kind of "divisiveness" which the majority foresees here has only been noted in those cases where the religious activity has been in some manner required. It is logically difficult to imagine how a completely voluntary program could be divisive.

## NOTES AND QUESTIONS

1. Would the Court's decision have been the same if, instead of meeting "to know God better so that they will be better persons . . . by prayerfully studying the Bible," the students wanted to meet and

subject the Bible to intellectual and empirical analysis in order to identify its historical validity? After this case could the high school offer a course entitled: "The Bible as Literature"? Is the Bible a secular or religious book? Does its characterization vary with the method and purpose of instruction?

2. Does the Court's decision give appropriate consideration to Healy v. James, *Tinker* and *Papish*? Is it necessarily implicit in the Court's reasoning that the prohibition against Establishing Religion takes priority over a person's right to have a school recognize his continuing association? Do you agree with this ordering of constitutional values in a high school context?

## PUBLIC AID TO PAROCHIAL SCHOOLS

--------

About five million students attend private or parochial schools in the United States. About ninety percent of these students attend Roman Catholic parochial schools. All these schools, private and parochial, have a constitutional right to exist under Pierce v. Society of Sisters, supra. But parents of students attending these schools must pay tuition to these private schools, relief from which many parents, and their representatives, want. They seek to obtain this relief through a variety of legislative devices that would channel public tax funds to private and parochial schools thereby relieving parents of their need to pay tuition, in full or in part.

--------

### JACKSON v. CALIFORNIA

United States Court of Apepals, 1972.
460 F.2d 282 (9th Cir.).

PER CURIAM.

Appellants brought this action seeking injunctive relief from the operation of California's constitutional and statutory provisions limiting appropriation of public funds for education to the support of public schools. They seek to require the state to establish a system of "tuition grants" to parents of school-age children which the parents could then utilize to provide education for their children in nonpublic elementary and secondary schools. Appellants essentially contend that the present state provisions violate their right to free exercise of religion as granted by the First Amendment, and that they also violate the equal protection clause of the Fourteenth Amendment. They sought the convening of a three-judge District Court. This was denied on the ground that no substantial federal question was presented, and judgment was rendered for the state.

The precise questions noted above which are presented by this appeal have been decided adversely to appellants by a three-judge District Court convened in the Eastern District of Missouri. Brusca v.

Missouri ex rel. State Board of Education, 332 F.Supp. 275 (E.D.Mo. 1971). We have deferred decision in this case awaiting the outcome of the appeal in *Brusca*. The Supreme Court has now affirmed the judgment of the District Court in that case. 405 U.S. 1050, 92 S.Ct. 1493, 31 L.Ed.2d 786 (1972).

On the authority of *Brusca*, judgment is affirmed.

## NOTES AND QUESTIONS

1. Bound by precedent to follow the U.S. Supreme Court's decision in Brusca, the Jackson court ruled that the constitution's free-exercise clause did not require California "to establish a system of 'tuition grants' to parents of school-age children which the parents could then utilize to provide education for their children in nonpublic elementary and secondary schools." Can you construct the free-exercise argument that the parents relied upon and which the courts rejected?

2. Brusca and Jackson do not deal with the question whether the constitution permits (as distinguished from requires) a state to establish a system of tuition grants. If a state should establish such a system it would not violate the free-exercise clause. But, would it raise "establishment" problems? Would such a system go beyond the "verge" identified in Everson, the next case?

---

## EVERSON v. BOARD OF EDUCATION

Supreme Court of the United States, 1947.
330 U.S. 1, 67 S.Ct. 504, 91 L.Ed. 711.

Mr. Justice BLACK delivered the opinion of the Court.

A New Jersey statute authorizes its local school districts to make rules and contracts for the transportation of children to and from schools.[1] The appellee, a township board of education, acting pursuant to this statute, authorized reimbursement to parents of money expended by them for the bus transportation of their children on regular busses operated by the public transportation system. Part of this money was for the payment of transportation of some children in the community to Catholic parochial schools. These church schools give their students, in addition to secular education, regular religious instruction conforming to the religious tenets and modes of worship of

[1] "Whenever in any district there are children living remote from any schoolhouse, the board of education of the district may make rules and contracts for the transportation of such children to and from school, including the transportation of school children to and from school other than a public school, except such school as is operated for profit in whole or in part.

"When any school district provides any transportation for public school children to and from school, transportation from any point in such established school route to any other point in such established school route shall be supplied to school children residing in such school district in going to and from school other than a public school, except such school as is operated for profit in whole or in part." New Jersey Laws, 1941, c. 191, p. 581; N.J.R.S.Cum.Supp., tit. 18, c. 14, § 8.

the Catholic Faith.   The superintendent of these schools is a Catholic priest.

The appellant, in his capacity as a district taxpayer, filed suit in a state court challenging the right of the Board to reimburse parents of parochial school students.  He contended that the statute and the resolution passed pursuant to it violated both the State and the Federal Constitutions.  .  .  .

Since there has been no attack on the statute on the ground that a part of its language excludes children attending private schools operated for profit from enjoying State payment for their transportation, we need not consider this exclusionary language; it has no relevancy to any constitutional question here presented.[2]  Furthermore, if the exclusion clause had been properly challenged, we do not know whether New Jersey's highest court would construe its statutes as precluding payment of the school transportation of any group of pupils, even those of a private school run for profit.  Consequently, we put to one side the question as to the validity of the statute against the claim that it does not authorize payment for the transportation generally of school children in New Jersey.

The only contention here is that the state statute and the resolution, insofar as they authorized reimbursement to parents of children attending parochial schools, violate the Federal Constitution in these two respects, which to some extent overlap.  *First.*  They authorize the State to take by taxation the private property of some and bestow it upon others, to be used for their own private purposes.  This, it is alleged, violates the due process clause of the Fourteenth Amendment.  *Second.*  The statute and the resolution forced inhabitants to pay taxes to help support and maintain schools which are dedicated to, and which regularly teach, the Catholic Faith.  This is alleged to be a use of state power to support church schools contrary to the prohibition of the First Amendment which the Fourteenth Amendment made applicable to the states.

*First.*  The due process argument that the state law taxes some people to help others carry out their private purposes is framed in two

[2] Appellant does not challenge the New Jersey statute or the resolution on the ground that either violates the equal protection clause of the Fourteenth Amendment by excluding payment for the transportation of any pupil who attends a "private school run for profit." Although the township resolution authorized reimbursement only for parents of public and Catholic school pupils, appellant does not allege, nor is there anything in the record which would offer the slightest support to an allegation, that there were any children in the township who attended or would have attended, but for want of transportation, any but public and Catholic schools.  It will be appropriate to consider the exclusion of students of private schools operated for profit when and if it is proved to have occurred, is made the basis of a suit by one in a position to challenge it, and New Jersey's highest court has ruled adversely to the challenger.  Striking down a state law is not a matter of such light moment that it should be done by a federal court *ex mero motu* on a postulate neither charged nor proved, but which rests on nothing but a possibility. Cf. Liverpool, N. Y. & P. S. S. Co. v. Comm'rs of Emigration, 113 U. S. 33, 39.

phases. The first phase is that a state cannot tax A to reimburse B for the cost of transporting his children to church schools. This is said to violate the due process clause because the children are sent to these church schools to satisfy the personal desires of their parents, rather than the public's interest in the general education of all children. This argument, if valid, would apply equally to prohibit state payment for the transportation of children to any non-public school, whether operated by a church or any other non-government individual or group. But, the New Jersey legislature has decided that a public purpose will be served by using tax-raised funds to pay the bus fares of all school children, including those who attend parochial schools. The New Jersey Court of Errors and Appeals has reached the same conclusion. The fact that a state law, passed to satisfy a public need, coincides with the personal desires of the individuals most directly affected is certainly an inadequate reason for us to say that a legislature has erroneously appraised the public need.

.  .  . Changing local conditions create new local problems which may lead a state's people and its local authorities to believe that laws authorizing new types of public services are necessary to promote the general well-being of the people. The Fourteenth Amendment did not strip the states of their power to meet problems previously left for individual solution. .  .  .

It is much too late to argue that legislation intended to facilitate the opportunity of children to get a secular education serves no public purpose. Cochran v. Louisiana State Board of Education, 281 U.S. 370 .  .  . The same thing is no less true of legislation to reimburse needy parents, or all parents, for payment of the fares of their children so that they can ride in public busses to and from schools rather than run the risk of traffic and other hazards incident to walking or "hitchhiking." .  .  . Nor does it follow that a law has a private rather than a public purpose because it provides that tax-raised funds will be paid to reimburse individuals on account of money spent by them in a way which furthers a public program. .  .  . Subsidies and loans to individuals such as farmers and home-owners, and to privately owned transportation systems, as well as many other kinds of businesses, have been commonplace practices in our state and national history.

Insofar as the second phase of the due process argument may differ from the first, it is by suggesting that taxation for transportation of children to church schools constitutes support of a religion by the State. But if the law is invalid for this reason, it is because it violates the First Amendment's prohibition against the establishment of religion. .  .  .

This Court has previously recognized that the provisions of the First Amendment, in the drafting and adoption of which Madison and Jefferson played such leading roles, had the same objective and were intended to provide the same protection against governmental intrusion on religious liberty as the Virginia state [Virginia's Bill for Religious Liberty] Reynolds v. United States, supra, at 164; Watson v. Jones, 13 Wall. 679; Davis v. Beason, 133 U.S. 333, 342. . . .

The "establishment of religion" clause of the First Amendment means at least this: Neither a state nor the Federal Government can set up a church. Neither can pass laws which aid one religion, aid all religions, or prefer one religion over another. Neither can force nor influence a person to go to or to remain away from church against his will or force him to profess a belief or disbelief in any religion. No person can be punished for entertaining or professing religious beliefs or disbeliefs, for church attendance or non-attendance. No tax in any amount, large or small, can be levied to support any religious activities or institutions, whatever they may be called, or whatever form they may adopt to teach or practice religion. Neither a state nor the Federal Government can, openly or secretly, participate in the affairs of any religious organizations or groups and *vice versa*. In the words of Jefferson, the clause against establishment of religion by law was intended to erect "a wall of separation between Church and State." Reynolds v. United States, supra at 164.

We must consider the New Jersey statute in accordance with the foregoing limitations imposed by the First Amendment. But we must not strike that state statute down if it is within the State's constitutional power even though it approaches the verge of that power. . . New Jersey cannot consistently with the "establishment of religion" clause of the First Amendment contribute tax-raised funds to the support of an institution which teaches the tenets and faith of any church. On the other hand, other language of the amendment commands that New Jersey cannot hamper its citizens in the free exercise of their own religion. Consequently, it cannot exclude individual Catholics, Lutherans, Mohammedans, Baptists, Jews, Methodists, Non-believers, Presbyterians, or the members of any other faith, *because of their faith, or lack of it,* from receiving the benefits of public welfare legislation. While we do not mean to intimate that a state could not provide transportation only to children attending public schools, we must be careful, in protecting the citizens of New Jersey against state-established churches, to be sure that we do not inadvertently prohibit New Jersey from extending its general state law benefits to all its citizens without regard to their religious belief.

Measured by these standards, we cannot say that the First Amendment prohibits New Jersey from spending tax-raised funds to pay the bus fares of parochial school pupils as a part of a general program under which it pays the fares of pupils attending public and other schools. It is undoubtedly true that children are helped to get to church schools. There is even a possibility that some of the children might not be sent to the church schools if the parents were compelled to pay their children's bus fares out of their own pockets when transportation to a public school would have been paid for by the State. The same possibility exists where the state requires a local transit company to provide reduced fares to school children including those attending parochial schools, or where a municipally owned transportation system undertakes to carry all school children free of charge. Moreover, state-paid policemen, detailed to protect children going to and from church schools from the very real hazards of traffic, would serve much the same purpose and accomplish much the same result as state provisions intended to guarantee free transportation of a kind which the state deems to be best for the school children's welfare. And parents might refuse to risk their children to the serious danger of traffic accidents going to and from parochial schools, the approaches to which were not protected by policemen. Similarly, parents might be reluctant to permit their children to attend schools which the state had cut off from such general government services as ordinary police and fire protection, connections for sewage disposal, public highways and sidewalks. Of course, cutting off church schools from these services, so separate and so indisputably marked off from the religious function, would make it far more difficult for the schools to operate. But such is obviously not the purpose of the First Amendment. That Amendment requires the state to be a neutral in its relations with groups of religious believers and non-believers; it does not require the state to be their adversary. State power is no more to be used so as to handicap religions than it is to favor them.

This Court has said that parents may, in the discharge of their duty under state compulsory education laws, send their children to a religious rather than a public school if the school meets the secular educational requirements which the state has power to impose. See Pierce v. Society of Sisters, 268 U.S. 510. It appears that these parochial schools meet New Jersey's requirements. The State contributes no money to the schools. It does not support them. Its legislation, as applied, does no more than provide a general program to help parents get their children, regardless of their religion, safely and expeditiously to and from accredited schools.

The First Amendment has erected a wall between church and state. That wall must be kept high and impregnable. We could not approve the slightest breach. New Jersey has not breached it here.

Affirmed.

Mr. Justice JACKSON, dissenting.

I find myself, contrary to first impressions, unable to join in this decision. I have a sympathy, though it is not ideological, with Catholic citizens who are compelled by law to pay taxes for public schools, and also feel constrained by conscience and discipline to support other schools for their own children. Such relief to them as this case involves is not in itself a serious burden to taxpayers and I had assumed it to be as little serious in principle. Study of this case convinces me otherwise. The Court's opinion marshals every argument in favor of state aid and puts the case in its most favorable light, but much of its reasoning confirms my conclusions that there are no good grounds upon which to support the present legislation. In fact, the undertones of the opinion, advocating complete and uncompromising separation of Church from State, seem utterly discordant with its conclusion yielding support to their commingling in educational matters. The case which irresistibly comes to mind as the most fitting precedent is that of Julia who, according to Byron's reports, "whispering 'I will ne'er consent,'—consented."

I

The Court sustains this legislation by assuming two deviations from the facts of this particular case; first, it assumes a state of facts the record does not support, and secondly, it refuses to consider facts which are inescapable on the record.

The Court concludes that this "legislation, as applied, does no more than provide a general program to help parents get their children, regardless of their religion, safely and expeditiously to and from accredited schools," and it draws a comparison between "state provisions intended to guarantee free transportation" for school children with services such as police and fire protection, and implies that we are here dealing with "laws authorizing new types of public services. . . . " This hypothesis permeates the opinion. The facts will not bear that construction.

The Township of Ewing is not furnishing transportation to the children in any form; it is not operating school busses itself or contracting for their operation; and it is not performing any public service of any kind with this taxpayer's money. All school children are left to ride as ordinary paying passengers on the regular busses operated by the public transportation system. What the Township does, and what the taxpayer complains of, is at stated intervals to reimburse parents for the fares paid, provided the children attend either public schools or Catholic Church schools. This expenditure of tax funds has no possible effect on the child's safety or expedition in transit. As passengers on the public busses they travel as fast and no faster, and are as safe and no safer, since their parents are reimbursed as before.

In addition to thus assuming a type of service that does not exist, the Court also insists that we must close our eyes to a discrimination which does exist. The resolution which authorizes disbursement of this taxpayer's money limits reimbursement to those who attend public schools and Catholic schools. That is the way the Act is applied to this taxpayer.

The New Jersey Act in question makes the character of the school, not the needs of the children, determine the eligibility of parents to reimbursement. The Act permits payment for transportation to parochial schools or public schools but prohibits it to private schools operated in whole or in part for profit. Children often are sent to private schools because their parents feel that they require more individual instruction than public schools can provide, or because they are backward or defective and need special attention. If all children of the state were objects of impartial solicitude, no reason is obvious for denying transportation reimbursement to students of this class, for these often are as needy and as worthy as those who go to public or parochial schools. Refusal to reimburse those who attend such schools is understandable only in the light of a purpose to aid the schools, because the state might well abstain from aiding a profit-making private enterprise. Thus, under the Act and resolution brought to us by this case, children are classified according to the schools they attend and are to be aided if they attend the public schools or private Catholic schools, and they are not allowed to be aided if they attend private secular schools or private religious schools of other faiths. . . .

If we are to decide this case on the facts before us, our question is simply this: Is it constitutional to tax this complainant to pay the cost of carrying pupils to Church schools of one specified denomination?

## II

Whether the taxpayer constitutionally can be made to contribute aid to parents of students because of their attendance at parochial schools depends upon the nature of those schools and their relation to the Church. The Constitution says nothing of education. It lays no obligation on the states to provide schools and does not undertake to regulate state systems of education if they see fit to maintain them. But they cannot, through school policy any more than through other means, invade rights secured to citizens by the Constitution of the United States. West Virginia State Board of Education v. Barnette, 319 U.S. 624. . . .

The function of the Church school is a subject on which this record is meager. It shows only that the schools are under superintendence of a priest and that "religion is taught as part of the curriculum." But we know that such schools are parochial only in name— they, in fact, represent a world-wide and age-old policy of the Roman Catholic Church. Under the rubric "Catholic Schools," the Canon Law of the Church, by which all Catholics are bound, provides:

> "1215. Catholic children are to be educated in schools where not only nothing contrary to Catholic faith and morals is taught, but rather in schools were religious and moral training occupy the first place. . . . (Canon 1372.)"

"1216. In every elementary school the children must, according to their age, be instructed in Christian doctrine.

"The young people who attend the higher schools are to receive a deeper religious knowledge, and the bishops shall appoint priests qualified for such work by their learning and piety. (Canon 1373.)"

"1217. Catholic children shall not attend non-Catholic, indifferent, schools that are mixed, that is to say, schools open to Catholics and non-Catholics alike. The bishop of the diocese only has the right, in harmony with the instructions of the Holy See, to decide under what circumstances, and with what safeguards to prevent loss of faith, it may be tolerated that Catholic children go to such schools. (Canon 1374.)"

"1224. The religious teaching of youth in any schools is subject to the authority and inspection of the Church.

"The local Ordinaries have the right and duty to watch that nothing is taught contrary to faith or good morals, in any of the schools of their territory.

"They, moreover, have the right to approve the books of Christian doctrine and the teachers of religion, and to demand, for the sake of safeguarding religion and morals, the removal of teachers and books. (Canon 1381.)" (Woywod, Rev. Stanislaus, The New Canon Law, under imprimatur of Most Rev. Francis J. Spellman, Archbishop of New York and others, 1940.)

It is no exaggeration to say that the whole historic conflict in temporal policy between the Catholic Church and non-Catholics comes to a focus in their respective school policies. The Roman Catholic Church, counseled by experience in many ages and many lands and with all sorts and conditions of men, takes what, from the viewpoint of its own progress and the success of its mission, is a wise estimate of the importance of education to religion. It does not leave the individual to pick up religion by chance. It relies on early and indelible indoctrination in the faith and order of the Church by the word and example of persons consecrated to the task.

Our public school, if not a product of Protestantism, at least is more consistent with it than with the Catholic culture and scheme of values. It is a relatively recent development dating from about 1840. It is organized on the premise that secular education can be isolated from all religious teaching so that the school can inculcate all needed temporal knowledge and also maintain a strict and lofty neutrality as to religion. The assumption is that after the individual has been instructed in worldly wisdom he will be better fitted to choose his religion. Whether such a disjunction is possible, and if possible whether it is wise, are questions I need not try to answer.

I should be surprised if any Catholic would deny that the parochial school is a vital, if not the most vital, part of the Roman Catholic Church. If put to the choice, that venerable institution, I should expect, would forego its whole service for mature persons before it would give up education of the young, and it would be a wise choice. Its growth and cohesion, discipline and loyalty, spring from its schools. Catholic education is the rock on which the whole structure rests, and to render tax aid to its Church school is indistinguishable to me from rendering the same aid to the Church itself.

### III

It is of no importance in this situation whether the beneficiary of this expenditure of tax-raised funds is primarily the parochial school and incidentally the pupil, or whether the aid is directly bestowed on the pupil with indirect benefits to the school. The state cannot maintain a Church and it can no more tax its citizens to furnish free carriage to those who attend a Church. The prohibition against establishment of religion cannot be circumvented by a subsidy, bonus or reimbursement of expense to individuals for receiving religious instruction and indoctrination.

The Court, however, compares this to other subsidies and loans to individuals and says, "Nor does it follow that a law has a private rather than a public purpose because it provides that tax-raised funds will be paid to reimburse individuals on account of money spent by them in a way which furthers a public program. . . . Of course, the state may pay out tax-raised funds to relieve pauperism, but it may not under our Constitution do so to induce or reward piety. It may spend funds to secure old age against want, but it may not spend funds to secure religion against skepticism. It may compensate individuals for loss of employment, but it cannot compensate them for adherence to a creed.

It seems to me that the basic fallacy in the Court's reasoning, which accounts for its failure to apply the principles it avows, is in ignoring the essentially religious test by which beneficiaries of this expenditure are selected. A policeman protects a Catholic, of course—but not because he is a Catholic; it is because he is a man and a member of our society. The fireman protects the Church school—but not because it is a Church school; it is because it is property, part of the assets of our society. Neither the fireman nor the policeman has to ask before he renders aid "Is this man or building identified with the Catholic Church?" But before these school authorities draw a check to reimburse for a student's fare they must ask just that question, and if the school is a Catholic one they may render aid because it is such, while if it is of any other faith or is run for profit, the help must be withheld. To consider the converse of the Court's reasoning will best disclose its fallacy.  That there is no parallel between police and fire protection and this plan of reimbursement is apparent from the incongruity of the limitation of this Act if applied to police and fire service.  Could we sustain an Act that said the police shall protect pupils on the way to or from public schools and Catholic schools but not while going to and coming from other schools, and firemen shall extinguish a blaze in public or Catholic school buildings but shall not put out a blaze in Protestant Church schools or private schools operated for profit?  That is the true analogy to the case we have before us and I should think it pretty plain that such a scheme would not be valid.

The Court's holding is that this taxpayer has no grievance because the state has decided to make the reimbursement a public purpose and therefore we are bound to regard it as such.  I agree that this Court has left, and always should leave to each state, great latitude in deciding for itself, in the light of its own conditions, what shall be public purposes in its scheme of things.  .  .  .  But it cannot make public business of religious worship or instruction, or of attendance at religious institutions of any character.  There is no answer to the proposition, more fully expounded by Mr. Justice RUTLEDGE, that the effect of the religious freedom Amendment to our Constitution was to take every form of propagation of religion out of the realm of things which could directly or indirectly be made public business and thereby be supported in whole or in part at taxpayers' expense.  That is a difference which the Constitution sets up between religion and almost every other subject matter of legislation, a difference which goes to the very root of religious freedom and which the Court is overlooking today.  This freedom was first in the Bill of Rights because it was first in the forefathers' minds; it was set forth in absolute terms, and its strength is its rigidity.  It was intended not only to keep the states' hands out of religion, but to keep religion's hands off the state, and, above all, to keep bitter religious controversy out of public life by denying to every denomination any advantage from getting control of public policy or the public purse.  Those great ends I cannot but think are immeasureably compromised by today's decision.

This policy of our Federal Constitution has never been wholly pleasing to most religious groups.  They all are quick to invoke its protections; they all are irked when they feel its restraints.  This Court has gone a long way, if not an unreasonable way, to hold that public business of such paramount importance as maintenance of public order, protection of the privacy of the home, and taxation may not be pursued by a state in a way that even indirectly will interfere with religious proselytising.  .  .  .

But we cannot have it both ways.  Religious teaching cannot be a private affair when the state seeks to impose regulations which infringe on it indirectly, and a public affair when it comes to taxing citizens of one faith to aid another, or those of no faith to aid all. If these principles seem harsh in prohibiting aid to Catholic education, it must not be forgotten that it is the same Constitution that alone assures Catholics the right to maintain these schools at all when predominant local sentiment would forbid them. Pierce v. Society of Sisters, 268 U.S. 510. Nor should I think that those who have done so well without this aid would want to see this separation between Church and State broken down. If the state may aid these religious schools, it may therefore regulate them. Many groups have sought aid from tax funds only to find that it carried political controls with it. Indeed this Court has declared that "It is hardly lack of due process for the Government to regulate that which it subsidizes." Wickard v. Filburn, 317 U.S. 111, 131.

. . . I cannot read the history of the struggle to separate political from ecclesiastical affairs . . . without a conviction that the Court today is unconsciously giving the clock's hands a backward turn.

Mr. Justice RUTLEDGE, with whom Mr. Justice FRANKFURTER, Mr. Justice JACKSON and Mr. Justice BURTON agree, dissenting.

. . . .

[The first portion of this opinion is printed supra.]

Does New Jersey's action furnish support for religion by use of the taxing power? Certainly it does, if the test remains undiluted as Jefferson and Madison made it, that money taken by taxation from one is not to be used or given to support another's religious training or belief, or indeed one's own. Today as then the furnishing of "contributions of money for the propagation of opinions which he disbelieves" is the forbidden exaction; and the prohibition is absolute for whatever measure brings that consequence and whatever amount may be sought or given to that end.

The funds used here were raised by taxation. The Court does not dispute, nor could it, that their use does in fact give aid and encouragement to religious instruction. It only concludes that this aid is not "support" in law. But Madison and Jefferson were concerned with aid and support in fact, not as a legal conclusion "entangled in precedents." . . . Here parents pay money to send their children to parochial schools and funds raised by taxation are used to reimburse them. This not only helps the children to get to school and the parents to send them. It aids them in a substantial way to get the very thing which they are sent to the particular school to secure, namely, religious training and teaching.

Believers of all faiths, and others who do not express their feeling toward ultimate issues of existence in any creedal form, pay the New Jersey tax. When the money so raised is used to pay for transportation to religious schools, the Catholic taxpayer to the extent of his proportionate share pays for the transportation of Lutheran, Jewish and otherwise religiously affiliated children to receive their non-Catholic religious instruction. Their parents likewise pay proportionately for the transportation of Catholic children to receive Catholic instruction. Each thus contributes to "the propagation of opinions which he disbelieves" in so far as their religions differ, as do others who accept no creed without regard to those differences. Each thus pays taxes also to support the teaching of his own religion, an exaction equally forbidden since it denies "the comfortable liberty" of giving one's contribution to the particular agency of instruction he approves.

New Jersey's action therefore exactly fits the type of exaction and the kind of evil at which Madison and Jefferson struck. Under the test they framed it cannot be said that the cost of transportation is no part of the cost of education or of the religious instruction given. That it is a substantial and a necessary element is shown most plainly by the continuing and increasing demand for the state to assume it. Nor is there pretense that it relates only to the secular instruction given in religious schools or that any attempt is or could be made toward allocating proportional shares as between the secular and the religious instruction. It is precisely because the instruction is religious and relates to a particular faith, whether one or another, that parents send their children to religious schools under the *Pierce* doctrine. And the very purpose of the state's contribution is to defray the cost of conveying the pupil to the place where he will receive not simply secular, but also and primarily religious, teaching and guidance. . .　.

.　.　. transportation, where it is needed, is as essential to education as any other element. Its cost is as much a part of the total expense, except at times in amount, as the cost of textbooks, of school lunches, of athletic equipment, of writing and other materials; indeed of all other items composing the total burden. Now as always the core of the educational process is the teacher-pupil relationship. Without this the richest equipment and facilities would go for naught. .　.　.

For me, therefore, the feat is impossible to select so indispensable an item from the composite of total costs, and characterize it as not aiding, contributing to, promoting or sustaining the propagation of beliefs which it is the very end of all to bring about. Unless this can be maintained, and the Court does not maintain it, the aid thus given is outlawed. Payment of transportation is no more, nor is it any the less essential to education, whether religious or secular, then payment for tuitions, for teachers' salaries, for buildings, equipment and necessary materials. Nor is it any the less directly related, in a school giving religious instruction, to the primary religious objective all those essential items of cost are intended to achieve. No rational line can be drawn between payment for such larger, but not more necessary, items and payment for transportation. The only line that can be so drawn is one between more dollars and less. Certainly in this realm such a line can be no valid constitutional measure. . . . Now, as in Madison's time, not the amount but the principle of assessment is wrong. . . .

### IV

. . . We have here then one substantial issue, not two. To say that New Jersey's appropriation and her use of the power of taxation for raising the funds appropriated are not for public purposes but are for private ends, is to say that they are for the support of religion and religious teaching. Conversely, to say that they are for public purposes is to say that they are not for religious ones.

This is precisely for the reason that education which includes religious training and teaching, and its support, have been made matters of private right and function, not public, by the very terms of the First Amendment. That is the effect not only in its guaranty of religion's free exercise, but also in the prohibition of establishments. It was on this basis of the private character of the function of religious education that this Court held parents entitled to send their children to private, religious schools. Pierce v. Society of Sisters, supra. Now it declares in effect that the appropriation of public funds to defray part of the cost of attending those schools is for a public purpose. If so, I do not understand why the state cannot go farther or why this case approaches the verge of its power.

In truth this view contradicts the whole purpose and effect of the First Amendment as heretofore conceived. The "public function"—"public welfare"—"social legislation" argument seeks, in Madison's words, to "employ Religion [that is, here, religious education] as an engine of Civil policy." . . . It is of one piece with the Assessment Bill's preamble, although with the vital difference that it wholly ignores what that preamble explicitly states. . . .

It is not because religious teaching does not promote the public or the individual's welfare, but because neither is furthered when the state promotes religious education, that the Constitution forbids it to do so. . . . In failure to observe [this distinction] lies the fallacy of the "public function"—"social legislation" argument, a fallacy facilitated by easy transference of the argument's basing from due process unrelated to any religious aspect to the First Amendment. . . .

The reasons underlying the Amendment's policy have not vanished with time or diminished in force. Now as when it was adopted the price of religious freedom is double. It is that the church and

religion shall live both within and upon that freedom.  There cannot
be freedom of religion, safeguarded by the state, and intervention
by the church or its agencies in the state's domain or dependency on
its largesse.  .  .  .  The great condition of religious liberty is
that it be maintained free from sustenance, as also from other interferences, by the state.  For when it comes to rest upon that secular
foundation it vanishes with the resting.  .  .  .  Public money devoted to payment of religious costs, educational or other, brings the
quest for more.  It brings too the struggle of sect against sect for the
larger share or for any.  Here one by numbers alone will benefit
most, there another.  That is precisely the history of societies which
have had an established religion and dissident groups.  .  .  .  It
is the very thing Jefferson and Madison experienced and sought to
guard against, whether in its blunt or in its more screened forms.
.  .  .  The end of such strife cannot be other than to destroy the
cherished liberty.  The dominating group will achieve the dominant
benefit;  or all will embroil the state in their dissensions.  .  .  .

This is not therefore just a little case over bus fares.  In para-
phrase of Madison, distant as it may be in its present form from a
complete establishment of religion, it differs from it only in degree;
and is the first step in that direction.  .  .  .  Today as in his
time "the same authority which can force a citizen to contribute three
pence only  .  .  .  for the support of any one [religious] establishment, may force him" to pay more;  or "to conform to any other establishment in all cases whatsoever."  And now, as then, "either  .  .  .  we must say, that the will of the Legislature is the
only measure of their authority;  and that in the plenitude of this
authority, they may sweep away all our fundamental rights;  or, that
they are bound to leave this particular right untouched and sacred."
.  .  .

Short treatment will dispose of what remains.  Whatever might
be said of some other application of New Jersey's statute, the one
made here has no semblance of bearing as a safety measure or, indeed, for securing expeditious conveyance.  The transportation supplied is by public conveyance, subject to all the hazards and delays
of the highway and the streets incurred by the public generally in
going about its multifarious business.

Nor is the case comparable to one of furnishing fire or police
protection, or access to public highways.  These things are matters
of common right, part of the general need for safety.  Certainly the
fire department must not stand idly by while the church burns.  Nor
is this reason why the state should pay the expense of transportation
or other items of the cost of religious education.  .  .  .

I have chosen to place my dissent upon the broad ground I think
decisive, though strictly speaking the case might be decided on narrower issues.  The New Jersey statute might be held invalid on its

face for the exclusion of children who attend private, profit-making schools.  .  .  .

Two great drives are constantly in motion to abridge, in the name of education, the complete division of religion and civil authority which our forefathers made.  One is to introduce religious education and observances into the public schools.  The other, to obtain public funds for the aid and support of various private religious schools.  .  .  .    In my opinion both avenues were closed by the Constitution.  Neither should be opened by this Court.  The matter is not one of quantity, to be measured by the amount of money expended.  Now as in Madison's day it is one of principle, to keep separate the separate spheres as the First Amendment drew them;  to prevent the first experiment upon our liberties;  and to keep the question from becoming entangled in corrosive precedents.  We should not be less strict to keep strong and untarnished the one side of the shield of religious freedom than we have been of the other.

The judgment should be reversed.

## NOTES AND QUESTIONS

1.  The legal department of the National Catholic Welfare Conference states: "The rule of Everson   .   .   .   is plainly this: (1) Government may support the education of citizens in various ways.  (2) 'Education of citizens' may take place in church-related schools.  (3) Government may not support a religion or church, as such, but so long as its program confers directly and substantially a benefit to citizen education, that program is constitutionally unobjectionable, although benefit is at the same time incidentally conferred upon a religion or a church.  .   .   ."  Do you agree?  The full position of the Legal Department is printed in 50 Geo.L.J. 397 (1961).  How would you have voted in Everson if you had been a member of the U.S. Supreme Court?  Why?

2.  Consider the interplay of the "neutrality" and "public welfare" rationales.  The Everson majority interpreted the constitution to require that government "be a neutral in its relations with groups of religious believers and non-believers."  However, "it does not require the state to be their adversary," and "state power is no more to be used so as to handicap religions than it is to favor them."  The Everson court also ruled that if government was engaged in a general public welfare program, such as promoting the safety of children by paying the public bus fares of pupils attending private and public schools, then the state's purpose and primary effect were secular and neutral, not religious, and the establishment clause was not violated.

3.  Under the public welfare theory of Everson, is either the "purpose or primary effect" of New Jersey's statute considered to be (1) the actual transportation of the children to school, or (2) the protection of their "safety" when going to school?  What other state public welfare goals would be equally acceptable?  Health?  Morals?  Education?  Is Everson different in principle from the situation presented

when police officers are required to be at street corners near parochial and private schools as well as public schools?

4.  According to dissenting opinions, would the expenditure of tax funds for public sidewalks that lead to a parochial school be a violation of the First Amendment? Should it be? Why or why not? What proposition of the majority does Mr. Justice Jackson dispute? Is he correct or incorrect? Why? Do you agree with Mr. Justice Rutledge that there is only one substantial issue in this case, and not two? Why or why not? Mr. Justice Rutledge argues (1) that it is impossible to separate out items of a school budget, all of which are thought essential for a child's education, and (2) that the public welfare or "child benefit" theory of the majority violates the intended purpose of the First Amendment; do you agree? Why or why not? What role should history play in the interpretation of the First Amendment? Did it play that role in the decision in this case?

5.  Applying the rationale of decision of the Everson majority, could a state constitutionally use public funds to provide all public and private schools, including parochial schools, with: (1) fire extinguishers; (2) police officers to control traffic near the school; (3) school lunches; (4) public health nurses and doctors; (5) speech, hearing, and psychological diagnostic services; (6) repairs to the plaster on classroom ceilings; (7) non-sectarian textbooks, film projectors, maps and other similar materials; (8) non-sectarian teachers of non-sectarian subjects such as mathematics, physics, etc., and (9) standardized examinations for non-sectarian subjects?

---

## Rev. Francis J. Connell, C. S. S. R., CENSORSHIP AND THE PROHIBITION OF BOOKS IN THE CATHOLIC CHURCH

Copyright © 1954 by Columbia Law Review
Selections from Vol. 54, Columbia Law Review, pp. 699–709.

The Catholic Church approaches the problem of man's right to knowledge with the realization that in settling concrete problems relative to human freedom two fundamental principles must be observed: First, liberty is a most precious possession, based on the dignity of every human person as a creature of God destined to an everlasting existence; hence it must be respected and protected. Second, for the good of society as well as for the welfare of individuals, personal liberty must be curtailed in certain circumstances. This is particularly true when the limitation of liberty is required as a means of protecting individuals from sin or moral evil, which would constitute an impediment to the attainment of their final goal, eternal happiness with God. In determining the extent of man's rights in particular cases a just and reasonable mean must be observed between these two principles. If the first is overemphasized, liberty degenerates into license. If the second is stressed too much, authority becomes tyranny and the way is open to totalitarianism.

These two principles must be properly coordinated in one of the problems which the Church treats in detailed legislation—the problem of the right to read certain books and other forms of published literature, a problem with a direct bearing on the right to knowledge and its free use.  .   .   .

The notion that people should be allowed to read everything they wish is quite common in our land, for we are a freedom-loving people, resenting any restriction of our freedom.  How often do we hear the statement that reading will never cause the reader any harm!  An example of this is a statement made by Verner W. Clapp, Acting Librarian of Congress:

> The notion that mankind is corrupted by books is, I believe, a notion held by those whose own reading has been largely of that enforced and unselective kind which the mass media provide.  Books are corruptive only to those who seek to be corrupted; but they are already corrupt.

Despite the dogmatic assurance with which this statement is made, the fact is that people can be influenced to evil as well as to good by what they read.  And while we justly uphold the ideals of freedom we must admit that freedom has its limitations.  Catholics believe that the laws of their Church in regard to censorship and the prohibition of books represent a reasonable limitation of their freedom.  And before passing an unfavorable judgment on the Church's legislation on this matter, one should examine the principles on which the Church bases its policy in restricting the right to read for those who are subject to the authority of the Church.

The Catholic Church believes that the chief purpose of man's earthly life is to prepare for an eternal life after death.  Happiness in this everlasting existence is merited by living in this world a life in conformity with the commands of God; and it is supremely important to live this life in such a manner as to attain this goal.  Whatever advantages may accrue through the exercise of personal freedom, they can have no real value if they impede or imperil the attainment of one's eternal destiny.  Hence it is not an evil but a good when those in authority, whether parents, civil rulers or ecclesiastical authorities, regulate the exercise of freedom by those subject to their jurisdiction so as to aid them to observe God's law and to reach the eternal happiness which the Creator has appointed to every human being.

Everyone admits that it is perfectly reasonable to limit the freedom of individuals when the purpose of such limitations is to prevent them from doing physical harm to themselves or to others.  If I refuse to give a person a gun with which he is likely to shoot himself or others I am indeed limiting his freedom, but no reasonable person will accuse me of doing wrong.  Instead of hampering his proper use of freedom, I am preventing him from abusing it.  The Catholic Church applies this same principle to the unrestricted right to read. There are books which would cause spiritual and moral harm to many persons if they were permitted to read them indiscriminately; hence the Church forbids the reading of such books.

Naturally it will be asked by what authority the Church claims the right to do this. The Church replies that it has received from God Himself the right to teach officially the truths of religion and morality and the right to legislate on matters pertinent to the spiritual welfare of those subject to its jurisdiction. . . .

Anyone who admits the existence of an intelligent and all-powerful Deity must grant that if He wills, He can authorize an organization on earth to represent Him in proposing to mankind the doctrines of religion and the principles of morality. For such a person, therefore, the vital question is whether or not the Almighty has acted thus in respect to the Catholic Church. . . .

As to the matter of religious belief, the Catholic Church is convinced that its duty of preserving in its members the faith in the truths which God has communicated to men calls for legislation against books that might endanger that faith. The Church is not motivated by a fear that the arguments brought against its teachings are sufficiently cogent in themselves to discredit Catholic teaching. Rather, the Church recognizes that many Catholics do not possess sufficient technical knowledge of the Catholic doctrine or of history to meet all the arguments that can be brought against Catholic belief; hence the Church legislates against books with such a purpose. . . .

----

### BOARD OF EDUC. v. ALLEN

Supreme Court of the United States, 1968.
392 U.S. 236, 88 S.Ct. 1923, 20 L.Ed.2d 1060.

Mr. Justice WHITE delivered the opinion of the Court.

A law of the State of New York requires local public school authorities to lend textbooks free of charge to all students in grade seven through 12; students attending private schools are included. This case presents the question whether this statute is a "law respecting an establishment of religion, or prohibiting the free exercise thereof," and so in conflict with the First and Fourteenth Amendments to the Constitution, because it authorizes the loan of textbooks to students attending parochial schools. We hold that the law is not in violation of the Constitution.

Until 1965, § 701 of the Education Law of the State of New York authorized public school boards to designate textbooks for use in the public schools, to purchase such books with public funds, and to rent or sell the books to public school students. In 1965, the Legislature amended § 701, . . . Beginning with the 1966–1967 school year, local school boards were required to purchase textbooks and lend them without charge "to all children residing in such district who are enrolled in grades seven to twelve of a public or private school which complies with the compulsory education law." The books now loaned are "textbooks which are designated for use in any public, elementary or secondary schools of the state or are approved by any boards of education," and which—according to a 1966 amendment—"a pupil is required to use as a text for a semester or more in a particular class in the school he legally attends."

Appellant Board of Education of Central School District No. 1 in Rensselaer and Columbia Counties, brought suit in the New York courts against appellee James Allen. The complaint alleged that § 701 violated both the State and Federal Constitutions; that if appellants, in reliance on their interpretation of the Constitution, failed to lend books to parochial school students within their counties appellee Allen would remove appellants from office; and that to prevent this, appellants were complying with the law and submitting to their constituents a school budget including funds for books to be lent to parochial school pupils. Appellants therefore sought a declaration that § 701 was invalid, an order barring appellee Allen from removing appellants from office for failing to comply with it, and another order restraining him from apportioning state funds to school districts for the purchase of textbooks to be lent to parochial students. . . .

Everson v. Board of Education, . . . is the case decided by this Court that is most nearly in point for today's problem. . . .

Everson and later cases have shown that the line between state neutrality to religion and state support of religion is not easy to locate. . . . "The test may be stated as follows: what are the purpose and the primary effect of the enactment? If either is the advancement or inhibition of religion then the enactment exceeds the scope of legislative power as circumscribed by the Constitution. That is to say that to withstand the strictures of the Establishment Clause there must be a secular legislative purpose and a primary effect that neither advances nor inhibits religion. . . ."

This test is not easy to apply. . . . The statute upheld in Everson would be considered a law having "a secular legislative purpose and a primary effect that neither advances nor inhibits religion." We reach the same result with respect to the New York law requiring school books to be loaned free of charge to all students in specified grades. The express purpose of § 701 was stated by the New York Legislature to be furtherance of the educational opportunities available to the young. Appellants have shown us nothing about the necessary effects of the statute that is contrary to its stated purpose. The law merely makes available to all children the benefits of a general program to lend school books free of charge. Books are furnished at the request of the pupil and ownership remains, at least technically, in the State.  Thus no funds or books are furnished to parochial schools, and the financial benefit is to parents and children, not to schools.  Perhaps free books make it more likely that some children choose to attend a sectarian school, but that was true of the state-paid bus fares in Everson and does not alone demonstrate an unconstitutional degree of support for a religious institution.

Of course books are different from buses.  Most bus rides have no inherent religious significance, while religious books are common.  However, the language of § 701 does not authorize the loan of religious books, and the State claims no right to distribute religious literature.  Although the books loaned are those required by the parochial school for use in specific courses, each book loaned must be approved by the public school authorities; only secular books may receive approval.  .  .  .  Absent evidence, we cannot assume that school authorities, who constantly face the same problem in selecting textbooks for use in the public schools, are unable to distinguish between secular and religious books or that they will not honestly discharge their duties under the law.  In judging the validity of the statute on this record we must proceed on the assumption that books loaned to students are books that are not unsuitable for use in the public schools because of religious content.

The major reason offered by appellants for distinguishing free textbooks from free bus fares is that books, but not buses, are critical to the teaching process, and in a sectarian school that process is employed to teach religion.  However, this Court has long recognized that religious schools pursue two goals, religious instruction and secular education.  .  .  .

.  .  .  private education has played and is playing a significant and valuable role in raising national levels of knowledge, competence, and experience.  Americans care about the quality of the secular education available to their children.  They have considered high quality education to be an indispensable ingredient for achieving the kind of nation, and the kind of citizenry, that they have desired to create.  Considering this attitude, the continued willingness to rely on private school systems, including parochial systems, strongly suggests that a wide segment of informed opinion, legislative and otherwise, has found that those schools do an acceptable job of providing secular education to their students.  This judgment is further evidence that parochial schools are performing, in addition to their sectarian function, the task of secular education.

Against this background of judgment and experience,  .  .  .  we cannot agree with appellants either that all teaching in a sectarian school is religious or that the processes of secular and religious training are so intertwined that secular textbooks furnished to students by the public are in fact instrumental in the teaching of religion.  This case comes to us after summary judgment entered on the pleadings.

Nothing in this record supports the proposition that all textbooks, whether they deal with mathematics, physics, foreign languages, history, or literature, are used by the parochial schools, to teach religion. No evidence has been offered about particular schools, particular courses, particular teachers, or particular books. We are unable to hold, based solely on judicial notice, that this statute results in unconstitutional involvement of the State with religious instruction or that § 701, for this or the other reasons urged, is a law respecting the establishment of religion within the meaning of the First Amendment.

Appellants also contend that § 701 offends the Free Exercise Clause of the First Amendment. However, "it is necessary in a free exercise case for one to show the coercive effect of the enactment as it operates against him in the practice of his religion," . . . and appellants have not contended that the New York law in any way coerces them as individuals in the practice of their religion.

The judgment is affirmed.

Mr. Justice Harlan, concurring. . . .

The attitude of government toward religion must, as this Court has frequently observed, be one of neutrality. Neutrality is, however, a coat of many colors. It requires that "government neither engage in nor compel religious practices, that it effect no favoritism among sects or between religion and nonreligion, and that it work deterrence of no religious belief." . . . Realization of these objectives entails "no simple and clear measure," . . . or which this or any case may readily be decided, but these objectives do suggest the principles which I believe to be applicable in the present circumstances. I would hold that where the contested governmental activity is calculated to achieve nonreligious purposes otherwise within the competence of the State, and where the activity does not involve the State "so significantly and directly in the realm of the sectarian as to give rise to . . . divisive influences and inhibitions of freedom," . . . it is not forbidden by the religious clauses of the First Amendment.

In my opinion, § 701 of the Education Law of New York does not employ religion as its standard for action or inaction, and is not otherwise inconsistent with these principles.

Mr. Justice BLACK, dissenting. . . .

The Everson and McCollum cases plainly interpret the First and Fourteenth Amendments as protecting the taxpayers of a State from being compelled to pay taxes to their government to support the agencies of private religious organizations the taxpayers oppose. To authorize a State to tax its residents for such church purposes is to put the State squarely in the religious activities of certain religious groups that happen to be strong enough politically to write their own religious preferences and prejudices into the laws. This links state and churches together in controlling the lives and destinies of our citizenship—a citizenship composed of people of myriad religious faiths, some of them bitterly hostile to and completely intolerant of the others.  It was to escape laws precisely like this that a large part of the Nation's early immigrants fled to this country.  It was also to escape such laws and such consequences that the First Amendment was written in language strong and clear barring passage of any law "respecting an establishment of religion."

It is true, of course, that the New York law does not as yet formally adopt or establish a state religion.  But it takes a great stride in that direction and coming events cast their shadows before them.  The same powerful sectarian religious propagandists who have succeeded in securing passage of the present law to help religious schools carry on their sectarian religious purposes can and doubtless will continue their propaganda, looking toward complete domination and supremacy of their particular brand of religion.  And it nearly always is by insidious approaches that the citadels of liberty are most successfully attacked.

I know of no prior opinion of this Court upon which the majority here can rightfully rely to support its holding this New York law constitutional.  In saying this, I am not unmindful of  .  .  .  Everson  .  .  .  in which this Court, in an opinion written by me, upheld a New Jersey law authorizing reimbursement to parents for the transportation of children attending sectarian schools.  That law did not attempt to deny the benefit of its general terms to children of any faith going to any legally authorized school.  Thus, it was treated in the same way as a general law paying the streetcar fare *of all school children,* or a law providing midday lunches for all children or all school children, or a law to provide police protection for children going to and from school, or general laws to provide police and fire protection for buildings, including, of course, churches and church school buildings as well as others.

As my Brother Douglas so forcefully shows, in an argument with which I fully agree, upholding a State's power to pay bus or streetcar fares for school children cannot provide support for the validity of a state law using tax-raised funds to buy school books for a religious school.  The First Amendment's bar to establishment of religion must preclude a State from using funds levied from all of its citizens to purchase books for use by sectarian schools, which, although "secular," realistically will in some way inevitably tend to propagate the religious views of the favored sect.  Books are the most essential tool of education since they contain the resources of knowledge which the educational process is designed to exploit.  In this sense it is not difficult to distinguish books, which are the heart of any school, from bus fares, which provide a convenient and helpful general public transportation service.  .  .  .

. . . It requires no prophet to foresee that on the argument used to support this law others could be upheld providing for state or federal government funds to buy property on which to erect religious school buildings or to erect the buildings themselves, to pay the salaries of the religious school teachers, and finally to have the sectarian religious groups cease to rely on voluntary contributions of members of their sects while waiting for the Government to pick up all the bills for the religious schools. Arguments made in favor of this New York law point squarely in this direction, namely, that the fact that government has not heretofore aided religious schools with tax-raised funds amounts to a discrimination against those schools and against religion. And that there are already efforts to have government supply the money to erect buildings for sectarian religious schools is shown by a recent Act of Congress which apparently allows for precisely that. See Higher Education Facilities Act of 1963, 77 Stat. 363, 20 U.S.C.A. § 701 et seq.

I still subscribe to the belief that tax-raised funds cannot constitutionally be used to support religious schools, buy their school books, erect their buildings, pay their teachers, or pay any other of their maintenance expenses, even to the extent of one penny. The First Amendment's prohibition against governmental establishment of religion was written on the assumption that state aid to religion and religious schools generates discord, disharmony, hatred, and strife among our people, and that any government that supplies such aids is to that extent a tyranny. And I still believe that the only way to protect minority religious groups from majority groups in this country is to keep the wall of separation between church and state high and impregnable as the First and Fourteenth Amendments provide. The Court's affirmance here bodes nothing but evil to religious peace in this country.

Mr. Justice DOUGLAS, dissenting. . . .

The statute on its face empowers each parochial school to determine for itself which textbooks will be eligible for loans to its students, for the Act provides that the only text which the State may provide is "a book which a pupil is required to use as a text for a semester or more in a particular class in the school he legally attends." . . . This initial and crucial selection is undoubtedly made by the parochial school's principal or its individual instructors, who are, in the case of Roman Catholic schools, normally priests or nuns.

The next step under the Act is an "individual request" for an eligible textbook (§ 701, subd. 3), but the State Education Department has ruled that a pupil may make his request to the local public board of education through a "private school official." Local boards have accordingly provided for those requests to be made by the individual or "by groups or classes." And forms for textbook requisitions to be filled out by the head of the private school are provided.

The role of the local public school board is to decide whether to veto the selection made by the parochial school. This is done by determining first whether the text has been or should be "approved" for use in public schools and second whether the text is "secular," "non-religious," or "non-sectarian." The local boards apparently have broad discretion in exercising this veto power.

Thus the statutory system provides that the parochial school will ask for the books that it wants. Can there be the slightest doubt that the head of the parochial school will select the book or books that best promote its sectarian creed? . . .

Whatever may be said of Everson, there is nothing ideological about a bus. There is nothing ideological about a school lunch, or a public nurse, or a scholarship. The constitutionality of such public aid to students in parochial schools turns on considerations not present in this textbook case. The textbook goes to the very heart of education in a parochial school. It is the chief, although not solitary, instrumentality for propagating a particular religious creed or faith. How can we possibly approve such state aid to a religion? A parochial school textbook may contain many, many more seeds of creed and dogma than a prayer. Yet we struck down in Engel v. Vitale, . . . even though it was not plainly denominational. For we emphasized the violence done the Establishment Clause when the power was given religious-political groups "to write their own prayers into law." . . . That risk is compounded here by giving parochial schools the initiative in selecting the textbooks they desire to be furnished at public expense.

. . . The New York Legislature felt that science was a non-sectarian subject. . . . Does this mean that any general science textbook intended for use in grades 7–12 may be provided by the State to parochial school students? May John M. Scott's Adventures in Science (1963) be supplied under the textbook loan program? This book teaches embryology in the following manner:

> "To you an animal usually means a mammal, such as a cat, dog, squirrel, or guinea pig. The new animal or embryo develops inside the body of the mother until birth. The fertilized egg becomes an embryo or developing animal. Many cell divisions take place. In time some cells become muscle cells, others nerve cells, or blood cells, and organs such as eyes, stomach, and intestine are formed.
>
> "The body of a human being grows in the same way, but it is much more remarkable than that of any animal, for the embryo has a human soul infused into the body by God. Human parents are partners with God in creation. They have very great powers and great responsibilities, for through their cooperation with God souls are born for heaven." (At 618–619.)

Comparative economics would seem to be a nonsectarian subject. Will New York, then, provide Arthur J. Hughes' general history text, Man in Time (1964), to parochial school students? It treats that topic in this manner:

> "Capitalism is an economic system based on man's right to private property and on his freedom to use that property in producing goods which will earn him a just profit on his investment. Man's right to private property stems from the Natural Law implanted in him by God. It is as much a part of man's nature as the will to self-preservation." (At 560.)

> "The broadest definition of socialism is government ownership of all the means of production and distribution in a country. . . . Many, but by no means all, Socialists in the nineteenth century believed that crime and vice existed because poverty existed, and if poverty were eliminated, then crime and vice would disappear. While it is true that poor surroundings are usually unhealthy climates for high moral training, still, man has the free will to check himself. Many Socialists, however, denied free will and said that man was a creation of his environment. . . . If Socialists do not deny Christ's message, they often ignore it. Christ showed us by His life that this earth is a testing ground to prepare man for eternal happiness. Man's interests should be in this direction at least part of the time and not always directed toward a futile quest for material goods." (At 561–564.)

Mr. Justice JACKSON said, ". . . I should suppose it is a proper, if not an indispensable, part of preparation for a wordly life to know the roles that religion and religions have played in the tragic story of mankind." . . . Yet, as he inquired, what emphasis should one give who teaches the Reformation, the Inquisition, or the early effort in New England to establish " 'a Church without a Bishop and a State without a King?' " . . . What books should be chosen for those subjects? . . .

Is the dawn of man to be explained in the words, "God created man and made man master of the earth" (P. Furlong, The Old World and America 5 (1937), or in the language of evolution (see T. Wallbank, Man's Story 32–35 (1961))? . . .

Is Franco's revolution in Spain to be taught as a crusade against anti-Catholic forces (see R. Hoffman, G. Vincitorio, & M. Swift, Man and His History 666–667 (1958)) or as an effort by reactionary elements to regain control of that country (see G. Leinwand, The Pageant of World History, supra, at 512)? Is the expansion of communism in select areas of the world a manifestation of the forces of Evil campaigning against the forces of Good? See A. Hughes, Man in Time, supra, at 565–568, 666–669, 735–748.

It will be often difficult, as Mr. Justice Jackson said, to say "where the secular ends and the sectarian begins in education." . . . But certain it is that once the so-called "secular" textbook is the price to be won by that religious faith which selects the book, the battle will be on for those positions of control. . . . It must be remembered that the very existence of the religious school—whether Catholic or Mormon, Presbyterian or Episcopalian—is to provide an education oriented to the dogma of the particular faith.

Father Peter O'Reilly put the matter succinctly when he disclosed what was happening in one Catholic school: "On February 24, 1954, Rev. Cyril F. Meyer, C. M., then Vice President of the University, sent the following letter to all the faculty, both Catholics and non-Catholics, even those teaching law, science, and mathematics:

" 'Dear Faculty Member"

" 'As a result of several spirited discussions in the Academic Senate, a resolution was passed by that body that a self-evaluation be made of the effectiveness with which we are achieving in our classrooms the stated objectives of the University. . . . The primacy of the spiritual is the reason for a Christian university. Our goal is not merely to equip students with marketable skills. It is far above this—to educate man, the whole man, the theocentric man. As you are well aware, we strive to educate not only for personal and social success in secular society, but far more for leadership toward a theocentric society. . . .

" 'May I, therefore, respectfully request that you submit answers as specific as possible to the following questions:

" '1. What do you do to make your particular courses theocentric?

" '2. Do you believe there is anything the Administration or your colleagues can do to assist you in presenting your particular courses more "according to the philosophical and theological traditions of the Roman Catholic Church"? Do not hesitate to let us know. There is no objective of our University more fundamental than this. We must all be aware that "the classroom that is not a temple is a den."

" 'Please try to have your answers, using this size paper, returned to me by March 10.' "

This tendency is no Catholic monopoly:

"The Presbyterian-affiliated Lewis and Clark College seems to have a similar interest in appearances of autonomy, with a view to avoiding possible legal bars to both federal funds and gifts from some foundations. The change, which legitimizes the college as an autonomous educational institution, removes the requirement that each presbytery in Oregon have at least one representative on the board, but it was made clear 'The college wishes to change *only its legal relationship* to the synod and *not its purposes,*' and promised that it still will elect a minister from each presbytery to the board on nomination of the synod, and will consult the synod before making any change in its statement of purpose, which defines it as a Presbyterian-related college."

The challenged New York law leaves to the Board of Regents, local boards of education, trustees, and other school authorities the supervision of the textbook program.

The Board of Regents (together with the Commissioner of Education) has powers of censorship over all textbooks that contain statements seditious in character, or evince disloyalty to the United States or are favorable to any nation with which we are at war. New York Education Law § 704. Those powers can cut a wide swath in many areas of education that involve the ideological element.

In general textbooks are approved for distribution by "boards of education, trustees or such body or officer as perform the functions of such boards. . . . " . . . These school boards are generally elected, . . . though in a few cities they are appointed. . . . Where there are trustees they are elected. . . . And superintendents who advise on textbook selection are appointed by the board of education or the trustees. . . .

The initiative to select and requisition "the books desired" is with the parochial school. Powerful religious-political pressures will therefore be on the state agencies to provide the books that are desired.

These then are the battlegrounds where control of textbook distribution will be won or lost. Now that "secular" textbooks will pour into religious schools, we can rest assured that a contest will be on to provide those books for religious schools which the dominant religious group concludes best reflect the theocentric or other philosophy of the particular church.

The states are now extremely high . . . to obtain approval of what is "proper." For the "proper" books will radiate the "correct" religious view not only in the parochial school but in the public school as well. . . .

. . . however the case be viewed—whether sectarian groups win control of school boards or do not gain such control—the principle of separation of church and state, inherent in the Establishment Clause of the First Amendment, is violated by what we today approve.

What Madison wrote in his famous Memorial and Remonstrance against Religious Assessments is highly pertinent here:

"Who does not see that the same authority which can establish Christianity, in exclusion of all other Religions, may establish with the same ease any particular sect of Christians, in exclusion of all other Sects? That the same authority which can force a citizen to contribute three pence only of his property for the support of any one establishment, may force him to conform to any other establishment in all cases whatsoever?" . . .

Mr. Justice FORTAS, dissenting.

The majority opinion of the Court upholds the New York statute by ignoring a vital aspect of it. Public funds are used to buy, for students in sectarian schools, textbooks which are selected and prescribed by the sectarian schools themselves. . . . the transparent camouflage that the books are furnished to students, the reality is that they are selected and their use is prescribed by the sectarian authorities. The child must use the prescribed book. He cannot use a different book prescribed for use in the public schools. The State cannot choose the book to be used. It is true that the public school boards must "approve" the book selected by the sectarian authorities; but this has no real significance. The purpose of these provisions is to hold out promise that the books will be "secular" . . . but the fact remains that the books are chosen by and for the sectarian schools. . . .

This case is not within the principle of Everson. . . . Apart from the differences between textbooks and bus rides, the present statute does not call for extending to children attending sectarian schools the same service or facility extended to children in public schools. This statute calls for furnishing special, separate, and particular books, specially, separately, and particularly chosen by religious sects or their representatives for use in their sectarian schools. This is the infirmity, in my opinion. . . .

I would reverse the judgment below.

## NOTES AND QUESTIONS

1. With which opinion of Everson and Board of Educ. v. Allen do you agree? Why? What is the rule of law established by Allen?

   Are the Everson and Allen cases fully consistent? Was the view of the court in Everson necessarily founded on the facts of that case, which were that administered public funds paid on a non-discriminatory basis to all citizens who sent their children to school via public transportation systems owned and operated by public authorities with all funds ultimately residing back in the public treasury. But, as Mr. Justice Fortas emphasized in Allen, the books supplied to private schools are not the same books supplied to the public schools; whereas, in Everson, the same public bus transportation was supplied to all children. Is this difference important? Why?

2. The Supreme Court read New York's law as "merely making available secular textbooks" and not as authorizing the loan of sectarian or re-

ligious books.   Thus, the approval or disapproval of a textbook loan by public officials (who often are elected public officials) depends on the character of the book and the ability of the public official to perceive that character.   The public official does not have to inquire into the use to which a book will be put because the Supreme Court's assumption in Allen was that secular books will be put to secular uses. One author states that "whether one talks of religious and secular *books* or religious and secular *uses*, the assumption that workable distinctions between 'secular' and 'religious' can be made is highly questionable."   Note, Sectarian Books, The Supreme Court and the Establishment Clause, 7 Yale L.J. 114 (1969).   Do you agree?   The author continues:

"It is clear that any book favoring the views of one sect over another should be rejected.   .   .   .   The most difficult theoretical problems in attempting to define 'where the secular ends and the sectarian begins' in textbook review arise in answering the preliminary question of what is a religion or religious sect. Would a text advocating the tenets of the League of Spiritual Discovery be classified as a secular or sectarian book?   What is the difference between a religion and an ideology?   Would a book placing capitalism or democracy or individualism at the center of a world view run afoul of the Establishment Clause?   Would a textbook advocating black separatism as a tenet of the Black Muslim religion be treated differently from a textbook advocating black separatism as the political philosophy of a black nationalist group?   Is morality ever separable from religion?   If a moral view is historically rooted in a religion, can its advocacy within a textbook ever escape the charge of being religious?   Whose definition of religion should be controlling?

"Identifying overt references to religious doctrines, events, or objects which are not universally shared requires knowledge of the subject matter of the textbook and a thorough knowledge of religious doctrines.   This expertise is usually not to be found in the New York officials charged with textbook review.   .   .   . There is no reason to assume that the identification of even overt sectarian references is being competently done when it is entrusted by this Law to officials without needed qualifications and with extensive other duties.

"Religious beliefs can be advanced in a textbook by a sectarian moral or ethical undertone.   .   .   .   Given the constraints on the New York reviewers—limited time and lack of special knowledge—it is impossible for their inspections of contents consistently to expose the impermissible undertones which may be present. Certainly a cleric is capable of authoring a non-sectarian textbook. However, religious authorship does tend to indicate a sectarian content: there is a likelihood of at least subconscious bias, and a possibility that the fact of clerical authorship indicates that the book was written and published in the hope of having a particular appeal to parochial schools.   But the regulations under the Textbook Loan Law declare that the reviewers' decisions must depend 'entirely on content'; authorship cannot be considered   .   .   .".

3.  It is possible that a textbook loan program, like the one approved in Bd. of Ed. v. Allen, would be unconstitutional under a state's constitution. See, Dickman v. School Dist., 232 Or. 238, 366 P.2d 533 (1961) certiorari denied 371 U.S. 823, 83 S.Ct. 41, 9 L.Ed.2d 62 (1962).

4.  Do Everson and Allen authorize the payment of tax funds by public officials to hospitals run by religious orders so long as those hospitals perform a "public welfare" function?

Under Everson and Allen, could the federal government or a state pay tuition for students enrolled in institutions of higher education, including those enrolled in Schools of Theology?

Under Everson and Allen, could the federal government allow a full income tax deduction to all persons who paid tuition, whether it be to public or non-profit private schools, common or higher education?

If a textbook loan program can comply with the First Amendment, could a teacher loan program? Are there any constitutional differences between making available bussing, textbooks or teachers for parochial school students? If a teacher loan program can comply with the First Amendment, could a program that paid parochial school salaries or provided funds for parochial school construction?

5.  In 1970, by a vote of 8 to 1, in Walz v. Tax Commission, 397 U.S. 664, 90 S.Ct. 1409, 25 L.Ed.2d 697 (1970), the Supreme Court rejected an attack on New York's law that allowed a property tax exemption for property used solely for religious purposes. Chief Justice Burger's majority opinion stated that "the Court has struggled to find a neutral course between the two Religion Clauses both of which are cast in absolute terms, and either of which, if expanded to a logical extreme, would tend to clash with the other." After considering the Court's cases, he said that "the general principle deducible [from the Court's past precedents] is this: that we will not tolerate either governmentally established religion or governmental interference with religion." The Court's majority opinion found that New York's tax exemption passed the "purpose" and "primary effect" tests of Abington v. Schempp, supra. But, this was not the end of the case, because the Court added a new and third test: "We must also be sure that the end result— the effect—is not an excessive government entanglement with religion. The test is inescapably one of degree." New York's law passed this test as well. When analyzing a problem under this test, the Court said "the questions are whether the involvement is excessive, and whether it is a continuing one calling for official and continuing surveillance lending to an impermissible degree of entanglement." If the tests of purpose, primary effect and excessive entanglement had been in effect at the time of decision in Everson or Allen, would those cases have been decided differently?

## LEMON v. KURTZMAN

Supreme Court of the United States, 1971.
403 U.S. 602, 91 S.Ct. 2105, 29 L.Ed.2d 745,
rehearing denied 404 U.S. 876, 92 S.Ct. 24, 30 L.Ed.2d 123.

Mr. Chief Justice BURGER delivered the opinion of the Court.

These two appeals raise questions as to Pennsylvania and Rhode Island statutes providing state aid to church-related elementary and secondary schools. Both statutes are challenged as violative of the Establishment and Free Exercise Clauses of the First Amendment and the Due Process Clause of the Fourteenth Amendment. . . .

### The Rhode Island Statute

The Rhode Island Salary Supplement Act was enacted in 1969. It rests on the legislative finding that the quality of education available in nonpublic elementary schools has been jeopardized by the rapidly rising salaries needed to attract competent and dedicated teachers. The Act authorizes state officials to supplement the salaries of teachers of secular subjects in nonpublic elementary schools by paying directly to a teacher an amount not in excess of 15% of his current annual salary. As supplemented, however, a nonpublic school teacher's salary cannot exceed the maximum paid to teachers in the State's public schools, and the recipient must be certified by the state board of education in substantially the same manner as public school teachers.

In order to be eligible for the Rhode Island salary supplement, the recipient must teach in a nonpublic school at which the average per-pupil expenditure on secular education is less than the average in the State's public schools during a specified period. Appellant State Commissioner of Education also requires eligible schools to submit financial data. If this information indicates a per-pupil expenditure in excess of the statutory limitation, the records of the school in question must be examined in order to assess how much of the expenditure is attributable to secular education and how much to religious activity.

The Act also requires that teachers eligible for salary supplements must teach only those subjects that are offered in the State's public schools. They must use "only teaching materials which are used in the public schools." Finally, any teacher applying for a salary supplement must first agree in writing "not to teach a course in religion for so long as or during such time as he or she receives any salary supplements" under the Act. . . .

### The Pennsylvania Statute

Pennsylvania has adopted a program that has some but not all of the features of the Rhode Island program. The Pennsylvania Nonpublic Elementary and Secondary Education Act was passed in 1968 in response to a crisis that the Pennsylvania Legislature found existed in the State's nonpublic schools due to rapidly rising costs. The statute affirmatively reflects the legislative conclusion that the State's educational goals could appropriately be fulfilled by government support of "those purely secular educational objectives achieved through nonpublic education. . . ."

The statute authorizes appellee state Superintendent of Public Instruction to "purchase" specified "secular educational services" from nonpublic schools. Under the "contracts" authorized by the statute, the State directly reimburses nonpublic schools solely for their actual expenditures for teachers' salaries, textbooks, and instructional materials. A school seeking reimbursement must maintain prescribed accounting procedures that identify the "separate" cost of the "secular educational services." These accounts are subject to state audit. The funds for this program were originally derived from a new tax on horse and harness racing, but the Act is now financed by a portion of the state tax on cigarettes.

There are several significant statutory restrictions on state aid. Reimbursement is limited to courses "presented in the curricula of the public schools." It is further limited "solely" to courses in the following "secular" subjects: mathematics, modern foreign languages, physical science, and physical education. Textbooks and instructional materials included in the program must be approved by the state Superintendent of Public Instruction. Finally, the statute prohibits reimbursement for any course that contains "any subject matter expressing religious teaching, or the morals or forms of worship of any sect." . . .

## II

In Everson . . . Mr. Justice Black, writing for the majority, suggested that the decision carried to "the verge" of forbidden territory under the Religion Clauses. . . . Candor compels acknowledgment, moreover, that we can only dimly perceive the lines of demarcation in this extraordinarily sensitive area of constitutional law. . . .

Every analysis in this area must begin with consideration of the cumulative criteria developed by the Court over many years. Three such tests may be gleaned from our cases. First, the statute must have a secular legislative purpose; second, its principal or primary effect must be one that neither advances nor inhibits religion, . . . finally, the statute must not foster "an excessive government entanglement with religion." . . .

Inquiry into the legislative purposes of the Pennsylvania and Rhode Island statutes affords no basis for a conclusion that the legislative intent was to advance religion. . . . A State always has a legitimate concern for maintaining minimum standards in all schools it allows to operate. As in Allen, we find nothing here that undermines the stated legislative intent; it must therefore be accorded appropriate deference. . . .

. . . We need not decide whether these legislative precautions restrict the principal or primary effect of the programs to the point where they do not offend the Religion Clauses, for we conclude that the cumulative impact of the entire relationship arising under the statutes in each State involves excessive entanglement between government and religion. . . .

Our prior holdings do not call for total separation between church and state; total separation is not possible in an absolute sense. Some relationship between government and religious organizations is inevitable. . . .

In order to determine whether the government entanglement with religion is excessive, we must examine the character and purposes of the institutions that are benefited, the nature of the aid that the State provides, and the resulting relationship between the government and the religious authority. . . . Here we find that both statutes foster an impermissible degree of entanglement. . . .

## (a) *Rhode Island program*

The District Court made extensive findings on the grave potential for excessive entanglement that inheres in the religious character and purpose of the Roman Catholic elementary schools of Rhode Island, to date the sole beneficiaries of the Rhode Island Salary Supplement Act.

The church schools involved in the program are located close to parish churches. This understandably permits convenient access for religious exercises since instruction in faith and morals is part of the total educational process. The school buildings contain identifying religious symbols such as crosses on the exterior and crucifixes, and religious paintings and statutes either in the classrooms or hallways. Although only approximately 30 minutes a day are devoted to direct religious instruction, there are religiously oriented extracurricular activities. Approximately two-thirds of the teachers in these schools are nuns of various religious orders. Their dedicated efforts provide an atmosphere in which religious instruction and religious vocations are natural and proper parts of life in such schools. Indeed, as the District Court found, the role of teaching nuns in enhancing the religious atmosphere has led the parochial school authorities to attempt to maintain a one-to-one ratio between nuns and lay teachers in all schools rather than to permit some to be staffed almost entirely by lay teachers.

On the basis of these findings the District Court concluded that the parochial schools constituted "an integral part of the religious mission of the Catholic Church." The various characteristics of the schools make them "a powerful vehicle for transmitting the Catholic faith to the next generation." This process of inculcating religious doctrine is, of course, enhanced by the impressionable age of the pupils, in primary schools particularly. In short, parochial schools involve substantial religious activity and purpose.

The substantial religious character of these church-related schools gives rise to entangling church-state relationships of the kind the Religion Clauses sought to avoid. . . .

The dangers and corresponding entanglements are enhanced by the particular form of aid that the Rhode Island Act provides. Our decisions from Everson to Allen have permitted the States to provide church-related schools with secular, neutral, or nonideological services, facilities, or materials. Bus transportation, school lunches, public health services, and secular textbooks supplied in common to all students were not thought to offend the Establishment Clause. We note that the dissenters in Allen seemed chiefly concerned with the pragmatic difficulties involved in ensuring the truly secular content of the textbooks provided at state expense.

In Allen the Court refused to make assumptions, on a meager record, about the religious content of the textbooks that the State would be asked to provide. We cannot, however, refuse here to recognize that teachers have a substantially different ideological character from books. In terms of potential for involving some aspect of faith or morals in secular subjects, a textbook's content is ascertainable, but a teacher's handling of a subject is not. We cannot ignore the danger that a teacher under religious control and discipline poses to the separation of the religious from the purely secular aspects of precollege education. The conflict of functions inheres in the situation.

In our view the record shows there dangers are present to a substantial degree. The Rhode Island Roman Catholic elementary schools are under the general supervision of the Bishop of Providence and his appointed representative, the Diocesan Superintendent of Schools. In most cases, each individual parish, however, assumes the ultimate financial responsibility for the school, with the parish priest authorizing the allocation of parish funds. With only two exceptions, school principals are nuns appointed either by the Superintendent or the Mother Provincial of the order whose members staff the school. By 1969 lay teachers constituted more than a third of all teachers in the parochial elementary schools, and their number is growing. They are first interviewed by the superintendent's office and then by the school principal. The contracts are signed by the parish priest, and he retains some discretion in negotiating salary levels. Religious authority necessarily pervades the school system.

The schools are governed by the standards set forth in a "Handbook of School Regulations," which has the force of synodal law in the diocese. It emphasizes the role and importance of the teacher in parochial schools: "The prime factor for the success or the failure of the school is the spirit and personality, as well as the professional competency, of the teacher. . . ." The Handbook also states that "Religious formation is not confined to formal courses; nor is it restricted to a single subject area." Finally, the Handbook advises teachers to stimulate interest in religious vocations and missionary work. Given the mission of the church school, these instructions are consistent and logical. . . .

We need not and do not assume that teachers in parochial schools will be guilty of bad faith or any conscious design to evade the limitations imposed by the statute and the First Amendment. We simply recognize that a dedicated religious person, teaching in a school affiliated with his or her faith and operated to inculcate its tenets, will inevitably experience great difficulty in remaining religiously neutral. Doctrines and faith are not inculcated or advanced by neutrals. With the best of intentions such a teacher would find it hard to make a total separation between secular teaching and religious doctrine. . . .

A comprehensive, discriminating, and continuing state surveillance will inevitably be required to ensure that these restrictions are obeyed and the First Amendment otherwise respected. Unlike a book, a teacher cannot be inspected once so as to determine the extent and intent of his or her personal beliefs and subjective acceptance of the limitations imposed by the First Amendment. These prophylactic contacts will involve excessive and enduring entanglement between state and church.

There is another area of entanglement in the Rhode Island program that gives concern. The statute excludes teachers employed by nonpublic schools whose average per-pupil expenditures on secular education equal or exceed the comparable figures for public schools. In the event that the total expenditures of an otherwise eligible school exceed this norm, the program requires the government to examine the school's records in order to determine how much of the total expenditures is attributable to secular education and how much to religious activity. This kind of state inspection and evaluation of the religious content of a religious organization is fraught with the sort of entanglement that the Constitution forbids. It is a relationship pregnant with dangers of excessive government direction of church schools and hence of churches. The Court noted "the hazards of government supporting churches" . . ., and we cannot ignore here the danger that pervasive modern governmental power will ultimately intrude on religion and thus conflict with the Religion Clauses.

### (b) *Pennsylvania program*

The Pennsylvania statute also provides state aid to church-related schools for teachers' salaries. The complaint describes an educational system that is very similar to the one existing in Rhode Island. According to the allegations, the church-related elementary and secondary schools are controlled by religious organizations, have the purpose of propagating and promoting a particular religious faith, and conduct their operations to fulfill that purpose. Since this complaint was dismissed for failure to state a claim for relief, we must accept these allegations as true for purposes of our review.

As we noted earlier, the very restrictions and surveillance necessary to ensure that teachers play a strictly nonideological role give rise to entanglements between church and state. The Pennsylvania statute, like that of Rhode Island, fosters this kind of relationship. Reimbursement is not only limited to courses offered in the public schools and materials approved by state officials, but the statute excludes "any subject matter expressing religious teaching, or the morals or forms of worship of any sect." In addition, schools seeking reimbursement must maintain accounting procedures that require the State to establish the cost of the secular as distinguished from the religious instruction.

The Pennsylvania statute, moreover, has the further defect of providing state financial aid directly to the church-related school. This factor distinguishes both Everson and Allen, for in both those cases the Court was careful to point out that state aid was provided to the student and his parents—not to the church-related school. . . .
. . ., the Court warned of the dangers of direct payments to religious organizations:

"Obviously a direct money subsidy would be a relationship pregnant with involvement and, as with most governmental grant programs, could encompass sustained and detailed administrative relationships for enforcement of statutory or administrative standards. . . ."

The history of government grants of a continuing cash subsidy indicates that such programs have almost always been accompanied by varying measures of control and surveillance. The government cash grants before us now provide no basis for predicting that comprehensive measures of surveillance and controls will not follow. In particular the government's post-audit power to inspect and evaluate a church-related school's financial records and to determine which expenditures are religious and which are secular creates an intimate and continuing relationship between church and state.

A broader base of entanglement of yet a different character is presented by the divisive political potential of these state programs. In a community where such a large number of pupils are served by church-related schools, it can be assumed that state assistance will entail considerable political activity. Partisans of parochial schools, understandably concerned with rising costs and sincerely dedicated to both the religious and secular educational missions of their schools, will inevitably champion this cause and promote political action to achieve their goals. Those who oppose state aid, whether for constitutional, religious, or fiscal reasons, will inevitably respond and employ all of the usual political campaign techniques to prevail. Candidates will be forced to declare and voters to choose. It would be unrealistic to ignore the fact that many people confronted with issues of this kind will find their votes aligned with their faith.

Ordinarily political debate and division, however vigorous or even partisan, are normal and healthy manifestations of our democratic system of government, but political division along religious lines was one of the principal evils against which the First Amendment was intended to protect. . . . The potential divisiveness of such conflict is a threat to the normal political process. . . . To have States or communities divide on the issues presented by state aid to parochial schools would tend to confuse and obscure other issues of great urgency. We have an expanding array of vexing issues, local and national, domestic and international, to debate and divide on. It conflicts with our whole history and tradition to permit questions of the Religion Clauses to assume such importance in our legislatures and in our elections that they could divert attention from the myriad issues and problems that confront every level of government. The highways of church and state relationships are not likely to be one-way streets, and the Constitution's authors sought to protect religious worship from the pervasive power of government. The history of many countries attests to the hazards of religion's intruding into the political arena or of political power intruding into the legitimate and free exercise of religious belief. . . .

The potential for political divisiveness related to religious belief and practice is aggravated in these two statutory programs by the need for continuing annual appropriations and the likelihood of larger and larger demands as costs and populations grow. . . .

In Walz it was argued that a tax exemption for places of religious worship would prove to be the first step in an inevitable progression leading to the establishment of state churches and state religion. That claim could not stand up against more than 200 years of virtually universal practice imbedded in our colonial experience and continuing into the present.

The progression argument, however, is more persuasive here. We have no long history of state aid to church-related educational institutions comparable to 200 years of tax exemption for churches. Indeed, the state programs before us today represent something of an innovation. We have already noted that modern governmental programs have self-perpetuating and self-expanding propensities. These internal pressures are only enhanced when the schemes involve institutions whose legitimate needs are growing and whose interests have substantial political support. Nor can we fail to see that in constitutional adjudication some steps, which when taken were thought to approach "the verge," have become the platform for yet further steps. A certain momentum develops in constitutional theory and it can be a "downhill thrust" easily set in motion but difficult to retard or stop. Development by momentum is not invariably bad; indeed, it is the way the common law has grown, but it is a force to be recognized and reckoned with. The dangers are increased by the difficulty of perceiving in advance exactly where the "verge" of the precipice lies. As well as constituting an independent evil against which the Religion Clauses were intended to protect, involvement or entanglement between government and religion serves as a warning signal.

Finally, nothing we have said can be construed to disparage the role of church-related elementary and secondary schools in our national life. Their contribution has been and is enormous. Nor do we ignore their economic plight in a period of rising costs and expanding need. Taxpayers generally have been spared vast sums by the maintenance of these educational institutions by religious organizations, largely by the gifts of faithful adherents.

The merit and benefits of these schools, however, are not the issue before us in these cases. The sole question is whether state aid to these schools can be squared with the dictates of the Religion Clauses. Under our system the choice has been made that government is to be entirely excluded from the area of religious instruction and churches excluded from the affairs of government. The Constitution decrees that religion must be a private matter for the individual, the family, and the institutions of private choice, and that while some involvement and entanglement are inevitable, lines must be drawn. . . .

Mr. Justice DOUGLAS, whom Mr. Justice BLACK joins, concurring. . . .

The analysis of the constitutional objections to these two state systems of grants to parochial or sectarian schools must start with the admitted and obvious fact that the raison d'etre of parochial schools is the propagation of a religious faith. They also teach secular subjects; but they came into existence in this country because Protestant groups were perverting the public schools by using them to propagate their faith. The Catholics naturally rebelled. If schools were to be used to propagate a particular creed or religion, then Catholic ideals should also be served. Hence the advent of parochial schools.

By 1840 there were 200 Catholic parish schools in the United States. By 1964 there were 60 times as many. Today 57% of the 9,000 Catholic parishes in the country have their church schools. "[E]very diocesan chancery has its school department, and it enjoys a primacy of status." The parish schools indeed consume 40% to

65% of the parish's total income.  The parish is so "school centered"
that "[t]he school almost becomes the very reason for being."

Early in the 19th century the Protestants obtained control of the
New York school system and used it to promote reading and teaching
of the Scriptures as revealed in the King James version of the Bible.
The contests between Protestants and Catholics, often erupting into
violence including the burning of Catholic churches, are a twice-told
tale;  the Know-Nothing Party, which included in its platform "daily
Bible reading in the schools," carried three States in 1854—Massachusetts, Pennsylvania, and Delaware.  Parochial schools grew, but not
Catholic schools alone.  Other dissenting sects established their own
schools—Lutherans, Methodists, Presbyterians, and others.  But the
major force in shaping the pattern of education in this country was
the conflict between Protestants and Catholics.  The Catholics logically
argued that a public school was sectarian when it taught the King
James version of the Bible.  They therefore wanted it removed from
the public schools;  and in time they tried to get public funds for their
own parochial schools.  .   .   .

The story of conflict and dissension is long and well known.  The
result was a state of so-called equilibrium where religious instruction
was eliminated from public schools and the use of public funds to
support religious schools was deemed to be banned.

But the hydraulic pressures created by political forces and by
economic stress were great and they began to change the situation.
Laws were passed—state and federal—that dispensed public funds to
sustain religious schools and the plea was always in the educational
frame of reference: education in all sectors was needed, from languages to calculus to nuclear physics.  And it was forcefully argued
that a linguist or mathematician or physicist trained in religious
schools was just as competent as one trained in secular schools.

And so we have gradually edged into a situation where vast
amounts of public funds are supplied each year to sectarian schools.

And the argument is made that the private parochial school
system takes about $9 billion a year off the back of government—as
if that were enough to justify violating the Establishment Clause.

While the evolution of the public school system in this country
marked an escape from denominational control and was therefore
admirable as seen through the eyes of those who think like Madison
and Jefferson, it has disadvantages.  The main one is that a state
system may attempt to mold all students alike according to the views
of the dominant group and to discourage the emergence of individual
idiosyncrasies.

Sectarian education, however, does not remedy that condition.
The advantages of sectarian education relate solely to religious or

doctrinal matters.  They give the church the opportunity to indoctrinate its creed delicately and indirectly, or massively through doctrinal courses.  . . .

. . . we have never faced, until recently, the problem of policing sectarian schools.  Any surveillance to date has been minor and
has related only to the consistently unchallenged matters of accredita-
tion of the sectarian school in the State's school system.

The Rhode Island Act allows a supplementary salary to a teacher
in a sectarian school if he or she "does not teach a course in religion."

The Pennsylvania Act provides for state financing of instruction
in mathematics, modern foreign languages, physical science, and physical education, provided that the instruction in those courses "shall
not include any subject matter expressing religious teaching, or the
morals or forms of worship of any sect."

Public financial support of parochial schools puts those schools
under disabilities with which they were not previously burdened.
For  .  .  .   governmental activities relating to schools "must be
exercised consistently with federal constitutional requirements."
.   .   .

Sectarian instruction in which, of course, a State may not indulge,
can take place in a course on Shakespeare or in one on mathematics.
No matter what the curriculum offers, the question is, what is *taught*?
We deal not with evil teachers but with zealous ones who may use
any opportunity to indoctrinate a class.

It is well known that everything taught in most parochial schools
is taught with the ultimate goal of religious education in mind.  .  .  .

One can imagine what a religious zealot, as contrasted to a civil
libertarian, can do with the Reformation or with the Inquisition.
Much history can be given the gloss of a particular religion.  I would
think that policing these grants to detect sectarian instruction would
be insufferable to religious partisans and would breed division and dissension between church and state.  .  .  .

. . . In the present cases we deal with the totality of instruction destined to be sectarian, at least in part, if the religious character
of the school is to be maintained.  A school which operates to com-
mingle religion with other instruction plainly cannot completely secu-
larize its instruction.  Parochial schools, in large measure, do not
accept the assumption that secular subjects should be unrelated to
religious teaching.

Lemon [the Pennsylvania case] involves a state statute that
prescribes that courses in mathematics, modern foreign languages,
physical science, and physical education "shall not include any subject matter expressing religious teaching, or the morals or forms of
worship of any sect."  The subtleties involved in applying this stand-

ard are obvious. It places the State astride a sectarian school and gives it power to dictate what is or is not secular, what is or is not religious. I can think of no more disrupting influence apt to promote rancor and ill-will between church and state than this kind of surveillance and control. They are the very opposite of the "moderation and harmony" between church and state which Madison thought was the aim and purpose of the Establishment Clause.

The DiCenso cases have all the vices which are in Lemon, because the supplementary salary payable to the teacher is conditioned on his or her not teaching "a course in religion."

Moreover, the DiCenso cases reveal another, but related, knotty problem presented when church and state launch one of these educational programs. The Bishop of Rhode Island has a Handbook of School Regulations for the Diocese of Providence.

The school board supervises "the education, both spiritual and secular, in the parochial schools and diocesan high schools."

The superintendent is an agent of the bishop and he interprets and makes "effective state and diocesan educational directives."

The pastors visit the schools and "give their assistance in promoting spiritual and intellectual discipline."

Community supervisors "assist the teacher in the problems of instruction." . . .

These are only highlights of the handbook. But they indicate how pervasive is the religious control over the school and how remote this type of school is from the secular school. Public funds supporting that structure are used to perpetuate a doctrine and creed in innumerable and in pervasive ways. Those who man these schools are good people, zealous people, dedicated people. But they are dedicated to ideas that the Framers of our Constitution placed beyond the reach of government.

If the government closed its eyes to the manner in which these grants are actually used it would be allowing public funds to promote sectarian education. If it did not close its eyes but undertook the surveillance needed, it would, I fear, intermeddle in parochial.affairs in a way that would breed only rancor and dissension.

We have announced over and over again that the use of taxpayers' money to support parochial schools violates the First Amendment, applicable to the States by virtue of the Fourteenth. . . .

Yet in spite of this long and consistent history there are those who have the courage to announce that a State may nonetheless finance the *secular* part of a sectarian school's educational program. That, however, makes a grave constitutional decision turn merely on cost accounting and bookkeeping entries. A history class, a literature class, or a science class in a parochial school is not a separate institute; it is part of the organic whole which the State subsidizes. The funds are used in these cases to pay or help pay the salaries of teachers in parochial schools; and the presence of teachers is critical to the essential purpose of the parochial school, viz., to advance the religious endeavors of the particular church. It matters not that the teacher receiving taxpayers' money only teaches religion a fraction of the time. Nor does it matter that he or she teaches no religion. The school is an organism living on one budget. What the taxpayers give for salaries of those who teach only the humanities or science without any trace of proseletyzing enables the school to use all of its own funds for religious training. As Judge Coffin said, 316 F.Supp. 112, 120, we would be blind to realities if we let "sophisticated bookkeeping" sanction "almost total subsidy of a religious institution by assigning the bulk of the institution's expenses to 'secular' activities." And sophisticated attempts to avoid the Constitution are just as invalid as simple-minded ones. . . .

In my view the taxpayers' forced contribution to the parochial schools in the present cases violates the First Amendment.

Mr. Justice BRENNAN. . . .

I continue to adhere to the view that to give concrete meaning to the Establishment Clause "the line we must draw between the permissible and the impermissible is one which accords with history and faithfully reflects the understanding of the Founding Fathers. It is a line which the Court has consistently sought to mark in its decisions expounding the religious guarantees of the First Amendment. What the Framers meant to foreclose, and what our decisions under the Establishment Clause have forbidden, are those involvements of religious with secular institutions which (a) serve the essentially religious activities of religious institutions; (b) employ the organs of government for essentially religious purposes; or (c) use essentially religious means to serve governmental ends, where secular means would suffice. When the secular and religious institutions become involved in such a manner, there inhere in the relationship precisely those dangers—as much to church as to state—which the Framers feared would subvert religious liberty and the strength of a system of secular government." . . .

The common feature of all three statutes before us is the provision of a direct subsidy from public funds for activities carried on by sectarian educational institutions. . . .

The statutory schemes before us, however, have features not present in either the Everson or Allen schemes. For example, the reimbursement or the loan of books ended government involvement in Everson and Allen. In contrast each of the schemes here exacts a promise in some form that the subsidy will not be used to finance courses in religious subjects—promises that must be and are policed to assure compliance. Again, although the federal subsidy, similar to the Everson and Allen subsidies, is available to both public and non-public colleges and universities, the Rhode Island and Pennsylvania subsidies are restricted to nonpublic schools, and for practical purposes to Roman Catholic parochial schools. These and other features I shall mention mean for me that Everson and Allen do not control these cases. Rather, the history of public subsidy of sectarian schools, and the purposes and operation of these particular statutes must be examined to determine whether the statutes breach the Establishment Clause. . . .

Our opinion in Allen recognized that sectarian schools provide both a secular and a sectarian education. . . .

. . . I do not read Pierce or Allen as supporting the proposition that public subsidy of sectarian institution's secular training is permissible state involvement. I read them as supporting the proposition that as an identifiable set of skills and an identifiable quantum of knowledge, secular education may be effectively provided either in the religious context of parochial schools, or outside the context of religion in public schools. The State's interest in secular education may be defined broadly as an interest in ensuring that all children within its boundaries acquire a minimum level of competency in certain skills, such as reading, writing, and arithmetic, as well as a minimum amount of information and knowledge in certain subjects such as history, geography, science, literature, and law. Without such skills and knowledge, an individual will be at a severe disadvantage both in participating in democratic self-government and in earning a living in a modern industrial economy. But the State has no proper interest in prescribing the no precise forum in which such skills and knowledge are learned since acquisition of this secular education is neither incompatible with religious learning, nor is it inconsistent with or inimical to religious precepts.

When the same secular educational process occurs in both public and sectarian schools, Allen held that the State could provide secular textbooks for use in that process to students in both public and sectarian schools. Of course, the State could not provide textbooks giving religious instruction. But since the textbooks involved in Allen would, at least in theory, be limited to secular education, no aid to sectarian instruction was involved.

More important, since the textbooks in Allen had been previously provided by the parents, and not the schools, . . . no aid to the institution was involved. Rather, as in the case of the bus transportation in Everson, the general program of providing all children in the State with free secular textbooks assisted all parents in schooling their children. And as in Everson, there was undoubtedly the possibility that some parents might not have been able to exercise their constitutional right to send their children to parochial school if the parents were compelled themselves to pay for textbooks. However, as my Brother Black wrote for the Court in Everson, "[C]utting off church schools from these [general] services, so separate and so indisputably marked off from the religious function, would make it far more difficult for the schools to operate. But such is obviously not the purpose of the First Amendment. That Amendment requires the state to be a neutral in its relations with groups of religious believers and non-believers; it does not require the state to be their adversary. State power is no more to be used so as to handicap religions than it is to favor them." . . .

Allen, in my view, simply sustained a statute in which the State was "neutral in its relations with groups of religious believers and nonbelievers. The only context in which the Court in Allen employed the distinction between secular and religious in a parochial school was to reach its conclusion that the textbooks that the State was providing could and would be secular. The present cases, however, involve direct subsidies of tax monies to the schools themselves and we cannot blink the fact that the secular education those schools provide goes hand in hand with the religious mission that is the only reason for the schools' existence. Within the institution, the two are inextricably intertwined. . . .

I conclude that, in using sectarian institutions to further goals in secular education, the three statutes do violence to the principle that "government may not employ religious means to serve secular interests, however legitimate they may be, at least without the clearest demonstration that nonreligious means will not suffice." . . .

I, therefore, agree that the two state statutes that focus primarily on providing public funds to sectarian schools are unconstitutional. . . .

Mr. Justice WHITE, concurring. . . .

. . . , while the decision of the Court is legitimate, it is surely quite wrong in overturning the Pennsylvania and Rhode Island statutes on the ground that they amount to an establishment of religion forbidden by the First Amendment.

No one in these cases questions the constitutional right of parents to satisfy their state-imposed obligation to educate their children by sending them to private schools, sectarian or otherwise, as long as those schools meet minimum standards established for secular instruction. The States are not only permitted, but required by the Constitution, to free students attending private schools from any public school attendance obligation. Pierce v. Society of Sisters. . . . The States may also furnish transportation for students, Everson, . . . and books for teaching secular subjects to students attending parochial and other private as well as public schools, Board of

Education v. Allen  .   .   . ;  we have also upheld arrangements whereby students are released from public school classes so that they may attend religious instruction.  Zorach v. Clauson,  .   .   .

Our prior cases have recognized the dual role of parochial schools in American society:  they perform both religious and secular functions.  .   .   .  Our cases also recognize that legislation having a secular purpose and extending governmental assistance to sectarian schools in the performance of their secular functions does not constitute "law[s] respecting an establishment of religion" forbidden by the First Amendment merely because a secular program may incidentally benefit a church in fulfilling its religious mission.  That religion may indirectly benefit from governmental aid to the secular activities of churches does not convert that aid into an impermissible establishment of religion.  .   .   .

It is enough for me that the States  .   .   .  are financing a separable secular function of overriding importance in order to sustain the legislation here challenged.  That religion and private interests other than education may substantially benefit does not convert these laws into impermissible establishments of religion.  .   .   .

The Court  .   .   .  creates an insoluable paradox for the State and the parochial schools.  The State cannot finance secular instruction if it permits religion to be taught in the same classroom;  but if it exacts a promise that religion not be so taught—a promise the school and its teachers are quite willing and on this record able to give—and enforces it, it is then entangled in the "no entanglement" aspect of the Court's Establishment Clause jurisprudence.  .   .   .

NOTES AND QUESTIONS

1.  Note the critical finding of fact regarding K–12 parochial schools made by the U.S. District Court.  The Supreme Court accepted the District Court's conclusion "that the parochial schools constituted 'an integral part of the religious mission of the Catholic Church.'"  The Supreme Court continued saying that the "process of inculcating religious doctrine is, of course, enhanced by the impressionable age of the pupils, in primary schools particularly;" that "in short, parochial schools involve substantial religious activity and purpose" and that the "substantial religious character of these church-related schools gives rise to entangling church-state relationships of the kind the Religion Clauses sought to avoid."  Contrast the opposite factual view regarding church-related institutions of higher learning found in Tilton v. Richardson, 403 U.S. 672, 91 S.Ct. 2091, 29 L.Ed.2d 790 (1971).  The case involved constitutional issues about federal aid, in the form of construction grants, to church-related colleges and universities:  "Appellants' position depends on the validity of the proposition that religion so permeates the secular education provided by church-related colleges and universities that their religious and secular educational functions are in fact inseparable.  [The record] provides no basis for any such assumption here.  The schools were characterized by an atmosphere

of academic freedom rather than religious indoctrination.  .  .  .
Individual projects can be properly evaluated if and when challenges
arise." In Roemer v. Maryland, 426 U.S. 736, 96 S.Ct. 2337, 49 L.Ed.
2d 179 (1976), by a 5 to 4 decision, the Supreme Court sustained a
broader program of state aid to church-related colleges, but the majority could not agree on any one rationale. Thus, it appears the
Supreme Court has created a pattern of finding fewer barriers in the
Establishment Clause to state aid to church-related colleges and universities than to K–12 parochial schools.

2.  Lemon identifies three types of "excessive entanglement": (1) the
continuing need for teacher surveillance; (2) the continuing need for
state inspection of school records, and (3) "the divisive political potential of these state programs." Would there be "excessive entanglement" if bus transportation, school lunches, fire extinguishers, school
nurses and secular textbooks are supplied to parochial school students?
Do Everson and Allen survive after the decision and reasoning in
Lemon?

## GOVERNMENTAL AID TO PAROCHIAL SCHOOLS
### SINCE LEMON AND TILTON

---

The Supreme Court decided five cases in 1973, four of which will
be digested here and the fifth, Norwood v. Harrison, appears with
the race relations materials. They and earlier cases are excellently
discussed in Morgan, The Establishment Clause and Sectarian Schools:
A Final Installment?, 1973 Supreme Ct.Rev. 57. In 1975, the Court
decided Meek v. Pittinger, and, in 1976, Roemer v. Maryland, supra.
Only brief digests of these cases are presented here because the issues
involved in them either have been discussed or are fully discussed in
the 1977 case of Wolman v. Walter, which involved a state's legislative response to Meek v. Pittinger and is set forth below.

---

## COMMITTEE FOR PUBLIC EDUCATION v. NYQUIST

Supreme Court of the United States, 1973.
413 U.S. 756, 93 S.Ct. 2955, 37 L.Ed.2d 948.

This was the major 1973 case, and it ruled unconstitutional New
York's tripartite program of aid to private K–12 schools: (1) direct
per-pupil money grants to non-public schools serving a high concentration of low-income families for the "maintenance and repair" of
facilities; (2) tuition reimbursements grants to non-public school parents earning less than $5,000 annually, and (3) tax credit relief to
non-public school parents in the middle incomes. The first part of
New York's program was stricken by a vote of 8 to 1, and the remainder by votes of 6 to 3. Justice White was the only dissenter on the
"maintenance and repair" provision, and was joined by Chief Justice
Burger and Justice Rehnquist on the remainder.

Justice Powell's majority opinion restated "the now well-defined three-part test" of the First Amendment, and concentrated on the part requiring a law to "have a primary effect that neither advances nor inhibits religion" in order to "pass muster under the Establishment Clause." The primary effect of the "maintenance and repair" provision "inevitably is to subsidize and advance the religious mission of sectarian schools," and therefore, advanced religion. The state was not neutral. The tuition-grants provision had been defended as a method whereby the state promoted the free exercise of religion by low-income parents. The Court rejected this argument saying that New York had "taken a step which can only be regarded as one 'advancing' religion." Thus, it, too, was stricken because of its "primary effect," although the Court indicated that state aid for transportation of students to school and police and fire protection "provided in common to all citizens" was sufficiently separate from the religious function of schools to be considered neutral, public welfare aid. There was little practical difference in effect between the tax credit provision and tuition reimbursements. But the Court also commented that the tax credit provision carried "grave potential for entanglement in the broader sense of continuing political strife over aid to religion."

## SLOAN v. LEMON

Supreme Court of the United States, 1973.
413 U.S. 825, 93 S.Ct. 2982, 37 L.Ed.2d 939.

Sloan was an easy case for the Court after its precedential decision in Nyquist. Pennsylvania, responding to the Court's decision in Lemon, enacted a tuition reimbursement law similar to New York's except that reimbursements were authorized for all parents irrespective of their income level. The argument in support of the reimbursement program was that the program clearly would not be unconstitutional if it applied only to parents of children in non-sectarian private schools and that by extending it to parents of children attending sectarian schools, Pennsylvania was merely affording all private school parents "the equal protection of the laws." The Supreme Court rejected this argument; it was unable to see any "constitutionally significant difference" between the primary effect of this program and that of New York.

## LEVITT v. COMMITTEE FOR PUBLIC EDUCATION

Supreme Court of the United States, 1973.
413 U.S. 472, 93 S.Ct. 2814, 37 L.Ed.2d 736.

Levitt ruled another New York program unconstitutional. It authorized an annual lump-sum state reimbursement of costs incurred by non-public schools for discharging state-mandated duties such as recordkeeping and testing. The tests were prepared by non-public school teachers. Chief Justice Burger wrote the majority opinion saying that the internally-prepared tests were "an integral part of the teaching process;" that the amount of the state's "aid that will be devoted to secular functions is not identifiable and separable from aid to sectarian activities;" that a "substantial risk" exists that tests will be prepared "with an eye, unconsciously or otherwise, to inculcate students in the religious precepts of the sponsoring church;" that here the state was supporting "activities of a substantially different character from bus rides or state-provided [secular] textbooks," and that the constitution's "primary purpose or effect" test "would be irreversibly frustrated if the Establishment Clause were read as permitting a state to pay for whatever it requires a private school to do." Justices Brennan, Douglas and Marshall concurred in the result, and Justice White dissented.

---

## HUNT v. McNAIR

Supreme Court of the United States, 1973.
413 U.S. 734, 93 S.Ct. 2868, 37 L.Ed.2d 923.

This case involved state aid to higher education and it, like Tilton, passed constitutional muster, indicating that the wall separating church and state is not as high in a higher education context as in a K–12 context. South Carolina authorized a scheme whereby a private college might use the state's capacity to borrow money at low interest rates (a state has this capacity because the federal income tax law exempts from taxation interest received from state bonds). The Act created a state authority to assist higher educational institutions in issuing bonds for financing the site preparation and construction of classroom buildings and other facilities except those to be used for sectarian education or religious worship. Hunt involved an attack on the law as applied to financing the construction of a dining hall on a Baptist college campus. Justice Powell's opinion for the Court upheld the Act after applying the "purpose, effect and entanglement" tests. The purpose of the Act was secular and on its primary effect, the Court ruled: "Aid normally may be thought to have a primary effect of advancing religion when it flows to an institution in which religion is so pervasive that a substantial portion of its functions are subsumed in the religious mission or when it funds a specifically religious activity in an otherwise substantially secular setting." But, here, religion was not pervasive. The college had no religious tests for faculty or for its student body which was about 60% Baptist, about equal to the number of Baptists in the surrounding community. The "entanglement" test gave the Court the most trouble because the state's Authority had rights of continuing inspection of projects and of participating in management decisions if, in the future, the college defaulted on the bonds, in which event the Authority could either foreclose on the mortgage or participate in management decisions on fees, rules and other charges. The Court said that "it may be argued that only the former would be consistent with the Establishment Clause, but we do not have that situation before us."

---

## MEEK v. PITTINGER

Supreme Court of the United States, 1975.
421 U.S. 349, 95 S.Ct. 1753, 44 L.Ed.2d 217.

This case involved Pennsylvania's new program, legislatively enacted after Lemon v. Kurtzman. Basically, this program also failed to pass constitutional muster. It was a tripartite program as follows: (1) textbooks were to be loaned to non-public K–12 students; (2) "instructional materials and equipment," defined as periodicals, photographs, maps, charts, sound recordings, films, and projection, recording and laboratory equipment, were to be "loaned" to non-public schools, and (3) "auxilliary services," identified as counseling, testing, speech and hearing therapy and "such other secular, neutral and non-ideological services" that are "provided for public school children," were supplied so long as the auxilliary services were provided by public school personnel in the non-public schools.

The Court invalidated most of the Act and applied four, not three, tests: (1) "secular legislative purpose;" (2) "primary effect;" (3) "excessive [continuing administrative] entanglement," and (4) "divisive political potential." The portions ruled unconstitutional carried a vote of 6 to 3. Justices Stewart, Blackmun, Powell, Brennan, Douglas and Marshall joined to rule two parts (the "instructional materials" and "auxilliary services" components) of the program unconstitutional. Justice Stewart wrote the opinion for the Court and was joined by Blackmun and Powell throughout. He emphasized that the "instructional material and equipment" loans had the "unconstitutional [primary] effect of advancing religion because of the predominantly religious character of the schools" benefiting from the state aid. In striking the "auxilliary services" provision, he focused on the "entanglement" and "political divisiveness" tests. Justices Brennan, Douglas, and Marshall emphasized the "political divisiveness" factor in a separate concurring opinion, and voted against the constitutionality of all three components of the program. Justices Rehnquist, White and Chief Justice Burger dissented from the two rulings of unconstitutionality, indicating that they thought the Court had gone beyond "neutrality" and had placed "its weight on the side of those who believe that our society as a whole should be a purely secular one." But, they joined with Justices Stewart, Powell and Blackmun, making a majority of six, to uphold the textbook loan provision. In doing so, the six Justices applied none of the tests of the Establishment Clause, but relied instead solely on precedent finding

Pennsylvania's program "constitutionally indistinguishable from the New York textbook loan program upheld in Board of Education v. Allen," supra.  Justices Brennan, Douglas and Marshall dissented from this third ruling stating that the Court had ignored the "political divisiveness" test which would have invalidated the textbook loan program.

Just as the Lemon case in 1971 created circumstances leading to a state legislative response which came before the Court in 1975 in Meek v. Pittinger, so, too, did the Court's decision in Meek create circumstances that led to a state's legislative response which, in turn, came before the Court in 1977 in Wolman v. Walter, printed below.

———

## WOLMAN v. WALTER

Supreme Court of the United States, 1977.
433 U.S. 229, 97 S.Ct. 2593, 53 L.Ed.2d 714.

[After Meek v. Pittinger, and in "an attempt to conform to the teachings of that decision," Ohio enacted a law authorizing "the State to provide nonpublic school pupils with books, instructional materials and equipment, standardized testing and scoring, diagnostic services, therapeutic services, and field trip transportation."  The Ohio legislature made an "initial biennial appropriation . . . for implementation of the statute . . . of $88,800,000."  The money was paid to the state's public school districts.  They, in turn, disbursed it, "and the amount expended per pupil in nonpublic schools may not exceed the amount expended per pupil in the public schools."  All but 29 of Ohio's 720 nonpublic schools were sectarian, with "more than 96% of the nonpublic enrollment attended sectarian schools, and more than 92% attended Catholic schools."  The U. S. District Court ruled that "although the stipulations of the parties evidence several significant points of distinction, the character of these schools is substantially comparable to that of the schools involved in Lemon v. Kurtzman."

The Supreme Court struck down some provisions of Ohio's law and sustained others, but the opinions of the Justices differed sharply, ranging along a broad spectrum.  On one hand Justice Brennan would have ruled the entire Ohio program unconstitutional, but on the other hand Justices White and Rehnquist would have upheld Ohio's entire package.  The parts ruled unconstitutional were invalidated by votes of 6 to 3 and 5 to 4 divisions.  The not unconstitutional parts of the program were sustained by votes ranging from 6 to 3 to 8 to 1.  Mr. Justice Blackmun summarized the Court's result as: "we hold constitutional those portions of the Ohio statute authorizing the State to provide nonpublic school pupils with books, standardized testing and scoring, diagnostic services, and therapeutic and remedial services. We hold unconstitutional those portions relating to instructional materials and equipment and field trip services."]

Mr. Justice BLACKMUN delivered the opinion of the Court (Parts I, V, VI, VII, and VIII), together with an opinion (Parts II, III, and IV), in which The Chief Justice, Mr. Justice STEWART, and Mr. Justice POWELL joined. . . .

## II.

The mode of analysis for Establishment Clause questions is defined by the three-part test that has emerged from the Court's decisions. In order to pass muster, a statute must have a secular legislative purpose, must have a principal or primary effect that neither advances nor inhibits religion, and must not foster an excessive government entanglement with religion.

In the present case we have no difficulty with the first prong of this three-part test. We are satisfied that the challenged statute reflects Ohio's legitimate interest in protecting the health of its youth and in providing a fertile educational environment for all the school-children of the State. As is usual in our cases, the analytical difficulty has to do with the effect and entanglement criteria.

We have acknowledged before, and we do so again here, that the wall of separation that must be maintained between church and state "is a blurred, indistinct, and variable barrier depending on all the circumstances of a particular relationship." Nonetheless, the Court's numerous precedents "have become firmly rooted," and now provide substantial guidance. We therefore turn to the task of applying the rules derived from our decisions to the respective provisions of the statute at issue.

## III.   TEXTBOOKS

The parties' stipulations reflect operation of the textbook program in accord with the dictates of the statute. In addition, it was stipulated:

> "The secular textbooks used in nonpublic schools will be the same as the textbooks used in the public schools of the state. Common suppliers will be used to supply books to both public and nonpublic school pupils."

> "Textbooks, including book substitutes, provided under this Act shall be limited to books, reusable workbooks, or manuals, whether bound or in looseleaf form, intended for use as a principal source of study material for a given class or group of students, a copy of which is expected to be available for the individual use of each pupil in such class or group."

This system for the loan of textbooks to individual students bears a striking resemblance to the systems approved in Board of Education v. Allen, and in Meek v. Pittenger . . . [A]ppellants urge that we overrule *Allen* and *Meek*. This we decline to do. Accordingly, we conclude that [the textbook loan program] is constitutional.

## IV.   TESTING AND SCORING

Section 3317.06 authorizes expenditure of funds:

> "(J) To supply for use by pupils attending nonpublic schools within the district such standardized tests and scoring services as are in use in the public schools of the state."

These tests "are used to measure the progress of students in secular subjects." Nonpublic school personnel are not involved in either the drafting or scoring of the tests. The statute does not authorize any payment to nonpublic school personnel for the costs of administering the tests.

In *Levitt* this Court invalidated a New York statutory scheme for reimbursement of church-sponsored schools for the expenses of teacher-prepared testing. The reasoning behind that decision was straightforward. The system was held unconstitutional because "no means are available, to assure that internally prepared tests are free of religious instruction."

There is no question that the State has a substantial and legitimate interest in insuring that its youth receive an adequate secular education. The State may require that schools that are utilized to fulfill the State's compulsory-education requirement meet certain standards of instruction, *Allen*, and may examine both teachers and pupils to ensure that the State's legitimate interest is being fulfilled. Under the section at issue, the State provides both the schools and the school district with the means of ensuring that the minimum standards are met. The nonpublic school does not control the content of the test or its result. This serves to prevent the use of the test as a part of religious teaching, and thus avoids that kind of direct aid to religion found present in *Levitt*. Similarly, the inability of the school to control the test eliminates the need for the supervision that gives rise to excessive entanglement. We therefore agree with the District Court's conclusion that § 3317.06(J) is constitutional.

## V.   DIAGNOSTIC SERVICES

Section 3317.06 authorizes expenditures of funds:

> "(D) To provide speech and hearing diagnostic services to pupils attending nonpublic schools within the district. Such service shall be provided in the nonpublic school attended by the pupil receiving the service.

"(F) To provide diagnostic psychological services to pupils attending nonpublic schools within the district. Such services shall be provided in the school attended by the pupil receiving the service."

It will be observed that these speech and hearing and psychological diagnostic services are to be provided within the nonpublic school. It is stipulated, however, that the personnel (with the exception of physicians) who perform the services are employees of the local board of education; that physicians may be hired on a contract basis; that the purpose of these services is to determine the pupil's deficiency or need of assistance; and that treatment of any defect so found would take place off the nonpublic school premises.

Appellants asserts that the funding of these services is constitutionally impermissible. They argue that the speech and hearing staff might engage in unrestricted conversation with the pupil and, on occasion, might fail to separate religious instruction from secular responsibilities. They further assert that the communication between the psychological diagnostician and the pupil will provide an impermissible opportunity for the intrusion of religious influence.

The District Court found these dangers so insubstantial as not to render the statute unconstitutional. We agree. This Court's decisions contain a common thread to the effect that the provision of health services to all schoolchildren—public and nonpublic—does not have the primary effect of aiding religion. In Lemon v. Kurtzman, the Court stated:

"Our decisions from *Everson* to *Allen* have permitted the States to provide church-related schools with secular, neutral, or nonideological services, facilities, or materials. Bus transportation, school lunches, *public health services,* and secular textbooks supplied in common to all students were not thought to offend the Establishment Clause."

The reason for considering diagnostic services to be different from teaching or counseling is readily apparent. First, diagnostic services, unlike teaching or counseling, have little or no educational content and are not closely associated with the educational mission of the nonpublic school. Accordingly, any pressure on the public diagnostician to allow the intrusion of sectarian views is greatly reduced. Second, the diagnostician has only limited contact with the child, and that contact involves chiefly the use of objective and professional testing methods to detect students in need of treatment. The nature of the relationship between the diagnostician and the pupil does not provide the same opportunity for the transmission of sectarian views as attends the relationship between teacher and student or that between counselor and student.

We conclude that providing diagnostic services on the nonpublic school premises will not create an impermissible risk of the fostering of ideological views. It follows that there is no need for excessive surveillance, and there will not be impermissible entanglement. We therefore hold that §§ 3317.06(D) and (F) are constitutional.

## VI. THERAPEUTIC SERVICES

Sections 3317.06(G), (H), (I), and (K) authorize expenditures of funds for certain therapeutic, guidance, and remedial services for students who have been identified as having a need for specialized attention. Personnel providing the services must be employees of the local board of education or under contract with the State Department of Health. The services are to be performed only in public schools, in public centers, or in mobile units located off the nonpublic school premises. The parties have stipulated: "The determination as to whether these programs would be offered in the public school, public center, or mobile unit will depend on the distance between the public and nonpublic school, the safety factors involved in travel, and the adequacy of accommodations in public schools and public centers."

Appellants concede that the provision of remedial, therapeutic, and guidance services in public schools, public centers, or mobile units is constitutional if both public and nonpublic school students are served simultaneously. Their challenge is limited to the situation where a facility is used to service only nonpublic school students. They argue that any program that isolates the sectarian pupils is impermissible because the public employee providing the service might tailor his approach to reflect and reinforce the ideological view of the sectarian school attended by the children. Such action by the employee, it is claimed, renders direct aid to the sectarian institution. Appellants express particular concern over mobile units because they perceive a danger that such a unit might operate merely as an annex of the school or schools it services.

At the outset, we note that in its present posture the case does not properly present any issue concerning the use of a public facility as an adjunct of a sectarian educational enterprise. The District Court construed the statute, as do we, to authorize services only on sites that are "neither physically nor educationally identified with the functions of the nonpublic school." Thus, the services are to be offered under circumstances that reflect their religious neutrality.

We recognize that, unlike the diagnostician, the therapist may establish a relationship with the pupil in which there might be opportunities to transmit ideological views. In *Meek* the Court acknowledged the danger that publicly employed personnel who provide services analogous to those at issue here might transmit religious instruction and advance religious beliefs in their activities. But, the Court emphasized that this danger arose from the fact that the services were performed in the pervasively sectarian atmosphere of the church-related school.  421 U.S., at 371.

The fact that a unit on a neutral site on occasion may serve only sectarian pupils does not provoke the same concerns that troubled the Court in *Meek*.  The influence on a therapist's behavior that is exerted by the fact that he serves a sectarian pupil is qualitatively different from the influence of the pervasive atmosphere of a religious institution.  The dangers perceived in *Meek* arose from the nature of the institution, not from the nature of the pupils.

Accordingly, we hold that providing therapeutic and remedial services at a neutral site off the premises of the nonpublic schools will not have the impermissible effect of advancing religion.  Neither will there be any excessive entanglement arising from supervision of public employees to insure that they maintain a neutral stance.  It can hardly be said that the supervision of public employees performing public functions on public property creates an excessive entanglement between church and state.  Sections 3317.06(G), (H), (I), and (K) are constitutional.

## VII.  INSTRUCTIONAL MATERIALS AND EQUIPMENT

Sections 3317.06(B) and (C) authorize expenditures of funds for the purchase and loan to pupils or their parents upon individual request of instructional materials and instructional equipment of the kind in use in the public schools within the district and which is "incapable of diversion to religious use."  Section 3317.06 also provides that the materials and equipment may be stored on the premises of a nonpublic school and that publicly hired personnel who administer the lending program may perform their services upon the nonpublic school premises when necessary "for efficient implementation of the lending program."

Although the exact nature of the material and equipment is not clearly revealed, the parties have stipulated: "It is expected that materials and equipment loaned to pupils or parents under the new law will be similar to such former materials and equipment except that to the extent that the law requires that materials and equipment capable of diversion to religious issues will not be supplied." Equipment provided under the predecessor statute included projectors, tape recorders, record players, maps and globes, science kits, weather forecasting charts, and the like.  The District Court, found the new statute, as now limited, constitutional because the court could not distinguish the loan of material and equipment from the textbook provisions upheld in *Meek*, and in *Allen*.

In *Meek*, however, the Court considered the constitutional validity of a direct loan to nonpublic schools of instructional material and equipment, and, despite the apparent secular nature of the goods, held the loan impermissible. Mr. Justice Stewart, in writing for the Court, stated:

> "The very purpose of many of those schools is to provide an integrated secular and religious education; the teaching process is, to a large extent, devoted to the inculcation of religious values and belief. Substantial aid to the educational function of such schools, accordingly, necessarily results in aid to the sectarian school enterprise as a whole. '[T]he secular education those schools provide goes hand in hand with the religious mission that is the only reason for the schools' existence. Within the institution, the two are inextricably intertwined.' Id., at 657 (opinion of Brennan, J.)."

Thus, even though the loan ostensibly was limited to neutral and secular instructional material and equipment, it inescapably had the primary effect of providing a direct and substantial advancement of the sectarian enterprise.

Appellees seek to avoid *Meek* by emphasizing that it involved a program of direct loans to nonpublic schools. In contrast, the material and equipment at issue under the Ohio statute are loaned to the pupil or his parent. In our view, however, it would exalt form over substance if this distinction were found to justify a result different from that in *Meek* . . . . In view of the impossibility of separating the secular education function from the sectarian, the state aid inevitably flows in part in support of the religious role of the schools.

Indeed, this conclusion is compelled by the Court's prior consideration of an analogous issue in Committee for Public Education v. Nyquist. There the Court considered, among others, a tuition reimbursement program whereby New York gave low-income parents who sent their children to nonpublic schools a direct and unrestricted cash grant of $50 to $100 per child (but no more than 50% of tuition actually paid). The State attempted to justify the program, as Ohio does here, on the basis that the aid flowed to the parents rather than to the church-related schools. The Court observed, however, that, unlike the bus program in Everson v. Board of Education, and the book program in *Allen*, there "has been no endeavor 'to guarantee the separation between secular and religious educational functions and to ensure that State financial aid supports only the former.'" The Court thus found that the grant program served to establish religion. If a grant in cash to parents is impermissible, we fail to see how a grant in kind of goods furthering the religious enterprise can fare any better. Accordingly, we hold §§ 3317.06(B) and (C) to be unconstitutional.

Field Trips

Section 3317.06 also authorizes expenditures of funds:

"(L) To provide such field trip transportation and services to nonpublic school students as are provided to public school students in the district. Schools districts may contract with commercial transportation companies for such transportation service if school district busses are unavailable."

There is no restriction on the timing of field trips; the only restriction on number lies in the parallel the statute draws to field trips provided to public school students in the district. The parties have stipulated that the trips "would consist of visits to governmental, industrial, cultural, and scientific centers designed to enrich the secular studies of students." The choice of destination, however, will be made by the nonpublic school teacher from a wide range of locations.

The District Court, held this feature to be constitutionally indistinguishable from that with which the Court was concerned in *Everson.* We do not agree. In *Everson* the Court approved a system under which a New Jersey board of education reimbursed parents for the cost of sending their children to and from school, public or parochial, by public carrier. The Court analogized the reimbursement to situations where a municipal common carrier is ordered to carry all schoolchildren at a reduced rate, or where the police force is ordered to protect all children on their way to and from school. The critical factors in these examples, as in the *Everson* reimbursement system, are that the school has no control over the expenditure of the funds and the effect of the expenditure is unrelated to the content of the education provided. Thus, the bus fare program in *Everson* passed constitutional muster because the school did not determine how often the pupil traveled between home and school—every child must make one round trip every day—and because the travel was unrelated to any aspect of the curriculum.

The Ohio situation is in sharp contrast. First, the nonpublic school controls the timing of the trips and, within a certain range, their frequency and destinations. Thus, the schools, rather than the children, truly are the recipients of the service and, as this Court has recognized, this fact alone may be sufficient to invalidate the program as impermissible direct aid. Second, although a trip may be to a location that would be of interest to those in public schools, it is the individual teacher who makes a field trip meaningful. The experience begins with the study and discussion of the place to be visited; it continues on location with the teacher pointing out items of interest and stimulating the imagination; and it ends with a discussion of the experience. The field trips are an integral part of the educational experience, and where the teacher works within and for a sectarian institution, an unacceptable risk of fostering of religion is an inevitable byproduct. In *Lemon* the Court stated:

> "We need not and do not assume that teachers in parochial schools will be guilty of bad faith or any conscious design to evade the limitations imposed by the statute and the First Amendment. We simply recognize that a dedicated religious person, teaching in a school affiliated with his or her faith and operated to inculcate its tenets, will inevitably experience great difficulty in remaining religiously neutral."

Funding of field trips, therefore, must be treated as was the funding of maps and charts in *Meek*, the funding of buildings and tuition in *Nyquist*, and the funding of teacher-prepared tests in *Levitt*; it must be declared an impermissible direct aid to sectarian education.

Moreover, the public school authorities will be unable adequately to insure secular use of the field trip funds without close supervision of the nonpublic teachers. This would create excessive entanglement:

> "A comprehensive, discriminating, and continuing state surveillance will inevitably be required to ensure that these restrictions are obeyed and the First Amendment otherwise respected. Unlike a book, a teacher cannot be inspected once so as to determine the extent and intent of his or her personal beliefs and subjective acceptance of the limitations imposed by the First Amendment. These prophylactic contacts will involve excessive and enduring entanglement between state and church."

We hold § 3317.06 (L) to be unconstitutional.

The Chief Justice dissents from Parts VII and VIII of the Court's opinion.

For the reasons stated in Mr. Justice Rehnquist's separate opinion in Meek v. Pittenger, and Mr. Justice White's dissenting opinion in *Nyquist*, Mr. Justice White and Mr. Justice Rehnquist concur in the judgment with respect to textbooks, testing and scoring, and diagnostic and therapeutic services (Parts III, IV, V and VI of the opinion) and dissent from the judgment with respect to instructional materials and equipment and field trips (Parts VII and VIII of the opinion).

Mr. Justice BRENNAN, concurring and dissenting.

I join Parts I, VII, and VIII of the Court's opinion, and the reversal of the District Court's judgment insofar as that judgment upheld the constitutionality of [Ohio's law].

I dissent however from Parts II, III, IV, V, and VI of the opinion insofar as it sustained the constitutionality of §§ 3317.06 (A), (D),

(F), (G), (H), (I), (J), and (K).  The Court holds that Ohio has managed in these respects to fashion a statute that avoids an effect or entanglement condemned by the Establishment Clause.  But "[t]he [First] Amendment nullifies sophisticated as well as simple-minded . . ." attempts to avoid its prohibitions, and, in any event, ingenuity in draftsmanship cannot obscure the fact that this subsidy to sectarian schools amounts to $88,800,000 . . . just for the initial biennium.  The Court nowhere evaluates this factor in determining the compatibility of the statute with the Establishment Clause, as that Clause requires.  Its evaluation, even after deduction of the amount appropriated to finance compels in my view the conclusion that a divisive political potential of unusual magnitude inheres in the Ohio program.  This suffices without more to require the conclusion that the Ohio statute in its entirety offends the First Amendment's prohibition against laws "respecting an establishment of religion."

Mr. Justice MARSHALL, concurring in part and dissenting in part.

I join Parts I, V, VII, and VIII of the Court's opinion.  For the reasons stated below, however, I am unable to join the remainder of the Court's opinion or its judgment upholding the constitutionality of [Ohio's law].

The Court upholds the textbook loan provision on the precedent of Board of Education v. Allen.  It also recognizes, however, that there is "a tension" between *Allen* and the reasoning of the Court in *Meek*.  I would resolve that tension by overruling *Allen*.  I am now convinced that *Allen* is largely responsible for reducing the "high and impregnable" wall between church and state erected by the First Amendment, Everson v. Board of Education, to "a blurred, indistinct, and variable barrier," incapable of performing its vital functions of protecting both church and state.

By overruling *Allen*, we would free ourselves to draw a line between acceptable and unacceptable forms of aid that would be capable of consistent application . . . .  That line, I believe, should be placed between general welfare programs that serve children in sectarian schools because the schools happen to be a convenient place to reach the programs' target populations and programs of educational assistance.  General welfare programs, in contrast to programs of educational assistance, do not provide "[s]ubstantial aid to the educational function" of schools, whether secular or sectarian, and therefore do not provide the kind of assistance to the religious mission of sectarian schools we found impermissible in *Meek*.  Moreover, because general welfare programs do not assist the sectarian functions of denominational schools, there is no reason to expect that political disputes over the merits of those programs will divide the public along religious lines.

In addition to  . . .  the textbook loan program, paragraphs (B), (C), and (L), held unconstitutional by the Court, clearly fall on the wrong side of the constitutional line I propose. Those paragraphs authorize, respectively, the loan of instructional materials and equipment and the provision of transportation for school field trips. There can be no contention that these programs provide anything other than educational assistance.

I also agree with the Court that the services authorized by paragraphs (D), (F), and (G) are constitutionally permissible. Those services are speech and hearing diagnosis, psychological diagnosis, and psychological and speech and hearing therapy. Like the medical, nursing, dental, and optometric services authorized by paragraph (E) and not challenged by appellants, these services promote the children's health and well-being, and have only an indirect and remote impact on their educational progress.

The Court upholds paragraphs (H), (I), and (K), which it groups with paragraph (G), under the rubric of "therapeutic services." I cannot agree that the services authorized by these three paragraphs should be treated like the psychological services provided by paragraph (G). Paragraph (H) authorizes the provision of guidance and counseling services. The parties stipulated that the functions to be performed by the guidance and counseling personnel would include assisting students in "developing meaningful educational and career goals," and "planning school programs of study." In addition, these personnel will discuss with parents "their children's (a) educational progress and needs, (b) course selections, (c) educational and vocational opportunities and plans, and (d) study skills." The counselors will also collect and organize information for use by parents, teachers, and students. This description makes clear that paragraph (H) authorizes services that would directly support the educational programs of sectarian schools. It is, therefore, in violation of the First Amendment.

Paragraphs (I) and (K) provide remedial services and programs for disabled children. The stipulation of the parties indicates that these paragraphs will fund specialized teachers who will both provide instruction themselves and create instructional plans for use in the students' regular classrooms. These "therapeutic services" are clearly intended to aid the sectarian schools to improve the performance of their students in the classroom. I would not treat them as if they were programs of physical or psychological therapy.

Finally, the Court upholds paragraph (J), which provides standardized tests and scoring services, on the ground that these tests are clearly nonideological and that the State has an interest in assuring that the education received by sectarian school students meets minimum standards. I do not question the legitimacy of this interest, and if Ohio required students to obtain specified scores on certain tests before being promoted or graduated, I would agree that it could administer those tests to sectarian school students to ensure that its standards were being met. The record indicates, however, only that the tests "are used to measure the progress of students in secular subjects." It contains no indication that the measurements are taken to assure compliance with state standards rather than for internal administrative purposes of the schools. To the extent that the testing is done to serve the purposes of the sectarian schools rather than the State, I would hold that its provision by the State violates the First Amendment.

Mr. Justice POWELL, concurring in part, concurring in the judgment in part, and dissenting in part.

. . . Parochial schools, quite apart from their sectarian purpose, have provided an educational alternative for millions of young Americans; they often afford wholesome competition with our public schools; and in some States they relieve substantially the tax burden incident to the operation of public schools. The State has, moreover, a legitimate interest in facilitating education of the highest quality for all children within its boundaries, whatever school their parents have chosen for them. . . . The risk of significant religious or denominational control over our democratic processes—or even of deep political division along religious lines—is remote, and when viewed against the positive contributions of sectarian schools, any such risk seems entirely tolerable in light of the continuing oversight of this Court. Our decisions have sought to establish principles that preserve the cherished safeguard of the Establishment Clause without resort to blind absolutism. If this endeavor means a loss of some analytical tidiness, then that too is entirely tolerable. Most of the Court's decision today follows in this tradition, and I join Parts I through VI of its opinion.

With respect to Part VII, I concur only in the judgment. I am not persuaded that all loans of secular instructional material and equipment "inescapably [have] the primary effect of providing a direct and substantial advancement of the sectarian enterprise."

. . . .

The Ohio statute includes some materials such as wall maps, charts, and other classroom paraphernalia for which the concept of a loan to individuals is a transparent fiction. A loan of these items is indistinguishable from forbidden "direct aid" to the sectarian institution itself, whoever the technical bailee. Since the provision makes no attempt to separate these instructional materials from others meaningfully lent to individuals, I agree with the Court that it cannot be sustained under our precedents. But I would find no constitutional defect in a properly limited provision lending to the individuals themselves only appropriate instructional materials and equipment similar to that customarily used in public schools.

I dissent as to Part VIII, concerning field trip transportation. . . . As I find this aid indistinguishable in principle from that upheld in *Everson*, supra, I would sustain the District Court's judgment approving this part of the Ohio statute.

Mr. Justice STEVENS, concurring in part and dissenting in part.

The line drawn by the Establishment Clause of the First Amendment must also have a fundamental character. It should not differentiate between direct and indirect subsidies, or between instructional materials like globes and maps on the one hand and instructional materials like textbooks on the other. For that reason, rather than the three-part test described in Part II of the plurality's opinion, I would adhere to the test enunciated for the Court by Mr. Justice Black:

> "No tax in any amount, large or small, can be levied to support any religious activities or institutions, whatever they may be called, or whatever form they may adopt to teach or practice religion." *Everson.*

Under that test, a state subsidy of sectarian schools is invalid regardless of the form it takes. The financing of buildings, field trips, instructional materials, educational tests, and schoolbooks are all equally invalid. For all give aid to the school's educational mission, which at heart is religious. On the other hand, I am not prepared to exclude the possibility, that some parts of the statute before us may be administered in a constitutional manner. The State can plainly provide public health services to children attending nonpublic schools. The diagnostic and therapeutic services described in Parts V and VI of the Court's opinion may fall into this category. Although I have some misgivings on this point, I am not prepared to hold this part of the statute invalid on its face.

This Court's efforts to improve on the *Everson* test have not proved successful. "Corrosive precedents" have left us without firm principles on which to decide these cases. As this case demonstrates, the States have been encouraged to search for new ways of achieving forbidden ends. What should be a "high and impregnable" wall between church and state, has been reduced to a " 'blurred, indistinct, and variable barrier.' " . . .

Accordingly, I dissent from Parts II, III, and IV of the plurality's opinion.

### NOTES AND QUESTIONS

1. What is the current precedential force of Allen? Can it be relied upon to control analogous situations, or is its precedential force strictly restricted to loans of secular textbooks? Must the textbooks be those used in the public schools? The Supreme Court drew a line of unconstitutionality between a state supplying secular textbooks and a state supplying other instructional materials, such as maps, to nonpublic schools. Does this line have a rational foundation? What would have

been the result in Wolman if the Court had applied the "divisive political potential" test, as urged by Justice Brennan?

2.  What has happened to the "divisive political potential" test? Mr. Justice Blackmun set forth "the three-part test" in Part II of the Court's plurality opinion. In Roemer, supra, Mr. Justice White, joined by Justice Rehnquist, rejected the "three-part test" of the Establishment Clause, and especially the "entanglement" criterion as "superfluous": "As long as there is a secular legislative purpose, and as long as the primary effect  .  .  .  is neither to advance nor inhibit religion, I see no reason [to] take the constitutional inquiry further." Apparently, Chief Justice Burger joined them in Wolman. Justice Stevens appears to have rejected the three-part test in Wolman; and Justice Brennan dissented from Part II and other portions of Blackmun's plurality opinion because it did not apply the political divisiveness test. Do these views indicate that either the "divisive political potential" test or the "excessive administrative entanglement" test is no longer part of constitutional law? State the current doctrinal tests of the constitution's prohibition on the establishment of religion.

3.  Identify carefully the types of aid that constitutionally might be supplied by a State to a nonpublic school. Can you think of any types that are new and haven't been involved in any of the cases in this section? The Packwood-Moynihan-Roth tuition tax credit bill provided a $250 federal income tax credit for tuition payments made to public and private colleges, universities and post-secondary vocational schools. The Bill also provided that in 1980 the tax credit would be raised to $500 and also made to apply to tuition payments for K–12 education. (H.R. 3946, 95th Cong., 2nd Sess.) Is any part of this Bill unconstitutional? By what set of constitutional tests should it be judged?

## THE FREE EXERCISE OF RELIGION AND SCHOOLS

———

[Reconsider Wisconsin v. Yoder, supra.]

———

## VALENT v. STATE BOARD OF EDUCATION

Superior Court of New Jersey, 1971.
114 N.J.Super. 63, 274 A.2d 832.

STAMLER, J. S. C.  .  .  .  Generally, plaintiffs [Valent] allege that a course entitled "Human Sexuality" given in the Parsippany-Troy Hills public schools requiring the attendance of their children violates the First, Ninth, Tenth and Fourteenth Amendments of the United States Constitution and Art. I, pars. 3 and 4 of the New Jersey Constitution. [Defendants moved for summary judgment.]

Collating the allegations of the verified complaint in each of its seven counts with the answers, there is but one area in which denials are found. . . . The local board does deny that the questioned course includes teachings and discussions of sexual intercourse, masturbation and contraception, contrary to religious beliefs of plaintiffs; that the course is critical of parental authority; that a *de facto* religion is created. . . .

We come through the years from 1878 to *Sherbert,* [374 U.S. 398] in 1963. A startling instruction by the United States Supreme Court for trial court conduct in "free exercise" cases appears between the lines. Mrs. Sherbert, a Seventh Day Adventist, was denied unemployment compensation because of her unwillingness to accept employment which required her to work on Saturday, a religious day. Mr. Justice Brennan, speaking for the Supreme Court, stated:

> It is basic that no showing merely of a rational relationship to some colorable state interest would suffice [to justify the denial]; in this highly sensitive constitutional area, "[o]nly the gravest abuses, endangering paramount interests, give occasion for permissible limitation." (374 U.S. at p. 406, 83 S.Ct. at p. 1795.)

Because the state had failed to carry its burden of showing clearly that an essential state interest would be jeopardized by non-compliance, Mrs. Sherbert prevailed. To put it another way, the impact of the questioned regulation upon her amounted to the loss of her living allowance, and the interest of the state was not particularly endangered. Additionally, an unquestioned, sincere religious belief was protected. . . .

The infant plaintiffs, speaking through their parents, state that they are sincere in their beliefs; that the program in "Human Sexuality" is derogatory to the beliefs that their religion requires them to entertain.

The questions to be answered in the present case are the extent of the governmental interest in promoting this program of "Human Sexuality" and whether permitting a student to be excused therefrom will detract substantially from or prevent the success of an essential program. Plaintiffs' assertion of a right of conscience is more impressive than the scorecard which was presented by the defendant local board, that 70% of the Junior Chamber of Commerce poll thought sex education was a good idea.

Defendants attempt to persuade the court that because in the recent school board elections the "pro-sex-education" candidates defeated the "anti-sex-education" candidates, an over-riding governmental interest and necessity is clearly demonstrated. This is completely unacceptable. If majority rule were to govern in matters of religion and conscience, there would be no need for the First Amendment.

The First Amendment, and particularly the "free exercise clause," was adopted to protect the one percent, one individual, one person, who is sincere in a conscientious religious conviction. . . .

The case of Epperson v. Arkansas, [supra,] the successor case to the Scopes trial, in which the Arkansas statute prohibiting the teaching of evolution was struck down, does not sustain defendants' position here.

There is nothing inherently evil from a constitutional standpoint in teaching evolution or comparative religions as historical fact. The disputed area of evolution, still disputed after all these years, is a matter of one belief in a scientific fact which does not intrude as long as other doctrine of genesis is given to the children. . . . *Epperson* does clearly state that the First Amendment mandate is absolute and "forbids alike the preference of a religious doctrine or the prohibition of theory which is deemed antagonistic to a particular dogma." . . .

In the case at bar what is taught is operational—how best to plan a future life and what conduct is acceptable—and which, according to plaintiff, is in direct conflict with or derogatory of plaintiffs' religious belief. The First Amendment stands ready, in the "free exercise" clause, to protect that person. Once it is shown that the state intrudes upon one's religious belief, the state, according to *Sherbert,* has the burden of showing an overriding need and that it has no other way to satisfy that need.

If the state can demonstrate that no satisfactory alternative exists, then the interest of the state and individual must be balanced. It may be that the individual's conscience may be fully protected by excusal from the program, or it may be that attendance is required because failure to perform the imposed duty has a harmful effect upon society generally and therefore involves a detriment to others. For example, a person may be required to take a smallpox or measles inoculation because failure to submit to injection may affect the health and welfare of many others in the community. There the state program is found to have an overriding purpose.

However, in dealing with persons who are fully consenting it may be that if an act is against religious belief and harms no other person, that person may be excused from submitting. For example, in the area of injections of penicillin and surgical procedures upon those people who practice Christian Science. It should be apparent that, in a "free exercise" case requiring a balancing approach, judicial determinations are not solely answers to questions of law on summary judgment. Facts must either be proven or stipulated and then balanced before a legal standard can be applied and judgment rendered.

The motion of defendants for summary judgment is denied. . . .

## NOTES AND QUESTIONS

1. In this case the court denied a motion for summary judgment. A motion for summary judgment is a procedure used to determine whether there is an issue of any material fact in a lawsuit, and, if not, whether any of the parties is entitled to a judgment as a matter of law without going through a trial. In ruling on a motion for summary judgment the court does not resolve factual issues; rather, it determines whether there are any factual issues the resolution of which would materially effect the outcome of a trial. The court has no discretionary power to grant a motion for summary judgment but may do so only when, after weighing all the evidence most heavily against the moving party, it can state as a matter of law that one party must prevail. The purpose of the summary judgment procedure is to expedite the judicial process by disposing of frivolous law suits. A denial of a motion for summary judgment does not mean necessarily that at a subsequent trial on the merits the opposing party will prevail. Such denial only means that the court cannot rule as a matter of law that the moving party must prevail before factual issues are resolved by the triers of fact—jury or judge.

2. How do you think this case ought to be decided when tried on the merits?

3. In Valent, religious parent-taxpayers claimed that a compulsory sex-education program violated only their individual rights under the free-exercise clause. The consequence of such a claim, if valid, is the excusal of Valent's child from class but the sex-education program continues. Could Valent have made a valid claim against the entire program under the Establishment Clause; namely, that the sex-education class aided in the establishment of the religion of Secular Humanism? Cornwell v. Board of Educ., 314 F.Supp. 340 (D.Md.1969) aff'd 428 F.2d 471 (4th Cir. 1970) certiorari denied, 400 U.S 942, 91 S.Ct. 240, 27 L.Ed.2d 246, involved a claim of establishment made against a law requiring "a comprehensive program of family life and sex education in every elementary and secondary school for all students as an integral part of the curriculum including a planned and sequential program of health education." What cases support the establishment claim of the parents? Barnette? Epperson? Abington v. Schempp? The District Court ruled in Cornwell that "the purpose and primary effect of the law is not to establish any particular religious dogma or precept, and the by-law does not directly or substantially involve the state in a religious exercise or in the favoring of religion or any particular religion. The law may be considered   .   .   .   simply as a public health measure   .   .   . .   The State's interest in the health of its children outweighs claims based on religious freedom and the right of parental control." Similar Establishment Clause claims were rejected in Citizens for Parental Rights v. San Mateo County, cited in note 5, immediately below.

4. Suppose a non-religious parent objects to his child being taught the official, school-district approved version of proper "family life" or "human sexuality," on what nonreligious grounds might he object?

Does he have any legal recourse? In Carroll v. Lucas, 39 Ohio Misc. 5, 313 N.E.2d 864, 68 O.O.2d 75 (Ct.Com.Pleas 1974) the court rejected parental claims of liability against school officials and the school district for confronting their child through assignments and sex education courses with "a side of life which her parents had sought to protect her from, in a manner tending to make it seem acceptable, and was thus causing serious emotional conflict, damage to her and damage to her relationship with her parents, in that the book [and sex education classes] confused her and put her in the middle of the antithesis between the values her parents had taught her, and the school's apparent values, interfering with the worth of her companionship and service to her parents." Although the court found no liability, it did indicate that school officials might be liable for malicious or deliberate injuries. Query: If a teacher of such a course did not teach it in accordance with the principles underlying Barnette, but as a set of doctrinal truths not to be challenged, would a court be willing to find liability against the teacher or against school officials knowing of the teacher's method, especially after Wood v. Strickland, infra?

5. Consider California's approach to the question. Is it a proper approach in your opinion? Why?

"Whenever any part of the instruction in 'health,' family life education, and sex education conflicts with the religious training and beliefs of the parent or guardian of any pupil, the pupil on written request of the parent or guardian, * * * shall be excused from part of the training which conflicts with such religious training and beliefs.

"As used in this section, 'religious training and beliefs' includes personal moral convictions." West's Ann.Educ.Code of Calif. § 51240.

A careful consideration of the problems raised by this and related statutes is found in Citizens for Parental Rights v. San Mateo County Board of Educ., 51 Cal.App.3d 1, 124 Cal.Rptr. 68 (1975), appeal dismissed, 425 U.S. 908, 96 S.Ct. 1502, 47 L.Ed.2d 759, rehearing denied 425 U.S. 1000, 96 S.Ct. 2217, 48 L.Ed.2d 825 (1976). See also, Hirschoff, Parents And The Public School Curriculum: Is There A Right To Have One's Child Excused From Objectionable Instruction? 50 Cal.L.Rev. 871 (1977).

6. Reconsider the court's decision in Archie Cude v. Arkansas, printed in Chapter II, and identify whether it was correctly decided.

## Chapter VI

# CONSTITUTIONAL FREEDOM AND GOVERNMENT CONTROLS OVER STUDENTS

### INTRODUCTION

The last three chapters focused on the First Amendment and explored the state's powers to mold its childrens' minds when they are in school. This chapter continues the exploration of a state's powers over its children when they are in school. But, the focus of this chapter is on a student's privacy and other substantive rights, on the types of procedures that the state must observe when dealing with students, and on some of the sanctions it may impose. Thus, in a significant sense, this chapter continues to explore an important related theme; i. e., the type of school governance system that may be required by the Constitution.

The doctrine of in loco parentis, by which state school officials stand in a parental relationship to students, plays a more significant role in this chapter than in previous ones, in part, because this chapter includes materials on student discipline. Blackstone's classic statement of the doctrine of in loco parentis is valid today: A parent, he wrote, "may . . . delegate part of his parental authority, during his life, to the tutor or schoolmaster of his child; who is then in loco parentis, and has such a portion of the power of the parent committed to his charge, viz. that is restraint and correction, as may be necessary to answer the purposes for which he is employed." Note that the doctrine limits the powers of a school official to do only that which "may be necessary to answer the purposes for which he is employed." The doctrine is further limited to K–12 education, and it plays no role in higher education discipline.

The doctrine presupposes a voluntary delegation of authority from parent to school official. Obviously, compulsory attendance laws vitiate this element. Moreover, school officials are agents of the government and seldom display the protective concern for a student which is an expected characteristic of a parent. This is especially true in the area of search and seizure. The school official acts as a representative of government—not as a representative of parents—when he takes a child in hand and turns him over to the police. Nevertheless, courts continue to rely on the in-loco-parentis doctrine in a public school discipline context. Furthermore, that doctrine frequently is used as a background for interpreting and supplementing state statutes, found in all states, that delegate power to school officials to make rules governing student behavior. "In making these rules school authorities are not restricted to fulfilling parental desires: the duty of public school authorities to educate and protect the children placed in their charge gives them the authority to adopt rules of conduct necessary to carry out that duty even though a parent may object to the application of a particular rule to his child." Goldstein, The Scope and Sources of School Board Authority To Regulate Student Conduct and Status: A Nonconstitutional Analysis, 117 U. of Pa.L.Rev. 373, 379 (1969). Again note that the power of school officials is limited to that power "necessary to carry out" their duties of education and of protecting children while educating them.

---

## I. PRIVACY AND OTHER SUBSTANTIVE RIGHTS— FREEDOM FROM UNREASONABLE SEARCHES AND SEIZURES

---

The Fourth Amendment has been incorporated into the Fourteenth Amendment and applies to all the States and their subdivisions. It provides: "The right of the people to be secure in their persons, houses, papers, and effects against unreasonable searches and seizures, shall not be violated, and no warrants shall issue, but upon probable cause, supported by Oath or Affirmation, and particularly describing the place to be searched, and the person or things to be seized." The Fourth Amendment is substantive in that once a search or seizure is characterized as "unreasonable," it automatically becomes prohibited as unconstitutional. Clearly, privacy is one of the values protected by the Fourth Amendment. But, the question is: by what criteria can unreasonable searches and seizures be distinguished from reasonable ones? Plainly, a search or seizure made pursuant to a valid warrant is reasonable, as is one made on the basis of voluntary consent. But many other searches are also considered "reasonable," and they are not made pursuant to consent or a warrant. But in each instance sufficient evidence of "probable cause" to search or seize must be present before it will be considered "reasonable." For example, a police officer/bank guard who has just captured a bank robber "reasonably," and without a warrant, or the robber's consent, could search the robber for concealed weapons in order to protect himself from harm and in order to protect against the robber's escape. But, if the robber were captured inside of the bank building, would it be "reasonable" for the police officer to make a warrantless search of the robber's knapsack lying on the bank's floor? Or, the robber's car parked in the bank's parking lot? Or, the robber's rented room located three miles away from the bank? "Probable cause," and hence, "reasonableness," obviously varies with the totality of the circumstances.

Generally speaking, a lower standard of "probable cause" applies when school officials search a student in the performance of their in loco parentis function.  See, e. g., Picha v. Wielgos, 410 F.Supp. 1214 (N.D. Ill.1976) and Frels, Search and Seizure In The Public Schools, 11 Houston Law Rev. 876 (1976).

---

## PEOPLE v. OVERTON

Court of Appeals, New York, 1967.

20 N.Y.2d 360, 283 N.Y.S.2d 22, 229 N.E.2d 596, vacated 393 U.S. 85, 89 S.Ct. 252, 21 L.Ed.2d 218 (1968) reinstated 24 N.Y.2d 522, 301 N.Y.S.2d 479, 249 N.E.2d 366 (1969).

KEATING, Judge.

Three detectives of the Mount Vernon Police Department having obtained a search warrant went to the Mount Vernon High School. The warrant directed a search of the persons of two students and, also, of their lockers.

The detectives presented the warrant to the vice-principal, Dr. Panitz, who sent for the two students, one of whom was the defendant, Carlos Overton.  The detectives searched them and found nothing. A subsequent search of Overton's locker, however, revealed four marijuana cigarettes.

The defendant moved to invalidate that portion of the search warrant which directed a search of his locker, on the ground that the papers were defective upon which it was based.  This motion was granted.  The court denied the motion to suppress, however, on the grounds that the vice-principal had consented to the search and that he had a right to do so.  The Appellate Term reversed and dismissed the information, holding that the consent of the vice-principal could not justify an otherwise illegal search.  The People have appealed from this order of the Appellate Term.

It is axiomatic that the protection of the Fourth Amendment is not restricted to dwellings.  A depository such as a locker or even a desk is safeguarded from unreasonable searches for evidence of a crime.

There are situations, however, where someone other than the defendant in possession of a depository may consent to what otherwise would have been an illegal search.  Such a case was United States v. Botsch, 364 F.2d 542 [2d Cir., 1966], cert. den. 386 U.S. 937, 87 S. Ct. 959, 17 L.Ed.2d 810.  In that case, the defendant had rented a shed from one Stein.  Stein retained a key to the shed and accepted deliveries on behalf of the defendant.  When the police approached Stein and informed him of their suspicion that the defendant was receiving goods obtained through fraud, Stein consented to a search of the shed.

In upholding the search, the court noted two significant factors. First, Stein had a key to the shed and, second, more than a mere land-lord-tenant relationship existed, since Stein was empowered to take deliveries on behalf of the defendant. The court also noted that Stein had a right to exculpate himself from implication in the defendant's scheme.

Considering all these factors cumulatively, the court concluded that, in this situation, Stein could give consent to the search. Thus, the search was not unreasonable in contravention of the Fourth Amendment.

Dr. Panitz, in this case, gave his consent to the search of Overton's locker. The dissenting opinion suggests, however, that Dr. Panitz' consent was not freely given, because he acted under compulsion of the invalid search warrant. If this were the case, his consent might be rendered somewhat questionable. However, Dr. Panitz testified that: "Being responsible for the order, assignment, and maintenance of the physical facilities, if *any* report were given to me by *anyone* of an article or item of the nature that does not belong there, or of an illegal nature, I would inspect the locker."

This testimony demonstrates beyond doubt that Dr. Panitz would have consented as he did regardless of the presence of the invalid search warrant.

The power of Dr. Panitz to give his consent to this search arises out of the distinct relationship between school authorities and students.

The school authorities have an obligation to maintain discipline over the students. It is recognized that when large numbers of teenagers are gathered together in such an environment, their inexperience and lack of mature judgment can often create hazards to each other. Parents, who surrender their children to this type of environment, in order that they may continue developing both intellectually and socially, have a right to expect certain safeguards.

It is in the high school years particularly that parents are justifiably concerned that their children not become accustomed to antisocial behavior, such as the use of illegal drugs. The susceptibility to suggestion of students of high school age increases the danger. Thus, it is the affirmative obligation of the school authorities to investigate any charge that a student is using or possessing narcotics and to take appropriate steps, if the charge is substantiated.

When Overton was assigned his locker, he, like all the other students at Mount Vernon High School, gave the combination to his home room teacher who, in turn, returned it to an office where it was kept on file. The students at Mount Vernon are well aware that the school authorities possess the combinations of their lockers. It appears understood that the lock and the combination are provided in order that each student may have exclusive possession of the locker vis-a-vis other students, but the student does not have such exclusivity over the locker as against the school authorities. In fact, the school issues regulations regarding what may and may not be kept in the lockers and presumably can spot check to insure compliance. The vice-principal testified that he had, on occasion, inspected the lockers of students.

Indeed, it is doubtful if a school would be properly discharging its duty of supervision over the students, if it failed to retain control over the lockers. Not only have the school authorities a right to inspect but this right becomes a duty when suspicion arises that something of an illegal nature may be secreted there. When Dr. Panitz learned of the detectives' suspicion, he was obligated to inspect the locker. This interest, together with the nonexclusive nature of the locker, empowered him to consent to the search by the officers.

Accordingly, the order of the Appellate Term should be reversed and the matter remitted to that court for consideration of the other points raised by the defendant which were not decided on the prior appeal.

BERGAN, Judge (dissenting).

The District Attorney concedes the search warrant was bad, i. e., "We acknowledge, to take as many issues out of the case as possible, that the search warrant was properly vacated". Defendant had paid for personal use of the locker and, as far as he was concerned the People also admit, a search of the locker by police without a warrant "would be invalid".

No doubt the principal of the school had a supervisory power to inspect the locker. But if an invalid warrant was used to compel him to exercise this power, and if it adversely affected the constitutional right of the defendant to be secure against unlawful search and seizure, this invalid compulsion under a bad search warrant was as much an invasion of defendant's rights as if the police, under the purported authority of the warrant, had broken the door of the locker or compelled the defendant himself to open it.

There can be no doubt, reading this record, that the principal opened the door, not because he was exercising a free supervisory control over the locker in the interest of the school program, but because he felt the invalid search warrant compelled him to do so. He affirmatively answered the question that in opening the door he was "honoring the search warrant".

Nor does United States v. Botsch, support the People in this case. There, the owner of a rented shed, having a key and requested by the tenant to deposit certain deliveries of goods in the shed, became concerned about his own involvement in a crime, and invited postal inspectors, without a warrant, to come into the premises. This has no relevance to the effect of compulsion exerted by an invalid warrant on the rights of a person affected by such compulsion.

The order should be affirmed.

VAN VOORHIS, BURKE, SCILEPPI and BREITEL, JJ., concur with KEATING, J.

BERGAN, J., dissents and votes to affirm in an opinion in which FULD, C. J., concurs.

Order of Appellate Term reversed and matter remitted to that court for further proceedings in accordance with the opinion herein.

----

## PEOPLE v. OVERTON

Court of Appeals of New York, 1969.
24 N.Y.2d 522, 301 N.Y.S.2d 479, 249 N.E.2d 366.

BURKE, Judge.  We ordered reargument in this case so that we might reconsider our initial determination   .   .   .   in light of the recent Supreme Court decision in Bumper v. North Carolina, 391 U.S. 543   .   .   .   The single issue before us is whether the search that was conducted in this case may be sustained without a warrant.

Following our decision, the Supreme Court decided Bumper v. North Carolina   .   .   .   .   Thereafter, a petition for certiorari was filed in the Supreme Court of the United States [which]   .   .   .   vacated the judgment and remanded this case for further consideration in light of the *Bumper* decision.   .   .   .

We are of the opinion that our initial decision, holding that the defendant is not entitled to suppress the cigarettes, was proper when rendered and is unaltered by the spirit, if not the language of Bumper v. North Carolina (supra).

The facts in *Bumper* illustrate the true meaning of what was written therein.  In *Bumper,* an elderly Negro woman, living in a house located in a rural area at the end of an isolated mile-long dirt road in North Carolina, was confronted by four white law enforcement officials—the County Sheriff, two deputies and a State investigator— who claimed the right to enter her premises pursuant to a search warrant.  The 66-year-old woman did not attempt to prevent them, as she meekly replied "Go ahead".  In that case, as in the present situation, the prosecutor later attempted to sustain the search on the ground of consent.  It was also argued that the search was valid because of what was uncovered.   .   .   .   The Supreme Court rejected both arguments.  In refusing to find a consent to the search, the court recited in detail the factual setting of the case and then declared that "When a law enforcement officer claims authority to search a home under a warrant, he announces that the occupant has no right to resist the search. The situation is instinct with coercion—albeit colorably lawful coercion. Where there is coercion there cannot be consent." . . . As we indicated before, it is undisputed that these words, as presented in *Bumper*, seem applicable and thus determinative here.

A close analysis of the facts in this case, however, discloses that there is lacking here even the "lawful coercion" which was found objectionable in *Bumper*. In the City of Mount Vernon, title to all school buildings and properties is in the Board of Education. The administrators of the various schools operate them as representatives of the owner. Dr. Panitz, an experienced administrator and educator, is that representative in the Mount Vernon High School. Under his direction and supervision, desks and lockers are assigned to students for their use, under predetermined conditions, one of which prohibits the storage of material which violates the law. In this case, the detectives approached him and requested his permission to speak with the defendant. With his assistance, they first questioned the defendant and after the colloquy described above—wherein the defendant indicated that there was marijuana in his locker—Dr. Panitz opened the defendant's locker. Were we to apply *Bumper* literally to this situation, we would have to conclude, as the dissenters do, that Dr. Panitz was coerced into opening the locker. Should we do so, I feel we would be extending *Bumper* far beyond its logical applicability.

Dr. Panitz was in charge of the Mount Vernon High School and it was his duty to enforce the rules and regulations which were in existence. As we earlier observed, "this right becomes a duty when suspicion arises." Dr. Panitz expressed his awareness of the duties of his position when he testified that: "Being responsible for the order, assignment, and maintenance of the physical facilities, if any report were given to me by anyone of an article or item of the nature that does not belong there, or of an illegal nature, I would inspect the locker." As the designated representative of the people of Mount Vernon, Dr. Panitz opened the locker, which was certainly not the private property of the defendant, in fulfillment of the trust and responsibility given him by the city residents through the Board of Education. Coercion is absent in this setting, having been displaced by the performance of a delegated duty. While we did state in our prior opinion that Dr. Panitz was empowered to consent to the search, in retrospect, it should be noted that this consent was equated to a nondelegable duty, which had to be performed to sustain the public trust. Contrasting the facts in this case with those in *Bumper,* it does not require extensive analysis to conclude that the "situation instinct with coercion" which characterized the plight of Bumper's 66-year-old grandmother can not be discerned where we find a public official performing a delegated duty by permitting an inspection of public property. In sum, the factual disparities render the decision in *Bumper* inapplicable.

Accordingly, upon reargument, we should adhere to this court's original decision of July 7, 1967 reversing the order of Appellate Terms.

BERGAN, Judge (dissenting). The police presented to Dr. Panitz, the school vice-principal, a search warrant. The People concede it was a bad warrant. Possessed of the warrant they searched a locker which defendant had rented and which had been assigned personally to him.

The court is again holding, as it did when the case was here before, . . . that, notwithstanding the purported authority of a bad search warrant, the search of defendant's locker was good because the principal who had general control of the school premises "consented" to the search.

No matter how the record is read, the coercive effect of this [illegal] search warrant on the principal as well as on the defendant is inescapable. Dr. Panitz himself testified that in permitting the search of defendant's locker he was "honoring the search warrant." . . .

There can be no doubt, therefore, that this was a search "in reliance upon a warrant" within the language of Bumper v. North Carolina. . . . It must equally be said of this present situation, as it was said in *Bumper*, that "the situation is instinct with coercion". . . .

This means that if the bad search warrant played an effective role in the invasion of defendant's privacy, the result is unlawful even though the vice-principal also gave his "consent" to the search and had a general authority in the school premises. . . .

Even if, on our own independent evalution of *Bumper,* we might think it quite distinguishable from the present problem, there can be no doubt that the Supreme Court saw an analogy between the cases because, in vacating the judgment of the Appellate Term entered on the remission from this court . . . it remanded the case back to New York "for further consideration in the light of" its *Bumper* decision. . . .

## NOTES AND QUESTIONS

1. Does the court in this case hold that the Fourth Amendment applies to a student's locker but that the search was reasonable, or does it hold that the Fourth Amendment does not apply to student lockers?

2. Do the majority and minority agree that the Fourth Amendment applies to the locker and that Dr. Panitz legally could have given his voluntary, uncoerced consent to search Overton's locker, but disagree on whether his consent was voluntary? If so, why should a vice-principal have the legal right voluntarily to consent to the search of a student's locker? Isn't he merely an agent of the government, seeking to carry out governmental policies and to realize governmental interests? Is this, and the government's policy against marijuana and other drugs, why Dr.

Panitz had a "duty" to open the locker? If he had a "duty" to open the locker, how could his consent have been "voluntary"? Does the in loco parentis doctrine adequately account for the vice-principal's legal right or should it have been restricted, especially to conform to the Tinker-Healy line of cases? That line of cases indicates that "students in school as well as out of school are 'persons' under our Constitution," and that "they are possessed of fundamental rights." Implicit in the Tinker-Healy model of school governance is a rejection of the authority-disciplinarian model. But, isn't that model of governance implicitly imbedded in a full-bodied doctrine of in loco parentis, which holds that school officials have plenary power over children while they are in school? Did New York's Court of Appeals apply a sweeping in-loco-parentis doctrine in order to justify the vice-principal's right voluntarily to consent to a search of Overton's locker? If so, should the court have analyzed and discussed that doctrine in light of Tinker et al., and moved New York's school governance systems closer to the pluralistic, democratic model?

3. Would the decision in this case have been different if the students had rented the lockers for $30.00 for the school year and under the school rules no one else had access to them? Does this decision apply to a teacher's desk or locker or office?

Suppose a student were wearing a jacket with marijuana cigarettes in a pocket (instead of in the locker), do the opinions hold that the principal could have consented to a search of the jacket? A student's pants pockets or purse? A faculty member's? Why or why not? Suppose the student's jacket were hanging up in the locker? Is Overton the proper way for a school to deal with the problem of marijuana and other drugs? Suppose a school had an early intervention program whereby it sought to identify potential drug abusers among its student body and to help them avoid becoming drug abusers. Could the school require a urine sample from all of its students in order to identify candidates for its program?

Suppose the principal refused to cooperate until after the police officers "ordered" him to open the locker, would the decision have been different? Why? Does the principal have a "duty" to open the locker and investigate after the police present him with uncorroborated but suspicious information? Will any "suspicion" do, or must it be supported by evidence? If so, how much evidence? Does a principal have a "duty" to frisk students? Faculty? Cf. Kansas v. Stein, 203 Kan. 638, 456 P.2d 1 (1969).

What is the legal status of a faculty member's locker, closet, desk or chests that may be in the school building? Are they subject to the rule of this case? Why or why not?

## PEOPLE v. BOWERS

Supreme Court of New York, Appellate Term, 1974.
77 Misc.2d 697, 356 N.Y.S.2d 432.

MEMORANDUM.

In this appeal by the People, defendant, a student at a high school, had moved to suppress certain evidence obtained by a school security officer. The officer had been informed by a dean of the school that a watch had been reported stolen from a student. Although no particular person was suspected, the defendant was found wearing a coat that fit the general description of the perpetrator. The defendant was taken to the dean's office where the victim stated that defendant was not the thief. Defendant was never interrogated concerning the stolen watch. However, the officer noticed a slight bulge and a brown manila envelope protruding from defendant's pants pocket. After defendant emptied his pocket pursuant to request, alleged marijuana was discovered within the envelope.

In our opinion, the evidence seized was properly excluded by the trial court.

As held by the Supreme Court of the United States in Tinker v. Des Moines, students do not shed their constitutional rights "at the school house gate". Although the Supreme Court in that case specifically addressed itself to First Amendment rights, the doctrine enunciated therein should be applicable to Fourth Amendment rights as well. This does not mean that such a doctrine is without exception. Indeed, as a general rule, a teacher, to a limited extent at least, stands *in loco parentis* to pupils under his charge. As such, the courts have held that it would not be "unreasonable or unwarranted that he [a coordinator of discipline] be permitted to search the person of a student where the school official has reasonable suspicion that narcotics may be found on the person of his juvenile charge" (People v. Jackson, 65 Misc.2d 909, 911, 319 N.Y.S.2d 731, 733, aff'd 30 N.Y. 2d 734, 333 N.Y.S.2d 167, 284 N.E.2d 153). In People v. Overton, the Court of Appeals after remand by the United States Supreme Court affirmed its prior decision which permitted a police officer to search a high school student's locker based upon the consent of a school official. The court stated:

> " . . . In summarizing the supervisory position retained by the school, Judge Keating observed, 'Not only have the school authorities a right to inspect but *this right becomes a duty when suspicion arises* that something of an illegal nature may be secreted there. When Dr. Panitz [school vice principal] learned of the detectives' suspicion, *he was obligated to inspect the locker.* This interest, together with the nonexclusive nature of the locker, empowered him to consent to the search by the officers.' "

In People v. Duka, (N.Y.L.J., March 14, 1974, p. 19, col. 7 [App. Term, 2d Dept.]) the court upheld a search by a school security officer pursuant to the direction of the principal who had reasonable suspicion. The courts have thus far limited the doctrine of *loco parentis*, including the right to search a student upon reasonable suspicion to the professional staff of the school, as in People v. Jackson, *supra*. The court, therein, applied the doctrine of *loco parentis* to a co-ordinator of discipline. It is important to note, however, that co-ordinators of discipline are faculty members of the schools in which they are employed.

School security officers although not considered peace officers within the contemplation of CPL 1.20(33) are appointed pursuant to section 434a–7.0(e) of the Administrative Code of the City of New York. These officers are appointed by the Police Commissioner at the request of the Board of Education and paid by the Board of Education but remain "subject to the orders of the commissioner and shall obey the rules and regulations of the department and conform to its general discipline and to such special regulations as may be made and shall during the term of their holding appointment possess all the powers and discharge all the duties of a peace officer while in the performance of their official duties."

It is clear that the security officer is, at least, a governmental agent clothed with the authority of a peace officer and ultimately responsible to the Police Commissioner. He was placed in the school solely for security purposes and served no educational function.

In the instant case, Taylor is a law enforcement officer and should not be equated with a teacher. People v. Brown (N.Y.L.J., December 15, 1970, p. 19, col. 2 [App.Term, 1st Dept.]), held that a security officer in a municipal hospital may act only on probable cause. It is worth noting that in the *Brown* case, the security officer, although he did not wear a uniform nor possess a badge, was still required to act only on probable cause. The court therein, stated:

> "It is, in fact, cynical to hold that the Fourth Amendment protections apply to searches by police officers but not to other agents of the City who are required to perform like governmental functions and clothed with the color of authority to make arrests. The government may not appoint agents to perform governmental functions, as here, and at the same time claim that they are immune from constitutional restrictions placed upon governmental authority."

With this in mind, it is difficult to justify attaching the doctrine of *loco parentis* to a security officer, since that is a doctrine that has, thus far, been limited to legitimate school personnel. Therefore, unlike a faculty member of a school who can search a student on the grounds of reasonable suspicion, a security officer, acting without direction of the school authorities, must premise such a search upon probable cause. Such a rule is not without logic; indeed, a member of the faculty views his role in disciplining a student in a different context than that of a security officer. The faculty member will use his experience, education, and unique relationship with the student to discipline him in such a manner as will best benefit the individual and school in general. A security officer, however, is employed for the purpose of maintaining school safety, handling disturbances and acts of crime.

Under the circumstances of the case at bar, the search of the defendant by the security officer violated the student's Fourth Amendment rights. Therefore, the evidence obtained was properly suppressed by the lower court.

Order affirmed.

## NOTES AND QUESTIONS

1. The Bowers court cited, but did not follow, People v. Jackson, 65 Misc.2d 909, 319 N.Y.S.2d 731, affirmed 30 N.Y.2d 734, 284 N.E.2d 153 (1972), which involved a "Coordinator of Discipline" who was a member of the school's teaching staff. New York's Court of Appeals approved the lower court's characterization of the Coordinator as a governmental officer who came within the in-loco-parentis doctrine, and not as a law enforcement officer who did not. On the in-loco-parentis doctrine New York's lower court stated:

"A school official, standing in loco parentis to the children entrusted to his care, has, inter alia, the long honored obligation to protect them while in his charge, so far as possible, from harmful and dangerous influences, which certainly encompasses the bringing to school by one of them of narcotics and 'works', whether for sale to other students or for administering such to himself or other students.

"What the Constitution (Fourth Amendment) forbids is not all searches and seizures, but unreasonable searches and seizures. Each search must be determined in its own setting. The Amendment, as it relates to seized property, after search, does not apply to private persons. Classifying the Coordinator as a governmental official, in his capacity and sphere of responsibility embracing the purpose and duties he is called upon to perform with respect to his charges, it would not be unreasonable or unwarranted that he be permitted to search the person of a student where the school official has reasonable suspicion that narcotics may be found on the person of his juvenile charge. Such action, of an investigatory nature, would and should be expected of him. Being justified, he would still be performing this important function, though three blocks from school, necessitated by the flight of this errant boy. As I view the incident, the Coordinator's function and responsibility went with him during the chase that took him and the boy away from the school. In loco parentis purpose did not end abruptly at the school door. The need to fulfill that purpose—including the making of a search—extended uninterruptedly beyond the school limits since the defendant chose to run away. This is a far cry from a situation not stemming from the school, without the nexus existing here. Absent that nexus, the search and seizure by the Coordinator would be unreasonable and unlawful for the obvious reason that his duties and responsibilities originate within the school."

On the general problem of searches conducted by school officials, see, Annotation, 49 A.L.R.3d 978 (1973).

2. Is the major difference between Overton and Bowers that the Bowers court took cognizance of Tinker and the Overton court did not? What role does (should) the in loco parentis doctrine play in Bowers? Overton? In Bowers would the court's decision on consent have been different if a vice-principal or a teacher, or a "Coordinator of Discipline" (a member of the teaching staff), instead of a security guard, had been involved?

3. With respect to consent, what is a description of the relevant constitutional difference between the security guard in this case and the vice-principal, Dr. Panitz, in Overton such that Dr. Panitz was constitutionally permitted to give consent in Overton but not the security guard? Did the student in Bowers give his voluntary consent for a search or was the situation like that in Bumper; i. e., "instinct with coercion—albeit colorably lawful coercion"? Why?

4. Assume you are a judge and that you must decide whether the search described below is "reasonable;" i. e., on "probable cause," and hence, without any possibility of legal liability for the searchers or whether it is unreasonable; hence, unconstitutional, with the searchers subject to legal liability. Assume further that there were only nine girls in a chemistry class and one of them removed her ring to conduct an experiment. After the experiment, the ring could not be found. (Suggested by Potts v. Wright, 357 F.Supp. 215 (E.D.Pa.1973)):

"Plaintiffs are eight female students who were subjected to a strip search on March 3, 1972, while attending Pulaski Junior High School in Chester, Pennsylvania. The search was conducted on the complaint of a fellow student that her ring was missing. The defendants are the principal and assistant principal of the school and the two police officers who responded to the school official's phone call reporting the theft of the ring.

"The complaint, the allegations of which we must accept as true for purposes of deciding these motions to dismiss, alleges that on March 3, 1972, a fourteen year old discovered while in class at Pulaski that her ring was missing. She told the principal, defendant S. Wesley Rhoades, Jr., who was in the classroom at the time. When the ring was not found after a search of the room where the girl thought she might have left the ring, the principal announced that the police would be called if the ring was not returned. The ring was not returned, and the principal and the assistant principal, Raymond J. Hagy, Jr., requested the aid of the police.

"Police officers Wright and Charleston, employees of the City of Chester Police Department, arrived at the school at one o'clock in the afternoon in response to the call from school officials.  After questioning the students, the police officers called defendant La-verne Rambo and asked that defendant Bonita Collins be sent to the school to conduct a search.  Over protests from the minor plaintiffs, policewoman Collins searched each plaintiff requiring them to strip to their bras and panties.  It is alleged that the search was carried out by the defendant Collins after threats of physical coercion were made to the plaintiffs by the defendants.  Among the threats al-legedly made was that Collins had a black belt in karate and that, therefore, plaintiffs should not cause Collins any difficulties.  After the search, which proved to be fruitless, plaintiffs were taken to their homes by members of the Chester Police Department.  It is al-leged that no search warrant had been issued to conduct the search and that there existed no probable cause for the search."

Would your answer have been different if the search had been conducted by a female vice-principal?

## STUDENT RECORDS

American schools gather, create and keep more information about their students than do the schools of any other country.  School records typically contain two types of information:  (1) a record of a pupil's activities and performance in school, and (2) data concerning a pupil's background, characteristics of his family, his out-of-school activities, his basic intellectual and personal qualities, including health, intellectual capabilities and personality dispositions plus statements about his family or other factors that affect these qualities.  Collec-tion and maintenance of this second type of information poses many constitutional concerns about privacy because students repeatedly are asked to reveal themselves or their families.  The uses to which both categories of information are put can also create severe constitutional questions.  Because of the total amount of information and the bureaucratic growth of centralized school systems in this country, there is danger that public school students in grades K–12 may be caught in a "records prison" that threatens them for life with per-sonality, intellectual, behavior, medical and other labels, many of which rest on dubious and highly questionable techniques.  (On the life-time importance of school labeling, see, C. Jenks, WHO GETS AHEAD—THE DETERMINANTS OF ECONOMIC SUCCESS IN AMERICA (1979); E. Van Allen, THE BRANDED CHILD (1964), and Kirp, Schools As Sorters: The Constitutional and Policy Im-plications Of Student Classification, 121 U. of Pa.L.Rev. 705 (1973)).  Often, assessments of their children have been withheld from parents (and children as well), and the consequences of parental ignorance can be a seriously diminished parental capacity for discharging their responsibilities in raising their children.

In 1969 the Russell Sage Foundation published a study of the record-keeping practices of 54 school districts in 29 states, ranging from major urban to rural farm school systems.  S. Wheeler (ed.), ON RECORD: FILES AND DOSSIERS IN AMERICAN LIFE, Ch. 2, "Record-Keeping In Elementary and Secondary Schools" (1969). The study showed that "most school systems keep informal teacher observation and comments regarding pupils in the permanent file even though space may not be provided on the record form;" that "errors are a normal part of every clerical procedure;" that "many, if not most, school systems have tended to deal with the recurrent controversy over standardized testing by doing everything possible to avoid calling undue attention to the school testing program;"  that with respect to "measures of character and personality development that find their way into pupil records  .  .  .  problems of standardization, accuracy and comparability of judgments and completeness of records abound," and that "school records usually contain an assortment of data concerning nonintellectual characteristics of pupils, the validity of at least some of which may be questioned, in part because of its source and in part because of the lack of adequate standards and techniques of measurement."  The study showed that 20 of the 54 school districts surveyed denied parents all access to their children's files;  14 denied them access to various parts of the files, and 8 granted access but only under certain circumstances.  On the other hand, 29 school districts granted full file access to the FBI and CIA; 23 allowed access to Juvenile Courts without any subpoena, and 14 granted full or partial access to prospective employers.  Only 4 of the 54 school districts permitted parents to challenge, delete or correct the contents of files they believed inaccurate;  in short, "most children or their parents have no choice about the kinds of records that are maintained about them and the information that goes into those records."

---

### EINHORN v. MAUS

Civ. A. No. 69–1403
United States District Court, 1969.
300 F.Supp. 1169 (E.D.Pa.).

KRAFT, District Judge.  This is a civil rights action brought by twelve minor plaintiffs and their parents to enjoin the defendant school officials from placing any notation upon the school record of any student who distributed literature or wore an arm band bearing the legend "HUMANIZE EDUCATION" at the graduation ceremonies of Springfield Township Senior High School on June 5, 1969.

Plaintiffs also seek to restrain defendants from communicating to any school, college, university, institution of higher learning or employer the fact that any student wore such an arm band or distributed such literature at the graduation ceremonies or that such students ignored an order of the school authorities not to engage in such activities.

Now before us is plaintiffs' motion for a preliminary injunction. At the hearing, the parties stipulated that for the purposes of this motion, the facts alleged in plaintiffs' complaint were to be taken as true. The Court approves the stipulation and adopts the allegations of fact in the complaint as its findings of fact.

At the hearing, the parties further stipulated that the only communication intended to be transmitted by defendants to the colleges and universities at which the minor plaintiffs hope to matriculate, respectively, in the fall is as follows:

> This letter is submitted to supplement the information we have furnished concerning _____. He/she was one of 22 seniors who wore arm bands at our Commencement Exercises *bearing the legend "Humanize Education"* as an indication of his/her concern regarding certain aspects of our educational program.

> These students wore arm bands even though they had been requested not to wear any insignia which deviated from the formal graduation attire. There was no disorder at the Commencement Exercises.

Counsel for the plaintiffs, at the hearing, agreed, in response to a question from the Court, that, if the defendants simply communicated to any such school a true factual account of what occurred at the graduation exercises, without expression of opinion as to the lawfulness or propriety of the demonstration, no constitutional invasion of plaintiffs' rights would occur. The proposed letter, supra, was first exhibited to the plaintiffs and their counsel at the hearing.

Since this is a motion for preliminary injunction it is fundamental that plaintiffs, in order to prevail, must demonstrate the likelihood of immediate, irreparable harm flowing from the defendants' proposed conduct.

An expression of opinion by students through the medium of arm bands in an orderly demonstration is constitutionally protected and cannot be circumscribed. Tinker v. Des Moines Independent Community School District. . . .

The students here demonstrated in an orderly manner and simply publicized their views upon the humanizing of education by wearing arm bands. No disciplinary action whatsoever was taken by the school officials against the students, although they had been instructed not to deviate from the formal graduation attire.

We perceive no threatened irreparable harm flowing from the proposed letter nor have the plaintiffs offered any evidence to demonstrate any likelihood thereof. School officials have the right and, we think, a duty to record and to communicate true factual information about their students to institutions of higher learning, for the purpose of giving to the latter an accurate and complete picture of applicants for admission.

The contention that the defendant school officials *may* attempt to prevent succeeding graduates from expressing their views in graduation exercises in June, 1970 or thereafter does not warrant a grant now of extraordinary relief by this Court in the form of a preliminary injunction, since the action of the school officials alleged by plaintiffs *to be anticipated* does not pose a threat of immediate irreparable harm.    What future graduating students may do or refrain from doing neither the Court nor the defendant school officials can forecast.    When such student action or inaction becomes reasonably determinable we think, in light of the present suit, that the school officials then in charge will be guided in their actions by Tinker v. Des Moines Independent Community School District, supra, and any relevant interim decisions.    If they fail so to do a remedy is not lacking.

.    .    .

## NOTES AND QUESTIONS

1.  Do you agree with the reasons of court in this case?   Can school officials place anything they want onto a student's record?   If not, why not?

2.  Do you think that private and, perhaps, public institutions of higher learning would tend to refuse admission to these plaintiffs because they are "troublemakers"?   If so, why should a person be denied admission for exercising his constitutional rights?   Could a state institution constitutionally deny admission on this ground?   If not, of what value will this information be to the institution?   How may it be used constitutionally?

3.  Is there any way, at the time of this case, that plaintiffs could have met the requirement of the court and "offered any evidence to demonstrate any likelihood" of threatened irreparable harm because of the letter?

4.  Will the practice of sending this letter deter other students in the future from exercising their First Amendment rights?   If so, what overriding justification is presented by the school district?   What did the court say?

5.  Could the Board of Education refuse to have issued the students a diploma because of their actions?

6.  Does this case apply to teachers' employment files?

7.  In Merrikan v. Cressman, 364 F.Supp. 913 (E.D.Pa.1973), plaintiffs, a junior high school student and his mother sued to enjoin a program the student was scheduled to participate in.   Only after bringing suit did school officials offer to make parental consent a prerequisite for participation in the program, but no student consent was contemplated.   The

program envisaged the collection of considerable data gathered by asking the participating students questions about their family religion, race or skin color, family composition and "whether one or both parents 'hugged and kissed me good night when I was small,' 'tell me how much they love me,' 'enjoyed talking about current events with me,' and 'make me feel unloved.' " Teachers were supposed to identify students who made "odd or unusual" remarks, got into fights or made "unusual or inappropriate" responses, but was not given any definition of these terms to guide them. The Court granted the injunction, expressing concern about confidentiality, but ruling more broadly that the "program will violate plaintiff's right to privacy inherent in the penumbras of the Bill of Rights of the United States Constitution."

After reviewing the *Merrikan* case, Senator Buckley suggested that it was "a microcosm of the problems addressed by my amendment—the violation of privacy by personal questionnaires, violation of confidentiality and abuse of personal data—with its harm to the individual—and the dangers of ill-trained persons trying to remediate the alleged personal behavior or values of students. It describes the potential harm that can result from poorly regulated testing, inadequate provisions for the safeguarding of personal information, and ill-advised or administered behavior modification programs." 120 Cong.Rec. 8067 (daily ed. May 14, 1974). "My amendment" became the Family Educational Rights and Privacy Act of 1974 which provides federal guidelines for schools for the collection and dissemination of information.

---

## SELECTIONS FROM THE FAMILY EDUCATIONAL RIGHTS AND PRIVACY ACT

20 U.S.C.A. § 1232g and h.

Pub.L. No. 93–380, § 513 (Aug. 21, 1974), adding § 438 to Part C of the General Education Provisions Act, 20 U.S.C. § 1232 (1970), as amended by Pub.L. 95–561, Title XII, § 1250 (Nov. 1, 1978), 92 Stat. 2355.

No funds shall be made available under any applicable program to any educational agency or institution which has a policy of denying, or which effectively prevents, the parents of students who are or have been in attendance at a school of such agency or at such institution, as the case may be, the right to inspect and review the education records of their children. If any material or document in the education record of a student includes information on more than one student, the parents of one of such students shall have the right to inspect and review only such part of such material or document as relates to such student or to be informed of the specific information contained in such part of such material. Each educational agency or institution shall establish appropriate procedures for the granting of a request by parents for access to the education records of their children within a reasonable period of time, but in no case more than forty-five days after the request has been made. . . . .

No funds shall be made available under any applicable program to any educational agency or institution unless the parents of students who are or have been in attendance at a school of such agency or at such institution are provided an opportunity for a hearing by such agency or institution, in accordance with regulations of the Secretary, to challenge the content of such student's education records, in order to insure that the records are not inaccurate, misleading, or otherwise in violation of the privacy or other rights of students, and to provide an opportunity for the correction or deletion of any such inaccurate, misleading, or otherwise inappropriate data contained therein and to insert into such records a written explanation of the parents respecting the content of such records.

For the purposes of this section the term "educational agency or institution" means any public or private agency or institution which is the recipient of funds under any applicable program.

For the purposes of this section, the term "education records" means  .   .   .  those records, files, documents, and other materials which—

(i) contain information directly related to a student; and

(ii) are maintained by an educational agency or institution or by a person acting for such agency or institution.

The term "education records" does not include—

(i) records of instructional, supervisory, and administrative personnel and educational personnel ancillary thereto which are in the sole possession of the maker thereof and which are not accessible or revealed to any other person except a substitute  .   .   ..

No funds shall be made available under any applicable program to any educational agency or institution which has a policy or practice of permitting the release of education records  .   .   .  of students without the written consent of their parents to any individual, agency, or organization, other than to the following—

(A) other school officials, including teachers within the educational institution or local educational agency, who have been determined by such agency or institution to have legitimate educational interests;

(B) officials of other schools or school systems in which the student seeks or intends to enroll, upon condition that the student's parents be notified of the transfer, receive a copy of the record if desired, and have an opportunity for a hearing to challenge the content of the record;

(C) authorized representatives of (i) the Comptroller General of the United States, (ii) the Secretary, (iii) an administrative head of an education agency  .  .  .  or (iv) State educational authorities  .  .  . ;

(D)  in connection with a student's application for, or receipt of, financial aid;

(E)  State and local officials or authorities to whom such information is specifically required to be reported or disclosed pursuant to State statute adopted prior to November 19, 1974;

(F)  organizations conducting studies for, or on behalf of, educational agencies or institutions for the purpose of developing, validating, or administering predictive tests, administering student aid programs, and improving instruction, if such studies are conducted in such a manner as will not permit the personal identification of students and their parents by persons other than representatives of such organizations and such information will be destroyed when no longer needed for the purpose for which it is conducted;

(G)  accrediting organizations in order to carry out their accrediting functions;

(H)  parents of a dependent student of such parents .  .  . ; and

(I)  subject to regulations of the Secretary, in connection with an emergency, appropriate persons if the knowledge of such information is necessary to protect the health or safety of the student or other persons.

Nothing in clause (E) of this paragraph shall prevent a State from further limiting the number or type of State or local officials who will continue to have access thereunder.

No funds shall be made available under any applicable program to any educational agency or institution which has a policy or practice of releasing, or providing access to, any personally identifiable information in education records other than directory information, .  .  .  unless—

(A)  there is written consent from the student's parents specifying records to be released, the reasons for such release, and to whom, and with a copy of the records to be released to the student's parents and the student if desired by the parents, or

(B)  such information is furnished in compliance with judicial order, or pursuant to any lawfully issued subpoena, upon condition that parents and the students are notified of all such orders or subpoenas in advance of the compliance therewith by the educational institution or agency.

.  .  .

Each educational agency or institution shall maintain a record, kept with the education records of each student, which will indicate all individuals   .   .   ., agencies, or organizations which have requested or obtained access to a student's education records maintained by such educational agency or institution, and which will indicate specifically the legitimate interest that each such person, agency, or organization has in obtaining this information.   Such record of access shall be available only to parents, to the school official and his assistants who are responsible for the custody of such records, and to persons or organizations authorized   .   .   .   as a means of auditing the operation of the system.

With respect to this subsection, personal information shall only be transferred to a third party on the condition that such party will not permit any other party to have access to such information without the written consent of the parents of the student.

## SURVEYS OR DATA–GATHERING ACTIVITIES; REGULATIONS

The Secretary shall adopt appropriate regulations to protect the rights of privacy of students and their families in connection with any surveys or data-gathering activities conducted, assisted, or authorized by the Secretary or an administrative head of an education agency.   Regulations established under this subsection shall include provisions controlling the use, dissemination, and protection of such data.   No survey or data-gathering activities shall be conducted by the Secretary, or an administrative head of an education agency under an applicable program, unless such activities are authorized by law.

## STUDENTS' RATHER THAN PARENTS' PERMISSION
## OR CONSENT

For the purposes of this section, whenever a student has attained eighteen years of age, or is attending an institution of postsecondary education the permission or consent required of and the rights accorded to the parents of the student shall thereafter only be required of and accorded to the student.

## INFORMING PARENTS OR STUDENTS OF RIGHTS
## UNDER THIS SECTION

No funds shall be made available under any applicable program to any educational agency or institution unless such agency or institution informs the parents of students, or the students, if they are eighteen years of age or older, or are attending an institution of postsecondary education, of the rights accorded them by this section.

## INSPECTION BY PARENTS OR GUARDIANS OF INSTRUCTIONAL MATERIAL

All instructional material, including teacher's manuals, films, tapes, or other supplementary instructional material which will be used in connection with any research or experimentation program or project shall be available for inspection by the parents or guardians of the children engaged in such program or project. For the purpose of this section "research or experimentation program or project" means any program or project in any applicable program designed to explore or develop new or unproven teaching methods or techniques.

## PSYCHIATRIC OR PSYCHOLOGICAL EXAMINATIONS, TESTING, OR TREATMENT

No student shall be required, as part of any applicable program, to submit to psychiatric examination, testing, or treatment, or psychological examination, testing, or treatment, in which the primary purpose is to reveal information concerning:

(1) political affiliations;

(2) mental and psychological problems potentially embarrassing to the student or his family;

(3) sex behavior and attitudes;

(4) illegal, anti-social, self-incriminating and demeaning behavior;

(5) critical appraisals of other individuals with whom respondents have close family relationships;

(6) legally recognized privileged and analogous relationships, such as those of lawyers, physicians, and ministers; or

(7) income (other than that required by law to determine eligibility for participation in a program or for receiving financial assistance under such program), without the prior consent of the student (if the student is an adult or emancipated minor), or in the case of unemancipated minor, without the prior written consent of the parent.

### NOTES AND QUESTIONS

1. The regulations implementing the law are found in 45 C.F.R. § 99 (1978).

2. Would Einhorn v. Maus, supra, have been decided differently if the above law had been in effect at the time of decision? Merrikan v. Cressman?

3. Are psychological and other reports of school counsellors "educational records"? If a K–12 student is having dificulties at home with his parents, can he confide in the school counsellor with the expectation that the substance of his remarks cannot be made available to his parents?

For discussion, see, Note, A Student Right of Privacy: The School Records Controversy, 6 Loyola U.L.J. 430 (1975).

4.  As a general rule, the statute requires parental consent before records of K–12 students can be seen by third parties. But there are exceptions. Should any teacher in a school have across-the-board access to any student's record, or should a teacher be required to have a "legitimate educational interest" before having access? Should a teacher be allowed to follow a policy whereby he reads all of his prospective students' files before the first day of class?

5.  Does the law prohibit the following type of cooperation? "Using federal funds, the California Council on Criminal Justice computerizes and centralizes all juvenile records of children six and older who have been identified as 'in danger of becoming delinquent.' One C.C.C.J. program trained kindergarten teachers to identify students whose social and academic profiles were similar to those of teenagers brought before the juvenile court." Comment, Protecting The Privacy Of School Children And Their Families Through The Family Educational Rights Act of 1974, 14 J.Fam.Law 255, 256 (1975).

6.  The law allows a challenge to information which is "inaccurate, misleading, or otherwise in violation of the privacy or other rights of students." Does this mean that the challenge must be limited to deleting inaccurately recorded information or can a challenge seek to delete correctly recorded but inaccurate substantive information? Can a parent seek to add information to the file? Is a parent's challenge limited to information about his child or may the parent attack inaccurate information about himself? Can he attack accurate but damaging information such as a characterization of the parent as an alcoholic?

---

## MARMO v. NEW YORK CITY BD. OF EDUCATION

New York Supreme Court, 1968.
56 Misc.2d 517, 289 N.Y.S.2d 51.

BENJAMIN BRENNER, Justice. This is a proceeding, in the nature of mandamus, in which the petitioner seeks to compel the Board of Education to allow him to inspect the names and addresses of students who were in a particular class with him at Grover Cleveland High School in the academic year 1963–64, for the purpose of allowing him to prepare a defense in a pending criminal action.

The Board opposes on the grounds that such lists are privileged and confidential, and that an administrative ruling contained in the Board's Manual of School Office Procedures and Practices states:

"No information may be given to private detectives, solicitors, collectors or investigators for mercantile agencies, and the like, seeking to trace families through the medium of school records. * * * In cases where persons seek to trace families for personal reasons or where insurance agents are trying to prevent lapse of policy, the principal may authorize the mailing of a letter to the last known address of the family."

At common law the right to inspect records of a public nature, not detrimental to the public interest, exists as to persons who have sufficient interest in the subject matter. . . . It has even been held that one's interest in public records need not be of personal concern. . . . In certain instances, however, the policy of free inspection may be superseded by statute or otherwise to preserve the confidentiality of the records sought to be inspected where confidentiality weighs more heavily in the public interest than the right to inspect . . . .

Section 51 of the General Municipal Law provides for taxpayers' actions against and inspection of public records of subdivisions of the State. In 1951 the Court of Appeals held that school districts were not within the purview of the section. . . . In 1962 the Section was amended to extend the right of inspection to the records of other "bodies corporate" possessing certain powers. . . . It is not clear whether the amendment effectively granted the right of inspection of school records, and thus the question remains whether petitioner's interest in the subject matter is sufficient under common-law rules to establish his right to the inspection . . .

It should be observed that we are dealing with a record that may be helpful in defense of a criminal prosecution. Thus, in Matter of Werfel v. Fitzgerald (supra), the Appellate Division, Second Department, said, with reference to the inspection of a record in a criminal proceeding by one not a party to the proceeding . . . :

> "Indeed, as already noted, in the one specific instance which the petitioner alleges in his petition, the paper desired was a docket book which contained an entry of importance to a client represented by the petitioner—an address of a witness whose testimony would assist in the client's defense. Based on this allegation, we think that for a reason apart from the general right to inspect public records, the petitioner was entitled to examine the docket book. *Where the defense of a person accused of a crime requires access to public records or even to records sealed from general examination, the right of inspection has a greater sanction and must be enforced* . . ." (emphasis supplied).

It would seem, therefore, that in the case at hand the right of inspection to prepare a defense in a criminal prosecution has greater sanction than the right to close the record, based on the claim of confidentiality asserted by the Board of Education. I must add that the policy of the Board of Education as enunciated in the administrative ruling quoted is sound and ordinarily should be given sanction, even if it defeat the common-law right to inspect. However, that policy must yield in situations where, as here, an individual wishes a limited inspection of a specific class roll to obtain the name and address of a fellow classmate to assist him in defending a criminal indictment. Accordingly, petitioner's motion is granted.

### NOTES AND QUESTIONS

1. Did the court follow the rule of the Board of Education? If not, did the court hold the rule invalid? What is the difference between "the common law rule" and the rule of the Board?

2. If the court held the rule of the Board of Education valid, why didn't the court follow the rule? State several other exceptions to the rule that the court would uphold. Why?

3. What would have been the decision of the court, if instead of names and addresses of students, the request had been for the reports and records of the school counselor? Why?

4. Would this case have been decided differently if the Family Educational Rights and Privacy Act had been in effect at the time of decision? Cf. Rios v. Read, 73 F.R.D. 589 (E.D.N.Y.1977).

## FREEDOM OF MARRIAGE AND PARENTHOOD

———

The U.S. Supreme Court in Loving v. Virginia, 338 U.S. 1, 87 S.Ct. 1817, 18 L.Ed.2d 1010 (1967), ruled that "the freedom to marry has long been recognized as one of the vital personal rights essential to the orderly pursuit of happiness by free men" and that "marriage is one of the 'basic civil rights of man,' fundamental to our very existence and survival." As such, it is protected by the Due Process and Equal Protection Clauses of the Fourteenth Amendment. Eleven years later, in Zablocki v. Redhail, 434 U.S. 374, 98 S.Ct. 673, 54 L.Ed.2d 618 (1978), the U.S. Supreme Court confirmed its prior decisions "that the right to marry is of fundamental importance for all individuals;" that "it would make little sense to recognize a right of privacy with respect to other matters of family life and not with respect to the decision to enter the relationship that is the foundation of the family in our society," and that only "reasonable regulations that do not significantly interfere with decisions to enter into the marital relationships may legitimately be imposed."

## CARROLLTON–FARMERS BRANCH INDEPENDENT SCHOOL DISTRICT v. KNIGHT

Court of Civil Appeals of Texas, 1967.
418 S.W.2d 535, ref. n. r. e.

FANNING, Justice. On January 13, 1967, Sallye Anne Thompson and Tex Lloyd Knight were married under a valid marriage license. Sallye Anne, a female, eighteen years of age, was under the laws of Texas authorized to marry; Tex Lloyd Knight, a male, seventeen years of age, and having the required statutory parental consent to obtain a marriage license, was also duly authorized to marry. Such marriage was in all respects a valid and lawful marriage under the laws of Texas.

At said time Sallye Anne and Tex were students at R. L. Turner High School, which high school was under the jurisdiction of appellant school district.

On January 16, 1967, Sallye Anne and Tex were suspended from school because of their marriage on January 13, 1967, based upon certain regulations of the school board.

On January 18, 1967, the judge of the 68th District Court issued a temporary restraining order directed to appellant school district and the President of its Board of Trustees, permitting appellees Sallye Anne Thompson Knight and Tex Lloyd Knight to attend school for *scholastic purposes only.* . . .

The principal question involved here is whether the trial court did or did not abuse its discretion in granting the temporary injunction under the record in this case. Involved here is the question of whether marriage alone is sufficient grounds to suspend appellee students from attendance at a public free school in Texas, for scholastic purposes only, wherein appellee students were unquestionably carried as lawful scholastics for which the State of Texas had furnished funds in accordance with the laws of Texas. . . .

In Bd. of Education of Harrodsburg, Kentucky v. Bentley, 383 S.W.2d 677, . . . a student was required to withdraw from school for a year because of marriage. The court held the regulation was invalid and stated:

"In 47 Am.Jur., Schools, § 155, it is said:

" 'However, a pupil may not be excluded from school because married, where no immorality or misconduct of the pupil is shown, nor that the welfare and discipline of the pupils of the school is injuriously affected by the presence of the married pupil.' " . . .

One of the first Texas cases dealing with married students was the case of Kissick v. Garland Independent School Dist., Tex.Civ.App.,

330 S.W.2d 708  .  .  .  (1959).  This case involved the marriage of a sixteen year old boy and a fifteen year old girl.  After his marriage Kissick was barred from further participation in athletic activities, but was allowed to continue his classroom work, pursuant to a regulation which provided that "married students or previously married students be restricted wholly to classroom work;  that they be barred from participating in athletics or other exhibitions, and that they not be permitted to hold class offices or other positions of honor."  The Dallas Court of Civil Appeals held that such regulation was reasonable in that the student was allowed to continue his classroom work.  Although the court in the Kissick case did not deal directly with complete suspension from school due to marriage, it said by way of dicta:

> "Apart from these considerations Jerry Kissick, Jr., had a *constitutional right* to attend the Garland School and take part in its functions subject to such reasonable rules and regulations as might be adopted by the School Board from time to time."  (Emphasis added.)  .  .  .

The latest Texas case dealing with aspects of the question here involved is Anderson v. Canyon Independent School Dist., by the Amarillo Court of Civil Appeals, Tex.Civ.App., 412 S.W.2d 387, no writ (1967), majority opinion by Chief Justice Denton, with Justice Northcutt dissenting.  The majority opinion held that the school board was without authority to adopt a rule that students who marry during the school term must withdraw from school for the remainder of the school year and that the board could not deny admission to the student because of the fact that she was married.  .  .  .

.  .  .  appellees were lawfully enrolled scholastics in R. L. Turner High School in appellant school district and possessed all the statutory requirements to attend said school as scholastics.  Their marriage was in all respects a legal marriage under the laws of Texas and such marriage being in all respects proper, legal and in compliance with the statutes of Texas could not be considered in any way to be against the public policy of the State of Texas.  The girl was 18 years of age and was of lawful age to marry;  the boy was 17 years of age, and had the required statutory parental consent to marry and secure a valid marriage license.

There was no evidence that either of appellees were guilty of any "incorrigible" or improper conduct in any manner.  They were suspended from school merely because they married while being students at said school.

We think the weight of authority in Texas and in the United States is to the effect that marriage alone is not a proper ground for a school district to suspend a student from attending school for scholastic purposes only.

We hold that the trial court did not abuse its discretion in granting the temporary injunction against the appellant under the record in this cause. All of appellant's points have been considered and are overruled. . . .

## DISQUALIFICATION

DAVIS, Justice. The writer honestly feels that he should disqualify himself from the decision in the above and foregoing case for the following reasons:

I was one of seven children of tenant farmers. My Mother passed away when I was only nine years of age. It was always her ambition, and it became mine, to get an education and become a lawyer. I finshed Glenwood, unaffiliated, High School when I was 18 years old. I tried to enter college, but, met with two most embarrassing situations, and could not do so. I worked as a common laborer. Finally, I decided to get married, accumulate enough wealth to attend college, get a law degree and pursue my profession. I married on October 26, 1929. The Crash of 1929 was really felt in 1930. I was a tenant farmer and, although I was plagued with my difficulties, I managed to hold my own.

When I decided it was impossible for me to attend college, I decided to get my law degree by home study. I traded two "frying size chickens and a mess of turnip greens" for my first lawbook.

The only law that I know is what I have read from the lawbooks at home (many nights I have studied all night without any sleep), and have gained from experience. In 1934, I notified the Board of Legal Examiners that I was ready to take the examination for a license. In return, I was notified that I would have to finish an "AFFILIATED HIGH SCHOOL DIPLOMA", file an application, and then wait 27 months before I would be permitted to take the Bar Exams. No one can imagine the depressed feeling that was brought upon me. I was married, then the father of two children, and was too poor to think about going to school. After much serious consideration, and a talk with Superintendent Henry McClelland and Principal John W. Avery of the Gilmer Affiliated High School, I decided to make the race for Justice of the Peace. While serving as Justice of the Peace, I would get an affiliated high school diploma. To my surprise, they told me that I could attend the school without any payment of tuition whatever, if I had the ambition and the "Guts" to do it. I made the race and was elected. I entered Gilmer High School in the fall of 1935 and received my AFFILIATED HIGH SCHOOL DIPLOMA on June 1, 1936, at which time I was 27 years old, the father of three children and had another one on the way. I did not receive my license to practice law until April 29, 1940, at which time I was 31 years old.

I have always been taught that the best education that you can get, the better off you will be. To me, there is nothing immoral, wrong, or degrading about a legal and moral marriage. Of course, no one approves of the marriage of teen-agers, unless there is a good reason. My wife and I were teen-agers when we married. The school trustees of the Gilmer Affiliated Independent School District were so proud of the fact that I was attending the school because of my ambition that they did not charge any tuition. I was permitted the same privileges that were permitted all other school children. In the beginning, it was an awful experience. To me, any Board of Trustees who would do anything to punish or delay anyone that does not do anything that is morally wrong is not thinking in the terms of the Gospel.

As a result of my being permitted to attend High School, after I was married, I have served one term in the Texas Legislature, and I am now serving my third term on the Court of Civil Appeals. Although, I am not a perfect man, I am quite proud of the experience that I have had, and am still married to a wonderful woman and we have four children of whom we are justly proud.

Where would I be today if I had not been permitted to attend a high school because of my marriage? For this reason, I disqualify myself.

### NOTES AND QUESTIONS

1.  State v. Priest, 210 La. 389, 27 So.2d 173 (1946) raised the unique question whether a state had power to compel a married 15-year old to attend school. The Louisiana Supreme Court ruled that marriage "emancipates" a minor female and releases her from all duties under the State's compulsory school attendance laws. In re State in Interest of Goodwin, 214 La. 1062, 39 So.2d 731 (1949) ruled that after the precedent established by the Priest case, a married 14-year old could not be a "truant" because she had been "irrevocably emancipated by this marriage as a matter of right."

2.  As Carrollton-Farmers indicates, courts are virtually unanimous in holding that married students cannot be excluded from the public schools simply because they are married. Although mentioned but not actually litigated in Carrollton-Farmers, do school officials have power to exclude all married pupils from participation in extracurricular activities?

---

### INDIANA HIGH SCHOOL ATHLETIC ASS'N v. RAIKE

Court of Appeals of Indiana, 2nd District, 1975.
164 Ind.App. 169, 329 N.E.2d 66.

BUCHANAN, Judge.

This is an appeal by Defendants-Appellants, Indiana High School Athletic Association (IHSAA) and Rushville Consolidated School Corporation (Rushville) from a declaratory judgment and permanent injunction prohibiting the Appellants from denying Plaintiff-Appellee Jerry W. Raike (Raike), a married high school student, from participating in Rushville's athletic and extra-curricular program, the Appellants claiming: (1) constitutionality of IHSAA's and Rushville's rules prohibiting married students from participating in athletics as violative of the equal protection clause of the U. S. and Indiana Constitutions  .  .  ..

.  .  .

On November 27, 1971, Raike was a senior in good standing enrolled in the Rushville High School in Rushville, Indiana.  On that date, Raike, being seventeen years of age, married a sixteen-year-old Rush County female and approximately two weeks later, a child was born to Mrs. Raike.  .  .  .

Prior to this marital union Raike actively participated in Rushville's athletic program, including football, wrestling and baseball.

Being aware of certain rules adopted by IHSAA and Rushville prohibiting married students from participating in athletics, Raike sought unsuccessfully prior to his marriage to avoid operation of these rules.

He then filed, on December 16, 1971, a complaint against Rushville and IHSAA seeking a Declaratory Judgment and a Temporary Restraining Order (with Affidavits).  The Temporary Restraining Order was granted the same day (*ex parte*) and on September 21, 1972, the Superior Court of Marion County, Room No. 6, made findings of fact and conclusions of law and entered a Declaratory Judgment and Permanent Injunction against IHSAA and Rushville enjoining them from enforcing their restrictive rules prohibiting married high school students from engaging in athletic competition and extra-curricular activities.  In granting injunctive relief the trial court specifically found that the rules in question violated equal protection of the laws guaranteed Raike under the Fourteenth Amendment to the Constitution of the United States and that the same rules were also violative of due process of law as guaranteed Raike by the Fourteenth Amendment of the Constitution of the United States.

The parties have stipulated that enforcement of the rules in question constitutes State action.

.  .  .

Do the Rules of Rushville and IHSAA prohibiting married high school students from participating in athletics and extra-curricular activities deny Raike equal protection of the laws as guaranteed by the Fourteenth Amendment of the U.S. Constitution?

Raike attacks these rules as being discriminatory:

*The Rushville Rule*:

> "Married students, or those who have been married, are in school chiefly to meet academic needs and they will be disqualified from participating in extra-curricular activities and Senior activities except Commencement and Baccalaureate."

*The IHSAA Rule*:

"Students who are or have been at any time married are not eligible for participating in intraschool athletic competition." . . .

The trial court found that Rushville was subject to the rules and regulations of IHSAA and evidence was introduced showing IHSAA's avowed purpose to be:

*"The purpose of this Association shall be to encourage and direct wholesome amateur athletics in the schools of Indiana.* In keeping with this purpose the Association shall regulate, supervise, and administer interscholastic athletic activities among its member schools. *All such activities shall remain an integral factor in the total secondary educational program."* . . .

High school principals, teachers, coaches and consultants testified to the reasons justifying the existence of the Rules. Their testimony may be summarized as follows:

1.  Married students need time to discharge economic and family responsibilities, and participating in athletics and extracurricular activities would interfere with these responsibilities;

2.  Teenage marriages should be discouraged so as to reduce the high percentage of divorce and school dropout rates among married students;

3.  Athletes serve as models or heroes to other students and teenage marriages are usually the result of pregnancy so that immorality is encouraged if married students participate without sanction in athletics.

4.  If married students participate in athletics, a double standard must be applied, thereby causing discipline, training and administrative problems.

5.  Unwholesome interaction between married and non-married students is prevented by avoidance of undesirable "locker room talk".

After Raike was permitted to participate in athletics as a married person, his athletic and academic career showed marked improvement. He won the sectional wrestling championship and was elected captain of the wrestling team. Similarly, in baseball Raike's batting average improved by almost 100 points from the prior year and the baseball team's record improved from the prior year.

Raike was able to maintain a B average, hold down a part-time job, engage in athletics and at the same time discharge his family responsibilities.

## CONTENTIONS OF THE PARTIES

Rushville and IHSAA assert that . . . there is neither a fundamental right nor suspect criteria presented which require "strict judicial scrutiny". The constitutionality of the Rules is supported by a rational basis and justified by the evidence under the low scrutiny standard of review.

Raike claims the Rules impair and infringe upon the fundamental right to marry and that no compelling state interest is satisfied under the strict scrutiny test. Secondly, these Rules fail to satisfy even the rational basis standard and this contention is fully supported by the evidence. . . .

Obviously a "suspect" classification is not involved (is not based on race, alienage or national origin). Not so obvious, however, is whether the Rules impinge upon a "fundamental right".

In determining a fundamental right, . . . .

. . .

. . . clouds of uncertainty surround the question of whether a married high school student can be denied the participation in athletics and extra-curricular activities solely because of marital status.

There is little doubt that the Rules affect Raike's right to marry. Regardless of his age or other circumstances he no longer can participate in athletics if he marries. Has a fundamental right . . . been violated?

> Concerning the institution of marriage, it has been said:
> "Freedom of personal choice in matters of marriage and family life is one of the liberties protected by the Due Process Clause of the Fourteenth Amendment. Loving v. Virginia, Griswold v. Connecticut, supra; Pierce v. Society of Sisters, supra; Meyer v. Nebraska, supra."

Freedom to marry has also been described as "one of the vital personal rights essential to the orderly pursuit of happiness by free men" [*Loving,* supra,] and is therefore "fundamental to our very existence and survival."

In Griswold v. Connecticut, the right to marital privacy was described as

> "lying within the zone of privacy created by several fundamental constitutional guarantees . . . . [Marriage] is an association for as noble a purpose as any involved in our prior decisions."

Justice Goldberg in his concurring opinion in *Griswold* found the right to marry a right similar in magnitude to "the fundamental rights specifically protected":

"The entire fabric of the Constitution and the purposes that clearly underlie its specific guarantees demonstrate that the rights to marital privacy and to marry and raise a family are of similar order and magnitude as the fundamental rights specifically protected.

"Although the Constitution does not speak in so many words the right of privacy in marriage, I cannot believe that it offers these fundamental rights no protection.  The fact that no particular provision of the Constitution explicitly forbids the state from disrupting the traditional relation of the family—a relation as old and as fundamental as our entire civilization—surely does not show that the government was meant to have the power to do so.  Rather  .   .   . there are fundamental personal rights such as this one, which are protected from the abridgement by the Government though not specifically mentioned in the Constitution."

Other descriptions of the rights emanating from marriage have been phrased in terms of being within the "penumbra" of the Bill of Rights or within the concept of "liberty" guaranteed by the first section of the Fourteenth Amendment, or being a "basic civil right of man."

.   .   .

High school students, with some limitations, also enjoy "the vital personal right(s)" of marriage (*Loving*), which is considered by some to rise to the level of a fundamental right.

A classification which prohibits participation in athletic competition solely because of the marital status of the high school student shackles two important rights  .   .   .. To withstand constitutional challenge, then, the classification:

"' "must be reasonable  .   .   . and must rest upon some ground of difference having a *fair and substantial relation to the object of the legislation,* so that all persons similarly circumstanced shall be treated alike." ' "

So our next task is to ascertain the objective of the Rules.  If the classification created bears a fair and substantial relation to the objective treating all persons similarly situated alike, then the classification is not violative of equal protection.

Article Two of the Constitution of IHSAA declares that:

"*The purpose* of this Association *shall be to encourage and direct wholesome amateur athletics* in the schools of Indiana. In keeping with this purpose the Association shall regulate, supervise and administer interscholastic athletic activities among its member schools."   (Emphasis supplied.)

.   .   .   we arrive at the conclusion that the objective of the
Rules is to preserve the integrity and wholesome atmosphere of amateur high school athletics by prohibiting married students from participating therein because they are bad examples and their participation interjects an unwholesome influence.  The unwholesome influence is said to result from discussion of marital intimacies and other
corrupting "locker room talk", and further, from hero worship of married students (who may or may not have engaged in premarital sex
with resultant pregnancy and forced marriage).

It is obvious that the classification used to attain the desired objective is one prohibiting *all* married high school students from participating in athletics solely on the basis of their present or previous
married status; i e., dissimilar treatment is afforded married and
unmarried students   .   .   .   all in the name of preventing married
students from exerting an unwholesome effect on high school athletics.

While the Rules as drawn may reasonably contribute in some
measure to the realization of that goal, they are unreasonable in that
the classification is not narrowly drawn—it is both over- and under-
inclusive.

The classification is over-inclusive in that it includes some married students of good moral character who would not corrupt the morality of their fellow students or contribute to an unwholesome atmosphere.

It is under-inclusive in that it includes neither unmarried high
school students who participate in athletics as team members, student
managers or trainers, and yet may engage in premarital sex nor unmarried high school students who may be of a depraved nature, all of
whom are as likely to be a corrupting influence as married high school
students.

The classification simultaneously catches too many fish in the
same net and allows others to escape.

In effect, those similarly situated are not similarly treated, and
therefor there is no fair and substantial relation between the classification and the objective sought.

.   .   .

Insofar as the classification discourages teenage marriages resulting from pregnancies, it is also defective in that it contravenes established public policy allowing teenage high school students of Raike's
age to legitimate offspring resulting from premarital sex.

The court in Romans v. Crenshaw, 354 F.Supp. 868 (S.D.Tex.
1972) put it this way:

"A rule that would punish the necessary legitimation of an
offspring [by getting married] *would* in its purblind application *effectively reward the bastardizing of the offspring*
[if marriage was not consummated]."  (Emphasis supplied.)

## THE "MARRIAGE" RULES VIEWED
## BY OTHER JURISDICTIONS

No Indiana court has considered the so-called "Marriage" rules prohibiting married students from participating in athletics and extra-curricular activities.  Other jurisdictions have treated the constitutionality of similar rules.  We find the cases are divided as to:  the result, the basis for the decision, and the date of the decision.

Prior to 1970 (the transitional period), courts appeared reluctant to intervene in disputes involving the propriety of regulations prohibiting married students from participating in extra-curricular activities:

> "It is not for the courts to be concerned with the wisdom or propriety of a [school board] resolution [prohibiting married students from participating in extra-curricular school activities] as to its social desirability, nor whether it best serves the objectives of education, nor the application to the plaintiff in his particular circumstances.  So long as the resolution is deemed by the Board of Education to serve the purpose of best promoting the objectives of a school, and the standards of eligibility are based upon uniformly applied classification which bear some reasonable relationship to the objectives, it cannot be said to be capricious, arbitrary, or unjustly discriminatory."

Starkey v. Board of Education, 14 Utah 2d 227, 381 P.2d 718, 720 (1963).

On the basis of some "reasonable relationship," courts did uphold the reasonableness and constitutionality of such rules.  [citations omitted]

Subsequent to 1970, these decisions appear not to have been followed or have been overruled. [citations omitted]

The recent trend does support our conclusion of unconstitutionality, and in our opinion, expresses "the more acceptable view at this time" and implies that courts are "beginning to develop the conception that school children are the intended beneficiaries of public education . . . not its prisoners or servants." . . .

### HOLDING

For the reasons stated the Rules are a constitutionally impermissible classification denying Raike equal protection of the laws by excluding him from athletic and other extra-curricular activities *solely* because of his marital status.  Insulating athletic competition from the baleful influence of high school students who may or may not have married in haste will not pass constitutional muster, because there is no fair and substantial relationship between such a prohibition and the desired objective of wholesomeness in interscholastic competition.

## DECISION

CONCLUSION—It is our opinion that the Rules prohibiting a married high school student from participating in athletics and extra-curricular activities do not bear a fair and substantial relation to the objective sought, and therefore deny Raike equal protection of the laws contrary to the Fourteenth Amendment of the U. S. Constitution.

————

## PERRY v. GRENADA MUNICIPAL SEPARATE SCHOOL DIST.

United States District Court, 1969.
300 F.Supp. 748 (N.D.Miss.).

ORMA R. SMITH, District Judge.   On September 18, 1967, Clydie Marie Perry filed a complaint in the case sub judice seeking a preliminary and permanent injunction compelling the school district to admit her to the public schools of Grenada, Mississippi.   The population of Grenada County, where the municipality of Grenada is located, is approximately 18,733 people.   The plaintiff brought the action on behalf of all unwed mothers of school age residing in Grenada County who are affected by the policy of the school board of denying admission to unwed mothers.   On November 30, 1967, an amended complaint was filed, adding another unwed mother, Emma Jean Wilson, as a party plaintiff.  .  .  .

There are three issues before the Court:  .  .  .

3) Whether the policy of the school board in excluding unwed mothers violates the Due Process Clause or the Equal Protection Clause of the Fourteenth Amendment of the Constitution.  .  .  .

The crux of this cause is whether the policy of the school board of denying admission to unwed mothers violates the Equal Protection Clause of the Fourteenth Amendment of the Constitution.   The case does not involve the curtailment of first amendment rights which has produced much litigation in recent years.  .  .  .   Neither does it fall within the ambit of cases involving whether a student received due process of law before being expelled from a school or university. .  .  .   The case sub judice falls within the category of cases involving whether there is invidious discrimination which violates the Equal Protection Clause of the Fourteenth Amendment.

The standards of the Equal Protection Clause are broad;  the generalities of the subject are not in dispute;  the application of the Equal Protection Clause turns peculiarly on the particular circumstances of each case.  .  .  .   The Equal Protection Clause does not force the laws of each state in the Union into the same mold.  A state may classify people but the classification must have some purpose and must not contain the kind of discrimination against which the Equal Protection Clause affords protection,   .   .   .   "Equal protection of the laws is something more than an abstract right."  It is a command which the state must respect, the benefits of which every person may demand. Not the least merit of our constitutional system is that its safeguards extend to all—the least deserving as well as the most virtuous."   .   .   .

The Supreme Court has laid down certain rules to test invidious discrimination:

> "The rules for testing a discrimination have been summarized as follows: 1.  The equal protection clause of the Fourteenth Amendment does not take from the State the power to classify in the adoption of police laws, but admits of the exercise of a wide scope of discretion in that regard, and avoids what is done only when it is without any reasonable basis and therefore is purely arbitrary.  2.  A classification having some reasonable basis does not offend against that clause merely because it is not made with mathematical nicety or because in practice it results in some inequality. 3.  When the classification in such a law is called in question, if any state of facts reasonably can be conceived that would sustain it, the existence of that state of facts at the time the law was enacted must be assumed.  4.  One who assails the classification in such a law must carry the burden of showing that it does not rest upon any reasonable basis, but is essentially arbitrary.   .   .   .

> "To these rules we add the caution that 'Discriminations of an unusual character especially suggests careful consideration to determine whether they are obnoxious to the constitutional provision.'   .   .   ."   .   .   .

In the present age of enlightenment no one can deny the importance of education to our youth.  As was stated in the Dixon case: "It requires no argument to demonstrate that education is vital and, indeed, basic to civilized society.  Without sufficient education the plaintiffs would not be able to earn an adequate livelihood, to enjoy life to the fullest, or to fulfill as completely as possible the duties and responsibilities of good citizens."  Dixon v. Alabama State Bd. of Education, 294 F.2d at 157.

The plaintiffs have introduced evidence which tends to show that unwed mothers, who are allowed to continue their education, are less likely to have a second illegitimate child.  In effect the opportunity to pursue their education gives them a hope for the future so that they are less likely to fall into the snare of repeat illegitimate births.  On the other hand the Court is aware of the defendants' fear that the presence of unwed mothers in the schools will be a bad influence on the other students vis-a-vis their presence indicating society's approval or acquiescence in the illegitimate births or vis-a-vis the association of the unwed mother with the other students.

The Court can understand and appreciate the effect which the presence of an unwed pregnant girl may have on other students in a school. Yet after the girl has the baby and has the opportunity to realize her wrong and rehabilitate herself, it seems patently unreasonable that she should not have the opportunity to go before some administrative body of the school and seek readmission on the basis of her changed moral and physical condition. Certainly this would be the cause if a girl had been raped and forced to bear the child of another.

Certainly school officials recognize the importance of education and the effect of a rigid rule which forever bars an individual from obtaining an education. The Court can appreciate that the Grenada School District might not have the funds to set up separate facilities for the education of pregnant girls. The purpose of excluding such girls is practical and apparent. But after the girl has the child, she should have the opportunity for applying for readmission and demonstrating to the school that she is qualified to continue her education. The continued exclusion of a girl without a hearing or some other opportunity to demonstrate her qualification for readmission serves no useful purpose and works an obvious hardship on the individual. It is arbitrary in that the individual is forever barred from seeking a high school education. Without a high school education, the individual is ill equipped for life, and is prevented from seeking higher education.

The Court would like to make manifestly clear that lack of moral character is certainly a reason for excluding a child from public education. But the fact that a girl has one child out of wedlock does not forever brand her as a scarlet woman undeserving of any chance for rehabilitation or the opportunity for future education. . . . the school is free to take reasonable and adequate steps to determine the moral character of a girl before she is readmitted to the school. If the board is convinced that a girl's presence will taint the education of the other students, then exclusion is justified. Nevertheless, the inquiry should be thorough and weighed in keeping with the serious consequences of preventing an individual from attaining a high school education.

In sum, the Court holds that plaintiffs may not be excluded from the schools of the district for the sole reason that they are unwed mothers; and that plaintiffs are entitled to readmission unless on a fair hearing before the school authorities they are found to be so lacking in moral character that their presence in the schools will taint the education of other students. . . .

## ORDWAY v. HARGRAVES

United States District Court, 1971.
323 F.Supp. 1155 (D.C.Mass.).

CAFFREY, District Judge.   This is a civil action brought on behalf of an 18-year old pregnant, unmarried, senior at the North Middlesex Regional High School, Townsend, Massachusetts.   The respondents are the Principal of the High School, Robert Hargraves, the seven individual members of the North Middlesex Regional High School Committee, and the School Committees of Pepperell and Townsend. The cause of action is alleged to arise under the Civil Rights Act, 42 U.S.C.A. § 1983, and jurisdiction of this court is invoked under 28 U.S.C.A. § 1343.   The matter came before the court for hearing on plaintiff's application for preliminary injunctive relief in the nature of an order requiring respondents to re-admit her to the Regional High School on a full-time, regular-class-hour, basis.

At the hearing, eight witnesses testified.  On the basis of the credible evidence adduced at the hearing, I find that the minor plaintiff, Fay Ordway, resides at East Pepperell, Massachusetts, and is presently enrolled as a senior in the North Middlesex Regional High School; and that plaintiff informed Mr. Hargraves, approximately January 28, 1971, that she was pregnant and expected to give birth to a baby in June 1971.   There is outstanding a rule of the Regional school committee, numbered Rule 821, which provides: "Whenever an unmarried girl enrolled in North Middlesex Regional High School shall be known to be pregnant, her membership in the school shall be immediately terminated."   Because of the imminence of certain examinations and the fact that school vacation was beginning on February 12, Mr. Hargraves informed plaintiff that she was to stop attending regular classes at the high school as of the close of school on February 12.  This instruction was confirmed in writing by a letter from Mr. Hargraves to plaintiff's mother, Mrs. Iona Ordway, dated February 22, 1971, in which Mr. Hargraves stated that the following conditions would govern Fay Ordway's relations with the school for the remainder of the school year:

(a) Fay will absent herself from school during regular school hours.

(b) Fay will be allowed to make use of all school facilities such as library, guidance, administrative, teaching, etc., on any school day after the normal dismissal time of 2:16 P.M.

(c) Fay will be allowed to attend all school functions such as games, dances, plays, etc.

(d) Participation in senior activities such as class trip, reception, etc.

(e) Seek extra help from her teachers during after school help sessions when needed.

(f) Tutoring at no cost if necessary; such tutors to be approved by the administration.

(g) Her name will remain on the school register for the remainder of the 1970–71 school year (to terminate on graduation day-tentatively scheduled for June 11, 1971).

(h) Examinations will be taken periodically based upon mutual agreement between Fay and the respective teacher.

Thereafter, plaintiff retained counsel, a hearing was requested, and was held by the school committee on March 3, 1971. The school committee approved the instructions and proposed schedule set out in Mr. Hargraves' letter of February 22, and a complaint was filed in this court on March 8.

It is well-established that in order to obtain a preliminary injunction, the plaintiff must satisfy two requirements, (1) that denial of the injunction will cause certain and irreparable injury to the plaintiff, and (2) "that there is a reasonable probability that (she) will ultimately prevail in the litigation."

At the hearing, Dr. F. Woodward Lewis testified that he is plaintiff's attending physician and that she is in excellent health to attend school. He expressed the opinion that the dangers in attending school are no worse for her than for a non-pregnant girl student, and that she can participate in all ordinary school activities with the exception of violent calisthenics. An affidavit of Dr. Charles R. Goyette, plaintiff's attending obstetrician, was admitted in evidence, in which Dr. Goyette corroborated the opinions of Dr. Lewis and added his opinion that "there is no reason that Miss Ordway could not continue to attend school until immediately before delivery."

Dr. Dorothy Jane Worth, a medical doctor, employed as Director of Family Health Services, Massachusetts Department of Public Health, testified that in her opinion exclusion of plaintiff will cause plaintiff mental anguish which will affect the course of her pregnancy. She further testified that policies relating to allowing or forbidding pregnant girls to attend high school are now widely varying within the state and throughout the United States. She testified that both Boston and New York now allow attendance of unmarried pregnant students in their high schools. She further testified that she was not aware of any reason why any health problems which arose during the day at school could not be handled by the registered nurse on duty at the high school.

Dr. Mary Jane England, a medical-doctor and psychiatrist attached to the staff of St. Elizabeth's Hospital, expressed the opinion that young girls in plaintiff's position who are required to absent themselves from school become depressed, and that the depression of the mother has an adverse effect on the child, who frequently is born depressed and lethargic. She further testified that from a psychiatric point of view it is desirable to keep a person in the position of plaintiff in as much contact with her friends and peer group as possible, and that they should not be treated as having a malady or disease.

Mrs. Janice Montague, holder of a Master's degree in social work from Simmons Graduate School, testified that on the basis of her eleven years experience working with Crittenton House, she has learned that the consensus among social workers who specialize in working with pregnant unwed girls is to give to the individual the choice of whether to remain in class or to have private instruction after regular class hours.

Plaintiff testified that her most recent grades were an A, a B-plus, and two C-pluses, and that she strongly desires to attend school with her class during regular school hours. She testified that she has not been subjected to any embarrassment by her classmates, nor has she been involved in any disruptive incidents of any kind. She further testified that she has not been aware of any resentment or any other change of attitude on the part of the other students in the school. This opinion of plaintiff as to her continuing to enjoy a good relationship with her fellow students was corroborated by the school librarian, Laura J. Connolly.

The remaining witness for plaintiff was Dr. Norman A. Sprinthall, Chairman of the Guidance Program, Harvard Graduate School of Education, who testified that in his opinion the type of program spelled out in Mr. Hargraves' letter of February 22, for after-hours instruction, was not educationally the equal of regular class attendance and participation.

It is clear, from the hearing, that no attempt is being made to stigmatize or punish plaintiff by the school principal or, for that matter, by the school committees. It is equally clear that were plaintiff married, she would be allowed to remain in class during regular school hours despite her pregnancy. Mr. Hargraves made it clear that the decision to exclude plaintiff was not his personal decision, but was a decision he felt required to make in view of the policy of the school committee which he is required to enforce as part of his duties as principal. In response to questioning, Mr. Hargraves could not state any educational purpose to be served by excluding plaintiff from regular class hours, and he conceded that plaintiff's pregnant condition has not occasioned any disruptive incident nor has it otherwise interfered with school activities. Cf. Tinker v. Des Moines Independent Community School District, where the Supreme Court limited school officials' curtailment of claimed rights of students to situations involving "substantial disruption of or material interference with school activities."

Mr. Hargraves did imply, however, his opinion is that the policy of the school committee might well be keyed to a desire on the part of the school committee not to appear to condone conduct on the part of unmarried students of a nature to cause pregnancy. The thrust of his testimony seems to be: the regional school has both junior and senior high school students in its student population; he finds the twelve-to-fourteen age group to be still flexible in their attitudes; they might be led to believe that the school authorities are condoning pre-marital relations if they were to allow girl students in plaintiff's situation to remain in school.

It should be noted that if concerns of this nature were a valid ground for the school committee regulation, the contents of paragraph b), c) and d) of Mr. Hargraves' letter of February 22 to plaintiff's mother substantially undercut those considerations.

In summary, no danger to petitioner's physical or mental health resultant from her attending classes during regular school hours has been shown; no likelihood that her presence will cause any disruption of or interference with school activities or pose a threat of harm to others has been shown; and no valid educational or other reason to justify her segregation and to require her to receive a type of educational treatment which is not the equal of that given to all others in her class has been shown.

It would seem beyond argument that the right to receive a public school education is a basic personal right or liberty. Consequently, the burden of justifying any school rule or regulation limiting or terminating that right is on the school authorities. Cf. Richards v. Thurston, 424 F.2d 1281, at 1286 (1 Cir. 1970), where the court ruled:

"In the absence of an inherent, self-evident justification on the face of the rule, we conclude that the burden was on the defendant."

On the record before me, respondents have failed to carry this burden. Accordingly, it is

Ordered:

Respondents are to re-admit plaintiff to regular attendance at North Middlesex Regional High School until further order of this court.

## NOTES AND QUESTIONS

1. Among other matters, Perry focuses on protecting classmates from possible moral, psychological and other harms because a pregnant student would be in the classroom. Ordway partially focuses on protecting the pregnant student from embarrassment of expulsion and other matters. Are these considerations relevant? If they are in conflict, which set of interests should prevail and be reflected in a school's set of regulations? Why shouldn't school attendance decisions be left to the pregnant student?

2.  In Alvin Independent School Dist. v. Cooper, 404 S.W.2d 76 (Tex.Civ. App.1966), the court was confronted by a claim for readmission to high school made by a 16-year old divorced mother who had been excluded from readmission on the basis of school board policy. The court struck the policy ruling that school officials "were without legal authority to adopt the rule or policy that excludes the mother of a child from admission to the school if she is of the age for which the state furnishes school funds."

3.  Title IX of the Educational Amendments of 1972 (§§ 901–907, Educ. Amds. of 1972, P.L. 92–318, 20 U.S.C.A. § 1681), with certain exceptions, provides that "no person in the United States shall on the basis of sex, be excluded from participation in, be denied the benefits of, or be subjected to discrimination under any education program or activity receiving federal financial assistance  .  .  .".

The federal regulations implementing this provision deal directly with student marital and parental status (45 C.F.R. § 86.40): "A recipient [school] shall not apply any rule concerning a student's actual or potential parental family or marital status which treats students differently on the basis of sex" and "A recipient [school] shall not discriminate against any student, or exclude any student from its education program or activity, on the basis of such student's pregnancy, childbirth, false pregnancy, termination of pregnancy or recovery therefrom, unless the student requests voluntarily to participate in a separate portion of the program or activity of the recipient  .  .  .".

## FREEDOM OF DRESS AND APPEARANCE

### BISHOP v. COLAW

United States Court of Appeals, 1971.
450 F.2d 1069 (8th Cir.).

BRIGHT, Circuit Judge.  The school administration of St. Charles, Missouri, a suburb of St. Louis, Missouri, in March 1970, suspended fifteen year old Stephen Bishop from school attendance solely because his hairstyle violated provisions of the school dress code. Stephen and his parents brought this action seeking to obtain his readmission, and a declaratory judgment overturning the dress code regulations governing the hair length and style of male students. Plaintiffs assert that these regulations violate Stephen's, and his parents', personal rights guaranteed by the United States Constitution.  .  .  .

The St. Charles high school administration incorporated the hair-length regulations into a dress code during the 1969–70 school year. The pertinent regulations in effect at the time of Stephen's expulsion provided as follows:

Section 4.  HAIR:

A.  All hair is to be worn clean, neatly trimmed around the ears and back of the neck, and no longer than the top of the collar on a regular dress or sport shirt when standing erect. The eyebrows must be visible, and no part of the ear can be covered. The hair can be in a block cut.

B. The maximum length for sideburns shall be to the bottom of the ear lobe.

A few days after school opened in September 1969, the physical education teacher objected to Stephen's hairstyle because it was not tapered in the back and above the ears as was then required by the existing regulations. Following several conferences involving Stephen, his parents, the principal, and the assistant principal, Stephen's hair was trimmed to conform to the regulations. In November, the same teacher protested the length of Stephen's hair, and following additional conferences with the administration, Stephen again cut his hair. In January 1970, after the hair-length regulations had been modified to allow for a block cut, Stephen's mathematics teacher complained that Stephen's hair was too long in the back and over the ears. In response, Stephen trimmed his hair in back, and after additional conferences between the assistant principal and Stephen's father, Stephen's hair was made to comply with the regulations by also trimming it over the ears. Finally, in February 1970, Stephen and his parents refused to acquiesce in the further demands of the school administration that Stephen's hair be trimmed again. Stephen was suspended a few days later, and the instant litigation followed.

In recent years, the federal courts have found themselves increasingly embroiled in hair-length controversies resulting from the enforcement of regulations similar to that promulgated by the school administration of St. Charles High School. The Supreme Court has, on several occasions, refused to review the constitutional questions raised in this area. . . . What little guidance we have from the Court in this area is conflicting. Justice Black, writing as Circuit Justice in Karr v. Schmidt, 401 U.S. 1201 . . . took the position that state regulation of matters such as hair length raises no issue of constitutional dimensions calling for review by federal courts. On the other hand, Justice Douglas, dissenting from a denial of certiorari, argued that state regulation of hair length raises a serious equal protection question. Ferrell v. Dallas Independent School District, 393 U.S. 856 . . . In addition, several courts of appeals have considered the validity of hair regulations similar to those presented here against a broad range of constitutional attacks.

The Seventh Circuit has ruled in favor of the students, holding that a student's right to govern the style and length of his hair is a personal freedom protected under the Ninth Amendment and the Due Process Clause of the Fourteenth Amendment. Crews v. Cloncs, 432 F.2d 1259 (7th Cir. 1970); Breen v. Kahl, 419 F.2d 1034 (7th Cir. 1969), cert. denied 398 U.S. 937, 90 S.Ct. 1836, 26 L.Ed.2d 268 (1970). Under that circuit's decisions, the state carries a "substantial burden of justification" for regulations which infringe upon this freedom. . . .

The First Circuit has also concluded that students possess a constitutional right to wear their hair as they choose. Richards v. Thurston, 424 F.2d 1281 (1st Cir. 1970). The First Circuit's approach differed slightly, however, from that of the Seventh Circuit. In *Richards*, the court found that the right of students to determine their personal appearance is "implicit in the 'liberty' assurance of the Due Process Clause." . . . The court said:

> We do not say that the governance of the length and style of one's hair is necessarily so fundamental as those substantive rights already found implicit in the "liberty" assurance of the Due Process Clause, requiring a "compelling" showing by the state before it may be impaired. Yet "liberty" seems to us an incomplete protection if it encompasses only the right to do momentous acts, leaving the state free to interfere with those personal aspects of our lives which have no direct bearing on the ability of others to enjoy their liberty. * * *

> We think the Founding Fathers understood themselves to have limited the government's power to intrude into this sphere of personal liberty, by reserving some powers to the people. The debate concerning the First Amendment is illuminating. The specification of the right of assembly was deemed mere surplusage by some, on the grounds that the government had no more power to restrict assembly than it did to tell a man to wear a hat or when to get up in the morning. The response by Page of Virginia pointed out that even those "trivial" rights had been known to have been impaired —to the Colonists' consternation—but that the right of assembly ought to be specified since it was so basic to other rights. The Founding Fathers wrote an amendment for speech and assembly; even they did not deem it necessary to write an amendment for personal appearance. We conclude that within the commodious concept of liberty, embracing freedoms great and small, is the right to wear one's hair as he wishes.

The court went on to note that, although this right is not a "fundamental" freedom which can be impaired only by showing a compelling state interest, the burden of justifying restrictions on this freedom still rests with the state.

The Fifth, Sixth, and Ninth Circuits have sustained school codes regulating hair. Ferrell v. Dallas Independent School Dist., 392 F.2d 697 (5th Cir.), cert. denied . . . Gfell v. Rickelman, 441 F.2d 444 (6th Cir. 1971); Jackson v. Dorrier, 424 F.2d 213 (6th Cir.), cert. denied   .   .   .   King v. Saddleback Junior College Dist., 445 F.2d 932 (9th Cir. 1971). Each has adopted a different approach in sustaining these regulations.

In *King,* supra, 445 F.2d at 940, the Ninth Circuit held that students have no "substantial constitutional right" to wear their hair as they desire. As a consequence, school authorities need not present proof of actual classroom disruptions to support hair regulations. Mere opinion evidence of teachers or school administrators that long hair interferes with the educational process will suffice.

The Sixth Circuit, although not recognizing a specific constitutional right to determine one's hair length and style, requires proof that the appearance of the students caused classroom or other school disruptions. Implicit in these decisions is a recognition of the principle that the state has the burden of establishing the reasonableness of its regulations.   .   .   .

The Fifth Circuit's decisions have turned on the reasonableness and necessity of the regulations. In *Ferrell*   .   .   .   the court, while recognizing the right of students to govern their personal appearance, held that this right was not unreasonably infringed because the school board was able to demonstrate a need for the regulations to control disruptions attributable to controversies over student hair lengths which departed from the more conventional styles. The court carefully disinguished a district court decision which had struck down a similar regulation because "[n]o suggestion was made that such [hairstyles] had any effect upon the health, discipline, or decorum of the institution."

In a subsequent decision, another panel of the Fifth Circuit did not hesitate to strike down a regulation restricting the style, rather than the length of hair. Griffin v. Tatum, 425 F.2d 201 (5th Cir. 1970). Later, in Stevenson v. Board of Education of Wheeler County, Georgia, 426 F.2d 1154 (5th Cir.), cert. denied   .   .   .   the court made clear that "[t]he touchstone for sustaining such regulations is the demonstration that they are necessary to alleviate interference with the educational process."   .   .   .

Federal district courts generally, as well as those of this circuit, have disagreed about the validity of hair-length regulations. Aside from the instant case, two district courts in this circuit have upheld hair regulations against constitutional challenges. Carter v. Hodges, 317 F.Supp. 89 (W.D.Ark.1970); Giangreco v. Center School District, 313 F.Supp. 776 (W.D.Mo.1969). In both cases, however, the courts proceeded from the premise that the state carries the burden of demonstrating the reasonableness of the regulation. And, in both cases, the courts found that the students' appearance had, in fact, caused school disruptions.

The other district courts of this circuit which have considered the issue have followed the rationale of the First and Seventh Circuits in holding that students possess a constitutionally protected right to govern their personal appearance, and that the state must justify any infringement of this right. . . . In a comment typical of those made by other district judges of this circuit in rejecting the validity of hair regulations, Judge Eisele, in *Fry,* supra, said:

> The sincerity of the [school administrators] is not in in doubt. The Court believes that the "hair" rule was adopted because of the conviction of school authorities that to permit extreme hair styles would result in disruption or distraction in the classrooms.

> * * * But the facts do not appear to sustain the fear. Generally this fear is based upon the idea as stated by Mr. Swift, the superintendent, that anything out of the ordinary attracts attention and therefore could be disruptive of the educational process. This appears, however, to be more of an educational philosophy than an established scientific fact. Students in our high schools and colleges must have some room within which to express their individual personalities.

With this background, we turn to the arguments advanced by appellants in this case. The Bishops assert that the regulations violate: 1) Stephen's First Amendment right to "symbolic expression"; 2) his Fourteenth Amendment right to equal protection; 3) his Ninth and Fourteenth Amendment rights to govern his personal appearance; and 4) his parents' Ninth and Fourteenth Amendment rights to govern the raising of their family.

### First Amendment

We deem the First Amendment contention to be without merit in the context of this case, since the record contains no evidence suggesting that Stephen's hairstyle represented a symbolic expression of any kind. The appellants concede that Stephen never considered his hairstyle to be symbolic of any idea. They argue, however, that a "[non-conforming hairstyle] need not symbolize anything at all * * * to be a constitutionally protected expression." We cannot accept this unusually broad reading of the First Amendment. Since all conduct cannot be labeled speech even when "the [actor] intends thereby to express an idea," United States v. O'Brien, 391 U.S. 367, 376, . . . certainly conduct not intended to express an idea cannot be afforded protection as speech.

### Equal Protection

Dissenting in *Ferrell,* supra . . . Judge Tuttle propounded an equal protection argument which Justice Douglas subsequently reiterated in dissenting from the Supreme Court's denial of certiorari. Justice Douglas said:

> It comes as a surprise that in a country where the States are restrained by an Equal Protection Clause, a person can

be denied education in a public school because of the length of his hair.  I suppose that a nation bent on turning out robots might insist that every male have a crew cut and every female wear pigtails.  But the ideas of "life, liberty, and the pursuit of happiness," expressed in the Declaration of Independence, later found specific definition in the Constitution itself, including of course freedom of expression and a wide zone of privacy.  I had supposed those guarantees permitted idiosyncrasies to flourish, especially when they concern the image of one's personality and his philosophy toward government and his fellow men.

The equal protection theory has been adopted in one circuit court decision.  In *Crews*, supra   .    ., the Seventh Circuit found that male students were denied equal protection since females, who participated in substantially the same school activities as males, were not subject to the same hairstyle restrictions.  Appellants have raised no question of sex discrimination.  Their argument, cast as it is in terms of discrimination between males with differing hairlengths, does not fall within traditional concepts of invidious discrimination subject to the proscription of the Equal Protection Clause.  Since we find in favor of appellants on other grounds, we do not pass upon this equal protection argument.

### Parents' Rights

Stephen's parents argue that the regulations violate their constitutional right to govern the raising of their family.  The thrust of their argument is that, although school authorities are vested with certain powers to maintain discipline, some room must be left for the exercise of parental control over a child's lifestyle.  They assert that the Fourteenth Amendment forbids state intrusion, such as that attempted here, into the parent-child relationship.  While there may be some merit to this assertion, we believe that this case is an inappropriate vehicle for making that determination.  There is no indication in the record that Stephen's parents were responsible for his choice of hairstyle.  Their role throughout has been limited to supporting Stephen's right to govern his personal appearance.  The record, therefore, fails to establish any direct invasion of the parents' rights.  We believe such a showing necessary to support a successful attack upon the regulations in question.

### Stephen's Rights

We hold that Stephen possessed a constitutionally protected right to govern his personal appearance while attending public high school.  In reaching this conclusion we find it necessary to determine the nature and source of this right.  Among those courts which agree that this right exists, there is some disagreement as to its nature and source.   .    .    Some have referred to the right as "fundamental", others as "substantial", others as "basic", and still others as simply a "right". The source of this right has been found within the Ninth Amendment, the Due Process Clause of the Fourteenth Amendment, and the privacy penumbra of the Bill of Rights. A close reading of these cases reveals, however, that the differences in approach are more semantic than real. The common theme underlying decisions striking down hairstyle regulations is that the Constitution guarantees rights other than those specifically enumerated, and that the right to govern one's personal appearance is one of those guaranteed rights.

The existence of rights other than those specifically enumerated in the Constitution was recognized by the Supreme Court in Griswold v. Connecticut, 381 U.S. 479, . . . . Much of the present divergence of opinion as to the source of the right asserted here can be traced to the different approaches adopted by the Justices in *Griswold*. We see no point in rehashing these different approaches, since under any one of them, the conclusion follows that certain additional rights exist.

We believe that, among those rights retained by the people under our constitutional form of government, is the freedom to govern one's personal appearance. As a freedom which ranks high on the spectrum of our societal values, it commands the protection of the Fourteenth Amendment Due Process Clause. . . . The importance attached to such personal freedom has been long recognized. Writing in 1891, Justice Gray said:

> No right is held more sacred, or is more carefully guarded, by the common law, than the right of every individual to the possession and control of his own person, free from all restraint or interference of others, unless by clear and unquestionable authority of law. As well said by Judge Cooley, "The right to one's person may be said to be a right of complete immunity: to be let alone." [Union Pacific Ry. Co. v. Botsford, 141 U.S. 250, 251 . . . ]

Our determination that Stephen possesses this personal freedom, however, does not end our inquiry into the constitutionality of the challenged regulations. Personal freedoms are not absolute; they must yield when they intrude upon the freedoms of others. Our task, therefore, is to weigh the competing interests asserted here. In doing so, we proceed from the premise that the school administration carries the burden of establishing the necessity of infringing upon Stephen's freedom in order to carry out the educational mission of the St. Charles High School. . . . Since our decision must turn on the necessity of the regulations, we review the evidence adduced in their support.

The record discloses that the St. Charles high school administrators believed that the wearing of long hair caused disruption in the educational process. They asserted that the male students with long hair tended to be rowdy, created a sanitation problem in the swimming pool, caused a safety problem in certain shop classes, and tended to make poorer grades than those with shorter hair.

Mr. Lauer, the principal, testified that a group of about twenty-five boys and girls, who opposed the dress code, generally congregated at one table in the school cafeteria. According to Mr. Lauer, this group has been noisy and boisterous, and, on one occasion, disrespectful to a teacher. The boys in this group apparently wear their hair longer than most others in the school.

The principal expressed the opinion that without a dress code the students would polarize into camps of "long hairs" and "short hairs". Mr. Lauer also indicated that, in his opinion, if boys were allowed to wear long hair so as to look like girls, it would create problems with the continuing operation of the school because of confusion over appropriate dressing room and restroom facilities.

The school administrators offered evidence which indicated that a fight had occurred between a student with long hair and one with short hair at a nonschool function. The athletic director suggested that, although he had encountered no problems, long hair might affect sanitation in the swimming pool. He further commented that a boy wearing long hair and somewhat unusual attire had attracted attention and caused a commotion in the hallway of the school on one occasion. The shop teacher interjected that there was a risk of injury in his classes for a student wearing long hair. Another teacher testified that, in her opinion, students wearing long hair did not possess as good an attitude toward their studies as those with short hair. The school superintendent stressed in his testimony the possible reaction of other students, teachers, and the public as possibly jeopardizing the St. Charles educational program. He noted that the community favored the dress code and felt that this justified its imposition.

We find virtually no evidence in this record to support the school board's contention that the hair regulations are necessary to prevent disruptions at St. Charles High School. The primary weakness in the state's case is that the cited student behavorial problems existed even though all of the students, except Stephen, were in compliance with the regulations, albeit grudgingly in some instances. It is conceded that Stephen was not involved in any conduct which caused a disturbance. There was testimony that one young lady refused to wear a driving helmet which Stephen had previously worn, but there was no indication that this refusal was prompted by sanitary considerations. Stephen testified that he frequently washed his hair, and the school produced no evidence that his hair caused sanitation problems.

Passing to the other evidence presented, we note that much of the board's case rests upon conclusionary assertions that disruptions would occur without the hair regulations. Although we have construed the evidence most favorably to the trial court's findings in support of the regulations' validity, it is apparent that the opinion testimony of the school teachers and administrators, which lacks any empirical foundation, likely reflects a personal distaste of longer hairstyles, which distaste is shared by many in the older generation. We do not feel that the suggestion that a correlation exists between the length of a student's hair and his classroom performance requires a response. The assertion that the emergence of long hairstyles will lead to co-educational restrooms is equally untenable. Nor does the acceptance of the dress code by the majority of the St. Charles community and students justify the infringement of Stephen's liberty to govern his personal appearance. Toleration of individual differences is basic to our democracy, whether those differences be in religion, politics, or life-style. Finally, we cannot accept the argument that uniformity of appearance must be maintained in order to prevent "polarization" in the St. Charles student body.

We find only two instances of actual disruption cited in the record. The misconduct in the school cafeteria by students wearing longer hair than other students, but not longer than the school administration's edict, represents an isolated incident. Moreover, its connection with long hair seems, at best, tenuous. The disturbance in the hall related to a young man, wearing long hair and bizarre dress, who was not enrolled in school. Of the justifications advanced by the school administrators in support of the regulations, only those relating to swimming pool sanitation and shop class safety bear any rational relation to the length of a student's hair. The school administration has failed to show why these particular problems cannot be solved by imposing less restrictive rules, such as requiring students to wear swimming caps or shop caps.

In summary, the case presented by the school administrators fails to demonstrate the necessity of its regulation of the hair length and style of male students. We hold this regulation invalid and its terms unenforceable.

We reverse and remand this case for the entry of judgment in conformity with this opinion.

ALDRICH, Circuit Judge (concurring).

A recent law review has concluded, after summarizing the cases,

> "What is disturbing is the inescapable feeling that long hair is simply not a source of significant distraction, and that school officials are often acting on the basis of personal distaste amplified by an overzealous belief in the need for regulations." 84 Harv.L.Rev. 1702 at 1715 (1971).

The connection between long hair and the immemorial problems of misdirected student activism and negativisim, whether in behavior or in learning, is difficult to see. No evidence has been presented that hair is the cause, as distinguished from a possible peripheral consequence, of undesirable traits, or that the school board, Delilah-like, can lop off these characteristics with the locks. Accepting as true the testimony that in St. Charles, Missouri, the longer the student's hair, the lower his grade in mathematics, it does not lead me to believe that shortening the one will add to the other. Indeed, the very fact that such evidence is offered would seem to support the periodical's conclusion.

The area of judicial notice is circumscribed, but I cannot help but observe that the city employee who collects my rubbish has shoulder-length hair. So do a number of our nationally famous Boston Bruins. Barrel tossing and puck chasing are honorable pursuits, not to be associated with effeteness on the one hand, or aimlessness or indolence on the other. If these activities be thought not of high intellectual calibre, I turn to the recent successful candidates for Rhodes Scholarships from my neighboring institution. A number of these, according to their photographs, wear hair that outdoes even the hockey players. It is proverbial that these young men are chosen not only for their scholastic attainments, but for their outstanding character and accomplishments. What particularly impresses me in their case is that they feel strongly enough about their chosen appearance to risk the displeasure of a scholarship committee doubtless including establishmentarians who may be expected to find it personally distasteful.

It is bromidic to say that times change, but perhaps this is a case where a bromide is in order.

LAY, Circuit Judge (concurring).

I concur.

This case for me is not one of easy decision. On the surface, one can be somewhat troubled with the fact that overloaded federal dockets are further burdened with cases which center their controversies on the length of a school boy's hair. It may well seem appropriate that this issue does not involve a question of substantial constitutional dimension. Freeman v. Flake, 448 F.2d 258 (10 Cir. 1971), or that such problems should be left to local authorities, King v. Saddleback Jr. College District, 445 F.2d 932 (9 Cir. 1971). Nevertheless, a state's invasion into the personal rights and liberty of an individual, of whatever age or description, should present a justiciable issue worthy of federal review. There is little doubt that this regulation seeks to restrict a young persons' personal liberty to mold his own lifestyle through his personal appearance. To say that the issue is not "substantial" turns a deaf ear to the basic values of individual privacy and the freedom to caricature one's own image. Our institutions do not rely on submerging individual personality in order to create an "idealized" citizen. Cf. Meyer v. Nebraska, . . . . The abhorrence of such treatment stems from the enlightened philosophy that school children must be given every feasible opportunity to grow in independence, to develop their own individualities and to initiate and thrive on creative thought.

Moreover, to say simply that the problem is best left to local authorities bemeans the intrinsic constitutional issue involved.  Such a rationale could sustain any school prohibition of the recognized constitutional rights of students.  Tinker v. Des Moines Independent Community School District,  .  .  .

The question confronting us is whether there exists any real educational purpose or societal interest to be served in the discipline the school has adopted.  After due consideration I fail to find any rational connection between the health, discipline or achievement of a particular child wearing a hair style which touches his ears or curls around his neck, and the child who does not.  The gamut of rationalizations for justifying this restriction fails in light of reasoned analysis.  When school authorities complain variously that such hair styles are inspired by a communist conspiracy, that they make boys look like girls, that they promote confusion as to the use of restrooms and that they destroy the students' moral fiber, then it is little wonder even moderate students complain of "getting up tight."  In final analysis, I am satisfied a comprehensive school restriction on male student hair styles accomplishes little more than to project the prejudices and personal distastes of certain adults in authority on to the impressionable young student.

———

## BANNISTER v. PARADIS

United States District Court, D.N.H., 1970.
316 F.Supp. 185.

BOWNES, District Judge.  This action was brought  .  .  . by Kevin Bannister, a student at the Pittsfield Junior High School, through his mother  .  .  .  against the principal of the Pittsfield High School and the members of the Pittsfield School Board.  The controversy centers on that portion of the Pittsfield dress code which provides as to boys: "Dungarees will not be allowed."

### STIPULATED FACTS

Prior to hearing, the parties entered into a stipulation of facts as follows.  Kevin Bannister is twelve years old and is a student in the sixth grade of the Pittsfield High School which runs from the fifth through the twelfth grades, and is a public school.  The present version of the dress code was adopted unanimously by the School Board on April 27, 1970, and the only section of the dress code in issue is the section quoted above referring to dungarees.  The plaintiff, however, does not agree that the dress code is constitutional as to its other provisions. Kevin was sent home for violation of the dress code because he was wearing blue jeans. At no time was force used to require Kevin to leave school.

## FINDINGS

At the outset, the Court has had some difficulty defining the word "dungarees." The principal of the school defined "dungarees" as working clothes made of a coarse cotton blue fabric. The Chairman of the School Board defined "dungarees" as a denim fabric pant used for work with color of no significance. Webster's Third International Dictionary defines "dungarees" as heavy cotton work clothes usually made of blue dungaree. For purposes of this case, the Court finds that blue jeans and dungarees are synonymous and that Kevin Bannister deliberately violated the school dress code on at least two occasions by wearing blue jeans to school. These violations were with the full knowledge and consent, if not the actual urging, of Kevin's parents. At the time the violations occurred, the blue jeans were neat and clean, as was all of Kevin's ensemble.

There was no evidence that the wearing of dungarees of any color had ever caused any disturbance at the school or given rise to any disciplinary problems. Kevin's wearing of blue jeans did not cause any disturbance and there was no disciplinary problem involved except the one involving Kevin himself. It can be fairly concluded that wearing clean blue jeans does not constitute a danger to the health or safety of other pupils and that wearing them does not disrupt the other pupils.

The principal of the school, Mr. Paradis, who has had a total of seven years' experience in teaching and school administration, testified that discipline is essential to the educational process, and that proper dress is part of a good educational climate. It was his opinion that if students wear working or play clothes to school, it leads to a relaxed attitude and such an attitude detracts from discipline and a proper educational climate. Mr. Paradis stated further that students with patches on their clothes and students with dirty clothes, regardless of the type of clothing, should be sent home. The Court notes here that there is nothing in the dress code specifically stating that clothes should be neat and clean. The dress code, as to the boys, is directed primarily to specific prohibitions and does not promulgate any positive standards to follow. On cross-examination, the principal stated: "I apply the dress code as I see it. We don't define the term dungarees as to what it is."

The Chairman of the School Board, E. Windsor Burbank, testified that it was his opinion, and the opinion of the School Board, that the relaxed atmosphere induced by wearing work or play clothes to school does not fit into the atmosphere of discipline and learning. This opinion was based on the Chairman's assertion that California students had poor academic records and that this was due to the sloppy and casual attire worn by them to school.  The Chairman is a full time pilot for TWA Airlines and his knowledge of the type of school dress worn by students in California was based on his observations at the times that his airplane schedule took him to various sections of California.  The Chairman did not explain the basis for his assertion that California high school students have poor academic records.

Prior to the adoption of a revised dress code in 1970, the Student Council had recommended that the prohibition against dungarees be eliminated.  The School Board did not accede to this request, but no reasons were given for its refusal.

## RULINGS

.   .   .   New Hampshire Revised Statutes Annotated, Chapter 189, Section 15 provides:

> *Regulations.*  The school board may, unless otherwise provided by statute or state board regulations, prescribe regulations for the attendance upon, and for the management, classification and discipline of, the schools; and such regulations, when recorded in the official records of the school board, shall be binding upon pupils and teachers.

There is no question, therefore, that the Pittsfield dress code is action by the State of New Hampshire.  The serious question is whether or not the prohibition of wearing dungarees is a deprivation of any rights, privileges, or immunities secured by the Constitution of the United States.  The Court has been unable to find any cases brought under the Civil Rights Act where the issue has been wearing apparel.  Students and school boards seem to have become entangled in the hirsute aspect of school dress codes to the exclusion of almost everything else.  The only case that comes close to the case before the Court is Westley v. Rossi, 305 F.Supp. 706 (D.Minn.1969), in which the plaintiff started out by violating several prohibitions of the dress code, but asserted in court that he was perfectly willing to comply with all of the rules and dress codes of his high school except for the length of his hair.  This dearth of cases relative to wearing apparel in the Civil Rights field may be an indication that neither pupils nor school boards look on clothes with the same emotion and fervor with which they regard the length of a young man's hair or it may indicate, as the Court believes it does, that most school boards are no longer concerned with what a student wears to school as long as it is clean and covers adequately those parts of the body that, by tradition, are usually kept from public view.

There was no suggestion that the wearing of blue jeans, clean or otherwise, in any way constitutes a right of expression.  The First Amendment, therefore, does not apply and is not an issue.

Certainly, the prohibition against the wearing of blue jeans or dungarees cannot by any stretch of the imagination touch the right of privacy as delineated in Griswold v. Connecticut, 381 U.S. 479,  . .

If it were not for the case of Richards v. Thurston, 424 F.2d 1281 (1st Cir. 1970), the Court might be tempted to dispose of this matter on the ground that there was no deprivation of any constitutional rights.  The language and reasoning of that case, however, convinces us that a person's right to wear clothes of his own choosing provided that, in the case of a schoolboy, they are neat and clean, is a constitutional right protected and guaranteed by the Fourteenth Amendment. Judge Coffin, in writing the opinion, quoted Union Pac. Ry. Co. v. Botsford, 141 U.S. 250, 251  . . .  which stated:

> No right is held more sacred, or is more carefully guarded, by the common law, than the right of every individual to the possession and control of his own person, free from all restraint or interference of others, unless by clear and unquestionable authority of law.

Surely, the commodious concept of liberty invoked by Judge Coffin, embracing freedoms great and small, is large enough to include within its embrace the right to wear clean blue jeans to school unless there is an outweighing state interest justifying their exclusion.  . . .

Since we have determined that a personal liberty is involved . . . we now consider the second question, and that is whether or not the regulations against the wearing of dungarees is justified under these circumstances.  Going again to Richards v. Thurston, supra, for our guidelines, we take into account the nature of the liberty asserted, the context in which it is asserted, and the extent to which the intrusion on the liberty is confined to the legitimate public interest to be served.

On the scale of values of constitutional liberties, the right to wear clean blue jeans to school is not very high.  There was no suggestion by the plaintiff that he could not afford pants other than blue jeans, although there was testimony by another parent that she had sent her son to school at the end of the year in blue jeans because she could not afford to buy him a pair of dress pants.

On the other hand, there was no showing that the wearing of dungarees in any way inhibited or tended to inhibit the educational process.  The Court is, of course, mindful of the testimony of the principal and the Chairman of the School Board that wearing work clothes or play clothes is subversive of the educational process because students tend to become lax and indifferent.  The Court confesses, however, that it has considerable difficulty accepting this proposition.  There was no expert testimony to this effect with the exception of that of Mr. Paradis.  While the Court realizes that Mr. Burbank's experience on the School Board of eight years' standing does give him certain credentials, it does not qualify him as an expert in the field of education and teaching. There was no evidence as to how many other school boards in the state followed a similar dress code nor, with the exception of Mr. Burbank's rather casual observations of the California school system, was there any testimony as to the type of dress worn by other pupils in any other schools.

In Breen v. Kahl, 419 F.2d 1034 (7th Cir. 1969), the Court pointed out at page 1037:

> Although schools need to stand in place of a parent, in regard to certain matters during the school hours, the power must be shared with the parents, especially over intimately personal matters such as dress and grooming.

Quoting *Breen* again:

> To uphold arbitrary school rules which "sharply implicate basic constitutional values" for the sake of some nebulous concept of school discipline is contrary to the principle that we are a government of laws which are passed pursuant to the United States Constitution.

We realize that a school can, and must, for its own preservation exclude persons who are unsanitary, obscenely or scantily clad. Good hygiene and the health of the other pupils require that dirty clothes of any nature, whether they be dress clothes or dungarees, should be prohibited. Nor does the Court see anything unconstitutional in a school board prohibiting scantily clad students because it is obvious that the lack of proper covering, particularly with female students, might tend to distract other pupils and be disruptive of the educational process and school discipline.

While the Court recognizes that school boards do have power to adopt reasonable restrictions on dress as part of its educational policy and as an educational device, the school board's power must be limited to that required by its function of administering public education. The observation in Westley v. Rossi, supra, is pertinent.

> The standards of appearance and dress of last year are not those of today nor will they be those of tomorrow. Regulation of conduct by school authorities must bear a reasonable basis to the ordinary conduct of the school curriculum or to carrying out the responsibility of the school.

The Court rules that the defendants have not justified the intrusion on the personal liberty of Kevin Bannister, small as that intrusion may be, and that the prohibition against wearing dungarees is unconstitutional and invalid. The School Board and the principal of the Pittsfield High School are permanently enjoined from enforcing that portion of the dress code which prohibits boys from wearing dungarees. . . .

## NOTES AND QUESTIONS

1.  As a general proposition do courts endorse the view that local school boards have power to adopt reasonable rules and regulations governing students? Must these rules be reasonably related to proper functioning and welfare of the school? Give some examples that would and would not qualify. Does their reasonableness depend upon the circumstance; thus, a rule reasonable for a school's cafeteria would not be reasonable in its art class? Do the courts presume the validity of a rule or regulation of a local school board and require that the complaining party show that the rule is unreasonable? How can rules and regulations governing student behavior off school premises be justified as being reasonably related to the proper functioning and welfare of the school? Give some examples. In Sullivan v. Houston Ind. School Dist., 307 F.Supp. 1328 (S.D.Tex.1969) the court said:

    "It is not clear whether the law allows a school to discipline a student for his behavior during free time away from the campus. . . . In this court's judgment, it makes little sense to extend the influence of school administration to off-campus activity under the theory that such activity might interfere with the function of education. School officials may not judge a student's behavior while he is in his home with his family nor does it seem to this court that they should have jurisdiction over his acts on a public street corner. A student is subject to the same criminal laws and owes the same civil duties as other citizens, and his status as a student should not alter his obligations to others during his private life away from the campus.

    "Arguably, misconduct by students during non-school hours and away from school premises could, in certain situations, have such a lasting effect on other students that disruption could result during the next school day. Perhaps then administrators should be able to exercise some degree of influence over off-campus conduct. This court considers even this power to be questionable.

    "However, under any circumstances, the school certainly may not exercise more control over off-campus behavior than over on-campus conduct. Serious disciplinary action concerning first amendment activity on or off campus must be based on the standard of substantial interference with the normal operations of the school."

2.  Do you agree with the decisions and reasons in the above two opinions? Why or why not? Would these two cases have been decided differently by courts in the Fifth, Sixth and Ninth Circuits? Why? Is this result justifiable? Would the decisions have been the same if a teacher, rather than a student, had been involved? See, e. g., Finot v. Bd. of Ed., 250 Cal.App.2d 189, 58 Cal.Rptr. 520 (1967).

3.  Does either court in Bishop or Bannister, supra, base its opinion on a constitutional provision? Is it the First Amendment? If not, which provision? Do you agree?

4.  What reason(s) can you give justifying a school's interest in the way in which its students dress and in their overall appearance?

5.  Suppose a school's regulation on hair styles pertains only to all students enrolled in either its shop, laboratory or art courses, requiring that (a) the ears shall not be covered below the lower parts of the earlobes; (b) hair at the back of the head shall not fall below the top of the dress shirt or blouse collar; (c) sideburns shall not extend below the bottom of the ear; and (d) the top of the eyebrow shall be the lower limit for the forehead, would this regulation be upheld? Suppose the school also required that all students take at least one shop, laboratory or art course, would this factor affect your reasoning? Why? See, Stull v. School Board, 459 F.2d 339 (3rd Cir. 1972).

6.  Suppose a school's dress code provided that (1) students who ride bicycles to school shall not wear bell-bottomed slacks; (2) students who wear slacks shall not wear slacks that are so skintight and, therefore, revealing as to provoke or distract students of the same or opposite sex; (3) no student shall wear bells, or other distractive devices, attached to the bottoms of slacks or other attire; (4) shirts and blouses must be tucked in at all times unless they are square cut in which case they can be left out; (5) metal cleats or taps are destructive of floor surfaces, and must not be worn; (6) no hairclips, hairrollers, haircurlers, kerchiefs or similar items may be worn; (7) sandals are not allowed; (8) neither micromini nor maxi skirts shall be worn; (9) all girls in high school shall wear brassieres, and (10) no partially bleached clothing shall be worn. Is any section of this code unenforceable because of constitutional reasons? If so, which one; why? See, e. g., Scott v. Board of Education, 61 Misc.2d 333, 305 N.Y.S.2d 601 (1969); Stromberg v. French, 60 N.D. 750, 236 N.W. 477 (1931); and Pugsley v. Sellmeyer, 158 Ark. 247, 250 S.W. 538 (1923).

7.  Could a local board legally refuse to issue a diploma to a student on the ground that he would not wear a cap and gown, and did not participate in graduation ceremonies? See, Valentine v. School Dist., 191 Iowa 1100, 183 N.W. 434 (1921), and Ryan v. Board of Education, 124 Kan. 89, 257 P. 945 (1927).

8.  In Zeller v. Donegal School Dist. Bd. of Educ., 517 F.2d 600 (3rd Cir. 1975), a student claimed damages alleging he was unconstitutionally excluded from the soccer team because of his noncompliance with an athletic code regulating hair styles. The court stated that "there are areas of state school regulation in which the federal courts should not intrude." Then, expressing concern about its workload and "a genuine fear of 'trivialization' of the Constitution," the court ruled "that student hair cases fall on the side where the wisdom and experience of school authorities must be deemed superior and preferable to the federal judiciary's" with the result that the student's "asserted claim is not one for which relief can be granted in a federal forum."

In Ferrara v. Hendry County School Bd., 362 So.2d 371 (Fla.App.1978), the court upheld a dress code requiring that "students are to be clean shaven," saying "that regulations such as involved here that do not affect fundamental freedoms are subject to a much less rigorous standard of judicial review than is applicable when such fundamental rights are at stake." See also, Hatch v. Goerke, 502 F.2d 1189 (10th Cir. 1974).

9.  Kelley v. Johnson, 425 U.S. 238, 96 S.Ct. 1440, 47 L.Ed.2d 708 (1976), involved a regulation limiting the length of a policeman's hair. The U. S. Supreme Court emphasized that, when organizing its police force, a county rationally could "give weight to the overall need for discipline, esprit de corps, and uniformity." Because of the rationality of such a policy, and because "similarity in appearance of police officers is desirable," the court could not declare the hair-length regulation "so irrational that it may be branded 'arbitrary,' and therefore a deprivation of respondent's 'liberty' interest in freedom to choose his own hair style." The court's characterization of the police was as a para-military force. Do Pierce, Barnette and Meyer preclude a direct application of this precedent to school regulations of grooming? Also see, Quinn v. Muscare, 425 U.S. 560, 96 S.Ct. 1752, 48 L.Ed.2d 165 (1976) rehearing denied 426 U.S. 954, 96 S.Ct. 3183, 49 L.Ed.2d 1194.

## FREEDOM OF OFF CAMPUS ACTIVITY

### WOODS v. WRIGHT

United States Court of Appeals, 5th Cir., 1964.
334 F.2d 369.

JONES, Circuit Judge. The appellant, Linda Cal Woods, a Negro girl living in Birmingham, Alabama, was a pupil in Washington School, a public school of that City. . . . The complaint alleges that Linda Cal Woods participated in a peaceful demonstration against racial segregation on May 4, 1963, which was a Saturday and a school holiday. She was arrested and charged under Section 1159 of the Code of the City of Birmingham with parading without a license. On May 20, 1963, Linda Cal Woods was given a letter at her school directed to her father, Calvin Woods, signed by the school principal, suspending Linda and stating that she was requested not to return to school for the remainder of the school term. The letter stated that the action was taken under the terms of a letter to the principal from the Superintendent, who was the defendant below and is the appellee here. . . .

The appellant has specified as error that (a) the suspensions and expulsions without notice or hearing violated due process rights, (b) that the Superintendent's directive is a restraint upon First and Fourteenth Amendment rights of liberty of expression, and (c) that the suspension is a denial of due process because it results from an alleged violation of an unconstitutional ordinance. These questions, we think, are not properly before us for decision. The case comes to us on appeal from the refusal of the district court to grant a temporary restraining order. Our holding that this order has finality of a kind which gives it appealability, does not make the district court's ruling dispositive of the case or operative as a final judgment. These issues are, in the first instance, for the district court.

We are fully aware of the reluctance with which Federal Courts should contemplate the use of the injunctive power to interfere with the conduct of state officers.  But when there is a deprivation of a constitutionally guaranteed right the duty to exercise the power cannot be avoided.  See Dixon v. Alabama State Bd. of Education, 294 F.2d 150 (5th Cir. 1961), cert. den. 368 U.S. 930, 82 S.Ct. 368, 7 L.Ed. 2d 193.  Where there is a clear and imminent threat of an irreparable injury amounting to manifest oppression it is the duty of the court to protect against the loss of the asserted right by a temporary restraining order.  We think such an order should have been entered in this cause by the district court.  .  .  .

The order denying a temporary restraining order will be reversed, and upon receipt of the mandate of this Court, a temporary restraining order will be entered by the district court enjoining, until its further order, Theo R. Wright, Superintendent of Schools of the City of Birmingham, his agents, employees, subordinates, successors, and all persons in active concert with him from enforcing and carrying into effect the order of the Board of Education issued by letter on May 20, 1963, which suspended or expelled the Negro minor plaintiff, Linda Cal Woods, and other pupils of the named class who received said letter, for parading without a permit.  It will not be appropriate to say, at this juncture, that if the facts recited in the affidavit of Calvin Woods and filed in the district court on May 21, 1963, are established, the plaintiffs will be entitled to a preliminary injunction of substantially the same tenor as the preliminary injunction until the final disposition of the cause.  .  .  .

------

## SHANLEY v. NORTHEAST INDEPENDENT SCHOOL DIST.

United States Court of Appeals, 1972.
462 F.2d 960 (5th Cir.).

GOLDBERG, Circuit Judge.  It should have come as a shock to the parents of five high school seniors in the Northeast Independent School District of San Antonio, Texas, that their elected school board had assumed suzerainty over their children before and after school, off school grounds, and with regard to their children's rights of expressing their thoughts.  We trust that it will come as no shock whatsoever to the school board that their assumption of authority is an unconstitutional usurpation of the First Amendment.

Appellants, Mark S. Shanley, Clyde A. Coe, Jr., William E. Jolly, John A. Alford, and John Graham, were seniors at MacArthur High School in the Northeast Independent School District of San Antonio.  At least they were students there save for a period of three days during which they were suspended for violating a school board "policy."  Each of the students here was considered a "good" or "excellent" student.  All were in the process of applying for highly competitive slots in colleges or for scholarships. The three days of zeros that resulted from the suspensions substantially affected their grade averages at a critical time of their educational careers.

The occasion of the suspension was the publication and distribution of a so-called "underground" newspaper entitled "Awakening." The newspaper was authored entirely by the students, during out-of-school hours, and without using any materials or facilities owned or operated by the school system. The students distributed the papers themselves during one afternoon after school hours and one morning before school hours. At all times distribution was carried on near but outside the school premises on the sidewalk of an adjoining street, separated from the school by a parking lot. The students neither distributed nor encouraged any distribution of the papers during school hours or on school property, although some of the newspapers did turn up there. There was absolutely no disruption of class that resulted from distribution of the newspaper, nor were there any disturbances whatsoever attributable to the distribution. It was acknowledged by all concerned with this case that the students who passed out the newspapers did so politely and in orderly fashion.

The "Awakening" contains absolutely no material that could remotely be considered libelous, obscene, or inflammatory. In fact, the content of this so-called "underground" paper is such that it could easily surface, flower-like, from its "underground" abode. As so-called "underground" newspapers go, this is probably one of the most vanilla-flavored ever to reach a federal court.

The five students were suspended by the principal for violation of school board "policy" 5114.2 which reads in pertinent part:

> "Be it further resolved that *any* attempt to avoid the school's established procedure for administrative approval of activities such as the production for distribution and/or distribution of petitions or printed documents of *any* kind, sort, or type without the specific approval of the principal shall be cause for suspension and, if in the judgment of the principal, there is justification, for referral to the office of the Superintendent with a recommendation for expulsion. . . . "

That courts should not interfere with the day-to-day operations of schools is a platitudinous but eminently sound maxim which this court has reaffirmed on many occasions. This court laid to rest more than a decade ago the notion that state authorities could subject students at public-supported educational institutions to whatever conditions the state wished. And of paramount importance is the constitutional imperative that school boards abide constitutional precepts:

> "The Fourteenth Amendment, as now applied to the States, protects the citizen against the State itself and all of its creatures—Boards of Education not excepted."

West Virginia State Board of Education v. Barnette.  The school board insists that "policy" 5114.2 is constitutional both "on its face" and "as applied" to the suspensions meted out under the circumstances of this case.

When the *Burnside/Tinker* standards are applied to this case, it is beyond serious question that the activity punished here does not even approach the "material and substantial" disruption that must accompany an exercise of expression, either in fact or in reasonable forecast.  As a factual matter there were no disruptions of class; there were no disturbances of any sort, on or off campus, related to the distribution of the "Awakening."  Disruption in fact is an important element for evaluating the reasonableness of a regulation screening or punishing student expression.  In a companion case to *Burnside,* this court held that conduct presumptively-protected in *Burnside* itself was not protected by the First Amendment when it was accompanied by disorderly and raucous distribution.  One week after *Tinker* the Supreme Court denied certiorari in a case that had involved rather violent and disruptive activity by some college students.  The district court found that the students had exceeded their constitutional privileges of free expression, Barker v. Hardway.  In the Supreme Court's denial of review, Mr. Justice Fortas, who wrote for the majority in *Tinker,* observed in concurrence that "the petitioners  .  .  . engaged in an aggressive and violent demonstration, and not in peaceful nondisruptive expression."

*Tinker's* dam to school board absolutism does not leave dry the fields of school discipline.  This court has gone a considerable distance with the school boards to uphold its disciplinary fiats where reasonable.  *Tinker* simply irrigates, rather than floods, the fields of school discipline.  It sets canals and channels through which school discipline might flow with the least possible damage to the nation's priceless topsoil of the First Amendment.  Perhaps it would be well if those entrusted to administer the teaching of American history and government to our students began their efforts by practicing the document on which that history and government are based.  Our eighteen-year-olds can now vote, serve on juries, and be drafted; yet the board fears the "awakening" of their intellects without reasoned concern for its effect upon school discipline.  The First Amendment cannot tolerate such intolerance.  This case is therefore reversed for entry of an order not inconsistent with this opinion.

Reversed.

## O'ROURKE v. WALKER

Supreme Court of Errors of Connecticut, 1925.
102 Conn. 130, 128 A. 25.

[A mother, Julia Walker, brought an unsuccessful action for damages against a principal because of his infliction of corporal punishment upon her son who had annoyed female students on their way home from school.]

KEELER, J. It is conceded . . . that the school board or other proper authority may make reasonable rules concerning the conduct of pupils, and inflict reasonable corporal punishment for the infraction of such rules, and that in the absence of rules so established, the teacher may make all necessary and proper rules for the regulation of the school. . . .

Counsel argue that the teacher stands in loco parentis while pupils are under his control and oversight in the school room; but when by a return to his home he has again come under parental control neither the teacher nor any other educational authority has any authority to follow him thither and to govern his conduct thereafter.

The authorities upon this point would not ordinarily be numerous, since it is a narrow one and restricted to transactions not usually forming the subject of litigation, and still less of consideration by appellate tribunals. In Lander v. Seaver, 32 Vt. 114, 76 Am.Dec. 156, a teacher whipped a pupil, who, after he had returned home from school, passed with other boys the home of the teacher, and made remarks insulting to the latter. The punishment was inflicted the next day in school. The court held that while ordinarily the control of pupils and the right of a teacher to use disciplinary measures with them ceased after they had reached home, yet where the acts done have a direct and immediate tendency to injure the welfare of the school and its usefulness, punishment may be inflicted upon a pupil for acts done after school hours and after his return home. In Hutton v. State, 23 Tex.App. 386, 5 S.W. 122, 59 Am.Rep. 776, defendant, a teacher, was convicted of assault and battery for whipping a pupil with a switch "about nine licks on the legs" for fighting after school hours in disobedience to a rule of the school. The court held that the fact that the fighting occurred after school hours did not deprive the teacher of his legal right to punish the pupil. In Burdick v. Babcock, 31 Iowa 562, the court says:

"The view that acts, to be within the authority of the school board and teachers for discipline and correction, must be done within school hours, is narrow, and without regard to the spirit of the law and the best interest of our common schools. It is in conflict, too, with authority."

In this case the penalty inflicted was suspension by virtue of a rule to that effect.

We find no cases in point to the contrary of those cited above. There are many cases concerned with the power of school authorities to make and enforce rules forbidding activities and conduct outside of school hours and after the return of pupils to their homes, made punishable by expulsion or suspension, where the acts are likely to injuriously affect the proper operation and conduct of the school, and such rules have been upheld by the courts where adjudged to be reasonable. . . .

Examination of the authorities clearly reveals the true test of the teacher's right and jurisdiction to punish for offenses not committed on the school property or going and returning therefrom, but after the return of the pupil to the parental abode, to be not the time or place of the offense, but its effect upon the morale and efficiency of the school, whether it in fact is detrimental to its good order, and to the welfare and advancement of the pupils therein. If the conduct punished is detrimental to the best interests of the school, it is punishable, and in the instant case, under the rules of the school board, by corporal infliction. The effect of the rule claimed by the plaintiff, if applied, would result in a serious loss of discipline in school, and possible harm to innocent pupils in attendance. Supposing that some strong-armed juvenile bully attending school lived upon the next block and sought for a brief moment the asylum of his home, and thence sallied forth and beat, abused, and terrorized his fellow pupils as they passed by returning home; then by the claim urged by plaintiff he would be immune from punishment by the school authorities, while if he began his assaults before he had passed within the bounds of his own front yard he would be liable to proper punishment for any harm done. Now the harm done to the morale of the school is the same. The injured and frightened pupils are dismayed and discouraged in going to and coming from the school, and demoralized while in attendance. It will not do to say, as plaintiff's counsel argue, that the proper resort to correct such an abuse is the parents of such offenders, or the public prosecutors. Some parents would dismiss the matter by saying that they could give no attention to children's quarrels; many would champion their children as being all right in their conduct. The public authorities would very properly say, unless the offense resulted in quite serious injury, that such affrays were too trifling to deserve their attention. Yet the harm to the school has been done, and its proper conduct and operation seriously harmed, by such acts. Correction will usually be sought in vain at the hands of parents; it can only be successfully applied by the teacher. It is not likely that any milder punishment than corporal infliction would act as a deterrent in cases like the present. The abuse of little girls by young bullies is a base and brutal offense.

In the instant case it will be observed that while the plaintiff had reached his home after school, his victims had not. This is an important fact, even if the rule claimed by plaintiff should be upheld as a general statement. The claim made in argument that the small girls who were abused were trespassers upon the property of plaintiff's mother is of no avail. There is nothing in the record to show that plaintiff was acting under direction of his mother, and even if he were, such conduct as the court has found to exist would not be lawful.

There is no error.

---

## HOWARD v. CLARK

New York Supreme Court, 1969.
59 Misc.2d 327, 299 N.Y.S.2d 65.

W. VINCENT GRADY, Justice. This is an article 78 proceeding to compel respondents to reinstate the  .  .  . petitioners as full time students in the New Rochelle High School. The  .  .  . petitioners were suspended indefinitely pursuant to the New Rochelle School Board Resolution No. 69–323 on March 17, 1969, on the grounds that they had been arrested on March 10, 1969, by the Mamaroneck police and charged with the criminal possession of a hypodermic instrument. It is apparent that the Superintendent of Schools relied upon that portion of Board of Education Resolution No. 69–323 which mandates suspension of "any student upon his indictment or arraignment in any court * * * for any criminal act of a nature injurious to other students or school personnel. * * * "

Education Law Section 3214(6)(a) provides that suspension can only be invoked upon the following minors:

"The school authorities, the superintendent of schools, or district superintendent of schools may suspend the following minors from requiring attendance upon instruction:

"(1) A minor who is insubordinate or disorderly;

"(2) A minor whose physical or mental condition endangers the health, safety, or morals of himself or of other minors;

"(3) A minor who, as determined in accordance with the provisions of part one of this article, is feebleminded to the extent that he cannot benefit from instruction."

The respondents contend that the validity of the challenged resolution may not be lawfully determined in an article 78 proceeding and that petitioners have not exhausted their administrative remedies of appeal to the Commissioner of Education under Education Law Section 310.  .  .  .

The question which is raised in this proceeding is whether the respondents in suspending the  .  .  .  petitioners under Resolution 69–323 of the New Rochelle Board of Education went beyond the powers conferred upon by the Superintendent of Schools and the Board of Education under section 3214(6)(a) of the Education Law.

Respondents argue that the Resolution was within the powers conferred by section 2503(2), (3) of the Education Law which gives power to the Board of Education to prescribe such regulations as may be necessary to make effectual the provisions of the Education Law for the general management operation, control maintenance and discipline of the schools.  Since section 3214(6)(a) Education Law specifically defines the grounds for suspension of a student, the powers of the Board of Education are limited in suspension cases to these grounds.

The respondents allege that the Superintendent of Schools suspended petitioners for the reason that: "possession by a high school student of heroin and of a hypodermic syringe for injection of the drug into the blood stream regardless of where offense is committed identified offender as a person whose conduct and mental condition endanger the safety, morals, health and welfare of other high school students with whom he would associate in the school."

While the use of heroin by students off the high school premises bears a reasonable relation to and may endanger the health, safety and morals of other students, the bare charges against petitioners of possession of heroin do not justify suspension of petitioners on the grounds set forth in section 3214(6)(a) that they are insubordinate or disorderly; nor that their physical or mental condition endangers the health, safety or morals of themselves or other minors.

The court finds that the respondents have exceeded the powers conferred upon them by the Education Law in suspending the  .  .  . petitioners on the ground that they have been accused of possession of heroin.  Until the legislature amends the Education Law, suspension of a student should be done pursuant to a strict interpretation and application of section 3214(6)(a) of the Education Law.

The court need not decide the constitutional issues raised by petitioners since petitioners are entitled to the relief they seek on the ground that the New Rochelle Board of Education exceeded its powers under the Education Law in suspending the  .  .  .  petitioners.

The application of the intervenors to intervene in this proceeding is denied.  However, since it appears that  .  .  .  Douglas Herman was suspended for five (5) days for being charged with possession of marijuana off school grounds, and his suspension has terminated, his intervention herein is now moot, but based on the within decision, the record of his suspension should be expunged from the school records.

The petition is granted and the Board of Education of the City of New Rochelle is ordered to permit petitioners to attend New Rochelle

High School forthwith as full time students and the record of their suspensions should be expunged from the school records.

---

PROBLEM

## R. R. v. BOARD OF EDUCATION

Superior Court of New Jersey, 1970.
109 N.J.Super. 337, 263 A.2d 180.

LANE, J. S. C.   .   .   .   The essential facts are not in dispute. On January 20, 1970 R. R., aged 15, was a sophomore at the high school which is located in West Long Branch, New Jersey.  After his dismissal from the high school at the end of the class day, he went to his home in a neighboring municipality, arriving about 3:30 P. M. Finding the door locked and no one at home, R. R. went across the street to the home of W. O. to see if his parents had left the key to the house there.  When R. R. rang the doorbell, L. O., about 15 years old, came to the door and let R. R. in.  It is not clear exactly what happened at this point.  R. R. alleges that he was provoked into striking L. O. on the back of her head with a piece of wood that he was carrying.  He claims that L. O. then picked up a knife and that during the ensuing scuffle in which he tried to get the knife away from her, she was cut in four places.  Her version is that R. R. deliberately tried to stab her.

On January 21, 1970 Elbert M. Hoppenstedt, superintendent of the high school, was informed by the principal of the incident.  Mr. Hoppenstedt immediately contacted the neighboring municipality's police department and was read a statement of L. O. which set forth her version of the incident.  Based on this information and information from the principal and vice-principal of the school that R. R. had been engaged in less serious conflicts with other students (which R. R. denies), it was decided that R. R. should be suspended until the next meeting of the board of education.  There was no specification as to such alleged "less serious conflicts."  There was no hearing afforded to R. R.

On January 22, 1970 a complaint was signed by a representative of the neighboring municipality's police department against R. R. alleging a violation of N.J.S.A. 2A:90–1.  The complaint was forwarded to the Juvenile and Domestic Relations Court on January 29, 1970. A plea of not guilty was entered on February 25, 1970.  The matter is now scheduled before that court for a formal hearing on April 9, 1970.

On January 23, 1970 M. R., R. R.'s father, who had been out of the State on business before this date, called the vice-principal of the high school who informed him of R. R.'s suspension from the high school until further notice.   The vice-principal told M. R. that the high school would try to get home instruction for R. R. during the period of his suspension.   On his own initiative, M. R. had his son examined on January 26, 1970 by Dr. Frank Husserl, a well-qualified psychiatrist.   Dr. Husserl requested that R. R. be examined by Dr. Edward Dengrove.   This examination was completed but Dr. Dengrove requested an electroencephalograph.   As a result of the report of Dr. Dengrove and the report of the electroencephalograph, which was normal, and based on his examination, Dr. Husserl under date of February 6, 1970 addressed a letter:

> To Whom It May Concern:
>
> I have examined the above named [R. R.] in my office on January 26, 1970.
>
> It is my professional opinion that he may return to school without risk to the safety and security of others or himself.   .   .   .

The court is informed that the board of education again considered the matter on February 25, 1970 and decided to keep the suspension in effect.   No hearing was afforded to R. R.

The question before the court is whether public school officials can deprive a student of his right to attend school because of acts committed off school property and totally unrelated to school activities, and, if so, what procedural due process must the school officials afford to the student.   .   .   .

Assume that you are the judge in this case, what decision will you render and for what reason(s)?


## NOTES AND QUESTIONS

1.   Like the laws of many states Kentucky Revised Statutes § 161.180, provide that "each teacher in the public schools shall hold pupils to a strict account for their conduct in school, on the way to and from school, on the playgrounds and during intermission or recess."   Would the following properly come within such a statute: (a) teacher disciplining students for fist-fighting after they returned home and went out to play; (b) a school board regulation requiring that students go directly home at the close of the school day; (c) the disciplining of a student for smoking (drinking) (uttering profanities) while on a public street; or (d) a rule prohibiting students from attending films, shows or social events on any nights except Friday or Saturday?

2.   Suppose a school board requires that students go directly home after school, but the custom, for years, has been for the students to "hang out" at a local business establishment after school, upon strict enforcement of the rule by a new principal the owner of the business sues the principal for loss of profits, what decision?   See, Jones v. Cody, 132 Mich. 13, 92 N.W. 495 (1902).

3. Repeated drinking of alcohol, smoking and late hours curtail or destroy an athlete's ability. Does a coach have the right to apply sanctions to these kinds of off-campus behavior?

4. Suppose a proprietor, Mr. Russell, opened a cafe on land adjacent to the school playground where students could be served without leaving school grounds. Also suppose the local board's regulation was designed to protect its lunchroom business: "No one, while in school, shall be allowed to enter the restaurant of Mr. Russell or any other business establishment in the town without permission from 8:45 a.m. until 3:00 p.m." and suppose the father of two students persisted in either taking them, or allowing them, to go to the Russell Cafe for lunch, could the students be subjected to discipline for this "off campus" activity? See, Casey County Board of Education v. Luster, 282 S.W.2d 333 (Ky.1955).

5. Suppose a local school board rule states that "No one shall leave the campus without permission or unless accompanied by a teacher from 9:00 a.m. until 3:00 p.m." and suppose a student was scheduled to take music lessons off-campus once a week during the school hours, but the school authorities refused to give permission; after being suspended, he now appeals—what decision for what reason(s)? See, Christian v. Jones, 211 Ala. 161, 100 So. 99 (1924).

6. Does O'Rourke v. Walker correctly apply the in-loco-parentis doctrine? It seems to, because the court restricted that doctrine to applications having a reasonable relationship to a school's educational and related host functions. The female students were where they were because of their compliance with the state's compulsory attendance laws. The court recognized the school's legitimate host interest in caring for them and in protecting them from harm by other students while on their way home. But a school's host-function power is limited. It does not imply that schools have power under the in-loco-parentis doctrine to act as general law enforcement agencies. For example, suppose the Walker boy only annoyed the female children on Sundays when they walked in front of his home on their way home from church; surely, the school would have no legal, host-function right to impose corporal punishment in such circumstances. Thus, the in-loco-parentis doctrine is restricted to applying to situations where the school has a valid educational or related host-function interest in controlling the behavior of its students. Does this reasoning explain why the doctrine was not applied in Woods v. Wright or Shanley which involved students exercising First Amendment rights?

## II.  PROCEDURAL DUE PROCESS RIGHTS

### OUR NATION'S SCHOOLS—A REPORT CARD: "A" IN SCHOOL VIOLENCE AND VANDALISM

U.S. Senate Comm. on the Judiciary, Subcomm. To Investigate Juvenile Delinquency, Report, 94th Cong., 1st Sess., April 1975.
Excerpt from pp. 3–13.

It is alarmingly apparent that student misbehavior and conflict within our school system is no longer limited to a fist fight between individual students or an occasional general disruption resulting from a specific incident.  Instead our schools are experiencing serious crimes of a felonious nature including brutal assaults on teachers and students, as well as rapes, extortions, burglaries, thefts and an unprecedented wave of wanton destruction and vandalism.  Moreover our preliminary study of the situation has produced compelling evidence that this level of violence and vandalism is reaching crisis proportions which seriously threaten the ability of our educational system to carry out its primary function.

Quite naturally the rising tide of violence in our schools has engendered an increasing awareness and concern among the American people.  In a 1974 Gallup poll most adults and high school students surveyed cited the lack of discipline as the chief problem confronting schools today.  In fact three of the top four problems cited by most of those polled were directly related to various problems of student behavior.

Our recently completed nationwide survey of over 750 school districts demonstrates that this concern is well founded.  The statistics gathered by the Subcommittee indicate that violence in our schools affects every section of the nation and, in fact, continues to escalate to even more serious levels.  The preliminary Subcommittee survey found that in the three years between 1970 and 1973:

(A)  Homicides increased by 18.5 percent;

(B)  Rapes and attempted rapes increased by 40.1 percent;

(C)  Robberies increased by 36.7 percent;

(D)  Assaults on students increased by 85.3 percent;

(E)  Assaults on teachers increased by 77.4 percent;

(F)  Burglaries of school buildings increased by 11.8 percent;

(G)  Drug and alcohol offenses on school property increased by 37.5 percent;  and

(H)  Dropouts increased by 11.7 percent.

An even more ominous statistic for the future course of school safety is the fact that by the end of the 1973 school year the number of weapons confiscated by school authorities had risen by 54.4 percent in three years.  These weapons include knives, clubs, pistols and even sawed-off shotguns designed to be easily concealed within a student's locker.

The conclusions to be drawn from the Subcommittee survey are supported by other studies of these problems.  Simply put, the trend in school violence over the last decade in America has been, and continues to be, alarmingly and dramatically upward.

There are indications that student violence and vandalism occurs more often in larger urban secondary schools.  A survey of newspaper articles between October 1969 and February 1970 revealed that 63 percent of the major school disruptions occurred in urban areas.  A Vandalism and Violence study published by the School Public Relations Association estimated that 55 percent of the major incidents of disruption occurred in cities larger than one million people and 26 percent occurred in cities of less than 100,000 population.  .  .  .

.  .  .  the principal victims of the rising tide of crime in our schools are not the teachers, but the students.  The Subcommittee's survey found that violent assaults on students increased by 85.3 percent over a three year period, while reported robberies of students increased by 36.7 percent.

The Subcommittee survey found that incidents involving the use of drugs and alcohol on public school property went up 37.5 percent.  .  .  .

.  .  .  tre principal victims of the rising tide of crime in our

The National Highway Safety Administration estimates that 50 percent of the nation's high school students go to drinking parties every month and that 61 percent of that group gets drunk once a month.  The Highway Safety Administration also found that these students represent a remarkable cross-section of our schools:

> They are not far out, drop out alienated or under achieving types.  On the contrary, they represent all levels of scholastic achievement and aspiration.  They report the same range of sport and extracurricular activities as the students who are not involved with drinking.

It is important to stress that the Subcommittee survey findings, as well as those of other surveys on violence within the school system, are only estimates of the nature and extent of the problem.  A report on the New York City school system found that the rate of unreported incidents ranged between 30 percent and 60 percent.  Albert Shanker, President of the American Federation of Teachers, explained teachers' reluctance to fully report such incidents as follows:

> Teachers find that if they report to the principal an assault, the principal who feels that his own reputation or her

reputation or the school's reputation is at stake here, will very frequently turn around and start harassing the teacher by saying, "Well, if you had three assaults, how come you are the one always complaining. You must have more observation or better planning, or this or that." So the teacher soon finds out that bringing these reports to the attention of the principal is something that is not wanted and tends to suppress that information.

.  .  .

In addition to the violence directed against both teachers and students within the school system, there is also a continuing and rapidly increasing level of destruction and theft of school property. A survey conducted by the Baltimore, Maryland, public schools of 39 cities across the country found that in 1968–69 these cities had reported vandalism losses of over $12,000,000. In a 1971 report prepared by Education U.S.A. and the National School Public Relations Association, it was estimated that vandalism was costing $200 million annually. Barely two years later Dr. Norman Scharer, President of the Association of School Security Directors, stated: "A conservative estimate of the cost of vandalism, thefts and arson to schools in this country this year will reportedly be over a half a billion dollars. I say conservative because out of the almost 15,000 school systems the top five account for $15–20 million dollars of this cost."

This $500 million vandalism cost represents over $10 per year for every school student, and in fact equals the total amount expended on textbooks throughout the country in 1972. Almost 60 percent of all vandalism takes place in larger districts with an average cost per district in 1973 at $135,297.

The source of this destruction ranges from broken windows, found in over 90 percent of our districts, to fires reported by 35 percent of the districts. Significant incidents of theft and malicious destruction of educational equipment occurs in 80 percent of the school districts in the country.

Staggering as these figures are they undoubtedly represent a very conservative estimate of economic loss attributable to school vandalism. A study of school vandalism by Bernard Greenberg of the Stanford Research Institute found: "It should be noted that the cost figure is grossly understated because it does not include in all instances losses attributable to burglary, theft and property damage repaired by resident maintenance staffs. Nor does it take into account costs to equip and maintain special security forces, which are considerable for the larger school districts, and law enforcement costs to patrol and respond to calls reporting school incidents. Many school districts carry theft insurance, but the costs are exceedingly high. Where data on selected school districts theft losses are available, the dollar amounts are significantly high."

Spiraling insurance rates are a significant, but often overlooked, factor in the overall cost of vandalism.   .   .   .

The overall impact of violence and vandalism on our educational system cannot, of course, be adequately conveyed by a recitation of the numbers of assaults and the dollars expended.  Every dollar spent on replacing a broken window or installing an alarm system cannot be spent on the education of students.  J. Arlen Marsh, editor of a study on school security costs estimates that:

> "The cost of replacing broken windows in the average big city would build a new school every year."

The School Public Relations Association study found that a $60,-000 loss, approximately the average loss for a school district, could pay for eight reading specialists or finance a school breakfast program for 133 children for a year.  It is quite clear that in some areas of the country the high costs of vandalism is resulting in the reduction or elimination of needed educational programs.

The natural reaction to these enormous amounts of wasted money is to wonder over the apparently senseless nature of this destruction. A study entitled Urban School Crisis, however, questions whether vandalism is as irrational as it may appear:  "Perhaps the most serious aspect of vandalism is the set of messages it conveys:  that students look upon the school as alien territory, hostile to their ambitions and hopes;  that the education which the system is attempting to provide lacks meaningfulness;  that students feel no pride in the edifices in which they spend most of their days."

In addition to requiring the diversion of funds from academic and scholastic projects to security and repair programs, the atmosphere of violence and vandalism has a devastating impact on the ability of our educational system to continue with the instruction of its students.
.   .   .

Few students can be expected to learn in an atmosphere of fear, assaults and disorder.  There can be little doubt that the significant level of violent activity, threats and coercion revealed by the Subcommittee's preliminary survey would have a detrimental effect on the psychological and educational development of children and young adults.  Moreover a continuous pattern of destruction of school equipment and buildings naturally makes nearly impossible the already challenging process of education.  The extent and continued growth of this chaotic and threatening climate in our schools is a serious threat to our educational system.

Not surprisingly, the underlying causes for this wave of violence and vandalism in our schools is a subject of intense debate and disagreement.  In a certain sense the school system may be viewed as merely a convenient battleground for the pervasive societal problem of juvenile crime.  As this Subcommittee pointed out in its recent Annual

Report, violent juvenile crime has increased by 246.5 percent in the last thirteen years. Over the same period crimes directed against property by youths increased by 104.6 percent. Today persons under 25 years old are committing 50 percent of all violent crimes and 80 percent of all property crimes. Since our school systems are charged with the care and custody of a large percentage of our young people it is reasonable to assume that the incidents of violence and vandalism within our educational institutions would follow patterns similar to those developing in the society at large. A study conducted in 1973 by Paul Ritterbrand and Richard Silberstein concluded that the roots of school problems could be traced to problems existing in the general American society rather than to conditions or failures within the school system itself.

Other studies, however, while acknowledging the substantial effect general societal conditions would have on the conduct of school behavior, have indicated the existence of several "in school" conditions which may contribute to the level of youthful disorder. One possible contributing factor is the various methods of excluding students from school. A 1974 report entitled, "Children Out of School in America," prepared by the Children's Defense Fund, estimates that hundreds of thousands of students are removed from schools each year by short-term, long-term or indefinite expulsions and suspensions. While most educators concur in the necessity for the exclusion of seriously disruptive troublemakers from the school environment, the Children's Defense Fund study found the numbers of students being suspended were far in excess of those who must be removed as a means of maintaining order. There are in fact so many students being subjected to expulsive disciplinary practices that the phenomena has been referred to as the "Pushout" problem.

Another facet of the pushout problem which may operate as a contributing factor to school disorders was revealed in a report recently released by the Department of Health, Education, and Welfare. In statistics gathered at the end of the 1973 school year it was demonstrated that while Blacks represent only 27 percent of the total student enrollment in the 3,000 school districts surveyed, they accounted for 37 percent of the expulsions and 42 percent of the suspensions from those districts. The disparity among these figures raises serious questions concerning possible widescale bias in the administration of suspension and expulsion. Such policies can only result in anger and hostility on the part of students.

In addition to these forms of compulsive absence from schools there are the related problems of "force outs" and truancy which contribute to the large numbers of children and young adults who attend school in only a very irregular fashion. The "force out" concept is the educational system's version of a plea bargain, so common in our criminal justice system. A student involved in academic or behavioral difficulty may be informally presented with the options of failing courses, facing expulsion or voluntary removal from school. In many instances the student will opt for "dropping out" and therefore be removed temporarily or permanently. Truancy, of course, is an accepted and traditional fact of life in schools, but the modern rates of truancy especially in the large urban systems, reveal numerous students attend school only in the most erratic fashion.

At first glance it might appear that the expulsion, suspension, pushout, force out and truancy phenomenon, although certainly tragic for those involved, might at least create a somewhat more orderly atmosphere for those remaining in school as a result of the absence of youngsters evidently experiencing problems adjusting to the school environment. The opposite, however, appears to be the case. The Syracuse study, for instance, found that in schools where the average daily attendance was lower, the disruptions, violence and vandalism rates were higher. This may be explained by the fact that the vast majority of students who are voluntarily or compulsively excluded from schools do, in time, return to those schools. In many instances their frustrations and inadequacies which caused their absence in the first place have only been heightened by their exclusion and the school community will likely find itself a convenient and meaningful object of revenge.

As the Subcommittee's statistics reveal, the use of drugs and alcohol by students in secondary schools continues to increase. These trends cannot be ignored as a contributing factor to the problems confronting the schools.   .   .   .

Another cause of disruption and violence found mainly in large urban centers on the East and West Coasts is the presence of youthful, but highly organized, gangs within the school system. A school which finds itself being used as the center of a gang's illegal activities can quickly develop a very hostile environment. A security director for a metropolitan school system in a letter to the Subcommittee states:

> Although the number of gang members, in proportion to the overall student population in most schools is minimal, the trouble they cause is at times, cataclysmic. Students are robbed, intimidated, raped, bludgeoned and sometimes fatally wounded. Teachers and other adults in the schools are threatened and on occasions, physically assaulted. The peace of any school is breached and the learning climate seriously polluted by gang activity, however slight.

> In some schools, gang activity is so intense that it is necessary for school security officers and the local police to escort one gang through the territory of a rival gang at dismissal time. At certain schools, Safety Corridors have been established which provide safe passage for neutral students under the protection of school security personnel and police, through the hostile territory. Needless to say, these meas-

ures provide at best, temporary relief.  They do not begin to attack the root causes of the problem.

.   .   .

One common thread of particular interest to the Subcommittee running through many of the underlying causes of school violence and vandalism is what may be called the crisis of Due Process.  Quite naturally schools, like other institutions, are compelled to issue rules and regulations concerning the conduct of persons within their jurisdiction.  It is clear that without fair and meaningful control and discipline the schools would quickly lose their ability to educate students.  Increasingly, though, educators and administrators are finding that the extent of student conduct which is sought to be regulated, as well as the methods of regulation, are causing more problems than they are controlling.  A 1975 NEA study interviewed a large number of students from different schools and found that, "Many students spoke of the need for consistent, fair discipline."

For example, the Subcommittee found that in numerous institutions across the country, students, administrators and teachers are embroiled in constant ongoing disputes over restrictions on dress, hair style, smoking, hall passes, student newspapers and a myriad of other aspects of school life.  The Syracuse study observes that intense efforts to control clothes or hair styles may, in fact, be counterproductive to a well ordered environment:

> This remains a constant bone of contention between students and staff, and when it takes on racial or ethnic features, the contention becomes far more serious.  We suspect that everyone would agree that nakedness at school is prohibited because, by itself, it disrupts education.  On the other hand, restrictions against bell bottom pants, long hair, 'Afros', and beads are probably useless and offensive.

In another area, administrative attempts to control student publications have at times appeared to be overly restrictive and conducted in a capricious manner.  A 1974 report by the Commission of Inquiry Into High School Journalism found that:

> Censorship and the systematic lack of freedom to engage in open, responsible journalism characterize high school journalism.  Unconstitutional and arbitrary restraints are so deeply embedded in high school journalism as to overshadow its achievements, as well as its other problems.

As discussed earlier, the manner in which suspensions and expulsions are administered have in some instances been arbitrary and discriminatory.  Students in some schools are suspended without being given an opportunity to answer or explain charges against them, while other students are suspended for improper conduct which results only in a reprimand for other students engaging in identical activity.  A study of the student pushout phenomena undertaken by the Southern Regional Council and the Robert F. Kennedy memorial found that:

> Most observers acknowledge the need for rules and the power to enforce them. The pragmatic observer will concede that there are those individual students, just as some older citizens, who finally will not or cannot conform to any societal standards. The misuse of discipline, however, often occurs because racial, cultural and generation differences cloud the judgment and actions of teachers and administrators alike.

On a more positive level certain efforts have been made to rationalize and reform the rule making and disciplinary functions in our schools. The Supreme Court held recently in Goss v. Lopez, 95 S.Ct. 729 (1975) that student expulsion or suspension procedures must be governed by at least the minimal standards of Due Process. The Court stated:

> In holding as we do, we do not believe that we have imposed procedures on school disciplinarians which are inappropriate in a classroom setting. Instead we have imposed requirements which are, if anything, less than a fair minded school principal would impose upon himself in order to avoid unfair suspensions.

The NEA has developed a Student Rights and Responsibility statement which recommends that the standards of conduct to be followed at a particular school be drawn up with participation by student representatives, and that they be distributed to all members of the school community in written form. This practice would insure that students as well as teachers have a clear and understandable statement of the rules and regulations governing their conduct while in school. Many schools have in fact amended or instituted written student codes which contain a statement of student rights and responsibilities and which set forth the grounds for suspension and expulsion along with whatever procedural protections are to be used prior to such action. The mere practice of committing school regulations to writing helps insure an even-handed administration of student discipline within the institution.

In addition to students, many teachers are anxious for clear and closely followed disciplinary codes within schools. Following the shooting death of a teacher in Philadelphia by a junior high school student who had continuously caused trouble at the school, both principals and teachers within that system demanded a new and stricter code for dealing with repeatedly disruptive students. Many teachers feel that only when seriously disruptive students are properly controlled can the remainder of the school community continue the task of education.

The proper response to the problem of the seriously disruptive student is a difficult and complex issue. On the one hand, a small group of disruptive and violent students can create conditions which make the task of education impossible and dangerous for both teachers and other students. On the other hand, however, several studies indicate that mass expulsions of these students from schools often creates groups of resentful youngsters who return to the school community to seek vengeance.

Unfortunately, not all the sources of school violence and vandalism discussed in this report are as amenable to solution as the promulgation and fair administration of rules and regulations affecting both teachers and students. Some of these causes are obviously beyond the direct control of administrators or teachers, while others no doubt remain largely unidentified. Many school districts are attempting to identify and confront those problems, but their nature and cure are not readily treatable solely by teachers or administrators. What is shockingly apparent from the Subcommittee survey, however, is that our school system is facing a crisis of serious dimensions, the solutions to which must be found if the system is to survive in a meaningful form. It is essential that the American public school becomes a safe and secure environment where education, rather than disruption, violence, and vandalism, is the primary concern.

---

## KNIGHT v. BOARD OF EDUCATION

United States District Court, E.D.N.Y., 1969.
48 F.R.D. 108.

WEINSTEIN, District Judge. This is a class action against the Board of Education of the City of New York and some of its officials by the seven named plaintiffs individually and on behalf of hundreds of fellow students allegedly dismissed from Franklin K. Lane High School on January 27, 1969. Two months after the event, March 28, the complaint was filed. It was not until April 17th that a proposed order was presented to this Court directing the defendants to show cause why a temporary injunction should not issue requiring the immediate readmission of these students. On request of the attorneys for the plaintiffs the order is not returnable until April 25, three months after the class was allegedly expelled. By telegram to counsel and individual defendants, the Court, on its own motion, ordered an appearance in Court at 9:00 A. M. today, Monday, April 21, for a conference pursuant to Rule 23 of the Federal Rules of Civil Procedure.

Allegations in the complaint and motion papers make out a prima facie failure by defendants to comply with elementary concepts of equal protection and due process in denying one of the necessities of our society—a sound high school education, important both for its own value and as a predicate for college. Defendants deny the charge, asserting that no students have been dismissed, that the school system has been, and is, making a determined and good faith attempt to provide meaningful education for all members of the class who wish it; and that it is providing intensive rehabilitative training and guidance to those members of the class, deficient in scholarship and delinquent in attendance, who are willing to prepare themselves to benefit from regular and full day-time high school attendance. The following statements of facts, except where specifically indicated, is based upon plaintiffs' contentions—strenuously controverted by defendants—and is intended only for purposes of the preliminary determinations made in this memorandum and order.

Franklin K. Lane High School (Lane) is an academic high school operated by the New York City Board of Education. On January 27, 1969, a total of 670 students were expelled from that school. Of this number, 412 were 17 years of age on April 1, 1969. Most of these 17-year olds have been discharged from the New York City Public School System and are presently receiving no public education; 258, who are under 17, were transferred to the jurisdiction of the Bureau of Attendance, an agency of the Board of Education. Many of those under 17 years of age are presently receiving instruction at an "annex" to Lane. This "annex" is inferior to Lane in physical facilities and educational exposure; it operates only three hours per day; no homework, examinations or grades are given.

It is the defendants' contention that approximately 600 students were involved; that each of them and their parents were contracted through a number of letters; and that many of the others were seen in repeated personal visits and interviews. Defendants submit that 165 students, who are over the age of 17, were voluntarily withdrawn from the school at the request of their parents; that 50 could not be located by mail or personal visitations although attempts are still being made to locate them; that 18 have returned to full-time instruction at Lane; that 70 are attending an annex of Lane where they are receiving intensive personal instruction in order to prepare them for full academic work at Lane; that 44, who are over 17, are now attending night high school; that 139, who are over 17, are still being investigated by the Bureau of Attendance although each has already received two letters and one visit; and that 112, who are under 17, are still being investigated, although each has already received two letters and one visit.

Plaintiffs assert that the only reason for this mass expulsion was the desire to relieve overcrowded conditions. No other high school in the City has found it necessary to embark upon a similar course. In effectuating the plan to relieve overcrowding, the following criteria were embodied in a mechanical rule: all students absent 30 days or more during the present school year and who had maintained an unsatisfactory academic record in the Autumn, 1968 semester, were to be dismissed from Lane.

Allegedly, no procedures were established to challenge the criteria or their application.  No opportunity to adduce any mitigating circumstances or to appeal the decisions of the administrators was provided.

Among the seven named plaintiffs, the criteria were applied without regard to specific circumstances, and in a non-uniform manner. In several instances, the administrators of this program failed to adhere to their own criteria:

(1)  Plaintiff Oscar Gonzalus had been absent less than 30 days in the Autumn, 1968 semester;

(2)  Plaintiff Marcine Chestnut had maintained a satisfactory academic record during the Autumn, 1968 semester;

(3)  Plaintiff Altamese Washington had maintained a satisfactory academic record, and had been absent less than 30 days during the Autumn, 1968 semester.

In addition, there was at least one instance in which the administrators of the program failed to take into account mitigating circumstances:  Plaintiff Arthur Knight was absent from Franklin K. Lane High School for the entire Autumn, 1968 semester because of a kidney ailment.

Three named plaintiffs meet the criteria and offer no mitigating circumstances.  Plaintiffs Willie Chestnut, Joel Barry Shiggs, and Jacqueline Andrews did experience academic difficulties during the Autumn, 1968 semester, and each was absent for more than 30 days during that period.

Plaintiffs Knight and Shiggs are the only named plaintiffs under the age of 17; both are assigned to the "annex."  Five of the named plaintiffs are above the age of 17.  Of these, four are presently receiving no public education.  Plaintiff Washington, a 17-year old senior, was readmitted to Lane on March 12, 1969.  Her eligibility for June, 1969 graduation is now in doubt because of schooling she lost during her exclusion.

Plaintiffs allege that the Autumn, 1968 semester is not an appropriate time period to use in formulating criteria designed to measure desire for an education.  During that semester there was a series of City-wide strikes by public school teachers; a disruptive student boycott of Lane; and disputes in several schools, among them Lane, about the propriety of establishing additional class days to compensate for those lost during the City-wide teachers' strike.  Absences on "make-up" days were counted as absences on students' attendance records.  During the Fall of 1968 there was also a severe influenza epidemic resulting in a large number of justifiable absences. . . .

Children have a right to due process and equal protection under the Constitution. . . .  The right to attend a public school may not be denied without due process. . . .

Constitutional requirements of due process in the administration of public school systems are violated by the expulsion of students without affording them an opportunity for a hearing.  .  .  .

Even if the criteria for expulsion were valid, lack of procedural due process, it is alleged, resulted in misapplication of the standards used.  In the case of three of the named plaintiffs an opportunity to be heard might have revealed that they did not come within even the letter of the expulsion criteria; a fourth named plaintiff might well have been able to show that strict application of the guidelines would have been unjustified.

Once a state undertakes to provide free public education, it may not arbitrarily discriminate among its citizens in making it available. Brown v. Board of Education  .  .  .  New York State has assumed the task of providing free education to all those between the ages of five and 21 who wish to take advantage of the opportunity; attendance in New York City is compulsory between the ages of seven and 16.  .  .  .

Beyond the issue of procedural due process, the facts alleged by the plaintiffs strongly suggest that hundreds of high school students may have been discriminated against by being denied the opportunity to obtain the free public education that is extended to other school-age youths in New York City.  Some rational basis justifying this discrimination must be shown by the state.  Hobson v. Hansen, 269 F. Supp. 401, 426, 429 (D.D.C.1967).  None has yet been offered except that this action was taken to prevent overcrowding.  Yet, other schools in New York City are apparently at least equally overcrowded.  With the expulsion of these students, Lane has become only the second of all New York City's high schools which do not require the scheduling of "multiple sessions" to meet the demands of large numbers of students.  Such discrimination, if it is proven—especially when no effective alternate educational opportunity is provided—must be considered invidious, and in violation of the requirements of the Equal Protection Clause of the Fourteenth Amendment.

The question of whether a case has been stated for a constitutionally prohibited discrimination within Lane between those students who have been retained and those who have been expelled, is closer. If it were really necessary to take such a drastic step to relieve overcrowding, it would be difficult to classify as unreasonable, arbitrary, or capricious a determination that only those who may benefit the most and who have shown the greatest interest may continue.

If, however, a determination based upon interest is made, it must be made in a reasonable manner and upon reasonable premises.  The facts upon which the distinction has been based cannot be said, at this stage of the litigation, to be of unquestionable relevance.  The disruptions that took place during the Fall period—a fact of which this

Court must take judicial notice—were hardly conducive to the development of typical academic performances. Since the choice of a period upon which to base the figures which formed the criteria for expulsion may have been constitutionally irrational, productive of untypical and distorted results, the actions of the school authorities may have resulted in an invidious discrimination in violation of the Fourteenth Amendment guarantees of equal protection.

In sum, in addition to the legal problems created by the alleged denial of due process to those students who allegedly have been expelled, there are questions of denial of equal protection raised by the action of the school authorities. Serious questions arise on two levels. First, has the action of the Board of Education resulted in an arbitrary and forbidden discrimination between the students at Lane and the students of other high schools in the City of New York? Second, has there been an invidious discrimination within Lane, between those students expelled and those continued as pupils? Plaintiffs have asserted a valid cause of action entitling them to immediate consideration of their claim that unless this Court acts at once they will be seriously harmed by denial of their constitutional rights. . . .

## NOTES AND QUESTIONS

1. Assuming the excluded students win the Knight case, their original expulsion still would have denied them their constitutional rights to procedural due process in that they would have been expelled without any hearing. Could the students sue the school officials for monetary compensation for having deprived them of their constitutional rights?
In Wood v. Strickland, 420 U.S. 308, 95 S.Ct. 992, 43 L.Ed.2d 214, rehearing denied 421 U.S. 921, 95 S.Ct. 1589, 43 L.Ed.2d 790 (1975), the U.S. Supreme Court held that school officials are not immune from law suits in the federal courts under 42 U.S.C.A. § 1983. They also can be subjected to law suits in state courts if the state law permits. The Supreme Court ruled that school officials could not be held liable in federal courts for actions undertaken in good faith. But, it also ruled that school officials can be subjected to liability if they knew or reasonably should have known that the action they took within their sphere of official responsibility would violate the constitutional rights of the students affected, or if they took the action with the malicious intention to cause a deprivation of such rights or other injury to the student. Carey v. Piphus, 435 U.S. 247, 98 S.Ct. 1042, 55 L.Ed.2d 252 (1978), spoke to the measure of damages that would be appropriate in a federal court under 42 U.S.C.A. § 1983. The case involved a claim for damages by students who had been suspended from public schools without procedural due process. Justice Powell's opinion for the Court ruled that "in the absence of proof of actual injury, the students are entitled to recover only nominal damages," not to exceed one dollar. Actual damages include emotional distress and similar harms actually incurred. Thus, if successful, the students in the Knight case probably could sue in a federal court and recover their actual damages. See also, Monell v. Dept. of Social Services, 436 U.S. 658, 98 S.Ct. 2018, 56 L.Ed. 2d 611 (1978).

2. Do short suspensions, expulsions for up to the end of a school term, or dismissals have a legitimate role? If so, what is that role? What educational purpose does it have? Do you agree or disagree with the following testimony of Albert Shanker, President, Am.Fed. of Teachers, AFL–CIO (U.S.Comm. On The Judiciary, Subcomm. to Investigate Juvenile Delinquency, Hearings, The Nature, Extent and Costs of Violence and Vandalism In Our Nation's Schools, 94th Cong., 1st Sess., April and June 1975, pp. 8–10):

In addition, on January 22nd, the United States Supreme Court ruled in Goss et al. v. Lopez et al.,[1] that students have a constitutional right not to be suspended for misbehavior unless they are first afforded due process rights—the right to be informed of the reason for the proposed suspension, and the right to a hearing.

In the context which I have been talking about, this ruling applies to suspensions of under 10 days. It may very well be that additional due process protections would be required for longer suspensions. There is good reason to believe that in this context this ruling will serve to create further difficulties for teachers and students who are victims as well and schools that are already overwhelmed by discipline problems.

A third factor is that the courts are powerless to act, because even when they find that a student is dangerous to himself and to those around him, there are no special school or institutional facilities available.

Those engaging in repeated acts of violence know that this lack exists and that, except for the most violent of actions, they are free to do as they please.

What is needed as a long-range solution for the disruptive and/or violent student is not expulsion, but rather a different educational setting—one that caters to his special needs, distinct from the usual setting. The other children can then go about their studies free of constant disturbance.

The only reason we are faced with the problem of pupil suspensions and expulsions is that, while we seem to care enough about the child to preserve even a single day's schooling, we do not seem to care enough to provide the funds for schooling that will work. What the disruptive student needs is alternative facilities where his individual needs are given sympathetic and skillful attention.

We have paid a cruel and unconscionable price by accepting violence as a way of life in our schools. The price includes physical and psychological injury to countless thousands of parents, teachers and pupils. It includes the social burden of many emotionally disturbed or disruptive students who have not been given the alternate educational settings they needed and who are now supported by the public—in jails or other State or Federal institutions.

[1] See "Models and Strategies for Change," hearing of Sept. 17, 1975; appendix.

It includes the many children, eager to learn, but deprived of a decent education by disruption and disorder in their classrooms and fear of physical harm.

Therefore we urge the Congress to take a number of steps.

Now what you are doing here is certainly a very necessary and important first step, which is to bring to the attention of the public the problems of victims of assault in the schools and the legal procedures which prevent effective prosecution of criminals who terrorize our schools.

## NEED ALTERNATIVE EDUCATIONAL OPPORTUNITIES

We need to appropriate additional funds so that the youngster who cannot adjust in the regular school situation can be helped in alternative educational settings in the public schools. And here I want to say that there is a whole segment of youngsters where the disruptive behavior is connected with the failure to learn.

When a child has been to kindergarten, first grade, second grade, third grade, fourth grade, and has still not learned to read, to write, and to figure, the child each year has a greater and greater belief that he will never learn these things. He has been in a classroom setting with a blackboard, chalk, books, teachers, and other students for 3 or more years and still is unable to read, to write, to figure. That child loses hope of ever being able to do those things in a regular educational setting.

There are two basic adjustments or adaptations children like this make. Some of them just retreat. They sit in the back of the room and they fall asleep or read comic books. They are sort of saying to the teacher, you leave me alone and I will leave you alone; I know I am just not going to make it.

The other group is very resentful of being compelled to sit in school in an atmosphere that reminds them of failure, year after year, and those students become rather violent and rather rebellious.

Now, sitting still and listening essentially from 8:40 in the morning until 3 in the afternoon is a most difficult thing. Most adults could not sit still and listen for that period of time. For those students who view the classroom as a place where they have not made it during all of these years, where they cannot participate in most of the work because they do not have the basic skills that were provided for the many students in the earlier years, a new atmosphere needs to be provided. We need educational settings that look different to the student and gives the student the feeling he is going to have a second chance in a different atmosphere. The normal school approach to the child who has been in school for five or six years and who has failed to make it by all these standards, compelling him to come back to that same atmosphere over and over again, is a kind of a provocation to disruption.

## EARLY CHILDHOOD EDUCATION

In addition, to this need for alternative settings, we ought to be placing a great emphasis on early childhood education. And here I am not just talking about extending education downward, but with the students that we now have.

We know when a student has been in a school for 4 years and has not made it, a large proportion of these students do become disruptive and violent. Therefore, we ought to be concentrating our efforts in the kindergarten, first, second and third grades, to make sure we provide whatever is necessary to reach students during those years so they can have these basic skills and basic foundations, so they get skills before they develop negative feelings about themselves—feelings that they will never learn and that they are bound to fail.

We also need additional funds to provide more security personnel in the Nation's schools so that criminals will not regard the schools as fair game for robbery and assault.

Another thing which would be extremely helpful is action which would require school systems to keep accurate records of crimes and vandalism. The terrible thing now is that there is a good deal of covering up. The fact is, without hearings of this sort, most would not know about school violence and vandalism except for an occasional headline here and there.

Just as we keep national figures on crime in other areas, we ought to be keeping figures on these problems in the schools so that we have a notion as to whether the methods that we are using are succeeding and whether the problem is increasing or decreasing.

We should also provide additional funds for narcotics education, because drug addiction is one of the key causes of violence in the schools.

The Congress must make a commitment, both moral and financial, to restore and preserve the productivity and safety of our schools.

Finally, I want to thank you for bringing these facts to the attention of the American public, and your continuing interest. I do, however, wish to share with you one final concern. That concern is that we have gone through a period of 15 or 20 years unique in American educational history, in that volumes and volumes have been written that are very negative about the public schools.

I hope that the overall tone of these hearings and of the pursuit here for solutions to a very serious problem do not result in adding to that voluminous negative material. We do not need another public outcry that the public schools are terrible, that the schools are failing, and that the schools cannot be salvaged.

I submit to you that part of the responsibility for the increasing violence lies with some of these very books and writers themselves. Over the last 20 years they have helped create some ideological support for crime and violence, in viewing students as a kind of colonial minority who are oppressed by teachers and principals and school systems, and who are subjected to all sorts of "torture," namely, to traditional learning. Some say the student who acts out, who is violent and is absent from school, who rebels against and rejects the regulations of the institution, is a great revolutionary hero who is performing a service for the students. We should not neglect that ideological atmosphere which tended to glorify lawlessness and disorder in the name of some sort of revolutionary gains.

This is one of the contributing factors here and I hope that in bringing all of these facts to the public's attention, it also be brought out that, overall, in fact our public schools are doing an excellent job for the overwhelming majority of our students.

I know what we are examining here involves something that is a real problem, and a growing problem, but we should not create the impression that parents should not send their children to schools because they are unlikely to come home someday in one piece, because that is just not true.

Thank you.

3. Under the Federal Education of the Handicapped Act (20 U.S.C.A. § 1401 et seq.), a handicapped child has a right to an education in the "least restrictive environment" which is implemented, in part, by requiring schools to provide a continuum of alternative placements, including regular classes, special classes, private schools, the child's home and other institutions. "The expulsion of handicapped children not only jeopardizes their right to an education in the least restrictive environment, but is inconsistent with . . . the Handicapped Act . . . [which] prescribes a procedure whereby disruptive children are transferred to more restrictive placements when their behavior significantly impairs the education of other children." Stuart v. Nappi, 443 F.Supp. 1235 (D.Conn.1978).

Do behaviorally disruptive children suffer from handicaps which may not be physical? Is there any reason for not treating all disruptive children the way in which handicapped children must be treated? If a behaviorally disruptive child is to be transferred from a school to a center especially designed to meet the needs of behaviorally disruptive children, does Goss v. Lopez, infra, apply? A federal Court of Appeals has ruled that the hearing and due process requirements of Goss, infra, must be met. Jordan v. Erie School Dist., 583 F.2d 91 (3d Cir. 1978).

4. Are Connecticut's new suspension and expulsion laws desirable? Do they handle the problem fully? Permanent dismissals? Are they constitutionally required? On suspension, Connecticut provides: "Any pupil who is suspended shall be given the opportunity to complete any classwork including, but not limited to, examinations which such pupil missed during the period of suspension." On expulsion it is provided that "Any pupil who is expelled shall be offered an alternative educational opportunity during the period of expulsion . . ." and

such "alternative may include, but shall not be limited to, the placement of such pupil in a regular classroom program of a school other
than the one from which such pupil has been excluded." Conn.Gen.
Stat.Ann. §§ 10–233c(c) and 10–233d(c) (1978).

## WHAT IS DUE PROCESS?

The Fifth and Fourteenth Amendment provide that government
may not deprive a person of "life, liberty or property without due
process of law." The exact type of process, i. e., procedure of law
due to a student varies. However, at a minimum, "due process of
law" generally requires: (1) notice, and (2) some kind of hearing.
The basic necessity of notice means that, generally, pre-existing rules
governing behavior must be enacted. The pre-existing rules must be
of sufficient clarity and detail such that an ordinary student would
be able to conform his actions to the rules, and thereby be capable of
steering himself clear of trouble. For example, In re John Meyer,
9 E.D.R. 8, Decision No. 8021 (July 25, 1969), involved a coach who
at the beginning of the season lectured his basketball squad generally
about their behavior and grooming, including long hair. Later, the
coach told a player that he no longer was on the team or he must cut
his hair if he wished to continue playing basketball, and the student
objected. New York's Commissioner of Education held the coach's
order invalid, emphasizing the need for pre-existing rules that would
give fair notice: "Even where valid rule-making power is involved,
the exercise of that power cannot be left to the untrammeled discretion of an individual on a case-to-case basis—some standards must
be promulgated." The importance of this last requirement—pre-existing, clear and detailed rules—was emphasized in Mitchell v. King,
169 Conn. 140, 363 A.2d 68 (1975). Connecticut's disciplinary exclusion law was typical of many existing state statutes, simply authorizing expulsion for student "conduct inimical to the best interests of
the school." Connecticut's Supreme Court stated that "what the
phrase 'inimical to the best interests' may mean to different persons
is virtually unlimited." It then relied on *Tinker* and Goss v. Lopez,
infra, and held:

> Section 10–234, when read in the light of the legal principles
> enunciated, is unconstitutionally vague on its face. It does
> not give fair notice that certain conduct is proscribed; it
> makes no distinction between student conduct on or off
> school property, during school hours or while school is not in
> session. It fails to provide any meaningful indication as to
> what range of behavior would legitimately subject a student
> to expulsion. Thus, the time, the place, and the nature of
> student conduct that might be deemed "inimical to the best
> interests of the school" would lie entirely within the subjec-

tive discretion of the board of education. A more specific standard is required.

The second item generally required by "due process of law" is some kind of hearing. The degree of detail necessary for the pre-existing rules and the characteristics of the hearing depend upon what is at stake; for example, stricter requirements of procedure must be met when permanent student expulsion is at stake than when a student is merely kept after school for ten minutes. The Supreme Court identified relevant consideration in Hannah v. Larche, 363 U.S. 420, 80 S.Ct. 1502, 4 L.Ed.2d 1307 (1960):

> "Due process" is an elusive concept. Its exact boundaries are indefinable, and its content varies according to specific factual contexts. Thus when governmental agencies adjudicate or make binding determinations which directly affect the legal rights of individuals, it is imperative that those agencies use the procedures which have traditionally been associated with the judicial process. On the other hand, when governmental action does not partake of an adjudication, as for example, when a general fact-finding investigation is being conducted, it is not necessary that the full panoply of judicial procedures be used. Therefore, as a generalization, it can be said that due process embodies the differing rules of fair play, which through the years, have become associated with differing types of proceedings.

Whether the Constitution requires that a particular right [be] obtain[ed] in a specific proceeding depends upon a complexity of factors. The nature of the alleged right involved, the nature of the proceeding, and the possible burden on that proceeding are all considerations which must be taken into account.

---

## GOSS v. LOPEZ

Supreme Court of the United States, 1975.
419 U.S. 565, 95 S.Ct. 729, 42 L.Ed.2d 725.

Mr. Justice WHITE delivered the opinion of the Court.

This appeal by various administrators of the Columbus, Ohio, Public School System (CPSS) challenges the judgment of a three-judge federal court, declaring that appellees—various high school students in the CPSS—were denied due process of law contrary to the command of the Fourteenth Amendment in that they were temporarily suspended from their high schools without a hearing either prior to suspension or within a reasonable time thereafter, and enjoining the administrators to remove all references to such suspensions from the students' records.

## I

Ohio law, Rev.Code Ann. § 3313.64 (1972), provides for free education to all children between the ages of six and 21. Section 3313.66 of the Code empowers the principal of an Ohio public school to suspend a pupil for misconduct for up to 10 days or to expel him. In either case, he must notify the student's parents within 24 hours and state the reasons for his action. A pupil who is expelled, or his parents, may appeal the decision to the Board of Education and in connection therewith shall be permitted to be heard at the board meeting. The Board may reinstate the pupil following the hearing. No similar procedure is provided in § 3313.66 or any other provision of state law for a suspended student. Aside from a regulation tracking the statute, at the time of the imposition of the suspensions in this case the CPSS itself had not issued any written procedure applicable to suspensions. Nor, so far as the record reflects, had any of the individual high schools involved in this case. Each, however, had formally or informally described the conduct for which suspension could be imposed.

The proof below established that the suspensions arose out of a period of widespread student unrest in the CPSS during February and March 1971.   .   .   .

Two named plaintiffs, Dwight Lopez and Betty Crome, were students at the Central High School and McGuffey Junior High School, respectively. The former was suspended in connection with a disturbance in the lunchroom which involved some physical damage to school property. Lopez testified that at least 75 other students were suspended from his school on the same day. He also testified below that he was not a party to the destructive conduct but was instead an innocent bystander. Because no one from the school testified with regard to this incident, there is no evidence in the record indicating the official basis for concluding otherwise. Lopez never had a hearing.

Betty Crome was present at a demonstration at a high school other than the one she was attending. There she was arrested together with others, taken to the police station, and released without being formally charged. Before she went to school on the following day, she was notified that she had been suspended for a 10-day period. Because no one from the school testified with respect to this incident, the record does not disclose how the McGuffey Junior High School principal went about making the decision to suspend Crome, nor does it disclose on what information the decision was based. It is clear from the record that no hearing was ever held.   .   .   .

## II

At the outset, appellants contend that because there is no constitutional right to an education at public expense, the Due Process

Clause does not protect against explusions from the public school system. This position misconceives the nature of the issue and is refuted by prior decisions. The Fourteenth Amendment forbids the State to deprive any person of life, liberty, or property without due process of law. Protected interests in property are normally "not created by the Constitution. Rather, they are created and their dimensions are defined" by an independent source such as state statutes or rules entitling the citizen to certain benefits.

Here, on the basis of state law, appellees plainly had legitimate claims of entitlement to a public education. Ohio Rev.Code Ann. §§ 3313.48 and 3313.64 (1972 and Supp.1973) direct local authorities to provide a free education to all residents between five and 21 years of age, and a compulsory-attendance law requires attendance for a school year of not less than 32 weeks. It is true that § 3313.66 of the Code permits school principals to suspend students for up to 10 days; but suspensions may not be imposed without any grounds whatsoever. All of the schools had their own rules specifying the grounds for expulsion or suspension. Having chosen to extend the right to an education to people of appellees' class generally, Ohio may not withdraw that right on grounds of misconduct, absent fundamentally fair procedures to determine whether the misconduct has occurred.

Although Ohio may not be constitutionally obligated to establish and maintain a public school system, it has nevertheless done so and has required its children to attend. Those young people do not "shed their constitutional rights" at the schoolhouse door. Tinker v. Des Moines School Dist. "The Fourteenth Amendment, as now applied to the States, protects the citizen against the State itself and all of its creatures—Boards of Education not excepted." West Virginia Board of Education v. Barnette. The authority possessed by the State to prescribe and enforce standards of conduct in its schools although concededly very broad, must be exercised consistently with constitutional safeguards. Among other things, the State is constrained to recognize a student's legitimate entitlement to a public education as a property interest which is protected by the Due Process Clause and which may not be taken away for misconduct without adherence to the minimum procedures required by that Clause.  .  .  .

Appellants proceed to argue that even if there is a right to a public education protected by the Due Process Clause generally, the Clause comes into play only when the State subjects a student to a "severe detriment or grievous loss." The loss of 10 days, it is said, is neither severe nor grievous and the Due Process Clause is therefore of no relevance. Appellants' argument is again refuted by our prior decisions; for in determining "whether due process requirements apply in the first place, we must look not to the 'weight' but to the *nature* of the interest at stake." Appellees were excluded from school only temporarily, it is true, but the length and consequent severity of a deprivation, while another factor to weigh in determining the appropriate form of hearing, "is not decisive of the basic right" to a hearing of some kind. The Court's view has been that as long as a property deprivation is not *de minimis*, its gravity is irrelevant to the question whether account must be taken of the Due Process Clause. A 10-day suspension from school is not *de minimis* in our view and may not be imposed in complete disregard of the Due Process Clause.

A short suspension is, of course, a far milder deprivation than expulsion. But, "education is perhaps the most important function of state and local governments," and the total exclusion from the educational process for more than a trivial period, and certainly if the suspension is for 10 days, is a serious event in the life of the suspended child. Neither the property interest in educational benefits temporarily denied nor the liberty interest in reputation, which is also implicated, is so insubstantial that suspensions may constitutionally be imposed by any procedure the school chooses, no matter how arbitrary.

### III

"Once it is determined that due process applies, the question remains what process is due." We turn to that question, fully realizing as our cases regularly do that the interpretation and application of the Due Process Clause are intensely practical matters and that "[t]he very nature of due process negates any concept of inflexible procedures universally applicable to every imaginable situation." We are also mindful of our own admonition:

"Judicial interposition in the operation of the public school system of the Nation raises problems requiring care and restraint. . . . By and large, public education in our Nation is committed to the control of state and local authorities."

There are certain bench marks to guide us, however. Mullane v. Central Hanover Trust Co., 339 U.S. 306 (1950), a case often invoked by later opinions, said that "[m]any controversies have raged about the cryptic and abstract words of the Due Process Clause but there can be no doubt that at a minimum they require that deprivation of life, liberty or property by adjudication be preceded by notice and opportunity for hearing appropriate to the nature of the case." "The fundamental requisite of due process of law is the opportunity to be heard," a right that "has little reality or worth unless one is informed that the matter is pending and can choose for himself whether to . . . contest." At the very minimum, therefore, students facing suspension and the consequent interference with a protected property interest must be given *some* kind of notice and afforded *some* kind of hearing. "Parties whose rights are to be affected are entitled to be heard; and in order that they may enjoy that right they must first be notified."

It also appears from our cases that the timing and content of the notice and the nature of the hearing will depend on appropriate accommodation of the competing interests involved. The student's interest is to avoid unfair or mistaken exclusion from the educational process, with all of its unfortunate consequences. The Due Process Clause will not shield him from suspensions properly imposed, but it disserves both his interest and the interest of the State if his suspension is in fact unwarranted. The concern would be mostly academic if the disciplinary process were a totally accurate, unerring process, never mistaken and never unfair. Unfortunately, that is not the case, and no one suggests that it is. Disciplinarians, although proceeding in utmost good faith, frequently act on the reports and advice of others; and the controlling facts and the nature of the conduct under challenge are often disputed. The risk of error is not at all trivial, and it should be guarded against if that may be done without prohibitive cost or interference with the educational process.

The difficulty is that our schools are vast and complex. Some modicum of discipline and order is essential if the educational function is to be performed. Events calling for discipline are frequent occurrences and sometimes require immediate, effective action. Suspension is considered not only to be a necessary tool to maintain order but a valuable educational device. The prospect of imposing elaborate hearing requirements in every suspension case is viewed with great concern, and many school authorities may well prefer the untrammeled power to act unilaterally, unhampered by rules about notice and hearing. But it would be a strange disciplinary system in an educational institution if no communication was sought by the disciplinarian with the student in an effort to inform him of his dereliction and to let him tell his side of the story in order to make sure that an injustice is not done. "[F]airness can rarely be obtained by secret, one-sided determination of facts decisive of rights. . . ." "Secrecy is not congenial to truth-seeking and self-righteousness gives too slender an assurance of rightness. No better instrument has been devised for arriving at truth than to give a person in jeopardy of serious loss notice of the case against him and opportunity to meet it."

We do not believe that school authorities must be totally free from notice and hearing requirements if their schools are to operate with acceptable efficiency. Students facing temporary suspension have interests qualifying for protection of the Due Process Clause, and due process requires, in connection with a suspension of 10 days or less, that the student be given oral or written notice of the charges against him and, if he denies them, an explanation of the evidence the authorities have and an opportunity to present his side of the story. The Clause requires at least these rudimentary precautions against unfair or mistaken findings of misconduct and arbitrary exclusion from school.

There need be no delay between the time "notice" is given and the time of the hearing. In the great majority of cases the disciplinarian may informally discuss the alleged misconduct with the student minutes after it has occurred. We hold only that, in being given an opportunity to explain his version of the facts at this discussion, the student first be told what he is accused of doing and what the basis of the accusation is. Lower courts which have addressed the question of the *nature* of the procedures required in short suspension cases have reached the same conclusion. Since the hearing may occur almost immediately following the misconduct, it follows that as a general rule notice and hearing should precede removal of the student from school. We agree   .   .   . that there are recurring situations in which prior notice and hearing cannot be insisted upon. Students whose presence poses a continuing danger to persons or property or an ongoing threat of disrupting the academic process may be immediately removed from school. In such cases, the necessary notice and rudimentary hearing should follow as soon as practicable   .   ..

We stop short of construing the Due Process Clause to require, countrywide, that hearings in connection with short suspensions must afford the student the opportunity to secure counsel, to confront and cross-examine witnesses supporting the charge, or to call his own witnesses to verify his version of the incident. Brief disciplinary suspensions are almost countless. To impose in each such case even truncated trial-type procedures might well overwhelm administrative facilities in many places and, by diverting resources, cost more than it would save in educational effectiveness. Moreover, further formalizing the suspension process and escalating its formality and adversary nature may not only make it too costly as a regular disciplinary tool but also destroy its effectiveness as part of the teaching process.

On the other hand, requiring effective notice and informal hearing permitting the student to give his version of the events will provide a meaningful hedge against erroneous action. At least the disciplinarian will be alerted to the existence of disputes about facts and arguments about cause and effect. He may then determine himself to summon the accuser, permit cross-examination, and allow the student to present his own witnesses. In more difficult cases, he may permit counsel. In any event, his discretion will be more informed and we think the risk of error substantially reduced.

Requiring that there be at least an informal give-and-take between student and disciplinarian, preferably prior to the suspension, will add little to the factfinding function where the disciplinarian himself has witnessed the conduct forming the basis for the charge. But things are not always as they seem to be, and the student will at least have the opportunity to characterize his conduct and put it in what he deems the proper context.

We should also make it clear that we have addressed ourselves solely to the short suspension, not exceeding 10 days. Longer suspensions or expulsions for the remainder of the school term, or permanently, may require more formal procedures. Nor do we put aside the possibility that in unusual situations, although involving only a short suspension, something more than the rudimentary procedures will be required.

## IV

The District Court found each of the suspensions involved here to have occurred without a hearing, either before or after the suspension, and that each suspension was therefore invalid and the statute unconstitutional insofar as it permits such suspensions without notice or hearing. Accordingly, the judgment is affirmed.

Mr. Justice POWELL, with whom The Chief Justice, Mr. Justice BLACKMUN, and Mr. Justice REHNQUIST join, dissenting. . . .

The Court's decision rests on the premise that, under Ohio law, education is a property interest protected by the Fourteenth Amendment's Due Process Clause and therefore that any suspension requires notice and a hearing. In my view, a student's interest in education is not infringed by a suspension within the limited period prescribed by Ohio law. Moreover, to the extent that there may be some arguable infringement, it is too speculative, transitory, and insubstantial to justify imposition of a *constitutional* rule . . . .

No one can foresee the ultimate frontiers of the new "thicket" the Court now enters. Today's ruling appears to sweep within the protected interest in education a multitude of discretionary decisions in the educational process. Teachers and other school authorities are required to make many decisions that may have serious consequences for the pupil. They must decide, for example, how to grade the student's work, whether a student passes or fails a course, whether he is to be promoted, whether he is required to take certain subjects, whether he may be excluded from interscholastic athletics or other extracurricular activities, whether he may be removed from one school and sent to another, whether he may be bused long distances when available schools are nearby, and whether he should be placed in a "general," "vocational," or "college-preparatory" track. . . .

## NOTES AND QUESTIONS

1. In U. of Missouri v. Horowitz, 435 U.S. 78, 98 S.Ct. 948, 55 L.Ed.2d 124 (1978), the U.S. Supreme Court was confronted with the dismissal of a medical student "during her final year of study for failure to meet academic standards." The Supreme Court granted review "to consider what procedures must be accorded to a student [dismissed on academic grounds from] a state educational institution . . . .". Assuming "the existence of a liberty or property interest," the Court, in an opinion by Mr. Justice Rehnquist, ruled that the student "has

been awarded as much due process as required by the Fourteenth Amendment." The student had been notified by a medical school committee that her " 'performance was below that of her peers in all clinical patient-oriented settings,' that she was erratic in her attendance at clinical sessions, and that she lacked a critical concern for personal hygiene." Students "are not typically allowed to appear before the [committee] on the occasion of their review of the student's academic performance."

"The school fully informed respondent of the faculty's dissatisfaction with her clinical progress and the danger that this posed to timely graduation and continued enrollment. The ultimate decision to dismiss respondent was careful and deliberate. These procedures were sufficient under the Due Process Clause of the Fourteenth Amendment. We agree with the District Court that respondent "was afforded full procedural due process by the [school]. In fact, the Court is of the opinion, and so finds, that the school went beyond [constitutionally] procedural due process by affording [respondent] the opportunity to be examined by seven independent physicians in order to be absolutely certain that their grading of the [respondent] in her medical skills were correct."

"In Goss v. Lopez, we held that due process requires, in connection with the suspension of a student from public school for disciplinary reasons, 'that the student be given oral or written notice of the charges against him and, if he denies them, an explanation of the evidence the authorities have and an opportunity to present his side of the story.' The Court of Appeals apparently read Goss as requiring some type of formal hearing at which respondent could defend her academic ability and performance. All that Goss required was an 'informal give-and-take' between the student and the administrative body dismissing him that would, at least, give the student 'the opportunity to characterize his conduct and put it in what he deems that proper context.' But we have frequently emphasized that '[t]he very nature of due process negates any concept of inflexible procedures universally applicable to every imaginable situation.' The need for flexibility is well illustrated by the significant difference between the failure of a student to meet academic standards and the violation by a student of valid rules of conduct. This difference calls for far less stringent procedural requirements in the case of an academic dismissal.

"Since the issue first arose 50 years ago, state and lower federal courts have recognized that there are distinct differences between decisions to suspend or dismiss a student for disciplinary purposes and similar actions taken for academic reasons which may call for hearings in connection with the former but not the latter . . . . .

"Reason, furthermore, clearly supports the perception of these decisions. A school is an academic institution, not a courtroom or administrative hearing room. In Goss, this Court felt that suspensions of students for disciplinary reasons have a sufficient resemblance to traditional judicial and administrative factfinding to call for a 'hearing' before the relevant school authority . . . . .

"Academic evaluations of a student, in contrast to disciplinary determinations, bear little resemblance to the judicial and administrative factfinding proceedings to which we have traditionally attached a full-hearing requirement.    In Goss, the school's decision to suspend the students rested on factual conclusions that the individual students had participated in demonstrations that had disrupted classes, attacked a police officer, or caused physical damage to school property. The requirement of a hearing, where the student could present his side of the factual issue, could under such circumstances 'provide a meaningful hedge against erroneous action.'    The decision to dismiss respondent, by comparison, rested on the academic judgment of school officials that she did not have the necessary clinical ability to perform adequately as a medical doctor and was making insufficient progress toward that goal.    Such a judgment is by its nature more subjective and evaluative than the typical factual questions presented in the average disciplinary decision.    Like the decision of an individual professor as to the proper grade for a student in his course, the determination whether to dismiss a student for academic reasons requires an expert evaluation of cumulative information and is not readily adapted to the procedural tools of judicial or administrative decision-making    .    .    .".

.    .    .

Except possibly for private schools, Horowitz may not have a major impact on K–12 education because there are few, if any, academic dismissals.    Under compulsory school attendance laws, K–12 students must go to school until they reach the maximum statutory age.    If students become academic failures, they are not dismissed, but required to repeat the grade.    Suppose a K–12 student fails a course because he is a "behavior problem," would Horowitz or Goss apply?    Horowitz might be important in a K–12 situation where the question, on academic grounds, is whether a student must repeat a grade.    Goss will probably remain the important case in K–12 education.    Goss holds that due process, in connection with a suspension of 10 days or less, requires that the student be given oral or written notice of the charges against him, and, if he denies them, an explanation of the evidence the authorities have and an opportunity to present his version of the matter.

2.    Under Goss, is a student entitled "to know the charges" and "to an informal hearing" before a teacher can require a student (1) to stand in the corner; (2) to write one hundred times something like "I will not throw erasers;" (3) to sit in the hallway for a given number of minutes; (4) to stay after school; (5) to report to the principal's office for discipline; or (6) to forego a recess period?    If not, then what process is due a student in such circumstances?

3.    The Supreme Court is careful in Goss to indicate that more formal procedures might be required in cases of suspension for more than 10 days or in expulsion cases.    "Longer suspensions or expulsions for the remainder of the school term, or permanently, may require more formal procedures."    Such cases could result in the U.S. Supreme Court finding more student rights.    Also, state constitutions and state statutes might require stricter, more formal procedures in cases involving long suspensions and expulsions.    Stricter procedural requirements by states are permissible under Goss.    Reasoning from Goss and Horowitz, what more do you think the U.S. Constitution requires in such cases?    Why?

Does it require the right to be represented by a lawyer? The right to confront one's accusers? To cross examine them? To present voluntary witnesses? The right to compel witnesses to appear on behalf of the student? The right to a neutral, unbiased judge? To an open hearing? To proof against a student beyond a reasonable doubt or by clear and convincing evidence or only by a mere preponderance of the evidence? The right to have access to all relevant student and other school files? The right, at school expense, to a transcript of the hearing?

---

## TIBBS v. BOARD OF EDUCATION

Superior Court of New Jersey, 1971.
114 N.J.Super. 287, 276 A.2d 165.

PER CURIAM.

The expulsions of appellants are reversed and set aside for failure to produce the accusing witnesses for testimony and cross-examination.

The matters are remanded to the Commissioner of Education for rehearing *de novo* of the charges on which appellants were expelled should the local school authorities choose to prosecute them. No costs.

CONFORD, P. J. A. D. (concurring).

The *per curiam* opinion of the court represents what all the members of the court can agree upon. I herewith supplement that determination with my own reasons for joining therein and my own more specific views as to what the Commissioner of Education should do and the local school authorities may do at this juncture.

We granted leave to appeal an interlocutory decision of the State Commissioner of Education, but denied appellants' request for *ad interim* readmission to classes at Franklin High School from which they had theretofore been expelled or suspended for an alleged physical assault upon other students said to have occurred October 7, 1970. (All were ultimately expelled.) The Supreme Court on motion thereafter directed the appellants to be readmitted to school, subject to good behavior, pending determination of this appeal.

The sole issue presented is whether a high school student may be expelled from school on the charge of physical assault upon another student where the hearing conducted by the local board of education on the charge is not preceded by identification to the accused of the accusing student witnesses whose *ex parte* statements the school administration has relied on in bringing the disciplinary proceedings and where such witnesses do not appear to testify at the hearing. My view, and I believe that of the court, is that this procedure denies due process to the student so expelled, and this notwithstanding a determination by the local board, held warranted by the State Commissioner, that the student witnesses were afraid to testify because of fear of physical reprisal and should not be compelled to do so against their will.

On October 7, 1970, according to hearsay testimony adduced before the local board and the Commissioner, two students at the school, sisters, were assaulted by a group of others, all or mostly girls, while all were walking home after classes, a short distance from the school exits. They were struck with a stick, pushed to the ground and jumped upon or kicked, and some of their possessions were taken from them and purloined or scattered. One of them sustained the destruction of her eyeglasses. Both had minor injuries. They ran, crying, back to the guidance office at the school. It appears that neither could, or was willing to, identify any of the attackers. But a number of student witnesses volunteered statements to the school authorities identifying appellants and others (about ten in all) as involved in the episode. They were apparently assured, upon request, that they would not be identified to the accused students because of fear of physical retaliation.

The alleged assailants were, so far as available, called in for interviews, and generally denied complicity. But some stated they were in the vicinity and had seen part of the events. In the case of appellant Tanya Tibbs, statements of other students supporting her defense that she had seen but not participated in the occurrence were proffered to the school authorities by her parents, but investigation thereof failed to satisfy the authorities that the *prima facie* case against her had been impaired. We are informed that initial suspensions were imposed upon a total of ten students. After informal hearings the suspensions were lifted as to five of the accused, but the other five, including the four present appellants, were expelled by the board of education after hearings substantially of the kind afforded Tanya, and described hereafter.

Tanya was originally notified of a suspension to begin October 13, 1970 and to terminate November 16. (She remained out of school until the Supreme Court order of January 25, 1971.) Tanya's parents were given notice October 27, 1970 by the superintendent of schools that the board of education would meet November 2, 1970 for a full hearing to consider the recommendation of the school principal and himself that the girl be expelled from school for "assault upon a student of Franklin High School"; that they could be represented by an attorney; that the vice-principal and principal would testify and be subject to cross-examination, and that signed statements of student witnesses would be presented but that such students would not appear at the hearing. The accused pupil would have the right to present testimony of witnesses or a signed statement by any witness not desiring or able to attend.

The hearing was postponed to November 9, 1970 at the request of Tanya's attorney but the latter was informed that the statements of the student witnesses to be provided would not be signed or identified.

At the hearing before the board the principal and vice-principal of the high school testified concerning their investigation and the informal hearings they conducted as to the incident, resulting in findings and conclusions by them substantially to the effect indicated above, including that of Tanya's guilt. The principal also testified that he had received a telephone call from the mother of one of the accused students threatening the life of one of the prospective student witnesses. There was testimony that the student witnesses were in terror of retaliation if their identity was revealed to the accused students. The principal explained that the problem he faced in deciding whether to produce the children to testify was "a two-fold one: What happens within the confines of a racially tense school; and my own concern for the continued safety of the students involved." (It seems agreed there has been a history of racial conflicts at the school.) The board voted to accept into evidence unsigned and unidentified statements by student witnesses, and three such were read into the record. In each such statement Tanya was identified as one of those "doing the hitting." A statement by the victims, identified as the Cornwell sisters, was also read. This described the occurrence but omitted identification of any assailant.

The attorney for Tanya objected throughout the hearing to the failure to identify and produce and subject to cross-examination any of the accusing witnesses whose statements were read. On the basis of that deficiency he refused to adduce defensive testimony by or on behalf of his client. He had also at the outset of the hearing moved that two members of the board disqualify themselves as prejudiced because of public statements previously made by them concerning the incident and alleged antecedent related occurrences. The motion was denied.

The board of education thereupon voted Tanya guilty and then took testimony concerning her prior disciplinary record in school. This was generally poor. After argument by counsel against expulsion the board voted that determination.

Tanya filed an appeal against the expulsion with the Commissioner of Education and petitioned him for *ad interim* relief of admission to classes pending adjudication. A hearing on the petition was conducted November 20, 1970 before the Division of Controversies and Disputes at which the school principal testified to the substance of what had been adduced before the local board. On December 1, 1970 the Commissioner of Education denied *ad interim* relief. He expressly decided that the procedure used by the local board comported with due process and that he was satisfied by the testimony of the principal "that school officials had sufficient cause for concern regarding the safety of potential student witnesses" so as to justify not "releasing the students' names" or permitting their cross-examination.

It is not necessary here to pursue in detail the long and uneven development of the law over the past century concerning appropriate procedures in school and college student disciplinary proceedings. . . .

To summarize briefly, the early cases, particularly in relation to proceedings below the college level, generally did not recognize due process concepts as appropriate to the exercise of discipline of students, even in the case of expulsion. The idea of the school administrators being *in loco parentis* to students of secondary and primary grade level held some sway. In the course of time, however, when the sanction applied for misconduct was expulsion or suspension of severe duration, especially in college-level cases, the decisions began to speak in terms of hearing requirements of due process. But a variety of expressions can be found in the cases as to the specifics of fair hearings or due process, particularly in relation to such claimed incidents as the right of counsel, personal appearances of accusing witnesses, and the right of cross-examination of such witnesses by the defense. The variations are probably explainable on the basis of the diversity of attendant circumstances in different cases—the nature of the offense; nature of the prosecuting and adjudicating entities; ages of the accused students and of witnesses; stage of the proceedings in the entirety of the process of investigation, punishment-treatment and review; and effect of statutory provisions, e. g., as to right to subpoena witnesses or to counsel, or the absence thereof, etc. See Madera v. Board of Education, City of New York, 386 F.2d 778 (2 Cir. 1967) cert. den. . . . Schwartz v. Schuker, 298 F.Supp. 238 (E.D.N.Y. 1969).

Our own statutes are rudimentary. N.J.S.A. 18A:37–2 provides that certain types of pupil misbehavior, including "d. physical assault upon another pupil * * *" may be attended by "suspension or expulsion from school." A principal may suspend any pupil "for good cause" but must report it forthwith to the superintendent of schools. The superintendent must report the suspension to the board of education at its next regular meeting. Either the principal or superintendent may reinstate the pupil prior to the second regular meeting of the board thereafter unless the board does so at its first meeting. N.J.S.A. 18A:37–4. No suspension may continue beyond the second regular meeting of the board after the suspension unless the board continues it, "and the power to reinstate, continue any suspension reported to it or expel a pupil shall be vested in each board." N.J.S.A. 18A:37–5. No hearing procedures attendant upon suspensions or expulsions are specified.

The leading decision of the modern era relating to fair procedures in college expulsion cases is Dixon v. Alabama State Board of Education, 294 F.2d 150 (5 Cir. 1961), cert. den. 368 U.S. 930, 82 S.Ct. 368, 7 L.Ed.2d 193 (1961). The guidelines there stated were quoted in full in R. R. v. Board of Education, Shore Reg. H.S., supra, (109 N.J.Super at 349, 263 A.2d 180) and need not be repeated here. . . . In contrast with the particular procedures followed here, the *Dixon* guidelines require affording the accused student in advance the names of the witnesses against him and a report of the facts they attest to. Cross-examination of witnesses and a "full-dress judicial hearing" is said not to be necessary. . . . Some cases, however, seem to suggest the desirability of production of the accusatory witnesses at the hearing and allowance of their cross-examination. Esteban v. Central Missouri State College, 277 F.Supp. 649, 651–652 (W.D.Mo. 1967) . . .

In R. R. v. Board of Education, Shore Reg. H.S., supra, our Chancery Division held a *Dixon*-type hearing mandatory as a condition for suspension of indefinite duration of a high school student charged with an assault on another child (off school premises). The New Jersey State Department of Education has heretofore recognized the general requirements of procedural due process in relation to school students facing severe disciplinary sanctions. Scher v. Board of Education, West Orange, 1968 School Law Decisions 92, 95.

There is no issue in the present case as to the necessity for a "fair hearing procedure" antecedent to imposition by a local board of education of the sanction of expulsion of a student for misconduct. Both sides agree on it. The issue is whether student witnesses against the accused must be identified to the accused and be produced and be subject to cross-examination, either (a) generally, or (b) under the circumstances of this case.

It is apparent from the decided cases that due process in the school or college context does not, by the weight of authority, require the production in person and right of cross-examination of adverse witnesses. It does call for identification of such witnesses and for supplying the accused with statements or affidavits by them verifying the charges in advance of the hearing. That much is minimally essential, in an issue over controverted objective conduct, as here, to give the accused a fair opportunity to meet and refute possibly mistaken or unfounded assertions of fact. If, despite the witnesses' fears, their identify must be revealed as a matter of minimum due process to the accused, there would seem little point in precluding the availability of the substantially more revealing personal testimony of the witnesses for the benefit both of the triers of the fact and the defense of the accused children in the search for the truth of the matter. Common experience, moreover, establishes that the right of cross-examination is almost always essential for assurance of an enlightened determination of a contested issue of fact. I therefore conclude that in the context of such a case as this not only should the accusing witnesses be identified in advance but also, as a general matter and absent the most compelling circumstances bespeaking a different course, be produced to testify and to be cross-examined.

Cross-examination of school children witnesses in proceedings like these should, however, be carefully controlled by the hearing officer or body, limited to the material essentials of the direct testimony and not be unduly protracted. Such a proceeding is decidedly not in the nature of a criminal trial nor to be encrusted with all the ordinary procedural and evidential concomitants of such a trial.

It remains to consider the particular objections raised by respondents to identification and examination at the hearing of the accusatory witnesses. I have no inclination to gainsay the determination of the local and state educational officials that these children were in a genuine state of fear over having their identity revealed. Whether the procedural policy adopted and approved at the administrative level for the handling of this matter would be justified, in the attendant circumstances, were the ultimate sanctions imposed substantially less than that of expulsion of the accused, is not the immediate issue here. I discuss that particular contingency later herein. We here confront a decision for expulsion—action which constitutes deprivation of a most drastic and potentially irreparable kind. In that setting compromise with punctilious procedural fairness becomes inacceptable. As was recently stated by a writer on the subject:

> The problem can be put in greater perspective by considering the importance of fair procedure to the student involved. He may have as much to fear from the arbitrary use of power at the secondary level as at the college or university level. This is particularly true where the misconduct may result in an expulsion or a lengthy suspension. The stigma of compulsory withdrawal may follow even a high school student for many years after the institution has considered the incident closed. Expulsion or suspension always involves a permanent notation on the student's record which may have long term effects on his ability to achieve entry into college or the job market. Moreover, if the child is unable to return to school, the economics of a premature withdrawal are startling and more tangible evidence of the burden that he must shoulder. . . .

At oral argument respondent conceded there was no assurance of early or favorable action on any application for reinstatement after expulsion which might be made by appellants, and it is apparent that admission to schools in other districts, if obtainable at all, would entail payment of a substantial nonresident fee these students could probably ill afford.

As against the interests of the pupils here accused in remaining in school, the school community must be content to deal with threats or intimidation of the kind allegedly encountered by invoking the jurisdiction of the law enforcement authorities who must be presumed equal to their responsibilities. . . .

KOLOVSKY, J. A. D. (concurring).

The State Commissioner of Education has heretofore recognized that in proceedings before a local board of education which may lead to the expulsion or suspension of a public school student for alleged misconduct—as contrasted with scholastic failure—due process requires, among other things, that the accused student be given at least the names of the witnesses against him and copies of the statements and affidavits of those witnesses. . . .

In my view, due process also requires that there be added to these minimal rights the right to demand that any such witness appear in person to answer questions. If the witness does not do so, his statement should not and may not be considered or relied on by the board.

. . . in this case the local board did not have to identify the witnesses against the accused students and could act on the basis of unsigned statements obtained from the witnesses. Justification therefor was found in the determination by the local board, based on the testimony of its investigatory staff, that the witnesses were afraid to testify for fear of physical reprisal.

In my opinion such fears afford no justification in any case for depriving the accused students of their constitutional right to be confronted by and to examine the witnesses against them. An ordered society cannot accept the view that the police and prosecuting authorities will be impotent to prevent and punish unlawful conduct of the kind which the witnesses allegedly fear, and on that basis deny the accused students their constitutional right to demand confrontation by the witnesses against them.

Such right is a fundamental aspect of due process, whatever other variant in the form of the hearing may be permitted where a public school student is charged with misconduct. . . .

It must be borne in mind that the action sought to be reviewed here is administrative action by a governmental agency, an agency which has the power to compel the attendance of witnesses. See N.J. S.A. 18A:6–20. Cases upholding expulsions or suspensions from schools or colleges that are not governmental agencies and whose administrators lack such power . . . are therefore of no precedential significance.

Rather, what is of controlling significance is the constitutional rule which mandates that a respondent charged with misconduct in a hearing before a governmental agency be given the opportunity to confront and cross-examine adverse witnesses where the decision of the governmental agency will turn on questions of fact. Goldberg v. Kelly, 397 U.S. 254, 269–270. . . .

My brother CONFORD suggests that such right of confrontation does not exist if the local board should decide that the penalty to be imposed on the accused students for the assaults and batteries with which they are charged is less than "expulsion or severe term of suspension."

I cannot agree. The constitutional rights of the accused students may not be dissipated by a decision by the local board in advance of a hearing that the penalty will not be "expulsion or a severe term of suspension." Moreover, it is evident that any suspension beyond the preliminary period of suspension which, under N.J.S.A. 18A:37–4, a principal may lawfully impose without a hearing, is a "severe term of suspension." . . .

CARTON, J. A. D. (concurring). . . .

I concur generally with the view expressed by Judge KOLOVSKY that in a disciplinary proceeding such as this which may result in expulsion, due process requires that the accused student be afforded an opportunity to confront and cross-examine adverse witnesses. However, I am concerned that our recognition of that right may be construed to mean that such a full-dress hearing is a necessary ingredient of procedural due process at the *local board level* or that our decision be interpreted to lay down the requirements of all such proceedings conducted at that level.

I would hold only that any procedures conducted by the local board must comply with the minimum requirements set forth in Dixon v. Alabama State Board of Education, 294 F.2d 150 (5 Cir. 1961), . . . The board should not be compelled, and due process does not require, the in-person production of adverse witnesses and the right of cross-examination at the local board hearing. Although cross-examination is a valuable method of developing the entire factual situation in a given case, it must be borne in mind that the proceeding is an administrative one conducted and controlled by boards of nine lay citizens ordinarily unfamiliar with legal procedures.

The courts cannot envision the whole range of situations which might arise in this administrative area. On the other hand, the Commissioner has an expertise in this field and by reason thereof is in an excellent position to develop and formulate workable and comprehensive procedures. Consequently, we should leave to his office the responsibility of determining the specific format of the hearings and the safeguards required at the board level in cases of this kind, subject of course to the fundamental requirements set forth in *Dixon.* . . .

---

## TIBBS v. BOARD OF EDUCATION

Supreme Court of New Jersey, 1971.
59 N.J. 506, 284 A.2d 179.

PER CURIAM.

The judgment of the appellate Division is affirmed substantially for the reasons expressed in the opinion of Judge Kolovsky. (114 N.J. Super. 287, 276 A.2d 165.) . . .

## MODEL SCHOOL DISCIPLINARY CODE
prepared by **Jeff Kobrick** with **Pat Lines**
Center for Law and Education, Harvard University.

Reprinted from INEQUALITY IN EDUCATION, #12, 1972, pp. 47–49,
a publication of the Center for Law and Education, Cambridge, Mass.

The model code which follows was prepared by lawyers at the Center for Law and Education as a guide to procedural due process . . . [for elementary and secondary schools]. It . . . would require some modification if it were to be used as state legislation. We thank Sue Martinez of the Youth Law Center and Ralph Faust of the Juvenile Law Center for their comments on earlier drafts.

**Section 1.**  The imposition of serious discipline upon any student including, but not limited to, suspension, transfer and expulsion, shall be governed by the provisions of this Code.

**Section 2.**  No student shall be suspended, transferred, expelled or otherwise seriously disciplined except on the basis of published and clear rules which reasonably inform students.

(a) of the specific kinds of conduct which can form the basis for punishment or discipline, and

(b) of the nature, and, in the case of a separation from school, duration of the punishment which can be imposed for each type of conduct which is prohibited by the rules.

**Section 3.**  Any rules which form the basis for discipline shall be distributed to students and their parents at the beginning of each school year and shall be posted in conspicuous places within each school throughout the school year.  Changes in the rules shall not take effect until they are distributed to students and parents.

**Section 4.**  No student shall be disciplined for, and no school rule or policy shall prohibit, impede or discourage, the exercise of constitutionally protected rights.

**Section 5.**  The principal or head administrative officer of each school shall have the sole power to initiate proceedings to suspend, transfer or expel any student.  If, upon receiving a complaint of possible student misconduct, the principal believes the matter is a potential disciplinary one, he shall fully investigate the facts.  Whenever possible, facts shall be obtained from those who directly observed them, and the student shall be allowed fully to explain his side of the story (although the student shall be advised that he has a right to remain silent if he wishes.)  The principal may hold a post-investigation conference with the student and his parents.

**Section 6.**  If, after full investigation, discussion, and attempted resolution of a complaint against a student, the principal finds

(a) that there is evidence that the student has actually committed the conduct charged, and

(b) that the matter cannot be handled through discussion or counselling, he may initiate the hearing procedure, as provided below, to suspend, transfer, or expel any student.

The principal shall make every effort to resolve potential disciplinary matters through discussion and counselling.

Section 7.   Prior to the suspension, transfer, or expulsion of any student, except as provided in section 16 below, the student shall be accorded a due process hearing.   The hearing shall be before an impartial panel which shall consist of

(a) an assistant superintendent, designated by the school committee;

(b) a student designated by the student council or some other fairly representative student group within the school;

(c) a teacher designated by the student who is charged with misconduct.

The principal shall be the charging party, and the assistant superintendent shall convene the hearing panel.   The principal shall not discuss the merits of the case with any member of the hearing panel prior or subsequent to the hearing.

Section 8.   The principal shall furnish the student written notice of the hearing sufficiently in advance to allow him adequately to prepare his defense.   The notice shall contain the following:

(a) the time and place of the hearing;

(b) a statement of the specific facts alleged against the student, the school rule(s) allegedly violated, and the proposed discipline;

(c) the student's right to be represented by an advocate of his choosing (including counsel);

(d) the student's right to present evidence, call witnesses, and cross-examine adverse witnesses;  and

(e) a copy of the school code of discipline.

Section 9.   All hearings shall be conducted as follows:

(a) it shall be private, unless the student requests that it be public;

(b) no evidence shall be offered against a student unless prior to the hearing the student is allowed to inspect written evidence and is informed of the names of witnesses against him and the substance of their testimony;

(c) all parties shall have the right to present evidence, call witnesses, cross-examine adverse witnesses, and submit rebuttal evidence.   All testimony shall be given under oath;

(d) the student shall have the right to be represented by an advocate of his choice (including counsel);

(e) the student shall have the right to confront any witnesses against him;

(f) the hearing panel or committee shall not be required to observe the same rules of evidence observed by the courts, but evidence may be admitted and given probative effect only if it is the kind of evidence on which reasonable persons are accustomed to rely in the conduct of serious affairs. The scope of the hearing shall be confined to the charges contained in the notice required by section 8;

(g) the hearing panel or committee shall make a verbatim transcript or tape recording of the hearing, a copy of which shall be made available to the student;

(h) the hearing panel or committee shall issue a written decision stating its findings of fact and the evidence upon which the findings are based. Findings shall be based solely on relevant evidence presented at the hearing.

Section 10.  No decision that disciplinary action is warranted shall be made unless the hearing panel first finds, upon the basis of clear and convincing evidence,

(a) that the student has, in fact, committed the conduct charged;

(b) that the student's conduct violated a published school rule; and

(c) that the student had reasonable notice that his conduct was prohibited by a school rule.

If the panel so finds against the student, it shall, by majority vote, take such disciplinary action as it may deem appropriate; provided, however, that such action shall not be more severe than that recommended by the principal.

Section 11.  In any case where the hearing panel imposes a suspension or transfer of ten or more school days, or expulsion, the student shall have a right, upon request, to a hearing before the school committee, which shall be conducted according to the rules set forth in section 9.

The scope of the school committee hearing shall be confined to the charges contained in the notice required by section 8.

The student shall be allowed to attend his regularly-assigned school pending the school committee hearing unless the hearing panel below finds, on the basis of clear and substantial evidence, that his continued presence presents a threat to the physical safety of others or that his conduct is so extremely disruptive as to make his removal necessary to preserve the right of other students to pursue an education.

Where the student is out of school, the hearing before the school committee shall be held within seven days from the day of his exclusion or transfer, unless the student or his representative move for an extension of time to allow adequate preparation.

Section 12. No student shall be expelled from school unless both the hearing panel and the school committee find, beyond a reasonable doubt, that he has engaged in frequent and repetitive conduct of such an extreme and serious nature as to make his removal for the rest of the school year necessary to protect the physical safety of others or to preserve the right of other students to pursue an education.

Section 13. In expulsion cases the student shall be represented by counsel, and the school committee shall pay for, or retain counsel to represent the student at all stages of the proceedings where the student is, himself, unable to retain or pay for counsel (for whatever reason). The school committee shall also compel the attendance, both at the initial hearing and at the school committee hearing, of witnesses requested by the student who are employed in the school system.

Section 14. No expulsion shall last beyond the school year in which it is made. The school committee shall notify an expelled student by registered mail of his right to re-enroll in school at the beginning of the school year following the expulsion.

Section 15. In the event that disciplinary action is not found warranted by either the hearing panel or the school committee, all notations relating thereto shall be completely removed from all school records. Students shall have the right to inspect their school records to ensure that such matters are removed, and also so that they will have reasonable opportunity to bring to the attention of school authorities and to rebut or correct any mistaken or incorrect information or notation thereon.

Section 16. The principal of a school (or an impartial person designated by a school committee to take his place where he is a complaining party) may take emergency action, including temporary suspension, after making a finding, that

(a) the student's conduct presents a clear threat to the physical safety of others, or is so extremely disruptive as to make the student's temporary removal necessary to preserve the right of other students to pursue an education;

(b) it is impossible to hold the hearing described in section 9 because of the emergency nature of the situation.

The principal or impartial person shall do everything feasible to assure that the temporary action is based upon a clear factual situation warranting it, including questioning the student and the complaining party in the student's presence.

A temporary suspension or removal shall last no longer than necessary to avoid the dangers described in (a) of this section, and in such cases the principal or impartial person shall make a written report of his findings to the student and to the school committee. In no event shall a student be temporarily suspended under this section for more than three consecutive school days or more than a total of six school days in a school year without the full hearing provided for in sections 7–10 above.

### NOTES AND QUESTIONS

1. Should any of the provisions in the above statement be revised? If so, how and why?

## III.  SANCTIONS OTHER THAN SUSPENSIONS, EXPULSIONS OR DISMISSALS

### CORPORAL PUNISHMENT

### INGRAHAM v. WRIGHT

Supreme Court of the United States, 1977.
430 U.S. 651, 97 S.Ct. 1401, 51 L.Ed.2d 711.

Mr. Justice POWELL delivered the opinion of the Court.

This case presents questions concerning the use of corporal punishment in public schools: First, whether the paddling of students as a means of maintaining school discipline constitutes cruel and unusual punishment in violation of the Eighth Amendment; and, second, to the extent that paddling is constitutionally permissible, whether the Due Process Clause of the Fourteenth Amendment requires prior notice and an opportunity to be heard.

I

Petitioners' [Ingraham and Andrews] evidence may be summarized briefly. In the 1970–1971 school year many of the 237 schools in Dade County used corporal punishment as a means of maintaining discipline pursuant to Florida legislation and a local school board regulation. The statute then in effect authorized limited corporal punishment by negative inference, proscribing punishment which was "degrading or unduly severe" or which was inflicted without prior consultation with the principal or the teacher in charge of the school. The regulation, Dade County School Board Policy 5144, contained explicit directions and limitations. The authorized punishment consisted of paddling the recalcitrant student on the buttocks with a flat wooden paddle measuring less than two feet long, three to four inches wide, and about one-half inch thick. The normal punishment was limited to one to five "licks" or blows with the paddle and resulted in no apparent physical injury to the student. School authorities viewed corporal punishment as a less drastic means of discipline than suspension or expulsion. Contrary to the procedural requirements of the statute and regulation, teachers often paddled students on their own authority without first consulting the principal.

Petitioners focused on Drew Junior High School, the school in which both Ingraham and Andrews were enrolled in the fall of 1970. In an apparent reference to Drew, the District Court found that "[t]he instances of punishment which could be characterized as severe, accepting the students' testimony as credible, took place in one junior high school." The evidence, consisting mainly of the testimony of 16 students, suggests that the regime at Drew was exceptionally harsh. The testimony of Ingraham and Andrews, in support of their individual claims for damages, is illustrative. Because he was slow to respond to his teacher's instructions, Ingraham was subjected to more than 20 licks with a paddle while being held over a table in the principal's office. The paddling was so severe that he suffered a hematoma requiring medical attention and keeping him out of school for several days. Andrews was paddled several times for minor infractions. On two occasions he was struck on his arms, once depriving him of the full use of his arm for a week.

## II

In addressing the scope of the Eighth Amendment's prohibition on cruel and unusual punishment, this Court has found it useful to refer to "[t]raditional common-law concepts," and to the "attitude[s] which our society has traditionally taken." So, too, in defining the requirements of procedural due process under the Fifth and Fourteenth Amendments, the Court has been attuned to what "has always been the law of the land," and to "traditional ideas of fair procedure." We therefore begin by examining the way in which our traditions and our laws have responded to the use of corporal punishment in public schools.

The use of corporal punishment in this country as a means of disciplining schoolchildren dates back to the colonial period. It has survived the transformation of primary and secondary education from the colonials' reliance on optional private arrangements to our present system of compulsory education and dependence on public schools. Despite the general abandonment of corporal punishment as a means of punishing criminal offenders, the practice continues to play a role in the public education of schoolchildren in most parts of the country. Professional and public opinion is sharply divided on the practice, and has been for more than a century. Yet we can discern no trend toward its elimination.

At common law a single principle has governed the use of corporal punishment since before the American Revolution: Teachers may impose reasonable but not excessive force to discipline a child. . . . The prevalent rule in this country today privileges such force as a teacher or administrator "reasonably believes to be necessary for [the child's] proper control, training, or education." To the extent that the force is excessive or unreasonable, the educator in virtually all States is subject to possible civil and criminal liability.

Although the early cases viewed the authority of the teacher as deriving from the parents, the concept of parental delegation has been replaced by the view—more consonant with compulsory education laws—that the State itself may impose such corporal punishment as is reasonably necessary "for the proper education of the child and for the maintenance of group discipline." All of the circumstances are to be taken into account in determining whether the punishment is reasonable in a particular case. Among the most important considerations are the seriousness of the offense, the attitude and past behavior of the child, the nature and severity of the punishment, the age and strength of the child, and the availability of less severe but equally effective means of discipline.

Of the 23 States that have addressed the problem through legislation, 21 have authorized the moderate use of corporal punishment in public schools. Of these States only a few have elaborated on the common-law test of reasonableness, typically providing for approval or notification of the child's parents, or for infliction of punishment only by the principal or in the presence of an adult witness. Only two States, Massachusetts and New Jersey, have prohibited all corporal punishment in their public schools. Where the legislatures have not acted, the state courts have uniformly preserved the common-law rule permitting teachers to use reasonable force in disciplining children in their charge.

Against this background of historical and contemporary approval of reasonable corporal punishment, we turn to the constitutional questions before us.

### III

The Eighth Amendment provides: "Excessive bail shall not be required, nor excessive fines imposed, nor cruel and unusual punishments inflicted." Bail, fines, and punishment traditionally have been associated with the criminal process, and by subjecting the three to parallel limitations the text of the Amendment suggests an intention to limit the power of those entrusted with the criminal-law function of government. An examination of the history of the Amendment and the decisions of this Court construing the proscription against cruel and unusual punishment confirms that it was designed to protect those convicted of crimes. We adhere to this longstanding limitation and hold that the Eighth Amendment does not apply to the paddling of children as a means of maintaining discipline in public schools.

.   .   .

The prisoner and the schoolchild stand in wholly different circumstances, separated by the harsh facts of criminal conviction and incarceration. The prisoner's conviction entitles the State to classify him as a "criminal," and his incarceration deprives him of the freedom "to be with family and friends and to form the other enduring attachments of normal life." Prison brutality is "part of the total punishment to which the individual is being subjected for his crime and, as such, is a proper subject for Eighth Amendment scrutiny." . . .

The schoolchild has little need for the protection of the Eighth Amendment. Though attendance may not always be voluntary, the public school remains an open institution. Except perhaps when very young, the child is not physically restrained from leaving school during school hours; and at the end of the school day, the child is invariably free to return home. Even while at school, the child brings with him the support of family and friends and is rarely apart from teachers and other pupils who may witness and protest any instances of mistreatment.

The openness of the public school and its supervision by the community afford significant safeguards against the kinds of abuses from which the Eighth Amendment protects the prisoner. In virtually every community where corporal punishment is permitted in the schools, these safeguards are reinforced by the legal constraints of the common law. Public school teachers and administrators are privileged at common law to inflict only such corporal punishment as is reasonably necessary for the proper education and discipline of the child; any punishment going beyond the privilege may result in both civil and criminal liability. As long as the schools are open to public scrutiny, there is no reason to believe that the common-law constraints will not effectively remedy and deter excesses such as those alleged in this case.

We conclude that when public school teachers or administrators impose disciplinary corporal punishment, the Eighth Amendment is inapplicable. The pertinent constitutional question is whether the imposition is consonant with the requirements of due process.

## IV

The Fourteenth Amendment prohibits any state deprivation of life, liberty, or property without due process of law. Application of this prohibition requires the familiar two-stage analysis: We must first ask whether the asserted individual interests are encompassed within the Fourteenth Amendment's protection of "life, liberty or property"; if protected interests are implicated, we then must decide what procedures constitute "due process of law." Following that analysis here, we find that corporal punishment in public schools implicates a constitutionally protected liberty interest, but we hold that the traditional common-law remedies are fully adequate to afford due process.

### A

While the contours of this historic liberty interest in the context of our federal system of government have not been defined precisely, they always have been thought to encompass freedom from bodily restraint and punishment. It is fundamental that the state cannot hold and physically punish an individual except in accordance with due process of law.

This constitutionally protected liberty interest is at stake in this case. There is, of course, a *de minimis* level of imposition with which the Constitution is not concerned. But at least where school authorities, acting under color of state law, deliberately decide to punish a child for misconduct by restraining the child and inflicting appreciable physical pain, we hold that Fourteenth Amendment liberty interests are implicated.

### B

"[T]he question remains what process is due." Were it not for the common-law privilege permitting teachers to inflict reasonable corporal punishment on children in their care, and the availability of the traditional remedies for abuse, the case for requiring advance procedural safeguards would be strong indeed. But here we deal with a punishment—paddling—within that tradition, and the question is whether the common-law remedies are adequate to afford due process.

Because it is rooted in history, the child's liberty interest in avoiding corporal punishment while in the care of public school authorities is subject to historical limitations. Under the common law, an invasion of personal security gave rise to a right to recover damages in a subsequent judicial proceeding. But the right of recovery was qualified by the concept of justification. Thus, there could be no recovery against a teacher who gave only "moderate correction" to a child. To the extent that the force used was reasonable in light of its purpose, it was not wrongful, but rather "justifiable or lawful."

The concept that reasonable corporal punishment in school is justifiable continues to be recognized in the laws of most States. It represents "the balance struck by this country" between the child's interest in personal security and the traditional view that some limited corporal punishment may be necessary in the course of a child's education. Under that longstanding accommodation of interests, there can be no deprivation of substantive rights as long as disciplinary corporal punishment is within the limits of the common-law privilege.

This is not to say that the child's interest in procedural safeguards is insubstantial. The school disciplinary process is not "a totally accurate, unerring process, never mistaken and never unfair. . . ." Goss v. Lopez. In any deliberate infliction of corporal punishment on a child who is restrained for that purpose, there is some risk that the intrusion on the child's liberty will be unjustified and therefore unlawful. In these circumstances the child has a strong interest in procedural safeguards that minimize the risk of wrongful punishment and provide for the resolution of disputed questions of justification.

It still may be argued, of course, that the child's liberty interest would be better protected if the common-law remedies were supplemented by the administrative safeguards of prior notice and a hearing. We have found frequently that some kind of prior hearing is necessary to guard against arbitrary impositions on interests protected by the Fourteenth Amendment. But where the State has preserved what "has always been the law of the land," the case for administrative safeguards is significantly less compelling.

.   .   .

But even if the need for advance procedural safeguards were clear, the question would remain whether the incremental benefit could justify the cost. Acceptance of petitioners' claims would work a transformation in the law governing corporal punishment in Florida and most other States. Given the impracticability of formulating a rule of procedural due process that varies with the severity of the particular imposition, the prior hearing petitioners seek would have to precede *any* paddling, however moderate or trivial.

Such a universal constitutional requirement would significantly burden the use of corporal punishment as a disciplinary measure. Hearings—even informal hearings—require time, personnel, and a diversion of attention from normal school pursuits. School authorities may well choose to abandon corporal punishment rather than incur the burdens of complying with the procedural requirements. Teachers, properly concerned with maintaining authority in the classroom, may well prefer to rely on other disciplinary measures—which they may view as less effective—rather than confront the possible disruption that prior notice and a hearing may entail. Paradoxically, such an alteration of disciplinary policy is most likely to occur in the ordinary case where the contemplated punishment is well within the common-law privilege.

Elimination or curtailment of corporal punishment would be welcomed by many as a societal advance. But when such a policy choice may result from this Court's determination of an asserted right to due process, rather than from the normal processes of community debate and legislative action, the societal costs cannot be dismissed as insubstantial. We are reviewing here a legislative judgment, rooted in history and reaffirmed in the laws of many States, that corporal punishment serves important educational interests. This judgment must be viewed in light of the disciplinary problems commonplace in the schools. As noted in Goss v. Lopez: "Events calling for discipline are frequent occurrences and sometimes require immediate, effective action." Assessment of the need for, and the appropriate means of maintaining, school discipline is committed generally to the discretion of school authorities subject to state law. "[T]he Court has repeatedly emphasized the need for affirming the comprehensive authority of the States and of school officials, consistent with fundamental constitutional safeguards, to prescribe and control conduct in the schools." Tinker v. Des Moines School Dist.

"At some point the benefit of an additional safeguard to the individual affected   .   .   .   and to society in terms of increased assurance that the action is just, may be outweighed by the cost." We think that point has been reached in this case. In view of the low incidence of abuse, the openness of our schools, and the common-law safeguards that already exist, the risk of error that may result in violation of a schoolchild's substantive rights can only be regarded as minimal. Imposing additional administrative safeguards as a constitutional requirement might reduce that risk marginally, but would also entail a significant intrusion into an area of primary educational responsibility. We conclude that the Due Process Clause does not require notice and a hearing prior to the imposition of corporal punishment in the public schools, as that practice is authorized and limited by the common law.

Affirmed.

Mr. Justice WHITE, with whom Mr. Justice BRENNAN, Mr. Justice MARSHALL, and Mr. Justice STEVENS join, dissenting.

Today the Court holds that corporal punishment in public schools, no matter how severe, can never be the subject of the protections afforded by the Eighth Amendment. It also holds that students in the public school systems are not constitutionally entitled to a hearing of any sort before beatings can be inflicted on them. Because I believe that these holdings are inconsistent with the prior decisions of this Court and are contrary to a reasoned analysis of the constitutional provisions involved, I respectfully dissent.

I

The Eighth Amendment places a flat prohibition against the infliction of "cruel and unusual punishments." This reflects a societal judgment that there are some punishments that are so barbaric and inhumane that we will not permit them to be imposed on anyone, no matter how opprobrious the offense. If there are some punishments that are so barbaric that they may not be imposed for the commission of crimes, designated by our social system as the most thoroughly reprehensible acts an individual can commit, then, a fortiori, similar punishments may not be imposed on persons for less culpable acts, such as breaches of school discipline. Thus, if it is constitutionally impermissible to cut off someone's ear for the commission of murder, it must be unconstitutional to cut off a child's ear for being late to class. Although there were no ears cut off in this case, the record reveals beatings so severe that if they were inflicted on a hardened criminal for the commission of a serious crime, they might not pass constitutional muster.

Nevertheless, the majority holds that the Eighth Amendment "was designed to protect [only] those convicted of crimes," relying on a vague and inconclusive recitation of the history of the Amendment. Yet the constitutional prohibition is against cruel and unusual *punishments*; nowhere is that prohibition limited or modified by the language of the Constitution. Certainly, the fact that the Framers did not choose to insert the word "criminal" into the language of the Eighth Amendment is strong evidence that the Amendment was designed to prohibit all inhumane or barbaric punishments, no matter what the nature of the offense for which the punishment is imposed.

. . . The Court would have us believe that there is a recognized distinction between criminal and noncriminal punishment for purposes of the Eighth Amendment. This is plainly wrong. "[E]ven a clear legislative classification of a statute as 'non-penal' would not alter the fundamental nature of a plainly penal statute." The relevant inquiry is not whether the offense for which a punishment is inflicted has been labeled as criminal, but whether the purpose of the deprivation is among those ordinarily associated with punishment, such as retribution, rehabilitation, or deterrence.

If this purposive approach were followed in the present case, it would be clear that spanking in the Florida public schools is punishment within the meaning of the Eighth Amendment. . . .

Without even mentioning the purposive analysis applied in the prior decisions of this Court, the majority adopts a rule that turns on the label given to the offense for which the punishment is inflicted. Thus, the record in this case reveals that one student at Drew Junior High School received 50 licks with a paddle for allegedly making an obscene telephone call. The majority holds that the Eighth Amendment does not prohibit such punishment since it was only inflicted for a breach of school discipline. . . .

. . . the majority adheres to its view that any protections afforded by the Eighth Amendment must have something to do with criminals, and it would therefore confine any exceptions to its general rule that only criminal punishments are covered by the Eighth Amendment to abuses inflicted on prisoners. Thus, if a prisoner is beaten mercilessly for a breach of discipline, he is entitled to the protection of the Eighth Amendment, while a schoolchild who commits the same breach of discipline and is similarly beaten is simply not covered. . . .

The essence of the majority's argument is that schoolchildren do not need Eighth Amendment protection because corporal punishment is less subject to abuse in the public schools than it is in the prison system.   However, it cannot be reasonably suggested that just because cruel and unusual punishments may occur less frequently under public scrutiny, they will not occur at all.   The mere fact that a public flogging or a public execution would be available for all to see would not render the punishment constitutional if it were otherwise impermissible.   .   .   .

Nor is it an adequate answer that schoolchildren may have other state and constitutional remedies available to them.   Even assuming that the remedies available to public school students are adequate under Florida law, the availability of state remedies has never been determinative of the coverage or of the protections afforded by the Eighth Amendment.   The reason is obvious.   The fact that a person may have a state-law cause of action against a public official who tortures him with a thumbscrew for the commission of an antisocial act has nothing to do with the fact that such official conduct is cruel and unusual punishment prohibited by the Eighth Amendment.   .   .   I only take issue with the extreme view of the majority that corporal punishment in public schools, no matter how barbaric, inhumane, or severe, is never limited by the Eighth Amendment.   Where corporal punishment becomes so severe as to be unacceptable in a civilized society, I can see no reason that it should become any more acceptable just because it is inflicted on children in the public schools.

## II

The majority concedes that corporal punishment in the public schools implicates an interest protected by the Due Process Clause— the liberty interest of the student to be free from "bodily restraint and punishment" involving "appreciable physical pain" inflicted by persons acting under color of state law.   The question remaining, as the majority recognizes, is what process is due.

The reason that the Constitution requires a State to provide "due process of law" when it punishes an individual for misconduct is to protect the individual from erroneous or mistaken punishment that the State would not have inflicted had it found the facts in a more reliable way.   In Goss v. Lopez, the Court applied this principle to the school disciplinary process, holding that a student must be given an informal opportunity to be heard before he is finally suspended from public school.

The Court now holds that these "rudimentary precautions against unfair or mistaken findings of misconduct," are not required if the student is punished with "appreciable physical pain" rather than with a suspension, even though both punishments deprive the student of a constitutionally protected interest.   Although the respondent school authorities provide absolutely *no* process to the student before the punishment is finally inflicted, the majority concludes that the student is nonetheless given due process because he can later sue the teacher and recover damages if the punishment was "excessive."

This tort action is utterly inadequate to protect against erroneous infliction of punishment for two reasons. First, under Florida law, a student punished for an act he did not commit cannot recover damages from a teacher "proceeding in utmost good faith . . . on the reports and advice of others;" the student has no remedy at all for punishment imposed on the basis of mistaken facts, at least as long as the punishment was reasonable from the point of view of the disciplinarian, uninformed by any prior hearing. The "traditional common-law remedies" on which the majority relies, thus do nothing to protect the student from the danger that concerned the Court in *Goss* —the risk of reasonable, good-faith mistake in the school disciplinary process.

Second, and more important, even if the student could sue for good-faith error in the infliction of punishment, the lawsuit occurs after the punishment has been finally imposed. The infliction of physical pain is final and irreparable; it cannot be undone in a subsequent proceeding. There is every reason to require, as the Court did in *Goss*, a few minutes of "informal give-and-take between student and discipinarian" as a "meaningful hedge" against the erroneous infliction of irreparable injury. . . .

. . .

Mr. Justice STEVENS, dissenting.

Mr. Justice WHITE's analysis of the Eighth Amendment issue is, I believe, unanswerable. I am also persuaded that his analysis of the procedural due process issue is correct. . . .

The constitutional prohibition of state deprivations of life, liberty, or property without due process of law does not, by its express language, require that a hearing be provided *before* any deprivation may occur. To be sure, the timing of the process may be a critical element in determining its adequacy—that is, in deciding what process is due in a particular context. Generally, adequate notice and a fair opportunity to be heard in advance of any deprivation of a constitutionally protected interest are essential. The Court has recognized, however, that the wording of the command that there shall be no deprivation "without" due process of law is consistent with the conclusion that a postdeprivation remedy is sometimes constitutionally sufficient.

When only an invasion of a property interest is involved, there is a greater likelihood that a damages award will make a person completely whole than when an invasion of the individual's interest in freedom from bodily restraint and punishment has occurred. In the property context, therefore, frequently a postdeprivation state remedy may be all the process that the Fourteenth Amendment requires. . . .

## NOTES AND QUESTIONS

1.  In Footnote 22, Justice Powell wrote: "Today, corporal punishment in school is conditioned on parental approval only in California. . . . This Court has held in a summary affirmance that parental approval of corporal punishment is not constitutionally required. Baker v. Owen, 423 U.S. 907, 96 S.Ct. 210, 46 L.Ed.2d 137, affirming 395 F.Supp. 294 (M.D.N.C.1975)." Should the Court have required parental authorization before allowing school officials to administer corporal punishment, the authorization could consist of a general authorization executed by parents at the beginning of each school year?

2.  What is the impact of Ingraham on Goss? What is the proper area of application of Goss after Ingraham?

3.  In another footnote (12) the Court stated that it denied review of a third question: "Is the infliction of severe corporal punishment upon public school students arbitrary, capricious and unrelated to achieving any legitimate educational purpose and therefore violative of the Fourteenth Amendment?" What is you answer to this question? Is corporal punishment a useful alternative to suspension? Does it deter "bad" behavior by increasing student fears of punishment? If so, is an atmosphere of fear conducive to learning? What legitimate educational purpose, if any, does corporal punishment achieve.

4.  Teachers and school officials can concoct disciplinary punishments which can be more objectionable or more permanent than corporal punishment. Valentine v. Independant School Dist., 191 Iowa 1100, 183 N.W. 434 (1921), is an example of the latter, and it illustrates the way courts rule on this type of problem. A school board directive required that "caps and gowns be worn [at graduation], and the same were furnished by the board." Three girls refused to wear the caps because they either did not fit or because of their offensive odor due to a recent fumigation with formaldehyde. School officials characterized the girls as "defiant;" refused to permit them to "occupy seats on the platform," and therefore, "diplomas were not granted to them." One girl sued, and the court upheld the student saying: "The issuance of a diploma by the school board to a pupil who satisfactorily completed the prescribed course of study and who is otherwise qualified is mandatory, and, although such duty is not expressly enjoined upon the board by statute, it does arise by necessary and reasonable implication."

---

### Aron & Katz

### CORPORAL PUNISHMENT IN THE PUBLIC SCHOOLS

Vol. 6, Harv.Civ.Rts. & Civ.Lib.L.Rev. 583, 1971.

. . . The Common law does not protect students against all corporal punishment, the administration of which is governed in many jurisdictions by state statute or school board regulation. . . . Statutes prohibiting cruelty to children and, more often, the common law of assault and battery provide some protection against abuses.

Courts have held that corporal punishment of children must be administered without malice, be reasonable in light of the age, sex, size, and physical strength of the child; be proportional to the gravity of the offense; and be performed to enforce reasonable rules. In holdings governing corporal punishment, some courts have presumed the reasonableness of the teacher's actions. Permissible "unabusive" beatings with a ratan, strap, paddle, or hand, however, as well as beatings impermissible under common law, produce degradation and psychological reactions that provide the rationale for declaring all such punishments violative of the eighth and fourteenth amendments.

Corporal punishment in the public schools is ineffective and harmful. If mildly and irregularly applied, it is useless in controlling behavior. In order to prevent the recurrence of unwanted behavior, corporal punishment must either be applied continually, or its exemplary application must have a "terrifying and traumatic" effect. Not surprisingly, the National Education Association has concluded that corporal punishment is ineffective in reducing behavioral problems. Furthermore, an English study found that a deterioration of behavior and an increase in delinquency accompany increased use of corporal punishment.

Corporal punishment has further deleterious effects on children. Insofar as it relies on fear, it disrupts the learning process by repressing the natural tendency of children to explore. This fear may be channeled into aggression against the teacher, against the school, or against society. At the extreme, juvenile delinquency may result. Finally, and perhaps most seriously, the use of corporal punishment may inhibit the development of self-criticism and self-direction in the child. Corporal punishment may drive students to concentrate their energies on conflict with the teacher instead of encouraging them to adjust to their classroom situation.

While theoretically corporal punishment need not be brutal, there is no assurance that it will be inflicted moderately or responsibly. In the heat of anger, especially if provoked by personal abuse, some teachers are likely to exceed legal bounds. Moreover, if limited corporal punishment were permitted, controls would be unlikely to prevent the "really unmistakable kind of satisfaction which some teachers feel in applying the rattan." A total ban of this punishment would provide far more effective control.

Finally, corporal punishment undermines human dignity. Students are placed at the mercy of teachers who have the power to beat them without explanation or justification. In an institution which purports to inculcate the value of reason in human affairs and the worth of each individual in society, it is antithetical to educate by brutality and unreason.

. . .

If corporal punishment is to be allowed at all, it must be administered only within the constraints of appropriate safeguards. Before taking certain disciplinary measures, public schools must provide students with an opportunity at least to hear and rebut charges before the proper authorities. Both colleges and public schools must accord students a hearing before suspending or dismissing them. Likewise, students subjected to disciplinary transfer, denied the right to participate in interscholastic athletics, or forbidden from taking a college qualifying examination, are entitled to hearings. Consideration of the procedural requisites of due process which should accompany disciplinary action necessitates an examination of the governmental function involved and the private interests affected.

As against a school's educational function, the interest of the student who is expelled or suspended is the impairment of his reputation, with serious economic and social consequences, especially when the action taken will be noted on his permanent record. The interest of the student subjected to corporal punishment involves his physical integrity and human dignity. The interest in each case is equally fundamental. Procedural safeguards in both, therefore, should prevent unwarranted punishment and those excessively administered.

Because tempers often flare in the classroom, it is important that the accuser, judge, and executioner not be the same person. The Supreme Court has recognized that the emotional involvement of the judge who declares a defendant in contempt disqualifies him from presiding when the contempt issue is tried. Similarly, the school official who prescribes corporal punishment, if it is permitted at all, should not be the one who applies it. At a minimum, for any offense serious enough to warrant corporal punishment, a child should have the opportunity to disclaim or justify his conduct before a teacher, parent, and impartial school officer, and the determination of the punishment should result from collaboration of the adults present. Such a requirement should be maintained because it is a guarantee of fairness and rationality which should be imported to an area in which students can be treated harshly.

The delay engendered by the imposition of procedural requirements between the misconduct and the punishment need not reduce the efficacy of the sanction, so long as the student fully comprehends the reason for his punishment. Even if the effectiveness were reduced, it might be the necessary cost of providing fair treatment. Schools would thereby demonstrate to their students that sound justifications should precede the use of physical force.

Once prevalent as a generally accepted means of controlling behavior, corporal punishment is officially sanctioned today only against children. It is inconsistent with modern educational theory and methods, which have progressed from a strict authoritarian concept of education to one emphasizing communication and rapport between teacher and student. The reliance on force, abusive and brutal at times, is a counterproductive means of achieving order in the schools. With an understanding of the effects of corporal punishment and an appreciation for the recently recognized status of students, courts should find corporal punishment cruel and unusual and a denial of due process of law.

## PROBLEM

1. Assume that you are a member of a state legislature and must vote on the two statutes set forth below. How would you vote on them and for what reason(s)? For further discussion see, N.E.A. Report Of The Task Force On Corporal Punishment (1972).

New Jersey Statutes Annotated, sec. 18:19–1:

No person employed or engaged in a school or educational institution, whether public or private, shall inflict or cause to be inflicted corporal punishment upon a pupil attending such school or institution. But any such person may, within the scope of his employment, use and apply such amounts of force as is reasonable and necessary: (1) to quell a disturbance, threatening physical injury to others; (2) to obtain possession of weapons or other dangerous objects upon the person or within the control of a pupil; (3) for the purpose of self-defense; and (4) for the protection of persons and property; and such acts, or any of them shall not be construed to constitute corporal punishment within the meaning and intendment of this section. Every resolution, by-law, rule, ordinance, or other act or authority permitting or authorizing corporal punishment to be indicted upon a pupil attending a school or educational institution shall be void.

Code of Virginia, sec. 22–231.1:

In the maintenance of order and discipline, and in the exercise of a sound discretion, a principal or teacher in a public school or a school maintained by the state, may administer reasonable corporal punishment on a pupil under his authority, provided he acts in good faith and such punishment is not excessive.

## TRANSCRIPT NOTATION AND GRADE REDUCTION

---

[Review Einhorn v. Maus, supra.]

---

### DORSEY v. BALE

Court of Appeals of Kentucky, 1975.
521 S.W.2d 76.

STEPHENSON, Justice. This appeal presents the question whether a board of education can by regulation reduce a student's grade for an unexcused absence as an additional punishment for conduct leading to a suspension from classes for a period of time. The trial court adjudged the regulation to be invalid and ordered the Caverna Independent School District Board to restore the deducted points to appellee's grades and to the grades of all other students similarly situated. The board appeals. We affirm . . . . .

The Caverna Board of Education promulgated a set of regulations incorporated into the Caverna High School Student Handbook. One of the regulations pertains to "unexcused absences":

"Absences for any other reason and failure to follow the outlined procedure will constitute an unexcused absence and work will not be allowed to be made up and furthermore five (5) points will be deducted from the total nine-weeks grade for each unexcused absence from each class during the grading period."

The handbook further provides that absence resulting from suspension "will constitute an unexcused absence."

The appellee, Tommy Bale, was suspended from school on two separate occasions for possession and consumption of alcoholic beverages on school property in violation of regulations of the Caverna High School. The unexcused-absence rule was not invoked for the first offense, but it was for the second offense on which he was suspended from school for four days. In accordance with the unexcused-absence rule, Bale's grades were reduced by five percentage points for each of the four days. As a result, his semester grades were reduced one letter in three of the five courses being taken.

Bale based his lawsuit against the board of education on lack of legal authority to invoke the unexcused-absence rule. The trial court agreed and issued a permanent mandatory injunction ordering the board to restore the deducted points to Bale's grades, and further to restore deducted points to the grades of all other students theretofore affected by the rule.

The appellants argue that the unexcused-absence rule is a reasonable regulation which promotes the school's educational philosophy. Their testimony is to the effect that prior to the adoption of the regulation there existed in the school turmoil, disruption, and disorder, and that suspension, expulsion, detention, and corporal punishment proved to be ineffective to maintain order. According to the testimony of the appellants, the regulation has rid the school system of the turmoil, disruption, and disciplinary problems existing before the adoption of the unexcused-absence rule.

Appellants rely on KRS 160.160, which empowers each board of education to "do all things necessary to accomplish the purpose for which it is created," and KRS 160.290(2), which provides that each board of education may make and adopt rules and regulations for the conduct of pupils.

The trouble with appellants' argument is that KRS 160.290(2) is directed to rules and regulations for the *conduct* of pupils, not to the disciplinary measures taken for the breach of such rules and regulations. We agree with their argument that courts should be reluctant to substitute their judgment for that of the school officials who promulgate the rules and regulations. However, the General Assembly has by statute enunciated legislative intent regarding discipline of students in public schools for serious breaches of school regulations.

KRS 158.150 provides:

"All pupils admitted to the common schools shall comply with the lawful regulations for the government of the schools. Wilful disobedience or defiance of the authority of the teachers, habitual profanity or vulgarity, or other gross violations of propriety or law constitutes cause for suspension or expulsion from school. The superintendent, principal or head teacher of any school may suspend a pupil for such misconduct, but shall report such action in writing immediately to the superintendent. The board of education of any school district may expel any pupil for misconduct as defined in this section, but such action shall not be taken until the parent, guardian or other person having legal custody or control of the pupil has had an opportunity to have a hearing before the board. The decision of the board shall be final."

We are of the opinion that this statute, under which Tommy Bale was suspended, clearly preempts the right of school officials to promulgate disciplinary regulations that impose additional punishment for the conduct that results in suspension. If the conduct of the student in the judgment of the school authorities warrants invoking the statutory authority to suspend, and school authorities do suspend, they have the right to determine the duration of suspension so that such action constitutes a complete punishment for the offense.

We express no opinion as to whether the unexcused-absence rule is a reasonable regulation as applied to students generally.

. . .

The judgment is affirmed as to Tommy Bale    .    . ..

## NOTES AND QUESTIONS

1. How could Bale have complied with the unexcused-absence rule during the time of his suspension?

2. Does the decision in Dorsey affect the school's unexcused-absence rule in situations where a suspension is not involved, but where a student is absent without excuse? If not, what is your opinion of the academic validity of the unexcused-absence rule? Is there an academic relationship between attendance and grades? Can the rule be attacked successfully on constitutional grounds, or would Horowitz, supra, preclude any attack? Was an administrative rule that automatically affected grades involved in Horowitz, or did that case presuppose an exercise of judgment directly by a teacher? Is this distinction important?

3. Compare Fisher v. Burkburnett Independent School Dist., 419 F.Supp. 1200 (N.D.Tex.1976), which was brought in a U.S. District Court, and involved a girl who seriously overdosed on Elavil in violation of the school's anti-drug rule. She was given a ten day suspension which was followed by an "expulsion for the balance of the school term and loss of all grades and credits for the school term." Under a temporary restraining order issued by a state court, she took and passed her final exams. "The only question [in the case] is whether she will be allowed credit for the completed term." The court ruled:

"The plaintiff finally urges that her punishment was so grossly excessive that it violates substantive due process. The court does not doubt that the power of the school board to punish is not without limit and that such a case could exist. See Dixon v. Alabama State Board of Education, 294 F.2d 150, 157 (5th Cir. 1961). Having said this, however, the court cannot find the loss of a trimester constitutionally unreasonable under the facts in this case. The loss of credit was undoubtedly a bitter pill for plaintiff to swallow; the court does not find it a particularly therapeutic dose of justice. Such an academic forfeiture will not demonstrably make the plaintiff a better person. But the plaintiff's interests in rehabilitation and personal development are not the sole considerations before the School Board.

"School administrators have a pressing interest in discouraging drug abuse at school. They may propagandize against such behavior, but the efficacy of strict punishment is surer. This concern with general deterrence explains the harshness of the Burkburnett I.S.D. policy on drugs. Stripping the plaintiff of academic credit does not serve any academic purpose, but it does affect school discipline. The school's policy of suspension for a trimester thus furthers a legitimate interest in a rational if severe manner.

"The school's interest in general deterrence cannot justify any punishment in any circumstance. The disparity between misconduct and punishment would be considerably greater had the plaintiff been caught with a joint of marijuana or a bottle of wine in her purse.　A great enough disparity between the offense and punishment in an individual case might render the punishment an unreasonable means to attain the legitimate end of general deterrence of drug abuse by others.　In the present case, however, the harshness of the punishment is tempered by the non-trivial nature of the incident.　The plaintiff flirted with death.　The punishment meted out to her is severe, but the court does not find it unconstitutionally excessive."

Would, or should, the Dorsey decision be different if the court had considered the general deterrent effect of the unexcused-absence rule? If the rule had been upheld do you think it would deter drinking alcohol on campus?　Truancy?

---

### GUTIERREZ v. SCHOOL DIST. R–1

Colorado Court of Appeals, Div. III, 1978.
585 P.2d 935.

VanCISE, Judge.　Based on the "attendance-tardies" policy adopted by La Junta High School and by the East Otero School District R–1 Board of Education, plaintiffs Artie and Carlos Gutierrez (the students) were denied academic credit for the fall semester of the 1977–1978 school year at La Junta High School.　The students and their parents then brought this action in the district court seeking a declaratory judgment and judicial review of the order of the board of education.　The court decreed that the attendance policy was contrary to state law and thus null and void insofar as the policy denied academic credit to the students for having failed to meet the attendance requirements established by that policy.　It further ordered that the students be allowed academic credit for the fall semester upon completion of any remaining necessary academic requirements. The defendants (collectively the school district) appeal.　We affirm.

The case was tried to the court on a stipulation of facts and issue, and on admissions in the pleadings.　The issue for decision was whether the school district could lawfully promulgate and enforce the attendance-tardies policy within the scope of the rule-making authority delegated to local school boards pursuant to § 22–32–109(1)(w), C.R.S.1973 (1976 Cum.Supp.)　That statute authorizes a school board:

"To adopt written policies, rules and regulations, not inconsistent with law, which may relate to the study, discipline, conduct, safety, and welfare of all pupils, or any classification of pupils, enrolled in the public schools of the school district and to adopt written procedures, not inconsistent with article 33 of this title, for the suspension and expulsion of, or denial of admission to, a pupil, which procedures shall afford due process of law to pupils, parents, and school personnel."

The attendance-tardies policy of the school district provided that a student will be denied academic credit for all classes in which more than seven "absences" occur in a semester. "The seven (7) days of absence are to accommodate such things as:

    a.   Personal illness.

    b.   Professional appointments that could not be scheduled outside the regular school day.

    c.   Serious personal or family problems.

    d.   Or any other reason."

An attendance review board is created, "to meet when requested by a student, teacher, parent, or counselor to examine the specific conditions relating to an individual case  .   .. Disciplinary suspension days will be included in the total days absent."  The review board "may extend the absence limit, continue the student's enrollment in the class(es) on a probationary basis, or take such action as is indicated."

During the fall semester of the 1977–78 school year, the students accumulated in excess of seven "absences."  These included tardies, truancies, suspension days, and excused absences.  Thereafter, after the specified administrative procedures and reviews had been completed, the school board ultimately affirmed the school administration's determination that pursuant to the school attendance policy, Artie was to be denied academic credit in all of his classes and Carlos was to be denied credit in all but one of his classes for the semester.

Plaintiffs contend that the attendance policy is invalid because inconsistent with state law and that, therefore, the denials of academic credit to these students cannot stand.  We agree.

Assuming, without deciding, that the School Attendance Law, § 22–33–101, et seq., C.R.S.1973, does not preclude the school district from adopting *an* attendance policy, any policy adopted must be consistent with that statute.

By § 22–33–104, C.R.S.1973, students are required to attend school for at least 172 days during the school year.  Days on which a student is "temporarily ill or injured," or "has been suspended [or] expelled," are, however, counted as part of the 172 mandatory attendance days.  The statute thus discloses a legislative policy that non-attendance sanctions not be imposed for these types of absences.  The school district's policy, however, denies academic credit to students with more than seven absences, even if, as here, the absences are due partially to suspensions and excused absences.  This is inconsistent with the statute, and is thus invalid.  .   .   .   The denial of academic credit to the plaintiffs based on this policy was in excess of the school district's authority.

.  .  .

Judgment affirmed.

---

## HUMILIATION AND MISCELLANEOUS PUNISHMENTS

---

### CELESTINE v. LAFAYETTE PARISH SCHOOL BD.

Court of Appeals of Louisiana, Third Cir., 1973.
284 So.2d 650.

HOOD, Judge. Allen Celestine instituted this action for judgment ordering that he be re-instated as a classroom teacher in the Lafayette Parish School System as of March 17, 1970 the date he was dismissed, with all of the emoluments and benefits of that employment. The defendant is the Lafayette Parish School Board. The trial judge rendered judgment in favor of the defendant School Board, dismissing plaintiff's suit. Plaintiff has appealed.

The issues are whether the evidence is sufficient to support the School Board's finding that plaintiff is incompetent, whether defendant acted arbitrarily or unreasonably in dismissing plaintiff, and whether plaintiff has been denied due process of law.

On March 16, 1970, plaintiff Celestine was serving as a fifth grade teacher in the N. P. Moss Elementary School in Lafayette Parish, pursuant to a contract of employment previously entered into between him and the Lafayette Parish School Board. He had been working as a classroom teacher for defendant for eleven years prior to that date, and he thus was a "permanent teacher," within the meaning of LSA–R.S. 17:442.

Shortly after his class reconvened following the noon lunch period on the above mentioned date, plaintiff was confronted by several students who told him that two of his girl students had been using "bad words." Plaintiff thereupon asked the two girls in the presence of other members of the class whether they had been using vulgar language, and when they responded that they had, he instructed each of them to write the vulgar word 1,000 times and to turn that work in to the principal for his signature, and to their parents for their signatures. One of the two girls to whom this assignment was given was eleven years of age at that time.

Pursuant to the instructions given to them by plaintiff, each of these girls began writing a four letter word, beginning with the letter "F," being an extremely vulgar word meaning sexual intercourse. They spent the rest of that day carrying out the assignment of writing that word 1,000 times.  .  .  .  A full public hearing was held by the School Board at the time scheduled for it, and at the conclusion of that hearing the School Board, by unanimous vote, formally dismissed plaintiff as a teacher in the Lafayette Parish School System. Plaintiff then instituted this suit.

Plaintiff contends, first, that he did not assign the "word" which was written by the two girl students. He testified that after his students informed him that the two girls had been using bad words, he asked the girls shortly after the class reconvened if they had used vulgar language again, and when they admitted that they had he instructed each of them to write the vulgar word they had used 500 times. The one who completed the assignment testified that she was instructed to write the word 1,000 times, and the record shows that she did write it that many times. Celestine maintains that he did not ask and did not know what the word was until after the assignment had been completed by one student and her paper on which the word had been written many times had been handed to him.

The girl who finished the assignment testified that immediately before the punishment was imposed the word which she wrote 1,000 times was spelled out to the plaintiff by another student in the classroom, and that although it was spelled in a low voice, she could hear it easily while sitting on the second or third row of seats in that class. Plaintiff does not deny that a student spelled the word for him before he gave the assignment, but he stated that if the student spelled it he didn't hear it. He concedes that he used poor judgment in giving that type punishment to a pupil, and that he would not require his own child to write the word which these two young girls wrote.

The evidence shows that the two students who were subjected to this punishment spent the rest of the day writing this vulgar word in the classroom in the presence of the other students, while classes were being conducted in the same room. At least some of the other students knew the word which was being written, because one of them testified that another student had told her what it was while the assignment was being carried out.

We do not feel that plaintiff's unawareness of the exact word which he required the girls to write relieves him of the responsibility of having assigned that specific word to them. According to his own testimony, he knew that he was requiring them to write a vulgar word. If he did not know or bother to inquire as to what the word was, then the assignment by chance could have involved a word which was even more vulgar than the one actually used in this instance, if such a word exists.

We can understand how upsetting the type of punishment administered by plaintiff in this instance may have been to the parents of all of the children in that school. We will not speculate as to the effect which such a punishment may have on the children who were given this assignment, or on the other pupils in the class, but it at least is conceivable that the effect would be harmful to them and to the school. . . .

When there is a rational basis for an administrative board's discretionary determinations which are supported by substantial evidence insofar as factually required, the Court has no right to substitute its judgment for the administrative board's or to interfere with the latter's bona fide exercise of its discretion. . . .

Plaintiff contends, however, that the action of the School Board should be set aside because it deprives him of his rights under the due process of law clauses of the State and Federal Constitutions. He assigns two grounds which he feels supports that contention.

He pointed out, first, that the School Board have never forbidden teachers from requiring students to write words as a method of disciplining them, and that the School Superintendent had "accepted in principle" this form of discipline. He argues that the School Board has "violated out concept of fair play which is embodied in the due process clauses" by dismissing plaintiff on the grounds that he used a form of discipline which had been accepted and had not been forbidden.

It is true that neither the School Board nor the Superintendent had ever forbidden teachers from using the form of punishment described by plaintiff. Celestine, however, was not dismissed because of the *form* or *method* of disciplining students which he used. He was dismissed because of his extremely poor judgment in requiring an eleven year old girl to write a very vulgar word many times, particularly in the presence of the other members of the class. It was the bad judgment, or the incompetency, of the teacher in requiring that a vulgar word be used which brought about his dismissal. It was not merely his selection of a form or method of punishment. We thus find no merit to plaintiff's argument that he has been denied due process because of the form of punishment which he used.

. . .

Plaintiff contends, finally, that his right to academic freedom as a teacher is protected by the First Amendment to the Federal Constitution, and that this right entitles him to administer the punishment which was administered to the two young girls in his class. He relies on Keefe v. Geanakos, which involved the use of a much less offensive word in teaching high school students. The court held, in effect, that the use of the word involved there, under those circumstances, would not justify dismissal of the teacher. The court also stated, however, that:

> "We of course agree with defendants that what is to be said or read to students is not to be determined by obscenity standards for adult consumption. . . . Furthermore, as in all other instances, the offensiveness of language and the

particular propriety or impropriety is dependent on the circumstances of the utterance.

"We accept the conclusion of the court below that 'some measure of public regulation of classroom speech is inherent in every provision of public education.' "

We do not believe that the right of academic freedom entitles a public school teacher to require his students, particularly very young people, to use and be exposed to vulgar words, particularly when no academic or educational purpose can possibly be served. In the instant suit, we agree with the School Board and the trial court that plaintiff did not have the right, under the principle of academic freedom or any other theory, to require an eleven year old girl to write the very vulgar word which was involved here even once, when no valid purpose conceivably could be served by the use of that word. He certainly had no right to require her to write such a word many times in the presence of her classmates. His very poor judgment in imposing such a requirement is sufficient to support the action of the School Board in dismissing him.

---

## WEXELL v. SCOTT

Appellate Court of Illinois, Third District, 1971.
2 Ill.App.3d 646, 276 N.E.2d 735.

GUILD, Justice.    The father of Paul Wexell an eleven year old boy, filed suit against the Board of Education of School District 202, Knox County and against a teacher, Juanita Scott, alleging that the teacher Juanita Scott humiliated, embarrassed, degraded and shamed the student by calling him "worthless, undependable, incompetent" and further that he was unfit to ever marry and that if he did, his children would be ashamed of him.    Plaintiff contended that he suffered great mental anguish, requiring the care of a physician as a result of this.    The second count of the complaint against the Board of Education alleged that the Board was negligent in assigning Juanita Scott as teacher of the class;  that it was negligent in failing to remove her as teacher when the complaint was made, and lastly, that the school board was negligent in failing to "take reasonable measures to safeguard the physical and mental welfare of the plaintiff." The trial court upon motion of the defendants, dismissed the complaint and in a written opinion held that the complaint failed to state a cause of action.

The basic question presented to this court, as stated by the trial court is whether or not verbal abuse by a teacher to a minor student is actionable in a civil suit for damages.

Counsel for the plaintiff agrees with the contention of the defendants that the Tort Immunity Act (C. 85 pps. 1–202, 1–206 and 1–207 IRS 1969) applies in the instant situation in the absence of wilful and wanton misconduct. Counsel also agrees that a teacher stands in loco parentis in the disciplining of children in the class room. The complaint herein does not allege that the actions of the teacher were wilful or malicious, but counsel contends that her actions were an "intentional tort."

The law in Illinois and in many, if not most states is succinctly stated in City of Macomb v. Gould, 104 Ill.App.2d 361, 244 N.E.2d 634 (1969):

> "We have no doubt of the right of a teacher to inflict corporal punishment in the process of enforcing discipline.
> .   .   . He may not wantonly or maliciously inflict corporal punishment and may be guilty of battery if he does so."

The question then becomes if a teacher may inflict corporal punishment does the same principle apply in the use of verbal chastisement? We think it does.

Without belaboring the term, we do believe that the teacher does stand in loco parentis, and in the absence of malice or wantonness, it may well be that disparaging comments about a pupil may be necessary and perhaps conducive to proper educational discipline. While we may not agree with the teacher's choice of words of approbation, nonetheless there are but few students who in the course of their education have not been chastised by the teacher! And few indeed, who have not been belittled by their parents for their shortcomings. And as indicated above, the same applies during that part of the day where the teacher assumes the role of parent.

.   .   .

The second count of the plaintiff's complaint seeks damages from the School Board for its negligence in assigning the teacher in question to the class, and its failure to remove the teacher from that class when a complaint was made as to her conduct. Plaintiff contends that if he cannot prevail against the teacher that the School Board should be responsible. With this we do not agree. As we have held that a teacher has the right to verbally chastise her pupil in the absence of alleged or proven malice or wantonness, a cause of action based on those actions against the employer of the teacher obviously must fail. For these reasons we affirm the judgment of the trial court.

Judgment affirmed.

## OWENS v. KENTUCKY

Court of Appeals of Kentucky, 1971.
473 S.W.2d 827.

STEINFELD, Judge.    Appellant Ethel Owens, a 69-year-old schoolteacher of forty-eight years' experience, was adjudged guilty of assault and battery of a high school girl.  She has appealed from the judgment, claiming only that the trial court erred in not instructing the jury that KRS 161.180 applies.  We reverse.

The teacher had been warned of threats by certain pupils to injure her;  wherefore, she carried a "sneeze gun", a small pencil-like device which, when activated, discharges a substance which causes temporary eye irritation to the person affected.

On the day preceding the alleged assault, Miss Owens had taken Brenda Hopkins to the office of the principal because she violated a school rule.  The next morning the teacher arrived early at the school for the purpose of discussing the incident with the principal before classes started.  Shortly thereafter, Brenda Hopkins and another girl stationed themselves at the door to Miss Owens' school room.  On several occasions when the teacher passed through the door to ascertain whether the principal had arrived, there were incidents of bodybumping with the two girls.  Finally, the general area was disturbed by loud remarks made by Miss Owens and by Brenda; whereupon, a large number of children gathered and other faculty and administrative personnel appeared.  Brenda was directed to go to the office in the company of a secretary and it was suggested that Miss Owens "quiet down".  Claiming that Miss Owens made vile remarks about her, Brenda left the secretary and returned to the place where Miss Owens was standing and almost immediately Brenda was sprayed with the "sneeze gun".

At the conclusion of the evidence, the court gave the jury the usual instructions in an assault and battery prosecution.  .   .   .
One of the grounds asserted on the motion for a new trial was the failure of the court to  " *   *   *  advise the jury under KRS 161.180 that the defendant was empowered  *   *   *  to exercise such disciplinary force as was necessary to restrain and to hold the prosecuting witness, Brenda Hopkins, in strict account for her conduct at the Gallatin School building  *   *   * "  KRS 161.180 reads:

> "Each teacher in the public schools shall hold pupils to a strict account for their conduct in school, on the way to and from school, on the playgrounds, and during intermission or recess."

A companion statute, KRS 161.190, provides:

> "No person shall upbraid, insult or abuse any teacher of the public schools in the presence of the school or in the presence of a pupil of the school."

It is our opinion that at all times related to this incident a student-teacher relationship existed between Brenda Hopkins and Miss Owens; therefore, the mandate of KRS 161.180 required that Miss Owens hold Brenda " * * * to a strict account for (her) conduct * * *" Carr v. Wright, 423 S.W.2d 521 (Ky.1968). While we admit that the use of a weapon such as a "sneeze gun" is unusual and not to be encouraged, nevertheless, in this instance, threats of bodily harm being claimed, it may be justified. It therefore appears that information with respect to the statutory duty of the teacher should have been given to the jury.

If this case is again tried and the evidence warrants, the court will repeat the instructions given in the first trial, except that Instruction No. 2 shall be given substantially as follows:

> Instruction No. 2: It is the duty of each teacher in the public school to hold pupils to a strict account for their conduct in school, on the way to and from school, on the playgrounds, and during intermission or recess. If the jury believe from the evidence in this case that at the time the defendant sprayed, or caused to be sprayed the irritating substance as stated in Instruction No. 1, if she did so, the defendant was making a reasonable attempt to carry out that duty with respect to Brenda Hopkins; or if the jury believe from the evidence that the defendant had reasonable grounds to believe and did believe she was then and there about to be assaulted or have bodily harm inflicted on her and that it reasonably appeared to her to be necessary for her to so spray or cause to be sprayed the irritating substance in order to repeal such assault or prevent such infliction of such personal injury, the jury shall find the defendant not guilty. . . .

# Chapter VII

## CONSTITUTIONAL FREEDOM AND GOVERNMENTAL CONTROLS OVER TEACHERS

### CERTIFICATION

### INTRODUCTION

Before a teacher lawfully can teach in a state's common schools that teacher must first be certified by that state. Thus, for example, Washington's law typically provides that "no person shall be accounted as a qualified teacher within the meaning of the school law who is not the holder of a valid teacher's certificate or permit issued by lawful authority of this state." RCW 28A.67.010. State legislatures and/or state boards of education have enacted laws governing the entire certification process. Immediately, a question is raised concerning student "practice teaching" because students do not meet the necessary conditions to be certificated, the purpose of which is to insure a minimum competency in classroom instructors and for which the student-teacher is preparing. Usually, this problem is met by statutes or rules and regulations of State Boards of Education that allow properly supervised practice teaching. In such situations the practicing teacher is considered to have volunteered his services and is entitled to no pay. See, Floyd County Board of Education v. Slone, 307 S.W.2d 912 (Ky.1957). The teaching certificate is a license, and is generally held not to be a contract between the teacher and the state. A valid certificate is evidence of teaching competency, and its absence is sufficient to uphold a finding of incompetency. Kobylski v. Board of Education, etc., 33 A.D.2d 603, 304 N.Y.S.2d 453 (1969).

A person is a "qualified teacher," in a legal sense, when that person has been certified and has a license to teach in the state's schools. Licenses can be restricted in various ways, and so may a teacher's "qualifications." Thus, a person can be certified to teach for only a period of time, or only to teach certain subjects, or only to teach in certain grades, etc. Furthermore, a state legislature can impose new or additional conditions that a teacher must satisfy in order to teach, and moreover, a teacher's license to teach can be revoked on prescribed grounds, so long as the grounds are constitutional. See, e. g., Keller v. Hewitt, 109 Cal. 146, 41 P. 871 (1895). Additionally, many states have a certificate renewal statute like California's which requires that a teacher have five years of successful teaching as a condition of renewal. These laws frequently lead to litigation because of differing opinions on what amounts to a "successful" teaching experience. For example, a California principal stated that he considered the performance of a teacher in his school to have been unsatisfactory, and her certificate was not renewed by the agency. She was dismissed. But California's court ruled that since she had been in that school system for ten years, and since no charges of incompetency had been brought against the teacher, her "successful" teaching experience would be presumed. Matteson v. State Bd. of Education, 57 Cal.App.2d 991, 136 P.2d 120 (1943).

While all states have laws requiring teacher certification, the laws vary greatly, from the overly specific to the broadly general. Thus, as with other matters, the same situation might receive different legal treatment in different states under different laws. It is essential that teachers know the specific law of their states. Nevertheless, one rule applicable in all states is that if a teacher meets all the conditions set forth for a certificate, the certifying agency has no power arbitrarily to refuse to issue the certificate, even though that agency might have discretionary powers delegated to it by the state legislature. Where states have delegated discretionary powers to a certifying agency, they sometimes include those allowing the agency to prescribe conditions for a teaching certificate in addition to those set forth by the legislature, and, of course, so long as the additionally prescribed conditions are properly within the agency's powers and are constitutional, they must be met before a certificate will issue. As in other matters, courts generally do not supervise the certification process, and tend not to interfere with the exercise of the discretionary powers of the certifying agency.

Can a certifying agency change its standards and then apply them to a person who began teacher training under the old standards? A Maryland case, Metcalf v. Cook, 168 Md. 475, 178 A. 219 (1935), is instructive. Maryland's legislature provided that a high school teacher's certificate "may be granted to persons who are graduates of a standard college or university, or who have had the equivalent in scholastic preparation." Under its discretionary powers, the state board of education promulgated a rule adding requirements to the state statute that "only such graduates as rank academically in the upper four-fifths of the Class and who make a grade of 'C' or better in practical teaching, shall be issued Maryland Teachers' Certificates." An applicant for a certificate ranked only in the lowest fifth of his class, and sued in the courts for a certificate after his application was refused by the state superintendent. The Court of Appeals of Maryland held:

> ". . . The provision . . . that a high school teacher's certificate 'may be granted,' to persons of the specified experience, is construed by the [applicant] as the equivalent of 'shall be granted,' and therefore as prohibiting a

choice among such persons by the board, limiting eligibility to those in the upper four-fifths of the classes.  With this construction, too, the court is in disagreement.  There seems to the court to be no intention manifested other than that of setting a minimum requirement for the board's selection of teachers.  That seems to be a reasonable construction, in accord with the evident plan of the whole statute that the board shall be depended upon largely to make the educational system work properly.  Discretion in selection from eligibles, whose fitness must differ greatly, would seem to be a very likely intention.  And if the discretion is given, as we think it is, then when exercised it acquires by the express terms of the statute the force of law, not to be interfered with by the courts.  .  .  .

"The [applicant] argues that exercise of the authority retroactively could not be intended, so that after a student has started on his preparation a higher test than that with which he was faced at the start could be imposed.  The by-law makes no change in courses of study and preparation; it concerns only the diligence and ability of the student in it, and the contention seems to be that the student had a right to take his work more easily.  We see no vested rights in the standards of work which might restrict retroactive by-laws.  Before the student is selected as a teacher he has no contract with the state, and no vested rights.  He is only the recipient of the state's bounty, with the state left unrestrained in adopting requirements it might find desirable at any time.

"A further objection, that no notice was given the [applicant] of the adoption of this by-law, is subject to the same criticisms.  There is no requirement of notice to individuals.  Publication of the by-law is required by the statute, and it is not denied that there was publication; and in that the full measure of the statutory requirements was met.  Upon publication the by-law acquired the force of law."

In your opinion, could, and should, the new standard of the board of education constitutionally be applied to those teachers previously certified but who ranked only in the lowest fifth of their class?  Why?

In addition to meeting required academic qualifications in most states an applicant must be of "good moral character," and that character must continue after certification otherwise the teacher may not be eligible for a renewal or continuation of his certificate.  In the following case, was good moral character exhibited?  Why or why not?

## BAY v. STATE BOARD OF EDUCATION

Supreme Court of Oregon, 1963.
233 Or. 601, 378 P.2d 558.

PERRY, Justice. Dean Norman Bay petitioned the circuit court of Union County for judicial review of the decision of appellant State Board of Education denying him issuance of a five-year elementary teacher's certificate. From the decree of the circuit court reversing the Board's decision for lack of competent evidence, appeal is made to this court.

In December of 1953 petitioner was tried and convicted in the state of Washington for his acts of breaking, entering, and grand larceny of several stores, the American Legion Club, and the local high school, committed while employed as a night policeman. At the time these acts were perpetrated, petitioner was 24 years old. After serving 18 months of a two-year sentence, he was paroled. He moved to La Grande, Oregon, where, in the fall of 1956 he enrolled at the Eastern Oregon College of Education. In 1958 the state of Washington restored to him his full civil rights.

In 1960 petitioner was granted a one-year elementary teacher's emergency certificate by the Superintendent of Public Instruction, and taught elementary school while completing his fourth year at the college. Following graduation he applied for a five-year elementary teacher's certificate, but his application was denied on June 14, 1961.

On September 13, 1961 a hearing was conducted before the Board, the primary purpose of which was to determine whether petitioner had furnished the evidence of good moral character which ORS 342.060(2) authorizes the superintendent to require of an applicant. Whereas numerous witnesses appeared at the hearing to testify of petitioner's good character and over-all reputation in the community, the sole evidence of bad character introduced was the record of the prior conviction. The Board concluded that petitioner had not met his burden of furnishing satisfactory evidence of good moral character and he thereupon petitioned the circuit court of Union County for review of the administrative order pursuant to ORS 183.-480. The court held that evidence as to a prior conviction was irrelevant and immaterial in determining present character where not accompanied by other evidence which related the prior act to the present, and therefore adjudged there was no competent evidence to support the Board's findings. The Board was ordered to issue petitioner the certificate, from which order this appeal is taken. . . .

In order to properly discuss the issues presented it is first necessary to discuss the powers of the trial court in reviewing the Board's determination.

While the statute uses the language "as a suit in equity," it is quite clear that this language refers only to the fact that the review shall be made by the court, not a jury, and does not grant to a trial court the right on appeal to try the cause de novo. That is, the reviewing court is not granted the power to weigh the evidence and substitute its judgment as to the preponderance thereof for that of the agency. The extent to which a reviewing court should review the action of an administrative agency has been expressed by this court, as follows:

> " * * * Generally, they go no further than to determine whether the agency (1) acted impartially; (2) performed faithfully the duties delineated in the legislative acts which conferred jurisdiction upon it; (3) stayed within its jurisdiction; (4) committed no error of law; (5) exercised discretion judiciously and not capriciously; and (6) arrived at no conclusion which was clearly wrong." . . .

The learned trial court recognized these guide posts and reached the conclusion that the finding of the Board as to lack of good moral character could not be sustained by the record. This conclusion of the court is based upon a finding that there was no evidence of bad moral character at the time of application and therefore the Board's conclusion was clearly wrong.

Whether or not the Board arrived at a conclusion which was clearly wrong depends upon whether a review of the entire record discloses any facts from which the conclusion drawn by the Board could be reached by reasonable minds. . . . There must be evidence that is "more than a mere scintilla. It means such relevant evidence as a reasonable mind might accept as adequate to support a conclusion." . . . These thoughts are contained in and usually expressed as the "substantial evidence rule." . . .

The Board made the following findings of fact which are pertinent to this appeal:

> "1. That the applicant on December 9, 1953, was convicted of grand larceny on four counts in the Superior Court for Klickitat County, State of Washington and received a one to fifteen-year sentence by the said Court. That thereafter his sentence was fixed at a term of two years by the State Board of Terms and Parole of the State of Washington, and the applicant served an eighteen-month term at the Monroe Reformatory in the State of Washington.

> "2. Thereafter upon his release he was placed on parole for approximately a year and moved to the City of La Grande, Oregon, and in the fall of 1956 entered the Eastern Oregon College of Education and enrolled in a teacher education course.

"3.  That by act of the Governor of the State of Washington full civil rights were restored to him on July 3, 1958.

\*     \*     \*     \*     \*     \*     \*     \*     \*

"8.  The Board further finds the offenses committed by Mr. Bay consisted of breaking and entering various stores in Goldendale, Washington and grand larceny, and included safe burglaries at the American Legion Club, the Goldendale High School.  That at the time he committed the offenses for which he was imprisoned he had reached the age of 24 years;  that his offenses numbered not one but several; that he was a man of superior intelligence as evidenced by his scores on intelligence tests in his subsequent college record.

"9.  The Board further finds that at the time of the thefts he occupied a position of trust as a night policeman in the community and that while so engaged he committed the acts resulting in his conviction.

"10.  That a teacher in a public school is the key factor in teaching by precept and example the subjects of honesty, morality, courtesy, obedience to law, and other lessons of a steadying influence which tend to promote and develop an upright and desirable citizenry, as required by ORS 336.240 and related statutes.

"11.  That there has been no evidence submitted to the Board of any violations of law or deviations from normally considered moral conduct from the time of his release from the Monroe Reformatory to the present time."

The Board then made the following conclusions of law:

"1.  That the applicant has not furnished evidence of good moral character deemed satisfactory and necessary by the Board to establish the applicant's fitness to serve as a teacher."

In resolving the question of moral character there must be kept in mind the distinction between character and reputation.  "Character is what a man or woman is morally, while reputation is what he or she is reputed to be."   .   .   .

"A person's 'character' is usually thought to embrace all his qualities and deficiencies regarding traits of personality, behavior, integrity, temperament, consideration, sportsmanship, altruism, etc. which distinguish him as a human being from his fellow men.  His disposition toward criminal acts is only one of the qualities which constitute his character. The statute subjects an applicant's 'character' to scrutiny by the Commission; in the absence of a legislative directive to the narrow interpretation advanced by plaintiffs, courts must give to words their commonly understood definitions and in this case 'character' certainly embraces involvement in the litigation proved against the plaintiffs and their disposition not to be ingenuous and truthful concerning it."

.   .   .

Since the crux of the question before the Board was good moral character, the fact that he had been guilty of burglarizing properties while he held a position of trust was most pertinent. These actions of petitioner clearly evidenced a lack of the moral fiber to resist temptation. The trial court therefore erred in holding there was no evidence of lack of good moral character.

The petitioner offered numerous witnesses from which a conclusion might properly be reached that this lack of moral fiber no longer exists. However, this condition, having been shown to have existed, it became a matter of judgment as to whether it had been overcome.

The power to decide such an issue was delegated by the legislature to the Board of Education, therefore, as previously pointed out, the courts are not permitted to substitute their judgment for that of the Board where there is substantial evidence to support the agency.

The judgment of the trial court is reversed with instructions to enter findings of fact and conclusions of law sustaining the action of the Board of Education.

## NOTES AND QUESTIONS

1. What was the scope of review by the Oregon Supreme Court? Why? Did its scope of review and the matters it considered within it differ from the scope of decision and the matters considered by the State Board of Education? Why? Do you agree with this procedure? Why or why not?

2. Do you agree with the decision of the State Board of Education? Do people change? Had the applicant changed? Is a conviction itself sufficient to show a lack of good moral character? Any conviction? Who among you has not committed a crime? Suppose the applicant had been convicted repeatedly of trespass, vagrancy and disorderly conduct because he repeatedly engaged in non-violent, civil-rights sit-in demonstrations against racial discriminators, or suppose he had been convicted of the private possession of marijuana, or of reckless driving, or of driving while intoxicated, would the decision have been the same? Should it be? Is it constitutionally required that in all cases the certifying agency must carefully consider (1) the nature of the conviction and whether it reveals items that would otherwise disallow the person from being a successful teacher, and (2) if so, whether that person has changed, or should the courts allow any conviction to support a certifying agency's decision of a lack of good moral character? If so, why? Is this what the Oregon Supreme Court did?

3. Define, precisely, what is meant by "good moral character" for a teacher. Should this standard be kept or eliminated? If a sexually active pedophile meets all the academic requirements for a teaching certificate, should he be issued one? Why or why not?

4. What is your legal opinion of the constitutionality of California's provision that:

"Whenever the holder of any credential, life diploma, or document issued by the State Board of Education has been convicted of any sex offense as defined in Section 12912 or narcotics offense as defined in Section 12912.5, the State Board of Education shall forthwith suspend the credential, life diploma, or document. If the conviction is reversed and the holder is acquitted of the offense in a new trial or the charges against him are dismissed, the Board shall forthwith terminate the suspension of the credential, life diploma, or document. When the conviction becomes final or when imposition of sentence is suspended the Board shall forthwith revoke the credential, life diploma, or document." West's Ann.Educ. Code of California § 13207. See, Vogulkin v. State Board of Education, 194 Cal.App.2d 424, 15 Cal.Rptr. 335 (1961), and State of Minnesota ex rel. Pearson v. Probate Court, 309 U.S. 270, 60 S.Ct. 523, 84 L.Ed. 744 (1940).

5. California also provides that:

"Except as provided in this code, no certification document shall be granted to any person unless and until he has subscribed to the following oath or affirmation: 'I solemnly swear (or affirm) that I will support the Constitution of the United States of America, the Constitution of the State of California, and the laws of the United States and the State of California, and will promote respect for the flag and respect for law and order and allegiance to the government of the United States of America.' The oath or affirmation shall be subscribed before any person authorized to administer oaths or before any member of the governing board of a school district or of any county board of education and filed with the commission or with the Board of Governors of the California Community Colleges, as the case may be. Any certificated person who is a citizen or subject of any country other than the United States, and who is employed in any capacity in any of the public schools of the state shall, before entering upon the discharge of his duties, subscribe to an oath to support the institutions and policies of the United States during the period of his sojourn within the state. Upon the violation of any of the terms of the oath or affirmation, the commission or the Board of Governors of the California Community Colleges, as the case may be, shall suspend or revoke the credential which has been issued." West's Ann.Educ.Code of California § 13165.

If a citizen refused to subscribe to this oath, does he lack good moral character? Is any part of this statute unconstitutional? Why or why not?

6. Could a state require a written, oral or performance examination of a prospective teacher as a condition of certification? A physical or

psychological examination? See, e. g., Crofts v. Board of Education, 105 Ill.App.2d 139, 245 N.E.2d 87 (1969); Corsover v. Board of Examiners, 59 Misc.2d 251, 298 N.Y.S.2d 757 (1968); Board of Trustees v. Porini, 263 Cal.App.2d 784, 70 Cal.Rptr. 73 (1968), and Nelson v. Board of Examiners, 21 N.Y.2d 408, 288 N.Y.S. 454, 235 N.E.2d 433 (1968).

7. Could the state require a personality test as a condition of certification? Why or why not? Is personality part of "good moral character"? Would Griswold v. Conn., supra, be relevant?

8. In 1967, a New York court required that an unsuccessful candidate for certification as a high school departmental chairman be given a model answer to the written examination questions on which his denial was based so the unsuccessful applicant would have some "objective" grounds for judging whether he was rightly denied the license. Schwartz v. Bogen, 28 A.D.2d 692, 281 N.Y.S.2d 279, modified 21 N.Y.2d 1020, 291 N.Y.S.2d 4, 238 N.E.2d 496 (1967). See also, Lubell v. Nyquist, 31 A.D.2d 569, 294 N.Y.S.2d 961 (1968).

## DECERTIFICATION

———

Several states have statutes requiring the revocation of a teaching certificate under certain circumstances. So long as the decertifying grounds pass constitutional muster, decertification can take place. However, fair procedures must be followed. In Florida, for example, before decertifying can occur, the State board of education must conduct a preliminary investigation and a separate fair hearing before deciding whether a teacher is guilty of conduct amounting to "moral turpitude." Neal v. Bryant, 149 So.2d 529 (Fla.1962). Compare carefully the following two cases decided under the same statute. Are they consistent? What are the reasons accounting for the way in which California's Supreme Court, in Morrison, construed the statute? If the statute had not been construed this way, would a serious constitutional problem be presented? Why? If so, state the problem, and its probable resolution. Was this problem present in Sarac? If so, what was the court's resolution of it? With which case opinion do you agree? Why? What is the validity of Sarac after Morrison?

———

## SARAC v. STATE BOARD OF EDUCATION

Court of Appeals, Second District, 1967.
249 Cal.App.2d 58, 57 Cal.Rptr. 69.

COBEY, Associate Justice. This is an appeal from a judgment denying appellant's petition under Code of Civil Procedure,   .   .   .

for a writ of mandate against respondent compelling it to rescind its revocation of his general secondary teaching credential.

In reviewing this action of respondent, in proceedings in administrative mandamus, the trial court exercised its independent judgment on the weight of the evidence and its decision must be sustained if there is any credible competent evidence to support its findings. . . . Furthermore, all conflicts in evidence must be resolved in favor of respondent and all reasonable and legitimate inferences must be indulged in order to uphold the findings of the trial court. In short, the evidence must be viewed by us in light most favorable to respondent. . . . Likewise, respondent's determination of the penalty will not be disturbed unless an abuse of discretion in this respect is established. . . .

. . . All of the foregoing is, however, subject to the limitation that if appellant can show denial of an essential constitutional guaranty of fair trial or due process of law, the judgment of the trial court may become subject to reversal. . . .

The administrative proceedings under review began with the filing of an accusation by and before respondent against appellant, who is a male teacher. This pleading charged him in substance with having engaged in immoral and unprofessional conduct within the meaning of Education Code, section 13202, in having, on or about July 28, 1962, at a public beach in or about the City of Long Beach, "rubbed, touched and fondled the private sexual parts of one L. A. Bowers, a person of the masculine sex, with the intent to arouse and excite unnatural sexual desires in said L. A. Bowers and in the [appellant]." The accusation then went on to recite that by reason of this conduct appellant was arrested and charged with violation of Penal Code, section 647a and was on September 4, 1962, convicted in the Long Beach Municipal Court of violation of section 4130(a) of the Long Beach Municipal Code (Disorderly Conduct) upon his plea of guilty thereto. Lastly, the accusation charged that appellant was unfit for service in the public school system within the meaning of the just-mentioned statute because of this conduct by him on the beach, because of the just-mentioned criminal proceedings against him occasioned by such conduct, and because of two admissions he had made to the said Bowers on or about the said July 28, 1962, that he had had a homosexual problem since he was 20 years old and that the last time he had had sexual relations with a man was approximately three weeks earlier.

A hearing was thereafter duly held. . . . Following a decision and order adverse to appellant these mandamus proceedings were duly initiated. . . .

The trial court concluded as a matter of law that appellant had committed "a homosexual act involving moral turpitude" which conduct constituted both immoral and unprofessional conduct within the meaning of said Education Code, section 13202; that the decision of respondent revoking his general secondary teaching credential was correct in that appellant had demonstrated that he was unfit for service in the public school system within the meaning of the just-mentioned statute; that respondent's decision was supported by its findings of fact and that its findings of fact were supported by the weight of the evidence before it and that appellant had been afforded full and complete due process of law at all stages of the administrative proceedings before respondent.

On this appeal we are concerned solely and exclusively with the legal correctness of the judgment of the trial court in this case. Appellant attacks such judgment as being unconstitutional. More specifically he claims that the trial court relied in part upon appellant's conviction of a violation of a Long Beach municipal ordinance, which he asserts is unconstitutional for vagueness and uncertainty and because, as applied to the type of conduct involved here, its field of operation has been preempted by the State. He further contends that all three triers of fact found erroneously in accordance with the accusation that he had pled guilty to a violation of this ordinance, when in fact he had merely refrained from contesting the prosecution's case against him for such violation because he and his then counsel had made a deal with the prosecutor under which, in exchange for such conduct, he obtained a dismissal of the much more serious criminal proceedings against him charging violation of the above stated section of the Penal Code. He argues that this treatment of a nonadmission of guilt as if it had been an admission of guilt unconstitutionally prejudiced the three triers of fact against his credibility in view of the sharp conflict in the evidence between the two police officers on the one hand and himself, his psychiatric expert witness and his 23 character witnesses on the other. He also objects to the findings of fact below insofar as they found true the making by him of two admissions to the said L. A. Bowers of prior homosexual experience on his part. Finally, he says that respondent acted unconstitutionally in revoking his teaching credential because it failed to establish any rational connection between the homosexual conduct on the beach, of which he was found guilty by respondent, and immorality and unprofessional conduct as a teacher on his part and his fitness for service in the public schools; and as a consequence the penalty imposed upon him by respondent, the revocation of his general secondary teaching credential, deprived him of both liberty and property without due process of law, and constituted cruel, unusual and double punishment for the same offense.

We have pointed out that the trial court limited its conclusions of law, insofar as appellant's conduct was concerned, to his one homosexual act on the beach. This renders immaterial and irrelevant appellant's claims respecting the constitutionality of the Long Beach ordinance and the erroneous finding of what happened in the Long

Beach Municipal Court with respect to the basis of his conviction there of its violation. The same may be said in regard to his objections as to the inclusion in the court's findings of fact of his two admissions of prior homosexual experience. . . .

Our review of the record before us, under the rules of law enunciated at the outset of this opinion, convinces us that the testimony of Police Officer, L. A. Bowers, in and of itself, constitutes more than ample credible and competent evidence to support the findings of the trial court that on July 28, 1962, appellant committed a homosexual act on the public beach in Long Beach. Homosexual behavior has long been contrary and abhorrent to the social mores and moral standards of the people of California as it has been since antiquity to those of many other peoples. It is clearly, therefore, immoral conduct within the meaning of Education Code, section 13202. It may also constitute unprofessional conduct within the meaning of that same statute as such conduct is not limited to classroom misconduct or misconduct with children. . . . It certainly constitutes evident unfitness for service in the public school system within the meaning of that statute. . . . In view of appellant's statutory duty as a teacher to "endeavor to impress upon the minds of the pupils the principles of morality" (Ed. Code, § 7851) and his necessarily close association with children in the discharge of his professional duties as a teacher, there is to our minds an obvious rational connection between his homosexual conduct on the beach and the consequent action of respondent in revoking his secondary teaching credential on the statutory grounds of immoral and unprofessional conduct and evident unfitness for service in the public school system of this State. Needless to say, we find no abuse of discretion by respondent in the penalty it here imposed on appellant, nor any constitutional questions whatsoever with respect to such action on its part. . . .

-------

## MORRISON v. STATE BD. OF EDUC.

Supreme Court of California, 1969.
1 Cal.3d 214, 82 Cal.Rptr. 175, 461 P.2d 375.

TOBRINER, Justice. . . . For a number of years prior to 1964 petitioner worked as a teacher for the Lowell Joint School District. During this period, so far as appears from the record, no one complained about, or so much as criticized, his performance as a teacher. Moreover, with the exception of a single incident, no one suggested that his conduct outside the classroom was other than beyond reproach.

Sometime before the spring of 1963 petitioner became friends with Mr. and Mrs. Fred Schneringer. Mr. Schneringer also worked as a teacher in the public school system. To the Schneringers, who were involved in grave marital and financial difficulties at the time, petitioner gave counsel and advice. In the course of such counseling Mr. Schneringer frequently visited petitioner's apartment to discuss his problems. For a one-week period in April, during which petitioner and Mr. Schneringer experienced severe emotional stress, the two men engaged in a limited, non-criminal physical relationship which petitioner described as being of a homosexual nature. Petitioner has never been accused or convicted of any criminal activity whatever, and the record contains no evidence of any abnormal activities or desires by petitioner since the Schneringer incident some six years in the past. Petitioner and Schneringer met on numerous occasions in the spring and summer after the incident and nothing untoward occurred. When Schneringer later obtained a separation from his wife, petitioner suggested a number of women whom Schneringer might consider dating.

Approximately one year after the April 1963 incident, Schneringer reported it to the Superintendent of the Lowell Joint School District. As a result of that report petitioner resigned his teaching position on May 4, 1964.

Some 19 months after the incident became known to the superintendent, the State Board of Education conducted a hearing concerning possible revocation of petitioner's life diplomas. Petitioner there testified that he had had some undefined homosexual problem at the age of 13, but that, with the sole exception of the Schneringer incident, he had not experienced the slightest homosexual urge or inclination for more than a dozen years. Mr. Cavalier, an investigator testifying for the board, stated that the Schneringer incident "was the only time that [petitioner] ever engaged in a homosexual act with anyone." No evidence was presented that petitioner had ever committed any act of misconduct whatsoever while teaching.

The Board of Education finally revoked petitioner's life diplomas some three years after the Schneringer incident. The board concluded that that incident constituted immoral and unprofessional conduct, and an act involving moral turpitude, all of which warrant revocation of life diplomas under section 13202 of the Education Code.

*Petitioner's actions cannot constitute immoral or unprofessional conduct or conduct involving moral turpitude within the meaning of section 13202 unless those actions indicate his unfitness to teach.*

Section 13202 of the Education Code authorizes revocation of life diplomas for "immoral conduct," "unprofessional conduct," and "acts involving moral turpitude." . . . [W]e have given those terms more precise meaning by referring in each case to the particular profession or the specific governmental position to which they were applicable. . . .

Board of Education v. Swan (1953) 41 Cal.2d 546, 261 P.2d 261, and Board of Trustees v. Owens (1962) 206 Cal.App.2d 147, 23 Cal. Rptr. 710, dealt with the term "unprofessional conduct" as applied to teachers. In *Swan* we stressed: "One employed in public service does not have a constitutional right to such employment and is subject to reasonable supervision and restriction by the authorized governmental body or officer *to the end that proper discipline may be maintained, and that activities among the employees may not be allowed to disrupt or impair the public service."* . . . In *Owens* the Court of Appeal held that in deciding whether certain conduct by a teacher constituted unprofessional conduct which warranted discipline, a trial court must inquire whether that conduct had produced "any disruption or impairment of discipline or the teaching process * * *."

. . .

In Orloff v. Los Angeles Turf Club (1951) 36 Cal.2d 734, 227 P.2d 449, we dealt with a statute authorizing the exclusion from theaters, museums, and race courses of persons of "immoral character." We reasoned that the objective of the statute was "the protection of others on the premises." (Id. at p. 740, 227 P.2d at p. 454.) Accordingly we held that a person might be excluded if, for example, he committed a lewd act or an act inimical to the public safety or welfare after gaining admittance to the place of entertainment. But we stressed that no sweeping inquiry could be made into the background and reputation of each person seeking admission. "[T]he private business, the personal relations with others, the past conduct not on the premises, of a person applying for or admitted to the [race] course, whether or not relevant to indicate his character, are immaterial in the application of the statutory standards * * *." . . .

In Jarvella v. Willoughby-Eastlake City School District (1967) 12 Ohio Misc. 288, 233 N.E.2d 143, the court faced the issue of whether a teacher could be dismissed for "immorality" merely because he had written a private letter to a friend containing language which some adults might find vulgar and offensive. The court held that Ohio Revised Code section 3319.16, authorizing dismissal for "immorality" did not cover the teacher's actions, and that he could not therefore be dismissed. The court explained, "Whatever else the term 'Immorality' may mean to many, it is clear that when used in a statute it is inseparable from 'conduct.' * * * But it is not 'immoral conduct' considered in the abstract. It must be considered in the context in which the Legislature considered it, as conduct which is hostile to the welfare of the general public; more specifically in this case, conduct which is hostile to the welfare of the school community. * * * In providing standards to guide school boards in placing restraints on conduct of teachers, the Legislature is concerned with the welfare of the school community. Its objective is the protection of students from corruption. This is a proper exercise of the power of a state to abridge personal liberty and to protect larger interests. But reasonableness must be the governing criterion. * * * Orloff v. Los Angeles Turf Club, Inc., 36 Cal.2d 734, 227 P.2d 449. * * * The private conduct of a man, who is also a teacher, is a proper concern to those who employ him only to the extent it mars him as a teacher * * *. Where his professional achievement is unaffected, where the school community is placed in no jeopardy, his private acts are his own business and may not be the basis of discipline." . . .

By interpreting these broad terms to apply to the employee's performance on the job, the decisions . . . give content to language which otherwise would be too sweeping to be meaningful. Terms such as "immoral or unprofessional conduct" or "moral turpitude" stretch over so wide a range that they embrace an unlimited area of conduct. In using them the Legislature surely did not mean to endow the employing agency with the power to dismiss any employee whose personal, private conduct incurred its disapproval. Hence the courts have consistently related the terms to the issue of whether, when applied to the performance of the employee on the job, the employee has disqualified himself.

In the instant case the terms denote immoral or unprofessional conduct or moral turpitude of the teacher which indicates unfitness to teach. Without such a reasonable interpretation the terms would be susceptible to so broad an application as possibly to subject to discipline virtually every teacher in the state. In the opinion of many people laziness, gluttony, vanity, selfishness, avarice, and cowardice constitute immoral conduct. . . . A recent study by the State Assembly reported that educators differed among themselves as to whether "unprofessional conduct" might include "imbibing alcoholic beverages, use of tobacco, signing petitions, revealing contents of school documents to legislative committees, appealing directly to one's legislative representative, and opposing major-[ity] *opinions* * * *." . . . We cannot believe that the Legislature intended to compel disciplinary measures against teachers who committed such peccadillos if such passing conduct did not affect students or fellow teachers. Surely incidents of extramarital heterosexual conduct against a background of years of satisfactory teaching would not constitute "immoral conduct" sufficient to justify revocation of a life diploma without any showing of an adverse effect on fitness to teach.

Nor is it likely that the Legislature intended by section 13202 to establish a standard for the conduct of teachers that might vary widely with time, location, and the popular mood. One could expect a reasonably stable consensus within the teaching profession as to what conduct adversely affects students and fellow teachers. No such consensus can be presumed about "morality." "Today's morals may be tomorrow's ancient and absurd customs." . . . And conversely, conduct socially acceptable today may be anathema tomorrow. Local boards of education, moreover, are authorized to revoke their own certificates and dismiss permanent teachers for immoral and unprofessional conduct  .   .   .   an overly broad interpretation of that authorization could result in disciplinary action in one country for conduct treated as permissible in another.   .   .   .   A more constricted interpretation of "immoral," "unprofessional," and "moral turpitude" avoids these difficulties, enabling the State Board of Education to utilize its expertise in educational matters rather than having to act "as the prophet to which is revealed the state of morals of the people or the common conscience."   .   .   .

That the meaning of "immoral," "unprofessional," and "moral turpitude" must depend upon, and thus relate to, the occupation involved finds further confirmation in the fact that those terms are used in a wide variety of contexts.   .   .   .

We therefore conclude that the Board of Education cannot abstractly characterize the conduct in this case as "immoral," "unprofessional," or "involving moral turpitude" within the meaning of section 13202 of the Education Code unless that conduct indicates that the petitioner is unfit to teach.  In determining whether the teacher's conduct thus indicates unfitness to teach the board may consider such matters as the likelihood that the conduct may have adversely affected students or fellow teachers, the degree of such adversity anticipated, the proximity or remoteness in time of the conduct, the type of teaching certificate held by the party involved, the extenuating or aggravating circumstances, if any, surrounding the conduct, the praiseworthiness or blameworthiness of the motives resulting in the conduct, the likelihood of the recurrence of the questioned conduct, and the extent to which disciplinary action may inflict an adverse impact or chilling effect upon the constitutional rights of the teacher involved or other teachers.  These factors are relevant to the extent that they assist the board in determining a teacher's fitness to teach, i. e., in determining whether the teacher's future classroom performance and overall impact on his students are likely to meet the board's standards.

*If interpreted in this manner section 13202 can be constitutionally applied to petitioner.*

Petitioner urges three substantive reasons to support his contention that section 13202 upon its face or as construed by the board deprived him of his constitutional rights.  As we shall show, however, that section, as we have interpreted it, could constitutionally apply to petitioner.

Petitioner first suggests that the terms "unprofessional," "moral turpitude," and particularly "immoral" are so vague as to constitute a denial of due process.  Civil as well as criminal statutes must be sufficiently clear as to give a fair warning of the conduct prohibited, and they must provide a standard or guide against which conduct can be uniformly judged by courts and administrative agencies.   .   .   .
The knowledge that he has erred is of little value to the teacher when gained only upon the imposition of a disciplinary penalty that jeop-

ardizes or eliminates his livelihood. . . . Courts and commentators have exposed and condemned the uncertainty of words such as "unprofessional," "immoral," and "moral turpitude." Indeed, in Orloff v. Los Angeles Turf Club, supra . . . this court recognized that the term "immoral" might well be unconstitutionally vague. . .

. . . As we have explained above, the prohibitions against immoral and unprofessional conduct and conduct involving moral turpitude by a teacher constitutes a general ban on conduct which would indicate his unfitness to teach. This construction gives section 13202 the required specificity. Teachers, particularly in the light of their professional expertise, will normally be able to determine what kind of conduct indicates unfitness to teach. Teachers are further protected by the fact that they cannot be disciplined merely because they made a reasonable, good faith, professional judgment in the course of their employment with which higher authorities later disagreed. . . .

Petitioner secondly contends that the ban on immoral conduct in section 13202 violates his constitutionally protected right to privacy. It is true that an unqualified proscription against immoral conduct would raise serious constitutional problems. Conscientious school officials concerned with enforcing such a broad provision might be inclined to probe into the private life of each and every teacher, no matter how exemplary his classroom conduct. Such prying might all too readily lead school officials to search for "telltale signs" of immorality in violation of the teacher's constitutional rights. (Griswold v. Connecticut). . . . The proper construction of section 13202, however, minimizes the danger of such sweeping inquiries. By limiting the application of that section to conduct shown to indicate unfitness to teach, we substantially reduce the incentive to inquire into the private lives of otherwise sound and competent teachers.

Finally, petitioner urges that the board cannot revoke his life diplomas because his questioned conduct does not rationally relate to his duties as a teacher. No person can be denied government employment because of factors unconnected with the responsibilities of that employment. . . . Again, however, the proper construction of section 13202 avoids this problem, for that interpretation would bar disciplinary action against petitioner unless the record demonstrated that petitioner's conduct did indicate his unfitness to teach.

*The record contains no evidence that petitioner's conduct indicated his unfitness to teach.*

As we have stated above, the statutes, properly interpreted, provide that the State Board of Education can revoke a life diploma or other document of certification and thus prohibit local school officials from hiring a particular teacher only if that individual has in some manner indicated that he is unfit to teach. Thus an individual can be removed from the teaching profession only upon a showing that his retention in the profession poses a significant danger of harm to either students, school employees, or others who might be affected by his actions as a teacher. . . . Accordingly, we must inquire whether any adverse inferences can be drawn from that past conduct as to petitioner's teaching ability, or as to the possibility that publicity surrounding past conduct may in and of itself substantially impair his function as a teacher.

As to this crucial issue, the record before the board and before this court contains no evidence whatsoever. . . .

This lack of evidence is particularly significant because the board failed to show that petitioner's conduct in any manner affected his performance as a teacher. There was not the slightest suggestion that petitioner had ever attempted, sought, or even considered any form of physical or otherwise improper relationship with any student. There was no evidence that petitioner had failed to impress upon the minds of his pupils the principles of morality as required by section 13556.5 of the Education Code. There is no reason to believe that the Schneringer incident affected petitioner's apparently satisfactory relationship with his co-workers.

The board revoked petitioner's license three years after the Schneringer incident; that incident has now receded six years into the past. Petitioner's motives at the time of the incident involved neither dishonesty nor viciousness, and the emotional pressures on both petitioner and Schneringer suggest the presence of extenuating circumstances. Finally, the record contains no evidence that the events of April 1963 have become so notorious as to impair petitioner's ability to command the respect and confidence of students and fellow teachers in schools within or without the Lowell Joint School District.

Before the board can conclude that a teacher's continued retention in the profession presents a significant danger of harm to students or fellow teachers, essential factual premises in its reasoning should be supported by evidence or official notice. In this case, despite the quantity and quality of information available about human sexual behavior, the record contains no such evidence as to the significance and implications of the Schneringer incident. Neither this court nor the superior court is authorized to rectify this failure by uninformed speculation or conjecture as to petitioner's future conduct. . . .

Respondent relies heavily on Sarac v. State Bd. of Education. . . . The facts involved in *Sarac* are clearly distinguishable from the instant case; the teacher disciplined in that case had pleaded guilty to a criminal charge of disorderly conduct arising from his homosexual advances toward a police officer at a public beach; the teacher admitted a recent history of homosexual activities. The court's discussion in that case includes unnecessarily broad language suggesting that all homosexual conduct, even though not shown to relate to fitness to teach, warrants disciplinary action. . . . The proper construction of section 13202, however, as we have demonstrated, is more restricted than indicated by this dicta in *Sarac,* and to the extent that *Sarac* conflicts with this opinion it must be disapproved. . . .

*Conclusion.*

In deciding this case we are not unmindful of the public interest in the elimination of unfit elementary and secondary school teachers. . . . But petitioner is entitled to a careful and reasoned inquiry into his fitness to teach by the Board of Education before he is deprived of his right to pursue his profession. . . . "The right to practice one's profession is sufficiently precious to surround it with a panoply of legal protection" . . . and terms such as "immoral," "unprofessional," and "moral turpitude" constitute only lingual abstractions until applied to a specific occupation and given content by reference to fitness for the performance of that vocation. . . .

Our conclusion affords no guarantee that petitioner's life diplomas cannot be revoked. If the Board of Education believes that petitioner is unfit to teach, it can reopen its inquiry into the circumstances surrounding and the implications of the 1963 incident with Mr. Schneringer. The board also has at its disposal ample means to discipline petitioner for future misconduct.

Finally, we do not, of course, hold that homosexuals must be permitted to teach in the public schools of California. As we have explained, the relevant statutes, as well as the applicable principles of constitutional law, require only that the board properly find, pursuant to the precepts set forth in this opinion, that an individual is not fit to teach. . . .

SULLIVAN, Justice.

I dissent. . . .

. . . The precise question before us is this: Did the Board properly revoke petitioner's life diplomas upon determining that petitioner, while employed as a teacher, had committed homosexual acts and engaged in a homosexual relationship with a fellow teacher and that such acts constituted immoral and unprofessional conduct within the meaning the sections 13202 and 13209 of the Education Code? . . .

. . . Homosexual behavior has long been contrary and abhorrent to the social mores and moral standards of the people of California as it has been since antiquity to those of many other peoples. It is clearly, therefore, immoral conduct within the meaning of Education Code, section 13202. It may also constitute unprofessional conduct within the meaning of that same statute as such conduct is not limited to classroom misconduct or misconduct with children. . . . It certainly constitutes evident unfitness for service in the public school system within the meaning of that statute. . . . In view of appellant's statutory duty as a teacher to 'endeavor to impress upon the minds of the pupils the principles of morality' (Ed.Code, § 7851) and his necessarily close association with children in the discharge of his professional duties as a teacher, there is to our minds an obvious rational connection between his homosexual conduct on the beach and the consequent action of respondent in revoking his secondary teaching credential on the statutory grounds of immoral and unprofessional conduct and evident unfitness for service in the public school system of this State." . . .

The majority argue that *Sarac* is distinguishable from the instant case on its facts. It is asserted that the teacher's homosexual conduct occurred on a public beach, whereas this petitioner's conduct occurred in the privacy of his apartment. Apparently this asserted difference reflects the view that, absent a criminal offense, petitioner's private life is his own business and the state " * * * must not arbitrarily impair the right of the individual to live his private life, apart from his job, as he deems fit. * * * " But the clandestine character of petitioner's acts did not render them any the less homosexual acts. These still remained, to borrow the language of *Sarac* " * * * contrary and abhorrent to the social mores and moral standards of the people of California * * *." . . . It would be fatuous to assume that such acts became reprehensible only if committed in public. One would not expect petitioner and Schneringer to commit the acts here involved (which, as I have said, need not be detailed) in full view of the citizenry.

It is also asserted by the majority that the teacher in *Sarac* pleaded guilty to and was convicted of a criminal charge. However, as I have pointed out, the accusation filed with the Board in that case was based primarily on the teacher's homosexual conduct, apart from his subsequent arrest, which fell within the compass of section 13202 and warranted revocation of his credentials. . . .

The court in *Sarac* also sustained the trial court's finding that the homosexual act there committed was one involving moral turpitude. As already stated, a similar finding and determination were made in the instant matter not only in the administrative proceedings but also in the superior court proceedings on review. The determination is unassailable. Although we have recognized on occasion that the problem of defining moral turpitude is not without difficulty . . . nevertheless this court has for many years . . . defined moral turpitude as " * * * everything done contrary to justice, honesty, modesty, or good morals. * * * " . . .

In sum, the majority opinion boils down to this: " * * * the Board failed to show that petitioner's conduct in any manner affected his performance as a teacher" and "petitioner is entitled to a careful and reasoned inquiry into his fitness to teach by the Board of Education before he is deprived of his right to pursue his profession." Taking this position, the majority remand this case to the superior court presumably, although they do not say so, to be remanded by that court in turn to the Board.

I feel it my duty to observe, with all due respect to the majority, that this action is taken without proper recognition of our function of review in cases of administrative boards. . . . To recapitulate: The Board in this case found on overwhelming evidence, indeed on the frank but unrepentent admissions of petitioner, that he had committed homosexual acts with another teacher and concluded that these acts constituted immoral and unprofessional conduct and acts involving moral turpitude. The trial court reached the same conclusion. The majority opinion is silent on this point. Yet I would respectfully suggest that it is an essential step in any process of reasoning which seeks to strike down the Board's action. Were petitioner's acts immoral or not? Or was he perhaps correct after all in maintaining they were not? The majority do not answer this question; nevertheless they reverse the judgment and remand the cause to the trial court for further proceedings. I would think that under the circumstances the question should be answered for the guidance of the court below on retrial; that court, as well as the Board, should be told whether or not they were in error in concluding that petitioner's homosexual acts were immoral and involved moral turpitude. As I said at the beginning, this is the pivotal question and I think it was correctly answered by the Board, the trial judge and the three appellate justices. . . .

In the instant case, both the Board and the trial court concluded that petitioner was unfit. I cannot say there is no rational connection between petitioner's homosexual acts and his fitness to teach. . . .

BURKE, Justice. . . .

. . . This case, and other recent cases, have involved the courts in the untenable position of attempting to assess factual issues of conduct, motive and intent that could better be left to the governmental agencies upon whom the discretion has been conferred by the Legislature. . . .

## THE TEACHER'S CONTRACT

### INTRODUCTION

If a person has been certified to teach in the common schools that does not mean he will automatically get a teaching position. It does mean that he has become a member of a "qualified" group, and can receive an offer of a job. In all states, statutes locate the power to make teaching contracts with qualified teachers in a school board, usually local boards. Similar to the certification process, school boards generally have power to promulgate legally valid rules and regulations that set forth the conditions under which a previously certified person becomes eligible for a contract. Thus, local boards establish qualifications for teachers through the contracting process that are in addition to those required for certification. Of course, the contractual conditions must themselves be constitutional; e. g., no local board could validly promulgate a rule denying contracts solely on the grounds of race, religion or political affiliation. But, what about union activities?

Only the board of education can enter into a binding contract. In the absence of a statute permitting that power to be delegated to someone else neither a State Superintendent, nor any other person, can validly make a contract with a teacher. Moreover, if there is no delegation of the power to contract, it follows that the Superintendent cannot terminate a contract, only the school board has the power to do so. Snider v. Kit Carson School District, 166 Colo. 180, 442 P.2d 429 (1968). The subject matter of teacher's contracts varies to a greater extent than certification requirements. A teacher can be employed to engage in a variety of activities that can be set forth in the contract. Thus, the contract is most important because it sets forth the rights and duties of the teacher and the school district. Moreover, contracts may be limited to a fixed period; thus, a teacher might have a lifetime certificate but only a one or three year contract. In such situations, after the time period has expired and both parties to the contract have performed, their relationship is at an end. The contract has expired.

At least two formal, legal requirements must be met before the teacher can be said to have a legally binding contract. First, the school board itself must have proceeded in such a way as to meet all the requirements for valid, legal action, thereby binding the school district. This means that the school board meeting where the action is taken to make an offer to a person, or to delegate that power (where permitted by statute), must conform to all the requirements of law, such as, having given proper notice; having a quorum present; having the meeting open, if required; following the technically correct procedures on the presentation of school board business, voting, etc. If the school board meeting does not comply with the requirements of law, then the school board, or its agent, has no lawful power to act, and in such circumstances, it cannot make a binding contract, and a teacher will not have a valid contract. Secondly, the teacher's contract must comply with the same general requirements of law that all contracts must satisfy. There must be (1) a specific and definite offer meeting the requirements of law and an unqualified acceptance of that offer; (2) legally competent persons capable of contracting, for example, a teacher without a valid teaching certificate may not be a competent person to contract with a board of education, this requirement can cause difficulty for persons who are graduating from a college or university and have obtained a teaching position before being certified; (3) consideration, i. e., something that is valuable, for example: the rendering of specified teaching services in exchange for money; (4) a legal subject matter, teaching is a lawful subject, but if it were not the contract would be declared void—could a school board validly contract with a minister to conduct religious services in school?; (5) a proper legal form; frequently States require that before a teacher's contract will be legally valid it must be in writing, especially tenure contracts.

If contracts required to be in writing are oral, then they are not enforceable; however, in such event, if a qualified teacher renders teaching services, courts allow him to recover a fair compensation for them, but not because he has a valid contract. See, e. g., Goose River Bank v. Willow Lake School Township, 1 N.D. 26, 44 N.W. 1002 (1890). Finally, in addition to the rules and regulations governing the qualifications for a contract, courts tend to hold that so long as the rules and regulations of the board of education do not conflict with the constitution, or other higher law, they, as well as the statutes of the state governing teacher behavior, are all part of the contract between the teacher and the school district. This last item can come as a surprise to many teachers who are ignorant of a local board's governing rules and regulations; for example, could a local board constitutionally provide that a teacher's contract would be terminated if he is absent from school for three months (Elder v. Board of Education, 60 Ill.App.2d 56, 208 N.E.2d 423 (1965)), or if he refused to sever his financial interests with a liquor store (Romeike v. Houston Independent School Dist., 368 S.W.2d 895 (Tex.1963)), or if he refused to engage in further professional training (Last v. Board of Education, 37 Ill.App.2d 159, 185 N.E.2d 282 (1962))?

At times local school boards, by contract, try to require that teachers go to rather drastic lengths in satisfying conditions that the board deems necessary for the efficient operation of the schools:

"I promise to take a vital interest in all phases of Sunday-school work, donating of my time, service, and money without stint for the benefit and uplift of the community.

"I promise to abstain from dancing, immodest dressing, and any other conduct unbecoming a teacher and a lady.

"I promise not to go out with any young men except insofar as it may be necessary to stimulate Sunday-school work.

"I promise not to fall in love, to become engaged or secretly married.

"I promise to remain in the domitory or on the school grounds when not actively engaged in school or church work elsewhere.

"I promise not to encourage or tolerate the least familiarity on the part of any of my boy pupils  .  .  ."

The above, taken from a teacher's contract in a North Carolina town, is set forth in Odegard, The American Public Mind 83 (1930), printed in Williams et al., Labor Relations and the Law. Boston: Little, Brown and Company, 1965, p. 751. Is such a contract constitutional? Is this type of contract a good argument for teachers' unions?

---

## BIG SANDY SCHOOL DISTRICT NO. 100–J v. CARROLL

Supreme Court of Colorado, 1967.
164 Colo. 173, 433 P.2d 325.

McWILLIAMS, Justice.   The central issue presented by this writ of error is whether a school board may delegate to its superintendent of schools the "power" and "duty" to employ teachers.

Before detailing some of the facts, it is deemed advisable to set forth at the very outset the particular statute with which we are here concerned.  C.R.S.1963, 123–10–19, which pertains generally to the "powers of a school board," provides in part as follows:

"(1) *Every school board*, unless otherwise especially provided by law, *shall have power, and it shall be their duty:*

"(2) *To employ* or discharge *teachers,* mechanics and laborers, *and to fix* and order paid *their wages;*  *  *  * "
(Emphasis added.)

The essential facts in the instant case are not really in dispute, although as to some peripheral matters there are some rather marked disputes.  Sometime in June 1963 the five members of the school board for the Big Sandy School District No. 100–J "authorized" the superintendent of schools to "contact and employ" a combination principal and teacher for the high school in Simla.  This "authorization" did not result from any formal action of the school board, but nonetheless was apparently acquiesced in by all five board members. The superintendent was advised as to the "salary limits" within which he could then fix the salary of the new principal-teacher, once he was located.  Otherwise, there were no additional limitations or restrictions placed on the superintendent, and it was strictly up to him to find and hire a combination principal and teacher for the high school.

To facilitate the entire process, the President and Secretary of the school board signed "in blank" an employment contract form used by the District.  In other words, the employment contract form signed by the President and Secretary of the Board did not, of course, designate the other contracting party, whose identity as of that time was unknown, or did it fix the salary or the dates the employment would either start or end.

In mid-August of 1963 Carroll first contacted the superintendent about possible employment as both the principal and a teacher in the Simla High School. On that occasion, Carroll and the superintendent conferred at some length about the teaching vacancy, and the two of them generally "came to terms" although Carroll said that he wanted to talk the matter over with his wife before he made any final decision. On this occasion the superintendent, in the presence of Carroll, typed in the "blanks" in the employment contract form theretofore signed in blank by the President and Secretary of the school board. Specifically, the superintendent typed in the name of "Barney Carroll" as the other party to the contract. The superintendent also typed in the salary as being "sixty-five hundred $6,500 dollars," payable in twelve monthly installments, as well as typing in the period of employment as "beginning August 21, 1963 and ending August 20, 1964."

According to Carroll, though this was denied by the superintendent, he (Carroll) called the superintendent on the following day and "accepted" the offer. Carroll testified that immediately thereafter he signed the original contract, and a copy thereof, both of which had been given him on the preceding day by the superintendent. Carroll retained the original of this contract and upon trial the document was offered and received into evidence. As concerns the copy of the aforementioned contract, Carroll testified that a few days after his telephone conversation with the superintendent he left the copy, signed by him, on the superintendent's desk. The superintendent testified, however, that he never found any such signed copy on his desk.

Without going into any great detail as to why he was relieved of his duties, Carroll was purportedly "discharged" by the superintendent some ten days later. It should be noted that the purported discharge occurred on the day before classes were to commence and was triggered by the fact that Carroll had "missed" the schools' registration day. However, no hearing was ever held as to whether this so-called discharge was "for cause," or not.

Carroll immediately brought suit against the District, alleging a contract of employment between himself and the District and a breach of that contract by the District when he was wrongfully discharged "without good cause shown or a hearing."

Upon trial of this matter the basic contention of the District was that the school board could not lawfully delegate to its superintendent the power to employ teachers and that accordingly there never was a valid contract between Carroll and the District. Though this case was tried to a jury, at the conclusion of all the evidence the trial court took the case from the jury on the premise that there were no issues of fact, only issues of law. The trial court then ruled that there was a valid contract of employment between Carroll and the District and that the District had breached the contract by summarily discharging Carroll without the benefit of any hearing as to whether there was "good cause" for his discharge. Judgment was then entered in Carroll's favor in the sum of $6,500 and interest from August 21, 1963. . . . Our study of the matter convinces us that under the circumstances there never was a valid and binding contract between Carroll and the District, and that the trial court therefore erred in its entry of judgment in behalf of Carroll.

The applicable statute not only empowers the school board to employ teachers and fix their wages, but goes on to declare that such is the *duty of the school board.* C.R.S.1963, 123–10–19. In other words, the power to employ teachers is exclusively vested by the legislature in the school board, and not in any other body or official. It being, then, the *duty* of the school board to employ teachers and fix their wages, the question is then raised as to whether the duty which has been thus placed by the legislature in the school board may be delegated, or on the contrary whether this is a non-delegable duty.

.   .   .

In our view the power to employ teachers and fix their wages is not a mere ministerial or administrative matter, where little or no judgment or discretion is involved, but on the contrary is a legislative or judicial power involving the exercise of considerable discretion. Hence, under the general rule, such power cannot be delegated. The power to employ teachers has been conferred by the legislature exclusively on the school board, and therefore it cannot be delegated. To hold to the contrary would thwart the obvious intent of the legislature and would amount to nothing more than pure judicial legislation. . . .

.   .   . if this should be deemed a "hard" case, hard cases should not be allowed to make bad law. To permit Carroll to recover against the District would make some very bad law and would open the door to great abuse. In short, by statute the school board is empowered to hire teachers and while it may well want to act on the recommendation of its superintendent, it cannot escape this statutory duty by completely shifting the responsibility to its superintendent. This is so because that is the way the legislature wanted it.

The judgment is reversed.   .   .   .

## CLEVELAND BD. OF ED. v. LaFLEUR

## COHEN v. CHESTERFIELD CTY. SCH. BD.

Supreme Court of the United States, 1974.
414 U.S. 632, 94 S.Ct. 791, 39 L.Ed.2d 52.

Mr. Justice STEWART delivered the opinion of the Court.    .    .    .

I

Jo Carol LaFleur and Ann Elizabeth Nelson are junior high school teachers employed by the Board of Education of Cleveland, Ohio. Pursuant to a rule first adopted in 1952, the school board requires every pregnant school teacher to take a maternity leave without pay, beginning five months before the expected birth of her child. Application for such leave must be made no later than two weeks prior to the date of departure. A teacher on maternity leave is not allowed to return to work until the beginning of the next regular school semester which follows the date when her child attains the age of three months. A doctor's certificate attesting to the health of the teacher is a prerequisite to return; an additional physical examination may be required. The teacher on maternity leave is not promised re-employment after the birth of the child; she is merely given priority in reassignment to a position for which she is qualified. Failure to comply with the mandatory maternity leave provisions is grounds for dismissal.

Neither Mrs. LaFleur nor Mrs. Nelson wished to take an unpaid maternity leave; each wanted to continue teaching until the end of the school year. Because of the mandatory maternity leave rule, however, each was required to leave her job in March of 1971. The two women then filed separate suits in the United States District Court for the Northern District of Ohio    .    .    .    challenging the constitutionality of the maternity leave rule. The District Court tried the cases together, and rejected the plaintiffs' arguments. A divided panel of the United States Court of Appeals for the Sixth Circuit reversed, finding the Cleveland rules in violation of the Equal Protection Clause of the Fourteenth Amendment.

Susan Cohen, was employed by the School Board of Chesterfield County, Virginia. That school board's maternity leave regulation requires that a pregnant teacher leave work at least four months prior to the expected birth of her child. Notice in writing must be given to the school board at least six months prior to the expected birth date. A teacher on maternity leave is declared re-eligible for employment when she submits written notice from a physician that she is physically fit for re-employment, and when she can give assurances that care of the child will cause minimal interferences with her job responsibilities. The teacher is guaranteed re-employment no later than the first day of the school year following the date upon which she is declared re-eligible.

Mrs. Cohen informed the Chesterfield County School Board in November 1970, that she was pregnant and expected the birth of her child about April 28, 1971. She initially requested that she be permitted to continue teaching until April 1, 1971. The school board rejected the request, as it did Mrs. Cohen's subsequent suggestion that she be allowed to teach until January 21, 1971, the end of the first school semester. Instead, she was required to leave her teaching job on December 18, 1970. She subsequently filed this suit in the United States District Court for the Eastern District of Virginia. The District Court held that the school board regulation violates the Equal Protection Clause, and granted appropriate relief. A divided panel of the Fourth Circuit affirmed, but, on rehearing *en banc*, the Court of Appeals upheld the constitutionality of the challenged regulation in a 4–3 decision.

We granted certiorari in both cases in order to resolve the conflict between the Courts of Appeals regarding the constitutionality of such mandatory maternity leave rules for public school teachers.

## II

This Court has long recognized that freedom of personal choice in matters of marriage and family life is one of the liberties protected by the Due Process Clause of the Fourteenth Amendment. . . . there is a right "to be free from unwarranted governmental intrusion into matters so fundamentally affecting a person as the decision whether to bear or beget a child."

By acting to penalize the pregnant teacher for deciding to bear a child, overly restrictive maternity leave regulations can constitute a heavy burden on the exercise of these protected freedoms. Because public school maternity leave rules directly affect "one of the basic civil rights of man," . . . the Due Process Clause of the Fourteenth Amendment requires that such rules must not needlessly, arbitrarily, or capriciously impinge upon this vital area of a teacher's constitutional liberty. The question before us in these cases is whether the interests advanced in support of the rules of the Cleveland and Chesterfield County School Boards can justify the particular procedures they have adopted.

The school boards in these cases have offered two essentially overlapping explanations for their mandatory maternity leave rules. First, they contend that the firm cut-off dates are necessary to maintain continuity of classroom instruction, since advance knowledge of when a pregnant teacher must leave facilitates the finding and hiring of a qualified substitute. Secondly, the school boards seek to justify their maternity rules by arguing that at least some teachers become physically incapable of adequately performing certain of their duties during the latter part of pregnancy. By keeping the pregnant teacher out of the classroom during these final months, the maternity leave rules are said to protect the health of the teacher and her unborn child, while at the same time assuring that students have a physically capable instructor in the classroom at all times.

It cannot be denied that continuity of instruction is a significant and legitimate educational goal. Regulations requiring pregnant teachers to provide early notice of their condition to school authorities undoubtedly facilitate administrative planning toward the important objective of continuity. But, as the Court of Appeals for the Second Circuit noted in Green v. Waterford Board of Education, 472 F.2d 629, 635:

> "Where a pregnant teacher provides the Board with a date certain for commencement of leave, however, that value [continuity] is preserved; an arbitrary leave date set at the end of the fifth month is no more calculated to facilitate a planned and orderly transition between the teacher and a substitute than is a date fixed closer to confinement. Indeed, the latter   .   .   .   would afford the Board more, not less, time to procure a satisfactory long-term substitute." (Footnote omitted.)

Thus, while the advance notice provisions in the Cleveland and Chesterfield County rules are wholly rational and may well be necessary to serve the objective of continuity of instruction, the absolute requirements of termination at the end of the fourth or fifth month of pregnancy are not. Were continuity the only goal, cut-off dates much later during pregnancy would serve as well or better than the challenged rules, providing that ample advance notice requirements were retained. Indeed, continuity would seem just as well attained if the teacher herself were allowed to choose the date upon which to commence her leave, at least so long as the decision were required to be made and notice given of it well in advance of the date selected.

In fact, since the fifth or sixth months of pregnancy will obviously begin at different times in the school year for different teachers, the present Cleveland and Chesterfield County rules may serve to hinder attainment of the very continuity objectives that they are purportedly designed to promote. For example, the beginning of the fifth month of pregnancy for both Mrs. LaFleur and Mrs. Nelson occurred during March of 1971. Both were thus required to leave work with only a few months left in the school year, even though both were fully willing to serve through the end of the term. Similarly, if continuity were the only goal, it seems ironic that the Chesterfield County rule forced Mrs. Cohen to leave work in mid-December 1970 rather than at the end of the semester in January, as she requested.

We thus conclude that the arbitrary cut-off dates embodied in the mandatory leave rules before us have no rational relationship to the valid state interest of preserving continuity of instruction. As long as the teacher is required to give susbtantial advance notice of her condition, the choice of firm dates later in pregnancy would serve the boards' objectives just as well, while imposing a far lesser burden on the women's exercise of constitutionally protected freedom.

The question remains as to whether the fifth and sixth month cut-off dates can be justified on the other ground advanced by the school boards—the necessity of keeping physically unfit teachers out of the classroom. There can be no doubt that such an objective is perfectly legitimate, both on educational and safety grounds. And, despite the plethora of conflicting medical testimony in these cases, we can assume *arguendo* that at least some teachers become physically disabled from effectively performing their duties during the latter stages of pregnancy.

The mandatory termination provisions of the Cleveland and Chesterfield County rules surely operate to insulate the classroom from the presence of potentially incapacitated pregnant teachers. But the question is whether the rules sweep too broadly. . . . That question must be answered in the affirmative, for the provisions amount to a conclusive presumption that every pregnant teacher who reaches the fifth or sixth month of pregnancy is physically incapable of continuing. There is no individualized determination by the teacher's doctor—or the school board's—as to any particular teacher's ability to continue at her job. The rules contain an irrebuttable presumption of physical incompetency, and that presumption applies even when the medical evidence as to an individual woman's physical status might be wholly to the contrary.

. . . "permanent irrebuttable presumptions have long been disfavored under the Due Process Clauses of the Fifth and Fourteenth Amendments." . . .

> "[I]t is forbidden by the Due Process Clause to deny an individual the resident rates on the basis of a permanent and irrebuttable presumption of nonresidence, when that presumption is not necessarily or universally true in fact, and when the state has reasonable alternative means of making the crucial determination."

Similarly, in Stanley v. Illinois, 405 U.S. 645, the Court held that an Illinois statute containing an irrebuttable presumption that unmarried fathers are incompetent to raise their children violated the Due Process Clause. Because of the statutory presumption, the State took custody of all illegitimate children upon the death of the mother, without allowing the father to attempt to prove his parental fitness.

Hence, we held that the State could not conclusively presume that any particular unmarried father was unfit to raise his child; the Due Process Clause required a more individualized determination.  .  .  .

These principles control our decision in the cases before us.  While the medical experts in these cases differed on many points, they unanimously agreed on one—the ability of any particular pregnant woman to continue at work past any fixed time in her pregnancy is very much an individual matter.  .  .  .  The conclusive presumption embodied in these rules  .  .  .  is neither "necessarily nor universally true," and is violative of the Due Process Clause.

The school boards have argued that the mandatory termination dates serve the interest of administrative convenience, since there are many instances of teacher pregnancy, and the rules obviate the necessity for case-by-case determinations.  Certainly, the boards have an interest in devising prompt and efficient procedures to achieve their legitimate objectives in this area.  .  .  .

While it might be easier for the school boards to conclusively presume that all pregnant women are unfit to teach past the fourth or fifth month or even the first month, of pregnancy, administrative convenience alone is insufficient to make valid what otherwise is a violation of due process of law.  The Fourteenth Amendment requires the school boards to employ alternative administrative means, which do not so broadly infringe upon basic constitutional liberty, in support of their legitimate goals.

We conclude, therefore, that neither the necessity for continuity of instruction nor the state interest in keeping physically unfit teachers out of the classroom can justify the sweeping mandatory leave regulations that the Cleveland and Chesterfield County School Boards have adopted.  While the regulations no doubt represent a good-faith attempt to achieve a laudable goal, they cannot pass muster under the Due Process Clause of the Fourteenth Amendment, because they employ irrebuttable presumptions that unduly penalize a female teacher for deciding to bear a child.

### III

In addition to the mandatory termination provisions, both the Cleveland and Chesterfield County rules contain limitations upon a teacher's eligibility to return to work after giving birth.  Again, the school boards offer two justifications for the return rules—continuity of instruction and the desire to be certain that the teacher is physically competent when she returns to work.  As is the case with the leave provisions, the question is not whether the school board's goals are legitimate, but rather whether the particular means chosen to achieve those objectives unduly infringe upon the teachers' constitutional liberty.

Under the Cleveland rule, the teacher is not eligible to return to work until the beginning of the next regular school semester following the time when her child attains the age of three months. A doctor's certificate attesting to the teacher's health is required before return; an additional physical examination may be required at the option of the school board.

[LaFleur does] not seriously challenge either the medical requirements of the Cleveland rule or the policy of limiting eligibility to return to the next semester following birth. The provisions concerning a medical certificate or supplemental physical examination are narrowly drawn methods of protecting the school board's interest in teacher fitness; these requirements allow an individualized decision as to teacher's condition, and thus avoid the pitfalls of the presumptions inherent in the leave rules. Similarly, the provision limiting eligibility to return to the semester following delivery is a precisely drawn means of serving the school board's interest in avoiding unnecessary changes in classroom personnel during any one school term.

The Cleveland rule, however, does not simply contain these reasonable medical and next-semester eligibility provisions. In addition, the school board requires the mother to wait until her child reaches the age of three months before the return rules begin to operate. The school boards have offered no reasonable justification for this supplemental limitation, and we can perceive none. To the extent that the three months provision reflects the school board's thinking that no mother is fit to return until that point in time, it suffers from the same constitutional deficiencies that plague the irrebuttable presumption in the termination rules. The presumption, moreover, is patently unnecessary, since the requirement of a physician's certificate or a medical examination fully protects the school's interests in this regard. And finally, the three month provision simply has nothing to do with continuity of instruction, since the precise point at which the child will reach the relevant age will obviously occur at a different point throughout the school year for each teacher.

Thus, we conclude that the Cleveland return rule, insofar as it embodies the three months age provision, is wholly arbitrary and irrational, and hence violates the Due Process Clause of the Fourteenth Amendment. The age limitation serves no legitimate state interest, and unncessarily penalizes the female teacher for asserting her right to bear children.

We perceive no such constitutional infirmities in the Chesterfield County rule. In that school system, the teacher becomes eligible for reemployment upon submission of a medical certificate from her physician; return to work is guaranteed no later than the beginning of the next school year following the eligibility determination. The medical certificate is both a reasonable and narrow method of protecting the school board's interest in teacher fitness, while the possible deferring of return until the next school year serves the goal of preserving continuity of instruction.  In short, the Chesterfield County rule manages to serve the legitimate state interests here without employing unnecessary presumptions that broadly burden the exercise of protected constitutional liberty. . . .

Mr. Justice DOUGLAS concurs in the result.

Mr. Justice POWELL, concurring in the result.

I concur in the Court's result, but I am unable to join its opinion. In my view these cases should not be decided on the ground that the mandatory maternity leave regulations impair any right to bear children or create an "irrebuttable presumption."  It seems to me that equal protection analysis is the appropriate frame of reference.

These regulations undoubtedly add to the burdens of childbearing. But certainly not every government policy that burdens childbearing violates the Constitution.  Limitations on the welfare benefits a family may receive that do not take into account the size of the family illustrate this point. .    .    .    Undoubtedly Congress could, as another example, constitutionally seek to discourage excessive population growth by limiting tax deductions for dependents.  That would represent an intentional governmental effort to "penalize" childbearing. .  .  .    The regulations here do not have that purpose.  Their deterrent impact is wholly incidental. . . .

I am also troubled by the Court's return to the "irrebuttable presumption" line of analysis  .  .  .    As a matter of logic, it is difficult to see the terminus of the road upon which the Court has embarked under the banner of "irrebuttable presumptions."  If the Court nevertheless uses "irrebuttable presumption" reasoning selectively, the concept at root often will be something else masquerading as a due process doctrine.  That something else, of course, is the Equal Protection Clause. .  .  .

To be sure, the boards have a legitimate and important interest in fostering continuity of teaching.  And, even a normal pregnancy may at some point jeopardize that interest.  But the classifications chosen by these boards, so far as we have been shown, are either contraproductive (sic) or irrationally overinclusive even with regard to this significant, nonillusory goal.  Accordingly, in my opinion these regulations are invalid under rational basis standards of equal protection review.

.  .  .    I think it important to emphasize the degree of latitude the Court, as I read it, has left the boards for dealing with the real and recurrent problems presented by teacher pregnancies.  Boards may demand in every case "substantial advance notice of [pregnancy] .  .  .  ."  Subject to certain restrictions, they may require all pregnant teachers to cease teaching "at some firm date during the last few weeks of pregnancy. . . ." The Court further holds that boards may in all cases restrict re-entry into teaching to the outset of the school term following delivery.

In my opinion, such class-wide rules for pregnant teachers are constitutional under traditional equal protection standards. School boards, confronted with sensitive and widely variable problems of public education, must be accorded latitude in the operation of school systems and in the adoption of rules and regulations of general application. . . . A large measure of discretion is essential to the effective discharge of the duties vested in these local, often elective, governmental units. My concern with the Court's opinion is that, if carried to logical extremes, the emphasis on individualized treatment is at war with this need for discretion. Indeed, stringent insistence on individualized treatment may be quite impractical in a large school district with thousands of teachers. . . .

Mr. Justice REHNQUIST, with whom The Chief Justice joins, dissenting.

The Court rests its invalidation of the school regulations involved in these cases on the Due Process Clause of the Fourteenth Amendment, rather than on any claim of sexual discrimination under the Equal Protection Clause of that Amendment. My Brother STEWART thereby enlists the Court in another quixotic engagement in his apparently unending war or irrebuttable presumptions. . . .

Countless state and federal statutes draw lines such as those drawn by the regulations here which, under the Court's analysis, might well prove to be arbitrary in individual cases. The District of Columbia Code, for example, draws lines with respect to age for several purposes. The Code requires that a person to be eligible to vote be 18 years of age, that a male be 18 and a female be 16 before a valid marriage may be contracted, that alcoholic beverages not be sold to a person under age 21 years, or beer or light wines to any person under the age of 18 years. A resident of the District of Columbia must be 16 years of age to obtain a permit to operate motor vehicle, and the District of Columbia delegate to the United States Congress must be 25 years old. Nothing in the Court's opinion clearly demonstrates why its logic would not equally well sustain a challenge to these laws from a 17-year-old who insists that he is just as well informed for voting purposes as an 18-year-old, from a 20-year-old who insists that he is just as able to carry his liquor as a 21-year-old, or from the numerous other persons who fall on the outside of lines drawn by these and similar statutes.

More closely in point is the jeopardy in which the Court's opinion places long-standing statutes providing for mandatory retirement of government employees.    5 U.S.C. § 8335 provides with respect to Civil Service employees:

> "(a) Except as otherwise provided by this section, an employee who becomes seventy years of age and completes fifteen years of service shall be automatically separated from the service    .    .    .    ."

.    .    .    In Truax v. Reich, the Court said:

> "It requires no argument to show that the right to work for a living and the common occupations of the community is of the very essence of the personal freedom and opportunity that it was the purpose of the Amendment to secure."    239 U.S. 33, 41.

Since this right to pursue an occupation is presumably on the same lofty footing as the right of choice in matters of family life, the Court will have to strain valiantly in order to avoid having today's opinion lead to the invalidation of mandatory retirement statutes for governmental employees.    In that event federal, state, and local governmental bodies will be remitted to the task, thankless both for them and for the employees involved, of individual determinations of physical impairment and senility.

It has been said before, Williamson v. Lee Optical Co., 348 U.S. 483, but it bears repeating here:    All legislation involves the drawing of lines, and the drawing of lines necessarily results in particular individuals who are disadvantaged by the line drawn being virtually indistinguishable for many purposes from those individuals who benefit from the legislative classification.    The Court's disenchantment with "irrebuttable presumptions," and its preference for "individualized determination," is in the last analysis nothing less than an attack upon the very notion of lawmaking itself.

The lines drawn by the school boards in the city of Cleveland and Chesterfield County in these cases require pregnant teachers to take forced leave at a stage of their pregnancy when medical evidence seems to suggest that a majority of them might well be able to continue teaching without any significant possibility of physical impairment.    But so far as I am aware, the medical evidence also suggests that in some cases there may be physical impairment at the stage of pregnancy fastened on by the regulations in question, and that the probability of physical impairment increases as the pregnancy advances.    If legislative bodies are to be permitted to draw a general line anywhere short of the delivery room, I can find no judicial standard of measurement which says the ones drawn here were invalid. I therefore dissent.

### NOTES AND QUESTIONS

1.  The records in these cases indicate that the maternity leave regulations originally may have been inspired by other considerations.

Would any of the following have served to justify the regulations: (1) that they were adopted to save pregnant teachers from the embarrassment of giggling children saying such things as "my teacher swallowed a watermelon"; (2) that their cut-off date at the end of the fourth month was chosen because that is when a teacher "begins to show", or (3) that the regulations insulate the school children from seeing conspicuously pregnant teachers?

2. In footnote 13 the Court states: "We are not dealing in these cases with maternity leave regulations requiring a termination of employment at some firm date during the last few weeks of pregnancy." Suppose medical evidence showed that pregnancy generally impaired a teacher's job performance during the last six or four weeks, would a mandatory cut-off rule for the last six or four weeks be constitutional?

3. Suppose psychological evidence showed that children of mothers who return to work within the first three months develop less rapidly and less well, having feelings of rejection and alienation, would this evidence have justified the return-to-work regulations?

4. The Court did not say that Virginia's rule requiring that the teacher give assurances that care of the child will not unduly interfere with her job duties is unconstitutional. Is it?

5. What are the constitutional requirements of these cases in the situations posed by Mr. Justice REHNQUIST? The United States Court of Appeals for the Second Circuit has held that the New York state compulsory retirement system for teachers is immune from constitutional attack as discriminatory on the basis of age in violation of the equal protection and due process guarantees of the Fourteenth Amendment. A state may prescribe mandatory retirement for teachers in order to open up employment opportunities for young teachers, to open more places for minorities, to bring young people with fresh ideas and techniques in contact with school children, or to assure predictability and ease in establishing and administering pension plans. Palmer v. Ticcione, 576 F.2d 459 (2d Cir. 1978).

6. Restrictive school policies regarding pregnancy leaves have been stricken in Driessen v. Freborg, 431 F.Supp. 1191 (D.N.D.1977); State Div. of Human Rights v. Board of Educ., 54 A.D.2d 1115, 388 N.Y.S.2d 785 (1976); Shirley v. Chagrin Falls Board of Educ., 521 F.2d 1329 (6th Cir. 1975), certiorari denied 424 U.S. 913, 96 S.Ct. 1111, 47 L.Ed.2d 317 (1976); Goetz v. Norristown School Dist., 16 Pa.Cmwlth. 389, 328 A.2d 579 (1974).

7. Pregnancy leaves may also be controlled by a statute, Title VII of the Civil Rights Act of 1964, which is beyond the scope of this book. The statute applies to school employers and prohibits sex-discrimination against employees. In Nashville Gas Co. v. Satty, 434 U.S. 136, 98 S.Ct. 347, 54 L.Ed.2d 356 (1977), the U.S. Supreme Court struck down an employer's "practice of denying accumulated seniority to female employees returning to work following disability caused by childbirth." That policy, the Court ruled, "acts both to deprive [formerly pregnant employees] 'of employment opportunities' and to 'adversely affect [their] status as an employee'" on the basis of sex, and in violation

of Title VII.  The leave policy was neutral on its face in its treatment of male and female employees (only some but not all females became pregnant; thus, perhaps no sex-classification is involved, and the policy may not, therefore, violate the Constitution's equal-protection clause). On this reasoning, in part, in Geduldig v. Aiello, 417 U.S. 884, 94 S.Ct. 2485, 41 L.Ed.2d 256 (1974), the U. S. Supreme Court held that a distinction between, and a different treatment of, pregnancy-related and other disabilities did not involve a sex-based classification, and in General Electric Co. v. Gilbert, 429 U.S. 125, 97 S.Ct. 401, 50 L.Ed.2d 343 (1976) that the company's disability benefits plan not covering pregnancy-related disabilities did not violate Title VII.  (See French, All Things Being Equal  .   .   .   General Electric Co. v. Gilbert: An Analysis, 7 J. of L. & Ed. 21 (1978)).  Nevertheless, the court held that the policy in Satty was discriminatory in its disproportionate impact (only females were affected) and so it was invalid under Title VII and the decision in Griggs v. Duke Power Co., 401 U.S. 424, 91 S.Ct. 849, 28 L.Ed.2d 158 (1971).

8.  The Equal Pay Act of 1963 (29 U.S.C.A. § 206(d)), was added as an amendment to the Fair Labor Standards Act of 1938 (29 U.S.C.A. § 201 et seq.).  It prohibits an employer from discriminating "between employees on the basis of sex by paying wages to employees  .   .   .   at a rate less than the rate at which he pays wages to employees of the opposite sex  .   .   .   for equal work on jobs the performance of which requires equal skill, effort, and responsibility, and which are performed under similar working conditions, except where such payment is made pursuant to  .   .   .   (IV) a differential based on any other factor than sex  .   .   .".  This Act carries a complicated definition of wage discrimination which has limited its industrial impact and focussed litigation on seemingly endless details of particular work.  See, e. g., Shultz v. Wheaton Glass Co., 421 F.2d 259 (3rd Cir.), certiorari denied 398 U.S. 905, 90 S.Ct. 1696, 26 L.Ed.2d 64 (1970).  The problem is not as severe in an educational context;  see, Board of Regents v. Dawes, 522 F.2d 380 (8th Cir. 1975), certiorari denied 424 U.S. 914, 96 S.Ct. 1112, 47 L.Ed.2d 318 (1976).

## TEACHER FREEDOM OF EXPRESSION AND OTHER RIGHTS

———

The doctrine of academic freedom and their First Amendment protections appear in Chapter III.  This section focuses on additional constitutional rights of teachers other than rights to academic freedom.  Constitutional rights of teachers (to free expression, privacy, etc.) serve to limit a state's power to dismiss; i. e., a state has no constitutional power to terminate a teacher simply because he exercised one of his constitutional rights, even though school officials may not have liked the way in which the constitutional right was exercised.

———

## PICKERING v. BOARD OF EDUC.

Supreme Court of the United States, 1968.
391 U.S. 563, 88 S.Ct. 1731, 20 L.Ed.2d 811.

Mr. Justice MARSHALL delivered the opinion of the Court.

Appellant Marvin L. Pickering, a teacher in Township High School District 205, Will County, Illinois, was dismissed from his position by the appellee Board of Education for sending a letter to a local newspaper in connection with a recently proposed tax increase that was critical of the way in which the Board and the district superintendent of schools had handled past proposals to raise new revenue for the schools. Appellant's dismissal resulted from a determination by the Board, after a full hearing, that the publication of the letter was "detrimental to the efficient operation and administration of the schools of the district" and hence, under the relevant Illinois statute . . . that "interests of the school require[d] [his dismissal]."

Appellant's claim that his writing of the letter was protected by the First and Fourteenth Amendments was rejected. . . . For the reasons detailed below we agree that appellant's rights to freedom of speech were violated and we reverse.

In February of 1961 the appellee Board of Education asked the voters of the school district to approve a bond issue to raise $4,875,000 to erect two new schools. The proposal was defeated. Then, in December of 1961, the Board submitted another bond proposal to the voters which called for the raising of $5,500,000 to build two new schools. This second proposal passed and the schools were built with the money raised by the bond sales. In May of 1964 a proposed increase in the tax rate to be used for educational purposes was submitted to the voters by the Board and was defeated. Finally, on September 19, 1964, a second proposal to increase the tax rate was submitted by the Board and was likewise defeated. It was in connection with this last proposal of the School Board that appellant wrote the letter to the editor (which we reproduce in an Appendix to this opinion) that resulted in his dismissal.

Prior to the vote on the second tax increase proposal a variety of articles attributed to the District 205 Teachers' Organization appeared in the local paper. These articles urged passage of the tax increase and stated that failure to pass the increase would result in a decline in the quality of education afforded children in the district's schools. A letter from the superintendent of schools making the same point was published in the paper two days before the election and submitted to the voters in mimeographed form the following day. It was in response to the foregoing material, together with the failure of the tax increase to pass, that appellant submitted the letter in question to the editor of the local paper.

The letter constituted, basically, an attack on the School Board's handling of the 1961 bond issue proposals and its subsequent allocation of financial resources between the schools' educational and athletic programs. It also charged the superintendent of schools with attempting to prevent teachers in the district from opposing or criticizing the proposed bond issue.

The Board dismissed Pickering for writing and publishing the letter. Pursuant to Illinois law, the Board was then required to hold a hearing on the dismissal. At the hearing the Board charged that numerous statements in the letter were false and that the publication of the statements unjustifiably impugned the "motives, honesty, integrity, truthfulness, responsibility and competence" of both the Board and the school administration. The Board also charged that the false statements damaged the professional reputations of its members and of the school administrators, would be disruptive of faculty discipline, and would tend to foment "controversy, conflict and dissension" among teachers, administrators, the Board of Education, and the residents of the district. Testimony was introduced from a variety of witnesses on the truth or falsity of the particular statements in the letter with which the Board took issue. The Board found the statements to be false as charged. No evidence was introduced at any point in the proceedings as to the effect of the publication of the letter on the community as a whole or on the administration of the school system in particular, and no specific findings along these lines were made. [The Illinois Supreme Court upheld the action of the board] . . .

To the extent that the Illinois Supreme Court's opinion may be read to suggest that teachers may constitutionally be compelled to relinquish the First Amendment rights they would otherwise enjoy as citizens to comment on matters of public interest in connection with the operation of the public schools in which they work, it proceeds on a premise that has been unequivocally rejected in numerous prior decisions of this Court. E. g., Wieman v. Updegraff, 344 U.S. 183 (1952); Shelton v. Tucker, 364 U.S. 479 (1960); Keyishian v. Board of Regents, 385 U.S. 589 (1967). "[T]he theory that public employment which may be denied altogether may be subjected to any conditions, regardless of how unreasonable, has been uniformly rejected." Keyishian v. Board of Regents, supra, at 605–606. At the same time it cannot be gainsaid that the State has interests as an employer in regulating the speech of its employees that differ significantly from those it possesses in connection with regulation of the speech of the citizenry in general. The problem in any case is to arrive at a balance between the interests of the teacher, as a citizen, in commenting upon matters of public concern and the interest of the State, as an employer, in promoting the efficiency of the public services it performs through its employees.

The Board contends that "the teacher by virtue of his public employment has a duty of loyalty to support his superiors in attaining the generally accepted goals of education and that, if he must speak out publicly, he should do so factually and accurately, commensurate with his education and experience." Appellant, on the other hand, argues that the test applicable to defamatory statements directed against public officials by persons having no occupational relationship with them, namely, that statements to be legally actionable must be made "with knowledge that [they were] . . . false or with reckless disregard of whether [they were] . . . false or not," New York Times Co. v. Sullivan, 376 U.S. 254, 280 (1964), should also be applied to public statements made by teachers. Because of the enormous variety of fact situations in which critical statements by teachers and other public employees may be thought by their superiors, against whom the statements are directed, to furnish grounds for dismissal, we do not deem it either appropriate or feasible to attempt to lay down a general standard against which all such statements may be judged. However, in the course of evaluating the conflicting claims of First Amendment protection and the need for orderly school administration in the context of this case, we shall indicate some of the general lines along which an analysis of the controlling interests should run.

An examination of the statements in appellant's letter objected to by the Board reveals that they, like the letter as a whole, consist essentially of criticism of the Board's allocation of school funds between educational and athletic programs, and of both the Board's and the superintendent's methods of informing, or preventing the informing of, the district's taxpayers of the real reasons why additional tax revenues were being sought for the schools. The statements are in no way directed towards any person with whom appellant would normally be in contact in the course of his daily work as a teacher. Thus no question of maintaining either discipline by immediate superiors or harmony among coworkers is presented here. Appellant's employment relationships with the Board and, to a somewhat lesser extent, with the superintendent are not the kind of close working relationships for which it can persuasively be claimed that personal loyalty and confidence are necessary to their proper functioning. Accordingly, to the extent that the Board's position here can be taken to suggest that even comments on matters of public concern that are substantially correct—such as statements (1)–(4) of appellant's letter, see Appendix, infra, may furnish grounds for dismissal if they are sufficiently critical in tone, we unequivocally reject it.

We next consider the statements in appellant's letter which we agree to be false. The Board's original charges included allegations that the publication of the letter damaged the professional reputations of the Board and the superintendent and would foment controversy and conflict among the Board, teachers, administrators, and the residents of the district. However, no evidence to support these allegations was introduced at the hearing. So far as the record reveals, Pickering's letter was greeted by everyone but its main target, the Board, with massive apathy and total disbelief.  The Board must, therefore, have decided, perhaps by analogy with the law of libel, that the statements were *per se* harmful to the operation of the schools.

However, the only way in which the Board could conclude, absent any evidence of the actual effect of the letter, that the statements contained therein were *per se* detrimental to the interest of the schools was to equate the Board members' own interests with that of the schools.  Certainly an accusation that too much money is being spent on athletics by the administrators of the school system (which is precisely the import of that portion of appellant's letter containing the statements that we have found to be false,  . . .) cannot reasonably be regarded as *per se* detrimental to the district's schools.  Such an accusation reflects rather a difference of opinion between Pickering and the Board as to the preferable manner of operating the school system, a difference of opinion that clearly concerns an issue of general public interest.

In addition, the fact that particular illustrations of the Board's claimed undesirable emphasis on athletic programs are false would not normally have any necessary impact on the actual operation of the schools, beyond its tendency to anger the Board.  For example, Pickering's letter was written after the defeat at the polls of the second proposed tax increase.  It could, therefore, have had no effect on the ability of the school district to raise necessary revenue, since there was no showing that there was any proposal to increase taxes pending when the letter was written.

More importantly, the question whether a school system requires additional funds is a matter of legitimate public concern on which the judgment of the school administration, including the School Board, cannot, in a society that leaves such questions to popular vote, be taken as conclusive.  On such a question free and open debate is vital to informed decision-making by the electorate.  Teachers are, as a class, the members of a community most likely to have informed and definite opinions as to how funds allotted to the operation of the schools should be spent.  Accordingly, it is essential that they be able to speak out freely on such questions without fear of retaliatory dismissal.

In addition, the amounts expended on athletics which Pickering reported erroneously were matters of public record on which his position as a teacher in the district did not qualify him to speak with any greater authority than any other taxpayer.  The Board could easily have rebutted appellant's errors by publishing the accurate figures itself, either via a letter to the same newspaper or otherwise. We are thus not presented with a situation in which a teacher has carelessly made false statements about matters so closely related to the day-to-day operations of the schools that any harmful impact on the public would be difficult to counter because of the teacher's presumed greater access to the real facts. Accordingly, we have no occasion to consider at this time whether under such circumstances a school board could reasonably require that a teacher make substantial efforts to verify the accuracy of his charges before publishing them.

What we do have before us is a case in which a teacher has made erroneous public statements upon issues then currently the subject of public attention, which are critical of his ultimate employer but which are neither shown nor can be presumed to have in any way either impeded the teacher's proper performance of his daily duties in the classroom or to have interfered with the regular operation of the schools generally. In these circumstances we conclude that the interest of the school administration in limiting teachers' opportunities to contribute to public debate is not significantly greater than its interest in limiting a similar contribution by any member of the general public.

The public interest in having free and unhindered debate on matters of public importance—the core value of the Free Speech Clause of the First Amendment—is so great that it has been held that a State cannot authorize the recovery of damages by a public official for defamatory statements directed at him except when such statements are shown to have been made either with knowledge of their falsity or with reckless disregard for their truth or falsity. . . . It is therefore perfectly clear that, were appellant a member of the general public, the State's power to afford the appellee Board of Education or its members any legal right to sue him for writing the letter at issue here would be limited by the requirement that the letter be judged by the standard laid down in *New York Times*. . . .

While criminal sanctions and damage awards have a somewhat different impact on the exercise of the right to freedom of speech from dismissal from employment, it is apparent that the threat of dismissal from public employment is nonetheless a potent means of inhibiting speech. We have already noted our disinclination to make an across-the-board equation of dismissal from public employment for remarks critical of superiors with awarding damages in a libel suit by a public official for similar criticism. However, in a case such as the present one, in which the fact of employment is only tangentially and insubstantially involved in the subject matter of the public communication made by a teacher, we conclude that it is necessary to regard the teacher as the member of the general public he seeks to be.

In sum, we hold that, in a case such as this, absent proof of false statements knowingly or recklessly made by him, a teacher's exercise of his right to speak on issues of public importance may not furnish the basis for his dismissal from public employment. Since no such showing has been made in this case regarding appellant's letter

. . . his dismissal for writing it cannot be upheld and the judgment of the Illinois Supreme Court must, accordingly, be reversed. . . .

### APPENDIX TO OPINION OF THE COURT

#### A. *Appellant's letter*

### LETTERS TO THE EDITOR

Graphic Newspapers, Inc.

Thursday, September 24, 1964, Page 4

Dear Editor:

I enjoyed reading the back issues of your paper which you loaned to me. Perhaps others would enjoy reading them in order to see just how far the two new high schools have deviated from the original promises by the Board of Education. First, let me state that I am referring to the February thru November, 1961 issues of your paper, so that it can be checked.

One statement in your paper declared that swimming pools, athletic fields, and auditoriums had been left out of the program. They may have been left out but they got put back in very quickly because Lockport West has both an auditorium and athletic field. In fact, Lockport West has a better athletic field than Lockport Central. It has a track that isn't quite regulation distance even though the board spent a few thousand dollars on it. Whose fault is that? Oh, I forgot, it wasn't supposed to be there in the first place. It must have fallen out of the sky. Such responsibility has been touched on in other letters but it seems one just can't help noticing it. I am not saying the school shouldn't have these facilities, because I think they should, but promises are promises, or are they?

Since there seems to be a problem getting all the facts to the voter on the twice defeated bond issue, many letters have been written to this paper and probably more will follow, I feel I must say something about the letters and their writers. Many of these letters did not give the whole story. Letters by your Board and Administration have stated that teachers' salaries total $1,297,746 for one year. Now that must have been the total payroll, otherwise the teachers would be getting $10,000 a year. I teach at the high school and I know this just isn't the case. However, this shows their "stop at nothing" attitude. To illustrate further, do you know that the superintendent told the teachers, and I quote, "Any teacher that opposes the referendum should be prepared for the consequences." I think this gets at the reason we have problems passing bond issues. Threats take something away; these are insults to voters in a free society. We should try to sell a program on its merits, if it has any.

Remember those letters entitled "District 205 Teachers Speak," I think the voters should know that those letters have been written and agreed to by only five or six teachers, not 98% of the teachers in the high school. In fact, many teachers didn't even know who was writing them. Did you know that those letters had to have the approval of the superintendent before they could be put in the paper? That's the kind of totalitarianism teachers live in at the high school, and your children go to school in.

In last week's paper, the letter written by a few uninformed teachers threatened to close the school cafeteria and fire its personnel. This is ridiculous and insults the intelligence of the voter because properly managed school cafeterias do not cost the school district any money. If the cafeteria is losing money, then the board should not be packing free lunches for athletes on days of athletic contests. Whatever the case, the taxpayer's child should only have to pay about 30¢ for his lunch instead of 35¢ to pay for free lunches for the athletes.

In a reply to this letter your Board of Administration will probably state that these lunches are paid for from receipts from the games. But $20,000 in receipts doesn't pay for the $200,000 a year they have been spending on varsity sports while neglecting the wants of teachers.

You see we don't need an increase in the transportation tax unless the voters want to keep paying $50,000 or more a year to transport athletes home after practice and to away games, etc. Rest of the $200,000 is made up in coaches' salaries, athletic directors' salaries, baseball pitching machines, sodded football fields, and thousands of dollars for other sports equipment.

These things are all right, provided we have enough money for them. To sod football fields on borrowed money and then not be able to pay teachers' salaries is getting the cart before the horse.

If these things aren't enough for you, look at East High. No doors on many of the classrooms, a plant room without any sunlight, no water in a first aid treatment room, are just a few of many things. The taxpayers were really taken to the cleaners. A part of the sidewalk in front of the building has already collapsed. Maybe Mr. Hess would be interest to know that we need blinds on the windows in that building also.

Once again, the board must have forgotten they were going to spend $3,200,000 on the West building and $2,300,000 on the East building.

As I see it, the bond issue is a fight between the Board of Education that is trying to push tax-supported athletics down our throats with education, and a public that has mixed emotions about both of these items because they feel they are already paying enough taxes, and simply don't know whom to trust with any more tax money.

I must sign this letter as a citizen, taxpayer and voter, not as a teacher, since that freedom has been taken from the teachers by the administration.  Do you really know what goes on behind those stone walls at the high school?

Respectfully,

Marvin L. Pickering.  .  .  .

Mr. Justice WHITE, concurring in part and dissenting in part.

The Court holds that truthful statements by a school teacher critical of the school board are within the ambit of the First Amendment.  So also are false statements innocently or negligently made. The State may not fire the teacher for making either unless, as I gather it, there are special circumstances, not present in this case, demonstrating an overriding state interest, such as the need for confidentiality or the special obligations which a teacher in a particular position may owe to his superiors.  The core of today's decision is the holding that Pickering's discharge must be tested by the standard of New York Times Co. v. Sullivan, 376 U.S. 254 (1964).  To this extent I am in agreement.  .  .  .

.  .  .  As I see it, a teacher may be fired without violation of the First Amendment for knowingly or recklessly making false statements regardless of their harmful impact on the schools. As the Court holds, however, in the absence of special circumstances he may not be fired if his statements were true or only negligently false, even if there is some harm to the school system.  .  .  .  If Pickering's false statements were either knowingly or recklessly made, injury to the school system becomes irrelevant, and the First Amendment would not prevent his discharge.  .  .  .

Nor can I join the Court in its findings with regard to whether Pickering knowingly or recklessly published false statements.  .  .  .

NOTES AND QUESTIONS

1.  What is the precise scope of the decision in Pickering and for what reason(s). Do you agree or disagree?  State the principle of constitutional law that this case stands for.  Should Pickering have been discharged?

2.  Were the statements of Pickering made recklessly?  Negligently?  What difference would it make?

3.  The Court stated that it would not "lay down a general standard against which all such statements [critical of school operation] may be judged" because there are an "enormous [possible] variety of fact situations." Present some hypothetical fact situations involving criticism that would be upheld by courts on the basis of the Pickering decision and other examples that would not.

4.  Suppose Pickering had been dismissed for "incompetence," and the evidence of incompetence was the factual errors in the letter, would the Court's decision have been different?  Why or why not?

5.  Suppose a grievance procedure rule of the school board required teachers to submit complaints about school operations to their superiors for

action thereon before bringing their complaints to the public, and suppose Pickering published his letter without first going through the grievance procedure, would the case have been decided the same way? Why or why not? At what point should a teacher be professionally free publicly to criticize the operations of his school?

6. Does the Supreme Court's decision in the Pickering case rest on the view that with respect to outside activities, even though involving a school, a teacher is to be treated like any other citizen, or does the Court's decision rest on the view that in such circumstances the teacher should be held to an exemplar standard and that Pickering met it?

---

### GIVHAN v. WESTERN LINE CONSOLIDATED SCHOOL DIST.

Supreme Court of the United States, 1979.
439 U.S. 410, 99 S.Ct. 693, 58 L.Ed.2d 619.

Mr. Justice REHNQUIST delivered the opinion of the Court.

Petitioner Bessie Givhan was dismissed from her employment as a junior high English teacher at the end of the 1970–1971 school year. At the time of petitioner's termination, respondent Western Line Consolidated School District was the subject of a desegregation order entered by the United States District Court for the Northern District of Mississippi. Petitioner filed a complaint in intervention in the desegregation action, seeking reinstatement on the . . . ground that nonrenewal of her contract . . . infringed her right of free speech secured by the First and Fourteenth Amendments of the United States Constitution. In an effort to show that its decision was justified, respondent school district introduced evidence of . . . a series of private encounters between petitioner and the school principal in which petitioner allegedly made "petty and unreasonable demands" in a manner variously described by the principal as "insulting," "hostile," "loud," and "arrogant." After a two-day bench trial, the District Court held that petitioner's termination had violated the First Amendment. Finding that petitioner had made "demands" on but two occasions and that those demands "were neither 'petty' nor 'unreasonable,' insomuch as all of the complaints in question involved employment policies and practices at [the] school which [petitioner] conceived to be racially discriminatory in purpose or effect," the District Court concluded that "the primary reason for the school district's failure to renew [petitioner's] contract was her criticism of the policies and practices of the school district, especially the school to which she was assigned to teach." Accordingly, the District Court held that the dismissal violated petitioner's First Amendment rights . . . and ordered her reinstatement.

The Court of Appeals for the Fifth Circuit reversed. Although it found the District Court's findings not clearly erroneous, the Court of Appeals concluded that because petitioner had privately expressed her complaints and opinions to the principal, her expression was not protected under the First Amendment. . . . The Court of Appeals also concluded that there is no constitutional right to "press even 'good' ideas on an unwilling recipient," saying that to afford public employees the right to such private expression "would in effect force school principals to be ombudsmen, for damnable as well as laudable expressions." We are unable to agree that private expression of one's views is beyond constitutional protection, and therefore reverse the Court of Appeals' judgment and remand the case so that it may consider the contentions of the parties freed from this erroneous view of the First Amendment.

This Court's decisions in *Pickering, Perry* and *Mt. Healthy* do not support the conclusion that a public employee forfeits his protection against governmental abridgment of freedom of speech if he decides to express his views privately rather than publicly. While those cases each arose in the context of a public employee's public expression, the rule to be derived from them is not dependent on that largely coincidental fact.

In *Pickering* a teacher was discharged for publicly criticizing, in a letter published in a local newspaper, the school board's handling of prior bond issue proposals and its subsequent allocation of financial resources between the schools' educational and athletic programs. Noting that the free speech rights of public employees are not absolute, the Court held that in determining whether a government employee's speech is constitutionally protected, "the interests of the [employee], as a citizen, in commenting upon matters of public concern" must be balanced against "the interest of the State, as an employer, in promoting the efficiency of the public services it performs through its employees." Pickering v. Board of Education, supra. The Court concluded that under the circumstances of that case "the interest of the school administration in limiting teachers' opportunities to contribute to public debate [was] not significantly greater than its interest in limiting a similar contribution by any member of the general public." Here the opinion of the Court of Appeals may be read to turn in part on its view that the working relationship between principal and teacher is significantly different from the relationship between the parties in *Pickering*. But we do not feel confident that the Court of Appeals' decision would have been placed on that ground notwithstanding its view that the First Amendment does not require the same sort of *Pickering* balancing for the private expression of a public employee as it does for public expression.[4]

---

[4] Although the First Amendment's protection of government employees extends to private as well as public expression, striking the *Pickering* balance in each context may involve different considerations. When a teacher speaks publicly, it is generally the *content* of his statements that must be assessed to determine whether they "in any way either impeded the teacher's proper performance of his daily duties in the classroom or . . . interfered with the regular

. . . . Nor is the Court of Appeals' view supported by the "captive audience" rationale. Having opened his office door to petitioner, the principal was hardly in a position to argue that he was the "*unwilling* recipient" of her views.

The First Amendment forbids abridgment of the "freedom of speech." Neither the Amendment itself nor our decisions indicate that this freedom is lost to the public employee who arranges to communicate privately with his employer rather than to spread his views before the public. We decline to adopt such a view of the First Amendment.

. . . .

Accordingly, the judgment of the Court of Appeals is vacated and the case remanded for further proceedings consistent with this opinion.

## NOTES AND QUESTIONS

1. What is the holding of Givhan? Is it only that the "private expression of one's views" receives constitutional protection? Or is it that Givhan's private expression of her views is constitutionally protected, and her contract cannot be non-renewed solely because she exercised her constitutional rights? Suppose she exercised her constitutional rights and also did more (was "insubordinate"), and her contract was not renewed for both reasons, would her non-renewal be valid? If the "insubordination" were sufficient by itself for non-renewal?

2. What is the impact of Givhan on "insubordination"? The District Superintendent gave the following reasons for not renewing Givhan's contract: (1) a flat refusal to administer standardized tests to her pupils; (2) an announced intention not to cooperate with the Administration of an Attendance Center, and (3) an antagonistic and hostile attitude to the Administration of the Attendance Center "demonstrated throughout the school year." Was Givhan "insubordinate"? Does the Supreme Court's ruling mean that the above-described facts cannot count as "insubordination" because they are constitutionally protected expression of one's private views? Or does the Court's ruling protecting private expression reach only Givhan's expressions allegedly made during her private encounters with the principal?

Most school district rules provide that teachers may be discharged for "insubordination" which has been defined as a "willful disregard of express or implied directions, or such a defiant attitude as to be equivalent thereto." (" 'Rebellious,' 'mutinous,' and 'disobedient' are often quoted as definitions or synonyms of 'insubordination' "). State v. Board of Regents, 70 Nev. 347, 269 P.2d 265 (1954). For example, one teacher

operation of the schools generally." Pickering v. Board of Education, supra, 391 U.S., at 572–573, 88 S.Ct., at 1737. Private expression, however, may in some situations bring additional factors to the *Pickering* calculus. When a government employee personally confronts his immediate superior, the employing agency's institutional efficiency may be threatened not only by the content of the employee's message, but also by the manner, time, and place in which it is delivered.

was legally dismissed for insubordination for refusing to attend a meeting called for the purpose of giving him the opportunity to resign, Millar v. Joint School Dist., 2 Wis.2d 303, 86 N.W.2d 455 (1957), and another "insubordinate" teacher was legally dismissed for refusing (because no witness was permitted) to attend a meeting with the principal at which there was to be discussion about leaflets derogatory to the school distributed by the teacher.  Gilbertson v. McAlister, 403 F.Supp. 1 (D. Conn.1975).  Do these two cases survive Givhan?  Can Givhan now be non-renewed for insubordination?

3.  In James v. Board of Educ., 385 F.Supp. 209 (D.C.N.Y.1974), a U. S. District Court relied on Tinker, and upheld the right of a teacher to wear a black armband, while teaching class, as a protest against the war in Vietnam.  Query:  If a teacher properly can be held to be an exemplar, was James an exemplar?  As an example of protest?  As an example of exercising one's rights to free expression?

4.  Greminger v. Seaborne, 584 F.2d 275 (8th Cir. 1978), involved several non-renewed teachers, active in the local Community Teachers Organization, who "were leaders in an effort to secure for teachers' salaries, certain funds known as 'the windfall money' which had been allocated to the school district above the usual appropriation."  The record indicated "that the principal, the school superintendents during this period, and the school board members believed plaintiffs had improperly bypassed the usual 'chain of command,' initially by seeking information about the windfall money from the school superintendent and ultimately by taking their cause to the community."  Noting that "plaintiff's activities were clearly within the scope of the First Amendment" and that the "allocation of funds for increased teachers' salaries is a subject of public concern upon which teachers may certainly comment," the court cited Pickering and ruled:  "Despite plaintiff's probationary or nontenured status, the school board could not constitutionally refuse to renew their contracts in retaliation for the exercise of their First Amendment rights."

---

## EAST HARTFORD EDUC. ASS'N v. BOARD OF EDUC.

United States Court of Appeals, 1977.
562 F.2d 838 (2d Cir.).

MESKILL, Circuit Judge.  Although this case may at first appear too trivial to command the attention of a busy court, it raises important issues concerning the proper scope of judicial oversight of local affairs.  The appellant here, Richard Brimley, is a public school teacher reprimanded for failing to wear a necktie while teaching his English class.  Joined by the teachers union, he sued the East Hartford Board of Education, claiming that the reprimand for violating the dress code deprived him of his rights of free speech and privacy.  Chief Judge Clarie granted summary judgment for the defendants.  A divided panel of this Court reversed and remanded for trial.  At the request of a member of the Court, a poll of the judges in regular active service was taken to determine if the case should be reheard *en banc*.  A majority voted for rehearing.  We now vacate the judgment of the panel majority and affirm the judgment of the district court.

The facts are not in dispute.  In February, 1972, the East Hartford Board of Education adopted "Regulations For Teacher Dress." At that time, Mr. Brimley, a teacher of high school English and filmmaking, customarily wore a jacket and sportshirt, without a tie. His failure to wear a tie constituted a violation of the regulations, and he was reprimanded for his delict.  Mr. Brimley appealed to the school principal and was told that he was to wear a tie while teaching English, but that his informal attire was proper during filmmaking classes.  He then appealed to the superintendent and the board without success, after which he began formal arbitration proceedings, which ended in a decision that the dispute was not arbitrable.  This lawsuit followed.  Although Mr. Brimley initially complied with the code while pursuing his remedies, he has apparently returned to his former mode of dress.  The record does not disclose any disciplinary action against him other than the original reprimand.

## I

In the vast majority of communities, the control of public schools is vested in locally-elected bodies.  This commitment to local political bodies requires significant public control over what is said and done in school.  It is not the federal courts, but local democratic processes, that are primarily responsible for the many routine decisions that are made in public school systems.  Accordingly, it is settled that "[c]ourts do not and cannot intervene in the resolution of conflicts which arise in the daily operation of school systems and which do not directly and sharply implicate basic constitutional values."  Epperson v. Arkansas.

Federal courts must refrain, in most instances, from interfering with the decisions of school authorities.  Even though decisions may appear foolish or unwise, a federal court may not overturn them unless the standard set forth in *Epperson* is met.  . . .

Because the appellant's clash with his employer has failed to "directly and sharply implicate basic constitutional values," we refuse to upset the policies established by the school board.

## II

Mr. Brimley claims that by refusing to wear a necktie he makes a statement on current affairs which assists him in his teaching. In his brief, he argues that the following benefits flow from his tielessness:

> (a) He wishes to present himself to his students as a person who is not tied to "establishment conformity."

(b) He wishes to symbolically indicate to his students his association with the ideas of the generation to which those students belong, including the rejection of many of the customs and values, and of the social outlook, of the older generation.

(c) He feels that dress of this type enables him to achieve closer rapport with his students, and thus enhances his ability to teach.

Appellant's claim, therefore, is that his refusal to wear a tie is "symbolic speech," and, as such, is protected against governmental interference by the First Amendment.

We are required here to balance the alleged interest in free expression against the goals of the school board in requiring its teachers to dress somewhat more formally than they might like. . . .

Obviously, a great range of conduct has the symbolic, "speech-like" aspect claimed by Mr. Brimley. To state that activity is "symbolic" is only the beginning, and not the end, of constitutional inquiry. Even though intended as expression, symbolic speech remains conduct, subject to regulation by the state. . . .

As conduct becomes less and less like "pure speech" the showing of governmental interest required for its regulation is progressively lessened. In those cases where governmental regulation of expressive conduct has been struck down, the communicative intent of the actor was clear and "closely akin to 'pure speech.'" Thus, the First Amendment has been held to protect wearing a black armband to protest the Vietnam War, Tinker v. Des Moines School District, supra, burning an American Flag to highlight a speech denouncing the government's failure to protect a civil rights leader, or quietly refusing to recite the Pledge of Allegiance, Russo v. Central School District, 469 F.2d 623 (2d Cir. 1972), cert. denied, 411 U.S. 932, 93 S.Ct. 1899, 36 L.Ed.2d 391 (1973).

In contrast, the claims of symbolic speech made here are vague and unfocused. Through the simple refusal to wear a tie, Mr. Brimley claims that he communicates a comprehensive view of life and society. It may well be, in an age increasingly conscious of fashion, that a significant portion of the population seeks to make a statement of some kind through its clothes. However, Mr. Brimley's message is sufficiently vague to place it close to the "conduct" end of the "speech-conduct" continuum described above. While the regulation of the school board must still pass constitutional muster, the showing required to uphold it is significantly less than if Mr. Brimley had been punished, for example, for publicly speaking out on an issue concerning school administration. Pickering v. Board of Education.

### III

At the outset, Mr. Brimley had other, more effective means of communicating his social views to his students. He could, for example, simply have told them his views on contemporary America; if he had done this in a temperate way, without interfering with his teaching duties, we would be confronted with a very different First Amendment case. The existence of alternative, effective means of communication, while not conclusive, is a factor to be considered in assessing the validity of a regulation of expressive conduct.

Balanced against appellant's claim of free expression is the school board's interest in promoting respect for authority and traditional values, as well as discipline in the classroom, by requiring teachers to dress in a professional manner. A dress code is a rational means of promoting these goals. As to the legitimacy of the goals themselves, there can be no doubt. In James v. Board of Education, Chief Judge Kaufman stated:

> The interest of the state in promoting the efficient operation of its schools extends beyond merely securing an orderly classroom. Although the pros and cons of progressive education are debated heatedly, a principal function of all elementary and secondary education is indoctrinative—whether it be to teach the ABC's or multiplication tables or to transmit the basic values of the community.

This balancing test is primarily a matter for the school board. Were we local officials, and not appellate judges, we might find Mr. Brimley's arguments persuasive. However, our role is not to choose the better educational policy. We may intervene in the decisions of school authorities only when it has been shown that they have strayed outside the area committed to their discretion. If Mr. Brimley's argument were to prevail, this policy would be completely eroded. Because teaching is by definition an expressive activity, virtually every decision made by school authorities would raise First Amendment issues calling for federal court intervention.

The very notion of public education implies substantial public control. Educational decisions must be made by someone; there is no reason to create a constitutional preference for the views of individual teachers over those of their employers. . . . In contrast to *James* and *Russo,* the First Amendment claim made here is so insubstantial as to border on the frivolous. We are unwilling to expand First Amendment protection to include a teacher's sartorial choice.

### IV

Mr. Brimley also claims that the "liberty" interest grounded in the due process clause of the Fourteenth Amendment protects his choice of attire. This claim will not withstand analysis.

The Supreme Court dealt with a similar claim in Kelley v. Johnson, 425 U.S. 238, 96 S.Ct. 1440, 47 L.Ed.2d 708 (1976). That case involved a challenge to the hair-grooming regulations of a police department. The Court was careful to distinguish privacy claims made by government employees from those made by members of the public:

> Respondent has sought the protection of the Fourteenth Amendment, not as a member of the citizenry at large, but on the contrary as an employee of the police force of Suffolk County, a subdivision of the State of New York. While the Court of Appeals made passing reference to this distinction, it was thereafter apparently ignored. We think, however, it is highly significant. In Pickering v. Board of Education after noting that state employment may not be conditioned on the relinquishment of First Amendment rights, the Court stated that "[a]t the same time it cannot be gainsaid that the State has interests as an employer in regulating the speech of its employees that differ significantly from those it possesses in connection with regulation of the speech of the citizenry in general." More recently, we have sustained comprehensive and substantial restrictions upon activities of both federal and state employees lying at the core of the First Amendment. If such state regulations may survive challenges based on the explicit language of the First Amendment, there is surely even more room for restrictive regulations of state employees where the claim implicates only the more general contours of the substantive liberty interest protected by the Fourteenth Amendment.

The same distinction applies here. The regulation involved in this case affects Mr. Brimley in his capacity as a public school teacher. Of course, as he points out, the functions of policemen and teachers differ widely. Regulations well within constitutional bounds for one occupation might prove invalid for another. Nonetheless, we can see no reason why the same constitutional test should not apply, no matter how different the results of their constitutional challenges.

*Kelley* goes on to set forth the standard to be applied in such cases:

> We think the answer here is so clear that the District Court was quite right in the first instance to have dismissed respondent's complaint. Neither this Court, the Court of Appeals, nor the District Court is in a position to weigh the policy arguments in favor of and against a rule regulating hairstyles as a part of regulations governing a uniformed civilian service. The constitutional issue to be decided by these courts is whether petitioner's determination that such regulations should be enacted is so irrational that it may be branded "arbitrary," and therefore a deprivation of re-

spondent's "liberty" interest in freedom to choose his own hairstyle.

If Mr. Brimley has any protected interest in his neckwear, it does not weigh very heavily on the constitutional scales. As with most legislative choices, the board's dress code is presumptively constitutional. It is justified by the same concerns for respect, discipline and traditional values described in our discussion of the First Amendment claim. Accordingly, appellant has failed to carry the burden set out in *Kelley* of demonstrating that the dress code is "so irrational that it may be branded 'arbitrary,'" and the regulation must stand.

The rights of privacy and liberty in which appellant seeks refuge are important and evolving constitutional doctrines. To date, however, the Supreme Court has extended their protection only to the most basic personal decisions. Nor has the Supreme Court been quick to expand these rights to new fields. . . . As with any other constitutional provision, we are not given a "roving commission" to right wrongs and impose our notions of sound policy upon society. There is substantial danger in expanding the reach of due process to cover cases such as this. By bringing trivial activities under the constitutional umbrella we trivialize the constitutional provision itself. If we are to maintain the vitality of this new doctrine, we must be careful not to "cry wolf" at every minor restraint on a citizen's liberty.

The two other Courts of Appeals which have considered this issue have reached similar conclusions. In Miller v. School District, 495 F.2d 658 (7th Cir. 1974), the Seventh Circuit upheld a grooming regulation for teachers. Mr. Justice Stevens, then a member of the Court of Appeals, wrote:

Even if we assume for purposes of decision that an individual's interest in selecting his own style of dress or appearance is an interest in liberty, it is nevertheless perfectly clear that every restriction on that interest is not an unconstitutional deprivation.

From the earliest days of organized society, no absolute right to an unfettered choice of appearance has ever been recognized; matters of appearance and dress have always been subjected to control and regulation, sometimes by custom and social pressure, sometimes by legal rules. A variety of reasons justify limitations on this interest. They include a concern for public health or safety, a desire to avoid specific forms of antisocial conduct, and an interest in protecting the beholder from unsightly displays. Nothing more than a desire to encourage respect for tradition, or for those who are moved by traditional ceremonies, may be sufficient in some situations. Indeed, even an interest in teaching respect for (though not necessarily agreement with) traditional manners, may lend support to some public grooming requirements. Therefore, just as the individual has an interest in a choice among different styles of appearance and behavior, and a democratic society has an interest in fostering diverse choices, so also does society have a legitimate interest in placing limits on the exercise of that choice.

The First Circuit reached the same result in Tardif v. Quinn, 545 F.2d 761 (1st Cir. 1976), where a school teacher was dismissed for wearing short skirts. In upholding the action of the school district, the Court stated:

> [W]e are not dealing with personal appearance in what might be termed an individual sense, but in a bilateral sense—a contractual relationship. Whatever constitutional aspect there may be to one's choice of apparel generally, it is hardly a matter which falls totally beyond the scope of the demands which an employer, public or private, can legitimately make upon its employees. We are unwilling to think that every dispute on such issues raises questions of constitutional proportions which must stand or fall, depending upon a court's view of who was right.

Both *Miller* and *Tardif* are stronger cases for the plaintiff's position than the instant case. Both involved dismissals rather than, as here, a reprimand. Moreover, *Miller* involved a regulation of hair and beards, as well as dress. Thus, Miller was forced to appear as his employers wished both on and off the job. In contrast, Mr. Brimley can remove his tie as soon as the school day ends. If the plaintiffs in *Miller* and *Tardif* could not prevail, neither can Mr. Brimley.

Each claim of substantive liberty must be judged in the light of that case's special circumstances. In view of the uniquely influential role of the public school teacher in the classroom, the board is justified in imposing this regulation. As public servants in a special position of trust, teachers may properly be subjected to many restrictions in their professional lives which would be invalid if generally applied. We join the sound views of the First and Seventh circuits, and follow *Kelley* by holding that a school board may, if it wishes, impose reasonable regulations governing the appearance of the teachers it employs. There being no material factual issue to be decided, the grant of summary judgment is affirmed.

OAKES, Circuit Judge (with whom Judge SMITH concurs) (dissenting):

In an area as fraught with uncertainty as constitutional law, it is particularly incumbent upon judges to explain carefully each analytical step they are making toward a particular conclusion and to evaluate searchingly each contention put forward by the parties. Reasoned analysis is particularly critical in a case of this nature, in which a school board, carrying the legitimacy of popular election, is claimed to infringe upon the liberty and expression interests of an individual employee who after exhausting mediation remedies seeks redress, in the time-tested constitutional framework, from the institution that has historically been charged with the task of guarding the individual's most precious freedoms against undue infringement by the majority. The en banc opinion, by downplaying the individual's interests here as "trivial" and giving weight to a school board interest not advanced as such, adds, it seems to me, an unfortunate chapter to this history. I dissent, with regret, not so much at the difference in value judgments that evidently underlies the majority's opinion but because the case apparently involves so little in the majority's view.

The panel majority opinion sought to follow a rather straightforward analysis: (1) appellant Brimley has a Fourteenth Amendment liberty interest in his personal appearance; (2) appellant also has a First Amendment interest, involving the right to teach; (3) the school board asserts three interests, two of which are invalid because *ultra vires* and the third of which (discipline) is not rationally furthered by this teacher dress code; (4) balancing these interests, appellant prevails. This dissent will discuss in the above order the treatment of each of these points in the en banc majority opinion.

First, since the en banc majority purports to follow Kelley v. Johnson, it presumably assumes, as did the Court in *Kelley,* that appellant *does* have a Fourteenth Amendment liberty interest in his personal appearance, even if not a "fundamental" one. If the school board cannot put a proper purpose that is rationally related to its regulation on the other side of the scales, this liberty interest alone, however, "trivial," will carry the day for appellant.

Second, the en banc majority baldly states in a footnote, without citation of authority, that appellant's asserted First Amendment right to teach is not a constitutionally cognizable interest. But this established constitutional right will not disappear because the en banc majority simply chooses to ignore it. Teaching methods in public high schools are in many instances protectible under the First Amendment, . . . While serious questions arise in measuring the parameters of the right in the context of public high school teaching, . . . answers to those questions are not aided by the ostrich-like presumption that they do not exist.

To be sure, the en banc majority does discuss at length symbolic speech, a concept quite separate from the right to teach. I do not disagree with the majority's conclusion that, to the limited extent that appellant is making a symbolic speech claim, it is close to the conduct end of the speech-conduct continuum. But even this conclusion still leaves appellant with a First Amendment constitutional interest that can be overcome only by a state regulation rationally related to a valid purpose.

Third, the en banc majority abandons two of the interests asserted by the school board, [these were establishing "a professional image for teachers" and promoting "good grooming among students."] Presumably agreeing with the panel [and] concurs with the panel in identifying a third interest; and makes up a fourth of its own. I agree fully with the en banc majority that the third and last interest asserted by the board—involving discipline, respect, and decorum in the classroom—is a proper one. The point made by the panel majority was that this interest did not seem furthered in any rational way by the teacher dress code at issue here. The en banc majority opinion makes no attempt whatever to address this critical analytical point. Instead, its logic appears to be: "The interest is furthered by the dress code because the school board says that it is." Whatever argument might be made that the school board's ends are furthered by its means, the en banc majority does not make it, and certainly the essential connection betwen means and ends is not here self-evident. The majority's less than rigorous inquiry is well short of the least demanding formulation of the inquiry necessary to determine the rationality of a state regulation.

The en banc majority also makes up an interest, respect for traditional values, that is not put forward by the school board. I understand it to be settled constitutional doctrine that only objectives articulated by the State are to be used in considering whether a regulation is rational. I had imagined that the day when courts supplied imaginary purposes for state regulations had passed.

The reason that the school board never asserted this interest, of course, is clear: the tie requirement is not related in any rational way to the admitted responsibility of a school board to inculcate traditional values in its students. The en banc majority does not enlighten us as to which value it has in mind, but in any event a necktie is a mere conventional fashion, with no connection of which I am aware to any traditional value. I fear that the majority simply confuses traditional values with mindless orthodoxy. The inculcation of the latter, of course, as the panel majority pointed out, is constitutionally forbidden.

Finally, the process by which the en banc majority balances the interests involved is defective.   .   .   . "responsible" balancing requires careful identification and separate evaluation of "each analytically distinct ingredient of the contending interests." This the en banc majority fails to do. Rather, at the end of the majority's discussion of each of appellant's two interests, it simply states that a teacher dress code rationally promotes the two interests identified as those of the school board and hence overcomes the interests of appellant. Even if a rational connection between the tie regulation and board interests did exist, the majority's assumption that both of appellant's interests can be disposed of separately under a rational relationship test is in my view not well-founded. If only a Fourteenth Amendment liberty interest were at stake, such a test might be the proper one to apply. When, instead, a First Amendment interest is asserted, there must in addition be some inquiry by the court into whether the state had available " 'less drastic means for achieving the same basic purpose.' " The necessary implication of *James* is that a less drastic means test must be applied even when it is a public employee who is asserting the First Amendment claim.

When an individual has more than one constitutional interest at stake, at least when one involves the First Amendment, a higher degree of scrutiny is required. . . .

I think the en banc majority gives away the real basis for its simple bow in the direction of balancing when it suggests that to hold otherwise is to give federal judges "a 'roving commission' to right wrongs and impose our notions of sound policy upon society." I had always thought that the federal courts were given by Article III of the Constitution and the doctrine of judicial review not a "roving commission" but a sworn duty to interpret and uphold that document equally for all who come before them. Constitutional doctrines have evolved that we may be aided in this awesome task, and, in my view, we must strive with as much intellectual clarity as possible to apply those doctrines to the case at hand. It is when we do not do this that we are truly imposing our own notions of sound policy on society, for our conclusions are then rooted in the shifting sands of our own prejudices and not in the rich, well-furrowed soil of the Document we are sworn to interpret. An individual's rights in this sense can never be "trivial." They are constitutionally based or they are not; they are opposed by rational state interests or they are not; they prevail in the balancing process or they do not. Here, they should prevail.

I dissent.

## PROBLEM

### SULLIVAN v. MEADE INDEPENDENT SCHOOL DIST.

United States Court of Appeals, 1976.
530 F.2d 799 (8th Cir.).

"This appeal presents the primary question of whether the school board of a small rural community violated the constitutional rights of a single young woman elementary teacher by discharging her in midterm as incompetent to continue teaching because she insisted upon sharing her dwelling located within the school community with a single man.

"The school district is predominantly rural, containing only two organized municipalities—Sturgis, population about 5,000 and Whitewood, population 600. Union Center lies approximately 60 miles east of Sturgis. Union Center, within this school district, is an unincorporated community of approximately 100 persons and contains approximately 17 dwellings including units located in a mobile home park which is about one-eighth mile from the Union Center Elementary School.  Ms. Sullivan lived in the mobile home park in a mobile home furnished by the school board.

"Ms. Sullivan began her teaching duties on August 27, 1974.  In October, a male friend, Donald Dragon, also from New York, came to visit her.  Thereafter and until her dismissal on November 29, 1974, Ms. Sullivan and Mr. Dragon lived together in the trailer home without any attempt to conceal their living arrangements.  Ms. Sullivan's students and their parents soon became aware that she and Mr. Dragon were living in the same trailer, and the community recognized that the couple were not married.

"This lifestyle offended the traditional mores followed by residents of this rural South Dakota community and provoked protests from some parents of children attending the school and others in the school community.  An initial protest by parents of a student attending Ms. Sullivan's class came to the attention of the school board, the school principal, and the school superintendent.  School officials first sought to resolve the complaint informally with Ms. Sullivan.  This effort failed when Ms. Sullivan, on October 29, 1974, advised the school principal that her living arrangement with Mr. Dragon was private, not subject to the scrutiny of the school authorities.  The principal advised Ms. Sullivan that the continuance of her living arrangement could jeopardize her job.

"In early November, the Board caused a notice to be delivered to Ms. Sullivan advising her of a hearing on the school superintendent's recommendation that she be dismissed on grounds of 'gross immorality and incompetency as the alleged immoral conduct affects the teacher's competency to teach.'

"During the hearing, the Board asked Ms. Sullivan on several occasions whether she would be willing to have Dragon live elsewhere but she responded negatively.  Finally, the Board adopted its decision to dismiss after giving Ms. Sullivan the opportunity to cease living with a man to whom she was not married during the balance of the school year.  When Ms. Sullivan rejected this option, the Board's decision became effective.

"These facts raise very difficult constitutional issues.  The Constitution affords a right of privacy, and a right of association with other persons for a variety of purposes.  Ms. Sullivan did not seek to hide her relationship with Mr. Dragon, an impossibility while living in the community trailer court of Union Center, but neither did she flaunt it.  She told the Board, in essence, that her decision to marry Dragon or to live with him without doing so was her personal business.  There is no suggestion that she ever interjected these personal beliefs concerning this relationship into the classroom.  Any knowledge of her conduct which her children possessed was simply the inevitable result of small town life.

"On the other hand, the Board had before it evidence that Ms. Sullivan's conduct violated local mores, that her students were aware of this, and that, because of the size of the town, this awareness would continue. The Board considered the unrefuted testimony of a professional educator that teachers teach by example as well as by lecture. Ms. Sullivan was shown to have generated deep affection from her students, increasing the probability of emulation. Also, it was shown that because of the isolation of Union Center, students are required to leave home at age 14 to attend high school in Sturgis, some 60 miles away. Thus, local parents believe that early proper moral training for youngsters is particularly crucial in Union Center.

"The Supreme Court has recognized that

'a teacher works in a sensitive area in a schoolroom. There he shapes the attitude of young minds towards the society in which they live. In this, the state has a vital concern.'

"The courts have held that, within constitutional limits, the state is entitled to require teachers to maintain a 'properly moral scholastic environment.' This reflects both an independent state interest in the well-being of youth and the state's interest in preserving the right of parents to control the upbringing of their children.

"None of these rights are absolute. When they come into conflict, a balance must be struck."

Assume you are an assistant to the Judge in this case, and that he asks you to finish writing this opinion.

## NOTES AND QUESTIONS

1.  East Hartford represents the trend of authority in the U.S. federal courts. Some state courts have held just the opposite. In Finot v. Pasadena City Bd. of Educ., 250 Cal.App.2d 189, 58 Cal.Rptr. 520 (1967), California's Court of Appeals held that a teacher had "a constitutional right [under the Ninth and Fourteenth Amendments] to wear his beard while engaged in classroom teaching. . . ." See also, Ball v. Kerrville Independent School Dist., 529 S.W.2d 792 (Tex.Civ.App.1975). Under the rule of these cases, allowing the expression of one's personality, would a teacher have a constitutional right to wear dungarees, a daishiki, an Afro hairdo, a micro-mini skirt, or to teach braless? In Morrison v. Hamilton County Bd. of Educ., 494 S.W.2d 770 (Tenn.1973), certiorari denied 414 U.S. 1044, 94 S.Ct. 548, 38 L.Ed.2d 335. Tennessee's Supreme Court upheld the dismissal of a tenured teacher for wearing a beard.

2.  The East Hartford majority judged the teacher's constitutional interest to be "so insubstantial as to border on the frivolous." Suppose the teacher's interest had been more substantial, would the majority decision have been different? In New Mexico State Bd. of Educ. v. Stoudt, 91 N.M. 183, 571 P.2d 1186 (1977), a teacher's contract could be terminated "for cause, including . . . incompetency, insubordination . . . or for any other good and just cause." An unmarried, preg-

nant teacher, whose "work performance ha[d] been satisfactory or better," was terminated under the standard of "other good and just cause." Her pregnancy "was evidence of her having engaged in premarital sexual intercourse which is considered immoral in the Taos community." Holding that the Bd. of Educ. had failed to meet its burden of showing that a prima facie case of good cause existed, it ruled that the teacher's termination "was arbitrary, unreasonable and not supported by substantial evidence." Would, or should, the decision have been different if New Mexico had a statute making fornication a crime?

## TEACHER TENURE

### INTRODUCTION

Today, most state legislatures have passed teacher tenure laws which provide that after having served a satisfactory probationary period either a teacher's "position" or his "contract" will be a continuing one without a periodic need for renewal. In McSherry v. City of St. Paul, 202 Minn. 102, 277 N.W. 541 (1938), Minnesota's Supreme Court discussed the general history and purpose of tenure legislation:

> "The education of our youth to fit them for the duties and responsibilities of citizenship in our state and nation was a matter of vital concern to our pioneers. This seems clear as we find that immediately upon statehood constitutional provision was made to accomplish that end. By article 8, §§ 1 to 7, inclusive, thereof provision was made for the establishment and maintenance of public education as a state system under its direction and control. Thus section 1 provides: 'The stability of a republican form of government depending mainly upon the intelligence of the people, it shall be the duty of the legislature to establish a general and uniform system of public schools.' . . .

> "Teachers' tenure, like civil service and other similar movements, dates back now over a period of many years. The abuses existing by reason of the 'spoils system' which came into prominence during Jackson's administration, later followed by national and other administrations, led to much-deserved criticism. That is why on January 16, 1883 ('An act to regulate and improve the civil service of the United States,' 22 Stat. 403), the first civil service act was passed. In 1885, the National Education Association brought forth the question of tenure of school officials. A committee of that association studied the matter and later submitted a report. Generally speaking the tenure so sought was interpreted to mean, in substance, the application of the principles of civil service to the teaching profession. It was

thought that for the good of the schools and the general public the profession should be made independent of personal or political influence, and made free from the malignant power of spoils and patronage. In 1886 the state of Massachusetts enacted a law 'relating to the tenure of office of teachers.' St.Mass.1886, c. 313. Thereunder school districts were permitted to enter into contracts with teachers for a longer period than one year. In 1889 the committee on rules of the Boston School Committee suggested a tenure law providing for a probationary period of one year, four years of annual elections, and thereafter permanent tenure subject to removal for cause after proper hearing. The bases for recommendations were that better talent would be attracted to the teaching profession; that annual contracts theretofore in vogue had not resulted in the elimination of poor, incompetent, and inefficient teachers; that the principle of annual election or appointment was not generally applied to policemen, firemen, or judicial officers, and in the very nature of things should not apply to teachers; that not infrequently the best teachers were discharged for inadequate reasons. (See report of Committee on Tenure of National Education Association for the year 1921.) Foreign countries have long recognized the principle of teachers' tenure. (See report of Committee on Tenure of National Education Association for the year 1936.) Since 1900 the principle of teachers' tenure in this country has developed more rapidly. In a general way it has followed the civil service plan. The objectives sought have been to protect the teachers against unjust removal after having undergone an adequate probationary period; that the movement itself has for its basis public interest, in that most advantages go to the youth of the land and to the schools themselves, rather than the interest of the teachers as such. (See report of Committee on Civil Service for Teachers of National Education Association for July, 1934.)

"Many states have adopted teachers' tenure acts. We shall not stop to enumerate them. The general purposes and advantages of these acts and the reasons therefor are interestingly set forth in 'Bulletin of National Education Association on Teachers' Tenure for 1937.'

"We refrain from making further comment on this phase, as every citizen knows and recognizes, not only as a matter of history, but also as a matter of personal experience, the great importance our schools have played and are playing in the furtherance of good citizenship by affording, generally, and to all our youth, opportunity to gain an education. . . .

"Plainly, the legislative purposes sought were stability, certainty, and permanency of employment on the part of those who had shown by educational attainment and by probationary trial their fitness for the teaching profession. By statutory direction and limitation there is provided means of prevention of *arbitrary* demotions or discharges by school authorities. The history behind the act justifies the view that the vicissitudes to which teachers had in the past been subjected were to be done away with or at least minimized. It was enacted for the *benefit and advantage of the school system* by providing such machinery as would tend to minimize the part that malice, political or partisan trends, or caprice might play. It established *merit* as the essential basis for the *right* of permanent employment. On the other hand, it is equally clear that the act does not impair *discretionary* power of school authorities to make the best selections consonant with the public good; but their conduct in this behalf is strictly circumscribed and must be kept within the boundaries of the act. The provision for a probationary period is intended for that very purpose. The right to demote or discharge provides remedies for safeguarding the future against incompetence, insubordination, and other grounds stated in the act. The act itself bespeaks the intent. Provisions for notice and hearing, the requirements of specified causes for discharge or demotion, are indicative of the general purpose. With these considerations in mind, it is our duty so to construe such parts of the act which on their face do not clearly delineate the legislative intent as will bring about a result in harmony with the expressed legislative policy. . . ."

Excerpts from Minnesota's current law applying to cities of the first class is an example of teacher tenure:

"All teachers in the public schools in cities of the first class during the first three years of consecutive employment shall be deemed to be in a probationary period of employment during which period any annual contract with any teacher may, or may not, be renewed as the school board shall see fit. The school board may, during such probationary period, discharge or demote a teacher for any of the causes as specified in this code. A written statement of the cause of such discharge or demotion shall be given to the teacher by the school board at least 30 days before such removal or demotion shall become effective, and the teacher so notified shall have no right of appeal therefrom.

"After the completion of such probationary period, without discharge, such teachers as are thereupon re-employed shall continue in service and hold their respective position during good behavior and efficient and competent service and shall not be discharged or demoted except for cause after a hearing.

"Any probationary teacher shall be deemed to have been re-employed for the ensuing school year, unless the school board in charge of such school shall give such teacher notice in writing before April 1 of the termination of such employment. In event of such notice the employment shall terminate at the close of the school sessions of the current school year.

"Causes for the discharge or demotion of a teacher either during or after the probationary period shall be:

(1) Immoral character, conduct unbecoming a teacher, or insubordination;

(2) Failure without justifiable cause to teach without first securing the written release of the school board having the care, management, or control of the school in which the teacher is employed;

(3) Inefficiency in teaching or in the management of a school;

(4) Affliction with active tuberculosis or other communicable disease shall be considered as cause for removal or suspension while the teacher is suffering from such disability; or

(5) Discontinuance of position or lack of pupils." M. S.A. § 125.17.

State tenure statutes may be broadly classified into three groups. One general type creates a "legislative status" for teachers by regulating the behavior of boards of education, but creates no contractual rights. Minnesota's statute, supra, is an example of this type of law. Its key word is "position," which refers to a teacher's relative rank, place or standing within a school system. Under it, local school boards have the power to transfer or assign teachers to positions for which they are qualified within the system so long as they act within their own rules and regulations and state law. This type of tenure statute confers a "position," not a contract right. In this circumstance, a state legislature is free to pass new laws amending the teacher-tenure statute; e. g., reducing salaries of tenured teachers or introducing new grounds for dismissal, without running afoul of Article I, section 10, of the United States Constitution, declaring that "No State shall . . . pass . . . any law impairing the obligation of contracts." See, Phelps v. Board of Education, 300 U.S. 319, 57 S.Ct. 483, 81 L.Ed.

674 (1937) and Dodge v. Board of Education, 302 U.S. 74, 58 S.Ct. 98, 82 L.Ed. 57 (1937).

A second general type of tenure statute creates a "contract status" for teachers, under which teachers have vested rights and state legislatures must conform all their future legislation to the requirements of Article I, section 10, of the Constitution of the United States. In 1927 Indiana's legislature passed a statute providing that "any person who has served . . . as a teacher in any school corporation in the State . . . for five or more successive years and who shall hereafter enter into a teacher's contract for further service with such corporation shall become a permanent teacher of such school corporation. . . . Upon the expiration of any contract between such school corporation and a permanent teacher, such contract shall be deemed to continue in effect for an indefinite period and shall be known as an indefinite contract . . .". Burns' Ind.Stat.Ann.Supp., 1929, § 6967.1. In 1933, Indiana's legislature tried to amend this statute by eliminating all township school corporations from its coverage, but not other types of school corporations. A teacher coming within the 1927 and 1933 laws brought suit, arguing that Indiana's 1933 amending statute was a violation of the constitutional clause prohibiting states from impairing the obligation of contracts. The Supreme Court of the United States agreed, holding that the teacher had a valid contract and that Indiana's 1933 amendment was an unconstitutional attempt to impair the obligation of that contract. State of Indiana ex rel. Anderson v. Brand, 303 U.S. 95, 58 S.Ct. 443, 82 L.Ed. 685 (1938). The Supreme Court did not say that a state legislature was fully disabled from passing all laws affecting teachers' contracts under tenure statutes. To the contrary, it stated:

> "Our decisions recognize that every contract is made subject to the implied condition that its fulfillment may be frustrated by a proper exercise of the police power [a state's legislative power] but we have repeatedly said that, in order to have this effect, the exercise of the power must be for an end which is in fact public and the means adopted must be reasonably adapted to that end, and the Supreme Court of Indiana has taken the same view in respect of legislation impairing the obligation of the contract of a state instrumentality. The causes of cancellation provided in the Act of 1927 and the retention of the system of indefinite contracts in all municipalities except townships by the Act of 1933 are persuasive that the repeal of the earlier Act by the latter was not an exercise of the police power for the attainment of ends to which its exercise may properly be directed."

Thus, the Court drew a line between the constitutional rights of a person and the rights of all the people. If a new statute was passed affecting Indiana's tenure statute and the contracts under it, but whose purpose implemented the general welfare of the whole public of the state then that new law would, presumably, be upheld as a reasonable and constitutional exercise of the legislature's powers.

A third general type of teacher tenure statute is one that expresses public policy. It neither creates a vested contract interest nor a legislative position. It is a mere declaration of sentiment. Obviously, in this situation a state legislature is not bound by the clause prohibiting the impairment of the obligation of contracts, and, perhaps, can repeal the law completely. See, Malone v. Hayden, 329 Pa. 213, 197 A. 344 (1938). Could the "practice" or "custom" of Boards of Education under a statute merely declaring a public policy in favor of tenure give rise to a legal interest similar to a property interest, which is the teacher's? Why or why not?

---

## PERRY v. SINDERMANN

Supreme Court of the United States, 1972.
408 U.S. 593, 92 S.Ct. 2694, 33 L.Ed.2d 570.

Mr. Justice STEWART delivered the opinion of the Court.

From 1959 to 1969 the respondent, Robert Sindermann, was a teacher in the state college system of the State of Texas. After teaching for two years at the University of Texas and for four years at San Antonio Junior College, he became a professor of Government and Social Science at Odessa Junior College in 1965. He was employed at the college for four successive years, under a series of one-year contracts. He was successful enough to be appointed, for a time, the cochairman of his department.

During the 1968–1969 academic year, however, controversy arose between the respondent and the college administration. The respondent was elected president of the Texas Junior College Teachers Association. In this capacity, he left his teaching duties on several occasions to testify before committees of the Texas Legislature, and he became involved in public disagreements with the policies of the college's Board of Regents. In particular, he aligned himself with a group advocating the elevation of the college to four-year status—a change opposed by the Regents. And, on one occasion, a newspaper advertisement appeared over his name that was highly critical of the Regents.

Finally, in May 1969, the respondent's one-year employment contract terminated and the Board of Regents voted not to offer him a new contract for the next academic year. The Regents issued a press release setting forth allegations of the respondent's insubordination. But they provided him no official statement of the reasons for the nonrenewal of his contract. And they allowed him no opportunity for a hearing to challenge the basis of the nonrenewal.

The respondent then brought this action in a federal district court. He alleged primarily that the Regents' decision not to rehire him was based on his public criticism of the policies of the college administration and thus infringed his right to freedom of speech. He also alleged that their failure to provide him an opportunity for a hearing violated the Fourteenth Amendment's guarantee of procedural due process. The petitioners—members of the Board of Regents and the president of the college—denied that their decision was made in retaliation for the respondent's public criticism and argued that they had no obligation to provide a hearing. On the basis of these bare pleadings and three brief affidavits filed by the respondent, the District Court granted summary judgment for the petitioners. It concluded that the respondent had "no cause of action against the [petitioners] since his contract of employment terminated May 31, 1969, and Odessa Junior College has not adopted the tenure system.

The Court of Appeals reversed the judgment of the District Court. . . . First, it held that, despite the respondent's lack of tenure, the nonrenewal of his contract would violate the Fourteenth Amendment if it in fact was based on his protected free speech. Since the actual reason for the Regents' decision was "in total dispute" in the pleadings, the court remanded the case for a full hearing on this contested issue of fact. . . . Second, the Court of Appeals held that, despite the respondent's lack of tenure, the failure to allow him an opportunity for a hearing would violate the constitutional guarantee of procedural due process if the respondent could show that he had an "expectancy" of re-employment. . . .

The first question presented is whether the respondent's lack of a contractual or tenure right to re-employment, taken alone, defeats his claim that the nonrenewal of his contract violated the First and Fourteenth Amendments. We hold that it does not.

For at least a quarter century, this Court has made clear that even though a person has no "right" to a valuable governmental benefit and even though the government may deny him the benefit of any number of reasons, there are some reasons upon which the government may not act. It may not deny a benefit to a person on the basis that infringes his constitutionally protected interests—especially, his interest in freedom of speech. For if the government could deny a benefit to a person because of his constitutionally protected speech or associations, his exercise of those freedoms would in effect be penalized and inhibited. This would allow the government to "produce a result which [it] could not command directly."

.   .   .   Such interference with constitutional rights is impermissible.

We have applied this general principle to denials of tax exemptions, . . . unemployment benefits, . . . and welfare payments, . . . But, most often, we have applied the principle to denials of public employment. . . . We have applied the principle regardless of the public employee's contractual or other claim to a job. . . .

Thus the respondent's lack of a contractual or tenure "right" to re-employment for the 1969–1970 academic year is immaterial to his free speech claim. Indeed, twice before, this Court has specifically held that the nonrenewal of a non-tenured public school teacher's one-year contract may not be predicated on his exercise of First and Fourteenth Amendment rights. . . .

In this case, of course, the respondent has yet to show that the decision not to renew his contract was, in fact, made in retaliation for his exercise of the constitutional right of free speech. The District Court foreclosed any opportunity to make this showing when it granted summary judgment. Hence, we cannot now hold that the Board of Regents' action was invalid.

But we agree with the Court of Appeals that there is a genuine dispute as to "whether the college refused to renew the teaching contract on an impermissible basis—as a reprisal for the exercise of constitutionally protected rights." . . . The respondent has alleged that his nonretention was based on his testimony before legislative committees and his other public statements critical of the Regents' policies. And he has alleged that this public criticism was within the First and Fourteenth Amendments' protection of freedom of speech. Plainly, these allegations present a *bona fide* constitutional claim. For this Court has held that a teacher's public criticism of his superiors on matters of public concern may be constitutionally protected and may, therefore, be an impermissible basis for termination of his employment. . . .

For this reason we hold that the grant of summary judgment against the respondent, without full exploration of this issue, was improper.

The respondent's lack of formal contractual or tenure security in continued employment at Odessa Junior College, though irrelevant to his free speech claim, is highly relevant to his procedural due process claim. But it may not be entirely dispositive.

We have held . . . that the Constitution does not require opportunity for a hearing before the nonrenewal of a nontenured teacher's contract, unless he can show that the decision not to rehire him somehow deprived him of an interest in "liberty" or that he had a "property" interest in continued employment, despite the lack of tenure or a formal contract. . . .

Similarly, the respondent here has yet to show that he has been deprived of an interest that could invoke procedural due process protection.    As in *Roth,* the mere showing that he was not rehired in one particular job, without more, did not amount to a showing of a loss of liberty.    Nor did it amount to a showing of a loss of property.

But the respondent's allegations—which we must construe most favorably to the respondent at this stage of the litigation—do raise a genuine issue as to his interest in continued employment at Odessa Junior College.    He alleged that this interest, though not secured by a formal contractual tenure provision, was secured by a no less binding understanding fostered by the college administration.    In particular, the respondent alleged that the college had a *de facto* tenure program, and that he had tenure under that program.    He claimed that he and others legitimately relied upon an unusual provision that had been in the college's official Faculty Guide for many years:

> *"Teacher Tenure:* Odessa College has no tenure system. The Administration of the College wishes the faculty member to feel that he has permanent tenure as long as his teaching services are satisfactory and as long as he displays a cooperative attitude toward his co-workers and his superiors, and as long as he is happy in his work."

Moreover, the respondent claimed legitimate reliance upon guidelines promulgated by the Coordinating Board of the Texas College and University System that provided that a person, like himself, who had been employed as a teacher in the state college and university system for seven years or more has some form of job tenure.    Thus the respondent offered to prove that a teacher, with his long period of service, at this particular State College had no less a "property" interest in continued employment than a formally tenured teacher at other colleges, and had no less a procedural due process right to a statement of reasons and a hearing before college officials upon their decision not to retain him.

We have made clear  .  .  .  that "property" interests subject to procedural due process protection are not limited by a few rigid, technical forms.    Rather, "property" denotes a broad range of interests that are secured by "existing rules or understandings."  .  .  . A person's interest in a benefit is a "property" interest for due process purposes if there are such rules or mutually explicit understandings that support his claim of entitlement to the benefit and that he may invoke at a hearing.

A written contract with an explicit tenure provision clearly is evidence of a formal understanding that supports a teacher's claim of entitlement to continued employment unless sufficient "cause" is shown.    Yet absence of such an explicit contractual provision may not always foreclose the possibility that a teacher has a "property" interest in re-employment.    For example, the law of contracts in most, if not all, [states] long has employed a process by which agreements, though not formalized in writing, may be "implied." . . . Explicit contractual provisions may be supplemented by other agreements implied from "the promisor's words and conduct in the light of the surrounding circumstances." . . . And, "[t]he meaning of [the promisor's] words and acts is found by relating them to the usage of the past." . . .

A teacher, like the respondent, who has held his position for a number of years, might be able to show from the circumstances of this service—and from other relevant facts—that he has a legitimate claim of entitlement to job tenure. Just as this Court has found there to be a "common law of a particular industry or of a particular plant" that may supplement a collective-bargaining agreement, . . . there may be an unwritten "common law" in a particular university that certain employees shall have the equivalent of tenure. This is particularly likely in a college or university, like Odessa Junior College, that has no explicit tenure system even for senior members of its faculty, but that nonetheless may have created such a system in practice. . . .

In this case, the respondent has alleged the existence of rules and understandings, promulgated and fostered by state officials, that may justify his legitimate claim of entitlement to continued employment absent "sufficient cause." We disagree with the Court of Appeals insofar as it held that a mere subjective "expectancy" is protected by procedural due process, but we agree that the respondent must be given an opportunity to prove the legitimacy of his claim of such entitlement in light of "the policies and practices of the institution." . . . Proof of such a property interest would not, of course, entitle him to reinstatement. But such proof would obligate college officials to grant a hearing at his request, where he could be informed of the grounds for his nonretention and challenge their sufficiency.

Therefore, while we do not wholly agree with the opinion of the Court of Appeals, its judgment remanding this case to the District Court is affirmed.

Affirmed.

Mr. Justice MARSHALL, dissenting in part. . . .

. . . I would modify the judgment of the Court of Appeals to direct the District Court to enter summary judgment for respondent entitling him to a statement of reasons why his contract was not renewed and a hearing on disputed issues of fact.

## NOTES AND QUESTIONS

1. Would this case have been decided differently if the person involved had been a teacher in the "common schools"? Why or why not?

2. Is this case terminated, or is there another legal step? If so, what is it? What will be the issue(s) to be resolved?

3. This opinion addresses itself to two issues and has two major parts, one dealing with constitutionally protected free expression, and the other dealing with a quasi-property interest founded upon a reasonable and objective "expectancy" by the teacher. Carefully analyze the reasoning in each part. Do you agree or disagree? Why? What is the nature of the "expectancy"?

4. Does the Court hold that it would be constitutional to refuse to renew a teacher's contract on the ground that he published a paid advertisement highly critical of the Board of Regents or does it hold only that the teacher must be afforded a hearing in order to determine whether such non-renewal would be constitutional? Why? Suppose the teacher's contract were not renewed solely because he left his teaching duties in order to testify before a legislative committee, would the non-renewal be upheld without a hearing? Would a hearing have to be afforded? Would it be important whether the teacher was testifying on a school-related matter, or not? Suppose he was opposing federal aid to public schools? To private schools?

5. What type of tenure statute governed Odessa Jr. College? Did the Court say that this law did, or could, give rise to a legal interest in the teacher? If so, what would that interest be? What proof would have to be shown before the legal interest would be present? State what might be the "common law" of Odessa Jr. College. What is its relationship to the "expectancy" requirement set forth by the Court? Suppose the situation were one that a reasonably-minded teacher in the same or similar circumstances would reasonably and objectively believe that he had an expectancy of tenure, but in a specific case with a specific and skeptical teacher who subjectively did not have that belief, would the quasi-property interest exist? Why or why not?

6. A companion case decided with Sindermann, Board of Regents v. Roth, 408 U.S. 564, 92 S.Ct. 2701, 33 L.Ed.2d 584 (1972), involved the right to a hearing of a probationary teacher without tenure and on a one year contract at Wisconsin State University–Oshkosh. There was no statutory or administrative standards defining eligibility for re-employment. The Court stated that:

"There might be cases in which a State refused to re-employ a person under such circumstances that interests in liberty would be implicated. But this is not such a case.

"The State, in declining to rehire the respondent, did not make any charge against him that might seriously damage his standing and associations in his community. It did not base the nonrenewal of his contract on a charge, for example, that he had been guilty of dishonesty, or immorality. Had it done so, this would be a different case. For '[w]here a person's good name, reputation, honor, or integrity is at stake because of what the government is doing to him, notice and an opportunity to be heard are essential.' . . . In such a case, due process would accord an opportunity to refute the charge before University officials. In the present case, however, there is no suggestion whatever that the respondent's interest in his 'good name, reputation, honor or integrity' is at stake.

"Similarly, there is no suggestion that the State, in declining to re-employ the respondent, imposed on him a stigma or other disability that foreclosed his freedom to take advantage of other employment opportunities. The State, for example, did not involve any regulations to bar the respondent from all other public employment in State universities. Had it done so, this, again, would be a different case. . . .

"Hence, on the record before us, all that clearly appears is that the respondent was not rehired for one year at one University. It stretches the concept too far to suggest that a person is deprived of 'liberty' when he simply is not rehired in one job but remains as free as before to seek another. . . .

"The Fourteenth Amendment's procedural protection of property is a safeguard of the security of interests that a person has already acquired in specific benefits. These interests—property interests—may take many forms. . . .

". . . To have a property interest in a benefit, a person clearly must have more than an abstract need or desire for it. He must have more than a unilateral expectation of it. He must, instead, have a legitimate claim of entitlement to it. It is a purpose of the ancient institution of property to protect those claims upon which people rely in their daily lives, reliance that must not be arbitrarily undermined. It is a purpose of the constitutional right to a hearing to provide an opportunity for a person to vindicate those claims.

". . . the respondent's 'property' interest in employment at the Wisconsin State University-Oshkosh was created and defined by the terms of his appointment. Those terms secured his interest in employment up to June 30, 1969. But the important fact in this case is that they specifically provided that the respondent's employment was to terminate on June 30. They did not provide for contract renewal absent 'sufficient cause.' Indeed, they made no provision for renewal whatsoever.

"Thus the terms of the respondent's appointment secured absolutely no interest in re-employment for the next year. They supported absolutely no possible claim of entitlement to re-employment. Nor, significantly, was there any state statute or University rule or policy that secured his interest in re-employment, or that created any legitimate claim to it. . . ."

7. Should a school district or a state legislature adopt the following rule? Why or why not? "In the event of a decision not to renew his contractual appointment, every faculty member shall be informed of the decision in writing by the State Superintendent and, if he so requests, he shall be advised of the reasons on which that decision is based".

8. Roth is clear, however, that if charges of dishonesty or immorality are the basis of a school board's decision not to rehire, then, if requested, the teacher must be given a hearing to determine the validity of the non-reappointment grounds as a matter of procedural due process of law. Since Roth, there have been very few non-renewals of contracts because of dishonesty or immorality of the teacher, and when involved, these charges now tend to be found in dismissal cases. In discharge cases, a hearing is uniformly required when requested by the teacher, irrespective of the ground for discharge.

9. Give several examples that would constitute improper grounds for non-renewal of a contract, or which would require a hearing. Would any or all of the following require that a hearing be granted to a non-reappointed teacher, or be proper grounds for non-renewal, assuming they are part of a letter to the teacher from the State Superintendent: (a) we no longer have the necessary funds to employ you; (b) a majority of the tenured faculty, by secret ballot, voted not to retain you; (c) the staff I inherited from my predecessor was lazy and ineffective, and I had hoped that you would stimulate them to emulate your fine teaching practices, but instead, they have influenced you into bad habits, more of which I cannot afford, therefore, you will not be retained; (d) you have consistently annoyed parents, students and members of the Board of Education, and even though you have very high standards and are quite competent, I cannot retain you; (e) your teaching colleagues and I think you're a phony; we haven't collected the evidence, but we can if we have to; anyway, you're fired; (f) according to the two department scoreboards, last year you got twenty-two student demerits and four stars and fifteen administrative demerits and only two stars; as you know, you must have eight stars per year to be retained  .  .  . ; (g) a more competent individual has applied for your job; and (h) all of the above!

---

## MT. HEALTHY CITY SCHOOL DIST. BD. OF EDUC. v. DOYLE

Supreme Court of the United States, 1977.
429 U.S. 274, 97 S.Ct. 568, 50 L.Ed.2d 471.

Mr. Justice REHNQUIST delivered the opinion of the Court.

.  .  .

Doyle was first employed by the Board in 1966. He worked under one-year contracts for the first three years, and under a two-year contract from 1969 to 1971. In 1969 he was elected president of the Teachers' Association, in which position he worked to expand the subjects of direct negotiation between the Association and the Board of Education. During Doyle's one-year term as president of the Association, and during the succeeding year when he served on its executive committee, there was apparently some tension in relations between the Board and the Association.

Beginning early in 1970, Doyle was involved in several incidents not directly connected with his role in the Teachers' Association. In one instance, he engaged in an argument with another teacher which culminated in the other teacher's slapping him. Doyle subsequently refused to accept an apology and insisted upon some punishment for the other teacher. His persistence in the matter resulted in the suspension of both teachers for one day, which was followed by a walkout by a number of other teachers, which in turn resulted in the lifting of the suspensions.

On other occasions, Doyle got into an argument with employees of the school cafeteria over the amount of spaghetti which had been served him; referred to students, in connection with a disciplinary complaint, as "sons of bitches"; and made an obscene gesture to two girls in connection with their failure to obey commands made in his capacity as cafeteria supervisor. Chronologically the last in the series of incidents which respondent was involved in during his employment by the Board was a telephone call by him to a local radio station. It was the Board's consideration of this incident which the court below found to be a violation of the First and Fourteenth Amendments.

In February 1971, the principal circulated to various teachers a memorandum relating to teacher dress and appearance, which was apparently prompted by the view of some in the administration that there was a relationship between teacher appearance and public support for bond issues. Doyle's response to the receipt of the memorandum—on a subject which he apparently understood was to be settled by joint teacher-administration action—was to convey the substance of the memorandum to a disc jockey at WSAI, a Cincinnati radio station, who promptly announced the adoption of the dress code as a news item. Doyle subsequently apologized to the principal, conceding that he should have made some prior communication of his criticism to the school administration.

Approximately one month later the superintendent made his customary annual recommendations to the Board as to the rehiring of nontenured teachers. He recommended that Doyle not be rehired. The same recommendation was made with respect to nine other teachers in the district, and in all instances, including Doyle's, the recommendation was adopted by the Board. Shortly after being notified of this decision, respondent requested a statement of reasons for the Board's actions. He received a statement citing "a notable lack of tact in handling professional matters which leaves much doubt as to your sincerity in establishing good school relationships." That general statement was followed by references to the radio station incident and to the obscene-gesture incident.

The District Court found that all of these incidents had in fact occurred. It concluded that Respondent Doyle's telephone call to the radio station was "clearly protected by the First Amendment," and that because it had played a "substantial part" in the decision of the Board not to renew Doyle's employment, he was entitled to reinstatement with backpay.  The District Court did not expressly state what test it was applying in determining that the incident in question involved conduct protected by the First Amendment, but simply held that the communication to the radio station was such conduct.  The Court of Appeals affirmed in a brief *per curiam* opinion.

Doyle's claims under the First and Fourteenth Amendments are not defeated by the fact that he did not have tenure.  Even though he could have been discharged for no reason whatever, and had no constitutional right to a hearing prior to the decision not to rehire him, Board of Regents v. Roth, he may nonetheless establish a claim to reinstatement if the decision not to rehire him was made by reason of his exercise of constitutionally protected First Amendment freedoms. Perry v. Sindermann.

That question of whether speech of a government employee is constitutionally protected expression necessarily entails striking "a balance between the interests of the teacher, as a citizen, in commenting upon matters of public concern and the interest of the State, as an employer, in promoting the efficiency of the public services it performs through its employees."  Pickering v. Board of Education. There is no suggestion by the Board that Doyle violated any established policy, or that its reaction to his communication to the radio station was anything more than an ad hoc response to Doyle's action in making the memorandum public.  We therefore accept the District Court's finding that the communication was protected by the First and Fourteenth Amendments.  We are not, however, entirely in agreement with that court's manner of reasoning from this finding to the conclusion that Doyle is entitled to reinstatement with backpay.

The District Court made the following "conclusions" on this aspect of the case:

"(1) If a non-permissible reason, e. g., exercise of First Amendment rights, played a substantial part in the decision not to renew—even in the face of other permissible grounds—the decision may not stand (citations omitted).

"(2) A non-permissible reason did play a substantial part.  That is clear from the letter of the Superintendent immediately following the Board's decision, which stated two reasons—the one, the conversation with the radio station clearly protected by the First Amendment.  A court may not engage in any limitation of First Amendment rights based on 'tact'—that is not to say that the 'tactfulness' is irrelevant to other issues in this case."

At the same time, though, it, stated that "[i]n fact, as this Court sees it and finds, both the Board and the Superintendent were faced with a situation in which there did exist in fact reason . . . independent of any First Amendment, rights or exercise thereof, to not extend tenure."

Since respondent Doyle had no tenure, and there was therefore not even a state-law requirement of "cause" or "reason" before a decision could be made not to renew his employment, it is not clear what the District Court meant by this latter statement. Clearly the Board legally *could* have dismissed respondent had the radio station incident never come to its attention. On plausible meaning of the court's statement is that the Board and the Superintendent not only could, but in fact *would* have reached that decision had not the constitutionally protected incident of the telephone call to the radio station occurred. We are thus brought to the issue whether, even if that were the case, the fact that the protected conduct played a "substantial part" in the actual decision not to renew would necessarily amount to a constitutional violation justifying remedial action. We think that it would not.

A rule of causation which focuses solely on whether protected conduct played a part, "substantial" or otherwise, in a decision not to rehire, could place an employee in a better position as a result of the exercise of constitutionally protected conduct than he would have occupied had he done nothing. The difficulty with the rule enunciated by the District Court is that it would require reinstatement in cases where a dramatic and perhaps abrasive incident is inevitably on the minds of those responsible for the decision to rehire, and does indeed play a part in that decision—even if the same decision would have been reached had the incident not occurred. The constitutional principle at stake is sufficiently vindicated if such an employee is placed in no worse a position than if he had not engaged in the conduct. A borderline or marginal candidate should not have the employment question resolved against him because of constitutionally protected conduct. But that same candidate ought not to be able, by engaging in such conduct, to prevent his employer from assessing his performance record and reaching a decision not to rehire on the basis of that record, simply because the protected conduct makes the employer more certain of the correctness of its decision.

This is especially true where, as the District Court observed was the case here, the current decision to rehire will accord "tenure." The long-term consequences of an award of tenure are of great moment both to the employee and to the employer. They are too significant for us to hold that the Board in this case would be precluded, because it considered constitutionally protected conduct in deciding not to rehire Doyle, from attempting to prove to a trier of fact that quite apart from such conduct Doyle's record was such that he would not have been rehired in any event.

In other areas of constitutional law, this Court has found it necessary to formulate a test of causation which distinguishes between a result caused by a constitutional violation and one not so caused.

. . . . [C]ases do suggest that the proper test to apply in the present context is one which likewise protects against the invasion of constitutional rights without commanding undesirable consequences not necessary to the assurance of those rights.

Initially, in this case, the burden was properly placed upon respondent to show that his conduct was constitutionally protected, and that this conduct was a "substantial factor"—or to put it in other words, that it was a "motivating factor" in the Board's decision not to rehire him.   Respondent having carried that burden, however, the District Court should have gone on to determine whether the Board had shown by a preponderance of the evidence that it would have reached the same decision as to respondent's reemployment even in the absence of the protected conduct.

We cannot tell from the District Court opinion and conclusions, nor from the opinion of the Court of Appeals affirming the judgment of the District Court, what conclusion those courts would have reached had they applied this test.   The judgment of the Court of Appeals is therefore vacated, and the case remanded for further proceedings consistent with this opinion.

So ordered.

## NOTES AND QUESTIONS

1.  In Doyle, a unanimous Supreme Court held that a nontenured teacher initially must bear the burden of proving that he engaged in constitutionally protected conduct and that this conduct was "a 'substantial factor'—or, to put it in other words, that it was a 'motivating factor'" in the decision against reappointment.   If the teacher carries this burden, then the school board must show "by a preponderance of the evidence" that its decision not to reappoint would have been the same "even in the absence of the protected conduct."   Will this standard have a major impact in First Amendment cases like Pickering and Givhan, supra?   How does one separate out the tainted from the untainted evidence?   Will school officials tend to testify that they would have made the same decision even if they had not considered a teacher's constitutionally protected activity?

2.  Do you think Doyle, like Perry v. Sindermann, applies to a tenured teacher's dismissal hearing?

----

## AYERS v. LINCOLN COUNTY SCHOOL DIST.

Supreme Court of Oregon, 1967.
248 Or. 31, 432 P.2d 170.

WOODRICH, Justice (pro tempore).   This is an appeal by the defendant school district from a judgment holding invalid the dismissal of a tenure teacher.   Hereafter, the word defendant will refer to the school district. . . .

Plaintiff had been a regular teacher with the school district for a number of years. She was subject to the Teacher Tenure Law. On February 10, 1966, the district school superintendent, by letter to the plaintiff, advised her that he intended to recommend to the school board that she be dismissed as a permanent teacher and advised her of her right to have the proposed recommendation reviewed by a panel of the Professional Review Committee.

The teacher requested a review of the district superintendent's proposed recommendation by the Professional Review Committee pursuant to ORS 342.895(3). Thereafter, the State Superintendent of Public Instruction designated the members of the panel to review the proposed recommendation of the district superintendent.

The Professional Review Committee met, heard witnesses, and examined documentary evidence. The plaintiff and her attorney were excluded from the proceedings before the review panel, except for the specific time when she was allowed to present evidence and argument. The teacher and her attorney were not permitted to hear the testimony of the witnesses nor to cross-examine them. Witnesses and evidence were presented and considered by the panel both before and after the teacher's testimony and argument.

Following the meeting of the Professional Review Committee, it entered its report on March 17, 1966, determining that the district superintendent was justified in recommending to the school board that plaintiff be dismissed for reason of physical incapacity, as authorized by ORS 342.865(1)(e), and that the grounds therefor were true and substantiated.

Thereafter, the plaintiff requested and was granted a hearing before the district school board, at which time testimony and documentary evidence was received by the board. Following this hearing the board entered its resolution terminating the teacher. The trial court on writ of review held the dismissal invalid.

This case involves the interpretation of ORS 342.905(2) and (3). These sections are a portion of the statute providing for the review of the superintendent's dismissal recommendation of a five-man panel of the Professional Review Committee, hereinafter called the "panel." The pertinent sections read, in part, as follows:

"* * *

"(2) As soon as possible after the time of designation, the panel shall elect a chairman and shall conduct such investigation as it may consider necessary for the purpose of determining whether the grounds for the recommendation are true and substantiated * * *.

"(3) The permanent teacher involved shall *have the right to meet with the panel accompanied by counsel* or other person of his choice *and to present any evidence and arguments which he considers pertinent.*"  (Emphasis supplied.)

This court is of the opinion that the legislature intended that the teacher's "right to meet with the panel" includes the right to be present throughout the hearing, personally and with counsel, to subpoena and cross-examine witnesses, present other evidence, and make arguments to the panel.

The type of hearings provided for in an administrative process is either an "adversary," trial-type hearing, or an "auditive," speech-making hearing. . . . One indicia of the legislature's choice of hearing type is the nature of powers conferred on the agency in conducting its hearing.  In this case the statutory powers conferred on the panel are those usually associated with the exercise of a judicial function.

" * * *  [T]he panel shall be furnished appropriate professional and other special assistance  * * *  shall be empowered to subpoena and swear witnesses and to require them to give testimony and to produce books and papers relevant to its investigation."  ORS 342.905(2).

The function that the panel performs is essentially judicial.  The panel is not called upon to make a policy decision or exercise discretion.  It merely determines if the evidence substantiates the existence of one of several statutory grounds for dismissal.  ORS 342.905(4).

The statute provides that a specific party, as distinguished from the public in general, has a right to appear and be heard.  A provision for a general notice by publication stating that all who are interested may appear and be heard was held to evidence an intent to create an "auditive" type hearing.  Mohr v. State Board of Education, supra.

Defendant contends that the panel proceedings are "investigatory" only, and because of that plaintiff may not complain over her exclusion.  This argument would be more persuasive if plaintiff were given an effective opportunity at a later stage to test the basis for the panel's decision.  The statutory procedure subsequent to the panel's decision does not protect that opportunity.

After the panel concludes its inquiry it must formalize its conclusions in a written report.  ORS 342.905(4).  Thereafter, the statutes provide two alternatives, depending on the findings of the panel.  If the panel's report is unfavorable to the teacher, the report *must* be considered by the school board at its hearing, which hearing may be informal.  At this informal hearing no explicit provision is made for subpoenaing witnesses, cross-examining witnesses, or making a record of the proceedings.  ORS 342.925.  There is no requirement that the report contain an accurate record of the evidence the panel considered.

There is no provision for a transcript of the panel proceedings. If the panel report is favorable to the teacher, the report may, but need not necessarily, be considered by the board; it is merely made competent evidence at the board hearing.

The foregoing summary demonstrates the importance of the panel hearing and report in determining the ultimate outcome of the dismissal procedure. It is obviously of more significance to the teacher when adverse. In that event, unless the teacher has the right to participate fully in the proceedings before the panel, the teacher is effectively denied any opportunity to test the credibility and authenticity of the evidence which quite likely will be determinative of the ultimate result. The teacher is denied the right to know precisely what evidence has occasioned the dismissal. The teacher could not rebut by evidence or argue effectively against dismissal without such knowledge.

Because the statute was intended to afford the teacher the right to be present with counsel throughout all of the panel proceedings, it was error for the panel to exclude plaintiff and her attorney.

The judgment of the trial court is affirmed.

## NOTES AND QUESTIONS

1. Oregon's Supreme Court ruled "that the legislature intended that the teacher's 'right to meet with the panel' includes the right to be present throughout the hearing, personally and with counsel, to subpoena and cross-examine witnesses, present other evidence, and make arguments to the panel." If Oregon's legislature really intended this, why didn't it say so in the statute? Why did Oregon's Supreme Court interpret this statute in this way? Did it avoid having to declare the statute unconstitutional by interpreting it in this manner?

---

## BOARD OF EDUC. v. WILLIAMS

Court of Appeals of Arizona, 1965.
1 Ariz.App. 389, 403 P.2d 324.

MALLOY, Judge. . . . The petitioner, prior to the institution of these proceedings, had been employed by the Board of Education of High School District No. 1, Pima County, for a number of year (sic). Under applicable law, we are concerned with four consecutive annual contracts, the first of such being for the 1959–1960 school year and the last one being for the 1962–1963 school year. In each of these documents it was stated that the contract was one between "John Wesley Williams, Teacher-Counselor" and the respondent, that the annual salary included a certain amount for "counseling," and that the time of employment was from a date approximately in mid-August until the end of the first week in June of the following calendar year. In the last of these contracts, the petitioner was employed at an annual salary of $8,731.00, which included $406.00 for counseling.

On March 22, 1963, the petitioner was asked to come to a conference at which the principal of his school and the respondent, Dr. Thomas Lee, Assistant Superintendent of Schools for Tucson High School District No. 1, were present. At this conference, the petitioner was told, and this communication was subsequently confirmed by a written memorandum, that:

> "In view of the numerous instances of difficulties this year in your counseling and teaching work, to be effective with the 1963–64 school year we are relieving you of counseling duties and transferring you to another high school."

The written communication continued by saying that the action being taken:

> " * * * should be regarded in the nature of a probationary move, because if your quality of teaching next year doesn't measure up to the quality expected in this district, we will recommend your termination."

Neither at this meeting, nor at a subsequent one with Dr. Lee called at the request of petitioner's counsel, were any specific written charges made against the petitioner nor were any witnesses called to substantiate any charges, though this was requested by the petitioner through counsel at the second conference.

Subsequently the petitioner was tendered a contract for the school year 1963–1964 at an annual salary of $8,675.00 ($56.00 less than the prior contract), which described the petitioner as a "teacher," and which, contrary to the previous contracts, did not have any indication that there was any special allowance for counseling. The new contract gave date of commencement as August 27, 1963, which was approximately two weeks later than the other contracts mentioned above. . . .

The trial court found, and this court holds correctly, that the proffered contract which contained a salary reduction was a violation of the subject act. Two pertinent provisions are these:

A.R.S. § 15–252:

> "Subject to the provisions of § 15–257, the contract of employment of a probationary or continuing teacher for a school year shall be deemed *automatically renewed* for the next ensuing school year, unless, on or before March 15 immediately preceding the ensuing school year, the school board, a member thereof acting on behalf of the board, or the superintendent of the school district, gives notice to the teacher of the termination of his contract." [Emphasis supplied]

A.R.S. § 15–257 [in part]:

"Nothing in this article shall be interpreted to prevent a
school board from reducing salaries or eliminating teachers
in a school district in order to effectuate economies in the
operation of the district or to improve the efficient conduct
and administration of the schools of the district, *but no reduction in the salary of a continuing teacher shall be made
except in accordance with a general salary reduction in the
school district by which he is employed,* and in such case the
reduction shall be applied equitably among all such teachers.
*  *  *".  [Emphasis supplied]

In this case, the petitioner was not notified prior to March 15
that his contract was not being renewed and there was no general
salary reduction in the school district.

This court holds, therefore, that the petitioner was entitled to
a renewal of his contract without a salary reduction.  .  .  .

The tenure granted by the Act does not include the right to teach
any particular class or classes nor to teach at any particular school.
.  .  .

Under teacher's tenure statutes in other states, which do not contain an explicit prohibition against a salary reduction, several courts
have come to the conclusion that the reduction in the "rank and
grade" of a teacher, when attendant with a salary reduction, is a
"dismissal," prohibited by the Act.  .  .  .  In a state such as ours,
where there is a specific prohibition against reduction of salary, this
court sees no need to extend the language of the Act so as to carry this
implied prohibition against reduction in rank or grade.  However,
even if this be the law of this state, there is no showing here that a
teacher is of any lower rank or grade than a counselor.  The testimony of the petitioner was unequivocal that the additional pay was
solely for the additional two weeks work.  There is no showing that
a counselor has any supervisory authority over other teachers nor
that a counselor is regarded as of a higher professional stature than
an ordinary teacher.  Accordingly there has been no reduction in
"rank and grade" of the petitioner.  .  .  .

[A] "decision" in the "nature of a probationary move" is not
one that is subject to being reviewed by a writ of certiorari.  A writ
of certiorari both at the common law and under our statute  .  .  .
is one that reviews the actions of an inferior tribunal while exercising
judicial or quasi-judicial functions.  .  .  .  There was nothing judicial or quasi-judicial about [a teacher having a conference with a
school administrator]  .  .  .  It [is] purely an administrative procedure.  It must be remembered that a school board exercises administrative, legislative and quasi-judicial functions.  The "triple

personality" of such a board has been commented upon in this language:

> "A school board is a part of the executive department, but, in the operation of our public school system, it exercises not only purely administrative functions but others of a legislative character, and still others of a quasi judicial character. Of the administrative type are the hiring of teachers, their assignment in the school system, and their discharge, once the grounds therefor are established. Of the legislative type are the making of rules and the determination of policies governing such hiring, assignment, and discharge of teachers. Of the quasi judicial type is the power to hear and determine proceedings for the removal of teachers for cause. * * *" State ex rel. Ging v. Board of Education of City of Duluth, 213 Minn. 550, 7 N.W.2d 544, 555 [1943].

Were the court to review "decisions" such as that taken at the subject conference, the court believes there would be no end to the judicial review of the multifarious administrative problems arising in school districts on a day-to-day basis. It is not felt that the judgment of the courts in connection with these problems of school administration would be any better than that of the officials elected to the positions of responsibility as to the particular school districts. The following additional quotation from the case of State ex rel. Ging v. Board of Education of City of Duluth, supra, is deemed pertinent:

> "The adoption of a liberal construction to combat the evils to which the law [Minnesota Teacher's Tenure Act] was directed does not permit a construction so benevolent toward teachers that, by eliminating one evil, we create another: that of transferring from the school boards, the duly elected representatives of the parents, taxpayers and other electors of the school district, to the teachers and the courts the management, supervision, and control of our school systems vested in such boards by other statutes." . . .

---

### ROSENTHAL v. ORLEANS PARISH SCHOOL BD.

Court of Appeals of Louisiana, 1968.
214 So.2d 203, app. den. 252 La. 963, 215 So.2d 130.

YARRUT, Judge. . . . Plaintiff is a tenured teacher. . .

In September, 1964, she was transferred by the School Board to the position of teacher of Biology at Benjamin Franklin Senior High School. On July 17, 1967, the Superintendent of The Orleans Parish School Board, notified Plaintiff, by letter, he planned to recommend to the School Board that she be transferred from the position of teacher of Biology at Franklin, to the position of teacher of Biology at Easton, reading:

"At my request, Mr. Daniel A. Allain, Jr., Assistant Superintendent, conferred with you concerning your student grading procedures. During this conference, Mr. Allain brought to your attention the following facts:

"1. Of the 55 pupils enrolled in your four sections of Biology during this past session, a total of 28 or 51 percent received final session grades of less than 80 percent.

"2. At the start of the school session 67 pupils were enrolled in your classes. At the close of the year only 55 pupils remained. Twelve of the 23 Tenth Grade pupils to withdraw from Franklin during the school year were assigned your course in Biology.

"3. The pupil-teacher ratio in your classes averaged 14.2 pupils per teacher.

"4. There was little improvement in the number of pupils receiving grades under 80 during the second semester in comparing the mid-year and final grades. The mid-term percentage was 56 percent and the final session percentage was 51 percent.

"5. During the 1965–1966 school session 41 percent of the pupils in your classes received final session grades of under 80 percent.

"It was your judgment in this conference that you do not have expectations of your students at Franklin which are unreasonable.

"After carefully weighing both perspectives and after reviewing your judgment in the context of the grades given by other teachers at Franklin, I conclude that your grading procedures do differ significantly from what is expected by both the administration of the school system and the great majority of the faculty at Franklin.

"The students at Franklin are required to maintain an overall average of 80, and are subject to removal if they do not. Consequently, if the grading procedures of any one teacher differs significantly from the grading procedures of the majority of the faculty, that one teacher will have an inordinate influence upon whether or not her students are allowed to remain at Franklin.

"For the foregoing reasons it is my opinion, and the opinion of the Director of Personnel, that the best interests of the school system will be served if you are transferred from the Benjamin Franklin Senior High School, to a position of equal rank, dignity and salary in another Senior High School in the system. . . .

. . . The general rule is:

"In the absence of constitutional or statutory limitations or restrictions, the employing school authorities usually have the power to assign, reassign, or transfer teachers, principals, and superintendents. * * *" . . .

Plaintiff contends that her transfer from the position of teacher of Biology at Franklin to the position of teacher of Biology at Easton, constitutes a removal from office which can be accomplished only if the provisions of [the teacher tenure code] are first complied with. . . .

The jurisprudence has established what does constitute such a removal under the above cited statute. In the case of State ex rel. McNeal v. Avoyelles Parish School Board, 199 La. 859, 7 So.2d 165, plaintiff resisted his transfer by the School Board from his position of a high school principal to the position of a teacher in a high school, at a reduced salary. The Court held that the School Board was without authority to demote plaintiff; and said:

" 'Removed from office' is much broader in its scope than 'discharge' or 'dismiss.' It is well recognized in the jurisprudence of this country that the word 'removal' as used in statutes similar to our Teachers' Tenure Act includes a demotion in office by assigning the employee to a lower position in the same service at a lower rate of compensation. . . ."

The Supreme Court also cited with approval case of Board of Education of Richmond County v. Young, 187 Ga. 644, 1 S.E.2d 739, which held:

" 'However, a demotion from one position to another, if and when accompanied by a substantial salary reduction, being in effect a removal from the original position . . . the board had no right, without assigning any cause and without a hearing, to accompany the demotion of this petitioner with a reduction in her salary from $2,200.00 to $1,400.00 per annum.' " . . .

Our jurisprudence established that the transfer of a teacher from one position to another, by a Parish School Board, does not constitute a removal from office, as prohibited by the Teachers' Tenure Law, unless: (1) A reduction in salary is involved; (2) the new position requires the teaching of subjects for which the teacher is not qualified; (3) the teacher must undergo additional training, at his expense, in order to obtain permanent certification in his new post; and (4) the transfer follows a dismissal without formal charges, or a hearing, and thus leaves a blot on the teacher's record. None of the foregoing exceptions are present in the instant case. . . .

The School Board has the duty to properly administer the Public School System, and necessarily has the right to transfer teachers from one school to another in the best interests of the pupils. This is the effect of the decision below for, if a teaching position at Franklin is of greater rank and dignity than a teaching position in the other Parish schools, then teachers assigned to Franklin cannot be transferred to any other school, for such a transfer would be a transfer to a position of lower rank and dignity. . . .

The only issue here is the relative rank and dignity of the positions of teacher of Biology at Franklin and at Easton. . . .

The students are selected for admission to Franklin based upon I.Q. and achievement, and are dismissed if they fail to mtaintain a high level of achievement. The teachers at Franklin are not selected on the basis of either their I.Q. or achievement. The tenure of teachers is not graded. Their transfer indicates nothing more nor less than the fact that those charged with the responsibility of running the School System feel that the service of such a teacher is needed more at some other school than at Franklin.

When Franklin was originally started the degree and experience requirements of teachers were higher than those required of teachers at other schools. However, some years before this suit was filed this differential in requirements was abolished.

While Franklin is an "exceptional school," since its students are required to have a minimum I.Q. and a minimum level of achievement, there is no evidence that the faculty at Franklin is any more exceptional than the faculty at any of the other senior high schools in the Orleans Parish School System. . . .

The Teachers' Tenure Act prevents a teacher from being "removed from office," without formal charges and a hearing. The Courts have found that being demoted constitutes being "removed from office." Before a teacher can be considered as having been demoted, she must have been assigned to a position of lower rank or dignity. It is submitted that the two teaching positions pay the same salary, and have the same rank and dignity. . . .

Accordingly, we must hold that the proposed transfer of Plaintiff from the position of teacher of Biology at the Benjamin Franklin Senior High School, to the position of teacher of Biology at the Warren Eastern Senior High School, does not amount to a demotion; and is not a removal from office; nor does it violate the Teachers' Tenure Act, nor any other statute of the State of Louisiana. . . .

REGAN, Justice (dissenting). . . .

. . . there is a very significant and pertinent letter in the record which also served to provoke this dissent. It is dated July 17, 1967, and it emanates from the Superintendent of the Orleans Parish School Board, Dr. Carl J. Dolce, and it is addressed to the plaintiff, Mrs. Rosenthal, wherein she is castigated and reprimanded in five distinct paragraphs of that letter for her "student grading procedure". In concluding this letter, Dr. Dolce was of the opinion that the best interests of the school system will be served if Mrs. Rosenthal is transferred from the Benjamin Franklin Senior High School to the Warren Easton Senior High School, and he finally expressed the hope that in her new assignment she would reexamine her "teaching techniques".

The only reasonable interpretation which can be drawn from the words forming the context of this letter is that Mrs. Rosenthal's transfer was simply a disciplinary measure neatly disguised in legalistic mumbo jumbo. A cursory reading of that letter will serve to confirm and emphasize this conclusion.

Hence, she is entitled to a hearing in conformity with the provisions of the Teachers' Tenure Law, . . .

### NOTES AND QUESTIONS

1. Identify the role played by tenure in the *Williams* and *Rosenthal* cases.

2. The *Williams* case involved a typical automatic renewal statute. It also involved a statute prohibiting individual salary reductions. How might the court have treated this case if the statute prohibiting individual salary reductions had not been part of the law? Might the court have followed the lead of other courts and extended the protection of the teacher tenure statute, holding that when a salary reduction is coupled with a reduction in grade or rank it is tantamount to a dismissal?

3. Did Louisiana's court find that Carolyn Rosenthal had a constitutional right, and then engage in a balancing process? If so, what was balanced?

Was the case decided correctly? Why or why not? Should the court substitute its judgment for that of the school district if there is some substantial evidence supporting the finding of facts and decisions of the school district?

Suppose Rosenthal had prevailed and the court decided that this case was one of a teacher being "removed from office" or "demotion," what would the court have required under the teacher's tenure act before she could be either demoted or removed from office?

4. Newman v. Board of Educ., 594 F.2d 299 (2nd Cir. 1979), involved a tenured teacher who, involuntarily, was placed on leave of absence without pay and was required to exhaust her 200 days of sick leave. "When her involuntary leave of absence terminated on June 30, 1971, she was

not allowed to resume work. Instead the Board in September, 1971, directed that she submit to further medical examinations. Two medical doctors (Drs. Lazarus and Cinque) examined her on October 18, 1971, at the Board's request and found her fit to return to duty. However, pursuant to the Board's direction she was then examined on November 18 and 29, 1971, by a psychiatrist (Dr. Schnee), who concurred in the earlier diagnosis by Dr. Isenberg, also a psychiatrist, and concluded that her 'mental status is passive-aggressive personality, agressive type, severe and is not fit to perform the duties of a teacher.' As a result she was found to be unfit for return to duty and her involuntary leave was extended.   .   .   .

"In an effort to rebut the Board's evaluation of her competency to teach, appellant consulted two private psychiatrists (Drs. Valicenti and Shea) and a psychologist (Dr. Fisher) for an independent appraisal of her condition. In contrast to the doctors designated by the Board, each of whom had examined appellant once (except for Dr. Schnee who interviewed her twice), one of the psychiatrists consulted by appellant (Dr. Valicenti) interviewed her once a week over a seven-week period in September-October 1970, and the other (Dr. Shea) examined her three times in November, 1971, and once in February, 1972. Each of the two psychiatrists reported that he found no neurotic or psychotic trends or any problems that would interfere with her performance of her duties as a teacher. Their reports were confirmed by the findings of the psychologist after testing. These reports were submitted to the Board and read by the Assistant Director of the Medical Division of the Board, who 'did not give them much weight.' "

After reviewing the facts, the Court stated that "due process under some circumstances may require a full scale trial-type pre-removal evidentiary hearing, but under others may be satisfied by much more informal procedures."

"Here the private interest at stake—the right of a tenured teacher to continue practicing her profession, free of any stigma flowing from an indefinite suspension attributable to mental unfitness—is substantial indeed. .   .   .   In view of the inexactness of psychiatry as a science, it would be unrealistic not to recognize the risk of loss of this valuable interest on the basis of one or two interviews with psychiatrists which might result in irreparable harm to an individual placed on 'inactive status,' regardless of whether he or she may have the right to seek restoration to an active status. Although the public clearly has an interest in ridding classrooms of mentally unfit teachers promptly and without undue burden or expense, this is counterbalanced not only by the due process interests of the teacher but also by the public's interest in attracting competent instructors to assume teaching positions in our public schools by the assurance that they will not be suspended unfairly or through error.

"In weighing these factors here we are satisfied that appellant, important as was her interest in retaining her position, was not entitled as a matter of due process to an adversarial hearing before being placed on leave of absence for mental unfitness; the risk of harm that might occur if a teacher believed to be mentally unfit were permitted to continue teaching is too great to insist on retention while the issue of mental fitness is being resolved. The situation is one where the teacher's due process interest should be satisfiable through post-suspension procedures.  Indeed, this was implicitly recognized by the New York Court of Appeals' holding  .  .  . that the interest of a teacher placed on inactive status for mental unfitness was adequately protected by his or her right to petition the Board for restoraton to active status and to obtain state court review of a denial by way of an Article 78 proceeding.  In this case appellant did follow that route, achieving success to the extent that she obtained from the State Supreme Court a remand to the Board of her claim to the extent that it was not time-barred.  .  .  .

"We believe that as a matter of fundamental fairness, access to the detailed evidence relied upon by the Board is essential to enable a suspended teacher (1) to demonstrate possible erroneous assumptions by the Board with respect to material facts, or errors in reasoning or analysis on the part of the Board's doctors, (2) to offer pertinent contrary evidence, and (3) to have a fair opportunity to persuade the Board that continuation of the teacher on an inactive status for mental unfitness is unjustified.  The Board of Education has conceded before this court that appellant was denied procedural due process by the failure of the Board to make available to her 'a more detailed statement of the reasons for her being involuntarily placed on unpaid leave status' and by its failure to provide her 'a subsequent meaningful opportunity to be heard on and to controvert the evidence relied upon' by the Board.

"In short, a terminated teacher's right to submit her doctors' reports is of extremely limited value without their first having in hand the findings, analyses and conclusions of the Board's medical experts, together with the evidence relied upon by them.  We believe that the Board, having assumed the burden of proving appellant to be medically unfit, should as a matter of fundamental fairness and rudimentary due process have made available to appellant's doctors copies of the medical reports received from its own doctors."

## THE HEARING AND HEARING PROCEDURES

### INTRODUCTION

Under the rulings of the Supreme Court of the United States, if a teacher insists, he clearly has a constitutional right to a hearing in the following situations: (1) decertification; (2) dismissal during a contractual term, and (3) dismissal if tenured.  The hearing and the hearing procedures need not be those followed in a court of law.  While variations of detail are permitted among the states in the three above situations, Supreme Court interpretation of the constitution requires: (1) that the teacher be given a clear statement of the charges against him and adequate opportunity to prepare his case; (2) that the standards under which he has been charged have been made publicly available to him and written in such a way that a man of ordinary intelligence can understand it, and (3) that a hearing be afforded where the teacher can be represented by a lawyer and have the opportunity to explain fully his side of the case.  Following a hearing the hearing board must make specific findings of fact based upon the evidence presented during the hearing, indicating what evidence is relied upon to support which findings of fact. If the teacher relies on a constitutional right during the hearing, then that hearing must be of sufficient scope to allow for the full development of all the necessary facts and law in order to judge whether that constitutional right exists in the specific circumstances and whether it has been infringed. Automatic dismissal for exercising a constitutional right is clearly unconstitutional. The overall impartiality and fairness of the hearing are the key considerations.

Most states have statutes affording a hearing in the case of decertification; dismissal during a contractual term or dismissal of a tenured teacher, and, of course, these statutes must be fully complied with. Deviation from the statute means that the proceeding is not in accordance with law, and is invalid. In such event, if a teacher has been suspended during this time, the school district must pay his salary. The hearing is usually conducted by a state board of education, and if its findings of fact are later reviewed by a court, they are usually reviewed only to see whether they are supported by substantial evidence. Courts generally prefer not to substitute their processes for those of the administrative agency's. On the other hand, one of the major problems inherent in this procedure is insuring that the teacher has received an impartial and fair hearing. The reason is that the board of education acts as prosecutor, judge and jury, and this situation sensitizes most courts. Wherever courts doubt the overall fairness or impartiality of the hearing they will reverse the decision of the board of education. The trend of court decision is toward requiring a hearing in a court of law rather than having the board of education function as prosecutor, judge and jury in the three types of circumstances mentioned above. See, Osborne v. Bullitt County Board of Education, 415 S.W.2d 607 (Ky.1967). In some states, statutes allow a "de novo" review in court to a teacher who has been decertified or dismissed. This is a new trial, the court hearing is original, not appellate.

------

## COMMENTS ON THE MODEL CODE OF PROCEDURES FOR ACADEMIC FREEDOM AND TENURE CASES

Draftsman of Model Code, Professor Arval A. Morris
School of Law, University of Washington
Seattle, Washington
Vol. 22 Journal of Legal Education pp. 222–234 (1968).

Any fair appraisal of the adequacy of any set of procedures in this area must proceed from one prime perspective: How well do the procedures actually protect academic freedom? What is desired is a fair, clear and orderly set of model procedures that allow for calm, clear and non-emotional decision making. This means, of course, that these procedures should be looked upon as "safeguards" or "procedural guarantees" conserving the interests of society and the faculty member in academic freedom; that is, both the "rights" and "duties" of academic freedom should be considered. Consequently, the procedures should be set forth in clear and consistent detail, and they should be incorporated into the governing code of the institution, and thereby, made mandatory.  .  .  .

## BACKGROUND EXPLANATION OF THE CODE
### Informal Procedures

After failure of unstructured attempts satisfactorily to resolve a faculty personnel problem, the first phase of any faculty dismissal is, and should be, informal. Although this be true, it is wise, and necessary, that the procedures allowing for informal adjustment and settlement be structured and formally set forth. What should they be?

1.    There should be a specific provision directing that a discussion, with the goal of amiable conciliation, be held between the faculty member and a representative of the administration. The code provision should specify that the purpose of this meeting is conciliatory, but that this end can only be reached if there is an honest and frank assessment of the situation followed by a sincere attempt to solve common problems. Naturally, such a conference must be held in good faith. Conducive to these ends is a code provision requiring that the administration representative produce a written statement of the facts so that a clear discussion can be had on this point. Also, a provision allowing a faculty member to present his view is necessary (this will, sometimes, persuade the administration not to review the faculty member's competence and integrity), and, conversely, there should be a provision whereby the administration presents its views to the faculty member (this may persuade a faculty member to cooperate with the administration).

2.    There should be a code provision to the effect that, before the structured and informal conference is held, the administration must inform the faculty member, in writing, that any information or arguments yielded in the informal conference can be later used against him at a formal hearing.

3.    The code should have a provision governing suspension during the hearing processes. A faculty member should be suspended from his assigned academic duties if, and only if, immediate harm to himself or others is threatened by his continuance. Suspension as an act to prevent immediate harm surely must be seldom, if ever. Suspension for any other reason profoundly affects the placing of burden of proof, etc., by prejudicing the minds of most persons with this question: "If faculty member 'X' really isn't guilty, then why was he immediately suspended, etc.?"

## Formal Procedures

The procedures that are meant to govern formal hearings constitute the very heart of Academic Due Process.  They are of extreme importance, and they should be carefully considered from all possible perspectives.  What, in principle, ought they be?

## The Hearing Committee

The hearing committee should be a standing committee of full-time teaching colleagues, without any administrative status or duties, who are democratically chosen by, and representative of the faculty, and selected by pre-established rules.  The administration which is the "charging authority," i. e., by analogy only, "the prosecution," should completely disassociate itself from those performing a judicial function at the tenure hearing.  The reason why the board must be all-faculty and all-faculty-elected is not that the faculty has greater wisdom, but rather that faculty points of view and judgment are needed, untinged by the appropriate but different contexts and value systems which might be applied by the administration and/or the ultimate perspectives play a role at a later stage.  The problem of bias in the committee should be handled in the usual manner of peremptory challenges and challenges for cause.

## Formal Procedures Prior to Hearing

The faculty member should receive from the administration an official statement that sets the formal machinery into operation, and this statement, the "complaint," should, in all particulars, meet the full demands of the principles of notice and confrontation.  Within this framework the charge, or complaint, performs several other critical functions: it determines the boundaries of the hearing, usually dictating what can, and cannot, be contested, and, of course, it performs the function of adequate notice;  thus, the complaint should embody:

1. A statement of the charges in the particular case, made in plain and simple English.

2. A detailed summary of the evidence upon which the charges are based.

3. A first list of witnesses to be called.

4. A statement setting forth the procedures the hearing body will follow, including a statement of the nature of the hearing body.

5. A formal invitation to the accused to attend the hearing with advisers and counselors.

6. A copy of relevant legislation, board or trustees bylaws and rulings, administrative rulings, faculty legislation, and so forth.

7.  Assurance of adequate time for preparation of a defense.

8.  An invitation to appropriate professional associations to send an observer.

*Counsel*: A faculty member (and administration) has need of two types of advice during a tenure hearing. One type, obviously, is legal, and for this service the faculty member needs a lawyer, or lawyers. Secondly, a faculty member (and administration) has need of advice on academic affairs, as well as a lawyer, and, like the lawyer, the academic adviser should be permitted to be present at all times. The same rights, of course, should apply to the administration as well as the faculty member in question.

*Open or closed hearing*? The tenure hearing should be private unless the faculty member requests otherwise. The decision about an open or closed hearing should be placed solely in the hands of the faculty member. His professional life, perhaps the whole future for himself and his family, may be at stake. These are great concerns and outweigh any consideration of possible embarrassment or pain to the institution, or to possible witnesses.

## The Hearing

The main questions here are what, in principle, ought to be the procedures governing evidence and evidence gathering and testing techniques. I shall elaborate the major principles:

1.  *Presence*: A faculty member and the administration, accompanied by their legal and academic adviser(s) ought to have full rights to be present at all times.

2.  *Confrontation*: Faculty member and administration alike should not only be accorded full rights under the principle of notification, but, also, under the principle of confrontation, and each should have the fullest opportunity to present, deny, refute and rebut all the evidence produced by the other; this expressly includes the full and complete rights of cross-examination.

3.  *Witnesses and Other Evidence*: Administration and faculty members should have complete rights to call witnesses and produce evidence in support of their position. The usual rules of evidence in law courts should not govern. The administration should make available to the faculty member whatever authority it possesses, under law, to require the presence of witnesses, production of other evidence, etc.

4.  *Expert Witnesses*: If the charge is one of professional incompetency, there should be admitted as evidence, in addition to individual testimony, a formal report on the work of the faculty member by his departmental col-

leagues, and of cognate departments in the University, and, if the faculty member so requests, a report by a committee of fellow-specialists from other institutions, appointed by the Committee on Faculty Affairs, and, if the charges include one of classroom incompetency, then, in this event, and, only to the extent of classroom competency, testimony from students taught by the faculty member may be elicited. Furthermore, any hearing committee judgment or professional competency must be restricted to the evidence described herein and cannot properly rest on any other considerations.

5. *The Hearing Committee Acting on Its Own Authority:* Prior to commencement of the hearing, the hearing committee should determine the order of proof; it may interrogate witnesses on its own when it believes either side has left a relevant matter lie dormant, and it may secure the presentation of evidence important to the case.

6. *Evidence Exempt from Cross-Examination*: The principle of confrontation should apply throughout the hearing and all evidence should be subjected to cross-examination. (There is only one conceivable ground that might be conceded here, and it is doubtful, but it is with respect to formal statements, depositions, of distant witnesses placed under oath, introduced under strict and exact rules of weight, openness to challenge, and every other safeguard needed to protect the faculty member).

7. *Burden of Proof*: The burden of proving the charges found in the complaint rests upon those who bring them, and that the burden of proving the charge shall be by a preponderance of the evidence relevant to each charge.

8. *The Record*: A full verbatim record of the proceedings shall be kept, the cost borne by the Institution, and that one full copy of said record be made available, at the same time, to the administration, to the faculty member involved and to the hearing committee.

9. *The Opinion*: In every case the tenure committee must write a full and adequate opinion setting forth its disposition of each issue in the case with its accompanying reasons relied upon to justify such disposition, and that one copy of this opinion be made available to the administration and the faculty member at the time when the tenure committee formally announces its decision in the case.

### Appellate Review

The decision of the Hearing Committee, if it is to have effect, should be final and binding (not "advisory") on the faculty member and the administration, unless either party elects to appeal. If there is an appeal, there should only be an appeal directly to the governing board of the institution, the ultimate authority.

If the Board chooses to review the case, its first review should strictly be confined to the record made at the hearing, accompanied by argument, oral or written, or both, as the administration and faculty member, in their discretion, choose to make. The decision of the Hearing Committee should either be sustained by the Board, or the entire proceedings should then be returned to the Hearing Committee along with a statement of the objections specified in writing, and with certain instructions to that committee. In such event, the Hearing Committee should reconsider, taking into account the stated objections and receiving new evidence if necessary. It should render a new decision and a new opinion which then shall be binding and final, and the case returned to the Board. After study of the committee's reconsideration, plus arguments, oral or written, by the parties, the Board should make its final ruling in the case. Any subsequent recourse should be to the courts. This is the procedure that ought to be followed. It guarantees both faculty perspectives in the procedures governing academic due process, and leaves the final decision with the Board.

## GROUNDS FOR DISMISSAL

### INTRODUCTION

Decertification and teacher dismissal statutes set forth specific grounds for decertifying and dismissing teachers. These grounds usually apply not only to tenured teachers, but also to non-tenured probationary teachers. They too, may be dismissed during their contractual period on similar grounds. The courts tend to hold to the view that where a statute sets forth specific grounds, they are exclusive, and other grounds are precluded by implication. In other words, local school boards cannot discharge, and states may not decertify, on any other ground. From a practical point of view, this protection is slight because many state statutes, and many rules and regulations of state boards of education, specifically include such broad grounds as "immorality," "conduct unbecoming a teacher," "behavior detrimental to the efficient operation and administration of the schools," "insubordination" or "other just cause." These generalized and conclusory types of discharge provisions run a serious risk of being applied unconstitutionally, or of being declared unconstitutional by courts either because they are so broad that they include behavior that is constitutionally protected or because they are so vague that they fail to give an ordinary teacher an adequate appreciation of what is forbidden, thereby effectively disallowing him from conforming his behavior to the requirement of law. If the constitutionality of a statutory ground is challenged as being conclusory and indefinite as to time, place and circumstance, some courts may distinguish between probationary and tenured teachers. For example, Arizona's statute requires "a statement of reasons" to be given in the case of non-renewal of a contract of a probationary teacher. In the case of a probationary teacher whose contract was not renewed on the grounds of "lack of cooperation," and "insubordination," Arizona's Supreme Court distinguished tenured from probationary teachers, saying that in this case these grounds were constitutionally valid because the purpose of Arizona's statute requiring "a statement of reasons" for probationary teachers is "simply to point out the teacher's inadequacies in order that she may prevent them in the event of subsequent employment. Accordingly, a specification of details, such as time, place and circumstances, are unnecessary." One might wonder how a teacher can correct his inadequacies without a specification of the details. Arizona's court specifically commented on two reasons given for non-renewal, saying that:

> "Insubordination imports a willful disregard of express or implied directions of the employer and a refusal to obey reasonable orders, McIntosh v. Abbot, 231 Mass. 180, 120 N.E. 383, and lack of cooperation is characteristically a subtle species of insubordination. Both terms are descriptive of a class of censurable practices destructive of the efficiency of the employer's organization. Accordingly, where, as here, a probationary teacher's right to remain in public service is dependent upon whether the appointing officers are satisfied with the teacher's conduct and capacity, and they are, in law, the sole judges, we are reluctant to place an unduly narrow construction on the legislative language lest it defeat the salutary purpose of determining the fitness of a probationer to serve a school district." School Dist. v. Superior Ct. of Pinal Cty., 102 Ariz. 478, 433 P.2d 28 (1968).

The range of application of these generalized types of "grounds" can be wide indeed; for example, what type of behavior might fall within the category "lack of cooperation"?

## IMMORALITY

---

### BURTON v. CASCADE SCHOOL DIST.

United States District Court, 1973.
353 F.Supp. 254 (D.C.Ore.).

SOLOMON, District Judge.    Plaintiff was dismissed from her teaching position at Cascade High School because she is a homosexual.    She seeks relief under 42 U.S.C.A. § 1983.    The case is before me on her motion for summary judgment.

Plaintiff began to teach in the Cascade High School on July 1, 1970.    She was a full-time teacher during the 1970–1971 school year. In October, 1971, after she commenced her second year of teaching, the principal of the High School learned that plaintiff was a homosexual from the mother of a student.    There is no allegation that plaintiff was derelict in her teaching duties or that she made any homosexual advances toward any student.    After she acknowledged that she was a "practicing homosexual," the Cascade School Board terminated her teaching contract pursuant to ORS 342.530(1)(b), which provides:

> *Dismissal of Teachers.*    (1) During the period of the contract
> .    .    .    the district school board shall dismiss teachers only
> for:
>
> .    .    .
>
> (b) Immorality;
>
> .    .    .

I find this statute unconstitutionally vague.    "A statute which either forbids or requires the doing of an act in terms so vague that men of common intelligence must necessarily guess at its meaning and differ as to its application violates the first essential of due process of law."

This statute vests in the school board the power to dismiss teachers for immorality.    However, the statute does not define immorality. Immorality means different things to different people, and its definition depends on the idiosyncracies of the individual school board members.    It may be applied so broadly that every teacher in the state could be subject to discipline.    The potential for arbitrary and discriminatory enforcement is inherent in such a statute.    "It would certainly be dangerous if the legislature could set a net large enough to catch all offenders, and leave it to the courts to step inside and say who would be rightfully detained and who should be set at large."

A statute so broad makes those charged with its enforcement the arbiters of morality for the entire community.    In doing so, it subjects the livelihood of every teacher in the state to the irrationality and irregularity of such judgments. The statute is vague because it fails to give fair warning of what conduct is prohibited and because it permits erratic and prejudiced exercises of authority. No amount of statutory construction can overcome the deficiencies of this statute.

.  .  .

## NOTES AND QUESTIONS

1. Review Morrison v. State Bd. of Educ., supra. As that case indicates, courts are reluctant to declare "immorality" statutes unconstitutional, and occasionally have tried to define the term. For example, Michigan's Supreme Court said that " 'Immorality' is not necessarily confined to matters sexual in their nature; it may be that which is contra bonos mores, or not moral, inconsistent with rectitude, purity or good morals; contrary to conscience or moral law; wicked; vicious; licentious, as, an immoral man or deed.  .  .  . That may be moral which is not decent." Schuman v. Pickert, 277 Mich. 225, 269 N.W. 152 (1936). Does this definition help any?

2. Other courts, like Morrison, have stated that immorality "is inseparable from 'conduct,' " and then imposed a linkage requirement such that immorality is "conduct which is hostile to the welfare of the school community." Jarvella v. Willoughby-Eastlake City School Dist. Bd. of Educ., 12 Ohio Misc. 288, 41 O.O.2d 423, 233 N.E.2d 143 (1967).

Should teacher conduct at home be grounds for dismissal? Would a linkage requirement prohibit the discharge of a teacher who at home performed cunnilingus on his nine-year-old stepdaughter? Florida's court said that the teacher's "conduct is an incident of a perverse personality which makes him a danger to school children and unfit to teach them," that "mothers and fathers would question the safety of their children; children would discuss [his] conduct and morals," and that "all of these relate to [his] job performance." Tomerlin v. Dade County School Bd., 318 So.2d 159 (Fla.Ct.App.1975). Was the teacher fired because he set a bad example? If so, was the "linkage" requirement of the "immorality" standard met because the court interpreted it in accordance with the notion of the teacher as exemplar? Why should teachers held to be good examples any more than any other citizen?

In another case a teacher was fired for immorality because she and her husband participated in "The Swingers Club." She had "engaged in acts of oral copulation with men other than her husband" and other similar activities. California's Supreme Court upheld the dismissal on the exemplar ground: "A teacher in the public school system is regarded by the public and pupils in the light of an exemplar, whose words and actions are likely to be followed by the children coming under her care and protection" and in the instant case, school officials were entitled to conclude that the teacher's "illicit and indiscreet actions disclosed her unfitness to teach in public elementary schools." Pettit v. State Bd. of Educ., 10 Cal.3d 29, 109 Cal.Rptr. 665, 513 P.2d 889 (1973). One judge dissented saying that "the majority is blind to the reality of sexual behavior" and that the majority view was "that teachers in their private lives should exemplify Victorian principles of sexual morality, and in the classroom should subliminally indoctrinate the pupils in such principles, is hopelessly unrealistic and atavistic." Under the exemplar interpretation of the immorality "linkage" requirement, was the teacher fired because of her "swinging" or because mothers, fathers and pupils knew of her "swinging"?

3. One of the fundamental premises is that the teacher properly can be held to meet the standard of the exemplar; he should serve as a model even in his out-of-school activities. Is this premise consistent with the analysis of the Supreme Court of the United States in Pickering? The constitutional right to privacy? Does the Supreme Court say that the "teacher-as-exemplar" standard can never be used? If not, under what circumstances is it appropriate to hold a teacher to standards that are higher than those applied to citizens at large? Can the exemplar standard be applied to a teacher's activities outside of school? Should it be? See, Emerson & Haber, Academic Freedom of the Faculty Member As Citizen, 28 LAW & CONTEMP. PROBS. 525 (1963).

## INCAPACITY OR OTHER "JUST CAUSE"

### IN RE GROSSMAN

Superior Court of New Jersey, 1974.
127 N.J.Super. 13, 316 A.2d 39.

SEIDMAN, J. A. D. The principal issue in this novel case is whether a male tenured teacher who underwent sex-reassignment surgery to change his external anatomy to that of a female can be dismissed from a public school system on the sole ground that his retention would result in potential emotional harm to the students.

Paul Monroe Grossman, now 54 years of age, married, and the father of three children, was engaged as a teacher by the Bernards Township Board of Education in 1957 and received tenure in 1960. He taught vocal music in one of the elementary schools, primarily to fourth, fifth and sixth grade children between the ages of 10 and 12.

For many years Grossman had had a gender identity problem which worsened with the passage of time until, shortly after his fiftieth birthday, he sought medical advice, commenced a course of treatment, and, in March 1971, had sex-reassignment surgery performed. He had been diagnosed as a transsexual; that is, one who anatomically is born with the genitalia of one sex but who believes himself (or herself) to be a member of the other sex.

Although Grossman had notified his superiors of his impending absence for surgery, he did not disclose its nature until his return in late April or May of 1971, when he informed the township superintendent of schools and made known his intention of remaining in the school system as a female. After completing the academic year in male attire, he assumed the name of Paula Miriam Grossman and began to live openly as a woman.

.   .   .

Mrs. Grossman now appeals to this court from the order of dismissal and the denial of back pay.   .   .   .

I

The scope of our review is clear with respect to the Commissioner's disposition   .   .   . .   The governing standard is, of course, whether the findings made could reasonably have been reached on sufficient credible evidence present in the record, considering the proofs as a whole, with due regard to the opportunity of the one who heard the witnesses to judge of their credibility. If the factual findings are supported by competent evidence, they will be upheld. It is not ordinarily our function to weigh the evidence, to determine the credibility of witnesses, to draw inferences and conclusions from the evidence, and to resolve conflicts therein. We have, though, the responsibility of determining whether pertinent principles of law were properly interpreted and applied to the facts as found by the trier thereof.

.   .   .

.   .   . the Commissioner found from the evidence that Mrs. Grossman was "incapacitated to teach children in the situation described herein because of the potential her presence in the classroom presented for psychological harm to the students of Bernards Township." His decision must be measured by the same standard—that is, whether it was supported by sufficient credible evidence considering the entire record.

The testimony on that issue was in sharp conflict. Dr. Charles W. Socarides, a psychiatrist and psychoanalyst with extensive qualifications and experience in the treatment of sexual disorders, appeared in behalf of the board, as did Dr. Harvey Martin Hammer, a psychiatrist specializing in the treatment of children. Dr. Charles L. Ihlenfeld, a physician who described himself as board eligible but not certified in the field of internal medicine, appeared for Mrs. Grossman, and Dr. Robert W. Laidlaw, a well-qualified psychiatrist, testified in her behalf by deposition. Although much of what they said dealt with the nature and treatment of transsexualism as well as the propriety of sex-reassignment surgery, we are primarily concerned here with their views on the impact upon students of a teacher who has undergone such surgery.

.   .   .

The Commissioner, acknowledging the conflicting evidence on the issue, found that the testimony of the experts was predicated on their differing concepts of the role of the teacher, with Dr. Socarides and Dr. Hammer both viewing the teacher as a "paradigmatic" person whose very presence in the classroom is instructive, whereas, to Dr. Ihlenfeld, a teacher in the classroom was merely another person from the outside world.   He chose to accept Dr. Socarides's description of the role of a teacher, and he relied heavily on the testimony of Dr. Hammer in reaching his conclusion that Mrs. Grossman's presence in the classroom could potentially result in psychological harm to the students.

Mrs. Grossman argues that there was a lack of substantial evidence to support the Commissioner's conclusion and that the proofs did not warrant the removal of a teacher otherwise "found to be capable, efficient, and physically able to perform her duties."   It is urged that there is little or no empirical data or evidence to indicate that psychological or emotional harm would result to the students of Bernards Township if Mrs. Grossman were allowed to teach in the school system.

It is not within our competency to balance the persuasiveness of the evidence on one side as against the other.   The choice of accepting or rejecting the testimony of the witnesses rests with the administrative agency subject to our oversight of whether there was substantial, legal evidence to support the conclusions reached.   The issue was thoroughly presented and argued by both sides.   The Commissioner resolved the conflicting medical evidence in favor of the board.   Understandably, in a case of this nature, most of the supporting evidence was in the form of opinions given by medical experts, as, indeed, was the opposing evidence.   We do not believe that those opinions were based on conjecture or speculation.   We are convinced that the evidence adduced sustained as reasonably probable the board's hypothesis that there would be emotional harm to the students if Mrs. Grossman were retained in the school system.   Consequently, we will not disturb the Commissioner's finding.

## II

Having reached the above conclusion, we must now determine whether the finding that Mrs. Grossman's retention as a teacher in Bernards Township schools would have an adverse emotional effect upon her students justifies her dismissal "for reason of just cause due to incapacity."   Central to this issue is N.J.S.A. 18A:6–10, which provides in pertinent part that no person under tenure shall be dismissed "during good behavior and efficiency" except "for inefficiency, incapacity, unbecoming conduct, or other just cause."   In the context of this case, the focal point among these grounds is "incapacity."

Mrs. Grossman's counsel argues that the word "incapacity," as used in the tenure statute, relates to the teacher's inability to teach in the classroom and not to his or her purported impact upon the "psyche" of the students as individuals.   He further argues that since Mrs. Grossman did not lack the ability, professionally, physically or mentally, to continue to function as a teacher, and since no illegal, immoral or deviant act or conduct had been established, she cannot be dismissed under the statute notwithstanding the finding that her presence in the classroom would have an adverse effect on the students. We think counsel's view of the statute is too narrow.

The term "incapacity," within the purview of the statute, has not received either precise definition or specific standards in this jurisdiction. However, in construing it we should not confine our attention to the term itself. We must examine it in the light of the statutory surroundings and objectives. It should receive a reasonable and sensible interpretation, and should, moreover, be considered in conjunction with the words "just cause."

Dismissal of teachers for "inefficiency, incapacity, conduct unbecoming a teacher or other just cause," has been held to provide a sufficient standard which, though "general in terms but measured by common understanding . . . fairly and adequately conveys its meaning to all concerned." It is clear . . . that the touchstone is fitness to discharge the duties and functions of one's office or position.

It is true that Mrs. Grossman's proficiency as a teacher is not in question and, as noted previously, she had been found physically and mentally competent to teach. It is also true that misconduct on her part has not been established. . . .

The problem to be resolved is whether "incapacity" of a teacher, as that term is used in the statute, can be established solely by a finding that the teacher will have an adverse effect upon the students in the classroom.

"Incompetency," [is] a term closely allied to "incapacity," . . . .
. . .

. . . "incapacity," like "incompetency," is directly related to fitness to teach, . . . . But fitness to teach is not based exclusively on a teacher's classroom proficiency or the absence of misconduct. It depends upon a broad range of factors. One of those factors, we have no doubt, must be the teacher's impact and effect upon his or her students . . . .

We think it would be wrong to measure a teacher's fitness solely by his or her ability to perform the teaching function and to ignore the fact that the teacher's presence in the classroom might, nevertheless, pose a danger of harm to the students for a reason not related to academic proficiency. We are convinced that where, as has been found in this case, a teacher's presence in the classroom would create a potential for psychological harm to the students, the teacher is unable properly to fulfill his or her role and his or her incapacity has been established within the purview of the statute. In fairness to Mrs. Grossman, we emphasize that the Commissioner's conclusions relate only to her fitness to continue teaching in the Bernards Township school system. We express no opinion with respect to her fitness to teach elsewhere and under circumstances different from those revealed in the present case.

. . .

## NOTES AND QUESTIONS

1. In a later case, the Superior Court of New Jersey held that if Paula Grossman "cannot teach because of that physical condition she is obviously incapacitated both for tenure and pension purposes." In re Grossman, 157 N.J.Super. 165, 384 A.2d 855 (1978).

2. What specific physical capacity did Paula Grossman lack, and/or what detrimental physical capacity did she have? In what precise way would Mrs. Grossman's physical capacities harm a child's emotional development? Does this decision ultimately turn on the teacher-as-exemplar requirement and on notions of sexual identity, like "boys not only learn their lessons in school but they learn how to be men from their teachers and they learn how to be men of certain types of character or personality or aspirations or they learn in a negative fashion"?

3. Compare Powell v. Board of Trustees, 550 P.2d 1112 (Wyo.1976) involving the issue of "whether or not a failure [of a teacher] to establish 'rapport' with the students is ground for dismissal." The court held:

> "We make one final observation concerning the 'good cause' facts necessary to support the discharge of a teacher. 'Good cause' cannot be just any reason that the Board deems sufficient for the discharge of the teacher.
>
> "Not only must there be 'good cause' and substantial evidence in support of the charge, but in order for the facts to sustain a charge they must bear reasonable relationship to the teacher's fitness or capacity to perform his duties in that position. Where a teacher's discharge was the concern of the court, it was said in Stiver v. State, 211 Ind. 380, 1 N.E.2d 1006, 1008 (1936): '. . . "other good and just cause" would include any cause which bears a reasonable relation to the teacher's "fitness or capacity to discharge the duties of his position. . . ." '
>
> "We find the test of good cause with respect to public officers generally to be facts which are related to the office and affect the administration thereof.
>
> "Therefore, it is the decision of this court that the 'good cause' to which the statute refers when the term 'any other good or just cause' is used in § 21.1–160, W.S.1957, 1975 Cum.Supp., these terms assume facts which bear a relationship to the teacher's ability and fitness to teach and discharge the duties of his or her position.
>
> "For the reasons above stated, we hold that a general charge of 'inability to establish rapport with his students,' unsupported by definition and specific facts going straight to the charge, is insufficient, standing alone, to constitute 'other good or just cause' under the statute, or the good cause which is necessary to insulate the order of termination or dismissal against capriciousness and arbitrariness. We repeat—in coming to this conclusion *we*

*place heavy emphasis upon the fact that the Board failed to find the contestant to have been deficient in his administration of the Board's disciplinary policy and there was no specificity of the rapport charge as required by the notice statute so that the contestant could know that the rapport allegation was an additional student-discipline charge which he would be required to overcome.* In any case—and within the four corners of this record—we cannot come to a conclusion that an 'inability to establish rapport with the students' is in all cases—and indeed in this case—an 'other good and just cause' under the statute which provides grounds for dismissing teachers."

4. As the last paragraph shows, the court in Powell was concerned with problems of notice, vagueness and overall fairness. DiLeo v. Greenfield, 541 F.2d 949 (2nd Cir. 1976), rejected a vagueness and overbreadth attack on a statute authorizing teacher discharge for "other due and sufficient cause." The court ruled that "due process requires *prior* notice of what constitutes forbidden behavior" but that the teacher "must have known beforehand that the conduct for which he was terminated fell within the proscriptions of the statute."

    "The test of a statute's vagueness for due process purposes is to be made with respect to the actual conduct of the actor who attacks the statute and not with respect to hypothetical situations at the periphery of the statute's scope or with respect to the conduct of other parties who might not be forwarned by the broad language. The evidence presented to the Board of Education allowed it to conclude that [the teacher] had engaged in a persistent pattern of neglecting his professional duties and harassing and humiliating students. There was evidence that his conduct continued and worsened after [the teacher] met with school administrators to resolve complaints received from parents and students regarding his classroom performance. In these circumstances it cannot be said that [the teacher] did not or should not reasonably have known that such behavior constituted due and sufficient cause for dismissal. Nor can he successfully contend that he had to guess whether the challenged statute would apply to such derelictions and bizarre conduct."

The court believed such conduct fell within the very "core" of the notion of "other due and sufficient cause." Query: suppose the facts of a different case, like Powell, fell at the periphery, would the statute survive a constitutional attack?

## INCOMPETENCY AND "OTHER GOOD CAUSE"

———

    Like "other just cause" and "immorality," "incompetency" and "other good cause" can be open-ended and catch-all categories. Courts allow many things to count as incompetency, ranging from inadequate teaching to physical or mental incapacity to a lack of self-control. Guthrie v. Board of Educ., 298 S.W.2d 691 (Ky.1957) upheld a teacher's discharge for reasons of "incompetency and inefficiency" primarily because she was unable to maintain discipline:

"A summary of the evidence is that Miss Guthrie, during much of her teaching career, was a poor disciplinarian.  Not only was she unable to preserve proper order in the classrooms over which she presided, but she was deficient in controlling pupils placed under her care on the playground.  Her pupils were unhappy and ill at ease, her classroom was full of tension and confusion, with the result that group work and individual incentive were lacking.  She was transferred from school to school, five in all, in an effort to adjust her to a general atmosphere in which she could instruct effectively, but such transfers failed to bring about any beneficial results.  Whereever she taught, demands by telephone and by letter were made by parents that she be transferred out of that school, or their children be moved to another teacher."

Suppose, at a dismissal hearing on incompetency, the testimony established "complaints as that some children were not allowed to go to the restrooms without facing loss of recess time;  a child who complained of excessive school bus speed was placed in the back of the bus;  a child was taken from school property to the home of another parent in an attempt to resolve a disciplinary problem;  a teacher under her supervision was allowed to spank a child on numerous occasions;  and an alleged immoral act of one of the pupils was discussed with members of the community," and the "evidence disclosed that the [teacher] became the focus of a community squabble. This arose out of the several incidents which are not sufficient to justify the discharge of a continuing teacher and in which the community apparently chose sides, some for and some against the teacher.  The critical question in this appeal is whether being the 'center of controversy' constitutes 'good cause' under the Teacher Tenure Act. . . ."    Kersey v. Maine Consolidated School Dist., 96 Ariz. 266, 394 P.2d 201 (1964), should this teacher be dismissed as incompetent?

Suppose, at a dismissal hearing, "three police officers testified to different times they had arrested the plaintiff, and that she was intoxicated at those times, the last two being within the past school year.  Their description included statements that plaintiff's clothing, general appearance and hair were mussed, breath strong with liquor, equilibrium abnormal, speech vague, had to have assistance to keep from falling.  On one occasion, she spent the night in jail and missed three days of school.  There was some other testimony that she had been seen unkempt, and that the arrests had been discussed by parents, teachers and pupils" (Scott v. Board of Educ., 20 Ill.App.2d 292, 156 N.E.2d 1 (1969)).  Should this teacher be dismissed as incompetent or as having engaged in "unprofessional conduct" ?  Why or why not?

Would the following testimonial evidence justify discharging the teacher on any of the following grounds: immorality, incompetency, intemperance, cruelty, willful and persistent negligence, mental derangement, persistent and willful violation of school laws or unprofessional conduct?

"A witness testified as follows:

"Q. What, if anying, did you see Miss Horosko do with relation to this slot machine?

"Mr. Reedy: We object to that as irrelevant and immaterial.

"The Court: Objection overruled, with exception.

"Mr. Reedy: Answer the question. A: Well, she showed us how to put the nickels into the slot machine and how the machine paid for itself.

"Q: Were the school children present when this was done? A: Yes.

"The record shows that November 12, 1936, a warrant issued for Kearney's arrest on the oath of a constable charging that he did "possess, promote or encourage a game or device of address or hazard, namely: 1 King Six Jr. 5 cent-25 cent dice game and 1 "Bally" Pin-Ball Machine at which money or other valuable things were betted upon, staked, striven for, won or lost . . .' and that on December 24, 1936, Kearney pleaded guilty and paid a fine of $14. The evidence of this conviction, the learned trial judge said, he disregarded; when offered, it was received as affecting the teacher's credibility.

"A witness testified:

"Q: Whether or not there were any games played in this establishment, Mr. Flynn? A: Yes, sir.

"Mr. Reedy: Objected to as irrelevant and immaterial and the witness having answered we ask the answer be stricken out.

"The Court: Objection overruled, with exception.

"Q: What was the nature of the games played?

"Mr. Reedy: We object to that too.

"The Court: Same ruling. A: Shaking dice.

"Q: Did you ever see Miss Horosko shake dice during this period? A: I have.

"Q: Ever shake dice with her? A: I have.

"Q: For what? A: Drinks.

"She [the teacher] testified that she never gambled but that: The only machine I know was in there was one of these pin-ball machines or amusement machines.

"Q: Were there any prizes offered for playing that? A: No, not the one I saw there.

"Q: Was it one of skill? A: Well, it was more of skill; amusement.

"Q: Did you ever play that in the presence of Mrs. Carley or anybody else? A: I don't believe I did in her presence.

"Q: You recall Mrs. Carley testifying you showed her how to play it. Do you recall doing that? A: No, I do not.

"Q: If such a thing did occur was it played for money or anything of that kind? A: No." Horosko v. School Dist., 335 Pa. 369, 6 A.2d 866 (1939). (She was discharged as incompetent.)

## INSUBORDINATION AND WILLFUL NEGLECT OF DUTY

Some courts define insubordination as "the willful refusal of a teacher to obey the reasonable rules and regulations of his or her employing board of education." State v. Board of Educ., 252 Ala. 254, 40 So.2d 689 (1949). Generally, however, an isolated refusal by a teacher will not result in a dismissal for insubordination because most courts consider insubordination as a "constant or continuing intentional refusal to obey a direct or implied order, reasonable in nature, and given by and with proper authority." Shockley v. Board of Educ., 51 Del. (1 Storey) 537, 541, 149 A.2d 331, 334, rev'd on other grounds, 52 Del. (2 Storey) 277, 155 A.2d 323 (1959). An example of the latter approach is provided by Ray v. Minneapolis Bd. of Educ., 295 Minn. 13, 202 N.W.2d 375 (1972):

"Appellant is a well-qualified Minneapolis high school teacher. He entered that system in 1964 and taught Russian and social studies at Edison High School until the date of his discharge. His discharge was precipitated by the fact that the North Central Association of College and Secondary Schools was conducting an evaluation of foreign languages and social studies departments in Minneapolis and St. Paul high schools. As part of this study, all teachers in each of those departments were required to fill out an 8-page form.

"Appellant was first requested in the fall of 1970 to complete and return the forms. In January 1971, he was asked by Mr. Frank Janes, who was in charge of the North

Central program for the Minneapolis district, to turn in his form for foreign languages. In filling out that form, appellant attacked Janes for requesting that the form be completed. In addition, appellant did not respond to all of the questions. He failed to answer questions regarding 'Teacher Load and Assigned Duties,' 'Preparation and Experience,' and 'Professional Activities.' In February 1971, appellant told the North Central evaluation team that if the team attended his class, he would leave the room. As a result, the team did not visit his class. When his principal asked him to complete the social studies form, he again did not fill it out completely, leaving some questions blank, answering some in an unresponsive fashion and in a way not useful to the evaluation. When requested, he refused to complete the form, asking his supervisor not to harass him again. Appellant was finally advised by Mr. Nathaniel Ober, associate superintendent of schools, that his failure to comply with the requirements would be regarded as an act of insubordination and dealt with accordingly. Subsequently, Dr. Harry N. Vakos, assistant superintendent, warned him that insubordination was one of the statutory grounds for dismissal. In April, appellant again refused to fill out and make available his social studies form. He was thereafter notified of his discharge. A public hearing by the school board followed, after which the board made findings of fact, conclusions of law, and its decision of discharge for insubordination.  .   .   .

"There is no question but that appellant had ample opportunity to fill out the evaluation forms and that his responses were purposely and intentionally incomplete, uncooperative, unresponsive, and argumentative. The decision of the school board and the concurrence of the trial court that such conduct was insubordination is a proper determination and must be affirmed."

---

## HARRAH INDEPENDENT SCHOOL DIST. v. MARTIN

Supreme Court of the United States, 1979.
440 U.S. 194, 99 S.Ct. 1062, 59 L.Ed.2d 248.

PER CURIAM. Respondent Martin was employed as a teacher by petitioner school district under a contract that incorporated by reference the school board's rules and regulations. Because respondent was tenured, Oklahoma law required the school board to renew her contract annually unless she was guilty of, among other things, "willful neglect of duty." The same Oklahoma statute provided for hearing and appeal procedures in the event of nonrenewal. One of the regulations incorporated into respondent's contract required teachers holding only a bachelor's degree to earn five semester hours of college credit every three years. Under the terms of the regulation, noncompliance with the continuing education requirement was sanctioned by withholding salary increases.

Respondent, hired in 1969, persistently refused to comply with the continuing education requirement and consequently forfeited the increases in salary to which she would have otherwise been entitled during the 1972–1974 school years. After her contract had been renewed for the 1973–1974 school term, however, the Oklahoma Legislature enacted a law mandating certain salary raises for teachers regardless of the compliance with the continuing educational policy. The school board, thus deprived of the sanction which it had previously employed to enforce the provision, notified respondent that her contract would not be renewed for the 1974–1975 school year unless she completed five semester hours by April 10, 1974. Respondent nonetheless declined even to enroll in the necessary courses and appearing before the Board in January 1974, indicated that she had no intention of complying with the requirement in her contract. Finding her persistent noncompliance with the continuing education requirement "willful neglect of duty," the Board voted at its April 1974 meeting not to renew her contract for the following school year. After unsuccessfully pursuing administrative and judicial relief in the Oklahoma state courts, respondent brought this action in the United States District Court for the Western District of Oklahoma. She claimed that the Board's action had denied her liberty and property without due process of law and equal protection of the laws, as guaranteed by the Fourteenth Amendment to the United States Constitution.

.   .   .   respondent's claim is simply that she, as a tenured teacher, cannot be discharged under the school board's purely prospective rule establishing contract nonrenewal as the sanction for violations of the continuing education requirement incorporated into her contract.

The school board's rule is endowed with a presumption of legislative validity, and the burden is on respondent to show that there is no rational connection between the Board's action and the school district's conceded interest in providing its students with competent, well-trained teachers. Respondent's claim that the Board acted arbitrarily in imposing a new penalty for noncompliance with the continuing education requirement simply does not square with the facts. By making pay raises mandatory, the state legislature deprived the Board of the sanction that it had earlier used to enforce its teachers' contractual obligation to earn continuing education credits. The Board thus turned to contract nonrenewal, but applied this sanction purely prospectively so that those who might have relied on its past practice would nonetheless have an opportunity to bring themselves into compliance with the terms of the contracts. Indeed, of the four teachers in violation of the continuing education requirement when the state legislature mandated salary increases, only respondent persisted in refusing to enroll in the necessary courses. Such a course of conduct on the part of a school board responsible for the public education of students within its jurisdiction, and employing teachers to perform the principal portion of that task, can scarcely be described as arbitrary. Respondent's claim of a denial of substantive due process under these circumstances is wholly untenable.

The Court of Appeals' reliance upon the equal protection guaranty of the Fourteenth Amendment was likewise mistaken. Since respondent neither asserted nor established the existence of any suspect classification or the deprivation of any fundamental constitutional right, the only inquiry is whether the State's classification is "rationally related to the State's objective." The most cursory examination of the agreed facts demonstrates that the Board's action met this test.

The school district's concern with the educational qualifications of its teachers cannot under any reasoned analysis be described as impermissible, and respondent does not contend that the Board's continuing education requirement bears no rational relationship to that legitimate governmental concern. Rather, respondent contests "the permissibility of the classification by which [she] and three other teachers were required to achieve [by April of 1974] the number of continuing education credits that all other teachers were given three years to achieve."

.   .   . There is no suggestion here that the Board enforces the continuing education requirement selectively; the Board refuses to renew the contracts of those teachers and only those teachers who refuse to comply with the continuing education requirement.

That the Board was forced by the state legislature in 1974 to penalize noncompliance differently than it had in the past in no way alters the equal protection analysis of respondent's claim. Like all teachers employed in the school district, respondent was given three years to earn five continuing education credits. Unlike most of her colleagues, however, respondent refused to comply with the requirement, thus forfeiting her right to routine pay raises. Had the legislature not mandated salary increases in 1974, the Board presumably would have penalized respondent's continued refusal to comply with the terms of her contract by denying her an increase in salary for yet another year. The Board, having been deprived by the legislature of the sanction previously employed to enforce the continuing education requirement, merely substituted in its place another, albeit more onerous, sanction. The classification created by both sanctions, however, was between those who had acquired five continuing education credits within the allotted time and those who had not.

At bottom, respondent's position is that she is willing to forego routine pay raises, but she is not willing to comply with the continuing education requirement or to give up her job.   The constitutional permissibility of a sanction imposed to enforce a valid governmental rule, however, is not tested by the willingness of those governed by the rule to accept the consequences of noncompliance.   The sanction of contract nonrenewal is quite rationally related to the Board's objective of enforcing the continuing education obligation of its teachers.   Respondent was not, therefore, deprived of equal protection of the laws.

The petition for certiorari is granted and the judgment of the Court of Appeals is

Reversed.

————

Excessive absence from teaching duties can result in a dismissal on insubordination grounds.   For example, in Fernald v. City of Ellsworth, 342 A.2d 704 (Me.1975) a teacher wrote to her superintendent: "This letter is to inform you that I plan to take a one-week leave . . .. During this time my husband and I will be taking a trip to Jamaica sponsored by the Grand Lodge. . . . Mrs. B_____ M_____ will substitute for me and I am sure my classes will be very capably covered."   The superintendent wrote the teacher that her plan was "not approved," but she was intentionally absent from class during the beginning of the relevant period.   Upholding her dismissal the court stated that the teacher's "conduct has the marks of a persistent, sustained, and unreasonable course of defiance;" that "such an attitude, over a course of time, breaches harmonious relations among colleagues and administrators," and "that the . . . School Committee was entitled to conclude that [the teacher's] usefulness in the school had become impaired and that the good of the school required dismissal."   On the other hand, a court reversed a school board's order dismissing a teacher who missed the first day of his teaching duties in order to enroll for an evening course at a University.   Although the teacher "missed the better part of one school day, his pupils did not suffer in his absence, because they were not scheduled to attend classes until later."   His "unexcused absence best might be described as an error in judgment, resulting in no harm to his employers."   Beverlin v. Board of Educ., —— W.Va. ——, 216 S.E.2d 554 (1975).

A teacher's continuous refusal to undertake non-classroom assignments, without added compensation, can raise the question of insubordination or willful neglect of duties.   The first, and much-cited, case is Parrish v. Moss, 200 Misc. 375, 106 N.Y.S.2d 577, affirmed 279 App.Div. 608, 107 N.Y.S.2d 580 (1951), where the court set forth the following guidelines:

> "Any teacher may be expected to take over a study hall; a teacher engaged in instruction in a given area may be expected to devote part of his day to student meetings where supervision of such teacher is, in the opinion of the board, educationally desirable. Teachers in the fields of English and Social Studies and undoubtedly in other areas may be expected to coach plays; physical training teachers may be required to coach both intramural and inter-school athletic teams; teachers may be assigned to supervise educational trips which are properly part of the school curriculum.
> .  .  . The board may not impose upon a teacher a duty foreign to the field of instruction for which he is licensed or employed. A board may not, for instance, require a *mathematics* teacher to coach intramural teams."

With respect to extracurricular assignments the basic question seems to be whether the teacher's assignment is sufficiently related to the school's program as to justify School Officials in making it? In other words, an elementary school teacher might be assigned to maintain order during recess but not to clean the mimeograph machine. Thus, a court ruled that a high school social studies teacher could not be assigned to oversee a bowling club that met once a week off school grounds at a local bowling alley. Pease v. Millcreek School Dist., 412 Pa. 378, 195 A.2d 104 (1963). But, another court has ruled that an English teacher can be required to take tickets at a football game. Todd Coronway v. Landsdowne School Dist. No. 785, (Court of Com. Pl. of Delaware Co. Pa., 1951). See also, District 300 Educ. Ass'n v. Board of Educ., 31 Ill.App.3d 550, 334 N.E.2d 165 (1975) holding that on Saturday afternoon or evening (1) an Industrial Arts teacher could be assigned to ride a "Pep" bus, (2) a Mathematics teacher could be assigned to supervise an afternoon football game and/or wrestling matches, and (3) a Biology teacher could be assigned to supervise a basketball game. Holding the assignments to be "within the discretion of the school authorities," the court said that "the duties assigned  .  .  . were necessary adjuncts to normal school activities and were neither demeaning in character nor unreasonably burdensome."

.   .   .

The definitions of the various grounds for dismissal, where they are not controlled by state law, and other procedures, such as reduction in force (rif), as well as many additional items, can be controlled or substantially affected by a collectively bargained agreement. Most courts and labor boards have ruled generally that a public employer cannot be required to bargain collectively with respect to the size of its work force or regarding the decision to lay off (rif) employees.  It is not an unfair labor practice if the employer refuses to bargain on such subjects.  Notwithstanding their general rulings, courts and labor boards typically enforce collectively bargained contracts on such matters, including binding arbitration, whenever the items voluntarily have been made the subject of negotiation.  Thus, it is always wise to begin to solve a law-and-education problem involving teachers by thoroughly checking the collectively bargained agreement.

---

## TEACHER ORGANIZATION

---

### McLAUGHLIN v. TILENDIS

United States Court of Appeals, Seventh Circuit, 1968.
398 F.2d 287.

CUMMINGS, Circuit Judge.  This action was brought under Section 1 of the Civil Rights Act of 1871 (42 U.S.C.A. § 1983) by John Steele and James McLaughlin who had been employed as probationary teachers by Cook County, Illinois, School District No. 149.  Each sought damages of $100,000 from the Superintendent of School District No. 149 and the elected members of the Board of Education of that District.

Steele was not offered a second-year teaching contract and McLaughlin was dismissed before the end of his second year of teaching. Steele alleged that he was not rehired and McLaughlin alleged that he was dismissed because of their association with Local 1663 of the American Federation of Teachers, AFL–CIO.  Neither teacher had yet achieved tenure.

In two additional Counts, Local 1663 and the parent union, through their officers and on behalf of all their members, sought an injunction requiring the defendants to cease and desist from discriminating against teachers who distribute union materials and solicit union membership.

The District Court granted the defendants' motion to dismiss the complaint, holding that plaintiffs had no First Amendment rights to join or form a labor union, so that there was no jurisdiction under the Civil Rights Act.  The District Court's memorandum opinion did not consider the alternative defense presented in the motion that defendants were immune from suit under the Illinois Tort Immunity Act (Ill.Rev.Stats.1967, Ch. 85, Sec. 2–201).  Concluding that the First Amendment confers the right to form and join a labor union, we reverse on the ground that the complaint does state a claim under Section 1983.

It is settled that teachers have the right of free association, and unjustified interference with teachers' associational freedom violates the Due Process clause of the Fourteenth Amendment. Shelton v. Tucker, 364 U.S. 479, 485–487. . . . Public employment may not be subjected to unreasonable conditions, and the assertion of First Amendment rights by teachers will usually not warrant their dismissal. Keyishian v. Board of Regents . . ., Pickering v. Board of Education. . . . Unless there is some illegal intent, an individual's right to form and join a union is protected by the First Amendment. Thomas v. Collins, 323 U.S. 516 . . ., Hague v. C.I.O., 307 U.S. 496 . . ., Griswold v. State of Connecticut . . ., Stapleton v. Mitchell, 60 F.Supp. 51, 59–60, 61 (D.Kan.1945; opinion of Circuit Judge Murrah), appeal dismissed, Mitchell v. McElroy, 326 U.S. 690, 66 S.Ct. 172, 90 L.Ed. 406. As stated in N.A.A.C.P. v. State of Alabama, 357 U.S. 449, 460, 78 S.Ct. 1163, 1171, 2 L.Ed.2d 1488:

> "It is beyond debate that freedom to engage in association for the advancement of beliefs and ideas is an inseparable aspect of the 'liberty' assured by the Due Process Clause of the Fourteenth Amendment, which embraces freedom of speech."

Even though the individual plaintiffs did not yet have tenure, the Civil Rights Act of 1871 gives them a remedy if their contracts were not renewed because of their exercise of constitutional rights.
. . .

Just this month the Supreme Court held that an Illinois teacher was protected by the First Amendment from discharge even though he wrote a partially false letter to a local newspaper in which he criticized the school board's financial policy. Pickering v. Board of Education. . . . There is no showing on this record that plaintiffs' activities impeded "[the] proper performance of [their] daily duties in the classroom." . . . If teachers can engage in scathing and partially inaccurate public criticism of their school board, surely they can form and take part in associations to further what they consider to be their well-being.

The trial judge was motivated by his conclusion that more than free speech was involved here, stating:

> "The union may decide to engage in strikes, to set up machinery to bargain with the governmental employer, to provide machinery for arbitration, or may seek to establish working conditions. Overriding community interests are involved. The very ability of the governmental entity to function may be affected. The judiciary, and particularly this Court, cannot interfere with the power or discretion of the state in handling these matters."

It is possible of course that at some future time plaintiffs may engage in union-related conduct justifying their dismissal. But the Supreme Court has stated that

> "Those who join an organization but do not share its unlawful purposes and who do not participate in its unlawful activities surely pose no threat, either as citizens or as public employees."  Elfbrandt v. Russell, 384 U.S. 11, 17, . . .

Even if this record disclosed that the union was connected with unlawful activity, the bare fact that membership does not justify charging members with their organization's misdeeds. Idem. A contrary rule would bite more deeply into associational freedom than is necessary to achieve legitimate state interests, thereby violating the First Amendment.

Illinois has not prohibited membership in a teachers' union, and defendants do not claim that the individual plaintiffs engaged in any illegal strikes or picketing. Moreover, collective bargaining contracts between teacher's unions and school districts are not against the public policy of Illinois. . . . Illinois even permits the automatic deduction of union dues from the salaries of employees of local governmental agencies. . . . These very defendants have not adopted any rule, regulation or resolution forbidding union membership. Accordingly, no paramount public interest of Illinois warranted the limiting of Steele's and McLaughlin's right of association. Of course, at trial defendants may show that these individuals were engaging in unlawful activities or were dismissed for other proper reasons, but on this record we hold that the complaint sufficiently states a justifiable claim under Section 1983. There is nothing anomalous in protecting teachers' rights to join unions. Other employees have long been similarly protected by the National Labor Relations Act. . . .

The second ground of defendants' motion to dismiss was that they are protected against suit by the Illinois Tort Immunity Act (Ill. Rev.Stats.1967, Ch. 85, Sec. 2–201). Under the Supremacy Clause, that statute cannot protect defendants against a cause of action grounded, as here, on a federal statute. Legislators and judges have broad immunity under Section 1983 because in enacting that statute Congress did not intend to overturn their pre-existing defense. . . . However, other officials, such as present defendants, retain only a qualified immunity, dependent on good faith action. . . . In this Court and in their brief below the defendants also rely on common law immunity, but we rejected a similar contention in Progress Development Corp. v. Mitchell, 286 F.2d 222, 231 (7th Cir. 1961), where it was held that common law immunity did not extend to members of the Deerfield, Illinois, Park Board charged with discriminating against Negroes. Unless they can show good faith action, the reach of that decision extends to the present defendants who are alleged to have discriminatorily discharged Steele and McLaughlin for their union

membership.  To hold defendants absolutely immune from this type
of suit would frustrate the very purpose of Section 1983.  .  .  .
At best, defendants' qualified immunity in this case means that they
can prevail only if they show that plaintiffs were discharged on justifiable grounds.  Thus here a successful defense on the merits merges
with a successful defense under the qualified immunity doctrine.
.  .  .

The judgment of the District Court is reversed and the cause is
remanded for trial.

## NOTES AND QUESTIONS

1.  Were tenured teachers involved in this case?

2.  Did the court hold that teachers have a constitutional right to organize
into unions in order to engage in lawful activities?  If so, what activities?  If so, what part of the constitution affords this right?  Do
you agree with the decision and the court's reasoning?  Why or why
not?

3.  Could a tenured teacher, or a probationary teacher during the term of
his contract, constitutionally be dismissed on the ground (1) that he
is a member of a union; (2) that he is a member of a union that called
for an illegal strike; or (3) that he is a member of a union that called
for an illegal strike in which he participated?

4.  What does the term "limited immunity from suit" mean?

5.  What will be the issues to be resolved at the trial of this case?  Suppose the school board shows by evidence other than union activities that
the teachers were "insubordinate" or engaged in "unprofessional" activities, what result?

6.  While essential to a complete understanding of the role of teacher organizations in education, a full development of all aspects of the law
pertaining to teacher organization, collective bargaining, the right of
public employees to strike, and their related considerations, is beyond
the scope of this book.  Only an introduction of the law will be set
forth here.  At present public employees do not come within the National Labor Relations Act; thus, teacher organization is dependent
upon state statutes where they exist and upon the common law in the
absence of state statutes.  The usual steps of organizing are these.
First of all are the initial organizing activities.  They are usually carried on by rival organizations; e. g., the National Education Association and the American Federation of Teachers.  The purpose of the
organizing activity is to obtain approval from a majority of teachers
in the district for the specific organization to represent them in negotiations with the school board.  In some states, statutes lump teachers
together with all other public employees, and allow only public-em-
ployee unions.  In these situations, it still may be possible for teachers
to obtain a separate union, or a separate division of a union, to represent them.  Generally, an election is held to determine which organization shall be certified by the appropriate state agency as the collective
bargaining representative.  Assuming that a majority votes for one

union and that state law is silent on the matter, a question can arise whether that organization shall be the exclusive bargaining agent or merely one of several. If the latter situation prevails then a board of education has the opportunity of pitting one group against another during negotiations and other activities. If one organization is designated the exclusive bargaining representative of the teachers then it will have the duty of fairly and honestly representing all the teachers, and not only those teachers who voted for it. Once the bargaining representative is selected the next step is to negotiate a collective agreement with the school board. This can be tricky, depending upon the exact way in which the law is worded and other factors. For example, suppose there is no legal authorization for a school board to negotiate, or if authorized, suppose there is no legal requirement that a school board negotiate and suppose it refuses to do so, or suppose it negotiates but refuses to do so in good faith? These are only some of the many problems that can arise. If the parties negotiate in good faith but an impasse develops, and the parties fail to resolve their differences, a specific problem can be submitted to mediation, and in some circumstances, to arbitration. Mediation involves bringing a powerless third party into the negotiations for the purposes of helping the negotiating parties modify their positions and reaching a voluntary agreement. Arbitration involves submitting the problem to arbitrators who, after a hearing on the issue, will decide the matter, and their decision will be binding, because, beforehand, the parties have agreed to be bound by it. Mediation and arbitration can also come into play when dealing with grievance concerns and other matters under a collective agreement. Assuming that a collective agreement is negotiated and that it comes into legal effect, it will create many rights and obligations between and among the school board, the teacher's organization and individual teachers. Basically, the style of decision-making within the district will change to meet the requirements of the collective agreement, affecting management decisions on such items as working conditions, salary levels, teacher assignment, transfer and dismissal. Additionally, collective agreements usually set up some type of grievance machinery through which teachers, the teacher organization and boards of education have access in order to complain. Many questions can arise; for example (1) what is the legal impact of an existing collective agreement on the power of the teachers to change their representative organization; (2) what is the legal validity of the existing collective agreement if the teachers change to another representative, or if there is a change in the employer because of school district reorganization? These and similar questions are beyond the scope of this book. The following materials illustrate some of the legal problems. Moreover, questions of constitutional freedom probably will also arise in the area of collective organization. For example, would a bargained for school board rule, or collective agreement provision be constitutional if it required all teachers to become members of and to contribute dues to a union that a majority of the teachers in that district selected as their bargaining representative? Could a teacher's union constitutionally contribute funds collected from all its members and then make contributions to support the election of a school board member who favored teacher unions or to support a political cause, both of which are opposed by some of the organization's members? Generally see, Wollett, The Coming Revolution In Public School Management, 67 Mich.L.Rev. 1017 (1969).

---

## CITY OF MADISON JOINT SCHOOL DIST. v. WISCONSIN EMPLOYMENT RELATIONS COMM.

Supreme Court of the United States, 1976.
429 U.S. 167, 97 S.Ct. 421, 50 L.Ed.2d 376.

Mr. Chief Justice BURGER delivered the opinion of the Court.

The question presented on this appeal from the Supreme Court of Wisconsin is whether a State may constitutionally require that an elected board of education prohibit teachers, other than union representatives, to speak at open meetings, at which public participation is permitted, if such speech is addressed to the subject of pending collective-bargaining negotiations.

The Madison Board of Education and Madison Teachers, Inc. (MTI), a labor union, were parties to a collective-bargaining agreement during the calendar year of 1971. In January 1971 negotiations commenced for renewal of the agreement and MTI submitted a number of proposals. One among them called for the inclusion of a so-called "fair-share" clause, which would require all teachers, whether members of MTI or not, to pay union dues to defray the costs of collective bargaining. Wisconsin law expressly permits inclusion of "fair share" provisions in municipal employee collective-bargaining agreements. Another proposal presented by the union was a provision for binding arbitration of teacher dismissals. Both of these provisions were resisted by the school board. The negotiations deadlocked in November 1971 with a number of issues still unresolved, among them "fair share" and arbitration.

During the same month, two teachers, Holmquist and Reed, who were members of the bargaining unit, but not members of the union, mailed a letter to all teachers in the district expressing opposition to the "fair share" proposal. Two hundred teachers replied, most commenting favorably on Holmquist and Reed's position. Thereupon a petition was drafted calling for a one-year delay in the implementation of "fair share" while the proposal was more closely analyzed by an impartial committee. The petition was circulated to teachers in the district on December 6, 1971. Holmquist and Reed intended to present the results of their petition effort to the school board and to MTI at the school board's public meeting that same evening.

Because of the stalemate in the negotiations, MTI arranged to have pickets present at the school board meeting. In addition, 300 to 400 teachers attended in support of the union's position. During a portion of the meeting devoted to expression of opinion by the public, the president of MTI took the floor and spoke on the subject of the ongoing negotiations. He concluded his remarks by presenting to the board a petition signed by 1,300–1,400 teachers calling for the expeditious resolution of the negotiations. Holmquist was next given the floor, after John Matthews, the business representative of MTI, unsuccessfully attempted to dissuade him from speaking. Matthews had also spoken to a member of the school board before the meeting and requested that the board refuse to permit Holmquist to speak. Holmquist stated that he represented "an informal committee of 72 teachers in 49 schools" and that he desired to inform the board of education, as he had already informed the union, of the results of an informational survey concerning the "fair share" clause. He then read the petition which had been circulated to the teachers in the district that morning and stated that in the 31 schools from which reports had been received, 53% of the teachers had already signed the petition.

Holmquist stated that neither side had adequately addressed the issue of "fair share" and that teachers were confused about the meaning of the proposal. He concluded by saying: "Due to this confusion, we wish to take no stand on the proposal itself, but ask only that all alternatives be presented clearly to all teachers and more importantly to the general public to whom we are all responsible. We ask simply for communication, not confrontation." The sole response from the school board was a question by the president inquiring whether Holmquist intended to present the board with the petition. Holmquist answered that he would. Holmquist's presentation had lasted approximately 2½ minutes.

Later that evening, the board met in executive session and voted a proposal acceding to all of the union's demands with the exception of "fair share." During a negotiating session the following morning, MTI accepted the proposal and a contract was signed on December 14, 1971.

(1)

In January 1972, MTI filed a complaint with the Wisconsin Employment Relations Commission (WERC) claiming that the board had committed a prohibited labor practice by permitting Holmquist to speak at the December 6 meeting. MTI claimed that in so doing the board had engaged in negotiations with a member of the bargaining unit other than the exclusive collective-bargaining representative, in violation of Wis.Stat. §§ 111.70(3)(a)1, 4 (1973). Following a hearing the Commission concluded that the board was guilty of the prohibited labor practice and ordered that it "immediately cease and desist from permitting employes, other than representatives of Madison Teachers Inc., to appear and speak at meetings of the Board of Education, on matters subject to collective bargaining between it and

Madison Teachers Inc." The Commission's action was affirmed by the Circuit Court of Dane County.

The Supreme Court of Wisconsin affirmed. . . . The court held that abridgment of the speech in this case was justified in order "to avoid the dangers attendant upon relative chaos in labor management relations."

(2)

The Wisconsin court perceived "clear and present danger" based upon its conclusion that Holmquist's speech before the school board constituted "negotiation" with the board. Permitting such "negotiation," the court reasoned, would undermine the bargaining exclusivity guaranteed the majority union under Wis.Stat. § 111.70(3)(a)4 (1973). From that premise it concluded that teachers' First Amendment rights could be limited. Assuming, *arguendo*, that such a "danger" might in some circumstances justify some limitation of First Amendment rights, we are unable to read this record as presenting such danger as would justify curtailing speech.

The Wisconsin Supreme Court's conclusion that Holmquist's terse statement during the public meeting constituted negotiation with the board was based upon its adoption of the lower court's determination that, " '[e]ven though Holmquist's statement superficially appears to be merely a "position statement," the court deems from the total circumstances that it constituted "negotiating." ' " This cryptic conclusion seems to ignore the ancient wisdom that calling a thing by a name does not make it so. Holmquist did not seek to bargain or offer to enter into any bargain with the board, nor does it appear that he was authorized by any other teachers to enter into any agreement on their behalf. Although his views were not consistent with those of MTI, communicating such views to the employer, could not change the fact that MTI alone was authorized to negotiate and to enter into a contract with the board.

Moreover, the school board meeting at which Holmquist was permitted to speak was open to the public. He addressed the school board not merely as one of its employees but also as a concerned citizen, seeking to express his views on an important decision of his government. We have held that teachers may not be "compelled to relinquish the First Amendment rights they would otherwise enjoy as citizens to comment on matters of public interest in connection with the operation of the public schools in which they work." Pickering v. Board of Education. Where the State has opened a forum for direct citizen involvement, it is difficult to find justification for excluding teachers who make up the overwhelming proportion of school employees and who are most vitally concerned with the proceedings. It is conceded that any citizen could have presented precisely the same points and provided the board with the same information as did Holmquist.

Regardless of the extent to which true contract negotiations between a public body and its employees may be regulated—an issue we need not consider at this time—the participation in public discussion of public business cannot be confined to one category of interested individuals. To permit one side of a debatable public question to have a monopoly in expressing its views to the government is the antithesis of constitutional guarantees. Whatever its duties as an employer, when the board sits in public meetings to conduct public business and hear the views of citizens, it may not be required to discriminate between speakers on the basis of their employment, or the content of their speech.

(3)

The WERC's order is not limited to a determination that a prohibited labor practice had taken place in the past; it also restrains future conduct. By prohibiting the school board from "permitting employes . . . to appear and speak at meetings of the Board of Education" the order constitutes an indirect, but effective, prohibition on persons such as Holmquist from communicating with their government. The order would have a substantial impact upon virtually all communication between teachers and the school board. The order prohibits speech by teachers "on matters subject to collective bargaining." As the dissenting opinion below noted, however, there is virtually no subject concerning the operation of the school system that could not also be characterized as a potential subject of collective bargaining. Teachers not only constitute the overwhelming bulk of employees of the school system, but they are the very core of that system; restraining teachers' expressions to the board on matters involving the operation of the schools would seriously impair the board's ability to govern the district. . . . The challenged portion of the order is designed to govern speech and conduct in the future, not to punish past conduct, and as such it is the essence of prior restraint.

The judgment of the Wisconsin Supreme Court is reversed, and the case is remanded to that court for further proceedings not inconsistent with this opinion.

Reversed and remanded.

Mr. Justice BRENNAN, with whom Mr. Justice MARSHALL joins, concurring in the judgment.

By stating that "the extent to which true contract negotiations . . . may be regulated [is] an issue we need not consider at this time," the Court's opinion treats as open a question the answer to which I think is abundantly clear. Wisconsin has adopted, as unquestionably the State constitutionally may adopt, a statutory policy that authorizes public bodies to accord exclusive recognition to representatives for collective bargaining chosen by the majority of an appropriate unit of employees. In that circumstance the First Amendment plainly does not prohibit Wisconsin from limiting attendance at a collective-bargaining session to school board and union bargaining representatives and denying Holmquist the right to attend and speak at the session. That proposition is implicit in the words of Mr. Justice Holmes, that the "Constitution does not require all public acts to be done in town meeting or an assembly of the whole." Certainly in the context of Wisconsin's adoption of the exclusivity principle as a matter of state policy governing relations between state bodies and unions of their employees, "[t]here must be a limit to individual argument in such matters if government is to go on." For the First Amendment does not command "that people who want to [voice] their views have a constitutional right to do so whenever and however and wherever they please." For example, this Court's "own conferences [and] the meetings of other official bodies gathered in executive session" may be closed to the public without implicating any constitutional rights whatever. Thus, the Wisconsin Supreme Court was correct in stating that there is nothing unconstitutional about legislation commanding that in closed bargaining sessions a government body may admit, hear the views of, and respond to only the designated representatives of a union selected by the majority of its employees.

But the First Amendment plays a crucially different role when, as here, a government body has either by its own decision or under statutory command, determined to open its decision making processes to public view and participation. In such case, the state body has created a public forum dedicated to the expression of views by the general public. "Once a forum is opened up to assembly or speaking by some groups, government may not prohibit others from assembling or speaking on the basis of what they intend to say. Selective exclusions from a public forum may not be based on content alone, and may not be justified by reference to content alone." . . . The State could no more prevent Holmquist from speaking at this public forum than it could prevent him from publishing the same views in a newspaper or proclaiming them from a soapbox.

I therefore agree that the judgment of the Wisconsin Supreme Court be reversed.

———

### CARY v. BOARD OF EDUC.

United States District Court, 1977.
427 F.Supp. 945 (D.C.Colo.).

MATSCH, District Judge.

This case has been submitted on stipulated facts with both plaintiffs and defendants moving for summary judgment.

Each of the plaintiffs is a senior high school English teacher employed by the defendant school district under a tenure system established by state statute. The plaintiffs have taught or are teaching elective courses designated as "Contemporary Literature," "Contemporary Poetry," and "American Masters" for eleventh and twelfth grade students, using contemporary literature and poetry as course material.

Three of the plaintiffs have structured these courses to permit the students to select almost all of the material to be read, individually. The others teach the same courses but assign most of the reading, with some electives. All of these teachers use group and class discussion of the books and poems read by the students.

The individual defendants are the incumbent members of the Board of Education governing Adams-Arapahoe School District 28–J. In Colorado, school board members are elected at regularly scheduled elections for fixed terms of office, and they are also subject to recall at a special election initiated by petition. With some exceptions, which are not relevant here, local school districts in Colorado are autonomous in the control and management of their public schools through twelfth grade. Colorado also has a compulsory attendance law which requires all persons to attend public schools from age seven to their sixteenth birthday, with certain statutory exceptions.

In January, 1975, the defendants formed a committee of teachers, students, parents and school board members, called the "High School Language Arts Text Evaluation Committee" to review text material. That committee met publicly, solicited comments from the public, and submitted a report on January 6, 1976. A minority report was also submitted.

At a regularly scheduled public meeting on January 12, 1976 the defendants, by a majority vote, approved a list of 1275 textbooks for use in the high schools and they disapproved the following ten books:

*A Clockwork Orange* by Anthony Burgess

*The Exorcist* by William P. Blatty

*The Reincarnation of Peter Proud* by Max Ehrlich

*New American Poetry* by Donald Allen

*Starting from San Francisco* by Lawrence Ferlinghetti

*The Yage Letters* by William Burroughs and Allen Ginsberg

*Coney Island of the Mind* by Lawrence Ferlinghetti

*Kaddish and Other Poems* by Allen Ginsberg

*Lunch Poems* by Frank O'Hara

*Rosemary's Baby* by Ira Levin

Each of these books had been included in reading lists used by the plaintiffs in their courses and none of them has been ordered removed from the school libraries.

The parties agreed that these ten books are not legally obscene; that they do not represent any system of thought or philosophy; and that the exclusion of these books could not be considered to be an abuse of discretion or otherwise contrary to any constitutional standards applicable to an appropriate decision-maker.

On January 13, 1976, the school board issued a memorandum, directing that the subject ten books "will not be purchased, nor used for class assignment, nor will an individual be given credit for reading any of these books." That memorandum also cautioned that any materials not included in the approved list of books could be used in the subject courses only with prior approval of the Division of Instructional Services. At all times the plaintiffs and defendants have followed a policy of permitting students, with parental approval, to request alternatives to assignments of material which offends them.

The Aurora Education Association (AEA), a non-profit Colorado corporation, acting as the representative of all teachers employed in the defendant school district, conducted negotiations with the school board, resulting in a collective bargaining agreement, dated February 13, 1976, effective for the years 1975–1978. One item of disagreement during those negotiations was the issue of final authority on matters relating to curriculum and selection of instructional material. The initial AEA proposal provided for final determination of questioned materials by a committee of the Teachers Advisory Council. It also provided that the recommendations of the Teachers Advisory Council could be rejected by the school board only for "good and just cause shown."

That proposal was rejected and the provisions agreed upon in the signed agreement include the following:

*Academic Freedom.* The parties seek to educate young people in the democratic tradition, to foster a recognition of individual freedom and social responsibility, to inspire meaningful awareness of and respect for the Constitution and the Bill of Rights.

Freedom of individual conscience, association, and expression will be encouraged and fairness in procedures will be observed both to safeguard the legitimate interests of the schools and to exhibit by appropriate examples the basic objectives of a democratic society as set forth in the Constitution of the United States and the State of Colorado.

The final responsibility in the determination of the above rests with the Board.

Article V, "Board Rights", at pages 7–8 of the agreement, provides that the board shall have the right to "[d]etermine the processes, techniques, methods and means of teaching any and all subjects."

The collective bargaining agreement includes a grievance procedure, with nonbinding arbitration.

Each of the plaintiffs is an active member of the AEA.  .  .  .

The professional judgment of the plaintiffs is that the ten excluded books should be available for use in teaching the subject courses.

The defendants agree that the following activities by the plaintiffs would be a violation of the January 13, 1976 directive:

> (a) Adding any of the subject textbooks to the reading list in their courses;
>
> (b) Assigning the reading of any of the subject textbooks;
>
> (c) Giving any student any credit in courses for reading any of the subject textbooks;
>
> (d) Reading aloud or causing to be read aloud any of the subject textbooks in the classroom during class time;
>
> or (e) Discussing with students in the classroom during class time any of these materials at such length so as to amount to a constructive assignment of the materials.

.  .  .  the plaintiffs assert that they have a constitutionally-protected right to select teaching materials for these elective courses for the eleventh and twelfth grades on the basis of their professional judgment as to the appropriateness of the materials for the subject of the courses and the ability of the students. The logical extension of plaintiffs' contention is that they can teach without accountability to their employer.

.  .  .

This case involves the issue of academic freedom in its purest form. The plaintiffs are not seeking to avoid restriction of any rights which they share with all other citizens. They are asserting a freedom peculiar to their positions as teachers. While such a right has been recognized here, for jurisdictional purposes, as a specific application of the general freedom of communication protected by the First Amendment, it is now important to acknowledge limitations in its scope and the manner of its exercise.

Teachers are employees who do not differ from other employees in their obligations to the employers in matters involving the administration and operation of the place of employment. Maintaining the schools as a special marketplace of ideas does not require the immunization of teachers from such controls as school boards exercise in common with other kinds of employers.

What separates teachers from production workers is the difference in the products which are the end results of their efforts. While an automobile manufacturer can compel adherence to such directions as may be necessary to make uniform models of vehicles according to strict design specifications, there can be no comparable power for a school board to design and specify uniformity in the graduates of its schools.

Academic freedom as the protection of open communication in the processes of teaching does not restrict the public authority to control the educational program and the place where it occurs. We will have such schools operating at such times and places with such curricula as the elected representatives of the people shall determine; but involuntary restrictions on the individual liberty of teachers and students to communicate, directly and indirectly, where such open expression is consistent with the attained level of educational development, are matters of constitutional concern.

The collective bargaining agreement is the central fact in this case. That is what alters the controversy from the abstraction of academic freedom to the specific commitment of a contractual obligation. Through the AEA the teachers in the defendant school district have elected to surrender their individual freedom of professionalism for the security of protectionism by collective action and a group contract. In so doing, they have voluntarily submitted themselves to the employer-employee model of the teacher's relationship to the school board for everything which is within the scope of the contract and that includes the authority to control communication through the assignment of reading material.

But for the bargained agreement, the plaintiffs would prevail here. The selection of the subject books as material for these elective courses in these grades is clearly within the protected area recognized as academic freedom. Additionally, the school board's policy directive of January 13, 1976, prohibiting the use of any material not included in the list of 1275 books without first obtaining approval of the Division of Instructional Services is the kind of broad prior restraint which is particularly offensive to First Amendment freedom.

Because of the bargained agreement, the plaintiffs' claims must be denied. Whatever may be the scope of the protection of the First and Fourteenth Amendments for a freedom to communicate with students, directly in classroom speech or indirectly through reading assignments, such protection does not present a legal impediment to the freedom to contract. Thus, a teacher may bargain away the freedom to communicate in her official role in the same manner as an editorial writer who agrees to write the views of a publisher or an actor who contracts to speak the author's script. One can, for consideration, agree to teach according to direction.

The combination of teachers into bargaining units with the coercive power of group action is a contradiction of the kind of individual freedom protected by the First Amendment. Conformity to the consensus of a peer group is the essence of a labor organization, and if teachers seek to enjoy the benefits of such concert they must respect the contract which results from the bargaining process and the rights which it gives to the employer. Teachers may elect to subject themselves to employer control through such contracts and thereby abandon the protection of their professionalism. Here the plaintiffs are acknowledged members of the AEA and that organization, acting as their agent, has yielded final authority to the Board of Education for the choice of instructional material. Each of these plaintiffs is bound by that agreement and none of them can act in contradiction of it. In full context, that contract says that while the school board agrees to respect their professional views, in the event of a conflict the Aurora teachers will accept the directions of their employer. The plaintiffs are bound by that commitment and they may not now seek to avoid it by calling upon a constitutional freedom to act independently and individually. Accordingly, it is concluded that the action of the defendants was taken pursuant to contractual authority and does not infringe upon any rights of plaintiffs. It is therefore,

ORDERED, that the defendants' motion for summary judgment is granted, and judgment shall enter for the defendants with costs to be taxed.

---

## ASSOCIATED TEACHERS OF HUNTINGTON v. BOARD OF EDUC.

New York Supreme Court, 1969.
60 Misc.2d 443, 303 N.Y.S.2d 469.

WILLIAM R. GEILER, Justice. Application by respondent, Board of Education to stay arbitration proceedings commenced by claimant Associated Teachers of Huntington.

The respondent and claimant entered into a contract on June 10, 1968 with reference to the employment of teachers in the Union Free School District No. 3 within the Town of Huntington, Suffolk County.

The contract includes a procedure for the submission of grievances to arbitration and defines a grievance in Article II A (1) in the following terms:

"A grievance is a claim which involves the interpretation and application of the terms and provisions of this contract."

The contract also includes a provision for giving notice of termination of employment to non-tenure teachers. This provision is contained in Article XVIII, Section A, paragraph 3 of the agreement and provides:

"Non-tenure teachers will be notified of termination of employment not later than March 1st, except that for the third year, the teacher will be notified not later than January 1."

The respondent, of May 1, 1969, sent a notice of termination of employment to a Samuel Grenz, a non-tenure teacher in his initial year of employment and a member of the claimant Teacher's Association. This notice was admittedly sent two months after the contractual requirement that all such notices be sent no later than March 1, 1969.

The claimant filed a demand for arbitration in accordance with Article II of the subject contract on the ground that there has been a violation of Article XVIII, Section A, paragraph 3 of the contract dealing with notice of termination of employment.

The respondent contends that this particular provision, governing the timing of termination notices to non-tenure teachers, is outside the scope of the grievance procedure and thus not subject to arbitration. The respondent Board, in support of this contention, cites Article XVIII, Section C of the contract, which provides:

"No tenure teacher shall be disciplined, reprimanded, reduced in rank or compensation, suspended, demoted, transferred, terminated or otherwise deprived of any professional advantage without just cause. In no case shall this be done publicly unless so requested by the teacher. Any such action, including adverse evaluation of teacher performance or a violation of professional ethics asserted by the Board or any agent thereof, shall be subject to the grievance procedure set forth in this Agreement, provided that in the case of a non-tenure teacher, termination shall not be grievable."

The respondent Board also implies that Article XVIII, Section A paragraph 3 is contrary to certain statutory provisions of the State of New York and therefore is void.

Does the subject contract preclude arbitration with reference to the procedure used in terminating the employment of a non-tenure teacher?

The respondent, in arguing that the language of the contract precludes arbitration, relies primarily on Section C of Article XVIII, which deals not with the procedure to be followed in terminating employment of non-tenure teacher but with the right of the School Board to terminate a tenure teacher's employment for just cause. This particular provision, as indicated above, also provides that the

Board may terminate the employment of a non-tenure teacher without having to demonstrate just cause in an arbitration proceeding.

There is no question that a non-tenure teacher, under Paragraph C of Article XVIII, is prohibited from challenging in arbitration the grounds for termination of employment and the claimant readily admits this fact.  However, this prohibition, in and of itself, does not mean that a non-tenure teacher is barred from challenging the "procedure" used in terminating employment.  Otherwise, Section A of Article XVIII would be meaningless and there is no language in the contract which declares or implies that this section dealing with notice of termination of employment of a non-tenure teacher was meant to be moot and unenforceable.  The Court has been unable to find any language in the broad arbitration provisions set forth in Article II of the subject contract which would imply that the procedure used in the termination of a non-tenure teacher was prohibited from being the subject of an arbitration proceeding.

It has been the established law in this State that questions concerning arbitrability are to be resolved in arbitration and not in a court, unless there is a clear and unquestionable exclusion from arbitration.  This basic rule of law was clearly enunciated  .   .   .  in the following language:

> "It is now a familiar rule that, where a labor agreement contains an arbitration provision, the presumption is that questions of arbitrability are for the arbitrator  *  *  *.  In the last analysis, arbitrations are the result of agreements between the parties and they draw their essence from those agreements.  It is only where the parties have employed language which clearly rebuts the presumption of arbitrability  *  *  *  that the matter may be determined by the courts.  In the absence of such unmistakably clear language  *  *  *  the matter is sent to the arbitrator for his determination on the merits."

The Court finds that there is no prohibition against submitting the question of the procedure used in terminating employment of a non-tenure teacher and the best that can be said for respondent's position herein is that there is doubt as to whether the provisions in question may or may not be arbitrable.  In such circumstances, the question of arbitrability must be submitted to an arbitrator for resolution.  .   .   .

Are school boards prohibited by law from agreeing to provide a notice of termination to non-tenure teachers?  Is such an agreement unenforceable?

The respondent Board has advanced the argument that the notice of termination provision for non-tenure teachers is, even though freely agreed to by them, void on the following basis:

1) Section 3012 of the Education Law does not require notice by March 1, and therefore any such requirement in the subject contract is illegal.

2) The arbitration provisions under the subject contract, if they cover the subject grievance, is broader than Section 684 of the General Municipal Law and is therefore void.

Section 3012 of the Education Law provides in part:

"1. Teachers * * * shall be appointed by the board of education * * * for a probationary period of three years. The service of a person appointed to any of such positions may be discontinued at any time during such probationary period * * *.

"2. * * * Each person who is not to be recommended for appointment on tenure, shall be notified by the superintendent of schools in writing not later than sixty days immediately preceding the expiration of his probationary period."

There can be no dispute that this section allows termination of employment of a non-tenure teacher at any time during his probationary period without a hearing. It is also undisputable that this section does not forbid providing a non-tenure teacher with prior notice of termination. In fact, Paragraph 2 of Section 3012 supra, mandates sixty days notice of termination where the non-tenure teacher's employment is to be terminated after the full three year period. The statute, by requiring notice of termination "not later than sixty days" before termination, impliedly permits notice before that day. Certainly this statutory provision does not bar earlier notice.

The respondent seems to imply that any provision which is broader than the statutory benefits is invalid. In other words, the statutory minimum according to respondent's reasoning is also the maximum. Is a contract of employment invalid because it provides for a wage in excess of the minimum wage set by the State of New York? The position of the respondent is without legal foundation or rational basis.

There is also no legal basis for respondent's contention that Section 684 of the General Municipal Law prohibits the negotiation of a better or broader grievance procedure. In fact, Section 684 was never intended to provide the exclusive machinery for the resolution of grievances concerning public employees as can be seen from the following language contained in Section 684 of the General Municipal Law:

"Each government which, on or before October first, nineteen hundred sixty-three, has not established and does not thereafter maintain a two stage grievance procedure for all its employees shall, acting through the chief executive officer of each government establish and administer a basic grievance procedure for the employees of such government in accordance with the provisions of this section and section six hundred three of this article."

Thus, under this section, a board of education is free to adopt its own grievance procedure.

Certainly, after 1967, not only is the subject type of arbitration permissible, but it was mandated by the public policy of this State. In 1967 . . . the public policy of this State was set forth as follows in Section 200 of the Civil Service Law as amd.:

"The legislature of the state of New York declares that it is the public policy of the state and the purpose of this act to promote harmonious and cooperative relationships between government and its employees * * * These policies are best effectuated by * * * (b) requiring the state, local governments and other political subdivisions to negotiate with, and enter into written agreements with employee organizations representing public employees * * * "

This Court would be remiss if it stayed the arbitration proceeding herein which is not prohibited by statute and which is in accordance with the public policy of this State. . . .

---

## HORTONVILLE JOINT SCHOOL DIST. v. HORTONVILLE EDUC. ASS'N

Supreme Court of the United States, 1976.
426 U.S. 482, 96 S.Ct. 2308, 49 L.Ed.2d 1.

Mr. Chief Justice BURGER delivered the opinion of the Court.

We granted certiorari in this case to determine whether School Board members, vested by state law with the power to employ and dismiss teachers, could, consistent with the Due Process Clause of the Fourteenth Amendment, dismiss teachers engaged in a strike prohibited by state law.

I

The petitioners are a Wisconsin school district, the seven members of its School Board, and three administrative employees of the district. Respondents are teachers suing on behalf of all teachers in the district and the Hortonville Education Association (HEA), the collective-bargaining agent for the district's teachers.

During the 1972–1973 school year Hortonville teachers worked under a master collective-bargaining agreement; negotiations were conducted for renewal of the contract, but no agreement was reached for the 1973–1974 school year. The teachers continued to work while negotiations proceeded during the year without reaching agreement. On March 18, 1974, the members of the teachers' union went on strike, in direct violation of Wisconsin law. On March 20, the district superintendent sent all teachers a letter inviting them to return to work; a few did so. On March 23, he sent another letter, asking the 86 teachers still on strike to return, and reminding them that strikes by public employees were illegal; none of these teachers returned to work. After conducting classes with substitute teachers on March 26 and 27, the Board decided to conduct disciplinary hearings for each of the teachers on strike. Individual notices were sent to each teacher setting hearings for April 1, 2, and 3.

On April 1, most of the striking teachers appeared before the Board with counsel. Their attorney indicated that the teachers did not want individual hearings, but preferred to be treated as a group. Although counsel agreed that the teachers were on strike, he raised several procedural objections to the hearings. He also argued that the Board was not sufficiently impartial to exercise discipline over the striking teachers and that the Due Process Clause of the Fourteenth Amendment required an independent, unbiased decision-maker. An offer of proof was tendered to demonstrate that the strike had been provoked by the Board's failure to meet teachers' demands, and respondents' counsel asked to cross-examine Board members individually. The Board rejected the request, but permitted counsel to make the offer of proof, aimed at showing that the Board's contract offers were unsatisfactory, that the Board used coercive and illegal bargaining tactics, and that teachers in the district had been locked out by the Board.

On April 2, the Board voted to terminate the employment of striking teachers, and advised them by letter to that effect. However, the same letter invited all teachers on strike to reapply for teaching positions. One teacher accepted the invitation and returned to work; the Board hired replacements to fill the remaining positions.

## II

The sole issue in this case is whether the Due Process Clause of the Fourteenth Amendment prohibits this School Board from making the decision to dismiss teachers admittedly engaged in a strike and persistently refusing to return to their duties. The Wisconsin Supreme Court held that state law prohibited the strike and that termination of the striking teachers' employment was within the Board's statutory authority. We are, of course, bound to accept the interpretation of Wisconsin law by the highest court of the State. The only decision remaining for the Board therefore involved the exercise of its discretion as to what should be done to carry out the duties the law placed on the Board.

Respondents' argument rests in part on doctrines that have no application to this case. They seem to argue that the Board members had some personal or official stake in the decision whether the teachers should be dismissed, and that the Board has manifested some personal bitterness toward the teachers, aroused by teacher criticism of the Board during the strike.

. . . the teachers did not show, and the Wisconsin courts did not find, that the Board members had the kind of personal or financial stake in the decision that might create a conflict of interest, and there is nothing in the record to support charges of personal animosity. The Wisconsin Supreme Court was careful "not to suggest . . . that the board members were anything but dedicated public servants, trying to provide the district with quality education . . . within its limited budget." That court's analysis would seem to be confirmed by the Board's repeated invitations for striking teachers to return to work, the final invitation being contained in the letter that notified them of their discharge.

The only other factor suggested to support the claim of bias is that the School Board was involved in the negotiations that preceded and precipitated the striking teachers' discharge. Participation in those negotiations was a statutory duty of the Board. The Wisconsin Supreme Court held that this involvement, without more, disqualified the Board from deciding whether the teachers should be dismissed.

. . . Respondents' claim and the Wisconsin Supreme Court's holding reduce to the argument that the Board was biased because it negotiated with the teachers on behalf of the school district without reaching agreement and learned about the reasons for the strike in the course of negotiating. From those premises the Wisconsin court concluded that the Board lost its statutory power to determine that the strike and persistent refusal to terminate it amounted to conduct serious enough to warrant discharge of the strikers. Wisconsin statutes vest in the Board the power to discharge its employees, a power of every employer, whether it has negotiated with the employees before discharge or not. The Fourteenth Amendment permits a court to strip the Board of the otherwise unremarkable power the Wisconsin Legislature has given it only if the Board's prior involvement in negotiating with the teachers means that it cannot act consistently with due process.

Due process, as this Court has repeatedly held, is a term that "negates any concept of inflexible procedures universally applicable to every imaginable situation." Determining what process is due in a given setting requires the Court to take into account the individual's stake in the decision at issue as well as the State's interest in a particular procedure for making it. Our assessment of the interests of the parties in this case leads to the conclusion that . . . the Board's prior role as negotiator does not disqualify it to decide that the public interest in maintaining uninterrupted classroom work required that teachers striking in violation of state law be discharged.

The teachers' interest in these proceedings is, of course, self-evident. They wished to avoid termination of their employment, obviously an important interest, but one that must be examined in light of several factors. Since the teachers admitted that they were engaged in a work stoppage, there was no possibility of an erroneous factual determination on this critical threshold issue. Moreover what the teachers claim as a property right was the expectation that the jobs they had left to go and remain on strike in violation of law would remain open to them. . . .

. . . The Board's decision whether to dismiss striking teachers involves broad considerations, and does not in the main turn on the Board's view of the "seriousness" of the teachers' conduct or the factors they urge mitigated their violation of state law. It was not an adjudicative decision, for the Board had an obligation to make a decision based on its own answer to an important question of policy: What choice among the alternative responses to the teachers' strike will best serve the interests of the school system, the interests of the parents and children who depend on the system, and the interests of the citizens whose taxes support it? The Board's decision was only incidentally a disciplinary decision; it had significant governmental and public policy dimensions as well.

State law vests the governmental, or policymaking, function exclusively in the School Board and the State has two interests in keeping it there. First, the Board is the body with overall responsibility for the governance of the school district; it must cope with the myriad day-to-day problems of a modern public school system including the severe consequences of a teachers' strike; by virtue of electing them the constitutents have declared the Board members qualified to deal with these problems, and they are accountable to the voters for the manner in which they perform. Second, the state legislature has given to the Board the power to employ and dismiss teachers, as a part of the balance it has struck in the area of municipal labor relations; altering those statutory powers as a matter of federal due process clearly changes that balance. Permitting the Board to make the decision at issue here preserves its control over school district affairs, leaves the balance of power in labor relations where the state legislature struck it, and assures that the decision whether to dismiss the teachers will be made by the body responsible for that decision under state law.

### III

Respondents have failed to demonstrate that the decision to terminate their employment was infected by the sort of bias that we have held to disqualify other decisionmakers as a matter of federal due process. A showing that the Board was "involved" in the events preceding this decision, in light of the important interest in leaving with the Board the power given by the state legislature, is not enough to overcome the presumption of honesty and integrity in policymakers with decisionmaking power. Accordingly, we hold that the Due Process Clause of the Fourteenth Amendment did not guarantee respondents that the decision to terminate their employment would be made or reviewed by a body other than the School Board.

Reversed and remanded.

Mr. Justice STEWART, with whom Mr. Justice BRENNAN and Mr. Justice MARSHALL join, dissenting.

The issue in this case is whether the discharge of the respondent teachers by the petitioner School Board violated the Due Process Clause of the Fourteenth Amendment because the Board members were not impartial decisionmakers. It is now well established that "a biased decisionmaker [is] constitutionally unacceptable [and] 'our system of law has always endeavored to prevent even the probability of unfairness.'"

In order to ascertain whether there is a constitutionally unacceptable danger of partiality, both the nature of the particular decision and the interest of the decisionmaker in its outcome must be examined. . . .

. . .

. . . I would . . . remand this case to the Wisconsin Supreme Court for it to determine whether, on the one hand, the School Board is charged with considering the reasonableness of the strike in light of its own actions, or is, on the other, wholly free, as the Court today assumes, to exercise its discretion in deciding whether to discharge the teachers.

Under the petitioners' view of the Wisconsin law, the discharge determination is purely a policy judgment involving an assessment of the best interest of the school system. Since that judgment does not require the Board to assess its own conduct during the negotiations, and since there is no indication that the Board members have a financial or personal interest in its outcome, the only basis for a claim of partiality rests on the Board's knowledge of the events leading to the strike acquired through its participation in the negotiation process. As the Court notes, however, "[m]ere familiarity with the facts of a case gained by an agency in the performance of its statutory role does not . . . disqualify a decisionmaker."

But a distinctly different constitutional claim is presented if, as the respondents contend, the School Board members must evaluate their own conduct in determining whether dismissal is a reasonable sanction to impose on the striking teachers. Last Term in *Withrow v. Larkin,* the Court noted that "[a]llowing a decisionmaker to review and evaluate his own prior decisions raises problems that are not present" where the bias issue rests exclusively on familiarity with the facts of a case. Apart from considerations of financial interest or personal hostility, the Court has found that officials "directly involved in making recommendations cannot always have complete objectivity in evaluating them."

"[U]nder a realistic appraisal of psychological tendencies and human weakness," I believe that there is a constitutionally unacceptable danger of bias where school board members are required to assess the reasonableness of their own actions during heated contract negotiations that have culminated in a teachers' strike. If, therefore, the respondents' interpretation of the state law is correct, then I would agree with the Wisconsin Supreme Court that "the board was not an impartial decision maker in a constitutional sense and that the [teachers] were denied due process of law."

For the reasons stated, I would vacate the judgment before us and remand this case to the Supreme Court of Wisconsin.

## NOTES AND QUESTIONS

1. What did the union want? Why? The school board? Why?

2. What was the issue(s) in this case and the reasons given by the court? Do you agree? Why or why not?

3. Suppose after this case, the teacher organization, through its parent organization, "sanctioned" the school district by black-listing it, would such action be lawful? In the first appellate court opinion discussing blacklisting the Supreme Court of New Jersey said:

> "And with respect to blacklisting of the school district and the scheme of 'sanctions' upon teachers who offer or take employment with a 'sanctioned' school board, it can escape no one that the purpose is to back up a refusal of others to continue to work. At a minimum the object is to withhold additional services a school district may need to discharge its public duty, which, as we have said, is no less illegal. Such an illegal agreement may come into being at time of the strike or may antedate it. If individuals enter into a union or association on terms that upon the occurrence of some stipulated event or signal they will impede government in its recruitment of services, that very arrangement constitutes an agreement the law denounces. An agreement not to seek, accept, or solicit employment in government whenever the upper echelon of the union makes a prescribed pronouncement is, no less, than an accomplished shutdown, a thrust at the vitality of government, and comes within the same policy which denounces a concerted strike or quit or slowdown or other obstruction of the performance of official duties." Board of Education v. New Jersey Ed. Assoc., 53 N.J.2d 29, 247 A.2d 867 (1969).

Do you agree? Should work stoppages, work slowdowns or blacklisting be treated, in law, like a strike? If so, what other powers do teacher's organizations possess to coerce recalcitrant school boards? Should they have any? Could the problem presented by strikes of public employees be correctly and constitutionally resolved by a state statute requiring that in the event the teacher organization and the school board reach an impasse and fail to agree on a matter, then that matter shall be submitted to compulsory, not voluntary, arbitration, and both parties shall be bound by the arbitrators' decision? Would it make any difference who the arbitrators were? Suppose there were a three member panel, and the teachers organization and the school board, in its discretion, selected one member each and the third member were selected by them jointly, or suppose all three members had to be selected jointly, which scheme is better; why? Is some other procedure better?

4.   Connecticut General Statutes, Title 10, provide:

"Sec. 10.153d. DUTY TO NEGOTIATE. The town or regional board of education and the organization designated or elected as the exclusive representative for the appropriate unit, through designated officials or their representatives, shall have the duty to negotiate with respect to salaries and other conditions of employment about which either party wishes to negotiate and such duty shall include the obligation of such board of education to meet at reasonable times, including meetings appropriately related to the budget-making process, and confer in good faith with respect to salaries and other conditions of employment, or the negotiation of an agreement, or any question arising thereunder and the execution of a written contract incorporating any agreement reached, if requested by either party, but such obligation shall not compel either party to agree to a proposal or require the making of a concession. The board of education of any town school district shall file forthwith a signed copy of any such contract with the town clerk. Any regional board of education shall file a signed copy of any such contract with the town clerk in each member town. The terms of such contract shall be binding on the legislative body of the town or regional school district, unless such body rejects such contract at a regular or special meeting called for such purpose within thirty days of the signing of the contract. Any regional board of education shall call a district meeting to consider such contract within such thirty-day period if the chief executive officer of any member town so requests in writing within fifteen days of the receipt of the signed copy of the contract by the town clerk in such town. The body charged with making annual appropriations in any school district shall appropriate to the board of education whatever funds are required to implement the terms of any contract not rejected pursuant to this section. If the legislative body rejects such contract within such period, the parties shall renegotiate the terms of the contract in accordance with the procedure in this section. The town or regional board of education, and its representatives, agents and superintendents shall not interfere, restrain or coerce employees in derogation of the rights guaranteed by sections 2 through 5 of this act and section 10–153c of the 1967 supplement to the general statutes, and, in the absence of any recognition or certification as the exclusive representative as provided by section 2 of this act, all organizations seeking to represent members of the teaching profession shall be accorded equal treatment with respect to access to teachers, principals, members of the board of education, records, mail boxes and school facilities and participation in discussions with respect to salaries and other conditions of employment.

"Sec. 10–153e.  STRIKE PROHIBITED.  No certified professional employee shall, in an effort to effect a settlement of any disagreement with his employing board of education, engage in any strike or concerted refusal to render services.  This provision may be enforced in the Superior Court for any county in which said board of education is located by an ex parte temporary injunction issued by said court or a judge thereof; provided, however, that if such injunction is issued, such employee may file a motion to dissolve said injunction and a hearing upon said motion shall be held by the superior court not later than three days after service of said motion upon said board of education pursuant to an order of court or a judge thereof.

"Sec. 10f–153f.  MEDIATION AND ARBITRATION OF DISAGREEMENTS.  (a) The governor shall appoint not less than ten or more than twenty-five persons to serve on an arbitration panel as provided in subsection (c) of this section from the effective date of this act through December 31, 1970.  Except as provided above, the governor shall appoint before the first day of December in the year of his election ten persons to serve on such panel, and he may appoint additional persons to the panel at any time provided the total number of persons serving on the panel shall not exceed twenty-five.  Each appointee shall serve until the last day of December following the first gubernatorial election after his appointment.  Persons appointed to the arbitration panel shall serve without compensation but each shall receive the per diem fee in lieu of expenses provided for arbitrators in section 31–94 for each day during which he is engaged in the arbitration of a dispute pursuant to this act.  The parties to the dispute so arbitrated shall pay the fee in accordance with subsection (c) of this section.  (b) If any town or regional board of education can not agree with the exclusive representatives of a teachers' or administrators' unit after negotiation concerning the terms and conditions of employment applicable to the employees in such unit, either party may submit the issues to the secretary for mediation.  If the parties fail to initiate mediation and such failure is, in the opinion of the secretary, jeopardizing the education of the children in such school district, the secretary may order the parties to appear before him for mediation of the dispute.  In either case, the parties shall meet with him or his agents or a mediator designated by him from a panel of mediators selected by state board of education to assist him.  For such purposes, the secretary may enter contracts for services with members of such panel, the terms of which shall be subject to approval by the state board of education. The parties shall provide such information as the secretary may require. The secretary may recommend a basis for settlement but such recommendations shall not be binding upon the parties. (c) If after mediation the parties have not reached agreement, the secretary may order the parties to appear before him on the fourth day next following the end of the mediation session. At such time the parties shall report their settlement of the dispute or each select and bring an arbitrator to such meeting. Such arbitrators may be members of the arbitration panel. Unless the parties have agreed to submit their dispute to one arbitrator, their designated arbitrators shall select a third arbitrator. If either party fails to bring an arbitrator, the secretary shall designate a member of the arbitration panel to serve and the two arbitrators shall select a third. If in either case the two arbitrators fail to agree on the selection of a third during such meeting, the secretary shall select the third from the arbitration panel. If both parties fail to bring an arbitrator and have not settled their dispute, the secretary shall designate one member of the arbitration panel to arbitrate the dispute. The arbitrators shall set the time and place for the hearing one week from the day on which the parties reported to the secretary except that if such day is Saturday, Sunday or a holiday, the hearing shall be held on the next Monday or the day following the holiday. After hearing all the issues, the arbitrators shall, within fifteen days, render a decision in writing, signed by a majority of the arbitrators, which states in detail the nature of the decision and the disposition of the issues by the arbitrators. The arbitrators shall file one copy of the decision with the secretary, each town clerk in the school district involved and the board of education and organization which are parties to the dispute. The decision of the arbitrators shall be advisory and shall not be binding upon the parties to the dispute. The parties shall each pay the fee of the arbitrator selected by or for them and share equally the fee of the third arbitrator and all other costs incidental to the hearing. . . . "

Is this a better solution to the problem than others? Why or why not? What happens if the report of the arbitrators is not accepted?

5.  Suppose all the teachers in the *Hortonville* case, supra, resigned after the decision in the case, and later the school board agreed to re-hire them, so long as each one "contributed" $100.00 to the school district's library fund, and suppose this condition of re-hiring were contested in court, what should be the court's decision; why?

---

## NATIONAL EDUCATIONAL ASS'N v. LEE COUNTY BD. OF PUBLIC INSTRUCTION

United States Court of Appeals, 5th Cir., 1972.
467 F.2d 447.

JOHN R. BROWN, Chief Judge. Having previously certified this case to the Supreme Court of Florida for an authoritative resolution of perplexingly difficult State law issues, we can now conclude with absolute assurance that despite a commendable effort the District Court incorrectly decided them. Since we are also convinced that the circumstances revealed by this record present no problem of Federal constitutional proportions, we reverse. . . .

Generally stated, the question is whether the Board of Public Instruction of Lee County, Florida may require individual payments of $100 as a condition for the reemployment with tenure of 425 public school teachers who had voluntarily submitted simultaneous mass resignations as a result of their disagreement with the State's educational policies. Deciding that the unilateral imposition of such a requirement violated both Florida law and the due process clause of the Fourteenth Amendment, the District Court granted the teachers' motion for summary judgment, directed the repayment of $100 to those teachers who had complied with the Board's demand, and ordered the reinstatement with back pay of those teachers who had not been rehired because of their refusal to comply. . . .

We agree with the District Court that those teachers who accepted reemployment neither waived nor were thereafter estopped from asserting their right to contest the legality of the disputed payments. . . . But we do not agree that the Board's imposition of the $100 condition violated the teachers' Federal constitutional rights.

Essentially the teachers' theory is that the forced exaction of a $100 payment from each of them in exchange for their returning to work with their pre-resignation status intact amounted to a fine or penalty for a legislatively undefined wrong, violative of their right to procedural due process because they were afforded no hearing or other opportunity to protest the payments or to contest their legality. Phrased another way, the argument is that the teachers were "punished" for their prior concerted efforts to effect changes in State school policies and that such "punishment," in the absence of traditional procedural safeguards, could not be made a condition for reemployment because it compelled the surrender of Fourteenth Amendment rights in return for a job in the Lee County school system.

Concededly it is now established to a point beyond all dispute that "public employment, including academic employment, may [not] be conditioned upon the surrender of constitutional rights which could not be abridged by direct governmental action." Keyishian v. Board of Regents . . . Denial of a government job solely because an individual refuses to abjure the protection afforded by the United States Constitution amounts to nothing more than an attempt to accomplish indirectly an otherwise impermissible objective—penalization of conduct which is constitutionally insulated against punishment. . . . Consequently, this Court has encountered no difficulty in holding that a Federal claim based upon the allegation that a State has denied public employment solely because of the exercise of a constitutional right will, if proven, entitle the plaintiff to appropriate relief. . . .

However, none of these cases have any application here unless the teachers were in fact compelled to forego the exercise of a Federal constitutional right in return for reemployment. The critical flaw in their argument is the uncritical (and, on this record, insupportable) assumption that the $100 payments constituted a *deprivation* of property without due process of law within the prohibition of the Fourteenth Amendment. The agreement clearly provided that the teachers would receive a benefit to which concededly they were not otherwise entitled—reemployment with full tenure rights and other accompanying privileges which they had enjoyed before their resignations— in return for a payment of $100. In substance, they were offered an opportunity to surrender one "property right" in order to acquire another "property right" that was plainly of greater value to them. Such a mutually advantageous exchange cannot be characterized as a *deprivation* of property, regardless of whether the teachers' payments are pejoratively denominated as "fines" and regardless of whether the subjective intention of the Board members who voted for it was to "punish" alleged past misconduct.

We do not dispute the District Court's conclusion that the payments were not "voluntary" in any meaningful sense. For that matter *all* exchanges of contractual consideration are "involuntary" to the extent that the contracting parties would much prefer to secure the benefits of the agreement without bearing the inevitable burdens. Likewise we may concede that the teachers here were involuntarily subjected to choosing between paying consideration for an employment benefit of at least equivalent value and foregoing employment altogether. The choice between these options was admittedly coerced. But regardless of whether it was accepted or rejected the Board's offer did not entail a deprivation of property. Accordingly, the payment of the $100 could not have involved the surrender of the right to protection of that property guaranteed by the due process clause of the Fourteenth Amendment.

Obviously the teachers would be in an entirely different position if they were somehow able to establish that they were legally entitled to tenure without payment of $100 and were therefore unilaterally deprived of that money without due process. Instead they are forced to concede that they had effectively resigned their positions and that the Board was not even legally obligated to rehire them at all. In such circumstances their claim fares no better than that of a teacher who, having neither *de facto* tenure nor an objective expectancy of reemployment, is discharged for unspecified reasons without notice or a hearing. . . . Absent the invasion of some protected Fourteenth Amendment right, neither notice nor hearing is required.

The same result obtains if approached outside of a concept of "exchange" of valuable rights. The key to decision, of course, is whether the teachers were forced to give up a constitutional right. Under Florida law they had no right to reemployment, either with or without tenure. Indeed, they had no right to reemployment with tenure. The loss of this right was not due to an exercise of First Amendment rights. It was the result of the purposeful resignations— a right which the earlier state court injunction expressly recognized was theirs. The school authorities did not accede to the demands of the teachers, but it did not prior to the resignations or thereafter deny them any federal constitutional right or impede in any way the unrestricted assertion of them. The teachers sought reemployment and a return to the status of former tenure privileges, a status lost by the resignations. The Florida Supreme Court's obligatory ruling accords to the requirement of a $100 payment the exercise of reasonable judgment on the part of the school authorities and in its exercise we find no element of a denial of a federal right.

The judgment of the District Court is reversed and the cause remanded for entry of judgment in favor of the Lee County Board of Public Instruction.

Reversed and remanded.


## NOTES AND QUESTIONS

1. Was the $100.00 payment a fine, an inducement for the board to rescind the resignations retroactively, or an "exchange of valuable rights"? If a fine, does a school board constitutionally have the power to "prosecute" a case, decide guilt or innocence, and levy a "fine"?

2. Under this case could a school board require that every teacher pay it $1,000.00 as a condition of obtaining tenure? Why or why not? Could a school board constitutionally require that all teachers annually pay it $100.00 before obtaining their contracts to teach? Is a school board in the business of selling tenure or teacher's contracts?

3. Does this case raise a question of "the equal protection of laws"?


## In the Matter of NEWARK TEACHERS UNION, LOCAL 481 AMERICAN FEDERATION OF TEACHERS AFL–CIO

Superior Court of New Jersey, 1972.
118 N.J.Super. 215, 287 A.2d 183.

PER CURIAM. During the 1971 Newark teachers strike which commenced February 2, 1971 and lasted until April 8, 1971, defendants were charged with contempt in that they willfully violated a final judgment of the Superior Court entered on February 27, 1970 which permanently enjoined the Newark Teachers Union, Local 481, its members, officers and directors, including certain named individuals, from participating in any strike, work stoppage, picketing, etc., against the Board of Education of Newark.

Hearings were held on the charges of contempt. At the conclusion thereof the trial court found in essence that each defendant had actual knowledge of the terms and conditions of the final judgment of February 27, 1970 but had nevertheless intentionally and deliberately participated in the 1971 strike activities and was guilty of the contempt charged. A fine, which ultimately amounted to $270,000, was imposed on the union. Twelve of the 15 individuals received six-month jail sentences and fines of $500. Defendant Fiorito, who was convicted of two separate contempts during the 1971 strike, was sentenced to two consecutive six-month jail terms and fined a total of $1,000. Defendants Bizzaro and Del Grosso received three-month terms and fines of $250.

We have carefully reviewed the entire record of proceedings *de novo,* and reach the following independent findings and conclusions as to guilt and punishment.

It is clear that each defendant had actual knowledge of the terms and provisions of the February 27, 1970 final judgment. That judgment in clear language manifested the intention of the court to prohibit participation in future strikes as well as the one then recently in progress. That that interpretation was not inadvertent is evidenced by the colloquy between the court and counsel for defendants at the time it was entered. The entry on February 3, 1971 of the cease and desist order and its subsequent service on the union and various individual defendants further emphasized and brought home to them the fact that the injunction was intended to apply to the 1971 strike. Nevertheless, they continued to defy its mandate. Thus, each of the defendants willfully and knowingly violated its terms by actually supporting and participating in the 1971 strike and is guilty of contempt. The record also establishes Fiorito's guilt of two separate contempts.

Defendants contend that regardless of their knowledge concerning its scope, the injunction was unconstitutional because (1) it was overbroad in that it barred future strikes, and (2) they were not given a hearing on the enforceability of the injunction where they might present new evidence. Both arguments are without merit.

We recognize that in the sensitive area of labor disputes the scope of the injunction should be carefully tailored to the factual situation from which the litigation sprang. Otherwise such injunctive orders may become overbroad or stale in their application to a later strike. Consequently, the better practice is for the employer to seek fresh relief. Thus, in the present case, when the 1971 strike materialized, it would have been better practice to file a new complaint with supporting affidavits setting forth the new factual situation and on this basis to seek a new injunction. However, we conclude that the 1970 final judgment, entered less than a year before the 1971 strike against the same union and its members, officers and directors, was efficacious in the particular circumstances here presented.

Defendants contend that they were entitled to a hearing on the enforceability of the injunction where they could present evidence that, in the negotiations for a new contract, the board of education was not bargaining in good faith and was using a strategy of forcing the teachers to strike so that they would lose public support.

If this was the board's plan it was reprehensible. However, assuming there was some basis for the teachers' contention, that was no excuse to violate the final judgment of February 27, 1970. The matter was not between private parties where issues of clean hands and good faith would be material. It concerned a public school system, and the continued public interest in having the schools remain open and the children educated.

As we have already noted, defendants had actual knowledge that the 1970 injunction was deemed applicable to the 1971 strike. If defendants intended to challenge its applicability to the 1971 context and, more specifically, to assert that a new situation had arisen with respect to the bargaining negotiations under the new contract, their remedy was to apply to the court to make that challenge before violating the outstanding injunction and to seek the court's assistance in requiring the board to negotiate in good faith. They were not free to defy the court order and take the law in their own hands. Walker v. City of Birmingham, 388 U.S. 307, 87 S.Ct. 1824, 18 L.Ed.2d 1210 (1967). . . .

We turn to the fines and jail sentences imposed by the trial court. It is clear that those participating in the 1971 strike have had brought home directly and emphatically the disastrous consequences of their illegal strike activity. However, of the 15 individual defendants herein, ten of them were also convicted of contempt in the 1970 strike proceedings. The union, of course, was also convicted in both the 1970 and 1971 contempt proceedings. We concur in the sentence imposed on the union by the trial court and adopt it as our own. Accordingly, a fine of $270,000 is hereby imposed on appellant Newark Teachers Union. Defendants Nicholas, Graves, Lasus, Lerman, Tur, Kirschbaum, Zimmer, Watkins and Washington, who were also convicted of contempt in 1970, are each hereby sentenced to three months in the Essex County Penitentiary and fined $500. Defendants Dasher, Koplin and Volpe, who, as officers of the union, were specifically named in the February 27, 1970 final judgment, are each hereby sentenced to three months in the Essex County Penitentiary and fined $500. Appellant Fiorito, who has been found guilty of two separate contempts during the 1971 strike and was also convicted of contempt during the 1970 strike, is hereby sentenced to a term of three months in the Essex County Penitentiary and fined $500 on each contempt. The jail terms hereby imposed on him run consecutively.

His sentence will aggregate six months in jail and a total fine of $1,000. Defendants Bizzaro and Del Grosso are each hereby sentenced to one month in the Essex County Penitentiary and fined $250. Each individual defendant is placed on probation for one year. The only condition will be that the person refrain from participating in any illegal activity, including but not limited to striking or work stoppage in connection with his or her employment by the board of education.

It is unfortunate that resort must be had to contempt of court procedure in this type of situation. Jailing teachers is not the answer to school strikes. The solution is legislative. Public employees have the right to bargain collectively as to the terms and conditions of their employment but cannot do so on equal terms with their employment unit since they have no means of negotiating from a position of strength. If the present policy prohibiting strikes by public employees is to be continued, machinery for the compulsory settlement of deadlocked labor disputes involving public employees should be established. For a discussion of the problem and suggestions as to possible alternatives, see Comment, "Alternatives to the Strike in Public Labor Relations," 85 Harv.L.Rev. 459 (Dec.1971).

Judgment accordingly.

## Chapter VIII

## CONSTITUTIONAL FREEDOM AND RACIAL
## DESEGREGATION

---

## INTRODUCTION

---

The next three chapters primarily will be concerned with an exploration of equal educational opportunity as it is defined and protected by the provision of the Fourteenth Amendment that prohibits states from denying "to any person within its jurisdiction the equal protection of the laws." A similar requirement limits the federal government. The focus in this chapter will be on racial considerations, and the focus of the next chapter will be on gender considerations. Each will be considered as it affects equal educational opportunity. The third chapter will focus on additional considerations such as securing equal educational opportunity for handicapped and gifted children, and for language minorities.

The "equal-protection" clause poses many analytical difficulties. The notion of "equality" is at the core of the guarantee. We know that equality requires like cases to be treated in a like manner. Moreover, unequal treatment consists in treating unlike cases in a like manner, or similar cases in a different manner. But, how can we identify cases that are alike, or unlike? Cases can be alike in one respect and unlike in another; for example, John and Mary can be alike in that they both have brown hair but unlike because they are of different sexes. The point is that a property, trait or standard (i. e., brown hair or sex) must be supplied before we can judge whether two cases are alike or unlike. Where does that trait or standard come from? Who supplies it? Does it come from the "equal-protection" clause, or does that clause only require that the formal elements of equality be observed, allowing the trait or standard to come from an outside source, say the legislature? Obviously, the equal-protection guarantee cannot be taken to mean that every law must apply equally to every person, because modern government would come to a halt. Government must classify, and that means that government will classify in accordance with some trait, standard or property. All legislation that classifies means that on the basis of some trait or standard some people are treated different from others, placing special burdens on some persons or granting benefits to others.

Membership in a class is determined by identifying whether one possesses the class-defining trait. But, if laws may classify on the basis of a trait, then what is required of a classification by the constitution's equal-protection clause? This question is explored in this chapter as it relates to classifications that are based on race.

Generally, the equal-protection clause requires that a legislative classification must bear a reasonable relationship to the underlying natural class, as the natural class is determined by the purpose of the law. How does one determine the natural class? If, for example, the purpose of a law is to promote vehicle safety by prohibiting all signs and advertising from the sides of all vehicles on streets and highways that may distract a driver, then the natural class would consist of all vehicles on streets or highways capable of carrying any sign or advertising. Driver distraction is to be minimized. Perfect equal protection would prohibit all signs and advertising and would require a legislative classification cast in descriptive words that would include all vehicles on streets or highways capable of carrying such signs, but only those vehicles. In this situation there would be a perfect "fit"—in light of the purpose of the law, the legislative class would include all members of the natural class and no others—and perfect equal protection is the result. But suppose the law's purpose is to promote vehicle safety by protecting drivers from additional kinds of distractions that are external to their vehicles, including bill boards as well as signs carried on the sides of vehicles. Suppose further, that the law prohibiting display of such signs and advertising was amended in the legislature so that it would not apply to any sign or advertising attached to an owner's property that promoted the business of the owner of the vehicle or bill board. This classification is underinclusive; that is, the legislative classification is not as broad as it should be in order to include all of the members of the natural class. The opposite situation would involve an overly broad legislative classification, including more than the members of the natural class; it would be overinclusive. But, whether underinclusive or overinclusive, the law may achieve a good part of its purpose of promoting safety by eliminating driver-distractions. Does it unconstitutionally deny equal protection of the laws? The answer depends on court judgments and on how perfect a "fit" courts require between legislative and natural classes. Today, courts require a much tighter "fit" where important human values are at stake, such as freedom from racial discrimination, than where economic matters are involved. Thus, legislative classifications based on race, nationality and alienage have been held to be "suspect," which requires courts to scrutinize them carefully and to uphold them only if the state can show that they demonstrate a close "fit" and are based on a "compelling" governmental interest. Classifications based on race, nationality and alienage are not forbidden, *per se,* but they are strongly disfavored.

## THE CONCEPT OF RACE

———

"Race" is not a sufficiently descriptive concept to be very helpful to physical anthropologists and to other physical scientists who study human populations from a genetic point of view. "Race" may be an important concept that can be culturally defined in various ways by sociologists, cultural historians or others who study people because people act in accordance with their cultural attitudes, whether their attitudes are well founded or not. But, as put by one eminent scholar:

> "The scientific study of human races is at least two centuries old. There are nevertheless few natural phenomena, and probably no other aspect of human nature, the investigation of which has so often floundered in confusion and misunderstanding." Dobzhansky, Mankind Evolving, 253 (Yale University Press, 1962).

The past history of racial classifications in the United States demonstrates that differently defined racial classifications were enacted into law during the height of this country's confusions and misunderstandings about race at a time of extreme social prejudice, and with the most deleterious social consequences. See, e. g., G. Myrdal, An American Dilemma: The Negro Problem and Modern Democracy (1944), and A. Montagu, Man's Most Dangerous Myth: The Fallacy of Race (1964).

It is now generally agreed that man, the genus *Homo,* is not more than a single specie to which all living races belong. Species are groups of inbreeding natural populations, reproductively isolated from other such groups. "Reproductive isolation" does not refer to spatial or geographical isolation, but rather to physical capacity. It refers to the *inability* to mate with other species and produce fertile progeny. A species, therefore is a genetically closed system since new genes, the biological units of inheritance, cannot be obtained from other groups and passed on through fertile hybrids. Thus, the species is the basic group for biological and anthropological classification. See generally, Simpson, Principles of Animal Taxonomy 18, 148–152 (1961); Dobzhansky, supra (1962).

Between the individual organism—which is the basic unit of the species—and the species itself, is another layer of cultural, but not physical, classification known as race. These racial classifications are classifications based on population groups within the species, which because of social or geographical boundaries, have tended to inbreed among themselves over long periods of time. As a result of this endogamy, they tend to express certain similar physical and genetic characteristics.   See Johnston, The Population Approach to Human Variation, 134 Annals of the New York Academy of Sciences, 507–515 (Feb. 28, 1966).

The process of classification and of the variability of racial classification has recently been described in this manner:

> "A race of *Homo sapiens* is a Mendelian population, a reproductive community of individuals sharing a common gene pool.  The level at which the reproductive community is defined depends upon the problem one is interested in investigating.  There is no absolute, final or 'true' level at which these reproductive communities are defined.  All members of our species belong to one Mendelian population, and its name is *Homo sapiens*.  This large specie-wide Mendelian population may be divided into smaller Mendelian populations, for all practical purposes an infinitely large number of them   .   .   .   Races are open genetic systems, and as such they are quite different from species."  Beuttner-Janusch, Book Review, American Journal of Physical Anthropology, 25:2, September 1966, p. 184.

The practical truth of the statement that the number of races can be infinite depending upon who is the classifier, is shown by Garn and Coon in an article, *On the Number of Races of Mankind.*  (57 American Anthropologist 996 (1955))  Differing classificatory systems have listed as few as two races and as many as two hundred.  The difference depends upon whether the classifier is a "lumper", one who groups a number of varieties into one broad category because the differences are considered too trivial to warrant special classification, or a "splitter", one who believes that distinctness and variety merit attention, but even in the latter case each minute distinction is not separately classed.  Garn, Human Races 15 (3rd. ed. 1971).  The usual approach to racial classifications is to focus on geography, either on a few geographical races, or on many local or microgeographical races.

A geographical race may be defined as "a collection of similar populations inhabiting a broad continental area or island chain."  A local race is a more neatly circumscribed physically or socially isolated inbreeding population group.  If the classifier uses the geographical races, then depending upon the criteria used, the number can be "approximately six or seven."  If the classifier uses local races, the number can be "upwards of thirty."  Garn & Coon, supra 999.  In other words, even at the level of greatest organization, the number is only an approximation.  There is, of course, no agreement on the precise number of geographical races or of the peoples that properly should be included within them.  See classifications noted in

Comas, Manual of Physical Anthropology, 18–19, 303–309 (1960) and Dobzhansky, supra, 262–265. Geographical races, the type of concept that has been used most often in the United States, are merely "collections of convenience." Garn and Coon, supra, 1000. They have insufficient scientific accuracy for the population geneticist. This is not to say that racial classifications have had an unimportant social history in the United States.

Moreover, when an individual leaves his population group and mates with an individual in another group, the racial classification of the offspring is immediately put in question. When miscegenation —which within the last five centuries has risen to rates unprecedented in human history—becomes widespread, "classifications of convenience" become even more blurred, loose and inexact. This is the situation in the United States today. The point is that there is only one "race"—the human race. For excellent analysis of this subject, see, L. Morris, Human Populations, Genetic Variation and Evolution (1971); S. M. Garn, Human Races (3rd. ed., 1971), and R. A. Goldsby, Race and Races (1971).

## RACIAL SEGREGATION

Although the concept of race lacks scientific validity, the Supreme Court of the United States approved the use of legislatively defined racial classification in 1896. In Plessy v. Ferguson, 163 U.S. 537, 16 S.Ct. 1138, 41 L.Ed. 256 (1896), the Court sustained the constitutional validity of a Louisiana statute requiring "equal but separate accommodations" for white and Negro railway passengers. The statute had been attacked as violative of the Fourteenth Amendment's prohibition that no state shall " . . . deny to any person within its jurisdiction the equal protection of the laws." In his Opinion for the Court, Mr. Justice Brown approved of the "separate but equal doctrine" holding that:

> "The object of the [Fourteenth] Amendment was undoubtedly to enforce the absolute equality of the two races before the law, but in the nature of things it could not have been intended to abolish distinctions based upon color, or to enforce social, as distinguished from political equality, or a commingling of the two races upon terms unsatisfactory to either. Laws permitting, and even requiring, their separation in places where they are liable to be brought into contact do not necessarily imply the inferiority of either race to the other, and have been generally, if not universally, recognized as within the competency of the state legislatures in the ex-

ercise of their police power. The most common instance of this is connected with the establishment of separate schools for white and colored children, which has been held to be a valid exercise of the legislative power even by courts of States where the political rights of the colored race have been longest and most earnestly enforced. . . .

"[This] case reduces itself to the question whether the statute of Louisiana is a reasonable regulation, and with respect to this there must necessarily be a large discretion on the part of the legislature. In determining the question of reasonableness it is at liberty to act with reference to the established usages, customs and traditions of the people, and with a view to the promotion of their comfort, and the preservation of the public peace and good order. Gauged by this standard, we cannot say that [this law] is unreasonable, or more obnoxious to the Fourteenth Amendment than the acts of Congress requiring separate schools for colored children in the District of Columbia, the constitutionality of which does not seem to have been questioned, or the corresponding acts of state legislatures.

"We consider the underlying fallacy of the plaintiff's argument to consist in the assumption that the enforced separation of the two races stamps the colored race with a badge of inferiority. If this be so, it is not by reason of anything found in the act, but solely because the colored race chooses to put that construction upon it. The argument necessarily assumes that if, as has been more than once the case, and is not unlikely to be so again, the colored race should become the dominant power, and should enact a law in precisely similar terms, it would thereby relegate the white race to an inferior position. We imagine that the white race, at least, would not acquiesce in this assumption. The argument also assumes that social prejudices may be overcome by legislation, and that equal rights cannot be secured to the negro except by an enforced commingling of the two races. We cannot accept this proposition. If the two races are to meet upon terms of social equality, it must be the result of natural affinities, a mutual appreciation of each other's merits and a voluntary consent of individuals. . . . Legislation is powerless to eradicate racial instincts or to abolish distinctions based upon physical differences, and the attempt to do so can only result in accentuating the difficulties of the present situation. If the civil and political rights of both races be equal one cannot be inferior to the other civilly or politically. If one race be inferior to the other socially, the Constitution of the United States cannot put them upon the same plane."

The first Mr. Justice Harlan dissented, saying:

". . . It was said in argument that the statute of Louisiana does not discriminate against either race, but prescribes a rule applicable alike to white and colored citizens. But this argument does not meet the difficulty. Every one knows that [Louisiana's law] had its origin in the purpose, not so much to exclude white persons from railroad cars occupied by blacks, as to exclude colored people from coaches occupied by or assigned to white persons. . . . The thing to accomplish was, under the guise of giving equal accommodation for whites and blacks, to compel the latter to keep to themselves while travelling in railroad passenger coaches. No one would be so wanting in candor as to assert the contrary. The fundamental objection, therefore, to the statute is that it interferes with the personal freedom of citizens. . . .

"The white race deems itself to be the dominant race in this country. And so it is, in prestige, in achievements, in education, in wealth and in power. So, I doubt not, it will continue to be for all time, if it remains true to its great heritage and holds fast to the principles of constitutional liberty. But in view of the Constitution, in the eye of the law, there is in this country no superior, dominant, ruling class of citizens. There is no caste here. Our Constitution is color-blind, and neither knows nor tolerates classes among citizens. There is no caste here. . . . The destinies of the two races, in this country, are indissolubly linked together, and the interests of both require that the common government of all shall not permit the seeds of race hate to be planted under the sanction of law. What can more certainly arouse race hate, what more certainly create and perpetuate a feeling of distrust between these races, than state enactments, which, in fact, proceed on the ground that colored citizens are so inferior and degraded that they cannot be allowed to sit in public coaches occupied by white citizens? That, as all will admit, is the real meaning of such legislation as was enacted in Louisiana. . . .

"The arbitrary separation of citizens, on the basis of race, while they are on a public highway, is a badge of servitude wholly inconsistent with the civil freedom and the equality before the law established by the Constitution. It cannot be justified upon any legal grounds. . . . The thin disguise of 'equal' accommodations for passengers in railroad coaches will not mislead anyone, nor atone for the wrong this day done.   .   .   .   ."

## NOTES AND QUESTIONS

1. What reason did the Court give as justification for its decision?   Do you agree?

2. By what criteria can one accurately judge who is "white" or "Negro"? Plessy was alleged to have been "seven-eighths Caucasian and one-eighth African blood" and that "the mixture of colored blood was not discernible in him."   Was Plessy "white" or "Negro"?

3. The Court drew a line between "social" and "political" equality, indicating that the Fourteenth Amendment's "equal protection" clause only applies to the latter.   Is this distinction workable?   Could the separate but equal doctrine be applied to a mixed jury, or would it require that the jury be of one "race"?   Could the doctrine be applied and still allow for a mixed faculty?

4. What promotion of the public's welfare was achieved by Louisiana's law?

5. Is it possible for two educational facilities, one for black students and one for whites, ever to be equal?   In faculty?   In Library?   In scientific laboratories?   In other facilities?   In equality of classroom instruction?   In student populations?   If not, what does "equal" in "separate but equal" mean?   If one "race" is dominant in political and social power, will the "inferior race" actually enjoy "equal" educational, or other, opportunities?

6. How would you have decided this case and for what reason(s)?

## "THE EQUAL PROTECTION OF THE LAWS"

### BROWN v. BOARD OF EDUC. (BROWN I)

Supreme Court of the United States, 1954.
347 U.S. 483, 74 S.Ct. 686, 98 L.Ed. 873.

Mr. Chief Justice WARREN delivered the opinion of the Court.

These cases come to us from the States of Kansas, South Carolina, Virginia, and Delaware.   .   .   .

In each of the cases, minors of the Negro race, through their legal representatives, seek the aid of the courts in obtaining admission to the public schools of their community on a nonsegregated basis.   In each instance, they had been denied admission to schools attended by white children under laws requiring or permitting segregation according to race.   This segregation was alleged to deprive the plaintiffs of the equal protection of the laws under the Fourteenth Amendment.   In each of the cases other than the Delaware case, a three-judge federal district court denied relief to the plaintiffs on the so-called "separate but equal" doctrine announced by this Court in Plessy v. Ferguson, 163 U.S. 537. Under that doctrine, equality of treatment is accorded when the races are provided substantially equal facilities, even though these facilities be separate. In the Delaware case, the Supreme Court of Delaware adhered to that doctrine, but ordered that the plaintiffs be admitted to the white schools because of their superiority to the Negro schools.

The plaintiffs contend that segregated public schools are not "equal" and cannot be made "equal", and that hence they are deprived of the equal protection of the laws. . . .

. . . The most avid proponents of the post-[Civil] War Amendments undoubtedly intended them to remove all legal distinctions among "all persons born or naturalized in the United States." Their opponents, just as certainly, were antagonistic to both the letter and the spirit of the Amendments and wished them to have the most limited effect. What others in Congress and the state legislatures had in mind cannot be determined with any degree of certainty.

An additional reason for the inconclusive nature of the Amendment's history, with respect to segregated schools, is the status of public education at that time. In the South, the movement toward free common schools, supported by general taxation, had not yet taken hold. Education of white children was largely in the hands of private groups. Education of Negroes was almost nonexistent, and practically all of the race were illiterate. In fact, any education of Negroes was forbidden by law in some states. Today, in contrast, many Negroes have achieved outstanding success in the arts and sciences as well as in the business and professional world. It is true that public school education at the time of the Amendment had advanced further in the North, but the effect of the Amendment on Northern States was generally ignored in the congressional debates. Even in the North, the conditions of public education did not approximate those existing today. The curriculm was usually rudimentary; ungraded schools were common in rural areas; the school term was but three months a year in many states; and compulsory school attendance was virtually unknown. As a consequence, it is not surprising that there should be so little in the history of the Fourteenth Amendment relating to its intended effect on public education.

. . . The doctrine of "separate but equal" did not make its appearance in this Court until 1896 in the case of Plessy v. Ferguson, supra, involving not education but transportation. American courts have since labored with the doctrine for over half a century. In this Court, there have been six cases involving the "separate but equal" doctrine in the field of public education. In Cumming v. County Board of Education, 175 U.S. 528, and Gong Lum v. Rice, 275 U.S. 78, the validity of the doctrine itself was not challenged. In more recent cases, all on the graduate school level, inequality was found in that specific benefits enjoyed by white students were denied to Negro students of the same educational qualifications. Missouri ex rel. Gaines v. Canada, 305 U.S. 337; Sipuel v. Oklahoma, 332 U.S. 631; Sweatt v. Painter, 339 U.S. 629; McLaurin v. Oklahoma State Regents, 339 U.S. 637. In none of these cases was it necessary to re-examine the doctrine to grant relief to the Negro plaintiff. And in Sweatt v. Painter, supra, the Court expressly reserved decision on the question whether Plessy v. Ferguson should be held inapplicable to public education.

In the instant cases, that question is directly presented. Here, unlike Sweatt v. Painter, there are findings below that the Negro and white schools involved have been equalized, or are being equalized, with respect to buildings, curricula, qualifications and salaries of teachers, and other "tangible" factors. Our decision, therefore, cannot turn on merely a comparison of these tangible factors in the Negro and white schools involved in each of the cases. We must look instead to the effect of segregation itself in public education.

In approaching this problem, we cannot turn the clock back to 1868 when the Amendment was adopted, or even to 1896 when Plessy v. Ferguson was written. We must consider public education in the light of its full development and its present place in American life throughout the Nation. Only in this way can it be determined if segregation in public schools deprives these plaintiffs of the equal protection of the laws.

Today, education is perhaps the most important function of state and local governments. Compulsory school attendence laws and the great expenditures for education both demonstrate our recognition of the importance of education to our democratic society. It is required in the performance of our most basic public responsibilities, even service in the armed forces. It is the very foundation of good citizenship. Today it is a principal instrument in awakening the child to cultural values, in preparing him for later professional training, and in helping him to adjust normally to his environment. In these days, it is doubtful that any child may reasonably be expected to succeed in life if he is denied the opportunity of an education. Such an opportunity, where the state has undertaken to provide it, is a right which must be made available to all on equal terms.

We come then to the question presented: Does segregation of children in public schools solely on the basis of race, even though the physical facilities and other "tangible" factors may be equal, deprive the children of the minority group of equal educational opportunities? We believe that it does.

In Sweatt v. Painter, supra, in finding that a segregated law school for Negroes could not provide them equal educational opportunities, this Court relied in large part on "those qualities which are incapable of objective measurement but which make for greatness in a law school."  In McLaurin v. Oklahoma State Regents, supra, the Court, in requiring that a Negro admitted to a white graduate school be treated like all other students, again resorted to intangible considerations: ".  .  .  his ability to study, to engage in discussions and exchange views with other students, and, in general, to learn his profession."  Such considerations apply with added force to children in grade and high schools.  To separate them from others of similar age and qualifications solely because of their race generates a feeling of inferiority as to their status in the community that may affect their hearts and minds in a way unlikely ever to be undone.  The effect of this separation on their educational opportunities was well stated by a finding in the Kansas case by a court which neverthless felt compelled to rule against the Negro plaintiffs:

> "Segregation of white and colored children in public schools has a detrimental effect upon the colored children. The impact is greater when it has the sanction of the law; for the policy of separating the races is usually interpreted as denoting the inferiority of the negro group.  A sense of inferiority affects the motivation of a child to learn.  Segregation with the sanction of law, therefore, has a tendency to [retard] the educational and mental development of negro children and to deprive them of some of the benefits they would receive in a racial[ly] integrated school system."

Whatever may have been the extent of psychological knowledge at the time of Plessy v. Ferguson, this finding is amply supported by modern authority.[11]  Any language in Plessy v. Ferguson contrary to this finding is rejected.

We conclude that in the field of public education the doctrine of "separate but equal" has no place.  Separate educational facilities are inherently unequal.  Therefore, we hold that the plaintiffs and others similarly situated for whom the actions have been brought are, by reason of the segregation complained of, deprived of the equal protection of the laws guaranteed by the Fourteenth Amendment.

---

[11] K. B. Clark, Effect of Prejudice and Discrimination on Personality Development (Midcentury White House Conference on Children and Youth, 1950); Witmer and Kotinsky, Personality in the Making (1952), c. VI; Deutscher and Chein, The Psychological Effects of Enforced Segregation: A Survey of Social Science Opinion, 26 J.Psychol. 259 (1948); Chein, What are the Psychological Effects of Segregation Under Conditions of Equal Facilities?, 3 Int.J.Opinion and Attitude Res. 229 (1949); Brameld, Educational Costs, in Discrimination and National Welfare (MacIver, ed., 1949), 44–48; Frazier, The Negro in the United States (1949), 674–681.  And see generally Myrdal, An American Dilemma (1944).

This disposition makes unnecessary any discussion whether such segregation also violates the Due Process Clause of the Fourteenth Amendment.

Because these are class actions, because of the wide applicability of this decision, and because of the great variety of local conditions, the formulation of decrees in these cases presents problems of considerable complexity. On reargument, the consideration of appropriate relief was necessarily subordinated to the primary question—the constitutionality of segregation in public education. We have now announced that such segregation is a denial of the equal protection of the laws. In order that we may have the full assistance of the parties in formulating decrees, the cases will be restored to the docket, and the parties are requested to present further argument on [the question of an adequate remedy].

---

## BROWN v. BOARD OF EDUC. (BROWN II)

Supreme Court of the United States, 1955.
349 U.S. 294, 75 S.Ct. 753, 99 L.Ed. 1083.

Mr. Chief Justice WARREN delivered the opinion of the Court.

These cases were decided on May 17, 1954. The opinions of that date, declaring the fundamental principle that racial discrimination in public education is unconstitutional, are incorporated herein by reference. All provisions of federal, state, or local law requiring or permitting such discrimination must yield to this principle. There remains for consideration the manner in which relief is to be accorded.

Because these cases arose under different local conditions and their disposition will involve a variety of local problems, we requested further argument on the question of relief. In view of the nationwide importance of the decision, we invited the Attorney General of the United States and the Attorneys General of all states requiring or permitting racial discrimination in public education to present their views on that question. The parties, the United States, and the States of Florida, North Carolina, Arkansas, Oklahoma, Maryland, and Texas filed briefs and participated in the oral argument. . . .

Full implementation of these constitutional principles may require solution of varied local school problems. School authorities have the primary responsibility for elucidating, assessing, and solving these problems; courts will have to consider whether the action of school authorities constitutes good faith implementation of the governing constitutional principles. Because of their proximity to local conditions and the possible need for further hearings, the courts which originally heard these cases can best perform this judicial appraisal. Accordingly, we believe it appropriate to remand the cases to those courts.

In fashioning and effectuating the decrees, the courts will be guided by equitable principles.  Traditionally, equity has been characterized by a practical flexibility in shaping its remedies and by a facility for adjusting and reconciling public and private needs.  These cases call for the exercise of these traditional attributes of equity power.  At stake is the personal interest of the plaintiffs in admission to public schools as soon as practicable on a nondiscriminatory basis.  To effectuate this interest may call for elimination of a variety of obstacles in making the transition to school systems operated in accordance with the constitutional principles set forth in our May 17, 1954, decision.  Courts of equity may properly take into account the public interest in the elimination of such obstacles in a systematic and effective manner.  But it should go without saying that the vitality of these constitutional principles cannot be allowed to yield simply because of disagreement with them.

While giving weight to these public and private considerations, the courts will require that the defendants make a prompt and reasonable start toward full compliance with our May 17, 1954, ruling.  Once such a start has been made, the courts may find that additional time is necessary to carry out the ruling in an effective manner.  The burden rests upon the defendants to establish that such time is necessary in the public interest and is consistent with good faith compliance at the earliest practicable date.  To that end, the courts may consider problems related to administration, arising from the physical condition of the school plant, the school transportation system, personnel, revision of school districts and attendance areas into compact units to achieve a system of determining admission to the public schools on a nonracial basis, and revision of local laws and regulations which may be necessary in solving the foregoing problems.  They will also consider the adequacy of any plans the defendants may propose to meet these problems and to effectuate a transition to a racially nondiscriminatory school system.  During this period of transition, the courts will retain jurisdiction of these cases.

The judgments below, except that in the Delaware case, are accordingly reversed and the cases are remanded to the District Courts to take such proceedings and enter such orders and decrees consistent with this opinion as are necessary and proper to admit to public schools on a racially nondiscriminatory basis with all deliberate speed the parties to these cases.  The judgment in the Delaware case—ordering the immediate admission of the plaintiffs to schools previously attended only by white children—is affirmed on the basis of the principles stated in our May 17, 1954, opinion, but the case is remanded to the Supreme Court of Delaware for such further proceedings as that Court may deem necessary in light of this opinion.

It is so ordered.

## NOTES AND QUESTIONS

1. Identify precisely the specific reason(s) given by the Court as justification for its decision on the merits. Do you agree? Was the decision based on the social science information cited in footnote 11? Does it rest on accepted standards of right or wrong plus the view that racial segregation by law necessarily inflicts humiliation?

2. State the principle of law in Brown v. Board of Education. What set of circumstances must be present before it can apply to future cases?

3. Does the ruling in Brown prohibit: (1) all forms of racial segregation in education; (2) only all forms that are enforced by law; (3) only all forms that are enforced by law in the public schools; or (4) only pupil assignment to public schools on the basis of race, whether such assignment is required by law or not?

4. What is the nature of a child's constitutional right? Is it a right: (1) to an integrated education; (2) to a desegregated education; (3) to require that a school board create a desegregation plan; (4) to one of the above but only "with all deliberate speed"?

5. Is the phrase "with all deliberate speed" a contradiction? Does it really call for a speedy but orderly transition to be supervised by the federal courts? If so, a transition from a dual school system to what: (1) a unitary school system, meaning only that action must be taken to produce the absence of a dual school system, or (2)a unitary school system, meaning action must be taken to produce a fully integrated system? By what criteria would you judge a school system completely to be racially integrated? How would you recognize one if you saw it?

6. Do you agree with one court's interpretation of Brown v. Board of Education? In Briggs v. Elliott, 132 F.Supp. 776 (D.C.S.1955) the court said:

"Whatever may have been the views of this court as to the law when the case was originally before us, it is our duty now to accept the law as declared by the Supreme Court.

"Having said this, it is important that we point out exactly what the Supreme Court has decided and what it has not decided in this case. It has not decided that the federal courts are to take over or regulate the public schools of the states. It is not decided that the states must mix persons of different races in the schools or must require them to attend schools or must deprive them of the right of choosing the schools they attend. What it has decided, and all that it has decided, is that a state may not deny to any person on account of race the right to attend any school that it maintains. This, under the decision of the Supreme Court, the state may not do directly or indirectly; but if the schools which it maintains are open to children of all races, no violation of the Constitution is involved even though the children of different races voluntarily attend different schools, as they attend different churches. Nothing in the Constitution or in the decision of the Supreme Court takes away from the people freedom to choose the schools they attend.

"It does not forbid such segregation as occurs as the result of voluntary action. It merely forbids the use of governmental power to enforce segregation. The Fourteenth Amendment is a limitation upon the exercise of power by the state or state agencies, not a limitation upon the freedom of individuals."

7. The best treatment of Brown is R. Kluger, SIMPLE JUSTICE (1976).

---

## BOLLING v. SHARPE

Supreme Court of the United States, 1954.
347 U.S. 497, 74 S.Ct. 693, 98 L.Ed. 884.
[This case was decided on the same day as Brown I, supra.]

Mr. Chief Justice WARREN delivered the opinion of the Court.

This case challenges the validity of segregation in the public schools of the District of Columbia. The petitioners, minors of the Negro race, allege that such segregation deprives them of due process of law under the Fifth Amendment. They were refused admission to a public school attended by white children solely because of their race. They sought the aid of the District Court for the District of Columbia in obtaining admission. That court dismissed their complaint. . . .

We have this day held that the Equal Protection Clause of the Fourteenth Amendment prohibits the states from maintaining racially segregated public schools. The legal problem in the District of Columbia is somewhat different, however. The Fifth Amendment, which is applicable in the District of Columbia, does not contain an equal protection clause as does the Fourteenth Amendment which applies only to the states. But the concepts of equal protection and due process, both stemming from our American ideal of fairness, are not mutually exclusive. The "equal protection of the laws" is a more explicit safeguard of prohibited unfairness than "due process of law," and, therefore, we do not imply that the two are always interchangeable phrases. But, as this Court has recognized, discrimination may be so unjustifiable as to be violative of due process.

Classifications based solely upon race must be scrutinized with particular care, since they are contrary to our traditions and hence constitutionally suspect. As long ago as 1896, this Court declared the principle "that the Constitution of the United States, in its present form, forbids, so far as civil and political rights are concerned, discrimination by the General Government, or by the States, against any citizen because of his race." And in Buchanan v. Warley, 245 U.S. 60, the Court held that a statute which limited the right of a property owner to convey his property to a person of another race was, as an unreasonable discrimination, a denial of due process of law.

Although the Court has not assumed to define "liberty" with any great precision, that term is not confined to mere freedom from bodily restraint. Liberty under law extends to the full range of conduct which the individual is free to pursue, and it cannot be restricted except for a proper governmental objective. Segregation in public education is not reasonably related to any proper governmental objective, and thus it imposes on Negro children of the District of Columbia a burden that constitutes an arbitrary deprivation of their liberty in violation of the Due Process Clause.

In view of our decision that the Constitution prohibits the states from maintaining racially segregated public schools, it would be unthinkable that the same Constitution would impose a lesser duty on the Federal Government. We hold that racial segregation in the public schools of the District of Columbia is a denial of the due process of law guaranteed by the Fifth Amendment to the Constitution.

For the reasons set out in Brown v. Board of Education, this case will be restored to the docket for reargument.   .   .   .

It is so ordered.

## NOTES AND QUESTIONS

1. In what way(s) is Bolling different from Brown I?

2. What justifying reason(s) is given by the Court for its decision? Do you agree? Is it that schools segregated by law are "so unjustifiable as to be violative of due process?" If so, what is the relationship between the equal protection clause and the due process clause? Is every violation of equal protection thereby a violation of due process? Is the justifying reason that "segregation in public education is not reasonably related to *any* proper governmental objective?" What about the governmental objective of maintaining the public peace approved in Plessy?

3. What is the status of Plessy after Brown v. Board of Education and Bolling v. Sharpe?

4. Would a desegregation plan meet the requirements of Brown if it permitted a student of a minority race voluntarily to transfer back to a school, where previously, his race was in the majority? Why? See, Goss v. Knoxville Board of Education, 373 U.S. 683, 83 S.Ct. 1405, 10 L.Ed.2d 632 (1963).

5. Would a desegregation plan meet Brown's requirements of "deliberate speed" if it desegregated one grade a year, assigning pupils in the non-desegregated grades on the basis of race? See, Rogers v. Paul, 382 U.S. 198, 86 S.Ct. 358, 15 L.Ed.2d 265 (1965).

6. Would a desegregation plan meet the requirements of Brown if students, or their parents, voluntarily could choose the school at which the child would attend?

## BROWN IN THE SOUTH: ENTRENCHED SEGREGATION
## AND DUAL SCHOOL SYSTEMS

---

During the mid-50s, by per curiam orders, usually simply by citing Brown, the Supreme Court declared racial segregation unconstitutional in places other than schools. See, e. g., New Orleans v. Detiege, 358 U.S. 54, 79 S.Ct. 99, 3 L.Ed.2d 46 (1958) (parks); Gayle v. Browder, 352 U.S. 903, 77 S.Ct. 145, 1 L.Ed.2d 114 (1956) (buses); Holmes v. Atlanta, 350 U.S. 879, 76 S.Ct. 141, 100 L.Ed. 776 (1955) (golf courses), and Mayor & City Council of Biltmore v. Dawson, 350 U.S. 877, 76 S.Ct. 133, 100 L.Ed. 774 (1955) (beaches).

---

## GREEN v. COUNTY SCHOOL BOARD

Supreme Court of the United States, 1968.
391 U.S. 430, 88 S.Ct. 1689, 20 L.Ed.2d 716.

Mr. Justice BRENNAN delivered the opinion of the Court.

The question for decision is whether, under all the circumstances here, respondent School Board's adoption of a "freedom-of-choice" plan which allows a pupil to choose his own public school constitutes adequate compliance with the Board's responsibility "to achieve a system of determining admission to the public schools on a nonracial basis. . . ." Brown v. Board of Education, 349 U.S. 294, 300–301 (*Brown II*).

Petitioners brought this action in March 1965 seeking injunctive relief against respondent's continued maintenance of an alleged racially segregated school system. New Kent County is a rural county in Eastern Virginia. About one-half of its population of some 4,500 are Negroes. There is no residential segregation in the county; persons of both races reside throughout. The school system has only two schools, the New Kent school on the east side of the county and the George W. Watkins school on the west side. In a memorandum filed May 17, 1966, the District Court found that the "school system serves approximately 1,300 pupils, of which 740 are Negro and 550 are White. The School Board operates one white combined elementary and high school [New Kent], and one Negro combined elementary and high school [George W. Watkins]. There are no attendance zones. Each school serves the entire county." The record indicates that 21 school buses—11 serving the Watkins school and 10 serving the New Kent school—travel overlapping routes throughout the county to transport pupils to and from the two schools.

The segregated system was initially established and maintained under the compulsion of Virginia constitutional and statutory provisions mandating racial segregation in public education, Va.Const., Art. IX, § 140 (1902); Va.Code § 22–221 (1950). These provisions were held to violate the Federal Constitution in Davis v. County School Board of Prince Edward County, decided with Brown v. Board of Education, 347 U.S. 483, 487 (*Brown I*). The respondent School Board continued the segregated operation of the system after the *Brown* decisions, presumably on the authority of several statutes enacted by Virginia in resistance to those decisions. Some of these statutes were held to be unconstitutional on their face or as applied. One statute, the Pupil Placement Act, Va.Code § 22–232.1 et seq. (1964), not repealed until 1966, divested local boards of authority to assign children to particular schools and placed that authority in a State Pupil Placement Board. Under that Act children were each year automatically reassigned to the school previously attended unless upon their application the State Board assigned them to another school; students seeking enrollment for the first time were also assigned at the discretion of the State Board. To September 1964, no Negro pupil had applied for admission to the New Kent school under this statute and no white pupil had applied for admission to the Watkins school.

The School Board initially sought dismissal of this suit on the ground that petitioners had failed to apply to the State Board for assignment to New Kent school. However on August 2, 1965, five months after the suit was brought, respondent School Board, in order to remain eligible for federal financial aid, adopted a "freedom-of-choice" plan for desegregating the schools. Under that plan, each pupil, except those entering the first and eighth grades, may annually choose between the New Kent and Watkins schools and pupils not making a choice are assigned to the school previously attended; first and eighth grade pupils must affirmatively choose a school. . . .

The pattern of separate "white" and "Negro" schools in the New Kent County school system established under compulsion of state laws is precisely the pattern of segregation to which *Brown I* and *Brown II* were particularly addressed, and which *Brown I* declared unconstitutionally denied Negro school children equal protection of the laws. Racial identification of the system's schools was complete, extending not just to the composition of student bodies at the two schools but to every facet of school operations—faculty, staff, transportation, extracurricular activities and facilities. In short, the State, acting through the local school board and school officials, organized and operated a dual system, part "white" and part "Negro".

It was such dual systems that 14 years ago *Brown I* held unconstitutional and a year later *Brown II* held must be abolished; school boards operating such school systems were *required* by *Brown II* "to effectuate a transition to a racially nondiscriminatory school system." 349 U.S., at 301. It is of course true that for the time immediately after *Brown II* the concern was with making an initial break in a long-established pattern of excluding Negro children from schools attended by white children.　The principal focus was on obtaining for those Negro children courageous enough to break with tradition a place in the "white" schools.　See, e. g., Cooper v. Aaron, 358 U.S. 1. Under *Brown II* that immediate goal was only the first step, however. The transition to a unitary, nonracial system of public education was and is the ultimate end to be brought about; it was because of the "complexities arising from the transition to a system of public education freed of racial discrimination" that we provided for "all deliberate speed" in the implementation of the principles of *Brown I*. . . . Thus we recognized the task would necessarily involve solution of "varied local school problems."　. . .　In referring to the "personal interest of the plaintiffs in admission to public schools as soon as practicable on a nondiscriminatory basis," we also noted that "[t]o effectuate this interest may call for elimination of a variety of obstacles in making the transition. . . ."　. . .　Yet we emphasized that the constitutional rights of Negro children required school officials to bear the burden of establishing that additional time to carry out the ruling in an effective manner "is necessary in the public interest and is consistent with good faith compliance at the earliest practicable date."　. . .　We charged the district courts in their review of particular situations to

> "consider problems related to administration, arising from the physical condition of the school plant, the school transportation system, personnel, revision of school districts and attendance areas into compact units to achieve a system of determining admission to the public schools on a nonracial basis, and revision of local laws and regulations which may be necessary in solving the foregoing problems.　They will also consider the adequacy of any plans the defendants may propose to meet these problems and to effectuate a transition to a racially nondiscriminatory school system."　. . .

It is against this background that 13 years after *Brown II* commanded the abolition of dual systems we must measure the effectiveness of respondent School Board's "freedom-of-choice" plan to achieve that end.　The School Board contends that it has fully discharged its obligation by adopting a plan by which every student, regardless of race, may "freely" choose the school he will attend.　The Board attempts to cast the issue in its broadest form by arguing that its "freedom-of-choice" plan may be faulted only by reading the Fourteenth Amendment as universally requiring "compulsory integration," a reading it insists the wording of the Amendment will not support. But that argument ignores the thrust of *Brown II*.　In the light of the command of that case, which is involved here is the question whether the Board has achieved the "racially nondiscriminatory school system" *Brown II* held must be effectuated in order to remedy the established

unconstitutional deficiencies of its segregated system.   In the context
of the state-imposed segregated pattern of long standing, the fact that
in 1965 the Board opened the doors of the former "white" school to
Negro children and of the "Negro" school to white children merely
begins, not ends, our inquiry whether the Board has taken steps adequate to abolish its dual, segregated system.   *Brown II* was a call for
the dismantling of well-entrenched dual systems tempered by an
awareness that complex and multifaceted problems would arise which
would require time and flexibility for a successful resolution.   School
boards such as the respondent then operating state-compelled dual systems were nevertheless clearly charged with the affirmative duty to
take whatever steps might be necessary to convert to a unitary system
in which racial discrimination would be eliminated root and branch.
.   .   .   The constitutional rights of Negro school children articulated
in *Brown I* permit no less than this;   and it was to this end that *Brown
II* commanded school boards to bend their efforts.

In determining whether respondent School Board met that command by adopting its "freedom-of-choice" plan, it is relevant that this
first step did not come until some 11 years after *Brown I* was decided
and 10 years after *Brown II* directed the making of a "prompt and
reasonable start."   This deliberate perpetuation of the unconstitutional dual system can only have compounded the harm of such a system.
Such delays are no longer tolerable, for "the governing constitutional
principles no longer bear the imprint of newly enunciated doctrine."
.   .   .   Moreover, a plan that at this late date fails to provide meaningful assurance of prompt and effective disestablishment of a dual
system is also intolerable.   "The time for mere 'deliberate speed' has
run out," Griffin v. County School Board, 377 U.S. 218, 234;   "the
context in which we must interpret and apply this language [of *Brown
II*] to plans for desegregation has been significantly altered."   .   .   .
The burden on a school board today is to come forward with a plan
that promises realistically to work, and promises realistically to work
*now*.

The obligation of the district courts, as it always has been, is to
assess the effectiveness of a proposed plan in achieving desegregation.
There is no universal answer to complex problems of desegregation;
there is obviously no one plan that will do the job in every case.   The
matter must be assessed in light of the circumstances present and the
options available in each instance.   It is incumbent upon the school
board to establish that its proposed plan promises meaningful and
immediate progress toward disestablishing state-imposed segregation.
It is incumbent upon the district court to weigh that claim in light
of the facts at hand and in light of any alternatives which may be
shown as feasible and more promising in their effectiveness.   Where
the court finds the board to be acting in good faith and the proposed
plan to have real prospects for dismantling the state-imposed dual

system "at the earliest practicable date," then the plan may be said to provide effective relief. Of course, the availability to the board of other more promising courses of action may indicate a lack of good faith; and at the least it places a heavy burden upon the board to explain its preference for an apparently less effective method. Moreover, whatever plan is adopted will require evaluation in practice, and the court should retain jurisdiction until it is clear that state-imposed segregation has been completely removed. . . .

We do not hold that "freedom of choice" can have no place in such a plan. We do not hold that a "freedom-of-choice" plan might of itself be unconstitutional, although that argument has been urged upon us. Rather, all we decide today is that in desegregating a dual system a plan utilizing "freedom of choice" is not an end in itself. As Judge Sobeloff has put it,

> " 'Freedom of choice' is not a sacred talisman; it is only a means to a constitutionally required end—the abolition of the system of segregation and its effects. If the means prove effective, it is acceptable, but if it fails to undo segregation, other means must be used to achieve this end. The school officials have the continuing duty to take whatever action may be necessary to create a 'unitary, nonracial system'." Bowman v. County School Board, 382 F.2d 326, 333 (C.A.4th Cir. 1967) (concurring opinion).

. . . Where it offers real promise of aiding a desegregation program to effectuate conversion of a state-imposed dual system to a unitary, nonracial system there might be no objection to allowing such a device to prove itself in operation. On the other hand, if there are reasonably available other ways, such for illustration as zoning, promising speedier and more effective conversion to a unitary, nonracial school system, "freedom of choice" must be held unacceptable.

The New Kent School Board's "freedom-of-choice" plan cannot be accepted as a sufficient step to "effectuate a transition" to a unitary system. In three years of operation not a single white child has chosen to attend Watkins school and although 115 Negro children enrolled in New Kent school in 1967 (up from 35 in 1965 and 111 in 1966) 85% of the Negro children in the system still attend the all-Negro Watkins school. In other words, the school system remains a dual system. Rather than further the dismantling of the dual system, the plan has operated simply to burden children and their parents with a responsibility which *Brown II* placed squarely on the School Board. The Board must be required to formulate a new plan and . . . fashion steps which promise realistically to convert promptly to a system without a "white" school and a "Negro" school, but just schools.

. . . .

## NOTES AND QUESTIONS

1. Green holds, inter alia, that all deliberate speed has run out and that the constitutional duty of a school board is to produce a unitary, "nondiscriminatory school system." Assume you are a local board member charged with describing to the board and to the public exactly what constitutes a unitary, "nondiscriminatory school system," what will you say?

2. How urgent is the constitutional duty of Green? Must a school board take *"whatever* steps might be necessary" to achieve a unitary, nondiscriminatory school system, or must it only approve of "alternatives which may be shown as feasible"?

3. Is the interpretation of the requirements of the equal protection clause in Green consistent with Brown I and II? Is the appropriate interpretation one that forbids only the use of a racial classification as the basis for student assignment to schools (a de jure approach), or is it one that focuses on the result requiring that a unitary, nondiscriminatory school system be achieved in fact (a de facto approach)?

4. Does Green require that boards of education create educational programs for educationally deprived children because of previous segregation? If so, can these programs be segregated? See, United States by Clark v. Plaquemines Parish School Board, 291 F.Supp. 841 (E.D. La.1967), mod. 415 F.2d 817 (5th Cir.).

5. Are the requirements of Green met by school board action to build a new school at a site that fails to make progress toward desegreation? See, Broussard v. Houston, 395 F.2d 817 (5th Cir. 1968) and United States v. Board of Public Instr. of Polk County, 395 F.2d 66 (5th Cir. 1968).

6. Does Green's constitutional duty apply to school boards that never operated a dual school system?

7. Could a state constitutionally pass a law allowing any or all counties to close any or all county schools if counties wanted to rather than comply with Brown and Green? See, Griffin v. County School Board, 377 U.S. 218, 84 S.Ct. 1226, 12 L.Ed.2d 256 (1964). Suppose instead of closing its schools a county simply gave large amounts of aid to nonsectarian, non-profit "private" schools, most of which were segregated?

---

## ALEXANDER v. HOLMES COUNTY BOARD OF EDUC.

Supreme Court of the United States, 1969.
396 U.S. 19, 90 S.Ct. 29, 24 L.Ed.2d 19, reh. den. 396 U.S. 976, 90 S.Ct. 437, 24 L.Ed.2d 447.

PER CURIAM. This case comes to the Court on a petition for certiorari to the Court of Appeals for the Fifth Circuit. The petition was granted on October 9, 1969, and the case set down for early argument. The question presented is one of paramount importance, involving as it does the denial of fundamental rights to many thousands of school children, who are presently attending Mississippi schools under segregated conditions contrary to the applicable decisions of this Court. Against this background the Court of Appeals should have denied all motions for additional time because continued operation of segregated schools under a standard of allowing "all deliberate speed" for desegregation is no longer constitutionally permissible. Under explicit holdings of this Court the obligation of every school district is to terminate dual school systems at once and to operate now and hereafter only unitary schools. Griffin v. County School Board, 377 U.S. 218, 234 (1964); Green v. County School Board of New Kent County, 391 U.S. 430, 438–439, 442 (1968). Accordingly, *It is hereby adjudged, ordered, and decreed*:

1. The Court of Appeals' order of August 28, 1969, is vacated, and the case is remanded to that court to issue its decree and order, effective immediately, declaring that each of the school districts here involved may no longer operate a dual school system based on race or color, and directing that they begin immediately to operate as unitary school systems within which no person is to be effectively excluded from any school because of race or color.

2. The Court of Appeals may in its discretion direct the schools here involved to accept all or any part of the August 11, 1969, recommendations of the Department of Health, Education, and Welfare, with any modifications which that Court deems proper insofar as those recommendations insure a totally unitary school system for all eligible pupils without regard to race or color.

The Court of Appeals may make its determination and enter its order without further arguments or submissions.

3. While each of these school systems is being operated as a unitary system under the order of the Court of Appeals, the District Court may hear and consider objections thereto or proposed amendments thereof, provided, however, that the Court of Appeals' order shall be complied with in all respects while the District Court considers such objections or amendments, if any are made. No amendment shall become effective before being passed upon by the Court of Appeals.

4. The Court of Appeals shall retain jurisdiction to insure prompt and faithful compliance with its order, and may modify or amend the same as may be deemed necessary or desirable for the operation of a unitary school system.

5. The order of the Court of Appeals dated August 28, 1969, having been vacated and the case remanded for proceedings in conformity with this order, the judgment shall issue forthwith and the Court of Appeals is requested to give priority to the execution of this judgment as far as possible and necessary.

## SINGLETON v. JACKSON MUNICIPAL SEPARATE SCHOOL DIST.

United States Court of Appeals, 1970.
419 F.2d 1211 (5th Cir.), cert. den. 402 U.S. 944, 91 S.Ct. 1611, 29 L.Ed.2d 112.

PER CURIAM. These appeals, all involving school desegregation orders, are consolidated for opinion purposes. They involve, in the main, common questions of law and fact. They were heard en banc on successive days.

Following our determination to consider these cases en banc, the Supreme Court handed down its decision in Alexander v. Holmes County Board of Education . . . That decision supervened all existing authority to the contrary. It sent the doctrine of deliberate speed to its final resting place . . .

The rule of the case is to be found in the direction to this court to issue its order "effective immediately declaring that each of the school districts . . . may no longer operate a dual school system based on race or color, and directing that they begin immediately to operate as unitary school systems within which no person is to be effectively excluded from any school because of race or color." We effectuated this rule and order in United States v. Hinds County School Board (5 Cir. (1969)), 417 F.2d 852. It must likewise be effectuated in these and all other school cases now being or which are to be considered in this or the district courts of this circuit.

The tenor of the decision in Alexander v. Holmes County is to shift the burden from the standpoint of time for converting to unitary school systems. The shift is from a status of litigation to one of unitary operation pending litigation. The new modus operandi is to require immediate operation as unitary systems. Suggested modifications to unitary plans are not to delay implementation. Hearings on requested changes in unitary operating plans may be in order but no delay in conversion may ensue because of the need for modification or hearing.

In Alexander v. Holmes County, the court had unitary plans available for each of the school districts. In addition, this court, on remand, gave each district a limited time within which to offer its own plan. It was apparent there, as it is here, that converting to a unitary system involved basically the merger of faculty and staff, students, transportation, services, athletic and other extra-curricular school activities. We required that the conversion to unitary systems in those districts take place not later than December 31, 1969. It was the earliest feasible date in the view of the court. United States v. Hinds County supra. In three of the systems there (Hinds County, Holmes County and Meridian), because of particular logistical difficulties the Office of Education (HEW) had recommended two-step plans. The result was, and the court ordered, that the first step be implemented not later than December 31, 1969, and the other beginning with the fall 1970 school term.

## I

Because of Alexander v. Holmes County, each of the cases here, as will be later discussed, must be considered anew, either in whole or in part, by the district courts. It happens that there are extant unitary plans for some of the school districts here, either Office of Education or school board originated. Some are operating under freedom of choice plans. In no one of the districts has a plan been submitted in light of the precedent of Alexander v. Holmes County. That case resolves all questions except as to mechanics. The school districts here may no longer operate dual systems and must begin immediately to operate as unitary systems. The focus of the mechanics question is on the accomplishment of the immediacy requirement laid down in Alexander v. Holmes County.

Despite the absence of plans, it will be possible to merge faculties and staff, transportation, services, athletics and other extra-curricular activities during the present school term. It will be difficult to arrange the merger of student bodies into unitary systems prior to the fall 1970 term in the absence of merger plans. The court has concluded that two-step plans are to be implemented. One step must be accomplished not later than February 1, 1970, and it will include all steps necessary to conversion to a unitary system save the merger of student bodies into unitary systems. The student body merger will constitute the second step and must be accomplished not later than the beginning of the fall term 1970.[2] The district courts, in the respective cases here, are directed to so order and to give first priority to effectuating this requirement.

To this end, the district courts are directed to require the respective school districts, appellees herein, to request the Office of Education (HEW) to prepare plans for the merger of the student bodies into unitary systems. These plans shall be filed with the district courts not later than January 6, 1970, together with such additional plan or modification of the Office of Education plan as the school district may wish to offer. The district court shall enter its final order not later than February 1, 1970, requiring and setting out the details of a plan

---

[2] Many faculty and staff members will be transferred under step one. It will be necessary for final grades to be entered and for other records to be completed, prior to the transfers, by the transferring faculty members and administrators for the partial school year involved. The interim period prior to February 1, 1970, is allowed for this purpose.

The interim period prior to the start of the fall 1970 school term is allowed for arranging the student transfers. Many students must transfer. Buildings will be put to new use. In some instances it may be necessary to transfer equipment, supplies or libraries. School bus routes must be reconstituted. The period allowed is at least adequate for the orderly accomplishment of the task.

designed to accomplish a unitary system of pupil attendance with the start of the fall 1970 school term.  Such order may include a plan designed by the district court in the absence of the submission of an otherwise satisfactory plan.  A copy of such plan as is approved shall be filed by the clerk of the district court with the clerk of this court.[3]

The following provisions are being required as step one in the conversion process.  The district courts are directed to make them a part of the orders to be entered and to also give first priority to implementation.

The respective school districts, appellees herein, must take the following action not later than February 1, 1970:

### DESEGREGATION OF FACULTY AND OTHER STAFF

The school board shall announce and implement the following policies:

1.  Effective not later than February 1, 1970, the principals, teachers, teacher-aides and other staff who work directly with children at a school shall be so assigned that in no case will the racial composition of a staff indicate that a school is intended for Negro students or white students.  For the remainder of the 1969–70 school year the district shall assign the staff described above so that the ratio of Negro to white teachers in each school, and the ratio of other staff in each, are substantially the same as each such ratio is to the teachers and other staff, respectively, in the entire school system.

The school district shall, to the extent necessary to carry out this desegregation plan, direct members of its staff as a condition of continued employment to accept new assignments.

2.  Staff members who work directly with children, and professional staff who work on the administrative level will be hired, assigned, promoted, paid, demoted, dismissed, and otherwise treated without regard to race, color, or national origin.

[3] In formulating plans, nothing herein intended to prevent the respective school districts or the district court from seeking the counsel and assistance of State departments of education, university schools of education or of others having expertise in the field of education.

It is also to be noted that many problems of a local nature are likely to arise in converting to and maintaining unitary systems.  These problems may best be resolved on the community level.  The district courts should suggest the advisability of biracial advisory committees to school boards in those districts having no Negro school board members.

3. If there is to be a reduction in the number of principals, teachers, teacher-aides, or other professional staff employed by the school district which will result in a dismissal or demotion of any such staff members, the staff member to be dismissed or demoted must be selected on the basis of objective and reasonable nondiscriminatory standards from among all the staff of the school district. In addition if there is any such dismissal or demotion, no staff vacancy may be filled through recruitment of a person of a race, color, or national origin different from that of the individual dismissed or demoted, until each displaced staff member who is qualified has had an opportunity to fill the vacancy and has failed to accept an offer to do so.

Prior to such a reduction, the school board will develop or require the development of nonracial objective criteria to be used in selecting the staff member who is to be dismissed or demoted. These criteria shall be available for public inspection and shall be retained by the school district. The school district also shall record and preserve the evaluation of staff members under the criteria. Such evaluation shall be made available upon request to the dismissed or demoted employee.

"Demotion" as used above includes any reassignment (1) under which the staff member receives less pay or has less responsibility than under the assignment he held previously, (2) which requires a lesser degree of skill than did the assignment he held previously, or (3) under which the staff member is asked to teach a subject or grade other than one for which he is certified or for which he has had substantial experience within a reasonably current period. In general and depending upon the subject matter involved, 5 years is such a reasonable period.

## MAJORITY TO MINORITY TRANSFER POLICY

The school district shall permit a student attending a school in which his race is in the majority to choose to attend another school, where space is available, and where his race is in the minority.

## TRANSPORTATION

The transportation system, in those school districts having transportation systems, shall be completely reexamined regularly by the superintendent, his staff, and the school board. Bus routes and the assignment of students to buses will be designed to insure the transportation of all eligible pupils on a nonsegregated and otherwise nondiscriminatory basis.

### SCHOOL CONSTRUCTION AND SITE SELECTION

All school construction, school consolidation, and site selection (including the location of any temporary classrooms) in the system shall be done in a manner which will prevent the recurrence of the dual school structure once this desegregation plan is implemented.

### ATTENDANCE OUTSIDE SYSTEM OF RESIDENCE

If the school district grants transfers to students living in the district for their attendance at public schools outside the district, or if it permits transfers into the district of students who live outside the district, it shall do so on a nondiscriminatory basis, except that it shall not consent to transfers where the cumulative effect will reduce desegregation in either district or reenforce the dual school system.

See United States v. Hinds County, supra, decided November 6, 1969. The orders there embrace these same requirements.

## II

In addition to the foregoing requirements of general applicability, the order of the court which is peculiar to each of the specific cases being considered is as follows:

### No. 26285—JACKSON, MISSISSIPPI

This is a freedom of choice system. The issue presented has to do with school building construction. We enjoined the proposed construction pending appeal.

A Federal appellate court is bound to consider any change, either in fact or in law, which has supervened since the judgment was entered. . . . We therefore reverse and remand for compliance with the requirements of Alexander v. Holmes County and the other provisions and conditions of this order. Our order enjoining the proposed construction pending appeal is continued in effect until such time as the district court has approved a plan for conversion to a unitary school system.

### No. 28261—MARSHALL COUNTY

\*     \*     \*     \*     \*     \*     \*     \*     \*     \*

## III

In the event of an appeal or appeals to this court from an order entered as aforesaid in the district courts, such appeal shall be on the original record and the parties are encouraged to appeal on an agreed statement as is provided for in rule 10(d), Federal Rules of Appellate Procedure (FRAP). Pursuant to rule 2, FRAP, the provisions of rule 4(a) as to the time for filing notice of appeal are suspended and it is ordered that any notice of appeal be filed within 15 days of the date of entry of the order appealed from and notices of cross-appeal within 5 days thereafter. The provisions of rule 11 are suspended and it is ordered that the record be transmitted to this court within 15 days after filing of the notice of appeal. The provisions of rule 31 are suspended to the extent that the brief of the appellant shall be filed within 15 days after the date on which the record is filed and the brief of the appellee shall be filed within 10 days after the date on which the brief of appellant is filed. No reply brief shall be filed except upon order of the court. The times set herein may be enlarged by the court upon good cause shown.

The mandate in each of the within matters shall issue forthwith. No stay will be granting pending petition for rehearing or application for certiorari.

Reversed as to all save Mobile and St. John The Baptist Parish; affirmed as to Mobile with direction; affirmed in part and reversed in part as to St. John The Baptist Parish; remanded to the district courts for further proceedings consistent herewith.

---

## SWANN v. CHARLOTTE–MECKLENBURG BOARD OF EDUCATION

Supreme Court of the United States, 1971.
402 U.S. 1, 91 S.Ct. 1267, 28 L.Ed.2d 554, cert. den. 403 U.S. 912, 91 S.Ct. 2200, 29 L.Ed.2d 689.

[These cases considered desegregation plans involving Charlotte, N. C. and its environs. In 1969–70 the federal district court rejected three plans that had been proposed by the board of education (respondent) and then accepted a plan prepared at the court's request by "an expert in education administration," and issued a decree which later was partially modified by the court of appeals. Later still, the district court rejected a plan prepared by HEW concluding that either the plan submitted by a minority of the school board or the one submitted by the court's expert was "reasonable and acceptable."]

Mr. Chief Justice BURGER delivered the opinion of the Court.

. . .

This case and those argued with it arose in States having a long history of maintaining two sets of schools in a single school system deliberately operated to carry out a governmental policy to separate pupils in schools solely on the basis of race. That was what Brown v. Board of Education was all about. These cases present us with the problem of defining in more precise terms than heretofore the scope of the duty of school authorities and district courts in implementing *Brown I* and the mandate to eliminate dual systems and establish unitary systems at once. . . .

.   .   .   we should now try to amplify guidelines, however in-complete and imperfect, for the assistance of school authorities and courts.   The failure of local authorities to meet their constitutional obligations aggravated the massive problem of converting from the state-enforced discrimination of racially separate school systems. This process has been rendered more difficult by changes since 1954 in the structure and patterns of communities, the growth of student population, movement of families, and other changes, some of which had marked impact on school planning, sometimes neutralizing or negating remedial action before it was fully implemented.   Rural areas accustomed for half a century to the consolidated school systems im-plemented by bus transportation could make adjustments more readily than metropolitan areas with dense and shifting population, numerous schools, congested and complex traffic patterns.

The objective today remains to eliminate from the public schools all vestiges of state-imposed segregation.   .   .   .

If school authorities fail in their affirmative obligations   .   .   . judicial authority may be invoked.   Once a right and a violation have been shown, the scope of a district court's equitable powers to remedy past wrongs is broad, for breadth and flexibility are inherent in equita-ble remedies.

> "The essence of equity jurisdiction has been the power of the Chancellor to do equity and to mould each decree to the necessities of the particular case.   Flexibility rather than rigidity has distinguished it.   The qualities of mercy and practicality have made equity the instrument for nice adjust-ment and reconciliation between the public interest and pri-vate needs as well as between competing private claims."

.   .   .

This allocation of responsibility once made, the Court attempted from time to time to provide some guidelines for the exercise of the district judge's discretion and for the reviewing function of the courts of appeals.   However, a school desegregation case does not differ fundamentally from other cases involving the framing of equitable remedies to repair the denial of a constitutional right.   The task is to correct, by a balancing of the individual and collective interests, the condition that offends the Constitution.

In seeking to define even in broad and general terms how far this remedial power extends it is important to remember that judicial powers may be exercised only on the basis of a constitutional viola-tion.   Remedial judicial authority does not put judges automatically in the shoes of school authorities whose powers are plenary.   Judicial authority enters only when local authority defaults.

School authorities are traditionally charged with broad power to formulate and implement educational policy and might well conclude, for example, that in order to prepare students to live in a pluralistic society each school should have a prescribed ratio of Negro to white students reflecting the proportion for the district as a whole. To do this as an educational policy is within the broad discretionary powers of school authorities; absent a finding of a constitutional violation, however, that would not be within the authority of a federal court. As with any equity case, the nature of the violation determines the scope of the remedy. In default by the school authorities of their obligation to proffer acceptable remedies, a district court has broad power to fashion a remedy that will assure a unitary school system.

The school authorities argue that the equity powers of federal district courts have been limited by Title IV of the Civil Rights Act of 1964, 42 U.S.C. § 2000c. The language and the history of Title IV show that it was enacted not to limit but to define the role of the Federal Government in the implementation of the *Brown I* decision. It authorizes the Commissioner of Education to provide technical assistance to local boards in the preparation of desegregation plans, to arrange "training institutes" for school personnel involved in desegregation efforts, and to make grants directly to schools to ease the transition to unitary systems. It also authorizes the Attorney General, in specified circumstances, to initiate federal desegregation suits. Section 2000c(b) defines "desegregation" as it is used in Title IV:

> " 'Desegregation' means the assignment of students to public schools and within such schools without regard to their race, color, religion, or national origin, but 'desegregation' shall not mean the assignment of students to public schools in order to overcome racial imbalance."

Section 2000c–6, authorizing the Attorney General to institute federal suits, contains the following proviso:

> "nothing herein shall empower any official or court of the United States to issue any order seeking to achieve a racial balance in any school by requiring the transportation of pupils or students from one school to another or one school district to another in order to achieve such racial balance, or otherwise enlarge the existing power of the court to insure compliance with constitutional standards."

On their face, the sections quoted purport only to insure that the provisions of Title IV of the Civil Rights Act of 1964 will not be read as granting new powers. The proviso in § 2000c–6 is in terms designed to foreclose any interpretation of the Act as expanding the *existing* powers of federal courts to enforce the Equal Protection Clause. There is no suggestion of an intention to restrict those powers or withdraw from courts their historic equitable remedial powers. The legislative history of Title IV indicates that Congress was concerned that the Act might be read as creating a right of action under the Fourteenth Amendment in the situation of so-called "de facto segregation," where racial imbalance exists in the schools but with no showing that this was brought about by discriminatory action of state authorities. In short, there is nothing in the Act that provides us material assistance in answering the question of remedy for state-imposed segregation in violation of *Brown I.* The basis of our decision must be the prohibition of the Fourteenth Amendment that no State shall "deny to any person within its jurisdiction the equal protection of the laws."

We turn now to the problem of defining with more particularity the responsibilities of school authorities in desegregating a state-enforced dual school system in light of the Equal Protection Clause. . . .

In *Green*, we pointed out that existing policy and practice with regard to faculty, staff, transportation, extracurricular activities, and facilities were among the most important indicia of a segregated system. . . . Independent of student assignment, where it is possible to identify a "white school" or a "Negro school" simply by reference to the racial composition of teachers and staff, the quality of school buildings and equipment, or the organization of sports activities, a *prima facie* case of violation of substantive constitutional rights under the Equal Protection Clause is shown.

When a system has been dual in these respects, the first remedial responsibility of school authorities is to eliminate invidious racial distinctions. With respect to such matters as transportation, supporting personnel, and extracurricular activities, no more than this may be necessary. Similar corrective action must be taken with regard to the maintenance of buildings and the distribution of equipment. In these areas, normal administrative practice should produce schools of like quality, facilities, and staffs. Something more must be said, however, as to faculty assignment and new school construction.

In the companion *Davis* case . . . the Mobile school board has argued that the Constitution requires that teachers be assigned on a "color blind" basis. It also argues that the Constitution prohibits district courts from using their equity power to order assignment of teachers to achieve a particular degree of faculty desegregation. We reject that contention.

In United States v. Montgomery County Board of Education, 395 U.S. 225 (1969), the District Court set as a goal a plan of faculty assignment in each school with a ratio of white to Negro faculty members substantially the same throughout the system. This order was predicated on the District Court finding that:

> "The evidence does not reflect any real administrative problems involved in immediately desegregating the substitute teachers, the student teachers, the night school faculties,

and in the evolution of a really legally adequate program for the substantial desegregation of the faculties of all schools in the system commencing with the school year 1968–69." Quoted at 395 U. S., at 232. . . .

We [held] that the order of the District Judge

"was adopted in the spirit of this Court's opinion in *Green* . . . in that his plan 'promises realistically to work, and promises realistically to work *now*'." . . .

The construction of new schools and the closing of old ones are two of the most important functions of local school authorities and also two of the most complex. . . . Over the long run, the consequences of the choices will be far reaching. People gravitate toward school facilities, just as schools are located in response to the needs of people. The location of schools may thus influence the patterns of residential development of a metropolitan area and have important impact on composition of innercity neighborhoods.

In the past, choices in this respect have been used as a potent weapon for creating or maintaining a state-segregated school system. In addition to the classic pattern of building schools specifically intended for Negro or white students, school authorities have sometimes, since *Brown*, closed schools which appeared likely to become racially mixed through changes in neighborhood residential patterns. This was sometimes accompanied by building new schools in the areas of white suburban expansion farthest from Negro population centers in order to maintain the separation of the races with a minimum departure from the formal principles of "neighborhood zoning." Such a policy does more than simply influence the short-run composition of the student body of a new school. It may well promote segregated residential patterns which, when combined with "neighborhood zoning," further lock the school system into the mold of separation of the races. Upon a proper showing a district court may consider this in fashioning a remedy.

In ascertaining the existence of legally imposed school segregation, the existence of a pattern of school construction and abandonment is thus a factor of great weight. In devising remedies where legally imposed segregation has been established, it is the responsibility of local authorities and district courts to see to it that future school construction and abandonment are not used and do not serve to perpetuate or re-establish the dual system. When necessary, district courts should retain jurisdiction to assure that these responsibilities are carried out. . . .

The central issue in this case is that of student assignment, and there are essentially four problem areas: . . .

(1) *Racial Balances or Racial Quotas.*

. . . . It would not serve the important objection of *Brown I* to seek to use school desegregation cases for purposes beyond their scope, although desegregation of schools ultimately will have impact on other forms of discrimination. We do not reach in this case the question whether a showing that school segregation is a consequence of other types of state action, without any discriminatory action by the school authorities, is a constitutional violation requiring remedial action by a school desegregation decree. This case does not present that question and we therefore do not decide it.

Our objective in dealing with the issues presented by these cases is to see that school authorities exclude no pupil of a racial minority from any school, directly or indirectly, on account of race; it does not and cannot embrace all the problems of racial prejudice, even when those problems contribute to disproportionate racial concentrations in some schools.

In this case it is urged that the District Court has imposed racial balance requirements of 71%–29% on individual schools. . . .

. . . If we were to read the holding of the District Court to require, as a matter of substantive constitutional right, any particular degree of racial balance or mixing, that approach would be disapproved and we would be obliged to reverse. The constitutional command to desegregate schools does not mean that every school in every community must always reflect the racial composition of the school system as a whole.

. . . the use made of mathematical ratios was no more than a starting point in the process of shaping a remedy, rather than an inflexible requirement. From that starting point the District Court proceeded to frame a decree that was within its discretionary powers, as an equitable remedy for the particular circumstances. As we said in *Green*, a school authority's remedial plan or a district court's remedial decree is to be judged by its effectiveness. Awareness of the racial composition of the whole school system is likely to be a useful starting point in shaping a remedy to correct past constitutional violations. In sum, the very limited use made of mathematical ratios was within the equitable remedial discretion of the District Court.

(2) *One-race Schools.*

The record in this case reveals the familiar phenomenon that in metropolitan areas minority groups are often found concentrated in one part of the city. In some circumstances certain schools may remain all or largely of one race until new schools can be provided or neighborhood patterns change. . . .

. . . No *per se* rule can adequately embrace all the difficulties of reconciling the competing interests involved; but in a system with a history of segregation the need for remedial criteria of sufficient specificity to assure a school authority's compliance with its constitutional duty warrants a presumption against schools that are substantially disproportionate in their racial composition. Where the school authority's proposed plan for conversion from a dual to a unitary system contemplates the continued existence of some schools that are all or predominately of one race, they have the burden of showing that such school assignments are genuinely nondiscriminatory. The court should scrutinize such schools, and the burden upon the school authorities will be to satisfy the court that their racial composition is not the result of present or past discriminatory action on their part.

An optional majority-to-minority transfer provision has long been recognized as a useful part of every desegregation plan. Provision for optional transfer of those in the majority racial group of a particular school to other schools where they will be in the minority is an indispensable remedy for those students willing to transfer to other schools in order to lessen the impact on them of the state-imposed stigma of segregation. In order to be effective, such a transfer arrangement must grant the transferring student free transportation and space must be made available in the school to which he desires to move.

. . .

### (3) *Remedial Altering of Attendance Zones.*

The maps submitted in these cases graphically demonstrate that one of the principal tools employed by school planners and by courts to break up the dual school system has been a frank—and sometimes drastic—gerrymandering of school districts and attendance zones. An additional step was pairing, "clustering," or "grouping" of schools with attendance assignments made deliberately to accomplish the transfer of Negro students out of formerly segregated Negro schools and transfer of white students to formerly all-Negro schools. More often than not, these zones are neither compact nor contiguous; indeed they may be on opposite ends of the city. As an interim corrective measure, this cannot be said to be beyond the broad remedial powers of a court.

Absent a constitutional violation there would be no basis for judicially ordering assignment of students on a racial basis. All things beng equal, with no history of discrimination, it might well be desirable to assign pupils to schools nearest their homes. But all things are not equal in a system that has been deliberately constructed and maintained to enforce racial segregation. The remedy for such segregation may be administratively awkward, inconvenient, and even bizarre in some situations and may impose burdens on some; but all awkwardness and inconvenience cannot be avoided in the interim period when remedial adjustments are being made to eliminate the dual school systems.

No fixed or even substantially fixed guidelines can be established as to how far a court can go, but it must be recognized that there are limits. The objective is to dismantle the dual school system. "Racially neutral" assignment plans proposed by school authorities to a district court may be inadequate; such plans may fail to counteract the continuing effects of past school segregation resulting from discriminatory location of school sites or distortion of school size in order to achieve or maintain an artificial racial separation. When school authorities present a district court with a "loaded game board," affirmative action in the form of remedial altering of attendance zones is proper to achieve truly nondiscriminatory assignments. In short, an assignment plan is not acceptable simply because it appears to be neutral.

In this area, we must of necessity rely to a large extent, as this Court has for more than 16 years, on the informed judgment of the district courts in the first instance and on courts of appeals.

We hold that the pairing and grouping of noncontiguous school zones is a permissible tool and such action is to be considered in light of the objectives sought. Judicial steps in shaping such zones going beyond combinations of contiguous areas should be examined in light of what is said in subdivisions (1), (2), and (3) of this opinion concerning the objectives to be sought. Maps do not tell the whole story since noncontiguous school zones may be more accessible to each other in terms of the critical travel time, because of traffic patterns and good highways, than schools geographically closer together. Conditions in different localities will vary so widely that no rigid rules can be laid down to govern all situations.

(4) *Transportation of Students.*

. . . No rigid guidelines as to student transportation can be given for application to the infinite variety of problems presented in thousands of situations. Bus transportation has been an integral part of the public education system for years, and was perhaps the single most important factor in the transition from the one-room schoolhouse to the consolidated school. Eighteen million of the Nation's public school children, approximately 39%, were transported to their schools by bus in 1969–1970 in all parts of the country. . . .

The decree provided that the buses used to implement the plan would operate on direct routes. Students would be picked up at schools near their homes and transported to the schools they were to attend. The trips for elementary school pupils average about seven miles and the District Court found that they would take "not over 35 minutes at the most." This system compares favorably with the transportation plan previously operated in Charlotte under which each day 23,600 students on all grade levels were transported an average of 15 miles one way for an average trip requiring over an hour. In these circumstances, we find no basis for holding that the local school authorities may not be required to employ bus transportation as one tool of school desegregation. Desegregation plans cannot be limited to the walk-in school.

An objection to transportation of students may have validity when the time or distance of travel is so great as to either risk the health of the children or significantly impinge on the educational process. District courts must weigh the soundness of any transportation plan in light of what is said in subdivisions (1), (2), and (3) above. It hardly needs stating that the limits on time of travel will vary with many factors, but probably with none more than the age of the students. The reconciliation of competing values in a desegregation case is, of course, a difficult task with many sensitive facets but fundamentally no more so than remedial measures courts of equity have traditionally employed. . . .

. . . we are unable to conclude that the order of the District Court is not reasonable, feasible and workable. However, in seeking to define the scope of remedial power or the limits on remedial power of courts in an area as sensitive as we deal with here, words are poor instruments to convey the sense of basic fairness inherent in equity. Substance, not semantics, must govern, and we have sought to suggest the nature of limitations without frustrating the appropriate scope of equity.

At some point, these school authorities and others like them should have achieved full compliance with this Court's decision in *Brown I*. The systems would then be "unitary" in the sense required by our decisions in *Green* and *Alexander*.

It does not follow that the communities served by such systems will remain demographically stable, for in a growing, mobile society, few will do so. Neither school authorities nor district courts are constitutionally required to make year-by-year adjustments of the racial composition of student bodies once the affirmative duty to desegregate has been accomplished and racial discrimination through official action is eliminated from the system. This does not mean that federal courts are without power to deal with future problems; but in the absence of a showing that either the school authorities or some other agency of the State has deliberately attempted to fix or alter demographic patterns to affect the racial composition of the schools, further intervention by a district court should not be necessary. . . .

### NOTES AND QUESTIONS

1. Do you agree with the opinion of the Supreme Court?
2. Is the constitution "color blind"?
3. Does this opinion indicate that the proper approach when deciding school desegregation cases is a result-oriented, de facto approach? If so, what standard should be used to judge whether the end sought has been achieved? Is it a "unitary" school system, or a unitary "non-discriminatory school system"? Does it make any difference whether the stress is on one or the other aspect of the formula?
4. Is Swann rigorously consistent with Green and Brown I and II?

5. Mr. Chief Justice Burger, speaking for the Court in Swann, states that "[a]n objection to transportation of students may have some validity when the time or distance of travel is so great as to  .  .  .  significantly impinge on the educational process." Suppose the following facts appear in a case before the Supreme Court: Past racial segregation in the schools of your school district has resulted in large discrepancies in educational achievement between students of the same grade but attending different de facto or de jure segregated schools within the district and that a bussing plan such as that offered in Swann was mandated. Suppose further that it was shown that because of the sudden integration of previously segregated students (who though in the same grade bring widely differing academic achievement to the now integrated classroom) the better prepared students will be slowed in their academic progress because of the presence of others who are less well prepared. Thus, integration may "significantly impinge on the educational process" as it affects the better prepared group. Proponents of the bussing plan, citing the above language from Swann, have appealed to the Supreme Court from a ruling of the federal circuit court of appeals holding the bussing plan invalid. Assume you are a member of the Supreme Court, what decision would you render and for what reason(s)?

6. What does the court say about de facto segregation?

7. The constitutional viability of a neighborhood school policy which causes, perpetuates or simply fails to eliminate racial imbalance has been the topic of considerable discussion. See generally, 1 U. S. Comm'n on Civil Rights, Racial Isolation in the Public Schools 219–29 (1967). If a school board follows a neighborhood school policy when drawing local school district lines, and it results in segregated schools, is this situation de jure segregation, coming within Brown I and II and Green?

---

## SCHOOL DESEGREGATION FROM BROWN TO SWANN

---

School desegregation in the South has been divided into three phases: (1) the "Muted Response" to Brown—1955–1963; (2) the "Search For Standards"—1963–1967, and (3) "Massive Integration" —1968–1972. See, Read, Judicial Evolution of the Law of School Integration Since Brown v. Board of Education, 39 Law & Contemp. Probs. 7 (1975). Green v. County Sch. Bd., supra, opened the final period and Alexander and Swann, supra, closed it. The following tables, printed in the Congressional Record for June 18, 1976, indicate that large amounts of school desegregation have taken place in the South. If the goal of Brown v. Board of Educ. is to eliminate the intentional and official segregation of races in schools, has that goal been achieved? If the goals of Brown are to produce an integrated school system and an integrated society, have they been achieved? Can they be achieved without eliminating de facto segregation? Can school desegregation produce an integrated society where there is widespread de facto segregation?

TABLE 1.—*Proportion of black children in predominantly minority public schools, 1970–74*

(Percent)

| | 1970 | 1972 | 1974 |
|---|---|---|---|
| National | 70.6 | 67.6 | 66.8 |
| South | 62.1 | 56.2 | 55.5 |
| Border and D.C. | 78.5 | 75.1 | 71.9 |
| Northeast | 78.7 | 79.6 | 81.0 |
| Midwest | 83.2 | 81.5 | 80.6 |
| West | 74.3 | 73.6 | 73.4 |

Source.—HEW Office for Civil Rights, May 1976.
Note.—The statistics in this table are based on enrollment reports from districts estimated to contain approximately 92 percent of the nation's black students in 1972–73.

TABLE 2.—*Proportion of black children in intensely segregated schools (90 to 100 percent minority enrollment)*

(Percent)

| | 1970 | 1972 | 1974 |
|---|---|---|---|
| South | 34.2 | 25.7 | 23.4 |
| Border and D.C. | 63.9 | 61.8 | 58.4 |
| West | 50.5 | 46.9 | 45.1 |
| Northeast | 52.5 | 54.6 | 57.8 |
| Midwest | 64.4 | 62.9 | 62.2 |
| National | 46.4 | 42.0 | 40.5 |

Source.—HEW Office for Civil Rights, May 1976.
Note.—The statistics in this table are based on enrollment reports from districts which contained an estimated 92 percent of the nation's black enrollment according to universe projections based on 1972–73 enrollment reports.

TABLE 3.—*Percentage of Latino children in predominantly minority schools, 1970–74*

(Percent)

| | 1970 | 1972 | 1974 |
|---|---|---|---|
| National | 64.2 | 65.2 | 67.4 |
| Northeast | 84.2 | 83.1 | 84.2 |
| South | 72.6 | 72.3 | 72.8 |
| Midwest | 52.6 | 53.4 | 57.1 |
| West | 48.5 | 51.4 | 56.3 |

Source.—HEW Office for Civil Rights, May 1976.
Note.—The statistics in this and the following tables are based on enrollment figures from districts estimated to contain 74 percent of the nation's Latino students

at the time of HEW's last universe projections, covering the 1972–73 school year. The data covers an estimated 87 percent of Latino enrollment in the Northeast, 82 percent in the South, 66 percent in the West, and 62 percent in the Midwest.

TABLE 4.—*Proportion of Latino children in intensely segregated schools (90 to 100 percent minority enrollment)*

(Percent)

|  | 1970 | 1972 | 1974 |
|---|---|---|---|
| National | 29.0 | 29.2 | 30.0 |
| Northeast | 50.0 | 50.5 | 53.8 |
| Midwest | 11.7 | 15.0 | 20.9 |
| West | 14.6 | 14.2 | 15.7 |
| South | 36.1 | 35.5 | 34.1 |

TABLE 5.—*1974 enrollment of Latino children in schools with 70 percent or more minority children*

(Percent)

|  | 1974 |
|---|---|
| National | 50.0 |
| Northeast | 71.7 |
| South | 56.8 |
| Midwest | 40.8 |
| West | 34.9 |

Source.—HEW Office for Civil Rights, May 1976.

---

## RUNYON v. McCRARY

Supreme Court of the United States, 1976.
427 U.S. 160, 96 S.Ct. 2586, 49 L.Ed.2d 415.

Mr. Justice STEWART delivered the opinion of the Court.

The principal issue presented by these consolidated cases is whether a federal law, namely, 42 U.S.C.A. § 1981, prohibits private schools from excluding qualified children solely because they are Negroes.

I

The respondents, . . . Michael McCrary and Colin Gonzales, are Negro children. By their parents, they filed a class action against the petitioners Russell and Katheryne Runyon, who are the proprietors of Bobbe's School in Arlington, Va. Their complaint alleged that they had been prevented from attending the school because of the petitioners' policy of denying admission to Negroes, in violation of 42 U.S.C.A. § 1981.[1] They sought declaratory and injunctive relief and damages. On the same day Colin Gonzales, . . . filed a similar complaint by his parents against the petitioner, . . . Fairfax-Brewster School, Inc., located in Fairfax County, Va. . . . the Southern Independent School Association, sought and was granted permission to intervene as a party defendant in the suit against the Runyons. That organization is a nonprofit association composed of six state private school associations, and represents 395 private schools. It is stipulated that many of these schools deny admission to Negroes.

The suits were consolidated for trial. The findings of the District Court, which were left undisturbed by the Court of Appeals, were as follows. Bobbe's School opened in 1958 and grew from an initial enrollment of five students to 200 in 1972. A day camp was begun in 1967 and has averaged 100 children per year. The Fairfax-Brewster School commenced operations in 1955 and opened a summer day camp in 1956. A total of 223 students were enrolled at the school during the 1972–1973 academic year, and 236 attended the day camp in the summer of 1972. Neither school has ever accepted a Negro child for any of its programs.

In response to a mailed brochure addressed "resident" and an advertisement in the "Yellow Pages" of the telephone directory, Mr. and Mrs. Gonzales telephoned and then visited the Fairfax-Brewster School in May 1969. After the visit, they submitted an application for Colin's admission to the day camp. The school responded with a form letter, which stated that the school was "unable to accommodate [Colin's] application." Mr. Gonzales telephoned the school. Fairfax-Brewster's Chairman of the Board explained that the reason for Colin's rejection was that the school was not integrated. Mr. Gonzales then telephoned Bobbe's School, from which the family had also received in the mail a brochure addressed to "resident." In response to a question concerning that school's admissions policies, he was told that only members of the Caucasian race were accepted. In August 1972, Mrs. McCrary telephoned Bobbe's School in response to an advertisement in the telephone book. She inquired about nursery school facilities for her son, Michael. She also asked if the school was integrated. The answer was no.

Upon these facts, the District Court found that the Fairfax-Brewster School had rejected Colin Gonzales' application on account of his race and that Bobbe's School had denied both children ad-

---

[1] Title 42 U.S.C.A. § 1981 provides:
  "All persons within the jurisdiction of the United States shall have the same right in every State and Territory to make and enforce contracts, to sue, be parties, give evidence, and to the full and equal benefit of all laws and proceedings for the security of persons and property as is enjoyed by white citizens, and shall be subject to like punishment, pains, penalties, taxes, licenses, and exactions of every kind, and to no other."

mission on racial grounds. The court held that 42 U.S.C.A. § 1981 makes illegal the schools' racially discriminatory admissions policies. It therefore enjoined Fairfax-Brewster School and Bobbe's School and the member schools of the Southern Independent School Association from discriminating against applicants for admission on the basis of race. . . .

The Court of Appeals for the Fourth Circuit, sitting en banc, affirmed the District Court . . . .

## II

It is worth noting at the outset some of the questions that these cases do not present. They do not present any question of the right of a private social organization to limit its membership on racial or any other grounds. They do not present any question of the right of a private school to limit its student body to boys, to girls, or to adherents of a particular religious faith, since 42 U.S.C.A. § 1981 is in no way addressed to such categories of selectivity. They do not even present the application of § 1981 to private sectarian schools that practice *racial* exclusion on religious grounds. Rather, these cases present only two basic questions: whether § 1981 prohibits private, commercially operated, nonsectarian schools from denying admission to prospective students because they are Negroes, and, if so, whether that federal law is constitutional as so applied.

## A.   APPLICABILITY OF § 1981

It is now well established that § 1 of the Civil Rights Act of 1866, 14 Stat. 27, 42 U.S.C.A. § 1981, prohibits racial discrimination in the making and enforcement of private contracts.

In *Jones* [392 U.S. 409, 88 S.Ct. 2186, 20 L.Ed.2d 1189] the Court held that the portion of § 1 of the Civil Rights Act of 1866 presently codified as 42 U.S.C.A. § 1982 prohibits private racial discrimination in the sale or rental of real or personal property. Relying on the legislative history of § 1, from which both § 1981 and § 1982 derive, the Court concluded that Congress intended to prohibit "all racial discrimination, private and public, in the sale . . . of property," and that this prohibition was within Congress' power under § 2 of the Thirteenth Amendment "rationally to determine what are the badges and the incidents of slavery, and . . . to translate that determination into effective legislation."

As the Court indicated in *Jones,* supra, holding necessarily implied that the portion of § 1 of the 1866 Act presently codified as 42 U.S.C.A. § 1981 likewise reaches purely private acts of racial discrimination. The statutory holding in *Jones* was that the "[1866] Act was designed to do just what its terms suggest: to prohibit all racial discrimination, whether or not under color of law, with respect to the rights enumerated therein—including the right to purchase or lease property." One of the "rights enumerated" in § 1 is "the same right . . . to make and enforce contracts . . . as is enjoyed by white citizens . . . ." Just as in *Jones* a Negro's § 1 right to purchase property on equal terms with whites was violated when a private person refused to sell to the prospective purchaser solely because he was a Negro, so also a Negro's § 1 right to "make and enforce contracts" is violated if a private offeror refuses to extend to a Negro, solely because he is a Negro, the same opportunity to enter into contracts as he extends to white offerees.

It is apparent that the racial exclusion practiced by the Fairfax-Brewster School and Bobbe's Private School amounts to a classic violation of § 1981. The parents of Colin Gonzales and Michael Mc-Crary sought to enter into contractual relationships with Bobbe's School for educational services. Colin Gonzales' parents sought to enter into a similar relationship with the Fairfax-Brewster School. Under those contractual relationships, the schools would have received payments for services rendered, and the prospective students would have received instruction in return for those payments. The educational services of Bobbe's School and the Fairfax-Brewster School were advertised and offered to members of the general public. But neither school offered services on an equal basis to white and nonwhite students. As the Court of Appeals held, "there is ample evidence in the record to support the trial judge's factual determinations . . . [that] Colin [Gonzales] and Michael [McCrary] were denied admission to the schools because of their race." The Court of Appeals' conclusion that § 1981 was thereby violated follows inexorably from the language of that statute, as construed in *Jones*.

. . . .

The petitioning schools and school association argue principally that § 1981 does not reach private acts of racial discrimination. That view is wholly inconsistent with *Jones'* interpretation of the legislative history of § 1 of the Civil Rights Act of 1866. This consistent interpretation of the law necessarily requires the conclusion that § 1981, like § 1982, reaches private conduct.

It is noteworthy that Congress in enacting the Equal Employment Opportunity Act of 1972, specifically considered and rejected an amendment that would have repealed the Civil Rights Act of 1866, as interpreted by this Court in *Jones,* insofar as it affords private-sector employees a right of action based on racial discrimination in employment. There could hardly be a clearer indication of congressional agreement with the view that § 1981 *does* reach private acts of racial discrimination. In these circumstances there is no basis for deviating from the well-settled principles of *stare decisis* applicable to this Court's construction of federal statutes.

## B. CONSTITUTIONALITY OF § 1981 AS APPLIED

The question remains whether § 1981, as applied, violates constitutionally protected rights of free association and privacy, or a parent's right to direct the education of his children.

### 1. Freedom of Association

In *NAACP v. Alabama* and similar decisions, the Court has recognized a First Amendment right "to engage in association for the advancement of beliefs and ideas . . . ." That right is protected because it promotes and may well be essential to the "[e]ffective advocacy of both public and private points of view, particularly controversial ones" that the First Amendment is designed to foster.

From this principle it may be assumed that parents have a First Amendment right to send their children to educational institutions that promote the belief that racial segregation is desirable, and that the children have an equal right to attend such institutions. But it does not follow that the *practice* of excluding racial minorities from such institutions is also protected by the same principle. As the Court stated in *Norwood v. Harrison*, "the Constitution . . . places no value on discrimination," and while "[i]nvidious private discrimination may be characterized as a form of exercising freedom of association protected by the First Amendment . . . it has never been accorded affirmative constitutional protections. And even some private discrimination is subject to special remedial legislation in certain circumstances under § 2 of the Thirteenth Amendment; Congress has made such discrimination unlawful in other significant contexts." In any event, as the Court of Appeals noted, "there is no showing that discontinuance of [the] discriminatory admission practices would inhibit in any way the teaching in these schools of any ideas or dogma."

### 2. Parental Rights

In Meyer v. Nebraska, the Court held that the liberty protected by the Due Process Clause of the Fourteenth Amendment includes the right "to acquire useful knowledge, to marry, establish a home and bring up children," and, concomitantly, the right to send one's children to a private school that offers specialized training—in that case, instruction in the German language. In Pierce v. Society of Sisters, the Court applied "the doctrine of Meyer v. Nebraska," to hold unconstitutional an Oregon law requiring the parent, guardian, or other person having custody of a child between 8 and 16 years of age to send that child to public school on pain of criminal liability. The Court thought it "entirely plain that the [statute] unreasonably interferes with the liberty of parents and guardians to direct the upbringing and education of children under their control." In Wisconsin v. Yoder, the Court stressed the limited scope of *Pierce*, pointing out that it lent "no support to the contention that parents may replace state educational requirements with their own idiosyncratic views of what knowledge a child needs to be a productive and happy member of society" but rather "held simply that while a State may posit [educational] standards, it may not pre-empt the educational process by requiring children to attend public schools." And in Norwood v. Harrison, the Court once again stressed the "limited scope of Pierce," which simply "affirmed the right of private schools to exist and to operate . . . ."

It is clear that the present application of § 1981 infringes no parental right recognized in *Meyer, Pierce, Yoder,* or *Norwood.* No challenge is made to the petitioner schools' right to operate or the right of parents to send their children to a particular private school rather than a public school. Nor do these cases involve a challenge to the subject matter which is taught at any private school. Thus, the Fairfax-Brewster School and Bobbe's School and members of the intervenor association remain presumptively free to inculcate whatever values and standards they deem desirable. *Meyer* and its progeny entitle them to no more.

### 3.   The Right of Privacy

The Court has held that in some situations the Constitution confers a right of privacy.

While the application of § 1981 to the conduct at issue here—a private school's adherence to a racially discriminatory admissions policy—does not represent governmental intrusion into the privacy of the home or a similarly intimate setting, it does implicate parental interests. . . . A person's decision whether to bear a child and a parent's decision concerning the manner in which his child is to be educated may fairly be characterized as exercises of familial rights and responsibilities. But it does not follow that because government is largely or even entirely precluded from regulating the child-bearing decision, it is similarly restricted by the Constitution from regulating the implementation of parental decisions concerning a child's education.

The Court has repeatedly stressed that while parents have a constitutional right to send their children to private schools and a constitutional right to select private schools that offer specialized instruction, they have no constitutional right to provide their children with private school education unfettered by reasonable government regulation. . . .

Section 1981, as applied to conduct at issue here, constitutes an exercise of federal legislative power under § 2 of the Thirteenth Amendment fully consistent with *Meyer, Pierce,* and the cases that followed in their wake. . . .

For the reasons stated in this opinion, the judgment of the Court of Appeals is in all respects affirmed.

It is so ordered.

Mr. Justice POWELL, concurring.

If the slate were clean I might well be inclined to agree with Mr. Justice WHITE that § 1981 was not intended to restrict private contractual choices. Much of the review of the history and purpose of this statute set forth in his dissenting opinion is quite persuasive. It seems to me, however, that it comes too late.

The applicability of § 1981 to private contracts has been considered maturely and recently, and I do not feel free to disregard these precedents. . . .

Mr. Justice STEVENS, concurring.

For me the problem in these cases is whether to follow a line of authority which I firmly believe to have been incorrectly decided. . . . Were we writing on a clean slate, I would therefore vote to reverse.

But *Jones* has been decided and is now an important part of the fabric of our law. Although I recognize the force of Mr. Justice WHITE's argument that the construction of § 1982 does not control § 1981, it would be most incongruous to give those two sections a fundamentally different construction. The net result of the enactment in 1866, the re-enactment in 1870, and the codification in 1874 produced, I believe, a statute resting on the constitutional foundations provided by both the Thirteenth and Fourteenth Amendments. An attempt to give a fundamentally different meaning to two similar provisions by ascribing one to the Thirteenth and the other to the Fourteenth Amendment cannot succeed. I am persuaded, therefore, that we must either apply the rationale of *Jones* or overrule that decision.

. . .

The policy of the Nation as formulated by the Congress in recent years has moved constantly in the direction of eliminating racial segregation in all sectors of society. This Court has given a sympathetic and liberal construction to such legislation. For the Court now to overrule *Jones* would be a significant step backwards, with effects that would not have arisen from a correct decision in the first instance. Such a step would be so clearly contrary to my understanding of the mores of today that I think the Court is entirely correct in adhering to *Jones*.

With this explanation, I join the opinion of the Court.

Mr. Justice WHITE, with whom Mr. Justice REHNQUIST joins, dissenting.

We are urged here to extend the meaning and reach of 42 U.S. C.A. § 1981 so as to establish a general prohibition against a private individual's or institution's refusing to enter into a contract with another person because of that person's race. Section 1981 has been on the books since 1870 and to so hold for the first time would be contrary to the language of the section, to its legislative history, and to the clear dictum of this Court in the *Civil Rights Cases,* 109 U.S. 3, 16–17, 3 S.Ct. 18, 25–26, 27 L.Ed. 835 (1883), almost contemporaneously with the passage of the statute, that the section reaches only discriminations imposed by state law. The majority's belated discovery of a congressional purpose which escaped this Court only a decade after the statute was passed and which escaped all other federal courts for almost 100 years is singularly unpersuasive. I therefore respectfully dissent.

. . .

## NOTES AND QUESTIONS

1. Would the decision in this case have been the same if McCrary had been excluded because he failed to have an adequate command of English? Because he spoke "Black English"? Because his parents were in the lower income bracket? Or, because "it would be detrimental to the best interests of the school"?

   Bobbe's and the Fairfax-Brewster schools "were advertised and offered to members of the general public." The court relied strongly on this fact as a limiting feature of § 1981. Would § 1981 apply if the schools had not extended their invitations to deal with the general public? If not, what will be the probable impact of Runyon on the admission practices of racially discriminatory private schools?

2. What is the precedential meaning of Pierce after Runyon v. McCrary? The court stated that Pierce "simply 'affirmed the right to private schools to exist and to operate.'" Is Pierce now limited specially; that is, to restricting parents from preparing their children "for additional obligations" by inculcating racial prejudices, or is Pierce limited generally; that is, to guaranteeing the existence of private schools, having eliminated a general constitutional right of parents "to recognize and prepare [their children] for additional obligations"? Did the court rule on parental rights? Were the rights of any parents, other than McCrary and Gonzales, before the court? Who were the defendants?

3. In Cook v. Hudson, 511 F.2d 744 (5th Cir. 1975), public school teachers were not rehired by the county board of education pursuant to an unwritten board policy that prohibited hiring of any teachers whose own children were enrolled in racially segregated private school. The court upheld the school board's decision as related to job performance (an exemplar?) and as not violative of the teachers' rights to freedom of association or their Fourteenth Amendment rights to due process or equal protection:

   "Although the president of the school board testified that patronage of the Academy by public school teachers had been a source of controversy in the community, the keystone to defendants' justification of the policy (and the district court's approval) came from the testimony of two experts in the field of educational psychology.   Both were of the opinion 'that the challenged policy was significantly related to a teacher's effectiveness and job performance [because] students in desegregated classes are likely to perceive rejection, and experience a sense of inferiority from a teacher whose own children attend a nearby racially segregated school, and [such students will] be inclined to perform at a lower educational level.'   Neither expert had evaluated plaintiffs individually.   One had been director of a three-year project the aim of which was 'to increase the interaction between the school and the community and the student and the teacher in public schools in Mississippi.'   His investigation had included schools in Calhoun County, although not the Calhoun City Attendance Center at which plaintiffs taught.   Both experts agreed that the Board policy was 'reasonable,' based on psychological principles of 'negative reinforcement' and 'teacher expectation.'   One of them explained:

"A.   Okay.   The kind of thing that operates in a classroom is that a major variable in learning is how a teacher relates to a student.   There is ample indication from both research, my own and others, and just observation on my part that a teacher who is perceived by students as rejecting the public school system will have a difficult time, for example, reinforcing the learning that would go on in the classroom.   It would be a perception on the part of students of a difference from the students, and I think this would be particularly true with the black students.

"Q.   What would be the relationship of this rejection and perception to academic achievement?

"A.   The major thing is that a teacher is the major—or a major reinforcer of learning.   And so that if there is a discrepancy in the way that a student—or let's say if there is a negative perception on the part of the student of the teacher, this detracts from the teacher's ability to reinforce learning.

"Q.   Is this what educational psychologists would refer to as terms of this reinforcement?

"A.   It's an operational principle in psychology that holds that a teacher, by such things as paying attention to students, showing respect, trust, acceptance has the potential for increasing or having a positive effect on learning.

"Q.   Is this what—

"A.   That's basically what reinforcement is.

"Q.   Is this what educational psychologists would refer to as positive or negative social reinforcement?

"A.   Right.

"Q.   And what would be the effect of a negative social reinforcement?

"A. The negative social reinforcement is shown in situations where the possibility exists for a teacher not having the potential or the possibility as a functional teacher to reinforce what goes on in an appropriate way in the classroom.

"Q. Doctor Eicke, would a student perceive a teacher who sent their own children to a private school—a public school student, would this be perceived as a negative social reinforcement?

"A. I think it would.

"Q. Doctor Eicke, what do psychologists mean when they refer to teacher expectations?

"A. Teacher expectation is an area that has been studied in educational psychology dealing with a phenomenon in which what is expected of students is what they tend to do. And my contention would be that if a teacher expected less from students that the students would tend to perform at a lower level; and conversely, if the teacher expected more, the students would tend to perform better. This need not be a conscious kind of thing. In fact, it usually isn't. And I would think that a teacher that rejects the public school system as acceptable for [the teacher's] own children would set lower expectations [for the public school students] that [the teacher] would then come in contact with.

"He added that '[a]nything that detracts from a positive perception of [the] teacher may affect learning.' The other expert repeated and further explained similar opinions.

"The district court found in this evidence a sufficient 'rational relation' between the challenged policy and the goal of public school desegregation to answer plaintiffs' equal protection objection. However, while apparently conceding that the Board's policy infringed plaintiffs' First Amendment rights, the court noted that those rights 'may not be considered in isolation,' that they 'must be applied in the light of the special circumstances of the environment of the particular case,' and that 'where the exercise of First Amendment rights impairs the teacher's effectiveness, or conflicts with the performance of her job, the school board may lawfully refuse to rehire the teacher.' After quoting from the Supreme Court's opinion in Adler v. Board of Educ., the court concluded: 'It necessarily follows that if the board's policy is a reasonable and constitutional regulation, plaintiffs may not complain of the consequence of not being rehired as public school teachers for having exercised their right to send their children to a private school.' The court evidently implied a finding that the policy was constitutional within its determination that the rational relation test had been met."

## BROWN IN THE NORTH AND WEST: DE FACTO SEGREGATION

School segregation in the North and West does not rest on racial assignment of children to separate schools that is enforced by law.

Instead, it rests on underlying segregated residential patterns, many of which are consequences of racial prejudices and discrimination. This is called "de facto" segregation. It is unlikely that a case arising in the North or West will present facts identical to Brown where racial school assignments for an entire state were required by state law. But, given a pattern of residential separation of races, a school district can take advantage of the de facto segregation and achieve nearly one-race schools by manipulating its school boundaries, by building new schools in places that assure their population by one race and by other techniques. When this occurs, it is called "de jure" segregation, and it violates the principle of Brown v. Board of Educ.

## KEYES v. SCHOOL DIST. NO. 1

Supreme Court of the United States, 1973.
413 U.S. 921, 93 S.Ct. 2686, 37 L.Ed.2d 548.

[This statement of facts is taken from the opinion of the Court of Appeals, 445 F.2d 990 (1971):

"In substance, the trial court found and concluded . . . that the named schools in Northeast Denver were segregated by affirmative state action. In its findings, the trial court noted specific instances of boundary gerrymandering, construction of a new school and classrooms, minority-to-majority transfers, and excessive use of mobile classroom units in this section of the district, all of which amount to unconstitutional state segregation. . . . On the second count, the court found that although the core area schools were not segregated by state action, fifteen designated schools should be granted relief because it was demonstrated that they were offering their pupils an unequal educational opportunity in violation of the Fourteenth Amendment equal protection clause. . . .

"The schools . . . are located in Northeast Denver in what is generally referred to as the Park Hill area. The schools are: East High School, Smiley and Cole Junior High Schools, Barrett, Stedman, Hallett, Park Hill and Philips Elementary Schools. Prior to 1950, the Negro population was centered in the Five Points area, near the northwest corner of City Park. Since 1940, the Negro population has steadily increased from 8,000 to 15,000 in 1950, to 30,000 in 1960, and to approximately 45,000 by 1966. The residential movement reflecting this growth has been eastward, down a 'corridor' which has fairly well defined north-south boundaries. In the early 1950, York Street (some 16 blocks west of Colorado Boulevard) was the east boundary of the residential expansion. Ten years later, the movement had reached and crossed Colorado Boulevard to a limited degree, and now the corridor of Negro residences extends from the Five Points area to the eastern city limits. The schools of concern are in and adjacent to this narrow strip of Negro residences.

"Barrett Elementary is located one block west of Colorado Boulevard in the heart of the Negro community. When it opened in 1960, the attendance lines were drawn to coincide almost precisely with the then eastern boundary of the Negro residential movement—Colorado Boulevard. When the school was being planned in 1958 and the sites for construction were being considered, the area west of Colorado Boulevard was already predominantly Negro; by 1960, when the school opened, the racial composition of the neighborhood which it was to serve was reflected in the 89.6% Negro student enrollment. In 1970, the racial and ethnic composition of the school was approximately 93% Negro, 7% Hispano.

"In addition, Barrett was built to accommodate only 450 students, a factor which manifestly precluded its use to substantially relieve the overcrowded conditions at adjacent schools. In 1960, Stedman (then predominantly Anglo), which was eight blocks due east of Barrett, was well over its intended capacity. Rather than constructing a larger physical plant at Barrett to accommodate part of Stedman's overflow, Barrett's size was restricted to serve only those pupils west of Colorado Boulevard.

"The trial court held that 'the positive acts of the Board in establishing Barrett and defining its boundaries were the proximate cause of the segregated condition which has existed in that school since its creation, which condition exists at present. * * * The action of the Board * * * was taken with knowledge of the consequences, and these consequences were not merely possible, they were substantially certain. Under such conditions we find that the Board acted purposefully to create and maintain segregation at Barrett.' . . .

"In 1960, Stedman was 96% Anglo, 4% Negro and was 20% above capacity. By 1962, it was 35 to 50% Anglo and 50 to 65% Negro. In 1963, it was 87.4% Negro and 18.6% Anglo, and still overcrowded. By 1968, this school was 94.6% Negro and 3.9% Anglo. Stedman is eight blocks due east of Barrett, and in 1960 the residential trend all but insured that in a few years it would be predominantly Negro. In 1962, three boundary changes were proposed to the Board which would have transferred students from Stedman to Smith, Hallett and Park Hill, each of which was predominantly Anglo. These three proposals were refused by the Board. In 1964, the Board made two boundary changes which affected Stedman: (1) a predominantly Anglo section of Stedman's school zone was detached to Hallett, and (2) the Park Hill-Stedman optional zone (96% Anglo) was transferred to Park Hill. To facilitate an expanding population at Stedman, which was overwhelmingly Negro, mobile units were erected.

"The trial court held: 'The actions of the Board with respect to boundary changes, installation of mobile units and repeal of Resolution

1531 shows a continuous affirmative policy designed to isolate Negro children at Stedman and to thereby preserve the "white" character of other Park Hill schools.' . . .

"In 1960, Park Hill and Philips Elementary Schools were predominantly Anglo. In 1968, Park Hill was 71% Anglo, 23.2% Negro and 3.8% Hispano; Philips was 55.3% Anglo, 36.6% Negro and 5.2% Hispano. Notwithstanding the Negro movement into this area, these two schools have continued to maintain a majority of Anglos in the student body.

"The court stated: 'In light of the natural and probable segregative consequences of removing the stabilizing effect of Resolution 1531 on Park Hill and Philips and re-establishing the original district boundaries, the Board must be regarded as having acted with a purpose of approving those consequences.' . . .

"In 1960, Hallett Elementary was 99% Anglo; in 1968 it was 90% Negro, 10% Anglo. The school is about 12 blocks due east of Stedman. When the Stedman boundary changes were considered in 1962, Hallett was under capacity and was 80 to 95% Anglo. The results of the boundary changes, had they occurred, would have brought Hallett up to capacity and would have had an integrative effect on the latter school. The 1964 Stedman boundary change that sent the predominantly Anglo section of Stedman to Hallett resulted in a 80% Anglo section of Hallett's attendance area being transferred to Philips. The effect of the Hallett to Philips transfer was a reduction in Anglo pupils at Hallett from 68.5 to 41.5%. By 1965, when four mobile units were built and additional classrooms constructed, Hallett was 75% Negro.

"The court said: 'The effect of the mobile units and additional classrooms was to solidify segregation at Hallett increasing its capacity to absorb the additional influx of Negro population into the area.'

. . .

"The feeder schools for Smiley Junior High School are Hallett, Park Hill, Smith, Philips, Stedman, Ashley and Harrington. By the established residential trend, Smiley will soon be all Negro. In 1968 there were 23.6% Anglo, 71.6% Negro and 3.7% Hispano, and there were 23 minority teachers. Only one other school in the entire Denver system, Cole Junior High, had more than six minority teachers. The court held: 'The effect of this repeal [of Resolutions 1520 and 1524] was to re-establish Smiley as a segregated school by affirmative Board action. At the time of the repeal, it was certain that such action would perpetuate the racial composition of Smiley at over 75 percent minority and that future Negro population movement would ultimately increase this percentage. * * * We, therefore, find that the action of the Board in rescinding Resolutions 1520 and 1524 was wilful as to its effect on Smiley.' . . .

"In 1969, East High School was 54% Anglo, 40% Negro and 7% Hispano. The court held that neither before nor after the passage of Resolution 1520 could East be considered segregated. But '[r]escission of these Resolutions might, through the feeder system, result in a segregated situation at East in the future. . . . the trial court extended its findings of de jure segregation to East High and Cole Junior High: 'The effect of the rescission of resolution 1520 at East High was to allow the trend toward segregation * * * to continue unabated. The rescission of Resolution 1524 as applied to Cole Junior High was an action taken which had the effect of frustrating an effort at Cole which at least constituted a start toward ultimate improvement in the quality of the educational effort there. * * * We must hold then that this frustration of the Board plan which had for its purpose relief of the effects of segregation at Cole was unlawful.' "]

Mr. Justice BRENNAN delivered the opinion of the Court. . . .

Petitioners apparently concede for the purposes of this case that in the case of a school system like Denver's, where no statutory dual system has ever existed, plaintiffs must prove not only that segregated schooling exists but also that it was brought about or maintained by intentional state action. Petitioners proved that for almost a decade after 1960 respondent School Board had engaged in an unconstitutional policy of deliberate racial segregation in the Park Hill schools. Indeed, the District Court found that "[b]etween 1960 and 1969 the Board's policies with respect to those northeast Denver schools show an undeviating purpose to isolate Negro students" in segregated schools "while preserving the Anglo character of [other] schools." . . . This finding did not relate to an insubstantial or trivial fragment of the school system. On the contrary, respondent School Board was found guilty of following a deliberate segregation policy at schools attended, in 1969, by 37.69% of Denver's total Negro school population, including one-fourth of the Negro elementary pupils, over two-thirds of the Negro junior high pupils, and over two-fifths of the Negro high school pupils. In addition, there was uncontroverted evidence that teachers and staff had for years been assigned on a minority teacher-to-minority school basis throughout the school system. Respondent argues, however, that a finding of state-imposed segregation as to a substantial portion of the school system can be viewed in isolation from the rest of the district, and that even if state-imposed segregation does exist in a substantial part of the Denver school system, it does not follow that the District Court could predicate on that fact a finding that the entire school system is a dual system. We do not agree. We have never suggested that plaintiffs in school desegregation cases must bear the burden of proving the elements of *de jure* segregation as to each and every school or each and every student within the school system. Rather, we have held that where plaintiffs prove that a current condition of segregated schooling exists within a school district where a dual system was compelled or authorized by statute at the time of our decision in Brown v. Board of Education, . . . (*Brown I*), the State automatically assumes an affirmative duty "to effectuate a transition to a racially nondiscriminatory school system," . . . (*Brown II*), that is, to eliminate from the public schools within their school system "all vestiges of state-imposed segregation." . . .

This is not a case, however, where a statutory dual system has ever existed. Nevertheless, where plaintiffs prove that the school authorities have carried out a systematic program of segregation affecting a substantial portion of the students, schools, teachers and facilities within the school system, it is only common sense to conclude that there exists a predicate for a finding of the existence of a dual school system. Several considerations support this conclusion. First, it is obvious that a practice of concentrating Negroes in certain schools by structuring attendance zones or designating "feeder" schools on the basis of race has the reciprocal effect of keeping other nearby schools predominantly white. Similarly, the practice of building a school—such as the Barrett Elementary School in this case—to a certain size and in a certain location, "with conscious knowledge that it would be a segregated school," . . . has a substantial reciprocal effect on the racial composition of other nearby schools. So also, the use of mobile classrooms, the drafting of student transfer policies, the transportation of students, and the assignment of faculty and staff, on racially identifiable bases, have the clear effect of earmarking schools according to their racial composition, and this, in turn, together with the elements of student assignment and school construction, may have a profound reciprocal effect on the racial composition of residential neighborhoods within a metropolitan area, thereby causing further racial concentration within the schools. . . .

In short, common sense dictates the conclusion that racially inspired school board actions have an impact beyond the particular schools that are the subjects of those actions. This is not to say, of course, that there can never be a case in which the geographical structure of or the natural boundaries within a school district may have the effect of dividing the district into separate, identifiable and unrelated units. Such a determination is essentially a question of fact to be resolved by the trial court in the first instance, but such cases must be rare. In the absence of such a determination, proof of state-imposed segregation in a substantial portion of the district will suffice to support a finding by the trial court of the existence of a dual system. Of course, where that finding is made, as in cases involving statutory dual systems, the school authorities have an affirmative duty "to effectuate a transition to a racially nondiscriminatory school system." . . .

Plainly, a finding of intentional segregation as to a portion of a school system is not devoid of probative value in assessing the school authorities' intent with respect to other parts of the same school system. On the contrary, where, as`here, the case involves one school board, a finding of intentional segregation on its part in one portion of a school system is highly relevant to the issue of the board's intent with respect to other segregated schools in the system. This is merely an application of the well-settled evidentiary principle that "the prior doing of other similar acts, whether clearly a part of a scheme or not, is useful as reducing the possibility that the act in question was done with innocent intent."   .   .   .   "Evidence that similar and related offenses were committed   .   .   .   tend[s] to show a consistent pattern of conduct highly relevant to the issue of intent."   .   .   .   Similarly, a finding of illicit intent as to a meaningful portion of the item under consideration has substantial probative value on the question of illicit intent as to the remainder.   .   .   .   And "[t]he foregoing principles are equally as applicable to civil cases as to criminal cases,   .   .   ."

Applying these principles in the special context of school desegregation cases, we hold that a finding of intentionally segregative school board actions in a meaningful portion of a school system, as in this case, creates a presumption that other segregated schooling within the system is not adventitious. It establishes, in other words, a prima facie case of unlawful segregative design on the part of school authorities, and shifts to those authorities the burden of proving that other segregated schools within the system are not also the result of intentionally segregative actions. This is true even if it is determined that different areas of the school district should be viewed independently of each other because, even in that situation, there is high probability that where school authorities have effectuated an intentionally segregative policy in a meaningful portion of the school system, similar impermissible considerations have motivated their actions in other areas of the system. We emphasize that the differentiating factor between *de jure* segregation and so-called *de facto* segregation to which we referred in *Swann* is *purpose* or *intent* to segregate. Where school authorities have been found to have practiced purposeful segregation in part of a school system, they may be expected to oppose system-wide desegregation, as did the respondents in this case, on the ground that their purposefully segregative actions were isolated and individual events, thus leaving plaintiffs with the burden of proving otherwise. But at that point where an intentionally segregative policy is practiced in a meaningful or significant segment of a school system, as in this case, the school authorities can not be heard to argue that plaintiffs have proved only "isolated and individual" unlawfully segregative actions. In that circumstance, it is both fair and reasonable to require that the school authorities bear the burden of showing that their actions as to other segregated schools within the system were not also motivated by segregative intent.

This burden-shifting principle is not new or novel. There are no hard and fast standards governing the allocation of the burden of proof in every situation. The issue, rather, "is merely a question of policy and fairness based on experience in the different situations." . . . In the context of racial segregation in public education, the courts, including this Court, have recognized a variety of situations in which "fairness" and "policy" require state authorities to bear the burden of explaining actions or conditions which appear to be racially motivated. . . .

In discharging that burden, it is not enough, of course, that the school authorities rely upon some allegedly logical, racially neutral explanation for their actions. Their burden is to adduce proof sufficient to support a finding that segregative intent was not among the factors that motivated their actions. The courts below attributed much significance to the fact that many of the Board's actions in the core city area antedated our decision in *Brown*. We reject any suggestion that remoteness in time has any relevance to the issue of intent. If the actions of school authorities were to any degree motivated by segregative intent and the segregation resulting from those actions continues to exist, the fact of remoteness in time certainly does not make those actions any less "intentional."

This is not to say, however, that the prima facie case may not be met by evidence supporting a finding that a lesser degree of segregated schooling in the core city area would not have resulted even if the Board had not acted as it did. In *Swann*, we suggested that at some point in time the relationship between past segregative acts and present segregation may become so attenuated as to be incapable of supporting a finding of *de jure* segregation warranting judicial intervention. . . . We made it clear, however, that a connection between past segregative acts and present segregation may be present even when not apparent and that close examination is required before concluding that the connection does not exist. Intentional school segregation in the past may have been a factor in creating a natural environment for the growth of further segregation. Thus, if respondent School Board cannot disprove segregative intent, it can rebut the prima facie case only by showing that its past segregative acts did not create or contribute to the current segregated condition of the core city schools.

The respondent School Board invoked at trial its "neighborhood school policy" as explaining racial and ethnic concentrations within the core city schools, arguing that since the core city area population had long been Negro and Hispano, the concentrations were necessarily the result of residential patterns and not of purposefully segregative policies. We have no occasion to consider in this case whether a "neighborhood school policy" of itself will justify racial or ethnic concentrations in the absence of a finding that school authorities have committed acts constituting *de jure* segregation. It is enough that we hold that the mere assertion of such a policy is not dispositive where, as in this case, the school authorities have been found to have practiced *de jure* segregation in a meaningful portion of the school system by techniques that indicate that the "neighborhood school" concept has not been maintained free of manipulation. . . .

Thus, respondent School Board having been found to have practiced deliberate racial segregation in schools attended by over one-third of the Negro school population, that crucial finding establishes a prima facie case of intentional segregation in the core city schools. In such case, respondent's neighborhood school policy is not to be determinative "simply because it appears to be neutral." . . .

. . . the case is remanded to the District Court for further proceedings consistent with this opinion.

It is so ordered.

Mr. Chief Justice BURGER concurs in the result.

Mr. Justice WHITE took no part in the decision of this case.

Mr. Justice DOUGLAS.

While I join the opinion of the Court, I agree with my Brother POWELL that there is, for the purposes of the Equal Protection Clause of the Fourteenth Amendment as applied to the school cases, no difference between *de facto* and *de jure* segregation. The school board is a state agency and the lines that it draws, the locations it selects for school sites, the allocation it makes of students, the budgets it prepares are state action for Fourteenth Amendment purposes.

. . . segregated schools are often created, not by dual school systems decreed by the legislature, but by the administration of school districts by school boards. Each is state action within the meaning of the Fourteenth Amendment. "Here school authorities assigned students, faculty, and professional staff, employed faculty and staff; chose sites for schools; constructed new schools and renovated old ones; and drew attendance zone lines. The natural and foreseeable consequence of these actions was segregation of Mexican-Americans. Affirmative action to the contrary would have resulted in desegregation. When school authorities by their actions, contribute to segregation in education, whether by causing additional segregation or maintaining existing segregation, they deny to the students equal protection of the laws.

"We need not define the quantity of state participation which is a prerequisite to a finding of constitutional violation. Like the legal

concepts of 'the reasonable man,' 'due care,' 'causation,' 'preponderance of the evidence,' and 'beyond a reasonable doubt,' the necessary
degree of state involvement is incapable of precise definition and must
be defined on a case-by-case basis. Suffice it to say that school authorities here played a significant role in causing or perpetuating
unequal educational opportunities for Mexican-Americans, and did so
on a system-wide basis."

These latter acts are often said to create *de facto* as contrasted
with *de jure* segregation. But as Judge Wisdom observes, each is but
another form of *de jure* segregation.

I think it is time to state that there is no constitutional difference
between *de jure* and *de facto* segregation, for each is the product of
state actions or policies. If a "neighborhood" or "geographical" unit
has been created along racial lines by reason of the play of restrictive
covenants that restrict certain areas to "the elite," leaving the "un-
desirables" to move elsewhere, there is state action in the constitutional sense because the force of law is placed behind those covenants.

There is state action in the constitutional sense when public funds
are dispersed by urban development agencies to build racial ghettoes.

Where the school district is racially mixed and the races are
segregated in separate schools, where black teachers are assigned
almost exclusively to black schools, where the school board closed
existing schools located in fringe areas and built new schools in black
areas and in distant white areas, where the school board continued
the "neighborhood" school policy at the elementary level, these actions
constitute state action. They are of a kind quite distinct from the
classical *de jure* type of school segregation. Yet calling them *de facto*
is a misnomer, as they are only more subtle types of state action that
create or maintain a wholly or partially segregated school system.

. . .

Mr. Justice POWELL concurring in part and dissenting in part.

. . .

This is the first school desegregation case to reach this Court
which involves a major city outside the South. It comes from Denver,
Colorado, a city and a State which have not operated public schools
under constitutional or statutory provisions which mandated or permitted racial segregation. Nor has it been argued that any other
legislative actions (such as zoning and housing laws) contributed to
the segregation which is at issue. . . .

In my view we should abandon a distinction which long since
has outlived its time, and formulate constitutional principles of national rather than merely regional application. When Brown v. Board
of Education, . . . was decided, the distinction between *de jure*
and *de facto* segregation was consistent with the limited constitutional
rationale of that case. The situation confronting the Court, largely

confined to the southern States, was officially imposed racial segregation in the schools extending back for many years and usually embodied in constitutional and statutory provisions.

The great contribution of *Brown I* was its holding in unmistakable terms that the Fourteenth Amendment forbids state-compelled or authorized segregation of public schools.  .  .  .  Although some of the language was more expansive, the holding in *Brown I* was essentially negative: It was impermissible under the Constitution for the States, or their instrumentalities, to force children to attend segregated schools.  The forbidden action was *de jure*, and the opinion in *Brown I* was construed—for some years and by many courts—as requiring only state neutrality, allowing "freedom of choice" as to schools to be attended so long as the State itself assured that the choice was genuinely free of official restraints.

But the doctrine of *Brown I*, as amplified by *Brown II*,  .  .  . did not retain its original meaning.  In a series of decisions extending from 1954 to 1971 the concept of state neutrality was transformed into the present constitutional doctrine requiring affirmative state action to desegregate school systems.  The keystone case was Green v. County School Board,  .  .  .  where school boards were declared to have "the affirmative duty to take whatever steps might be necessary to convert to a unitary system in which racial discrimination would be eliminated root and branch."  The school system before the Court in *Green* was operating in a rural and sparsely settled county where there were no concentrations of white and black populations, no neighborhood school system (there were only two schools in the county), and none of the problems of an urbanized school district. The Court properly identified the freedom of choice program there as a subterfuge, and the language in *Green* imposing an affirmative duty to convert to a unitary system was appropriate on the facts before the Court.  .  .  .

Rather than continue to prop up a distinction no longer grounded in principle, and contributing to the consequences indicated above, we should ackowledge that whenever public school segregation exists to a substantial degree there is prima facie evidence of a constitutional violation by the responsible school board.  It is true, of course, that segregated schools—wherever located—are not solely the product of the action or inaction of public school authorities.  Indeed, as indicated earlier, there can be little doubt that principal causes of the pervasive school segregation found in the major urban areas of this country, whether in the North, West, or South, are the socio-economic influences which have concentrated our minority citizens in the inner cities while the more mobile white majority disperse to the suburbs. But it is also true that public school boards have continuing, detailed responsibility for the public school system within their district and, as

Judge John Minor Wisdom has noted, "where the figures [showing segregation in the schools] speak so eloquently, a *prima face* case of discrimination is established."   United States v. Texas Education Agency, 467 F.2d 848, 873 (C.A.5 *en banc* 1972).   Moreover, as aforeshadowed in *Swann* and as implicitly held today, school boards have a duty to minimize and ameliorate segregated conditions by pursuing an affirmative policy of desegregation.   It is this policy which must be applied consistently on a national basis without regard to a doctrinal distinction which has outlived its time.*

NOTES AND QUESTIONS

1.   What are the ways in which courts allocate "burdens" (1) when dealing with a district that openly had operated a dual school system, and (2) when dealing with a district that had never openly operated a dual school system?   What difference does the procedure make?   Do you agree?   Why?   See also, Cisneros v. Corpus Christi Independent School Dist., 467 F.2d 142 (5th Cir. 1972).

2.   What evidence in addition to defacto segregation would be required in order to show that a school offered educational opportunities inferior to those of other schools or intended to segregate?   What are the implications of Keyes for "de facto segregation"?

3.   In September 1976, Congress sought to restrict busing by attaching a rider to the Appropriation Act for the Departments of HEW and Labor.   The rider prohibited the use of funds to "force" any school district, meeting the desegregation definition in the Civil Rights Act of 1964, "to take any action to force the busing of students" or to require the "transportation of any student to a school other than the school which is nearest the student's home, and which offers the courses of study pursued by such student, in order to comply with [the 1964 Act]."   §§ 206–208, Public Law 94–439, 90 Stat. 1434.   This rider remained in effect until the end of fiscal year 1978.

4.   In 1976 the Supreme Court reaffirmed that the "central purpose of the Equal Protection clause   .   .   .   is the prevention of official conduct discriminating on the basis of race;" that "the basic equal protection principle [is] that the invidious quality of a law claimed to be racially discriminatory must ultimately be traced to a racially discriminatory purpose;" that while "disproportionate impact is not irrelevant, [it] is not the sole touchstone," and that the "essential element of *de jure* segregation is 'a current condition of segregation resulting from intentional state action   .   .   .   the differentiating factor between *de jure* segregation and so-called *de facto* segregation   .   .   .   is *purpose* or *intent* to segregate.'"   Washington v. Davis, 426 U.S. 229, 96 S.Ct. 2040, 48 L.Ed.2d 597 (1976).   Also see, Village of Arlington Heights v. Metropolitan Housing Dev. Corp., 429 U.S. 252, 97 S.Ct. 555, 50 L.Ed.2d 450 (1977).

5.   In Pasadena City Bd. of Educ. v. Spangler, 427 U.S. 424, 96 S.Ct. 2697, 49 L.Ed.2d 599 (1976), the court held that a federal court had no

* A dissenting opinion by Mr. Justice Rehnquist is omitted.

power to make any adjustments in a requirement of a desegregation plan once the requirement has been met, even though demographic changes have produced severe racial isolation in the schools.

6. In Milliken v. Bradley (Milliken II, 1977), supra Chapter II, the Supreme Court held for the first time that "federal courts can order remedial education programs as part of a school desegregation decree."

--------

## COLUMBUS BD. OF EDUC. v. PENICK

Supreme Court of the United States, 1979.
— U.S. —, 99 S.Ct. 2941, 61 L.Ed.2d 666.

Mr. Justice WHITE delivered the opinion of the Court.

The public schools of Columbus, Ohio, are highly segregated by race. In 1976, over 32% of the 96,000 students in the system were black. About 70% of all students attended schools that were at least 80% black or 80% white. Half of the 172 schools were 90% black or 90% white. Fourteen named students in the Columbus school system brought this case on June 21, 1973, against the Columbus Board of Education, the State Board of Education, and the appropriate local and state officials. The second amended complaint, filed on October 24, 1974, charged that the Columbus defendants had pursued and were pursuing a course of conduct having the purpose and effect of causing and perpetuating the segregation in the public schools, contrary to the Fourteenth Amendment. A declaratory judgment to this effect and appropriate injunctive relief were prayed. Trial of the case began a year later, consumed 36 trial days, produced a record containing over 600 exhibits and a transcript in excess of 6,600 pages, and was completed in June 1976. Final arguments were heard in September, and in March 1977 the District Court filed an opinion and order containing its findings of fact and conclusions of law.

The trial court summarized its findings:

"From the evidence adduced at trial, the Court has found earlier in this opinion that the Columbus Public Schools were openly and intentionally segregated on the basis of race when *Brown* was decided in 1954. The Court has found that the Columbus Board of Education never actively set out to dismantle this dual system. The Court has found that until legal action was initiated by the Columbus Area Civil Rights Council, the Columbus Board did not assign teachers and administrators to Columbus schools at random, without regard for the racial composition of the student enrollment at those schools. The Columbus Board even in very recent times . . . has approved optional attendance zones, discontiguous attendance areas and boundary changes which have maintained and enhanced racial imbalance in the Columbus Public Schools. The Board, even in very recent times and after promising to do otherwise, has adjured [*sic*] workable suggestions for improving the racial balance of city schools.

"Viewed in the context of segregative optional attendance zones, segregative faculty and administrative hiring and assignments, and other such actions and decisions of the Columbus Board of Education in recent and remote history, it is fair and reasonable to draw an inference of segregative intent from the Board's actions and omission discussed in this opinion."

The District Court's ultimate conclusion was that at the time of trial the racial segregation in the Columbus school system "directly resulted from [the Board's] intentional segregative acts and omissions," in violation of the Equal Protection Clause of the Fourteenth Amendment. . . . The Board subsequently presented a plan that complied with the District Court's guidelines and that was embodied in a judgment entered on October 7. The plan was stayed pending appeal to the Court of Appeals. Based on its own examination of the extensive record, the Court of Appeals affirmed the judgments entered against the local defendants. . . . Implementation of the desegregation plan was stayed pending our disposition of the case, . . . and we now affirm the judgment of the Court of Appeals.

## II

The Board earnestly contends that when this case was brought and at the time of trial its operation of a segregated school system was not done with any general or specific racially discriminatory purpose, and that whatever unconstitutional conduct it may have been guilty of in the past such conduct at no time had systemwide segregative impact and surely no remaining systemwide impact at the time of trial. A systemwide remedy was therefore contrary to the teachings of the cases that the scope of the constitutional violation measures the scope of the remedy.

We have discovered no reason, however, to disturb the judgment of the Court of Appeals, based on the findings and conclusions of the District Court, that the Board's conduct at the time of trial and before not only was animated by an unconstitutional, segregative purpose, but also had current, segregative impact that was sufficiently systemwide to warrant the remedy ordered by the District Court. . . .

## A

First, although at least since 1888 there had been no statutory requirement or authorization to operate segregated schools, the District Court found that in 1954, when *Brown I* was decided, the Columbus Board was not operating a racially neutral, unitary school system, but was conducting "an enclave of separate, black schools on the near east side of Columbus," and that "[t]he then-existing racial separation was the direct result of cognitive acts or omissions of those school board members and administrators who had originally intentionally caused and later perpetuated the racial isolation. . . . " Such separateness could not "be said to have been the result of racially neutral official acts."

Based on its own examination of the record, the Court of Appeals agreed with the District Court in this respect, observing that, "[w]hile the Columbus school system's dual black-white character was not mandated by state law as of 1954, the record certainly shows intentional segregation by the Columbus Board. As of 1954 the Columbus School Board had 'carried out a systematic program of segregation affecting a substantial portion of the students, schools, teachers and facilities within the school system.' " quoting Keyes v. School Dist.

The Board insists that, since segregated schooling was not commanded by state law and since not all schools were wholly black or wholly white in 1954, the District Court was not warranted in finding a dual system. But the District Court found that the "Columbus Public Schools were *offcially* segregated by race in 1954," and in any event, there is no reason to question the finding that as the "direct result of cognitive acts or omissions" the Board maintained "an enclave of separate, black schools on the near east side of Columbus." Proof of purposeful and effective maintenance of a body of separate black schools in a substantial part of the system itself is prima facie proof of a dual school system and supports a finding to this effect absent sufficient contrary proof by the Board, which was not forthcoming in this case. *Keyes,* supra.

### B

Second, both courts below declared that since the decision in Brown v. Board of Education (II), 349 U.S. 294 (1955), the Columbus Board has been under a continuous constitutional obligation to disestablish its dual school system and that it has failed to discharge this duty. Under the Fourteenth Amendment and the cases that have construed it, the Board's duty to dismantle its dual system cannot be gainsaid.

Where a racially discriminatory school system has been found to exist, *Brown II* imposes the duty on local school boards to "effectuate a transition to a racially non-discriminatory school system." "*Brown II* was a call for the dismantling of well-entrenched dual systems," and school boards operating such systems were "clearly charged with the affirmative duty to take whatever steps might be necessary to convert to a unitary system in which racial discrimination would be eliminated root and branch." Green v. County School Board. Each instance of a failure or refusal to fulfill this affirmative duty continues the violation of the Fourteenth Amendment.   .   .   .

As The Chief Justice's opinion for a unanimous Court in *Swann* recognized, *Brown* and *Green* imposed an affirmative duty to desegregate. "If school authorities fail in their affirmative obligations under those holdings, judicial authority may be invoked.   .   .   . In default by the school authorities of their obligation to proffer acceptable remedies, a district court has broad power to fashion a remedy that will assure a unitary school system."   .   .   .

In determining whether a dual school system has been disestablished, *Swann* also mandates that matters aside from student assignments must be considered:

> "[W]here it is possible to identify a 'white school' or a 'Negro school' simply by reference to the racial composition of teachers and staff, the quality of school buildings and equipment, or the organization of sports activities, a *prima facie* case of violation of substantive constitutional rights under the Equal Protection Clause is shown."

Further, *Swann* stated that in devising remedies for legally imposed segregation the responsibility of the local authorities and district courts is to ensure that future school construction and abandonment are not used and do not serve to perpetuate or re-establish the dual school system. As for student assignments, the Court said:

> "No *per se* rule can adequately embrace all the difficulties of reconciling the competing interests involved; but in a system with a history of segregation the need for remedial criteria of sufficient specificity to assure a school authority's compliance with its constitutional duty warrants a presumption against schools that are substantially disproportionate in their racial composition. Where the school authority's proposed plan for conversion from a dual to a unitary system contemplates the continued existence of some schools that are all or predominantly of one race, they have the burden of showing that such school assignments are genuinely nondiscriminatory."

The Board's continuing "affirmative duty to disestablish the dual school system" is therefore beyond question, and it has pointed to nothing in the record persuading us that at the time of trial the dual school system and its effects had been disestablished. The Board does not appear to challenge the finding of the District Court that at the time of trial most blacks were still going to black schools and most whites to white schools. Whatever the Board's current purpose with respect to racially separate education might be, it knowingly continued its failure to eliminate the consequences of its past intentionally segregative policies.  The Board "never actively set out to dismantle this dual system."

## C

Third, the District Court not only found that the Board had breached its constitutional duty by failing effectively to eliminate the continuing consequences of its intentional systemwide segregation in 1954, but also found that in the intervening years there had been a series of Board actions and practices that could not "reasonably be explained without reference to racial concerns," and that "intentionally aggravated, rather than alleviated," racial separation in the schools.  These matters included the general practice of assigning black teachers only to those schools with substantial black student populations, a practice that was terminated only in 1974 as the result of a conciliation agreement with the Ohio Civil Rights Commission; the intentionally segregative use of optional attendance zones, discontiguous attendance areas, and boundary changes; and the selection of sites for new school construction that had the foreseeable and anticipated effect of maintaining the racial separation of the schools.  The court generally noted that "[s]ince the 1954 *Brown* decision, the Columbus defendants or their predecessors were adequately put on notice of the fact that action was required to correct and to prevent the increase in" segregation, yet failed to heed their duty to alleviate racial separation in the schools.

## III

Against this background, we cannot fault the conclusion of the District Court and the Court of Appeals that at the time of trial there was systemwide segregation in the Columbus schools that was the result of recent and remote intentionally segregative actions of the Columbus Board.  While appearing not to challenge most of the subsidiary findings of historical fact, petitioners dispute many of the factual inferences drawn from these facts by the two courts below.  On this record, however, there is no apparent reason to disturb the factual findings and conclusions entered by the District Court and strongly affirmed by the Court of Appeals after its own examination of the record.

Nor do we discern that the judgments entered below rested on any misapprehension of the controlling law.  It is urged that the courts below failed to heed the requirements of *Keyes,* Washington v. Davis, and Village of Arlington Heights v. Metropolitan Housing Dev. Corp., that a plaintiff seeking to make out an equal protection violation on the basis of racial discrimination must show purpose.  Both courts, it is argued, considered the requirement satisfied if it were shown that disparate impact would be the natural and foreseeable consequence of the practices and policies of the Board, which, it is said, is nothing more than equating impact with intent, contrary to the controlling precedent.

The District Court, however, was amply cognizant of the controlling cases. It is understood that to prevail the plaintiffs were required to " 'prove not only that segregated schooling exists but also that it was brought about or maintained by intentional state action,' " quoting *Keyes,* supra,—that is, that the school officials had "intended to segregate." The District Court also recognized that under those cases disparate impact and foreseeable consequences, without more, do not establish a constitutional violation. Nevertheless, the District Court correctly noted that actions having foreseeable and anticipated disparate impact are relevant evidence to prove the ultimate fact, forbidden purpose. Those cases do not forbid "the foreseeable effects standard from being utilized as one of the several kinds of proofs from which an inference of segregative intent may be properly drawn." Adherence to a particular policy or practice, "with full knowledge of the predictable effects of such adherence upon racial imbalance in a school system is one factor among many others which may be considered by a court in determining whether an inference of segregative intent should be drawn." The District Court thus stayed well within the requirements of Washington v. Davis and Arlington Heights.

It is also urged that the District Court and the Court of Appeals failed to observe the requirements of our recent decision in *Dayton I,* which reiterated the accepted rule that the remedy imposed by a court of equity should be commensurate with the violation ascertained, and held that the remedy for the violations that had then been established in that case should be aimed at rectifying the "incremental segregative effect" of the discriminatory acts identified. In *Dayton I,* only a few apparently isolated discriminatory practices had been found; yet a systemwide remedy had been imposed without proof of a systemwide impact. Here, however, the District Court repeatedly emphasized that it had found purposefully segregative practices with current, systemwide impact. And the Court of Appeals, responding to similar arguments, said:

"School board policies of systemwide application necessarily have systemwide impact. (1) The pre-1954 policy of creating an enclave of five schools intentionally designed for black students and known as 'black' schools, as found by the District Judge, clearly had a 'substantial'—indeed, a systemwide—impact. (2) The post-1954 failure of the Columbus Board to desegregate the school system in spite of many requests and demands to do so, of course, had systemwide impact. (3) So, too, did the Columbus Board's segregative school construction and siting policy as we have detailed it above. (4) So too did its student assignment policy which,

as shown above, produced the large majority of racially identifiable schools as of the school year 1975–1976. (5) The
practice of assigning black teachers and administrators only
or in large majority to black schools likewise represented a
systemwide policy of segregation. This policy served until
July 1974 to deprive black students of opportunities for contact with and learning from white teachers, and conversely
to deprive white students of similar opportunities to meet,
know and learn from black teachers. It also served as discriminatory, systemwide racial identification of schools."

Nor do we perceive any misuse of *Keyes,* where we held that purposeful discrimination in a substantial part of a school system furnishes a sufficient basis for an inferential finding of a systemwide discriminatory intent unless otherwise rebutted, and that given the purpose
to operate a dual school system one could infer a connection between
such a purpose and racial separation in other parts of the school system. There was no undue reliance here on the inferences permitted
by *Keyes,* or upon those recognized by *Swann.* Furthermore, the
Board was given ample opportunity to counter the evidence of segregative purpose and current, systemwide impact, and the findings of
the courts below were against it in both respects.

Because the District Court and the Court of Appeals committed
no prejudicial errors of fact or law, the judgment appealed from must
be affirmed.

So ordered.

Mr. Chief Justice BURGER, concurring in the judgment.

I perceive no real difference in the legal principles stated in the
dissenting opinions of Mr. Justice Rehnquist and Mr. Justice Powell
on the one hand and the concurring opinion of Mr. Justice Stewart in
this case on the other; they differ only in their view of the District
Court's role in applying these principles in the finding of facts.

Like Mr. Justice REHNQUIST, I have serious doubts as to how
many of the post-1954 actions of the Columbus Board of Education
can properly be characterized as segregative in intent and effect. On
this record I might very well have concluded that few of them were.
However, like Mr. Justice Stewart, I am prepared to defer to the trier
of fact because I find it difficult to hold that the errors rise to the level
of "clearly erroneous" under Rule 52. The District Court did find
facts sufficient to justify the conclusion reached by Mr. Justice Stewart that the school "district was not being operated in a racially neutral fashion" and that the Board's actions affected "a meaningful portion" of the school system. Keyes v. School District, No. 1. . . .
For these reasons I join Mr. Justice Stewart's opinion.

Mr. Justice STEWART, with whom The Chief Justice joins,
. . .

Whether actions that produce racial separation are intentional within the meaning of Keyes v. School Dist. No. 1, Washington v. Davis, and Village of Arlington Heights v. Metropolitan Housing Dev. Corp., is an issue that can present very difficult and subtle factual questions. Similarly intricate may be factual inquiries into the breadth of any constitutional violation, and hence of any permissible remedy. See Milliken v. Bradley I. . . . Those tasks are difficult enough for a trial judge. The coldness and impersonality of a printed record, containing the only evidence available to an appellate court in any case, can hardly make the answers any clearer. I doubt neither the diligence nor the perservance of the judges of the Courts of Appeals, or of my Brethren, but I suspect that it is impossible for a reviewing court factually to know a case from a 6,600 page printed record as well as the trial judge knew it. In assessing the facts in lawsuits like these, therefore, I think appellate courts should accept even more readily than in most cases the factual findings of the courts of first instance.

My second disagreement with the Court in these cases stems from my belief that the Court has attached far too much importance in each case to the question whether there existed a "dual school system" in 1954. As I understand the Court's opinions in these cases, if such an officially authorized segregated school system can be found to have existed in 1954, then any current racial separation in the schools will be presumed to have been caused by acts in violation of the Constitution. Even if, as the Court says, this presumption is rebuttable, the burden is on the school board to rebut it. And, when the factual issues are as elusive as these, who bears the burden of proof can easily determine who prevails in the litigation.

I agree that a school district in violation of the Constitution in 1954 was under a duty to remedy that violation. So was a school district violating the Constitution in 1964, and so is one violating the Constitution today. But this duty does not justify a complete shift of the normal burden of proof.

Presumptions are sometimes justified because in common experience some facts are likely to follow from others. A constitutional violation in 1954 might be presumed to make the existence of a constitutional violation 20 years later more likely than not in one of two ways. First, because the school board then had an invidious intent, the continuing existence of that collective state of mind might be presumed in the absence of proof to the contrary. Second, quite apart from the current intent of the school board, an unconstitutionally discriminatory school system in 1954 might be presumed still to have major effects on the contemporary system. Neither of these possibilities seems to me likely enough to support a valid presumption.

Much has changed in 25 years, in the Nation at large and in Dayton and Columbus in particular. Minds have changed with respect to racial relationships. Perhaps more importantly, generations have changed. The prejudices of the school boards of 1954 (and earlier) cannot realistically be assumed to haunt the school boards of today. Similarly, while two full generations of students have progressed from kindergarten through high school, school systems have changed. Dayton and Columbus are both examples of the dramatic growth and change in urban school districts. It is unrealistic to assume that the hand of 1954 plays any major part in shaping the current school systems in either city. For these reasons, I simply cannot accept the shift in the litigative burden of proof adopted by the Court.

Because of these basic disagreements with the Court's approach, these two cases look quite different to me from the way they look to the Court. In both cases there is no doubt that many of the districts' children are in schools almost solely with members of their own race. These racially distinct areas make up substantial parts of both districts. The question remains, however, whether the plaintiffs showed that this racial separation was the result of intentional systemwide discrimination.

## THE *DAYTON* CASE

After further hearings following the remand by this Court in the first *Dayton* case, the District Court dismissed this lawsuit. It found that the plaintiffs had not proved a discriminatory purpose behind many of the actions challenged. It found further that the plaintiffs had not proved that any significant segregative effect had resulted from those few practices that the school board had previously undertaken with an invalid intent. The Court of Appeals held these findings to be clearly erroneous. I cannot agree.

As to several claimed acts of post-1954 discrimination, the Court of Appeals seems simply to have differed with the trial court's factual assessments, without offering a reasoned explanation of how the trial court's finding fell short. The Court of Appeals may have been correct in its assessment of the facts, but that is not demonstrated by its opinion. I would accept the trial judge's findings of fact.

Furthermore, the Court of Appeals relied heavily on the proposition that the Dayton School District was a "dual system" in 1954, and today this Court places great stress on the same foundation. In several instances the Court of Appeals overturned the District Court's findings of fact because of the trial court's failure to shift the burden of proof. Because I think this shifting of the burden is wholly unjustified, it seems to me a serious mistake to upset the District Court's findings on any such basis. If one accepts the facts as found by the District Judge, there is almost no basis for finding any constitutional violations *after* 1954. Nor is there any substantial evidence of the continuing impact of pre-1954 discrimination. Only if the defendant school board is saddled with the burdens of proving that it acted out of proper motives after 1954 *and* that factors other than pre-1954 policies led to racial separation in the district's schools, could these plaintiffs possibly prevail.

For the reasons I have expressed, I dissent from the opinion and judgment of the Court.

## THE *COLUMBUS* CASE

In contrast, the Court of Appeals did not upset the District Court's findings of fact in this case. In a long and careful opinion, the District Judge discussed numerous examples of overt racial discrimination continuing into the 1970's. Just as I would defer to the findings of fact made by the District Court in the *Dayton* case, I would accept the trial court's findings in this case.

The Court of Appeals did rely in part on its finding that the Columbus board operated a dual school system in 1954, as does this Court. But evidence of recent discriminatory intent, so lacking in the *Dayton* case, was relatively strong in this case. The particular illustrations recounted by the District Court may not have affected a large portion of the school district, but they demonstrated that the district was not being operated in a racially neutral manner. The District Court found that the Columbus board had intentionally discriminated against Negro students in some schools, and that there was substantial racial separation throughout the district. The question in my judgment is whether the District Court's conclusion that there had been a systemwide constitutional violation can be upheld on the basis of those findings, without reference to an affirmative duty stemming from the situation in 1954.

I think the Court's decision in Keyes v. School Dist. No. 1, provides the answer:

> "We hold that a finding of intentionally segregative school board actions in a meaningful portion of a school system, as in this case, creates a presumption that other segregated schooling within the system is not adventitious. It establishes, in other words, a prima facie case of unlawful segregative design on the part of school authorities, and shifts to those authorities the burden of proving that other segregated schools within the system are not also the result of intentionally segregative actions."

The plaintiffs in the *Columbus* case, unlike those in the *Dayton* case, proved what the Court in *Keyes* defined as a prima facie case.[9] The

---

[9] The Denver school district at the time of the trial in *Keyes* had 96,000 students, almost exactly the number of students in the Columbus system at the time of this trial. The Park Hill region of Denver had been the scene of the intentional discrimination that the Court believed justified a presumption of sys-

District Court and the Court of Appeals correctly found that the school board did not rebut this presumption. It is on this basis that I agree with the District Court and the Court of Appeals in concluding that the Columbus school district was operated in violation of the Constitution.

The petitioners in the *Columbus* case also challenge the remedy imposed by the District Court. Just two Terms ago we set out the test for determining the appropriate scope of a remedy in a case such as this:

> "If such violations are found, the District Court in the first instance, subject to review by the Court of Appeals, must determine how much incremental segregative effect these violations had on the racial distribution of the  . . .  school population as presently constituted, when that distribution is compared to what it would have been in the absence of such constitutional violations. The remedy must be designed to redress that difference, and only if there has been a systemwide impact may there be a systemwide remedy." Dayton Board of Education v. Brinkman I, 433 U.S. 406, 420.

In the context in which the *Columbus* case has reached us, I cannot say that the remedy imposed by the District Court was impermissible under this test. For the reasons discussed above, the District Court's conclusion that there was a systemwide constitutional violation was soundly based. And because the scope of the remedy is tied to the scope of the violation, a remedy encompassing the entire school district was presumptively appropriate. In litigating the question of remedy, however, I think the defendants in a case such as this should always be permitted to show that certain schools or areas were not affected by the constitutional violation.  . . .

For these reasons, I concur in the result in Columbus Board of Education v. Penick, and dissent in Dayton Board of Education v. Brinkman.

Mr. Justice POWELL, dissenting.

I join the dissenting opinions of Mr. Justice REHNQUIST and write separately to emphasize several points. The Court's opinions in these two cases are profoundly disturbing. They appear to endorse a wholly new constitutional concept applicable to school cases. The opinions also seem remarkably insensitive to the now widely accepted view that a quarter of a century after Brown v. Board of Education, the federal judiciary should be limiting rather than expanding the extent to which courts are operating the public school systems of our country. In expressing these views, I recognize, of course, that my

temwide violation. That region contained six elementary schools and one junior high school, educating a small portion of the school district's students, but a large number of the district's Negro students.

Brothers who have joined the Court's opinions are motivated by purposes and ideals that few would question. My dissent is based on a conviction that the Court's opinions condone the creation of bad constitutional law and will be even worse for public education—an element of American life that is essential, especially for minority children.

## I

The type of state-enforced segregation that *Brown* properly condemned no longer exists in this country. This is not to say that school boards—particularly in the great cities of the North, Midwest, and West—are taking all reasonable measures to provide integrated educational opportunities. . . .

## II

Holding the school boards of these two cities responsible for *all* of the segregation in the Dayton and Columbus systems and prescribing fixed racial ratios in every school as the constitutionally required remedy necessarily implies a belief that the same school boards—under court supervision—will be capable of bringing about and maintaining the desired racial balance in each of these schools. The experience in city after city demonstrates that this is an illusion. The process of resegregation, stimulated by resentment against judicial coercion and concern as to the effect of court supervision of education, will follow today's decisions as surely as it has in other cities subjected to similar sweeping decrees.

The orders affirmed today typify intrusions on local and professional authorities that affect adversely the quality of education. They require an extensive reorganization of both school systems, including the reassignment of almost half of the 96,000 students in the Columbus system and the busing of some 15,000 students in Dayton. They also require reassignments of teachers and other staff personnel, reorganization of grade structures, and the closing of certain schools. The orders substantially dismantle and displace neighborhood schools in the face of compelling economic and educational reasons for preserving them. This wholesale substitution of judicial legislation for the judgments of elected officials and professional educators derogates the entire process of public education. Moreover, it constitutes a serious interference with the private decisions of parents as to how their children will be educated. These harmful consequences are the inevitable byproducts of a judicial approach that ignores other relevant factors in favor of an exclusive focus on racial balance in every school.

These harmful consequences, moreover, in all likelihood will provoke responses that will defeat the integrative purpose of the courts' order. Parents, unlike school officials, are not bound by these decrees and may frustrate them through the simple expedient of withdrawing their children from a public school system in which they have lost confidence. In spite of the substantial costs often involved in relocation of the family or in resort to private education, experience demonstrates that many parents view these alternatives as preferable to submitting their children to court-run school systems. In the words of a leading authority:

> "An implication that should have been seen all along but can no longer be ignored is that a child's enrollment in a given public school is not determined by a governmental decision alone. It is a joint result of a governmental decision (the making of school assignments) and parental decisions, whether to remain in the same residential location, whether to send their child to a private school, or which school district to move into when moving into a metropolitan area. The fact that the child's enrollment is a result of two decisions operating jointly means that government policies must, to be effective, anticipate parental decisions and obtain the parents' active cooperation in implementing school policies." Coleman, New Incentives for Desegregation, 7 Human Rights 10, 13 (1978).

At least where inner-city populations comprise a large proportion of racial minorities and surrounding suburbs remain white, conditions that exist in most large American cities, the demonstrated effect of compulsory integration is a substantial exodus of whites from the system. See J. Coleman, S. Kelly, and J. Moore, Trends in School Segregation, 1968–1973, at 66, 76–77 (1975). It would be unfair and misleading to attribute this phenomenon to a racist response to integration *per se*. It is at least as likely that the exodus is in substantial part a natural reaction to the displacement of professional and local control that occurs when courts go into the business of restructuring and operating school systems.

Nor will this resegregation be the only negative effect of court-coerced integration on minority children. Public schools depend on community support for their effectiveness. When substantial elements of the community are driven to abandon these schools, their quality tends to decline, sometimes markedly. Members of minority groups, who have relied especially on education as a means of advancing themselves, also are likely to react to this decline in quality by removing their children from public schools. As a result, public school enrollment increasingly will become limited to children from families that either lack the resources to choose alternatives or are indifferent to the quality of education. The net effect is an overall deterioration in public education, the one national resource that traditionally has made this country a land of opportunity for diverse ethnic and racial groups.

## III

If public education is not to suffer further, we must "return to a more balanced evaluation of the recognized interests of our society in achieving desegregation with other educational and societal interests a community may legitimately assert."  The ultimate goal is to have quality school systems in which racial discrimination is neither practiced nor tolerated.  It has been thought that ethnic and racial diversity in the classroom is a desirable component of sound education in our country of diverse populations, a view to which I subscribe.  The question that courts in their single-minded pursuit of racial balance seem to ignore is how best to move toward this goal.

.   .   .  Experience in recent years, however, has cast serious doubt upon the efficacy of far-reaching judicial remedies directed not against specific constitutional violations, but rather imposed on an entire school system on the fictional assumption that the existence of identifiable black or white schools is caused entirely by intentional segregative conduct, and is evidence of systemwide discrimination. In my view, some federal courts—now led by this Court—are pursuing a path away from rather than toward the desired goal.   .   .   .
It is now reasonably clear that the goal of diversity that we call integration, if it is to be lasting and conducive to quality education, must have the support of parents who so frequently have the option to choose where their children will attend school.  Courts, of course, should confront discrimination wherever it is found to exist.  But they should recognize limitations on judicial action inherent in our system and also the limits of effective judicial power.  The primary and continuing responsibility for public education, including the bringing about and maintaining of desired diversity, must be left with school officials and public authorities.

Mr. Justice REHNQUIST, with whom Mr. Justice POWELL joins dissenting.

.   .   .

.   .   .   .  Given the similar approaches employed by the Court in this case and *Dayton II,* this case suffices for stating what I think are the glaring deficiencies both in the Court's new framework and in its decision to subject the Columbus school system to the District Court's sweeping racial balance remedy.

## I

The Court suggests a radical new approach to desegregation cases in systems without a history of statutorily mandated separation of the races:  if a district court concludes—employing what in honesty must be characterized as an irrebuttable presumption—that there was a "dual" school system at the time of *Brown I,* it must find post-1954 constitutional violations in a school board's failure to take every affirmative step to integrate the system.  Put differently, *racial imbalance* at the time the complaint is filed is sufficient to support a systemwide, racial balance school busing remedy if the district court can find *some* evidence of discriminatory purpose prior to 1954, without any inquiry into the causal relationship between those pre-1954 violations and current segregation in the school system.

This logic permeates the findings of the District Court and Court of Appeals, and the latter put it most bluntly.

"[T]he District Judge on review of pre-1954 history found that the Columbus schools were de jure segregated in 1954 and, hence, the Board had a continuing constitutional duty to desegregate the Columbus schools.  The pupil assignment figures for 1975–76 demonstrate the District Judge's conclusion that this burden has not been carried.  On this basis alone (if there were no other proofs), we believe we would be required to affirm the District Judge's finding of present unconstitutional segregation."  Penick v. Columbus Board of Education, 583 F.2d 787, 800 (1978).

In Brinkman v. Gilligan, 583 F.2d 243, 256 (1978), also affirmed today, this post-1954 "affirmative duty" is characterized a duty "to diffuse black and white students" throughout the system.

The Court in this case apparently endorses that view.  For the Court finds that "[e]ach instance of a failure or refusal to fulfill this affirmative duty continues the violation of the Fourteenth Amendment," and the mere fact that at the time of suit "most blacks were still going to black schools and most whites to white schools" establishes current effect.

.   .   .   The notion of an "affirmative duty" as acknowledged in *Keyes* is a remedial concept defining the obligation on the school board to come forward with an effective desegregation plan *after* a finding of a dual system.  This could not be clearer in *Keyes* itself.

"[P]roof of a state-imposed segregation in a substantial portion of the district will suffice to support a finding by the trial court of the existence of a dual system.  Of course, where that finding is made, as in cases involving statutory dual systems, the school authorities have an affirmative duty 'to effectuate a transition to a racially nondiscriminatory school system.'  *Brown II,* supra, at 301."

Indeed, *Keyes* did not discuss the complexion of the Denver school system in 1954 or in any other way intimate the analysis adopted by the Court today.  Rather it emphasized that the relevance of past actions was determined by their causal relationship to current racially imbalanced conditions.

Even so brief a history of our school desegregation jurisprudence sheds light on more than one point. As a matter of history, case law, or logic, there is nothing to support the novel proposition that the primary inquiry in school desegregation cases involving systems without a history of statutorily mandated racial assignment is what happened in those systems before 1954. As a matter of history, 1954 makes no more sense as a benchmark—indeed it makes *less* sense— than 1968, 1971 or 1973. Perhaps the latter year has the most to commend it, if one insists on a benchmark, because in *Keyes* this Court first confronted the problem of school segregation in the context of systems without a history of statutorily mandated separation of the races.

. . .

. . . the Court's decision today enunciates, without analysis or explanation, a new methodology that dramatically departs from *Keyes* by relieving school desegregation plaintiffs from any showing of a causal nexus between intentional segregative actions and the conditions they seek to remedy.

Causality plays a central role in *Keyes* as it does in all equal protection analysis. The *Keyes* Court held that before the burden of production shifts to the school board, the plaintiffs must prove "that the school authorities have carried out a systematic program of segregation *affecting a substantial portion of the students, schools, teachers and facilities within the school system."* . . . The relevance of past acts of the school board was to depend on whether "segregation resulting from those actions continues to exist." That inquiry is not central under the approach approved by the Court today. Henceforth, the question is apparently whether pre-1954 acts contributed in some unspecified manner to segregated conditions that existed in 1954. If the answer is yes, then the only question is whether the school board has exploited all integrative opportunities that presented themselves in the subsequent 25 years. If not, a systemwide remedy is in order, despite the plaintiff's failure to demonstrate a link between those past acts and current racial imbalance.

The Court's use of the term "affirmative duty" implies that integration by the pre-eminent—indeed, the controlling—educational consideration in school board decisionmaking. It takes precedence over other legitimate educational objectives subject to some vague feasibility limitation. That implication is dramatically demonstrated in this case. . . .

## II

In Washington v. Davis, Village of Arlington Heights v. Metropolitan Housing Development Corp., and Personnel Administrator of

Massachusetts v. Feeney, we have emphasized that discriminatory purpose as a motivating factor in governmental action is a critical component of an equal protection violation. Like causation analysis, the discriminatory purpose requirement sensibly seeks to limit court intervention to the rectification of conditions that offend the Constitution—stigma and other harm inflicted by racially motivated governmenal action—and prevent unwarranted encroachment on the autonomy of local governments and private individuals which could well result from a less structured approach.

This Court has not precisely defined the manner in which discriminatory purpose is to be proved. Indeed, in light of the varied circumstances in which it might be at issue, simple and precise rules for proving discriminatory purpose could not be drafted. The focus of the inquiry in a case such as this, however, is not very difficult to articulate: Is a desire to separate the races among the reasons for a school board's decision or particular course of action? The burden of proof on this issue is on the plaintiffs.

The best evidence on this score would be a contemporaneous explanation of its action by the school board, or other less dramatic evidence of the board's actual purpose, which indicated that one objective was to separate the races. Objective evidence is also probative. Indeed, were it not this case would warrant very little discussion, for all the evidence relied on by the courts below was of an "objective" nature.

But objective evidence must be carefully analyzed for it may otherwise reduce the "discriminatory purpose" requirement to a "discriminatory impact" test by another name. . . .

Indeed, reflection indicates that the District Court's test for segregative intent in *Columbus* is logically nothing more than the affirmative duty stated a different way. Under the test a "presumption of segregative purpose arises when plaintiffs establish that the natural, probable, and foreseeable result of public officials' . . . inaction was . . . perpetuation of public school segregation. The presumption becomes proof unless defendants affirmatively establish that their . . . inaction was a consistent and resolute application of racially neutral policies." If that standard were to be applied to the average urban school system in the United States, the implications are obvious. Virtually every urban area in this country has racially and ethnically identifiable neighborhoods, doubtless resulting from a melange of past happenings prompted by economic considerations, private discrimination, discriminatory school assignments, or a desire to reside near people of one's own race or ethnic background. It is likewise true that the most prevalent pupil assignment policy in urban areas is the neighborhood school policy. It follows inexorably that urban areas have a large number of racially identifiable schools.

Certainly "public officials' . . . inaction . . . perpetuates . . . public school segregation" in *this* context. School authorities could move to pairing, magnet schools or any other device to integrate the races. The failure to do so is a violation . . . unless the "inaction was a consistent and resolute application of racially neutral policies." The policy that most school boards will rely on at trial, and the policy which the Columbus School Board in fact did rely on, is the neighborhood school policy. According to the District Court in this case, however, not only is that policy not a defense, but in combination with racially segregated housing patterns, it is itself a factor from which one can infer segregative intent and a factor in this case from which the District Court did infer segregative intent, stating that "[t]hose who rely on it as a defense to unlawful school segregation fail to recognize the high priority of the constitutional right involved." But the Constitution does not command that school boards not under an affirmative duty to desegregate follow a policy of "integration über alles." .   .   .

## NOTES AND QUESTIONS

1. Before there can be a violation of the equal-protection clause, there first must be proof of a racially discriminatory purpose. What, precisely, was that proof in the Columbus case? Identify each component. What role in that proof was played by the "natural and foreseeable consequences" doctrine? Is it true, after Columbus, that the equal-protection clause is violated if it can be proved that a racially disparate impact was the natural and foreseeable consequence of the practices and policy of a school board? If not, what more must be proven? What more was actually proved in Columbus? Must there be proof of a pre-1954 violation? How does one prove such a violation in the 1980s?

Suppose, tomorrow, a school board evenhandedly applied a neighborhood school assignment policy to its students throughout its district which is strongly characterized by de facto residential segregation with the result that 51 of its 69 schools were either all-black or all-white, even though only 43% of the students in the system were black. In light of the Columbus case, has that school district engaged in de jure segregation? If not, suppose the school board decides to build a needed new school building to relieve overcrowding, which, on completion, will be 75% black. Is this an act of de jure segregation? If not, suppose, in an attempt to provide students with successful role models, the school board approves a teacher assignment policy whereby, if possible, two-thirds of the teachers in any school building will be of the same race as the students. Is this an act of de jure segregation?

2. Would the decision in Columbus have been the same if there had not been a finding of intentional racial segregation existing before 1954? Was there no finding of an intentional violation after 1954? If so, what was it, and what was the evidence it was based on? Is the Columbus case limited in its applications to school districts that in-

tentionally practiced racial segregation before 1954? What is the relationship of Columbus to Keyes?

3. Carefully consider Mr. Justice Powell's dissenting opinion. Do you agree or disagree with him? Is his dissenting opinion consistent with his concurring opinion in Keyes?

4. What are the basic points of Mr. Justice Rehnquist's dissent? Do you agree with them? How would you have voted in this case if you had been a member of the U.S. Supreme Court? Why?

5. In a companion case, Dayton Bd. of Educ. v. Brinkman, —— U.S. ——, 99 S.Ct. 2971, 61 L.Ed.2d 720 (1979), which was before the Supreme Court for the second time, the Court was confronted with a public school system that "was highly segregated by race." Forty-three percent of the students in the Dayton system were black, "but 51 of the 69 schools in the system were virtually all-white or all-black." The earlier case was sent back to the trial court for additional evidentiary hearings.

"The District Court held a supplemental evidentiary hearing, undertook to review the entire record anew, and entered findings of fact and conclusions of law and a judgment dismissing the complaint. In support of its judgment, the District Court observed that, although various instances of purposeful segregation in the past evidenced 'an inexcusable history of mistreatment of black students,' plaintiffs had failed to prove that acts of intentional segregation over 20 years old had any current incremental segregative effects. The District Court conceded that the Dayton schools were highly segregated but ruled that the Board's failure to alleviate this condition was not actionable absent sufficient evidence that the racial separation had been caused by the Board's own purposeful discriminatory conduct. In the District Court's eyes, plaintiffs had failed to show either discriminatory purpose or segregative effect, or both, with respect to the challenged practices and policies of the Board, which included faculty hiring and assignments, the use of optional attendance zones and transfer policies, the location and construction of new and expanded school facilities, and the rescission of certain prior resolutions recognizing the Board's responsibility to eradicate racial separation in the public schools.

"The Court of Appeals reversed. The basic ingredients of the Court of Appeals' judgment were that at the time of *Brown I*, the Dayton Board was operating a dual school system, that it was constitutionally required to disestablish that system and its effects, that it had failed to discharge this duty, and that the consequences of the dual system, together with the intentionally segregative impact of various practices since 1954, were of systemwide import and an appropriate basis for a systemwide remedy. In arriving at these conclusions, the Court of Appeals found that in some instances the findings of the District Court were clearly erroneous and that in other respects the District Court had made errors of law."

In upholding the Court of Appeals, the U.S. Supreme Court invoked Columbus's line of analysis, ruling:

"The Court of Appeals expressly held that, 'at the time of *Brown I*, defendants were intentionally operating a dual school system in violation of the Equal Protection Clause of the fourteenth amendment,' and that the 'finding of the District Court to the contrary is clearly erroneous.' On the record before us, we perceive no basis for petitioners' challenge to this holding of the Court of Appeals.

"Concededly, in the early 1950's, '77.6 percent of all students attended schools in which one race accounted for 90 percent or more of the students and 54.3 percent of the black students were assigned to four schools that were 100 percent black.' One of these schools was Dunbar High School, which, the District Court found, had been established as a districtwide black high school with an all-black faculty and a black principal, and remained so at the time of *Brown I* and up until 1962. The District Court also found that 'among' the early and relatively undisputed acts of purposeful segregation was the establishment of Garfield as a black elementary school. The Court of Appeals found that two other elementary schools were, through a similar process of optional attendance zones and the creation and maintenance of all-black faculties, intentionally designated and operated as all-black schools in the 1930's, in the 1940's, and at the time of *Brown I*. Additionally, the District Court had specifically found that in 1950 the faculty at 100% black schools was 100% black and that the faculty at all other schools was 100% white.

"These facts, the Court of Appeals held, made clear that the Board was purposefully operating segregated schools in a substantial part of the district, which warranted an inference and a finding that segregation in other parts of the system was also purposeful absent evidence sufficient to support a finding that the segregative actions 'were not taken in effectuation of a policy to create or maintain segregation' or were not among the 'factors . . . causing the existing condition of segregation in these schools.' Keyes v. School Dist. No. 1. The District Court had therefore ignored the legal significance of the intentional maintenance of a substantial number of black schools in the system at the time of *Brown I*. It had also ignored, contrary to Swann v. Charlotte-Mecklenburg Board of Education the significance of purposeful segregation in faculty assignments in establishing the existence of a dual school system; here the 'purposeful segregation of faculty by race was inextricably tied to racially motivated student-assignment practices.' Based on its review of the entire record, the Court of Appeals concluded that the Board had not responded with sufficient evidence to counter the inference that a dual system was in existence in Dayton in 1954. Thus, it concluded that the Board's 'intentional segregative practices cannot be confined in one distinct area'; they 'infected the entire Dayton public school system.'

B

"Petitioners next contend that, even if a dual system did exist a quarter of a century ago, the Court of Appeals erred in finding any widespread violations of constitutional duty since that time.

"Given intentionally segregated schools in 1954, however, the Court of Appeals was quite right in holding that the Board was thereafter under a continuing duty to eradicate the effects of that system, and that the systemwide nature of the violation furnished prima facie proof that current segregation in the Dayton schools was caused at least in part by prior intentionally segregative official acts. Thus, judgment for the plaintiffs was authorized and required absent sufficient countervailing evidence by the defendant school officials. At the time of trial, Dunbar High School and the three black elementary schools, or the schools that succeeded them, remained black schools; and most of the schools in Dayton were virtually one-race schools, as were 80% of the classrooms. '*Every* school which was 90 percent or more black in 1951–52 *or* 1963–64 *or* 1971–72 and which is still in use today remains 90 percent or more black. Of the 25 white schools in 1972–73, *all* opened 90 percent or more white and, if opened, were 90 percent or more white in 1971–72, 1963–64 and 1951–52.' 583 F.2d, at 254 (emphasis in original), quoting Brinkman v. Gilligan, 503 F.2d 683, 694–695 (CA6 1974). Against this background, the Court of Appeals held '[t]hat the evidence of record demonstrates convincingly that defendants have failed to eliminate the continuing systemwide effects of their prior discrimination and have intentionally maintained a segregated school system down to the time the complaint was filed in the present case.' At the very least, defendants had failed to come forward with evidence to deny 'that the current racial composition of the school population reflects the systemwide impact' of the Board's prior discriminatory conduct.

"Part of the affirmative duty imposed by our cases, as we decided in Wright v. Council of City of Emporia, 407 U.S. 451 (1972), is the obligation not to take any action that would impede the process of disestablishing the dual system and its effects. The Dayton Board, however, had engaged in many post-*Brown* actions that had the effect of increasing or perpetuating segregation. The District Court ignored this compounding of the original constitutional breach on the ground that there was no direct evidence of continued discriminatory purpose. But the measure of the post-*Brown* conduct of a school board under an unsatisfied duty to liquidate a dual system is the effectiveness, not the purpose, of the actions in decreasing or increasing the segregation caused by the dual system. As was clearly established in *Keyes* and *Swann*, the Board had to do more than abandon its prior discriminatory purpose. The Board has had an affirmative responsibility to see that pupil assignment policies and school construction and abandonment practices 'are not used and do not serve to perpetuate or re-establish the dual school system,' and the Board has a 'heavy burden' of showing that actions that increased or continued the effects of the dual system serve important and legitimate ends.

"The Board has never seriously contended that it fulfilled its affirmative duty or the heavy burden of explaining its failure to do so. Though the Board was often put on notice of the effects of its acts or omissions, the District Court found that 'with one [counterproductive] exception . . . no attempt was made to alter the racial characteristics of any of the schools.' The Court of Appeals held that far from performing its constitutional duty, the Board had engaged in 'post-1954 actions which actually have exacerbated the racial separation existing at the time of *Brown I.*' The court reversed as clearly erroneous the District Court's finding that intentional faculty segregation had ended in 1951; the Court of Appeals found that it had effectively continued into the 1970's. This was a systemwide practice and strong evidence that the Board was continuing its efforts to segregate students. Dunbar High School remained as a black high school until 1962, when a new Dunbar High School opened with a virtually all-black faculty and student body. The old Dunbar was converted into an elementary school to which children from two black grade schools were assigned. Furthermore, the Court of Appeals held that since 1954 the Board had used some 'optional attendance zones for racially discriminatory purposes in clear violation of the Equal Protection Clause.' The District Court's finding to the contrary was clearly erroneous. At the very least, the use of such zones amounted to a perpetuation of the existing dual school system. Likewise, the Board failed in its duty and perpetuated racial separation in the schools by its pattern of school construction and site selection, . . . that resulted in 22 of the 24 new schools built between 1950 and the filing of the complaint opening 90% black or white. The same pattern appeared with respect to additions of classroom space made to existing schools. Seventy-eight of a total of 86 additions were made to schools that were 90% of one race. We see no reason to disturb these factual determinations, which conclusively show the breach of duty found by the Court of Appeals."

---

## MILLIKEN v. BRADLEY

Supreme Court of the United States, 1974.
418 U.S. 717, 94 S.Ct. 3112, 41 L.Ed.2d 1069.

Mr. Chief Justice BURGER delivered the opinion of the Court.

We granted certiorari in these consolidated cases to determine whether a federal court may impose a multidistrict, areawide remedy to a single-district *de jure* segregation problem absent any finding that the other included school districts have failed to operate unitary school systems within their districts, absent any claim or finding that the boundary lines of any affected school district were established with the purpose of fostering racial segregation in public schools, absent any finding that the included districts committed acts which effected segregation within the other districts, and absent a meaningful opportunity for the included neighboring school districts to present evidence or be heard on the propriety of a multidistrict remedy or on the question of constitutional violations by those neighboring districts.

The District Court found that the Detroit Board of Education created and maintained optional attendance zones within Detroit neighborhoods undergoing racial transition and between high school attendance areas of opposite predominant racial compositions. These zones, the court found, had the "natural, probable, foreseeable and actual effect" of allowing white pupils to escape identifiably Negro schools. Similarly, the District Court found that Detroit school attendance zones had been drawn along north-south boundary lines despite the Detroit Board's awareness that drawing boundary lines in an east-west direction would result in significantly greater desegregation. Again, the District Court concluded, the natural and actual effect of these acts was the creation and perpetuation of school segregation within Detroit.

The District Court found that in the operation of its school transportation program, which was designed to relieve overcrowding, the Detroit Board had admittedly bused Negro Detroit pupils to predominantly Negro schools which were beyond or away from closer white schools with available space. This practice was found to have continued in recent years despite the Detroit Board's avowed policy, adopted in 1967, of utilizing transportation to increase desegregation. . . .

With respect to the Detroit Board of Education's practices in school construction, the District Court found that Detroit school construction generally tended to have a segregative effect with the great majority of schools being built in either overwhelmingly all-Negro or all-white neighborhoods so that the new schools opened as predominantly one-race schools. Thus, of the 14 schools which opened for use in 1970–1971, 11 opened over 90% Negro and one opened less than 10% Negro.

The District Court also found that the State of Michigan had committed several constitutional violations with respect to the exercise of its general responsibility for, and supervision of, public education. The State, for example, was found to have failed, until the 1971 Session of the Michigan Legislature, to provide authorization or funds for the transportation of pupils within Detroit regardless of their poverty or distance from the school to which they were assigned; during this same period the State provided many neighboring, mostly white, suburban districts the full range of state-supported transportation.

The District Court found that the State, through Act 48, acted to "impede, delay and minimize racial integration in Detroit schools." The first sentence of § 12 of Act 48 was designed to delay the April 7, 1970, desegregation plan originally adopted by the Detroit Board. The remainder of § 12 sought to prescribe for each school in the eight districts criteria of "free choice" and "neighborhood schools," which, the District Court found, "had as their purpose and effect the maintenance of segregation."

The District Court also held that the acts of the Detroit Board of Education, as a subordinate entity of the State, were attributable to the State of Michigan, thus creating a vicarious liability on the part of the State.   Under Michigan law,   .   .   .   school building construction plans had to be approved by the State Board of Education, and, prior to 1962, the State Board had specific statutory authority to supervise school-site selection.   The proofs concerning the effect of Detroit's school construction program were therefore, found to be largely applicable to show state responsibility for the segregative results.

Turning to the question of an appropriate remedy for these several constitutional violations, the District Court deferred a pending motion by intervening parent defendants to join as additional parties defendant the 85 outlying school districts in the three-county Detroit metropolitan area on the ground that effective relief could not be achieved without their presence.   The District Court concluded that this motion to join was "premature," since it "has to do with relief" and no reasonably specific desegregation plan was before the court. Accordingly, the District Court proceeded to order the Detroit Board of Education to submit desegregation plans limited to the segregation problems found to be existing within the city of Detroit.   At the same time, however, the state defendants were directed to submit desegregation plans encompassing the three-county metropolitan area despite the fact that the 85 outlying school districts of these three counties were not parties to the action and despite the fact that there had been no claim that these outlying districts had committed constitutional violations.   .   .   .

On June 12, 1973, a divided Court of Appeals, sitting en banc, affirmed in part, vacated in part, and remanded for further proceedings.   The Court of Appeals held, first, that the record supported the District Court's findings and conclusions on the constitutional violations committed by the Detroit Board, and by the state defendants. It stated that the acts of racial discrimination shown in the record are "causally related to the substantial amount of segregation found in the Detroit school system," and that "the District Court was therefore authorized and required to take effective measures to desegregate the Detroit Public School System."

The Court of Appeals also agreed with the District Court that "any less comprehensive a solution than a metropolitan area plan would result in an all black school system immediately surrounded by practically all white suburban school systems, with an overwhelming white majority population in the total metropolitan area."   The court went on to state that it could "[not] see how such segregation can be any less harmful to the minority students than if the same result were accomplished within one school district."

Accordingly, the Court of Appeals concluded that "the only feasible desegregation plan involves the crossing of the boundary lines between the Detroit School District and adjacent or nearby school districts for the limited purpose of providing an effective desegregation plan." It reasoned that such a plan would be appropriate because of the State's violations, and could be implemented because of the State's authority to control local school districts.   .   .   .   An interdistrict remedy was thus held to be "within the equity powers of the District Court."

<h2 style="text-align:center">II</h2>

Ever since Brown v. Board of Education, judicial consideration of school desegregation cases has begun with the standard:

> "[I]n the field of public education the doctrine of 'separate but equal' has no place. Separate educational facilities are inherently unequal."

This has been reaffirmed time and again as the meaning of the Constitution and the controlling rule of law.

.   .   .

The *Swann* case, of course, dealt

> "with the problem of defining in more precise terms than heretofore the scope of the duty of school authorities and district courts in implementing *Brown I* and the mandate to eliminate dual systems and establish unitary systems at once."   .   .   .

In further refining the remedial process, *Swann* held, the task is to correct, by a balancing of the individual and collective interests, "the condition that offends the Constitution." A federal remedial power may be exercised "only on the basis of a constitutional violation" and, "[a]s with any equity case, the nature of the violation determines the scope of the remedy."

Proceeding from these basic principles, we first note that in the District Court the complainants sought a remedy aimed at the *condition* alleged to offend the Constitution—the segregation within the Detroit City School District.   .   .   .

While specifically acknowledging that the District Court's findings of a condition of segregation were limited to Detroit, the Court of Appeals approved the use of a metropolitan remedy   .   .   ..

Viewing the record as a whole, it seems clear that the District Court and the Court of Appeals shifted the primary focus from a Detroit remedy to the metropolitan area only because of their conclusion that total desegregation of Detroit would not produce the racial balance which they perceived as desirable. Both courts proceeded on an assumption that the Detroit schools could not be truly desegregated—in their view of what constituted desegregation—unless the racial composition of the student body of each school substantially reflected the racial composition of the population of the metropolitan area as a whole.   .   .

In *Swann,* which arose in the context of a single independent school district, the Court held:

> "If we were to read the holding of the District Court to require, as a matter of substantive constitutional right, any particular degree of racial balance or mixing, that approach would be disapproved and we would be obliged to reverse."

The clear import of this language from *Swann* is that desegregation, in the sense of dismantling a dual school system, does not require any particular racial balance in each "school, grade or classroom."

Here the District Court's approach to what constituted "actual desegregation" raises the fundamental question, not presented in *Swann,* as to the circumstances in which a federal court may order desegregation relief that embraces more than a single school district. The court's analytical starting point was its conclusion that school district lines are no more than arbitrary lines on a map drawn "for political convenience."   Boundary lines may be bridged where there has been a constitutional violation calling for interdistrict relief, but the notion that school district lines may be casually ignored or treated as a mere administrative convenience is contrary to the history of public education in our country.   No single tradition in public education is more deeply rooted than local control over the operation of schools;  local autonomy has long been thought essential both to the maintenance of community concern and support for public schools and to quality of the educational process.   .   .   .   [L]ocal control over the educational process affords citizens an opportunity to participate in decision-making, permits the structuring of school programs to fit local needs, and encourages "experimentation, innovation, and a healthy competition for educational excellence."

.   .   .   The metropolitan remedy would require, in effect, consolidation of 54 independent school districts historically administered as separate units into a vast new super school district.   Entirely apart from the logistical and other serious problems attending large-scale transportation of students, the consolidation would give rise to an array of other problems in financing and operating this new school system.   Some of the more obvious questions would be: What would be the status and authority of the present popularly elected school boards?   Would the children of Detroit be within the jurisdiction and operating control of a school board elected by the parents and residents of other districts?   What board or boards would levy taxes for school operations in these 54 districts constituting the consolidated metropolitan area?   What provisions could be made for assuring substantial equality in tax levies among the 54 districts, if this were deemed requisite?   What provisions would be made for financing?

Would the validity of long-term bonds be jeopardized unless approved by all of the component districts as well as the State? What body would determine that portion of the curricula now left to the discretion of local school boards? Who would establish attendance zones, purchase school equipment, locate and construct new schools, and indeed attend to all the myriad day-to-day decisions that are necessary to school operations affecting potentially more than three-quarters of a million pupils?

   .  .  .  We  .  .  .  turn to address, for the first time, the validity of a remedy mandating cross-district or interdistrict consolidation to remedy a condition of segregation found to exist in only one district.

The controlling principle consistently expounded in our holdings is that the scope of the remedy is determined by the nature and extent of the constitutional violation. Before the boundaries of separate and autonomous school districts may be set aside by consolidating the separate units for remedial purposes or by imposing a cross-district remedy, it must first be shown that there has been a constitutional violation within one district that produces a significant segregative effect in another district. Specifically, it must be shown that racially discriminatory acts of the state or local school districts, or of a single school district have been a substantial cause of interdistrict segregation. Thus an interdistrict remedy might be in order where the racially discriminatory acts of one or more school districts caused racial segregation in an adjacent district, or where district lines have been deliberately drawn on the basis of race. In such circumstances an interdistrict remedy would be appropriate to eliminate the interdistrict segregation directly caused by the constitutional violation. Conversely, without an interdistrict violation and interdistrict effect, there is no constitutional wrong calling for an interdistrict remedy.

The record before us, voluminous as it is, contains evidence of *de jure* segregated conditions only in the Detroit schools; indeed, that was the theory on which the litigation was initially based and on which the District Court took evidence. See supra at 3117–3118. With no showing of significant violation by the 53 outlying school districts and no evidence of any interdistrict violation or effect, the court went beyond the original theory of the case as framed by the pleadings and mandated a metropolitan area remedy. To approve the remedy ordered by the court would impose on the outlying districts, not shown to have committed any constitutional violation, a wholly impermissible remedy based on a standard not hinted at in *Brown I* and *II* or any holding of this Court.

   .  .  .

### III

We recognize that the six-volume record presently under consideration contains language and some specific incidental findings thought by the District Court to afford a basis for interdistrict relief. However, these comparatively isolated findings and brief comments concern only one possible interdistrict violation and are found in the context of a proceeding that, as the District Court conceded, included no proof of segregation practiced by any of the 85 suburban school districts surrounding Detroit.

.   .   .

We conclude that the relief ordered by the District Court and affirmed by the Court of Appeals was based upon an erroneous standard and was unsupported by record evidence that acts of the outlying districts effected the discrimination found to exist in the schools of Detroit. Accordingly, the judgment of the Court of Appeals is reversed and the case is remanded for further proceedings consistent with this opinion leading to prompt formulation of a decree directed to eliminating the segregation found to exist in Detroit city schools, a remedy which has been delayed since 1970.

Reversed and remanded.

Mr. Justice DOUGLAS, dissenting.

The Court of Appeals has acted responsibly in these cases and we should affirm its judgment.   .   .   .

When we rule against the metropolitan area remedy we take a step that will likely put the problems of the blacks and our society back to the period that antedated the "separate but equal" regime of Plessy v. Ferguson. The reason is simple.

The inner core of Detroit is now rather solidly black; and the blacks, we know, in many instances are likely to be poorer,   .   .   . the poorer school districts must pay their own way. It is therefore a foregone conclusion that we have now given the States a formula whereby the poor must pay their own way.

Today's decision means that there is no violation of the Equal Protection Clause though the schools are segregated by race and though the black schools are not only "separate" but "inferior."

So far as equal protection is concerned we are now in a dramatic retreat from the 7-to-1 decision in 1896 that blacks could be segregated in public facilities, provided they received equal treatment.

As I indicated in Keyes, there is so far as the school cases go no constitutional difference between *de facto* and *de jure* segregation. Each school board performs state action for Fourteenth Amendment purposes when it draws the lines that confine it to a given area, when it builds schools at particular sites, or when it allocates students. The creation of the school districts in Metropolitan Detroit either maintained existing segregation or caused additional segregation. Restrictive covenants maintained by state action or inaction build black ghettos. It is state action when public funds are dispensed by housing agencies to build racial ghettos. Where a community is racially mixed and school authorities segregate schools, or assign black teachers to black schools or close schools in fringe areas and build new schools in black areas and in more distant white areas, the State creates and nurtures a segregated school system, just as surely as did those States involved in Brown v. Board of Education, when they maintained dual school systems.

All these conditions and more were found by the District Court to exist. The issue is not whether there should be racial balance but whether the State's use of various devices that end up with black schools and white schools brought the Equal Protection Clause into effect. Given the State's control over the educational system in Michigan, the fact that the black schools are in one district and the white schools are in another is not controlling—either constitutionally or equitably. . . . [S]ince Michigan by one device or another has over the years created black school districts and white school districts, the task of equity is to provide a unitary system for the affected area where, as here, the State washes its hands of its own creations.

Mr. Justice WHITE, with whom Mr. Justice DOUGLAS, Mr. Justice BRENNAN, and Mr. Justice MARSHALL join, dissenting.

.    .    .

Regretfully, and for several reasons, I can join neither the Court's judgment nor its opinion. The core of my disagreement is that deliberate acts of segregation and their consequences will go unremedied, not because a remedy would be infeasible or unreasonable in terms of the usual criteria governing school desegregation cases, but because an effective remedy would cause what the Court considers to be undue administrative inconvenience to the State. The result is that the State of Michigan, the entity at which the Fourteenth Amendment is directed, has successfully insulated itself from its duty to provide effective desegregation remedies by vesting sufficient power over its public schools in its local school districts. If this is the case in Michigan, it will be the case in most States.

There are undoubted practical as well as legal limits to the remedial powers of federal courts in school desegregation cases. The Court has made it clear that the achievement of any particular degree of racial balance in the school system is not required by the Constitution; nor may it be the primary focus of a court in devising an acceptable remedy for *de jure* segregation. A variety of procedures and techniques are available to a district court engrossed in fashioning remedies in a case such as this; but the courts must keep in mind that they are dealing with the process of *educating* the young, including the very young. The task is not to devise a system of pains and penalties to punish constitutional violations brought to light. Rather, it is to desegregate an *educational* system in which the races have been kept apart, without, at the same time, losing sight of the central *educational* function of the schools.

Viewed in this light, remedies calling for school zoning, pairing, and pupil assignments, become more and more suspect as they require that schoolchildren spend more and more time in buses going to and from school and that more and more educational dollars be diverted to transportation systems. Manifestly, these considerations are of immediate and urgent concern when the issue is the desegregation of a city school system where residential patterns are predominantly segregated and the respective areas occupied by blacks and whites are heavily populated and geographically extensive. Thus, if one postulates a metropolitan school system covering a sufficiently large area, with the population evenly divided between whites and Negroes and with the races occupying identifiable residential areas, there will be very real practical limits on the extent to which racially identifiable schools can be eliminated within the school district. It is also apparent that the larger the proportion of Negroes in the area, the more difficult it would be to avoid having a substantial number of all-black or nearly all-black schools.

The Detroit school district is both large and heavily populated.
.   .   .   If "racial balance" were achieved in every school in the district, each school would be approximately 64% Negro. A remedy confined to the district could achieve no more desegregation. .   .   .

Despite the fact that a metropolitan remedy, if the findings of the District Court accepted by the Court of Appeals are to be credited, would more effectively desegregate the Detroit schools, would prevent resegregation, and would be easier and more feasible from many standpoints, the Court fashions out of whole cloth an arbitrary rule that remedies for constitutional violations occurring in a single Michigan school district must stop at the school district line. Apparently, no matter how much less burdensome or more effective and efficient in many respects, such as transportation, the metropolitan plan might be, the school district line may not be crossed. Otherwise, it seems, there would be too much disruption of the Michigan scheme for managing its educational system, too much confusion, and too much administrative burden.

.   .   .   .

I am   .   .   .   mystified as to how the Court can ignore the legal reality that the constitutional violations, even if occurring locally, were committed by governmental entities for which the State is responsible and that it is the State that must respond to the command of the Fourteenth Amendment. An interdistrict remedy for the infringements that occurred in this case is well within the confines and powers of the State, which is the governmental entity ultimately responsible for desegregating its schools. The Michigan Supreme Court has observed that "[t]he school district is a State agency," and that " '[e]ducation in Michigan belongs to the State. It is no part of the local self-government inherent in the township or municipality, except so far as the legislature may choose to make it such.  The Constitution has turned the whole subject over to the legislature.  .  .  .' "  .  .  .

The Court draws the remedial line at the Detroit school district boundary, even though the Fourteenth Amendment is addressed to the State and even though the *State* denies equal protection of the laws when its public agencies, acting in its behalf, invidiously discriminate.  The State's default is "the condition that offends the Constitution," and state officials may therefore be ordered to take the necessary measures to completely eliminate from the Detroit public schools "all vestiges of state-imposed segregation."  I cannot understand, nor does the majority satisfactorily explain, why a federal court may not order an appropriate interdistrict remedy, if this is necessary or more effective to accomplish this constitutionally mandated task.  .  .  .

Mr. Justice MARSHALL, with whom Mr. Justice DOUGLAS, Mr. Justice BRENNAN, and Mr. Justice WHITE join, dissenting.

.  .  .

I

The great irony of the Court's opinion and, in my view, its most serious analytical flaw may be gleaned from its concluding sentence, in which the Court remands for "prompt formulation of a decree directed to eliminating the segregation found to exist in Detroit  .  .  ..

Nowhere in the Court's opinion does the majority confront, let alone respond to, the District Court's conclusion that a remedy limited to the city of Detroit would not effectively desegregate the Detroit city schools.  I, for one, find the District Court's conclusion well supported by the record and its analysis compelled by our prior cases.  .  .  .

Desegregation is not and was never expected to be an easy task. Racial attitudes ingrained in our Nation's childhood and adolescence are not quickly thrown aside in its middle years.  But just as the inconvenience of some cannot be allowed to stand in the way of the rights of others, so public opposition, no matter how strident, cannot be permitted to divert this Court from the enforcement of the constitutional principles at issue in this case.  Today's holding, I fear, is more a reflection of a perceived public mood that we have gone far enough in enforcing the Constitution's guarantee of equal justice than it is the product of neutral principles of law.  In the short run, it may seem to be the easier course to allow our great metropolitan areas to be divided up each into two cities—one white, the other black—but it is a course, I predict, our people will ultimately regret.  I dissent.

### NOTES AND QUESTIONS

1.  Is it true that segregated education is necessarily inferior education and that integrated education is necessarily superior education?  Is

"race the critical factor or socio-economic class? Consider the following: "Coleman on 'The Coleman Report'

"The following letter, by Professor James Coleman, was sent to to the *New York Times* on April 13th. The *Times* having failed to find space for it, we are here inserting it into the public record of the debate on busing and school integration:

"Dear Sirs:

"Although I make it a practice to stay away from reporters, some statements of mine were printed in Sunday's (April 9) *Times*. I want to clarify several things concerning the findings of the so-called 'Coleman Report,' and the use of those findings by governmental institutions, including the courts:

"1. The Report found, as I have testified in various court cases, and as has been confirmed by numerous further analyses of those same data, that the academic achievement of children from lower socio-economic backgrounds (black or white) was benefited by being in schools with children from higher socio-economic backgrounds (black or white).

"2. This achievement increment is not nearly sufficient to overcome the educational disadvantage of children from lower socio-economic backgrounds.

"3. This effect, however, was greater than those of other school resources of the kind ordinarily added by compensatory programs. The effects of these resources on achievement can hardly be found at all.

"My opinion, with which others who have more experience in constitutional law than I may disagree, is that the results stated in 1 and 3 above have been used inappropriately by the courts to support the premise that equal protection for black children is not provided unless racial balance is achieved in schools. I believe it is necessary to recognize that equal protection, in the sense of equal educational opportunity, cannot be provided by the State. Most of the inequality of opportunity originates in the home, through loving care and attention by parents—but differential care and attention, since parents differ—and the State can hope only to add opportunity in such a way that these inequalities are not increased but reduced. This does mean, of course, that actions of the State that have increased racial or socio-economic segregation should be corrected by the courts, but not on the mistaken assumption that they are thereby creating equal educational opportunity.

"While the issue of racial integration in schools does not, I believe, involve constitutional questions of equal protection for black children conditional upon increased achievement in integrated schools, it is a matter on which school boards and governmental authorities have a responsibility to take affirmative action—action with a less punitive and blunt quality than some court decisions, but affirmative action nevertheless. In the past 20 years, there has been an increasing self-segregation into homogeneous communities by those families that have greatest freedom to move. The result is an increasing social and economic segregation in the schools, which makes a mockery of the classic American conception of the common school attended by children of all social groups.

"Probably the most cogent recent statement on this issue is that made by the New York Board of Regents on March 24, in reaffirming its stand on school integration. The Board of Regents did not mention constitutional equal protection of black students because of greater achievement in integrated schools, but said rather, 'This Board cannot foresee any but the most sullen and corrosive scenarios of the future if the multicolored and multicultured children of this state and nation are not permitted to get to know one another as individuals.'

"James S. Coleman
"Professor of Social Relations"

From No. 28, the Public Interest 127–8 (Summer 1972), c. by National Affairs Inc., 1972, and see also, J. S. Coleman, et al., Equality of Educational Opportunity (1966).

2. Does a court have constitutional power to order socio-economic integration, as distinguished from racial desegregation? Does a school board? Why or why not? If most minority groups are poor does racial integration tend to produce socio-economic integration? Is this an objective school board should seek to accomplish? See, H. Walberg & A. Kopan, Rethinking Urban Education (1972).

3. Should school boards seek racial integration even if it could not be shown that students do better academically in racially integrated schools? Are there other proper objectives?

4. Can a school be desegregated in terms of its overall numbers, but segregated within its walls because of internal devices such as "ability grouping" or "tracking"?

---

## BLACK SCHOOLS THAT WORK

Newsweek Magazine, Jan. 1, 1973.
Reprinted with permission Copyright, © Newsweek, Inc., 1973.

The Windsor Hills Elementary School in Los Angeles had a big problem. When city school officials disclosed in 1969 that its pupils had the highest average IQ scores in Los Angeles, Windsor Hills was threatened with inundation by parents from other districts who tried to enroll their children, sometimes going to the length of faking their home addresses. In response, the neighborhood formed a Parents for

Quality Education committee to fight overcrowding. "We were out there every morning," recalls one of the parents, Mrs. Gwen Jackson, "taking down the license plates of those who didn't belong." That scene has been repeated many times in the unequal world of American education; at good schools, the "haves" always want to keep the "have-nots" out. What makes Windsor Hills extraordinary is the fact that its students body is 98 per cent black.

The school has gone through a racial transformation that is typical of many urban schools. A decade ago, most of its students were white. Then blacks began to move into the neighborhood, and in almost textbook fashion, the student body "tipped"; by 1965 it was half black, and three years later few whites were left. In most American schools, racial tipping is followed by a decline in educational quality . . . Instead, Windsor Hills improved dramatically. Once only average, it now ranks among the top 5 per cent of the city's schools in standard reading tests. Few predominantly black schools in the U. S. can match that record. But a handful do, and as black psychologist Kenneth Clark observes, "the fact that there are a few good black schools means that low quality is not inevitable."

*Success*: One of the things that make Windsor Hills a good school is that most of its pupils come from prosperous families. The parents are an upper-middle-class melange of doctors, lawyers and engineers, and the houses in the hilly neighborhood overlooking the Pacific are worth as much as $150,000. But there are other ingredients of the school's success, and these factors—unlike high family income—are common to all of the outstanding, predominantly black schools across the country.

One of the hallmarks is strict discipline and a strong focus on such fundamentals as reading and writing. "We are less permissive than other high schools," says Napoleon B. Lewis, the black principal of Howard D. Woodson High School in Washington, D. C. "I don't believe in crutches. The best thing you can do for a black kid is to have high expectations." "They need academic skills," adds Sondra Hirsch, a white teacher at P. S. 234 in New York's borough of the Bronx. "I'm a staunch supporter of innovation, but kids have to learn to read, and I expect them to do it." Father Paul Smith, the black principal of the Holy Angels Roman Catholic elementary school in Chicago, argues that permissive educators reflect "an Anglo-Saxon mentality of freedom. The black child in the inner city needs the tight system that we have here because of the chaos and disruption in the community where he lives." Father Smith's system is tight indeed. At Holy Angels, homework is mandatory every day, and the children are spanked when other forms of discipline fail.

Most children seem to respond well to such stern requirements. "The harder I work them, the more they like it," reports Mrs. Hirsch.

"Third graders come back for homework, and second graders moan when there isn't any." "I'm a slow learner," admits a member of the junior class at Woodson. "I was going to drop out of my old school, but coming here changed my thoughts a little." Although some 70 percent of his schoolmates hope to go on to college, Jones wants to be an electrician, which is one of the many vocational skills taught at Woodson.

*Sound*: Stressing the basics does not mean that up-to-date teaching methods are ignored. New York's P.S. 234 uses a system developed by British mathematician Caleb Gattegno to teach reading and math. The reading program revolves around a large word chart, on which each of the 47 sounds in the English language is color-coded. The *u* in "up" is yellow, for example, as are the similar-sounding *o* in "done," the *oe* in "does" and the *oo* in "blood."

Like most urban schools, the best of the black institutions have crowded classrooms. At Windsor Hills, the first three grades average 28 children to a class, and grades four through six have about 35. What sets the better schools apart is that most of them have superior facilities, often due to Federal aid. Woodson's new $10 million, eight-story building includes a rifle range and an Olympic-size swimming pool. The top schools also manage to give their students individual attention, despite crowded classrooms. At the Woodland Elementary School in Kansas City, students in the first three grades take a reading course that allows each child to work through nineteen books at his own pace. "The slow ones aren't forced to go too fast," says reading teacher Dan Reuter, "and the bright ones aren't frustrated by being held back."

Successful schools also work hard at involving parents in their activities. In addition to its PTA, the Captain Arthur Roth Elementary School in Cleveland has a fathers' club that organizes recreation and trips—pointedly including children who don't have fathers of their own. At Woodland, a salaried "parent visitor," Mrs. Rose Fowler, calls on other parents who are suspicious or apathetic about the school. "We start with little things," says Mrs. Fowler, "like keeping a supply of underwear and socks for children whose parents can't afford to buy them." The PTA at Windsor Hills has such *esprit de corps* that the school auditorium can barely contain the turnout at its monthly meetings. In addition, more than 100 parents take part in a volunteer program, performing such jobs as running the mimeograph machine, keeping order in the corridors and tutoring slow students. There is also an advisory council of parents that takes part in the selection of new teachers. "We are so interested," reports one member of the panel, "that we even sent representatives to sit in when a man was interviewed for a new custodial post."

Another essential requirement, of course, is a competent and dedicated faculty. And somehow, amid all the frustrations of the urban educational scene, a few predominantly black schools have succeeded in assembling an impressive array of teaching talent. Before P. S. 234 opened in the fall of 1971, the community school board placed an advertisement in The New York Times asking for imaginative teachers. Nearly 250 people applied for the 85 jobs at P. S. 234 and a neighboring school, and principal Peter Negroni was able to handpick his staff. One of the successful candidates was Sondra Hirsch, who had just obtained her master's degree and who turned down a position in pastoral Vermont to come to the Bronx. "It's the best school in the city," maintains Mrs. Hirsch, who commutes to her job from suburban Long Island. "I wish my own kids were here instead of in Great Neck."

## NOTES AND QUESTIONS

1. What factor(s) is responsible for the quality of these schools? Did the factor(s) play an important role in Brown v. Board of Education? Should it have?

2. What are the implications of these schools "that work" for desegregation? Socio-cultural integration? Headstart programs? Future court decisions?

3. In what way are these schools different from upper-middle class "white" schools?

4. Should these schools be desegregated?

———

## NOTE ON ALTERNATIVES TO INTEGRATION

White resistance in the North and West as well as in the South to the Supreme Court's decision in Brown v. Board of Education has not abated. In some parts of the United States the white resistance has intensified and has assumed more subtle forms. Faced with continuing white resistance to integration many minority-group parents and leaders have tired. They no longer pursue methods designed to achieve integration in schools. Instead, they are trying to identify alternative ways in which minority-group children can actually be afforded equal educational opportunity in quality schools without concern whether the schools are integrated. Among the methods that are being tried are community control, various kinds of compensatory education schemes, free schools and equalized school funding. These, and other, techniques promise some measure of success in certain circumstances, but they raise major questions of adequacy when they are offered as alternatives to fully integrated schools for all minority groups as a whole. They also raise new and different legal problems. See, Bell, School Litigation Strategies for the 1970's: New Phases in the Continuing Quest for Quality Schools, 1970 Wis.L.Rev. 257.

## Community Control

Many minority-group parents and leaders who are pursuing alternatives to integrated schools distinguish sharply between a "segregated" school and a school that is all, or predominantly, of one minority group; e. g., black. The ultimate difference between the two is said to be the quality of education offered. For example, some black parents and leaders hold that a "segregated" school is one that not only is populated with children who are all, or almost all, from one or more minority groups, but also, a "segregated" school is one that is controlled by whites. Blacks and other minority groups have no voice nor effective power over the substance of critical decisions, curriculum or other matters that count. Moreover, the white administrators and teachers in "segregated" schools are said not to understand fully their black, and other minority-group, children. All too often, the argument proceeds, the white faculty members and administrators operate on the basic belief that black children cannot be expected to learn very much because (1) black children are inferior in some basic way or (2) black children have suffered crippling blows from their culturally and economically deprived backgrounds. In both cases, the crucial consequences are identical. The teachers have low learning expectations for black and other minority group children which expectations, in turn, tend to fulfill themselves, because if the low expectations held by the teachers are conveyed to the children and they come to believe that they can't learn, then they do not, especially when combined with opinions of low self-esteem. See, e. g., R. Rosenthal & L. Jacobson, Pygmalian in the Classroom (1968).

There are at least three possible solutions to this problem. First, white administrators and teachers could change the message that they transmit. The feasibility of this solution is usually discounted on various grounds. Second, white children can be brought into the classrooms, thereby seeking to have the teachers and administrators elevate their expectations accordingly. This solution leads to integration strategies. As Dr. Kenneth Clark sees the matter: "It is not the presence of the white child per se that leads to higher achievement for the Negro child who associates with him in class; it is the quality of the education provided because the white child is there that makes the difference." (Clark, Fifteen Years of Deliberate Speed, *Saturday Review*, Dec. 20, 1969). This solution is discounted because of white resistance to integration. Third, black and other minority-group teachers and administrators can replace whites. The idea is that under community control, especially minority-group control of local school boards, the new teachers and administrators who will be appointed will be selected because they are sensitive to the needs of minority-group children and because they will create an atmosphere of mutual trust, pride and esteem that is more conducive to learning. This solution directly eliminates the low expectations and simultaneously affords minority-group school children with minority-group models of success which will serve to increase the children's pride and raise their low self-esteem which subverts their achievement potential. The community control solution is seen as providing the foundation for a "union of children, parents, teachers (specially trained to teach in such communities), social workers, psychologists, doctors, lawyers and community planners," which would "make the system a functioning, relevant part of the lives of the local people" and such "involvement is essential" to abate "the present situation of existing and growing alienation." Hamilton, Race and Education: A Search for Legitimacy, 38 Harv.Ed.Rev. 671 (1968). For further discussion see, M. Berobe and M. Gittell, Confrontation at Ocean Hill-Brownsville (1968); Edmonds, Judicial Assumptions on the Value of Integrated Education for Blacks, Proceedings, Nat'l Policy Conference on Education for Blacks 140 (1972); U.S. Senate Select Committee on Equal Educational Opportunity, Hearings, 5873–5874 (July 27, 1971); Kirp, Community Control, Public Policy and the Limits of Law, 68 Mich.L.Rev. 1355 (1970); Owens v. School Committee, 304 F.Supp. 1327 (D.Mass., 1969), and Oliver v. Donovan, 293 F.Supp. 958 (E.D. N.Y.1968).

## Compensatory Education

Compensatory education programs take many forms. But commonly, they provide for more teachers with specialized teaching skills; for more and specialized teaching aids, and for more and specialized programs aimed at the specific problems of minority children, especially ghetto children. Compensatory education programs are costly, and usually local communities will not, or cannot, tax themselves sufficiently to finance them. Some compensatory education programs have been financed by the federal government under the largest compensatory education program ever attempted, authorized by Title I of the Elementary and Secondary Education Act of 1965 (79 Stat. 27–35, as amended, 20 U.S.C. §§ 236–244 (1965).

But problems have arisen. There have been repeated reports of corruption, waste, misuse and mismanagement of the federal monies. Far too often monies have been used to equalize state funding of schools rather than to increase the funding of ghetto schools that already should be receiving their equal share of funds, or monies have been used to upgrade the physical aspects of target schools rather than their educational programs. See, 1969 Civil Rights Commission Report 32. But probably the greatest obstacle to realizing fully the promise of compensatory educational programs is a failure of national will and funds. The magnitude of the need is great, and compensatory education is expensive. The Chairman of the Senate's Select Committee on Equal Educational Opportunity, Walter Mondale, stated that "with few exceptions, an annual Federal investment of $1.5 billion in compensatory education has little perceptible impact on mounting educational disadvantages." (New York Times, Feb. 27, 1972, E. 13, col. 8). But, the large scale resistance by whites to integration indicates that there is probably insufficient solid support for the needed compensatory education programs that would spend four times as much money on the education of minority-group children than on white education. See, Cohen, Policies for the Public Schools: Compensation and Integration, 38 Harv.Ed.Rev. 114 (1968).

## Free Schools

Free schools, generally, are private schools that have been located in poor areas. They serve minority-group children primarily. They tend to be staffed by sensitive and committed teachers, to have exciting curricula especially designed for minority-group children, and they seem to be fun for the children and have a better-than-average rate of success. See, J. Kozol, Free Schools (1972), and G. Dennison, Lives of Children (1969). But free schools have many problems, probably the greatest of which is financing. Parents who are able to pay tuition pay it on a sliding scale basis, and sometimes there are additional funds that come from foundation grants and other sources. The free schools of the Black Muslims seek no outside sources of funds. These schools are characterized by strict segregation, strong discipline, attempts to generate feelings of racial pride and self-reliance, and the black children seem to achieve at, or above, their grade levels. See, The Muslim Way, *Newsweek*, 106 (Sept. 25, 1972). The Black Muslims, of course, have an intensity of commitment not easily duplicated. Dedication can be a second problem. In addition to funds, free schools also require large amounts of commitment, competence, courage and considerateness from their teachers which, often, are hard to sustain over long periods of time.

## Equalized School Funding

The idea here is that state authorities should undertake to eliminate financial differences between school districts, especially the under-financed ghetto schools. Much financing of the common schools comes from local property taxes. The amount of funds raised varies widely among school districts because valuable properties and their assessed valuations and their property tax rates vary widely. Equalized school funding is explored in Chapter 10.

## Voucher Education

Voucher education, or a system of tuition grants, has been proposed as an alternative to integrated education. See Sizer & Whitten, A Proposal for a Poor Children's Bill of Rights, Psychology Today 59 (Aug. 1968), and Sizer, The Case for a Free Market, Saturday Review 34 (Jan. 11, 1969). For a discussion of the constitutional and other problems presented by a voucher program compare King, Rebuilding the "Fallen House"—State Tuition Grants for Elementary and Secondary Education, 84 Harv.L.Rev. 1057 (1971) with Green, Education Vouchers, 6 Harv.Civ.Rights-Civ.Lib.L.Rev. 466 (1971), and see, Mecklenberger and Wilson, Learning C.O.D.—Can the Schools Buy Success?, *Saturday Review* 62 (Sept. 18, 1972); J. Coons & S. Sugarman, EDUCATION BY CHOICE (1978), and Cohen & Farrar, Power To The Parents, 48 The Public Interest 72 (1977).

## CONSTITUTIONAL LIMITATIONS ON STATE AID TO RACIALLY DISCRIMINATORY PRIVATE SCHOOLS

### NORWOOD v. HARRISON

Supreme Court of the United States, 1973.
413 U.S. 455, 93 S.Ct. 2804, 37 L.Ed.2d 723.

Mr. Chief Justice BURGER delivered the opinion of the Court.

. . .

Private schools in Mississippi have experienced a marked growth in recent years. As recently as the 1963–1964 school year, there were only 17 private schools other than Catholic schools; the total enrollment was 2,362 students. 916 students in these nonpublic schools were Negro, and 192 of these were enrolled in special schools for retarded, orphaned, or abandoned children. By September of 1970, the number of private non-Catholic schools had increased to 155 with a student population estimated at 42,000, virtually all white. Appellees do not challenge the statement, which is fully documented in appellants' brief, that "the creation and enlargement of these [private] academies occurred simultaneously with major events in the desegregation of public schools. . . ."

This case does not raise any question as to the right of citizens to maintain private schools with admission limited to students of particular national origins, race or religion or of the authority of a State to allow such schools. See Pierce v. Society of Sisters . . . The narrow issue before us, rather, is a particular form of tangible assistance the State provides to students in private schools in common with all other students by lending textbooks under the State's 33-year-old program for providing free textbooks to all the children of the State. The program dates back to a 1940 appeal for improved education facilities by the Governor of Mississippi to the state legislature. The legislature then established a state textbook purchasing board and authorized it to select, purchase, and distribute free textbooks for all school children through the first eight grades. In 1942, the program was extended to cover all high school students, and, as codified, the statutory authorization remains substantially unchanged. . . .

The District Court found that "34,000 students are presently receiving state-owned textbooks while attending 107 all-white, non-sectarian private schools which have been formed throughout the state since the inception of public school desegregation." During the 1970–1971 school year, these schools held 173,424 books for which Mississippi paid $490,239. The annual expenditure for replacement or new texts is approximately $6 per pupil or a total of approximately $207,000 for the students enrolled in the participating private segregated academies, exclusive of mailing costs which are borne by the state as well.

In dismissing the complaint the District Court stressed, first, that the statutory scheme was not motivated by a desire to further racial segregation in the public schools, having been enacted first in 1940, long before this Court's decision in Brown v. Board of Education, 347 U.S. 483 (1954), and consequently, long before there was any occasion to have a policy or reason to foster the development of racially segregated private academies. Second, the District Court took note that providing textbooks to private *sectarian* schools had been approved by this Court in Board of Education v. Allen, 392 U.S. 236 (1968), and that "the essential inquiry, therefore, is whether we should apply a more stringent standard for determining what constitutes state aid to a school in the context of the Fourteenth Amendment's ban against denial of equal protection that the Supreme Court has applied in the First Amendment cases." The District Court held no more stringent standard should apply on the facts of this case, since, as in *Allen,* the books were provided to the students and not to the schools. Finally, the District Court concluded that the textbook loans did not interfere with or impede the State's acknowledged duty to establish a unitary school system under this Court's holding in Green v. County School Board, . . .

This Court has consistently affirmed decisions enjoining state tuition grants to students attending racially discriminatory private schools. A textbook lending program is not legally distinguishable from the forms of state assistance foreclosed by the prior cases. Free textbooks, like tuition grants directed to private school students, are a form of financial assistance inuring to the benefit of the private schools themselves. An inescapable educational cost for students in both public and private schools is the expense of providing all necessary learning materials. When, as here, that necessary expense is borne by the State, the economic consequence is to give aid to the enterprise; if the school engages in discriminatory practices the State by tangible aid in the form of textbooks thereby gives support to such discrimination. Racial discrimination in state-operated schools is barred by the Constitution and "[i]t is also axiomatic that a state may not induce, encourage or promote private persons to accomplish what it is constitutionally forbidden to accomplish." . . .

We do not suggest that a State violates its constitutional duty merely because it has provided *any* form of state service that benefits private schools said to be racially discriminatory. Textbooks are a basic educational tool and, like tuition grants, they are provided only in connection with schools; they are to be distinguished from generalized services government might provide to schools in common with others. Moreover, the textbooks provided to private school students by the State in this case are a form of assistance readily available from sources entirely independent of the State—unlike, for example, "such necessities of life as electricity, water, and police and fire protection." . . . The State has neither an absolute nor operating monopoly on the procurement of school textbooks; anyone can purchase them on the open market.

The District Court laid great stress on the absence of showing by appellants that "any child enrolled in private school if deprived of free textbooks would withdraw from private schools and subsequently enroll in the public schools." We can accept this factual assertion; we cannot and do not know, on this record at least, whether state textbook assistance is the determinative factor in the enrollment of any students in any of the private schools in Mississippi. We do not agree with the District Court in its analysis of the legal consequences of this uncertainty, for the Constitution does not permit the State to aid discrimination even when there is no precise causal relationship between state financial aid to a private school and the continued well-being of that school. A State may not grant the type of tangible financial aid here involved if that aid has a significant tendency to facilitate, reinforce, and support private discrimination. "[D]ecisions on the constitutionality of state involvement in private discrimination do not turn on whether the state aid adds up to 51 per cent or adds up to only 49 per cent of the support of the segregated institution." . . .

The recurring theme of appellees' argument is a sympathetic one —that the State's textbook loan program is extended to students who attend racially segregated private schools only because the State sincerely wishes to foster quality education for all Mississippi children, and, to that end, has taken steps to insure that no sub-group of school children will be deprived of an important educational tool merely because their parents have chosen to enroll them in segregated private schools. We need not assume that the State's textbook aid to private schools has been motivated by other than a sincere interest in the educational welfare of all Mississippi children. But good intentions as to one valid objective do not serve to negate the State's involvement in violation of a constitutional duty. "The existence of a permissible purpose cannot sustain an action that has an impermissible effect." . . . The Equal Protection Clause would be a sterile promise if state involvement in possible private activity could be shielded altogether from constitutional scrutiny simply because its ultimate end was not discrimination but some higher goal. . . .

The District Court offered as further support for its holding the finding that Mississippi's public schools "were fully established as

unitary schools throughout the state no later than 1970–71 [and]
continue to attract 90% of the state's educable children." . . .
We note, however, that overall statewide attendance figures do not
fully and accurately reflect the impact of private schools in particular
school districts.  In any event, the constitutional infirmity of the
Mississippi textbook program is that it significantly aids the organization and continuation of a separate system of private schools which,
under the District Court holding, may discriminate if they so desire.
A State's constitutional obligation requires it to steer clear not only
of operating the old dual system of racially segregated schools but also
of giving significant aid to institutions that practice racial or other
invidious discrimination.  That the State's public schools are now
fully unitary, as the District Court found, is irrelevant.

Appellees and the District Court also placed great reliance on
our decisions in Everson v. Board of Education . . . and Board
of Education v. Allen  . . .  In *Everson,* we held that the Establishment Clause of the First Amendment did not prohibit New Jersey
from "spending tax-raised funds to pay the bus fares of parochial
school pupils as part of a general program under which it pays the
fares of pupils attending public and other schools." . . . *Allen,*
following *Everson,* sustained a New York law requiring school textbooks to be let free of charge to all students, including those in attendance at parochial schools, in specified grades.

Neither *Allen* nor *Everson* is dispositive of the issue before us
in this case.  Religious schools "pursue two goals, religious instruction and secular education." . . .  And, where carefully limited
so as to avoid the prohibitions of the "effect" and "entanglement"
tests, States may assist church-related schools in performing their
secular functions . . . not only because the States have a substantial interest in the quality of education being provided by private schools . . . but more importantly because assistance prop-
ly confined to the secular functions of sectarian schools does not substantially promote the readily identifiable religious mission of those
schools and it does not interfere with the free exercise rights of others.

Like a sectarian school, a private school—even one that discriminates—fulfills an important educational function; however, the difference is that in the context of this case the legitimate educational
function cannot be isolated from discriminatory practices—if such
in fact exist.  Under Brown v. Board of Education, supra, discriminatory treatment exerts a pervasive influence on the entire educational
process.  The private school that closes its doors to defined groups of
students on the basis of constitutionally suspect criteria manifests,
by its own actions, that its educational processes are based on private
belief that segregation is desirable in education.  There is no reason
to discriminate against students for reasons wholly unrelated to individual merit unless the artificial barriers are considered an essen-

tial part of the educational message to be communicated to the students who are admitted. Such private bias is not barred by the Constitution, nor does it invoke any sanction of laws, but neither can it call on the Constitution for material aid from the State.

Our decisions under the Establishment Clause reflect the "internal tension in the First Amendment between the Establishment Clause and the Free Exercise Clause,"  .   .   .  This does not mean, as we have already suggested, that a State is constitutionally obligated to provide even "neutral" services to sectarian schools. But the transcendent value of free religious exercise in our constitutional scheme leaves room for "play in the joints" to the extent of cautiously delineated secular governmental assistance to religious schools, despite the fact that such assistance touches on the conflicting values of the Establishment Clause by indirectly benefiting the religious schools and their sponsors.

In contrast, although the Constitution does not proscribe private bias, it places no value on discrimination as it does on the values inherent in the Free Exercise Clause. Invidious private discrimination may be characterized as a form of exercising freedom of association protected by the First Amendment, but it has never been accorded affirmative constitutional protections. And even some private discrimination is subject to special remedial legislation in certain circumstances under § 2 of the Thirteenth Amendment; Congress has made such discrimination unlawful in other significant contexts. However narrow may be the channel of permissible state aid to sectarian schools  .   .   .  it permits a greater degree of state assistance than may be given to private schools which engage in discriminatory practices that would be unlawful in a public school system.  .   .   .

The judgment of the District Court is vacated and the case is remanded for further proceedings consistent with this opinion.

So ordered.

Mr. Justice DOUGLAS and Mr. Justice BRENNAN concur in the result.

### NOTES AND QUESTIONS

1.  Identify the types of aid that a state constitutionally can provide to a racially discriminatory private school? To a non-racially discriminatory private school that is also a parochial school? To a non-racially discriminatory, non-parochial private school?

2.  Does the principle of this case apply to parochial schools that refuse to admit as students those persons who are not members of the school's religious faith?

3.  What would be the application of the principle of this case to a state program that awarded tuition grants to all students in the state so that they could go to "any school of their choosing, public or private"? Cf. Coffey v. State Educational Fin. Comm., 296 F.Supp. 1389 (S.D.

Miss.1969), app. dism., 398 U.S. 956, 400 U.S. 986.  Suppose the Commissioner of Internal Revenue has awarded the schools in Norwood a tax-exempt status under § 501(c)(3) of the Federal Internal Revenue Code thus ensuring donors the right to deduct contributions to these schools, would a plaintiff be successful under the rule of this case in obtaining an injunction prohibiting these schools from being classified as tax-exempt?  See, Green v. Kennedy, 309 F.Supp. 1127 (D.C.1970), and Comment, Segregation Academies And State Action, 82 Yale L.J. 1436 (1973).

4.  Private segregated schools tend to lack money for things like athletic fields, libraries, etc.  In Gilmore v. Montgomery, 417 U.S. 556, 94 S.Ct. 2416, 41 L.Ed.2d 304 (1974), the Supreme Court affirmed a lower court's judgment enjoining a city from permitting exclusive access and use of its recreational facilities by racially discriminatory private schools.  The Court's ruling stated that assistance by the City "significantly tended to undermine the federal court order mandating the establishment and maintenance of unitary school system in Montgomery" and emphasized that the City's action had "significantly enhanced the attractiveness of segregated private schools, formed in reaction against the federal court's school order, by enabling them to offer complete athletic programs."

Suppose the segregated private schools did not want exclusive use of public facilities for themselves, but now offer to allow their athletic teams to join and compete in a league against public schools in public facilities.  Can public school officials accept their offer?  If not, must the public library and public museum turn away students of private segregated schools whenever those schools seek to have their students use the facilities as part of their curriculum?

5.  After Norwood, does a state have constitutional power to certify that attendance at a private, racially segregated school is attendance that satisfies its compulsory attendance law in conformity with Pierce v. Society of Sisters?

---

## INTEGRATION OF FACULTY

---

### BAKER v. COLUMBUS MUNICIPAL SEPARATE SCHOOL DIST.

United States District Court, N.D.Miss.1971.
329 F.Supp. 706, aff'd 462 F.2d 1112.

ORMA R. SMITH, District Judge.

### FINDINGS OF FACT ON COUNT ONE

1.  Plaintiffs in Count One of this action are the National Education Association (NEA), the Mississippi Teachers Association (MTA), and eight Negro teachers who taught in the Columbus Municipal Separate School District during the academic year 1969–70  .   .   .

3.   The defendants are the Columbus Municipal Separate School District of Lowndes County, Mississippi  .   .   .

4.   Count One of the amended complaint alleges that defendants have unlawfully refused to reemploy black teachers and to hire black applicants for teaching positions.   .   .   .

6.   During the academic year 1969–70, the student enrollment in the Columbus Public School was 8,865 students.   The racial composition of the student body was approximately 5,392 white students or 61 per cent white, and approximately 3,473 black students or 39 per cent black.

7.   At least until the commencement of the 1970–71 school year, the defendants operated a dual school system.   .   .   .

9.   Defendants intended to reduce the size of the faculty by three positions for the 1970–71 school year.   On the day before school opened, however, Superintendent Goolsby advised the Court that there were 36 vacancies on his staff.   Thus, the 1970–71 school year commenced with a faculty that was 39 persons below the faculty for the preceding academic year, 1969–70.   In all, there were 376 faculty members in 1969–70 and 337 faculty members as of September 3, 1970.

10.   Between the academic years 1969–70 and 1970–71, the racial composition of the faculty changed substantially.   The number of black teachers dropped from 133 to 103 and the number of white teachers dropped from 243 to 234.   Thus, the number of black teachers on the faculty declined by 22 per cent and the number of white teachers on the faculty declined by 3 per cent.

11.   Through September 3, 1970, defendants had hired 44 new teachers for the 1970–71 academic year.   All but one were white.

12.   The marked changes in the racial composition of defendants' faculty between the academic years 1969–70 and 1970–71 coincide with the changes in defendants' hiring and retention policy.   On January 12, 1970, the Board of Trustees modified the procedures and requirements for hiring and reelection of teachers by adding to those procedures and requirements, effective for the 1970–71 academic year, the following:

> "Each classroom teacher that was employed to teach in the Columbus Public School System for the first time for the year 1969–1970 [shall] be required to have on file in the Superintendent's office a composite score of 1000 on the National Teachers Examination before they [shall] be considered for employment as a classroom teacher for the year 1970–71 and  *   *   *   all classroom teachers that were not employed by the Columbus Public Schools during the 1969–70 school year and all future classroom teachers that are employed [shall] be required to meet the above standards."

.   .   .

18.  Also on or about March of each year, each principal has evaluated the teachers in his school on the basis of a rating form used throughout the school district.  The principals rated the teachers on a scale of 0 to 5 with respect to each of 25 criteria:

Wholesome Personality
Appearance
Poise
Desirable Work Habits
Good Command of English
Good Physical and Mental Health
Proper Ethical Conduct
Interest in Self Improvement
Knowledge of Subject Matter and Methods of Instruction
Academic Requirements of Subject Matter or Grade Level
Willingness to Accept and Execute Policies and Assignments
Readiness to Share Ideas and Methods
Skill in Evaluating Pupils and Reporting to Parents
Willingness to Ask for and Accept Help
Participation in Professional Organizations and School Activities
Competency in Record Keeping
Follows Philosophy of Education for Columbus Public Schools
Concern for Physical Aspects of Room
Self-Discipline and Classroom Control
Consistency in Lesson Planning
Energy and Enthusiasm in Presenting Lesson
Skill in Giving Directions, Questioning and Testing
Use of Teaching Aids
Skill in Making Reasonable Homework and Research Assignments
Providing for Individual Instruction During Supervised Study
Period  .  .  .

22.  The NTE cutoff score requirement had its origins in a merit pay program of defendants known as the "Voluntary Professional Enrichment Program" or "PEP".

23.  .  .  .  The PEP program was formulated by the Superintendent, who consulted with a committee of teachers belonging to the local white teacher association.  No black teachers were consulted.

24.  Under PEP no teacher was eligible for merit pay unless he had filed an NTE score with the school district.  In addition, a teacher had to earn 70 points to qualify for the minimum pay increment of $300;  75 points for an increment of $400;  and 80 points for the maximum increment of $500.  .  .  .

27.  During the first year of PEP (1966–67), 59 teachers applied for merit pay and filed NTE scores.  Five of the applicants were black.  Fifty-two white teachers and one black teacher posted

scores of 500 or more on one of the NTE examinations. Twenty-six applicants, all of whom were white, received merit pay.

28. In the second year (1967–68) of PEP, 77 teachers applied for merit pay. Seven of these applicants were black. Sixty-eight white teachers and one black teacher posted scores of 500 or more on one of the NTE examinations. Forty-three of the applicants, all of whom were white, received merit pay.

29. In the third year (1968–69) of PEP, 98 teachers applied for merit pay. Fifteen of these applicants were black. Seventy-nine white teachers and eight black teachers posted scores of 500 or more in one of the NTE examinations. Fifty-six teachers, of whom four were black, received merit pay. . . .

33. On April 14, 1969, Mrs. Holloman moved the Board of Trustees "to require new teachers elected to the Columbus Public Schools faculty for the first time for the 1969–70 school session to file their National Teacher Examination scores by January 1, 1970." The motion carried. . . .

36. The NTE cutoff score requirement was invoked by defendants without investigating or studying the validity and reliability of the examination and the particular cutoff score as a means of selecting teachers for hiring and reelection for the Columbus system, and without consulting with the developer of the NTE. The Superintendent disavows any expertise with respect to the NTE.

37. The Board of Trustees, in adopting the cutoff score on January 12, 1970, was aware of the racially disparate results worked by the NTE requirements of the PEP program. The Superintendent also expected that the percentage of black teachers or applicants who would not qualify would be greater than the percentage of whites. . . .

### The National Teachers Examination

39. Educational Testing Service (ETS), a non-profit corporation, produces and administers the National Teachers Examination. It also designs, produces and administers a broad range of other standardized testing programs, including the College Board Examinations, the Law School Aptitude Test, and the Graduate Record Examinations. ETS annually administers test programs to about five million individuals who are in or moving toward professional careers.

40. There are two major sections of the NTE: the Common Examination and the Teaching Area Examination. The Common Examination consists of a professional education test and a set of three general education tests which provide a general appraisal of the prospective teacher's basic professional preparation and general academic attainment. The Teaching Area Examinations test the candidate with respect to a particular academic discipline. There are

about 20 different Teaching Area Examinations.  Separate scores are reported by ETS for the Common Examination and for the Teaching Area Examination.

41.    Plaintiffs presented as their expert witness Dr. James R. Deneen, Senior Program Director for Teacher Examinations of the ETS.  Prior to joining ETS in 1969, Dr. Deneen was a full-time consultant to the Ford Foundation in matters of school administration. In earlier years, he was the Codirector of Education Study in the Catholic Archdiocese of New York; an Adjunct Professor at Fordham University, teaching school personnel administration; and Executive Secretary for the Superintendent of the National Catholic Education Association;  and between 1957 and 1966 the Superintendent of Schools for the Catholic Diocese of Evansville, Indiana, a system of 16,000 pupils.

42.    Defendants presented as their expert witness Dr. Stephen Knezevich, Professor of Education Administration at the University of Wisconsin.  Prior to serving at the University of Wisconsin, Dr. Knezevich was associated with the American Association of School Administrators.  In earlier years, he served as Professor and Department Head at Florida State University;  Professor of Education at the University of Iowa;  Associate Professor of Education at University of Tulsa;  and Superintendent of Schools in Algoma, Wisconsin.

43.    Dr. Deneen's experience with the NTE has been in his present capacity as the supervisor of the program in which the NTE is developed and administered.  Dr. Knezevich's direct experience with the NTE was in 1960 when he reviewed the test and prepared a paper on the subject.  Since that time, his contact with the NTE has been limited to that stemming from his relationship to the process for admission of students for the Florida State Graduate School of Administration Supervision and Curriculum between 1961 and 1965. In admitting students, that graduate school relied in part on standardized test scores, most extensively the Graduate Record Examination score, but sometimes the NTE score.  With the exception of a review of some NTE booklets in preparation for his testimony in this case, Dr. Knezevich has not had any contact with the NTE since 1965.

### What the NTE Is Designed to Measure

44.    The primary purpose of the NTE is to measure the academic achievement of college seniors completing four years of teacher education.  It is limited to the assessment of those aspects of teacher education which are validly and reliably measured by well-constructed, objective paper-and-pencil tests.  The NTE are used primarily by state and local school systems, teacher education institutions, and other agencies concerned with the guidance, preparation, certifica-

tion and employment of teachers for elementary and secondary schools.

45. It is not known whether there is a relationship between academic preparation, as measured by the NTE, and effective teaching. Dr. Deneen testified that "We cannot demonstrate such a relationship," and Dr. Knezevich generally agreed with the conclusion. Thus, the reliability and validity of the NTE as a means of identifying effective teachers is unknown. There is no evidence developed to date of a correlation, positive or negative, between the NTE score and teacher effectiveness. The NTE does not claim predictive validity—i. e., "the ability to forecast teaching performance."

### Defendants' Use of the NTE—Absence of Validation

46. Defendants rely exclusively on the NTE in refusing to reemploy first-year teachers and to hire applicants who have not satisfied the 1000 cutoff score requirement.

47. Use of the NTE with a cutoff score as a means of selecting teachers cannot be considered reasonable unless steps are first taken to relate the score to experience and needs in the particular school district. These steps include identification of the strengths and weaknesses of the school district's present staff; determination of the characteristics of teacher preparation programs in those colleges from which the district draws most of its teachers; determination of the composition and needs of the district's student body in relation to national and local education goals; and consultation with ETS regarding the uses to which the examination can be put in meeting the districts' goals and the tests' limitations.

48. In making a decision not to reemploy an in-service teacher or not to employ an applicant solely on the basis of the NTE, an administrator runs great risks of arbitrary and unreasonable results in the absence of information which relates academic qualities to teaching success in his district.

49. The defendants did not take the steps necessary to guard against arbitrary results in using cutoff scores on the NTE as a means of selecting teachers for reemployment and employment.

51. The likelihood of arbitrary results from use of the NTE with a cutoff score is enhanced because the NTE measures only a fraction of the characteristics required for effective classroom performance.

52. The NTE examinations are not measures of classroom teaching performance. Dr. Deneen testified: "The test does not get at, does not examine, * * * many areas which school superintendents or a state may wish to know about prospective teacher candidates. It cannot, for example, supply what one can learn uniquely through a personal interview." Among the qualities required of teachers which the NTE does not measure are: possession of manual

skills, attitudes about children, personal and social characteristics, ability to communicate with students, ability to motivate students, ability to discipline students, ability to evaluate students, capability to maintain satisfactory relationships with parents of students, capability to maintain satisfactory relationships with fellow teachers and, most important, whether the teacher can function effectively in the classroom.

53. In his paper on the subject, Dr. Knezevich observed:

"The examinations do not purport to measure such things as personal and social characteristics. Those responsible for the examinations are quick to point these things out and urge the National Teacher Examinations result be supplemented with the result of other evaluations of techniques before any final decision is made to the prospective teacher's qualifications.

"The National Teacher Examinations were constructed to provide objective measures of some of the intellectual, academic, and cultural factors basis [sic] for teacher success. Any school official or other person who is judging the teacher fitness of a candidate should not use the National Teacher Examinations result as a sole basis for selection. Due cognizance should be taken of such factors as personality, social characteristics, training, experience, and classroom effectiveness. These should be evaluated independently by local school officials through interviews, observations of classroom procedures, and careful consideration of records and credentials."

54. The NTE tests in some degree for only four of the 25 criteria used by defendants to evaluate in-service teachers—namely, knowledge of subject matter and methods of instruction; academic requirements of subject matter or grade level; skill in giving directions, questioning and testing; and use of teaching aids. . . .

55. With respect to new hires, it was unreasonable for defendants to exclude teacher applicants on the sole basis of a score on the NTE which had never been validated.

56. With respect to in-service teachers, it was even less justifiable for defendants to exclude teachers from reemployment on the sole basis of a score on the NTE because other, more probative means of evaluation were available. As Dr. Deneen testified:

The best indication that a teacher can teach well is that he has taught well. . . .

58. ETS made a computer check of the NTE scores achieved by students reporting attendance at predominately white and black in-

stitutions of higher learning in Mississippi during the four most recent administrations of the examination prior to the hearing in this case—July and November 1969, and January and April 1970. The racial make-up of these institutions was determined from the Department of Health, Education and Welfare's publication reporting the enrollment by race in Mississippi institutions.

59. ETS's study of scores at Mississippi institutions show that about 90 per cent of the students graduating from predominately white institutions score 1000 or better on the NTE, while 89 percent of the students graduating from predominately black institutions fail to attain a score of 1000.

60. Roughly 75 per cent of the teachers hired by defendants are graduates of Mississippi institutions of higher education.

61. The NTE cutoff score requirement will continue to disqualify substantially more black applicants for teaching positions in defendants' system than white applicants for the next few years. . . .

### Unequal Application of the NTE Requirement

67. The NTE cutoff requirement has been applied in a racially discriminatory manner. One first-year white teacher who failed to attain the cutoff score was reemployed for the 1970–71 school year. No black teacher who failed to attain the NTE cutoff score was reemployed for 1970–71.

68. Two black teachers—plaintiffs Prowell and Hubbard—were nonrenewed on the basis of the NTE requirement, although they were not within the class of teachers to which the requirement applied. . . .

69. Defendants, on the day before school opened, had hired 43 new white teachers and one new black teacher. At that time, there were 36 vacancies on defendants' staff.

70. Five black applicants had filed satisfactory NTE scores with their applications to the Columbus School District prior to July 14, 1970. The number had increased from five to nine by September 3, 1970. None of the applicants had been employed by defendants prior to the time when this Court entered its preliminary injunction on September 3, 1970.

### Conclusion

71. The facts surrounding the adoption and application of the NTE requirement demonstrate that defendants acted for the purpose of barring proportionately more black teachers than white teachers from reemployment and hiring by the Columbus School district.

72. The effect of the NTE cutoff score requirement has been to bar proportionately more black teachers than white teachers from reemployment and hiring by the Columbus School District. . . .

CONCLUSIONS OF LAW . . .

3. It is unconstitutional for public officials to discriminate on the basis of race in the hiring and retention of teachers in the public schools. . . .

4. In cases where discrimination is in issue, "statistics often tell much, and Courts listen." . . .

5. In the case at bar there has been a long history of racial discrimination by defendants in the conduct of the Columbus Municipal Separate School District. . . .

6. The inference that defendants acted with a racially discriminatory purpose in setting the requirement for a 1000 score on the NTE is concretely reinforced in this case by other facts. First, defendants knew from the experience with the PEP program that a 1000 cutoff score would eliminate proportionately a much higher percentage of black than white teachers and applicants. Second, defendants applied the NTE score requirement in an uneven fashion. Two black teachers who were employed prior to the 1969–70 school year and therefore were not subject to the NTE requirement were refused reemployment because they allegedly failed to qualify with a score of 1000. One white teacher in his first year was retained even though he did not attain a score of 1000. Third, defendants hired 44 new teachers, only one of whom was black. On the day before school opened, defendants have not offered jobs to nine black applicants who had attained and submitted NTE scores of 1000 or more even though there were 36 vacancies in defendants' system.

7. The inference of racial discrimination arising from the circumstances of this case "thrust[s] upon the School Board the burden of justifying its conduct by clear and convincing evidence." . . .

8. Defendants have not shown by "clear and convincing evidence" that their failure to rehire black first-year teachers and to hire black applicants was not racially discriminatory. . . .

9. The Court concludes that defendants in formulating and applying the NTE cutoff score requirement have purposely discriminated against black teachers and black applicants on account of their race.
. . .

13. In the case at bar, defendants have not discharged their "very heavy burden of justification" . . . and the Court, therefore, concludes that the NTE cutoff score requirement is an unconstitutional racial classification. . . .

18. In the case at bar, defendants have failed to show a "manifest relationship" between the cutoff score used and job performance.

19. Although plaintiffs do not have the burden of proving that there is no "manifest relationship," the proof demonstrates as much.

The NTE does not predict classroom effectiveness and does not even test for the great majority of factors that defendants believe are important in good teaching. The relationship between the test and teaching effectiveness is even more attenuated because defendants have used a cutoff score of 1000. There is no convincing evidence in the record showing any relationship between 1000 on the NTE and effective classroom teaching, and results worked by the use of the cutoff score indicate that no relationship can be established. The Superintendent admitted that the NTE would bar some good teachers and all the plaintiffs at bar were recommended for reelection by their principals, who made their evaluations on the basis of classroom performance. One of these plaintiffs ranked first on the faculty at his school.   .   .   .

21. It is unlawful for public officials to exclude a person from practicing his profession in a manner or for reasons that contravene the Due Process or Equal Protection Clauses of the Fourteenth Amendment. In this connection, the Supreme Court has ruled that "any qualification must have a rational connection with the applicant's fitness or capacity" to perform his occupation or profession.   .   .   .
The Court concludes that, apart from its discriminatory aspects, the NTE cutoff score requirement is an arbitrary and unreasonable qualification for reemployment and employment as a teacher in the Columbut system and therefore violates the Due Process Clause   .   .   .   .

## NOTES AND QUESTIONS

1. Does the court say that NTE scores could never be used for purposes of salary increases and teacher retention, or not used in the way they were in this case? If they can be used constitutionally, describe how.

2. See also, United States v. Texas Ed. Agency, 459 F.2d 600 (5th Cir. 1972), and Armstead v. Starkville Mun. Sch. Dist., 461 F.2d 276 (5th Cir. 1972).

3. The Court relied, in part, on the fact that the tests used had not been job validated: "The NTE does not predict classroom effectiveness and does not even test for the great majority of factors that defendants believe are important in good teaching."

In Griggs v. Duke Power Co., 401 U.S. 424, 91 S.Ct. 849, 28 L.Ed.2d 158 (1971), a statutory Title VII case, the U. S. Supreme Court ruled that, under the statute, tests must be validated and shown to be job related before they can be used: "Under the [Civil Rights] Act, practices, procedures, or tests neutral on their face, and even neutral in terms of intent, cannot be maintained if they operate to 'freeze' the status quo of prior discriminatory employment practices." The long and the short of the matter under Title VII is that "if an employment practice which operates to exclude Negroes cannot be shown to be related to job performance, the practice is prohibited." Thus, any non-validated test or employment practice having a disproportionate or differential impact on a specific racial, sexual or religious group violates Title VII, and is prohibited by federal statute.

But, Title VII does not control constitutional interpretation. Baker was decided under the constitution's equal-protection clause which requires that more than differential impact be shown before there is a constitutional violation; i. e., while "disproportionate impact is not irrelevant, [it] is not the sole touchstone of an invidious racial discrimination forbidden by the Constitution" because "the basic equal protection principle [is] that the invidious quality of a law claimed to be racially discriminatory must ultimately be traced to a racially discriminatory purpose," or intent. Washington v. Davis, supra. The Baker court concluded that defendants "purposely discriminated against black teachers and black applicants on account of their race," and found a constitutional violation. What were the facts the Baker court relied on other than the facts showing a differential racial impact of the NTE scores?

4.    Baker was decided under the Constitution, but federal statutes can also apply to teacher employment. Title VII of the Civil Rights Act of 1964 (42 U.S.C.A. § 2000e et seq.) creates the right to be free from racial, sexual and religious discrimination by employers, employment agencies and labor organizations. As indicated in the preceding note, this law is violated when an employer's unvalidated test or employment practice has a disproportionate differential impact on a racial group. Under the Constitution's Supremacy Clause, state laws and regulations must give way to this federal law. It also provides that the U. S. Attorney General can sue on behalf of persons if they have been injured by a "pattern or practice" of employment discrimination in violation of Title VII.

Hazelwood School Dist. v. United States, 433 U.S. 299, 97 S.Ct. 2736, 53 L.Ed.2d 768 (1977) was such a case. It shows that the hiring practices of a school can be a significant factor in determining whether a school is segregated. The United States brought an action against the Hazelwood School District, located in St. Louis County, Mo., and various officials, alleging that they were engaged in a "pattern or practice" of teacher employment discrimination in violation of Title VII of the Civil Rights Act of 1964, as amended, which became applicable to petitioners as public employers on March 24, 1972. The District Court ruled that the Government had failed to establish a pattern or practice of discrimination. The Court of Appeals reversed, in part on the ground that the trial court's analysis of statistical data rested on an irrelevant comparison of Negro teachers to Negro pupils in Hazelwood, instead of on a comparison of Negro teachers in Hazelwood to Negro teachers in the relevant labor market area, which it found to consist of St. Louis County and the city of St. Louis, where 15.4% of the teachers are Negro. In the 1972–1973 and 1973–1974 school years only 1.4% and 1.8%, respectively, of Hazelwood's teachers were Negroes, and this statistical disparity, particularly when viewed against the background of Hazelwood's teacher hiring procedures, was held to constitute a prima facie case of a pattern or practice of racial discrimination. The school district contended that the statistical data on which the Court of Appeals relied cannot sustain a finding of a violation of Title VII. But, the U. S. Supreme Court held that the Court of Appeals erred in disregarding the statistical data in the record dealing with Hazelwood's hiring after it became subject to Title VII, and the court should have remanded the case to the District Court for further findings as to the relevant labor market area and for an ultimate determination whether Hazelwood has engaged in a pattern or practice of employment discrimination since March 24, 1972. Though the Court of Appeals was correct in the view that a proper comparison was between the racial composition of Hazelwood's teaching staff and the racial composition of the qualified public school teacher population in the relevant labor market, it erred in disregarding the possibility that the prima facie statistical proof in the record might at the trial court level be rebutted by statistics dealing with Hazelwood's post-Act hiring practices such as the number of Negroes hired compared to the total number of Negro applicants. For, once a prima facie case has been established by statistical work-force disparities, the employer must be given an opportunity to show that "the claimed discriminatory pattern is a product of pre-Act hiring rather than unlawful post-Act discrimination," International Bhd. of Teamsters v. United States, 431 U.S. 324, 360, 97 S.Ct. 1843, 52 L.Ed.2d 396 (1977). The record showed, but the Court of Appeals in its conclusions ignored, that for the two-year period, 1972–1974, 3.7% of the new teachers hired in Hazelwood were Negroes. The court accepted the Government's argument that the relevant labor market was St. Louis County and the city of St. Louis without considering the school district's contention that St. Louis County alone (where the figure was 5.7%) was the proper area because the city of St. Louis attempts to maintain a 50% Negro teaching staff. The difference between the figures may well be significant since the disparity between 3.7% and 5.7% may be sufficiently small to weaken the Government's other proof, while the disparity between 3.7% and 15.4% may be sufficiently large to reinforce it. In determining what figures provide the most accurate basis for comparison to the hiring figures at Hazelwood, numerous other factors, moreover, must also be evaluated by the trial court.

---

## AFFIRMATIVE ACTION PROGRAMS

---

### PORCELLI v. TITUS

United States Court of Appeals, 3rd Cir., 1970.
431 F.2d 1254, cert. den. 402 U.S. 944, 91 S.Ct. 1612, 29 L.Ed.2d 112.

PER CURIAM.

The plaintiffs herein, Victor Porcelli et al., ten white teachers employed by the Newark Board of Education, brought suit under the Civil Rights Act alleging that as of May 28, 1968, the defendant, Superintendent of Schools in the City of Newark, Franklyn Titus, acting under color of law for the Newark School System, subjected the plaintiffs to deprivation of their rights, privileges or immunities secured to them by the Constitution of the United States of America. This allegedly was accomplished by the abolition of a promotional list which had been in existence since 1953, which provided for oral and written examinations for anyone wishing to aspire to be principals or vice-principals in the System and which, it was contended by so doing, racially discriminated against whites whose names appeared on the promotional list for appointment.  At the time of the abolition or suspension of the said promotional list, the first fifteen thereon had been appointed, but Porcelli, Bigley and Shapiro, plaintiffs herein, though eligible, had not yet been appointed.

The school population in the City of Newark in October, 1961, was 67,134, of which the Negro population was 55.1%.  In September, 1968, the total school population was 75,876, with a Negro student population of 72.5% reflecting an increase in seven years of 8,742 students and a percentage increase of Negro students of 17.4%.  During the school year 1967–1968, there were 249 administrative and supervisory positions (superintendents, principals and vice-principals, senior and junior high school principals, etc.), of which 27, or 10%, were held by Negroes.  On August 22, 1968, only one Negro each for principal and vice-principal was eligible on the promotional list and of the 72 principals in the system none were Negro and of 67 vice-principals, 64 were white and 3 Negro.  .   .   .

Under date of May 28, 1968, defendant Board of Education passed a resolution suspending and abolishing the making of appointments from this list and instead the defendant, Franklyn Titus, Superintendent of the School System in Newark, presented certain recommendations for the appointments of principals, vice-principals, senior and junior high school principals, which the Board adopted, representing a total of 35 white appointments and 20 Negro appointments.  The appointments were designated as temporary appointments and the Board was to later review the appointments recommended, the criteria to be used by the Board having not as yet been finalized.  In his recommendation to the Board the Superintendent candidly admitted that color was one of the criteria which he utilized, contending that the pattern by which principals, vice-principals and others were appointed reflected an era in 1953, when the promotional list was adopted, and as of 1968, conditions had so changed in the Newark School System that the promotional list had become outmoded by virtue of the changing population, community-wise and in the school system, which had occurred since its adoption.

This action was begun by a motion for summary judgment on the pleading, but the lower court denied it and ordered a full evidentiary hearing at which both sides were heard at great length.  Superintendent Titus, one of the defendants, stated as one of his reasons for the abolition of the promotional list the fact that the Newark Public School System, especially in reading, was well below the national norm which obtained throughout the country;  that there was such a great imbalance in the principal and vice-principal positions that, in his professional judgment, he felt that by adding a Negro who was qualified to these important positions, thus making the faculty more integrated, would the more readily lend itself to an upgrading of the Public School System in Newark. Although, as has been indicated, color was frankly admitted by all the witnesses for the appellees as being one of the factors in the selection of the principals and vice-principals, and one Simeon Moss, who was the assistant superintendent for elementary education who made the recommendations to the Superintendent for the appointments, stated that color was a prime factor, it was not the only factor, as the procuring of qualified individuals was the real objective. Plaintiffs' position was that this use of color in the selection of principals and vice-principals and the device used to achieve that selection by abolition or suspension of the promotional list was a violation of their Constitutional rights under the Fourteenth Amendment.

With this contention we do not agree. State action based partly on considerations of color, when color is not used per se, and in furtherance of a proper governmental objective, is not necessarily a violation of the Fourteenth Amendment. Proper integration of faculties is as important as proper integration of schools themselves. . . . In Kemp v. Beasley, 389 F.2d 178, at 189 (8 Cir. 1968), the court held, where race was a consideration in the selection of teachers and faculties, "We reaffirm the principle that faculty selection must remain for the board and sensitive expertise of the School Board and its officials." . . . "The question thus becomes, when is there such faculty distribution as to provide equal opportunities to all students and to all teachers—whether white or Negro? Students in each school should have the same quality of instruction as in any other school. Every predominantly Negro school should have, wherever possible, substantially as integrated a faculty as the predominantly white school."

. . .

It would therefore seem that the Boards of Education have a very definite affirmative duty to integrate school faculties and to permit a great imbalance in faculties—as obtained on August 22, 1968, when a new plan was proposed to the School Board in Newark for the increasing of qualified Negro administrators—would be in negation of the Fourteenth Amendment to the Constitution and the line of cases which have followed Brown v. Board of Education, supra.

. . .

The judgment of the lower court will be affirmed.

## NOTES AND QUESTIONS

1. Was this case one of de jure or de facto segregation? Did the board of education come within the affirmative duty imposed by Brown I and II and Green supra? Did Newark ever operate a dual school system?

2. Is the Porcelli case an example of an affirmative action program by a board of education; a program having been designed to relieve racial imbalances which the board did not create?

3. *Problem:* A school district's special operative budget levy fails, requiring a 25% reduction in teaching staff within the district. The school board's established policy for not renewing teaching contracts in such an eventuality has been to decline to renew all the contracts of that 25% of the teaching staff most recently hired. However, the board of education observes that if such a practice is adopted now virtually all the present minority teachers will not be renewed because they were the most recently hired in the school because of the district's recent affirmative action program and so, under the old scheme, they would be the first to go. In the past minorities had been under represented on the teaching faculty; there has been no past practice of racial discrimination in hiring. Now, wanting to maintain its newly increased minority representation on its staff, the school board has decided to divide the teaching staff into two classes, non-minority and minority, and not to renew 25% of those persons in each class who have the least seniority. Winefred White has four years seniority, and Betty Black has three years of seniority. But, because more than 25% of the minority staff has less than three years seniority, Betty Black's teaching contract is renewed. However, Winefred White's contract is not renewed because the 25% of non-minority staff most recently hired include all those with four years seniority or less. White brings an action against the school district in federal district court under the Civil Rights Act (42 U.S.C.A. §§ 1983 and 1985(3)), asking that her contract be renewed, claiming that she has been denied the due process and equal protection of the laws solely on the basis of her or another's race. You are the federal district court judge. What decision do you render and for what reasons?

This problem is not controlled by two much-popularized affirmative-action cases. It is not controlled by Regents of the University of California v. Bakke, 483 U.S. 265 (1978) which resulted in six opinions without any commanding a majority, and without the case having any precedential rationale. Nor is the problem controlled by United Steelworkers v. Weber, —— U.S. ——, 99 S.Ct. 2721, 61 L.Ed.2d 480 (1979) which involved a private, not a public, employer, for as the Court stated in Weber: "Since the Kaiser-USWA plan does not involve state action, this case does not present an alleged violation of the Equal Protection Clause of the Constitution."

# Chapter IX

## CONSTITUTIONAL FREEDOM AND GENDER DISCRIMINATION

### INTRODUCTION

This chapter continues the exploration of the equal-protection clause in an equal educational context that was begun in the last chapter. That chapter focussed on race, while this chapter focusses on sex-based discrimination. The prior chapter indicated that race-based classifications are "suspect" and will be upheld only if there is a close "fit" or congruence between the natural and legislative classes, and then only if the government's interest in using the race-based classification is "compelling;" i. e., no reasonable alternative is available. In short, courts subject racial classifications to the most rigid judicial scrutiny. Sex-based classifications are not "suspect" but they are subjected to "substantial" scrutiny. They must show a substantial congruence between the legislative and natural classes and rest on substantial government interest. The Supreme Court has adopted the rule that to "withstand constitutional challenge . . . classifications by gender must serve important governmental objectives and must be substantially related to achievement of those objectives." Craig v. Boren, 429 U.S. 190, 97 S.Ct. 451, 50 L. Ed.2d 397 (1976).

The Equal Rights Amendment would impose a stricter standard on sex-based classifications. It provides that "equality of rights under the law shall not be denied or abridged by the United States or by any State on account of sex." It carries a significant privacy exception to its general mandate; thus, concerns about such matters as unisex bathrooms and public sleeping rooms are unfounded. The ERA's basic principle would require that law classify on the basis of attributes or traits of an individual other than sex, and would virtually eliminate gender-based classifications.

### SEX DISCRIMINATION AND CURRICULAR ACTIVITIES

#### VORCHHEIMER v. SCHOOL DIST. OF PHILADELPHIA

United States Court of Appeals, 1976.
532 F.2d 880 (3d Cir.), affirmed by an equally divided U.S. Supreme Court,
430 U.S. 703, 97 S.Ct. 1671, 51 L.Ed.2d 750 (1977).

##### OPINION OF THE COURT

JOSEPH F. WEIS, JR., Circuit Judge. Do the Constitution and laws of the United States require that every public school, in every public school system in the Nation, be coeducational? Stated another way, do our Constitution and laws forbid the maintenance by a public school board, in a system otherwise coeducational, of a limited number of single-sex high schools in which enrollment is voluntary and the educational opportunities offered to girls and boys are essentially equal? This appeal presents those questions and, after careful consideration, we answer negatively. Accordingly, we vacate the district court's judgment which held that the school board policy was impermissible.

Plaintiff is a teen-age girl who graduated with honors from a junior high school in Philadelphia. She then applied to Central High School, a public school in the city, but was refused admission because that institution is restricted to male students. After that setback, she filed this class action in the United States District Court seeking relief under 42 U.S.C.A. § 1983 from alleged unconstitutional discrimination. After a trial, the district court granted an injunction, ordering that she and other qualified female students be admitted to Central.

The Philadelphia School District offers four types of senior high schools: academic, comprehensive, technical and magnet. Although this suit is aimed at only an academic school, it is necessary to review the roles of other schools as well.

Comprehensive schools provide a wide range of courses, including those required for college admission, and offer advanced placement classes for students who are intellectually able to progress at a faster than average rate. The criterion for enrollment in the comprehensive schools is residency within a designated area. Although most of these schools are co-ed, two admit only males and one is restricted to female students. At the time the injunction was granted, plaintiff was enrolled at George Washington High School, a coeducational comprehensive school.

Academic high schools have high admission standards and offer only college preparatory courses. There are but two such schools in Philadelphia, and they accept students from the entire city rather than operating on a neighborhood basis. Central is restricted to males, and Girls High School, as the name implies, admits only females.

Central High School was founded in 1836 and has maintained a reputation for academic excellence. For some years before 1939, it was designated a comprehensive rather than an academic high school as it is presently. Its graduates both before and after 1939 have made notable contributions to the professions, business, government and academe.

Girls High has also achieved high academic standing. It was founded in 1848 and became an academic school in 1893. Its alumnae have compiled enviable records and have distinguished themselves in their chosen diverse fields. It now has a faculty of more than 100 and a student body of approximately 2,000, about the same as those of Central.

Enrollment at either school is voluntary and not by assignment. Only 7% of students in the city qualify under the stringent standards at these two schools, and it is conceded that plaintiff met the scholastic requirements of both. The Philadelphia school system does not have a co-ed academic school with similar scholastic requirements for admission.

The courses offered by the two schools are similar and of equal quality. The academic facilities are comparable, with the exception of those in the scientific field where Central's are superior. The district court concluded "that [generally] the education available to the female students at Girls is comparable to that available to the male students at Central." Moreover, "[g]raduates of both Central and Girls High, as well as the other senior high schools of Philadelphia," have been and are accepted by the most prestigious universities.

The plaintiff has stipulated that "the practice of educating the sexes separately is a technique that has a long history and world-wide acceptance." Moreover, she agrees that "there are educators who regard education in a single-sex school as a natural and reasonable educational approach." In addition to this stipulation, the defendants presented the testimony of Dr. J. Charles Jones, an expert in the field of education. Dr. Jones expressed a belief, based on his study of New Zealand's sex-segregated schools, that students in that educational environment had a higher regard for scholastic achievement and devoted more time to homework than those in co-ed institutions. The district judge commented that even had the parties not stipulated to the educational value of the practice, "this Court would probably have felt compelled to validate the sex-segregated school on the basis of Dr. Jones' hypotheses concerning the competition for adolescent energies in a coed school and its detrimental effect on student learning and academic achievement."

. . .

The trial judge found the gender based classification of students at the two schools to lack a "fair and substantial relationship to the School Board's legitimate interest" and enjoined the practice. The court [found] that Girls and Central are academically and functionally equivalent . . ..

A fair summary of the parties' positions, therefore, is that:

    1. the local school district has chosen to make available on a voluntary basis the time honored educational alternative of sexually-segregated high schools;

    2. the schools for boys and girls are comparable in quality, academic standing, and prestige;

     3.  the plaintiff prefers to go to the boys' school because of its academic reputation and her personal reaction to Central.  She submitted no factual evidence that attendance at Girl's High would constitute psychological or other injury;

     4.  the deprivation asserted is that of the opportunity to attend a specific school, not that of an opportunity to obtain an education at a school with comparable academic facilities, faculty and prestige.

With this factual background, we now turn to a review of the legal issues.  We look first to federal statutory law to determine if it resolves the question raised here.

.   .   .

In 1972 Congress provided that the benefits of educational programs funded through federal monies should be available to all persons without discrimination based on sex.  20 U.S.C.A. §§ 1681 et sec.  The statute applies, however, to only specified types of educational institutions and excludes from its coverage the admission policies of secondary schools.  .  .  .

.   .   .  [Congress] passed  .   .   .  "The Equal Educational Opportunities Act," legislation aimed against busing as a means of securing racial balance in schools.  .  .  .

The Act's policy declaration is that children are entitled to "equal educational opportunity" without regard to race, color, or sex.  The finding of the district court discloses no inequality in opportunity for education between Central and Girls High Schools.  We cannot, therefore, find that language applicable here.

Section 204(c), 20 U.S.C.A. § 1703(c), is intelligible if read against the background of the busing controversy which spawned it.  That subsection prohibits the assignment of a student to a school other than the one closest to his residence if the assignment results in a greater degree of segregation in the schools based on race, color, sex or national origin.  The thrust is directed toward the "neighborhood school" concept, which was so much a part of the busing dispute, and against assignment of students to non-neighborhood schools to achieve segregation on any of the forbidden bases.  We do not here face an attempt by a school board to assign "a student to a school, other than the one closest to his or her place of residence within the district in which he or she resides  .   .," 20 U.S.C.A. § 1703(c).

We conclude the legislation is so equivocal that it cannot, control the issue in this case.  .   .   .

Finding no Congressional enactments which authoritatively address the problem, we must consider the constitutional issues which provided the impetus for issuance of the injunction.

The district court reviewed the line of recent cases dealing with sex discrimination . . .. As a result of that analysis, the district judge reasoned that, while the Supreme Court has not held sex to be a suspect classification, a stricter standard than the rational relationship test applies and is denominated "fair and substantial relationship."

.  .  .

.  .  .

In each instance where a statute was struck down, the rights of the respective sexes conflicted, and those of the female were found to be inadequate. None of the cases was concerned with a situation in which equal opportunity was extended to each sex or in which the restriction applied to both. And, significantly, none occurred in an educational setting.

The nature of the discrimination which the plaintiff alleges must be examined with care. She does not allege a deprivation of an education equal to that which the school board makes available to boys. Nor does she claim an exclusion from an academic school because of a quota system, or more stringent scholastic admission standards. Moreover, enrollment at the single-sex schools is applicable only to high schools and is voluntary, not mandatory. The plaintiff has difficulty in establishing discrimination in the school board's policy. If there are benefits or detriments inherent in the system, they fall on both sexes in equal measure.

Plaintiff cites Sweatt v. Painter, and Brown v. Board of Education, which prohibit racial segregation in the educational process. Those cases are inapplicable here. Race is a suspect classification under the Constitution, but the Supreme Court has declined to so characterize gender. We are committed to the concept that there is no fundamental difference between races and therefore, in justice, there can be no dissimilar treatment. But there are differences between the sexes which may, in limited circumstances, justify disparity in law. As the Supreme Court has said: "[g]ender has never been rejected as an impermissible classification in all instances."

Equal educational opportunities should be available to both sexes in any intellectual field. However, the special emotional problems of the adolescent years are matters of human experience and have led some educational experts to opt for one-sex high schools. While this policy has limited acceptance on its merits, it does have its basis in a theory of equal benefit and not discriminatory denial.

.  .  .

The record does contain sufficient evidence to establish that a legitimate educational policy may be served by utilizing single-sex high schools. The primary aim of any school system must be to furnish an education of as high a quality as is feasible. Measures which would allow innovation in methods and techniques to achieve that goal have a high degree of relevance. Thus, given the objective of a quality education and a controverted, but respected theory that adolescents may study more effectively in single-sex schools, the policy of the school board here does bear a substantial relationship.

We need not decide whether this case requires application of the rational or substantial relationship tests because, using either, the result is the same. We conclude that the regulations establishing admission requirements to Central and Girls High School based on gender classification do not offend the Equal Protection Clause of the United States Constitution.

The gravamen of plaintiff's case is her desire to attend a specific school based on its particular appeal to her. She believes that the choice should not be denied her because of an educational policy with which she does not agree.

We are not unsympathetic with her desire to have an expanded freedom of choice, but its cost should not be overlooked. If she were to prevail, then all public single-sex schools would have to be abolished. The absence of these schools would stifle the ability of the local school board to continue with a respected educational methodology. It follows too that those students and parents who prefer an education in a public, single-sex school would be denied their freedom of choice. The existence of private schools is no more an answer to those people than it is to the plaintiff.

It is not for us to pass upon the wisdom of segregating boys and girls in high school. We are concerned not with the desirability of the practice but only its constitutionality. Once that threshold has been passed, it is the school board's responsibility to determine the best methods of accomplishing its mission.

The judgment of the district court will be reversed.

GIBBONS, Circuit Judge (dissenting).

.   .   .   No doubt had the issue in this case been presented to the Court at any time from 1896 to 1954, a "separate but equal" analysis would have carried the day. I was under the distinct impression, however, that "separate but equal" analysis, especially in the field of public education, passed from the fourteenth amendment jurisprudential scene over twenty years ago. See, e. g., Brown v. Board of Education. The majority opinion, in establishing a twentieth-century sexual equivalent to the *Plessy* decision, reminds us that the doctrine can and will be invoked to support sexual discrimination in the same manner that it supported racial discrimination prior to *Brown*.

But the resurrection of the "separate but equal" analysis is not my most serious quarrel with the majority opinion. What I find most disturbing is the majority's deliberate disregard of an express Congressional finding that the maintenance of dual school systems in which students are assigned to schools solely on the basis of sex violates the equal protection clause of the fourteenth amendment. § 203 (a)(1), Equal Educational Opportunities Act of 1974, 20 U.S.C.A. § 1702(a)(1). So long as Congress has acted within the sphere of its legislative competence in making such a finding, I submit, we are not free to substitute a "separate but equal" legislative judgment of our own. Because I conclude that Congress has acted to prohibit the maintenance of single-sex public schools pursuant to its powers under § 5 of the fourteenth amendment, I dissent from the majority's substitution of a "separate but equal" legislative judgment. I would affirm the decision below.

.   .   .

## II

On August 21, 1974, Congress passed a series of amendments to the Elementary and Secondary Education Act of 1965, 20 U.S.C.A. §§ 241a et seq. One of these amendments was the Equal Educational Opportunities Act of 1974 (hereinafter E.E.O.A.), 20 U.S.C.A. §§ 1701–1758. Section 202(a)(1) of this Act declared it to be the public policy of the United States that "all children enrolled in public schools are entitled to equal educational opportunity without regard to race, color, sex, or national origin." 20 U.S.C.A. § 1701(a)(1). Had Congress stopped there one could argue, as the majority does, that a policy of "equal educational opportunity" does not preclude a "separate but equal" analysis, at least outside the racial context. But Congress went further. Relying specifically on the legislative authority conferred by § 5 of the fourteenth amendment, it made a series of legislative findings in § 203, the most important of which for the purpose of this appeal was that:

> (1) the maintenance of dual school systems in which students are assigned to schools solely on the basis of .   .   . sex   .   .   . denies those students the equal protection of the laws guaranteed by the fourteenth amendment. 20 U.S.C.A. § 1702(a)(1).

We are thus confronted with an explicit legislative finding that the maintenance of a dual school system on the basis of sex violates the equal protection clause. Philadelphia operates such a system in its senior academic high schools. We need look no further than this legislative finding in order to find a violation for which 42 U.S.C.A. § 1983 provides a remedy. But Congress was not content, as the majority suggests, merely to assert broad legislative findings that might later prove to be inconsistent with or unrelated to its specific statutory scheme, for it defined in § 204 of the amendment a number of unlawful practices based on its findings. 20 U.S.C.A. § 1703.

Section 204 states in pertinent part that:

> No State shall deny equal educational opportunity to an individual on account of his or her . . . sex . . . by—

> (c) the assignment by an educational agency of a student to a school, other than the one closest to his or her place of residence within the district in which he or she resides, if the assignment results in a greater degree of segregation of students on the basis of . . . sex . . . among the schools of such agency than would result if such student were assigned to the school closest to his or her place of residence within the school district of such agency providing the appropriate grade level and type of education for such student. 20 U.S.C.A. § 1703(c).

This subsection says that a pupil assignment system which results in increased segregation by sex, as well as race, color or national origin, over what would result in a neighborhood assignment system, is unlawful. At first blush Philadelphia may not appear to operate a neighborhood school assignment system, as that term is used in § 204(c), for its academic high schools since eligibility for enrollment at those schools is determined by scholastic excellence rather than residence within a designated area. The majority opinion contends that § 204(c) is inapplicable to the factual setting of this case because the " 'neighborhood school' concept which was so much a part of the busing dispute" was not "an attempt to abolish single-sex schools." But this view fails to consider Congress' understanding of the meaning of neighborhood school assignment which is disclosed in another subsection of the E.E.O.A. Section 206, 20 U.S.C.A. § 1705, provides in pertinent part that:

> [T]he assignment by an educational agency of a student to the school nearest his place of residence *which provides the appropriate grade level and type of education* for such student is not a denial of equal educational opportunity or of equal protection of the laws *unless such assignment is for the purpose of segregating students* on the basis of . . . sex . . . .. (emphasis added).

It is clear that this subsection must be read in conjunction with § 204(c), for it further clarifies and reenforces the meaning of that provision. Section 206 states that the lawful neighborhood assignment system outlined in § 204(c) also includes the school nearest the student which provides the "appropriate grade level and type of education" unless assignment to that school is for the purpose of segregation on the basis of race, color, sex or national origin. Thus, by assigning academically gifted students to Central or Girls on the basis of sex, the Philadelphia School Board assigns students in a manner which results in greater segregation of students by sex than if it assigned students solely on the basis of the nearest senior academic high school. The Philadelphia dual system for scholastically superior students not only falls within the legislative finding of the denial of equal protection of the laws, but is also a specified unlawful practice under § 204(c).

While I agree with the majority that the language of § 204(c) must be read with an appreciation of the heated debate over the school busing issue, I cannot agree that this contextual background justifies ignoring the plain language of both the legislative finding in § 203(a)(1) and the specified unlawful practice in § 204(c). . . .

### III

Unlike the majority, I find it particularly difficult to say on the basis of the record in this case that the exclusion of females from Central bears a fair and substantial relationship to any of the Philadelphia School Board's legitimate objectives. Admittedly coeducation at the senior high school level has its supporters and its critics. The majority is also undoubtedly correct in suggesting that a legitimate educational policy may be served by utilizing single-sex high schools. But certainly that observation does not satisfy the substantial relationship test. Some showing must be made that a single-sex academic high school policy advances the Board's objectives in a manner consistent with the requirements of the Equal Protection Clause.

The Board, as the district court, emphasized, did not present sufficient evidence that coeducation has an adverse effect upon a student's academic achievement. Indeed, the Board could not seriously assert that argument in view of its policy of assigning the vast majority of its students to coeducational schools. Presumably any detrimental impact on a student's scholastic achievement attributable to coeducation would be as evident in Philadelphia's coeducational comprehensive schools which offer college preparatory courses as the Board suggests it would be in its exclusively academic high schools. Thus, the Board's single-sex policy reflects a choice among educational techniques but not necessarily one substantially related to its stated educational objectives. One of those objectives, in fact, is to provide "educational options to students and their parents." The implementation of the Board's policy excluding females from Central actually precludes achievement of this objective because there is no option of a coeducational academic senior high school.

Because I agree with the district court that the Board has not made the required showing of a substantial relationship between its single-sex academic high school policy and its stated educational objectives, I would affirm the decision below even if I were willing to ignore the pertinent provisions of the E.E.O.A.

### NOTES AND QUESTIONS

1. This case was affirmed on appeal by an equally-divided court. Because judgments of the U. S. Supreme Court by an equally-divided vote are

not entitled to precedential weight, Vorcheimer, technically, does not resolve the question, and technically it is still open. However, many analysts believe that since Mr. Justice Rehnquist was the non-participating Justice (making an eight-Justice court in Vorcheimer) that the Supreme Court's position is not unclear. Nevertheless, other federal courts have resolved the issue differently, see, e. g., United States v. Hinds County School Bd., 560 F.2d 619 (5th Cir. 1977).

2. Would it be constitutional for school authorities to permit a larger student enrollment (with its greater commitment of resources) at Girls High than at Central High? Suppose by using identical academic selection criteria, it turned out that twice as many girls as boys were qualified for superior academic work and wanted to go to Girls High, are school officials constitutionally required, under the Equal-Protection Clause, to have equal student populations at the two schools? If not, could school authorities constitutionally follow a policy of equal-sized high schools, even if it meant that the academic cut-off point would be much higher for girls than for boys, and with the result that some boys would get into Central High with lower qualifications than some girls excluded from Girls High? See, Bray v. Lee, 337 F.Supp. 934 (D.Mass. 1972). Are sex-segregated schools as "inherently unequal" as the race-segregated schools of Brown? If so, do they create inferiority feelings? If not, what makes them "inherently unequal"? See, Comment, Single-Sex Public Schools: The Last Bastion of "Separate But Equal"? 77 Duke L.J. 259 (1977).

3. Would the decision in Vorcheimer have been different if the student initially had been assigned by state officials to a non-coeducational school? If the program had not been voluntary? Could a school district constitutionally segregate *all* of its K–12 schools on the basis of sex? Would it be sound educational policy to do so? Do sound educational grounds exist for maintaining some, but not all, public schools on a sex-segregated basis? At the middle or high school level? At the elementary level? For all students or only for some students?

Should all classification of students by sex be declared unconstitutional?

---

## IT IS THE MALE WHO SUFFERS MOST

Robert Groeschell
Director of Program Development
Office of Superintendent of Public Instruction
Olympia, Washington
Reprinted with permission from Mr. Groeschell

Not too long ago I was a visitor in a new open design elementary school. As the enthusiastic principal showed us the building and its program, we entered the area designated for helping the hard to teach and hard to handle students. His expression changed. "I wish I understood this phenomenon," he said. We looked at the group of students.

Of the 32 in the area, 31 were boys. Unusual? Not too much. Estimates are that the ratio (across the state) in special education classes averages four boys to each girl. But that is just the beginning. Facts show that in school you are lucky to be a girl.

Recent news indicates that sex bias in schools is toward girls. Girls suffer from inequalities in such programs as sports and career stereotyping. What about other important manifestations of schooling?

For example: Since we don't hear about failure differences, is the rate of failure in school equal between the sexes? Do just as many boys drop out of school as girls? Are both sexes graded equally when achievement is equal? Are remedial reading, remedial speech and remedial hearing classes balanced in their enrollment of boys and girls? Do both sexes share equally in teacher rewards and punishments? Is achievement in learning to read equal? If disparities do exist in all of these areas, shouldn't drastic action be taken to remedy the situation?

Yes, gross disparities do exist in all these areas. In every case it is the male who suffers the most! In some cases the rates of incidence are as much as four to one. Perhaps the greatest injustice in the school setting is that dispite physical, behavioral and emotional differences of the sexes, we develop policies and practices which treat all children alike.

Walter Waetjen, University of Maryland, says, "The most unequal thing that happens in our schools is that unequals are treated as equals. We know that learning proceeds according to individual differences, and it follows logically teaching must take these differences into account. In short, our schools are sex neutral institutions operating on the assumption that all persons are alike with respect to the ways in which we learn and achieve. We wish to make crystal clear our position that it makes a significant difference whether the person we are teaching is a boy pupil or a girl and that instructional provisions should be made accordingly."

Why does this researcher in sex differences take such a position? Partially because of the amount of data that is available which indicates serious differences in results of schooling. For instance, many people are concerned about the 20 to 25 percent dropout rate in Washington schools. Last year for each 5.6 girls who left school, there were 8 boys. It is estimated that the national average is 2 to 1. While no figures are available for failure rates in Washington, a study in California reports a failure rate of 2.6 boys to 1 girl.

Walter Waetjen reports that in the school district in which he once worked a study of retention showed that of 110,000 pupils, there were 1,909 cases of retention in all grades. Of these, 1,431 or 75 percent, were boys. Obviously there is a close relationship of school failure; that is, having to repeat a grade or subject, with the drastic dropping of school completely before graduation.

Many of these success-failure elements are so closely interrelated that it is impossible to locate beginnings and endings. Grading, for example. Here the sex differences and how we treat them in the school are very marked and have been accurately measured. Where examinations of grading by sexes have taken place, the results are always the same; girls get the best grades.

Waetjen says, "Why is it that boys receive a higher proportion of low grades in every level of education whether it's elementary school, junior high school, high school, or indeed in colleges and universities? In every comparison you can make, girls as a group have a higher scholastic average than boys as a group."

Earl Hanson studied the grades of 3,000 students, elementary and secondary, comparing grades given in relationship to achievement. He found that of all students who received A and B in achievement, 48 percent of the girls were given A and B grades. Among the A and B boys, however, only 29 percent were given A and B grades.

There is an interesting study in grading junior high math that relates to the sex of the teachers. Both men and women teachers graded the girls higher than boys, but the men teachers graded the girls even higher than the women teachers. This investigation casts doubt on the idea that men are more understanding of boys, their interests, learning styles and classroom behavior characteristics.

One question that must be raised in this regard is, "why?" Why should boys receive lower grades and lesser rewards when achievement is equal? This investigator has found little direct research material but is led to speculative conclusions based on some closely related data.

There is evidence that teachers prefer to teach girls. In one study, Jo Stanchfield, Occidental College, Calif., reports that 70 percent of the primary teachers preferred girls. One reason seems to be that the most popular methods that schools use to teach beginning reading are more successful with girls. In addition, girls aren't likely to be aggressive and nonconforming, traits that are not assets when the environment is crowded. This position is further supported by the studies that have been conducted on pupil-teacher interaction.

In examining classroom behavior of teachers, it has been discovered that boys interact more frequently with teachers, but much of the interaction is negative. In one study by Jackson, for example, on personal communication, he discovered that in the area of classroom management and control, sixth-grade boys got into at least eight times more trouble with the teachers than girls.

There is also the variable of dependency versus independency of behavior. Investigations in this area tend to support the concept that boys and girls have different styles of presenting themselves as well as different sources of awareness. Boys, it is found, are more likely to look inwardly, thus deriving a more personal and independent orientation. They are more self-confident, assertive and aggressive. The female's orientation tends to be more external, more people oriented. They are not so certain about their accomplishments and their popularity means much. Popularity and conformity in school tend to be like kissing cousins.

Patricia Minuchin, researcher at Banks Street College, investigated the physchological development of children and writes, "We might note also that boys and girls generally had quite different attitudes toward school. Boys were more resistant and negative about school and education, less concerned about achievement. Girls were concerned about achievement and recognition, more positively identified with school, more apt to find the entire experience of school life more comfortable, pleasant and meaningful."

Upon examination of the behavior characteristics of the sexes, the learning styles and attitudes of students toward self and school, one is forced to this conclusion: Grades are determined by more than achievement and female behavior characteristics bring higher rewards than those practiced by the males.

Teachers are generally hesitant about stating their reactions to boys. Most believe that they are neutral, do not have a preference, that they enjoy and appreciate independence and deviant thinking. The evidence suggests, however, that schools are operated by standards reflecting a female culture and value system. Behavior standards and not learning accomplishment alone are reflected in the reward system. Girls get the best grades, are failed less often and stay in school longer.

Success in school is closely related to the child's reading ability. With a preponderance of reading as a learning activity, a child's ability to handle books becomes essential. In no area of instruction in the school is the difference of achievement more marked than in the first R. While boys score only slightly lower than girls in reading readiness tests in September, by June a noticeable gap in achievement has emerged. This gap is consistent throughout the grades. As early as the '30s, a research project conducted by St. John of 1,000 first to fourth graders showed that girls markedly excelled in reading, and that boys showed 75 percent more nonpromotions than girls.

What really caused concern of educational researchers was a project conducted with 50,000 students in 300 schools in Iowa in the '40s. Students in grades three through eight were tested by Stroud and Lindquist in reading comprehension, vocabulary, work study skill, basic language skills and arithmetic skills. They found that girls were significantly superior over boys in every category except arithmetic.

For years, the achievement disparity has been known by educators. Most frequently it was explained as a difference in maturity
rates. This explanation lacks credence, however, for it ignores the
fact that boys scored equally with the girls on readiness tests, that
mental ages are equal, or that boys are superior in math. Upon
analysis we must realize that the immaturity concept places all the
blame on the child.

In 1961, Gates began to raise questions regarding the school environment and the social setting rather than maturity alone as the
cause. He analyzed the reading test scores of 6,676 boys and 6,468
girls, grades two to eight. The girls' scores were significantly higher.
His feelings were, however, that the poorer scores of the boys indicated
an environmental rather than hereditary explanation. Research by
Towell and Robinson further supports Gates' conclusion. The school
setting is more conducive to helping girls achieve. For example, the
teaching methods usually call for long periods of quiet, sitting behavior, a condition for which boys have a low aptitude.

The seriousness of the disparity of reading achievement cannot
be underestimated. When we investigate the students who are assigned to remedial reading instruction, we find once again the 4 boys
to 1 girl ratio.

So far it has been established that boys are not as successful in
school in terms of grades, promotions and graduation. Further, boys
are not taught to read as well as the girls, affecting their success in
school in all areas where reading is necessary to the learning process.
About this time we can imagine what is happening to the male's self-
concepts, feelings of worth, and attitudes toward school. A loser is
in the making. As a boy develops feelings or views of his world that
are negative, disruptive behavior is certain to emerge.

As if these were not enough, the male has to recognize that he is
also on the short end of the stick in matters of health. Frances Bent-
zen, writing from the Journal of Orthopsychiatry, says "I shall establish as fact that pathological conditions, including learning and behavior disorders, are three to ten times more frequent among males
than females of the same chronological age." The health factors
which led to this opinion are staggering.

First of all is the realization that the school girl of today will live
a ten percent longer life than her male classmate (7.5 years). That
is, those that have survived the prenatal period. Fetal death rates
show that 78 percent of the stillborn fetuses delivered before the
fourth month are male. Death rates during the first year are 56.5
percent male and 43.5 percent female. The higher mortality rate for
males begins at conception and continues throughout life.

Studies by Pasamanick and his colleagues indicate that not only
are there higher fetal and neonatal death rates as well as still-birth
rates for males, but that throughout life males also show higher

illness rates due to brain injury. Strauss and Lehtinen, as well as a number of others, have pointed out that there is a probable relationship between the fact that many more boys than girls suffer brain injury because of the greater birth weight of males, and the fact that more boys than girls are among the first born.

What does this mean in terms of human functioning? Of school success? It means that the chances are boys will have more emotional and behavior problems, that problems of learning to talk will be greater, that speech malfunctions, such as stuttering will be four times greater, that vision and hearing problems will be greater. All these play a part in the boy's learning and success in school.

This single report on sex differences can hardly begin to cover the amount of material that is available providing documentation that the sexes are different in many ways. It should be apparent by this time that the schools cannot be sexually neutral any more than they can be racially neutral. If boys are to enjoy equal success in school, drastic changes have to be made.

Schools need to adopt instructional practices that are more realistic with boys' learning aptitudes and behavior patterns. A few have made notable instructional adjustments, beginning with the adoption of specially prepared reading programs that follow instructional methods which counter the traditional stereotyping of rate of maturity. They are grouping students by sex as an additional process. Whittier School of Tacoma uses special materials in its primary grades, a variety of instructional methods which include physical involvement of the child and grouping by sex. Boys come to school an hour earlier than the girls and leave an hour sooner. Reading instruction takes place when the individual groups are present.

The results are similar to other places where the innovation has been tried. The Whittier teaching staff reports that boys work harder and feel less competitive pressure. The all-boy classes are not more difficult to manage under this arrangement. Both boys and girls have special feelings of comradeship in their groups. But most important of all, according to the test results at the end of the first grade, boys are achieving equal to the girls.

But a great deal still needs to be done, and at all levels. As it is now, the statistics are telling us a powerful message: that boys do have a tougher time.

### NOTES AND QUESTIONS

1. The unpopular view that schools tend to be girl-oriented institutions penalizing the natural inclination of boys was set forth again by Dianne McGuiness, a researcher in neuropsychology at Stanford University, in How Schools Discriminate Against Boys, 2 Human Nature 82 (1979). She bluntly states that "by the time they are 5 or 6, children in Western

classrooms are expected to behave like girls  .  .  .  In the early school years, children concentrate on reading and writing, skills that largely favor girls." "As a result, boys fill remedial reading classes, don't learn to spell, and are classified as dyslexic or learning-disabled four times as often as girls." Moreover, they are far more likely to be labeled "hyper-active" and put on "Ritalin." Ms. McGuiness says that sensitive, experienced teachers know these facts, but no one wants to say anything about them or sex-based classifications. "The sexes are supposed to be equal in every way, so information about inequity is suppressed or ascribed to a social conspiracy," she explains. Curiously, however, no one counts it as a sexist conspiracy, when one observes that girls easily outstrip boys in language development, fine motor skills and art, or suffer from "math anxieties."

The differences between the sexes, writes Ms. McGuiness, are significantly innate, with many of them easily observed in new-born infants: "Boys are awake more, show more low-intensity motor activity (head-turning, hand-waving, twitching and jerking) and more facial grimacing than girls." Girls, on the other hand, "speak sooner, with greater fluency and grammatical accuracy, and use more words per utterance than boys." She continues noting an astonishing range of sex differences, from color discernment and noise toleration to visual tracking and modes of play—all of which, she writes, "have profound implications for the development of intellectual abilities." Basically, girls tend to learn most easily through communication, while boys tend to learn through watching, manipulating and doing.

'A verbal command fades rapidly from (a boy's) attention, especially if new and exciting visual information comes along to erase it. Boys can not sit still; they are distractible; they test the properties of objects. Such behavior interferes with the concentration they need to learn to read and write, as well as their classmates' attempts to read and write.  .  .  .  Yet much of this behavior is precisely that which leads to excellence in mechanics, mathematics and the physical sciences."

Granting the validity of Ms. McGuiness' observations, what should schools realistically do? Should there be separate classes or schools for all or some girls and boys? Establish remedial classes in languages, reading and allied subjects primarily for boys? Quit forcing elementary level boys to sit still, remain quiet, and learn to manipulate only verbal symbols? Establish remedial classes in subjects like math and physics primarily for girls, or maybe in machine repair, for why should a woman be a dunce when confronted with a recalcitrant washing machine or a car that won't start? Do these suggestions raise any legal problems? If so, what are they?

If a school district recognized the views of Ms. McGuiness, could it institute an affirmative action program and legally assign an equal number of boys and girls to its academically superior high schools even if that meant that some girls with higher academic records than some boys would not be admitted?

## BERKELMAN v. SAN FRANCISCO UNIFIED SCHOOL DIST.

United States Court of Appeals, 1974.
501 F.2d 1264 (9th Cir.).

ALFRED T. GOODWIN, Circuit Judge.  The district court denied injunctive and other relief in this civil rights action challenging the San Francisco Unified School District's standards for admitting students to Lowell High School.  Appellants, claiming to represent a class of students denied admission, have appealed.

Lowell High School is an academic, or college-preparatory, public high school which accepts each year those applicants for admission whose prior academic achievement places them within approximately the top 15 per cent of the junior-high-school graduates in the district.

The issues on appeal, phrased broadly, are:  (1) whether a school district may admit students to a preferred high school on the basis of past academic achievement if the percentage of black, Spanish-American, and low-income students who qualify for admission is substantially disproportionate to the percentage of black, Spanish-American, and low-income students in the school district at large; [1]  (2) whether a school district, in order to maintain equal numbers of boys and girls in the school, may apply higher admission requirements to girls than to boys. [2]

I

The district operates eleven high schools.  Seven are "comprehensive" high schools, to which students are assigned substantially on the basis of residence.  The other four high schools have special educational objectives and accept qualified students from anywhere in the district.  Lowell, one of these special schools, offers advanced, college-preparatory courses.  Others serve students who need special help because of language or other problems, who work part-time, or who desire vocational training.

Except for students admitted under a pilot minority-admissions program (see n. 1), or under the balancing-of-the-sexes policy at issue in this case, admission to Lowell is based solely upon a student's

---

[1] The district has a modified admissions program for black and Spanish-American students which admits members of these groups who would not qualify under the normal admission standards in addition to those black and Spanish-American students who do qualify under the grade-point standard.  It is unclear what criteria were used in 1970 and 1971 to select students under this program.  Since 1972 a cutoff point one-half point (on a 4-point scale) below regular admissions requirements was used for selection of students in the minority admissions program. Plaintiffs have not attacked this program except to assert that it does not go far enough to bring more minority students into Lowell.

[2] A third issue—the unconstitutionality of any academic high school—was abandoned by appellants at oral argument.

junior-high-school grade-point average in four college-preparatory subjects. All applicants in the district are ranked numerically by their junior-high-school grade-point averages, and students are admitted in their numerical order until their class is filled. Grade averages are not weighted according to schools in which they were earned. All junior-high grades are accepted at face value, regardless of neighborhood or demographic factors that might produce non-uniformity of grading among junior-high schools.

The statistical data stipulated into this record indicate a lower proportion of low-income students at Lowell than in the high school population city-wide. The data also show that 7.5% of Lowell's students are black, while 25.9% of the district's high school students are black; 5.2% of Lowell's students are Spanish-American, and 13% of the district's high-school students are Spanish-American. The minority percentages in Lowell's student body would be even lower than they are but for the minority-admissions program instituted in 1970.

However, the district-court record reveals that Lowell has not become an exclusive province of the affluent and white. Chinese students contribute 29.8% of Lowell's student body, while they make up only 17.9% of the district's high-school population. Further, 3.2% of Lowell's students are Japanese, and 3.8% are Filipino, while the respective city-wide percentages are 1.9% and 4.5%.

There was no evidence that the Board's actions in connection with its administration of Lowell were racially motivated. The admission standard is neither an intentionally discriminatory standard, nor a neutral standard applied in an intentionally discriminatory manner. Nor do the Board's actions in moving the school building to the far southwest corner (described as a predominantly white area) of the city and in modifying the admission policy indicate intent to insure and increase the underrepresentation of black and Spanish-American students at Lowell. These actions, of themselves, give no evidence of discrimination, and appellants have not offered any additional evidence of racially discriminatory motivation. We note that the admission-policy changes of which appellants complain (e. g., abandoning a form of neighborhood, admission quotas in favor of city-wide admission standards) were accompanied by the development of a pilot minority admissions program. In the absence of proof, appellants' conclusory allegations were insufficient to make the Board's intent a triable question that would frustrate an otherwise appropriate summary judgment.

However, if an admission standard operates in fact to exclude a disproportionate number of black and Spanish-American students from Lowell, the court has a duty to test the constitutionality of that standard. Where a nonsuspect classification (past academic achievement) is alleged to operate to the detriment of a disadvantaged class or classes (black and Spanish-American students), neither "strict" nor "minimal" scrutiny provides useful guidance as a standard of review. The task is to examine the school district's assertion that the standard of past academic achievement substantially furthers the purpose of providing the best education possible for the public-school students in the district. If the past-achievement standard does substantially further that purpose, then the district has not unconstitutionally discriminated in its Lowell admission policy.

The advantages of an "academic" high school offering advanced courses to students who have excelled in a traditional curriculum are obvious. Lowell provides in one school a program which cannot be duplicated in ten other schools any more than special courses for students with specific educational needs can be economically taken from the other special high schools in the city and spread among all eleven schools. The student whose past performance has demonstrated ability to move at an advanced rate in an advanced program will receive a "better" education than he or she would receive if required to work in subject matter and at a pace which does not provide as great an educational challenge. Likewise, a student with an interest in vocational training receives a "better" education if permitted to take vocational courses than if required to continue against his wishes with the "traditional" high-school program. The school district has determined that it is educationally "better" to consolidate special offerings for the benefit of those who can meet the performance standards than to dispense with the effort entirely because budget considerations make it impossible to offer every program at every school.

Conditioning admission to Lowell upon the level of past academic achievement substantially furthers the district's purpose of operating an academic high school. Those students who have best mastered their junior-high-school courses are well prepared for more advanced courses at the high-school level. Of course, it does not necessarily follow that all applicants who fall below the cutoff line are educationally disqualified for Lowell's program. The cutoff is the result of space and budget limitations, not the result of a perfect determination of who can and who cannot benefit from the program.

Those students not admitted to Lowell are neither denied a quality education nor relegated to an inadequate school. Rather, they attend one of San Francisco's seven "comprehensive" high schools. Unlike a "tracking" system in which the challenged classifications are "predictive" and isolate students of "less promising" ability, the classification here is based upon past achievement impartially measured. There is slight potential for psychic injury to a student from attending a comprehensive high school with the majority of the city's high-school students. We conclude that the district's legitimate interest in establishing an academic high school, admission to which is based upon past achievement, outweighs any harm imagined or suffered by students whose achievement had not qualified them for admission to that school.

Our decision does not mean that we are not troubled by the underrepresentation of some racial and ethnic groups at Lowell. Uncertainty on this score, however, does not mean that the maintenance of Lowel High is itself unconstitutional or that conditioning admission on the basis of past academic achievement is unconstitutional.

Nor does the alleged underrepresentation at Lowell of students of low-income families render the admission policy unconstitutional. Low-income persons have no greater status under the equal-protection clause of the Fourteenth Amendment than members of racial minorities. It follows that since the admission policy is not made unconstitutional by its impact upon black students, it is likewise not made unconstitutional by a similar impact upon low-income students.

## II

Appellants also attack as discrimination on the basis of sex the school district's policy of requiring higher admission standards for girls than for boys. The school district asserts that the standards were designed to produce an equal number of boys and girls at Lowell. This policy has been in effect since 1970. In 1970 and 1971, male applicants were required to have a 3.0 (on a 4-point scale) average, while female applicants were required to have a 3.25 average. In 1972, the requirement for male applicants for admission was raised to 3.25 and the requirement for female applicants was raised to 3.50. Although the school district contends that if qualified males were, in any year, to outnumber qualified females the admission standards would be reversed, the situation has not yet arisen and the district consequently has not yet been put to the test. If the district's argument about maturation and achievement rates is sound, the situation is not likely to arise.

Appellants urge us to apply a stringent standard of review, while appellees urge the traditional rational-basis standard of review, in considering discrimination between females and males. Although a majority of the Supreme Court has not yet added sex to its list of suspect classifications, it has suggested that a classification based upon sex will have to be justified by more than the traditional "rational" connection between the classification and some valid legislative purpose. Frontiero v. Richardson, 411 U.S. 677, 93 S.Ct. 1764, 36 L.Ed. 2d 583 (1973); Reed v. Reed, 404 U.S. 71, 92 S.Ct. 251, 30 L.Ed.2d 225 (1971). Reed established, and Frontiero reiterated, that governments may not legislate classifications on the basis of criteria not shown to be related to the objective of the statute.

. . .

In both Reed and Frontiero, stereotypes as to the social roles of males and females formed the bases of the classifications. An unsupported notion that an equal number of male and female students is an essential element in a good high-school education was apparently the justification for the school district's policy requiring higher grade-point averages for females than for males. While that policy is not based upon an individual stereotype such as was present in *Reed* and *Frontiero*, we do not read those cases so narrowly as to sanction all other sex discrimination. No actual proof that a balance of the sexes furthers the goal of better academic education was offered by the school district.[9]

We note that had the advanced courses been offered in each high school, rather than in a separate high school, and had the school authorities applied the same or similar admission standards to such courses, the admission standards would have been an illegal discrimination on the basis of sex under Title IX of the Education Amendments of 1972, 20 U.S.C.A. § 1681. Although Congress condemned discrimination on the basis of sex in any education program, the prohibition with regard to sex discrimination in admissions to educational institutions was not extended to public secondary schools. 20 U.S.C.A. § 1681(a)(1). This omission, however, indicates nothing more than that Congress did not know the manner, extent, or rationale of separate education below the college level, and could not anticipate the effect of a prohibition upon such single-sex schools. See 118 Cong.Rec. 5804 (1972). On the other hand, its reasons for prohibiting sex discrimination in educational programs in general bears directly upon this case. Congress recognized that, because education provides access to jobs, sex discrimination in education is potentially destructive to the disfavored sex. 118 Cong.Rec. 5804. Lowell High, as a conduit to better university education and hence to better jobs is exactly that type of educational program with regard to which Congress intended to eliminate sex discrimination when it passed Title IX.

On the basis of the foregoing, we hold that the use of higher admission standards for female than for male applicants to Lowell High School violates the Equal Protection Clause of the Fourteenth Amendment.

The judgment of the district court is affirmed in part and reversed in part, and this case is remanded for disposition consistent with this opinion.

## NOTES AND QUESTIONS

1. Lowell High is coeducational. Could San Francisco solve its problem by creating another school similar to Lowell, thereby having one for boys and one for girls? A conclusion similar to Berkelman's was

---

[9] In a similar case, another court, without discussing the "equal numbers" theory, ordered the use of the same standard of admission for boys and girls to an academic high school operated by the Boston public school system. Bray v. Lee, 337 F.Supp. 934 (D.Mass.1972).

reached in Bray v. Lee, 337 F.Supp. 934 (D.Mass.1972). Boston's schools included Boston Latin (for boys) and Girls Latin which, like San Francisco's Lowell High, are devoted to university preparatory and high academic education. In 1970, a boy had to score 120 out of 200 points on the admission test in order to enter Boston Latin, but a girl had to score 133 or better in order to gain admission to Girls Latin. Some girls had been denied admission; they had scored higher than some boys who had been admitted, and the girls sued after having been refused entry to Boston Latin. The court ruled "that the use of separate and different standards to evaluate the examination results to determine the admissibility of boys and girls to the Boston Latin schools constitute a violation of the Equal Protection Clause. . . ." and that "female students seeking admission to Boston Latin School have been illegally discriminated against solely because of their sex and . . . denied . . . their constitutional right to an education equal to that offered to male students at the Latin school."

2. Some states resolve the entire sex-discrimination question directly by a statute. "Notwithstanding any general, special, local law or rule or regulation of the education department to the contrary, no person shall be refused admission into or be excluded from any course of instruction offered in the state public and high school system by reason of that person's sex. No person shall be disqualified from state public and high school athletic teams, by reason of that person's sex, except pursuant to regulations promulgated by the state commissioner of education." N.Y.Educ.Law (McKinney) § 3201-a (1979).

3. Title IX of the Education Act Amendments of 1972 (§§ 901–907 of the Ed.Amds. of 1972, PL 92–318, 20 U.S.C.A. § 1681) broadly declares that "No person in the United States shall, on the basis of sex, be excluded from participation in, be denied the benefits of, or be subjected to discrimination under any education program or activity receiving federal financial assistance . . .". But an exception is made for K–12 education: ". . . in regard to admissions to educational institutions, this section shall apply only to institutions of vocational education, professional education, and graduate higher education, and to public institutions of undergraduate higher education." Thus, situations like those in Vorcheimer and Berkelman fall within the exception.

4. The Educational Amendments of 1974 (P.L. 93–380) included a provision authorizing the Secretary of HEW "to prepare and publish . . . regulations implementing the provisions of Title IX . . .". On July 21, 1975, the Secretary published final regulations implementing Title IX, one of which relates to textbook and curricular material (45 C.F.R. § 86.42): "Nothing in this regulation shall be interpreted as requiring or prohibiting or abridging in any way the use of particular textbooks or curricular materials."

This regulation led one commentator to say: "Sex-stereotyping in educational materials, beginning with the first-grade primer 'Dick and Jane'—which portrays females as timid, unimaginative, and unproductive—and on through high school texts in history, which often do not mention female contributions at all, has been recognized as a serious problem by HEW.  However, HEW has declined to deal with this problem for fear that censorship of school materials might raise serious First Amendment questions.  The regulations do cover testing and counseling *materials*, which may not differ for the two sexes." Levin, Recent Developments In The Law of Equal Educational Opportunity, 4 J. of L. & Ed. 411, 427 (1975).

5.  Does New York's law, supra, prohibit schools from using materials containing sexual stereotypes?

California's law provides: "No teacher shall give instruction nor shall a school district sponsor any activity which reflects adversely upon persons because of their  .  .  .  sex  .  .  ." and "No textbook, or other instructional materials shall be adopted  .  .  .  for use in the public schools which contains any matter reflecting adversely upon persons because of their  .  .  .  sex  .  .  .". West's Ann.Educ.Code §§ 51500, 51501.  Another California provision, § 60044, provides that "no instructional materials shall be adopted by any governing board for use in the schools which, in its determination, contains  .  .  . any matter reflecting adversely upon persons because of their  .  .  . sex  .  .  .".  Do these statutes raise First Amendment problems? Are they wise?  Do these statutes prohibit the use of curricular materials and pedagogy involving sexual stereotypes?  Do sexual stereotypes "reflect adversely upon persons"?  See, Amyx, Sex Discrimination: The Textbook Case, 62 Cal.L.Rev. 1312 (1974), and Neiman, Teaching Woman Her Place, 24 Hastings L.J. 1087 (1973).

---

## SEX DISCRIMINATION AND EXTRA–CURRICULAR ACTIVITIES

---

## YELLOW SPRINGS SCHOOL DIST. v. OHIO HIGH SCHOOL ATHLETIC ASS'N

United States District Court, 1978.
443 F.Supp. 753 (S.D.Ohio).

CARL B. RUBIN, District Judge.  This matter is before the Court on cross motions for summary judgment.

### I.  FACTS

1.  Three groups of litigants are involved in this action:  The Ohio High School Athletic Association (Association);  Robert Holland, Assistant Director of Health, Physical Education and Recreation, Ohio Department of Education, Franklin B. Walter, Superintendent of Public Instruction, Ohio Department of Education, and the Ohio Board of Education (State Defendants);  and The Yellow Springs Exempted School District Board of Education (Board).

2.    The Association is a nonprofit organization which coordinates interscholastic athletic activity among secondary schools in Ohio.   It is composed of approximately 830 secondary schools, most of which are public, and it is supported by gate receipts collected at sports tournaments that are held at public school facilities.   Membership is voluntary and is available to any secondary school accredited by the Ohio Department of Education.

3.    The Association administers interscholastic athletic programs through its scheduling and rule-making functions.   The rules which it promulgates are binding upon its members and may not be waived. Members who disregard them are subject to suspension from the Association.   Such suspension, in effect, eliminates a school from any interscholastic athletic competition since Association members are prohibited from competing against nonmembers.

4.    The State defendants are charged with establishing and implementing minimum standards for secondary schools in Ohio.   The Ohio Board of Education exercises the "policy forming, planning and evaluative function for the public schools of the state."   Alternatively, the Ohio Department of Education is the administrative unit and organization through which the policies, directives, and powers of the state board of education   .   .   .   are administered.

5.    The State defendants do not exercise direct control over interscholastic athletic competition within Ohio.   Although an Assistant Director of the Ohio Department of Education is an *ex officio* member of the Association's governing board, he cannot vote.   The State defendants do not have a duty to enforce Association rules since athletics are not a minimum requirement for public schools.   Insofar as the Ohio Board of Education controls local school district policy through financial leverage, the State defendants can indirectly control Association policy since the Association's governing board is composed of representatives from the six District Boards of Education.

6.    The Board operates a public school system in Yellow Springs, Ohio.   It is given approximately 1.5 million dollars annually to educate 950 students.   Although local taxes are a major source of income, the State of Ohio contributes $375,000 per year to the Board, while between $40,000 and $50,000 is received from the federal government. Because the Board uses three-quarters of this latter sum to run general programs, including athletics, the Board is subject to the requirements of Title IX of the Education Amendments of 1972.   Since some of the schools within its jurisdiction belong to the Association, the Board is also sensitive to Association requirements.

7.    The activity which forged this dispute occurred in 1974.   Two female students, who were enrolled in a school within the Board's jurisdiction, competed for and were awarded positions on the school's interscholastic basketball team.   Because of their sex, the Board ex-

cluded them from the team and, instead, created a separate girls' basketball team on which they could participate.

By so doing, the Board complied with Association Rule 1, § 6, which prohibits mixed gender interscholastic athletic competition in contract sports, such as basketball. A failure of such exclusion would place in jeopardy membership in the Association and would exclude the basketball team from interscholastic competition.

## OPINION

### State Action

The determination of whether a State athletic association's conduct constitutes State action is factually based. Of the many indicia of State action, four are especially probative: association dependence upon the State for operating revenue; involvement by school officials in the decision-making process of the association; predominance of public schools within association membership; and association ability to impose sanctions upon State schools, i. e., State agencies, for non-compliance with association mandates.

Given these criteria, there can be no doubt that the Association has been acting as an instrumentality of the State. The Association's only source of revenue is the gate receipts from tournaments held at public school facilities. Thus the viability of the Association is very much a function of State policy. Association policy is determined by school officials and not by an independent board. Under Article 5 of the Association Constitution, Association decision-making functions are vested in six District Board representatives among others. The Association is primarily an agent for public schools. Of its approximately 950 members, at least three quarters are public schools. Finally, the State acquiesces in Association sanctions against member public schools; that is, it permits a technically non-governmental entity to dictate terms to a State entity. In view of the foregoing, it is clear that the State of Ohio is intimately involved in the administration of interscholastic athletics and the Association's conduct constitutes State action in the Constitutional sense.

### The Due Process Clause

The Association's exclusionary rule deprives school girls of liberty without due process of law. Freedom of personal choice in matters of "education and acquisition of knowledge," is a liberty interest protected by the Due Process Clause of the Fourteenth Amendment. By denying all girls the chance to compete against boys for positions on teams which participate in interscholastic contact sports, that right may be permanently foreclosed. The Due Process Clause permits such a deprivation only when it is predicated upon a sufficiently important governmental interest.

Two governmental objectives could be proffered to support the Association rule. First, the State arguably has an interest in preventing injury to public school children. Second, the State could contend that prohibiting girls from participating with boys in contact sports will maximize female athletic opportunities. Both are palpably legitimate goals. To achieve these goals, however, the State must assume without qualification that girls are uniformly physically inferior to boys. The exclusionary rule, as it relates to the objective of preventing injury, creates a conclusive presumption that girls are physically weaker than boys. The rule, as it relates to the objective of maximization of female opportunities, creates an equally conclusive presumption that girls are less proficient athletes than boys. However, these presumptions are in fact indistinguishable since both posit that girls are somehow athletically inferior to boys solely because of their gender.

A permanent presumption is unconstitutional in an area in which the presumption might be rebutted if individualized determinations were made. The athletic capabilities of females is such an area. Although some women are physically unfit to participate with boys in contact sports, it does not "necessarily and universally" follow that all women suffer similar disabilities. Babe Didrikson could have made anybody's team. Accordingly, school girls who so desire, must be given the opportunity to demonstrate that the presumption created by the rule is invalid. They must be given the opportunity to compete with boys in interscholastic contact sports if they are physically qualified.

The consequences of this determination carry beyond the State level. For the federal regulations also are unconstitutional insofar as they suggest that mixed gender competition, creation of separate teams for girls and boys in each sport, or creation of an all male team in contact sports are independent and wholly satisfactory methods of compliance. Separate teams may, in fact, be satisfactory if they ensure due process. However, their existence cannot serve as an excuse to deprive qualified girls positions on formerly all boy teams, regardless of the sport. The Due Process Clause of the Fifth Amendment necessarily forbids that which its counterpart prohibits under the Fourteenth Amendment.

.　.　.

In view of the foregoing, the Court considers it unnecessary to rule upon questions raised under either the Supremacy Clause or the Equal Protection Clause.

The foregoing is intended to set forth the precedential underpinnings of this Court's ruling. It is addressed to those who will scrutinize the legal reasoning of this opinion. However, it is not only legal scholars, commentators and appellate courts who might have occasion to review this matter. There are many who may also be affected who are not trained in the law and who likewise seek an explanation. For them, the following has been added.

It has always been traditional that "boys play football and girls are cheerleaders." Why so? Where is it written that girls may not, if suitably qualified, play football? There may be a multitude of reasons why a girl might elect not to do so. Reasons of stature or weight or reasons of temperament, motivation or interest. This is a matter of personal choice. But a prohibition without exception based upon sex is not. It is this that is both unfair and contrary to personal rights contemplated in the Fourteenth Amendment to the United States Constitution.

It may well be that there is a student today in an Ohio high school who lacks only the proper coaching and training to become the greatest quarterback in professional football history. Of course the odds are astronomical against her, but isn't she entitled to a fair chance to try?

. . .

The defendants' motions are hereby DENIED and the Board's motion is GRANTED insofar as it alleges violations of the Fourteenth Amendment by the Association, the Ohio Board of Education, and Robert Holland and the individual Association defendants, and is GRANTED insofar as it alleges violations of Section 1983 by the individual State defendants and the individual Association defendants. The defendants should be and are hereby permanently enjoined from continuing to enforce or to maintain Association Rule 1 § 6, or from enforcing, promulgating, or maintaining any rule, regulation, directive, custom or usage which bars physically qualified girls from participating with boys in interscholastic contact sports. The defendants should be and are further enjoined from disciplining, imposing sanctions, or otherwise penalizing the Morgan Middle School, any official thereof, its basketball team, any member thereof, or its coach because of participation on said team by females.

. . .

### NOTES AND QUESTIONS

1. "Contact" sport participation has given rise to significant litigation. Non-contact interscholastic sports, such as skiing or cross-country running, have not presented courts with many difficult problems. They have ordered that girls be allowed to participate. See, e. g., Brenden v. Independent School Dist. 742, 477 F.2d 1292 (8th Cir. 1973). The rule involved in the Yellow Springs case denied all girls the chance to compete against boys for positions on teams which participate in interscholastic contact sports. Did the judge in the Yellow Springs case make the correct decision? Should he have given greater consideration to physiological or psychological factors? To sexually erotic factors if the contact sport is wrestling? Did he allow a separate-but-equal option for contact sports?

Similar interscholastic athletic association rules have been stricken by state courts under State ERA provisions. See, e. g., Commonwealth v. Pennsylvania Interscholastic Athletic Ass'n, 18 Pa.Cmwlth. 45, 334 A.2d 839 (1975), and Darrin v. Gould, 85 Wash.2d 859, 540 P.2d 882 (1975) (football).

Federal courts have disapproved sex-based discrimination in circumstances involving females interested in participation in sports programs. Fortin v. Darlington Little League, Inc., 514 F.2d 344 (1st Cir. 1975) (ten-year-old girl in little league baseball). Brenden v. Independent School Dist. 742, 477 F.2d 1292 (8th Cir. 1973) (high school tennis and cross-country running and skiing where there were no female teams). Hoover v. Meiklejohn, 430 F.Supp. 164 (D.Colo.1977) (high school soccer team limited to males). Carnes v. Tennessee Secondary School Athletic Ass'n, 415 F.Supp. 569 (E.D.Tenn.1976) (high school baseball teams excluded females where there was no team for females). Clinton v. Nagy, 411 F.Supp. 1396 (N.D.Ohio 1974) (twelve-year-old girl excluded from football in recreational league). Gilpin v. Kansas State High School Activities Ass'n, 377 F.Supp. 1233 (D.Kan.1973) (high school cross-country team excluded females where there was no team for females).

2.  The result in the Yellow Springs case is typical. But, it is grounded in the Due Process of Law Clause. Many, perhaps most, of the cases are grounded in the Equal Protection Clause. Leffel v. Wisconsin Interscholastic Athletic Ass'n, 444 F.Supp. 1117 (E.D.Wisc.1978) is typical. The Wisconsin Interscholastic Athletic Association's rule prohibited "interscholastic activity involving boys and girls competing with or against each other." The court held the rule unconstitutional saying:

> "In its present posture, the case is therefore reduced to the following two issues: First, have the defendants violated the equal protection clause by denying female high school students the opportunity to qualify for a position on a boys varsity interscholastic team engaging in a contact sport where no separate team is provided for girls, or where the separate team provided does not have a comparable program? Secondly, as to both contact and noncontact sports, does the equal protection clause of the fourteenth amendment require that female high school students be permitted to attempt to qualify for a position on a boys varsity interscholastic team where the boys team has a higher level of competition than the corresponding girls team? The second issue will be addressed first.

> "A.  Equal Levels of Competition

> "There is no dispute that the WIAA rule in question and the defendants' application of the rule is an intentional discrimination, i. e., for what they deem to be legitimate purposes, the defendants intentionally treat boy and girl athletes differently. Since an intentional discrimination is involved, the fourteenth amendment's equal protection clause is implicated. Washington v. Davis . . . . .

> "However, there are no allegations in the instant complaints that the defendants have intentionally imposed different levels of competition on boys and girls. Any such differences arise from

the abilities of the team members themselves.  Thus, the plaintiffs'
claim for declaratory and injunctive relief cannot encompass the
concept of equal levels of competition.
"B.   Equal Opportunity to Participate in Contact Sports

"The most recent direction from the Supreme Court as to the
proper standard of review for gender-based classification appears
in Craig v. Boren  .  .  .

"To withstand constitutional challenge, previous cases establish that classifications by gender must serve important governmental objectives and must be substantially related to achievement
of those objectives.

"The governmental objective posited by the defendants is the
prevention of injury to female athletes.  The defendants argue that
'anatomical and physiological differences between boys and girls'
and 'differences in athletic abilities' justify the prohibition of coeducational teams in contact sports.  The defendants offer affidavits to support the proposition that anatomical and physiological
differences between boys and girls will leave girls exposed to an unreasonable risk of injury if they were to compete with or against
boys.

"The plaintiffs do not dispute that the defendants' stated objectives are legitimate, but they argue that the correlation between
gender and athletic ability is too weak to withstand equal protection
scrutiny.  Even if the defendants' generalizations are assumed to
be true, I nevertheless find that the exclusion of girls from all contact sports in order to protect female high school athletes from an
unreasonable risk of injury is not fairly or substantially related to
a justifiable governmental objective in the context of the fourteenth
amendment.

"The defendant advances no governmental objective whatsoever
to justify providing boys with the opportunity to participate in
varsity interscholastic competition in contact sports while *absolutely*
denying the same opportunity to girls.  It is doubtful that any such
legitimate governmental objective exists.  The defendants do not
argue that girls will be exposed to an unreasonable risk of injury
in a separate girls athletic program for contact sports; they argue
that girls will be exposed to an unreasonable risk of injury if allowed to compete on boys teams.  However, coeducational teams are
only one possible remedy for the defendants' constitutional violation.  The defendants have the other two alternatives of (1) dropping all varsity interscholastic competition, and (2) establishing
separate girls teams for contact sports.  As noted previously, the
demand for relief of the plaintiffs at bar would be met by the establishment of separate girls teams with a comparable program; thus,
I need not decide whether the concept of separate girls teams presents a problem of equal protection.

"The state public schools are under no constitutional compulsion to provide interscholastic competition in any sport, but once
they choose to do so, this educational opportunity must be provided
to all on equal terms.  Although the plaintiffs do not have a con-

stitutional right to compete on boys teams in contact or noncontact sports, the defendants may not afford an educational opportunity to boys that is denied to girls.  .  .  .

"The defendants' affidavits state that since the commencement of this litigation, sports programs for girls have been established where sufficient interest has been shown.  These considerations may properly be taken into account by the defendants in their future application of the WIAA rule in question."

3.  The Leffel court states that the Equal Protection claim "of the plaintiffs  .  .  .  would be met by the establishment of separate girls teams with a comparable program" Could the Due Process claim in Yellow Springs be satisfied in the same way?  Does approval of such a remedy mean that proof of the existence of "separate-but-equal" facilities defeats a claim of sex-discrimination?  Should it?  See, Lewis, Plessy Revived:  The Separate But Equal Doctrine And Sex-Segregated Education, 12 Harv.Civ.Rts. & Civ.Lib.L.Rev. 585 (1977).

In Cape v. Tennessee Secondary School Athletic Ass'n, 563 F.2d 793 (6th Cir. 1977), the court upheld different sets of rules for girls and boys basketball on the ground of general physical differences between boys and girls in high school.  If this ruling is correct, and if different rules justifiably can be applied to boys and girls participating in high school basketball because of their physical differences, then why is it unconstitutional on Due Process grounds (Yellow Springs, supra) or Equal Protection grounds (Leffel, supra) to prohibit girls from participating in mixed-contact sport competitions held under boys' rules?  Can you review the law in this area and formulate it into a single, coherent set of rules that account for all the cases?

Under the Leffel separate-but-equal option, or under the Yellow Springs ruling, does a qualified male have a right to play on an all-girl high school basketball team where the high school offered no separate male basketball team?  If so, would the male be entitled to participate under boys rules or girls rules?

------

## GOMES v. RHODE ISLAND INTERSCHOLASTIC LEAGUE

United States District Court, 1979.
469 F.Supp. 659 (D.R.I.).

PETTINE, Chief Judge.  In recent years dozens of federal courts have interpreted the equal protection clause of the fourteenth amendment as mandating equal athletic opportunities for high school females.  These rulings allowed girls to breach such previously all-male bastions as Little League baseball, high school soccer and cross-country skiing.  There were only some minor limitations upon this athletic revolution: schools had a sufficiently strong interest in safety to prohibit co-ed participation in "contact" sports, "separate but equal" sports teams were permissible, and a reluctant school committee could always avoid such constitutional requirements by eliminating its athletic program competely.

Congress further assured athletic equality for females by passing Title IX of the Education Amendments of 1972. The statute broadly assures that no person "shall, on the basis of sex, be excluded from participation in, be denied benefits of, or be subjected to discrimination under any educational program or activity receiving Federal financial assistance. . . ." 20 U.S.C.A. § 1681. Regulations promulgated under the statute assure that Title IX covers such educational activities as high school athletics. 45 C.F.R. § 86.41. Responding to these judicial and legislative mandates, many schools now provide increased athletic opportunities for women.

The present case requires this Court to face the unique, if inevitable, corollary to such advances against sex discrimination: may a qualified male play on an all-girls athletic team when the high school offers no separate male team. This issue is presented by a motion for a preliminary injunction filed by Donald Gomes, a senior at Rogers High School in Newport, Rhode Island, against the Rhode Island Interscholastic League, members of the Newport School Committee, and others. Gomes correctly premises his claim upon 42 U.S.C.A. § 1983 and alleges violations of Title IX and the fourteenth amendment. This Court need only decide the statutory issue. . . .

. . .

Donald Gomes is six feet tall and sincerely desires to play volleyball. Donald had played on an all-boys volleyball team in Harrisburg, Pennsylvania, before being transferred to Rogers High. The sole reason Donald cannot play at Rogers High is his sex. The Rhode Island Interscholastic League does not provide interscholastic volleyball competition for males and disqualifies any team on which a male plays. There are a few all-girl private schools in the League; their teams are necessarily restricted to females. Some Rhode Island high schools field all-male volleyball teams which play outside the League's jurisdiction; Rogers High is not one of these schools.

Rogers High School does offer a wide variety of athletic opportunities for males. Women and men compete for positions on such teams as cross country, tennis, track, basketball, and baseball. Males constitute the overwhelming majority on those teams open to co-ed participation. The school also provides teams exclusively for females in tennis, track, basketball, gymnastics, volleyball, and softball. Thus, a woman may choose to compete for a position on a co-ed tennis team or a position on the female tennis team; likewise, she may try out for the baseball team or the all-girls softball team. According to the league regulations adopted by the school, men are limited to the co-ed teams and, thus, may never participate in volleyball and gymnastics on a competitive basis. For safety reasons, women are not permitted to compete for positions on the all-male football team.

Not dissuaded by the League's rules, Donald tried out for and made the girls' volleyball team. He was the only male among the thirty-two individuals competing for the sixteen slots on the team. Apparently Donald's athletic interest was rather unique; the school's athletic director testified that there was not sufficient interest among the other boys at Rogers High to field a male volleyball team. Donald has been issued a uniform and has practiced steadily with the team but, because of his sex, he has not been allowed to play in the interscholastic games.

Despite Donald's size advantage over many of his female teammates, his coach, Mrs. Bryl Johnston, only ranks him between 9th and 6th in terms of comparative playing ability. Mrs. Johnston noted that girls volleyball rules differed in only one way from boys volleyball; i. e., the net height is approximately seven inches lower in girls volleyball. Mrs. Johnston also testified that in her experience of teaching co-ed gym classes in volleyball, the playing skills of boys and girls have been relatively equal. She admitted, however, that if volleyball became a popular sport among high school boys, males would begin to dominate a co-ed team. . . .

Plaintiff readily agrees that "separate but equal" teams are not only athletically beneficial, but also constitutionally permissible. It is the second strand of defendants' argument that plaintiff heatedly contests. The defendants assert that they are not required by Title IX or the equal protection clause to provide males such as Donald an opportunity to compete either on the present team or on a separate all-male team. Defendants concede that this approach bestows a benefit upon females and penalizes males such as Donald. This disparate treatment, however, is allegedly justified because it is a purposeful method of overcoming past athletic discrimination against females. The defendants claim that this "affirmative action" of conferring special athletic opportunities upon women is both statutorily and consitutionally justified because it is a deliberate attempt to redress "our society's longstanding disparate treatment of women". They point out that Title IX reflects this affirmative approach and explicitly authorizes their present course of conduct.

Plaintiff counters by arguing that the constitution protects males as well as females against sex-discrimination. . . . He also relies upon Title IX and its regulations, arguing that the statute mandates sexual equality in athletics and prohibits the complete denial of an opportunity to play a sport such as volleyball.

The dispute is resolved by interpreting and applying the regulation promulgated under Title IX which explicitly deals with athletics and separate sex teams. The regulation, 45 C.F.R. § 86.41(a), assures that:

> (a) *General.* No person shall, on the basis of sex, be excluded from participation in, be denied the benefits of, be treated differently from another person or otherwise be discriminated against in any interscholastic, intercollegiate,

club or intramural athletics offered by a recipient, and no recipient shall provide any such athletics separately on such basis.

The second paragraph of the regulation specifically addresses the issue of separate teams and attempts to reconcile such teams with the broad promise of equal athletic treatment:

(b) *Separate Teams*. Notwithstanding the requirements of paragraph (a) of this section, a recipient may operate or sponsor separate teams for members of each sex where selection for such teams is based upon competitive skill or the activity involved is a contact sport. *However, where a recipient operates or sponsors a team in a particular sport for members of one sex but operates or sponsors no such team for members of the other sex, and athletic opportunities for members of that sex have previously been limited, members of the excluded sex must be allowed to try-out for the team offered unless the sport involved is a contact sport.* For the purposes of this part, contact sports include boxing, wrestling, rugby, ice hockey, football, basketball and other sports the purpose of major activity of which involves bodily contact.

(Emphasis added).

Both sides agree that this regulation applies to this case but they dispute the interpretation of the phrase "and athletic opportunities for members of that [excluded] sex have previously been limited". Defendants argue that this phrase must be interpreted in a general sense and must refer to overall athletic opportunities for the sex. Thus, because only women have previously endured limited athletic opportunities, the phrase must only refer to the female sex. This interpretation would allow formation of separate female teams without male equivalents because overall athletic opportunities for males have never previously been limited; according to defendants' argument, male teams could not be established, except in contact sports, without female equivalents. Plaintiff takes a different approach and argues that the phrase must be interpreted in regard to the "particular sport" and team in question. Thus, because athletic opportunities have previously been limited for males in such sports as volleyball or field hockey, equivalent male teams must be established in these sports; such would not be the case in sports where males previously had equal or superior opportunities to participate.

This is a situation where both sides have offered equally intelligent, plausible and differing interpretations of an ambiguous phrase. This Court concedes that as a matter of linguistics both constructions are fully justified. If the Court accepts defendants' interpretation, however, serious questions arise concerning the constitutionality of the regulation. The defendants' approach would authorize schools to establish female teams in any sport without equivalent male teams because women have been generally deprived of athletic opportunities. Such a broadly focused remedial program may run afoul of the equal protection clause. The constitution does permit a legislature to bestow disproportionate benefits upon women if such legislative advantages are deliberately enacted to compensate for particular and provable economic and social disabilities suffered by women. Differences in treatment are not permissible if they are based on overbroad generalizations or are the "accidental byproduct of a traditional way of thinking about females".

Title IX and its regulations do evidence a deliberate intent to rid high school athletics of the sex discrimination that long plagued women athletes. Providing women with separate and exclusive teams in sports previously dominated by men appears a legitimate and narrowly drawn attempt to rectify past discrimination. Likewise, Rogers High School's decision to offer girls, but not boys, a choice between competing on an "open" team or on a single-sex team appears to be a legitimate attempt to encourage female athletics and rectify past discrimination. Both these alternatives provide women with some athletic advantages but assume that adequate opportunities will continue to exist in a particular sport for qualified males.

The practice challenged in this case is far different. Defendants would provide a single sex volleyball team for women while totally barring men from playing a sport in which males only have had limited opportunities to play. The athletic scheme is not directed toward the special disadvantages women have suffered in a particular sport and, thus, may be impermissibly overbroad.

More troublesome is the drastic affirmative action remedy that defendants assert. To completely deny one sex any opportunity to participate in a federally funded activity from which either sex could benefit is an unprecedented doctrine. As previously stated, courts interpret the Constitution to permit "separate but equal" athletic teams; but, "separate but equal" necessarily envisions two equal systems, not an exclusive opportunity for only one sex to participate. See, e. g., Vorchheimer School Dist. of Philadelphia. Further, the constitution permits a disadvantaged race or sex to receive some preferential treatment, but no affirmative action program has gone so far as to absolutely bar the other race or sex from participation.

Of course, Donald Gomes is not barred from all athletic opportunities because Rogers High continues to provide various athletic teams for both males and females; yet, this is small consolation for an individual whose skills and desires are particularly suited for the unique game of volleyball. The theoretical opportunity to play other sports has never been a justification for sexual discrimination which bars the door to a particular sport.[2]  Any interpretation of 45 C.F.R. § 86.41 that permits such a sexually exclusionary athletic program, raises serious question concerning the constitutional validity of that regulation.

A much wiser course, as Chief Justice Marshall observed, is to interpret legislation so as to avoid questions of its constitutional validity.  Plaintiff's narrower interpretation of the regulation avoids the serious constitutional problems raised by defendants' construction.  A separate and exclusive female team may be established only when males previously had, and presumably continue to have, adequate athletic opportunities to participate in that sport.[3]  At least in terms of volleyball at Rogers High, athletic opportunities for males have been severely limited.  Therefore, 45 C.F.R. is best read as requiring Rogers High School to provide Donald Gomes with the opportunity to play interscholastic volleyball either by establishing a separate volleyball team for boys or by allowing Donald to compete on the present girls' team, or by some other practical means.

This interpretation of the federal regulation convinces this Court that a preliminary injunction must issue.  Donald has successfully argued the merits of his case.  The irreparable harm he would suffer by missing the volleyball season is unquestioned.  In light of his relatively limited ability, there is little possibility that his participation will substantially disrupt League play or provide one team with a

---

[2] This does not mean that the sports offered males and females must be identical in every respect.  Rule differences between boys and girls sports are certainly legitimate, even if they change the nature of the game significantly.  Cape v. Tennessee Secondary School Athletic Ass'n, 563 F.2d 793 (6th Cir. 1977).  This is true even if the rules change the name of the game; thus, school administrators could legitimately decide to offer baseball for boys and softball for girls.  A federal court is no place to decide whether a particular sex should be allowed to dribble the full length of a basketball court or pitch underhand.  See Hoover v. Meiklejohn, 430 F.Supp. 164, 171 (D.Colo.1977).

This case, however, presents a different issue.  The plaintiff here is totally denied the opportunity to play a recognized sport on the interscholastic level.  No other sport combines the same combination of athletic skills as volleyball.  Different rules may change the pace, character and nature of the sport, but they still permit both sexes to utilize the unique combination of athletic skills characteristic of the sport.

[3] For example, the regulation would permit the establishment of an all-girls team without an equivalent all-male team in a sport where women have had limited athletic opportunities (baseball, for example).  In such a situation, an all-male equivalent would be unnecessary.  Males could (as they do at Rogers High School) compete on a "co-ed" or "open" team.  In the alternative, a school might arrange for their male students to participate on another school's male or co-ed baseball team.  Perhaps, in a sport long dominated by males, a school could even create only a female team without making any provisions for male participation; such a hypothetical situation might be constitutionally permissible because Congress could find that sufficient athletic opportunities existed in the private sector for males to play the particular sport.  In all these scenarios, women are given the advantage of nurturing their talents within the context of single-sex competition while male students are not completely denied the opportunity to compete in a particular sport.

disproportionate advantage. There is no evidence that this limited preliminary injunctive relief will lead to a sudden male influx or domination of Rhode Island interscholastic volleyball. Defendants admit that, at this time, there is little interest in volleyball among the general male population at Rogers High. Nor is there any evidence that any other male at any League affiliated school qualified for a position on a volleyball team during the time limits designated by the League rules. Therefore, a preliminary injunction can prevent plaintiff's irreparable harm without disrupting other students' rights to play in a competitive athletic league.

This conclusion in no way minimizes the expert athletic and medical evidence offered at the hearing. Separate but equal volleyball teams do appear the most advantageous athletic approach. But whether such teams are created at Rogers High School can only be decided by the school administrators, the coaches, and, ultimately, the political process. A court can only approach the problem in a more generalized fashion and interpret statutes in light of broad constitutional requirements. Within the broad commands of the constitution, there is certainly leeway to create fair and equal athletic opportunities for both sexes; the details of such plans are best formulated by the political process, not a federal court.

An order will be prepared accordingly.

## NOTES AND QUESTIONS

1. Massachusetts' Supreme Court ruled similarly in Attorney Gen. v. Massachusetts Interscholastic Athletic Ass'n, —— Mass. ——, 393 N.E.2d 284 (1979). This was an action by the Attorney General, acting on behalf of the State Board of Education, against the Massachusetts Interscholastic Athletic Association, which, by delegation from the local school committees, regulates and controls inter-high school athletic competition in the Commonwealth. The Attorney General sought a declaration that a 1978 rule of the Association—"No boy may play on a girls' team"—was invalid.

The Supreme Judicial Court held in a unanimous decision that this total ban on boys' participation with girls, which purported to apply even where no comparable boys' team was offered, was impermissible under the Equal Rights Amendment.

The action did not challenge the exclusion of boys from girls' teams where comparable boys' teams existed. And the court recognized that girls' teams could properly be protected against undue invasion by boys to the detriment of the progressive development of girls' athletic programs. However, the absolute exclusion of boys under any and all conditions was held to be improper.

Among the arguments in support of the rule was one identified as "sex as a proxy for function":

"The defendants seem to suggest in the course of their argument that the discrimination under attack is in reality not one based on sex but rather on functional differences deriving in the main from biology, and is thus not proscribed by the ERA. No doubt biological circumstance does contribute to some overall male advantages. But we think the differences are not so clear or uniform as to justify a rule in which sex is sought to be used as a kind of 'proxy' for a functional classification

A second argument in support of the rule was safety:

"The defendants argue that the gender-based absolute exclusion is necessary to achieve an important State interest, protection of players' safety. Indeed, 'protecting the . . . safety of all students' appears in the preamble of the rule (in company with the vague term 'welfare') as the rule's objective. It may be enough to say—as the plaintiffs do—that the defendants have not satisfied their burden of supporting the claim with facts. Nevertheless we analyze the claim by reference to law and common sense. The defendants' argument on the score of safety or health was implicitly rejected in Opinion of the Justices, where the proposed ban on girls' participation in football and wrestling was considered invalid. A girl is surely not less exposed to injury as a member of a predominantly male team, than as one of a team predominantly female but with some male players. In any case, a girl is entitled as much as a boy to choose to take a risk, subject always to safety rules and appropriate supervision and equipment."

A third argument in support of the rule was based on affirmative action considerations and protecting girls' participation in sports:

"Although the preamble seems otherwise directed, the prohibition of rule 17(d)(1) is now sought to be justified as a measure of 'affirmative action' needed, so it is alleged, to prevent the swamping of girls' teams by boys of skill and prowess superior to those of girls. But the rule is out of proportion to any looming danger. It represents a sweeping use of a disfavored classification when less offensive and better calculated alternatives appear to exist and have not been attempted. We neither know, nor are apprised by the record, that the apprehended peril is such as to require so sweeping a prohibition. But even if the claimed fear of inundation because of male advantages in many sports were more solidly based in fact, it would not justify the categorical exclusion of males from any sport, or divisions or 'events' of a sport, in which, overall, they enjoy no or only a slight advantage over females. Gymnastics and swimming (as well as riflery) may be examples. No less important is the fact that the rule overlooks approaches, short of broad prohibition, that could solve any anticipated problem of boys in substantial numbers displacing girls from competition to the serious detriment of the development of athletics for girls. Use of standards focussing on height, weight, or skill rather than solely on gender represents one such approach: males would thus be admitted who could not dominate the mixed teams or overwhelm the opposition. Admission could perhaps be regulated by handicapping in a sport like golf. On another level also, lesser measures than complete exclusion sug-

gest themselves.  Where boys' teams were not feasible, admission
of boys to girls' teams could be limited, not to exceed reasonable
numbers.  In particular situations, rotating systems might be
adopted by which qualified boys were admitted but only a certain
number could play in a given game.  We emphasize that resort
to a separate team for boys acts as a backstop for many if not all
alternatives which result in introducing boys into girls' teams.
That is to say, if enough boys are interested in a sport to try out
for, and threaten to oust girl players from, a particular team,
the school authorities are on notice that a boys' team may be in
order.  Should the number of boys be not quite enough for a
separate squad, the problem would sometimes be amenable to solution by forming a consolidated boys' team representing neighboring schools.  The legality of segregation in separate but equal
teams is not challenged here."

The court summed up its views as follows:

"The State Board of Education, through the Attorney General, has rightly questioned a rule of the MIAA which would bar
boys from playing on girls' interscholastic teams—an absolute
rule applying by its terms even when no comparable boys' team
exists.  Any rule which classifies by sex alone is subject to close
examination under the concept of equal protection of the laws, as
that has been strengthened by the popularly adopted ERA and
the statute on educational opportunity.  Upon such examination,
no current situation confronting MIAA has been pointed to that
would warrant so drastic a rule of exclusion.  An alleged 'safety'
justification for the prohibition must fail.  A further justification
alleged was that, without a total ban on all participation by boys,
girls' sports would be overrun by boys who as a class are physically
better equipped for athletic competition.  Undoubtedly, there is a
problem here which is entitled to sympathetic consideration and to
the extent necessary may even call for 'affirmative action.'  On
analysis, however, it appeared that the problem was marginal;
where it arises, it can be met by measures less offensive and less
sweeping than a complete sex barrier.

"It can be expected that the present decision will make little
practical differences in the traditional conduct of interscholastic
athletic competition, for that will proceed in the great majority
of instances on a basis of 'separate but equal' teams whose validity
is assumed here.  We do not believe our decision will interfere with
the development of competitive athletics for girls.  On the contrary, to immunize girls' teams totally from any possible contact
with boys might well perpetuate a psychology of 'romantic paternalism' inconsistent with such development and hurtful to it in
the long run.

"The present decision is addressed to the facts as they now
appear.  We acknowledge that future changes in the situation,
not now perceptible, may call hereafter for a different solution."

## A NOTE ON TITLE IX

§§ 901–907 of the Educ.Amds. of 1972, P.L. 92–318.
20 U.S.C.A. § 1681.

Strictly speaking, an exploration of Title IX is beyond the scope of this book, but it is so important that it must be touched on. As noted above, except for K–12 admissions and several other exceptions, Title IX applies fully to elementary and secondary educational institutions. It broadly declares that "no person in the United States shall, on the basis of sex, be excluded from participation in, be denied the benefits of, or be subjected to discrimination under any education program or activity receiving federal financial assistance . . . .". Each "Federal department and agency which is empowered to extend federal financial assistance to any education program or activity . . . is authorized and directed to effectuate the provisions" of Title IX. (20 U.S.C.A. § 1682) The ultimate sanction is withdrawal of federal funds. Moreover, the Secretary for HEW has been given authority to promulgate regulations implementing Title IX, and they are found in volume 45 of the Code of Federal Regulations, Part 86. Furthermore, the U.S. Supreme Court has held that, after exhausting administrative remedies, Title IX can be enforced in the courts by an individual through a private cause of action. Cannon v. University of Chicago, —— U.S. ——, 99 S.Ct. 1946, 60 L.Ed.2d 560 (1979).

HEW Regulation § 86.41 speaks directly to athletics, providing that "no person shall, on the basis of sex . . . be treated differently from another person . . . in any interscholastic, . . . club or intramural athletics offered by a recipient . . .". The same basic requirement has been made applicable to (1) all educational programs and activities (§ 86.31); (2) access to course offerings (§ 86.34); (3) counseling and counseling materials (§ 86.36); (4) student employment assistance (§ 86.38); and (5) student marital or parental status (§ 86.40). As indicated above, Title IX does not apply to textbooks and curricular materials, thereby avoiding First Amendment problems.

A recurring issue concerns the relationship of Title IX to Title VII of the Civil Rights Act of 1964, and particularly whether Title IX controls sex-based employment discrimination in educational institutions receiving federal funds? Romeo Community School v. United States Dept. of HEW, 438 F.Supp. 1021 (E.D.Mich.1977) held that Title IX applied only to students and other direct beneficiaries and participants of school programs receiving federal funds and that any regulation applying the law to any other persons was not authorized by Title IX, and hence, unenforceable. Thus, neither teachers nor other school employees come within Title IX, unless some program makes them direct beneficiaries of federal funds. Another federal court has reached the same conclusion; see, Brunswick School Bd. v. Califano, 449 F.Supp. 866 (D.C.Me.1978). Also see, Kuhn, Title IX: Employment and Athletics Are Outside HEW's Jurisdiction, 65 Geo. L.J. 49 (1976).

# Chapter X

## CONSTITUTIONAL FREEDOM AND EQUAL
## EDUCATIONAL OPPORTUNITY

---

### INTRODUCTION

---

This chapter completes the exploration of the equal-protection clause in an equal education context that was begun in the last two chapters. The focus here, however, is markedly different from that of the previous two chapters where it was on race and sex-based discrimination. In each of the two preceding chapters the basic concern was whether racial or sexual considerations justified separating otherwise equally qualified, otherwise equivalent students. The claim of the separated students was not that they were different, but that they were the same as others and entitled "to a piece of the same action" because they were just like the other children. In other words, ethnic minorities were entitled to share equally in whatever education the state provided, and no one was to be excluded or relegated to an inferior educational opportunity because of his race or sex. In an important sense, the students, whether male or female or of ethnic majority or minority, were looked upon as not having any significant differences, and therefore they were entitled to "equal" education. The meaning of "equal" in the equal-protection clause in the last two chapters was something like "same education," or "as identical as possible."

The focus of this chapter is different. Primarily, it is on children who are different in some important way from other children. They may be gifted or handicapped in one way or another, either physically or environmentally. They claim that, because of their differences, they are entitled to a significantly different kind of educational experience. They may wish desperately that they could be treated the "same" as all the other children, but they cannot be. Equality of educational opportunity in this context means treating certain children different from those others in the "mainstream." No one, on humanitarian grounds, wants to limit any of these children to exactly the same amount of school resources claimed by each of the other children. A greater input of school resources is necessary for each importantly different child, if any kind of reasonable educational result is to be achieved.

In an important sense, this chapter, along with the last two chapters, shares a fundamental common goal of education. That goal is

864

educationally achievable. It is that equal educational opportunity means that effective public schooling should, as much as possible, lead to equal adult opportunities of the highest kinds possible for all students, given their innate properties. This goal implies that public schooling should reduce the effects of handicaps, whether physical or environmental, including the handicap of ignorance.

A state is not obligated by the Constitution of the United States to provide any educational opportunity for its children. However, if a state does provide any type of educational opportunity for its children, then the equal protection clause of the Fourteenth Amendment requires that the state provide that educational opportunity "equally" to all its children. This requirement provided the foundation for decision in the desegregation cases. Brown I declared that a state-operated dual school system that is based on race deprived the minority children of equal educational opportunity because "separate educational facilities are inherently unequal." They stigmatize minority children, branding them as inferior, and this "impact is greater when it has the sanction of the law." Thus, we know that racially separated education, by law, is constitutionally unequal education. What other types of educational opportunity might or might not qualify as being "equal" or "unequal"? That is the primary question posed by this chapter.

A second concept of equal educational opportunity, not involving race or sex, derives from the principles of classical liberalism. According to this concept equal educational opportunity exists when each child has equal access to an equal amount of public school resources; i. e., when each child has equal educational facilities, an equal amount of school financing and equal services. The focus is on the schools and on an equality of inputs per student. In this sense, the input per student of the schools themselves is to be measured, and those inputs are to be made fully equal. But schools are not to be equalizers. The students are to be afforded equal access to equal amounts of public resources devoted to education, ignoring the unequal backgrounds and abilities that students may bring to the schools, unless they are gross.

A third concept of equal educational opportunity focuses primarily on the output of the schools, and schools are to be equalizers. According to this view, equal educational opportunity exists when each child is schooled in relation to his individual background and ability up to a minimum and when the consequences of schooling compensate for prior inequalities among students. Under this concept consequences are critical, and it would not be a violation of equal educational opportunity for one student to receive more school resources, finances and services than another student. A violation would occur when the constitutionally required minimum outcomes of schooling are unequal, and all school resources would be devoted to producing this minimum in all students. A variant of this concept does not require that all school resources be devoted exclusively to producing a constitutionally required minimum of education in each student. It does include the minimum outcome requirement, but also it allows for some school resources to be used for more than the minimum educational development of students of high ability who show promise. Under the variant concept, each student first is to be educated at least up to the constitutionally required minimum outcome, and, secondly, each student capable of it is to be educated beyond that minimum level in accordance with his innate capacities for educational growth and development. Thus, under the variant concept, the equality of consequence that is to be achieved beyond the minimum required of all, is the equally full educational development of the uniquely unequal talents that are innately found in each student whether he be rich or poor. Should the constitutionally required minimum, be defined as that education necessary for "good citizenship"? If so, what public justifications are there (1) for using the public's tax funds to educate some, but not all, students beyond that minimum, and (2) for requiring compulsory school attendance of students after they have attained the minimum level?

Three basic categories of equal educational opportunity can be identified which will include the alternative and competing concepts of equal educational opportunity: (1) equal treatment of races or sexes, (2) equal access to an equal amount of public school resources (input equality), and (3) equal outcomes from the effectiveness of school resources and processes (output equality). All present severe problems of accurate measurement. The latter two are the primary focus of this chapter. For discussion see, Yudoff, Equal Educational Opportunity and the Courts, 51 Texas L.Rev. 411 (1973), and Rand Corp., Report: How Effective Is Schooling? (1971), prepared for the President's Commission On School Finance, Dec. 1971.

## THE PROBLEM

What is within a state's power to equalize? Does J. S. Coleman provide a beginning answer in his Foreword to J. Coons, W. H. Clune III and S. Sugarman, Private Wealth and Public Education (1970): "There is, of course, a broader sense of the term 'equality of educational opportunity' [than financial equality] which should be kept in mind: equality of *all* the effective resource inputs into education, not merely the financial ones. This equality can only be measured by equal effects for children of equal ability; but it clearly consists of a variety of input resources, not merely financial ones. The question about the state's provision of equal education opportunity becomes a difficult one: over which of these resources does the state have control, or should the state have control? Which of the resources can the state, through legal means, demand be redistributed equally? Certainly not the attentive help that some parents give their children in learning to read, nor the discipline some parents exert in enforcing the homework assignments of the school, nor the reinforcements by parents of the performance rewards given by the school.  But the state has attempted to control the distribution of one educational resource, that is money—though, . . . this distribution is currently far from equal—and recently it has, in what might be seen as a radical venture into resource redistribution, attempted to control the distribution of educational resources embodied in classmates.  The means, of course, has been racial and social class integration.  In this second area of resources, it has been even more ineffective than in its attempt to redistribute financial resources.  This [is a] second kind of educational resource, in the form of other children in a school.  . . . Yet the attempt of the state to effect a redistribution focuses attention on the fact that financial resources are not the only ones. More fundamentally, it raises the question of just how far the state can go, and how far it should go, in redistributing educational resources to provide equal protection to the young in the form of equal educational opportunity.  It is not a question that is easily answered. . . ."

For an analysis concluding that the education actually received by students in American schools has failed to equalize Americans and to make us more equal in terms of income, social status and political power, see, Jencks et al., Inequality (1972).  Granting this conclusion, does it follow that equal educational opportunity in the sense of equal school inputs per child also would probably fail to equalize socioeconomic classes in this country?  If so, is this an acceptable argument against providing equal schools to all children?  Or is this an acceptable justification for constitutionally requiring an output measure of equal educational opportunity?

---

## TOWARD EQUAL EDUCATIONAL OPPORTUNITY

United States Senate Select Comm. On Equal Educational Opportunity,
Report, 92nd Cong., 2nd Sess. Dec. 31, 1972.
Excerpts from pp. 9–13.

. . .   About one-fifth, or 9.3 million of our Nation's 46.3 million students in public preschools and elementary and secondary schools, are members of minority groups.  At the same time another 20 percent are from families with incomes under $5,000 a year, and about 4 million are from families with annual incomes less than $3,-000 per year.  Also, 12.2 million students are in families where the head of the household has no more than 8 years of school, and 10.5 million are children with unemployed or underemployed parents. These and other statistics—the 8.7 million children who arrive at school each day without a nutritious breakfast, the fact that at least 5 million children live in substandard housing units, and the high incidence of inadequate health care for perhaps as many as 21 million children of all ages—indicate the magnitude of disadvantaged among our Nation's school- and preschool-age population. We estimate that at least 12 million and perhaps as many as 20 million of the Nation's school-age population of 59 million, between 3 and 17, are from either economically or educationally disadvantaged homes.

For most of these children formal education is a yearly repetition of accelerating failure. Our public education system has failed and continues to fail successive generations of children from disadvantaged and minority group backgrounds—millions of children who leave school years behind in achievement and without the skills, knowledge or motivation they need to succeed in life. The result is that our public schools not only perpetuate but often exacerbate rather than help overcome the economic, social and racial inequalities in our society.

The typical child who is black, Mexican American, Puerto Rican, American Indian, a member of another racial- or language-minority group, or poor white and living in a rural community, is likely to achieve in school at two-thirds the rate of the average child. On entering the third grade he is often already a year behind. By the 12th grade he is likely to be 4½ years behind.

But the real story of educational failure was related to the committee in the testimony of witnesses, many of them professional educators, from communities across the country. It is a tale of devastating personal tragedy of enormous consequences to individual children. Here is a sampling of some of the things we heard about the performance of disadvantaged children.

- In the ghetto schools of Hartford, Conn., the average IQ scores of black elementary schoolchildren show a steady decline between the 4th and the 8th grade from 94 to 86. This 8th grade score is only 6 points above the IQ level at which the laws of Connecticut permit institutionalization in special schools for the mentally retarded.

- Similarly, at the preschool level, in the Edgewood school district of San Antonio, Tex., Chicano children at the age of 3 score an average of 104 in IQ tests. At age 4 their average is 90. By the time they are 5, and ready to enter the first grade, it is 70.

- In the typical Philadelphia inner city elementary school, 65 percent of the students score in the 16th percentile in the Iowa Test of Basic Skills—so low they are simply not functioning as students.

- Of the Mexican-American students in Texas, 56.8 percent leave school before completing the 8th grade; 78.9 percent drop out before high school graduation. One expert estimated 20 percent of migrant children never attend school at all.

- There are 7,800 Puerto Rican students in the public schools of Newark, N. J. Only 96 are in the 12th grade: in Boston between 1965 and 1969, only 4 out of 7,000 Puerto Rican schoolchildren graduated from high school; and in Chicago, the Puerto Rican dropout rate before high school graduation is 60 percent.

- Two-thirds of all American Indian adults have never gone beyond elementary school; 10 percent of those over 14 never went to school at all; and probably as many as half the American Indian children enrolled in school today will not finish high school.

These are but a few examples of the tragic educational failure of minority group and disadvantaged children.

## THE ELEMENTS OF INEQUALITY IN EDUCATION

Today and throughout our history, where a person is born, his race, his native language, his cultural background and his parents' income and occupation are the principal factors that determine where he lives and the quality of his education. The child from a disadvantaged home usually enters school already behind in his ability to communicate and relate to the new world around him. He goes to school with others from similar backgrounds and often to a school with inadequate facilities. He is often taught by less-qualified teachers who are insensitive to his culture and background, and who label him as different, slow in learning and likely to fail. He is often tested and tracked in a class for slow learners. He is more likely than the child from an advantaged home to drop out before graduation. If he does graduate he is usually years behind in achievement; he seldom continues his education and is likely to return to all the handicaps of the environment into which he was born. This is the unequal life of the disadvantaged schoolchild.

There are three principal, interrelated ways in which the process of education in this Nation is unequal.

*First*, children from minority and economically disadvantaged families live their lives isolated from the rest of society. The fact is that education in this country is still—for the most part—segregated by race, economic and social class. By any reasonable measure, except in the 11 Southern States, we have hardly begun the task of eliminating the segregation of minority group and disadvantaged students in our Nation. Nationally, 5.9 million out of 9.3 million minority-group students, or more than 60 percent, still attend predominantly minority-group schools. At the same time 72 percent of the Nation's nonminority-group students attend schools which are at least 90 percent nonminority. Four million minority-group students attend schools which are 80 percent or more minority, and 2 million are in classes which are 99–100 percent minority. . . .

Minority-group children are more isolated in large school districts than in small ones. About one-half of the Nation's black students are in our 100 largest school districts. These school districts, which include all the Nation's large cities, are the most segregated in the Nation. Nearly 75 percent of the black students in these districts were in 80–100 percent minority schools, and 60 percent were in 95–100 percent minority schools in the Fall of 1971.

*Second,* minority and disadvantaged children are often treated in unequal ways by schools themselves.

Their performance, their aspirations and motivations are often adversely affected by the attitudes and expectations of their teachers—who often label them as inferior, and destined to fail. The disadvantaged child is often tracked in a class or other group of "slow learners" or "underachievers." In short, these children are subjected to a labeling process according to their background rather than their ability or potential—a process which deeply affects a child's attitudes about himself, his family, his culture and virtually assures school failure and a life of unequal opportunity after school.

One of our witnesses described these unequal practices as they affect Spanish-speaking children:

> The injuries of the Latin American child have been inflicted by those who have claimed to teach and motivate him, and who have, in reality, alienated him, and destroyed his identity through the subtle rejection of his language [which nobody speaks], his culture [which nobody understands], and ultimately him [whom nobody values].

*Third,* the financial resources for public elementary and secondary education are both raised and distributed inequitably so that the quality of a child's education is largely dependent upon the taxable wealth of each school district and its citizens. As a result, most children from low-income families and those who live in communities with low tax bases or high public service costs attend schools with fewer and lower quality educational services.

The disparities in school expenditures across the Nation can only be described as spectacular. They exist among States, among school districts within States and among schools within school districts. Among the 50 States the range of per-pupil expenditures is from $1,429 in Alaska to $489 in Alabama. Within almost every State the highest spending school district spends at least twice as much as the lowest spending school district and variations of 3-, 4-, and 5-to-1 are not uncommon.

In short, poor children usually attend poor schools.  They are the victims of the fact that most of the resources for education in this Nation are allocated in a manner which assures that the best education that money can buy is available to children in wealthy communities, and the lowest quality education goes to those in the poorest communities.

These three factors—segregation of minority-group and disadvantaged children in fact, if not in law;  the unequal practices and treatment to which they are subjected, and the inequality in educational resources—combine to produce inequality in American public elementary and secondary education.  Together they produce educational failure in the form of low aspirations and motivations, high dropout rates, and low achievement.

## THE PRIMARY CAUSES OF EDUCATIONAL INEQUALITY

What these elements of educational inequality—segregation, economic discrimination, malnutrition and the unequal treatment of, and unequal resources for, minority-group and poor children—add up to is a system which is failing millions of children.  The reasons for that failure are complex.  But they add up to a central finding of our work:

It is not that children fail.  It is our Nation that has failed them.

They are the victims—the victims of racial discrimination and class prejudice, poor schools, unfit housing, inadequate health care, malnutrition, unemployment and poverty.  They are the victims of virtually every institution in our society—of which our public education system is among the most important—institutions that are insensitive and unresponsive to the needs of racial minorities and disadvantaged groups.  The fact is that many of the school systems in this Nation that are confronted with children from families whose racial or cultural heritage or spoken language are different from those of most white middle-class American children are somehow institutionally unable to respond to their needs.  .   .   .

## RECOMMENDATIONS

We believe that any system designed to make schools more responsive must have four key elements:

*First,* parents and students should become directly involved in school affairs.

*Second,* the fullest possible, accurate information must be publicly available on school performance and other essential aspects of school life.

*Third,* school principals should be relieved of many of their present administrative burdens so they can be more active participants in the educational process and made more responsible for the outcomes of their schools.

*Fourth,* all teachers must become sensitive to diversity and to the backgrounds of different children and be free to innovate, experiment and develop new instructional techniques.

---

## CONSTITUTIONAL FREEDOM AND ABILITY GROUPING

---

### HOBSON v. HANSEN

United States District Court, 1967.
269 F.Supp. 401, cert. dism. 393 U.S. 801, 89 S.Ct. 40, 21 L.Ed.2d 85.

[The opinion in this case is 119 pages; only excerpted portions dealing with ability grouping are reprinted here. The entire opinion merits careful study and is recommended.)

J. SKELLY WRIGHT, Circuit Judge.   . . .

### IV. THE TRACK SYSTEM

The District of Columbia school system employs a form of ability grouping commonly known as the track system, by which students at the elementary and secondary level are placed in tracks or curriculum levels according to the school's assessment of each student's ability to learn. Plaintiffs have alleged that the track system—either by intent or by effect—unconstitutionally discriminates against the Negro and the poor. . . . . . As the evidence in this case makes painfully clear, ability grouping as presently practiced in the District of Columbia school system is a denial of equal educational opportunity to the poor and a majority of the Negroes attending school in the nation's capital, a denial that contravenes not only the guarantees of the Fifth Amendment but also the fundamental premise of the track system itself. What follows, then, is a discussion of that evidence—an examination of the track system: in theory and in reality.

B. *Track Theory.*

Basic to an understanding of the conflict between the parties in this lawsuit is an appreciation of the theory that motivates the track system as it operates in the District school system. The most comprehensive statement of that theory can be found in Dr. Hansen's book, FOUR TRACK CURRICULUM FOR TODAY'S HIGH SCHOOLS, published in 1964. Although Dr. Hansen disclaims full responsibility for creating the track system, a reading of his book leaves no doubt that it was his firm guiding hand that shaped that system in its essential characteristics. Thus, as principal architect of the track system and as Superintendent of Schools, Dr. Hansen presumably can be looked to as the authoritative spokesman on the subject.

*Purpose and philosophy.*  Dr. Hansen believes that the comprehensive high school (and the school system generally) must be systematically organized and structured to provide differing levels of education for students with widely differing levels of academic ability. This is the purpose of the track system.  In expressing the track system's philosophy Dr. Hansen has said, "Every pupil in the school system must have the maximum opportunity for self-development and this can best be brought about by adjusting curriculum offerings to different levels of need and ability as the pupil moves through the stages of education and growth in our schools."  .   .   .   And he has identified as the two objectives on which the track system is founded: "(1) The realization of the doctrine of equality of education and (2) The attainment of quality education."

*Student types.*  Within the student body Dr. Hansen sees generally four types of students: the intellectually gifted, the above-average, the average, and the retarded.  He assumes that each of these types of students has a maximum level of academic capability and, most importantly, that that level of ability can be accurately ascertained. The duty of the school is to identify these students and provide a curriculum commensurate with their respective abilities.  Dr. Hansen contends that the traditional school curriculum—including the usual two-level method of ability grouping—does a disservice to those at either end of the ability spectrum.

The gifted student is not challenged, so that he becomes bored, lazy, and perhaps performs far below his academic potential;  his intellectual talents are a wasted resource.  The remedy lies in discovering the gifted student, placing him with others of his own kind, thereby stimulating him through this select association as well as a rigorous, demanding curriculum to develop his intellectual talent.  Indeed, "the academically capable student should be required as a public necessity to take the academically challenging honors curriculum."

On the other hand, continues Dr. Hansen, the retarded or "stupid" student typically has been forced to struggle through a curriculum he cannot possibly master and only imperfectly comprehends.  Typically he is slow to learn and soon falls behind in class;  he repeatedly fails, sometimes repeating a grade again and again;  he becomes isolated, frustrated, depressed, and—if he does not drop out before graduation —graduates with a virtually useless education.  Here the remedy is seen as separating out the retarded student, directing him into a special curriculum geared to his limited abilities and designed to give him a useful "basic" education—one which makes no pretense of equalling traditionally taught curricula.

In short, Hansen views the traditional school curriculum as doing too little for some students and expecting too much of others.  As for the latter type, whom Dr. Hansen characterizes as "the blue-collar student," going to school—a "white-collar occupation"—can be an artificial experience.  .   .   .

*Tracking.*   In order to tailor the educational process to the level appropriate to each student.   Dr. Hansen adopted the track system. Each track is intended to be a separate and self-contained curriculum, with the educational content ranging from the very basic to the very advanced according to the track level.   In the elementary and junior high schools three levels are used: Basic or Special Academic (retarded students), General (average and above-average), and Honors (gifted).   In the senior high school a fourth level is added: The Regular Track, a college-preparatory track intended to accommodate the above-average student.

The significant feature of the track system in this regard is its emphasis on the ability of the student.   A student's course of instruction depends upon what the school system decides he is capable of handling.   "It took a while for everybody on the [working] committee to understand that *ability was to be the primary key to the placement in a curriculum sequence, and that this factor, not the subject-matter emphasis, was one of the unique characteristics of the four-track system.*"

*Flexibility.*   Dr. Hansen, while assuming that some students can be educated to their maximum potential in one of the four curricula, also anticipates that not all students will neatly or permanently fit into a track.   Thus a second important assumption underlying the track system is that tracking will be a flexible process.   Flexibility encompasses two things: First, although a student today may demonstrate an ability level which calls, for example, for placement in the General Track, a constant and continuing effort must be made to assure that he is at his true ability level.   This calls for instruction directed toward correcting any remedial educational problems which account for the student's present poor performance; and it calls for close analysis and counselling to determine whether these remediable deficiencies exist and when they have been sufficiently corrected. When the latter is determined, the student is to be upgraded to the next higher track.   Second, even though a student may not be in a position to make an across-the-board move from one track to another, his ability level may be such that he needs to take courses in two track levels on a subject-by-subject basis.   This process, known as cross-tracking, is critical: it is the mechanism the system relies upon to assure that students whose ability levels vary according to particular subjects are not thwarted in developing their strong areas because their weak areas result in their being placed in a lower curriculum level.   It also serves as a way of selectively raising the intensity of instruction on a subject-matter basis as a part of the process of gradually upgrading a student.

*Fundamental assumptions.* To summarize, the track system's approach is twofold. The separate curriculum levels are for some the maximum education their abilities permit them to achieve. For others, a track is supposed to be a temporary assignment during which a student's special problems are identified and remedied in whatever way possible. The express assumptions of this approach are three: *First*, a child's maximum educational potential can and will be accurately ascertained. *Second*, tracking will enhance the prospects for correcting a child's remediable educational deficiencies. *Third*, tracking must be flexible so as to provide an individually tailored education for students who cannot be pigeon-holed in a single curriculum. . . .

Having seen how the track system in practice has become a relatively rigid form of class separation, the court now turns to a discussion of the principal causes of this result. . . . Here the focus will be on the major institutional shortcomings that not only thrust the disadvantaged student into the lower tracks but tend to keep him there once placed. The first area of concern is the lack of kindergartens and Honors programs in certain schools; the second relates to remedial and compensatory programs for the disadvantaged and educationally handicapped student; and the third, and most important, involves the whole of the placement and testing process by which the school system decides who gets what kind of education. . . .

   3. *Placement and testing.*

What emerges as the most important single aspect of the track system is the process by which the school system goes about sorting students into the different tracks. This importance stems from the fact that the fundamental premise of the sorting process is the keystone of the whole track system: that school personnel can with reasonable accuracy ascertain the maximum potential of each student and fix the content and pace of his education accordingly. If this premise proves false, the theory of the track system collapses, and with it any justification for consigning the disadvantaged student to a second-best education. . . .

The court now turns to the crucial issue posed by plaintiffs' attack on defendants' use of tests: whether it is possible to ascertain with at least reasonable accuracy the maximum educational potential of certain kinds of schoolchildren. This question goes to the very foundation of the track system since . . . one of the fundamental premises of track theory is that students' potential can be determined. On this premise rests the practice of separating students into homogeneous ability groups; and most importantly, on this premise rests the sole justification for a student's being *permanently* assigned to lower track classes where the instructional pace and content have been scaled down to serve students of supposedly limited abilities. That is, according to track theory, those who remain in a lower curriculum remain *because they are achieving at their maximum level of ability*.  They are not admitted to—or are at least discouraged from seeking admission to—a higher instructional level because the school system has determined that they cannot "usefully" and "successfully" rise above their present level.  The evidence that defendants are in no position to make such judgments about the learning capacity of a majority of District schoolchildren is persuasive.  Because of the importance of testing to the process of evaluating and programming students, the evidence has focused primarily on tests.  However, necessarily bound up in the question of testing is the larger problem of the whole evaluation process—how the school goes about deciding who gets what kind of education.  Plaintiffs' attack strikes at the heart of this process.  .   .   .

*Test structure.*

(a)  *The nature of scholastic aptitude tests.*

There are essentially two types of tests used in educational evaluation, achievement tests and scholastic aptitude tests.  An *achievement* test is designed primarily to measure a student's level of attainment in a given subject, such as history, science, literature, and so on.  The test presumes the student has been instructed in the subject matter;  it seeks to find out how well he has learned that subject.  Although achievement test scores play an important role in placement decisions, their use has not been seriously questioned by plaintiffs except to the extent the test scores tend to reinforce already erroneous decisions.  Consequently, the discussion here will center on aptitude tests.

A *scholastic aptitude* test is specifically designed to predict how a student will achieve in the future in an academic curriculum.  It does this by testing certain skills which have come to be identified as having a high correlation with scholastic achievement.  Once a student's present proficiency in these skills is ascertained, an inference is drawn as to how well he can be expected to do in the future.

The skills measured by scholastic aptitude tests are verbal.  More precisely an aptitude test is essentially a test of the student's command of standard English and grammar.  The emphasis on these skills is due to the nature of the academic curriculum, which is highly verbal; without such skills a student cannot be successful.  Therefore, by measuring the student's present verbal ability the test makes it possible to estimate the student's likelihood of success in the future.

Some aptitude tests may include questions that are nonverbal in content so as to circumvent possible verbal handicaps.  Technically, nonverbal tests are nonlanguage tests of reasoning processes thought to be indicative of ability to handle academic tasks successfully. .   .   .   The usual type of question consists of geometric symbols or drawings, the student being required to perceive and analyze relationships among a group of symbols. The process is variously termed "abstract reasoning," "spatial perception," or the like. As with verbal tests, prediction is based on how well a student is able to answer non-verbal questions. . . .

Whether a test is verbal or nonverbal, the skills being measured are *not* innate or inherited traits. They are learned, acquired through experience. It used to be the prevailing theory that aptitude tests— or "intelligence" tests as they are often called, although the term is obviously misleading—do measure some stable, predetermined intellectual process that can be isolated and called intelligence. Today, modern experts in educational testing and psychology have rejected this concept as false. Indeed, the best that can be said about intelligence insofar as testing is concerned is that it is whatever the test measures. . . . In plain words, this means that aptitude tests can only test a student's present level of learning in certain skills and from that infer his capability to learn further.

Of utmost importance is the fact that, to demonstrate the ability to learn, a student must have had the opportunity to learn those skills relied upon for prediction. In other words, an aptitude test is necessarily measuring a student's background, his environment. It is a test of his cumulative experiences in his home, his community and his school. Each of these social institutions has a separate influence on his development; one may compensate for the failings of the others, or all may act in concert and reinforce each other—for good or for ill.

(b) *Causes of low test scores.*

A low aptitude test score may mean that a student is innately limited in intellectual ability. On the other hand, there may be other explanations possible that have nothing to do with native intelligence. Some of those reasons are pertinent here.

. . . one of the important factors that could account for a low test score is the student's *environment.* If a student has had little or no opportunity to acquire and develop the requisite verbal or non-verbal skills, he obviously cannot score well on the tests.

Another source of variation is the student's *emotional or psychological condition* when he takes the test. He may have a poor attitude toward the test or the testing situation, generally characterized as apathy. This may be due to lack of motivation; or it may be a defensive reaction caused by worry or fear—what has been called "test anxiety". Anxiety can also cause extremely nervous reactions. All of these behavior patterns will cause the student to perform poorly on a test, either because he panics and forgets what he knows or rushes through the test skipping questions, guessing at answers, or otherwise acting carelessly.

Some tests are constructed to take account of some behavior variations. In general, however, every test score must be interpreted by those who intend to rely on them for making decisions about the individual student. Test publishers warn that scores must be evaluated in terms of the individual so as to discover, if possible, any nonintellectual variables that could have influenced the student's test score. . . .

### Testing the Disadvantaged Child.

Having touched generally upon the technical aspects of scholastic aptitude testing, it is now possible to give attention to plaintiffs' specific arguments. At base they are focusing on an area of educational testing that has been given close attention only in recent years: the testing of the disadvantaged child. The issue plaintiffs have raised is whether standard aptitude tests are appropriate for making inferences about the innate intellectual capabilities of these children.

Although the term "disadvantaged" is by nature imprecise, a working definition adopted for purposes of discussing educational problems is commonly based on two factors: the child's socio-economic status, as measured by the family's annual income; and his cultural status, as measured by the number of years of schooling attained by his parents. Both of these factors have been identified as having a high correlation with achievement both in school and in society generally, since they tend to reflect the kinds of background more or less conducive to developing scholastic-type skills. There are also indications that racial factors may well have some separate bearing on whether a child can be considered disadvantaged. . . .

### (a) Handicaps to learning.

Disadvantaged children typically are saddled with tremendous handicaps when it comes to competing in the ethnocentric academic society of public schools. That society, mirroring American society generally, is strongly influenced by white and middle class experiences and values. While there is nothing necessarily wrong about this orientation, it does raise certain barriers for lower class and Negro children—barriers that are to be found in most aptitude tests as well.

1. *Environmental factors.* The chief handicap of the disadvantaged child where verbal tests are concerned is in his limited exposure to people having command of standard English. Communication within the lower class environment, although it may rise to a very complex and sophisticated level, typically assumes a language form alien to that tested by aptitude tests. Slang expressions predominate; diction is poor; and there may be ethnically based language forms. The language spoken by Negro children in the ghetto has been classified as a dialect. . . .

The disadvantaged child has little or no opportunity to range beyond the boundaries of his immediate neighborhood. He is unfamiliar, therefore, with concepts that will expand both his range of experiences and his vocabulary. He has less exposure to new things that he can reduce to verbal terms. For example, one defense witness, a principal of a low-income Negro elementary school, told of how most of the children had never been more than a few blocks from home; they had never been downtown, although some had been to a Sears department store; they did not know what an escalator was, had not seen a department-store Santa Claus, had not been to a zoo. These experiences, common in the subject matter of tests and textbooks, were alien to the lives of these children.

The way in which environmental factors affect the development of nonverbal skills is not quite as clear. There is evidence that such factors are less of a handicap to scoring well on a nonverbal aptitude test than they are to scoring well on a verbal test. . . . Nonetheless, the child's environment remains very much a factor in the development of nonverbal skills. Defendants' expert, Dr. Dailey, was of the opinion that a nonlanguage test of abstract reasoning tests the same intellectual process required to read a paragraph and answer questions about it. Thus the skill a child develops in the process of reducing life experiences to verbal terms is really but another aspect of the process by which a child reasons abstractly about geometric symbols in nonlanguage terms. The less a child is exposed to situations in which he has the stimulation or the opportunity to deal with complex experiences or concepts, the more retarded both his verbal and nonverbal development will be—although the retarding effect may be greater in the case of verbal skills.

2. *Psychological factors.* Although any student taking a test may be subject to psychological influences of various sorts, there is a good deal of evidence that disadvantaged children and Negro children are more likely than others to suffer from influences that have a depressing effect on test scores. The problem can generally be described as one of low self-esteem, or lack of self-confidence.

i. *Socio-economic causes.* There is evidence that disadvantaged children, black or white, are those most likely to lack self-confidence in the school situation. This is due to a complex of causes, many of them directly related to the environmental factors already discussed. The disadvantaged child is made profoundly aware of this academic shortcoming as soon as he enters school. There is a great risk of his losing confidence in his ability to compete in school with children who are "better off." A frequent manifestation of this is for the child to become a discipline problem, as he goes through the process of rejecting a situation in which he feels inadequate. All of this can have a direct and significant effect on test performance as much as on scholastic performance.

ii. *Racial causes.* Apart from factors related to socio-economic status, there is striking evidence that Negro children undergo a special kind of psychological stress that can have a debilitating effect on academic and test performance. . . . Because of their race and the ever present reminders of being "different", Negro children generally are subject to very serious problems of self-identification. By the time the Negro child is about to enter school he has become very much racially self-conscious, which causes considerable psychological turmoil as he attempts to come to terms with his status as a Negro. He tends to be imbued with a sense of worthlessness, of inferiority, of fear and despair which is transmitted to him primarily through his parents.

In this state of turmoil, many Negro children approach school with the feeling they are entering a strange and alien place that is the property of a white school system or of white society, even though the school may be all-Negro. And when the school *is* all-Negro or predominantly so, this simply reinforces the impressions implanted in the child's mind by his parents, for the school experience is then but a perpetuation of the segregation he has come to expect in life generally. Evidence of turmoil can be found in the inability of many Negro pre-schoolers and first graders to draw themselves as colored, or other than in an animal-like or caricature-like fashion. This general psychological phenomenon is not confined to the South but is common to Negroes throughout the country. . . .

When economically based deprivation is combined with the traumas suffered simply because of being Negro, the psychological impact can be crushing.

iii. *Manifestations of low self-esteem: anxiety and apathy.* When a child lacks confidence in himself or is self-degrading, he is likely to manifest this during the test-taking experience. One reaction that has been identified has been called "test anxiety." The child, apprehensive about his ability to score well and fearful about what others—especially his teacher or principal—might see in the test score, reacts in a self-defeating manner: He becomes highly nervous, even "wildly rampant"; or he withdraws. Either reaction lowers his test score. . . . Although both advantaged and disadvantaged children can experience test anxiety, in the opinion of Dr. Cline, plaintiffs' expert, the disadvantaged child—and particularly the disadvantaged Negro child—tend to be under much greater psychological stress in the testing situation and thus are more likely to show the effects in test performance. . . . Several empirical studies support Dr. Cline's conclusion. . . .

Aside from anxiety-caused withdrawal, a child may be apathetic about a test simply because he does not see it as important. Children who come from backgrounds lacking in parental and environmental support for academic achievement will be more prone to be apathetic about testing; and disadvantaged children are those most likely to have nonsupportive backgrounds. In general, the middle and upper class child is made aware of the importance and value of school and testing; this will make him take both more seriously in terms of his goals in life. The lower class child, and especially a Negro facing the fact of racial discrimination, is more likely to view school and testing as a waste of time. Those grown accustomed to lower horizons may find it hard to take seriously such things as aptitude tests.

### (3) *Empirical confirmation.*

Empirical confirmation of the disadvantaged child's handicaps on aptitude tests can be found in the remarkably high degree of correlation between test scores on standard aptitude tests and the socio-economic status of the child. The more disadvantaged the child, the lower his test score will be. . . .

Defendants, while acknowledging the handicaps of the disadvantaged child, have steadfastly maintained that the cause of low test scores is strictly a matter of socio-economic status, not race. In their view, the fact that a child is Negro is irrelevant to test performance. The evidence, however, does not support such a definitive conclusion. Dr. Lennon testified that, in constructing sampling groups, socio-economic and cultural factors seem to account for any significant variances. And Dr. Dailey testified to having conducted a multiple regression study of District test results, finding that the race of the child had no observable impact on those particular test scores. . . . Nevertheless, Dr. Dailey later admitted that he has not firmly ruled out race as a wholly irrelevant factor. . . . Thus, what both he and Dr. Lennon left open was the possibility of an overlap between socio-economic and racial factors, the former in many instances masking the effects of the latter.

Certainly, given the persuasive evidence of the psychological impact of segregation and other forms of discrimination on the Negro, defendants' evidence falls far short of successfully eliminating racial factors as influential in test performance.

### (4) *The influence of school.*

For the disadvantaged child, handicapped as he is by home and community circumstances, the school remains as the last hope for overcoming academic deficiencies. In recognition of this fact the urban schools, including the District school system, are giving more and more attention to providing compensatory education for these children, for it is the school that by definition is best suited to providing students with the opportunity to acquire and perfect the academic skills which the school itself demands. And if the school fails in this task, the disadvantaged child will remain handicapped both in class and in taking tests.

But the influence of the school is not confined to how well it can teach the disadvantaged child; it also has a significant role to play in shaping the student's emotional and psychological make-up. The formula for reaching a student who comes to school academically ill-equipped from the start, who is disposed to reject the whole educational complex because of feelings of fear, frustration and an abiding sense of futility, is still one of the unsolved problems in American education. What is clear is that the urban school treads a narrow and difficult path in trying to reach the disadvantaged child. If it missteps, the consequence can be a devastating reinforcement of the psychological handicaps that already plague these children. . . .

. . . The horrible consequence of a teacher's low expectation is that it tends to be a self-fulfilling prophecy. The unfortunate students, treated as if they were subnormal, come to accept as a fact that they *are* subnormal. They act out in their school behavior and in the testing situation what they have been conditioned to believe is their true status in life; and in conforming to expectations, they "confirm" the original judgment. A noted expert, Professor Kenneth Clark, has summed up the problem thusly:

> " * * * When a child from a deprived background is treated as if he is uneducable because he has a low test score, he becomes uneducable and the low test score is thereby reinforced. If a child scores low on an intelligence test because he cannot read and then is not taught to read because he has a low test score, then such a child is being imprisoned in an iron circle and becomes the victim of an educational self-fulfilling prophecy."

Aside from the influence of the teacher, the whole of the school experience will shape a student's behavior. If that experience is for one reason or another a negative one for the student, his performances will likewise be negative. . . .

d.  *Accuracy of test measurements.*

Plaintiffs charge that the disadvantaged child's handicaps—both environmental and psychological—are such that standard aptitude tests cannot serve as accurate measurements of innate ability to learn. In Dr. Cline's opinion these tests are worthless. The evidence that this is so is persuasive.

It will be recalled that a scholastic aptitude test is constructed to test present facility in verbal—and, sometimes, nonverbal—skills so as to make possible an inference about an individual's innate ability to succeed in school. The inference is expressed in the form of a test score which is a statement of how the individual student compares with the median score of the norming group. The median reflects an "average" ability to learn, a score above or below that average indicating superior or inferior ability. A crucial assumption in this comparative statement, however, is that the individual is fairly comparable with the norming group in terms of environmental background and psychological make-up; to the extent the individual is not comparable, the test score may reflect those differences rather than innate differences. For example, perhaps the most ideal circumstance for making an accurate estimate of innate ability from comparing test scores would be in the case of twins. If the twins were given the same test and one scored significantly higher than the other, a reasonable inference would be that the higher scoring twin had the superior innate ability; both children presumably would have had the same opportunity to learn the tested skills and both would probably have been subject to similar psychological influences.

Transferring this principle to standard aptitude tests in general, the best circumstance for making accurate estimates of ability is when the tested student is most like the typical norming student: white and middle class. Because the white middle class student predominates in the norming sample, it is possible to say the average student in that group will have had roughly the same opportunities to develop standard verbal and nonverbal skills as the rest of the group and will probably be psychologically similar as well. Thus the national median or norm is a reasonably accurate statistical statement of what the average American student ought to have learned in the way of verbal and nonverbal skills by a certain age and what can therefore be considered average intelligence or ability to learn. For this reason, standard aptitude tests are most precise and accurate in their measurements of innate ability when given to white middle class students.

When standard aptitude tests are given to low income Negro children, or disadvantaged children, however, the tests are less precise and less accurate—so much so that test scores become practically meaningless. Because of the impoverished circumstances that characterize the disadvantaged child, it is virtually impossible to tell whether the test score reflects lack of ability—or simply lack of opportunity. Moreover, the probability test scores of the Negro child or the disadvantaged child will be depressed because of somewhat unique psychological influences further compounds the risk of inaccuracy.

*Lorton study.* Striking evidence of the inaccuracy of standard tests is revealed in a study made in 1965 at the Lorton Youth Center, a penal institution set up under the Federal Youth Corrections Act and serving the District of Columbia. Inmates range in age from 18 to 26 years; 90% are dropouts from the District schools; and 95% of these are Negroes. Sixty-nine inmates enrolled in the Youth Center School pursuing a course of study leading to a high-school-equivalent diploma were examined as a follow-up to an earlier study to determine these inmates' educational progress under "ideal" educational circumstances. In the earlier study several factors had been identified as causing these inmates to underachieve in school and eventually to drop out; the second study was designed to measure achievement once those factors had been removed. . . . the major points of interest are these:

1) Two types of aptitude tests were used to measure ability, the Otis test used in District Schools, a verbal test; and the Revised Beta Examination, which is nonverbal. The IQ ranges for the two tests differed markedly. For the whole group of 69 inmates the range of IQ's obtained by using the Otis test was from 50 to 110; the average was 78, substantially below normal. Scores on the nonverbal Beta test, however, were higher, ranging from 71 to 118; the average was 98—20 points higher than the Otis average, and a level considered to indicate average intelligence.

Twenty-four of the 69 inmates scored at 75 or below on the Otis test, the IQ's ranging from 50 to 75; the average was 62. Yet on the Beta test the range was from 71 to 112, the average being 91—or 29 points higher than the Otis average.

2) Gains in achievement in reading and arithmetic over a one-year period were measured using the Stanford Achievement Tests, one of the series used in the District schools. The expected gain for a student of average intelligence, according to Stanford norms, is 1.0 (i. e., a progress equivalent to one grade level in one year).

*Reading.* The average gain for all 69 inmates was 1.3 years, increasing from an average grade level equivalent of 6.9 (ninth month of the sixth grade) to 8.2 (second month of the eight grade). For the 24 inmates in the 75 or below range (Otis), the average gain also was 1.3 years, increasing from a grade level equivalent of 3.9 to 5.2.

*Arithmetic.* The average gain for all inmates was 1.8 years, increasing from 5.6 to 7.4. For the 24 low-scoring inmates the average gain was 1.8, increasing from 4.2 to 6.0.

This study reveals in hard fact that a disadvantaged Negro student with a supposedly low IQ can, given the opportunity, far surpass what might be expected of a truly "subnormal" student. It illustrates the principle that a standard verbal aptitude test—in this case the Otis test—can be a faulty predictor of actual achievement for disadvantaged students, and confirms Dr. Clines assessment of the disabilities of such tests in making accurate inferences about innate ability.

*Local norms.* Two techniques have been cited by plaintiffs that might help give a more accurate estimation of the ability of the disadvantaged child. One of these is the development of a locally standardized test. The principle is the same as that applied to the nationally standardized test, except that the test questions are made appropriate to the students being tested and the norm is ascertained

from a group of similarly situated students—that is, those students within the local school system at the appropriate age levels. The purpose of the local norm is to produce test scores that will reflect what the child *has* had the opportunity to learn and to compare his achievement with that of others who have had comparable opportunities. Defendants have not availed themselves of this technique.
. . .

Another method of establishing a local norm is to use the standard aptitude test but to restandardize the median score according to local performances. . . .

*Empirical verification.* A second method designed to assure accuracy of measurements, strongly recommended by educational test experts and test publishers alike, is for the school system to conduct an empirical study of the predictive validity of the aptitude tests it uses. Since there is a probability of error in prediction for any school population, it is desirable to obtain evidence as to how accurate the test is for the local student body. When the student body is highly dissimilar to the standardizing group it becomes even more desirable to verify the accuracy of the test's predictions. This is done by making a follow-up study of a group of students to see how much correlation there is between actual scholastic achievement and the initial test score. The District has not made any empirical studies of this sort, even though the student body and the system itself are admittedly "unique". . . .

*Conclusion.* In light of the above evidence regarding the accuracy of aptitude test measurements, the court makes the following findings. First, there is substantial evidence that defendants presently lack the techniques and the facilities for ascertaining the innate learning abilities of a majority of District school children. Second, lacking these techniques and facilities, defendants cannot justify the placement and retention of these children in lower tracks on the supposition that they could do no better, given the opportunity to do so.

*Misjudgments and undereducation.* Plaintiffs have alleged that the harm in using standard aptitude tests is not simply a matter of technical inability to estimate innate learning capacities of disadvantaged children. They go further and say that the false images test scores can project because of this disability will lead teachers —and principals, when they are involved in making the decision about proper track placement—into misjudging the capabilities of these children. The consequence is to create a substantial risk of underestimating and thus undereducating the disadvantaged child. . . .

OPINION OF LAW

## VI.  THE TRACK SYSTEM

.   .   .   The evidence amassed by both parties with regard to
the track system has been reviewed in detail   .   .   .   the court
has already had occasion to note the critical infirmities of that system.   The sum result of those infirmities, when tested by the principles of equal protection and due process, is to deprive the poor and
a majority of the Negro students in the District of Columbia of their
constitutional right to equal educational opportunities.   .   .   .

Ability grouping is by definition a classification intended to discriminate among students, the basis of that discrimination being a
student's capacity to learn.   Different kinds of educational opportunities are thus made available to students of differing abilities.
Whatever may be said of the concept of ability grouping in general,
it has been assumed here that such grouping can be reasonably related to the purposes of public education.   .   .   .   the substance
of plaintiffs' complaint is that in practice, if not by design, the track
system—as administered in the District of Columbia public schools
—has become a system of discrimination founded on socio-economic
and racial status rather than ability, resulting in the undereducation of many District students.

As the court's findings have shown, the track system is undeniably an extreme form of ability grouping.   Students are early in
elementary school sorted into homogeneous groups or tracks (and
often into subgroups within a track) thereby being physically separated into different classrooms.   Not only is there homogeneity,
in terms of supposed levels of ability—the intended result—but as a
practical matter there is a distinct sameness in terms of socio-economic status as well.   More importantly, each track offers a substantially different kind of education, both in pace of learning and in
scope of subject matter.   At the bottom there is the slow-paced, basic
(and eventually almost purely low-skill vocational) Special Academic
Track;   at the top is the intense and challenging Honors program
for the gifted student.   For a student locked into one of the lower
tracks, physical separation from those in other tracks is of course
complete insofar as classroom relationships are concerned;   and the
limits on his academic progress, and ultimately the kind of life work
he can hope to attain after graduation, are set by the orientation of
the lower curricula.   Thus those in the lower tracks are, for the most
part, molded for various levels of vocational assignments;   those in
the upper tracks, on the other hand, are given the opportunity to
prepare for the higher ranking jobs and, most significantly, for college.

In theory, since tracking is supposed to be kept flexible, relatively few students should actually ever be locked into a single track or

curriculum. Yet, in violation of one of its principal tenets, the track system is not flexible at all. Not only are assignments permanent for 90% or more of the students but the vast majority do not even take courses outside their own curriculum. Moreover, another significant failure to implement track theory—and in major part responsible for the inflexibility just noted—is the lack of adequate remedial and compensatory education programs for the students assigned to or left in the lower tracks because of cultural handicaps. Although one of the express reasons for placing such students in these tracks is to facilitate remediation, little is being done to accomplish the task. Consequently, the lower track student, rather than obtaining an enriched educational experience, gets what is essentially a limited or watered-down curriculum.

These are, then, the significant features of the track system: separation of students into rigid curricula, which entails both physical segregation and a disparity of educational opportunity; and, for those consigned to the lower tracks, opportunities decidedly inferior to those available in the higher tracks.

A precipitating cause of the constitutional inquiry in this case is the fact that those who are being consigned to the lower tracks are the poor and the Negroes, whereas the upper tracks are the provinces of the more affluent and the whites. Defendants have not, and indeed could not have, denied that the pattern of grouping correlates remarkably with a student's status, although defendants would have it that the equation is to be stated in terms of income, not race. However, . . . to focus solely on economics is to oversimplify the matter in the District of Columbia where so many of the poor are in fact the Negroes. And even if race could be ruled out, which it cannot, defendants surely "can no more discriminate on account of poverty than on account of religion, race, or color." . . . As noted before, the law has a special concern for minority groups for whom the judicial branch of government is often the only hope for redressing their legitimate grievances; and a court will not treat lightly a showing that educational opportunities are being allocated according to a pattern that has unmistakable signs of invidious discrimination. Defendants, therefore, have a weighty burden of explaining why the poor and the Negro should be those who populate the lower ranks of the track system.

Since by definition the basis of the track system is to classify students according to their ability to learn, the only explanation defendants can legitimately give for the pattern of classification found in the District schools is that it does reflect students' abilities. If the discriminations being made are founded on anything other than that, then the whole premise of tracking collapses and with it any justification for relegating certain students to curricula designed for those of limited abilities. While government may classify persons and thereby effect disparities in treatment, those included within or excluded from the respective classes should be those for whom the inclusion or exclusion is appropriate; otherwise the classification risks becoming wholly irrational and thus unconstitutionally discriminatory. It is in this regard that the track system is fatally defective, because for many students placement is based on traits other than those on which the classification purports to be based.

The evidence shows that the method by which track assignments are made depends essentially on standardized aptitude tests which, although given on a system-wide basis, are completely inappropriate for use with a large segment of the student body. Because these tests are standardized primarily on and are relevant to a white middle class group of students, they produce inaccurate and misleading test scores when given to lower class and Negro students. As a result, rather than being classified according to ability to learn, these students are in reality being classified according to their socioeconomic or racial status, or—more precisely—according to environmental and psychological factors which have nothing to do with innate ability.

Compounding and reinforcing the inaccuracies inherent in test measurements are a host of circumstances which further obscure the true abilities of the poor and the Negro. For example, teachers acting under false assumptions because of low test scores will treat the disadvantaged student in such a way as to make him conform to their low expectations; this acting out process—the self-fulfilling prophecy —makes it appear that the false assumptions were correct, and the student's real talent is wasted. Moreover, almost cynically, many Negro students are either denied or have limited access to the very kinds of programs the track system makes a virtual necessity: kindergartens; Honors programs for the fast-developing Negro student; and remedial and compensatory education programs that will bring the disadvantaged student back into the mainstream of education. Lacking these facilities, the student continues hampered by his cultural handicaps and continues to appear to be of lower ability than he really is. Finally, the track system as an institution cannot escape blame for the error in placements, for it is tracking that places such an emphasis on defining ability, elevating its importance to the point where the whole of a student's education and future are made to turn on his facility in demonstrating his qualifications for the higher levels of opportunity. Aside from the fact that this makes the consequences of misjudgments so much the worse, it also tends to alienate the disadvantaged student who feels unequal to the task of competing in an ethnocentric school system dominated by white middle class values; and alienated students inevitably do not reveal their true abilities—either in school or on tests.

All of these circumstances, and more, destroy the rationality of the class structure that characterizes the track system. Rather than reflecting classifications according to ability, track assignments are for many students placements based on status. Being, therefore, in violation of its own premise, the track system amounts to an unlawful discrimination against those students whose educational opportunities are being limited on the erroneous assumption that they are capable of accepting no more.

## REMEDY

The remedy to be provided against the discriminatory policies of the defendants' school administration must center primarily on pupil assignment, teacher assignment and the track system. . . .

    .   .   .   with respect to the track system, the track system simply must be abolished. . . .

Even in concept the track system is undemocratic and discriminatory. Its creator admits it is designed to prepare some children for white-collar, and other children for blue-collar, jobs. Considering the tests used to determine which children should receive the blue-collar special, and which the white, the danger of children completing their education wearing the wrong collar is far too great for this democracy to tolerate. Moreover, any system of ability grouping which, through failure to include and implement the concept of compensatory education for the disadvantaged child or otherwise, fails in fact to bring the great majority of children into the mainstream of public education denies the children excluded equal educational opportunity and thus encounters the constitutional bar. . . .

## NOTES AND QUESTIONS

1.  Did the court say that ability group tracking was unconstitutional per se, in all circumstances, or that it was unconstitutional only within the circumstances of this case? If only within this case, identify the critical circumstances. How would it have to be changed so as to make ability group tracking constitutional in Washington, D. C.? Why did the court hold that "the track system simply must be abolished"?

2.  Did the court hold that ability group tracking is unconstitutional in Washington, D. C., because it denied equal educational opportunity irrespective of race, or because it was the functional equivalent of racial segregation enforced by public officials under law? What difference does the reason make? Did Washington, D. C., operate a dual school system before Brown I and II? If so, does this opinion merely extend Bolling v. Sharpe to ability group tracking?

3.  Are the vices of segregation and ability group tracking as set forth by Judge J. Skelly Wright found equally in schools where de facto segregation exists? If so, would his opinion apply equally to de facto situations? Why or why not? Should your answer be yes, is it based on the view that the reasoning in this case is ultimately grounded on an unconstitutional denial of equal educational opportunity irre-

spective of race?  How can equal educational opportunity be made available to all children?  What about the "gifted" child?  Shouldn't he have an honors program?

4.  Can you accurately measure and predict a student's "maximum educational potential" one month into the future?  Six months?  One year? Three years?  Five years?  How?  Do you agree with the court's reasoning on this point?  If not, how can you accurately identify the retarded child, the gifted child, the superior child or the ordinary child?

5.  In the Keyes case, supra, the court required proof that the racial imbalance "was caused by intentional state action," did the court require the same proof in Hobson v. Hansen?  If not, why not?  Do you agree?

6.  Is Hobson v. Hansen an "equal protection" or "due process" case, or both?  Why?  What concept of equal educational opportunity does the decision rest on?

7.  On appeal, the decision in Hobson v. Hansen was affirmed sub nom. in Smuck v. Hobsen, 408 F.2d 175 (D.C.Cir. 1969).  On tracking the appellate court said: "The simple decree enjoining the 'track system' does not interpose any realistic barrier to flexible school administration by a school board genuinely committed to attainment of more quality and equality of educational opportunity."  If you had been a member of the reviewing court, how would you have voted?  Why? State the way(s) in which it would be possible to attain "more quality and equality of educational oportunity."  See, Symposium, Equal Educational Opportunity, 61 Geo.L.J. 845 (1973).

8.  It has been said that the superior student wastes half his time in the typical American school; that the gifted child wastes it all, and that the upper five to ten percent of America's school-age children are the most underprivileged group.  For example at page 19 of The Gifted Child in the Regular Classroom (1953) Marian Scheifele states that "it is a shocking fact that many gifted children, in terms of [potential] achievement, are the most serious retarded pupils in our schools today."  Moreover, there is reason to believe that the characteristics denoted as "giftedness" are equally distributed in children throughout the "racial" and socio-economic spectra.  Thus, the minority or lower income class student who is "gifted" may be doubly at a disadvantage. The problem for our schools today is simply that of making available to ALL young people the sort of educational opportunity which an accurate appraisal of their capacities require, and boards of education (and teachers too) should see to it that universal education translates as honest educational opportunities commensurate with a child's genuine talent and potential.  Assuming that this goal is valid and desirable, how can it be achieved while also achieving desegregation and the elimination of unconstitutional tracking systems?

9.  Aptitude, scholastic achievement, and psychological testing are recognized tools for the correct placement of pupils to obtain maximum educational benefits.  See Green v. School Bd. of City of Roanoke, Virginia, 304 F.2d 118 (5th Cir. 1962), and Murray v. West Baton Rouge Parish School Bd., 472 F.2d 438 (5th Cir. 1973).  Does a spe-

cial problem arise if their use immediately follows the termination of a dual school system? See, McNeal v. Tate County School Dist., 508 F.2d 1017, 1020 (5th Cir. 1975). In this situation must a school system abolish these types of testing procedures altogether? What can be done if a remedial program maintains segregated classrooms? See, George v. O'Kelly, 448 F.2d 148, 150 (5th Cir. 1971).

10. In Hart v. Community School Bd. of Brooklyn, N.Y. School Dist. No. 21, 383 F.Supp. 699 (E.D.N.Y.1974), the court held that "[t]racking . . . must be reduced to the minimum required for sound education" and that "students may be selected by objective, racially and ethnically neutral criteria such as reading scores." Would Hobson hold that reading scores are "racially neutral"? Why or why not? See, Kirp, Schools As Sorters, 121 U. of Pa. L.Rev. 705 (1973).

In Board of Educ. v. Department of HEW, 396 F.Supp. 203 (S.D.Ohio 1975), the court referred to Hobson and stated that where racial imbalance is shown in the classroom, and the primary factor in assignment of students to classes is a testing procedure, "the burden shifts to the school authorities to demonstrate some 'substantial congruence' between the testing process and the purpose for which the assignments are allegedly used." How would school authorities be able to meet this burden? Would the recognized validity of standard tests be sufficient? What is a "locally standardized test" as referred to in Hobson? Would refusal to use such a test necessarily betray segregative intent?

11. In P. v. Riles, 343 F.Supp. 1306 (N.D.Cal.1972), affirmed 502 F.2d 963 (9th Cir. 1974), black, San Francisco elementary school children brought a lawsuit to enjoin their being placed in classes for the Educable Mentally Retarded (EMR) because, inter alia, they scored below 75 on the school district's I.Q. tests. Blacks constituted 28.5% of all the students, but 66% of the EMR students. The defendant school district did "not seem to dispute the evidence amassed by plaintiffs to demonstrate that the I.Q. tests in fact are culturally biased. Indeed, defendants have stated that they are merely awaiting the development of what they expect will be a minimally biased test. This test currently is being standardized; but the final product is not expected to be available for more than a year." Noting that alternatives to the I.Q. tests were available, the court ruled in favor of the black school children, "conclud[ing] that defendants have not sustained their burden of demonstrating that I.Q. tests are rationally related to the purpose of segregating students according to their ability to learn in regular classes, at least insofar as those tests are applied to black students."

Query: From a socio-economic class or culturally-biased point of view, are I.Q. tests more or less objectionable than teacher evaluations of minority children?

## HOFFMAN v. BOARD OF EDUC.

New York Supreme Court, 2d Dept., 1978.
64 A.D.2d 369, 410 N.Y.S.2d 99.

SHAPIRO, Justice. . . .

Shortly after starting kindergarten in September, 1956, plaintiff was placed in a class for Children with Retarded Mental Development (CRMD) based upon a determination by defendant's certified psychologist that the child had an intelligent quotient (I.Q.) of 74. *Seventy-five was the cut-off point fixed by the defendant, so that if plaintiff had been given a rating of 75 he would not have been found to be retarded and would not have been sent to a class for mentally retarded children. He remained in classes for the retarded for 11 years,* until he was 17 years of age. At that age he was transferred to the Occupational Training Center for the retarded. He remained there for one year; at the start of the second year, in September, 1969, he was advised that he would not be continued there because an I.Q. test administered in May, 1969 showed that he was not retarded.

. . . on May 12, 1969, . . . plaintiff was administered an I.Q. test by Dr. William F. Garber of the Bureau of Child Guidance. At that time, plaintiff was one month past his 18th birthday and he was approaching the end of his first year at the Queens Occupational Training Center. Dr. Garber's report explains the reasons for administering that I.Q. test as follows:

> "Danny is being re-evaluated as to intellectual status, following an interview with his mother, who came to the school very much disturbed because her son has been rejected by Social Security for continuance of payments after the age of 18, the S.S.A. feeling he was not sufficiently handicapped by his retarded status to pursue gainful employment. On January 9, 1957, the Bureau of Child Guidance found a Binet I.Q. of 74."

> Plaintiff was administered a Wechsler Intelligence Scale for Adults (W.A.I.S.) test. He scored a verbal I.Q. of 85 and a performance I.Q. of 107 resulting in a full scale I.Q. of 94.

The report of the test includes the following:

> "He is a tall, well-built boy, alert looking and charming in manner, who is so incapacitated by a speech defect that communication is difficult for him. He relates very well, displays humor, and appears reality oriented.

> *"On the W.A.I.S, he obtained a Verbal Scale I.Q. 85, Performance I.Q. 107, Full Scale I.Q. 94. This places him in the normal range.* However, his superior performance on tests of non-verbal intelligence, as well as the fact that his

extremely poor academic background, severely depreciated his scores on some verbal tests, make it very likely that *his intellectual potential is at least Bright Normal.*

*"Projective tests and tracings of geometric designs confirm the impression of good intelligence and contraindicate organicity.* He is however extremely compulsive, to a degree that sometimes reality testing suffers in his distribution of time for a task.

*"This boy has above average intellectual potential* and a good personality structure. Due to his being almost immobilized in the speech area as well as considering his extremely defective academic background he would find it difficult, if not impossible, to function in a regular high school. Psychomotor coordination is good, however. Referral to [Division of Vocational Rehabilitation of the State Education Department] is suggested for specialized training and alleviation of the speech problem." (Emphasis supplied.) . . .

Plaintiff had no additional schooling up to the time of the trial. In August, 1970, when he was 19 years old, he was interviewed by the State Division of Vocational Rehabilitation. Its records show that he was "outgoing, cheerful and desirous of the company of his peers. He misses the Queens Training Center. However, medical examination indicates that . . . [his] primary need is for speech training, since he is barely understandable. In addition to his handicap, his mother seems to have developed a deep need and a habit of doing all of . . . [his] communication for him; they have a warm relationship."

The Division of Vocational Rehabilitation provided a speech therapy program for him in the National Hospital for Speech Disorders. He was provided 40 weekly sessions of therapy and he showed slow improvement. In July, 1972, when he was 21 years old, he was referred by his rehabilitation counselor to Dr. Bernard Stillerman, who noted that plaintiff was "very dependent on his mother who not only made the appointment for him but his verbal contact, for the most part, with the world. . . . He described himself as being mildly anxious, nervous and tense when he is with people and I assume this was related to his . . . speech. He is also moderately depressed because of the speech problem which precludes him from having friends. In fact, he is preoccupied with the thought that he can make friends but cannot keep them because of his speech."

Dr. Kaplan testified that when he saw plaintiff in 1975 (apparently in preparation for the trial) he had progressed in improving his speech, although he continued to have "persistent language problems, chiefly with some stammering and articulatory difficulties".

Plaintiff was trained by the Division of Vocational Rehabilitation to be a messenger and it obtained his first job for him. Thereafter he had 11 different messenger jobs. At the time of the trial he had a part-time job as a messenger, earning $50 per week for 20 hours of work. He testified that he did not like this work. A record of the division, dated June 20, 1973 (when plaintiff was 22 years old) states:

> "Recent Psychological testing indicates that the client is capable of performance at a much higher level than was previously determined. The test material indicates that [the] client is capable of training in a skilled mechanical area. His motivation for doing better is extremely high. . . . He is unable at this time to relate to a specific vocational goal, and it is felt that a period of further evaluation would be appropriate prior to any lengthy training program."

At the age of 26 (as of the date of the trial) he had not made any advancement in his vocational life, nor any particular improvement in his social life.

*AS TO DEFENDANT'S FAILURE TO FOLLOW THE RECOMMENDATION OF DR. GOTTSEGEN THAT PLAINTIFF'S "INTELLIGENCE SHOULD BE RE-EVALUATED WITHIN A TWO YEAR PERIOD SO THAT A MORE ACCURATE ESTIMATION OF HIS ABILITIES CAN BE MADE".*

Defendant's principal argument for reversal is that Dr. Gottsegen's report of January 23, 1957 did *not* recommend that plaintiff be given another I.Q. test within two years, and that his testimony that it did was incredible *as a matter of law* and therefore could not act as a basis for the jury's verdict in favor of the plaintiff. Dr. Gottsegen testified that "we wanted him *retested* within two years" and that it was his "feeling there was retardation" but that he "doubted some of the results and *therefore I suggested a retesting*" (emphasis supplied). He also testified that he had followed the procedure of the Bureau of Child Guidance and "if we had doubts about what we were doing, that we recommend that he be *retested* and say it, and that's what happened here." *At no time was he cross-examined as to the propriety of his conclusion that that was what he had recommended.* Defendant argues . . . that Dr. Gottsegen's testimony cannot be given factual acceptance because, in his report, he used the words "should be *re-evaluated*" and not "should be *retested*". However, in so arguing, defendant entirely omits to note that the direction was that his "intelligence should be re-evaluated".

It is defendant's position that the words "retest" and "re-evaluate" are words of art with different meanings. "Retest", argues defendant, means to administer a further I.Q. test, while "re-evaluate" means observation of the child and noting his achievements as a basis for determining whether a new I.Q. test should be administered.

Defendant maintains that the continuous observation of plaintiff by his succeeding teachers, each of whom noted the scores on the semi-annual achievement tests, amounted to "a *constant* re-evaluation, with Dr. Gottsegen's report not overriding their own observations." Defendant asserts that the record amply supported their judgments and, further, that if there was a difference of opinion as to this it was no more than an error of professional judgment not severe enough to constitute negligence.

Defendant's analysis flies in the face of the testimony of the expert witnesses on both sides to the effect that intelligence of children is determined in schools (and elsewhere) *only* by I.Q. testing, and that achievement tests and classroom evaluations do not determine the intelligence of a child. Since Dr. Gottsegen's written recommendation was that plaintiff's "*intelligence* should be re-evaluated within a two year period", it could only mean that he was to be administered a new I.Q. test within that period. If it did not have that meaning, it meant nothing, since a CRMD child is always being observed by his teacher for signs of improvement, and achievement tests were being given semi-annually to *all* CRMD children. Actually, it would mean less than nothing for it would (absurdly) mean that (a) instead of the teachers observing him daily, they should do so only once in two years, and (b) instead of giving the required achievement tests twice a year, plaintiff (alone among all CRMDs) should be given such a test only once during the ensuing two years. Yet defendant argues, in effect, that such was the correct interpretation and that it is *incredible* to maintain otherwise.

. . .

On the facts in this record, we need not reach the question of whether plaintiff's teachers, on their own, should have recommended I.Q. testing or whether plaintiff's mother was remiss in not requesting it (or, and more to the point, whether defendant was remiss in not advising plaintiff's mother that she had the right to make such a request, in which case it would be granted) since it is not necessary to go any further than to note that the school psychologist's recommendation was totally ignored. Only the test result showing an I.Q. of 74 (and apparently the erroneous references to "Mongolian tendencies" and "Mongoloid features") was acted upon; the rest might as well have been written in sand. The consequences of defendant's failure to follow its own psychologist's recommendation were predictable. So little had to be done to avoid the awesome and devastating effect of that failure on plaintiff's life, and that little was not done.

. . .

Defendant's affirmative act in placing plaintiff in a CRMD class initially (when it should have known that a mistake could have devastating consequences) created a relationship between itself and plaintiff out of which arose a duty to take reasonable steps to ascertain whether (at least, in a borderline case) that placement was proper. We need not here decide whether such duty would have required "intelligence" retesting (in view of plaintiff's poor showing on achievement tests) had not the direction for such retesting been placed in the very document which asserted that plaintiff was to be placed in a CRMD class. It ill-becomes the Board of Education to argue for the untouchability of its own policy and procedures when the gist of plaintiff's complaint is that the entity which did not follow them was the board itself.

. . . Had plaintiff been improperly diagnosed or treated by medical or psychological personnel in a municipal hospital, the municipality would be liable for the ensuing injuries. There is no reason for any different rule here because the personnel were employed by a government entity other than a hospital. Negligence is negligence, even if defendant . . . prefer semantically to call it educational malpractice. Thus, defendant's rhetoric constructs a chamber of horrors by asserting that affirmance in this case would create a new theory of liability known as "educational malpractice" and that before doing so we must consider public policy and the effects of opening a vast new field which will further impoverish financially hard pressed municipalities. Defendant, in effect, suggests that to avoid such horrors, educational entities must be insulated from the legal responsibilities and obligations common to all other governmental entities no matter how seriously a particular student may have been injured and, ironically, even though such injuries were caused by their own affirmative acts in failing to follow their own rules.

I see no reason for such a trade-off, on alleged policy grounds, which would warrant a denial of fair dealing to one who is injured by exempting a governmental agency from its responsibility for its *affirmative* torts. Such a determination would simply amount to the imposition of private value judgments over the legitimate interests and legal rights of those tortiously injured. That does not mean that the parents of the Johnnies who cannot read may flock to the courts and automatically obtain redress. Nor does it mean that the parents of all the Janies whose delicate egos were upset because they did not get the gold stars they deserved will obtain redress. If the door to "educational torts" for nonfeasance is to be opened, it will not be by this case which involves *misfeasance* in failing to follow the individualized and specific prescription of defendant's own certified psychologist, whose very decision it was in the first place, to place plaintiff in a class for retarded children, or in the initial making by him of an ambiguous report, if that be the fact.

. . . "the thrust of the plaintiff's case is not so much a failure to take steps to detect and correct a weakness in a student, that is, a failure to provide a positive program for a student, but rather, affirmative acts of negligence which imposed additional and crippling burdens upon a student" . . ..

Judgment of the Supreme Court, Queens County entered November 3, 1976, reversed, on the law, and new trial granted with respect to the issue of damages only, with costs to abide the event, unless, within 20 days after entry of the order to be made hereon, plaintiff shall serve and file in the office of the clerk of the trial court, a written stipulation consenting to reduce the verdict in his favor to $500,000, and to the entry of an amended judgment accordingly, in which event the judgment, as so reduced and amended, is affirmed, without costs or disbursements.

COHALAN and O'CONNOR, JJ., concur.

MARTUSCELLO, J. P., and DAMIANI, J., dissent and vote to reverse the judgment and dismiss the complaint, with separate opinions.

————

## CONSTITUTIONAL FREEDOM AND LANGUAGE MINORITIES

————

### TOWARD EQUAL EDUCATIONAL OPPORTUNITY

United States Senate Select Comm. on Equal Educational Opportunity,
Report, 92nd Cong., 2nd Sess. Dec. 31, 1972.
Excerpts from Pp. 45–47, 49.

.　　.　　.　　The American child whose first language is other than English suffers a double disadvantage. Like the black child and poor white child he is probably isolated in a rural slum or urban ghetto community where he was born and lives and goes to school. If he is poor, he probably attends a school with other poor children of the same racial or ethnic background. And often it is an older school with less qualified teachers and fewer resources.

But when he arrives at school he faces a special disadvantage, for his language and culture are different and they are often neither valued nor understood by those who teach him and run his school. Often his language is considered alien, his culture unimportant, and his manner unusual. He is probably told he must learn in English, a language which may be alien to him or at least is seldom spoken at home. He enters a new world where the values his parents taught him are now often rejected, tacitly if not explicitly. He may be asked to change into something different. He is sometimes even forbidden to speak his native language in school.

Unable to conform to his new world, the language-minority child is often labeled and stamped as inferior. He is tested. But the test he takes was probably designed for middle-class English-speaking "Anglo" children. If he fails or does poorly, he is then often tracked into a class with slow learners. He may then see himself as inferior.

He soon learns that his heritage is not regarded by others as important, for there is little in his curriculum or his textbooks about his heroes or the history of his people. His world at home is simply excluded from this world at school.

This is the plight of hundreds of thousands of language-minority children—children whose heritage in Spanish, Mexican, Puerto Rican, Portuguese, Chinese, Japanese, Filipino, Korean, American Indian or whose forebears may be from any of a large number of other foreign lands.

Unfortunately, all too often fluency in a foreign language is looked upon by public school systems as a handicap for the child who is deficient in his ability to communicate in English. While detailed surveys have not been undertaken for language-minority groups, the U. S. Census Bureau estimates that of the 9.2 million Spanish-surnamed Americans in the United States, only half usually speak English at home. In a survey conducted by the U. S. Civil Rights Commission in 1969 it was estimated that nearly half the Mexican-American first graders in Arizona, California, Colorado, New Mexico and Texas are deficient in English when they arrive at school.

Even greater proportions of American Indian children are deficient in English. In its report, "Indian Education: A National Tragedy—A National Challenge," the Special Subcommittee on Indian Education concluded that more than half our Indian youths between the ages of 6 and 18 use their native language at home and that two-thirds of Indian children entering BIA schools have little or no skill in English.

The language-minority child not only arrives at school with this handicap, he is immediately subjected to practices and policies and sometimes even legal prohibitions which attempt to keep him from communicating in his native language. In fact, until recently, many States had legal prohibitions forbidding teaching in public schools in any language other than English.

But even in the absence of official State laws prohibiting foreign languages in schools there are still school districts which prohibit or discourage the speaking of foreign languages.

These rules are enforced, often rigidly, through various forms of punishment: Detention after school hours, the payment of a few pennies in fines for each word of Spanish spoken, suspension from school, and even, sometimes, corporal punishment.

The rejection of the minority child's language is also accompanied by the exclusion of his culture from the school curriculum. Most schools offer neither Spanish-surnamed, Indian, Oriental or other foreign language children an opportunity to learn about their heritage or folklore. Their textbooks either ignore the history of their people or present a distorted picture based on false stereotypes.

Witnesses before this and other committees described history texts with degrading characterizations of Hispanic, Oriental and American Indian peoples.  They also described school censorship practices which deprive language-minority children of the opportunity for exposure to the conditions of their people in America today.

These are among the unequal practices to which the language-minority child is subjected in school.  But they are perhaps only the symptoms of a more fundamental cause of educational inequality for the language-minority child—exclusion from the process by which decisions are made about the education of minority-group and disadvantaged children.  For the language minorities and for other disadvantaged groups most public school systems are a closed society. All too often educational decisions are made about disadvantaged children without consultation with or explanation to those who are affected and in some school districts school officials are openly hostile to language-minority groups.

It is clear from all the testimony we have heard—from the educators, students and other observers from both minority and non-minority groups that unless ways can be found to involve minority groups in their own education and in their own schools, for them public education will remain unequal and their lives will remain a series of lost opportunities.  .  .  .

*Bilingual Educational Personnel*—The effectiveness of any bilingual education effort depends largely on the availability of teachers, principals, counselors and other educational personnel who are capable of meeting the needs of language-minority children.  Only if educators are sensitive to the needs of these children, understand and respect the language they speak and the culture and heritage of which they are proud will education be a successful experience for minority-group children whose first language is not English.

There is presently a totally inadequate supply of trained teachers and other school personnel who are either themselves members of language-minority groups or who are adequately trained to meet the need for bilingual education.

There are a number of reasons for this lack of adequate personnel for bilingual education.

*First*, the recruitment and training of bilingual teachers and administrative personnel has been largely neglected by our public school systems and by teacher education institutions.

*Second*, there has been neither an adequate commitment nor sufficient resources for the recruiting and training of bilingual teacher aides and paraprofessionals from minority groups.

*Third*, State legal requirements which are designed to set minimum standards for the employment of educational personnel often operate to discriminate against language-minority educators.

We recommend that teacher training institutions in this country, particularly those in regions of the Nation containing substantial numbers of language-minority citizens, include in their curricula programs designed to acquaint prospective teachers with the culture and heritage of language-minority children. We recommend that teachers be encouraged to concentrate in this vital field and that a major effort be undertaken by teacher training institutions to recruit members of language-minority groups.

---

## LAU v. NICHOLS

Supreme Court of the United States, 1974.
414 U.S. 563, 94 S.Ct. 786, 39 L.Ed.2d 1.

Mr. Justice DOUGLAS delivered the opinion of the Court.

The San Francisco California school system was integrated in 1971 as a result of a federal court decree, 339 F.Supp. 1315. See Lee v. Johnson, 404 U.S. 1215. The District Court found that there are 2,856 students of Chinese ancestry in the school system who do not speak English. Of those who have that language deficiency, about 1,000 are given supplemental courses in the English language. About 1,800 however do not receive that instruction.

This class suit brought by non-English speaking Chinese students against officials responsible for the operation of the San Francisco Unified School District seeks relief against the unequal educational opportunities which are alleged to violate the Fourteenth Amendment. No specific remedy is urged upon us. Teaching English to the students of Chinese ancestry who do not speak the language is one choice. Giving instructions to this group in Chinese is another. There may be others. Petitioner asks only that the Board of Education be directed to apply its expertise to the problem and rectify the situation.

The District Court denied relief. The Court of Appeals affirmed, holding that there was no violation of the Equal Protection Clause of the Fourteenth Amendment nor of § 601 of the Civil Rights Act of 1964, which excludes from participation in federal financial assistance, recipients of aid which discriminate against racial groups, 483 F.2d 791. One judge dissented. A hearing *en banc* was denied, two judges dissenting.

We granted the petition for certiorari because of the public importance of the question presented . . . .

The Court of Appeals reasoned that "every student brings to the starting line of his educational career different advantages and disadvantages caused in part by social, economic and cultural background, created and continued completely apart from any contribution by the school system,". . . . Yet in our view the case may not be so easily decided. . . . § 571 of the California Education Code states that "English shall be the basic language of instruction in all schools." That section permits a school district to determine "when and under what circumstances instruction may be given bilingually." That section also states as "the policy of the state" to insure "the mastery of English by all pupils in the schools." And bilingual instruction is authorized "to the extent that it does not interfere with the systematic, sequential, and regular instruction of all pupils in the English language."

Moreover § 8573 of the Education Code provides that no pupil shall receive a diploma of graduation from grade 12 who has not met the standards of proficiency in "English," as well as other prescribed subjects. Moreover by § 12101 of the Education Code children between the ages of six and 16 years are (with exceptions not material here) "subject to compulsory full-time education."

Under these state-imposed standards there is no equality of treatment merely by providing students with the same facilities, text books, teachers, and curriculum; for students who do not understand English are effectively foreclosed from any meaningful education.

Basic English skills are at the very core of what these public schools teach. Imposition of a requirement that, before a child can effectively participate in the educational program, he must already have acquired those basic skills is to make a mockery of public education. We know that those who do not understand English are certain to find their classroom experiences wholly incomprehensible and in no way meaningful.

We do not reach the Equal Protection Clause argument which has been advanced but rely solely on § 601 of the Civil Rights Act of 1964, 42 U.S.C.A. § 2000(d) to reverse the Court of Appeals.

That section bans discrimination based "on the ground of race, color, or national origin," in "any program or activity receiving federal financial assistance." The school district involved in this litigation receives large amounts of federal financial assistance. HEW, which has authority to promulgate regulations prohibiting discrimination in federally assisted school systems, 42 U.S.C.A. § 2000(d), in 1968 issued one guideline that "school systems are responsible for assuring that students of a particular race, color, or national origin are not denied the opportunity to obtain the education generally obtained by other students in the system." 33 CFR § 4955. In 1970 HEW made the guidelines more specific, requiring school districts that were federally funded "to rectify the language deficiency in order to open" the instruction to students who had "linguistic deficiencies."   35 Fed. Reg. 11595.

By § 602 of the Act HEW is authorized to issue rules, regulations, and orders to make sure that recipients of federal aid under its jurisdiction conduct any federal financed projects consistently with § 601. HEW's regulations specify, 45 CFR § 80.3(b)(1), that the recipients may not:

> "Provide any service, financial aid, or other benefit to an individual which is different, or is provided in a different manner, from that provided to others under the program;

.        .        .        .        .

> "Restrict an individual in any way in the enjoyment of any advantage or privilege enjoyed by others receiving any service, financial aid, or other benefit under the program";

Discrimination among students on account of race or national origin that is prohibited includes "discrimination in the availability or use of any academic   .   .   .   or other facilities of the grantee or other recipient."

Discrimination is barred which has that *effect* even though no purposeful design is present: a recipient "may not   .   .   .   utilize criteria or methods of administration which have the effect of subjecting individuals to discrimination" or has "the effect of defeating or substantially impairing accomplishment of the objectives of the program as respect individuals of a particular race, color, or national origin."

It seems obvious that the Chinese-speaking minority receives less benefits than the English-speaking majority from respondents' school system which denies them a meaningful opportunity to participate in the educational program—all earmarks of the discrimination banned by the Regulations.   In 1970 HEW issued clarifying guidelines (35 Fed.Reg. 11595) which include the following:

"Where inability to speak and understand the English language excludes national origin-minority group children from effective participation in the educational program offered by a school district, the district must take affirmative steps to rectify the language deficiency in order to open its instructional program to these students."

"Any ability grouping or tracking system employed by the school system to deal with the special language skill needs of national origin-minority group children must be designed to meet such language skill needs as soon as possible and must not operate as an educational deadend or permanent track."

Respondent school district contractually agreed to "comply with title VI of the Civil Rights Act of 1964   .   .   .   and all requirements imposed by or pursuant to.the Regulations" of HEW (45 CFR Pt. 80) which are "issued pursuant to that title . . ." and also immediately to "take any measures necessary to effectuate this agreement." The Federal Government has power to fix the terms on which its money allotments to the States shall be disbursed. . . . Whatever may be the limits of that power . . . they have not been reached here. Senator Humphrey, during the floor debates on the Civil Rights Act of 1964, said:

"Simple justice requires that public funds, to which all taxpayers of all races contribute, not be spent in any fashion which encourages, entrenches, subsidizes, or results in racial discrimination."

We accordingly reverse the judgment of the Court of Appeals and remand the case for the fashioning of appropriate relief.

Reversed.

Mr. Justice WHITE concurs in the result.

Mr. Justice STEWART, with whom The Chief Justice and Mr. Justice BLACKMUN join, concurring in the result. . . .

The critical question is, . . . whether the regulations and guidelines promulgated by HEW go beyond the authority of § 601. Last Term, in Mourning v. Family Publications Service, Inc., 411 U.S. 356, 369, we held that the validity of a regulation promulgated under a general authorization provision such as § 602 of Tit. VI "will be sustained so long as it is 'reasonably related to the purposes of the enabling legislation.'" I think the guidelines here fairly meet that test. The Department has reasonably and consistently interpreted § 601 to require affirmative remedial efforts to give special attention to linguistically deprived children.

For these reasons I concur in the judgment of the Court.

Mr. Justice BLACKMUN, with whom The Chief Justice joins, concurring in the result. . . .

I merely wish to make plain that when, in another case, we are concerned with a very few youngsters, or with just a single child who speaks only German or Polish or Spanish or any language other than English, I would not regard today's decision, or the separate concurrence, as conclusive upon the issue whether the statute and the guideline require the funded school district to provide special instruction. For me, numbers are at the heart of this case and my concurrence is to be understood accordingly.

## NOTES AND QUESTIONS

1. Usually the term "bilingual" refers to a person who is competent in two languages, and, as such, being bilingual is readily approved throughout the world. In the United States, however, "bilingualism" carries another meaning as well, one that is linked to "educationally deprived,"

"disadvantaged," or "culturally deprived," and can refer to children whose first language is not English which is the essential language for effective social, economic and political intercourse in this country. "Bilingual education," the U. S. Office of Education has said, "is instruction in two languages and the use of those two languages as mediums of instruction for any part of or all of the school curriculum. Study of the history and culture associated with a student's mother tongue is considered an integral part of bilingual education." U. S. Office of Ed., Draft Guidelines To The Bilingual Education Program, in T. Anderson & M. Boyer, Bilingual Schooling In The United States, App.B. (1970). This definition includes biculturalism as well as bilingualism. The federal Bilingual Education Act, 20 U.S.C.A. § 880b (P.L. 90–247, Title VII, § 701, as amended by Educ.Amends. of 1974, P.L. 93–380, Title I, § 105) has been heavily funded; for example, in fiscal year 1973, $35,000,000 in Title VII funds were available; in F.Y. 1974, $60,000,000 was appropriated, and $85,000,000 in F.Y. 1975.

One author has identified three major groups of language minorities in the United States. First, there are the indigenous minorities such as Eskimos, Aleuts, native Hawaiians, American Samoans and American Indians, which at about one million, is probably the largest of this group. Second, there are localized or regionalized pockets of non-indigenous ethnic populations that either have been assimilated or rapidly are being assimilated, such as Italians, Greeks, Japanese, Poles and Germans. Finally, there is the category of non-indigenous groups having large populations which differ from the second group only in their lack of assimilation, particularly the 20-plus million "Spanish-surnamed" group. See, Foster, Bilingual Education: An Educational and Legal Survey, 5 J. of Law & Ed. 149 (1976).

Two distinctly different, and perhaps conflicting, purposes seem to dominate bilingual educational programs in the United States: (1) achieving the purpose of assimilating the minority into the dominant culture, and (2) achieving the purpose of establishing and maintaining a minority's culture, thereby promoting a culturally pluralistic society. This second purpose requires "bicultural" as well as bilingual education. Assimilation as a goal follows from the necessity of ameliorating or solving social and economic problems, such as problems caused by friction and hostility between ethnic and non-ethnic groups. Assimilation has been the path of Italians, French, Irish, Swiss, Greeks, Germans, Poles and other ethnic groups. Pluralism is opposed, at least in part, to assimilation and stresses societal diversity and the need of specific peoples to live out their own specific identity, culture and language.

Questions: Granting the general validity of the second goal, should cultural pluralism be achieved through the use of public tax funds? What ethnic populations currently qualify as target groups for the second goal? Which minority-group culture should be maintained and which allowed to die? Why should this second purpose be a governmentally financed goal in light of the fact that Greeks, Japanese, Italians, Poles and other immigrants have all significantly maintained their cultural identities in the United States without governmentally financed bilingual-bicultural educational programs? Why can't other groups do likewise? Is officially-promoted "biculturalism" dangerous to the nation? Doesn't Canada's situation with Quebec tragically demonstrate the awesome power of bilingualism (not to mention biculturalism) to create and perpetuate differences within a country, deepen antagonisms and make national politics an almost endless walk on an ethnic tightrope? Why should there be any accommodation to non-English speakers; that is, why shouldn't all children be treated like the immigrant children of the late Nineteenth and early Twentieth Centuries, who, simply, were placed in schools taught in English and left to sink or swim? Considering our history, is it clear that the "sink or swim" method is not effective? Does Justice Blackmun approve this method in Lau for small numbers of ethnic children? The "sink or swim" method may impair the ethnic minority's culture but does an ethnic minority have a constitutional right to have its culture maintained at the expense of taxpayers of other cultural groups? Carefully evaluate the differing goals and methods of various bilingual programs.

Foster, supra, identifies four basic models of bilingualism: (1) Assimilation with Mixed Classes. This is the traditional model whereby ethnic children are integrated into a school's regular classes; ethnic differences are ignored, and "bilingualism" consists in use of the child's first language to the extent necessary to work an effective transition into the English language and culture; i. e., assimilation; (2) Assimilation with Separate Classes. This model is found in school districts confronted with the need of absorbing large numbers of ethnic children; hence, separate classes are created for them in which subject-matter instruction in their native language takes place as well as instruction in English-as-a-second-language in order to integrate the ethnic children into the regular program as soon as possible; (3) Pluralism with Mixed Classes. This model stresses that each student group should learn the language and culture of the other, and subject-matter instruction takes place in two or more languages, and (4) Pluralistic with Separate Classes. This model is characterized by a desire to create a given ethnic cultural and psychological identity in the student. The ethnic language is the language of instruction with English, at best, a supplemental skill to be learned. The school becomes an ethnic enclave.

Questions: Which of the above models was approved by the U.S. Supreme Court in Lau v. Nichols? Did it opt for the bilingual programs as promoters of values of national unity; i. e., assimilation, or for values of cultural diversity; i. e., biculturalism? Is the focus of the Court in Lau on an equality of "inputs," on what the state initially provides its children, or is it on an equality "outputs," on equal capacities of the children as they leave school? Which of the above models is implicit in the U.S. Dept. of Education definition set forth above?

2.  Does Lau, or any other case or statute in this section, apply to black children whose first language is "black English"?

3.  Is bilingual-biculturalism with its stresses on separate and different languages and cultural identities consistent with the basic integration requirements of Brown v. Board of Educ.? Hobson v. Hansen?

4. Do language minority children have a constitutional right to a bilingual (bicultural?) program? See, comment, Bilingual Education: A Privilege or a Right, 24 DePaul L.Rev. 990 (1975). Would language-minority children have a constitutional right, if, as in Lau, the language barrier functioned effectively to exclude them from all education? What does "functional exclusion" mean? From what are they excluded? Assimilation? Biculturalism? Generally see, Grubb, Breaking The Language Barrier: The Right to Bilingual Education, 8 Harv.Civ.Rts.- Civ.Lib.L.Rev. 53 (1974).

5. Massachusetts' law identifies "Children of limited English-speaking ability" as those incapable of performing ordinary classwork in English and who either have been born in the U.S. to non-English speaking parents or have been born out of the U.S. and their native tongue is not English. These children are eligible for a "program in transitional bilingual education" which involves regular subject-matter instruction in the child's native tongue and English; instruction in English, and instruction in the history and culture of the native land of their parents and of the United States. Mass.Laws Ann., Ch. 71A (1971). If you had been a legislator, would you have voted for this law? Why?

---

## GUADALUPE ORGANIZATION, INC. v. TEMPE ELEMENTARY SCHOOL DIST.

United States Court of Appeals, 1978.
587 F.2d 1022 (9th Cir.).

SNEED, Circuit Judge. This appeal is from the district court's adverse determination of a civil rights class action filed by plaintiff-appellants to compel the Tempe Elementary School District No. 3 to provide all non-English-speaking Mexican-American or Yaqui Indian students attending district schools with bilingual-bicultural education. Appellants assert that their rights to equal educational opportunity have been disregarded in violation of the Equal Protection Clause of the Fourteenth Amendment and that the school district's failure to provide bilingual-bicultural education also violates rights granted by Section 601 of the Civil Rights Act of 1964, the Equal Education Opportunity Act of 1974 and Title 42 U.S.C.A. § 1983. The district court granted appellees' motion for summary judgment. . . . We affirm.

### I. FACTS

Appellants are elementary school children of Mexican-American and Yaqui Indian origin or their representatives of the community of Guadalupe, Arizona, a semi-rural community of approximately 5,000 people, most of whom are Mexican-American or Indian. Plaintiffs allege that of the approximately 12,280 students in the Tempe Elementary School District No. 3, approximately 18% are Mexican-American or Yaqui Indian, and that in the elementary school in

Guadalupe, approximately 554 of 605 students are Mexican-American or Yaqui Indian. Appellants allege four discriminatory acts constituting the violation of their rights:

(1) Failure to provide bilingual instruction which takes into account the special educational needs of Mexican-American and Yaqui Indian students;

(2) Failure to hire enough teachers of Mexican-American or Yaqui Indian descent who can adequately teach bilingual courses and effectively relate to the educational and cultural needs of the appellants;

(3) Failure to structure a curriculum that even minimally takes into account appellants' particular educational needs;

(4) Failure to structure a curriculum that even minimally reflects the historical contributions of people of appellants' descent to the State of Arizona and the United States.

The district court initially dismissed appellants' complaint on May 21, 1973 on the basis of this court's holding in Lau v. Nichols, 483 F.2d 791 (9th Cir. 1973), rev'd, 414 U.S. 563, 94 S.Ct. 786, 39 L. Ed.2d 1 (1974). This court, by an order dated April 5, 1975, remanded this action "for further consideration in accordance with the decision of the Supreme Court" in Lau v. Nichols. This court had held when Lau v. Nichols was before us that the Fourteenth Amendment Equal Protection Clause did not require the San Francisco Unified School District to provide compensatory English language instruction to students who spoke only Chinese. The Supreme Court, without reaching the constitutional question, held that 42 U.S.C.A. § 2000d and underlying HEW regulations require school districts to "take affirmative steps to rectify the language deficienc[ies]" of non-English-speaking students, and that the San Francisco Unified School District had not met this standard.

Upon remand, defendant-appellees made a motion for a more definite statement to clarify the distinction between the relief sought in this case and that ordered by the Supreme Court in Lau v. Nichols. In answer to interrogatories of the appellees and in argument before the district court appellants admitted that they did not complain of the school district's efforts to cure existing language deficiencies of non-English-speaking students. Instead, they contended below as well as here that the appellees have failed to provide them with a program of instruction that "has as its goal having a child graduate at each grade level from kindergarten to fourth year in high school competent and functional in reading, writing, and comprehension both in the child's own language, Spanish, and the language of the majority culture, English." The appellees allegedly also have failed to provide an educational program in which "all courses of instruction, testing procedures, instructional materials [are] bilingual and bicultural." Finally, appellants contend that the school district failed to reflect in its program of instruction the particular language, particular customs and particular history of the parents of each child attending the school.[1]

.  .  .

Appellants argue that the duties they seek to impose upon the appellees are required by the Fourteenth Amendment's Equal Protection Clause, the Civil Rights Act of 1964, and the Equal Education Opportunity Act of 1974. We shall consider separately each of these sources of the duties appellants seek to impose upon appellees. In doing this our effort joins a growing number of cases in which the federal courts have been called upon to trace the bounds of "equal educational opportunity" as required by the Constitution or statute. Decisions flowing from such an undertaking involve, *inter alia,* the question of "the proper role of the federal judiciary in overseeing the decisions of local administrative bodies in the field of public education." Responding to this question also involves considering the interests of the children being educated, their parents, and the local school authorities, the respective roles of the state and federal governments, the competency of the federal courts to undertake the requested education oversight, and, at least in this case, the nature of the social compact that binds this Nation together.

We now turn to those sources from which the appellants assert flow the duties they insist the appellees must discharge.

## II.  FOURTEENTH AMENDMENT

The Supreme Court in San Antonio Independent School District v. Rodriguez, taught us that education, although an important inter-

---

[1] The U. S. Office of Education has defined bilingual education as:

> instruction in two languages and the use of those two languages as mediums of instruction for any part of or all of the school curriculum. Study of the history and culture associated with a student's mother tongue is considered an integral part of bilingual education. . . .

Beginning with the passage of the Bilingual Education Act in 1968, 20 U.S. C.A. § 880b, legislators have recognized the desirability of encouraging bilingual education programs. Section 701 of Pub.L. 90–247, Title VII, provided as follows:

> The Congress hereby finds that one of the most acute educational problems in the United States is that which involves millions of children of limited English-speaking ability because they come from environ-

ments where the dominant language is other than English, that additional efforts should be made to supplement present attempts to find adequate and constructive solutions to this unique and perplexing educational situation ; and that the urgent need is for comprehensive and cooperative action now on the local, State, and Federal levels to develop forwardlooking approaches to meet the serious learning difficulties faced by this substantial segment of the Nation's schoolage population.

Beside's federal encouragement, as of 1977, 24 states expressly or implicitly permitted instruction in a language other than English. Since 1971, eight of the 24 states have stipulated certain conditions under which a school is required to offer such courses. C. Ovando, School Implications of the Peaceful Latino Invasion, Phi Delta Kappan, Dec. 1977, at 232.

est, is not guaranteed by the Constitution. Therefore, it is not a fundamental right. Differences in treatment of students in the educational process, which in themselves do not violate specific constitutional guarantees, do not violate the Fourteenth Amendment's Equal Protection Clause if such differences are rationally related to legitimate state interests. This was the approach we adopted in our Lau v. Nichols; the Supreme Court did not reject the approach in its reversal of that case. *Rodriguez* suggests that a rational relationship to legitimate state interests is absent when the educational "system fails to provide each child with an opportunity to acquire the basic minimal skills necessary for the enjoyment of the rights of speech and of full participation in the political process."

We hold that the appellees fulfilled their equal protection duty to children of Mexican-American and Yaqui Indian origin when they adopted measures, to which the appellants do not object, to cure existing language deficiencies of non-English-speaking students. There exists no constitutional duty imposed by the Equal Protection Clause to provide bilingual-bicultural education such as the appellants request. The decision of the appellees to offer the educational program attacked by appellants bears a rational relationship to legitimate state interests. Nor, so far as this record reveals, does the appellees' program fail "to provide each child with an opportunity to acquire the basic minimal skills necessary for the enjoyment of the rights of speech and of full participation in the political process."

We reach this conclusion fully aware of the serious nature of the appellants' contentions. Our analysis returns us to the foundations of organized society as manifested by the nation-state. We commence by recognizing that the existence of the nation-state rests ultimately on the consent of its people. The scope of this fundamental compact may be extensive or limited. Its breadth fixes the effective limits of government by the nation-state.

Linguistic and cultural diversity within the nation-state, whatever may be its advantages from time to time, can restrict the scope of the fundamental compact. Diversity limits unity. Effective action by the nation-state rises to its peak of strength only when it is in response to aspirations unreservedly shared by each constituent culture and language group. As affection which a culture or group bears toward a particular aspiration abates, and as the scope of sharing diminishes, the strength of the nation-state's government wanes.

Syncretism retards, and sometimes even reverses, the shrinkage of the compact caused by linguistic and cultural diversity. But it would be incautious to strengthen diversity in language and culture repeatedly trusting only in syncretic processes to preserve the social compact. In the language of eighteenth century philosophy, the century in which our Constitution was written, the social compact depends on the force of benevolence which springs naturally from the hearts of all men but which attenuates as it crosses linguistic and cultural lines. Multiple linguistic and cultural centers impede both the egress of each center's own and the ingress of all others. Benevolence, moreover, spends much of its force within each center, and, to reinforce affection toward insiders, hostility toward outsiders develops.

The fundamental nature of these tendencies makes clear that their scope varies from generation to generation and is fixed by the political process in its highest sense. The Constitution, aside from guaranteeing to individuals certain basic rights, privileges, powers, and immunities, does not speak to such matters; it merely evidences a compact whose scope and strength cannot be mandated by the courts but must be determined by the people acting upon the urgings of their hearts. The decision of the appellees to provide a predominantly monocultural and monolingual educational system was a rational response to a quintessentially "legitimate" state interest. The same perforce would be said were the appellees to adopt the appellants' demands and be challenged by an English-speaking child and his parents whose ancestors were Pilgrims.

Whatever may be the consequences, good or bad, of many tongues and cultures coexisting within a single nation-state, whether the children of this Nation are taught in one tongue and about primarily one culture or in many tongues and about may cultures cannot be determined by reference to the Constitution. We hold, therefore, that the Constitution neither requires nor prohibits the bilingual and bicultural education sought by the appellants. Such matters are for the people to decide.

The cases which have dealt with constitutional claims to bilingual and bicultural education are not inconsistent with our holding. Directly supportive is *Keyes* which refused to order bilingual-bicultural education as a remedy to eliminate the consequences of de jure segregation and expressly held that the "Cardenas Plan," a specific program of bilingual-bicultural education, was not required by the Fourteenth Amendment. On the other hand, in United States v. Texas Education Agency, 532 F.2d 380, 398 (5th Cir.), vacated sub nom. Austin Independent School District v. United States, 429 U.S. 990, 97 S.Ct. 517, 50 L.Ed.2d 603 (1976), a certain form of bilingual-bicultural education was held to be a proper part of a remedy fashioned by the district court to eliminate de jure segregation. A similar holding where de jure segregation had existed was made in United States v. Texas. Fashioning a remedy for de jure segregation, however, is a task quite distinct from determining whether there exists a constitutional right to bilingual-bicultural education in a desegregated system. The first involves a balancing of individual and collective interests having as its goal the correction of de jure segregation. Determining that a remedy is appropriate to further the correction of de jure segregation does not *a fortiori* make it a constitutional entitlement in the absence of de jure segregation. That must be determined by the analysis employed above. Supporting *Keyes* and our holding are two district court cases, Otero v. Mesa County Valley School District No. 51, 408 F.Supp. 162 (D.Colo.1975), vacated on other grounds, 568 F.2d 1312 (10th Cir. 1978) and Morales v. Shannon, 366 F.Supp. 813, 821–23 (W.D.Tex.1973), rev'd on other grounds, 516 F.2d 411 (5th Cir.), cert. denied, 423 U.S. 1034, 96 S.Ct. 566, 46 L.Ed.2d 408 (1975). A contrary position was taken in Serna v. Portales Municipal Schools, 351 F.Supp. 1279 (D.N.M.1972), aff'd on other grounds, 499 F.2d 1147 (10th Cir. 1974).[4]

Finally, our recent decision in De La Cruz v. Tormey, 582 F.2d 45 (9th Cir. 1978) provides no comfort to the appellants. There we held that a complaint that alleged "a course of conduct by defendants susceptible of an inference of intentional discrimination" on the basis of sex contrary to the Equal Protection Clause survived a motion to dismiss.[5] Appellants here alleged no course of conduct from which an inference of intentional discrimination can be drawn. They acknowledge that the remedial instruction in English is sufficient to allow Mexican-American and Yaqui students to participate effectively in the educational program. A failure to do more constitutes no intentionally discriminatory course of conduct condemned by the Equal Protection Clause. Assuming adequate remedial instruction, education in English reflecting American culture and values only is not a discriminatory course of conduct.

### III.   CIVIL RIGHTS ACT OF 1964

The appellants fare no better under the Civil Rights Act of 1964, 42 U.S.C.A. § 2000d. Section 601 states:

> No person in the United States shall, on the ground of race, color, or national origin, be excluded from participation in, be denied the benefits of, or be subjected to discrimination

[4] In *Serna*, the district court found an unconstitutional denial of equal educational opportunity and ordered more and better bilingual-bicultural education and the hiring of a greater number of Spanish-speaking teachers. The Tenth Circuit affirmed the decision on the non-constitutional ground of Section 601 of Title VI. The Court of Appeals supported its affirmance of the broad remedy with Fourteenth Amendment cases such as Swann v. Charlotte-Mecklenburg Board of Education, supra, and Green v. County School Board, 391 U.S. 430, 88 S.Ct. 1689, 20 L.Ed.2d 716 (1968). 499 F.2d at 1154. The court further stated that because § 601 gives a right to bilingual instruction, bilingual-bicul-

tural education can be ordered. Id. Because we find no violation of § 601 we need not decide whether the sweeping judicial remedies appropriate under the Fourteenth Amendment are available for statutory violations. The Tenth Circuit, moreover, has questioned seriously the remedy found appropriate in *Serna*. Keyes v. School District No. 1, 521 F.2d 465, 483 n. 22 (10th Cir. 1975), cert. denied, 423 U.S. 1066, 96 S.Ct. 806, 46 L. Ed.2d 657 (1976).

[5] In the present case, appellees presently are providing remedial language instruction intended to assure that appellants derive equivalent value from existing programs. . . .

under any program or activity receiving Federal financial assistance.

Under authority of Section 602 of the Act, HEW authorized regulation 45 C.F.R. § 80(b)(1), which provides that recipients may not:

(ii) Provide any service, financial aid, or other benefit to an individual which is different, or is provided in a different manner, from that provided to others under the program;

. . .

(iv) Restrict an individual in any way in the enjoyment of any advantage or privilege enjoyed by others receiving any service, financial aid, or other benefit under the program

. . . ..

In addition, HEW clarifying guidelines state:

Where inability to speak and understand the English language excludes national origin-minority group children from effective participation in the educational program offered by a school district, the district must take affirmative steps to rectify the language deficiency in order to open its instructional program to these students.

35 Fed.Reg. 11,595 (1970).

In Lau v. Nichols, supra, the Supreme Court, interpreting these regulations, emphasized that the failure of the San Francisco Unified School District to teach remedial English *excluded* Chinese-speaking students from any meaningful education. The Court stated: "[T]here is no equality of treatment merely by providing students with the same facilities, textbooks, teachers, and curriculum; for students who do not understand English are *effectively foreclosed from any meaningful education.*" (emphasis added). Under the Court's analysis of the Title VI requirements, non-English-speaking students received fewer benefits from the school system than did their English-speaking counterparts.

Appellants argue that the failure to implement a bilingual-bicultural education program staffed with bilingual instructors forecloses them from meaningful education and that they receive fewer benefits from the district's educational programs than do English-speaking children. We do not agree. Providing the appellants with remedial instruction in English which appellants appear to admit complies with *Lau's* mandate makes available the meaningful education and the equality of educational opportunity that Section 601 requires. There is no suggestion that appellees' remedial program operates "as an educational deadend or permanent track."

## IV. EQUAL EDUCATIONAL OPPORTUNITY ACT OF 1974

Congress enacted the Equal Educational Opportunity Act as a part of the Education Amendments of 1974. The portion of the Act applicable to the present case is Section 204, 20 U.S.C.A. § 1703, which states:

> No state shall deny equal educational opportunity to an individual on account of his or her race, color, sex, or national origin, by—
>
> . . .
>
> (f) the failure by an educational agency to take appropriate action to overcome language barriers that impede equal participation by its students in its instructional programs.

Because Section 1703(f) was proposed as an amendment from the floor of the House, there is very little legislative history. No previous decision has interpreted the scope of the "appropriate action" requirement. Inasmuch as, to repeat, the appellants do not challenge the appellees' efforts to cure existing language deficiencies we are not asked to decide whether their chosen program constitutes "appropriate action to overcome language barriers that impede equal participation by its students in its instructional program." Rather the issue is whether "appropriate action" *must* include the bilingual-bicultural education the appellants seek. We hold that it need not. To hold as appellants urge us to do would distort the relevant statutory language severely. The interpretation of floor amendments unaccompanied by illuminating debate should adhere closely to the ordinary meaning of the amendment's language. Deerfield Hutterian Association v. Ipswich Board of Education, 444 F.Supp. 159 (D.S.D. 1978) is not to the contrary. It merely holds that a complaint alleging that a board of education "made no plans or provisions to deal with the language handicap" states a claim under Section 1703(f). We agree. In this case plans were made and implemented and the effectiveness of these plans is not challenged. *Deerfield* did not address the issue which this case presents.

Affirmed.

### NOTES AND QUESTIONS

1. What is the major difference between Guadalupe and Lau v. Nichols? Is it that the Chinese children in Lau were functionally excluded from all meaningful education whereas the children in Guadalupe were not fully excluded? If that is the difference, do you believe the underlying facts actually bear out the court's decision in Guadalupe? If not, what accounts for it? Would you vote the same way? Assuming the difference noted above, would children have a constitutional right under the equal-protection clause to bilingual education whenever their lack of English language skills functioned to exclude them totally from a

school's educational program? One child or must there be a significant number? Suppose a Basque family with one six-year-old boy has just migrated to the United States from Spain, and the Basque boy is the only non-English speaker in the school district, is he constitutionally entitled to a bilingual program? If not, why not? Is there any reason not to believe that a child totally excluded from a school's educational program for reasons other than language; i. e., a mental, physical, emotional or environmental handicap, would equally have a constitutional right to a meaningful education?

2. Does the Guadalupe court believe that bilingual education in the sense of achieving assimilation is required by law but that bilingual education in the sense of biculturalism that seeks to create and maintain a cultural and psychological identity, is not required by law? If so, do you agree that this is the law? If so, should it include biculturalism?

3. Is the Guadalupe court's treatment of Title VI consistent with that of Lau v. Nichols? Did the rationale of the Supreme Court's decision in Lau require biculturalism?

4. In a footnote the Guadalupe court states that, on Title VI, "our holding is consistent with" the Serna case, which follows. Analyze Serna and determine whether the two cases are consistent.

---

## SERNA v. PORTALES MUNICIPAL SCHOOLS

United States Court of Appeals, 1974.
499 F.2d 1147 (10th Cir.).

HILL, Circuit Judge. Appellees in this class action are Spanish surnamed Americans seeking declaratory and injunctive relief against Portales Municipal School District for alleged constitutional and statutory violations committed under color of state law. In particular, appellees contend that appellant-school district has deprived them of their right to equal protection of the laws as guaranteed by the Fourteenth Amendment to the United States Constitution and of their statutory rights under Title VI of the 1964 Civil Rights Act, specifically § 601, 42 U.S.C.A. § 2000d. Jurisdiction is invoked under 28 U.S.C.A. § 1343.

Pertinent facts include the following. The City of Portales, New Mexico, has a substantial number of Spanish surnamed residents. Accordingly, a sizable minority of students attending the Portales schools are Spanish surnamed. Evidence indicates that many of these students know very little English when they enter the school system. They speak Spanish at home and grow up in a Spanish culture totally alien to the environment thrust upon them in the Portales school system. The result is a lower achievement level than their Anglo-American counterparts, and a higher percentage of school dropouts.

For the 1971–72 school year approximately 34 percent of the children attending Portales' four elementary schools, Lindsey, James,

Steiner and Brown, were Spanish surnamed.[1]  The junior high school and senior high school enrollments of Spanish surnamed students were 29 percent and 17 percent, respectively.  Unquestionably as Spanish surnamed children advanced to the higher grades a disproportionate number of them quit school.

Appellees in their complaint charge appellant with discriminating against Spanish surnamed students in numerous respects.  Allegedly there is discrimination in appellants' failure to provide bilingual instruction which takes into account the special educational needs of the Mexican-American student;  failure to hire any teachers of Mexican-American descent;  failure to structure a curriculum that takes into account the particular education needs of Mexican-American children;  failure to structure a curriculum that reflects the historical contributions of people of Mexican and Spanish descent to the State of New Mexico and the United States;  and failure to hire and employ any administrators including superintendents, assistant superintendents, principals, vice-principals, and truant officers of Mexican-American descent.  This failure to provide equal educational opportunities allegedly deprived appellees and all other similarly situated of their right to equal protection of the laws under the Fourteenth Amendment.

At trial appellees presented the following evidence to support their allegations.  Until 1970 none of the teachers in the Portales schools was Spanish surnamed, including those teaching the Spanish language in junior and senior high school;  there had never been a Spanish surnamed principal or vice-principal and there were no secretaries who spoke Spanish in the elementary grades.

Evidence was offered showing that in 1969 the report by Portales Municipal Schools to United States Commission on Civil Rights indicated that at Lindsey, the 86 percent Spanish surnamed school, only four students with Spanish surnames in the first grade spoke English as well as the average Anglo first grader.  During an evaluation of the Portales Municipal Schools by the New Mexico Department of Education in 1969, the evaluation team concluded that the language arts program at Lindsey School "was below average and not meeting the needs of those children."  Notwithstanding this knowledge of the plight of Spanish surnamed students in Portales, appellants neither applied for funds under the federal Bilingual Education Act, 20 U.S.C.A. § 880b, nor accepted funds for a similar purpose when they were offered by the State of New Mexico.

Undisputed evidence shows that Spanish surnamed students do not reach the achievement levels attained by their Anglo counterparts.  For example, achievement tests, which are given totally in

[1] Lindsey school's enrollment consisted of nearly 86 percent Spanish surnamed children while the ethnic composition of students at the other three elementary schools was 78 to 88 percent Anglo.

the English language, disclose that students at Lindsey are almost a full grade behind children attending other schools in reading, language mechanics and language expression. Intelligence quotient tests show that Lindsey students fall further behind as they move from the first to the fifth grade. As the disparity in achievement levels increases between Spanish surnamed and Anglo students, so does the disparity in attendance and school dropout rates.

Expert witnesses explained what effect the Portales school system had on Spanish surnamed students. Dr. Zintz testified that when Spanish surnamed children come to school and find that their language and culture are totally rejected and that only English is acceptable, feelings of inadequacy and lowered self esteem develop. Henry Pascual, Director of the Communicative Arts Division of the New Mexico Department of Education, stated that a child who goes to a school where he finds no evidence of his language and culture and ethnic group represented becomes withdrawn and nonparticipating. The child often lacks a positive mental attitude. Maria Gutierrez Spencer, a longtime teacher in New Mexico, testified that until a child developed a good self image not even teaching English as a second language would be successful. If a child can be made to feel worthwhile in school then he will learn even with a poor English program. Dr. Estevan Moreno, a psychologist, further elaborated on the psychological effects of thrusting Spanish surnamed students into an alien school environment. Dr. Moreno explained that children who are not achieving often demonstrate both academic and emotional disorders. They are frustrated and they express their frustration in lack of attendance, lack of school involvement and lack of community involvement. Their frustrations are reflected in hostile behavior, discipline problems and eventually dropping out of school.

Appellants' case centered around the testimony of L. C. Cozzens, Portales' superintendent of schools. Cozzens testified that for the 1971–72 school year out of approximately 80 applications for elementary school teaching positions only one application was from a Spanish surnamed person. Nevertheless, through aggressive recruiting Portales hired six Spanish surnamed teachers. At Lindsey a program was established to teach first graders English as a second language; and with the aid of federal funds a program was also established to serve the needs of pre-school Spanish surnamed children. At the high school level an ethnic studies program was initiated which would be directed primarily at the minority groups and their problems.

The faculty was encouraged to attend workshops on cultural awareness. Altogether over a third of the entire faculty attended one or more of these workshops.

After hearing all evidence, the trial court found that in the Portales schools Spanish surnamed children do not have equal educational opportunity and thus a violation of their constitutional right to equal protection exists.   The Portales School District was ordered to:

> reassess and enlarge its program directed to the specialized needs of its Spanish surnamed students at Lindsey and also to establish and operate in adequate manner programs at the other elementary schools where no bilingual-bicultural program now exists.
>
> .   .   .
>
> Defendant school district is directed to investigate and utilize whenever possible the sources of available funds to provide equality of educational opportunity for its Spanish-surnamed students.
>
> .   .   .
>
> It is incumbent upon the school district to increase its recruiting efforts and, if those recruiting efforts are unsuccessful, to obtain sufficient certification of Spanish-speaking teachers to allow them to teach in the district.

Appellants, in compliance with the court's order to submit a plan for remedial action within 90 days, thereafter filed a proposed plan.   In essence the plan provided bilingual education for approximately 150 Lindsey students in grades one through four.   Each group would be given instruction in Spanish for approximately 30 minutes daily.   A Title VII bilingual program would be instituted for approximately 40 pre-school children.   Practically all personnel employed for this program would be Spanish surnamed.   At the junior high one Spanish surnamed teacher aide would be employed to help Spanish surnamed children experiencing difficulty in the language arts.   At the high school a course in ethnic studies would be offered emphasizing minority cultures and their contribution to society.   In connection with this program appellants applied to the State Department of Education for state bilingual funds.   These funds would provide one bilingual-bicultural instructor for the school district's other three elementary schools, and one bilingual-bicultural teacher or teacher aide at the junior high school.   Seeking other sources of funding was also promised as long as the control and supervision of the programs remained with the local board of education.

Although complying with most of the court's order, appellants noted that because enrollment is declining in the Portales schools there would be fewer teachers employed next year.   Thus, very likely there would not be any positions to be filled.   If a position becomes vacant, however, the school district promised to make every reasonable effort to secure a qualified teacher with a Spanish surname.

Appellees thereafter filed a Motion for Hearing to hear appellees' objections to appellants' program.   The motion was granted and at the hearing, after stating their objections to appellants' proposed plan, appellees introduced their own proposed bilingual-bicultural program. After reviewing both parties' programs, the trial court entered final judgment, adopting and adding the following to its prior memorandum opinion:

## I.  Curriculum

### A.  Lindsey Elementary

All students in grades 1–3 shall receive 60 minutes per day bilingual instruction.  All students in grades 4–6 shall receive 45 minutes per day bilingual instruction.  These times are to be considered a minimum and should not be construed to limit additional bilingual training (i. e. the Title III self contained classroom for first graders with special English language problems).

A testing system shall be devised for determining the adequacy of the above established time periods with ensuing adjustments (either an increase or decrease in bilingual instruction) as needed.

### B.  James, Steiner and Brown Elementary

All Spanish-speaking students in grades 1–6 shall receive 30 minutes per day of bilingual instruction.  This program should be made available to interested non-Spanish speaking students as funding and personnel become available to expand the bilingual instruction.

A bicultural outlook should be incorporated in as many subject areas as practicable.

Testing procedures shall be established to test the results of the bilingual instruction and adjustments made accordingly.

### C.  Junior High

Students should be tested for English language proficiency and, if necessary, further bilingual instruction should be available for those students who display a language barrier deficiency.

### D.  High School

An ethnic studies course will be offered in the 1973–74 school year as an elective.  This course should be continued and others added in succeeding years.

The minimum curriculum schedule set forth in A through D above is not intended to limit other bilingual programs or course offerings currently available in the Portales school system or which will become available in the future.

## II.  RECRUITING AND HIRING

A special effort should be made to fill vacancies with qualified bilingual teachers.  Recruiting should be pursued to achieve this objective.

## III.  FUNDING

Defendants appear to have complied with the court's directive to investigate and utilize sources of available funding. Efforts should continue in seeking funding for present as well as future programs which will help achieve equality of educational opportunities for Spanish-surnamed students.

Appellants promptly appealed, positing  .  .  .  that failure to afford a program of bilingual instruction to meet appellees' needs does not deny them equal protection of the law when such needs are not the result of discriminatory actions.

.  .  .

Appellants  .  .  .  challenge the district court's holding that the Portales municipal schools denied appellees equal protection of the law by not offering a program of bilingual education which met their special educational needs.  In light of the recent Supreme Court decision in Lau v. Nichols, however, we need not decide the equal protection issue.  *Lau* is a case which appellants admit is almost identical to the present one.  .  .  .

.  .  .

.  .  .  Appellees are Spanish surnamed students who prior to this lawsuit were placed in totally English speaking schools.  There is substantial evidence that most of these Spanish surnamed students are deficient in the English language; nevertheless no affirmative steps were taken by the Portales school district to rectify these language deficiencies.

The trial court noted in its memorandum opinion that appellees claimed deprivation of equal protection guaranteed by the Fourteenth Amendment and of their statutory rights under Title VI of the 1964 Civil Rights Act, specifically § 601.  While the trial court reached the correct result on equal protection grounds, we choose to follow the approach adopted by the Supreme Court in *Lau*; that is, appellees were deprived of their statutory rights under Title VI of the 1964 Civil Rights Act.  As in *Lau,* all able children of school age are required to attend school.  N.M.Const. Art. XII, § 5.  All public schools must be conducted in English.  N.M.Const. Art. XXI, § 4.  While Spanish surnamed children are required to attend school, and if they attend public schools the courses must be taught in English, Portales school district has failed to institute a program which will rectify language deficiencies so that these children will receive a meaningful education. The Portales school curriculum, which has the effect of discrimination even though probably no purposeful design is present, therefore violates the requisites of Title VI and the requirement imposed by or pursuant to HEW regulations. *Lau,* supra.

Appellants argue that even if the school district were unintentionally discriminating against Spanish surnamed students prior to institution of this lawsuit, the program they presented to the trial court in compliance with the court's memorandum opinion sufficiently meets the needs of appellees. The New Mexico State Board of Education (SBE), in its Amicus Curiae brief, agrees with appellants' position and argues that the trial court's decision and the relief granted constitute unwarranted and improper judicial interference in the internal affairs of the Portales school district. After reviewing the entire record we are in agreement with the trial court's decision. The record reflects a long standing educational policy by the Portales schools that failed to take into consideration the specific needs of Spanish surnamed children. After appellants submitted a proposed bilingual-bicultural program to the trial court a hearing was held on the adequacies of this plan. At this hearing expert witnesses pointed out the fallacies of appellants' plan and in turn offered a more expansive bilingual-bicultural plan. The trial court thereafter fashioned a program which it felt would meet the needs of Spanish surnamed students in the Portales school system. We do not believe that under the unique circumstances of this case the trial court's plan is unwarranted. The evidence shows unequivocally that appellants had failed to provide appellees with a meaningful education. There was adequate evidence that appellants' proposed program was only a token plan that would not benefit appellees. Under these circumstances the trial court had a duty to fashion a program which would provide adequate relief for Spanish surnamed children. As the Court noted in Swann v. Charlotte-Mecklenburg Board of Education "[o]nce a right and a violation have been shown, the scope of a district court's equitable powers to remedy past wrongs is broad, for breadth and flexibility are inherent in equitable remedies." Under Title VI of the Civil Rights Act of 1964 appellees have a right to bilingual education. And in following the spirit of *Swann,* supra, we believe the trial court, under its inherent equitable power, can properly fashion a bilingual-bicultural program which will assure that Spanish surnamed children receive a meaningful education.   .   .   . We believe the trial court has formulated a just, equitable and feasible plan; accordingly we will not alter it on appeal.

The New Mexico State Board of Education stresses the effect the decision will have on the structure of public education in New Mexico. It is suggested that bilingual programs will now be necessitated throughout the state wherever a student is found who does not have adequate facility in the English language. We do not share SBE's fears. As Mr. Justice Blackmun pointed out in his concurring opinion in *Lau,* numbers are at the heart of this case and only when a substantial group is being deprived of a meaningful education will a Title VI violation exist.

## NOTES AND QUESTIONS

1. The court held that the "school district is not providing an equal educational program which affords equality of educational opportunity for all of its students." What concept of equal educational opportunity has the court embraced?

2. Imagine that you are the lawyer for the local Board of Education of Portales School District, what plan would you have submitted to the court?

3. What is the appropriate constitutional conception of equal educational opportunity? Is it appropriate to hold that equal educational opportunity exists whenever the educational opportunities afforded children by the state (1) are such that the opportunities do not depend upon the economic circumstances of the parents of the children nor upon the geographical location of the children within the state; or (2) are such that each child up to a certain age can fulfill all his potentialities regardless of race, creed, social standing or economic position; or (3) are such that they are expressed in dollars with each child representing an expenditure of an equal amount of state funds however allowing local communities to tax themselves further if they should elect to make additional educational opportunities available; or (4) are such that each child is afforded an equal minimum achievement level, although differing amounts of state funds must be allocated to different children in order to produce a common achievement level, but thereafter allowing local communities further to tax themselves in order to make additional educational opportunities available; or (5) are such that the distribution of all funds, state and local, are equal on a per child basis; or (6) are such that the distribution of all state and local funds are in an inverse proportion to the children's abilities in order to insure that all children leave school on an equal footing; or (7) are such that the distribution of all state and local funds are directly in proportion to the various talents and abilities of the children, thereby insuring that those best able to benefit will have the use of the funds; or (8) are such that all state and local funds are distributed equally on a per child basis within a classification, but children might be classified into various groups with differing amounts of state funds being allocated to various classifications even though each classification contains an equal number of children? What are the consequences of each concept? What are the appropriate criteria that should be used in order to select the correct constitutional concept of equal educational opportunity? For discussion see, Wise, Rich Schools, Poor Schools (1972).

4. In United States v. Texas, 342 F.Supp. 24 (E.D.Tex.1971), the court mandated bilingual education for Mexican-American and Anglo-American students in the San Felipe-Del Rio School District of Texas. However, the basis for the court's order was a prior determination that there had been de jure racial segregation and the purpose of the court's

order was to "eliminate discrimination root and branch" and to create a unitary school system without separate white and Mexican schools.

5. In Serna, the court stated that the Portales schools must "take into consideration the specific needs of Spanish surnamed children." Can this principle be limited to children with language deficiencies? Could children with other learning handicaps invoke it successfully, e. g., mentally, physically or emotionally handicapped children or those suffering from socio-cultural or economic deprivation, or those whose "first language" is black English? If "black English" qualifies, can schools hire teachers who speak black English without committing a de jure act of racial segregation?

6. Identifying who qualifies for a bilingual program can be difficult. In Aspira v. Board of Educ., 394 F.Supp. 1161 (S.D.N.Y.1975) the court held that Hispanic students scoring above the 20th percentile on a set of English language tests were not entitled to participate in a bilingual program.

7. In Otero v. Mesa County School Dist., 408 F.Supp. 162 (1975) vacated on other grounds 568 F.2d 1312 (10th Cir. 1977), the federal trial court found as a fact that there was no significant number of Hispanic children with substantial language problems, and hence, no justification for ordering a bilingual program under the Lau-Serna doctrine. See also, Comment, Bilingual Education—A Problem of "Substantial" Numbers?, 5 Fordham Urb.L.J. 561 (1977).

---

# CONSTITUTIONAL FREEDOM AND EDUCATION OF THE "GIFTED" AND "EXCEPTIONAL" CHILD

---

## MILLS v. BOARD OF EDUCATION

United States District Court, D.C.D.C., 1972.
348 F.Supp. 866.

### MEMORANDUM OPINION, JUDGMENT AND DECREE

WADDY, District Judge.

This is a civil action brought on behalf of seven children of school age by their next friends in which they seek a declaration of rights and to enjoin the defendants from excluding them from the District of Columbia Public Schools and/or denying them publicly supported education and to compel the defendants to provide them with immediate and adequate education and educational facilities in the public schools or alternative placement at public expense. They also seek additional and ancillary relief to effectuate the primary relief. They allege that although they can profit from an education either in regular classrooms with supportive services or in special classes adopted to their needs, they have been labelled as behavioral problems, mentally retarded, emotionally disturbed or hyperactive, and denied admission to

the public schools or excluded therefrom after admission, with no provision for alternative educational placement or periodic review.
. . . .

## THE PROBLEM

The genesis of this case is found (1) in the failure of the District of Columbia to provide publicly supported education and training to plaintiffs and other "exceptional" children, members of their class, and (2) the excluding, suspending, expelling, reassigning and transferring of "exceptional" children from regular public school classes without affording them due process of law.

The problem of providing special education for "exceptional" children (mentally retarded, emotionally disturbed, physically handicapped, hyperactive and other children with behavioral problems) is one of major proportions in the District of Columbia. The precise number of such children cannot be stated because the District has continuously failed to comply with Section 31–208 of the District of Columbia Code which requires a census of all children aged 3 to 18 in the District to be taken. Plaintiffs estimate that there are ". . . 22,000 retarded, emotionally disturbed, blind, deaf, and speech or learning disabled children, and perhaps as many as 18,000 of these children are not being furnished with programs of specialized education." According to data prepared by the Board of Education, Division of Planning, Research and Evaluation, the District of Columbia provides publicly supported special education programs of various descriptions to at least 3880 school age children. However, in a 1971 report to the Department of Health, Education and Welfare, the District of Columbia Public Schools admitted that an estimated 12,340 handicapped children were not to be served in the 1971–72 school year.

Each of the minor plaintiffs in this case qualifies as an "exceptional" child. . . .

## THERE IS NO GENUINE ISSUE OF MATERIAL FACT

Congress has decreed a system of publicly supported education for the children of the District of Columbia. The Board of Education has the responsibility of administering that system in accordance with law and of providing such publicly supported education to all of the children of the District, including these "exceptional" children.

Defendants have admitted in these proceedings that they are under an affirmative duty to provide plaintiffs and their class with publicly supported education suited to each child's needs, including special education and tuition grants, and also, a constitutionally adequate prior hearing and periodic review. They have also admitted that they failed to supply plaintiffs with such publicly supported education and have failed to afford them adequate prior hearing and periodic review. . . .

## PLAINTIFFS ARE ENTITLED TO RELIEF

Plaintiffs' entitlement to relief in this case is clear. The applicable statutes and regulations and the Constitution of the United States require it.

### *Statutes and Regulations*

Section 31–201 of the District of Columbia Code requires that:

"Every parent, guardian, or other person residing [permanently or temporarily] in the District of Columbia who has custody or control of a child between the ages of seven and sixteen years shall cause said child to be regularly instructed in a public school or in a private or parochial school or instructed privately during the period of each year in which the public schools of the District of Columbia are in session . . ."

Under Section 31–203, a child may be "excused" from attendance only when

" . . . upon examination ordered by . . . [the Board of Education of the District of Columbia], [the child] is found to be unable mentally or physically to profit from attendance at school: Provided, however, That if such examination shows that such child may benefit from specialized instruction adapted to his needs, he shall attend upon such instruction."

Failure of a parent to comply with Section 31–201 constitutes a criminal offense. . . . The Court need not belabor the fact that requiring parents to see that their children attend school under pain of criminal penalties presupposes that an educational opportunity will be made available to the children. The Board of Education is required to make such opportunity available. It has adopted rules and regulations consonant with the statutory direction. Chapter XIII of the Board Rules contains the following:

> 1.1—All children of the ages hereinafter prescribed who are bona fide residents of the District of Columbia are entitled to admission and free tuition in the Public Schools of the District of Columbia, subject to the rules, regulations, and orders of the Board of Education and the applicable statutes.

> 14.1—Every parent, guardian, or other person residing permanently or temporarily in the District of Columbia who has custody or control of a child residing in the

District of Columbia between the ages of seven and sixteen years shall cause said child to be regularly instructed in a public school or in a private or parochial school or instructed privately during the period of each year in which the Public Schools of the District of Columbia are in session, provided that instruction given in such private or parochial school, or privately, is deemed reasonably equivalent by the Board of Education to the instruction given in the Public Schools.

14.3—The Board of Education of the District of Columbia may, upon written recommendation of the Superintendent of Schools, issue a certificate excusing from attendance at school a child who, upon examination by the Department of Pupil Appraisal, Study and Attendance or by the Department of Public Health of the District of Columbia, is found to be unable mentally or physically to profit from attendance at school: Provided, however, that if such examination shows that such child may benefit from specialized instruction adapted to his needs, he shall be required to attend such classes.

Thus the Board of Education has an obligation to provide whatever specialized instruction that will benefit the child. By failing to provide plaintiffs and their class the publicly supported specialized education to which they are entitled, the Board of Education violates the above statutes and its own regulations.

### The Constitution—Equal Protection and Due Process

The Supreme Court in Brown v. Board of Education . . .

"Today, education is perhaps the most important function of state and local governments. Compulsory school attendance laws and the great expenditures for education both demonstrate our recognition of the importance of education to our democratic society. It is required in the performance of our most basic public responsibilities, even service in the armed forces. It is the very foundation of good citizenship. Today it is a principal instrument in awakening the child to cultural values, in preparing him for later professional training, and in helping him to adjust normally to his environment. In these days, it is doubtful that any child may reasonably be expected to succeed in life if he is denied the opportunity of an education. *Such an opportunity, where the state has undertaken to provide it, is a right which must be made available to all on equal terms.* (emphasis supplied)

Bolling v. Sharpe . . . decided the same day as *Brown*, applied the *Brown* rationale to the District of Columbia public schools by finding that:

> "Segregation in public education is not reasonably related to any proper governmental objective, and thus it imposes on Negro children of the District of Columbia a burden that constitutes an arbitrary deprivation of their liberty in violation of the Due Process Clause." . . .

In Hobson v. Hansen, *supra*, Judge Wright found that denying poor public school children educational opportunities equal to that available to more affluent public school children was violative of the Due Process Clause of the Fifth Amendment. *A fortiori*, the defendants' conduct here, denying plaintiffs and their class not just an equal publicly supported education but all publicly supported education while providing such education to other children, is violative of the Due Process Clause.

Not only are plaintiffs and their class denied the publicly supported education to which they are entitled many are suspended or expelled from regular schooling or specialized instruction or reassigned without any prior hearing and are given no periodic review thereafter. Due process of law requires a hearing prior to exclusion, termination of classification into a special program. . . .

### The Defense

The Answer of the defendants to the Complaint contains the following:

> "These defendants say that it is impossible to afford plaintiffs the relief they request unless:
>
> (a) The Congress of the United States appropriates millions of dollars to improve special education services in the District of Columbia; or
>
> (b) These defendants divert millions of dollars from funds already specifically appropriated for other educational services in order to improve special educational services. These defendants suggest that to do so would violate an Act of Congress and would be inequitable to children outside the alleged plaintiff class."

This Court is not persuaded by that contention.

The defendants are required by the Constitution of the United States, the District of Columbia Code, and their own regulations to provide a publicly-supported education for these "exceptional" children. Their failure to fulfill this clear duty to include and retain these children in the public school system, or otherwise provide them with publicly-supported education, and their failure to afford them due process hearing and periodical review, cannot be excused by the claim

that there are insufficient funds.  In Goldberg v. Kelly, 397 U.S. 254
.   .   .   the Supreme Court, in a case that involved the right of a welfare recipient to a hearing before termination of his benefits, held
that Constitutional rights must be afforded citizens despite the greater
expense involved.  The Court stated  .   .   .   that "the State's interest that his [welfare recipient] payments not be erroneously terminated, clearly outweighs the State's competing concern to prevent
any increase in its fiscal and administrative burdens."  Similarly the
District of Columbia's interest in educating the excluded children
clearly must outweigh its interest in preserving its financial resources.
If sufficient funds are not available to finance all of the services and
programs that are needed and desirable in the system then the available funds must be expended equitably in such a manner that no child
is entirely excluded from a publicly supported education consistent
with his needs and ability to benefit therefrom.  The inadequacies of
the District of Columbia Public School System whether occasioned by
insufficient funding or administrative inefficiency, certainly cannot
be permitted to bear more heavily on the "exceptional" or handicapped
child than on the normal child.  .   .   .

### NOTES AND QUESTIONS

1.   What concept of equal educational opportunity is implicit in this opinion?
     Do you agree?  For further discussion see, Weintraub and Abeson,
     Appropriate Education for All Handicapped Children:  A Growing
     Issue, 23 Syracuse L.Rev. 1037 (1972), and generally see, L. M. Dunn,
     Exceptional Children in the Schools (1963).

2.   Pennsylvania Ass'n for Retarded Children v. Commonwealth of Pa., 343
     F.Supp. 279 (E.D.Pa., 1972) involved a statute, common to many states,
     that students can be excluded from schools on the ground that the
     students are "uneducable and untrainable."  The efficacy of this type
     of statute turns on the existence of medical and educational facts.
     Plaintiffs claimed that "the premise of the statutes which necessarily
     assumes that certain retarded children are uneducable and untrainable
     lacks a rational basis in fact."  Unanimous expert opinion showed that
     "all mentally retarded persons are capable of benefitting from a program
     of education and training."  Accepting the expert opinion and plaintiff's
     claim the court held that plaintiffs presented a substantial constitutional
     issue of denial of equal protection of the law.  For additional discussion
     see, Schwartz, The Education of Handicapped Children: Emerging Legal
     Doctrine, 7 Clearinghouse Review 125 (1973).

3.   Would the decisions in the cases have been any different if instead of
     involving an "exceptional" child it had involved a "gifted" child of
     unusual ability who had not been recognized but who had been labelled
     "hyperactive," a "behavioral problem" or "uneducable and untrain-
     able," and had been excluded from school?  If not, what remedy could
     the court decree?  In the case of either an "exceptional" or "gifted"
     child can a court decree that teachers' salaries shall vary directly with
     the rate of educational progress shown by their students?

4.  For discussions of the constitutional dimensions of the "right of handi-
    capped children to education," see Haggerty & Sacks, Education of The
    Handicapped, 50 Temple L.Q. 961, 964–84 (1977); Handel, The Role
    of the Advocate In Securing the Handicapped Child's Right to an
    Effective Minimal Education, 36 Ohio State L.J. 349, 356–58 (1975),
    and Herr, The Children Who Wait, in THE MENTALLY RETARDED
    CITIZEN AND THE LAW, 252, 255–64 (1976).

## A NOTE ON THE EDUCATION FOR ALL HANDICAPPED CHILDREN ACT OF 1975

P.L. No. 94–142, 89 Stat. 773
(codified as 20 U.S.C.A. §§ 1401–1461 (1976)).

Basically, Congress treated this Act as a spending measure. The
Act sets forth general requirements that states must meet in order to
qualify for federal funds. Forty-nine states are currently receiving
federal funds. With minor exceptions, the Act requires states to provide a "free appropriate public education" (a FAPE) to all handicapped children between three and twenty-one. But it does not identify the specific educational programs local school districts must make
available in order to meet their federal obligations. Included within the definition of "handicapped" are children who are mentally retarded, learning disabled, physically handicapped, and emotionally
disturbed. The Act defines a FAPE as "special education and related services which  .  .  .  are provided in conformity with [an]
individualized education program." An individualized education program (IEP) is a "written statement for each child" which is developed at a meeting of school officials with the child's parent. The IEP
must include a description of the child's present level of performance,
the objectives of his special education program, the specific services
that make up the program, and "appropriate objective criteria" for
identifying whether the program's objectives are achieved. The Act
directs that handicapped and non-handicapped children should be educated together "to the maximum extent appropriate" (mainstreaming). In an attempt to reduce misclassification, the Act prohibits
culturally and racially biased tests and precludes reliance on any one
factor; e. g., I.Q., to determine a child's placement. Mainstreaming
handicapped children is the most controversial part of the Act.

Parents are the heart of the enforcement mechanism. The Act
creates detailed procedural safeguards, and specifically gives parents
the right to complain about "any matter relating to the identification, evaluation, or educational placement of the child, or the provision of a free appropriate education to such child." A complaining
parent is entitled to an "impartial due process hearing" at the local
level before a person who is not employed by the school district, and
if not satisfied, a parent is entitled to appeal to a state agency. Thereafter, the Act allows a party aggrieved by a state determination to
sue in either state or federal courts. For further discussion see, Com-

ment, Enforcing The Right To An "Appropriate" Education:   The Education For All Handicapped Children Act of 1975, 92 Harv.L.Rev. 1103 (1979).

On "mainstreaming," one federal judge has observed (Lora v. Board of Educ., 456 F.Supp. 1211 (E.D.N.Y.1978)):

> "Briefly, 'mainstreaming' involves the integration of handicapped children into the regular classroom to the greatest degree possible.  A discussion of this approach and the problems and legal implications it raises is essential
>
> .   .   ..
>
> "As a general proposition all agree that children with special educational needs, including the socially maladjusted and emotionally disturbed, should be served in regular classrooms and neighborhood schools insofar as these arrangements are conducive to good educational progress.  In addition, it is acknowledged that supplementary services for exceptional children, or their removal from part or all of the regular school environment may be required.  The continuum of acceptable educational programs designed to meet the needs of exceptional children, arranged from least to most restrictive, has traditionally been:  (1) regular classroom;  (2) regular classroom with specialist consultation;  (3) regular classroom with itinerant teachers;   (4) regular classroom plus resource room;  (5) part-time special class;  (6) full-time special class;  (7) special day school; and (8) residential institutions.  M. C. Reynolds, "A Framework for Considering Some Issues In Special Education," in J. P. Glavin, MAJOR ISSUE IN SPECIAL EDUCATION, 13 14 (1973).
>
> "A standard conceptual approach to the utilization of these resources has been the 'Cascade System.'  It has been described as follows:
>
>> The flow of service provisions in the cascade progresses from minimal to maximal.  The regular classroom is the level at which the least amount of special resources are needed.  There are, however, three modifications of the regular classroom which allow the minimally handicapped child the maximum opportunity to obtain and participate in a normal educational experience.
>>
>> Modification I provides the regular classroom teacher with the opportunity to obtain consultation with a number of educational and related specialists in instructional materials, reading, psychology, guidance, speech, and others.  In this situation, the regular classroom teacher, who is ultimately responsible for the child, is

searching for a better understanding of the child and his problems, and is seeking improved instructional and management techniques. Modification II involves itinerant specialists and differs from I in that these individuals actually work with the child. Modification III includes the placement of the child in a regular classroom, but with some time spent in a special resource area where specific remedial instruction occurs. Specialists working in this area confer with the classroom teacher, and together they plan appropriate programs for the child.

Children who cannot participate or achieve in one of the above modifications of the regular classroom can split their school day by spending part of it in the regular class and the remainder in a special class. In this program option, the special class is staffed by a trained special educator who works with the child in a special adaptation of the regular classroom program as well as other specialized instructional areas. Also in this situation, the special education and regular classroom teachers confer, and jointly plan to insure that the child is provided with a meaningful and coordinated education.

If a child is unable to participate successfully in most regular classroom activities, he may be placed in a full-time special education class where all of his education, with the exception of non-academic areas such as physical education, art, shop, and music, will be provided. In this placement the total curriculum is adapted to each child's individual needs. The special class teacher in this program is ultimately responsible for the children.

Special day schools for handicapped children offer facilities and programs generally unavailable in the regular school. These include . . . smaller pupil-teacher ratios, and the availability of greater amounts of supportive personnel. The children live at home and are frequently transported from large geographic areas extending beyond single school districts.

F. J. Weintraub and A. R. Abeson, 'Appropriate Education for All Handicapped Children: A Growing Issue,' 23 Syracuse L.Rev. 1037, 1040–41 (1972).

"Recently, this scheme has been challenged by increasing numbers of special educators who feel that special day schools and other programs that remove mildly handicapped children from the 'mainstream' may in many instances represent an unnecessary and undesirable educational tool, not part of a defensible and acceptable education scheme.

"The following definition is a useful starting point for a discussion of mainstreaming as it bears on the issue before us.

"Mainstreaming Is:

- providing the most appropriate education for each child in the least restrictive setting.

- looking at the educational needs of children instead of clinical or diagnostic labels such as mentally handicapped, learning disabled, physically handicapped, hearing impaired, or gifted.

- looking for and creating alternatives that will help general educators serve children with learning or adjustment problems in the regular setting. Some approaches being used to help achieve this are consulting teachers, methods and materials specialists, itinerant teachers, and resource room teachers.

- uniting the skills of general education and special education so all children may have equal educational opportunity.

"Mainstream Is Not:

- wholesale return of all exceptional children in special classes to regular classes.

- permitting children with special needs to remain in regular classrooms without the support services they need.

- ignoring the need of some children for a more specialized program than can be provided in the general education program.

- less costly than serving children in special self-contained classrooms.

J. L. Paul, A. P. Turnball, Wm. M. Cruickshank, MAINSTREAMING, A PRACTICAL GUIDE, vii–viii (1977) (citations omitted).

"The movement reflects dissatisfaction with the way that special education programs have been handled to permit regular teachers to avoid problems they should be capable of dealing with. The following criticisms are typical:

Special education is part of the arrangement for cooling out students. It has helped to erect a parallel system which permits relief of institutional guilt and humiliation stemming from the failure to achieve competence and effectiveness in the task given to it by society. Special education is helping the regular school maintain its spoiled identity when it creates special programs (whether psychodynamic or behavioral modification) for the 'disruptive child' and the 'slow learner,' many of whom, for some strange reason, happen to be Black or poor and live in the inner city.

J. L. Johnson, 'Special Education and the Inner City. A Challenge For the Future or Another Means for Cooling the Mark Out?,' The Journal of Special Education 241, 245 (1969).

The conscience of special educators needs to rub up against morality. In large measure we have been at the mercy of the general education establishment in that we accept problem pupils who have been referred out of the regular grades. In this way, we contribute to the delinquency of the general educators since we remove the pupils that are problems for them and thus reduce their need to deal with individual differences. Because of these pressures from the school system, we have been guilty of fostering quantity with little respect for quality of special education instruction. . . . Our first responsibility is to have an abiding commitment to the less fortunate children we aim to serve.

M. Dunn, 'Special Education for the Mildly Retarded—Is Much of It Justifiable?,' 35 Exceptional Children 5, 20 (1968) . . ..

"It should be noted that mainstreaming does not necessarily call for the eradication of all special education settings. Some educators do take an extreme position, sometimes termed a 'zero reject' model, aimed at making it virtually impossible to switch mildly disturbed or behaviorally disoriented children out of the regular classroom, but providing support and special training to the regular teacher. E. g., M. S. Lilly, 'A Training Based Model for Special Education,' in J. P. Glavin, MAJOR ISSUES IN SPECIAL EDUCATION, 219 (1973). See also testimony of Dr. Rachel Lauer, transcript at 1142–45. Most take a less absolutist stance, and are critical of the 'zero reject' model.

Some very peculiar things have happened in the name of education in the United States, and this movement toward integration into the regular grades is among them. Tens of thousands of children are involved as well as thousands of teachers. However, the literature is devoid of any reasonable research which demonstrates the positive gains to both exceptional and normal children under this arrangement. Overnight, educational leadership has advocated integration. No solid facts exist to support their claims. The literature is full of opinions, but not facts born of careful longitudinal research under relatively controlled conditions —essentials in this significant issue. . . .

Caution is recommended, for the needs of a generation of children are at stake. Those things which can be considered good in the special class should be retained and further perfected. Those elements which give rise to sound hope for integration should immediately be put to the test. The culling from both should provide the base for a rich educational plan for the next generation of exceptional children.

. . .

1. For the child, it is desirable to provide service outside the regular classroom . . . when his needs cannot reasonably be met within the flexibility possible in the regular classroom. Meeting needs does not include children who exist, even placidly in a regular class, but whose problems are such that educational growth fails. The fact that they present no problem to the group or the teacher is not enough. They must benefit by remaining.

2. It must be remembered that the normal pupils have rights too. The usual school operates on a large group basis and has goals which are set in terms of a broad normal range. The exceptional child with bizarre behavior, excessive aggression, or an all-out belligerent attitude may upset the group or require an inordinate amount of teacher time so that the other pupils are left with too little help. In other words, it may be asking the class to take on more than it can when a disturbed pupil remains. When the group is being sacrificed for the individual, resources outside the classroom are needed.

3. Some teachers handle a trying child well, others do not. Some have high tolerance, some low tolerance. There is nothing to be gained by saying that every teacher should be able to accept one such child or two. When the disturbed child takes up the teacher's psychic energy and reduces her effectiveness, removal is necessary.

Wm. M. Cruikshank, G. O. Johnson, EDUCATION OF EXCEPTIONAL CHILDREN AND YOUTH, 82, 84, 597–98 (3d Edition 1975). See also F. Christoplos, P. Renz, 'A Critical Examination of Special Education Programs,' 3 Journal of

Special Education 371, 373–74 (1969) (no reliable evidence either way as to effect on learning of 'normal' or exceptional children from inclusion of the latter in the regular class).

"Criticism and skepticism of mainstreaming has stemmed also from a fear that the process may advance without adequate changes in the system and that the results will be disastrous. A recent study of the impact of mainstreaming on deaf children pointed out the dangers incurred in forcing untrained teachers in overcrowded classrooms to deal with a new group of students who are tragically vulnerable educationally, psychologically and socially. 'The dream is equality and social acceptance. The fact is that nine out of ten deaf chidren will receive neither. For some, mainstreaming may be catastrophic.' J. Greenberg, G. Doolittle, 'Can Schools Speak the Language of the Deaf,' N.Y. Times Sunday Magazine, 50, Dec. 11, 1977.

"The controversy over mainstreaming of emotionally disturbed and behaviorally maladjusted students is especially intense. The disruptive behavior so often manifested by these children presents more of a threat to the integrity of the regular classroom than do under-achievement or physical handicaps. Unlike the latter problems, 'acting out' is not easily accommodated by special academic materials or adjustment of the physical plant. A. J. Pappanikou, J. L. Paul, MAINSTREAMING EMOTIONALLY DISTURBED CHILDREN, xii–xiii (1977); Wm. C. Morse 'The Psychology of Mainstreaming Socio-Emotionally Disturbed Children,' in A. J. Pappanikou and J. L. Paul, supra at 18, 22.  .  .  . "

.  .  .

This case, *Lora*, involved plaintiffs who had complained "that their constitutional and statutory rights are being denied by the procedures and facilities afforded by New York City for the education of children whose emotional problems result in severe acting-out and aggression in school, behavior which may produce danger to others as well as themselves. These children often have severe academic problems. They have been placed in special day schools for the education of the emotionally handicapped. The schools utilize smaller class size, specially trained teachers and support staff, and special facilities, designed to provide a 'generally therapeutic' atmosphere.

"Racial composition of the pupil population in these special day schools is 68% Black; 27% Hispanic; and 5% other, primarily White (figures as of October 31, 1977). The high percentage of 'minorities' in these schools is not a recent phenomenon; rather, a disparate racial composition has remained constant for nearly 15 years. The other major services for children with emotional disturbance, 'classes for emotionally handicapped' (CEH classes) have a higher proportion, 20%, of non-minority students. Still higher is the proportion of Whites in the New York City public school equivalent grades: 36% Black, 23% Hispanic and 41% 'other.'

"Starting from this striking racial disparity plaintiffs have added extensive evidence supporting their thesis. They contend that the special day schools are intentionally segregated 'dumping grounds' for minorities forced into inadequate facilities without due process. White students with the same problems, it is maintained, are treated more favorably in other settings. Defendants and their witnesses deny any racial bias. They point with considerable pride to the advantages afforded, at substantial taxpayers' expense, in an effort to bring these problem students into the mainstream of education and society.

"Laid bare by the dispute is one of the most excruciating issues of our democratic society. Almost every American agrees that the ringing words of the Declaration of Independence, 'all men are created equal,' mean at least that each person shall have an equal opportunity to develop and exercise his God-given talents. But many children born into deprived social, economic and psychological backgrounds lack the equality of real opportunity they would have had were their familial circumstances more fortunate. Unfavorable environment in such cases overwhelms favorable genes. To afford equality of opportunity so far as we can, we depend primarily on education. The free public system of education is the great equalizer, conceived to allow those born into the lowliest status the opportunity of rising as far as their potential talents, drive and luck will take them. But the system is—and perhaps by its nature must be—inadequate to lift fully the burden of poverty, of discrimination and of ignorance that so many of our children carry.

"Depressingly revealed by the record are some of the almost insoluble problems of educating certain of the products of this background—the socially and emotionally maladjusted children who present a physical danger to themselves and others, who cannot learn and who prevent others from learning in a regular school setting. Yet the evidence before us also illustrates how talented and devoted school personnel, sympathetic to this group of children and operating under federal, state and local laws and regulations, can help even those who appeared beyond redemption.

"Hope for substantial improvements lies not in the courts but in the hands of those who control society's resources and of those who are trained and dedicated to use pedagogic and therapeutic arts. Nevertheless, since the matter has been properly placed before us for adjudication, we have, under our legal system, no alternative but to address the issues in their limited legal context. The dismal facts, the enobling aspirations, and the encouraging portents for the future have been revealed by devoted and skillful counsel for both sides. . . ."

.   .   .

Judge Weinstein wrote an extensive opinion, holding that assigning emotionally handicapped students to special day schools without providing them adequate educational and therapeutic treatment violated their right to treatment under the due process and equal protection clauses of the United States Constitution and various federal statutes, including the EHA and the Rehabilitation Act. In addition, the court held that before a child can be removed from the educational mainstream and placed in a special education program, due process and federal and state statutes require the provision of adequate notice and an opportunity to be heard. Furthermore, the assignment of students to the special day schools was found to be racially discriminatory in violation of the equal protection clause and Title VI of the Civil Rights Act of 1964, 42 U.S.C.A. § 2000d. Significantly, the court held that Title VI did not require an intent to discriminate. For discussion, see, Comment, The Right To Treatment and Educational Rights of Handicapped Persons: Lora v. Board of Educ., 79 Col.L.Rev. 807 (1979).

————

Another federal law, Section 504 of the Rehabilitation Act of 1973, 87 Stat. 394, as amended, 29 U.S.C.A. § 794, provides that "No otherwise qualified handicapped individual . . . shall, solely by reason of his handicap, be excluded from the participation in, or be denied the benefits of, or be subjected to discrimination under any program or activity receiving federal financial assistance." In Southeastern Community College v. Davis, —— U.S. ——, 99 S.Ct. 2361, 60 L.Ed.2d 980 (1979), the U. S. Supreme Court interpreted this statute narrowly holding, contra to the Lau v. Nichols approach, that "neither the language, purpose nor history of § 504 reveals an intent to impose an affirmative action obligation on all recipients of federal funds" and that "even if HEW has attempted to create such an obligation itself, it lacks the authority to do so."

## THE OTHER MINORITY

A Preliminary Report on USOE's Effort To Help Our Most Promising Children
by
Dr. Harold C. Lyon, Jr.
Director of Education For The Gifted and Talented
U.S. Office of Education

.  .  .    there is another minority that has as much right to special attention—a minority denoted not by race, socio-economic background, ethnic origin or impaired faculties, but by their exceptional ability. They come from all levels of society, from all races and national origins, and are equally distributed among the sexes.

These children have an unusual endowment of talent. It may be intellectual. It may be aesthetic. It may be creative in an artistic or scientific or social way, or even in ways which neither the schools nor society yet understand. But whatever their talent, from their ranks will come the small percentage of humans who are truly great —not just capable performers in the sciences, the arts, and the professions, but those extraordinary few who will leave their disciplines, their societies, and perhaps even the human kind different because of their work. These are the future Beethovens; the Newtons, the Jeffersons, the Picassos, the Baldwins, the Ernesto Galarzas and the Martin Luther Kings.

These are gifted children—and, like the other minorities, they need help. Though the great men mentioned above had their painful struggles, history was generous to them, and it may be difficult to grasp why children with the potential to achieve a similar eminence should require special attention from our educational system. The explanation is that for every Einstein or Martin Luther King who emerges, it is likely that a dozen or more do not. Though it is impossible to offer scientific proof of this hypothesis—biographers, after all, do not study average men and women—the evidence that we have from the lives of great men and women as well as studies of school-age children back up this conclusion from a 1968 investigation of the gifted.

> "We would even go so far as to say that, to a very considerable extent, those individuals who constitute the 'creative minority' in our society (or in *any* society)  .  .  . have achieved their eminence *in spite of,* rather than because of, our school system."

Thomas Edison's mother withdrew him from school after three months of the first grade because, his teacher said, he was "unable." Gregor Mendel, founder of the science of genetics, flunked his teacher's examination four times and gave up trying. Newton, considered a poor student in grammar school, left at 14, was sent back at 19 because he read so much, and graduated from Cambridge without any distinction whatever.  Winston Churchill was last in his class at Harrow.  Charles Darwin dropped out of medical school.  Shelley was expelled from Oxford, James Whistler and Edgar Allen Poe from West Point.  Gibbon considered his education a waste of time, and Einstein found grammar school boring;  it was his uncle, showing the boy tricks with numbers, who stimulated his interest in mathematics.

For every genius who did poorly in school, one can cite another who did well.  Yet this random sampling of academic misfits indicates that traditional academic programs are sometimes poorly suited to humans of extraordinary potential.  One is left to wonder how many Churchills, how many Whistlers did not survive educational disaster —how many hatchlings (pronounced ugly ducklings) had the good luck and the persistence to continue seeking other ponds until they were recognized as swans.

Why should children with unusual ability experience trouble with ordinary school curricula?

Precisely because they are ordinary.  Education is a mass enterprise, geared by economic necessity as well as politics to the abilities of the majority—and the majority are, by definition, average, but just as a child of less-than-average mental ability frequently has trouble keeping up with his classmates, so a child of above average ability has trouble staying *behind* with them.  Mastering in a few days material that other children require weeks to understand, he or she becomes bored, restless, anxious to move on.  Prevented from moving ahead by the rigidity of normal school procedures—assigned to a class with others of the same age, expected to devote the same attention to the *same* textbooks, required to be present for the same number of hours in the same seat—the gifted youngster typically takes one of two tacks:  he or she conceals his or her ability, anxious not to embarrass others or draw their ridicule by superior performance;  or, not understanding his or her frustration, becomes a discipline problem.  Typical of the latter case was a troublesome seventh-grader whose baffled teacher reported that, while the girl claimed she could not understand simple fractions, she "delighted in working compound trigonometry fractions";  the same week that she failed a math test, this girl was caught in study hall "writing her own math textbook."

Uniformity of curriculum is not the only difficulty under which gifted children must work.  Others include:

—*Failure to be identified:*  The president of one State association for the handicapped reported that his staff members find "extremely gifted children among their target group *very* frequently," and another State found that 3.4 percent of its school dropouts had IQ's of 120 or higher.

Of schools surveyed by the U.S. Office of Education during the 1969–70 school year, 57.5 percent reported that they had no gifted pupils . . . an indication that teachers and other staff simply did not know how to identify them.

—*Hostility of school staff*: For quite human reasons, including an impatience with the "unusual" child and an assumption that the gifted are a favored elite who deserve even less than normal consideration, some educational personnel actually resent them. One study, surprisingly, found "significantly greater hostility toward the gifted among school psychologists" than among school personnel.

—*Lack of attention to the gifted*: In only 10 State departments of education is there a professional assigned full-time responsibility for education of the gifted and talented; it is estimated that fewer than four percent of the Nation's gifted and talented students have access to special programs. Of these, the great majority are in the 10 States with a full-time professional responsible for programs in this area.

—*Lack of trained teachers*: Only 12 American Universities offer graduate programs to train teachers in educating the gifted and talented.

Most Americans by now accept the reality of racial, linguistic, socio-economic, and physical handicaps, and back special educational efforts to help children overcome these obstacles to their self-realization. It is time for us to recognize that unusual ability can also prove a barrier to achievement, and that it is peculiarly in our national interest to assure the development of children who have potential to make extraordinary contributions to our common life.

---

### ACKERMAN v. RUBIN

Supreme Court, Special Term, Bronx County, 1962.
35 Misc.2d 707, 231 N.Y.S.2d 112, aff'd 17 A.D.2d 796, 232 N.Y.S.2d 872.

BERNARD NEWMAN, Justice. Petitioner seeks an order of the court (Civil Practice Act, art. 78) compelling respondents to admit his son, who has completed his sixth grade and is now eligible to enter the Junior High School Division, to a two-year special progress class in September of 1962, to be conducted at his Junior High School in The Bronx.

Respondents readily concede that the pupil is academically well qualified, but have denied him admission to the special class on the grounds (a) that he is not of the required age (11.3 years), and (b) that he had been previously "accelerated" in school. These grounds for refusal are in accordance with respondents' established criteria for admission to the special progress class. The latter objection was waived in several similar situations, and hence the respondents' refusal must be predicated on the former ground, viz., that the pupil is younger than the requisite age. Petitioner contends that this criterion applicable to his son (10.7 years of age) is arbitrary, capricious and without legal foundation.

It appears that the Board of Education initiated special progress classes more than forty years ago. Indeed, it has been the experience of the Board and of educators throughout the country that special progress classes and enriched program classes are of great benefit to gifted students, enabling them the better to develop their potential. From time to time the Board has revised the requirements for entrance to such special classes.

The last revision was promulgated by a Board of Education directive in July of 1962—after decades of study and trial by experienced educators—and the Board now offers three different courses comprising the Junior High School curriculum:

    (a) regular three-year classes;

    (b) three-year special progress classes, embodying a specially enriched curriculum;

    (c) two-year special progress classes, accelerated to cover the regular three-year course in two years.

The directive limits eligibility to the b and c courses to pupils with superior scholarship grades. Petitioner's son has been admitted to b, but has been denied admission to c, primarily because of the fact that he will be 10.7 years of age in September—the date of admission—as against the 11.3 years-age requirement. The Board freely acknowledges that the pupil meets all the other detailed requirements; but insists that the norms adopted are not arbitrary, and that the additional year required for younger students will serve to develop them emotionally, socially, and physiologically at the adolescent stage so as to eliminate stress and aid the child's development.

Petitioner, in effect, desires to substitute the judgment of a justly proud parent for that of experienced educators, who seek to apply their observations and experience for the benefit of his son. Contrary to petitioner's contentions, the standards adopted by respondents are based, not on whim or caprice, but on years of study and trial; they are derived from the experience of day-to-day dealings with children and their problems.

In the instant proceeding, it appears to be the considered opinion of those educators who are in close contact with petitioner's son that, although he is a gifted child, nevertheless for reasons specifically outlined in the Board's answering papers, further acceleration might be detrimental to this student's best interests. Indeed, the pupil's teacher for the last two years graciously avers that the pupil "has a great potential and will develop into an exceptional student, if his development is allowed to take a natural course".

Certainly, the court may not hold as arbitrary or capricious the respondents' determination that chronologically determined physical, social and emotional maturity are vital and proper factors to be considered in the development and education of a child. To thrust a youngster into an environment where all his classmates are older may well result in the consequent impairment of the necessary social integration of the child with his classmates. The court proceeds from the hypothesis that these respondents are dedicated to the proper educational development of the whole child; and nothing has been shown to cast the slightest doubt upon the validity of this assumption. It may be that respondents, in the exercise of their continuing concern for the proper development of all their charges, including petitioner's son, will find it possible to afford him all or some of the additional benefits of the accelerated special progress classes. It may be that continuing examination of the emotional, physiological and social maturity of petitioner's son will afford respondents, in the future, a basis for review of their determination challenged herein. Our educational system continually changes and re-examination of procedures and policies is a constant process. In the course of this process, perhaps the respondents will afford intellectually gifted, but chronologically younger children, such as petitioner's son, opportunities for advancement and enrichment supplementing those afforded in the three-year special progress program described above. However, the court will not attempt to invade that area; nor may the court seek to substitute its judgment in that area for respondents' expertise.

Consequently, the court finds the Board's directive (to which petitioner objects) to be proper and in accord with the applicable law (see Sec. 2554 [9], Education Law detailing the "Powers and duties of the board of education"). And the court sincerely believes that petitioner, upon objective reflection, will agree that respondents, in adopting these regulations, have acted in the best interests of his son and all other school children. Furthermore, it is axiomatic that a reasonable administrative determination will not be disturbed by the court. . . . Plainly, then, the directive comes within the familiar rule that the courts will apply the presumption of reasonableness to the acts of public officials taken for the general welfare . . .

Accordingly, the application is denied and the petition is dismissed.

### NOTES AND QUESTIONS

1. Is uniformity of age in grades beginning with the first grade a worthy educational goal? A useful administrative device? If you were an instructor in a course of beginning foreign language for adults would you first group them by age for instructional purposes? Can you

think of any educational or training program apart from the common schools where children are grouped according to age rather than by level of achievement? Is there justifying reason for schools to be different? Is ability grouping the answer?

## CONSTITUTIONAL FREEDOM AND EDUCATIONAL FINANCE

### INTRODUCTION

Local government districts raise over half of the school revenue in the United States. While they rely on income and sales taxes, as well as a variety of other type of taxes, the major levy used is the property tax. The property tax is collected from owners of property and is based on the value of that property; for example, a property tax base (say, $1,000) (statutory assessment formulas for property vary: "market value," "actual value," "fair value," "full value," "fair cash value," "true and fair market value," but, basically, they all mean "market value" which, in turn, generally refers to the last sales price), plus a tax (rate say, 1%) giving a tax yield ($10.00).

Usually the "property" that can be subjected to taxation by a local government unit is defined by state constitutions and statutes. Almost all "real property" (land and buildings, bulkheads and other improvements erected onto the land) is taxable. However, many states allow "homestead" and "veteran" tax exemptions. Moreover, since states are constitutionally disallowed from taxing federally owned real property without the consent of Congress, much real property, especially in the American west, escapes state and local taxation. A second category of property subject to the property tax is "tangible personal property." Tangible personal property includes almost everything that is movable, such as cars, trucks, railroad cars, clothing, furniture, business equipment, inventories, farm equipment and animals, jewelry, etc. Some states include tangible personal property under their general property laws and others have special laws applying only to this type of property. Tax exemptions exist here as well. Finally, there is intangible personal property, such as bank accounts, stocks and bonds and other valuable claims of ownership or control. Intangibles are extremely difficult to locate and to assess. Only few more than one-third of the states include intangible personal property in their general property tax. The remainder of the states tax intangibles by special statute and at very low rates or not at all. Clearly, the major type of taxable property subject to local government taxation is real estate.

While it is true that the property tax is "paid" by the owner, it is possible for some property owners to "shift" the tax burden onto others. For example, the owner of an apartment house may "shift" the tax burden onto his tenants by charging them higher apartment rental prices. In these circumstances the tenant bears the "incidence" of the tax while the property owner "pays" it and also receives a federal income tax deduction because he "paid" it. Taxes can be shifted only by manipulations in the market in one of two ways, either by charging a higher price ("shifting" forward) or by being economically strong enough to pay a lower price for what one buys ("shifting" backward). Since ordinary people who own houses do not function in the housing market, it is generally believed that they cannot shift their property tax burdens. They "pay" and they also suffer the "incidence" and burden of the property tax. On the other hand, when levied on business properties the property tax is generally believed to be shifted rather easily and quickly onto the consumer. The tax is simply viewed as a direct expense of doing business and added to the sales price, especially where sellers have any degree of market or monopoly power. Also, to the ordinary person the property tax, like the sales tax, is regressive, primarily because high-priced properties are underassessed. (A regressive tax is one that falls most heavily on those persons least capable of paying it.) Estates and mansions are put on the market less frequently than moderately priced housing; thus, their last "market" value for tax purposes tends to be lower. Peter Gruenstein ("What's Wrong With the Property Tax," THE NATION, p. 582, May 7, 1973) states that:

> A large part of the property tax morass stems from unprofessional or dishonest assessments which produce tremendous tax breaks for large corporations and the wealthy. For example, a study made by Texas University law students found that oil-producing properties in Hector County, Texas, were underassessed by about 56 per cent as opposed to about 7 per cent for home owners. Union Camp, a large South Carolina corporation, sold to the state for $2,000 per acre land that was being assessed at $20 per acre. Even after the sale, adjoining Union Camp land that was not sold continued to be assessed at $20 per acre. In Appalachia, rich coal lands are being assessed at $10 per acre or less, even though they sell for $200 to $500 per acre on the open market.

Moreover, the property tax properly can be viewed as an excise on housing, perhaps representing, on the average, a figure as high as twenty-five percent. Thus, the property tax is one of the heaviest taxes levied on any single item, or service, in the United States.

Because of the heavy reliance on the property tax local government units usually can get more money only in three ways (1) reassessing existing properties values upward; (2) raising the tax rates if they are not already at the statutory maximum, or (3) by levying taxes on newly built properties, especially industrial properties. The first two are highly unpopular which tends to leave only the third.

But the third alternative usually runs into obstacles because local government units compete with each other for the location of new industrial properties by offering prospective industries lower tax rates than those offered by another local government unit. This "beggar-my-neighbor" policy is well known. This type of "competition" produces the unfortunate consequence of concentrating taxable industries within the one or few local government districts that offer the lowest tax rates and of concentrating residential properties in the other districts which soon suffer from high taxes and low services. Given the flight of whites and new industry to the suburbs, more and more a diminishing tax base is becoming the fate of America's core cities. It is clear that equal educational opportunity is denied some children when there are major disparities in per-student expenditures among school districts within a single state.

## The Gap Between Rich and Poor Schools

State by State Ratio of Assessed Property Valuation per Pupil in School District with the Largest Figure to That in District with Smallest Figure, 1968–69.

[A8748]

## J. COONS, W. H. CLUNE III, S. SUGARMAN, PRIVATE WEALTH AND PUBLIC EDUCATION

Copyright 1970, Belknap Press of Harvard University Press.
Excerpts from pages xviii-xxii.

.   .   .   .   A brief tale of two schoolboys will illustrate. They could be any color, but suppose them white in a white neighborhood. One lives on 36th Street in Oakland, California; his friend lives across the street in Emeryville. Every weekday morning at 8:00 they separate, each to attend his assigned public school—one in the Oakland system, one in the Emeryville District. If the reader knows something of California public schools, this trivial event is worth recording. The separation is a fateful one for these children and the millions like them around the nation for whom the accidents of residence and boundary play a decisive role in the character of their formal education. The State of California, like most states, has provided a system guaranteeing to one child a superior education, while to the other it offers mediocrity or worse. Oakland will spend $600–700 on the first child; the Emeryville student will go first class at nearly three times that expense. [The Oakland tax rate is nearly twice that of Emeryville; *California Public Schools Selected Statistics 1967–68,* 24 (Sacramento: Department of Education, 1969).] This example is neither extreme nor extraordinary. The spectrum of school districts in California includes expenditures both higher and considerably lower than these. Nor is the picture radically different in other states: expenditures in Illinois range from under $400 up to $1,600 or more per pupil, and the disparities in Ohio are similar.

Differentials of these magnitudes in per-pupil expenditure within the same state should evoke nothing but outrage. Indeed, there is something incongruous about a differential of any magnitude the sole justification for which is an imaginary school district line between two children. It is the kind of phenomenon that forces its defenders into the dense refuge of "political realities" in search of a rationale. The plain fact is that our state governments have embraced the philosophy that, as a rule, the quality of public education should be in direct proportion to the wealth of the school district; in general this also means that the quality will be in inverse proportion to the needs of children. The primary dependence of public education upon the real property tax and the localization of that tax's administration and expenditure have combined to make the public school into an educator for the educated rich and a keeper for the uneducated poor. There exists no more powerful force for rigidity of social class and the frustration of natural potential than the modern public school system with its systematic discrimination against poor districts.

The remedy is not obvious. Political forces supporting the status quo no doubt vary in strength from state to state, but educational systems themselves are so structured as to be naturally protected from legislative drift toward an egalitarian form. Districts favored by a superior tax base are likely to be opposed to change on all grounds; districts of average affluence are apathetic but can also be opposed to change because they fear potential loss of local control. Poor districts alone have a clear stake in change, but their case is supported only by justice. Hence the persuasiveness of the argument from "reality." Little is to be expected from the political process in its legislative mode.

What, if anything, can be expected from the judicial process? The lawyer's instinct is to recoil from judicial intrusion into the structure of state government. The instinct is sound; but, like most instincts, it can also mislead. Its solid core lies in the mistrust of political change through nonmajoritarian decision-making. It is at ground a democratic impulse which prefers that questions of structure be submitted at least indirectly to the popular will. Under certain conditions its essential benevolence is self-defeating. Legislative malapportionment is a historic instance in which vox populi was simply unavailable in any effective form. The will of the majority required not judicial restraint but judicial rescue.

The goal of equal education may justify heroic judicial measures on a rationale similar in two respects to the reapportionment theme. First, as noted, the deprived child and his subsociety may be and frequently are in a position of political impotence, not because of limited numbers but because of districting structure and other factors organic to the system. Second, education shares with voting the quality of being logically and practically anterior to all other values in democratic society. In fact, as between the two, education arguably deserves precedence as the indispensable preamble of political life.

But there is a third and independent rationale for equality in public education in any capitalist society. At the pinnacle of our economic temple still flies the standard of universal access to the levers of opulence and mobility. Beyond argument, the prime mover in the modern labor market is education. In a free-enterprise system its differential provision by the public school marks the intrusion of economic (if not legal) heresy, for it means that certain participants in the economic race are hobbled at the gate—and hobbled by the public handicapper.

In assessing the propriety of judicial intervention under the Fourteenth Amendment these three factors and others will be elaborated in more detail. They are noted at this preliminary stage to suggest both that systematic discrimination in quality of public education may be viewed as a realistic constitutional issue and that the objection to it is in many respects an intensely conservative one. This latter observation is useful here to parry or at least postpone the natural reaction that equality is once more to become the leveler's stalking horse. The truth is not so simple. The case for equality in public education is a schizophrenic medley of Karl Marx and Barry Goldwater, St. Thomas and Saint-Simon. Reservation of judgment is all that can be asked, but nothing less will do.

The problem is complicated principally by the value that Americans place on local decision-making—a value we shall label "subsidiarity." Few would object in theory to equality of educational opportunity if that result did not seem necessarily to cast out local choice. Some argue simplistically that equality of educational opportunity is flatly inconsistent with local authority. [See, e. g., Phillip Kurland, "Equal Educational Opportunity: The Limits of Constitutional Jurisprudence Undefined," *University of Chicago Law Review*, 35:583 (1968). (See also A. E. Wise, *Rich Schools, Poor Schools: The Promise of Equal Educational Opportunity* (Chicago: University of Chicago Press, 1968).] We are convinced that this supposed antithesis between equality and subsidiarity is overdrawn: that both values can be preserved if only one is willing to struggle with the complexities and fine tuning required of any balanced system. Much of this book involves an analysis of the relation between the two values and of structures designed to achieve such a balance. A moment's reflection will suggest the significance of such structures for the movement toward greater decentralization of control in public education. Until it descends to the level of the family, the drift toward smaller units in education has no natural limit other than the ability of such units to finance themselves. . . .

## SAN ANTONIO INDEPENDENT SCHOOL DIST. v. RODRIGUEZ

Supreme Court of the United States, 1973.
409 U.S. 822, 93 S.Ct. 40, 34 L.Ed.2d 77.

Mr. Justice POWELL delivered the opinion of the Court.

This suit attacking the Texas system of financing public education was initiated by Mexican-American parents whose children attend the elementary and secondary schools in the Edgewood Independent School District, an urban school district in San Antonio, Texas. They brought a class action on behalf of school children throughout the State who are members of minority groups or who are poor and reside in school districts having a low property tax base. . . .

### I

The first Texas Constitution, promulgated upon Texas' entry into the Union in 1845, provided for the establishment of a system of free schools. Early in its history, Texas adopted a dual approach to the financing of its schools, relying on mutual participation by the local school districts and the State. . . .

Until recent times Texas was a predominantly rural State and its population and property wealth were spread relatively evenly across the State. Sizable differences in the value of assessable property between local school districts became increasingly evident as the State became more industrialized and as rural-to-urban population shifts became more pronounced. The location of commercial and industrial property began to play a significant role in determining the amount of tax resources available to each school district. These growing disparities in population and taxable property between districts were responsible in part for increasingly notable differences in levels of local expenditure for education. . . .

Recognizing the need for increased state funding to help offset disparities in local spending and to meet Texas' changing educational requirements, the state legislature in the late 1940's undertook a thorough evaluation of public education with an eye toward major reform. [After review, it] establish[ed] the Texas Minimum Foundation School Program. Today this Program accounts for approximately half of the total educational expenditures in Texas.

The Program calls for state and local contributions to a fund earmarked specifically for teacher salaries, operating expenses, and transportation costs. The State, supplying funds from its general revenues, finances approximately 80% of the Program, and the school districts are responsible—as a unit—for providing the remaining 20%. The districts' share, known as the Local Fund Assignment, is apportioned among the school districts under a formula designed to reflect each district's relative taxpaying ability. . . . In the years since this program went into operation in 1949, expenditures for education—from State as well as local sources—have increased steadily. Between 1949 and 1967 expenditures increased by approximately 500%. . . .

The school district in which appellees reside, the Edgewood Independent School District, has been compared throughout this litigation with the Alamo Heights Independent School District. This comparison between the least and most affluent districts in the San Antonio area serves to illustrate the manner in which the dual system of finance operates. . . . Edgewood is one of seven public school districts in the metropolitan area. Approximately 22,000 students are enrolled in its 25 elementary and secondary schools. The district is situated in the core-city sector of San Antonio in a residential neighborhood that has little commercial or industrial property. The residents are predominantly of Mexican-American descent: approximately 90% of the student population is Mexican-American and over 6% is Negro. The average assessed property value per pupil is $5,960—the lowest in the metropolitan area—and the median family income ($4,686) is also the lowest. At an equalized tax rate of $1.05 per $100 of assessed property—the highest in the metropolitan area—the district contributed $26 to the education of each child for the 1967–1968 school year above its Local Fund Assignment for the Minimum Foundation Program. The Foundation Program contributed $222 per pupil for a state-local total of $248. Federal funds added another $108 for a total of $356 per pupil.

Alamo Heights is the most affluent school district in San Antonio. Its six schools, housing approximately 5,000 students, are situated in a residential community quite unlike the Edgewood District. The school population is predominantly Anglo, having only 18% Mexican-Americans and less than 1% Negroes. The assessed property value per pupil exceeds $49,000 and the median family income is $8,001. In 1967–1968 the local tax rate of $.85 per $100 of valuation yielded $333 per pupil over and above its contribution to the Foundation Program. Coupled with the $225 provided from that Program, the district was able to supply $558 per student. Supplemented by a $36 per pupil grant from federal sources, Alamo Heights spent $594 per pupil.

Although the 1967–1968 school year figures provide the only complete statistical breakdown for each category of aid, more recent partial statistics indicate that the previously noted trend of increasing state aid has been significant. For the 1970–1971 school year, the Foundation School Program allotment for Edgewood was $356 per pupil. . . . Alamo Heights enjoyed a similar increase under the Foundation Program, netting $491 per pupil in 1970–1971. These recent figures also reveal the extent to which these two districts' allotments were funded from their own required contributions to the Local Fund Assignment. Alamo Heights, because of its relative wealth, was required to contribute out of its local property tax collections approximately $100 per pupil, or about 20% of its Foundation grant. Edgewood, on the other hand, paid only $8.46 per pupil, which is about 2.4% of its grant, . . . it was these disparities, largely attributable to differences in the amounts of money collected through local property taxation, that led the District Court to conclude that Texas' dual system of public school finance violated the Equal Protection Clause. The District Court held that the Texas system discriminates on the basis of wealth in the manner in which education is provided for its people. Finding that wealth is a "suspect" classification and that education is a "fundamental" interest, the District Court held that the Texas system could be sustained only if the State could show that it was premised upon some compelling state interest. On this issue the court concluded that "[n]ot only are defendants unable to demonstrate compelling state interests . . . they fail even to establish a reasonable basis for these classifications."

II

The wealth discrimination discovered by the District Court in this case, and by several other courts that have recently struck down school financing laws in other States, is quite unlike any of the forms of wealth discrimination heretofore reviewed by this Court. Rather than focusing on the unique features of the alleged discrimination, the courts in these cases have virtually assumed their findings of a suspect classification through a simplistic process of analysis: since, under the traditional systems of financing public schools, some poorer people receive less expensive educations than other more affluent people, these systems discriminate on the basis of wealth. This approach largely ignores the hard threshold questions, including whether it makes a difference for purposes of consideration under the Constitution that the class of disadvantaged "poor" cannot be identified or defined in customary equal protection terms, and whether the relative—rather than absolute—nature of the asserted deprivation is of significant consequence. Before a State's laws and the justifications for the classifications they create are subjected to strict judicial scrutiny, we think these threshold considerations must be analyzed more closely than they were in the court below.

The case comes to us with no definitive description of the classifying facts or delineation of the disfavored class. Examination of the District Court's opinion and of appellees' complaint, briefs, and contentions at oral argument suggests, however, at least three ways in which the discrimination claimed here might be described. The Texas system of school finance might be regarded as discriminating (1) against "poor" persons whose incomes fall below some identifiable level of poverty or who might be characterized as functionally "indigent," or (2) against those who are relatively poorer than others, or (3) against all those who, irrespective of their personal incomes, happen to reside in relatively poorer school districts. Our task must be to ascertain whether, in fact, the Texas system has been shown to discriminate on any of these possible bases and, if so, whether the resulting classification may be regarded as suspect.

The precedents of this Court provide the proper starting point. The individuals or groups of individuals who constituted the class discriminated against in our prior cases shared two distinguishing characteristics: because of their impecunity they were completely unable to pay for some desired benefit, and as a consequence, they sustained an absolute deprivation of a meaningful opportunity to enjoy that benefit. In Griffin v. Illinois, 351 U.S. 12, 76 S.Ct. 585, 100 L. Ed. 891 (1956), and its progeny, the Court invalidated state laws that prevented an indigent criminal defendant from acquiring a transcript, or an adequate substitute for a transcript, for use at several stages of the trial and appeal process. The payment requirements in each case were found to occasion *de facto* discrimination against those who, because of their indigency, were totally unable to pay for transcripts. And, the Court in each case emphasized that no constitutional violation would have been shown if the State had provided some "adequate substitute" for a full stenographic transcript.

Likewise, in Douglas v. California, 372 U.S. 353, 83 S.Ct. 814, 9 L.Ed.2d 811 (1963), a decision establishing an indigent defendant's right to court-appointed counsel on direct appeal, the Court dealt only with defendants who could not pay for counsel from their own resources and who had no other way of gaining representation. *Douglas* provides no relief for those on whom the burdens of paying for a criminal defense are relatively speaking, great but not insurmountable. Nor does it deal with relative differences in the quality of counsel acquired by the less wealthy.

Williams v. Illinois, 399 U.S. 235, 90 S.Ct. 2018, 26 L.Ed.2d 586 (1970), and Tate v. Short, 401 U.S. 395, 91 S.Ct. 668, 28 L.Ed.2d 130 (1971), struck down criminal penalties that subjected indigents to incarceration simply because of their inability to pay a fine. Again, the disadvantaged class was composed only of persons who were totally unable to pay the demanded sum. Those cases do not touch on the question whether equal protection is denied to persons with relatively less money on whom designated fines impose heavier burdens. The Court has not held that fines must be structured to reflect each person's ability to pay in order to avoid disproportionate burdens. Sentencing judges may, and often do, consider the defendant's ability to pay, but in such circumstances they are guided by sound judicial discretion rather than by constitutional mandate.

Finally, in Bullock v. Carter, 405 U.S. 134, 92 S.Ct. 849, 31 L.Ed. 2d 92 (1972), the Court invalidated the Texas filing fee requirement for primary elections. Both of the relevant classifying facts found in the previous cases were present there. The size of the fee, often runing into the thousands of dollars and, in at least one case, as high as $8,900, effectively barred all potential candidates who were unable to pay the required fee. As the system provided "no reasonable alternative means of access to the ballot" inability to pay occasioned an absolute denial of a position on the primary ballot.

.  .  . Even a cursory examination, however, demonstrates that neither of the two distinguishing characteristics of wealth classifications can be found here. First, in support of their charge that the system discriminates against the "poor," appellees have made no effort to demonstrate that it operates to the peculiar disadvantage of any class fairly definable as indigent, or as composed of persons whose incomes are beneath any designated poverty level. Indeed, there is reason to believe that the poorest families are not necessarily clustered in the poorest property districts. A recent and exhaustive study of school districts in Connecticut concluded that "[i]t is clearly incorrect  .  .  .  to contend that the 'poor' live in 'poor' districts .  .  .  . Thus, the major factual assumption of *Serrano*—that the educational finance system discriminates against the 'poor'—is simply false in Connecticut." Defining "poor" families as those below the Bureau of the Census "poverty level," the Connecticut study found, not surprisingly, that the poor were clustered around commercial and industrial areas—those same areas that provide the most attractive sources of property tax income for school districts. Whether a similar pattern would be discovered in Texas is not known, but there is no basis on the record in this case for assuming that the poorest people—defined by reference to any level of absolute impecunity—are concentrated in the poorest districts.

Second, neither appellees nor the District Court addressed the fact that, unlike each of the foregoing cases, lack of personal resources has not occasioned an absolute deprivation of the desired benefit. The argument here is not that the children in districts having relatively low assessable property values are receiving no public education; rather, it is that they are receiving a poorer quality education than that available to children in districts having more assessable wealth. Apart from the unsettled and disputed question whether the quality of education may be determined by the amount of money expended for it, a sufficient answer to appellees' argument is that at least where wealth is involved the Equal Protection Clause does not require absolute equality or precisely equal advantages.  Nor indeed, in view of the infinite variables affecting the educational process, can any system assure equal quality of education except in the most relative sense.  Texas asserts that the Minimum Foundation Program provides an "adequate" education for all children in the State.  By providing 12 years of free public school education, and by assuring teachers, books, transportation and operating funds, the Texas Legislature has endeavored to "guarantee, for the welfare of the state as a whole, that all people shall have at least an adequate program of education. This is what is meant by 'A Minimum Foundation Program of Education.' "  The State repeatedly asserted in its briefs in this Court that it has fulfilled this desire and that it now assures "every child in every school district an adequate education."  No proof was offered at trial persuasively discrediting or refuting the State's assertion.

For these two reasons—the absence of any evidence that the financing system discriminates against any definable category of "poor" people or that it results in the absolute deprivation of education—the disadvantaged class is not susceptible to identification in traditional terms.

As suggested above, appellees and the District Court may have embraced a second or third approach, the second of which might be characterized as a theory of relative or comparative discrimination based on family income.  Appellees sought to prove that a direct correlation exists between the wealth of families within each district and the expenditures therein for education.  That is, along a continuum, the poorer the family the lower the dollar amount of education received by the family's children. . . .  These questions need not be addressed in this case, however, since appellees' proof fails to support their allegations or the District Court's conclusions.

This brings us, then, to the third way in which the classification scheme might be defined—*district* wealth discrimination.  Since the only correlation indicated by the evidence is between district property wealth and expenditures, it may be argued that discrimination might be found without regard to the individual income characteristics of district residents. . . .  district except the district that has the most assessable wealth and spends the most on education. Alternatively, as suggested in Mr. Justice MARSHALL's dissenting opinion the class might be defined more restrictively to include children in districts with assessable property which falls below the statewide average, or median, or below some other artificially defined level.

However described, it is clear that appellees' suit asks this Court to extend its most exacting scrutiny to review a system that allegedly discriminates against a large, diverse, and amorphous class, unified only by the common factor of residence in districts that happen to have less taxable wealth than other districts. The system of alleged discrimination and the class it defines have none of the traditional indicia of suspectness: the class is not saddled with such disabilities, or subjected to such a history of purposeful unequal treatment, or relegated to such a position of political powerlessness as to command extraordinary protection from the majoritarian political process.

We thus conclude that the Texas system does not operate to the peculiar disadvantage of any suspect class. But in recognition of the fact that this Court has never heretofore held that wealth discrimination alone provides an adequate basis for invoking strict scrutiny, appellees have not relied solely on this contention. They also assert that the State's system impermissibly interferes with the exercise of a "fundamental" right and that accordingly the prior decisions of this Court require the application of the strict standard of judicial review. It is this question—whether education is a fundamental right, in the sense that it is among the rights and liberties protected by the Constitution—which has so consumed the attention of courts and commentators in recent years.

Nothing this Court holds today in any way detracts from our historic dedication to public education. We are in complete agreement with the conclusion of the three-judge panel below that "the grave significance of education both to the individual and to our society" cannot be doubted. But the importance of a service performed by the State does not determine whether it must be regarded as fundamental for purposes of examination under the Equal Protection Clause. . . . It is not the province of this Court to create substantive constitutional rights in the name of guaranteeing equal protection of the laws. Thus the key to discovering whether education is "fundamental" is not to be found in comparisons of the relative societal significance of education as opposed to subsistence or housing. Nor is it to be found by weighing whether education is as important as the right to travel. Rather, the answer lies in assessing whether there is a right to education explicitly or implicitly guaranteed by the Constitution.

Education, of course, is not among the rights afforded explicit protection under our Federal Constitution. Nor do we find any basis for saying it is implicitly so protected. As we have said, the undisputed importance of education will not alone cause this Court to depart from the usual standard for reviewing a State's social and economic legislation.  It is appellees' contention, however, that education is distinguishable from other services and benefits provided by the State because it bears a peculiarly close relationship to other rights and liberties accorded protection under the Constitution.  Specifically, they insist that education is itself a fundamental personal right because it is essential to the effective exercise of First Amendment freedoms and to intelligent utilization of the right to vote.  In asserting a nexus between speech and education, appellees urge that the right to speak is meaningless unless the speaker is capable of articulating his thoughts intelligently and persuasively.  The "marketplace of ideas" is an empty forum for those lacking basic communicative tools.  Likewise, they argue that the corollary right to receive information becomes little more than a hollow privilege when the recipient has not been taught to read, assimilate, and utilize available knowledge.

A similar line of reasoning is pursued with respect to the right to vote.  Exercise of the franchise, it is contended, cannot be divorced from the educational foundation of the voter.  The electoral process, if reality is to conform to the democratic ideal, depends on an informed electorate: a voter cannot cast his ballot intelligently unless his reading skills and thought processes have been adequately developed.

We need not dispute any of these propositions.  The Court has long afforded zealous protection against unjustifiable governmental interference with the individual's rights to speak and to vote.  Yet we have never presumed to possess either the ability or the authority to guarantee to the citizenry the most *effective* speech or the most *informed* electoral choice.  That these may be desirable goals of a system of freedom of expression and of a representative form of government is not to be doubted.  These are indeed goals to be pursued by a people whose thoughts and beliefs are freed from governmental interference.  But they are not values to be implemented by judicial intrusion into otherwise legitimate state activities.

Even if it were conceded that some identifiable quantum of education is a constitutionally protected prerequisite to the meaningful exercise of either right, we have no indication that the present levels of educational expenditure in Texas provide an education that falls short.  Whatever merit appellees' argument might have if a State's financing system occasioned an absolute denial of educational opportunities to any of its children, that argument provides no basis for finding an interference with fundamental rights where only relative differences in spending levels are involved and where—as is true in the present case—no charge fairly could be made that the system fails to provide each child with an opportunity to acquire the basic minimal skills necessary for the enjoyment of the rights of speech and of full participation in the political process.

Furthermore, the logical limitations on appellees' nexus theory are difficult to perceive. How, for instance, is education to be distinguished from the significant personal interests in the basics of decent food and shelter? Empirical examination might well buttress an assumption that the ill-fed, ill-clothed, and ill-housed are among the most ineffective participants in the political process and that they derive the least enjoyment from the benefits of the First Amendment.

.   .   . The present case, in another basic sense, is significantly different from any of the cases in which the Court has applied strict scrutiny to state or federal legislation touching upon constitutionally protected rights. Each of our prior cases involved legislation which "deprived," "infringed," or "interfered" with the free exercise of some such fundamental personal right or liberty. A critical distinction between those cases and the one now before us lies in what Texas is endeavoring to do with respect to education. Mr. Justice Brennan, writing for the Court in Katzenbach v. Morgan, 384 U.S. 641, 86 S.Ct. 1717, 16 L.Ed.2d 828 (1966), expresses well the salient point:

> "This is not a complaint that Congress   .   .   .   has unconstitutionally denied or diluted anyone's right to vote but rather that Congress violated the Constitution by not extending the relief effected [to others similarly situated]   .   .   .   .
>
> "[The federal law in question] does not restrict or deny the franchise but in effect extends the franchise to persons who otherwise would be denied it by state law.   .   .   . We need decide only whether the challenged limitation on the relief effected   .   .   .   was permissible. In deciding that question, the principle that calls for the closest scrutiny of distinctions in laws *denying* fundamental rights   .   .   . is inapplicable; for the distinction challenged by appellees is presented only as a limitation on a reform measure aimed at eliminating an existing barrier to the exercise of the franchise. Rather, in deciding the constitutional propriety of the limitations in such a reform measure we are guided by the familiar principles that a 'statute is not invalid under the Constitution because it might have gone farther than it did,'   .   .   .   that a legislature need not 'strike at all evils at the same time,'   .   .   . and that 'reform may take one step at a time, addressing itself to the phase of the problem which seems most acute to the legislative mind   .   .   .   .'" (Emphasis from original.)

The Texas system of school finance is not unlike the federal legislation involved in *Katzenbach* in this regard. Every step leading to the establishment of the system Texas utilizes today—including the decisions permitting localities to tax and expend locally, and creating and continuously expanding the state aid—was implemented in an effort to *extend* public education and to improve its quality. Of course, every reform that benefits some more than others may be criticized for what it fails to accomplish. But we think it plain that, in substance, the thrust of the Texas system is affirmative and reformatory and, therefore, should be scrutinized under judicial principles sensitive to the nature of the State's efforts and to the rights reserved to the States under the Constitution.

We need not rest our decision, however, solely on the inappropriateness of the strict scrutiny test. A century of Supreme Court adjudication under the Equal Protection Clause affirmatively supports the application of the traditional standard of review, which requires only that the State's system be shown to bear some rational relationship to legitimate state purposes. This case represents far more than a challenge to the manner in which Texas provides for the education of its children. We have here nothing less than a direct attack on the way in which Texas has chosen to raise and disburse state and local tax revenues. We are asked to condemn the State's judgment in conferring on political subdivisions the power to tax local property to supply revenues for local interests. In so doing, appellees would have the Court intrude in an area in which it has traditionally deferred to state legislatures. This Court has often admonished against such interferences with the State's fiscal policies under the Equal Protection Clause   .   .   .

Thus we stand on familiar grounds when we continue to acknowledge that the Justices of this Court lack both the expertise and the familiarity with local problems so necessary to the making of wise decisions with respect to the raising and disposition of public revenues. Yet we are urged to direct the States either to alter drastically the present system or to throw out the property tax altogether in favor of some other form of taxation. No scheme of taxation, whether the tax is imposed on property, income, or purchases of goods and services, has yet been devised which is free of all discriminatory impact. In such a complex arena in which no perfect alternatives exist, the Court does well not to impose too rigorous a standard of scrutiny lest all local fiscal schemes become subjects of criticism under the Equal Protection Clause.

In addition to matters of fiscal policy, this case also involves the most persistent and difficult questions of educational policy, another area in which this Court's lack of specialized knowledge and experience counsels against premature interference with the informed judgments made at the state and local levels. Education, perhaps even more than welfare assistance, presents a myriad of "intractable economic, social, and even philosophical problems." The very complexity of the problems of financing and managing a statewide public school system suggest that "there will be more than one constitution-ally permissible method of solving them," and that, within the limits of rationality, "the legislature's efforts to tackle the problems" should be entitled to respect. On even the most basic questions in this area the scholars and educational experts are divided. Indeed, one of the hottest sources of controversy concerns the extent to which there is a demonstrable correlation between educational expenditures and the quality of education—an assumed correlation underlying virtually every legal conclusion drawn by the District Court in this case. Re-lated to the questioned relationship between cost and quality is the equally unsettled controversy as to the proper goals of a system of public education. And the question regarding the most effective relationship between state boards of education and local school boards, in terms of their respective responsibilities and degrees of control, is now undergoing searching re-examination. The ultimate wisdom as to these and related problems of education is not likely to be de-vined for all time even by the scholars who now so earnestly debate the issues. In such circumstances the judiciary is well advised to refrain from interposing on the States inflexible constitutional re-straints that could circumscribe or handicap the continued research and experimentation so vital to finding even partial solutions to ed-ucational problems and to keeping abreast of ever changing condi-tions.

It must be remembered also that every claim arising under the Equal Protection Clause has implications for the relationship be-tween national and state power under our federal system.    .    .    .
it would be difficult to imagine a case having a greater potential im-pact on our federal system than the one now before us, in which we are urged to abrogate systems of financing public education presently in existence in virtually every State.

## III

The State's contribution, under the Minimum Foundation Pro-gram, was designed to provide an adequate minimum educational of-fering in every school in the State. Funds are distributed to assure that there will be one teacher—compensated at the state-supported minimum salary—for every 25 students. Each school district's other supportive personnel are provided for: one principal for every 30 teachers; one "special service" teacher—librarian, nurse, doctor, etc. —for every 20 teachers; superintendents, vocational instructors, counselors, and educators for exceptional children are also provided. Additional funds are earmarked for current operating expenses, for student transportation, and for free textbooks.

By virtue of the obligation to fulfill its local Fund Assignment, every district must impose an *ad valorem* tax on property located within its borders. The Fund Assignment was designed to remain sufficiently low to assure that each district would have some ability to provide a more enriched educational program. Every district supplements its foundation grant in this manner. In some districts the local property tax contribution is insubstantial, as in Edgewood where the supplement was only $26 per pupil in 1967. In other districts the local share may far exceed even the total Foundation grant. . . . In large measure, these additional local revenues are devoted to paying higher salaries to more teachers. Therefore, the primary distinguishing attributes of schools in property-affluent districts are lower pupil-teacher ratios and higher salary schedules. . . . In its reliance on state as well as local resources, the Texas system is comparable to the systems employed in virtually every other State.

. . . While assuring a basic education for every child in the State, it permits and encourages a large measure of participation in and control of each district's schools at the local level. In an era that has witnessed a consistent trend toward centralization of the functions of government, local sharing of responsibility for public education has survived. . . . In part, local control means, as Professor Coleman suggests, the freedom to devote more money to the education of one's children. Equally important, however, is the opportunity it offers for participation in the decision-making process that determines how those local tax dollars will be spent. Each locality is free to tailor local programs to local needs. Pluralism also affords some opportunity for experimentation, innovation, and a healthy competition for educational excellence. An analogy to the Nation-State relationship in our federal system seems uniquely appropriate. Mr. Justice Brandeis identified as one of the peculiar strengths of our form of government each State's freedom to "serve as a laboratory . . . and try novel social and economic experiments." No area of social concern stands to profit more from a multiplicity of viewpoints and from a diversity of approaches than does public education.

. . . While it is no doubt true that reliance on local property taxation for school revenues provides less freedom of choice with respect to expenditures for some districts than for others, the existence of "some inequality" in the manner in which the State's rationale is achieved is not alone a sufficient basis for striking down the entire system. Nor must the financing system fail because, as appellees suggest, other methods of satisfying the State's interest, which occasion "less drastic" disparities in expenditures, might be conceived. Only where state action impinges on the exercise of fundamental constitutional rights or liberties must it be found to have chosen the least restrictive alternative. It is also well to remember that even those districts that have reduced ability to make free decisions with respect to how much they spend on education still retain under the present system a large measure of authority as to how available funds will be allocated. They further enjoy the power to make numerous other decisions with respect to the operation of the schools. The people of Texas may be justified in believing that other systems of school finance, which place more of the financial responsibility in the hands of the State, will result in a comparable lessening of desired local autonomy. That is, they may believe that along with increased control of the purse strings at the state level will go increased control over local policies.

. . . But any scheme of local taxation—indeed the very existence of identifiable local governmental units—requires the establishment of jurisdictional boundaries that are inevitably arbitrary. It is equally inevitable that some localities are going to be blessed with more taxable assets than others. Nor is local wealth a static quantity. Changes in the level of taxable wealth within any district may result from any number of events, some of which local residents can and do influence. For instance, commercial and industrial enterprises may be encouraged to locate within a district by various actions—public and private.

Moreover, if local taxation for local expenditure is an unconstitutional method of providing for education then it may be an equally impermissible means of providing other necessary services customarily financed largely from local property taxes, including local police and fire protection, public health and hospitals, and public utility facilities of various kinds. We perceive no justification for such a severe denigration of local property taxation and control as would follow from appellees' contentions. It has simply never been within the constitutional prerogative of this Court to nullify statewide measures for financing public services merely because the burdens or benefits thereof fall unevenly depending upon the relative wealth of the political subdivisions in which citizens live.

. . . the system here challenged is not peculiar to Texas or to any other State. In its essential characteristics the Texas plan for financing public education reflects what many educators for a half century have thought was an enlightened approach to a problem for which there is no perfect solution. We are unwilling to assume for ourselves a level of wisdom superior to that of legislators, scholars, and educational authorities in 49 States, especially where the alternatives proposed are only recently conceived and nowhere yet tested. The constitutional standard under the Equal Protection Clause is whether the challenged state action rationally furthers a legitimate state purpose or interest. We hold that the Texas plan abundantly satisfies this standard.

### IV

. . . this Court's action today is not to be viewed as placing its judicial imprimatur on the status quo. The need is apparent for reform in tax systems which may well have relied too long and too heavily on the local property tax. And certainly innovative new thinking as to public education, its methods and its funding, is necessary to assure both a higher level of quality and greater uniformity of opportunity. These matters merit the continued attention of the scholars who already have contributed much by their challenges. But the ultimate solutions must come from the lawmakers and from the democratic pressures of those who elect them.

Reversed.

Mr. Justice STEWART, concurring.

The method of financing public schools in Texas, as in almost every other State, has resulted in a system of public education that can fairly be described as chaotic and unjust. It does not follow, however, and I cannot find, that this system violates the Constitution of the United States. I join the opinion and judgment of the Court because I am convinced that any other course would mark an extraordinary departure from principled adjudication under the Equal Protection Clause of the Fourteenth Amendment. . . .

Mr. Justice BRENNAN, dissenting.

Although I agree with my Brother WHITE that the Texas statutory scheme is devoid of any rational basis, and for that reason is violative of the Equal Protection Clause, I also record my disagreement with the Court's rather distressing assertion that a right may be deemed "fundamental" for the purposes of equal protection analysis only if it is "explicitly or implicitly guaranteed by the Constitution." As my Brother MARSHALL convincingly demonstrates, our prior cases stand for the proposition that "fundamentality" is, in large measure, a function of the right's importance in terms of the effectuation of those rights which are in fact constitutionally guaranteed. Thus, "[a]s the nexus between the specific constitutional guarantee and the nonconstitutional interest draws closer, the nonconstitutional interest becomes more fundamental and the degree of judicial scrutiny applied when the interest is infringed on a discriminatory basis must be adjusted accordingly."

Here, there can be no doubt that education is inextricably linked to the right to participate in the electoral process and to the rights of free speech and association guaranteed by the First Amendment. This being so, any classification affecting education must be subjected to strict judicial scrutiny, and since even the State concedes that the statutory scheme now before us cannot pass constitutional muster under this stricter standard of review, I can only conclude that the Texas school financing scheme is constitutionally invalid.

Mr. Justice WHITE, with whom Mr. Justice DOUGLAS and Mr. Justice BRENNAN join, dissenting.

. . . this case would be quite different if it were true that the Texas system, while insuring minimum educational expenditures in every district through state funding, extends a meaningful option to all local districts to increase their per-pupil expenditures and so to improve their children's education to the extent that increased funding will achieve that goal. The system would then arguably provide a rational and sensible method of achieving the stated aim of preserving an area for local initiative and decision.

The difficulty with the Texas system, however, is that it provides a meaningful option to Alamo Heights and like school districts but almost none to Edgewood and those other districts with a low per-pupil real estate tax base. In these latter districts, no matter how desirous parents are of supporting their schools with greater revenues, it is impossible to do so through the use of the real estate property tax. In these districts the Texas system utterly fails to extend a realistic choice to parents, because the proprety tax, which is the only revenue-raising mechanism extended to school districts, is practically and legally unavailable. . . .

Both the Edgewood and Alamo Heights districts are located in Bexar County, Texas. . . . In order to equal the highest yield in any other Bexar County district, Alamo Heights would be required to tax at the rate of 68¢ per $100 of assessed valuation. Edgewood would be required to tax at the prohibitive rate of $5.76 per $100. But state law places a $1.50 per $100 ceiling on the maintenance tax rate, a limit that would surely be reached long before Edgewood attained an equal yield. Edgewood is thus precluded in law, as well as in fact, from achieving a yield even close to that of some other districts.

The Equal Protection Clause permits discriminations between classes but requires that the classification bear some rational relationship to a permissible object sought to be attained by the statute. It is not enough that the Texas system before us seeks to achieve the valid, rational purpose of maximizing local initiative; the means chosen by the State must also be rationally related to the end sought to be achieved. . . . Requiring the State to establish only that unequal treatment is in furtherance of a permissible goal, without also requirig the State to show that the means chosen to effectuate that goal are rationally related to its achievement, makes equal protection analysis no more than an empty gesture. In my view, the parents and children in Edgewood, and in like districts, suffer from an invidious discrimination violative of the Equal Protection Clause. . . .

Perhaps the majority believes that the major disparity in revenues provided and permitted by the Texas system is inconsequential. I cannot agree, however, that the difference of the magnitude appearing in this case can sensibly be ignored, particularly since the State itself considers it so important to provide opportunities to exceed the minimum state educational expenditures. . . .

Mr. Justice MARSHALL, with whom Mr. Justice DOUGLAS concurs, dissenting.

The Court today decides, in effect, that a State may constitutionally vary the quality of education which it offers its children in accordance with the amount of taxable wealth located in the school districts within which they reside. The majority's decision represents an abrupt departure from the mainstream of recent state and federal court decisions concerning the unconstitutionality of state educational financing schemes dependent upon taxable local wealth. More unfortunately, though, the majority's holding can only be seen as a retreat from our historic commitment to equality of educational opportunity and as unsupportable acquiescence in a system which deprives children in their earliest years of the chance to reach their full potential as citizens. The Court does this despite the absence of any substantial justification for a scheme which arbitrarily channels educational resources in accordance with the fortuity of the amount of taxable wealth within each district.

In my judgment, the right of every American to an equal start in life, so far as the provision of a state service as important as education is concerned, is far too vital to permit state discrimination on grounds as tenuous as those presented by this record. Nor can I accept the notion that it is sufficient to remit these appellees to the vagaries of the political process which, contrary to the majority's suggestion, has proven singularly unsuited to the task of providing a remedy for this discrimination. I, for one, am unsatisfied with the hope of an ultimate "political" solution sometime in the indefinite future while, in the meantime, countless children unjustifiably receive inferior educations that "may affect their hearts and minds in a way unlikely ever to be undone." Brown v. Board of Education, . . . the issue in this case is not whether Texas is doing its best to ameliorate the worst features of a discriminatory scheme, but rather whether the scheme itself is in fact unconstitutionally discriminatory in the face of the Fourteenth Amendment's guarantee of equal protection of the laws. When the Texas financing scheme is taken as a whole, I do not think it can be doubted that it produces a discriminatory impact on substantial numbers of the schoolage children of the State of Texas.

. . . Authorities concerned with educational quality no doubt disagree as to the significance of variations in per pupil spending. Indeed, conflicting expert testimony was presented to the District Court in this case concerning the effect of spending variations on educational achievement. We sit, however, not to resolve disputes over educational theory but to enforce our Constitution. It is an inescapable fact that if one district has more funds available per pupil than another district, the former will have greater choice in educational planning than will the latter. In this regard, I believe the question of discrimination in educational quality must be deemed to be an objective one that looks to what the State provides its children, not to what the children are able to do with what they receive. That a child forced to attend an underfunded school with poorer physical facilities, less experienced teachers, larger classes, and a narrower range of courses than a school with substantially more funds—and thus with greater choice in educational planning—may nevertheless excel is to the credit of the child, not the State. . . . Indeed, who can ever measure for such a child the opportunities lost and the talents wasted for want of a broader, more enriched education? Discrimination in the opportunity to learn that is afforded a child must be our standard.

. . . it is difficult to believe that if the children of Texas had a free choice, they would choose to be educated in districts with fewer resources, and hence with more antiquated plants, less experienced teachers, and a less diversified curriculum. In fact, if financing variations are so insignificant to educational quality, it is difficult to understand why a number of our country's wealthiest school districts, who have no legal obligation to argue in support of the constitutionality of the Texas legislation, have nevertheless zealously pursued its cause before this Court.

At the very least, in view of the substantial interdistrict disparities in funding and in resulting educational inputs shown by appellees to exist under the Texas financing scheme, the burden of proving that these disparities do not in fact affect the quality of children's education must fall upon the appellants. Cf. Hobson v. Hansen, 327 F.Supp. 844, 860–861 (D.C.D.C.1971). Yet appellants . . . have argued no more than that the relationship is ambiguous. This is hardly sufficient to overcome appellees' prima facie showing of state created discrimination between the school children of Texas with respect to objective educational opportunity.

Nor can I accept the appellants' apparent suggestion that . . . the Equal Protection Clause cannot be offended by substantially unequal state treatment of persons who are similarly situated so long as the State provides everyone with some unspecified amount of education which evidently is "enough."

. . . this Court has never suggested that because some "adequate" level of benefits is provided to all, discrimination in the provision of services is therefore constitutionally excusable. The Equal Protection Clause is not addressed to the minimal sufficiency but rather to the unjustifiable inequalities of state action. It mandates nothing less than that "all persons similarly circumstanced shall be treated alike."

Even if the Equal Protection Clause encompassed some theory of constitutional adequacy, discrimination in the provision of educational opportunity would certainly seem to be a poor candidate for its application. Neither the majority nor appellants informs us how judicially manageable standards are to be derived for determining how much education is "enough" to excuse constitutional discrimination. . . .

In my view, then, it is inequality—not some notion of gross inadequacy—of educational opportunity that raises a question of denial of equal protection of the laws. I find any other approach to the issue unintelligible and without directing principle. Here appellees have made a substantial showing of wide variations in educational funding and the resulting educational opportunity afforded to the school children of Texas. This discrimination is, in large measure, attributable to significant disparities in the taxable wealth of local Texas school districts. This is a sufficient showing to raise a substantial question of discriminatory state action in violation of the Equal Protection Clause. . . . This is clear from our decision only last Term in Bullock v. Carter, 405 U.S. 134, 92 S.Ct. 849, 31 L.Ed.2d 92 (1972), where the Court, in striking down Texas' primary filing fees as violative of equal protection, found no impediment to equal protection analysis in the fact that the members of the disadvantaged class could not be readily identified. The Court recognized that the filing fee system tended "to deny some voters the opportunity to vote for a candidate of their choosing; at the same time it gives the affluent the power to place on the ballot their own names or the names of persons they favor." Id., at 144, 92 S.Ct., at 856. The Court also recognized that "[t]his disparity in voting power based on wealth cannot be described by reference to discrete and precisely defined segments of the community as is typical of inequities challenged under the Equal Protection Clause. . . ." Ibid. Nevertheless, it concluded that "we would ignore reality were we not to recognize that this system falls with unequal weight on voters . . . according to their economic status." Ibid. The nature of the classification in *Bullock* was clear, although the precise membership of the disadvantaged class was not. This was enough in *Bullock* for purposes of equal protection analysis. It is enough here.

I believe it is sufficient that the overarching form of discrimination in this case is between the school children of Texas on the basis of the taxable property wealth of the districts in which they happen to live. . . . the children of a district are excessively advantaged if that district has more taxable property per pupil than the average amount of taxable property per pupil considering the State as a whole. By contrast, the children of a district are disadvantaged if that district has less taxable property per pupil than the state average. Whether this discrimination, against the school children of property poor districts, inherent in the Texas financing scheme is violative of the Equal Protection Clause is the question to which we must now turn.

. . . The Court apparently seeks to establish today that equal protection cases fall into one of two neat categories which dictate the appropriate standard of review—strict scrutiny or mere rationality. But this Court's decisions in the field of equal protection defy such easy categorization. A principled reading of what this Court has done reveals that it has applied a spectrum of standards in reviewing discrimination allegedly violative of the Equal Protection Clause. This spectrum clearly comprehends variations in the degree of care with which the Court will scrutinize particular classifications, depending, I believe, on the constitutional and societal importance of the interest adversely affected and the recognized invidiousness of the basis upon which the particular classification is drawn. I therefore cannot accept the majority's labored efforts to demonstrate that fundamental interests, which call for strict scrutiny of the challenged classification, encompass only established rights which we are somehow bound to recognize from the text of the Constitution itself. . . .

The majority is, of course, correct when it suggests that the process of determining which interests are fundamental is a difficult one. But I do not think the problem is insurmountable. . . . Although not all fundamental interests are constitutionally guaranteed, the determination of which interests are fundamental should be firmly rooted in the text of the Constitution. The task in every case should be to determine the extent to which constitutionally guaranteed rights are dependent on interests not mentioned in the Constitution. As the nexus between the specific constitutional guarantee and the nonconstitutional interest draws closer, the nonconstitutional interest becomes more fundamental and the degree of judicial scrutiny applied when the interest is infringed on a discriminatory basis must be adjusted accordingly. . . .

. . . Procreation is now understood to be important because of its interaction with the established constitutional right of privacy. The exercise of the state franchise is closely tied to basic civil and political rights inherent in the First Amendment. And access to criminal appellate processes enhances the integrity of the range of rights implicit in the Fourteenth Amendment guarantee of due process of law. Only if we closely protect the related interests from state discrimination do we ultimately ensure the integrity of the constitutional guarantee itself. This is the real lesson that must be taken from our previous decisions involving interests deemed to be fundamental.

The effect of the interaction of individual interests with established constitutional guarantees upon the degree of care exercised by this Court in reviewing state discrimination affecting such interests is amply illustrated by our decision last Term in Eisenstadt v. Baird, 405 U.S. 438, 92 S.Ct. 1029, 31 L.Ed.2d 349 (1972). In *Baird*, the

Court struck down as violative of the Equal Protection Clause a state statute which denied unmarried persons access to contraceptive devices on the same basis as married persons. The Court purported to test the statute under its traditional standard whether there is some rational basis for the discrimination effected. In the contex of commercial regulation, the Court has indicated that the Equal Protection Clause "is offended only if the classification rests on grounds wholly irrelevant to the achievement of the State's objective. And this lenient standard is further weighted in the State's favor by the fact that "[a] statutory discrimination will not be set aside if any state of facts reasonably may be conceived [by the Court] to justify it." But in *Baird* the Court clearly did not adhere to these highly tolerant standards of traditional rational review. For although there were conceivable state interests intended to be advanced by the statute— e. g., deterrence of premarital sexual activity; regulation of the dissemination of potentially dangerous articles—the Court was not prepared to accept these interests on their face, but instead proceeded to test their substantiality by independent analysis. Such close scrutiny of the State's interests was hardly characteristic of the deference shown state classifications in the context of economic interests. Yet I think the Court's action was entirely appropriate for access to and use of contraceptives bears a close relationship to the individual's constitutional right of privacy.

A similar process of analysis with respect to the invidiousness of the basis on which a particular classification is drawn has also influenced the Court as to the appropriate degree of scrutiny to be accorded any particular case. The highly suspect character of classifications based on race, nationality, or alienage is well established. The reasons why such classifications call for close judicial scrutiny are manifold. Certain racial and ethnic groups have frequently been recognized as "discrete and insular minorities" who are relatively powerless to protect their interests in the political process. Moreover, race, nationality, or alienage is " 'in most circumstances irrelevant' to any constitutionally acceptable legislative purpose, Kiyoshi Hirabayashi v. United States, 320 U.S. 81, 100, 63 S.Ct. 1375, 87 L.Ed. 1774." McLaughlin v. Florida, 379 U.S., at 192, 85 S.Ct., at 288. Instead, lines drawn on such bases are frequently the reflection of historic prejudices rather than legislative rationality. It may be that all of these considerations, which make for particular judicial solicitude in the face of discrimination on the basis of race, nationality, or alienage, do not coalesce—or at least not to the same degree—in other forms of discrimination. Nevertheless, these considerations have undoubtedly influenced the care with which the Court has scrutinized other forms of discrimination.

In James v. Strange, 407 U.S. 128, 92 S.Ct. 2027, 32 L.Ed.2d 600 (1972), the Court held unconstitutional a state statute which provided for recoupment from indigent convicts of legal defense fees paid by the State. The Court found that the statute impermissibly differentiated between indigent criminals in debt to the state and civil judgment debtors, since criminal debtors were denied various protective exemptions afforded civil judgment debtors. The Court suggested that in reviewing the statute under the Equal Protection Clause, it was merely applying the traditional requirement that there be " 'some rationality' " in the line drawn between the different types of debtors. Yet it then proceeded to scrutinize the statute with less than traditional deference and restraint. Thus the Court recognized "that state recoupment statutes may betoken legitimate state interests" in recovering expenses and discouraging fraud. The Court, in short, clearly did not consider the problems of fraud and collection that the state legislature might have concluded were peculiar to indigent criminal defendants to be either sufficiently important or at least sufficiently substantiated to justify denial of the protective exemptions afforded to all civil judgment debtors, to a class composed exclusively of indigent criminal debtors.

Similarly, in Reed v. Reed, 404 U.S. 71, 92 S.Ct. 251, 30 L.Ed.2d 225 (1971), the Court, in striking down a state statute which gave men preference over women when persons of equal entitlement apply for assignment as an administrator of a particular estate, resorted to a more stringent standard of equal protection review than that employed in cases involving commercial matters. The Court . . . was unwilling to consider a theoretical and unsubstantiated basis for distinction—however reasonable it might appear—sufficient to sustain a statute discriminating on the basis of sex.

*James* and *Reed* can only be understood as instances in which the particularly invidious character of the classification caused the Court to pause and scrutinize with more than traditional care the rationality of state discrimination. Discrimination on the basis of past criminality and on the basis of sex posed for the Court the spectre of forms of discrimination which it implicitly recognized to have deep social and legal roots without necessarily having any basis in actual differences. Still, the Court's sensitivity to the invidiousness of the basis for discrimination is perhaps most apparent in its decisions protecting the interests of children born out of wedlock from discriminatory state action.

In summary, it seems to me inescapably clear that this Court has consistently adjusted the care with which it will review state discrimination in light of the constitutional significance of the interests affected and the invidiousness of the particular classification. In the context of economic interests, we find that discriminatory state action is almost always sustained for such interests are generally far removed from constitutional guarantees. . . . But the situation differs markedly when discrimination against important individual interests with constitutional implications and against particularly disadvantaged or powerless classes is involved. The majority suggests, however, that a variable standard of review would give this Court the appearance of a "superlegislature." I cannot agree. Such an approach seems to me a part of the guarantees of our Constitution and of the historic experiences with oppression of and discrimination against discrete, powerless minorities which underlie that Document. In truth, the Court itself will be open to the criticism raised by the majority so long as it continues on its present course of effectively selecting in private which cases will be afforded special consideration without acknowledging the true basis of its action.

Opinions such as those in *Reed* and *James* seem drawn more as efforts to shield rather than to reveal the true basis of the Court's decisions. Such obfuscated action may be appropriate to a political body such as a legislature, but it is not appropriate to this Court. Open debate of the bases for the Court's action is essential to the rationality and consistency of our decisionmaking process. Only in this way can we avoid the label of legislature and ensure the integrity of the judicial process.

. . . It is true that this Court has never deemed the provision of free public education to be required by the Constitution. Indeed, it has on occasion suggested that state supported education is a privilege bestowed by a State on its citizens. Nevertheless, the fundamental importance of education is amply indicated by the prior decisions of this Court, by the unique status accorded public education by our society, and by the close relationship between education and some of our most basic constitutional values. Education directly affects the ability of a child to exercise his First Amendment interest both as a source and as a receiver of information and ideas, whatever interests he may pursue in life. . . ., in the final analysis, "the pivotal position of education to success in American society and its essential role in opening up to the individual the central experiences of our culture lend it an importance that is undeniable."

. . . Education serves the essential function of instilling in our young an understanding of and appreciation for the principles and operation of our governmental processes. Education may instill the interest and provide the tools necessary for political discourse and debate. Indeed, it has frequently been suggested that education is the dominant factor affecting political consciousness and participation. A system of "[c]ompetition in ideas and governmental policies is at the core of our electoral process and of the First Amendment freedoms." Data from the Presidential Election of 1968 clearly demonstrates a direct relationship between participation in the electoral process and level of educational attainment.

. . . the issue is neither provision of the most *effective* speech nor of the most *informed* vote. Appellees do not now seek the best education Texas might provide. They do seek, however, an end to state discrimination resulting from the unequal distribution of taxable district property wealth that directly impairs the ability of some districts to provide the same educational opportunity that other districts can provide with the same or even substantially less tax effort. The issue is, in other words, one of discrimination that affects the quality of the education which Texas has chosen to provide its children; and, the precise question here is what importance should attach to education for purposes of equal protection analysis of that discrimination. . . .

    . . . We are told that in every prior case involving a wealth classification, the members of the disadvantaged class have "shared two distinguishing characteristics: because of their impecunity they were completely unable to pay for some desired benefit, and as a consequence, they sustained an absolute deprivation of a meaningful opportunity to enjoy that benefit." . . . at 1290. I cannot agree.
. . .

    . . . *Griffin* and *Douglas* refute the majority's contention that we have in the past required an absolute deprivation before subjecting wealth classifications to strict scrutiny. The Court characterizes *Griffin* as a case concerned simply with the denial of a transcript or an adequate substitute therefor, and *Douglas* as involving the denial of counsel. But in both cases the question was in fact whether "a State that [grants] *appellate review* can do so in a way that discriminates against some convicted defendants on account of their poverty." In that regard, the Court concluded that inability to purchase a transcript denies "the poor an adequate *appellate review* accorded to all who have money enough to pay the costs in advance," *ibid.* (emphasis added), and that "the type of an *appeal* a person is afforded . . . hinges upon whether or not he can pay for the assistance of counsel." The right of appeal itself was not absolutely denied to those too poor to pay; but because of the cost of a transcript and of counsel, the appeal was a substantially less meaningful right for the poor than for the rich. It was on these terms that the Court found a denial of equal protection, and those terms clearly encompassed degrees of discrimination on the basis of wealth which do not amount to outright denial of the affected right or interest.

This is not to say that the form of wealth classification in this case does not differ significantly from those recognized in the previous decisions of this Court. Our prior cases have dealt essentially with discrimination on the basis of personal wealth. Here, by contrast, the children of the disadvantaged Texas school districts are being discriminated against not necessarily because of their personal wealth or the wealth of their families, but because of the taxable property wealth of the residents of the district in which they happen to live. The appropriate question, then, is whether the same degree of judicial solicitude and scrutiny that has previously been afforded wealth classifications is warranted here.

.   .   .  That wealth classifications alone have not necessarily been considered to bear the same high degree of suspectness as have classifications based on, for instance, race or alienage may be explainable on a number of grounds.  The "poor" may not be seen as politically powerless as certain discrete and insular minority groups.  Personal poverty may entail much the same social stigma as historically attached to certain racial or ethnic groups.  But personal poverty is not a permanent disability; its shackles may be escaped.  Perhaps, most importantly, though, personal wealth may not necessarily share the general irrelevance as basis for legislative action that race or nationality is recognized to have.  While the "poor" have frequently been a legally disadvantaged group, it cannot be ignored that social legislation must frequently take cognizance of the economic status of our citizens.  Thus, we have generally gauged the invidiousness of wealth classifications with an awareness of the importance of the interests being affected and the relevance of personal wealth to those interests.

When evaluated with these considerations in mind, it seems to me that discrimination on the basis of group wealth in this case likewise calls for careful judicial scrutiny.  First, it must be recognized that while local district wealth may serve other interests, it bears no relationship whatsoever to the interest of Texas school children in the educational opportunity afforded them by the State of Texas.  Given the importance of that interest, we must be particularly sensitive to the invidious characteristics of any form of discrimination that is not clearly intended to serve it, as opposed to some other distinct state interest.  Discrimination on the basis of group wealth may not, to be sure, reflect the social stigma frequently attached to personal poverty.  Nevertheless, insofar as group wealth discrimination involves wealth over which the disadvantaged individual has no significant control, it represents in fact a more serious basis of discrimination than does personal wealth.  For such discrimination is no reflection of the individual's characteristics or his abilities.  And thus—particularly in the context of a disadvantaged class composed of children—we have previously treated discrimination on a basis which the individual cannot control as constitutionally disfavored.

The disability of the disadvantaged class in this case extends as well into the political processes upon which we ordinarily rely as adequate for the protection and promotion of all interests.  Here legislative reallocation of the State's property wealth must be sought in the face of inevitable opposition from significantly advantaged districts that have a strong vested interest in the preservation of the status quo, a problem not completely dissimilar to that faced by underrepresented districts prior to the Court's intervention in the process of reapportionment . . . our other prior cases have dealt with discrimination on the basis of indigency which was attributable to the operation of the private sector. But we have no such simple *de facto* wealth discrimination here. The means for financing public education in Texas are selected and specified by the State. At the same time, governmentally imposed land use controls have undoubtedly encouraged and rigidified natural trends in the allocation of particular areas for residential or commercial use, and thus determined each district's amount of taxable property wealth. In short, this case, in contrast to the Court's previous wealth discrimination decisions, can only be seen as "unusual in the extent to which governmental action *is* the cause of the wealth classifications."

. . . I do not question that local control of public education, as an abstract matter, constitutes a very substantial state interest. . . . But I need not now decide how I might ultimately strike the balance were we confronted with a situation where the State's sincere concern for local control inevitably produced educational inequality. For on this record, it is apparent that the State's purported concern with local control is offered primarily as an excuse rather than as a justification for interdistrict inequality. . . . If Texas had a system truly dedicated to local fiscal control one would expect the quality of the educational opportunity provided in each district to vary with the decision of the voters in that district as to the level of sacrifice they wish to make for public education. In fact, the Texas scheme produces precisely the opposite result. Local school districts cannot choose to have the best education in the State by imposing the highest tax rate. Instead, the quality of the educational opportunity offered by any particular district is largely determined by the amount of taxable property located in the district—a factor over which local voters can exercise no control.

The study introduced in the District Court showed a direct inverse relationship between equalized taxable district property wealth and district tax effort with the result that the property poor districts making the highest tax effort obtained the lowest per pupil yield. . . . Clearly, this suit has nothing to do with local decisionmaking with respect to educational policy or even educational spending. It involves only a narrow aspect of local control—namely, local control over the raising of educational funds. In fact, in striking down interdistrict disparities in taxable local wealth, the District Court took the course which is most likely to make true local control over educational decisionmaking a reality for *all* Texas school districts.

Nor does the District Court's decision even necessarily eliminate local control of educational funding. The District Court struck down nothing more than the continued interdistrict wealth discrimination inherent in the present property tax. Both centralized and decentralized plans for educational funding not involving such interdistrict discrimination have been put forward. The choice among these or other alternatives remains with the State, not with the federal courts.

The Court seeks solace for its action today in the possibility of legislative reform. The Court's suggestions of legislative redress and experimentation will doubtless be of great comfort to the school children of Texas' disadvantaged districts, but considering the vested interests of wealthy school districts in the preservation of the status quo, they are worth little more. The possibility of legislative action is, in all events, no answer to this Court's duty under the Constitution to eliminate unjustified state discrimination. In this case we have been presented with an instance of such discrimination, in a particularly invidious form, against an individual interest of large constitutional and practical importance. To support the demonstrated discrimination in the provision of educational opportunity the State has offered a justification which, on analysis, takes on at best an ephemeral character. Thus, I believe that the wide disparities in taxable district property wealth inherent in the local property tax element of the Texas financing scheme render that scheme violative of the Equal Protection Clause.

I would therefore affirm the judgment of the District Court.

## NOTES AND QUESTIONS

1. What concept of equal educational opportunity is rejected by the Court and which is accepted by it? By Mr. Justices White and Marshall?

2. According to the Supreme Court, how can one identify the interest that ranks as "fundamental"?

3. When considering whether wealth is a suspect class the Court reviewed prior precedents and concluded that a classification based on wealth is suspect only where it functions as a complete deprivation of education because of an absolute inability to pay (indigency), rather than a relative deprivation based on a relative inability to pay. Is the Court's reading of the prior cases correct? For example, in Griffin, Illinois granted a partial appellate review to an indigent but not a full appellate review because it refused to afford an indigent a free copy of the trial transcript of the testimony. Thus, an indigent had a partial review and suffered a relative deprivation. However, the Supreme Court struck Illinois' procedures and required that it afford an indigent a full review equal to that of any other appellant. Is Griffin a precedent for the Court's decision? If not, what should have been the decision based on Griffin? If so, would the decision have been different if Rodriguez had been indigent?

4. Does the *San Antonio School* case indicate that, under the federal Constitution, a state need not provide any public education, but if a state provides a school system, then the equal-protection clause requires that otherwise eligible children not be excluded? In other words, an otherwise eligible child has a constitutional right not to be totally excluded, functionally or directly, from a state's public school system? If so, does this part of the case corroborate the views of

Lau and similar cases?  On the other hand, does the case also hold that if a child is not totally excluded from a state's school system, but receives some, albeit inferior, meaningful education, then he has no constitutional right under the equal protection clause, to an equal quality education?  What is the Court's justification for this position?  If it is the Court's position, how inferior must a child's education become before the disparity is too great and amounts to a constitutional violation?  Could the inferiority ever be proved by gross financial differences between school districts?

5.  Is there really no direct relationship between financing and the quality of education?  Perhaps not when one considers only slight financial differences between school districts, but what about gross disparities?  If a school district is so poor that it cannot finance chemistry, physics and other similar laboratories and equipment, isn't the quality of its educational opportunity offered to children directly affected by the level of funding?

On the other hand, close to 80% of the operating budgets of most school districts go to salaries.  If the operations budget of a school district were increased by 20% would there also be an equal increase in the quality of the education available?

6.  Although the *San Antonio School District* case seemingly has ended attempts to use the U.S. Constitution to invalidate current school financing systems based largely on property taxes, it has not ended the battle over school financing.  The focus has shifted to state constitutions and to state courts.  Some state constitutions have provisions relating to education that are similar to Washington's: "It is the paramount duty of the state to make ample provision for the education of all children within its borders   .   .  .".  Wash.Const. Art. IX, Sec. 1. Other states have weaker provisions or only constitutional provisions which parallel the Fourteenth Amendment's equal-protection clause. But, on all state constitutional provisions, the state courts have the last word of interpretation.  State courts are not bound by U.S. Supreme Court interpretations of the U.S. Constitution when they interpret their own, individual state constitutions.  Thus, although the San Antonio School case holds there is no U.S. Constitutional right to an education, a state court may interpret its state constitution as providing a state constitutional right to an education.  Consequently, after the *San Antonio School* case, the legal battle over school finance has shifted to the state courts.

Litigants have achieved greater success in the state courts than in the U.S. Supreme Court.  Horton v. Meskill, 172 Conn. 615, 376 A.2d 359 (1977) is an example.  Connecticut's constitution provides that "There shall always be free public elementary and secondary schools in the state.  The general assembly shall implement this principle by appropriate legislation" (Conn.Const. Art. VIII, § 1); that "All men when they form a social compact, are equal in rights   .   .   .  ." (Conn.Const. Art. I, § 1), and that "No person shall be denied the equal protection of the law  .   .   .  ." (Conn.Const. Art. I, § 20).  In holding Connecticut's school financing system unconstitutional, its State Supreme Court said:

"In our consideration of the merits of the present appeals, we have not found material aid in the many decisions from the courts of other jurisdictions since most of them depend upon the controlling and differing provisions of the constitutions in the particular jurisdictions. Nor have we found the *Rodriguez* test for the fundamentality of the right to an education of particular help —although under that test it cannot be questioned but that in the light of the Connecticut constitutional recognition of the right to education (article eighth, § 1) it is, in Connecticut, a 'fundamental' right.

"As other courts have recognized, educational equalization cases are 'in significant aspects sui generis' and not subject to analysis by accepted conventional tests or the application of mechanical standards. The wealth discrimination found among school districts differs materially from the usual equal protection case where a fairly defined indigent class suffers discrimination to its peculiar disadvantage. The discrimination is relative rather than absolute. Further, the children living in towns with relatively low assessable property values are afforded public education but, as the trial court found, the education they receive is to a substantial degree narrower and lower in quality than that which pupils receive in comparable towns with a larger tax base and greater ability to finance education. True, the state has mandated local provision for a basic educational program with local option for a program of higher quality but, as the trial court's finding indicates, that option to a town which lacks the resources to implement the higher quality educational program which it desires and which is available to property-richer towns is highly illusory. As Mr. Justice Marshall put it in his dissent in *Rodriguez*: '[T]his Court has never suggested that because some "adequate" level of benefits is provided to all, discrimination in the provision of services is therefore constitutionally excusable. The Equal Protection Clause is not addressed to the minimal sufficiency but rather to the unjustifiable inequalities of state action. It mandates nothing less than that "all persons similarly circumstanced shall be treated alike." F. S. Royster Guano Co. v. Virginia, 253 U.S. 412, 415, 40 S.Ct. 560, 562, 64 L.Ed. 989 (1920).' With justification, the trial court found merit to the complaints of the plaintiffs about 'the sheer irrationality' of the state's system of financing education in the state on the basis of property values, noting that their argument ' "would be similar and no less tenable should the state make educational expenditures dependent upon some other irrelevant factor, such as the number of telephone poles in the district." Note . . . ['A Statistical Analysis of the School Finance Decisions: On Winning Battles and Losing Wars,' 81 Yale L.J. 1303, 1307].

"We find our thinking to be substantially in accord with the decisions of the New Jersey Supreme Court in Robinson v. Cahill,

62 N.J. 473, 303 A.2d 273 and the California Supreme Court in Serrano v. Priest, 18 Cal.3d 728, 135 Cal.Rptr. 345, 557 P.2d 929 (*Serrano II*), and whether we apply the 'fundamentality' test adopted by *Rodriguez* or the pre-*Rodriguez* test under our state constitution (as the California Supreme Court did in *Serrano II*) or the 'arbitrary' test applied by the New Jersey Supreme Court in Robinson v. Cahill, supra, 62 N.J. 473, 303 A.2d 273 we must conclude that in Connecticut the right to education is so basic and fundamental that any infringement of that right must be strictly scrutinized.

"Connecticut has for centuries recognized it as her right and duty to provide for the proper education of the young. . . . Education is so important that the state has made it compulsory through a requirement of attendance. As early as 1650, the General Court (as the General Assembly was then called) adopted a provision that 'euery Towneshipp within this Jurissdiction, after the Lord hath increased them to the number of fifty housholders, shall then forthwith appoint one within theire Towne to teach all such children as shall resorte to him, to write and read. . . . And it is further ordered, that where any Towne shall increase to the number of one hundred families or housholders, they shall sett vp a Grammer Schoole, the masters thereof being able to instruct youths so farr as they may bee fitted for the Vniversity.' This same basic educational system has continued to this date, the state recognizing that providing for education is a state duty and function now codified in the constitution, article eighth, § 1, with the obligation of overseeing education on the local level delegated to local school boards which serve as agents of the state. The General Assembly has by word, if not by deed, recognized in the enactment of § 10–4a of the General Statutes that it is the concern of the state that 'each child shall have . . . equal opportunity to receive a suitable program of educational experiences.' Indeed the concept of equality is expressly embodied in the constitutional provision for distribution of the school fund in the provision (article eighth, § 4) that the fund 'shall be inviolably appropriated to the support and encouragement of the public schools throughout the state, and for the equal benefit of all the people thereof.'

"The present-day problem arises from the circumstances that over the years there has arisen a great disparity in the ability of local communities to finance local education, which has given rise to a significant disparity in the quality of education available to the youth of the state. It was well stated in the memorandum of decision of the trial court, which noted that the present method [of financing education in the state] is the result of legislation in which the state delegates to municipalities of disparate financial capability the state's duty of raising funds for operating public schools within that municipality. That legislation gives no consideration to the financial capability of the municipality to raise funds sufficient to discharge another duty delegated to the municipality by the state, that of educating the children within that municipality. The evidence in this case is that, as a result of this duty-delegating to Canton without regard to Canton's financial capabilities, pupils in Canton receive an education that is in a substantial degree lower in both breadth and quality than that received by pupils in municipalities with a greater financial capability, even though there is no difference between the constitutional duty of the state to the children in Canton and the constitutional duty of the state to the children in other towns.

"We conclude that without doubt the trial court correctly held that, in Connecticut, elementary and secondary education is a fundamental right, that pupils in the public schools are entitled to the equal enjoyment of that right, and that the state system of financing public elementary and secondary education as it presently exists and operates cannot pass the test of 'strict judicial scrutiny' as to its constitutionality. These were the basic legal conclusions reached by the court. The remaining conclusions arise from the application of these legal principles to the facts which the court found. These we have already summarized and it is unnecessary to repeat them. It suffices to note that the exhaustive finding of facts amply supports the conclusions of the court that the present legislation enacted by the General Assembly to discharge the state's constitutional duty to educate its children, depending, as it does, primarily on a local property tax base without regard to the disparity in the financial ability of the towns to finance an educational program and with no significant equalizing state support, is not 'appropriate legislation' (article eighth, § 1) to implement the requirement that the state provide a substantially equal educational opportunity to its youth in its free public elementary and secondary schools."

---

## PROBLEM

## JOHNSON v. NEW YORK STATE EDUC. DEPT.

Supreme Court of the United States, 1972.
409 U.S. 75, 93 S.Ct. 259, 34 L.Ed.2d 290.

PER CURIAM. We granted certiorari to review the judgment of the United States Court of Appeals for the Second Circuit, . . . affirming the District Court's . . . dismissal of petitioners' complaint challenging the constitutionality of New York Education Laws § 701 et seq. (1971). . . . However, respondents' brief states that "[o]n May 3, 1972, the qualified voters of the respondent school district elected by majority vote to assess a tax for the purchase of *all* textbooks for grades one through six in the schools of the district." In light of this fact, and given the suggestion at oral argument that the books themselves have a life expectancy of five years, the judgment is vacated and the case is remanded to the United States District

Court for the Eastern District of New York to determine whether this case has become moot.

Mr. Justice MARSHALL, concurring.

While I join the Court's decision, I feel obliged to state somewhat more fully what I view to be the reasons for and meaning of this remand.

The New York statutory scheme here under attack effectively denies textbooks to indigent elementary public school children unless the voters of their district approve a tax especially for the purpose of providing the books.[1]  Petitioners who are indigent recipients of public assistance allege, *inter alia*, that the statute, as applied to their children, creates a wealth classification violative of the Equal Protection Clause.

When this action was initiated in September 1970, respondent Board of Education of Union Free School District No. 27 was not providing free textbooks to petitioners' children, although textbooks were available upon the payment of a fee, which petitioners were unable to afford.[2]  The practical consequence of this situation was that indigent children were forced to sit " 'bookless, side by side in the same classroom with other more wealthy children learning with purchase[d]  .  .  .  textbooks, [thus engendering] a [widespread] feeling of inferiority and unfitness in poor children [which] is psychologically, emotionally, and educationally disastrous to their well being.' "  Indeed, an affidavit submitted to the District Court indicated that in at least one case, an indigent child was told that "he will receive an 'F' for each day because he is without the required textbooks.  When the other pupils in the class read from text-books, the teacher doesn't let him share a book with another pupil, instead she gives him paper and tells him to draw."  Despite this evidence, the Court of Appeals, with one Judge dissenting, affirmed the District Court's dismissal of the complaint.  We granted certiorari.

This case obviously raises questions of large constitutional and practical importance.  For two full school years children in elementary grades were denied access to textbooks solely because of the indigency of their families while these questions were considered by the lower courts.  After we had granted certiorari, however, a majority of the voters in respondent school district finally agreed to levy a tax for the purchase of textbooks for the elementary grades, and we are told that free textbooks have now been provided.

[1] Under New York law, local school districts are required to loan textbooks free to students in grades seven through 12.  N.Y.Education Law § 701 (1971).  No such provision is made for children in grades one through six; free textbooks are to be made available to children in those grades only upon the vote of the majority of the district's eligible voters to levy a tax to provide funds for the purchase of the textbooks, N.Y.Education Law § 703 (1971).

[2] The fee imposed was $7.50 per child.

I join in the Court's decision to remand the case so that the District Court can assess the consequences of this new development. I do so because I believe that the Court acts out of a proper sense of our constitutional duty to decide only live controversies, and because I believe that the District Judge can best resolve the factual issues upon which proper resolution of the mootness question depends. Certainly, our mere act of remanding in no way suggests any particular view as to whether this case is in fact moot. That decision is for the District Judge in the first instance.

In reaching his decision, the District Judge will, of course, have to take into account the standards which we have previously articulated for resolving mootness problems. On the one hand, "[a] case [may be] moot if subsequent events [make] it absolutely clear that the allegedly wrongful behavior could not reasonably be expected to recur." . . . But on the other, "[m]ere voluntary cessation of [allegedly] illegal conduct does not moot a case; if it did, the courts would be compelled to leave '[t]he defendant . . . free to return to his old ways.' " . . . In the context of constitutional questions involving electoral processes, these principles have generally found expression in the proposition that a case is not moot if "[t]he problem is . . . 'capable of repetition, yet evading review.' " . . .

In applying these standards to this case, the District Judge should ascertain the nature of the textbook problem for the elementary grades in respondent school district. Respondents have not suggested that the problem has been resolved once and for all by the recent purchases. To be sure, they do contend that the new textbooks have a useful life of five years. But does this adequately account for destruction by extraordinary events, for loss due to theft, and for obsolescence due to curriculum changes? And, even accepting the five-year figure, does this make the problem a non-recurring one insofar as the continuing viability of this litigation is concerned?

The District Judge should also investigate the posture in which the legal issues presented by this case might again arise when the books begin to wear out. Will the respondent school district delay holding a new election until the new books are actually needed? Is it possible that litigation would again have to proceed for an entire school year, or more, while indigent children are deprived of books before the constitutionality of that deprivation is finally determined?

These seem to me essential questions for the District Court to consider on remand in disposing of the issue of mootness.

Assume that you are the judge. What decision would you render on the merits and for what reasons?

## IS REVENUE SHARING THE ANSWER?

Many people believe that the local tax burdens can be alleviated by the federal government sharing tax revenues with states. If the federal government through revenue sharing is to supply states with tax funds for education, public welfare and other purposes, the federal government will have to get the money through taxation. It is possible that the funds will be derived from the existing sources of federal revenue, primarily the income tax, but it is equally likely that a new source of revenue will be sought. One frequently named candidate is the value-added tax (VAT), which, in reality, is a sales tax. A general sales tax administered at the federal level would produce as much revenue as a greater reliance on the income tax, but its impact would be quite different. The reason is that the income tax is mildly progressive, but a value-added tax is regressive in its impact.

A value-added tax is a tax on consumption expenditures, just like a sales tax, except it is hidden. It would work something like the following hypothetical: a cattle raiser would pay one cent of tax on every ten cents' worth of cattle produced; the butcher would pay one cent on every ten cents' worth of value that he added in butchering, but he would be allowed to subtract the ten cents that he paid the cattle raiser before calculating his value-added basis. The meat packer would pay one cent on each of his ten cents' worth of value added during packing, but first he would be allowed a deduction for the amount paid to the butcher, and finally, the retailer pays one cent on each ten cents' worth of value that he adds during retail distribution. The consumer pays the full, final price. An example of the tax's regressiveness can be seen by comparing its impact on a poor husband and wife with four children and an income of $6,000 and on a more affluent husband and wife with four children and an income of $25,000. Assuming each family buys $5,000 worth of goods subject to the value added tax, the poor family has five-sixths of its income subjected to the value-added tax, but the richer family has only one-fifth. Thus, the general impact of the tax falls heavier on poorer families. The value-added tax is made politically appealing to voters because part of its legislative package includes property tax relief.

### David L. Kirp & Mark G. Yudof
### REVENUE SHARING AND ITS EFFECT ON THE POOR

Copyright © 1972, by Northwestern University.
Reprinted by permission from THE CLEARING HOUSE REVIEW, Vol. 5, No. 9.
Excerpts from pages 496–97, 529–32.

.   .   .   In the context of presidential rhetoric, revenue sharing is not a limited response to the nation's problems, but a necessary element in the revitalization of government: "Power [is] turned back to the people  .  .  .  [so that] government at all levels [is] refreshed and renewed, and made truly responsive."

The most interesting, because the most novel, of the administration's revenue sharing plans would turn back to the states on a population basis 1.3% of the income tax dollars collected by the Internal Revenue Service, an estimated $5 billion for the fiscal year 1972. The states could use those funds to meet their self-determined, self-described needs; they would be essentially unencumbered by federal restrictions.  .  .  .

The fiscal arguments for general revenue sharing are straightforward. Federal revenues, tied to the progressive income tax, rise rapidly as the gross national product increases. While the federal government has almost preempted income tax as a means of raising money (90% of all income tax dollars are collected by Washington, only 10% by other governmental units), state and local governments are forced to rely on regressive and relatively sluggish property and sales taxes to support their increasing needs. As a result, the argument continues, Washington rapidly collects dollars while the rest of the country verges on bankruptcy. Why not address that fiscal mismatch by using the federal government for the one thing it is unmistakably good at doing—raising revenue—while at the same time turning over a portion of that revenue to states, counties and cities so that they can maintain and expand their public services?  .  .  .

Behind the obliquity of the president's pronouncements lies a set of facts more complex and elusive. An analysis of the *impact* of revenue sharing yields conclusions not obvious on the face of the proposal and detrimental to the interests of the poor. Revenue sharing undermines the commitment of the national government to poor and minority groups, moving this country in a direction antithetical to their claim for a decent life. It jeopardizes the role of Washington as the advocate for innovation, reform, and equitable taxation. It submerges the federal presence to what is at best a revitalized parochialism, a reinforcement of the worst aspects of the status quo.  .  .  .

The most notable fiscal failing of general revenue sharing, is that it does not address serious *within-state* inequities in taxing and spending practices. Current state revenue-raising schemes are not merely sluggish. They are regressive: their burden falls unduly on those in our society least able to pay. Sales and excise taxes are relatively more detrimental to the poor than to the rich; even in those states and cities which have adopted income taxes, the practice has generally been to set a uniform rate and not to tax progessively. A revenue sharing bill could address this problem intelligently, providing a $5 billion carrot to coerce states into adjusting their own taxing practices  .  .  .

  .  .  .  If states employed an equitable formula for the distribution of state-collected dollars, a formula based on relative need or even parity, cities would be significantly better off than they are at present. Yet the administration's revenue sharing proposal does nothing to prevent a state from deliberately designing a revenue distribution plan to keep the cities poor. As in the case of the tax structure, revenue sharing could serve as a device to correct distribution inequities by requiring that state spending arrangements be reformed; the Nixon plan, however, provides only a *carte blanche* for states to continue acting as they have in the past.

    . . . the crucial question is not whether state and local governments are presently responsive to "the people," but to which people they respond. The answer to this question is clear: city and state governments are committed to those middle class constituents who have a political and economic interest in the status quo. State and local governmental control over unrestricted money would inevitably reward the affluent, for it is they who control state houses and city halls. There is little likelihood (and no requirement) that additional dollars would evoke novel behavior; indeed, infusions of new money seem more likely to reinforce their worst habits. With no incentive for these governments to behave otherwise, the David Riesman principle "the more, the more" would apply in full force.

    The poor and minority groups, to whom state and local governments have been unresponsive, are the political losers under revenue sharing. Whether measured in terms of welfare eligibility requirements, exclusionary zoning, education dollars, low-cost housing, or municipal services, the cities and states have not hitherto reflected the wishes and interests of these disadvantaged groups. Indeed, the chief impetus for innovation and reform has come from Washington, for poor and black people have historically turned to Washington for support against entrenched, unsympathetic local power structures. The Voting Rights Act, community action agencies, Title I of the Elementary and Secondary Education Act and the Model Cities Program are but a few of the positive federal responses. To be sure, that support has often been reluctant and unwilling. But under the administration's revenue sharing plan, even this impetus will be lost, and the disadvantaged "insular minorities" will once again be subject to the vagaries of state and local politics. . . .

    Nor is there much evidence that local school districts are using *local revenue* to provide compensatory programs for the poor or to experiment with new education models. Very few states provide supplemental services for disadvantaged students; none presently require that bilingual programs be offered the non-English speaking. Disparities between rich and poor schools and rich and poor districts abound. Poor and black students, north and south, find themselves locked into dead-end "vocational" or "remedial" groups. No effort is made to nourish non-sectarian alternatives to the public schools, to create the sort of educational diversity which might ultimately improve the quality of education for all children; instead, progress is inextricably linked to the fate of the public school monopoly. Urban school systems "decentralize" without granting any power to the decentralized governing units. Apart from North Dakota's state-wide effort and a handful of experiments in other parts of the country, efforts at informalizing and humanizing the classroom are submerged in a resurgent war against "permissiveness." Test scores continue to serve as the sole criterion for school-measured success. Student self-image, pluralism, diversity, experimentation and even income and status rewards become unimportant in the quest for good achievement test results and the "efficient" management of schools. . . .

It is not difficult to fathom a functional rationale for special revenue sharing. State governments are the big winners; they receive unrestricted dollars which they can divide much as they see fit. City and state education bureaucracies are given another opportunity to expend funds in accordance with their self-described interest, unfettered by the need to attend to the welfare of those without political power. Rich suburbs benefit also, for the relative need standard in practice means equal dollars per child for all districts regardless of need. Those who oppose education reform will also gain; for parochialism, undiminished by federal restraint or by a truly representative governing structure, will be strengthened.

The losers? Urban areas, once again, wil be shortchanged. Children whose native language is not English, or who come to school with physical, mental or emotional problems, will find fewer programs designed to meet their special needs. Poor children—white, black, Chicano, Puerto Rican, Indian—will continue to be discarded by the educational system run by and for the middle class. . . .

# INDEX

References are to Pages

**DESEGREGATION—Cont'd**
All deliberate speed, 716–718, 723–728
Boundary gerrymandering, 754–764
Compulsory school laws and, 101
De facto segregation, 736, 753–797
  De jure segregation, compared, 754–764
  Defined, 753–754
Desegregation plan,
  Remedial and compensatory educational programs, 139–146
Dual school systems, elimination of, 721 et seq.
Due process, 719–720
Faculty, of, 730–731, 809–820
  Affirmative action,
    Firing, 823
    Promotions, 820–827
Freedom-of-choice plan, 721–725, 732
Guidelines, 734–741
Integrated education,
  Alternatives, 797–803
    Community control, 801–802
    Compensatory education, 802–803
    Equalized school funding, 803
    Free schools, 803
    Voucher education, 803
  Integrated vs. segregated, discussion of merits, 795–800
Multidistrict or metropolitan remedy, 786–795
Plans, 721–742
Private schools, 744–751
  Constitutionality of, 81–82
Purpose, discrimination,
  Rebuttable presumption, 769–782
Segregated private schools,
  Constitutional limitations on state aid, 804–809
  Constitutionality, 748–751
  Public school's refusal to hire teachers with children in private schools, 751–753
Separate but equal doctrine, 709–712
  Rejection of, 712–716
Statistical analysis, 743–744
Student assignment,
  Attendance zones, remedial altering of, 739–740
  Busing, 740–741
  One-race schools, 738–739
  Quotas, 737–738
Suburbs,
  See Multidistrict or metropolitan remedy, this topic
Unitary nondiscriminatory system pending litigation, 728

**DICTA**
Judicial, 46
Obiter, 46

**DISCIPLINE**
See Student Rights

**DISCRETIONARY POWER**
Discretionary-ministerial distinction, 67, 128

**DISMISSAL OF TEACHERS**
See Teacher Rights

**DISTRICT COURTS**
See Federal Courts

**DUE PROCESS**
  See also Desegregation; Equal Educational Opportunity; Gender Discrimination; Student Rights
Generally, 495–534
Corporal punishment, 537–540
Damage suits against school officials, 507
Defined, 512–513, 516
Expulsion or suspension procedures, 501–534
  Alternative educational opportunities, 509, 511–512
  Hearing,
    Confrontation of accusing witnesses, 522–529
    Right to, 506, 508, 513–522
  Model school disciplinary code, 530–534
  Notice, right to, 512, 514–522
  Overcrowding, use of expulsion to relieve, 503–507
  Reasons, informed of, 508
Hearing, 513
  See also Teacher Rights, Hearings and hearing procedures
Paddling, 540
Notice, 512
Paddling, 540
Right to attend a public school, 503–505, 514–516

**DUE PROCESS CLAUSE OF FOURTEENTH AMENDMENT**
See Fourteenth Amendment

**EDUCATIONAL MALPRACTICE**
See Compulsory Schooling, Suits by parents or students

**ELEMENTARY AND SECONDARY EDUCATION ACT (ESEA)**
Description, 68–69

FREEDOM OF EXPRESSION—Cont'd
Censorship of class materials, 218–225, 241–249
  See also Expression of Ideas, Governmental Power to Control, Within curriculum
Collective-bargaining negotiations,
  Prohibition of nonunion representatives from speaking on subject of pending negotiations, 677–681
Constitution of the United States, 150–151
Declaration of Independence, 150
Demonstrations,
  Off campus,
    Suspension from school, 484–485
Flag salute, 194–203
John Stuart Mill,
  *On Liberty*, 151–157
Mind, freedom of the, 194–204
Opinions, expression of, 157–159
Procedural regulations, 149–150
System of, 160–164
Teachers, 596 et seq.
  See also Teacher Rights

FULL FAITH AND CREDIT CLAUSE
Limitations on, 19–20
Text, 9

GENDER DISCRIMINATION
Generally, 824–863
Admission requirements, 840, 843–844
Affirmative action,
  Athletics, 855–857, 860–861
Athletics, 846–863
  Exclusion of males from only interscholastic team in school, 853–861
  Mixed gender interscholastic competition in contact sports, 846–853
Curricular activities, 824–846
Educational materials, sex stereotyping in, 845–846
Employment discrimination,
  Title IX, application of, 862–863
Equal Rights Amendment, 824
Extra-curricular activities, 846–863
Males, discrimination against, 833–839
Maternity leave, mandatory,
  Constitutionality of, 586–596
Single-sex public schools, 824–833, 844–845
Statutes forbidding discrimination, 845–846
Title IX, pp. 862–863
Wages, 596

GIFTED CHILDREN
See Equal Educational Opportunity

HANDICAPPED CHILDREN
See Equal Educational Opportunity, Gifted and exceptional children

HEARINGS AND HEARING PROCEDURES
See Teacher Rights

HOME INSTRUCTION
See Compulsory Schooling, Equivalent education

IN LOCO PARENTIS
Defined, 425
Doctrine criticized, 425–426
Off campus activities, 484–494
School security officer, 435
Search and seizure, 425, 427, 434–436

INTEGRATION
See Desegregation

I.Q. TESTS
See Equal Educational Opportunity

JOHN STUART MILL
See Freedom of Expression

JUDICIAL REVIEW
Generally, 29–34
Standard, appropriate, 31–34

LANGUAGE MINORITIES
See Equal Educational Opportunity

LEGAL REASONING AND RESEARCH
Finding and reading case opinions, 44–48
  Briefing, 46–48

LEGAL SYSTEM OF THE UNITED STATES
  See also Court Systems; Federal Courts; Judicial Review; Supreme Court
Generally, 21–57

LEGISLATIVE COURTS
See Federal Courts

MAINSTREAMING
See Equal Educational Opportunity

MARRIAGE
See Compulsory Schooling; Student Rights

MATERNITY LEAVE
See Contracts, Teacher's

†